American Government and Politics in the New Millennium

Sixth Edition

American Government and Politics in the New Millennium

Sixth Edition

Virginia Stowitts
  Palo Alto College
  San Antonio, Texas

Christine Schultz
  Santa Monica College
  Santa Monica, California

Theresia Stewart
  Elizabethtown Community College
  Elizabethtown, Kentucky

Karen Sunshine
  SUNY Rockland Community College
  Suffern, New York

Abigail Press   Wheaton, IL 60187

Design and Production: Abigail Press
Typesetting: Abigail Press
Typeface: AGaramond
Cover Art: Sam Tolia

**American Government and Politics
in the New Millennium**

Sixth Edition, 2007
Printed in the United States of America
Translation rights reserved by the authors
ISBN 10: 1-890919-40-3
ISBN 13: 978-1-890919-40-5

Dedications

In memory of my father, Milton Vogel; in honor of my mother, Julia Vogel; with love to my children, Ken, Suzanne, Sari and Doug; and for my grandchildren, Andi, Lauren, Zoë, Jake, Alex, and Samantha, for the endless joy they bring.

Karen Vogel Sunshine

A special thank you is extended to two very important individuals in my life: my husband and son, Greg and Brian. I would also like to thank everyone who has demonstrated patience with me during this project: my parents, my friends, Beth and Bill Cahaney, and my colleagues in the Social and Behavioral Science Division at Elizabethtown Community College.

Terri Stewart

In memory of my father, George Churchill Stowitts, for his loving support and faith in me.

Ginny Stowitts

To my husband, Greg, and daughters, Katlain and Courtney, and to students the world over engaged in the pursuit of knowledge.

Christine Schultz

ABOUT THE AUTHORS

Karen Vogel Sunshine

Virginia Stowitts

Karen Vogel Sunshine, Professor of Political Science, has a Ph. D. in Politics from the Graduate School of Arts and Sciences of New York University. She is the head of the Political Science discipline in the Social and Behavioral Sciences division at Rockland Community College, State University of New York. Karen, whose specialization is political psychology, is a 1998 recipient of a national award (NISOD) for teaching excellence. Dr. Sunshine is the author of numerous articles.

Virginia (Ginny) Stowitts is an Assistant Professor of government at Palo Alto College in San Antonio, Texas. She serves as the Chairperson of the Social Sciences Department. She is the co-author of *Texas Politics: Roots, Culture and Reform* and recently completed *American Government: A Public Policy Reader.* She received her Masters Degree in Political Science from St. Mary's University in San Antonio, Texas. She is the immediate past president of the Women's Political Caucus of Bexar County and serves as vice president of the San Antonio Chapter of the League of Women Voters.

Christine Schultz

Theresia Stewart

Christine Schultz teaches in the political science department at Santa Monica College California. Christine graduated from the University of Southern California with a degree in Political Science in 1973. She received her Ph.D. from the University of California, Los Angeles in 1986. Christine's particular interest is in the role mass communications play in elections. Christine is also Coordinator of the campus Scholars Program.

Theresia Stewart is an Associate Professor of political science at Elizabethtown Community College. Theresia is a leader in the field of multicultural education, serving as chairperson of the multicultural committee at her institution since 1994 and assisting in the development of curriculum for teaching international relations, funded through a grant from the U.S. Institute of Peace. She shares her expertise by participating in workshops among individuals in the business and political community.

Contents in Brief

Table of Contents

Chapter Eight
Interest Groups 247

INTRODUCTION

HOW DO POLITICAL SCIENTISTS KNOW WHAT THEY KNOW? A BRIEF LOOK AT APPROACHES AND METHODS

Most consumers are probably well aware of the dictum "let the buyer beware," which is a reminder to examine merchandise carefully before buying it. This adage is an important one for students to keep in mind for, although they are not often categorized as such, they too are consumers. Students are buyers of knowledge or information, and information, just as any other commodity, requires inspection and evaluation.

HOW DO THEY KNOW?

To evaluate information is to determine whether the knowledge that is presented, be it in a radio or television report, a magazine, a journal, a newspaper, a lecture hall, or an academic text such as this one, is valid. That determination is made essentially by questioning how the information being conveyed was acquired. In short, "How do they know?" (which is another way of asking "Is this product worth buying?") is the question that all students, including those of American government and politics, should ask. The following nonpolitical but true story illustrates why.

The story begins on Sunday, October 30, 1938, at 8:00 P.M. when CBS went on the air with a radio program that was soon to make history.[1] The program, as *The New York Times* reported the next day, started with a weather report. Then:

> an announcer remarked that the program would be continued from a hotel, with dance music. For a few moments a dance program was given in the usual manner. Then there was a "break-in" with a "flash" about a professor at an observatory noting a series of gas explosions on the planet Mars.
>
> News bulletins and scene broadcasts followed, reporting, with the technique in which the radio had reported actual events, the landing of a "meteor" near Princeton, N. J., "killing" 1,500 persons, the discovery that the "meteor" was a "metal cylinder" containing strange creatures from Mars armed with "death rays" to open hostilities against the inhabitants of the earth

The casualties at the landing site in Grovers Mill, N. J., as reported by one of the radio announcers, were enormous. He broke the news to his listeners in graphic detail:

> Ladies and gentlemen, I have a grave announcement to make. Incredible as it may seem, both the observations of science and the evidence of our eyes lead to the inescapable assumption that those strange beings who landed in the Jersey farmlands tonight are the vanguard of an invading army from the planet Mars. The battle which took place tonight at Grovers Mill has ended in one of the most startling defeats ever suffered by an army in modern times; seven thousand men armed with rifles and machine guns pitted against a single fighting machine of the invaders from Mars. One hundred and twenty known survivors. The rest strewn over the battle area from Grovers Mill to Plainsboro crushed and trampled to death under the metal feet of the monster, or burned to cinders by its heat ray. The monster is now in control of the middle section of New Jersey and has effectively cut the state through its center. Communication lines are down from Pennsylvania to the Atlantic Ocean. Railroad tracks are torn and service from New York to Philadelphia discontinued except routing some of the trains through Allentown and Phoenixville. Highways to the north, south, and west are clogged with frantic human traffic. Police and army reserves are unable to control the mad flight. By morning the fugitives will have swelled Philadelphia, Camden and Trenton, it is estimated, to twice their normal population.
>
> At this time martial law prevails throughout New Jersey and eastern Pennsylvania. We take you now to Washington for a special broadcast on National Emergency . . . the Secretary of the Interior . . . .

The announcer of course was right. This was an incredible story. It was, in fact, as stated numerous times before, during and after the transmission, a work of fiction, a play, "Invasion From Mars," based on a classic novella by H. G. Wells entitled *The War of the Worlds*. However, many listeners did not seem to hear the disclaimers, or to question what one reporter called "a totally unreasonable, completely fantastic proposition." Instead, they joined the estimated 1,200,000 others who "took the program literally and reacted according to their natures and circumstances." The reactions, as can be seen in the samples reported by the Associated Press, can be summarized in a single word, "panic." (See "War's Over: How U. S. Met Mars.")

Without passing judgment on their behavior, it is reasonable, perhaps unavoidable, to ask why those individuals who panicked did not know the difference between fact and fiction. While there probably is no simple response to that question, nor single explanation for the mass hysteria, some understanding of what happened can be achieved by recognizing that people come to "know" things in a wide variety of ways.

If time permitted, a lot of space could be devoted to exploring the many ways of knowing. There is actually an entire field of study devoted to understanding how people know the world. The field, for those interested in exploring the subject more fully, is a branch of philosophy called **epistemology** (from the Greek word "epistéme" meaning knowledge).

According to experts in this area, knowledge may be based—and there is considerable overlap in this list—on: myths, superstitions, hunches, intuition, common sense, casual observations,

War's Over
How U. S. Met Mars

The radio's "end of the world," as some listeners understood it, produced repercussions throughout the United States. Samples, as reported by the Associated Press, follow:

Woman Tries Suicide

Pittsburg.—A man returned home in the midst of the broadcast and found his wife, a bottle of poison in her hand, screaming: "I'd rather die this way than like that."

Man Wants to Fight Mars

San Francisco.—An offer to volunteer in stopping an invasion from Mars came among hundreds of telephone inquiries to police and newspapers during the radio dramatization of H. G. Wells' story. One excited man called Oakland police and shouted: "My God! Where can I volunteer my services? We've got to stop this awful thing!"

Church Lets Out

Indianapolis.—A woman ran into a church screaming: "New York destroyed; it's the end of the world. You might as well go home to die. I just heard it on the radio." Services were dismissed immediately.

College Boys Faint

Brevard. N. C.—Five Brevard College students fainted and panic gripped the campus for a half hour with many students fighting for telephones to inform their parents to come and get them.

It's a Massacre

Providence, R. I.—Weeping and hysterical women swamped the switchboard of the Providence Journal for details of the "massacre." The electric company received scores of calls urging it to turn off all lights so that the city would be safe from the "enemy."

She Sees "the Fire"

Boston.—One woman declared she could "see the fire" and told the Boston Globe she and many others in her neighborhood were "getting out of here."

"Where Is It Safe?"

Kansas City.—One telephone informant said he had loaded all his children into his car, had filled it with gasoline, and was going somewhere. "Where it is safe?" he wanted to know. The Associated Press bureau received queries on the "meteors" from Los Angeles, Salt Lake City, Beaumont, Tex., and St. Joseph, Mo.

Prayers in Richmond

Richmond, Va.—The Times-Dispatch reported some of its telephone calls came from persons who said they were praying.

Atlanta's "Monsters"

Atlanta—Listeners throughout the Southeast called newspapers reporting that "a planet struck in New Jersey, with monsters and almost everything, and anywhere from 40 to 7,000 people were killed." Editors said responsible persons, known to them, were among the anxious information seekers.

unverified beliefs, opinions, imagination, custom, astrology, magic, dreams, faith, and so on. There is nothing wrong with any of these ways of knowing things. Most people, for example, have relied upon hunches and intuition when there is nothing else to base their actions upon. Students frequently do that when taking objective exams. Virtually everyone has acted on faith or what others have told them is true. Patients take the medicine the doctor prescribes not because they have tested the drugs in the laboratory but because they have confidence in the physician and in the medication that is recommended. At the very least, life would be a lot more complicated than it already is if all data received from others, such as that the earth is round or that broccoli and spinach are nutritious or even that one political party is superior to the other, was rejected.

In a similar way the panic of those individuals who believed the "information" being reported on the radio on the evening of October 30, 1938, can be understood in terms of their faith, intuition, and/or the reactions of those around them. As one analyst of the event explained, "We are ready to believe almost anything if it comes from a recognized authority. This man [the announcer] gave complete credibility to the "news bulletins.... He mentioned the 'Secretary of State' [by name] although it was actually the fictional Secretary of the Interior...whose voice came over the air. Instead of hearing what was actually said, the listener heard what accorded with his preconceptions."

Given this, why then was it that the majority of those who heard the broadcast, approximately 4,800,000 listeners, knew or very quickly learned that what they were hearing was not true? How did they know?

Perhaps they reasoned that what was being described—a large alien that emitted rays and had tentacles, serpent-like eyes, skin that glistened like wet leather, and a lipless, V-shaped mouth that dripped saliva—had never been seen before and therefore probably did not exist; or they might have been somewhat suspicious about the accelerated pace and illogical sequence in which events were said to have taken place. (Within minutes of announcing the monster's arrival, it was reported that three million people had already moved out of New York.) Or maybe the "facts" were checked, and it was found that the agency doing the reporting, the Intercontinental Radio News, was nonexistent; or, after changing the radio dial, it was discovered that no other station was reporting the catastrophic invasion of Martians; or, after consulting a published listing of radio programs, it was ascertained that a play based on *The War of the Worlds* had been scheduled. The individuals who used such logical reasoning and who made such direct observations had a particular way of "knowing" or explaining reality that is described as **empirical** (based on experience or observation) or scientific.

Sometimes, as it was in the case just examined, it is preferable to rely more on knowledge based on observation than on intuition. The answer to the "How do they know?" question, in other words, provides a sound basis for accepting or rejecting information.

As with most people, those who study and write about political phenomena come to know things in a variety of ways. Some, including two of the great political philosophers, Plato and Jean Jacques Rousseau, were rather mystical thinkers who relied more on subjective impressions than on objective experiences. Others, such as Aristotle and John Locke, are recognized as being systematic or scientific thinkers. The reader will probably find that although the full range of ways that knowledge may be derived is represented within the covers of this volume that scientific studies rather than intuitive or mystical speculations are the dominant sources of information.

The reason for the scientific slant, in this and in most current political science texts, is related to the fairly recent evolution of the study of politics. During the 1950s, in a period now referred to as the "behavioral revolution," a number of political scientists argued that the study of politics should become much more systematic and objective than it had been up to that point. By the mid-1960s the majority of political scientists had been persuaded, and their efforts to become more scientific led to the introduction of many new methods, techniques, and approaches.

METHODS, TECHNIQUES, AND APPROACHES: THE DIFFERENCES

Before beginning any discussion of methods, techniques, and approaches, which will be treated here as distinct but related concepts, it should be made clear that not all political scientists agree that there are any distinctions or, if they do think that they exist, about what the differences are. Disagreements about the meanings of terms, as will be more fully explained in Chapter 1, are not unusual among political scientists. However, most of them do recognize that "scientists" have to be quite specific about their meanings.

Methods and Techniques

A **method** refers to a generally accepted way of obtaining and explaining information. (Methodology is a subfield of epistemology.) As has been pointed out earlier, at present the generally accepted way for political scientists to obtain and analyze information is "empirically." That is to say that, to the extent it is possible to do so, the scientific method, which for political scientists consists of the systematic and objective investigation of political phenomena, is used.

A **technique** refers to the SPECIFIC empirical or scientific procedures used to obtain and analyze political information. To put it more plainly, a technique refers to how something (including empirical research) is explicitly "DONE."

Nonpolitical Techniques

If asked for some "nonpolitical" examples of techniques, the reader could probably list a large number. The procedures an automobile mechanic uses to tune an engine, a dentist's techniques for filling a cavity, the procedures that an architect uses to design a house or an apartment building, the techniques that a pastry chef uses to bake chocolate chip cookies, and the procedures a student follows to prepare for an exam in American government would all be good examples. To tune an engine, fill a tooth, design a house, bake cookies, or prepare for an exam, certain things will inevitably be done.

The chef, for instance, would probably begin by blending and mixing the appropriate quantities of butter, flour, sugar, and chips and would then shape the delectable morsels into portions of the desired size, place them on a cookie sheet, and, finally, would pop them into the oven and bake them at approximately 350 degrees for twenty minutes or until they were a golden color.

Each step in the process of preparation is physical and can be observed. The baker has DONE something, employed procedures or techniques that, in the case of the cookies, are set out precisely, step by step, in a recipe. Obviously, the recipe for chocolate chip cookies just given is not the only one there is. One might add nuts, raisins, or M & Ms, or might blend instead of mix, stir instead of blend, or bake for thirty minutes rather than twenty.

Political Techniques

Just as there is more than one method to bake cookies, tune engines, study for exams, fill teeth, and design houses, there is more than one way to investigate political phenomena. Political scientists who are interested in the field of American government could, for example, select from the following limited list of common empirical or scientific techniques: surveys, statistics and content analysis.

Surveys: The survey, or opinion poll, in which individuals are asked to respond to mailed questionnaires or to answer questions in telephone or personal interviews is probably the most widely used technique for obtaining and analyzing current information about the government and about the attitudes of American citizens.

Every incumbent politician such as Senator Clinton or Senator McCain; every candidate for public office such as Bush and Kerry in 2004; every topical issue including terrorism, health care, welfare, taxes, crime, and immigration policy; every political process including judicial decisions, legislative vetoes, and the influence of lobbyists; and every political institution such as the presidency, the bureaucracy, and interest groups are grist for the pollster's mill.

Some readers may have at one time or another actually participated as respondents in a poll and, in the future, many more are likely to. Among those that regularly conduct or commission these polls are:

1. local, state, or federal governments
2. government agencies
3. politicians
4. college and university faculty
5. political parties
6. survey research centers (Inter-University Consortium for Political and Social Research, University of Michigan; National Opinion Research Center, University of Chicago; Roper Center, University of Connecticut)
7. polling agencies (Gallup, Yankelovich Clancy Shulman)
8. the communications media (The ABC television network collaborates with the *Washington Post* on polls; CBS works in conjunction with *The New York Times*; and NBC news polls are associated with the *Wall Street Journal*.)

Media journalists are convinced that most of their audience thoroughly enjoys the juicy bits of gossipy-type information about political personalities that some polls report. However, it is reasonable, given their pervasiveness in society and the vast amount of more serious information that is often received from them, to ask whether knowledge derived from surveys is valid.

Should an individual decide to run or not to run for political office based on the reported results of popularity in a public opinion poll? Should citizens change their opinions about an issue or a policy, as they sometimes do, to conform to the attitudes that polls show most other Americans have? In other words should polls be trusted? Do researchers and reporters who rely on survey data really know what they think they know?

One expert on the survey method provides a checklist of eighteen specific questions that he believes have to be answered to evaluate the validity of survey findings. (See "Guide to Reading Survey Reports" p. 8.) The questions on the "Guide" list indicate that it is important to examine the procedures that have been followed by those who design the polls, those who administer them, and those who interpret the data.

Such a task is less daunting than it may initially seem, because at least some of that information is often made readily available to average readers of surveys. A responsible polling agency will explain, along with its published findings, how the poll was conducted. (See below "How the Poll Was Conducted.") The next table, "Summary of Polling Methodology," (pp. 10-11) describes the polling techniques of the four major national polling organizations in their efforts to find representative samples of the population to question during one election year. It is important, as can now be appreciated, to look for these explanations and descriptions before deciding to accept or to reject survey results.

How the Poll Was Conducted

The latest *New York Times*/CBS News Poll is based on telephone interviews conducted Aug. 5 to 9 with 1,478 adults throughout the United States.

The sample of telephone exchanges called was randomly selected by a computer from a complete list of active residential exchanges in the country. The list of more than 36,000 residential exchanges is maintained by Marketing Systems Group of Philadelphia.

Within each exchange, random digits were added to form a complete telephone number, thus permitting access to both listed and unlisted numbers. Within each household, one adult was designated by a random procedure to be the respondent for the survey.

The results have been weighted to take account of household size and number of telephone lines into the residence and to adjust for variations in the sample relating to geographic region, race, sex, age and education.

Source: R. W. Apple Jr., "Poll Shows Disenchantment With Politicians and Politics," *The New York Times*, 13 August 1995, A(8).

Guide to Reading Survey Reports

1. What general topic does the researcher wish to examine?

2. What was his motivation in designing and executing the study?

3. Is the researcher's main purpose one of exploration, description, explanation, or a combination of these?

4. What general population are the findings meant to represent?

5. What was the sampling frame used for purposes of selecting a sample to represent that population?

6. How was the sample actually selected?

7. How many respondents were initially selected in the sample and how many actually participated?

8. To what extent is sampling error likely to affect the results of the survey?

9. How were the data collected? Was the data collection method appropriate to the population and the subject matter of the study?

10. When did the data collection take place and how long did it take?

11. How were specific variables measured in the analysis? How were questionnaire items worded and/or how were responses combined into composite measures of variables? Does a given response pattern—imagining the orientations of persons giving it—reflect our common sensible interpretation of the summary term associated with the response pattern (for example, "very religious")?

12. Have composite measures been validated in such a way as to further ensure their adequate representation of the variables under consideration?

13. Are the methods of analysis used in the report appropriate both to the subject matter and the form of the data collected?

14. How strong are the associations discovered among variables? What do associations of that strength mean in understanding the real world?

15. Has the researcher adequately presented the logic of associations discovered empirically? Has he presented plausible reasons for those associations?

16. Has the researcher adequately tested for alternative explanations? Has he tested the possible spuriousness of the relationships?

17. Do the empirical relationships suggest further analyses that the researcher has neglected?

18. Could an independent reader replicate the survey on the basis of information presented in the report?

While these questions will not provide an exhaustive critique of all survey reports, they indicate the kinds of questions that a critical reader should ask and that the conscientious researcher should anticipate in the framing of his report.

Source: Earl R. Babbie, *Survey Research Methods* (Belmont, CA: Wadsworth Publishing Company, Inc., 1973), 3645.

Statistics: Statistics refer to the mathematical procedures that are used to interpret **data** (information) such as that collected in surveys. As students who have taken a "stat" (or as some have been known to call it "sadistics") course realize, some of the procedures used by statisticians can be quite complex and therefore somewhat intimidating. However, it's important to keep in mind that the reason for doing statistics in the first place is to simplify, not to complicate, the way information is analyzed and communicated.

Anyone who has ever calculated a college grade point average already knows that. Such a calculation is made by summing up all earned numerical scores (4.0 + 3.5 + 4.0 + 3.0 + 3.5) and then dividing the total by the number of grades received (five). The resulting number is the **mean** or average (a 3.6 using the numbers above), which is a statistical measure of **central tendency**. Why do students take the time to calculate the mean? Probably because it is easier to describe their academic performances with this single number than it is to communicate a long list of five, or ten, or twenty, or more individual grades. In short, statistics are used to simplify the communication of this information to others.

There are many, many other descriptive and inferential statistical procedures that allow people to measure data, make projections, test the strength of the **relationship** (association, dependence, covariance) between and among **variables** (the objects being examined or tested), validate or invalidate **hypotheses** (educated guesses about what a researcher expects to find), and so on. It is not necessary for purposes of this text to know how to mathematically perform all the tasks. It is enough just to be aware that these procedures do exist and that knowledge of them allows an individual to go beyond mere hunches or intuition in interpreting information and acquiring knowledge about American government. At some point in their academic careers those students who decide to pursue a bachelors degree in political science, or economics, or criminal justice, or just about any of the social and physical sciences will probably be required to take a least one course in statistics to complete their degree requirements.

Content Analysis: The name of this technique, **content analysis**, is fairly self-explanatory. What political scientists and others who use this technique do is to analyze the written record of the news media or to examine and "analyze" the "contents" of written remarks (in autobiographies, diaries, letters, etc.) and oral statements (formal speeches, casual remarks and conversations, press conferences, etc.) of individuals such as the President of the United States or a member of Congress.

The procedures used in the analysis, which are quite sophisticated, include: sampling, categorizing, coding, quantifying, and statistically evaluating the content being studied. A content analyst (To enhance reliability more than one coder is generally used.) might, for instance, want to determine the frequency with which a political leader uses a particular word or expression or calculate its **salience** (importance) to the user. If the leader's remarks and statements are found to be filled with abundant, fist-pounding references to acts of "war" or "terrorism" or are saturated with frequent tearful predictions of "economic collapse" or "doom," the utterings may be deemed to be significant.

Summary of . . .

Designing a "perfect" poll is a bit like creating the "perfect" spaghetti sauce: all cooks start with tomatoes, but each uses his own favorite combination of seasonings—sometimes with widely varied results. Presented below are the ingredients that went into the survey designs of four major national polling organizations during an election year.

CBS/New York Times

Population sampled from: National adult population telephone survey.

Household selection: Random digit dialing. Up to four attempts to contact household.

Respondent selection: Random selection, appointment made if designated respondent not at home.

Weighting: To correct for household size and to reflect demographics.

Identification of electorate: "Likelihood weight" based on past voting behavior and current intention and reported behavior of similar groups in 1976.

Actual choice: Choice among three major candidates, labeled by party. Leaners included in reported distributions.

Adjustments: None.

Gallup

Population sampled from: Registered voters. In-person interviews.

Household selection: Households randomly selected from sample precincts. No callbacks.

Respondent selection: Systematic selection based on age and sex.

Weighting: To correct for "times at home" and to reflect demographics.

Identification of electorate: "Likely voters" identified based on past behavior, interest, and intention to vote, and expected turnout.

Actual choice: "Secret ballot" for tickets, labeled by party. Undecided asked to mark ballot based on leaning.

Adjustments: Undecideds allocated; figures corrected for deviation of sample precincts from national results in 1976.

ABC/Harris*

Population sampled from: Expected electorate (based on 1976). Series of telephone surveys.

Household selection: Random digit dialing. Households not reached retained for one more survey.

Respondent selection: Systematic selection by modified sex quota.

Weighting: To reflect demographics.

Identification of electorate: "Likely voters" identified based on past behavior and intention to vote, and expected turnout.

Actual choice: Choice among three major candidates, labeled by party. Leaners included in reported distributions.

Adjustments: Survey results from last 12 days combined. (No day-to-day differences noted). Undecided allocated evenly between Carter and Reagan.

... Polling Methodology

NBC/AP**

Population sampled from: National adult population. Telephone survey.
Household selection: Random digit dialing. No callbacks (except for "busies").
Respondent selection: Systematic selection based on sex quota.
Weighting: None. Sample deemed "self-weighting."
Identification of electorate: "Likely voters" identified based on past behavior, interest, and intention to vote.
Actual choice: Choice among three major candidates, labeled by party (following questions on open-ended preferences and whether respondents had made up minds).
Adjustments: None

Glossary

National adult population. The sample is designed to reflect the characteristics, including geographic distribution, of the entire adult population.
Registered voters. The same, but the population is registered voters, instead of all adults.
Electorate. The same, but the actual electorate—i.e.,taking differential turnout on a geographic basis into account.
Random digit dialing. Procedures giving households (both listed and unlisted numbers) a fair chance to be reached.
Callbacks. Multiple attempts to reach a household.
Random selection. Procedures to give each potential respondent in a household a random chance to come into the sample.
Systematic selection. Selection according to same system, depriving the interviewer of the choice of respondent.
Likelihood weight. An estimate of how likely someone is to vote. Someone who is 80 percent likely will count twice as much in the final figures as someone only 40 percent.
Likely voters. An attempt to separate respondents into two groups: "likely voters" and "non-likely voters." Only the former enter into the reported distributions.
Allocation. Division of the undecided based on other information, such as their partisan preference, issue positions, or data from other surveys.

Note: This overview cannot capture the full details of procedures used—for example what precise "demographics" were used.
*ABC had conducted polls with Louis Harris and Associates at the time of this summary. **AP conducted a survey on its own after the last joint survey.

Source: C. Everett Ladd and G. Donald Ferree, "Were the Pollsters Really Wrong?" *Public Opinion*, vol. 3, no. 6 (December/January 1981): 18. Reprinted with permission of American Enterprise Institute.

Source: Herbert Asher, *Polling and the Public: What Every Citizen Should Know* (Washington, D. C. : CQ Press, 1988), 140-141.

One news correspondent, William Safire, who informally used the technique, found that in his second inaugural address President Ronald Reagan used the word "freedom" twelve times and the words "free" and "freely" an additional four times. Clearly, Safire states this president saw freedom (from excessive government at home and from tyranny abroad) "as the essence of his message and the mark of his administration."[2] An analysis of Mr. Safire's columns might reveal that his conclusions about President Reagan were either based on an objective analysis or were the product of Safire's personal bias.

Other analysts have found that the structure of a leader's communication, the syntax, whether she/he is subdued or ecstatic, stuttering or hesitating, speaking exceptionally rapidly or slowly, loudly or quietly, and so forth, may show emotional distress. Take a few moments and think about what, if anything, the following quotation taken from one of many secretly recorded presidential conversations might reveal about the emotional state of the speaker.

> The report was not frankly accurate. Well it was accurate but it was not full. And, he tells me the reason it wasn't full, was that he didn't know. Whether that is true or not, I don't know. Although it wasn't I'm told. But I'm satisfied with it.[3]

Although it is difficult, without formal training in psychology, to specify precisely what it is that is wrong here, it is likely that most readers did recognize that something seems to have been troubling the speaker of these words. Dr. Walter Weintraub, a psychiatrist who is an expert on verbal behavior, certainly thinks so. He argues that the statement, which is "full of vacillation and negative words," indicates that the president who spoke them, Richard Nixon, "may have been clinically depressed at the time the conversations were recorded" (during the Watergate investigations).[4]

Content analysis has also been used to predict the winner of presidential elections. In one study an examination of the nomination speeches made by candidates in every presidential election year from 1948 through 1988 was conducted. The analysts extracted expressions of "optimism" (defined as talking about global or personal problems as being temporary and correctable), and "pessimism" (marked by the taking of blame for the problems or by stating that they are intractable) from the speeches and found that with one exception (not named in the source), the most optimistic candidate won the election.[5]

Analyses, such as those described above, show that a careful examination of oral remarks or written records can provide interesting information about politicians. Such studies can also provide insight into the people who vote for and write about them.

Limitations of Political Techniques

It would not be right to leave the impression that each of the three techniques we have just briefly examined provides an infallible way of knowing about American government.

For example, statistics (including those used in content analysis) can intentionally or unintentionally be extremely misleading. A very short, humorous, classic book of "pretty little instances of [statistical] bumbling and chicanery," *How to Lie with Statistics* by Darrell Huff, provides excellent examples of how politicians (among others) can lead the unknowing and the unthinking astray.

Polls too have been wildly inaccurate. Both the infamous 1936 poll conducted by the *Literary Digest* that inaccurately predicted that the Republican presidential candidate, Alf Landon, would win a landslide victory over the Democratic challenger, Franklin Delano Roosevelt, and the notoriously wrong forecasts in 1948 of a sweeping victory for Republican candidate Thomas E. Dewey over the incumbent President Harry S. Truman are examples of such inaccuracies.

Having noted these limitations, it should also be pointed out that when the intentions of a researcher are not to mislead but to convey accurate information (and that is probably the case most of the time) and when research techniques are carefully and explicitly carried out, they yield valid, as well as interesting, knowledge. There is something else to keep in mind about research techniques and that is that they are related to "**approaches.**"

Approaches

Rather than beginning with the customary definition, this segment will start with an example—a nonpolitical one—and work back to a definition of an approach. The example that follows is based on an actual conversation that took place between two students who were sitting and talking in the cafeteria at their college (and who weren't aware that their conversation was overheard by a professor who would soon immortalize it in a textbook).

Student 1. It's hard to believe that another semester has started but I'm glad to be back.
Student 2. You're kidding.
Student 1. No, I like it here. I'm taking really interesting courses, and my instructors are great.
Student 2. You're kidding. Wouldn't you rather be watching the soaps?
Student 1. Nope. I think that being a Student Senator and a member of the Political Science Association is a lot more interesting than "The Young and the Restless."
Student 2. You're kidding. Are you forgetting about reading assignments, term papers, and exams? I can't wait to get out of this place!
Student 1. It's true that there is a lot of work. But after all, this is college, not nursery school. Besides, some of that stuff we read and study is pretty amazing.
Student 2. You're kidding.

This conversation is not an unusual one. In fact, at least one of the authors of this text recalls engaging in a similar exchange many years ago. It's hardly a revelation to say that attitudes about school, work, or just about anything else may range anywhere from intense dislike to rapturous enjoyment. People simply "approach" life differently.

An **approach** then is a way of looking at something. It is an orientation or a perspective (as opposed to a method or technique, which is something that is done). Just as there are many ways of looking at or approaching life, there are many ways to approach or look at American government.

Two Broad Approaches

Traditional Approaches

Traditional approaches to government tend to focus on what "was" and on what "should be"; they look at governmental institutions and tend to be "normative" or value-laden. The historical approach, the constitutional/legal approach, and the philosophical approach are a few of the traditional ways to look at American government. There will be places throughout this text in which one or more of these approaches will be taken.

Behavioral Approaches

Behavioral approaches tend to focus on what "is." They look at people (behavior) and tend to be "empirical" or scientific. Game theory and systems analysis are two important behavioral ways to look at American government.

Game Theory: In many ways it's easier to understand what game theory is all about, and to appreciate its usefulness, by actually playing a "game" before any of the details about the approach are discussed. The following nonpolitical game is a simple one, but it does explain this particular way of looking at things.

The Game: To begin, the reader is asked to suspend reality for a while and pretend that she/he is on a railroad station platform getting ready to board a train. At that moment,

> you meet a friend you are trying to avoid; he is going to coax you onto some committee. Your reservations are in different cars, but he suggests meeting in the diner. When the steward comes through [to take reservations for lunch], you discover to your relief that there are two diners, first-class and buffet, and if you choose correctly, you may "innocently" miss your friend. You have to be careful; he can guess that you'll evade him if you can. Normally you'd dine first class and he knows it. For which car [first-class or buffet] do you make your lunch reservation?[6]

Characteristics of Games: A few of the important attributes of games are illustrated, or implied, in this dining car example. So, before explaining what a game theorist might do in this situation, three of these characteristics should be noted.

1. A game, like the dining car game, (or chess, trivial pursuit, monopoly, or one of the many computer-generated games) involves making a choice or decision (to dine first class or buffet) after anticipating what the opponent might do. If he thinks that since you always eat in the first class diner that he can meet up with you there, he is likely to make a first class reservation. But, since he knows that you will try to avoid him, perhaps he will choose the buffet. However, if you think that he knows that you know that he knows that you will try to avoid him, then making the choice appears to be more problematic.

2. It is assumed that the players (at least two in a game) are rational, meaning that they are playing to win (or, in situations where winning is not possible, that they are trying to minimize

losses and maximize gains). Irrational players cannot be anticipated, and hence the theory of gaming becomes irrelevant.

3. Each of the participants in the game has to have full information about the options or choices that are available. If, for example, the steward taking lunch reservations forgot to mention that the train had two restaurants, there is no game being played. Whether the two do or do not meet in a dining car would then be simply a matter of fate.

Political Games: Before explaining how a game theorist could use game theory to make the best possible lunch reservation decision, it should be noted that there is a very strong connection between the somewhat frivolous nonpolitical dining car game and the more serious political games associated with politics and American government. For instance, political decisions and actions such as declaring and fighting in a war or running for a political office are often conceptualized or looked at as games because they generally involve the same assumptions and characteristics as the three listed above; they involve two or more rational (if they are playing to win) players (countries like the United States and Syria or people like Bush and Cheney) that formulate strategies and make decisions after anticipating the moves of an enemy or an opponent.

Both political and nonpolitical games then ultimately involve making calculations. Making calculations means following a procedure(s). A behavioral or scientific **approach**, such as Game Theory, may require the use of certain empirical **techniques**, such as mathematics. For purposes of explanation it is useful to separate the topics of approaches and techniques, but, in practice, they are closely associated.

Making the Decision: After considering the options in the dining car game, a decision or choice about where to eat must be made by each of the players. (Skipping lunch altogether may seem like a good idea, but that's not an option in this particular game.) Is it to be first class or buffet? How was the reader's decision reached? What might a game theorist do in this situation?

A game theorist would probably begin by calculating all the possible outcomes. In many decision-making situations such calculations are often highly complex, but the dining car game happens to be a relatively simple one. It is a game with only two players (you and your friend,) each having two choices (first class or buffet dining car).

These small numbers allow for a visual display of all the possible combinations of the choices the two players can make. This is done by constructing a **matrix** (a rectangular array of information). Two players with two choices result in a 2 x 2 matrix and looks like this.

FRIEND'S CHOICES

	First Class	Buffet
Y O U R ⇒ First Class		
C H O I C E S ⇒ Buffet		

It can be seen that this 2 x 2 matrix contains two rows that reflect the reader's possible choices (Rows go in this direction ⇒.) and two columns that reflect your friend's possible choices. (Columns go in this direction ⇓.) There are 4 squares, which are called **cells**, in a 2 x 2 matrix, and each cell reflects a different combination of the players' choices and indicates for each which player would win and which would lose the game if both players select the same option.

In the next matrix, letters are used to indicate the outcome or the results. From your point of view a successful outcome (indicated by the letter "S" in the lower left hand corner) is one in which you avoid your friend. Meeting with him results in a failure for you (indicated by the letter "F" in the lower left hand corner). The letters in the upper right corner of each cell indicate the outcome of the game (success [S] or failure [F]) from your friend's point of view. The matrix will then look like this.

FRIEND'S CHOICES

		First Class	Buffet
YOUR CHOICES	⇒ First Class	F · · S	S · · F
	⇒ Buffet	S · · F	F · · S

Possible Outcomes: A matrix is read by moving across the row (⇒) for the outcome of your decision and down (⇓) the column for your friend's. The four possible combinations are:

Possibility 1: You decide to dine, as always, in first class and so does your friend. This combination of choices is found in the cell in the upper left corner. This is a failure for you (F) and a success for him (S).

Possibility 2: You decide to dine in first class, but your friend, believing that you might try to avoid him, made his reservation where he expected to find you—in the buffet. This combination of choices is found in the cell in the upper right corner. These decisions result in a success for you (S) and a failure (F) for him.

Possibility 3: You decide to go to the buffet, and your friend decides to dine first class. This combination, a success (S) for you and a failure (F) for him is found in the cell in the lower left corner.

Possibility 4: The last combination of choices is displayed in the lower right corner. In this situation you have chosen to eat in the buffet dining car and so has your friend. This results in a failure (F) for you and a success (S) for him.

Since game theorists are more likely to use numbers than letters in calculating their options, the matrix will be adjusted accordingly by replacing each "S" with +1 and each "F" with -1. So the final matrix (sometimes referred to as a "payoff" matrix because the payoffs—the rewards and penalties for each player's decision—are given) will look like this.

FRIEND'S CHOICES

	First Class ⇓	Buffet ⇓
YOUR ⇒ First Class	+1 / -1	-1 / +1
CHOICES ⇒ Buffet	-1 / +1	+1 / -1

Reading the Matrix

What the matrix clearly shows is that no matter where the reader decides to eat, in first class or buffet, half of the time that will be a winning choice (S or +1) and half of the time it will not (F or -1). Since this was a simple win/lose or "zero-sum" (if all the +1 and the -1 numbers are added the result is zero) game, a matrix might not even have been needed to figure out that there is a fifty-fifty chance of meeting. The advantage of knowing these odds before making a reservation is that a decision to dine, as the reader usually does, in first-class elegance would not cause undue emotional angst.

The matrix also shows that until both of the players of the game make their decisions, there is no "right" choice or "wrong" choice. Choosing to dine first class turns out to be right only if your friend chooses buffet. It turns out to be wrong if he also chooses first class. In short, a decision becomes right or wrong **after** both of the players have made their choices. All that game theory helps the decision-makers to do is to make the best possible choice given the information that they have.

Why Government Leaders Play Games

Government leaders have to make decisions that are virtually always more complex than the game just played. Usually there are more players and more choices, and their games can be "non zero-sum" (involve cooperation among the players) as well as "zero-sum" (win or lose games in which cooperation is not an option).

Furthermore, a leader's decision, for example a president's decision to use troops rather than diplomacy to settle a domestic or international problem, can be a matter of life and death. It is essential then for him to make a rational decision, to get as much information about the possible choices as he can, to look at all of his and his opponents' options, to think clearly about the payoffs, and then to make the best possible decision given the information that he has. Playing out the "game" before making the actual decision is one way for a president, just as it was for the players in the dining car game, to accomplish these objectives.

Why Political Scientists Take This Approach

One important task for many political scientists has always been to analyze both the decisions that are made by government officials and the processes by which they are made. That used to be a more difficult job than it is now because game theory was not invented until 1944 and because the pioneering work in the field was done by economists who used it to analyze economic decisions. (Fifty years later, in 1994, three of the early pioneers were awarded the Nobel prize for their efforts.) However, it didn't take long for political scientists to begin to appreciate how useful game theory could be for their work, and so they borrowed it. Today researchers use this approach because it helps them to understand what a leader thought he "knew," how he "knew" it, and whether the decision (be it to raise taxes or to send troops to Iraq) he ultimately made was the best possible one that could have been made at the time.

Micro and Macro Approaches

The game theory approach is sometimes referred to as a "micro" approach. The next approach to be examined is often referred to as a "macro" approach. The differences between the two, as the following nonpolitical example illustrates, are fairly easy to spot.

To simplify matters imagine that there are only two ways of looking at the geographical features of the forty-eight contiguous states that comprise the United States. The first way, or approach, is to get on an airplane and look down as the jet flies from the northern U.S. border shared with Canada to the southern border that separates the United States from Mexico and then from the eastern Atlantic coast to the western Pacific coast. This approach will provide an overall view, a view of the land masses and rivers, of the urban cities and the rural farmlands, and of the mountains and the plains. This broad, widespread perspective is the "macro" view.

But for someone who wants to see more than vague shapes and the general features of the U.S., this broad aerial view would simply not be sufficient. An individual who wants to see the faces of people, the details of buildings, the variation of plants, and the major tourist attractions between Santa Monica and New York, or between San Antonio and Kentucky, would be better advised to get into an automobile and drive from one destination to the other. This more restricted or narrowly defined perspective is the "micro" approach. Game theory is the equivalent of traveling by car. It is a micro approach. Its focus is limited to "rational" decision-making. The next approach to be examined is like the view from the plane. It is a broad way of looking at politics that provides an overall perspective. This macro approach is called "systems analysis" (S/A).

Systems Analysis (S/A)

Anyone who has ever engaged in a conversation about the sound "system" in a car (or its exhaust, steering, braking, and suspension systems) or about the inadequate heating or air conditioning "system" in an uncomfortably hot or cold classroom, or made a reference to the solar "system," or to the grading or registration "system" used in a college, or to a computer "system," or even to their own digestive "system" after having consumed an entire pineapple-pepperoni pizza already has some understanding of what a system is.

What is that understanding? Exactly what is meant when people talk about such different entities as CD players and stereo radios, oil heaters and air conditioners, stars and planets, computers and printers, and the internal organs and tissues of the human body as "systems"? These are not easy questions to answer.

A System

A **system** is made up of two related components: (1) a set of interdependent parts and (2) an environment(s). This can be seen by analyzing a few of the nonpolitical systems mentioned above.
1. The sound "system" in a car:
    Parts: AM/FM radio, CD player, speakers, etc.
    Environments: (1) The interior of the car (upholstery that can muffle the sounds)
    (2) The exterior of the car (competing sounds and noises that come from people and traffic outside the car)

A radio is just a radio. A CD player is just a CD player. But when the two are looked at as interdependent parts, and when these parts are looked at in terms of their relation to, or interaction with, their environments, then they are referred to as a system.
2. The heating system in a college:
    Parts: Furnace, thermostat, ducts, etc.
    Environments: (1) The weather (subfreezing v. moderate temperature)
    (2) The school building (insulation, number of windows, number of people in it)

The furnace in the basement of a classroom building is one of the many interdependent parts that collectively provide heat. When the relationship between these parts and the environments with which they interact are discussed, then it is more accurate to refer to them as a heating system.
3. The solar system:
    Parts: Sun, nine planets, comets, satellites, meteoroids, interplanetary dust and gas, etc.
    Environments: (1) gravitational forces
    (2) electromagnetic forces
    (3) "strong" and "weak" nuclear forces

There are other solar systems, such as the Earth's, within the Milky Way galaxy, and that galaxy is only one of many. (Telescopes have identified at least 1000 million others!) It would be possible then to think of the solar system as one part, or a subsystem, of other systems. This holds true for all types of systems; the sound system of a car and the heating system in a building, for example, can each be looked at as a subsystem of an electrical system.
4. A computer system :
    Parts: Control unit, monitor, keyboard, cables, printer, mouse, modem, programs, etc.
    Environments: (1) Paper to print on
    (2) People (programmers and users)

Many, if not most, college students can probably see how the many parts are interdependent and how they are related to (affect and are affected by) their environments. Those who can look at the monitor or printer as interdependent parts of a whole rather than as separate entities, and those who recognize that the related parts have an impact on the environment and vice-verse, understand the concept of a system.

As the examples above indicate, virtually anything can be looked at as a system. The question is why one would want to. Perhaps the best way to answer that question is to recall the old Indian fable, "The Blind Men and the Elephant."

Six blind beggars sitting by a roadside as an elephant passed were told they might touch it so that they would know what an elephant was like. The first one touched only the elephant's side and said, "He is like a wall!" The second one felt only his tusk and said, "No, no, he is like a spear." The third one took hold of his trunk and said, "Surely he is like a snake." "No such thing," cried the fourth, grasping one of his legs, "he is like a tree." The fifth was a tall man and took hold of his ear and said, "All of you are wrong, he is like a fan." The sixth man happened to catch hold of his tail and cried, "O foolish fellows, he is not like a wall, nor a spear, nor a snake, nor a tree, nor a fan; he is exactly like a rope." So the elephant passed on while the six blind men stood there quarreling, each being sure he knew exactly how the elephant looked, and each calling the other hard names because the rest did not agree with him.

The point, or moral, of the story is that to understand the essence of an elephant one first has to know how all the parts are related. It has to be considered as an entity. And, it has to be seen as it relates to its environment. This is as true for CD players and radios, furnaces and thermostats, planets and comets, and modems and printers as it is for elephants. It is also true for politics.

A Political System

As in all systems, a political system is made up of interdependent parts and environments. These are:

Parts: Everything that constitutes **Government**, including
 a) **people**, such as the president, senators, representatives, and bureaucrats;
 b) **political institutions**, including the executive, legislative, and judicial branches of government, the bureaucracy, interest groups, and political parties;
 c) **political processes**, for instance the legislative and electoral processes;
 d) **interactions**, for example bargaining and negotiation.

These "parts" are interdependent. Just imagine how difficult it would be to make political decisions about "who gets what, when, how" if any one of these elements were missing!

Environments: Everything else! Something is either part of the government or it is in the government's environment. The U.S. government, as does every government, has two major environments:

 (1) a domestic environment: the people and events in the United States that are related to (affect and are affected by) the government;

 (2) an international environment: the people and events in another country(ies) that are related to (affect and are affected by) the United States government.

The close relationship between a government and its environment[s] is sometimes illustrated in a figure that looks like "The Political System" on the following page.

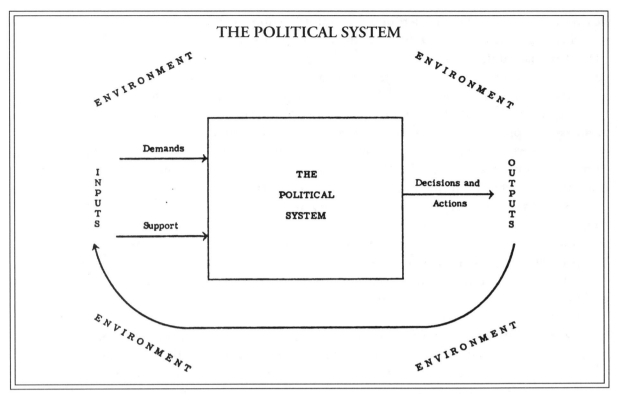

THE POLITICAL SYSTEM

Source: David Easton, *A Framework for Political Analysis* (Chicago: The University of Chicago Press, 1965), p. 112.

Consider where in this diagram a class of American government students would be found. Most of them are probably located out in the environment, more specifically, in the U.S. domestic environment. If some of them feel strongly enough about a given political issue such as health care, women's rights, or welfare, they might decide to express their opinions and to request that government take some action. That may be done by faxing a letter to Congress, by voting on election day for new representatives with different and more compatible points of view, by joining with others in a protest march, or in a myriad of other ways.

In systems analytic terms the requests made to government by those American government students (and others in the environment) are called **demands**. Demands are one type of **input** (information that comes from the environment and goes into the government). As the diagram shows, there is another type of input called **support**. Support reflects the degree of satisfaction or dissatisfaction with how the government responds to demands. For instance, if Congress passes a health-care bill that many citizens approve of, that would probably be reflected in an increased level of support for the government. If, on the other hand, they find a Supreme Court decision on affirmative action or on abortion undesirable, that might be reflected in a withdrawal of support. A government that experiences the withdrawal of support from large numbers of its citizens, as the United States did during the Vietnam War in the 1960s, may be in serious trouble.

Laws, executive orders, judicial decisions, bureaucratic rules and regulations—everything that comes from the government and goes out into the environment—are called **outputs**. These outputs, or governmental decisions, may then have an **impact** on the individuals out in the domestic environment. Some of the readers of this text, for example, might have been among the numerous students that felt the impact of the government's decision in many states to cut back the availability of student loans during the past few years. If the response to this impact will be to cast a vote in the next election against the office holders who advocated the financial cutbacks, or to join with the thousands of students who have already protested in their state capitals, they will be giving or "feeding" new information (called **feedback**) to the government in the form of new inputs (demands and support). The hope is that government will respond with different outputs to which students would be likely to react with new inputs and to which government would respond with different outputs and so on. This never-ending cycle of government converting inputs into outputs, through what is simply referred to as the **conversion process**, is the overall view of how politics works in the United States (and in every other country as well). It is a view of the "whole elephant."

Systems analysis was first used in the physical sciences and was introduced in the discipline of political science by a series of works written during the 1950s and 60s by one of its most respected theorists, David Easton.[7] In the second of these works, *A Framework for Political Analysis*, Easton explains the utility of the systems approach. It, he states,

> is a way of unveiling the basic processes through which a political system, regardless of its generic or specific type ["democratic, dictatorial, bureaucratic, traditional, imperial or otherwise"], is able to persist as a system of behavior in a world either of stability or of change.[8]

What Easton is saying is that by introducing systems analysis to political scientists he has given them an approach, the only approach to date, which explains how politics (who gets what, when, how; or, the authoritative allocations of values) works anywhere and at any time. In other words, inputs are converted into outputs by all governments. Those which can not or do not meet the demands of their citizens are probably doomed while those governments that are successfully carrying out the conversion process are more likely to persist.

The U.S. government has, with one notable exception, the Civil War era, always been able to meet the demands of enough of its citizens to insure its continuity. Systems analysis, a macro approach to politics, clearly shows us that.

CONCLUSION

The importance for the consumer of every academic text, every television and radio news report, news magazine, newspaper, and academic journal to critique, evaluate, and question how the information being communicated was acquired and to accept or reject it on that basis was made at the start of this chapter. The authors of this text would now like to reaffirm that conviction and to ask readers to keep just four general points in mind as they move on to examine the subsequent chapters in this book.

1. There are many approaches (traditional and behavioral, macro and micro) and many methods and techniques (empirical and non-empirical) that can be used to investigate American government.

2. It is preferable, when possible, for a researcher to use the scientific method, which is to empirically (objectively and systemically) examine American government using reliable and valid techniques.

3. The approach or way of looking at U.S. politics that is selected limits what the investigator finds and reports. Systems analysis is an approach that can yield information about various types of inputs but little, if any, data about how decisions are reached. The game theory approach gives some insight into the decision-making process but does not explain much about demands or supports.

4. While cynicism for the sake of being a cynic is not a particularly attractive quality, it is okay not only to question how political data or information is acquired but to accept or reject it on that basis. In fact, it is more than okay; it is expected. It is expected that as an educated citizen, the first reaction to all of what is read about American government, and seen and heard about it on the media and from friends and acquaintances (including instructors), is to ask "HOW DO THEY KNOW?" At the very least if this question is asked, the readers of this text are not likely to find themselves panicking in the streets of their hometowns because of a reported invasion by Martians!

CHAPTER NOTES

[1]All the data on the broadcast of "Invasion From Mars," the responses to it by the audience, the coverage by the news media, and the subsequent analysis of the events are taken from Howard Koch, *The Panic Broadcast: Portrait of an Event* (Boston: Little, Brown and Company, 1970).

[2]William Safire, "Grading the Speech," *The New York Times*, 24 January 1985, 25(A).

[3]Dava Sobel, "Language Patterns Reveal Problems in Personality," *The New York Times*, 27 November 1981, 1(C).

[4]Ibid.

[5]Daniel Goleman, "For Presidential Candidates, Optimism Appears a Winner," *The New York Times*, 8 May 1988, 1(A). The procedures used in the study are elaborated upon in this article; *The New York Times*, "Now That It's Over," 21 November 1988.

[6]T. C. Schelling, "What is Game Theory?" in *Contemporary Political Analysis*, ed. James C. Charlesworth (New York: The Free Press, 1967) 212. Thomas Schelling, an economist at the University of Maryland, is considered to be one of the founders of applied game theory.

[7]David Easton introduced systems theory in three works: *The Political System: An Inquiry into the State of Political Science* (New York: Alfred A. Knopf, 1953); *A Framework for Political Analysis*, (Chicago: The University of Chicago Press, 1965); *A Systems Analysis of Political Life* (Chicago: The University of Chicago Press, 1965). See also Easton's, "An Approach to the Analysis of Political Systems," *World Politics* 9 (1957): 383-400.

[8]Easton, *A Framework for Political Analysis*, Preface, xiv.

SUGGESTED READINGS

Crick, Bernard. *The American Science of Politics: Its Origins and Conditions.* Berkeley, CA: University of California Press, 1964.

Easton, David, John G. Gunnell, and Luigi Graziano, eds. *The Development of Political Science: A Comparative Survey.* New York: Routledge, 1991.

Katznelson, Ira and Helen Milner, eds. *Political Science: The State of the Discipline III.* Washington, D.C.: The American Political Science Association, 2002.

Hoover, Kenneth R. *The Elements of Social Scientific Thinking.* 7th ed. New York: Bedford/St. Martin's, 2001.

Chapter One

THE LANGUAGE OF
POLITICAL SCIENCE

> The irresponsible use of language leads to the destruction of the social, moral, and political structure that is our society, our culture, our nation.
>
> William Lutz[1]

A glossary is generally found in the back of a volume or at the end of a chapter. This placement is a convenient one both for knowledgeable readers who are already somewhat familiar with the subject of the text, and the language or specific terms used in it, and also for casual readers who may not need to have more than a general understanding of the material or the vocabulary. However, for college students who are beginning their formal study of a field, such as American government, it is logical to discuss at least some of the key terminology that will be used repeatedly throughout the text at the beginning.

The logic of this arrangement is probably very clear to any individual who has had the unsettling experience of attending a lecture or reading an article in which some of the terms used by the speaker or writer were not understood. In such cases the spoken or written words may have seemed to be nothing more than meaningless babble. Those, for example, who are unfamiliar with expressions such as a "popped-up bunt attempt" or a "power-play rebound" or a "360-degree spin move on a driving layup" or a "birdie putt from a tough lie" would probably find much of the Sports Section of a daily newspaper rough going. And how much more confusing it would be for those without the appropriate vocabulary to comprehend the following statement, written by a professor of English, which appeared in an academic journal.

Quintilian's uncertainty whether irony is included in allegory turns on whether antiphrasis is a sport of irony or its radical essence. If antiphrasis is irony's essence, then all forms of irony must threaten from their place on the inside of allegory the existence of what allegory cannot help affirming . . . the logocentric plurality of its meanings, grounded in the material unity of its signs—in a word, polysemy.[2]

The subject of inquiry for political scientists is, of course, politics. But just like their counterparts who write about "sports" or about "irony," they too have a unique language—one that may seem to be incomprehensible until it is learned. Until that language is learned, political dialogue or discourse between individuals is often quite difficult.

Complicating the matter of political discourse still further is the often highly subjective and emotional nature of much of what is discussed. Questions such as whether Republicans or Democrats make the best presidents and issues such as whether federal funds should be used for the development of military weapons or should be earmarked for social programs, including welfare and education, have sometimes brought those engaged in conversations about these matters almost to the point of physical combat.

There are, however, no absolute political "truths," and hence there is neither a "right" or a "wrong" response to such questions, nor a "good" or a "bad" side to take on such issues. And so, in the absence of universal political verities, it is not surprising that passionate feelings are aroused and that people—as was discussed in the introductory chapter of this text—rely heavily on myths, superstitions, hunches, intuition, stereotypes, and unverified beliefs to support those feelings. Perhaps this is why conventional wisdom has it that, as happens in the case of religion, which is largely based on faith, it is sometimes best to avoid talking about politics in polite company.

Nonetheless, in the "real," as well as in the academic, world it is frequently difficult, if not impossible, to avoid political discourse. And because it is, every attempt should be made to both use empirical data whenever feasible (See introductory chapter.) and to keep the language used in the discussion as clear and as precise as possible.

EVOLUTION, CONCEPTS, THEORIES, AND DEFINITIONS

Evolution

All political constructs occur within a particular time, place, and culture. Time, place, and culture, then, comprise the "context" within which political concepts, theories, and definitions emerge. It is important for students of politics to be aware of this for as time, place, and culture change so do political constructs. Political phenomena, for example, have been the subject of speculation and investigation in both the Eastern and the Western worlds for thousands of years. The very different nature of experiences in these two ancient worlds eventually led to two very different political traditions.

The roots of American political thought are found within the Western tradition and culture and are generally traced back in time and space to ancient Greece (c. 500 B.C.E.). Two of the early political philosophers from this era who wrote about and who influenced Western ideas about the nature of government were Plato and Aristotle. Plato (417-347 B.C.E.,) in his major work, *The Republic*, discussed the attributes of an ideal or utopian government (which is the "republic" referred to in the title) while his student Aristotle (384-322 B.C.E.) described existing or actual governments in *The Politics*. Interestingly, neither of these great thinkers, who started what is sometimes referred to by current philosophers as "The Great Conversation," formally defined the term government.

Over the subsequent twenty-five hundred years many scholars, all viewing and writing about the political world from the unique perspective determined by their particular era, place, and culture, entered into this Conversation. As they did, the language of politics, which includes its concepts and theories as well as the definitions of its terms, gradually evolved, developed, and became much more precise.

Concepts

Concepts are simply the words or names used to symbolize or represent ideas. "Warmth," to use a nonpolitical example, is simply the concept or the name given to, among other things, the feeling or experience of the sun on the skin.

Among some of the more frequently used concepts in the field of American government are: government, politics, democracy, and power. Concepts such as these are sometimes referred to as the building blocks of political science because they are the components that are used to construct theories.

Theories

Theories are the attempts made to explain, rather than just name, political phenomena. Using the concept of democracy as a starting point, for instance, an investigator might try to find out why some countries are democratic and some are not or why some democracies are stable or long-lasting and others are unstable. In the process of trying to understand and explain the conditions that are conducive to or promote the democratic process, the researcher is developing a theory of democracy. However, without first defining the concept "democracy," the effort to explain it or to theorize about it would be an exercise in futility.

Definitions

There are different types of definitions. For the most part political scientists use **nominal definitions**, "which indicate how a concept is to be used. In other words, we specify that for our purposes something is this and not that." Democracy, for instance, is according to some "rule by the people" and not "rule for the people."[3] (See "What Constitutes a Democracy is Subjective" p. 28.)

Such definitions do not claim to describe all of a concept's important qualities. There is often much disagreement among experts on precisely what those qualities are and, for that reason, there are frequently many definitions of the same concept. Since concepts are used in constructing theories, it follows that there are often also many competing theories or different explanations for the same political phenomena.

Some of the definitional and theoretical disagreements will become rather evident as a sample of the more frequently used political terms, including the concepts of "politics," "political science," "government," "American government," "democracy," "power," "authority," and "legitimacy," are discussed in the remainder of this chapter.

AMERICAN GOVERNMENT TERMINOLOGY

Politics

Politics is one of those concepts about which there is some disagreement. Although most of the hundreds of definitions of the term do acknowledge that "**governmental decision-making**" is the essence of the concept of politics, some of those definitions stress the importance of the people who make the decisions while others focus on the people who are the recipients of the decisions made. A look at two of the most widely used definitions, Harold D. Lasswell's and David Easton's, reflect these different perspectives.

"WHAT CONSTITUTES A DEMOCRACY IS SUBJECTIVE"

It was a grand pronouncement tucked into a long inaugural speech, the kind of sweeping statement that most people lump with the likes of "The Internet is expanding by leaps and bounds."

But when President Clinton declared that, "And for the first time in all of history, more people on this planet live under democracy than dictatorship," it begged the question: Is that right? And if so, well, just how many people are free?

The answer, according to a very rough estimate by *The New York Times*, is yes, Mr. Clinton is correct. According to 1996 United Nations population data, an estimated 3.1 billion people live in democracies, and 2.66 billion do not. This is a margin of 53.82 percent to 46.18 percent, a difference of 7.6 percentage points, or nearly the same as that of Mr. Clinton's popular vote count over Bob Dole, his Republican challenger.

The biggest democracies are India, with 944.58 million people, and the United States, with 269.44 million. On the flip side are China, with 1.232 billion, and Indonesia, with 200.453 million.

Of course, deciding what constitutes a democracy is subjective. Do you include countries in which voting irregularities are common? Do you exclude places like Pakistan, Bangladesh and Kenya that ambassadors would likely call democracies? (We did, but this is not scientific.)

The reason Mr. Clinton even mentioned this, presumably, is that the pendulum has swung sharply in favor of the democratic nations in the last few years, due largely to the 280 million people in the nations that comprised the Soviet Union. Then again, the numbers are always subject to a coup here or a pro-democracy outbreak there.

One thing that is certain in this first year of Mr. Clinton's second term, though, is that the pro-democracy population will slip a fraction on July 1 [1997.] That is when Hong Kong, population 6.2 million, reverts to China from Britain.

Source: David W. Chen, "The Numbers Favor Those Living in Democracies," *The New York Times*, 21 January 1997, 14 (A).

Lasswell's Definition

In 1936 Lasswell's book, *Politics: Who Gets What, When, How,* was published.[4] The catchy sounding second part of the title, "who gets, what, when, how," soon became one of the most frequently used responses to the question "what is politics?" For Lasswell, whose definition focuses on the recipients, those who have the most (the elite) get the most of what government has to give: the most "deference," the most "income," and the most "safety."[5]

Easton's Definition

Easton has defined politics as "the authoritative allocation of values for a society."[6] This definition, just as Lasswell's, refers to the object of political decisions, which is the "society." However, unlike Lasswell's, Easton's definition places an emphasis on the idea that the things that the individuals in a society want or "value" are "allocated" (distributed) by those with authority. In most instances, the authority to make decisions or allocate values for an entire society resides with government.

An examination of some of the major issues debated during the 2004 presidential election reveals what it is that the American people have considered to be of value in recent times. Among these are: security, lower taxes, protection of Social Security benefits, improved education, health care, a reduction in crime, and a clean environment.

The two candidates, George W. Bush and John Kerry, disagreed not about what the values were but to whom they were to be allocated. The positions they took about taxes clearly show this. Bush proposed a permanent tax cut to those who earn $200,000 or more a year while the Kerry proposal called for a rollback on tax cuts for the wealthy.

Whether the executive branch is headed by Bush or Kerry or by any other individual does not alter the fact that in the United States the "government" authoritatively allocates values for the entire society; it determines who gets what, when, how. Both Lasswell's and Easton's definitions accurately convey the essence of the concept of politics.

Political Science

Political science is the academic discipline or body of knowledge that is devoted to the study of politics ("who gets what" or the authoritative allocation of values"). It is classified, as are the disciplines of history, sociology, social psychology, economics, geography, and anthropology, as a "social" science. The social sciences share a common focus—a focus on human behavior—and for that reason they are sometimes referred to as "behavioral sciences."

Because they have a common subject, there is a lot of overlap in the material they examine. In fact, before political science emerged as a separate and distinct area of study, which was around the turn of the twentieth century, the study of politics was incorporated into the disciplines of sociology, economics, law, religion, and, particularly, history. Currently, however, each one of the social or behavioral sciences places its primary focus on a different aspect of human behavior, and for political science the emphasis is obviously on political conduct (everything related to the authoritative allocation of values).

It does not necessarily follow that because its focus is directed only to the subject of politics that the scope (fields and subjects) of political science is limited. Actually, as the number of fields of specialization enumerated in the list prepared by the American Political Science Association (APSA) in 1983 shows [See "APSA Fields of Specialization" p. 31.], the scope is actually rather extensive. However, it is also true that students who major in political science in the United States generally select their courses from approximately five to eight principal fields. Among these are:

1. Comparative Government/Politics
2. International Relations/Politics
3. Political Philosophy/Theory
4. Public Administration
5. American Government

Of these, this text introduces the reader to the fifth field on the list, American Government.

Government/American Government

If politics is defined as "who gets what, when, how" then **government** can be described as the people and the institutions who decide who gets what or, in Eastonian terms, as the people and institutions who authoritatively allocate values. American government then refers to the people and institutions that allocate or make political decisions for the inhabitants of the United States.

Political Institutions

Among the political institutions that allocate values in the U.S. are the:

a. Congress   b. presidency
c. courts   d. bureaucracy

Political parties, the media, elites, interest groups and their lobbyists, and big businesses and corporations and their Political Action Committees (PACs) are also, as will be described in later chapters, institutions that play a significant role in the process of determining who gets what.

The "People"

The people who allocate values occupy positions in these institutions. Their titles may vary depending upon the level of government (national, state, or local government) for which they work. So, for instance, the president is the chief decision maker in the executive branch of government at the national level; the governor is responsible for allocating values in the executive branch at the state level; and mayors, who are among the many executives at the local level (cities, counties, school districts, and special districts) of government, are among those who decide who gets what in sub-state communities.

At each of these different levels, the "**regime**" or the "way of governing" is essentially democratic, which is to say that while there are different types of regimes including communism, socialism, and fascism, the people and institutions that allocate values in the United States are expected to do so according to the principles of democracy.

APSA FIELDS OF SPECIALIZATION

Foreign and Cross-national Politics
1. Latin America
2. Western Europe
3. Eastern Europe
4. Russia
5. North Africa and Middle East
6. Sub-Sahara Africa
7. Southeast Asia
8. China
9. Far East
10. Other (specify)

Methodology
1. Computer techniques
2. Content analysis
3. Epistemology & philosophy of science
4. Experimental design
5. Field data collection
6. Measurement & index construction
7. Model building
8. Statistical analysis
9. Survey design and analysis
10. Other (specify)

Political Stability, Instability, and Change
1. Cultural modification & diffusion
2. Personality and motivation
3. Political leadership & recruitment
4. Political socialization
5. Revolution and violence
6. Schools of political education

Public Administration
1. Bureaucracy
2. Comparative administration
3. Organization & management analysis
4. Organization theory & behavior
5. Personnel administration
6. Planning, programming, & budgeting
7. Politics and administration
8. Systems analysis
9. Other (specify)

International Law, Organization, and Politics
1. Analyses of particular systems or sub-systems
2. Decision-making processes
3. Elites and their oppositions
4. Mass participation & communications
5. Parties, movements, & secondary associations
6. Political development & modernization
7. Politics of planning
8. Values, ideologies, belief systems, & culture
9. International law
10. International organization and administration
11. International politics
12. Other (specify)

Political Theory
1. Systems of political ideas in history
2. Ideological systems
3. Political philosophy (general)
4. Methodological & analytic systems
5. Other (specify)

Public Policy: Formation and Content
1. Policy theory
2. Policy measurement
3. Economic policy and regulation
4. Science and technology
5. Natural resources & environment
6. Education
7. Poverty and welfare
8. Foreign and military policy
9. Other substantive areas (specify)

U. S. Political Institutions, Processes, and Behavior
1. Courts and judicial behavior
2. Elections and voting behavior
3. Ethnic politics
4. Executives
5. Interest groups
6. Intergovernmental relations
7. Legislatures
8. Political & constitutional history
9. Political parties
10. Public law
11. Public opinion
12. State, local & metropolitan government
13. Urban politics
14. Other (specify)

Democracy

Although the term democracy was coined by the historian Herodotus in ancient Greece, it took, according to political scientist James David Barber, over two thousand years for a democratic government to come into existence. That government, he says, was in the United States—"the world's first true democracy."[7]

Perhaps it took so long because maintaining a democratic regime requires considerable effort and vigilance. At a minimum it entails following three basic principles or "essentials": (a) holding regular elections; (b) creating a constitution; and (c) protecting citizens' rights. As Barber explains,

a. Democracy is a **national government elected by the people**.

The chief executive and the legislature make the rules of the nation, but the citizens decide, through elections, who will be the chief executive and who will serve in the legislature. Those elections must be clear-cut, regular, and honest. When people vote for different candidates, the candidates who get the most votes must win the positions. The citizens need to know how to predict how the different candidates will operate once in office, so knowledge of candidates' political positions is essential. Thus democracy depends on citizens freely and knowledgeably selecting political governors who recognize that their power derives from popular election and may be removed in the next popular election.

b. Democracy requires a **constitution**.

The legislature makes laws, but the constitution is the law above all laws. Established at the birth of democracy, it sets forth procedures: how elections will be conducted and how the government must act. The constitution must be known to the public and truly implemented—not just asserted. The constitution can be changed, but only by a difficult procedure requiring far more discussion and votes than ordinary laws.

c. Democracy requires **human rights**.

The main constitution establishes rules of procedure, but a bill of rights gives the fundamental rights of the people, typically including freedom of religion, speech, and the press; the right of assembly; and equality of all citizens under the law. For example, the bill of rights should protect individuals from arrest and imprisonment because of their political beliefs. These rights are original and should be subject to change only by the same difficult procedure for changing the constitution.[8]

Besides adhering to these three principles, Barber continues, a democratic government **must** also control police and military violence; provide freedom, equality, and justice under law; and promote a knowledgeable citizenry that participates in "frequent public discourse."[9]

There is, of course, no guarantee that because the United States was the first country to meet all of these criteria or because it has continued to meet them for over two hundred years, that it will always do so. The fate of American democracy, in both its "direct" and "indirect" forms is, in short, dependent upon the will of an educated public to maintain it.

Direct and Indirect Democracy

As indicated earlier in this chapter, the term democracy, as it is translated from the original Greek, means government, or rule, by the people. In a **direct democracy**, or as it is sometimes referred to a **participatory democracy**, such as that which existed in ancient Athens, that definition is taken literally—the people (those who meet established criteria such as age, citizenship, etc.) actually make decisions about who gets what or allocate values for themselves.

Such an arrangement works well when the decisions to be made are for relatively small geographic areas, such as a Greek city-state, or more currently, in a Swiss canton or an American town or village. This is because the smallness makes it possible for the resident voters of the community to get together to discuss, debate, and decide.

Direct democracy is also practiced in some U. S. states, which are considerably larger in size, through such processes as the:

a) direct initiative: registered voters, by following specified state procedures, may propose new legislation or an amendment to the state constitution
b) recall: registered voters, by following specified state procedures, may vote to remove an official during his/her term of office
c) popular referendum: registered voters may vote their approval or disapproval of existing, or proposed, legislation or constitutional changes

It is important to note, however, that at present not every state has provisions for these three processes. Furthermore, the Constitution of the United States makes no provision for the referendum, initiative, or recall at the national level of government.

It is unlikely that the framers of the Constitution, who had little faith in the people's ability to make rational decisions, would have provided for direct democracy even if the technology to do so had existed in the eighteenth century. What they devised instead was a plan where citizens elect representatives, representatives make political decisions for the people, and the citizens control their representatives through regularly scheduled elections. A country that adheres to this system of **indirect rule** by the people is called a **representative democracy** or more simply a **republic**.

Identifying a country as a democracy, either direct or indirect, is to locate it on a linear representation often referred to as the "political spectrum."

The Political Spectrum

As explained by James B. Whisker, the editor of a dictionary of American political concepts, "the **political spectrum** is often divided into right, center, and left."[10] Those on the **political right**, which according to Whisker include "those who tend toward **conservatism** or other protectionist or reactionary political ideas" generally are predisposed in varying degrees, to accept ideas of nationalism and traditionalism. The past is a general guide to present and future action and change is generally destructive of the political system in rightist views. On the far end of the rightist side of the political spectrum are fascism and nazism. In Europe rightists may support the restoration of traditional monarchies.[11]

Those on the **political left**, which as Whisker points out include liberals, socialists, communists, and radicals, hold

> in varying degrees, to ideas of change and alteration in the political system. They generally favor, or pretend to favor, mass democracy and popular sovereignty. In Europe, the distinction is seen more clearly than in America. One might not speak of a "liberal" as a "leftist" here so frequently as one might in Europe.[12]

It is quite useful to place political parties along the linear spectrum described by Whisker especially if the reason for doing so is to make comparisons between and among the parties of different countries. Using the scale, for example, Whisker is able to communicate the idea that "Continental European parties tend more toward political extremes whereas American parties tend toward the political center."[13]

While American political parties and their members do tend toward the political center, there are both parties and people in the United States to be found at virtually each of the degrees along the spectrum. Furthermore, there are individuals who hold conservative views on some policy issues and take a liberal position on still others. Classifying or labeling an individual then is no easy matter. (See, "Who's A Liberal!" p. 36.) It may, therefore, be useful to think of the left and right positions not as isolated and rigid but as related and flexible categories. The following spectrum, a slight variation on the traditional left-center-right scale, is useful for examining and thinking about the relational ties that often exist.

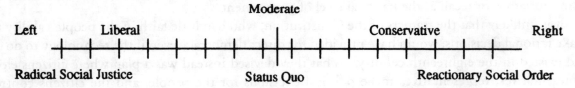

The "**status quo**" position on the scale refers simply to what the official governmental policy on any issue, such as health care, is at a given time. Health-care policy and hence the status quo may vary from country to country; Canada, for instance, currently has a national health-care system and the United States does not. And a policy may vary within a country over time; to say that the United States does not now have a national health-care system is not to say that it never will.

Political parties and individuals who are presently satisfied with the health-care policy of their country are situated squarely on the status quo line. Those that want to alter the policy would be located to the right of that line if they prefer a pre-existing or more conservative policy than that of the current one and to the left of that line if they prefer a more innovative or liberal policy. The degree to which an individual is placed to the right or the left of the status quo line is determined by the **intensity** (how strongly the change is wanted) and the **preferred speed** (how fast or slow the change is wanted) of the desired policy change. The further away from the status quo line, in either direction, that a person or party is located is also determined by the amount of change that is desired and the amount of resources, such as time and money, willing to be invested to cause that change.

The two amounts are usually highly correlated. Those individuals who are located at the extreme ends of the spectrum and who wish to drastically alter the status quo may, for example, even be willing to invest or sacrifice their lives to promote their causes (social justice, or political and economic equality, to the left of the spectrum and social order, or the adherence to traditional values and laws, to the right of the spectrum) and to bring about political change. However, in the U.S., as indicated earlier, the majority of people are not extremists. Today Americans, for the most part, neither desire profound changes in existing policies nor wish to invest very much time in facilitating those changes that they may want. As a consequence, policies do not tend to change dramatically in the United States.

That has not always been the case. It is an interesting mental exercise to look back in time to the founding of this country and to think about where on the political spectrum John Adams, John Hancock, Benjamin Franklin, Thomas Jefferson, and the other signers of the Declaration of Independence would have been placed in 1776 and where they would be placed today. A consideration of how yesterday's revolutionaries have become today's heroes might serve to both dispute stereotypical notions of extremism and to illustrate the importance of knowing the time, the place, and the cultural context within which political terms such as liberal, conservative, radical, and reactionary are used.

Power

It is frequently observed that the United States is the most "powerful" country in the world and that the president is the most "powerful" leader in both the domestic and international arenas. Such an observation implies that both the U. S. and the president are powerful because they are likely to get whatever it is they desire or want from another or others. It implies that the United States uses its great wealth and military strength to get what it wants from other countries and that the president uses the status of his office, his personal magnetism, and/or the force of the Constitution, among other things, to get his constituents, the Congress, and other world leaders to go along with his proposals.

These common-sense notions of power are actually pretty good descriptions of the term and are very much in keeping with the more formal definition proffered by the noted logician and moral philosopher Bertrand Russell. According to Russell, **power** is "the production of intended effects."[14] A country (or an individual), in other words, has power if it can get or "produce" what it wants or "intends" to get from another country (or another person).

As Russell goes on to explain, producing the intended effects usually involves the promise of rewards (such as economic, military, or humanitarian aid) or the threat of penalties (such as a trade embargo or a military action)—which he calls "sanctions." Clearly the more sanctions a country has at its disposal, the more powerful it is, and the more likely it is to get what it wants. Power, in short, is distinguished by the following qualities:

Who's a Liberal! Is Clinton One? Was Nixon?

How do you stump a liberal? Ask him or her whether President Clinton is one. The response will be momentary bewilderment and often a stammer, but almost never a definitive "yes."

"It's in the eye of the beholder, but I think he's a pragmatic progressive," said Michael S. Dukakis, the 1988 Democratic Presidential nominee who proclaimed his liberalism on the eve of that election—and lost.

"He's neither liberal or conservative—he is a progressive," agreed Harold M. Ickes, a deputy White House chief of staff and the most devoted liberal in Mr. Clinton's inner circle.

"We would have an internal debate about that question, especially after his decision to sign the welfare bill," said Robert J. Carolla, communications director of Americans for Democratic Action, the nation's oldest liberal organization....

Given [his] record, calling Mr. Clinton a liberal these days could be likened to calling Richard M. Nixon a liberal: a case can be made, but it does not easily stick. Despite his reputation as the hard-edged partisan who tried to weed out Communists, Mr. Nixon proposed universal health coverage and a guaranteed minimum income for all Americans, and he created the Environmental Protection Agency.

"If you peeled away Nixon's paranoia, basically I'd say they're not so far apart," Walter Dean Burnham, a professor of government at the University of Texas at Austin, said of Mr. Clinton and Mr. Nixon. As for Mr. Clinton, he said, "He's an Eisenhower Republican, brought up to date, of course."

Source: Richard L. Berke, "Who's a Liberal! Is Clinton One? Was Nixon?" *The New York Times*, 29 September 1996, Section 4, 1 (E) and 5 (E).

• **It is a relationship.** To exercise power there must be at least two people or two countries, one of which gets what is desired from the other. Power would be a meaningless concept in a world inhabited by only one individual or in which there was only one country. Clearly it would be foolish to call the U.S. powerful if there were no other country from which it could extract what it wanted. Power then is a relationship that exists between two or more entities.

• **It is predictable.** Because the **power base** or assets (wealth, a large military, abundant natural resources, status, etc.) possessed by one of the individuals or countries in a relationship are greater than that of the other, it can be predicted, with a "reasonable" degree of accuracy, that the one that has the most assets to use as sanctions (rewards/penalties) will be successful in producing the intended effects. However, as the Vietnam conflict, in which the United States did not succeed in stopping Hanoi from uniting its country under Communist rule, demonstrated—there are no guarantees. Power does not always ensure victory.

• **It costs.** Conflicts, such as that between the U.S. and North Vietnam, reveal another facet of power—that it "costs." In a military confrontation its costs may include the expenditure of money, raising taxes, the time and energy of political leaders, the loss of citizens' lives and possibly—as it did the U.S. in the case of Vietnam—public support for the government. There is little doubt that President Lyndon Johnson's decision not to run for re-election in 1968 was largely based on the calculation that he had lost so much support that he could not win. As one of his biographers concluded

> forced to confront a precipitous drop in his public standing, a sharp shift in editorial reaction, and the loss of support from key-interest-group leaders, Johnson finally accepted the fact that he was in a situation he could no longer control and that further escalation would produce only more uncontrollability. Faced at the same time with loss of love and gratitude on what seemed an irretrievable scale, Johnson had no choice but to withdraw.[15]

All in all it appears that in the case of Vietnam, the cost of exercising power was very high. Some have argued that it was too high.

• **It is sometimes exercised by the people.** The "vote," as was just discussed, is clearly one of the most important assets that citizens possess for use as a sanction. It can be used as a reward when it is given to a candidate or as a penalty when it is withheld. This sanction is a major component of the power base of the American people.

The notion that power resides with the people or, more precisely, with the majority of the people is referred to as the "majoritarian theory" of democracy. This theory is one of three popular theories of who holds "**actual**"—or largely nonelected—as opposed to "**formal**"—or governmental—power in a democratic country such as the United States. The other two power theories are the "group" and the "elite" theories.

Group Theories

Arthur F. Bentley, one of the earliest group theorists and author of the classic study on the subject, *The Process of Government* (1908), set forth the basic argument in support of actual power residing with groups. It is theorized that

• the United States is a pluralist country, that is a country that consists of many different or diverse populations
• the numerous religious, ethnic, racial, occupational, and cultural differences lead to the formation of organized groups
• some of the groups are considered to be "political" in that they compete with one another in an attempt to get whatever it is that they want from the government
• the government provides multiple access points for the groups to participate in policy making
• policies benefiting the general public are made through compromise and coalition building.

Some interest groups, including the tech companies that are discussed in Chapter 8, are so well organized and so wealthy that they have successfully pressured presidents, legislators, judges, bureaucrats, and other officials to shape governmental policies and to pass and enforce laws that suit their needs. These interest groups, then, according to group theorists, wield immense political power.

Some reject the optimistic vision of what has become known as the **pluralist theory**. Like Theodore Lowi, they argue that pluralism is out of control, that groups have become so powerful they can effectively dominate policy. This leads, according to these theorists, to **hyperpluralism** with conflicting sets of policies, stalemate, and gridlock.

Elite Theory

Those who have the **most** of whatever is valued in a society (wealth, education, power, etc.) are called the **elite**. By definition then an elite consists of relatively few individuals as compared with the large memberships found in the powerful interest groups. Thomas Dye has calculated that America's national elite consists of individuals in just over 7,300 corporate, public interest, and governmental positions and adds

> these top positions, taken collectively, control almost three quarters of the nation's industrial assets; one half of all assets in communication and utilities; over one half of all U.S. banking assets; over three quarters of all insurance assets; and they direct Wall Street's largest investment firms. They control the television networks, the influential news agencies, and the major newspaper chains. They control nearly 40 percent of all the assets of private foundations and two thirds of all private university endowments. They direct the nation's largest and best-known New York and Washington law firms as well as the nation's major civic and cultural organizations. They occupy key federal governmental positions in the executive, legislative, and judicial branches. And they occupy all the top command positions in the Army, Navy, Air Force and Marines.[16]

Dye naturally concludes, that these figures "are important indicators of the concentration of authority and control in American society."[17]

The three theories (majoritarian, group, and elite) briefly described above are competing theories. That means if one theory accurately describes the power reality in the U.S. then the other two can not. Which then provides the most accurate description? Unfortunately there is no definitive answer to that question. Scholars simply do not agree. However two observations can be made: (1) of these three contending theories, scholars generally adhere to either the group or the elite explanations of power and (2) while sociologists generally favor the elite theory, political scientists tend to support the group theory.

Authority and Legitimacy

Authority is a form of power. It is, more precisely, **"legitimate"** or **accepted** power. Although power, by definition, requires the promise or the threat of sanctions, it does not necessarily follow that those sanctions must be used to produce the intended effects.

When, for example, the government wants to conserve fuel or decrease traffic fatalities and attempts to do so by reducing highway speed limits, or when it raises taxes, or when it calls on Americans to fight in a war, voluntary citizen compliance indicates that the government has au-

"THE GOVERNMENT'S DOUBLESPEAK OF WAR"

In war the first casualty is language. And with the language goes the truth. It was the Vietnam "conflict," not the Vietnam War. It was the Korean "police action," not the Korean War....

The doublespeak of war consists, as Orwell wrote of all such language, 'of euphemism, question-begging, and sheer cloudy vagueness.' It is, fundamentally, the language of insincerity, where there is a gap between the speaker's real and declared aims. It is language as an instrument for concealing and preventing thought, not for expressing or extending thought. Such language silences dialogue and blocks communication.

During the Vietnam 'conflict' we learned that mercenaries paid by the U.S. government were 'civilian irregular defense soldiers,' refugees fleeing the war were 'ambient noncombatant personnel,' and enemy troops who survived bombing attacks were 'interdictional nonsuccumbers.' In Vietnam, American war planes conducted 'limited duration protective reaction strikes' during which they achieved an 'effective delivery of ordnance.' So it went too in the Persian Gulf.

Just as officially there was no war in Korea or Vietnam, so officially there was no war in the Persian Gulf. After all, Congress didn't declare war, it declared an authorization of the 'use of force,' a power clearly delegated to Congress in Article I, Section 8 of the Constitution, which now apparently reads: 'Congress shall have the power to authorize the use of force.' So now we have not war but Operation Desert Storm, or 'exercising the military option,' or, according to President Bush, an 'armed situation.'

During this 'armed situation' massive bombing attacks became 'efforts.' Thousands of war planes didn't drop tons of bombs; 'weapons systems' or 'force packages' 'visited a site.' These 'weapons systems' didn't drop their tons of bombs on buildings and human beings, they 'hit' 'hard' and 'soft targets.' During their 'visits,' these 'weapons systems' 'degraded,' 'attrited,' 'suppressed,' 'eliminated,' 'cleansed,' 'sanitized,' 'impacted,' 'decapitated,' or 'took out' targets, they didn't blow up planes, tanks, trucks, airfields, and the soldiers who were in them, nor did they blow up bridges, roads, factories, and other buildings and the people who happened to be there. A 'healthy day of bombing' was achieved when more enemy 'assets' were destroyed than expected.

If the 'weapons systems' didn't achieve 'effective results' (blow up their targets) during their first 'visit' (bombing attack), as determined by a 'damage assessment study' (figuring out if everything was completely destroyed), the 'weapons systems' will 'revisit the site' (bomb it again). Women, children, or other civilians killed or wounded during these 'visits,' and any schools, hospitals, museums, houses, or other 'nonmilitary' targets that were blown up were 'collateral damage,' which is the undesired damage or casualties produced by the effects from 'incontinent ordnance' or 'accidental delivery or ordnance equipment,' meaning the bombs and rockets that miss their targets.

To function as it should and as we expect it to, language must be an accurate reflection of that which it represents. The doublespeak of war is an instance of thought corrupting language, and language corrupting thought.

Source: Lutz, **The New Doublespeak**, 182-184.

thority. Their compliance does not mean that the people actually like the new legislation. It only indicates that they psychologically accept the right of the government to make such laws and thus no governmental sanctions, no force or physical coercion such as calling out the national guard, actually has to be used. As a popular couplet more succinctly explains the distinction between power and authority:

Power and might, Authority and right

Any government that has to rely on the use of sanctions because its people have not "internalized the social order," that is they do not accept its right to allocate values or to decide who gets what, is in trouble.[18] It is in trouble because its attempts to obtain compliance primarily by power are likely to be very costly and possibly unsustainable. Governmental authority, such as that which has long existed in the United States, hardly costs at all.

CONCLUSION

In an experiment conducted by Dr. J. Scott Armstrong, an actor was coached to deliver what was purported to be a scientific talk entitled "Mathematical Game Theory as Applied to Physician Education" to three separate groups of social workers, psychologists, psychiatrists, educators, and administrators. Far from being scientific, the lecture actually consisted entirely of "double talk, meaningless words, false logic, contradictory statements, irrelevant humor, and meaningless references to unrelated topics."[19] Surprisingly none of the knowledgeable listeners caught on to the hoax. In fact, most of the individuals in the three audiences who later responded to a poll taken by the experimenter went so far as to describe the lecture as being "clear and stimulating."[20]

One conclusion that can be drawn from Armstrong's rather amazing findings is that language can, intentionally or unintentionally, be used to deceive virtually everyone.

Politicians, for instance, seem quite adept at using language to obfuscate or befuddle the thinking of their constituents particularly about what they deem to be unpopular activities such as war and unpopular legislation such as raising taxes. (See, "The Government's Doublespeak of War" p. 39.) For example, rather than risk the wrath of the voters the term "tax increases" is sometimes simply replaced by legislators with such expressions as: "revenue enhancements," "receipts strengthening," "receipts proposals," "passenger facility charges," "user fees" and "wage-based premiums."[21] Students of American government, who have learned the language of politics, will not, however, be easily deceived.

CHAPTER NOTES

[1]William Lutz, *The New Doublespeak: Why No One Knows What Anyone's Saying Anymore* (New York: Harper Collins Publishers, 1996), xi.

[2]Stephen G. Bloom, and James L. Wunsch, "Prof Talk," *The New York Times Magazine*, 25 August 1996, 22.

[3]Alan S. Zuckerman, *Doing Political Science: An Introduction to Political Analysis* (Boulder, Colorado: Westview Press, 1991), 8.

[4]Harold D. Lasswell, *Politics: Who Gets What, When, How* (Cleveland, Ohio: The World Publishing Company, 1958.

[5]Ibid., 13.

[6]David Easton, *The Political System: An Inquiry into the State of Political Science* (New York: Alfred A. Knopf, 1971), 129.

[7]James David Barber, *The Book of Democracy* (Englewood Cliffs, New Jersey: Prentice Hall, Inc., 1995), 2.

[8]Ibid., 3.

[9]Ibid., 4-7.

[10]James B. Whisker, *A Dictionary of Concepts on American Politics* (New York: John Wiley & Sons, 1980), 9.

[11]Ibid., 16.

[12]Ibid., 9-10.

[13]Ibid., 10.

[14]Bertrand Russell, *Power: A New Social Analysis* (New York: W.W. Norton & Company, Inc., 1938), 35.

[15]Doris Kearns, *Lyndon Johnson and the American Dream* (New York: Harper & Row,

[16]Thomas R. Dye, *Who's Running America? The Clinton Years*. 6th ed. (Englewood Cliffs, New Jersey: Prentice Hall, 1995), 11.

[17]Ibid.

[18]Stanley Milgram, *Obedience to Authority: An Experimental View* (New York: Harper & Row, Publishers, 1974), 138.

[19]Malcolm W. Browne, "Wanted: Interpreters for the Frontiers of Science," *The New York Times*, 6 January 1987, 3.

[20]Ibid.

[21]Lutz, 13-14; 154-155; 185.

SUGGESTED READINGS

Elliot, Jeffrey M., and Sheikh R. Ali. *The Presidential-Congressional Political Dictionary*. Santa Barbara, Calif.: ABC-Clio Information Services, 1984.

Erickson, Paul D. *Reagan Speaks: The Making of an American Myth*. New York: New York University Press, 1985.

Hart, Roderick P. *The Sound of Leadership: Presidential Communication in the Modern Age*. Chicago, Ill.: The University of Chicago Press, 1987.

Lutz, William. *Doublespeak: From "Revenue Enhancement" to "Terminal Living": How Government, Business, Advertisers, and Others Use Language to Deceive You*. New York: Harper & Row Publishers, 1989.

Plano, Jack C., and Milton Greenberg. *The American Political Dictionary*. 10th ed. Fort Worth, Texas: Harcourt Brace Jovanovich College Publishers, 1996.

Safire, William. *The New Language of Politics: An Anecdotal Dictionary of Catchwords, Slogans and Political Usage*. New York: Random House, 1968.

Chapter Two

CONSTITUTIONAL BEGINNINGS

ABUSE OF POLITICAL POWER: The Case of England and America

The judgment of whether political power has been abused is a subjective one. For example, citizens today who are told that there will be even a slight increase in their taxes or a minor reduction in their benefits might contend that the government has abused its power. By July 4, 1776, a significant number of American colonists believed that the British government had become so abusive and oppressive that they stated their intent to declare their independence from the British Empire and establish their own sovereign state.

Declaring Independence

Declaring independence from Great Britain was not an easy decision for the colonists and was done only after great deliberation and after they believed they had no other options available to them. The events that led to rebellion were sometimes small and often seemingly unconnected, but each event furthered the breach between the colonies and the mother country.[1] Particularly offensive to the colonists was the ability of Great Britain to tax them without any American representation in Parliament. Direct taxes such as the **Sugar Act** (1764), which taxed molasses and other imported products, the **Stamp Act** (1765), which taxed legal documents and printed material, and the **Townshend Revenue Act** (1767), which contained among other items a resented tax on tea, were viewed as major abuses by the British Crown.

On July 2, 1776, after a year of debating the issue of separation, the Second Continental Congress, which was meeting in Philadelphia to resolve the British question, adopted the "Resolution of Independence." The first draft of the Declaration of Independence, which was already in progress, followed and was passed by the delegates to the Continental Congress two days later. Although we celebrate July 4th as "Independence Day," the final version of the document was not actually accepted by the members of the Congress until the nineteenth of July and was not signed by them until August 2, 1776. The time it took them to reach the decision to separate from England indicates how difficult a decision it was.

It is important to note that the deliberations among the members of the Continental Congress over the issue of independence were often long and heated. The delegates knew if they decided to declare independence from England, they would be committing an act of treason punishable by a gruesome death. Individuals such as Thomas Jefferson, Samuel Adams, John Adams, and John Hancock knew that while they were deliberating the issue of independence, their names had already been placed on a British "hanging" list. This meant that the judgment read to them might someday be the same one read by an English judge in 1775 to some Irish rebels.

> You are to be drawn on hurdles to the place of execution, where you are to be hanged by the neck, but not until you are dead; for, while you are still living your bodies are to be taken down, your bowels torn out and burned before your faces, your heads then cut off, and your bodies divided each into four quarters, and your heads and quarters to be then at the King's disposal.[2]

The Declaration of Independence: An Anatomy

The Declaration of Independence, written primarily by Thomas Jefferson, along with the Constitution and its Bill of Rights are considered America's three "charters of freedom." The contents of the Declaration can be divided into two major sections: the preamble or introduction, which contains a philosophical statement on natural rights, and a listing of twenty-seven specific grievances citing the abuses committed by the King against the American colonies.

Section 1. Introduction

The Americans knew that they were not going to receive economic and military support from foreign powers, or be able to make treaties and enter trade agreements with them, until their independence had been acknowledged and their sovereignty accepted. The Declaration of Independence was primarily an effort to explain to other countries that the reasons for the colonial separation from England were not frivolous. The Declaration outlines the reasons for separation in both pragmatic and philosophical terms.

Section 2. Abuses of Natural Rights by King George III

The second and largest section of the Declaration is composed of a list of the colonists' grievances against the British Crown. This list includes over twenty grievances including refusing assent to

This scene shows Americans' feelings toward taxation.

laws necessary for the public good, repeatedly dissolving Representative Houses, making judges dependent on his will, plundering seas, ravaging coasts, burning towns, and, of course, "imposing taxes" without consent.

At the conclusion of the long list of colonists' grievances, the document goes on to say that repeated attempts, through petitions, warnings, reminders, and appeals, to get Britain to "disavow these Usurpation's" had been unsuccessful. For that reason, there was no other recourse but to "solemnly Publish and Declare, That these United Colonies are, and of Right ought to be, Free and Independent States . . . ."

Significance of the Colonial Experience

In Chapter 4, "Public Opinion, Political Culture, and Political Socialization," the reasons behind Americans' negative attitudes towards authority will be explored. It is possible that the negative attitudes towards political power expressed in today's opinion polls have their roots in eighteenth century America and are expressed in the harsh words used in the Declaration of Independence to describe King George and his policies.

As a result of their experiences with the King, eighteenth century Americans tried through the Articles of Confederation, through the principles adhered to in the Constitution ratified in 1789, and through the inclusion of a Bill of Rights (1791) to control or manage governmental power. Each of these documents reflects the concern that the existence of a strong central government might again lead to tyrannical rule and the necessity to revolt. This concern is reflected in the governing documents left as a legacy from the colonists to the Americans of the twenty-first century.

THE FIRST CONSTITUTION: THE ARTICLES OF CONFEDERATION

What is a Constitution?

A **constitution** is the supreme law of the land. All other acts of governance must fall within its framework. Its major function is to establish the parameters of governmental power. In so doing, it limits the power of government and establishes its boundaries. A constitution, however, is not self-executing. It must be interpreted and administered by those in power. Consequently, a constitution alone cannot guarantee that those in power not abuse their positions, for example, Germany, under Adolph Hitler. However, a constitution, once accepted as legitimate, can act as a powerful mental barrier to those who desire to usurp governmental authority. The more a political culture accepts the legitimacy of a constitution, the more difficult it becomes to undermine its authority. Without a constitution no such barrier exists. Government power without formally established limits is virtually waiting to be usurped.

Framework for Governing

Since its inception, the United States has been governed by two constitutions: The Articles of Confederation and the present Constitution written in 1787. These two documents have in some way framed all political activity since independence.

It is important to examine these documents and the political events that surrounded them and place them within their proper historical perspective. This allows us to examine them in the context in which they were written and devise a framework for contextual awareness. Once accomplished, this will enable us to establish a baseline from which to evaluate current governmental policies and procedures. How does the context of the past impact the policies of the present?

Both documents reflect the prevailing political environment of a distinct period in the history of the United States. Within their historical and cultural framework both documents can be viewed as progressive for their time. However, this may be less true for the United States of the twentieth and twenty-first centuries, for example, both documents were written in what today would be considered sexist and racist language. Within a modern construct, both documents would be considered reactionary. Is it possible that progressive documents written in the past can be responsible for creating and/or sustaining reactionary institutions and/or policies in the future? Should the governing documents stand on their own merit or be placed simply in an historical context? It is often difficult to extract the past from the present because the two are so interrelated. Both documents were creations of their own time, place, and culture, and, as such, it is important to examine "their beginnings." Hidden in the problems and political quagmires that underscored the writing of the two documents are possible answers and insights into modern day America.

Articles of Confederation

The first constitution was the Articles of Confederation, and it lasted less than ten years. However, understanding its underlying philosophy and the reason for its almost inevitable demise provides insight into today's governing structure. Many of the fundamental political issues discussed during the writing of the Articles are still at the heart of many of the political questions that plague current policy makers. Although the writers of the Articles found much on which they found consensus, there remained many issues on which they disagreed. Many of these issues were settled through compromise; still others were simply found to be intractable and remained unresolved. These political questions and the answers to them drafted by the writers of the Articles of Confederation are all part of the legacy left to today's decision makers.

The Articles were written during a war and reflected the violence and political uncertainty of that time. They were written by the elite of the revolutionaries engaged in treason against the British Crown. Wanting to legitimize both their economic and political independence from England, the Second Continental Congress created a committee, chaired by John Dickenson of Maryland, to formally draft a governing document that would be implemented after militarily securing independence. The Congress completed the Articles in 1777 but they did not become effective as a governing instrument until 1781 when all the states finally adopted it. The fundamental task of the Articles was to form a "union" of states. Everything else was secondary. The central question was what would be the relationship between the newly independent states and the newly created central government? How would power be distributed among the governing institutions? Essentially, what would be the nature of the union? Would real political power rest with the states or with the newly formed national government? This question was not a new one as it had plagued the revolutionaries even before the war of independence had been won.

Today, the revolutionaries of 1776 are often portrayed as a group of men who shared one vision, based on common ideals and values. However, the war with Great Britain often disguised the serious differences that divided them, none more so than the issue of the nature of the union. The concept of state versus national power was at the center of their disagreements. How would the Articles fare once the war was over? Would the Articles serve as a unifying document capable of resolving their differences or would it merely be a stopgap measure, a tenuous agreement incapable of addressing the serious underlying problems that separated the revolutionaries?

Two Points of View

There were two fundamental positions to the basic political question regarding the nature of the union: the states' rights position and the nationalist perspective. The arguments on both sides of the issue were strong and persuasive. The states' rights position was clear. Political power would remain in the hands of the states. Supporters of this position were concerned about relinquishing political power to another political entity, especially a central government whose powers and goals were unclear at best. Their argument was simple and two-track. First, the traditional source of power at that time rested in the state legislatures. Those individuals who maintained this position wanted power to remain there. They were unwilling to relinquish what power they already possessed because their political interests would best be served by maintaining the status quo. Second, they were fighting a war of independence against what they considered a tyrannical centralized government. A major fear expressed by many of the states was that if the Continental Congress legitimized a strong national government it would just be replacing one tyranny for another. They wanted little, if anything, to do with another distant and unresponsive government. This argument was the precursor to the well-refined states' rights argument that is still used today. It maintains that the states must stand as bastions of freedom against the tyranny of the national government.

The nationalist argument was also clear. Its supporters claimed that a strong union of states was necessary to survive. It was also simple and two-track. First, the colonies had declared themselves an independent nation. It would behoove them to establish a strong national government to produce a formidable political unit vìs a vìs the established European nations. If the states remained thirteen independent entities, they could easily be individually devoured either economically or politically and reclaimed as part of a colonial empire either by England or another imperialist power, such as Spain. Second, a strong national government would eliminate interstate fighting such as had existed on the European continent for centuries. Peace and the combining of resources among neighboring states were viewed as constructive. The alternative, war among neighboring states, was seen as a useless waste of valuable and scarce resources. Interstate squabbling would also present an opportunity for the European states to re-acquire them through a "divide and conquer" policy. The newly independent states would be divided and poorly defended, and again the possibility for recolonization was a real concern.

Neither position was accepted in its entirety. Rather, a compromise was forged leaning more to the states' rights position but incorporating elements of the nationalist view. A loose confederation of states with a weak national government was established; most of the power remained with the traditional source of power, the state legislature.

Structure of National Government

All governments consist of elements of three branches of government: executive, legislative, and judicial. How those branches of government are structured and the various functions they perform differentiates one government from another. For example, in a dictatorship all three branches of government and its powers would be vested in one person. A democracy might attempt by constitutional measures to divide the power of government among the three branches so that no one branch could acquire all the power and become too powerful. Where and how the power is distributed will eventually determine its effectiveness and legitimacy.

As discussed earlier, the framers of the Articles of Confederation were not willing to invest too much power in the national government. Therefore, the executive, legislative, and judicial branches of the new central government were either extremely limited or nonexistent. The Articles of Confederation consciously did not provide for either a national executive to execute governmental principles or a central judiciary to adjudicate legal problems that might arise between the states. The legislative branch was the only functioning branch of the new central government, and it was severely limited. Four restrictions imposed by the Articles of Confederation on the national legislature left it virtually powerless:

1. no power to tax individuals
2. limited ability to requisition money from the states
3. no power to regulate interstate commerce
4. amendments required unanimous approval of all state legislatures

The legislative branch was incapable of acquiring either legitimacy or effectiveness. Distrust of the unknown and fear of a strong centralized government caused the framers of the Articles to be very conservative in their allocation of power to the only functioning branch of the national government. This left the national government virtually incapable of acting. The individual states then were powerful enough to promote their own self-interests, placing them before the national good. This combination was a catalyst for disaster.[3]

Problems Under the Articles of Confederation

National Debt

Problems began to develop quickly in the fledgling nation. These problems were political and economic in nature. Politically, the government was not capable of performing two major tasks: maintaining its legitimacy among its citizens and forging a strong national union among the states. Economically, the government was incapable of paying its debt, establishing a national economy, or regulating the relationship between creditors and debtors. These problems were all interrelated.

Wars are never cheap, and the Revolutionary War was no exception. The revolutionaries borrowed vast sums of money to finance their war of independence. The money was borrowed by the Continental Congress and by the individual states; it was amassed by issuing bonds and securities. By the end of the war, the Continental Congress was over forty million dollars in debt to its American investors and over ten million dollars to foreign investors. Using the same financial strategies, the individual states cumulatively borrowed over twenty million dollars.

People who invest in risky commodities, for instance revolutionary war securities and bonds, tend to be large creditors with disposable income. While not investing in war bonds, a modern day creditor with enough disposable income to "risk" hoping for a specific political outcome would be Steve Forbes, the 1996 Republican presidential candidate; Ross Perot, the Independent Party, would also fall into this category. Without any assurance of return on their money, these men were willing to invest their own personal fortunes to facilitate a particular political outcome. The creditors' motives for investing in the revolutionary war effort were often mixed and complex. Some creditors invested in the war effort because they believed in the independence movement. Other creditors believed they could make a profit on the war. Whatever the creditors' investment motives, a profit could only be made on the securities and bonds if the revolutionaries were successful in winning the war. If they failed, the chance that the revolutionaries would be hung as traitors was very real, and the securities and bonds that financed the war effort would become as worthless as Confederate money became after the Civil War. The money the revolutionaries borrowed became the first debt of the new government. The question was then, as it is today, how would the government pay it.

Since the revolutionaries won the war, the bonds and securities became viable commodities, and the creditors were ready to cash in their investment. Two roadblocks became immediately apparent. First, the national treasury was exhausted from the cost of the war. In addition, the government under the Articles could not tax individuals and could only requisition the states for contributions to run the national government. Needless to say, the states were not very generous or very forthcoming with dollars. For example, in 1781, Congress requisitioned eight million dollars from the states; they responded by sending less than half-a-million. While the Articles were in effect, the cumulative amount of money paid by all the states to the national treasury barely exceeded what was required to pay the interest on the debt for one year.[4]

The inability of the national government to pay its debt brought into question the credibility and legitimacy of the national government. The investors quickly lost faith in the government, and as a result the national government's ability to continue as a viable governing body was seriously challenged. Creditors feared they would lose their entire investment. To forestall financial ruin, many creditors sold their stocks and bonds on the open market for ten cents on the dollar. This meant that creditors were losing large sums of money due to the inability of the national government to pay its debt. This choked off the flow of capital in the country and eventually hurt the noninvestor, the debtor sector of the population. The economy was quickly deteriorating.

National Economy

Once the Revolutionary War ended, the reasons for cooperation among the states began to decline, particularly in the area of commerce. This was exacerbated by the fact that the national government was not capable of promoting good will in the area of commerce since the Articles of Confederation did not allow it to regulate interstate commerce. The states were not interested in developing a national economy; they were much more concerned in promoting the interests of their own state economy. States established trade barriers to promote their own merchants and provide them with special privileges. For example, the seaboard states levied taxes on their goods going inland.

Another method the states used to promote their own individual economies was printing their own currency, which led to problems not only between the states but also within them. Externally, using different currencies in the individual states made it difficult to establish its value and created financial confusion conducting business outside state borders. This monetary inconsistency made it difficult for the creditors, the financial elite, to invest and re-invest their capital holdings particularly across state lines in the form of interstate investment. Internally, the ability to print and regulate currency caused inflation, recession, and social unrest.

Creditors vs. Debtors

Conflict existed not only among states but within the two major economic classes within them, the creditors and the debtors. In many states, this conflict became bitter and in certain circumstances erupted into open rebellion by the debtor class. Capitalist theory maintains that the health of the economy is intricately tied to the well being of the creditor class. It claims that capital should be maintained in the hands of a few with the idea that resources will eventually trickle down to the masses; therefore, it is essential that the few are doing well. President Reagan espoused this view of capitalism almost 200 years later in his "trickle down" analysis of how the American economic system should function. This system obviously favors the elite for if the economy is to flourish, the elite must do well. The question both then and now might be "how well did and does capital trickle down to the masses?" Many of the laws passed by the state governments quickly became a direct threat to the creditor class. Two types of laws particularly affected it. First, the state governments exercised their power to coin money and issue paper currency. Second, they passed laws that altered the structure of contractual obligations. Both types of laws were originally designed to relieve the economic pressures felt by the debtor class by allowing debt repayment to be less painful during bad economic times. The results were quite the opposite.

The paper money printed by the state governments soon became known as "cheap money," because it was basically worthless paper and caused notable inflation in the states. The paper money flooded the market and allowed the debtors to pay back their loans to their creditors with inflated worthless dollars; the creditors were then incapable of recouping the full value of their loan. The restructuring of contractual obligations was designed to forestall repayment of outstanding debts and, in certain situations, negate them outright. In both cases, these new laws passed by the state governments cut off the flow of capital to the creditor class. Their loans were either repaid with worthless money over longer contractual periods or, in some instances, not at all. The creditors were quickly losing their resources.

Although the laws were initially designed to aid the debtors, in many circumstances they had the opposite effect. Particularly hard pressed by these economic developments were the debtor farmers who had invested heavily in land and equipment. As capital was either not repaid to the creditors or repaid with inflated currency, the creditors were incapable of re-investing their resources. As the creditors' resources dried up, the debtors had fewer resources available to them. They had fewer opportunities to finance or re-finance their loans. As a result, capital was not effectively flowing through the economy.

As economic times deteriorated, debtors began to rebel against the existing governmental authorities in the states. In several states, debtors became engaged in open rebellion against tax collectors and sheriffs attempting to repossess their farms on behalf of the creditors. The most serious of these rebellions, **Shays' Rebellion**, broke out in Massachusetts in 1786. By 1786 in the

Shays led a band of farmers in revolt against tax creditors attempting to repossess their farms.

city of Concord, Massachusetts, the site of one of the first battles of the Revolution, there were three times as many people in prison for debts as there were for all other crimes combined. In Worcester County, the ratio was even higher—twenty to one. Most of the prisoners were small farmers who were incapable of paying their debts because of the disorganized nature of the economy.[5] Within this economic environment, Daniel Shays, an ex-revolutionary war captain, led a band of rebels composed of farmers, artisans, and laborers whose land and possessions were scheduled for foreclosure by the local courthouses. Shays and his rebels captured several courthouses, burned records, and briefly held the city of Springfield.[6] These rebellions were seen as a direct military threat to the governing elite, the creditors.

As a result of these economic and political developments, a sense of nationalism began to emerge among the creditor class, even among those creditors who had initially either made or supported the states' rights argument during the writing of the Articles of Confederation. The desire to design interstate solutions to intrastate problems became evident as seen in their initiative to formulate interstate conferences, such as the Annapolis Conference. The creditors who had established the Articles of Confederation and had seen a strong national government as a threat began to see restructuring it as the only alternative to an impending debtor rebellion as witnessed in events such as Shays' Rebellion. The existing creditor class was afraid its power and very existence as a class was threatened. If the economic situation was not resolved, the very government the creditors had created would be destroyed. The elite were now more afraid of class warfare than a strong national government.

As early as 1785, a small but very important group of men began to articulate the need for a stronger national government. It is significant that George Washington, the most prominent American of the time, took an active role in this movement. In 1785, at Mt. Vernon, George Washington hosted what today might be considered an economic summit with delegates attending from Virginia and Maryland. Out of this meeting came the idea to hold a general economic summit for all the states. This meeting was to be held at Annapolis in 1786.

The conference in Annapolis was a disappointment as only five of the thirteen states sent delegates. This did not deter Alexander Hamilton as he and his ideas tended to dominate the meeting. In spite of poor attendance, he persuaded the delegates at the Annapolis convention to call for a constitutional solution to the prevailing social, political, and economic problems. In addition, the Annapolis convention adopted a report written by Hamilton that outlined the defects in the Articles of Confederation. That report requested that the states send delegates to a new convention in Philadelphia in May 1787, to address the problems that existed in the Articles. Rumors at the time suggested that Alexander Hamilton with the help of James Madison working behind the scenes had intended that the Annapolis convention would fail at its task. Their hope was that the conference was meant to be a stepping stone to a larger more inclusive convention that would significantly alter the substance of the Articles, transferring power from the states to the national government.[7]

Debtors' discontent continued to put pressure on the creditors. Shays' Rebellion in 1786 was the final blow. This outright challenge to the governing elite put the creditors and state legislatures on notice that something needed to be done, and on February 21, 1787, Congress called for a convention to meet in Philadelphia in the summer of 1787 for the specific purpose of revising the Articles of Confederation.

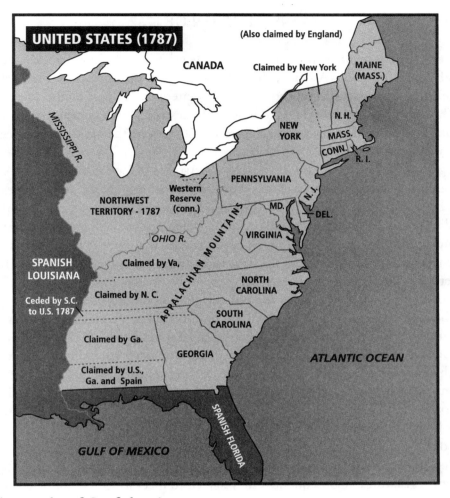

UNITED STATES (1787)

(Also claimed by England)

CANADA

Claimed by New York

MAINE (MASS.)

N. H.

NEW YORK

MASS.

CONN.

R. I.

MISSISSIPPI R.

PENNSYLVANIA

Western Reserve (conn.)

NORTHWEST TERRITORY - 1787

MD.

N.J.

DEL.

OHIO R.

VIRGINIA

APPALACHIAN MOUNTAINS

SPANISH LOUISIANA

Claimed by Va,

NORTH CAROLINA

Ceded by S.C. to U.S. 1787

Claimed by N. C.

SOUTH CAROLINA

Claimed by Ga.

GEORGIA

ATLANTIC OCEAN

Claimed by U.S., Ga. and Spain

SPANISH FLORIDA

GULF OF MEXICO

Failures of the Articles of Confederation

The convention in Philadelphia was a direct result of the inability of the revolutionaries to resolve the political problems that confronted them during the writing of the Articles of Confederation. The framers of the Articles established a governmental structure that constructed an untenable balance of power between the states and national government, creating a central government too weak to survive. The failure of the framers of the Articles to resolve these political problems led to economic distress for the creditors and the debtor class, causing class warfare that led to political unrest.[8] How would the Articles be revised so that the country could survive?

Even though the Articles were a failure, they should be viewed as an essential transitional document that forged a "union" of states during a politically tentative time in the fledgling nation's history. The political environment in 1777 was such that it was the best possible political solution that could be forged among the elite of the thirteen colonies. In fact, the document eventually written at the convention in 1787 would have been virtually impossible in 1777. The political environment of 1787 had changed significantly in the ten years following the implementation of the Articles, and the document written in Philadelphia reflected that change.

CONSTITUTION OF 1787

The Articles of Confederation assured that the state legislatures would remain the legitimate and real source of political power. As such, the delegates to the convention in Philadelphia were to represent their respective state legislatures and their interests. Twelve of the thirteen states sent delegates. The only state legislature not to send delegates was Rhode Island. It was the only state legislature totally controlled by the debtor class and as such more than reluctant to negotiate political solutions with members of the creditor class.

The delegates were given the task of revising the Articles of Confederation in such a way as to resolve the escalating economic and political problems in the new nation. All changes to the document had to be unanimously approved by the state legislatures. However, once the delegates convened in Philadelphia, they realized that the Articles were impossible to revise. The Articles needed more than minor changes. It needed a major overhaul. As written, the balance of power between the state and national government, and the definition of the "nature of the union," threatened not only the interests of the creditor class but the very survival of the union. Maintaining the union had become the political centerpiece for the political and economic elite; state and regional differences could be addressed after the survival of the union had been secured. This required that the basic tenets on which the union rested would need to be restructured. This required a major shift in political power. The delegates needed to create a stronger national government to save the union, and this would come at the expense of the existing state legislatures.

To accomplish this, the delegates redefined their mandate. They tossed the Articles aside and scripted a new governing document. In so doing, they worked outside the boundaries of their legitimate political authority. The state legislatures had empowered the delegates to revise the Articles of Confederation. It had not given the convention the power to destroy it.

The delegates knew their actions would spark great controversy and create much resistance from their state legislatures. Consequently, they agreed to meet in secret, taking an oath of silence not to leak their negotiations to the press. There were no official minutes taken at the convention. Much of what is known about what happened behind the closed doors at the convention in Philadelphia came from the unofficial notes kept by James Madison and the diaries of other delegates.

This document, written in virtual secrecy by the elite, became the supreme law of the land, and it still governs the United States today. The delegates were successful in resolving the pragmatic issues that plagued the new republic. They had saved the union. However, we can question if they were successful in resolving the underlying political debates surrounding the nature of the union. That question is still central to the distribution of power between the national government and the states. The merits of both sides of the question are still hotly debated in Washington D.C. and the corridors of the state governments.

Delegates to the Convention

Although seventy-four delegates were appointed by their states, only fifty-five actually attended the convention. However, the men who attended were some of the most prominent economic and political figures in the United States. Five men stand out as leaders of the convention: George

Washington, who was quickly made president of the convention, James Madison, Edmund Randolph, Benjamin Franklin, and Gouverneur Morris, one of the foremost business and financial leaders in the country. Conspicuous by their absence were Patrick Henry, Samuel Adams, John Adams, John Hancock, Thomas Paine, and Thomas Jefferson.[9]

Much has been written regarding the differences, debates, and compromises made at the convention; however, more important than the differences at the convention were the demographic and philosophical similarities of the delegates. Although there were delegates representing the extremes of the political spectrum, such as Luther Martin representing the ardent states' rights position and Alexander Hamilton representing the extreme nationalist perspective, most delegates' differences were more of degree than substance.[10]

First, demographically, the delegates were very similar. They were the elite of the American elite. They did not represent the population at large. The delegates were all white men who ranged in age from twenty-six to eighty-one; Ben Franklin was the eldest of the delegates. They were all well educated. More than half of the delegates had been educated at either Harvard, William and Mary, Yale, University of Pennsylvania, Columbia College, Princeton, or in England.[11] Many of them possessed past governing experience either at the state or national level. Seven had served as governors of their states; thirty-nine had served in Congress. Five delegates signed both the Declaration of Independence and the Constitution. All the men at the convention were creditors who represented the conservative interests of the creditor class. At least forty of the fifty-five men held revolutionary stocks or bonds; fourteen were land speculators; twenty-four were moneylenders and investors; eleven were engaged in commerce or manufacturing; fifteen owned large plantations.[12]

Most groups presently thought of today as politically significant were not represented at the convention. No women were present; there were no nonwhite or nonProtestants; there were no ethnic minorities of any nationality included. Representatives of the small farmer and the small businessman were also conspicuously absent. Not only were these groups not represented but they had no input into the process at all since one of the first actions taken by the delegates to the convention was to uphold an oath of silence regarding their activities at the convention. Most Americans at the time had virtually no idea of what was transpiring in Philadelphia. The white male creditor class working outside their boundaries of authority were constructing a new political reality establishing new political boundaries without any input from other sources.

Second, there was great consensus among the delegates as to their political values. Their demographic similarities may certainly have contributed to their almost virtual agreement on fundamental political values. Many of the views shared by the delegates on the role of government can be found in the writings of John Locke. His *Second Treatise on Civil Government* written in 1690 was widely accepted by the American leadership as the definitive study on government. Locke, a British philosopher, was considered to be one of the most notable and controversial liberal democratic writers of his time. He was known as a "**social contract**" theorist. Locke believed that men entered into a political society to establish a government, which was formed by tacitly establishing a contract. This contract was between those who govern and those who are governed. The ultimate legitimacy of government rests with the people themselves and not with gods or kings; the basis for this political society and government is the consent of the governed. The government would consist of a legislative body that should make laws and an executive that should enforce them. The ultimate end of government was to preserve liberty and property with the major emphasis on property. In his *Second Treatise on Civil Government* Locke wrote, "The preservation of their property is the great and chief end...of men's uniting into Commonwealths." Locke's writings supported two major concepts in the Articles of Confederation. First, the ultimate goal of government was to protect private property. Second, if a man did not own property, he would have no interest in government and therefore deserved no vote.[13] Since the Articles of Confederation was a government incapable of protecting property rights and since the end goal of government was to protect property, it was the duty of the delegates to create one that could accomplish that goal.

One of the most important of the delegates' shared beliefs was the concept of **nationalism**. This was the idea that the union of states must continue, that there would be a "united" states of America. Their vision was that individuals would begin to define their interests in terms of the national government rather than the narrow interests of their state or region. This could only happen if the national government was strengthened. Without a strong national government the United States would implode because of the failure of the state governments to cooperate and look beyond their parochial interests. The creditors realized that the states were incapable of building a national economy, and without this the creditor class was in danger of collapsing. The concept of nationalism was basically an elite one that was not universally accepted by the masses until well after the Civil War.

The delegates also shared a belief in **limited government**. Government was to perform very specific functions, the protection of liberty and property, and beyond that the government should not interfere in a person's life. Although the delegates were in Philadelphia to create a stronger national government, there was a great concern among them that concentration of power would lead to "unlimited" government. Part of their challenge was to design a strong and more effective national government with enough safeguards to prevent authoritarian rule.

The last major fundamental political value on which the delegates agreed was that of establishing a **republican** form of government. This did not mean the same in 1787 as it does today. The delegates were opposed to a governing elite that was based on heredity rather than accomplishments. In reality, a republican form of government meant non-hereditary rule. Since government's chief objective was to protect property, individuals who owned property should govern. Men of wealth and education should govern. Therefore, the delegates believed that the masses should have a very limited role in the selection of their governors; this role, if any, should be indirect. The delegates never meant for "the people" to govern either directly or indirectly in their national government. An example that illustrates the commitment and agreement to which the delegates shared excluding "the masses" from participation in their national government is the selection process for the constitutional officers to the new national government. The selection process virtually excludes the general population from directly participating. The chart on the following page illustrates the method of selection for constitutional officers to the national government stipulated by the Constitution written in 1787. The only constitutional officer to be "elected" by the people were the members of the House of Representatives. The other constitutional officers were not selected by direct voter participation. Their selection process was left either directly or indirectly in the hands of the state legislatures. The framers of the Constitution were essentially telling the state legislatures not to fear the new national government because they would be able to select the personnel for it.

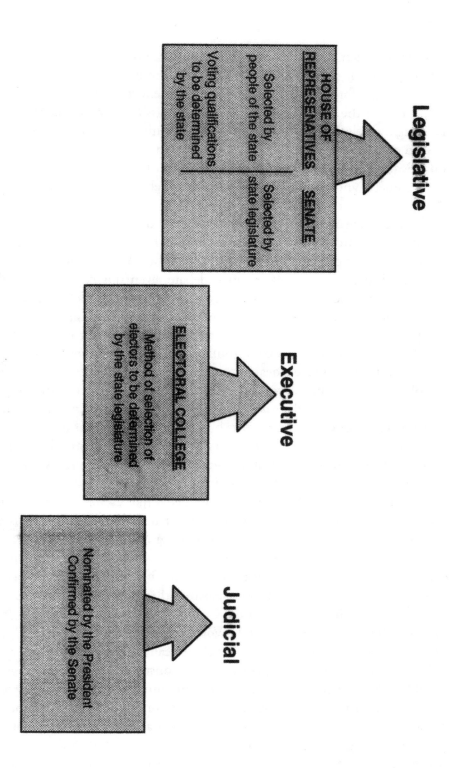

HOUSE OF REPRESENATIVES

Selected by people of the state

Voting qualifications to be determined by the state

SENATE

Selected by state legislature

Legislative

ELECTORAL COLLEGE

Method of selection of electors to be determined by the state legislature

Executive

Nominated by the President Confirmed by the Senate

Judicial

Methods of selection of the constitutional officers as designated by the original Constitution.

Compromises

Although there was much consensus on fundamental values among the delegates, there was disagreement among the delegates about how these values should be practically implemented. Consequently, there was cause for many compromises, and the effects of these are still evident today. One of the compromises at the convention centered on the issue of voter qualifications. There was a consensus among the delegates that men of property should govern and should be selected by their peers, men who owned property. John Dickinson exemplified the delegates' feelings stating that property qualifications were a "necessary defense against the dangerous influence of those multitudes without property and without principle, with which our country like all others, will in time abound."[14]

Yet, in spite of consensus on this issue, the delegates did not incorporate a property requirement for voter qualifications into the Constitution. This was because they could not come to an agreement on what the specific property requirement should be. A committee was established to determine property qualifications, and, after much debate, even this committee could not agree on property qualifications since they recognized that "property" from a non-traditional perspective assumed many forms. Madison pointed out in a July debate that establishing a traditional land ownership requirement would exclude the mercantile and manufacturing classes from membership in the House of Representatives.[15] A compromise resolving the property issue was finally reached in committee; it did not, however, deal with the nature of property or ownership. Rather, the compromise placed voter qualifications outside the jurisdiction of the national government. Instead of the national government determining voter qualifications, each state would have the power to determine not only property requirements but all the qualifications necessary for voting.

Since this compromise allowed the states to enfranchise voters rather than the national government, substantial inequalities in citizenship soon developed. An individual's ability to participate in the political process was determined by the state in which he lived.

Many states initially imposed property requirements that established a pattern of class voting that continues today. This compromise was also later used by states as a basis to exclude from voting not only non-propertied individuals but other groups as well. After the Civil War, states imposed poll taxes and literacy tests as voter qualifications to hinder not only the lower socioeconomic classes but also African Americans from participating in the political process. This systematic exclusion of participation in the process ensured that decision-making would remain in the hands of a privileged few. It was only after the Civil Rights movement of the 1950s and 1960s that spawned the Civil Rights Act of 1964 and the Voting Rights Act of 1965 that this compromise was effectively nullified. Today's political construct rhetorically presents democracy as "government of the people, by the people and for the people." This construct has its beginnings within a framework that established the selection process as elitist and much less democratic by today's standards.

The compromise regarding voter qualifications was only one of many negotiated in Philadelphia. The delegates came to Philadelphia with two agendas that may or may not have been mutually exclusive: first, design a stronger national government, and, second, protect personal, state, and regional interests. Many compromises were needed to reconcile these two agendas. The most famous, and perhaps the most important, compromise dealt with the structure of the legislative branch. The delegates believed that the legislative branch was to be the most powerful and the most important branch of government. As such, its structure was of the utmost importance to the delegates. Two major plans regarding the structure of the legislative branch were submitted to the convention. A compromise was ultimately struck incorporating elements of both thus laying the foundation for today's Congress.

Virginia Plan

James Madison and the Virginia delegation were extremely well prepared for the convention, and, by the time the other delegates arrived in Philadelphia, they had already prepared fifteen resolutions including one that dealt with the structure of the legislative branch. When Washington opened the convention, Governor Edmund Randolph of the Virginia delegation immediately presented their proposals to the other state delegations. This was an assertive tactical move on the part of the Virginians, which put them in the position of setting the agenda for the rest of the convention. The rest of the state delegations were constantly forced to respond and react to Virginia's proposals.[16]

Philosophically, it deconstructed the underlying premise of the Articles of Confederation. The Articles of Confederation were based on the equality of the states. The Virginia Plan rested on the equality of the individual voter. This diminished the importance of the state legislature vis a vis the national government. Structurally, the plan created a legislative branch that would be bicameral, two houses. The seats in each house would be allocated among the states in proportion to the state's population. The people of each state would directly select the representatives to the first or lower house; the lower house would then select the second house from a slate of nominees submitted by the state legislatures. This plan favored the larger states as representation in the legislature was ultimately based on the population of the individual states.

New Jersey Plan

The smaller states were very concerned that the new national government would be controlled by the larger states. They felt that they would always be outvoted in the legislature by the larger states. William Patterson of New Jersey became the spokesperson for the smaller states and introduced a counterproposal to the Virginia Plan. The New Jersey Plan rested on the premise of the equality of the individual states. Those who supported the New Jersey plan argued that the Articles of Confederation created all states equal, not all voters equal. Supporting the equality of the voter would violate the spirit of the Articles of Confederation. The plan argued that the Virginia resolutions were unfair in attempting to shift the focus from the "equality of the states" to the "equality of the voter." No matter how the voter qualifications would be determined, the larger states would always have more power because they would always have more voters. The Virginia resolutions would destroy the balance of power that currently existed among the states. The Articles of Confederation were well on the way to destroying the union of the United States, but, at least, under the Articles all the states were "equally" on the way to ruin.

Although the disagreements centered on the principle of the "equality of voters" versus the "equality of states," the real problem centered on how the states would be represented in the new

THE THIRTEEN COLONIES

national government. The delegates were all convinced that there needed to be a stronger national government to preserve the union. The Virginia Plan and the New Jersey Plan exemplify their resolve on this issue since each contained elements of national supremacy shifting the balance of power from the states to the national government. The New Jersey Plan, as well as the Virginia Plan, accepted the principle of national supremacy by stipulating that the national legislature would be the supreme legislative authority. It granted Congress the ability to levy taxes and regulate interstate commerce. This eliminated two of the major constraints on the legislative branch under the Articles that stood as major obstacles to developing a national economy. In so doing, this new legislative arrangement shifted economic policy-making from the states to the national government.

Shifting the power from the states to the national government focused the dialogue on exactly how strong the national government should be and who should control this new and stronger government. The more populous states, such as Massachusetts and Pennsylvania, favored the Virginia Plan because it would give them more seats in Congress. New Jersey, Connecticut, and

Delaware favored the New Jersey Plan because they believed it would preserve the present political balance. The smaller states believed that if the national government was strictly based on state population that the interests of the smaller states would be less important than those of the more populous ones.

Connecticut Compromise

New Jersey's Plan was rejected; however, it put the large states on notice that the small states would not be intimidated. Deliberations on the structure of the legislature continued, and the delegates became increasingly disgruntled with their inability to resolve this issue. Several delegations even threatened to withdraw from the convention. A committee was established to forge a compromise and break the deadlock. William Johnson of Connecticut proposed the results of that committee that became known as the **Great Compromise**. This compromise was overwhelmingly accepted by the delegates. The compromise fused the concepts of the "equality of the voter" with the "equity of the states" into a bicameral legislature.

The new national legislature would consist of two houses, the House of Representatives and the Senate. The House of Representatives was based on population. Representatives were to be selected by the people of their state; the state legislatures would determine the qualifications of the voters. The second house, the Senate, was based on equal representation. Each state, no matter what their population, would be entitled to two Senators. Senators were selected by their state legislatures. The compromise also provided that the equal representation of the states, secured in the Senate, could never be altered, not even by constitutional amendment. The compromise also required that both Houses of Congress would have to pass all legislation thereby granting both Houses of the legislature equal political power.

The Connecticut Compromise allowed both the small and large states to gain some concessions without either one acquiring everything it desired. The compromise ensured that the interests of all the states would have to be considered. It would be difficult for one state or any group of states to acquire complete control.

The legacy of the Connecticut Compromise is broad and complex. Balancing power to assure that no one group or interest could acquire power at any one time has resulted in a legislative process that is slow-paced, tedious, and open-ended. Facilitating change in Congress is slow. Thus, the process of passing legislation has made substantive change extremely difficult, for example, restructuring the health-care delivery system. The system focuses rather on making incremental changes or what has commonly become known as "band aid" solutions to problems. This has, in effect, maintained the status quo: policies, once made, tend to remain unchanged. Change only tends to occur when there is a significant public outcry to change the policies of the status quo as in the case of restructuring domestic policies concerning apartheid during the Civil Rights movement or re-examination of the foreign policy that led to the U.S. military involvement in Vietnam.

Maintaining the status quo produces political stability. The word "stability" usually carries with it a positive connotation, for example, a stable person is looked upon more favorably than an unstable person. However, stability does not necessarily translate into efficient governmental policy; it can often be the antithesis of efficiency. Since stability maintains the status quo, inefficient policies tend to remain in place. The safeguards built into the legislative process to balance power virtually mandate that legislation takes time, facilitates negotiation, and requires compromise. The legislative process is "messy" at best and virtually ensures inefficiency. Stability and inefficiency are the two blades of a double edged sword built into the legislative process. Citizens of a democracy often find their legislature to be their safeguard against tyranny and at the same time their biggest source of frustration.

Slavery

Slavery was a central issue at the convention, and it stimulated the most heated debates. Unlike the issue of representation, political alliances centered on regional interests rather than on the size of the states. The compromises secured by the delegates over slavery considered its abolition and limitation as two separate issues. However, actual abolition of slavery was only marginally considered as a viable possibility and quickly rejected. It was too sensitive an issue to warrant serious consideration. Although slavery was legal in every state but Massachusetts, northern states were more inclined to limit its practice with the idea that the institution would in time be abolished. Southern states, however, considered it vital to their economic and political interests and were willing to dissolve the union rather than abolish slavery. The end of slavery would have meant the end of the union. In fact, the institution of slavery was so central to the survival of the union that before the convention finished its work, it placed the prohibition on interference with the slave trade beyond the power of a constitutional amendment. As mentioned earlier, only the equal suffrage of states in the Senate shared this high sanctuary of immunity.[17] It is apparent that the framers of the Constitution never considered the abolition of slavery a real issue. The sanctity of the union was more important to the framers than the abolition of slavery.

Instead of abolishing slavery, the delegates focused on limiting it, a much less sensitive issue. Central to limiting slavery was the issue of the slave trade and who would ultimately control it. The issue of limiting slavery divided the ranks of the southern states. By 1787, some southern states, such as Virginia, already had a sufficient slave population and could indulge in the argument of whether to limit the boundaries of the importation of slaves. However, other southern states, such as South Carolina, had a smaller slave population. They strongly opposed any restrictions on the institution of slavery. Charles Pinckney of South Carolina led the strong southern opposition to any of these constraints. Ultimately, the delegates compromised. They agreed that the importation of slaves could continue for the time being. However, twenty years after the ratification of the Constitution, Congress would have the authority to limit the slave trade.[18]

The issue then became one of how to incorporate slavery into the new republic and limit its practice in a way that would best accommodate both regions. The issue of slavery was constructed in two ways: moral and economic. The moral argument was clear. None of the revolutionaries could reconcile the principles of the Declaration of Independence with human bondage.[19] Even so, many of them did not practice what they preached. The moral argument against slavery was often presented by slave-owners. For example, at the convention, the movement to abolish slavery was championed by such notables as George Washington. Washington, a slave-owner, stated that slavery debased not only the slaves but the slave owners. Although not present at the convention,

Thomas Jefferson, who penned the immortal words "all men are created equal," was also a slave-owner. However, the principle of equality put forth in the Declaration found itself squarely in conflict with the obligation of government to protect property rights. By the time of the convention, it has been estimated that the American Revolution for which the Declaration was penned only bequeathed civil rights on approximately 15 percent of the population, leaving not only the slaves but also poorer colonists, all women and Native Americans to the mercies of the propertied elite.[20] In many cases, this would translate leaving policy decisions regarding these groups up to the states.

In the end, the economic argument, the protection of property rights, took precedence over the moral debate. The debate centered on the right of states to control slave importation. This argument was part of the larger issue of the states' right to self-determination. Although many Southerners were ardent nationalists who wanted to create a strong central government, they also feared that the commerce clause of the Constitution, the right of Congress to "regulate commerce among the several states," could be used as a weapon against slavery and a way to exploit and eventually ruin the plantation economy.[21] The South feared that the North would use this against them in constructing policy and eventually control them politically, socially, and economically.

The economic discussion revolved around three important issues: representation, taxation, and the competitive vs. noncompetitive labor market. The first two issues are interrelated. Of primary importance was the question of how slaves were to be counted for the purpose of representation in the House of Representatives. The southern states wanted slaves to be counted for representation purposes. Since a large portion of the population in the South consisted of slaves, if only "free" men were counted for representation purposes, the southern states knew they would be seriously "underrepresented" in one house of the national legislature. The House of Representatives would not reflect the real population of the southern states but rather only the "free" population. Southerners were concerned that this would alter the balance of power not only between the individual states but also between the regions of the country.

The northern states did not want to count slaves for representation purposes. They claimed that slaves were considered property by their owners and, therefore, should not be counted as "free" people for representation purposes. Northerners wanted slaves considered for taxation purposes. The compromise reached by the delegates stipulated that slaves would be counted as three-fifths of a person for both representation purposes in the House of Representatives as well as in allocating the tax burden among the states.

The last economic question centered on the labor force: competitive labor market vs. noncompetitive labor market. The North relied on a competitive labor market. The plantation system was an economic system unique to the South, and it relied on noncompetitive labor, slavery. The South believed that if slavery was abolished, it would be forced to rely on competitive labor to operate their plantations, and this would cause financial ruin and destroy the plantation culture. Allowing slavery to continue maintained the two labor markets to exist in the different regions of the country.

The legacy of the slavery compromises was a racial hierarchy sanctioned by the supreme law of the land. The convention placed property rights and the "union" above the principles of equality. Counting each slave as three-fifths of a person for representation and taxation purposes explicitly established a racial hierarchy where one group of people is intrinsically worth more than another. The Constitution politically sanctioned dominant and subordinate racial groups within the culture. These compromises permeated all the institutions in the United States inevitably creating a system of institutionalized racism. The framers of the Constitution politically validated a racial hierarchy that had already existed before the writing of the Constitution and continues to frame the question of race relations in the United States to the present day. They established the political environment within which race relations would be discussed and constructed in the twenty-first century.

War, constitutional amendments, and subsequent legislation eventually eliminated the institution of slavery in the United States. However, the legacy of the unresolved political issue of slavery at the constitutional convention can be seen reflected in the political debate that continues today in the ongoing discussion of race relations illustrated by such high profile cases as the Rodney King and the O.J. Simpson trials. Issues such as affirmative action discussed in the chapter on civil rights continue to be both debated and divisive in the twenty-first century. The issue of race was as prevalent in the presidential campaign of 2000 as it was in the constitutional convention of 1787. The language of the debate has changed, but its essence remains the same.

How the Constitution Manages Power

"Every word of [the Constitution] decides a question between power and Liberty."
James Madison, *National Gazette*, January 19, 1792

There are four principles that the framers of the Constitution adhered to in their efforts to manage the power of the government they were about to create: federalism, separation of powers, checks and balances, and limited government. Of these four, federalism was the only original principle.

Federalism (National and State Levels of Government)

Of the four principles that guided the decisions of the framers, federalism was the only one that was a unique American invention. The framers were faced with a unique situation. They wanted to devise a national government that was much more powerful than that under the Articles of Confederation. At the same time they did not want to create one that was so strong that the states, concerned that most of their own power would be usurped and fearful of potentially tyrannical rule, were unlikely to ratify the new Constitution.

The solution was to delegate some powers, such as declaring war, solely to the central government; reserve some powers, those not granted to the national government including conducting elections, only for the states (See the Tenth Amendment.) and distribute some powers, such as taxation, to both. This distribution of power between levels of government (national and state), although not specifically designated as such in the Constitution, is what is meant by **federalism**.

Federalism will be more fully discussed in chapter three. For now it is sufficient to keep in mind that the Constitutional delegation of powers was one way of attempting to control governmental abuse and preserve the Union.

Separation of Powers (Branches of National Government)

The principle and the practice of separating governmental powers did not originate with the framers. However, the **doctrine of separation**, strongly advocated by Charles-Louis de Montesquieu in *The Spirit of the Laws* (1748), is made explicit in the Constitution of 1787.

Art. I, Sec. 1 states that   "all legislative powers herein granted shall be vested in a Congress of the United States, which shall consist of a Senate and a House of Representatives."

Art. II, Sec. 1 states that   "the executive power shall be vested in a president of the United States of America."

Art. III, Sec. 1 states that   "the judicial power of the United States shall be vested in one supreme court . . . ."

Writing in response to the "anti-federalists" who objected to the new Constitution, Madison (who frequently cites the "oracle" Montesquieu in *The Federalist Papers*) explains that the need for such separation is to prevent any one branch from dominating another and becoming too powerful:

the accumulation of all powers, legislative, executive, and judiciary, in the same hands, whether of one, a few, or many, and whether hereditary, self-appointed, or elective, may justly be pronounced the very definition of tyranny (*Federalist No. 47.*)

Madison continues, in *Federalist No. 51*, by observing that the maintenance of the three separate branches of government would be possible only if certain conditions are met. One of these is that each of the three is to be selected for a different term of office and by a different constituency. The provisions set forth by the framers were as follows:

BRANCH	TERM	CONSTITUENCY
Legislative (Representatives)	two years	citizens
Legislative (Senators)	six years	state legislators (repealed by 17th amendment)
Executive (Presidents)	four years	electoral college
Judicial (Supreme Court Justices)	life (based on good behavior)	(nominated by the president, confirmed by the Senate)

In *Federalist No. 48* Madison had set forth still another condition arguing that the separation of powers "can never in practice be duly maintained" unless each branch be given "a constitutional control over the others." In other words, the principle of separation of powers is contingent upon a third principle, that of **checks and balances**.

Checks and Balances

As just noted, Madison recognized that besides separating the government into three branches also having each branch responsible for some of the functions of the other two would, by reducing the concentration of power in each, lessen the likelihood of tyrannical leadership. This notion of a "balanced" government, one which checks or controls itself, first advocated by two Englishmen, Henry St. John Bolingbroke (1678-1751) and William Blackstone (1723-1780), was then still another way of managing power.

The Constitution is rather specific about these checks. It provides, for example, that:

a) the legislative branch of government, whose job it is to enact laws, must approve presidential appointments and treaties, can override presidential vetos (checks on the executive branch), and determines the number, the jurisdiction, and the location of federal courts (check on the judicial branch).

b) the executive branch of government, whose job it is to enforce laws, can propose and veto laws (checks on the legislative branch), can nominate government officers and officials, and pardon those convicted of federal crimes (checks on the judicial branch).

c) the judicial branch of government, whose primary function it is to interpret laws, can find that presidential actions and that laws passed by the Congress are unconstitutional (checks on the executive and legislative branches).

Such checks, among others, go a long way toward preventing any one branch of the government from running amok. While helping to reduce the possibility of the abuse of power, governmental checks create another problem: they can slow the operation of government down to a grinding halt. For example, there have been five governmental shutdowns since 1980. **Shutdowns** occur when the legislative branch of government checks the executive branch by refusing to approve its federal budget, which includes thirteen appropriation bills that fund the federal government. The congressional passage of a "continuing resolution" can, with presidential approval, keep the government running for a year or until a budget agreement is reached. But a confrontation between the two branches, such as the one that took place between the Republican Congress and the Democratic President in November 1995 during the first Clinton administration, can—and did—lead to a partial shutdown or temporary layoff of 800,000 "non-essential" federal employees and the closing of national parks, libraries, and passport offices.

The framers would not have been too surprised by either the shutdown or the name-calling between the adversaries. They knew that a government in which each branch has some control over the others is by design a government that will evoke some acrimony and promote some conflict. According to notes taken by Madison, who served as the unofficial recorder of the Constitutional Convention, the delegates were aware that they had set the stage for governmental animosity and gridlock, and they concluded that the tradeoff of inaction in exchange for liberty was worth it. "We have," as Madison put it, "engineered an inefficient government to keep men free."

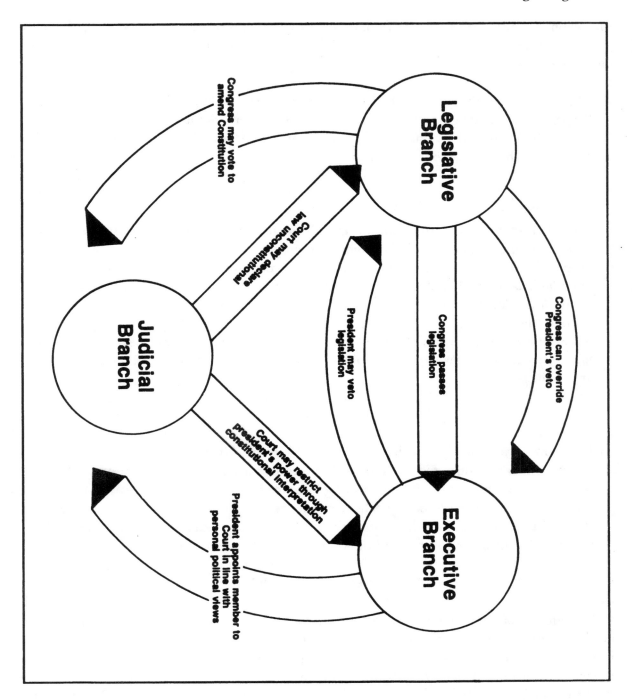

Limited Government and the Bill of Rights

The **Bill of Rights**, the first ten amendments to the Constitution, explicitly limits or restrains the actions of the national government upon individuals. These restraints were not included in the original Constitution, and there was much concern and discussion regarding this at the state level.

Impassioned statements of concern from citizens, such as those cited below, about the absence of defined liberties in the Constitution of 1787 indicate that the likelihood of its ratification was highly questionable.[22]

> The principles of this system [the Constitution] are extremely pernicious, impolitic, and dangerous . . . . The rights of conscience, trial by jury, liberty of the press, all your immunities and franchises, all pretensions to human rights and privileges, are rendered insecure, if not lost, by this change [of government . . . .]
>
> Patrick Henry, in Virginia Constitutional
> Convention, June, 1788

> Here we find no security for the rights of individuals, no security for the existence of our state governments; here is no bill of rights, nor proper restriction of power; our lives, our property, and our consciences, are left wholly at the mercy of the legislature, and the powers of the judiciary may be extended to any degree short of almighty . . . . Is this, sir, a government for freedom? Are we thus to be duped out of our liberties? . . . . We are told, sir, that a government is like a mad horse, which, notwithstanding all the curb you can put upon him, will sometimes run away with his rider . . . . Would he not, therefore, be deemed a mad man, and deserve to have his neck broken who should trust himself on this horse without any bridle at all?
>
> Thomas Tredwell, in New York Constitutional
> Convention, June-July, 1788

> I will now tell you what I do not like. First, the omission of a bill of rights, providing clearly . . . for freedom of religion, freedom of the press, protection against standing armies, restriction of monopolies, the eternal and unremitting force for the habeas corpus laws, and trials by jury . . . . I have a right to nothing, which another has a right to take away . . . . Let me add, that a bill of rights is what the people are entitled to against every government on earth, general or particular; and what no just government should refuse, or rest on inference.
>
> Thomas Jefferson, letter to James Madison,
> December 20, 1787

As Jefferson put it, inference was not enough. A promise that the first order of business for the new Congress would be to amend the Constitution to include the liberties of the citizens had to be made to insure the ratification of the document by the required nine states. The promise was kept. Twelve amendments, which provided for a limited government, were introduced by Madison in the first Congress and sent on to the state legislatures on September 25, 1789. Ten, the **Bill of Rights**, were approved by the required three-fourths of the states by December 1791.

Although there is no discussion in the Constitution of the four principles that guided its writing, it is helpful to keep in mind that it was the intent of the framers to manage the power of the new government they were creating by dividing, separating, checking and balancing, and limiting it. Furthermore, in choosing these ways of ensuring freedom from arbitrary power, the framers knew that they would be sacrificing the possibility of speedy governmental action. In other words, the U.S. government today is working just as it was designed to work over two hundred years ago: slowly, cautiously, and deliberately.

As frustrating as this may be, to have it work any other way would require changing or amending the Constitution. The framers, as will be seen in the next section of this chapter, made the formal process for bringing about a change both explicit and difficult to accomplish.

THE CONSTITUTION: An Anatomy

An examination of the Constitution's "physical attributes," or anatomy, besides a perusal of its words, provides some clues about what the framers had in mind while they were creating the new government. Two examples come to mind. The first is the most obvious feature of the Charter, its brevity.

The shortness of the document suggests that it was never intended to be all-inclusive. The Constitution is brief because it was written to provide a general rather than a detailed outline of how the government was to be organized and to work.

Observation also reveals a second noticeable feature. The Constitution ratified in 1788 consists of just two parts, the Preamble and seven Articles. The third part, the Bill of Rights, was added in 1791.

The Preamble

We the People of the United States, in Order to form a more perfect Union, establish Justice, insure domestic Tranquility, provide for the common defence, promote the general Welfare, and secure the Blessings of Liberty to ourselves and our Posterity, do ordain and establish this Constitution for the United States of America.

A **preamble**, which literally means "to walk before," precedes the body of a work and provides the context for, and sometimes a summary of, the material that follows. Although a preamble is an opening statement, it does not mean that it was the first part actually written. The framers, as many authors do today, completed their document and then, knowing what was said, went back to the beginning and wrote their introduction.

This bit of historical trivia takes on significance only because, as it is often observed, the first few words of the one-sentence preamble of the Constitution, **"We the People of the United States,"** could never have been written on May 25, 1787, when the delegates convened the first formal meeting of the convention in the East Room of the Pennsylvania State House. The conceptualization of citizenship in one single nation was still a new one for these Americans whose loyalty, up to this point, had primarily been to their respective states. The notion of national identity, and the acceptance of the "United States" in place of the "Federal Union of Sovereign States," evolved slowly over the 115 days that the delegates met, debated, compromised, and eventually produced a new Constitution.

The Preamble establishes four specific goals: to "**establish Justice, insure domestic Tranquility, provide for the common defence, promote the general Welfare, and secure the Blessings of Liberty . . . .**" These then were the objectives set forth for the government that was to be structured by the seven articles that followed.

An Overview of Articles I-VII

As discussed previously, it was the desire to prevent an accumulation of power that led the framers to separate and divide it among three branches that would check each other. These branches, the legislature, the executive and the judiciary, are established by the first three articles. Some of the sections and clauses of these three are summarized below.

ARTICLE I: THE LEGISLATIVE ARTICLE

Section 1: All legislative Powers herein granted shall be vested in a Congress of the United States, which shall consist of a Senate and House of Representatives.

Article 1, begins by establishing a bicameral, two-house, Congress. The two-house legislature provided additional insurance that the government would be a "balanced" one in which all interests of society would be represented: wealthier interests primarily in the upper house, Senate, and the interests of the rest of the population primarily in the lower house, House of Representatives. Having two houses also provided an additional opportunity for "checks" by each house of the other so that no one interest would dominate the others.

Section 2: House of Representatives

This section describes the term of office (two years), qualifications (age twenty-five or older, a citizen of the United States for at least seven years, a resident of the electing state), apportionment of representatives (establishment of congressional districts), and impeachment power. (The House of Representatives takes the first step in the removal of a government official by bringing formal charges against the individual.)

Section 3: Senate

Section 3 discusses the composition of the Senate (two senators from each state), term of office (six years with one third of the Senate up for re-election every two years), qualifications (age thirty or older, a citizen of the United States for at least nine years, a resident of the electing state), and the power to try impeachments. (The Senate trial is the second step in the removal of a government official.)

Section 4: Congressional Elections and Sessions

The first Tuesday after the first Monday in November in even-numbered years was established, by the Congress, as election day for representatives. Every state now elects their senators on that date. The Congress is required to meet at least once each year and, according to the Twentieth Amendment, their session begins at 12:00 P.M. on January 3.

Section 5: Powers and Duties of the Houses

The Houses determine which individuals are entitled to be seated and the rules for conducting their meetings. They are obliged to keep an official record of their proceedings and to agree on when to adjourn.

Section 6: Rights and Restrictions of Members

Members are entitled to compensation for their services, and their salaries have increased from the initial $6 per diem rate received by legislators in 1789 to $133,600 today. They may not be arrested for anything they say on the floor of Congress or in committee meetings and reports, and they have immunity from arrest for the commission of civil offenses while in the Capital Building.

Members are restricted from holding two federal government positions concurrently. This restriction is in keeping with and supports the principle of separation of powers.

Section 7: Bills and Vetoes

Revenue bills originate in the House of Representatives although the Senate may amend House bills or substitute a new one. All bills must be passed in identical form by both houses and then sent to the president. If the president does not sign the bill, he may either return it to the house in which it originated and a two-thirds majority in both houses is then required to pass it into law. He may hold the bill and, unless Congress adjourns, it becomes law at the end of ten days (excluding Sundays).

Section 8: Legislative Powers of Congress

Beginning with the words "**The Congress shall have Power to,**" this section goes on to delegate, in seventeen clauses, seventeen specific legislative powers many of which the Congress that functioned under the Articles did not have. These include, for example, the first—and weight should be given to that status —"**the Power To lay and collect Taxes . . . ,**" the fifth, "**to coin money . . . ,**" and the eleventh "**to declare War . . . .**"

Clause eighteen is sometimes referred to as the "**elastic**" or "**necessary-and-proper**" clause because it allows Congress to do whatever it deems necessary and proper to do to carry out its seventeen delegated powers. For instance, although Section 8 does not specifically give Congress the power to establish a national bank, the Supreme Court decided in the famous case *McCulloch v Maryland* (1819) that such a bank was necessary in order for Congress to execute its expressed powers to lay and collect taxes, regulate currency, and promote interstate commerce.

The expansion of congressional strength to include such "**implied powers**" was very controversial, but as Madison argued, in *Federalist 44*, that "without the **substance** of this power, the whole Constitution would be a dead letter . . . ." After all, to have attempted to enumerate every power "would have involved a complete digest of laws on every subject to which the Constitution relates; accommodated too, not only to the existing state of things, but to all the possible changes which futurity may produce . . . ." The future then was very much in the minds of those who advocated on behalf of Clause 18. They intended to, and did by its inclusion, create a "living" Constitution.

Section 9: Powers Denied to Congress

Among the eight powers denied to Congress are the powers to prohibit the importation of slaves (described in this section with the euphemism "persons") until the year 1808; to suspend the writ of *habeas corpus*; to discriminate against any state(s) in the regulation of interstate and foreign commerce; and to bestow a title of nobility.

Section 10: Powers Denied to the States

The powers denied to the States include making international treaties; coining money; maintaining troops during peacetime; and engaging in war.

ARTICLE II: THE EXECUTIVE ARTICLE

The second Article, which is comprised of four sections, is, when contrasted with the nine in Article I, rather succinct. This, in part, reflects the attempt to reduce the powers held by the person occupying the office of the presidency to that of executing or carrying out the laws made by Congress.

Section 1: Nature and Scope of Presidential Power

According to the provisions of this first section:

a. a president serves for a term of four years. After Franklin Delano Roosevelt died in the beginning of his fourth term as president, the Twenty-second Amendment (ratified in 1951) was proposed to limit future executives to two, four-year terms.

b. the selection of the president is to be carried out through an Electoral College, rather than by direct popular vote. The original procedures set down for selecting electors were changed in 1804 by the Twelfth Amendment.

c. Congress is given the power to designate the date for choosing electors. It has selected the first Tuesday after the first Monday in November in presidential election years. On the Monday following the second Wednesday in December, the electors cast their votes for president.

d. an individual must be a natural-born citizen, at least thirty-five years of age, and a resident of the United States for fourteen years to be eligible for election to the presidency.

e. in addition to the provisions summarized above, Section 1 of Article II provides for the succession of the vice president; prevents a cut in, or increase of, the president's salary (which today is $400,000 with an additional $50,000 for expenses) to keep the executive office independent from the Congress; and specifies the oath of office to be given, usually by the Chief Justice of the Supreme Court, on inauguration day (currently the twentieth day of January).

Section 2: Powers of the President

Once inaugurated the powers of the office are officially conferred upon the president.

a. To ensure civilian control of the military, the president (a civilian) is the Commander in Chief of the armed forces.

b. He is empowered to grant reprieves and pardons in cases that involve offenses against the United States and the president. (Gerald Ford did so when he pardoned former President Richard

Nixon for any crimes he might have committed during his term of office. This was probably the most controversial presidential pardon in American history although others, such as President Carter's pardon of those who violated the draft law during the Vietnam period, have also angered many people.)

c. The president is given the power to make treaties and to appoint ambassadors, justices of the Supreme Court, and other government ministers, consuls, and officers. However, Senate approval is required for treaty ratification (two-thirds vote) and the confirmation of many appointments (majority vote). This is a clear example of a check on the presidential branch of government.

d. When the Senate is in recess, the president may temporarily fill vacant federal offices.

Section 3: Duties of the President

a. This section requires the president to "**from time to time give the Congress Information of the State of the Union . . . .**" Although this directive does not explicitly say so, most presidents have delivered such information to Congress and the American people in an annual State of the Union address. With the advent of television coverage, it has become the custom for the opposition party to have air-time immediately following the speech to respond to the president's remarks.

b. Section 3 also allows the president to call a special session of Congress and states that it is his duty to receive Ambassadors from foreign countries, to commission officers, and to "**take Care that the Laws be faithfully executed.**" The last of these provisions requires the president to enforce all laws, all federal court decisions, and all regulations of the federal bureaucracy. Such a requirement raises the question of whether a president is expected to execute laws that she(he) believes to be unconstitutional.

Section 4: Impeachment

If **impeached** (formally accused) and convicted of "**Treason, Bribery, or other high Crimes and Misdemeanors**" the president, vice president, or other civil officers are removed from office. The Senate decided after one of its members was impeached in 1797 that members of Congress are not "civil officers," and they are not therefore now subject to the Constitution's impeachment clause.

ARTICLE III: THE JUDICIAL ARTICLE

The wording of this Article, which contains three sections, is sometimes vague because it reflects the difficulties the members of the Convention had in coming to an agreement about the nature of the third branch of government.

Section 1: Judicial Power, Term, and Compensation

a. Because the framers could not agree on the structure of the federal court system, they invested judicial power in one Supreme Court and left it to Congress to create "inferior" courts.

b. The judges, or as they have been called since 1789 "justices," of the Supreme Court serve for life during good behavior and receive compensation that, to maintain their independence, may not be reduced during their service.

Section 2: Scope of Judicial Power

a. Federal courts decide cases that concern the Constitution, federal laws, treaties, the admiralty, maritime, citizens of different states, and citizens of foreign countries.

b. The Supreme Court, which functions primarily as an appeal court, has original jurisdiction only in "**Cases affecting Ambassadors, other public Ministers and Consuls, and those in which a State shall be a party.**"

c. Individuals accused of committing a federal crime are guaranteed the right to a trial by jury in a federal court in the state in which the crime was committed.

Section 3: Treason

a. Treason is defined as "**levying war**" against the United States or in giving "**Aid and Comfort**" to U.S. enemies.

b. The Constitution gives Congress the power to determine the punishment for treason. It has determined that the punishment can be a prison sentence of no less than five years, a fine of $10,000, or death.

ARTICLE IV: RELATIONS AMONG THE STATES

Article IV requires each state to respect the laws, proceedings, and judicial decisions of the others. It forbids discrimination by any state against out-of-state citizens by entitling them to "**all Privileges and Immunities of Citizens in the several States**"; it provides for interstate rendition or extradition, and it gives Congress the power to admit new states to the union.

ARTICLE V: INSTRUCTIONS FOR AMENDING THE CONSTITUTION

Amending the Constitution is a two-step process. Amendments must be proposed, and they must be ratified. Although Article V describes two different methods of carrying out each of these steps, up to this time every amendment that has been added since the original ten that constitute the Bill of Rights has been proposed by a two-thirds vote of Congress rather than by the alternative method—a request from two-thirds of the state legislatures that Congress summon a national convention.

Congress determines which of the two ways of ratifying a proposed amendment will be used. As of today, all but one of the seventeen amendments that have been approved since 1791 have been ratified by three-fourths of the state legislatures. Only the Twenty-first Amendment, which repealed prohibition (Amendment Eighteen), was ratified following the other procedure—approval by state conventions in three-fourths of the states.

Although these procedures make it possible to change the Constitution, they clearly do not make it easy.

ARTICLE VI: THE SUPREMACY OF THE NATIONAL GOVERNMENT

This article, which addresses the issue of federalism, states that the Constitution and the laws of the national government "**shall be the supreme Law of the Land.**" To acknowledge acceptance of this premise, every national and state official is required to take an oath of office in which the promise, "to support this [the U.S.] Constitution" is made.

ARTICLE VII: RATIFICATION OF THE CONSTITUTION

"The Ratification of the Conventions of nine States shall, be sufficient for the Establishment of this Constitution between the States so ratifying the Same."

Ratification

Before the new document was even completed, the delegates realized that ratification of it by the state legislatures would be difficult at best. The state legislatures, the traditional source of power in the states, distrusted the results of the convention in Philadelphia. The delegates had already gone outside the boundaries of the authority granted to them by their state legislatures and redistributed governmental power in such a way as to consolidate power in the national government. This new governmental configuration was expected to meet much opposition in the state legislatures since they were the governing bodies that would be relinquishing power. More than merely being dis- gruntled about the new power relationships, the delegates were concerned that the state legislatures might hold the Constitution as a political hostage. The state legislatures were mired down with complex agendas. Each focused on the parochial interests of the individual states. Any faction within the legislature that wished to promote any part of its particular agenda might hold out voting either for or against ratification until its agenda was met.

The delegates needed to devise a ratification plan for the Constitution that would accomplish two objectives. First, the requirements for ratification would have to be much less stringent than the amendment process for the Articles of Confederation, which required the unanimous consent of the state legislatures. The delegates quickly eliminated the "unanimous" requirement, realizing that this would be impossible to accomplish since Rhode Island did not even send a state delegation to the convention in Philadelphia. In the spirit of "quick" ratification, the delegates stipulated that only nine out of the thirteen states would be required for ratification before the Constitution be- came the official governing document of the United States.

Second, since the delegates could not risk sending the Constitution to the state legislatures, they needed to devise an alternative "legitimate" ratifying institution. They devised an ingenious way to accomplish this objective. The delegates specified that "special ratifying conventions" would act as the agents of ratification. Voters in each state would select representatives to attend their state ratifying convention. These representatives would attend their conventions for the sole purpose of deciding whether to ratify the Constitution. Ostensibly the conventions would have no vested interest in the power struggles that currently raged in their individual state legislatures.

Two distinct groups formed around the ratification question. The **Federalists** were supporters of ratification, and their most notable spokespersons were James Madison and Alexander Hamilton. The **Anti-Federalists** were opposed to ratification, and their most vocal leaders were Samuel Adams and Patrick Henry. Economist Charles Beard argues that the ratification question was divided along class lines with the economic elite supporting ratification and the masses opposing it. While historians disagree on this point, clearly the ratification process itself was an elite event. Only approximately 160,000 voted for representatives to the state ratifying conventions and of those only approximately 100,000 supported ratification. This figure represents only approximately 5 percent of the population of the United States.[23]

The battle for ratification was bitter. One of the major battles focused on the lack of an explicit statement of rights in the document. The delegates did not even discuss the possibility of such a statement until the last week of the convention and had been brilliantly persuaded by such delegates as Hamilton and Madison that such a list would be more exclusive than inclusive. It was effectively argued that all the rights of man that needed to be protected from government could never be fully enumerated. Instead of a specific list of rights, it would be more efficient to create a set of structural guarantees against governmental abuses of liberty. These structural guarantees were considered to be insufficient barriers against tyranny by the state conventions. To avoid calling a new convention, the Federalists guaranteed that the first order of business of the new Congress would be to establish a Bill of Rights enumerating specific rights that government could not abuse. This guarantee cleared the way for ratification.

In December 1787, Delaware became the first state to ratify the Constitution, and nine months later, New Hampshire became the ninth and final state needed to activate the Constitution as the new governing document. Three other states ratified before 1788, but Rhode Island held out until May 1790, which was after the first Congress had convened, Washington had been inaugurated, and the Supreme Court established.[24] The new Congress met for the first time in March 1789. The Constitution that had been illegally constructed by the delegates to the convention in Philadelphia was now the official governing document of the United States and would continue to be so. This document currently frames the political environment of the United States and establishes the political construct in which the government of today is understood.

CONCLUSION

The political questions addressed by the writers of the Articles of Confederation and the delegates to the Constitutional Convention were never fully answered. For all practical purposes, the constitutional convention is still in session. If we listen carefully to the rhetoric in the corridors of the Capital in Washington D.C. today and to the speeches made by governors and state legislators we can hear the same rhetoric that was used to address the question of the "nature of the union" over 200 years ago.

CHAPTER NOTES

[1]Frederic A. Youngs, Jr., Henry L. Snyder, E.A. Reitan, *The English Heritage*, 2d ed. (Arlington Heights, Illinois: Forum Press, Inc., 1988), 274.

[2]Fawn M. Brodie, *Thomas Jefferson: An Intimate History*, (Toronto, Canada: Bantam Books, Inc., 1975), 120.

[3]Thomas R. Dye, and L. Harmon Zeigler, *The Irony of Democracy: An Uncommon Introduction to American Politics*, 5th ed., (Duxbury Press: Monterrey, Calif., 1981), 32.

[4]Ibid.

[5]Barbara A. Bardes, Mack C. Shelley II, and Steffen W. Schmidt, *American Government and Politics Today: The Essentials,* (St. Paul, Minn. West Publishing Co., 1986), 35.

[6]Thomas R. Dye, and Harmon Zeigler, *The Irony of Democracy: An Uncommon Introduction to American Politics,* (Belmont, Calif.: Wadsworth Publishing Co., 1993), 28.

[7]Ibid., 30.

[8]Michael Parenti, *Democracy for the Few*, 6th ed., (New York: St. Martins Press, 1995), 62.

[9]J.W. Peltason, *Corwin & Peltason's Understanding the Constitution*, 13th ed., (Forth Worth: Harcourt Brace College Publishers, 1994), 13.

[10]Ibid., 14.

[11]Dye, 1993, 32.

[12]Ibid.

[13]Clayton Roberts, and David Roberts, *A History of England: Prehistory to 1714*: Volume I, 3rd ed., (Englewood Cliffs: New Jersey: Prentice Hall, 1991), 411.

[14]Dye, 1981, 47.

[15]Bardes, 45.

[16]Ibid.

[17]David Brion Davis, "The Constitution and the Slave Trade," in *American Negro Slavery: A Modern Reader*, 3rd ed., (New York: Oxford University Press, 1979), 25.

[18]Ibid., 21-25.

[19]William W. Freehling, "The Founding Fathers and Slavery," in *American Negro Slavery: A Modern Reader*, 3rd ed., (New York: Oxford University Press, 1979), 17.

[20]Cedric J. Robinson, Black Movements in America, (New York: Routledge, 1997), 22.

[21]Davis, 24.

[22]Saul K. Padover, *The Living U.S. Constitution*, 2d ed. (New York: New American Library, 1983), 21-24.

[23]Dye, 1993, 47.

[24]Peverill Squire and others, *Dynamics of Democracy*, (Madison: Brown and Benchmark, 1995), 23.

SUGGESTED READING

Agel, Jerome, and Bernstein B. *Amending America*. New York: Random House, 1993.

Beard, Charles, H. *The Enduring Federalist*. Garden City, N.Y.: Doubleday and Co., Inc., 1948.

Brodie, Fawn M. *Thomas Jefferson: An Intimate History*. *Toronto*, Canada: Bantam Books, Inc., 1975.

Collier, Christopher, and Collier, James Lincoln. *Decision in Philadelphia*. New York: Random House, 1986.

Friendly, Fred W., and Martha J. H. Elliott. *The Constitution that Delicate Balance: Landmark Cases that Shaped the Constitution*. New York: Random House. 1984.

Mitchell, Ralph. *CQ's Guide to the U.S. Constitution*. Congressional Quarterly, 1988.

Paine, Thomas. *Rights of Man and Common Sense*, with an Introduction by Michael Foot. New York: Alfred A. Knopf, 1994.

CHARLESTON
MERCURY
EXTRA:

Passed unanimously at 1.15 o'clock, P. M., December
20th, 1860.

AN ORDINANCE

To dissolve the Union between the State of South Carolina and
other States united with her under the compact entitled "The
Constitution of the United States of America."

We, the People of the State of South Carolina, in Convention assembled, do declare and ordain, and
it is hereby declared and ordained,

That the Ordinance adopted by us in Convention, on the twenty-third day of May, in the
year of our Lord one thousand seven hundred and eighty-eight, whereby the Constitution of the
United States of America was ratified, and also, all Acts and parts of Acts of the General
Assembly of this State, ratifying amendments of the said Constitution, are hereby repealed;
and that the union now subsisting between South Carolina and other States, under the name of
"The United States of America," is hereby dissolved.

THE

UNION
IS
DISSOLVED!

Chapter Three

FEDERALISM: Theories of Governing

KATRINA: THE HUMAN FACE OF FEDERALISM
CRISIS MANAGEMENT OR EVERYDAY FEDERALISM?

Many Americans were riveted to their TV sets during the tragedy of Hurricane Katrina. What they were viewing was actually the human element of federalism, an element often forgotten when we discuss the formal definitions and constitutional explanations of that concept. A concept often taken for granted because it usually functions adequately until a situation occurs, which stresses the political system to its limit and demonstrates its flaws.

Hurricane Katrina devastated New Orleans and much of southern Louisiana, Mississippi and parts of Arkansas. More than 1,000 people died, and over 1.5 million residents throughout the Gulf Coast were displaced. Hardest hit was New Orleans. Although 80 percent of the population of New Orleans had been evacuated; over 100,000 people were left behind, mostly low income African Americans. It is still difficult to get the visual images of the initial devastation and human suffering out of one's mind. The image of 25,000 people stranded in the Superdome for over three days without food or water is seared in our memories as part of our political and institutional history.

The question of federalism is at the core of the discussion of Katrina, and it is the very essence of how our system operates as a whole political process. Federalism is essentially one of jurisdiction. Who gets to do what, when do they get to do it, and who pays for it? The national government? The state? The local government? Never was this more apparent in the intergovernmental jurisdictional wrangling, not only in the immediate aftermath of Katrina, which required quick response to the initial impact of the hurricane, but in the days and weeks that followed in the process of rebuilding the area.

During the crisis it often appeared that the dispute over governmental jurisdiction left no one willing to take action, leaving the victims stranded. Governmental officials at all levels took the position it was someone else's jurisdiction. Mayor Ray Nagin and Louisiana's Governor Kathleen Blanco criticized the disorganized responses of the Federal Emergency Management Agency (FEMA) which had been made part of the Department of Homeland Security, directly answerable to President Bush. They had their own views of the situation, their own views of their jurisdiction and their own views of what others should be responsible for doing. In the end, these conflicting views were unable to resolve the problems. Although within weeks of Katrina, Michael Brown, Director of FEMA, was forced to resign for his agency's inability to act quickly in the face of a natural disaster, state and local officials to include Nagin and Blanco were also criticized for their lack of action as "first responders" to the crisis.

Who is responsible? Who is accountable? Who pays for evacuation and reconstruction? The federalist system of government often makes it difficult to define and assess these elements of the concept. But federalism is more than jurisdiction; it is about responsibility within jurisdiction. As we examine these concepts, let us remember Katrina's human face.

THEORIES OF GOVERNANCE

There are two basic classifications of governmental structures: **federal** and **unitary**. Within each classification there are subsets, for example, a confederacy is a subset of the federal system. The United States has a federal system. Federalism, however, is not a particularly common form of government as only 11 out of the approximately 190 countries are structured in this manner. Countries that have selected federalist systems may have very little in common other than their governing structure. Federalism exists in many unique forms in such diverse political settings as Switzerland, Canada, India, Mexico, and Argentina.[1]

The theory of **federalism** is simple, but it is difficult to implement. Theoretically, it is a way of organizing government so that **power is shared**. This means that power is decentralized, and there are many sources, or **points of power**. It is designed so that no one group or person can ever acquire all the power. In a federal system, two or more units of government have formal control and authority over the same people and the same territory. Each unit of government sustains substantial and autonomous governing authority. Its decision-makers maintain power independent of the desires of those who control the other levels of government. Therefore, decentralization may also cause conflict.[2]

In a federal system, the constitution is the source of political power. It establishes the parameters of power for the various governing units. The U.S. Constitution stipulates that power will be shared by the national and state governments. Simultaneously, each exists as an autonomous governing authority. For example, the national government has the authority to make laws that have an affect on citizens in all fifty states. At the same time, each state has the authority to determine policies for individuals within its own geographic boundaries. Therefore, individuals in the states of New York and Kentucky are each concurrently governed by the policies and laws of their state and national governments.

Both the national and state governments receive their power from the Constitution; they do not receive their power from each other. They stand alone as independent governing bodies, each vested with its own political power. They exist because the Constitution says they do. Neither the national nor any state government has the authority to abolish the other. What the Constitution has given, the governing bodies may not take away.

In practice, federalism is much more complicated. Since federalism's concept of shared powers virtually assures that individuals will simultaneously be governed by a myriad of independent policies, the possibility for conflict is practically assured. In a perfect system, the national and state policies would coexist in harmony. The reality is that, more often than not, their policies, or at least the implementation of those policies, conflict. Federalism is one of five principles that were discussed in Chapter Two. To be effective, federalism requires that all units of government engage in cooperative policy-making. How that happens, or does not happen, defines the success or failure of a federalist system. The story of American federalism is in its implementation; the case of Hurricane Katrina exemplifies the worst-case scenario of the failure of federalism. However, not all examples are so dramatic or negative. Policy-makers deal with the concept of federalism everyday, often in such a way that most people do not notice its implementation and often have positive results.

Unitary System

The more common governing structure is the **unitary** system. It contrasts sharply from the federalist system. Unlike the federal system where power is shared, the unitary system vests all power in one governing body, the central government. This system, like federalism, also exists in many diverse forms. The most common model of unitary government allows the central government to create subunits or local governments. Subdividing the government into smaller units enables the central government to conduct its business more efficiently. However, in a unitary system, in contrast to a federal system, whatever power the central government grants, it may also take away. For example, Great Britain has a unitary system, and all power is vested in the central government, more specifically in Parliament, the legislative branch. Parliament passes legislation that creates local governments, establishing the physical and political boundaries of these subunits. It can, and has, changed or abolished them as it deemed necessary. In 1972, Great Britain passed the Local Government Act that reduced the number of local authorities, especially borough councils, and created six large new metropolitan councils.[3] In contrast, in the United States, Congress does not have the authority to pass legislation that could abolish San Francisco or Dallas.

Unitary Component of Federal System

Although the United States has a federal system, it actually contains elements of both the federal and unitary systems. The federal constitution defines the shared powers of the national and state governments; however, it makes no provision for local governments. Therefore, there is no inherent constitutional right for local governments, such as counties or cities, to exist. The reality of the American federal system is that there are three, rather than two, levels of government: national, state, and local. In fact, local governments make up the bulk of the governing structure of the U.S. federal system. Today, it is estimated that there are approximately 79,000 local governing units. However, if there is no provision for them in the federal constitution, how are local governments created, and from where do they receive their power?

State governments function in the capacity of a unitary system vìs a vìs their local governments. Power is centralized in the hands of the state, and it is not shared with the local governments. Local governing units are not autonomous governing units; rather, they are created by the state governments to administer state power. Local governments exist because the state says they may and, consequently, the states can choose to abolish them or create more of them as they see fit.

It is a state's constitution that determines both if and how local units will be created and under what conditions they may continue to exist. In most instances, state constitutions provide for legislative procedures that will allow the state's legislative body to enact statutes to empower local governments. Legislation will determine the parameters of local power and regulate its political functions. It will also determine the relationship the state will have with its local units and that the local units will have with each other. For example, the state of Kentucky has ratified four constitutions and is currently operating under the last one that was ratified in 1891. Under the first three constitutions, the General Assembly, or legislative body, exercised total control over the creation of cities, counties, and other units of local government and could adjust the boundaries of existing ones without limitation. Today, all local units of Kentucky government including cities, counties, special districts, and school districts are legal subdivisions of the state. They derive their powers from the state and can do only those things permitted by the Constitution and laws passed by the General Assembly. The 1891 Constitution established six classes of cities, based on population, so that all laws relating to a particular class of city would apply equally to all cities with the same population class. It provided for the election or appointment of city and county officers, established their qualifications, and prohibited them from having conflicts of interests. The General Assembly retained its authority to create new cities, counties, and other units of local governments.[4]

There is, however, one federal constitutional limit to what local governments may or may not do. Since local governments are agents of the state, they are governed by the federal as well as their state constitution. Whatever the federal constitution says states may or may not do, local governments also may or may not do. State governments can never grant more power to their local governments than they themselves have been granted by the federal constitution.

HISTORICAL ROOTS OF UNITED STATES FEDERALISM

Today it is difficult to find a federal system of government, and it was even more unusual to find such a system in 1787. So, incorporating the basic concept of federalism into the 1787 Constitution begs two interesting questions: first, "Why?" and, second, "Where did the concept originate?"

Historically, the foundations for the U.S. political system have been credited to Anglo-Saxon traditions stemming from ideas and practices inherited from the British. In many cases this was true. After all, most of the white population just prior to the American Revolution considered themselves to be British and quite naturally would adopt their governing practices albeit with an American spin. For example, in Great Britain, the legislative branch, Parliament, had replaced the monarch as the legitimate governing authority. The revolutionaries in writing the Articles of Confederation used the British model; however, their new government only consisted of a legislative branch. In 1787, again using the British model, the framers of the Constitution determined that the legislative branch, Congress, was to be the most powerful and significant branch of government.

However, as previously discussed, Great Britain has a unitary system. If the colonists were following British traditions and practices, would it have not been logical to assume that they would adopt a unitary system of government that concentrated power in the hands of the central government? This did not occur. The state legislatures were not going to relinquish all of their power to a central authority. The fledgling country needed to find an alternative governing structure to the British unitary system. It was a risky experiment in the process of governing but the Continental Congress adopted a federal system of government, virtually unheard of in Europe at the time, thus creating what appeared to be a unique American creation. However, adopting the federal system begs two questions. Since the roots of the federal system were not inherently British, how were the seeds of this idea planted in the colonies and how and why did it grow? What factors led the framers of the Constitution to adopt this unique concept as one of their fundamental governing principles?

Native American Influence

There is a growing body of scholarly research that suggests that the colonists borrowed several political and social concepts from the Native Americans. Federalism was one of those concepts. It was an idea that was deeply embedded in the traditions of several Indian political structures, and it is believed that the roots of American federalism can be traced back to them, most particularly, the Iroquois confederation of nations.

The British colonists were not the first to encounter the Iroquois Confederacy. Iroquois is a French term for the united nations of the "Haudenosaunee," meaning "people of the Longhouse." Although it is difficult to date the origin of the Iroquois League whose five original nations, Mohawk, Oneida, Onondaga, Cayuga, and Seneca, were joined by the Tuscaroras around 1700 CE, scholars agree that it existed well before contact with any European nation, around 1450-1500 CE. By the time the American revolutionaries encountered the Iroquois Confederacy, it was a well-established, strong and well-functioning political entity.[5]

The Iroquois nations and its confederation fired the imaginations of the American revolutionaries. The six nations that composed the Iroquois confederation were diverse in nature and yet worked together as a cohesive governing unit. Several of the American revolutionaries, including Jefferson and Franklin, viewed this as a viable working arrangement for the American colonies. Jefferson and Franklin believed that the Indians had what the colonists wanted, societies free of oppression and class stratification. Franklin and his fellow colonists learned from the American Indians and assimilated into their vision of the American future aspects of their political wisdom and governing structure.[6]

Benjamin Franklin more than any of the other constitutional writers promoted the integration of Iroquois social and political thought into the new U.S. government. Franklin became involved

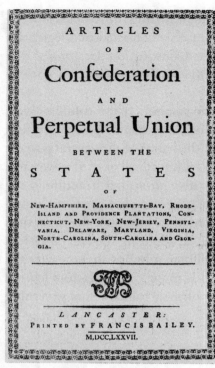

Benjamin Franklin
promoted the integration
of Iroquois thought.

The Articles of Confederation
became the first American
Constitution.

in Native American relations early in his political career. Most of his early experience derived from the periods of peace the colonists shared with the Native Americans, which until recently had been relatively unexplored in historical research. This is unfortunate because periods of peace often reveal more about society and the political process than do periods of war. Periods of peace between the colonists and the Native Americans were important because this was the time when positive cultural exchanges took place.

Periods of peace required peace councils. The councils brought together the leaders of both cultures. It was here that significant social and political ideas were exchanged between the colonists and the Native Americans. This was particularly important during the mid-eighteenth century when the seeds for political thought were being sewn in North America. Franklin first attended the peace councils as a note-taker, as a "printer" of the proceedings, and later as an official colonial envoy. It was during this period that Franklin first became impressed with Iroquois political thought. During the pre-Revolutionary period, he was looking for alternatives to a European order that he regarded as tyrannical. These councils provided the seeds of thought that grew into an early campaign by Franklin for a colonial Union based on a federal model, very similar to the Iroquois system.[7] Franklin hoped to unite the colonies not only in a revolutionary movement against the British but in implementing a successful governing structure after independence. Franklin and other revolutionaries realized that adopting a strictly European governing model was inadequate for their needs. The Iroquois nation offered them an alternative.

As early as 1750, Franklin began to envision a form of political confederation that would accommodate distinct, often mutually suspicious, political entities, the thirteen colonies. A confederal or governmental structure similar to the Iroquois Confederacy, which would allow each state in the Union to manage its own internal affairs while it empowered the central government with pursuing common external matters, was very appealing.[8] In 1754, Franklin presented his ideas regarding confederation in the Albany Plan of Union. Although originally rejected by the colonial legislatures, this plan was the precursor to the Articles of Confederation.[9]

According to Lewis Henry Morgan, known as the "father of American anthropology," the federalism of the Iroquois was similar to the newly united British colonies. He concluded that the six Iroquois nations sustained nearly the same relation to the Iroquois league that the American states had with the Union. He also claims that the Iroquois suggested to the colonists that their political organization might be appropriate for them:

> The people of the Longhouse commended to our forefathers a union of colonies similar to their own as early as 1755 . . . . The Iroquois saw in the common interests and common speech of the colonies the elements for a confederation.[10]

In July of 1744, Canasstego, Iroquois speaker at the council of Onondaga, a joint council meeting between the colonists and the Iroquois, advised American colonists that a confederation of states such as theirs would be a plausible, if not the ideal, form of government for them. He states:

> Our wise forefathers established union and amity between the Five Nations. This has made us formidable. This has given us great weight and authority with our neighboring Nations. We are a powerful Confederacy and by your observing the same methods our wise forefathers have taken you will acquire much strength and power; therefore, whatever befalls you, do not fall out with one another.[11]

In 1754, the colonists had rejected Franklin's Albany Plan. By 1777, circumstances had changed drastically in the colonies. The Revolutionary War had begun. Realizing that unity was a necessity, the Second Continental Congress appointed a committee to draw up a plan of perpetual union, resulting in the Articles of Confederation. Although not formally adopted by the states until 1781, the confederation established by the Articles presented a unified position not only to the British but the rest of the European world as well. As individual states, they would perish; as a confederacy, the Americans took on the British Empire.

By 1787, the political and economic situation in the United States had so deteriorated that the states were willing to relinquish still more power to a central government to preserve the Union. In structure, the Articles of Confederation much more resembled the Iroquois Confederacy than did the Constitution. The articles were intended as a "league of friendship" among sovereign states.[12] However, as discussed in Chapter Two, the Articles of Confederation did not create a strong enough national government for the Union to survive. The constitutional convention was forced to address the deficiencies in the Articles and established a stronger national government. By 1787, the concept of confederalism was no longer sufficient to hold the Union together. How the states and central government would share power needed to be renegotiated. The concept of shared power was now firmly embedded in the American political and legal tradition.

Implementation of Federalism

U.S. Constitution/Federalism

Federalism is one of the fundamental concepts that establishes the basic character of the American government. It is also the cause of one of the most intractable political problems in American politics. The core of the problem is the Constitution's inability to define the relationship between the states and national government. This has resulted in creating tension between the states and the national government, tearing at the very fiber of the Union. The solution to this political dilemma has always eluded decision-makers because it has required precisely defining the nature of the Union. In so doing, it would clearly define power relationships, something politicians were either unable or unwilling to do.

The history of federalism represents the political history of the United States. The debate over the nature of the Union has historically been framed in terms of state sovereignty versus the power of the national government. The debate over this issue has raged from the time of the Articles of Confederation to the Supreme Court decision, *Bush v Gore*, rendered during the presidential election in 2000, to the life threatening circumstances created by Hurricane Katrina. There have been times in American history when the debate over federalism became so serious that it erupted into violence, for example, the Civil War.

Federal systems by definition require that power be shared, and this inherently creates tension. In a perfect world, the Constitution would clearly define the relationship between the national government and the states. This would go a long way to diminishing the tensions between the two. However, the U.S. Constitution did not create a perfect world. Powers are not always clearly defined. The framers of the Constitution left the division of power vague and open to interpretation. The parameters of power are flexible and often difficult to determine. Consequently, the boundaries of state and national power are constantly shifting, continually altering the balance of power between the national and state governments, creating constant tension between the two. The tension has pulled the system in two different directions, one towards the national government, the other towards the states. Historically, the U.S. has moved towards eliminating that tension by concentrating power in the hands of the national government. However, when the national government becomes either too powerful or too economically weak, the system readjusts and recenters itself by returning some of that power back to the states.

GRANTS OF CONSTITUTIONAL POWER

Federalism permeates the very essence of the Constitution. However, it never explicitly mentions federalism nor formally defines the concept. Instead, it simply creates the framework for the distribution of power between the national government and the states. The framers of the Constitution attempted to maintain a balance between sovereign states and a sovereign national government. In so doing, they simultaneously granted and withheld a variety of powers to each level of government. The idea was to allocate powers in such a way as to create a strong national government without seriously weakening the states. The framers did not want to create states that were so powerful that they could undermine the national government. This was no easy task as the political history of the United States reveals.[13] The very nature of the task required ambiguous and/or contradictory grants of power to both levels of government.

The constitutional basis of American federalism is as follows:

1. The Constitution delegates explicit powers to the national government.
2. Article VI of the Constitution contains the "national supremacy" clause, asserting that the national government is supreme.
3. It reserves to the states powers not granted to the national government.
4. The Constitution denies some powers to both the national and state governments. It specifically denies some powers only to the national government and still other powers are denied only to the state governments.[14]

National Powers

Explicit or **enumerated** powers are specifically granted to the national government in the Constitution. Although they can be found scattered throughout the document, most congressional grants of power are in Article I, Section 8. These include such diverse powers as the ability to coin money, regulate commerce, establish federal courts, and declare war.

Implied powers are not particular grants of power such as those listed in Article I, Section 8. Rather, they are powers that may be reasonably inferred from the powers already expressly granted. Implied powers stem from the paragraph or last legislative grant of power in Article I, Section 8. This is known as the implied powers/elastic or "**necessary and proper clause.**" It states:

Congress shall have power . . . to make all Laws which shall be necessary and proper for carrying into Execution the foregoing powers, and all other Powers vested by this Constitution in the Government of the United States, or in any Department or Officer thereof.

The extent to which the national government may exercise its implied powers has always been in dispute and can be traced back to George Washington's first administration. The debate over implied powers went to the heart of the balance of power between the national and state governments. Supporters of the implied powers clause, such as Secretary of the Treasury, Alexander Hamilton, favored a strong national government. Hamilton believed the clause should be interpreted broadly, extending the powers of the national government. Secretary of State Thomas Jefferson believed in states' rights and believed that the clause should be strictly interpreted. Strict interpretation of the implied powers clause would limit the power of the national government thereby reallocating power to the states.

In 1819, in *McCulloch v. Maryland,* the Supreme Court first recognized that the national government did have the power to exercise the "necessary and proper" clause to expand its power. This landmark decision by the Court framed the development of the concept of implied powers. At issue was whether Congress had the power to establish a national bank even though it had not expressly been given that power in Article I, Section 8. Chief Justice John Marshall, speaking for the Court, gave his full support for what has become known as the "nationalist" position. This position broadly interprets the power of the national government. He said that although the power to establish a national bank is not among the powers expressly granted to Congress, they may find it is a useful and convenient method for executing such delegated powers such as regulating currency, borrowing money on the credit of the United States, or regulating commerce.[15] Marshall wrote:

> Let the end be legitimate, let it be within the scope of the Constitution, and all means which are appropriate, which are plainly adapted to the end, which are not prohibited, but consist with the letter and spirit of the Constitution are constitutional.[16]

This concept coupled with the **supremacy clause** in Article VI enabled the national government to extend the scope of its power. Not only did this sanction Congress to create the national bank but it subsequently allowed it to establish national parks, set the minimum wage, and determine the standards for clean air and water.

Inherent powers are a special category of national powers not delegated to the national government but also not covered by the "necessary and proper" clause. These are powers in the field of foreign affairs that the Supreme Court has declared derived from the very fact that there is a national government.[17] The United States is a sovereign power, one nation in the international arena, and, as such, its national government must be the only government that deals with other countries. Under international law, it is assumed that all countries, regardless of their size or power, have an inherent right to ensure their own survival. To do this, each country must have the ability to act in its own interest among and with the community of nations. Inherent powers are powers the national government would have even if the Constitution was silent, because they are powers all nations have under international law, including discovering and occupying territory and making treaties.[18] For example, in 1936, in *United States v. Curtiss-Wright Export Co.*, the Supreme Court upheld the validity of a joint resolution of Congress delegating the power to the president to prohibit arms shipments to foreign belligerents. Inherent powers are especially important today in

Chief Justice John Marshall dominated the Court and clarifed the Court's role.

dealing with the issue of terrorism. Much of the power granted to the newly created Cabinet Department of Home Land Security is grounded in the inherent grant of power to the national government.

Besides inherent powers, Congress also possesses **inherited powers**. These are powers it inherited from traditions of the British Parliament and early state legislatures. One important inherited power is the power to conduct investigations to gather information needed to legislate or perform other constitutional functions. The power to investigate allows Congress to subpoena witnesses, grant immunity, or punish those who refuse to produce documents or answer questions. The House of Representatives established its right to this power very early in U.S. history by invoking it in 1792. It reinforced its investigatory powers by summoning witnesses and punishing those who did not comply. [19] However, congressional investigations have been ruled by the Supreme Court as going too far. In 1957, the Supreme Court ruled that the House Committee on Un-American Activities was violating First Amendment rights by inquiring into and attempting to punish people for their beliefs and associations. Writing for the majority, Chief Justice Earl Warren acknowledged that "abuses of the investigative process may imperceptibly lead to abridgement of protected freedoms." [20]

More recently in 2001, Congress exercised its inherited powers to probe President Clinton's pardon of billionaire Marc Rich, who had been one of the Justice Department's most wanted international fugitives, indicted on tax evasion, racketeering, and violating trade sanctions with Iran. Although a presidential pardon is strictly an executive function outside the scope of legislative authority, the House Government Reform Committee and the Senate Judiciary Committee both held hearings on this matter. They sought to determine whether Clinton's pardon was linked to the more than one million dollars Rich's ex-wife, Denise Rich, donated to Democratic causes, including then-first lady Hillary Rodham Clinton's Senate campaign. The committees subpoenaed numerous witnesses, including Jack Quinn, former White House counsel during the Clinton administration, to explain the role they played in the president's decision to pardon Rich. Although the committee blustered that the president's pardon privileges should be constrained, the committee's investigation degenerated into political wrangling and accusations that may or may not produce any substantive or procedural changes regarding presidential pardons. Since the president's constitutional authority to grant pardons is virtually unfettered, there is little Congress can do, short of a constitutional amendment, to restrain the president. In this case, Congress sought to use its inherited powers to politically limit the power of the president.[21]

National Supremacy Clause

Article VI, or the **national supremacy clause**, of the Constitution states:

> This Constitution . . . all laws passed in pursuance thereof, and treaties of the United States are the supreme law of the land; and the Judges in every State shall be bound thereby, any Thing in the Constitution or laws of any State to the Contrary notwithstanding.

This clause goes directly to the heart of the debate surrounding the relationship between the national and state governments. The debate is usually framed as states' rights versus the national government. Individuals who support the states' rights position claim that the Constitution is an agreement between states and that the states created both the document and the national government. Therefore, states are supreme to the national government. National power is derived directly from the states and should be narrowly construed. Early supporters of states' rights were Thomas Jefferson and John C. Calhoun. Conversely, individuals who support the nationalist position, such as Alexander Hamilton and John Marshall, contended that the national government is not a creature of the states. Rather, it is supreme to the states. The Constitution is not an agreement between states but rather a social contract between the people of the United States. The states did not create the national government; therefore, they cannot determine its power. The people established a national government, and its power should be liberally interpreted.

The national supremacy clause has been significant in establishing the relationship between the national government and the states. Although not always popular, historically, the nationalist position has prevailed as the primary philosophy that has underpinned the relationship between the national government and the states. Numerous court decisions and political events, including the Civil War, have given the national government significant political power. Although the list is not all inclusive, many political scientists have identified that the following four major events have made a significant contribution to expanding the power of the national government.

1. The 1819 Supreme Court case of *McCulloch v. Maryland*
2. The 1824 Supreme Court case of *Gibbons v. Ogden*
3. The Civil War (1860-1865)
4. The 1954 Supreme Court case of *Brown v. Board of Education*

Other events not included in this list but that should be given equal weight concerning the expansion of national power are the New Deal, the cold war, and nuclear proliferation.

McCulloch v. Maryland

As previously mentioned, **McCulloch v. Maryland** was the first in a long line of Supreme Court decisions that validated the nationalist position. *McCulloch v. Maryland* determined that the national government had the right to create a national bank and, in so doing, defined and solidified the doctrine of implied powers. However, this case raised an equally important constitutional question of when and where states could exercise their power. The Court's response to this question was significant in the development of national power.

Specifically, *McCulloch v. Maryland* presented the Court with the problem of how and when a state could implement its constitutional power to tax. Maryland levied a tax against the Baltimore Branch of the Bank of the United States. McCulloch, the cashier, refused to pay the taxes on the grounds that a state could not use its power to thwart national policy, specifically taxing the national bank. In presenting its case before the Court, Maryland hedged its bet by presenting two possible scenarios. Maryland argued that the federal government did not have the power to establish a national bank; however, if the Court ruled that they did, the states would have the power to tax it.

Speaking for the Court, Chief Justice Marshall supported the nationalist position. Maryland lost both of its arguments. The Court reasoned that not only did the national government have the right to establish a national bank but that the states did not have the right to tax it. The Court determined that although the states did have the power to tax, they could not use it to tax instruments of the national government because "the power to tax involved the power to destroy."[22] The Court implied that Maryland had deliberately intended to thwart national policy and to destroy the national bank by exercising its right to tax. The Court found Maryland's actions to be unconstitutional.

Gibbons v. Ogden (1824)

In 1824, in *Gibbons v. Ogden*, the Supreme Court expanded national powers through its interpretation of the commerce clause. Article I, Section 8, grants to Congress the power "to regulate Commerce with foreign nations, and among the several States, and with the Indian Tribes." In *Gibbons v. Ogden*, the question before the court was "what does it mean to regulate commerce?" The Court's response gave the national government the power to develop a national economy that today has become the center piece of a modern global economy.

Gibbons v. Ogden centered on a relatively narrow issue of whether the state of New York could grant a monopoly to a business that operated between two states. In 1803, Robert Fulton, the inventor of the steamboat, and Robert Livingston, American minister to France, had secured a monopoly of steam navigation on the waters in New York state from the New York legislature. They hired Aaron Ogden to operate their steam-powered ferryboats between New York and New Jersey. Thomas Gibbons decided to compete with Ogden but did so without receiving the permission of the New York legislature. Ogden sued Gibbons in a New York court and contended that he did not have a right to operate his boat. As a result of Ogden's suit, a New York state court issued an injunction prohibiting Gibbons from operating in New York waters. Gibbons appealed to the Supreme Court. He countered that his boats were licensed under a 1793 act of Congress for vessels "employed in the coasting trade and fisheries" and that a state did not have the right to issue an injunction prohibiting him from operating his vessel between two states.[23]

John Marshall was still Chief Justice of the Supreme Court and as a staunch Federalist used this opportunity to increase the power of the national government. The Court unanimously held that the monopoly granted by New York to Aaron Ogden interfered with Congress' power to regulate interstate commerce.[24] The Court could have narrowly construed its decision, but it didn't. Instead, it used its power to establish broad public policy. Marshall delivered an opinion that was a classic statement of nationalism by "nationalizing" the definition of commerce. The Court concluded that commerce, in Article I Section 8, includes not only buying and selling but all forms of commercial dealings including transportation and communication. Marshall concluded that the power of the national government to regulate commerce virtually had no limitations. He states that power, "is complete in itself, may be exercised to its utmost extent and acknowledges no limitations other than are prescribed in the Constitution."[25]

Congress has used the commerce clause to provide extensive regulation of the workplace affecting almost every area of life in modern America. It has regulated how and why employees can be hired, promoted, and fired. It has established minimum wage laws, regulated child labor practices, and, more recently, established the Family Leave Bill. To safeguard interstate commerce from interruption by strikes, Congress has regulated employer-employee relations in businesses and industries that "affect" areas of commerce such as the potential strikes and slowdowns. The commerce clause was also the constitutional linchpin for most federal civil rights legislation. The 1964 Civil Rights Act forbids discrimination because of race, religion, or national origin in places of public accommodation or because of race, religion, gender, or national origin in matters of employment. Congress's rational in passing this legislation was not altruistic but rather practical. Racial discrimination in hiring practices was interfering with interstate travel that disrupted commerce. Consequently, Congress could outlaw discriminatory hiring practices.[26]

The Civil War

The nationalist interpretation rendered by the Supreme Court in 1819 has been sustained by many subsequent Court decisions. However, it did not resolve the conflict between the states' rights and national supremacy positions. Notwithstanding McCulloch, many have continued to champion the states' rights interpretation. Chief Justice Roger Taney, Marshall's immediate successor on the Court, was one such person. The Court's decisions began to reflect his position in its decisions. *Dred Scott v. Sanford* was just such a case. Many historians believe that the 1857 *Dred Scott* case made the Civil War inevitable and that it was one of the greatest tragedies in the history of the Court.[27]

The *Dred Scott* decision sustained the power of the southern states by striking down the 1820 Missouri Compromise passed by Congress prohibiting slavery in the Northwest Territory. This had been a tenuous political compromise forged in Congress to assuage both the North and the South and maintain a balance of power in the national government between the two regions of the country. In return for prohibiting slavery in the new territories, the rest of the country, specifically the South, was allowed to pursue their local policies vìs a vìs slavery. In declaring the Missouri Compromise unconstitutional, the Court had disrupted the balance of power between the northern and southern states. In addition, Taney went on to say that African Americans were not citizens of the United States and as such had no rights under the Constitution. He wrote:

> Negroes were not intended to be included, under the citizen' in the Constitution, and can therefore claim none of the rights and privileges which that instrument provides for and secured to citizens of the United States. On the contrary, they were at that time considered as a subordinate and inferior class of beings, who had been subjugated by the dominant race, and whether emancipated or not, yet remained subject to their authority, and had not rights or privileges but such as those who held the power and the government might choose to grant them.[28]

Although Taney had intended that this would resolve the slavery issue once and for all, it did quite the opposite. *Dred Scott* enraged the abolitionists, many of whom were more anti-Southern than they were anti-slavery. Taney's decision triggered resistance in northern states, which in turn underscored to the Southerners that their interests could not be preserved within the Union.[29] This wrecked the incoming administration of James Buchanan and fueled the flames that led to the Civil War.[30]

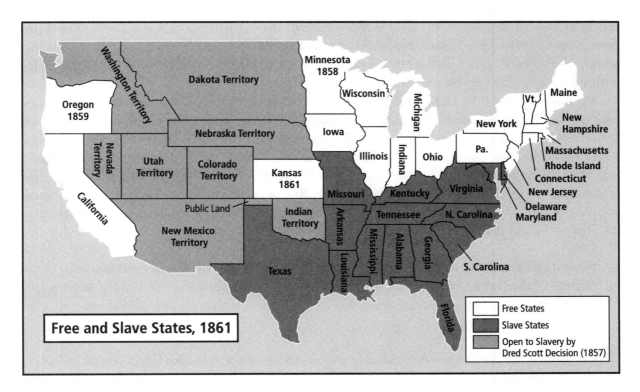

The Civil War was the ultimate challenge to federalism in the United States, because it challenged the very existence of the Union. The country went to war against itself because of its inability to reach a consensus on the fundamental question about the nature of the Union. Beginning with the Articles of Confederation, the ultimate political goal of the country's elite was to hold the Union together at all costs.

The early history of the U.S. was the continuing saga of a nation attempting to avert civil war. By 1860, the political struggle to maintain the Union had failed. The discussion surrounding the nature of federalism moved out of the political sphere to another arena, the battlefield. The southern states, champions of the doctrine of states' rights, claimed that they were free to secede from the Union. Since the states had created the Union, they had the right to dissolve it. The northern states defended the doctrine of national supremacy. They argued that the South did not have the right to dissolve the Union and that the citizens of the southern states were also citizens of the United States. The states did not have the right to strip them of their U. S. citizenship without the permission of the national government. Since the nationalists were not willing to allow the South to secede, the final question to be answered was, "Did a state have the right to oppose federal action by force of arms?"

What followed was the bloodiest war in U.S. history. More Americans died in the Civil War than in any other American war. The North won, and the nationalist position prevailed. The military had settled the political question of whether a state could constitutionally secede from the Union. The answer was "no," and the Union was preserved. The Supreme Court upheld the nationalist position when after the war it ruled on which government actually possessed the political jurisdiction for national reconstruction. Did the responsibility for it rest with the state governments or the national one? In *Texas v White* (1869), the Court held that the Constitution had created an indestructible Union composed of indestructible states. Chief Justice Chase held that secession was illegal. Since the Union was perpetual, reconstruction was a political problem that lay within the scope of congressional power.[31]

Reconstruction of the Union returned the question of federalism to the political sphere. After securing victory on the battlefield, the nationalists strove to institutionalize their newly won power and forever limit the power of the states. They hoped to destroy the underlying premise of the states' rights doctrine once and for all. Their tool of destruction was the Fourteenth Amendment, one of the three Reconstruction amendments the South was forced to ratify as a prerequisite for readmission to the Union. The Fourteenth Amendment was designed to institutionalize the supremacy of the national government. Under the Fourteenth Amendment, no state could deny to its citizens the rights they had been afforded under the federal Constitution. It states:

> No state shall make or enforce any law which shall abridge the privileges or immunities of citizens of the United States: nor shall any State deprive any person of life, liberty, or property, without due process of law: nor deny to any person within its jurisdiction the equal protection of the laws.

On the surface, the Fourteenth Amendment appears to be self-explanatory. The Constitution now firmly established the national government as supreme to the states. There now existed a definite hierarchy of power. Or was there? As with all issues regarding federalism, the Fourteenth Amendment first needed to be interpreted and then implemented. Much of the responsibility for this fell on the shoulders of the Supreme Court. The Court was left to determine the political reality of whether the Fourteenth Amendment would actually dismantle the concept of states' rights. The Court avoided this question until 1925, when, in *Gitlow v. New York*, the Supreme Court struck a severe blow to the concept of states' rights.

Gitlow v. New York was just the beginning of a process called the **incorporation doctrine** that nationalized the Bill of Rights. This process resulted in major changes in the modern law of civil liberties, affording citizens a federal remedy if the states deprived them of their "fundamental rights" established in the Bill of Rights.[32] This process greatly expanded the power of the national government, and a thorough discussion of it can be found in the chapter on civil liberties.

Brown v. Board of Education (1954)

Brown v. Board of Education was a watershed decision in federalism. This 1954 Supreme Court decision continued to support the nationalist position and expand the power of the national government. It placed the responsibility for the social and political construct of race in America squarely in the hands of the national government. *Brown v. Board of Education* signaled national recognition of the modern national civil rights movement and reaffirmed the intent of the Reconstruction Amendments. It signaled the "Second Reconstruction" of America.

The unanimous Supreme Court decision in the *Brown* case reversed its 1896 *Plessy v. Ferguson* decision. In 1896, *Plessy v. Ferguson* did for states' rights what *Brown v. Board of Education* did for the nationalist position. *Plessy v. Ferguson* was largely responsible for undermining the intent of the

Not all citizens are treated fairly in a federated system. The distribution of goods and services required by families for a healthy and meaningful existence usually comes from the state. But what happens if the state either refuses to provide such services or, worse yet, decides to distribute them unequally? Does this occur in America? Can you cite some examples?

Reconstruction Amendments, whose purpose was to free the slaves, grant them citizenship, and protect their rights, especially the right to vote, against infringement by the states. The Thirteenth, Fourteenth, and Fifteenth Amendments were designed to limit the power of the states and ensure that they would not impose restrictions on African Americans because of their race, color, or previous condition of servitude.

Plessy v. Ferguson established the "separate but equal" doctrine legally sanctioning the states to create two distinct societies: one African American, one white. It sanctioned legal segregation. The Supreme Court held that a state could compel racial segregation in the use of public facilities, provided equal facilities were available for all races. Justice Harlan, a former slave-owner, was the only justice who dissented. In his dissent he wrote that the Constitution was "colorblind, and neither knows nor tolerates classes among citizens."[33]

Justice Harlan's voice was soon lost in the flurry of Jim Crow, or segregation laws, passed by the states. These laws ensured separate but rarely equal facilities for African Americans and whites. *Plessy v Ferguson* gave states the authority to regulate all phases of life from birth to the grave and everything in between including restroom facilities, school attendance, and burial plots.

During the 1940s, the Court indicated that it was prepared to tackle the question of race. Its subsequent decisions insisted that states must either stop requiring segregation in the use of public facilities or start providing African Americans with truly equal facilities. The Court ruled that an African American with a first-class train ticket could not be legally ordered to sit in the second-class section and that an African-American applicant must be admitted to an all-white law school if there is no other law school in the state.[34] Although its decisions did not directly confront the "separate but equal" doctrine and the principle of racial discrimination, the Court began to affirm that the national government did have a responsibility to and authority in securing equal protection of its laws to all races under the Fourteenth Amendment. By 1954, the Court appeared ready to confront *Plessy*; all that was needed was the right case.

In 1954, the **National Association for the Advancement of Colored People** (NAACP), the most notable civil rights organization of that period, believed they had such a case. Oliver Brown was an African-American railroad worker who sued the Topeka, Kansas Board of Education for not allowing his daughter, Linda Brown, to attend the all white Sumner Elementary School. In so doing, Oliver Brown challenged the state and local segregation laws. Every day Linda Brown traveled approximately twenty blocks to the nearest all African-American school when Sumner Elementary was closer to the Brown's home. In September 1950, Oliver Brown took Linda to the closer all white Sumner school to enroll her in the third grade. When the state refused to admit Linda, the Browns took their case to the NAACP.

Thurgood Marshall, chief counsel for the NAACP Legal Defense and Educational Fund, later the first African American appointed to the Supreme Court, argued the case before the Court. Marshall directly challenged the issue of "separate but equal." As a result of Marshall's arguments, the Supreme Court ruled that "separate educational facilities are inherently unequal" and that segregation is in itself discrimination. The Court ruled that the public schools must desegregate at the earliest possible date. The doctrine of separate but equal was dead.

The *Brown* decision altered the constitutional framework and the concept of federalism in two fundamental ways. First, after *Brown*, the states no longer had the power to use race as a criterion of discrimination in law. Second, the national government now had the power and, perhaps what is even more important, the obligation to intervene against the discriminatory actions of state or local governments.[35] The national government had been given the ability to reconstruct the social, political, and economic dimensions of race relations in America, thus forcing the "Second Reconstruction" of American society.

The decision in *Brown* was very specific in that it only applied to public schools. Public schools had traditionally been the domain of the state governments. Now the national government had the green light to intervene in an area traditionally reserved to the states. However, the federal government moved slowly, often begrudgingly, to enforce the decision. In 1957, President Eisenhower, who was opposed to the *Brown* decision, reluctantly sent federal troops to Little Rock, Arkansas to desegregate their school system. This was the first time that federal troops were used to enforce a federal anti-discrimination policy.

The Court continued to reinforce the *Brown* decision. In subsequent years, the Supreme Court ruled that all forms of segregation in public facilities were unconstitutional. Furthermore, the Court ruled that the Constitution requires authorities not merely to cease discriminatory actions but also to provide mechanisms to remedy the consequences of their past segregative conduct.[36] This was the boldest move yet by the national government to impose its will on the states. These decisions eventually led to the controversial policy of affirmative action, which the Supreme Court has yet to resolve. In the field of higher education, the central issue regarding affirmative action has remained relatively constant since the 1970's: may race be used as a factor in undergraduate, graduate and professional school admissions? Two 2003 Supreme Court decisions, *Gratz v Bollinger* and *Grutter v. Bollinger*, both involving the University of Michigan's admissions policies, did little to put the issue to rest. In the first case, the Supreme Court struck down the university's affirmative action program; in the later, its policies were upheld. The implementation of affirmative action programs was central to the Court's rulings.

In a 6-3 decision in *Gratz v. Bollinger,* Chief Justice Rehnquist writing for the majority ruled that although diversity could be considered a compelling state interest, in this instance, the university did not implement "individualized consideration" in its undergraduate program as it added 20 points to admission scores for minorities. However, in a 5-4 ruling in *Grutter v. Bollinger* the Court upheld the University of Michigan's Law School policy stating that its program allowed for "flexible" consideration of race using it as one factor among others to "achieve critical mass of underrepresented minorities."[37]

Although *Brown* itself was narrowly interpreted, it opened the door to nullify Jim Crow laws and end legal segregation. Congress would take *Brown* a step further and move it from the public to the private sector. In 1964, Congress passed the Civil Rights Act, virtually affecting every business in the United States. Based on the commerce clause in the Constitution as interpreted in *Gibbons v. Ogden*, Congress determined that segregation negatively interfered with interstate commerce. Therefore, any business that employed over fifteen people or engaged in interstate commerce could not discriminate in their hiring practices based on race, sex, or national origin.

Even greater in scope was the Voting Rights Act of 1965. Its purpose was to fulfill the promise of the first Reconstruction and give African Americans the real right to vote that had previously been denied to them through disenfranchising strategies, such as literacy tests and poll taxes. President Johnson signed the bill into law on August 6, 1965, claiming, "I pledge we will not delay and we will not hesitate . . . until Americans of every race and color and origin in this country have the same rights as all others to share in the process of democracy."[38] Federal examiners were sent into the South with the full powers of the government to safeguard the registration and voting of African Americans. Within five years, the effects of the Voting Rights Act were truly startling. Between 1964 and 1969 the percentage of African-American adults registered to vote in the South soared: Alabama 19.3 percent to 61.3 percent; Georgia, 27.4 percent to 60.4 percent; Louisiana, 31.6 percent to 60.8 percent; Mississippi, 6.7 percent to 66.5 percent.[39]

In 1896, Justice Harlan wrote of a color blind society. However, the interpretation of federalism then enabled the states to construct a society based on color. *Brown v. Board of Education* altered the balance of power between the national and state governments in the area of race relations. However, it is easy to see that policies such as affirmative action continually challenge the system and that the issue of federalism and race is far from settled. Much will depend on whether these issues find friend or foe sitting in the White House or on the Supreme Court. It is clear from *Gratz* and *Gutter* that these will not be the last cases on race and affirmative action that find their way onto the high Court's docket.

States' Powers

Reserved Power/Tenth Amendment

The Tenth Amendment is called the **reserved powers** amendment. It states that "power not delegated to the United States by the Constitution nor prohibited by it to the States, are reserved to the States respectively, or to the people." The Antifederalists feared that a strong national government would encroach on individual liberty and repeatedly pressed for a substantial guarantee that would limit national power. In response to their concerns and to assure ratification of the Constitution, supporters of the Constitution promised that the first Congress would propose measures that would protect individual liberties from government intrusion. The protections the first Congress proposed and the states ratified became known as the Bill of Rights. The Bill of Rights contains the Tenth Amendment.

States' rights proponents have used the Tenth Amendment to foster their position vìs a vìs the national government. Taken to the extreme, they have claimed that the states did not have to submit to national laws when they believed that the national government had exceeded its authority. The Tenth Amendment was used to justify such historical events as the Nullification Crisis of 1832, South Carolina's attempt to nullify a national tax on the grounds that the national government had overstepped its limits of constitutional authority, and the Civil War. More recently it has been utilized by conservative groups, such as the Heritage Foundation, to justify their position that a strong national government encroaches on individual liberties. They believe such freedoms are better protected by maintaining power in the hands of the states.

Boundaries Established by the Tenth Amendment

The Tenth Amendment explicitly states that there are powers that belong to the state that the national government cannot deny to them. However, the Constitution never expressly lists what they are; consequently, questions often arise whether a power is actually delegated to the national government or reserved to the state. In exercising their reserved powers, states may not frustrate the national government's ability to make policy. Conversely, Congress is not to exercise its power in such a way that would diminish a state's integrity or ability to govern effectively.[40] It is easy to see why conflicts arise between the levels of government that are required to share power. The Tenth Amendment has facilitated an informal agreement as to what level of government retains authority over what policies. Since states are unitary political entities vìs a vìs their local governments, they retain control over their organization and political authority. Traditionally, states have generally retained control over property and contract law, criminal law, marriage and divorce, education, highways, and social welfare activities.[41] However, these specific areas of policy-making are always in the process of evolving, and the boundaries of federalism are constantly in flux and being challenged. For example, although the states maintain individual educational systems, the federal government provides funding to both state and local school districts. The criteria used to determine the distribution of federal funds is constantly in question. Most recently the controversy in the distribution of federal educational dollars and its control over curricula and the educational process is embedded in the No Child Left Behind Act, signed into law on January 8, 2002 and championed by the Bush administration. Although the federal law enables each state to construct its own criteria and testing, the act also requires schools to have 100 percent of their students scoring at the proficient level or higher on state tests by 2014. Schools that receive federal Title I money, dollars originally earmarked to service low income areas including bilingual communities and Native Americans, would be subjected to sanctions and the withholding of federal funds. By 2005, forty-seven states had challenged the No Child Left Behind in some way. Only three states have not challenged in some way this act's extension of federal supervision over education.

Establishing the boundaries of the Tenth Amendment has unwittingly fallen to the Supreme Court. The Court has often stated that it is not its job to do this, but when they do, the results have been inconsistent and have often produced conflictual rulings. For example, the 1976 case, *National League of Cities v. Usery,* for the first time since the New Deal struck down a federal law on the grounds that Congress had transgressed the permissible boundaries of federalism. It redefined the states traditional governmental functions and, in so doing, reestablished the boundaries of federalism. The Court struck down a 1974 federal statute that extended the maximum hours and minimum wage provisions of the Fair Labor Standards Act to most state and municipal employees.[42] It stated that Congress had interfered with the states' "freedom to structure integral operations in areas of traditional governmental functions—functions essential to separate and independent existence."[43] Although the *National League of Cities v. Usery* breathed new life into the Tenth Amendment, it left the boundaries of federalism unclear as to what was permissible federal intrusion on the states. The Court ruled that the federal government should treat "states as states," and they had the sovereign right to implement the "traditional operations of state and local governments."[44] One such attribute of state sovereignty is the states' power to determine the wages that shall be paid to those whom they employ to carry out their governmental functions.[45]

The *National League of Cities* had a short life-span. Nine years later in 1985, the Court reversed itself in *Garcia v. San Antonio Metropolitan Transit Authority.* The boundaries of federalism were again redrawn. *Garcia* also involved the application of the maximum hours and minimum wage provision of the Fair Labor Standards Act to a city owned and operated public transportation system. The San Antonio Metropolitan Transit Authority sought a judgment exempting it from FLSA provisions on the grounds that it violated the Tenth Amendment. The Transit Authority won in a federal district court, but Joe Garcia, a transit authority worker, appealed the decision to the Supreme Court. In this instance, the Court ruled that it was impossible to draw the boundaries of federalism for traditional governmental functions.[46]

Its ruling indicated that the Court was frustrated in its efforts to attempt to define the boundaries of federalism. As if throwing up its hands in disgust, the Court stated that federalism is a political structure in which the states' interests are represented, for better or worse, in the national political process.[47] The states need to look to the structure of federalism to define state sovereignty and the traditional areas of state authority. The boundaries of federalism are political and consequently the states need to look to their representatives within the constitutional framework to clarify and sustain their power. For example, individual states are represented in the Senate, and rather than depend on judicial interference to restrict the power of the national government, the states must find protection from congressional regulation from their representatives within the national political process. The Court said that the states have power within the national government to define the boundaries of federalism as they see fit. The political process was to define federalism. This position was reaffirmed in 1988. In *South Carolina v. Baker*, the Court not only upheld *Garcia* but appeared to shut the door on the possibility that there might be some categories of state activity constitutionally protected from national regulation. The Court concluded that there must be some evidence of "extraordinary defects in the national political process" before the Court will entertain a violation of the Tenth Amendment.[48]

The relationship between the national government and the states is always in flux; nothing is written in granite, particularly where the Supreme Court is concerned. In 1995, in the case of

United States v. Lopes, the Supreme Court took a position that differed from that reversed in *Garcia*. The Court ruled that Congress had actually overstepped its authority under the commerce clause and struck down the federal Gun-Free School Zones Act that made it a federal offense to possess firearms in school zones. The Court ruled that since this was not an economic activity that had an affect on interstate commerce, the law was unconstitutional.

In June of 1997 the Court again found fault with federal handgun restrictions. In the case of Jay Printz, Sheriff/Coroner, *Ravalli County Montana v. United States*, the Court further limited the power of the federal government by declaring part of the Brady Bill unconstitutional. The Brady Bill is a federal law that restricts the purchase of handguns, requiring a five-day waiting period before a federally licensed gun dealer can transfer a handgun to a purchaser. During the waiting period, local law enforcement officers must make a "reasonable" check of official records to find out if the buyer was a felon, a drug addict, a fugitive from justice, an illegal alien, a mental defective, a spouse under a court restraining order, or a dishonorably discharged member of the armed forces. Such a person is ineligible to receive a handgun. Two western sheriffs, one from Montana, another from Arizona, contested the law stating that not only was the expense of the law burdensome to the local governments but that the time it required them to do the background checks made it impossible to perform their regular duties.[49] The Court decided that the substance of the Brady Bill was constitutional but that the section requiring local governments to do background checks was an improper federal invasion of state and local powers. The Court ruled that state governments are not required to enforce federal mandates with their own funds.

In May 2000, in *Brzonkala v Morrison*, the Rehnquist Court, in a 5-4 decision, struck down parts of the Violence Against Women Act in yet another attempt to rein in federal laws that it viewed encroached on a state's authority. This case, which at first glance appears to be about sexual politics, is really about federalism and is just one in a series of recent Supreme Court decisions that favors states' rights over federal authority. The *Brzonkala* decision threw out a key section of the Violence Against Women Act ruling that Congress had exceeded its constitutional authority when it allowed rape victims to bypass state judicial systems and sue their alleged assailants in federal court. The Court stipulated that the 1994 law was a "sweeping intrusion" into matters traditionally handled by the states, and upheld a lower federal court's reasoning that violence against women had only an "indirect relationship with interstate commerce." Chief Justice Rehnquist wrote for the majority, "We regret the argument that Congress may regulate non-economic, violent criminal conduct based solely on its effect on interstate commerce." Justice Souter, writing in dissent, accused the majority of the Court to have an antiquated idea of "federalism of some earlier time." The main focus of this case appears not to be whether violence against women is a serious issue but rather how it should be addressed and who should have jurisdiction over it.

Concurrent Powers

Besides their reserved power, the states exercise **concurrent powers** with the national government. In certain circumstances the national and state governments have an equal right to pass legislation and regulate activities. Most concurrent powers are not explicitly stated in the Constitution. They are only implied, and, as with all other categories of constitutional powers, these are also ambiguous and left open to interpretation. An example of a concurrent power is the power to tax, for example, the income tax. Another example of concurrent powers is the ability of the national and state governments to establish courts. Whenever the concurrent policies of a state government conflict with the national, national policy prevails.

Powers Denied by the Constitution

The Constitution denies some powers to both the national and state governments; it denies some powers only to the national government; still other powers are denied only to the states. Denied powers are specifically listed in the Constitution. Powers that are denied to the national government are enumerated in Article I, Section 9. As we have seen, even explicit grants of power have evolved into ambiguous interpretations of federalism. The same case applies to denied powers. For example, Article I, Section 9 prohibits Congress from taxing any goods exported from a state. However, it can under its power to "regulate commerce with foreign nations," prohibit the state from exporting their goods.[50] The federal government is also limited by the Tenth Amendment and the reserved power of the states. Any power not delegated expressly or implicitly to the federal government by the Constitution is prohibited to it.

The Constitution also limits state power vìs a vìs the national government. These restrictions can be found in Article I, Section 10. States are prohibited from conducting independent foreign and monetary policies, coining their own money, imposing export duties, impairing the obligations of contracts, granting titles of nobility, and passing bills of attainder or ex post facto laws.[51]

The Thirteenth, Fourteenth, Fifteenth, Nineteenth, Twenty-fourth, and Twenty-sixth Amendments also limit state power. The Reconstruction Amendments, the Thirteenth, Fourteenth and Fifteenth Amendments, were ratified following the Civil War. They were designed to reassert the power of the national government and undermine the concept of states' rights. Of these three amendments, the Fourteenth has been the most effective in limiting state power as it is the one on which the Supreme Court has based its incorporation doctrine. The Nineteenth, Twenty-fourth and Twenty-sixth Amendments all in some way limited the power of the states in the area of determining voter qualifications. The Nineteenth Amendment extended voting rights to women thereby forbidding any state to deny anyone the right to vote based on gender; the Twenty-fourth Amendment outlawed the use of poll taxes by the states as a requirement for voting thereby striking down many southern laws that had used poll taxes as a strategy to deny African American and lower socio-economic whites the right to vote, and the Twenty-sixth Amendment required states to grant eighteen-year-olds the right to vote.

THE NATURE OF FEDERALISM TODAY

The construction of the federal system has been an evolutionary process, and it is certainly different today than it was in 1787. Or is it? The history of federalism has been the story of the ability of different levels of government to share power in a peaceful and productive way. As we have seen, this has not always been possible. Today, the debate about federalism is similar to the one heard in

1787; however, the implementation of federalism has significantly changed. Alexander Hamilton's and Thomas Jefferson's philosophical debate over the merits of a strong national government versus state sovereignty still can be heard today in the corridors of Washington and the state capitals. Instead of debating whether the national government has the power to establish a national bank, policy-makers discuss the Clean Air Act and/or the Americans with Disabilities Act vìs a vìs the Federal Unfunded Mandate Act of 1995. Does the federal government have the authority and obligation to enact its implied powers to provide an equitable quality of life across the fifty states and, if so, must the states comply? In modern political jargon, "Can the federal government pass legislation and then require the states to pay the bill?"

Since the days of Benjamin Franklin and the Iroquois Confederacy, several theories have evolved to lay the groundwork for the present system of federalism. Historically, they have created the constitutional foundations of federalism. These theories, however, have not followed a linear progression. Rather, they have come full circle. The nature of the debate is similar; only the terminology has changed. Instead of states' rights vs. national government, the nature of the Union is discussed in terms of the "devolution revolution." If one listens very carefully, one can hear the voices of Hamilton and Jefferson discussing "devolution revolution." The theories that have gotten us to where we are today are concurrent majorities, dual federalism, cooperative federalism, and the New Federalism, culminating in the "devolution revolution."

Concurrent Majorities

John C. Calhoun is usually credited with championing the concept of concurrent majorities. This vision of federalism would effectively give the states a veto power over the federal government. Calhoun was a statesman from South Carolina who spent many years in Congress, as well as serving as Andrew Jackson's vice president during the Nullification Crisis of 1832. Calhoun entered Congress in 1811. At that time he was a strong nationalist, supporting the War of 1812 and introducing measures that supported a combination of protective tariffs, internal transportation, and a national bank. By the 1830s Calhoun had become one of the strongest supporters of states' rights, writing the doctrine of concurrent majorities to protect the sectional interests of the South.

By the late 1820s, the South had lost considerable power in the national government and by the 1830s no longer controlled a majority of votes. Calhoun, as well as other Southerners, believed that they soon would be controlled by northern industrial interests and that eventually slavery would be abolished. The Southern planters believed that they were becoming an oppressed minority within the United States. The source of their oppression was the national government. They needed to protect their interests vìs a vìs the national government and the only institution that could effectively do this was the state legislatures. In 1828, Calhoun wrote the South Carolina Exposition and Protest that not only asserted the position that the South was an oppressed minority but as such that a state had the power of nullification over any federal law it deemed unconstitutional in order to protect the interest of that minority. To restore the South's power and maintain sectional equilibrium, Calhoun went on to propose that each section of the country, through its own majority, may veto the acts of the federal government. He also proposed a constitutional amendment that would allow three-quarters of the states to override the actions of another state. These proposals rejected the concept of majority rule and supported the minority interests of a particular region. The ability of a state to nullify an action of the federal government turned constitutional theory on its head. By the 1830s Calhoun was ready to sacrifice the Constitution for the sectional interests of the South.

Today, remnants of Calhoun's theory can be seen in the Council of State Governments' active and effective lobbying efforts. The Council of State Governments is an umbrella organization for state government associations. States are dues paying members. It was founded in 1933 and is a nonprofit, nonpartisan organization serving the executive, legislative and judicial branches of state government.

The organization is part of the "devolution revolution" movement to realign federalism. The Council of State Governments believes that there is currently an imbalance between the state and national governments and that this imbalance is causing a distortion of the constitutional balance of power intended in the federal system. It believes that the national government is exercising power it was never meant to have. The Council is currently exploring how states could unite to restore power to the states and to the people and carry out the intent of the Tenth Amendment. One of the four options the Council proposes indirectly reflects Calhoun's thinking of the 1830s. It is the "National Reconsideration" proposal. It proposed that the states need to devise "A mechanism to provide the people of the states, through their legislatures, the power to require Congress to reconsider laws, specific provisions of laws, or regulations that interfere with state authority."[52] Unlike Calhoun, this would not give the states the right to actually nullify an act of Congress, but it would require the federal government to reconsider legislation that the states deemed to be outside the scope of authority of the national government. This function has traditionally been reserved for the Supreme Court. However, as previously mentioned, the Court is not pleased to perform this function. Some organizations have proposed that the mechanism state legislatures should seek for implementing "national reconsideration" is a constitutional amendment. This amendment would allow two-thirds of the states to strike down any federal law or regulation until Congress is willing to "re-enact it." This would require Congress to re-work legislation to meet the states' criteria, whatever that might be. The states would virtually have veto power over Congress. This amendment would enable the states to monitor the activities of the federal government; however, it would seriously alter the existing system of checks and balances and separation of powers.

Dual Federalism

Allegedly, the Civil War resolved the question of the nature of the union. In reality, it redefined the scope of the discussion. The Civil War only temporarily silenced the proponents of states' rights, and the national government was left once again with the problem of how to successfully "divide" power. During Reconstruction, the Supreme Court sought to accommodate both the nationalist and the states' rights positions and developed the doctrine of dual federalism. It is the concept that the national and state governments are equal sovereigns, each with its own sphere of supremacy. This constitutional interpretation implied that the national government should not exceed its enumerated powers leading the states to assume that all other policy matters fall within their domain. The national government and the states would each have its own sphere of influence and never the twain shall meet. For example, in the case of *Texas v. White*, 1869, the Court ruled in favor of the nationalist position stating that "The Constitution looked to an indestructible Union composed of indestructible States." However, in the Slaughterhouse Cases in 1873, Justice Samuel Miller advanced the idea of dual citizenship that strengthened the states' right position by sharply limiting the Fourteenth Amendment's application to the states. Again in 1896 in *Plessy v. Ferguson*, the Court supported the concept of dual sovereignty when it placed civil liberties squarely in the hands of the state by declaring that "separate but equal facilities" were constitutional.[53]

Traditionally, dual federalism is described by political scientists in culinary terms as layer-cake federalism. The various layers or boundaries of the different levels of government are clearly defined as they are in a layer cake. In the United States, the cake has two layers. The first layer is the national government; the second layer is made up of the state governments. The national and state governments each have their own areas of policy making. Traditionally, the national government's layer consisted of defense, foreign policy, and interstate commerce. The states regulated important domestic issues such as voter qualifications, civil rights, and education. However, as time went on, it was apparent that the layers were very porous, and whenever the cake was cut, the frosting from the top layer seeps into the bottom. Dual federalism came to an abrupt end in the 1930s brought on by the economic and social problems of the Great Depression.

Cooperative Federalism

Like dual federalism, political scientists often describe the concept of cooperative federalism in culinary terms. It, too, is like a cake, but a marble cake rather than a layer one. A marble cake requires the chef to use two different batters of cake mix, for example, one chocolate and one vanilla, and to mix them together before baking. Once cooked, it is impossible to distinguish the layers as vanilla and chocolate because they have become one in the baking process. So it is with cooperative federalism. It is difficult to distinguish between the layers of government as they have been blended together. In dual federalism the power of the state and national governments are clearly defined and recognizable. In cooperative federalism that is not the case.

The main ingredient that has blended the two layers of government is money. Cooperative federalism was ushered in on the coattails of fiscal federalism that mushroomed during the New Deal of the 1930s. These programs provided financial assistance to the underclass. There was a proliferation of these programs during Lyndon Johnson's War on Poverty during the 1960s, to include the Elementary and Secondary Education Act of 1965, Title I, which offered grants and services to schools serving low income areas, including inner cities and bilingual communities. Acts such as this would require the national and state governments to cooperate in the area of education, a policy domain that traditionally rested with the states. However, if the states wanted the federal money for education, they would have to "cooperate" and follow federal guidelines and mandates to get them. The two layers of government also cooperated in implementing programs such as public housing and urban renewal, which had been understood to be areas of policy-making that traditionally belonged to the states. Congress had no explicit power to develop policies in these areas. Rather, it relied on its implied powers in Article I, Section 8 to "provide for the general welfare" of the people. Congress defined the goals of the programs and distributed grants-in-aid to the states and local governments to administer the programs and achieve the national government's objectives. This constitutional interpretation, clearly Hamiltonian in nature, signaled a shift in power to the national government. Federal money put the national government in the driver's seat, and the states and their local governments cooperated in order to get it. Although important partners in governing, the national and state governments were no longer equal partners with their own sphere of influence.

Grants are the backbone of "fiscal federalism." The administration of the grants, in large part, continues to define the parameters of federalism and the nature of the union. There are basically two types of grants: categorical and block. Categorical grants compose the majority of money distributed by the federal government. According to the Office of Management and Budget (OMB), in 1995 the federal government provided approximately 235 billion dollars in financial assistance to the state and local governments. Of the 235 billion, 90 percent of the money was allocated in the form of categorical grants. The OMB estimates that in 2006-2007 federal grants to state and local governments will exceed 460 billion dollars. In 2004, they accounted for approximately 25 percent of all the funds spent by state and local governments and for about 18 percent of all federal expenditures. Ninety-two percent of the estimated $460 billion the federal government is sending back to the states in 2006-2007 is for programs in the areas of health care, education, social services and transportation. However, according to the OMB, when adjusted for inflation, grants to the states and localities, other than for Medicaid, have been falling since 2005. While it appears that the states are receiving more aid for more programs, they are actually being required to do more for less dollars. These grants are used for specific purposes as designated by the national government. Categorical grants concentrate a lot of power in the hands of the national government, because Congress determines the purpose of the grant, who receives it, and exactly for what purpose the money can be used. The use of the money carries with it federal restrictions and control. If the states do not adhere to national governmental regulations, federal funds will be withheld. A project grant, a type of categorical grant, allows Congress to bypass the state governments. This grant awards money directly to local governments or even nongovernmental agencies willing to fulfill national policies. States complained that project grants not only bypassed the state governments but serviced narrowly defined interest groups that may or may not have influenced Congress.[54]

The second type of grant, the block grant, is not as restrictive as the categorical grant. They are given to states in a block of money to be used for a specific purpose. Block grants, unlike categorical grants, do not have strings attached to them. States prefer the block grant because it allows them more flexibility in administering programs. For example, a block grant is allocated to the state for law enforcement, and the state would then decide how best to use the money. The state could spend the money for law enforcement training, more vehicles, or computerized equipment. Block grants are also given directly to the states, and, as such, the states believe they did not service specific interest groups.

Although the national and state governments cooperated in executing public policy, in many instances, the state governments believed that they were simply irrelevant in the process and merely acted as pawns of the federal government. Conversely, the national government did not trust the states to carry out national policy particularly in the area of desegregation and civil rights. By the 1970s cooperation was beginning to wear thin, and the states were beginning to feel overburdened and overregulated. The states began to make noises about wanting reform.

New Federalism

Until the 1970s, the history of federalism had been a movement towards concentrating power in the hands of the federal government. This was exacerbated by the Civil Rights Movement and the social programs of the sixties. Beginning with the Nixon administration, the movement took a decisive shift in direction. Policy-makers began to explore the very real possibility that the federal programs were so inflexible that they could not realistically meet the needs of the people on the local levels. The federal programs would be better managed in the hands of the state. This would require a shift in philosophy and implementation. Power would have to be transferred from the national government back to the states. The federal government would have to give up control and some of its power, and the states would have to assume responsibility substantively and financially for programs they may or may not be equipped to implement.

A strong movement, New Federalism, started by the states to regain their former status, found substantial support in the White House. By the 1970s, the White House was looking for ways to trim the federal budget and divest itself of its financial responsibilities to the states. The states' interests in re-establishing their power and the federal government's desire to balance the budget led to yet another realignment of the federal system.

Although New Federalism began during the Nixon administration, Ronald Reagan is more commonly thought of as its "father." Reagan believed that the federal government exercised too much control over the states. This belief stemmed from his years as governor of California (1967-1974). As governor, he experienced frustrations that resulted from federal intervention in state business. During his presidency, Reagan planned to put the federal system back in balance by returning power to the states. President Reagan clearly told the American people his plans in his inaugural address when he said, "It is my intention to curb the size and influence of the Federal establishment and to demand recognition of the distinction between the powers granted to the states or to the people. All of us need to be reminded that the Federal government did not create the states: the states created the Federal government."[55] Reagan's philosophy was reminiscent of the Jeffersonian states' rights proponents of the new republic. His speech seemed to breath new life into the Tenth Amendment.

Reagan saw to it that the policies started in the Nixon administration came to fruition in his. Richard Nixon, in 1971, proposed a special revenue sharing program designed to shift the control of federal programs to the states. This would enable his administration to bypass congressional politics that targeted categorical grants for special constituencies. In 1981, the budget crunch of the 1980s forced the Reagan administration to all but eliminate revenue sharing. Instead, Reagan substituted block grants for categorical ones. This eliminated the "strings" associated with the categorical grants, cut the budget by placing more fiscal responsibility with the states, and avoided the categorical "pork" often incorporated into legislation.[56] The balance between the national and state governments, however, had shifted in favor of the states. The states wanted even more control over policy. They believed that there was another federal "monkey on their backs" that needed to be eliminated. This was what is known as regulatory federalism or unfunded mandates. This led to the "devolution revolution."

"Devolution Revolution"

The "devolution revolution" is an extension of New Federalism. The current "devolution revolution" is credited to Newt Gingrich's 1995 class of Republicans and their Contract of America. It is a belief that the national government has been and is currently acting in ways the Constitution never meant it to. One of the major issues of the "devolution revolution" is federally **unfunded mandates**. These are federal laws that require state and local governments to follow federal regulations without allocating them the money to do it. These laws have been designed to ensure that states would provide equal treatment and equal goods and services to their constituents. They cover such diverse policy issues as establishing clean air and water standards to providing standards for nursing homes. For example, in 1987 Congress passed legislation requiring the states to follow federal guidelines in the maintenance of nursing homes. These federal mandates included pre-admission screening, nurse aide training and competency programs, a nurse aid registry, resident assessment, review of mentally ill and mentally retarded residents, and alternatives for persons requiring active treatment. In seven years the cost of these mandates to the state of Michigan alone was over $137 million dollars.[57]

The growth of national standards has created new problems and raised questions about how far federal standardization should go, especially if the federal government is not willing to pay for their policies.[58] Both the national and state governments present convincing arguments to this policy question. The national government believes national standards are necessary. Over the years, the states have demonstrated an unwillingness to initiate and implement social policies. For example, implementing the intent of *Brown v. Board of Education* is still a work in progress. The national government has assumed the lion's share of the cost of the social and economic programs. The states became to depend on federal money to subsidize their many programs. For example, approximately 25 percent of Michigan's gross state budget is paid for by the federal government. Mandates can be seen as the "strings" attached to the goodies, and "he who pays the piper will call the tune."[59]

The states, however, detested the federal standards and mandates for two reasons. First, they claim that unfunded federal mandates strike at the very heart of the Constitution undermining the foundations of federalism. The states believe power should be returned to them and the intent of the Tenth Amendment should be fulfilled. Second, the states believe that they have been financially burdened by federal laws. The growth of unfunded mandates was the product of a Democratic Congress that wanted to achieve liberal social objectives and Republican presidents who opposed increased social spending. Unfunded mandates were ways to achieve both objectives. This placed an enormous financial burden on the states. States complained that mandates took up so much of their budgets that they were not able to set their own priorities.[60] The National Conference of State Legislatures recently identified 192 unfunded mandates, including Medicaid, regulations governing the use of underground storage tanks, the Clean Water Act, the Americans with Disabilities Act and the Fair Labor Standards Act. The U.S. Conference of Mayors and Price Waterhouse estimate that the 1994-1998 cost of these mandates (excluding Medicaid) on 314 cities at $54 billion or the equivalent of 11.7 percent of all local taxes.[61] In response to this, the Republican Congress passed the Mandates Reform Act of 1995. The law requires Congress to estimate the costs of proposals that may cost more than $50 million. Congress must then vote to pass the program, publicly taking responsibility for the cost. The law attempts to shift power to the states and to limit Congress's ability to pass unfounded mandates, but in reality it just makes members of Congress vote twice to enact such mandates; however, they have to do it publicly.

The Unfunded Mandate Act of 1995 had no teeth to it and failed to stop the federal government from shifting the fiscal burden of legislation to the states through the passage of more unfunded mandates. Both the Republicans and the Democrats did this. In addition to the already mentioned unfunded mandates passed by Congress, to include No Child Left Behind, it has passed a myriad of security legislation under the Homeland Security Act and its department. Much of this legislation has had a significant fiscal impact on the states. One of these laws, the Real ID law was passed in 2005. This law gave states two years to put in place standards of issuing drivers' licenses and other identity cards that will ensure that those in the country illegally cannot obtain legal means of identification. The National Council of State Legislatures claims that states unreimbursed start-up costs for this program will range from $50 million to $169 million and then cost millions to administer every year.[62]

The question is whether these federal mandates are necessary to fulfill the national government's constitutional directive ensuring to all citizens the "equal protection of the law," or are they a barrier to and infringement of states' rights? Do they reinforce the federal system or compromise it? States want to ensure that a proper balance is restored to the federal system, and they believe that if the national government is left to its own devices, this will never happen. The Council of State Governments issued a four-point program designed to rebalance the relationship between the national and state governments. The Council stated that the national government needed to enact the following:

1. A federalism act to enhance the political safeguards of federalism and give states a more effective voice in congressional deliberations.

2. A mechanism to provide the people of the states, through their legislatures, the power to require Congress to reconsider laws, specific provisions of laws, or regulations that interfere with state authority.

3. A mechanism that would allow the states to propose specific amendments to the U.S. Constitution subject to ratification by the United States Congress.

4. Appropriate statutory remedies and/or constitutional reforms to address the problems of conditions attached to spending grants, regulations, and mandates.[63]

Currently, there is a Federalism Act working its way through the halls of Congress. One element of the Federalism Act would require the national government to specify the constitutional power it used to justify the specific legislation it enacted and implemented. This coupled with the "national reconsideration" amendment would transfer enormous power back to the states. However, the Federalism Act is not high on any party's agenda and has for the time being been kept on the back burner.

CONCLUSION

The pendulum of federalism is alledgedly currently swinging in the direction of the state government. However, they are "paying" dearly for the shift in power. One might even describe the shift in power as an illusion as the federal government continues to write laws mandating that the states follow its guidelines while paying for its implementation. This may not be a shift in power but rather a shift in the burden of supporting programs the national government can no longer afford to support

However, federalism has been a work in progress since the days of the Articles of Confederation, and it is still evolving. Its evolution has developed into one of the most effective constitutional checks and balances. It provides additional meaning to the concept of "cooperative federalism" in that to accomplish policy, one level of government really must cooperate with another to get things done. This chapter started with an example of federalism in crisis, Hurricane Katrina. However, federalism is not always obvious, as it was with Katrina, but, rather, its process goes forward everyday all over the country in ways that many of us do not even realize. For example, in 1973, Congress passed the **Endangered Species Act** (ESA). Looking through a broad lens, its purpose was to conserve America's imperiled fish, wildlife, and plant resources. Since 1973, the conservation measures of the ESA have been credited with preventing the extinction of more than 1200 species in the United States including the bald eagle, grizzly bear, grey wolf, and wild stocks of Pacific and Atlantic salmon.[64] It would seem that saving the environment would naturally be a good thing and not raise much controversy. However, this act challenged many already standing vested interests and had a large impact on state and local governments, as well as the private sector where endangered populations lived. Consequently, the ESA has not move forward without serious political wrangling at all levels.

Focusing on only one issue within the ESA will demonstrate how federalism is a course in advanced citizenship. The grizzly bears of the lower 48 states are causing quite a growl out West these days. The grizzly population now faces its greatest challenge since it was first placed on the ESA list of threatened species in 1975. Later this year, wildlife officials will unveil a conservation strategy to guide bear management and will likely propose to declare the grizzlies a recovered population and want them delisted from the ESA list. Removing the grizzly from the endangered species list would require taking bear management out of the hands of the national government and placing it in the care of the state governments of Wyoming, Montana, and Idaho. Many, including the Sierra Club, believe that this would negatively impact the grizzly population because delisting would remove current prohibitions on the killing and harassing of grizzlies.[65] Although this concerns one small element in one act of Congress, many levels of government and the private sector are currently engaged in the political wrangling of this issue. They include the national government, five federal agencies, seven national forest areas, two national parks, three state governments, three state agencies, twenty county governments, numerous citizen action groups and lobby organizations, all with their own agendas.

Two issues central to the question of delisting are land usage and funding, both significantly impact the grizzlies in the area which surrounds Yellowstone National Park. The question of land usage has been hotly debated as 175,000 acres of Wyoming's Bridger-Teton National Forest were

The grizzly population now faces its greatest challenge since it was first placed on the ESA list of threatened species in 1975. Photo by Theresia Stewart.

recently designated to be leased for oil and gas development. Much of this land is roadless and prized for its wildlife. The leases have brought into question many "what ifs" as to the sustainability of a viable grizzly community if this land is used for commercial development. Funding, the other issue critical in the debate surrounding delisting, would impact state and local governmental budgets and their ability to implement sustainable wildlife habitat. Currently an estimated $3.5 million per year is needed to fund research, provide public education, and monitor grizzly population. At this time funding is $2M and falls short of what is necessary to sustain these activities. If the grizzlies are delisted, federal funds will be lost and more of the financial responsibility will fall to the already overburdened state and local governments.[66]

The question might be, what is best for the grizzly bear, and who best to decide that policy issue. Would it be the national government, state governments, or local interests? It will probably take all these groups to work out a compromise, hopefully in the best interest of the bears and all parties concerned. A delisting ruling is currently pending.

The Constitution established a government whose framework required its units to "share" power but left only vague guidelines as how to accomplish this difficult governing feat. How power is to be shared is still open to debate today exemplified in the discussion of New Federalism and the "devolution revolution." Recently the states have been successful in stating their case before Congress and the American people that they are more than "interest groups" in the governing process. They are demanding an equal share in the political process. However, in so doing, are they subverting the process? Would the passage of a Federalism Act be constitutional or in the words of Chief

Justice Marshall, "If the legislatures of the several states may, at will, annul the judgements of the courts of the United States and destroy the rights acquired under those judgements, the constitution itself becomes a solemn mockery."[67]

The world is moving towards global economic interdependence. If the devolution revolution is successful, is it realistic to assume that the states will be able to design and execute the difficult social and economic programs necessary not only for a nationalist capitalist economy but a global economy as well? More to the point, will the states be able to pay for the programs politically and financially and, if not, will the citizens have to pay for this in a cut in programs, some states more than others. Does a national and international economy demand that the federal government steer the course for the fifty states? Would the national government be abdicating its constitutional responsibility by devolving power to the states? Or is it possible that the national and state governments will continue to function as interdependent units and continue to share power as the Constitution intended? If so, the debate as to how that power is to be shared will continue in the new millennium.

CHAPTER NOTES

[1]George C. Edwards III, Martin P. Wattenberg, and Robert L. Lineberry, *Government in American*, (New York: Longman, 1997), 58.

[2]J. W. Peltason, Corwin & Peltason's *Understanding the Constitution*, (Fort Worth: Harcourt Brace College Publishers, 1994), 19.

[3]Clayton Roberts, and David Roberts, *A History of England: 1688 to the Present*, Volume II, 3rd edition, (Englewood Cliffs, N.J., 1991), 834.

[4]Kentucky Municipal Statutory Law, Informational Bulletin No. 145, (Frankfort, Kentucky: Legislative Research Commission, August, 1993), 1-5.

[5]Bruce E. Johansen, *Dating the Iroquois Confederacy*, Akwesasne Notes New Series, Fall 1995, 62-63.

[6]Bruce E. Johansen, *Forgotten Fathers*, (Ipswich, Massachusetts: Gambit, Inc., p. 1982), xvi.

[7]Ibid., xv, xvi.

[8]Ibid., 64.

[9]Ibid., 74.

[10]Ibid., 8, 9.

[11]Ibid., 61.

[12]Oren Lyons and others, *Exiled in the Land of the Free: Democracy, Indian Nations, and the U.S. Constitution*, (Santa Fe: Clear Light Publishers, 1992), 115.

[13]Barbara A. Bardes. Mack C. Shelley, II and Steffen W. Schmidt, *American Government and Politics Today: The Essentials*, 3rd edition, (St. Paul: West Publishing Co., 1990), 41.

[14]Peltason, 19.

[15]Ibid., 20.

[16]Ibid.

[17]Ibid., 21.

[18]Ibid.

[19]Ibid., 98.

[20]Sue Davis, Corwin and J.W. Peltason, *Understanding the Constitution,* 17th ed., (United States: Thomson Wadsworth, 2008), pp. 141-142.

[21]Carter, Yang, "Probing a Pardon," February 9, 2001, abcNEWS.com.

[22]Peltason, 20.

[23]O'Brien, 508.

[24]Ibid.

[25]Peltason, 77.

[26]Ibid.

[27]Daniel A Farber, Williams N. Eskridge, Jr., and Philip P. Frickey, *Constitutional Law: Themes for the Constitutions Third Century,* (St. Paul, Minn.: West Publishing Co., 1993), 10.

[28]Peltason, 347.

[29]David M. O'Brien, *Constitutional Law and Politics: Struggles for Power And Governmental Accountability,* Volume One, 2nd edition, (New York: W.W. Norton & Co., 1995), 586.

[30]Farber, 10.

[31]Kermit Hall, and others ed., *The Oxford Companion to the Supreme Court of the United States* (New York: Oxford University Press, 1992), 868.

[32]Ibid., 339.

[33]John C. Domino, *Civil Rights & Liberties: Toward the Twenty-first Century,* (Harper Collins College Publishers (1994), 226.

[34]Ibid., 227.

[35]Ginsberg, 683.

[36]Peltason, 365.

[37]Sue Davis and J.W. Peltason, *Understanding the Constitution, 16th ed.,* (Australia, United Kingdom and United States, et al: Thomson Wadsworth, 2004), p. 425.

[38]Manning Marable, *Race, Reform, and Rebellion: The Second Reconstruction in Black America,* 1945-1990, 2nd edition, (Jackson: University Press of Mississippi, 1991) 81-82.

[39]Ibid.

[40]Peltason, 173.

[41]Thomas R. Dye and Harmon Zeigler, *The Irony of Democracy: An Uncommon Introduction to American Politics,* 9th edition (Belmont, California: Wadsworth Publishing Co., 1993), 360.

[42]Hall, 573.

[43]Peltason, 173.

[44]Hall, 573-574.

[45]Farber, Eskridge and Frickey, 833.

[46]O'Brien, 633.

[47]Ibid., 628.

[48]Peltason, 174.

[49]Arron Epstein ,"High Court to Say If Brady Handgun Law Goes too Far," *Lexington Herald Leader,* 1996.

[50]Peltason, 105.

[51]O'Brien, 587.

[52]"States' Federalism Summit Statement," Council of State Government: Policy and Program Development, July, 1997, 1. http://www.csg.org/federalism.html.

[53]O'Brien, 587.

[54]Lewis Bender & James Stever, ed., *Administering The New Federalism,* (Boulder:Westview Press, 1986), 43.

[55]Ibid., 54.

[56]James Hosek & Robert Levine, "An Introduction to the Issues," in *The New Fiscal Federalism and the Social Safety Net: A View From California* (Rand, 1996), 1.

[57]Michael Lafaive, "Washington Should Kick the Mandate Habit," Mackinac Center for Public Policy, February 8, 1993, No 93-04. http://www.mackinac.org/viewpoin/1993cv/v9304.html.

[58]Ginsberg, 130.

[59]Lafaive, "Washington Should Kick the Mandate Habit."

[60]Ginsberg, 131-132.

[61]Douglas Seay and Wesley Smith, "Federalism," *Issues '96: The Candidate's Briefing Book*, (Heritage Foundation, 1996), Chapter, 14, 7. http://www.cpac.org/heritage/issues96/chpt14.html.

[62] "Mandate for ID Meets Resistance From States," *New York Times*, May 6, 2006

[63]States' Federalism Summit, 1-4.

[64]Sierra Club Foundation. *Grizzly Bear Project; The Delisting Threat*, www.tscf.org/foundation/programs/grizzly.asp

[65]Ibid.

[66]"The Good, The Bad and the Grizzly," 2004 Educational Broadcasting Corporation, http://www.pbs.org/wnet/nature/thegrizzly/print/delisting.html.

[67]Domino, 233.

SUGGESTED READINGS

Bender, Lewis, and James Stever, ed. *Administering The New Federalism.* Boulder: Westview, 1986.

Bruce E. Johansen. *Forgotten Fathers.* Ipswich, Mass.: Gambit, Inc., 1982. *False Patriots: The Threat of Antigovernment Extremists.* Montgomery, Ala.: Southern Poverty Law Center, 1996.

Hosek, James, and Robert Levine. *The New Fiscal Federalism and the Social Safety Net: A View From California.* Rand, 1996.

Kaplan, Marshall, and Sue O'Brien. *The Governors and the New Federalism.* Boulder: Westview Press, 1991.

Lyons, Oren, John Mohawk, Vine Deloria, Jr., Laurence Hauptman, Howard Berman,

Donald Grinde, Jr., Curtis Berkey, and Robert Venables. *Exiled in the Land of the Free: Democracy, Indian Nations, and the U.S. Constitution.* Santa Fe: Clear Light Publishers, 1992.

Chapter Four

PUBLIC OPINION, POLITICAL CULTURE, AND POLITICAL SOCIALIZATION

Consider the following scenario. Pollsters visit your college, among a number of other colleges and universities in the United States, and ask each student for his/her thoughts on the cost of higher education in the United States. Perhaps 65 percent say that education costs too much, 30 percent believe that the cost is fair, and 5 percent have no opinion. ("No opinion" is referred to as "**latent opinion**" when the response is given because the individual has not yet fully formed a judgment.) Suppose the pollsters then analyze the data and find:

(1) that while all the male students believe that the cost is too high, only a simple majority (50 percent plus 1) of the female students believes so,

(2) that responses to the cost question also varied according to the age, race, ethnicity, and political party affiliations of those polled.

These findings, the **distributions** (65 percent, 30 percent, 5 percent) and the other distributions or percentages of responses based on gender, age, race, etc., are commonly referred to as "public opinion."

Public opinion is so closely related to political culture and political socialization that it is sometimes difficult to talk about it, or about either of them, without reference to the other two. However, each will be considered in this chapter, and the connections among them should become rather apparent.

PUBLIC OPINION

Public opinion has been formally defined as "an aggregate of individual views, attitudes or beliefs shared by a portion of a community."[1] As this definition suggests, there may be more than one public and more than one opinion. In the community of college students the 65 percent who

115

expressed the view that a college diploma is too "pricey" is one public; the attitudes of male students who concurred on one side or the other is a second public; female students who shared the same position is a third, and so on.

The Importance of Public Opinion

Limited Range Importance

Knowledge about how people feel about specific issues may be of importance to relatively few individuals such as to politicians who want to be elected or re-elected. Armed with the information obtained from the fictitious poll described above, for example, candidates seeking to win the college-age vote in a presidential election would probably make some effort to argue for a reduction in tuition.

The extent of that effort would be partially dependent upon how important or **salient** students say the issue is, that is, whether the cost of tuition is more or less important to them than perhaps the issues of abortion or the economy. In part, the extent of the candidates' efforts to woo students will also be based on how strong or **intense** they say the tuition issue is to them. The greater the intensity, the more burning the issue, the less likely a smart candidate will be to ignore it.

When issues are both salient and intense, they are taken very seriously by politicians. Both Presidents Richard M. Nixon and Lyndon B. Johnson cut their political careers short because of the convictions expressed by the public. High negative ratings in public opinion polls contributed to the resignation of the former and caused the latter to reject a bid for a second term in office. In both instances young voters helped to generate the hostile political climate that brought these presidents down, and the opinions of young people have, therefore, continued to carry some weight. In the 1992 presidential campaign, voters between the ages of 18 and 24 were successfully courted by Bill Clinton and, probably because 37 percent of those young voters turned out at the polls for that election, they have been pursued by both parties ever since.

Candidates and politicians seeking to ascertain the public mood on various issues generally rely heavily on public opinion polls. As the following report shows, Clinton, who had always been concerned with his standing in the polls, monitored not only what young voters said to pollsters but what people of all ages had to say about even relatively insignificant activities.

Dick Morris once said that every time Bill Clinton had a problem, he got a poll in his head. That, as it turns out, was a sad understatement. Every time Bill Clinton had a vacation, he got a poll in his head.

In 1995, worried that the Clintons' last vacation sailing with Jackie O. in Martha's Vineyard had not been suitably populist, Mr. Morris recommended that the President go on a mountain vacation with high-tech gear. A White House poll on "life-style clusters" had shown that swing voters liked camping, hiking and technology.

The President dutifully went camping and hiking in a national park, but was grumpy afterward. "That's the first vacation I've taken that didn't help me in the polls," Mr. Clinton said irritably upon his return, according to Mr. Morris's new memoir [**Behind the Oval Office**]. "The first one. After all my **other** vacations, I've always risen a point or two. This vacation I didn't go up at all.[2]

Among the many life-style clusters that the president was interested in assessing were the women voters soon to be labeled by pollsters as the "soccer moms."

Soccer moms, or as one observer called them, the 1996 "electoral-bloc clichè," were frequently described in the media as affluent, middle-class, suburban, married women of the baby-boomer generation who spent their afternoons car pooling sports-oriented children to soccer games in mini-vans.[3] What they shared with each other, and with many other female voters, were their opinions about which political issues were the most important. Abortion rights, health care, Medicare, education, the environment, the economy, and family leave ranked high on their lists, and they voted for the man they believed would acknowledge their concerns and support the reforms that they advocated.

Because they did (54 percent voted for Clinton, 38 percent for Dole in 1996; and 53 percent for Gore and 45 percent for Bush in 2000), the issues that these women were concerned about were also addressed during the 2004 presidential campaign.

In this first post-9/11 presidential election some women voters headed their traditional list of concerns with the issue of national security and their worry about another terrorist attack in the United States. The media quickly labeled them "security moms."

Security moms have been identified as "an outgrowth of the soccer moms . . . . But soccer moms tended to live mainly in the suburbs and could vote either way. Security moms live[d] everywhere and [were] leaning Republican."[4] Also "leaning" Republican were the "Nascar moms" who were married to conservative, pro-Republican race-car fans ("Nascar dads").

Bush, who recognized that he had an opportunity to win over some of these voters, began to talk about terrorism and the war in Iraq in a way that resonates with women:

> I've held the children of the fallen, who are told their dad or mom is a hero, but would rather just have their dad or mom.[5]

The president's increased sensitivity to what the polls showed was an important issue for women voters resulted in a narrowing of the gender gap. (Kerry won the women's vote by 51 percent to Bush's 48 percent.)

The use of polls by candidates and by incumbent politicians is currently so widespread that it is a bit surprising to discover that the practice is a relatively recent one. Scientific public opinion polls first appeared in the 1930s. Table 4.1 cites some of the opinions about government held by Americans during that early period. The first politician to use such data was Governor Thomas E. Dewey in his unsuccessful bid for the Republican presidential nomination in 1940, and, twenty years later John F. Kennedy became the first candidate to actually hire a pollster.

Extended Range Importance

Knowledge of a public's opinion may be of interest to a much wider audience than just college students or political candidates. Many Americans, for instance, are concerned about the growing feeling of despair about the future among their fellow citizens and about the increasingly high levels of distrust of government because such expressions signal the potential for serious trouble for the regime and/or for the government. For example, a special report which appeared in *U.S. News & World Report* during the 1996 presidential election year found that

> never has the public felt so alienated from its leaders; Trust [sic] in the federal government has taken a nose dive from four decades ago, when 75 percent of Americans said they had faith in the folks in Washington to do the right thing most of the time. Today, three out of four people say they have no such faith. In fact, a third of those questioned in a recent Gallup poll say their faith is so low they think the federal government poses 'an immediate threat to the rights and freedoms of ordinary citizens.'[6]

The numbers haven't changed all that much over the years. Although 55 percent of those questioned shortly after 9/11 said that they trusted government, by the summer of 2003 only 36 percent of poll respondents said that they trusted the government in Washington D.C. to do what was right "just about always" or "most of the time."[7]

Two years later, a *New York Times*/CBS News Poll reported that "more Americans now distrust the Federal government to do the right thing than at any time since the attacks on the World Trade Center and the Pentagon.[8]

These public opinion findings of discontent among the electorate are obtained in a number of different ways in addition to polls, such as the Gallup and *Times*/CBS polls mentioned in the

---

TABLE 4.1

PUBLIC OPINION POLL DATA, CIRCA NEW DEAL ERA

Three-fourths believed "the government should see to it that any man who wants to work has a job."
Fortune: July 1935

Eight out of ten members of the public favored "an amendment to the Constitution prohibiting child labor."
Gallop: March 28, 1936

Six out of ten approved minimum wage regulations.
Gallop: June 6, 1937

Eight out of ten felt the Federal Government should "provide free medical care for those unable to pay."
Gallop: June 14, 1937

Six out of ten thought "the Federal Government ought to set a limit on the number of hours employees should work in each business and industry."
Gallop: July 26, 1937

Seven out of ten approved Government regulation of the stock exchanges.
Gallop: October 17, 1937

Seven out of ten thought "the Federal Government should give money to the states to help local schools."
Gallop: March 26, 1938

Seven out of ten thought "it is the government's responsibility to pay the living expenses of needy people who are out of work."
Gallop: April 5, 1939

Source: Cited in Lloyd A. Fred and Hadley Cantril, *The Political Beliefs of Americans: A Study of Public Opinion* (New York: Simon and Schuster, 1968), 10.

articles quoted above. They are also acquired by quantifying the frequency of large-scale political protests, demonstrations, and riots, such as those that took place in the 1960s over civil rights and the conflict in Vietnam; the growing numbers of negative articles and reports about the government in the media; and the decline in legitimate political participation, such as in voting, paying taxes, or volunteering for military service. All of these actions and negative expressions are reliable measures of public opinion.

Public Opinion and Democracy

Because American democracy embraces the notion that government rule should be in the public interest, it is necessary for official decision-makers to know both what that interest is and whether it is being satisfied. That doesn't necessarily mean that the government will always act on its knowledge. Neither the Equal Rights Amendment nor stricter gun control, both of which are currently favored by a majority of Americans, have become public policies. Nevertheless, keeping a finger on the pulse of public opinion is an important technique for monitoring—to put it in systems analysis terms—levels of "support."

It was noted in the introductory chapter of this text that an increase of public support shows a high degree of citizen satisfaction and acceptance of the government and the regime and suggests the continuing stability and persistence of a democratic system. The withdrawal of support by an extremely large number of individuals is, on the other hand, suggestive of the loss of a government's or a regime's legitimacy and may portend a government's fall in an upcoming election.

Such predictions were made during the second term of the Bush administration when the failure to provide adequate relief to the victims of Hurricane Katrina, the upwardly spiraling rise in gasoline prices and the persistence of fighting in Iraq all contributed to George W. Bush's plummeting public approval levels. His public approval average for 2004-2005 was 46 percent. By May 2006, his approval rating in the polls was down to 31 percent (Nixon and Carter were the only presidents that rated lower in the polls) and political pundits were already beginning to speculate that the Democrats would win seats in—if not control of— Congress during the 2006 mid-term elections and would win the presidency in 2008.

Public Opinion and Political Culture

Political culture is defined as "a people's predominant beliefs, attitudes, values, ideals, sentiments, and evaluations about the political system of its country, and the role of the self in that system."[9] The term "predominant" in the definition just quoted is one key to differentiating public opinion from political culture. Public opinion, as defined at the beginning of this chapter, refers to the beliefs or opinions that are "shared by a portion of a community." These beliefs may or may not be the same as those that prevail or "predominate" in the population as a whole. Another difference between the two concepts is that public opinion tends to be much more volatile and transitory in nature.

AMERICAN POLITICAL CULTURE

American political culture refers to the widely shared and enduring beliefs, attitudes, feelings and emotions, and values, etc., about government and about politics and about the role of citizens in the United States. These include: beliefs in freedom, liberty, equality, justice, citizen participation, and limited government; feelings of pride and respect for national heroes and martyrs such as George Washington, Susan B. Anthony, the "unknown soldier" buried in Arlington Cemetery, Neil Armstrong, Malcolm X, and Martin Luther King; emotional attachments to symbols including the U.S. flag, the Statue of Liberty, the White House, the bald eagle, and the three Charters of Freedom; and values such as peace, security, and prosperity.

All of these components of American political culture, which systems analysts refer to as the country's "domestic environment," transcend, for the most part, the ethnic, racial, religious, social, political, geographical, educational, and gender diversity of the population in this country. There are "subcultures" in the United States to be sure, but the long list of shared beliefs, feelings, attachments, and values given above itemizes just some of the things that unite the "majority" of Americans. Many of these items, as the next two statements made by eminent statesmen show, have united us for centuries.

A Few Selected Descriptions of U.S. Political Culture

Benjamin Franklin

Born in America in 1706, and a participant in the deliberations for both independence from England in 1776 and the new Constitution in 1787, Franklin recognized early on that a unique national spirit, character, and culture prevailed in America. He expressed these sentiments often and considered them to be valid reasons for the colonies to separate from England. Some of the special qualities that were uniquely American were later put forth in a humorous letter, written in 1784 to his daughter Sarah Bache, in which he described the reasons for his dismay about the choice of the Bald Eagle as the national symbol of the country. The eagle, he explained,

> is a Bird of bad moral Character; he does not get his living honestly; . . . too lazy to fish for himself, he watches the Labour of the Fishing-Hawk; and, when that diligent Bird has at length taken a Fish . . . the Bald Eagle pursues him, and takes it from him. With all this Injustice . . . . he is generally poor, and often very lousy. Besides, he is a rank Coward; the little KingBird, not bigger than a Sparrow, attacks him boldly and drives him out of the District. He is therefore by no means a proper emblem for the brave and honest [Americans] who have driven all the Kingbirds from our Country . . . .

A more suitable selection, one more representative of those unique American values Franklin suggested, was the turkey,

> a much more respectable Bird, and withal a true original Native of America . . . . He is, . . . a Bird of Courage, and would not hesitate to attack a Grenadier of the British Guards, who should presume to invade his FarmYard with a **red** Coat on.[10]

Alexis de Tocqueville

This Frenchmen, a nobleman and an assistant magistrate at Versailles, visited America in 1831 and kept a record of the trip including his conversations with John Quincy Adams, Sam Houston, Daniel Webster, and President Andrew Jackson. His notes, which filled the pages of many journals, were published in 1835 under the title *Democracy in America*. Like Franklin, he too recognized and wrote about the qualities that distinguish Americans.

Of all the aspects of American political culture, and Tocqueville uses the term "political character" rather than culture, he was perhaps most struck by the strong emphasis placed on "equality." This is the first thing he comments upon in the introduction to the book.

> Amongst the novel objects that attracted my attention during my stay in the United States, nothing struck me more forcibly than the general equality of condition among the people. I readily discovered the prodigious influence which this primary fact exercises on the whole course of society; it gives a peculiar direction to **public opinion** [emphasis added,] and a peculiar tenor to the laws; it imparts new maxims to the governing authorities, and peculiar habits to the governed.

Equality in Europe, he adds by way of comparison, has not "reached the extreme limit which it seems to have attained in the United States . . . ."[11]

Gabriel Almond and Sidney Verba

The expression "political culture" was popularized over a hundred years after Tocqueville's journals were published by these renowned political scientists in a groundbreaking book entitled *The Civic Culture* (1963). In this work, now considered to be a classic in political science, the authors, among many other things, describe the U.S. political culture and compare American "feelings toward government and politics" with those in four other countries. Americans were found to have the most pride in their government and political institutions.

> Eighty-five percent of the American respondents cited some feature of the American government or political tradition—the Constitution, political freedom, democracy, and the like—as compared with 46 percent for the British, 7 percent for the Germans, 3 percent for the Italians, and 30 percent for the Mexicans.[12]

In addition, Americans more strongly favored political participation and had more confidence in their ability to influence government and its laws. That, of course, was in the early 1960s. In a follow-up work, *The Civic Culture Revisited*, edited by Almond and Verba and published in 1980, American political culture was described as being "under stress." Americans, having experienced both the Vietnam War and Watergate, were found to be "more cynical about politicians, less confident in political institutions, and more politically sophisticated . . . ."[13] It was concluded, however, that these "changes in American political culture during the late 1960s and early 1970s were produced by short-term issues and events rather than fundamental changes in American society."[14]

In other words, while political culture is not changeless, it is very tenacious. The American values and beliefs identified so long ago by Franklin and Tocqueville have endured and, as one author explains, "have given us a common identity in the midst of incredible diversity . . . [and] have made us one people."[15] In fact, a core of fundamental cultural beliefs and values tends to be handed down or transmitted from one generation to the next relatively intact not only in the United States but in every country. It is this persistence of political values over time that makes the process by which they are transmitted an interesting one to so many students of American government today.

The Source of Political Culture

It has been said that the most basic question that can be asked about political culture is "where does it come from?"[16] The answer is probably already clear. Political culture is bequeathed (taught), and it is inherited (learned). The process by which this transferal or transmission takes place is called "political socialization."

POLITICAL SOCIALIZATION

Political socialization is defined in two ways. It is sometimes defined, as suggested above, as the process by which political cultures are passed on over the generations. The actual teaching and learning parts of the process, however, are not a collective one. It is one that takes place individual by individual and citizen by citizen in every local community in every state in every country. The child in eighteenth century America who listened to adults speak about the tyrant King George III was being socialized. So too is the twenty-first century college student whose tuition costs increase each semester because of cutbacks in government funding.

When the focus shifts away from the political culture in general and turns to the individuals—children or adults—that are being taught and are acquiring the political values and beliefs that predominate in the community and/or in the country, political socialization is defined in a second way. It is defined as the process by which individual political outlooks are acquired.

The two aspects and the two definitions of socialization are—like the chicken and the egg—closely related; the accumulation of individual beliefs in a country constitutes its political culture, and the political culture in turn shapes the beliefs acquired by the individual. Having already spent some time examining the first component, political culture, the second—the acquisition of individual political outlooks—will be explored in the remainder of this chapter.

Political Socialization and the Individual

In 1959 Herbert H. Hyman published the first major work on the subject of political socialization. His book, entitled *Political Socialization: A Study in the Psychology of Political Behavior*, set down a fundamental point to remember about when and how individuals are politically socialized: they are socialized over the entire span of their lifetimes by a wide variety of structures or sources Hyman called "agencies of socialization." Today these "agencies" are more commonly referred to as "agents."

Agents of Socialization

An agent of socialization is any formal or informal group or structure that intentionally or unintentionally sends out a political message. This description is so broad that virtually everyone at some point probably qualifies as an agent. But while there are many, some of them, including those discussed below, are considered to be more important than others.

The Family. "Foremost among agencies of socialization into politics," Hyman wrote over forty years ago, "is the family."[17] Given the current realities of everyday life, the notion of what a "family" is should probably be expanded to include any and all of the infant's and young child's primary caregivers. But Hyman's premise—which is that those that have the initial contacts and/or spend extended time with the child ("proximity") have the best opportunity to pass on fundamental beliefs and values—remains the same.

There is a certain common sense logic being employed by Hyman and those that agree with him. They begin with the assumption that since parents generally succeed in transmitting their own religious and social beliefs to their offspring, (Young children, for example, usually belong to the same faith and root for the same sports teams as the adult members of the family.) then the same should hold true for political beliefs and values.

While this assumption is a reasonable one, supporting empirical evidence only partially confirms it. The family does not seem to transmit specific political positions (on abortion or legalizing drugs, for example), but it does seem to excel at passing on general orientations, such as partisan values. That is to say that a child whose parents are Democrats or Republicans is likely to follow suit. This is especially the case when both of the parents and/or others in the family are members of the same political party, are strongly committed to it, and regularly engage in political conversations and express their beliefs in the child's presence.

In addition to party affiliation, general attitudes about authority and government are often passed on from the adults to the young children in a family. For example, David Easton, who has been referred to earlier in this text in connection with both his definition of politics and with the systems analysis approach, reports the following conversation with his three-and-a-half year old son that took place as the two were looking for a place to park their car.

> Child. "There's somewhere."
> Father. "I can't park there."
> Child. "Why?"
> Father. "It's not allowed."
> Child. "Who say so?"
> Father. "I'll get a ticket."
> Child. "Uh."
> Father. "A policeman will stop me."
> Child. "Oh."[18]

Easton goes on to explain that this "laconic" conversation was significant, because the child "learned if not his first political lesson at least the beginning of an important one. He was being introduced to the notion that his father is not omnipotent, that there is a power external to the family to which even his father has to submit, and that somehow the policeman represents this power."[19] In short, the child was being exposed to the ideas that politics both touches his daily life and that he is expected to obey the laws passed by the government.

These are certainly among the predominant views held today, and over the centuries, by most Americans. If a child, such as young Easton, does not happen to learn them from the family, another agent of socialization, the school, is expected to pick up the slack and deliver the message in an even more direct way.

The School.

> [Teachers] use very great endeavor and diligence to put into the heads of their children while they yet be tender and pliant, good opinions and profitable for the conservation of their weal public. Which when they be once rooted in children do remain with them all their life after, and be wondrous profitable for the defense and maintenance of the state of the commonwealth, which never decayeth but through vices rising of evil opinions.
>
> Sir Thomas More, *Utopia*, 1516

Schools, from kindergarten through college, make it their business to teach citizenship, patriotism, and obedience to authority. They have done so from the earliest days of the American republic when the curriculum included "civic training." By 1915, the term "civics" was regularly used to designate those high school courses that were expressly developed to teach students about citizenship and about political institutions and processes.[20]

Although "civics" is no longer a requirement in most educational institutions, memories of many readers' earliest school days probably include the efforts made by their teachers to instill patriotic values. These attempts usually started at the beginning of the day with the singing of the national anthem and the recitation of the pledge of allegiance and continued later on with instruction in American history and government. Lessons in these subjects, especially in the early grades, frequently centered around national holidays (Thanksgiving, Veterans Day, Presidents Day) and national heroes and heroines. (Is there anyone who did not hear about George Washington Carver and the peanut or Betsy Ross and the flag?)

Perhaps because teachers, as More put it, "use very great endeavor and diligence to put [patriotic ideas] into the heads of their children while they yet be tender and pliant," empirical studies have shown that they have been largely successful in instilling patriotic attitudes to even the youngest students. One of the most fascinating of the early studies, conducted by Easton and Dennis in 1961 and 1962, surveyed the feelings of 12,052 children in grades 2-8 about the president. An analysis of their findings showed that

> from the earliest grade the child sees the President as on a commanding height, far above adults as well as children. The President flies in on angel's wings, smiling, beneficent, powerful, almost beyond the realm of mere mortals . . . . He is seemingly a storehouse of inexhaustible virtues—wisdom, benevolence, power, trustworthiness, and exemplary leadership.[21]

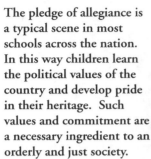

The pledge of allegiance is a typical scene in most schools across the nation. In this way children learn the political values of the country and develop pride in their heritage. Such values and commitment are a necessary ingredient to an orderly and just society.

"In all of our testing and interviewing," the researchers observed, "we were unable to find a child who did not express the highest esteem for the President. The descriptions of him were universally so approving that we must describe them as a form of idealization."[22] A little more than a decade later, after the Watergate scandal and the resignation of President Nixon, another researcher concluded that although children had negative judgments about Nixon they "still idealized the presidential role in the abstract."[23]

The ability to transmit feelings of patriotism and other political orientations is facilitated in that children in the United States, and in almost every other country, are required by law to attend school daily while it is in session. For many of them that means that more of their waking hours are spent there than at home. It is because so much of a child's life is spent in school that countries that have experienced a change in regime (the Soviet Union, Nazi Germany, Communist China, Cuba) have used this agent in a deliberate effort to "resocialize" children and to encourage loyalty to the new order.

Peers. While family and schools are apparently the most important agents of political socialization during childhood, by adolescence, and throughout the adult years, the individual's personal experiences play a larger and more significant role. These experiences, often in the form of peer pressure or influences from the peer environment, may either affirm or lead to the adjustment of existing political beliefs.

Peers are those who in some way, such as age, rank or position, share equal status. One's peers include friends, colleagues, and neighbors, as well as other individuals who may be known more casually, those, for instance, who attend the same place of worship, or belong to the same volunteer organization, or social or sports club.

The more overlap or agreement there is in the beliefs held by an individual's different peer groups, the stronger the potential to exert influence. Similarly, the more time that is spent with any one group of peers (proximity), the greater its impact is likely to be. Peer impact on some preferences such as the music an individual listens to or the type of clothes she/he wears can be immediately appreciated by taking a look at how the majority of students in the reader's American govern-

Schools as an Agency of Resocialization in Fascist Germany

Shortly after Hitler came to power in 1933 the National Socialist Party (the Nazis) assumed immediate control over the educational system and devoted itself to two goals: to remove all vestiges of democratic principles and to replace them with fascist doctrines. Speaking in May 1933, the German Minister of the Interior, issued many decrees for the redirection of education; "the schools," he was quoted as saying, "must be politicized and become centers for the political training of youth so that there will result an undivided political will as the basis of a strong and permanent nation; everything that menaces this national-political foundation must be excluded." And what was to be taught?

History and those subjects that are essential for national survival are the most important, for the task of the Revolution is to develop the highest patriotism and fanatical enthusiasm for the nation. The school should instill national pride; it should paint great discoverers as national heroes, who love their people and show this love through devotion and sacrifice. Nationalism and a feeling of national uprightness and righteousness should be combined without hesitation . . . .The greatest revolutions in history occurred as a result . . . of fanatical, hysterical passion. Finally, no boy or girl should leave school without realizing the significance of racial or blood purity. An education conducted from the point of view of race and nation must culminate in military service, the crown of the normal education of the average German.

Source: I. L. Kandel, *The Making of Nazis* (New York: Bureau of Publications Teachers College, Columbia University, 1934), 40-41, and 45.

ment course are attired the next time the class meets or by browsing through some friends' CD collections. Though less obvious to see at a glance, peers also have the potential to affect each others' political beliefs and behavior.

The extent of peer influence on the attitudes of college students during the politically turbulent years of the late 1960s and early 1970s was documented by a Columbia University professor and two graduate student researchers whose offices and laboratories had been occupied by student demonstrators. Using a variety of measures, including the New Left Scale, interviews, and survey questionnaires, they found that conservative freshmen students took on the political values of their peers and were radicalized during their first year at Columbia. When asked why they had changed their political beliefs, about one-half of a sample of students reported that their friends, rather than any other alternative—parents, political participation, communications media, books, or teachers—had influenced their political attitudes.[24]

The socialization/radicalization process at Columbia and throughout the country resulted in a "peer counterculture," one that was against the war in Vietnam, the deceptive practices of the national government, the profit-at-all-costs motivation of big businesses and corporations, existing college curricula (which was found to be largely irrelevant), and racial and sexual inequality. The media helped to disseminate all of these views to a generation of young people, one of whom was

George W. Bush. It is an interesting exercise to ponder the possible effects that those views may have had on the policy decisions of the Bush administration. The topic of the president's socialization will be brought up again in Chapter 12.

Mass Communication Media. The mass communication media—magazines, newspapers, television, cable, radio, and increasingly the information superhighway—primarily report topical political information, that is, facts and opinions about current political events and issues that help to shape the political attitudes and behavior of adults. When the political messages delivered by the media are fictionalized and presented in the form of cartoons and comic books, it serves primarily as an agent of childhood political socialization.

The Media and Children. Many children spend at least some of their after school hours and their weekend mornings in front of the television set watching cartoon programs. Aside from the violent content of many of these programs, there are some, which intentionally or not, also teach basic political values. Over the years cartoon programs such as "G.I. Joe," "He-Man," "She-Ra," "Rambo," "The Gobots," "Voltran," "Trans-Formers," and "The Defenders of the Earth" have presented, as one expert on the subject has pointed out, a view of the world in terms of "good countries" and "evil empires," a view in which the United States is always the good country and

- American heroes have only peaceful intentions;
- if not for the enemy, the world would remain at peace;
- the hero (American) rarely strikes first;
- it's the enemy attack that prompts the hero to respond with force; and
- the hero always acts in self-defense to insure freedom and uphold his moral convictions.[25]

There are a number of political messages that these cartoons convey but foremost among them is the value of "patriotism." Whether the media should teach this and other basic political values in a less biased fashion remains an ongoing subject of debate.

The Media and Adults. Except for when the news that it reports is cataclysmic in nature, the media does not usually play a significant role in changing the "predominant" political beliefs that adult Americans have long-held. More often, it helps to shape their opinions about political personalities (See "1960 Televised Debates," p. 126.) and, according to some in the case of Michael Moore's controversial movie about George W. Bush—*Fahrenheit 9/11*—to reaffirm their pre-existing beliefs. The media does, however, help to change attitudes about "specific" events or issues, and it has done so in this country ever since Thomas Paine's little pamphlet, *Common Sense*, swayed public opinion against King George III and toward independence in 1776. In more recent times it has been the reporting of newspaper columnists and television newscasters that has informed the public and shaped its opinions about particular issues, sometimes in rather unexpected ways. During the 1996 presidential campaign the *New York Times*, based on the results of a survey conducted by the Pew Research Center for the People and the Press, reported that 40 percent of young people (under age 30) and 25 percent of Americans over all said that they had learned something about the 1996 presidential campaign from late-night television comedy. Viewers probably learned something about the 2004 presidential candidates as well. Statistics from the Center for Media and Public Affairs show that Jay Leno, David Letterman, Conan O'Brien and Jon Stewart told a total of 285 jokes about George W. Bush and 102 about John Kerry from January 1 to April 9, 2004.[26]

1960 TELEVISED DEBATES BETWEEN RICHARD M. NIXON AND JOHN F. KENNEDY

Conventional wisdom has it that Richard M. Nixon lost the 1960 election on the evening of the first televised debate he had with John F. Kennedy. Why? Because

the TV candidate . . . is measured not against his predecessors—not against a standard of performance established by two centuries of democracy—but against Mike Douglas. How well does he handle himself? Does he mumble, does he twitch, does he make me laugh? Do I feel warm inside?

Into this milieu came Richard Nixon: grumpy, cold and aloof....[Marshall] McLuhan watched him debate Kennedy and thought he resembled 'the railway lawyer who signs leases that are not in the best interests of the folks in the little town.'

He nearly became President in 1960. . . . He failed because he was too few of the things a President had to be— and because he had no press to lie for him and did not know how to use television to lie about himself.

It was just Nixon and John Kennedy and they sat down together in a television studio and a little red light began to glow and Richard Nixon was finished. Television would be blamed but for all the wrong reasons.

They would say it was makeup and lighting, but Nixon's problem went deeper than that. His problem was himself. Not what he said but the man he was. The camera portrayed him clearly. America took its Richard Nixon straight and did not like the taste.

The content of the programs made little difference. Except for startling lapses, content seldom does. What mattered was the image the viewers received, though few observers at the time caught the point. . . . In McLuhan's opinion 'Without TV, Nixon had it made.'

Source: Joe McGinniss, *The Selling of the President 1968* (New York: Pocket Books, 1970), 23-26.

The Significance of Political Socialization

Individual by individual the major agents of socialization, family, schools, peers, and the media, transmit the predominate political beliefs, attitudes, and values from one generation to the next. The significance of understanding this never-ending process is twofold: it provides some concrete insights into what makes Americans tick politically, and it is used, as Tocqueville and Almond and Verba did, as a measure for comparing the United States with other countries.

Comparisons can help both scholars and citizens in the U.S. to understand the similarities that unite and the differences that separate them from those in other countries with different political cultures. Americans were reminded of this during the Russian run-off presidential election between President Boris N. Yeltsin and his Communist rival, Gennadi A. Zyuganov, which was held in June 1996.

Watching the conventions, seeing the campaign advertisements and posters, and listening to the speeches from a distance, some U.S. observers did not realize how superficial the trappings of American style democracy actually are in Russia. However, one of Boris Yeltsin's senior aides, Viktor Ilyushin, attempted to set the record straight. From the first meeting he had with foreign election specialists who were attempting to coach the Russians in campaigning techniques he realized, as he told a U.S. reporter, "that it was unlikely we could get many useful tips from our foreign colleagues. Because this is Russia. This is not Germany, not the United States, not Italy. Here we have the Russian people, Russian traditions, Russian habits and a Russian president. Elections in Russia will always take place in the Russian way."[27] This was just another way of saying that as long as Russians socialize Russians, the political culture will not be easily changed. It is as durable for them as it is for Americans.

In informing us about the durability of the beliefs and attitudes that are acquired over a lifetime, socialization theories and concepts provide an explanation for why Americans today distrust national government and executive leadership and why they believe in liberty and freedom and equality. These are among the two-hundred-year old legacies from their colonial past. The durability of beliefs also helps explain why the U.S. political system persists in spite of the many assaults upon it. It persists in the face of communist scares (1950s), youth movements that call for its destruction (1960s and 1970s), domestic and international terrorist attacks that are designed to alter its policies and dilute its legitimacy (beginning with the downing of Pan Am flight 103 over Lockerbie Scotland on December 21, 1988), and militia or paramilitary groups such as the Freemen and the Vipers that try to undermine its institutions (1990s). The system persists because the majority of Americans have been sufficiently socialized. They have been taught and they have learned to support it in good times when it's easy do so and in bad times when it is not and to support it when the system meets their demands and on the occasions (as long as they are not too frequent) when it does not. Easton calls this type of unequivocal support "**diffuse**" support.

CONCLUSION

In discussing public opinion, political culture, and political socialization we have come full circle. These concepts, to use a popular analogy, are like a doughnut—there is no beginning, there is no middle, and there is no end. It's okay then to pick up a round confection and to bite into it

Kennedy and Nixon debated on television.

anywhere. And so it is with the concepts covered in this chapter. Public opinion consists of political attitudes and beliefs; the predominant political attitudes and beliefs shared by a population is called its political culture; political culture is transmitted to each individual through the process of political socialization; and political socialization helps to shape political attitudes and beliefs and to transmit political cultures.

For political scientists the importance of understanding these concepts and processes is that they provide at least some tentative answers to some of the important political questions that have been asked ever since Western politics began back in ancient Greece. Questions about

the political orientations and behaviors of individuals: about who votes and who does not, about who participates in political life and who does not, about what accounts for citizen loyalty, obedience and patriotism and partisanship, liberalism and, conservatism, etc. and questions about political systems: about what accounts for democracy, authoritarianism, regime stability and instability, revolutions, peaceful change, development, legitimacy, etc.

It is because public opinion and political culture and socialization concepts provide some answers to these eternal questions that they may aptly be described as "mega-concepts."[28] They are among the most powerful explanatory concepts in the discipline of political science.

CHAPTER NOTES

[1]Jack C. Plano, and Milton Greenberg, *The American Political Dictionary*, 7th ed. (New York: Holt, Rinehart and Winston, 1985), 171-172.

[2]Maureen Dowd, "Leaders As Followers," *The New York Times*, 12 January 1997, Section 4, 17 (E).

[3]Terry Golway, "Life in the 90's," *America*, 9 November 15. John McCormick and John Leland, "The Fight Over the Soccer Moms," *Newsweek*, 26 August 1966, 28.

[4]Katharine Q. Seelye, "Kerry in a Struggle for a Democratic Base: Women," *The New York Times* 22 September 2004, 16 (A).

[5]Lance Tarrence and Leslie Sanchez, "What Women Voters Want," *The New York Times* 12 September 2004, 13 (WK).

[6]Joannie M. Schrof, David Fischer, Kenan Pollack, Beth Brophy and Linda Kulman, "Speak Up! You Can be Heard!," *U.S. News & World Report*, 19 February 1996, 42.

[7]Sam Roberts, "In Government We Trust (As Far as We Can Throw It)," *The New York Times* 4 January 2004, 4(WK).

[8]Todd S. Purdum and Majorie Connelly, "Support for Bush Continues to Drop as More Question his Leadership Skills, Poll Shows," *The New York Times*, 15 September 2005, 18(A).

[9]Larry Diamond, "Political Culture and Democracy," chap. in *Political Culture and Democracy in Developing Countries* (Boulder, Colorado: Lynne Rienner Publishers, Inc., 1994), 7.

[10]Benjamin Franklin, "Letter to Mrs. Sarah Bache, January 26, 1784," in *The Writings of Benjamin Franklin*, Volume IX, 1783-1788, ed. Albert Henry Smyth, (New York: The Macmillan Company, 1907), 166-167.

[11]Alexis de Tocqueville, *Democracy in America*, edited with an Introduction by Andrew Hacker (New York: Washington Square Press, Inc., 1964), 3.

[12]Gabriel A. Almond and Sidney Verba, *The Civic Culture: Political Attitudes and Democracy in Five Nations* (Princeton, New Jersey: Princeton University Press, 1963), 102.

[13]Alan I. Abramowitz, "The United States: Political Culture under Stress," in *The Civic Culture Revisited*, eds. Gabriel A. Almond and Sidney Verba (Boston, Massachusetts: Little, Brown and Company, 1980), 270.

[14]Ibid., 206.

[15]Frances Moore Lappe, *Rediscovering America's Values* (New York: Ballantine Books, 1989), 3.

[16]Larry Diamond, "Causes and Effects," chap. in *Political Culture & Democracy in Developing Countries* (Boulder, Colorado: Lynne Rienner Publishers, 1994), 229.

[17]Herbert H. Hyman, *Political Socialization: A Study in the Psychology of Political Behavior* (New York: The Free Press, 1959), 51.

[18]David Easton and Jack Dennis, *Children in the Political System: Origins of Political Legitimacy* (New York: McGraw-Hill Book Company, 1969), 3

[19]Ibid., 3 and 4.

[20]Kenneth P. Langton and M. Kent Jennings, "Political Socialization and the High School Civics Curriculum in the United States," in *Socialization to Politics: A Reader*, ed. Jack Dennis (New York: John Wiley & Sons, 1973), 365-366.

[21]Easton and Dennis, 171 and 178.

[22]Ibid., 177.

[23]Fred I. Greenstein, "The Benevolent Leader Revisited: Children's Images of Political Leaders In Three Democracies," *The American Political Science Review* 69 (December 1975): 1397.

[24]Alice Ross Gold, Richard Christie and Lucy Norman Friedman, *Fists and Flowers: A Social Psychological Interpretation of Student Dissent* (New York: Academic Press, Inc., 1976), 99-100, 138 and 149.

[25]Petra Hesse, *The World is a Dangerous Place: Images of the Enemy on Children's Television* (Cambridge, Massachusetts: Center for Psychological Studies in the Nuclear Age, 1989), video cassette.

[26]Jack Hitt, "No Laughing Matter," *The New York Times Magazine* 10 October 2004, 15.

[27]Michael Specter, "The Election Shows Russia is Russia," *The New York Times*, 7 July 1996, sec. 4, 1 and 4.

[28]Lucian W. Pye, "Political Culture Revisited," *Political Psychology* 12 (September 1991) 487-508.

SUGGESTED READINGS

Dennis, Jack, ed. *Socialization to Politics: A Reader*. New York: John Wiley & Sons, 1973.

Greenstein, Fred I. *Children and Politics*. New Haven, Conn.: Yale University Press, 1985.

Jacobson, Gary C., *A Divider, Not a Uniter: George W. Bush and the American People*. New York: Pearson Longman, 2007.

Milburn, Michael A. *Persuasion and Politics: The Social Psychology of Public Opinion*. Belmont, Calif.: Wadsworth, Inc., 1991.

Renshon, Stanley Allen, ed. *Handbook of Political Socialization: Theory and Research*. New York: The Free Press, 1977.

Sigel, Roberta S., and Marily B. Hoskin. *The Political Involvement of Adolescents*. New Brunswick, New Jersey: Rutgers University Press, 1981.

Will, George F. *The Leveling Wind: Politics, the Culture and Other News, 1990-1994*. New York: Viking, 1994.

Woshinsky, Oliver H. *Culture and Politics: An Introduction to Mass and Elite Political Behavior*. Englewood Cliffs, New Jersey: 1995.

Chapter Five

POLITICAL PARTIES

Revolution on Monday, independence on Tuesday, a constitution on Wednesday, political parties on Thursday, orderly elections on Friday, stable democratic government by Saturday, and rest on Sunday—any such conception of political creation is the stuff of dreams.

William Nisbet Chambers

William Nisbet Chambers implies that a democracy cannot be built in a day or even a week. It is a difficult process that takes time, compromise, mistakes, and continual rethinking to produce an end product that only "sometimes" works. Democracy in the United States today is still a work in progress. It officially began with the signing of the Declaration of Independence in 1776, established a viable confederation under the Articles of Confederation, and continued with the adoption of the Constitution of 1787. Not to diminish the importance of these accomplishments, but in hindsight that appears to have been the easy part. The following generations were left with the hard part—ensuring that "the work in progress" succeeds.

The success of a democracy can be measured by its ability to empower people through participation in their political process. One way to accomplish this is by establishing a fair and equitable election process. The foundation for this process has traditionally been functioning and effective political parties. Political parties have become an essential element in the process of "making it all work." They are the largest voluntary associations in a democratic society whose function is to control government through the process of winning elections. Political parties are considered linkage institutions that "link" people to their government.

In the best of all possible worlds, political parties link the needs of the people to the public policy of the government. If this link is either corroded, chipped, or broken the needs of the people cannot effectively be translated into governmental public policy.

The history and effectiveness of our democracy can be traced through the development of our political parties. It is the story of a struggling country, groping its way towards political stability and the democratic methods it now takes for granted. Political parties have been an essential component in the process of nation building, institutionalizing political beliefs and providing a vehicle for orderly political conduct. Our first national parties not only represented the conflicting interests of pluralism but, at the same time, attempted to organize them into viable political alternatives thereby assuring themselves a fundamental role in the dialogue of the American political process. They became a unifying symbol in an otherwise fragmented political system. They provided a political environment that enabled this democratic dialogue to develop and mature.[1]

POLITICAL PARTIES AND ELECTIONS

The goal of this chapter will be to examine what role American political parties play in today's political dialogue. The quote at the beginning of the chapter states "political parties on Thursday, orderly elections on Friday." It is significant to note that William Chambers specifies that party development precedes elections because it is a common misconception that democracies are created by elections. The reverse is true. Elections do not make a democracy; a democracy makes elections, and political parties are the foundation of elections. E. E. Schattschneider, a noted political scientist, stated, "political parties created democracy and that modern democracy is unthinkable save in terms of the parties."[2] Therefore, if you want to take the pulse of a democratic system to examine its overall health, it is critical to access the viability of the political parties within the process. Although the electoral process contains a myriad of interdependent parts, political parties are the glue that fixes the process in place. If the glue becomes old and receives no maintenance, it disintegrates, allowing the political parties to separate from the electoral process thereby creating a void in the democratic process. The political dialogue disintegrates, causing the process to fracture. This is what has happened to the political party system in the United States over the past forty years, and it has had serious consequences for the democratic system in the United States. The political system is no longer healthy and vibrant. It has been diagnosed with a chronic case of alienation and apathy. The eroding of the political parties has caused the political system's immune system to breakdown; its most obvious symptom is the decline of voter participation in the United States.

The following sections will examine how the system became infected, the present condition of the patient, possible cures, and a prognosis for the future. First, it is important to examine the foundations for and evolution of political parties in the United States. It is essential to today's dialogue to understand how political parties grew up within the constructs of the Constitution. Only after we understand how and why the parties developed the way that they did can we clearly evaluate where the U. S. political system is today and where it may be headed. Clearly any discussion about American political parties reflects a "work in progress."

Historical Roots

Political philosophers have been debating the nature of political parties almost as long as man has been debating the necessity for and the function of government. The Western debate began in ancient times with Aristotle around 350 B.C.E. and continued with such notable political writers as Machiavelli in the sixteenth century, Thomas Hobbes in the seventeenth century, and John Locke in the eighteenth century. As different systems of government evolved, the discussion surrounding political parties was altered to reflect these changes. However, through the centuries, all of the discussions in some way centered on the "perils" of political parties and the problems that "partisanship" could cause in a political system. From Aristotle to Locke, Western political philosophers were not apt to promote the virtues of a party system believing that in some sense they were a necessary evil that would in the end cause political division.[3]

The Framers of the Constitution expressed many of the same concerns of the earlier philosophers. Yet, as the concept of government changed, political parties were painted in a significantly different light. Democracy was no longer viewed as a myth but as a viable political process. Parties were now viewed not only as constructive but necessary institutions. E. E. Schattschneider states, "The most important distinction in modern political philosophy, the distinction between democracy and dictatorship, can be made best in terms of party politics."[4] The political systems of which Aristotle, Machiavelli, and Locke wrote were significantly different from the one we experience in the United States today. Nonetheless, U.S. politicians from James Madison and Thomas Jefferson to Bill Clinton and George W. Bush have worked to integrate past philosophers' ideas with present concepts and institutions to create a "modern" political party system.

Political institutions are not created in isolation. They are carefully constructed. This construction requires the careful use of building block skills usually associated with the ability to perform mathematics. Just as it is important to learn the fundamentals of addition and subtraction before moving on to calculus, the same is true of political institutions. They are constructed on experiences gained from the past, previous successes as well as failures. U.S. political parties are products of lessons learned from the past as well as building blocks for the future. What were some of the significant developments in the history of political parties that helped to shape the ones that exist in the U.S. today?

Development: Factions to Parties

Although early political philosophers addressed the concept of political parties, they did not really emerge as established institutions until the early 1700s in England. Even then they were still in the embryonic stage and were considered "factions" rather than parties. Factions and parties are related, yet two very distinct entities. However, it is often difficult to tell them apart because factions can easily be disguised as parties. This is just as true today as it was in eighteenth century England. A **faction** is fundamentally a divisive organization. Its power base is small because its needs are narrowly defined, such as the National Rifle Association (NRA) or the Environmental Defense Fund (EDF). Today, groups such as the NRA and EDF are not considered factions of political parties but rather fall under the category of interest groups, and, as such, most adhere to the governmental rules that regulate them. Factions can also consist of a group of people loyal to an individual, such as Ross Perot or Ralph Nader. This is often known as the "cult of the individual." Power rests with the individual's ability to command or maneuver his/her personal connections to secure specific goods or services for a small and narrowly defined group of individuals. Today, this type of faction does not tend to outlive the popularity of the individual and group loyalty will then be dispersed to other individuals or groups. A faction's agenda does not serve the good of the community, much like many of today's interests groups but, rather, pursues policies that only benefit themselves.

A party, unlike a faction that "separates" people, is a unifying force. It is a cohesive organization that is not based on personality but rather on a set of interests that would promote the good of the community. Its power rests with its ability to define the needs of the community and unite the diverse factions within that community for a common good.[5] Parties tend to take individuals with disparate interests and identify their common characteristics and bring them together under one "political umbrella" or "political label." In Federalist #10, James Madison describes a faction as "a number of citizens . . . who are united and actuated by some common impulse of passion, or of interest, adverse to the rights of other citizens, or to the permanent and aggregate interests of the community." Modern American political parties attempt to transcend Madison's definition by being more inclusive and extending their political agendas to include more issues and more diverse opinions all without destroying the cohesiveness of a much more heterogeneous group of people and their interests. The question might be whether or not U.S. political parties are successful in accomplishing this objective.

Four characteristics essential to the development of political parties are **loyal opposition, like-minded people getting together, formation of cohesive voting blocks**, and **coherent election campaigning**. These developments are psychological as well as political. A political culture needs to possess a mindset within its political psyche or culture that will allow these qualities to develop. They must exist before effective political parties can emerge providing the foundations for a fair and equitable election process. Although these four characteristics may seem elementary and obvious to citizens in countries where stable political parties currently exist, they are not so obvious in countries such as Haiti, Nigeria, and the Democratic Republic of the Congo.

The British Parliament was the birthplace of modern political parties, and they developed out of the helter-skelter *factional* fighting *within* the British Parliament. The conditions for parties developed as Parliament evolved into a viable governing institution. This did not happen overnight. Parliament existed as a recognizable body in 1307; however, it did not emerge as a viable governing institution until after the Glorious Revolution of 1688. This proved to be a watershed event in British history because it elevated the status of Parliament above that of the monarch and firmly established it as the predominant governing authority. Although the monarch still existed, it never again wielded executive authority. Once Parliament had established legislative prerogative, it passed a Bill of Rights that was tantamount to a "social contract" between the King and his subjects. This social contract was constructed on the basis of property rights, albeit unequally divided that would serve as the basis for a political contract between Parliament and the people. Once Parliament was firmly established as the legitimate governing authority, loyal opposition mounted within its ranks. **Loyal opposition** is the concept of competitive politics, the concept that groups can compete for power and resources and that this competition can be resolved in both a peaceful and systematic manner. The members of Parliament, MPs, supported the concept of parliamentary government but disagreed amongst themselves as to the implementation of specific policies. By 1679, two distinct parties, the Whig and the Tories, had emerged within Parliament.[6]

The "age of party" came to fruition during the reign of Queen Anne (1702-1714). The Whigs and Tories were clearly distinct groups of **like-minded people** in Parliament who opposed each other's policies but supported the concept of parliamentary rule. They quickly turned their like-mindedness into **cohesive voting blocks** to ensure that their policies would be implemented. Voting records of that period reveal that these voting blocks were very cohesive, demonstrating an extremely high correlation between voting and party identification. Records show that among those who voted, 85 percent cast votes solely along party lines. These statistics can be misleading and appear to be much like the congressional record of the 108th Congress. In reality, control of Parliament continually switched from one party to another. These contests for political control of Parliament were often tawdry affairs riddled with corruption. However, rudimentary these parties and their politics, they re-enforced the foundations of parliamentary legitimacy. The internal politics between Whigs and Tories within Parliament was eventually translated into **election campaigning**. Although the electorate was extremely limited during this period, only 4.3 percent of the population was granted the right to vote, the Whigs and Tories effectively transmitted their policies to their limited audience. Out of the 1,064 members returned to Parliament between 1702 and 1714 only 71 cannot be clearly identified as Whig or Tory.[7]

Although these parties were at best fledgling, they were the beginning. They could not have been considered "modern" by today's standards, because they did not have to concern themselves with either a mass electorate or the needs of "the people." They were factions evolving into parties. At this time, it was not a matter of the elite controlling government, for only they were allowed to participate in the process. As the electorate expanded, so did the parties. Political control remained in the hands of the elite, but as the parties grew, they framed the direction of the very process of democracy in England.

Constitution/The Early Days

In a broad sense, modern political parties in the United States, such as the Democrat and the Republican, have their roots in the British political system. Between 1765 and 1775, the thirteen colonies felt betrayed by the newly emerging political parties in England that were passing laws that they considered not only unfair but actual acts of tyranny. These parliamentary acts passed by the British political parties became the foundation of the American Revolution. They also established a framework for the revolutionaries' "feelings" about parties in general. The revolutionaries looked upon political parties with great suspicion and are usually portrayed as bitter opponents of political parties, finding them from their own personal experience to be divisive, oppressive, and self-serving. On the surface this is true. The principle piece of evidence in support of this position is James Madison's famous argument against "factions" presented in his *Federalist #10*. Madison states, "Among the numerous advantages promised by a well constructed Union, none deserves to be more accurately developed than its tendency to break and control the violence of factions." However, we must approach this conclusion with caution. Three reasons should give us pause: first, the Framers, who are so often portrayed as anti-party, were, in fact, the leaders and members of the first national political parties in the United States; second, the Framers were opposed to divisive "factions," not unifying parties; and, third, the Constitution they constructed allowed for parties to grow and develop.

First Parties

The Framers scarcely realized at the outset that they were building parties but build parties they did. The characteristics necessary for constructing political parties were already indigenous to the system. They merely needed to be given form and substance. The Constitution provided all the form and substance that was needed not only in the early days of the republic but also in the election of 2000 as loyalty to the Constitution has become the historic touchstone of America's party politics. Whatever parties did, they did ultimately in the name of guarding the Constitution. Although this reason could become a pretext for abuse of political power, it also provided the indispensable standards by which abuses could be judged. Serious partisan disputes were therefore constitutional disputes. American political parties operated to restrain the passions of ambitious political men by forcing them to vie with other ambitious men in support of the Constitution.[8] This is not merely an abstract concept as was clearly demonstrated in the disputed presidential election of 2000. Both the Democrats and the Republicans were careful to construct the arguments they used to secure the twenty-one disputed Floridian electoral votes within the framework of the Constitution. Al Gore, the Democratic candidate, and now President George "W" Bush, the Republican, claimed that all their political challenges were not for personal gain but rather to uphold the integrity of the Constitution. Their political dispute became a constitutional one.

Loyal opposition quickly developed in the United States. The Constitution was ratified in 1789, and by 1790 the Federalist Party led by Alexander Hamilton had begun to take form. Those that opposed the Federalists were considered Anti-federalists, and they eventually solidified their

American women had to campaign for the right to vote in the early 1900s.

loyal opposition in the form of the Democratic-Republican Party. Both the Federalists and the Democrat-Republicans were founded to protect the essence of the Constitution albeit their own interpretation of the document. The Federalist Party sought a strong federal government that would benefit the predominantly northern capitalist interests. The Anti-Federalists or Democrat-Republicans sought a weak federal government so that the agrarian interests of the south and the west would be able to prosper.[9] Both parties found sufficient grounds for their political claims in the body of the Constitution. The parties that they established did not necessarily violate the Framers' principles because in their eyes they were not factions. They did not seek to undermine the rights of their fellow citizens. Rather, they aimed at securing a goal that they believed was in the interests of the whole community. The first two parties were established to guard the principles of the Constitution from ambitious men for the good of the country.

The first political parties would be considered elitist by today's standards. They represented the interests of a small group of individuals. They were not grass roots organizations that either originated with or were representative of the interests of "the people." In many ways U.S. parties mirrored the first parties in Great Britain. The parties reflected the interests of those who participated in the process. Only a small portion of the population was granted the right to vote. The original Constitution does not establish voter qualifications, and, consequently, they were left open to the state. Although they differed on a state by state basis, the early years of the republic restricted voting rights to white men over the age of twenty-five who owned property. Finally, the early political parties evolved within the legislative branch as congressional factions. They were like-minded people who established cohesive voting blocks within Congress to protect their own vision of the Constitution. In the early years, these first parties had little recognition outside the capital. Parties in the United States began within the legislative branch and expanded and were modified as the democratic process developed. As the electorate expanded, the parties incorporated more people into their ranks and developed broader and more diverse issues into their agenda.

The Document

The Constitution itself reveals much about the mindset of the Framers. The Constitution is the supreme law of the land and was written to distribute political power in the United States. If the Framers of the Constitution were as rabidly anti-party as they are often portrayed, they had the perfect opportunity to ban political parties from the American process. They were well acquainted with the concept of political parties, and they had personally felt the effects of party development in England that resulted in their own armed conflict. Armed with this information, they still chose not to ban them. Instead, the language of the Constitution not only created a framework that allowed for the development of political parties but also established a system that would require political parties to emerge in order for it to function in an efficient and effective manner. How does the Constitution accomplish this? First, the Constitution's deafening silence made parties possible. Silence provided parties the window of opportunity to exist.

Nowhere in the Constitution are parties mentioned. Therefore, political parties were not constructed as formal governmental institutions. Instead, the Constitution's very silence allowed parties to grow and develop without any formal guidelines or restraints. The parties are only constrained by the system itself. Political parties evolved as extra-constitutional para-governmental institutions whose structures and functions were framed by the implicit and explicit concepts expressed in the Constitution. Two principles that generally influenced both the structure and function of political parties are separation of powers and federalism. Both of these will be described in detail in the next section.

Silence, however, was only one attribute of the Constitution that allowed political parties to emerge. There were other provisions of the document not directly related to political parties that also made them possible. One such provision is the First Amendment in the Bill of Rights passed by the first Congress on September 25, 1789, and ratified by the states on December 15, 1791. The Bill of Rights was the result of a political battle between the Federalists and the Antifederalists, and it centered on the constitutional issue of individual rights. The question was not only if but how the Constitution would guarantee individual liberties. The Federalists believed individual constitutional guarantees were unnecessary; the Antifederalists vehemently disagreed and believed they were an essential part of the document. The Antifederalists quickly branded the Federalists as "elitist" and threatened to thwart the ratification process unless constitutional guarantees would be forthcoming. To counter the "elitist" accusations hurled by the Antifederalists and to ensure ratification of the Constitution, the Federalists promised to propose constitutional amendments during the first congressional session that would guarantee individual liberties. The Federalists honored their promise, and the Bill of Rights was the result of a political battle between the first political parties. Ironically, individual rights guaranteed in the Bill of Rights assured that the institution of political parties would become permanent fixtures in the governmental process.

Two individual rights granted in the First Amendment that directly related to the development of political parties were the freedom of speech and the freedom to assemble. First, freedom of speech is particularly important to all Americans because it grants to them a sense of independence guaranteeing to all citizens the ability to express their personal beliefs. However, in a broader and more political sense, freedom of speech is essential to political parties and, consequently, to the survival of the democratic process. Freedom of speech extends beyond the individual to the collective. The very essence of a political party, "like-minded people," requires that individuals must be able to speak and meet collectively for political purposes. Political speech is the heart and soul of a political party and is given special constitutional consideration. In *Dun & Bradstreet v. Greenmosse Builders,* 1985, the Supreme Court stated that "Not all speech is of equal First Amendment concern . . . Political speech about matters of public concern is at the heart of the First Amendment's protection."[10] In 1988, in *Boos v. Barry,* the Supreme Court spoke out again on political speech stating that such speech is so important that "in public debate our own citizens must tolerate insulting, and even outrageous, speech in order to provide adequate breathing space to the freedoms protected by the First Amendment."[11] An individual is provided constitutional protection of their "freedom of speech" both as an individual and in a collective sense.

Second, the right to assemble is essential to the growth and development of political parties in that it has enabled like-minded people to congregate for political purposes. The Constitution protects an individual's right to assemble in public places and although the government may establish procedural regulations, such as requiring a parade permit, to preserve public order, it is unconstitutional for governing authorities to determine which groups will be allowed to hold public meetings and which will not. The ability to meet has resulted in the physical and ideological bonding necessary to facilitate political association. Although the right to associate is not specifically granted in the Constitution, it has long been held to be "implicit in the freedoms of speech, assembly and petition."[12] The Supreme Court has consistently supported the right of citizens to belong to and engage in political party activities. They have specifically applied the "freedom to associate" to decisions regarding the structures and functions of political parties. Recent Supreme Court decisions have applied the right to associate in such a fashion as to strengthen the autonomy of political parties vis-à-vis governmental control ruling unconstitutional state regulations directly related to restraining party independence. For example, it recently struck down a California law that restricted the terms of office for state central committee chairs. The Supreme Court has also been especially vigilant to protect the "right of citizens to create and develop new political parties." In *Norman v. Reed* (1992), the Supreme Court stipulated that "the right of citizens to create and develop new political parties" was paramount and "to the degree that a State would thwart this interest by limiting the access of new parties to the ballot," has been significantly curtailed. The Court ruled that the state must demonstrate a "corresponding interest sufficiently weighty to justify the limitation" of state regulations on the formations of new parties. States may not construct unjustifiable barriers restricting the development of political parties.[13] The Court has recognized the importance of political parties by securing for them the right to exist, to meet, and to speak. New parties must be allowed to develop in opposition to the existing power structure. Only then can loyal opposition, the very foundation of political parties, be allowed to flourish.

Not only did the Framers make political parties possible, certain procedural provisions of the Constitution also made them "necessary." The most important of these can be found in the method of selection for constitutional officers that mandates that an election process be formally established albeit operated and monitored by the state governments. An earlier chapter described the various methods of selection for constitutional officers to the national government and although most of them were not originally meant to be selected "by the people," the Framers did establish one office, the House of Representatives, that was to be "chosen every second Year by the People of the several States." In so doing, the original Constitution required elections be held for national officers. These elections necessitated the development of political organizations that would link the needs of the people to the policies of the government. Without such organizations, the elections would be a sham. The Framers established a small "electoral window" forever "necessitating" the existence of political parties.

GOVERNMENTAL STRUCTURES

Two Party Systems

The Constitution's silence on the issue of political parties not only made them possible but necessary. Once established, they have developed within the governing process constructed within the normative guidelines established by the Constitution. Through the years, the party system has become entrenched, having been reinforced by federal and state laws. Party systems are then reflections of their governmental structures. Therefore, the number of parties included in the system and their ideological strength are defined by the governmental structure. The theory of representation and its underlying electoral structure is significant in determining these qualities of the party system.

Traditionally there have always been two dominant, centrist parties in the United States that have volleyed for political power. In 1790, the Federalist and Anti-Federalist were the two major parties that controlled the process and since the presidential election of 1860, the Democrats and Republicans have performed that function. Although, the actual control of the government has seesawed between the two of them over the last one hundred and fifty years, there has been no significant challenge to them in the form of a viable third party. Many other democratic countries, however, have produced multiparty systems, consisting of a number of noncentrist ideological parties. The difference between having a two party system vs. a multiparty system is a direct result of the institutions, laws, and rules that govern the different countries. Political parties are reflections of their political structures. Although democracies appear very similar in principle, their structures can be very different making each party system unique. Consequently, "democratic" parts are not necessarily interchangeable, and it is difficult to superimpose parts of one system onto another. If you want to change how political parties operate within a system, it is very possible that the underlying structure of the system must be changed. For example, if a political system has a centralized system of government, the parties will tend to be centralized. If a system of government is decentralized (federal system), the parties will tend to be decentralized as well. In order for the parties to look and act differently, the underlying structure must change. Otherwise, changes to the political parties will merely be cosmetic and incremental.

America's two-party system is due largely in part to the fact that the country chooses its officials through plurality (whoever gets the most votes) voting system. The American system elects legislators from **single-member electoral districts**. To conduct elections under this system, Congress and state legislatures are divided into districts. For example, the House of Representatives has 435 individual districts. Each district services a particular geographic area and elects a single member to represent it. Only individuals who are citizens of that district may participate in the election. The winner in each district is the candidate who receives the plurality of votes in that district. This single-member district mandates that there will only be one winner per election. It is a **winner-take-all** system. The winner of the plurality of votes wins "the seat."

This system discourages minor or third parties from participating. Imagine that a third or minor party consistently won 20 percent of the vote in a particular district or even in congressional districts across the country. Even though 1 out of 5 voters supported this party, it would not win any representation in the legislature. The winning candidate would always be from one of the two major parties that received the larger proportion of the remaining 80 percent of the vote. Because of the expense of elections, third parties then do not often attempt to throw their hats into the electoral ring knowing that the system favors the two major parties and makes it almost impossible to overcome the political odds of winning in any district.

An alternative electoral structure is based on **proportional representation** predicated on the concept of proportional voting rather than a winner takes all system. This system exists in different forms in many European democracies and provides smaller parties an incentive to organize and compete for power. It does so because it provides them the possibility of winning seats in their legislative branch. One common system of proportional representation mandates that legislators be elected at large rather than from specific districts. Citizens are not required to live in a particular geographic area to participate in the election. This requires that parties put forth a list of candidates for the nation at large, and citizens vote for the entire list rather than for an individual candidate. The party will win a number of seats proportionate to the votes that it receives. If a party wins 30 percent of the vote, it will win 30 percent of the seats in the legislature. The candidates do not represent an individual district but their party and the nation as a whole.[14] Another form of proportional representation allows that more than one elected official may be sent to the national assembly from each legislative district. The number of representatives elected is directly proportional to the votes that each party received on election day. For example, if the Libertarian Party received 20 percent of the ballots on election day and a district has five members, then the Libertarians would send one member to the national legislature from that district.[15]

How does the structural difference of electoral representation in these two different democratic systems manifest itself in the number of political parties and their ideological strength? First, the actual number of parties in the system stems from the actual ability of a party to be successful within the electoral process and secure legislative seats. The single-member district system tends to limit the number of parties that participate in the electoral process because the prospect of success for minor parties is relatively small. The candidate with the most votes wins; the loser gets nothing. However, proportional voting tends to produce a multiparty system because minor parties have a better chance of being successful. This system is not based on a zero-sum, winner take all election. It also places the focus on the party rather than on the individual candidate. It is not necessary for a candidate from a party to win the "entire" election. It is not a candidate's responsibility to win "the district." A party can win an election by winning a proportion of the votes nationwide. Therefore, small parties can win enough votes to obtain seats within the legislative branch of government. For example, 10 percent of the national vote can win a party 10 percent of the seats in the legislative branch.

Second, ideologically, the single-member district facilitates centrist politics whereas proportional representation tends to support parties capable of fostering stronger ideological positions. The elections in single-member districts place the emphasis on the candidate rather than the party. Since only one person can win the election, the candidates tend to appeal to the center of the political spectrum hoping to solicit as many votes as possible. This requires simultaneously appealing to as many people in the district as possible regardless of ideology while alienating no one. This is no easy task. This election strategy forces the candidate to appeal to the center of the political spectrum making it very difficult to take a strong ideological position on any issue. Taking such a position could possibly alienate too many voters costing the candidate "the district" and the legislative seat. Proportional representation shifts the focus from the individual candidate to the party and, in so doing, allows minor parties to participate. These minor parties are exclusive in that they are more ideological in nature and appeal to a smaller population. Although these parties do not control the government, they definitely have input into public policy. This structure allows individuals to believe that they can have their needs met by minor parties just as well, if not better, than by the large all inclusive parties. The parties in the system of proportional voting need not appeal to the center to be elected. Consequently, they may take more electoral risks by presenting ideologies that may or may not appeal to a majority of people. They only need to win a proportion of the vote to participate in governing. This produces parties that are less centrist and more ideological in nature.[16]

Single-member districts are only part of the governmental structure that produces the existing party system. There are many other laws and customs in the United States that underpin a two-party system. These include both federal and state laws ranging from federal election campaign financing laws to state laws that set requirements for getting on the ballot. And although they are given the same legal status under the law as the major parties, the system discourages them at every turn from participating as full members of the political process.

Examples of third party discrimination exist throughout the entire system but no more so than the rules of the House of Representatives and the Senate. Once elected, the rules and customs that govern Congress and the state legislatures favor the two-party system because they dole out their committee seats based on the two major parties. This is no more evident than the defection in May 2001 of James Jeffords, Republican Senator from Vermont, from his party. His defection shifted control of the Senate to the Democrats, thus replacing all Republican committee chairpersons with prominent Democrats. The election of 2002 re-enforced the importance of the role of the party label and the rules of the system. Since the Republicans won the majority of seats in the Senate, control of that house shifted again, replacing all Democratic committee chairpersons in the Senate with prominent Republicans. Then in 2006, the Democrats recaptured control of the Senate and all the committee chairpersons switched back from Republicans to Democrats. However, the Democrats margin of victory was slim; they control the Senate by just one seat. Just recently, South Dakota Senator Tim Johnson underwent brain surgery after suffering a brain hemorrhage. Although his recovery is going well, no one knows at this juncture whether he will be able to return to work and assume his duties in the Senate. If he is unable to do so, the Democrats are in jeopardy of losing their majority in the Senate and the committee chairs will revert back to the Republicans once again. Moreover, other power positions, such as Speaker of the House, are based on party membership. In 2006, the Democrats not only recaptured the Senate but also won the majority of seats in the House of Representatives and consequently the privilege of selecting the Speaker of the House. History was made when the Democrats selected the first female Speaker, Representative Nancy Pelosi from the 8th District in California.

Separation of Powers/Federalism

According to E. E. Schattschneider, decentralization of power is by all odds the most important single characteristic of the American political party system. He states, "More than anything else this trait distinguishes it from all others. Indeed, once this truth is understood, nearly everything else about American parties is greatly illuminated."[17] Two important principles implicit in the Constitution, separation of powers and federalism, provide the foundation for the decentralized structure of the parties in the United States. Separation of powers and federalism have created a decentralized system of power distributing power not only among the various branches of the national government but between the national and state governments. The decentralized nature of government is reflected in the decentralized nature of the political parties. This is exhibited in two structural attributes of the American party system; parties tend to be nonhierarchical and non-ideological in form and substance.

Table 5.1

COMPARISON OF PARTY SYSTEMS

MULTI-PARTY SYSTEM	TWO-PARTY SYSTEM	ONE-PARTY SYSTEM
More than one major political party	Two major political parties	One major political party
Parties usually ideological	Parties either ideological or non-ideological	Party ideological
Parties usually disciplined, structured	Parties disciplined, organized, structured when ideological; not disciplined, nor highly organized when nonideological	Party highly organized, disciplined, structured
Compromises frequently take place between parties after an election; frequent coalition governments	Compromises occur within the parties before an election; coalitions within the party	Any differences of opinion are ironed out in the top levels of the party and are not publicized
Parties are frequently leader centered	Parties usually not leader centered	Party leader centered
Parties are frequently short lived	Parties exist indefinitely	Party exists indefinitely
Party organization and government organization easily distinguishable	Party organization and government organization easily distinguishable	Difficult to distinguish between party organization and government organization
Found in democratic countries	Found in democratic countries	Frequently found in nondemocratic countries - dictatorships
Governments frequently unstable	Governments stable	Governments stable unless overthrown

Hierarchical power relationships require centralization and distribute power and information from the top to the bottom. Decisions made at the top are disseminated to the bottom with the intent that they be carried out. American political parties are almost the antithesis of this. Federalism has required that state laws largely govern the party system, so the state and local levels of government are ultimately responsible for the process of elections. This creates a "bottom up" approach to politics, and the party structure is a reflection of this relationship. Although the national government often appears to dictate policy to the states, national policy is actually formulated in Congress by representatives of the states. Therefore, the top level of government does not maintain hierarchical control over the other units of government but rather, more often than not, reflects the policy wishes of the "lower" units of government. The party structure reflects this nonhierarchical approach to government, and the top of the party structure ultimately has very little control over the lower levels of the organization. It also reflects the ideological and policy considerations of its smaller units.

The American governmental system constructed political parties that are loose coalitions of their state and local political parties. The Democratic and Republican national parties are a coalition of its fifty state and local party affiliates. The decentralized nature of the party system creates an inconsistent ideological approach to politics. Each state and local organization has its own "spin" on issues created by and suited to the members of its constituents. Since the election process is "single-member" districts, the party does not need to appeal to the nation as a whole but rather to smaller "populations" at the state and local levels. Not only are national officials selected in state and local elections but so are all the state and local governmental officials from the school board and city council races to the state legislative and gubernatorial campaigns. This greatly empowers the lower units of the political parties. Local elections supply the majority of elected officials in the governmental system. Local governments in the United States consist of over 92,000 different units of government exclusive of the national government and the fifty states. These include 3043 counties, 18,000 municipalities, 17,000 townships, 34,700 school districts, and 18,000 special districts.[18]

The electoral structure necessitates that the state and local parties maintain their base of support, which requires sustaining local political loyalties. State and local party organizations are pivotal to electoral success. Parochial political loyalties in conjunction with the large number of state and local public offices has created an intricate system of provincial political rewards that operates outside the control of the two major national parties while maintaining party labels. Because local loyalties are more important than national ones, the national party has been relegated to a secondary position, thus hampering the development of a national political ideology. Frank Sorauf, an expert on political party organization in the United States, notes that the decentralization of American federalism has created "local political loyalties and stimulated generations of localized, often provincial, political traditions."[19] It is hard to image that the Mississippi Democratic Party and the Massachusetts Democratic Party share the same ideology or traditions. Within both of these organizations are a myriad of county and local Democratic and Republican Parties, each one formulating its ideology to suit its own constituents. These traditions do not necessarily parallel that of the national party but, yet in some way, actually make up the national party. The national party must attempt then to assemble the often disparate ideological preferences of its parts into a seemingly consistent ideology usually with fair to mixed results. Even with these structural problems, the national parties continue to be viable structures. Their longevity can be understood through an analysis of the structure of these various layers of the party system.

Illusion

Even though the reality is that separation of powers and federalism have created decentralized parties, there still exists today a public misconception that these parties are monolithic organizations that dictate policy from the national level down to the state and local parties, maintaining party cohesion and party discipline. What has created this disparity between illusion and reality? The illusion begins with the presidential election. This election is the most publicized one in the United States. The press presents it as an ongoing drama that takes anywhere from eighteen to twenty-four months to unfold. For example, presidential hopefuls from both parties start "testing the waters" almost 24 months before the election. Consequently, for the 2008 election, both potential candidates and the press gear up for the pending election season. Political pundits use this time to dissect "the possibilities" of each potential candidate's chances of winning by analyzing their personal foibles and examining their policy positions. This might even be helpful if the pundits actually had something to say after 24 months. However, after a year or two of speculating on "who might run, who has a chance of winning and why," the American public seems to become lulled into a political coma. With the increased use of television and the Internet as political vehicles for disseminating information, the public is often an unwilling participant is this lengthy process, exposing them to what appears to be a national election process controlled by the National Democratic Party and the National Republican Party. An illusion is created that the "national" election is the most important and, consequently, national parties must be the most important unit of the political party. Nothing can be further from the truth. Not only is the national level of the party system not the most important, but the presidential election is not even a "national" election. The presidential election is a state by state winner-take-all electoral college election so well illustrated by the controversy over the Floridian electoral votes in the presidential election of 2000. Again in the election of 2004 the Electoral College winner hinged on one state, Ohio. Its twenty electoral votes gave President Bush a re-election victory of 286 votes to 252 votes over Democratic challenger Senator John Kerry. The illusion is that it is run by the national party, but in reality it takes the effort of the state and local parties to get a candidate elected President of the United States. Separation of powers and federalism have created semiautonomous political organizations within the national framework of the two parties.[20] These semiautonomous units are beholden to the national party when they choose to be and separate in ideology and resources when they need to be. How do these individual parts of the political party puzzle come together to present the illusion of national cohesion? If one could separate illusion from reality, it would be easier to pursue more realistic expectations of the political parties, understanding that all the semiautonomous units are neither united in ideology nor address political issues with one voice. The two major political parties as a whole may not be able to accommodate the entire electorate, but the individual semiautonomous units may service their constituencies well.

Although the foundations of the political parties are grounded in the principles of the Constitution, the day to day operations of the party require a less esoteric and more practical political approach. Both parties' structures are similar and basically have parallel organizational structures. The key to understanding the daily party operations is the same as the theory that underpins them—decentralization. The party structure would be easy to dissect if it was as neatly constructed as the organizational diagram suggests. However, the pyramid is a simplistic representation of a complex structure. All the parts of the party system are interrelated just as all the parts of our governmental process are interrelated. Often it is difficult to distinguish one level or unit of the party from another. It is like taking a drop of ink and pouring it into a bottle of water and shaking it up. Once you shake it, you can't distinguish the water from the ink, and it is then impossible to pull the drop of ink back out of the water. That being said, we will make some generalizations as to the day to day workings of the party organizations. Remember, the Democrats and Republicans have parallel political structures, so the following organizational chart can be used for either party.

Organizational Chart

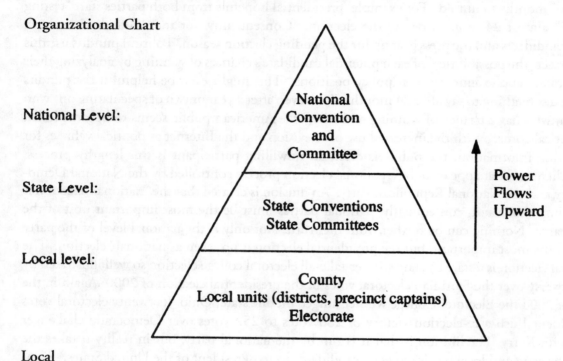

National Level: National Convention and Committee

State Level: State Conventions / State Committees

Local level: County / Local units (districts, precinct captains) / Electorate

Power Flows Upward

Local

The lowest level of the pyramid is the largest. This is the "**party of the electorate.**" It consists of the millions of individual registered voters in the United States who represent the amalgam of ideas, visions, and demographic backgrounds that construct the American political culture and their voting patterns. However, their relationship with the party is passive and their identification with it more of a "feeling" of belonging rather than any formal attachment or commitment to an organization. They are men and women who affiliate casually with the party, identify with it, and even vote habitually for it, but they do not actively participate in the party organization nor do they usually interact with the leaders and the activists of the party. The party of the electorate is not formally linked to the organization.[21] However, on election day, it is the "party of the electorate" that goes into the voting booth and casts their ballot to decide who will govern the country. Therefore, it is up to the party activists to organize and mobilize this disorganized, often disassociated, group of voters to cast their ballots for their party candidate. It is the challenge of the party leadership to convince the "party of the electorate" that their party is more capable of translating their needs into public policy. If they are successful in convincing the "party of the electorate," they will have taken over government through the process of winning elections.

Voters are divided into local electoral units called precincts. There are approximately 166,000 located throughout the United States.[22] The **precinct** is the place where voters go to cast their ballot for all elections whether it be to select a local school board or the President of the United States. In urban areas, a precinct usually is just a few adjacent city blocks. In rural areas, where the population is more dispersed, a precinct can extend for several, if not often, many miles. Consequently, the local party organization parallels the precinct structure and the cornerstone of the American party organization is at the precinct level. If the "party of the electorate" is to be mobilized to vote, it must start at the precinct level. If it doesn't work at the precinct level, it doesn't work at all. Elections are virtually won or lost at the precinct level. This includes all political races, including state-wide races as well as the presidential election. The local party committees are responsible for making it work at the local level and are considered the foot soldiers of the organization. These individuals are known as party activists, as they take an active role in ensuring the party's success. The people on these committees do a lot of thankless tasks to "get out the vote," including distributing campaign literature door to door, making phone calls, and essentially informing voters about the party's candidates. The committees are chaired by an individual who is selected from the ranks of party activists. The local chairperson then selects precinct captains. This is an important position because he/she is responsible for motivating voters within his/her precinct to "get out the party" vote on Election Day. They are literally responsible for the "party of the electorate." The precinct captains work hand-in-hand with the local committee, and often many of them serve on the local committee.

The local organizations have always been the heart and soul of the party structure because they are the closest to the voters. They traditionally control the flow of information to the voters and the turnout of the voters to the polls. County organizations provide the same basic organizational structure only encompass a larger geographic area.

Urban Political Machines

Local organizations in large cities were so effective at turning out the vote that they became known as **political machines**. These machines emerged during the post-civil war era due in large part to the weak municipal governments, the large influx of immigrants into the urban areas, and the tremendous migration to the cities. In 1850 only 15 percent of the country's population lived in urban areas, but by 1890 over 40 percent were city dwellers.[23] The machines were controlled by party loyalists and operated by precinct captains or county chairpersons who often used political patronage to insure voter loyalty at the polls. **Political patronage** is a system of inducements that would reward individuals for their political loyalty on election day. The rewards were in the form of government jobs and contracts. The jobs were not "big time" government jobs, such as Secretary of State or Attorney General. Rather, they included working on a highway crew or selling concessions in the city park district.

The political machine has often been criticized for buying an individual's vote in exchange for party support. However, these organizations were important to the poor and immigrant populations, many of whom came to the urban areas with little or no resources. The urban political machine was one of the few organizations that was capable of integrating the newly arrived city dwellers into American life and softened their desperate conditions in strange surroundings.[24] Traditionally the poor and immigrant populations were not part of the dominant political culture. Rather, they were either ethnic or religious minorities who had great difficulty integrating themselves into the power structure. The political machine provided important services and protections to the disenfranchised.[25] In fact, urban political machines became the instrument of popular democracy. It was the means by which the popular majorities, the poor, and the immigrant workers first won control of the cities from the old aristocratic and largely Anglo-Saxon elite.[26] An example of an effective political machine is the Democratic Party machine in Chicago, Illinois.

In Chicago, the Democratic Party machinery allowed the rapidly increasing Irish Catholic population to wrestle power away from the traditional Anglo-Saxon power elite. The machine was effectively controlled by Mayor Richard J. Daley until his death in 1976. His son, Richard J. Daley Jr., currently the mayor of Chicago, won election by forging a coalition among all ethnic groups effectively convincing them that the old line political machine could still provide goods and services to the disenfranchised of the city. Although the machine is not as well oiled as when his father ran it, it still hums along more than people would like to admit. For wherever there is local politics, there will be machines. Otherwise, politics at the local level would come to a grinding halt. However, for all practical purposes, large urban political machines, as well as other local political organizations, have lost much of the power they once had. Simply, they do not control the patronage system they once did. Progressive changes, such as the merit civil service exam, have taken the distribution of public jobs out of the hands of local politicians. As power became more concentrated in the hands of the national government, jobs that were once distributed at the local level in return for political loyalty were now controlled by state and national agencies. However, the "devolution revolution" has seen governmental reform shifting both power and programs back to the states and ultimately to the local level. It will be interesting to see if the return of government jobs to the local level will resurrect the sputtering political machine.

State

The next level of party organization is the state. The state organization has a well-structured system that looks good on paper. It usually consists of a state chairperson, a state central steering committee, and a state convention. Although the differences between state committees differ greatly from state to state depending on membership selection, size and function, it is possible to make some generalizations about them. The state committee is usually responsible for carrying out the directives of the state convention. Both organizations consist of powerful members of the local and county organizations. Whatever the state organization looks like on paper, political loyalty and power dissipate as you move up the organizational ladder. Whatever the formal structure of the state party system, most state party organizations are merely federations or loose confederations of their local and county chairpeople. In reality, the local and county organizations control the state organization, not the other way around. It is a rare exception when a state organization can manage

Kay Bailey Hutchison (R-TX) was one of the keynote speakers at the 2000 Republican National Convention. Convention speeches lavish praise and extol the virtues of the candidate. Prominent party leaders usually make an appearance to solidify party support.

to dominate the city and county organizations and issue mandates that will be followed at the local levels. Hierarchical state control usually only occurs when a particular state politician is so charismatic that he or she can command personal political loyalty and dominate the state's political arena, such as Senator Harry Byrd of Virginia or Huey Long of Louisiana. The usual scenario is that the state organization and the candidates running for state office still rely on the local and county organizations to organize the "party of the electorate."

National

The national organization sits at the pinnacle of the party structure. However, despite all the appearances of hierarchy in the party organization, there are no signs of hierarchical authority and control. In no important way does any national party unit limit the autonomy of the state and local party organizations.[27] Just as the state party organization is a loose confederation of local and county parties, the national organization is a loose confederation of state organizations. Except for the campaign finance area, virtually all governmental regulation of political parties is left up to the states.

The national party consists of a national chairperson, national committee, and a national convention. The national chairperson is traditionally selected by the party's presidential candidate and is the chief spokesperson for the party. His or her major responsibility is to manage the national election campaign, which entails fundraising and coordinating state and local organizations during the election process. The national committee is made up of representatives from all the states, the District of Columbia, and the territories and is formally approved by the national convention. Each state chooses their own method of selection for representation on the committee. Two popular methods of selection are the state central committee and the state convention. Its main job is to coordinate party activities for the next four years, which entails being a liaison between the national organization and the state and local structures. Along with the national chairperson, it promotes the national party, raises funds, and works on the upcoming presidential campaign. Much of its power in these matters is diminished by the fact that the individual candidate has their own campaign strategists and fund-raisers. The national chairperson is also ratified by the national convention.

The national convention meets every four years. It consists of delegates from every state, the District of Columbia, and the territories. Each state chooses its own method of selection for delegates to the convention. Popular methods of selection include either a state primary election, state caucus, or state convention. The convention's formal functions include ratification of the party platform, selection of the party's presidential and vice-presidential candidates, and voting on and ratification of the rules of the national party. However, the convention has many informal functions, the most important of which is to show that there is in both form and substance a "national" party. The convention is the time for the party to demonstrate to the "party of the electorate" that there is one unified organization and that all of its parts function as a whole. It is imperative to present the image of unity to convince the voters that the party is capable of governing the country as a single unit with a united purpose. This is the time when the Democratic Mississippi Party and the Massachusetts Democratic Party come together and put aside their parochial perspectives for the good of the whole. They are no longer merely parts of the whole; they *are* the Democratic Party. Although the convention performs very important functions, it is tantamount to a family reunion. This is a time to resolve intra-party squabbles, reminisce, and plan for the future.

The Republican convention in 2004 was a coronation for the incumbent president, George W. Bush. Perhaps its most noteworthy feature was its timing. It occurred in early September, much later than traditional national party conventions ordinarily take place. The reason for this was to take advantage of the third anniversary of the September 11 terrorist attacks, an especially potent symbol given that the convention was held in New York City. Since many viewed Bush's performance in the aftermath of 9/11 as his finest hour, framing the convention in these terms greatly advantaged the Republican Party as it went into campaigning for the November election.[28]

The Democratic convention was less successful in 2004. The Democrats were not convincing in projecting an image of unity and did not have a theme around which to showcase their candidate, John Kerry. However, one of the unexpected successes to come out of this convention was an Illinois politician, Senator

Barack Obama. He made a stirring keynote address, which catapulted him into the national limelight. In 2007, Obama announced his candidacy for president.[29]

Functions of Political Parties

The main function of political parties is to aggregate and mobilize people to vote to take over government through the process of winning elections. They serve to link people and government, transforming the needs of the people into public policy. Martin Wattenberg, a noted political scientist, has compiled a list secondary functions that parties perform to accomplish their major objective:

1. Generating symbols of identification and loyalty
2. Socializing voters and maintaining a popular following
3. Organizing dissent and opposition
4. Recruiting political leadership and seeking governmental offices
5. Institutionalizing, channeling, and socializing conflict
6. Overriding the dangers of sectionalism and promoting the national interest
7. Implementing policy objectives
8. Legitimizing decisions of government
9. Fostering stability in government[30]

Party Decline

Earlier in the chapter it was proposed that the U. S. party system was in ill-health. It is now time to examine the patient and make a prognosis. The parties are definitely in a state of decline. They are not in a state of realigning their constituent base; they are in the process of losing it. The reason for this decline is that the link between people and government provided by the political parties has been broken. Voters are treating parties as if they were obsolete and irrelevant institutions. Public affection for parties has declined not because of specific negative feelings about the Democrats or Republicans but rather because there is an increasing sense that the parties as an institution are no longer crucial to the governmental process.[31] The "party of the electorate" is beginning to view its party as irrelevant to the electoral process. The party has been replaced by other institutions that have proven to be ineffectual at connecting people to government. The party's functions have been taken over by other elements within the system with very little success. Consequently, there is no longer any organization capable of translating the needs of the people into public policy. The link has been broken; people feel disconnected, alienated and apathetic, not only to their parties but to the system as a whole.

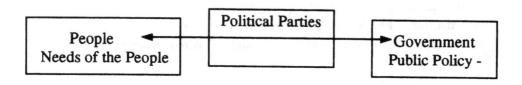

Indicators

There are two major indicators that suggest that the party is in a state of decline: decline in voter participation and the change in and decline of party identification among voters.

Voter Turnout

Voter turnout is an excellent indicator not only of the health of the party system but the democratic process as well because if a democratic society's success can be measured in its ability to empower people through the process of participation, it is important to evaluate if, and when, they are participating. If citizens are not participating in their political process, then the system has not been successful at empowering them. Voting is the most common and simplest form of political activity in which a citizen may engage and requires very little effort in the form of either time or money on the part of the public. It is the major form of participation of the "party of the electorate." Studies have shown that if a citizen does not participate in the process of voting, it is highly unlikely that he/she will participate in other political activities that require expending more of their resources, either tangible or intangible, such as writing letters to their governmental officials, financial contributions to a campaign, or attending a political function such as a candidate forum. If party officials are not successful in turning out the vote, they will not only be incapable of taking over government through the process of winning elections but their role in linking people to their government is in serious jeopardy. Declining voter turnout serves as a warning of potentially serious underlying systemic problems in the "democratic process" in the United States.

Since the early 1900s, voter turnout has been on a slow and albeit not always steady decline. In the early 1900s when party activity was at its height, political machines were well oiled and in operation, and party identification was strong. Voter turnout was approximately 85 percent. In the presidential election of 2000, only 50.1 percent of registered voters went to the polls. However, there was an increase in voter turnout in the 2004 election to 54.6 percent. It is still too soon to know if this is a new trend. In the past seventy to eighty years, there has been a drop of almost 35 percent in voter participation. This has been grim news for both the party system and the democratic process.

The decline in voter participation has perplexed scholars for years. It has been particularly troubling because over the past thirty years changes in voting laws have actually created the opportunity for more access to the system, theoretically increasing voter participation. Laws, such as the Voting Rights Act of 1965, and more recently the National Voter Registration Act of 1993 popularly known as the Motor Voter Act have been passed to eradicate institutional barriers that had been established previously to deny people access to the polls based on race, class, and gender. Many of these barriers had originally been established by the states and now required federal legislation to tear them down. The Voters Rights Act of 1965 finally extended the right to vote to African Americans that had previously been guaranteed to them in 1868 in the Fourteenth Amendment of the Constitution. The Motor Voter Act was designed to simplify the process of registration. Its intent was to reach minority voters and under-educated citizens traditionally barred from the process.

Over the past thirty years, demographics have also changed and done so in such a way that should have increased voter turnout at the polls. However, the reverse has occurred. There are many variables that serve as indicators for voter turnout, however they are not all equal. The best indicators of voter participation are those that reflect socioeconomic status, education income and occupation. Of these education is the most important. Research has shown that an individual's propensity to vote tends to increase as his/her education level increases. For example, if you are a college graduate the chances are about 70 percent that you will vote; if you have less than a high school education, the chances of voting drops to only about 30 percent.[32] In the past thirty years, the educational level of Americans has increased, which theoretically should have increased voter turnout. In 1952, approximately 65 percent of eligible voters cast their ballot in the presidential election. That year only 15 percent of the population had received some college education and 41 percent had only received a grammar school education. In the presidential election of 1980, only 55 percent of eligible voters cast their ballots. This represents a 10 percent decrease in voter turnout since 1952. However, while voter turnout declined in 1980, educational levels increased. In 1980, 37 percent of Americans had attended college and only 12 percent of the population had received only a grade school education.[33] Voter turnout decreased while educational levels increased. This trend continues today as over 50 percent of Americans claim to have some form of college credit.

Much research has been done and many solutions have been offered as to why voter participation is in such a state of decline. Many of the solutions that have been offered are superficial. For example, statistics indicate that U.S. voter participation is low when compared with other democratic countries in the world. In fact, as declines continue, the United States has become the "democracy" with the lowest voter turnout in the world. European voter turnout is extremely high compared to the United States. Depending on the country of origin and the perceived importance of a particular election, European countries produce anywhere from a 75 percent to 85 percent voter turnout. European democracies hold their elections on Saturday or Sunday; the U.S. holds their elections on Tuesday. Some scholars suggest that voting participation has declined because Tuesday is an inconvenient day to vote. It may be inconvenient, but it does not explain the decline in voter turnout since Americans have voted on Tuesdays since 1845.[34] Apparently Tuesday has just recently become inconvenient.

It is important to acknowledge that there could be many reasons why voter participation has declined drastically over the years. Many theories have been proposed to explain these phenomena, which range from economic and social alienation to complex voter registration laws and inconvenient voting times and places. Each of these theories may possess a legitimate explanation of the problem of declining voter participation. However, when the core of these arguments is exposed, problems with political parties usually stand at their center. Journalist David Broder sums up the problem when he states, "The governmental system is not working because the political parties are not working."[35]

Party Identification

Party identification has traditionally tied individuals not only to a specific party but to the system in general. Specifically, party identification is a form of political self identification and a declaration of political intent. This intent or identification is usually registered with one of the major parties. Political identification is often learned early in life usually from one's parents or members of the household and tends to grow stronger with age. It is a psychological attachment rather than a physical commitment. Party identification does not necessarily entail a legal commitment to or any contact with the party organization. Rather, it is a "feeling" of belonging to "the party." Generically, party identification is similar to religious affiliation. According to Warren Miller, "In both instances the institution, that is the group, is concerned with defining the proper relationship between the person and the group-relevant components of social life . . . the existence of the group with acknowledged leaders who articulate the group's values and interpret the group's interest in the stream of public affairs, is crucial to the group member's ability to relate to the larger world." Party identification serves as the primary source of an individual's political attitude just as religious denomination acts as an orientation for religious matters. It defines the individual in terms of their political environment.[36]

Generally, partisanship has also been viewed as expressing a belief in the fact that political parties should play a role in the political process.[37] Used in this manner, party identification can identify an individual's propensity to act in their political environment. The stronger an individual's party identification, the greater the probability that the individual will be active in politics.[38] Consequently, the stronger the party affiliation, the greater the propensity to vote. Conversely, lack of party affiliation is also an indicator of an individual's propensity to engage in political behavior. Lack of any party identification or a weak party affiliation tends to demonstrate less of a propensity to participate in the political process. An individual who does not identify with either of the major parties is known as an independent. This term means that a person is **independent** of a political identification. An independent's political identification does not rest with the party. However, since party identification tends to define the individual in terms of their political environment, claiming no party identification makes it difficult for them to relate to the political process. While specifically claiming no particular party identity, the independent voter is also generally denying the role that political parties should play in the political process. The independent must find other ways to identify themselves in the political process. Often this identification rests with an individual candidate or alternative institution. For example, an independent may claim that they "vote for the best person, not the party." However, more often than not, the independent voter has less of an attachment to the political system and generally demonstrates less interest in their political environment. The result is that independents are usually less well-informed and less likely to vote than an individual who claims party affiliation.[39]

Party identification with the two major parties has been on a steady decline for the past forty years. In 1936, approximately 85 percent of Americans claimed political identification with one of the two major parties; 50 percent identified themselves as Democrats and 35 percent as Republicans. Only 15 percent declared themselves to be undecided, meaning no identification with either of the two major parties. By 1988 political parties had significantly declined. Only 63 percent of Americans identified with either one of the two major parties; 35 percent of Americans identified themselves as Democrats, 28 percent as Republicans. The number of Americans who claimed to be undecided had more than doubled, increasing from 15 percent to 36 percent. In 1996, the trend continued, and only 64 percent of Americans claimed party affiliation; 27 percent of Americans identified themselves as Republicans, 37 percent as Democrats. By 1996, the number of Americans unwilling to identify with either political party remained at 35 percent.[40] In 2000, just prior to the presidential election, the number of voters who identified themselves as independents climbed to 40 percent.[41] Gallop poll data dated November 4, 2002, indicates that these numbers tended to remain constant for the 2002 off-year elections. These numbers reflected no significant shifts in the electorate over the past two years.

The election of 2004, however, did exhibit a shift in political identification. According to the National Annenberg Election Study, 2004, those claiming to be Independent decreased from 40 percent in 2000 to 34 percent in 2004. This seems to indicate a reversal in the trend to declare party identification. The biggest winner in this shift was the Republican Party. Those claiming Democratic Party identification remained relatively constant at 34 percent. Republican self-iden-tification increased from 24 percent to 31 percent. This could account for President Bush's re-election and the congressional victories for the Republicans in both the House of Representatives and the Senate. A May 2006 Gallop poll indicated little change in the 2004 data. Democratic identification remained constant at 34 percent and Republican identification dropped from 31 percent to 30 percent. The question is whether this shift in identification in favor of the Republi-cans is a permanent change or an aberration. Too soon too tell. Interestingly, the Annenberg Study reports that nearly 55 percent of the youngest voters claimed to be Independent. This is in contrast to only 28 percent of those age 65 and over. Committing younger voters to the party and/or the process might be the key to the health of the political parties.

Although the election of 2004 might challenge conventional theories, some scholars associate the declining party identifications with the fact that the two major parties are in a state of political flux, known as either **dealignment** and/or **realignment**. These two concepts imply an electorate that is in the process of changing identifications; disassociation from one party and re-identifica-tion with the other as perhaps indicated in the increase of Republican identification. Although some individuals may personally be involved in this process, systemically this is not the case. The "party of the electorate" is not currently in the process of party dealignment and realignment but rather in a state of **party disassociation**. It is more than mere disassociation or dissatisfaction with the two major parties. It indicates a general dissatisfaction for parties in the electoral process as much as it indicates dissatisfaction for any particular party. It reflects a general sense that parties are no longer legitimate institutions within the political environment. As more and more voters choose to be self-identified as either "independent" or "undecided" rather than affiliated with either major party, individuals lose their primary source or "center" for political attitudes. They also lose their ability to relate to the larger political unit, the state. Loss of party identification is a psychological loss and a very personal one. Disassociation reflects a general feeling of detachment from the system. Individuals have lost their "link" to government.[42]

Since party identification is an indicator of a person's propensity to vote, the stronger the iden-tification, the stronger their propensity to vote. This indicates a relationship between declining party identification and voter turnout. The lower the party identification, the lower the voter turnout. As more and more individuals declare themselves "independent" or "undecided," their propensity to vote declines. As fewer people participate in the process, there is a stronger sense of alienation and less party identification. Increasing party de-identification inevitably continues to create lower voter turnout. Declining voter turnout continues to indicate low association with the political system and a low sense of individual political efficacy or empowerment. The latest numbers from the election of 2004 appear to validate the inverse of the above theory. In 2004 more individuals claimed party identification, almost 6 percent, and voter participation rose almost 5 percent. As more people self-identified with a political party, more participated in the process. If more individuals continue to declare party identification as they did in 2004 and again in 2006, will we continue to see higher voter turnout in the future? Trend or aberration? Again, too soon too tell.

Reasons for Decline

Political parties have been replaced as the institution that traditionally has linked people to their government. Other institutions have recently emerged to assume the functions previously performed by them, and they have not been successful in fulfilling their role. The new institutions, while usurping party functions, have been incapable of maintaining a connection or "link" between the people and their government. In fact, the reverse has been true. The new institutions have broken the link between people and government and created a yet unfilled void in the political process. The link established by the political parties has been broken by several factors:

1. rise of the media
2. rise of the candidate
3. election reform

The role of the media is intricately connected to the two other areas of our discussion, the "rise of the candidate" and "election reform." It becomes impossible to factor out the media as it relates to the other two issues.

RISE OF THE MEDIA

> *It used to be, in the old days when I went around the state with my grandfather, that what you needed to get elected to office was a big cigar, a shadbelly vest, and a constitution that permitted you to stand out in the hot July sun and talk for two and a half hours or three hours. Well, that day is gone. There is a new way of communicating with people and that is television.*

Senator Thruston Morton, Republican, Kentucky

The nationally televised Kennedy/Nixon presidential debates in 1960 ushered in a new era in American politics forever changing the political landscape. The media era had arrived and the use of television in the political process redefined not only the nature of politics but the role of political parties within that process. Television usurped several important functions traditionally performed by the political parties: controlling the flow of political information and setting the political agenda. The party had traditionally controlled the flow of political information that enabled them to prioritize political issues thus setting the political agenda for both the party's candidates and the American public. However, television changed all of that, and it now controls the flow of information thereby establishing the parameters for political discussion. Media issues have effectively become political issues that have not only been placed on the public agenda for political action but given high priority by elected officials.

Doris Graber in her book, *Mass Media and American Politics,* states that in many instances the media goes beyond agenda setting to agenda building. The media sets the public agenda when they rivet attention on a news story that accentuates a political or social problem, making it seem important to many people. Individuals often quickly move from the micro news story to a macro political issue. However, the media often goes beyond setting the political agenda and actually "builds" or establishes the public agenda when they create the context in which citizens conceptualize issues that eventually shapes their opinions on political problems.[43]   Instead of simply presenting the facts, the media often conveys information in a way that presents an agenda that attempts to sway the masses about how they should feel about particular news events or issues. Although there is very little evidence that the media can change existing mass values, studies have shown that prolonged sustained media coverage on a single topic can significantly influence mass opinion about an individual event.[44] This influence was significant in the press coverage of the war in Iraq.

In matters of foreign policy, the mainstream media all too often tends to present the government's position and no more so than during the Bush administration's PR (public relations) campaign to invade Iraq. The mainstream media conveyed, with very little scrutiny, the Bush administration's assertions that there was a link between Saddam Hussein and the Al Qaeda attack on 9/11. For many people, this became a primary justification for the war. The media also presented the administration's position without examining the validity of its assertions that Iraq possessed weapons of mass destruction (WMD). This too became many people's justification for the war. And in 2003, when the United States invaded Iraq, the American media framed the war primarily as a defensive measure to rid the world of "the evil-doers" and weapons of mass destruction. According to a University of Maryland study,

> Too few stories proffered alternative perspectives to the official line, a problem exacerbated by the journalistic prioritizing of breaking-news stories . . . . many stories reported the incumbent administration's perspective giving too little critical examination of the way officials framed the events, issues, threats and policy options."[45]

The media had taken control of setting the agenda for the invasion of Iraq and helped gear up public support for the initial invasion. It wasn't until well into the war effort that facts revealed that the Hussein regime did not possess WMDs and there was no connection between Saddam Hussein and the attack of 9/11.

The question might be asked how television in general and the news departments in particular have been able to take the role of agenda setting away from the political parties. It is interesting to reflect on the early days of television, remembering that it was originally designed for entertainment, and its ultimate goal was to produce profits. Since its inception, however, television has become the prime source of news in the United States, replacing newspapers, radio and periodicals. Over time there has been a proliferation of news programming on television including news coverage on cable television. Americans, when surveyed, consistently claim they are most likely to get their news from television and that they tend to feel that television news is the most credible.

Television news, much like its entertainment counterpart, is for profit. Consequently, many issues find their way onto the political agenda because they are entertaining and provide profit for corporate America. News journalism has come under great criticism by some of its finest reporters for exactly this reason. Walter Cronkite, esteemed journalist and longtime CBS news anchor, highly criticized television journalism today as "profit centers," stating that news as well as entertainment programs were now designed to make money for the networks.[46]

News programs must compete for ratings just as any other entertainment program on television. As such, much of the news programming presented on television is done so in an entertainment format. News has become America's entertainment, and this has not always had a positive affect on political parties, the public agenda, or the democratic process. News programs such as *Dateline* and *48 Hours* must compete with entertainment programming for ratings. These programs continue to proliferate. In addition to hour-long news dramas, there has been an increase of talk shows, such as the *Jon Stewart's Daily Show* and Christ Matthew's *Hardball*, with each host setting his/her own agenda and presenting it as if it be considered as the ultimate political agenda. They must generate sufficient audiences to remain on the air, and the only way to accomplish this is to be entertaining. Therefore, political issues that entertain people become the political agenda. But it is not only the networks that air these programs. The networks themselves now have competition from Cable TV channels, as well as Satellite TV. The audience shares per show have dwindled simply because of the amount of programming that is available. The political message becomes more and more splintered. This is often called narrowcasting in contrast to the original term of broadcasting. This type of programming tends to attract smaller and more focused groups of viewers. Focused, however, leads to smaller shares in ratings. Consequently, many of these shows that were "narrowcasting," now needed to attract larger audiences. These programs, as well as talk shows that present issues as "trash-news," tend to concentrate on scandal, abuse, and corruption in the government. Stories exposing illegal activities in the CIA and FBI as well as sex and campaign scandals in Washington fill the airwaves. These stories were originally designed to inform as well as entertain. The information they provided could have developed a positive reform mentality among the viewing public that could have resolved serious political defects within the system. Instead, their presentation had an opposite effect. The media focused on only the sensational aspects of political issues, hoping to procure an audience and improve its ratings. Unfortunately, sensational information has translated into negative information about both the political agenda and the government's ability to address it. Consequently, the media's control of information has ultimately re-inforced negative feelings towards government. Over time, negative stories have produced negative feelings of general distrust and cynicism toward government and the political system.[47] Ironically, this general feeling of mistrust sustained by the media has been transferred to the political parties who long ago had been rendered technologically obsolete.

Media/Rise of Candidate

Besides setting the political agenda, television has become the principle link between the candidates and the voters. Candidates now take their campaign directly to the voter by passing the political party and its organizational structure. Some scholars have portrayed television as the dominant political institution in American culture:

Party organizations have little to say about who wins the party's nomination next to nothing to say about who wins in the general election. Aspiring candidates no longer begin their
quest for public office by calling on party leaders but start by hiring professional media
advertising firms.[48]

Television has redirected the focus of politics, centering the attention on the individual candidate and his/her particular issues. This has produced "candidate-centered" campaigns. Television
campaigns focus on the image of the candidates rather than on the substance of their campaign.
The main goal is re-election and the vehicle by which to accomplish this objective is television.
Consequently, in order to promote a candidate, highly paid professional public relations, advertising agencies and political consultants are hired to project the personal traits of the candidate as if
they were political issues. Personality traits such as warmth, youth, and vision replace policy positions and voting records. Elections are presented as struggles between competing personalities.[49] It
is the image of the candidate, not the party, who is transmitted over the airwaves. The candidate is
no longer an abstraction presented by the party but rather an individual created by his or her public
relations firm. The importance of public relations firms was never more obvious or important than
in the Congressional Resolution to allow President Bush to use military force in Iraq. According to
Marc Hetherington, a noted political parties scholar,

> Working for the Democratic members of Congress facing reelection in November, consult-
> ants advised the need to act swiftly on the war resolution in order to focus on domestic
> issues where Democrats had an advantage with voters. This advice seemed to be given with
> little regard for the profound consequences of war. For consultants, the focus was simply
> on the coming election and the best way to win it, irrespective of policy implications."[50]

So with regards to the issue of the invasion of Iraq, many Democrats simply deferred to their
political operatives rather than investigating the facts. This coupled with the images already portrayed of the WMDs and Saddam Hussein put candidates and political parties in an untenable
situation. The magic of the media portrays the image of reality and that image can have serious
consequences. Today, many candidates running both for Congress and the presidential nomination are having to justify their vote on the Iraqi War Resolution.

Foremost among the changes created by the televisual computer age is the declining influence
of political parties, particularly in presidential elections. During the 1940s party allegiance was the
most important determinant of the vote. Next in rank were voters' feelings of allegiance to a social
group, assessment of the candidate's personality, and consideration of issues. That ranking has now
been reversed. The candidate's character has become the prime consideration at the presidential
level. Issues associated with the candidate have become intertwined with considerations of character because issues are used to infer character traits. Party affiliation and group membership now are
ranked last as determinants when considering a presidential candidate. When voters base their
decisions on a candidate's personality and positions on issues, the media becomes more important
than political parties because it is the chief source of information about these matters.[51]

Television news coverage can also make or break a candidate depending on how and what they
choose to cover or not cover. A case in point is the candidacy or as it turns out non-candidacy of

Democratic presidential hopeful Howard Dean. At the time this happened, many considered Dean to be the front runner in the Democratic race for the presidential candidacy. It was expected that he might be the man to beat President Bush in 2004. However, in the primary and caucus campaigns, Howard Dean, depending on your perspective, either self-destructed or was destroyed by media coverage. In a speech to his loyal campaign workers after winning the Iowa caucus, he gave an exuberant speech that ended with an enthusiastic "YEEHA" or scream. The media then replayed this scream over 600 times within a 4-day period. Pundits began to question Dean's emotional stability and some even questioned whether anyone who got "that excited" should be so close to the nuclear button. From that point on, Dean lost his momentum in the campaign and was eventually forced to drop out. It was clear that whatever your perspective, media coverage had an impact on the political process.

The average American household now watches 7.21 hours of television per day. It is difficult to discern what part of that can be considered hard core news, political infomercials, political information or genuine entertainment, as these genres are becoming more and more difficult to distinguish. Political information is disseminated to the public in a variety of ways in ever increasing non-traditional formats such as Larry King Live, Jay Leno's, the *Tonight Show*, and the *David Letterman Show*.[52] Whether news anchors such as Katie Couric and Brian Williams are considered by Americans to be a more reliable source than Jay Leno is debatable; however, the fact that television dominates the process of disseminating political information is not.

The more Americans rely on television, the more candidates integrate it into their campaigns. Both the Republicans and Democrats designed campaign strategies for the presidential election including appearances on *Larry King Live* and the *Jay Leno Show*. The fact that television has become the centerpiece of modern day campaigning has given rise to the importance of ad specialists and public relations consultants. These people are the technocrats behind the candidates who craft a public image of the candidate in packaged commercials. Television is the perfect format to exploit a variety of themes, slogans and symbols that make it appear that the candidate is concerned and knowledgeable regarding issues important to each and every individual. The candidate seen in the commercials appears to possess the same values, beliefs and attitudes as the people themselves. It is beyond clever; it is a way to program the voters.[53]

These types of formats give voters the illusion of democracy and the people a sense of control over their government; however, in reality the use of television as the medium for deciding public policy creates a form of media authoritarianism. Television eliminates the need for interaction between each other, the candidate, the party, and ultimately the government. It presents a situation where individuals formulate ideas and contemplate policy decisions in isolation based on "images" created for them and presented to them by the media. The media creates a political image that is embraced by the American public. Jonathon Kozol in his book, *Illiterate America,* presents television as the embodiment of an "amputated present." It has no past and presents no future; television presents what is happening now and this presentation is formatted in "images." The use of television and its ability to generate and control the flow of information has not given the "government" back to the people but rather created a greater feeling of alienation on the part of the people towards their parties and their government. This is reflected in the declining voter turnout and the increasing disassociation from political parties as linkage institutions.

Television has created the illusion of intimacy between the political arena and the voter because it brings the campaign and the candidate into the intimacy of the voter's home. No longer are Americans required to venture outside the comfort of their living rooms to meet the candidate or interact with "like-minded" people. Instead Americans "invite" the candidate or rather the image of the candidate into their home when they turn on their television set. Although perhaps an often unwanted intrusion, the image of the candidate takes on a heightened importance because in reality the candidate is a guest in the voter's home. The candidate is now sharing the voter's intimate space. Depending on the location of the television set in the home, the candidate can relax in the living room with the voters after a hard day of work, share a meal with them at the dining room table, or actually be the last person they see at night as they turn out the lights in their bedroom. The perceived intimacy of a media campaign creates a bond between the individual candidate and the voter. The individual candidate becomes the "link" between people and government. The individual voter begins to bond with the "candidate" rather than the party. This artificial bonding is all facilitated by the images created by television. Media politics is truly the epitome of "a picture is worth a thousand words."

The Internet

Only the Internet looms as a potential rival to television as a primary source of political information, particularly the younger voter. This new format for accessing political information threatens the existence of parties as it allows the public to interact directly with the candidate. This, even more than television bypasses the political party, making the electoral process even more candidate-centered. Although the major parties have their own web sites, they seem to virtually be lost in cyberspace in that they are unable to compete with the individual candidate's web pages. Pollster and political consultant Dick Morris believes that the Internet will eventually "result in the death" of the political party.[54]

The Internet is used much more extensively than ever before. In 1999, as the campaign of 2000 began to heat up, estimates placed the number of Internet users at 76 million, with one million new users logging on the World Wide Web each month. One survey estimates that 70 percent of voting-age Americans were online by election day 2000.[55]

In the election of 2004, many Democratic hopefuls used the Internet to raise money for the primary efforts. In the first quarter of 2004, Senator John Edwards raised just under $1 million, Senator Kerry approximately $450,000 and Howard Dean raised $1 million. As the campaign continued and Kerry became the Democratic candidate for the presidency, his Internet fundraising skyrocketed. In June 2004, Kerry reported to the Federal Election Committee that he had raised $37 million, one-third of the donations were over the Internet.[56] Today, all major presidential candidates use the Internet for fundraising purposes.

However, the candidates were not alone on the Internet. There continues to be fierce competition for voters' attention. Candidates must compete with the traditional print and visual media that have gone online to attract new viewers. Politically oriented web sites such as CNN, NPR, *Congressional Quarterly, New York Times, Wall Street Journal*, ABC, and CBS cover the campaigns, candidates, and elections electronically. However, not only must the candidate contend with these web sites, but they must also compete with the Internet sites of interest groups, such as the National Organization of Women and the National Rifle Association.[57] All of these sites put forth their political agendas and strive to influence their constituents in a more effective manner. They also use the web to raise money, which is an essential tool to furthering their agendas. Their constituents access the candidates directly over the Internet to register their views. This process effectively bypasses the political party. There are also new voices on the Internet, such as the YouTube website, that do not represent any particular interest but are available for public posting. Just recently, March 2007, one posting "Hillary 1984" created quite a stir and scored over 2 million hits. It was posted by Philip de Vellis, a 33-year old strategist with Blue State Digital, a Washington company that advises Democratic candidates. In claiming authorship of the posting, deVellis wrote that he "wanted to show that an individual citizen can affect the process . . . . this shows that the future of American politics rests in the hands of the ordinary citizens."[58] If E.E. Schattschneder was correct that there could be no democracy without political parties, will the Internet be the death of both political parties and democracy? Daniel Shea, noted political scientist, states, "Parties organize and oversee elections, encourage political participation and educate vote . . . they are the channels through which demands of participation can be accommodated and new groups of citizens brought into the political system."[59] Can the parties effectively channel the Internet to remain a viable funnel of political ideas in the political process or will it soon become outdated? If so, what does that do for political participation and the democratic process?

ELECTION REFORM

Progressive reforms designed to improve the performance of government and in the process make it more "democratic" have assigned functions previously performed by the parties to other institutions. The shift in these functions away from the party has significantly diminished the role of the party in the electoral process. Two important functions altered by the reforms were candidate selection and the distribution of political patronage. Direct primaries now select candidates and the civil service merit exam seriously diminished the amount of political patronage available either to the candidate or the party.

Direct Primary

The **direct primary** was an effort to reform candidate selection. Prior to the direct primary election, candidates had been selected by party elite, first in the "smoke filled room," then by party caucus, and finally party conventions. The elite based their candidate selection not only on the person's ability to win public office but also as the supreme reward for party loyalty and service. Receiving the nomination from the party was the ultimate political prize and signified an individual's power and strength within the party structure. The party organization would then throw its weight behind the elite's selection and the campaign would begin.

The concept of the direct primary was simple; let the "party of the electorate" select their own candidate through the electoral process. It was the democratization of the nomination process.

Frank Sorauf states, "the history of the evolution of nominating methods in the United States above all is a story of the progressive triumph of the ethic and symbols of democracy."[60] The direct primary was the last step in this evolutionary process that moved candidate selection out of the hands of the elite and placed it squarely in the hands of the people. The first statewide primary was held in Wisconsin in 1902. Within fifteen years all but four states had adopted the concept at least in part. Today all states hold some form of primary elections.[61]

While the direct primary may have opened the nomination process to the people, it had a negative effect on the political party. On the surface this should have been a victory for the democratic process. In fact, it has crippled the political party, the traditional link between people and government. The nomination process is now carried out in the media. The candidates take their case directly to the people bypassing the party structure. The campaigns for nominations become "candidate-centered" rather than party centered and are conducted through the media. The candidate's "image" is designed by public relations firms who tend to focus their candidate's campaign around the media-generated issues. The candidate owes no loyalty to the party and requires little or no support from the party structure, sometimes only using the party label as a defining mechanism. The candidate's new loyalty is to the media and the image it can project. The candidate then becomes personally responsible for transforming the needs of the people into public policy. However, these needs are hard to comprehend as television presents a montage of images with very little opportunity for interaction by the voting public. The image of the candidate is again the centerpiece of the campaign facilitated by television. The party has again been rendered obsolete and its functions usurped.

Political Patronage

Political patronage, or the "**spoils system**," is the practice of hiring and firing government employees based on their party loyalty and electoral support. This placed government jobs almost exclusively under the control of the political parties. Andrew Jackson was one of the first presidents who openly fostered the "spoils system." He believed that most government jobs required little more than common sense and, consequently, made party loyalty the primary consideration in hiring people to work for the federal government. This system made the federal bureaucracy more responsive to his presidential leadership. "To the victor, goes the spoils," ultimately gave victorious political parties control over the federal bureaucracy. The promise of government employment was a strong incentive for an individual to be loyal to and work for the party organization.[62]

Political patronage solidified the political parties and gave them enormous power; however, the "spoils system" created inefficiency on two levels. First, as government grew and technology became more sophisticated, policy issues became more complex. Government agencies grew in size and number. It required more than "common sense" to work in a government bureaucracy. Technological skills on sophisticated equipment and expertise in areas of economics, medicine, and banking became prerequisites for effective government employment. Second, the "winner-take-all" spoils system meant that every time a different party "won" an election, there would be a complete turnover in personnel in the government agencies. Political parties would reward their own campaign workers by providing them with political jobs and contracts. Members of the

Although America is basically a two-party system, other political parties do exist. Here a member of the "Marxist-Leninist Party" distributes literature on apartheid (segregation in South Africa). This party has few followers and has never been listed on a national ballot.

defeated political party would lose their government jobs and be replaced by members of the victorious political party. Electoral victory for one party translated into "pink slips" for the other. This was a huge incentive for people to work for and be loyal to their party; however, it also caused disruption in government services. Bureaucracies, to run efficiently, require a stable and competent workforce. Political patronage jeopardized the stability of the government agencies.

The elimination of political patronage as a tool of the political party has severely undercut its ability to maintain loyalty among its membership. Reforms were legislated to eliminate as much patronage as possible to improve the efficiency and stability in the government bureaucracies. In 1883, Congress passed the Pendleton Act, which has become the basis for the **civil service system**. This act was based on the idea that government service should be based on a person's qualifications rather than on his or her political connections. The civil service system is based primarily on merit and requires applicants for most government positions to pass a civil service test to be hired. This system stresses *what* you know, instead of who you know. At first, the civil service jobs only comprised 10 percent of the federal work force. In 1993, 80 percent of the federal workforce was civil service or merit based. Today the percentage of civil service workers remains constant and since 1993 has not dropped below 80 percent. The remaining jobs are still subject to political appointment.[63] Although the Pendleton Act and subsequent congressional legislation only apply to the federal workforce, state governments have followed the national government's model in constructing its workforce by passing its own civil service legislation. Currently state and local governments' hiring practices are severely restricted by legislation. The days of political patronage on the local, state, and federal level are effectively over.

These reforms have wielded a double edged sword at the institutions of government significantly altering the process of government. One edge of the sword cut deeply into the inefficiency and instability of government agencies by professionalizing and streamlining government through the merit system of hiring. The civil service system has enabled the vast government bureaucracies to function in a more efficient and stable manner. No longer are there massive turnovers in government agencies every time a new party wins office. The infusion of merit into government hiring has required that competent individuals be hired to fill bureaucratic positions. Merit hiring has also altered the composition of the federal work force. Because of their party loyalty, the patronage system traditionally targeted white, Anglo-Saxon Protestant men for government service. Until 1970, women and other minorities had been grossly underrepresented in the federal workforce. The civil service acts redistributed government jobs among the population in two significant albeit different ways: adhering to affirmative action guidelines and modifying the merit exam to provide special benefits for certain groups.

Affirmative action in hiring requires that all candidates being considered for a government position have roughly equal merit when being considered for a position. If, however, several applicants prove to be essentially equal, women and minority candidates may be given either strong consideration of or preference for the position based on their gender or ethnic background. Before 1970 approximately 33 percent of the federal workforce were woman. By 1990, after implementing affirmative action guidelines, their numbers increased to 50 percent of the federal workforce. Minorities increased in the same period from 20 percent to 26 percent. According to the 2005 Annual Report on the Federal Workforce published by the U.S. Equal Employment Opportunity Commission, the number of women in the federal work force has remained constant since 1993 while the number of minorities has increased and now comprise 34 percent. Although women and minorities continue to be underrepresented in the upper positions of the government agencies, these percentages now roughly reflect their proportions in the general population.[64]

The civil service merit exam has also served to alter the federal workforce by providing "bonus points" on the exam for special groups. These bonus points grant special privilege to certain groups, allowing them to score higher on the exam than their merit would indicate. Unlike affirmative action that requires applicants to be to have "roughly equal qualifications," bonus points are granted for special circumstances. Groups covered under affirmative action, such as women and minorities, are not normally qualified to receive bonus points. The largest group to benefit from "bonus points" has been military veterans. The bonus system works in roughly the following manner. The original merit test was based on 100 points. From a strictly merit standpoint, the job applicants with the highest test scores are hired. Under the modified merit system, the federal civil service exam adds a bonus of between five and fifteen points to the test scores of all applicants who have served on active military duty. The number of bonus points increases with a veteran's war-related disabilities and with service in the Vietnam War. Spouses, widows, widowers, and mothers of military veterans also may have bonus points added to their test scores under certain circumstances. Not counting postal workers, military veterans now makeup one-third of the federal workforce.[65]

The other edge of the sword has cut into the structure of the political parties. The party function of providing government jobs for party loyalty had been usurped. No longer is political patronage available to the parties as it had been under the spoils system. This has struck at the very heart of the party's ability to maintain loyalty among its constituents. Loyalty to party is no longer a prerequisite for government service. As long as individuals could see no personal gain in working for the party, they deserted their ranks in alarming numbers. Their loyalty at the polling place had been replaced by the "candidate-centered" campaign and media issues. What do parties have to offer their followers? As individuals find that their loyalty is no longer rewarded by the party system, they look elsewhere for political satisfaction. As we have already seen, they apparently have had difficulty finding it elsewhere as has been demonstrated by the continually declining voter turnout. So while in the process of making government more efficient, people generally feel more alienated from it. Progressive reforms designed to improve the conditions of democracy have produced an unforeseen side effect, the erosion of the power of the political parties. Government civil service jobs have replaced one of the major functions of the political parties thereby continuing to corrode the link between people and government.

Third Parties

Third parties are nearly as old as the country itself. Perhaps the first serious threat of a third party occurred in 1806 when John Randolph of Virginia, a member of the Anti-Federalist/Democrat-Republican party of President Jefferson, opposed the president over his land policy. Randolph and his supporters sought a "tentative quid," a third position, and became known as the "Quids." As most third parties in the United States, Randolph and the Quids failed.[66]

Even though third parties are not an electoral success, it is not surprising that they appear frequently within our system. In a centrist two-party system, some citizens feel constricted by the two seemingly non-choices at election time. Since U.S. parties tend to be non-ideological in nature, and increasingly more so, it is inevitable that people will feel alienated from the parties and consequently from the structure that produces them. In their struggle to feel connected to the system, people will seek alternatives, in the form of third parties.

Because of institutional barriers, however, such as the winner-take-all, single-member district elections, third party candidates tend not to be elected. Therefore, their voices are not usually heard from within the power structure, but rather from without. However, as losers, third parties perform two major functions within the electoral process. First, third parties can alter the result of an election by pulling votes from one or the other or both of the major party candidates. Second, some third parties, if they are not able to impact election results, may redefine the parameters of political discussion. Third party candidates tend to speak loudly enough during the election process so that the candidates from the two major parties are forced to listen to them and often re-focus their campaigns on issues that might otherwise be ignore.

The most recent third party phenomenon is the Green Party. It has received much notoriety because it was capable of successfully fulfilling the two major functions of third parties in a very conspicuous manner in the 2000 presidential election. Ralph Nader was the Green Party's presidential candidate in 2000. Although Ralph Nader has virtually become the symbol of the Green Party, prior to the election Nader had no official role within it. In fact, even as Nader accepted the nomination for president, he did not officially join the party but rather choose to remain an independent. However, his goal as candidate for the Green Party was to return political power to the disenfranchised and nonvoting citizens by offering an alternative to the two-party system. Nader made it perfectly clear that he believed that neither Bush nor Gore was capable of being president. When asked about Governor Bush, Nader replied, "He's like his father, even less energetic. He doesn't know very much. He doesn't like controversy. He's not about to push toward significant new directions." When asked about Gore, "He's even more reprehensible . . . he knows better and doesn't do it. All during the campaign he has weaseled and waffled. He's between being a great pretender and a great imposter."[67]

Since political parties in the U.S. are non-hierarchical in nature, in order to be successful they must become entrenched at the state and local levels. The Green Party has attempted to do just that. The Green Party is a national party that pre-dates Nader and was inspired by Germany's Green Party, a pro-environment, antinuclear movement that flowered in the 1980s. For the past four years, the Green Party was a generic term that applied to two different national groups: the Association of State Green Parties and the Green Party USA. The state group is a loose affiliation of autonomous state-based parties. That group formally nominated Nader for president at its convention in Denver in June 2000. In contrast, the Green Party USA has functioned more as a think tank and less as a political party. The two groups have several important philosophical differences that have sometimes tripped up Nader supporters and reporters writing about Green Party candidates. Some writers, for example, have incorrectly associated Nader with the political platform espoused by the Green Party USA, which called for the abolition of the U.S. Senate and adoption of the national "maximum" wage.[68]

To end the confusion, leaders of the two parties adopted a resolution agreeing to change the names of the two groups. Green Party USA would drop the word party from its name. The state group would dissolve and re-emerge as the National Committee of the Green Party. This new group would then seek Federal Election Commission recognition as the official Green Party. The new group anticipated establishing a national political presence and headquarters in Washington D.C.[69]

The state Green Parties continued to have the last word on whether to run candidates for local, state, and congressional office. "It really boils down to who wants to run, and most states have rules about endorsements," noted Gary Wolf, a member of the platform committee of the Association of state Green Parties. Wolf said that many state groups are gearing up to field more state and local candidates in 2002. "That's where you win," Wolf said. "Then people start moving up in the political system, so that in 10 or 15 years we'd have somebody who would be a credible candidate for a major race."[70]

Gary Wolf's prediction was right on target for the elections of 2002. Although the majority of the press had focused on Nader's campaign, in the election of 2000 the Green Party ran a total of 56 candidates in congressional races in nineteen states. None of them won. However, in 2002, although no Green Party candidate won a congressional seat, the party ran 549 candidates in 40 states for 81 types of offices. Seventy-one of the Green Party candidates won their elections, to include capturing its first state legislative seat in Maine's 31st district. The Green Party opened a national office in Washington D.C. in 2002 and has officially been recognized by the Federal Election Commission as the Green Party of the United States.[71]

The Green Party received considerable attention from major national and statewide newspapers and broadcast media during Ralph Nader's run for the presidency under its banner in 2000. Many analysts believe that although Nader was successful in only capturing 3 percent of the vote nationally, and just under eight million dollars in campaign donations, he was successful in significantly altering the presidential election of 2000. Nader's candidacy greatly impacted the election returns in several of the key electoral states, the most important of which was Florida. Although the exact margin of victory is still in dispute in Florida, ranging from 193 to 1200 votes, depending on who did the counting and when, what is not up for debate is that Nader received 97,000 votes in that state.[72] Most analysts believe that many of these votes would have gone to Al Gore, winning him not only the state of Florida and its electoral votes but the presidency as well.

Many questions surround the survivability of the Green Party. Is it just a passing historical phenomenon that will fade from the political scene as other third parties before it, such as Ross Perot and the Reform Party in the 1990s? Was Nader's presidential race the "cult of the individual," or can the Green Party sustain itself as a national party running effective state and local races without the celebrity status of Nader? Some of these questions were answered in the election of 2004. Ralph Nader ran for president without the support of the Green Party and won less than 1 percent of the total vote nation-wide in contrast to the 3 percent he won running under the Green Party label. The Green Party, without Nader, ran David Cobb, who won only 112,000 votes nation-wide. Although neither Nader nor the Green Party was very effective at the national level, the Green Party is solidifying its power at the state and local levels. In 2004, the Green Party ran 433 candidates in 42 states for 74 different types of offices and had 70 victories including returning John Eder to the statehouse in Maine. To date, Nader does not have any effective state and local organizations. It appears that Nader is an example of the "cult of the individual," while the Green Party appears to be developing into a functioning viable third party option developing a power base at the state and local levels.[73] The Green Party once again proved itself to be viable, and in the midterm elections of 2006, the Greens won over 35 races nationwide including the mayoral race in Richmond, California, which is the first city with more than 100,000 residents to have a Green Party mayor. The Green Party currently has 57 candidates running for various offices in 11 states for the 2007 elections.[74]

CONCLUSION

Political parties have always been a prerequisite to elections, and elections have always been a prerequisite to empowerment, providing access to the democratic process. They have served as the link in the electoral process between people and their government. However, as we have seen, other institutions and circumstances have developed that have usurped the traditional functions of parties rendering them either dying or obsolete. Perhaps the patient should be allowed to expire. However, in the process of removing the support system from the patient, we don't want to kill the entire system. We have already witnessed serious decline in voter turnout among the electorate, indicating alienation and disassociation from their political system. Disassociation from the two major parties has caused less empowerment, not more. The faltering political parties have not been replaced by any alternative institutions effective at sustaining the democratic process.

New circumstances require a new paradigm or way of thinking. It is time to look at political parties and the electoral process in a different light. If not parties, then what new life forms must be allowed to grow and develop in its place. Some analysts have proposed that these new life forms would emerge in the form of "third" or alternative parties, such as the Green Party. However, the prevailing system does not allow third parties to be viable because it underpins the present two party system. The present governmental structure dooms third parties to failure. Third parties in the United States have merely tended to be constructed as factions rather than political parties. Factions were the groups most feared by the Framers of the Constitution because they were self-serving and not in the interest of the whole republic.

The existing system frames the present two-party centrist system. The new paradigm must provide for systemic changes and not merely cosmetic ones. These new changes must provide for alternative links to connect people to their government. This would necessitate the development of a new political paradigm that would allow third parties to develop as viable political alternatives. This would require serious changes to the existing political process. Since the Constitution establishes the framework for the party system, it would need to be examined. This would directly challenge the vested interests of the two major parties. The entire system of representation would be called into question, for example, the concept of single-member district representation vs. proportional representation would need to be examined. The entire system would need to be re-evaluated. This feat would be impossible without confronting the fundamental constitutional issues of federalism and separation of powers that underpin the entire system. However, without designing a new paradigm for political parties, the two major existing political parties appear that they will continue to erode. As it stands today, the institutions that have emerged to replace the functions of the political parties have been detrimental to the democratic process and, consequently, it is in serious jeopardy. Does the election of 2004 indicate new trends and perhaps new life for the political parties? Or, were increased party identification and voter turnout merely flashes in the pan? What will the election of 2008 tell us with regards to the life of the party system?

CHAPTER NOTES

[1]William Nisbet Chambers, *Political Parties in New Nation: The American Experience 1776-1809*, (New York: Oxford University Press, 1963), 1-25.

[2]E.E. Schattschneider, *Party Government* (New York: Rinehart, 1942), 1.

[3]Michael Allen Gillespie, "Political Parties and the American Founding" in *American Political Parties and Constitutional Politics*, (Rowman and Littlefield Publishers, Inc.1993), 20.

[4]Schattschneider, 1.

[5]Harvey C. Mansfield, 20.

[6]Clayton Roberts and David Roberts, *A History of England: Prehistory to 1714, Volume I*, 3rd edition, (Englewood Cliffs, New Jersey: Prentice Hall, 1991), 410.

[7]Ibid.

[8]Charles R. Kesler, "Political Parties, The Constitution, and the Future of American Politics," in *American Political Parties and Constitutional Politics*, (Rowman and Littlefield Publishers, Inc. 1993), 230.

[9]Peverill Squire and others, *Dynamics of Democracy*, (Madison: Brown & Benchmark Publishers, 1995), 223.

[10]J.W. Peltason, Corwin & Peltason's *Understanding the Constitution*, 13th edition, (Fort Worth: Harcourt Brace College Publishers, 1994), 207.

[11]Ibid.

[12]Ibid., 238.

[13]Ibid., 238-240.

[14]Squire, 219.

[15]John White and Daniel Shea, *New Party Politics: From Jefferson and Hamilton to the Information Age* (Boston:Bedford/ St. Martins, 2000), 267.

[16]Ibid.

[17]Schattschneider, 129.

[18]Cornelius P. Cotter, ed., *Practical Politics in the United States*, (Boston: Allyn and Bacon, 1969), 43.

[19]Frank J. Sorauf, *Party Politics in America*, (Boston: Little Brown and Company, 1968), 405.

[20]Ibid., 405.

[21]Ibid., 11.

[22]Cotter, 43.

[23]Edward F. Cooke, "Big City Politics," in *Practical Politics in the United States*, (Boston: Allyn and Bacon, Inc.), 78.

[24]Sorauf, 78.

[25]Barbara A. Bardes, Mack C. Shelley II, and Steffen W. Schmidt, *American Government and Politics Today: the Essentials,* (St. Paul: West Publishing Co., 1986), 232.

[26]Sorauf, 78.

[27]Ibid., 108.

[28]Marc J. Hetherington and William J. Keffer, *Parties, Politics and Public Policy in America*, 10th ed., (Washington, D.C.: CQ Press, 2007), p. 93.

[29]Ibid.

[30]Martin P. Wattenberg, *The Decline of American Political Parties: 1952-1988*, Cambridge, Mass.: Harvard University Press. 1990),2.

[31]Ibid., ix.

[32]Hetherington, p. 196.

[33]Information for voter turnout statistics are a composite from the following: Martin P. Wattenberg, *The Decline of American Political Parties: 1952-1992*, (Cambridge, Mass.: Harvard University Press, 1994).Barbara A. Bardes, Mack C. Shelley II, and Steffen W. Schmidt, *American Government and Politics Today: The Essentials, 1996-1997 edition*, (St. Paul: West Publishing Co., 1996). Peverill Squire and others, *Dynamics of Democracy*, (Madison: Brown & Benchmark, 1997).

[34]Sorauf, 233

[35]Wattenberg, 1988, 2.

[36]Wattenberg, 1994, 11-12.

[37]Ibid. 30.

[38]Sorauf, 161.

[39]Ibid. 166.

[40]Gallop poll 8-28-96. Received information from Gallop poll research assistant at Gallop Headquarters, November, 1996.

[41]Ibid., Information received April, 2001.

[42]Wattenberg, 1994, Chapters 1 and 2.

[43]Doris A Graber, *Mass Media and American Politics, 5th edition*, Washington D.C.: CQ Press: A Division of Congressional Quarterly, Inc., 1997), 168.

[44]Thomas R. Dye and Harmon Zeigler, *The Irony of Democracy: An Uncommon Introduction to American Politics,* (Belmont, California: Wadsworth Publishing Co., 1993), 154.

[45]Susan D. Moeller, *Media Coverage of Weapons of Mass Destruction*, Philip Merrill College of Journalism, (University of Maryland: Center for International and Security Studies at Maryland, March 9, 2004), p. 3.

[46]Interview with Walter Cronkite, *Good Morning America*, December 5, 1996.

[47]Ibid.

[48]Ibid., 185.

[49]Ibid., 184.

[50]Hetherington, p. 234.

[51]Graber, 231.

[52]W. Lance Bennett, *News: The Politics of Illusion*, 4th edition (New York: Longman, 2001), 11-29.

[53]Samuel J. Eldersveld and Hanes Walton Jr., *Political Parties in American Society*, 2nd edition (Boston: Bedford/St. Martins, 2000), 313.

[54]White, 7.

[55]Ibid, 4-11.

[56]"Kerry Sets Democratic Fundraising Record," *USA Today*, July, 21, 2004.

[57]Ibid.

[58]Gregg Keizer, "Hillary 1984" www.computerworld.com and Jim Kuhnhenn, "Mystery Creator of Anti-Clinton Ad ID'd," www.abcnews.com

[59]Ibid., 5.

[60]Sorauf, p. 202.

[61]Sorauf, 202-203.

[62]Squire, 373.

[63]Ibid.

[64]Ibid.

[65]Ibid.

[66]Eldersveld, 66.

[67]Godfrey Spearling, "When Good Feeling Ruled," *Christian Science Monitor*, November 21, 2000, p11.

[68]Margaret Kriz and Louis Jacobson, "Invasion of the Greens," *National Journal*, January 6, 2001, 22.

[69]Ibid.

[70]Ibid.

[71]Green Party Election Results, 2002, www.greens.org/election and www.greenpartyus.org/donate.html.

[72]"Election 2000," www.lawpubllish.com/election2000

[73]Green Party Election Results, November 3, 2004, http://www.gp.org/2004election/pr_11_03_04.html.

[74]"*Greens Advance on November 7, Prepare for 2008 National Run*," Green Party of the United States, www.gp.org.

SUGGESTED READINGS

Beard, Charles A. *The American Party Battle*. New York: The Macmillan Company, 1928.

Chambers, William Nisbet. *Political Parties in a New Nation: The American Experience 1776-1809*. New York: Oxford University Press, 1963.

Schattschneider, E.E. *Party Government*. New York: Rinehart, 1942.

Schramm, Peter W., and Bradford P. Wilson, eds. *American Political Parties and Constitutional Politics*. Rowman and Littlefield Publishers, 1993.

Sorauf, Frank J. *Party Politics in America*. 4th ed. Boston: Little Brown and Co., 1980.

Wattenberg, Martin. *The Decline of American Political Parties: 1952-1992.*. Cambridge, Mass.: Harvard University Press, 1994.

Chapter Six

CAMPAIGNS AND ELECTIONS

When the Constitution was written, it was assumed that the government would be run by citizen-politicians, men who would come together for perhaps only a few weeks to do the business of the country. Today, candidates are professional politicians engaged in a permanent campaign. The time between the completion of one election and the beginning of the next gets shorter and shorter. By spring 2001, only a few short months after the election of George W. Bush, candidates of both parties began looking towards the 2004 election, traveling to New Hampshire and other states that had early caucuses and primaries, assembling a field operation of consultants, pollsters, fund-raisers, and speechwriters. No longer does an election campaign start and end in an election years; now it is a permanent campaign with no beginning and no clear end.

Several factors are responsible for the dramatic changes in campaigns and elections. Most importantly, candidates must now win their party's nomination by competing for votes in primary elections. In the "old days," candidates had merely to appeal to party leaders. This was a less public, less expensive, and less time-consuming process. Now, candidates must win primaries by directly appealing to a large number of voters. Technology has made this possible.

Even in comparison to only twenty years ago, the media and information technology have revolutionized campaigning and contributed to the permanent campaign. Modern computer and phone technology enable the media and private organizations to continually poll the American public. The emphasis on polling has forced candidates to begin to campaign earlier so as to gain public recognition and front-runner status.

Gaining front-runner status is important because it places the candidate in a position to attract the campaign donations that fuel the permanent campaign. The incumbent politicians have an enormous advantage in achieving front-runner status. Their constituents recognize their name and they can use the postal system for free to communicate regularly with the voters. A challenger must buy media time to achieve similar levels of recognition. In the case of congressional campaigns, unless a challenger raises $500,000 or more they face a very low probability of beating an incumbent. Every $10,000 spent by a House challenger increases his or her vote total by more than 2 percent. As challengers spend more, so do the incumbents. The money chase then escalates.

The 2002 congressional election cost $2.2 billion, while the 2004 election, which included a presidential contest, cost $4.2 billion. In 2006, congressional candidates raised $1.3 billion with Republicans raising $586 million and Democrats raising an additional $567 million. With a final burst of fund-raising by candidates in late October 2006, spending by political parties and outside advocacy groups pushed the total price tag to a record for a nonpresidential election, $2.6 billion on the campaigns that determined control of Congress. That comes to an average of $59 per vote in Senate races and $35 per vote in the House of Representatives. And despite a 2002 law that aims to limit the impact of money on the political process, candidates and outside political groups raised more money than ever for television ads, travel, voter outreach efforts and other campaign activities. The $2.6 billion estimated cost of the 2006 campaign represents an 18 percent increase over 2002, outstripping the 13 percent inflation over the same period.

As in previous elections, the incumbent lawmakers in 2006 maintained a tremendous fund-raising advantage over their challengers. Sitting senators enjoyed a 4-to-1 advantage, while members of the House enjoyed a 7-to-2 advantage over those seeking to unseat them. This was because the business, labor and ideological interests that account for a large chunk of donations overwhelmingly continue to favor those already in power. Not surprisingly, incumbents also enjoyed an enormous electoral advantage, most of them winning by large margins. Rarely can a challenger raise enough money to successfully unseat a well-funded incumbent.[1]

It is an irony of modern American politics that campaigns have become extravagant, year-long events that produce hours of advertisements and media coverage, consume billions of dollars, exhaust candidates, their staff members, journalists, and the American public, and yet manage to return to office the same people over and over again.

THE CHANGING FACE OF AMERICAN CAMPAIGNS AND ELECTIONS

The 2006 state and midterm congressional elections saw a continued trend in voter dissatisfaction with the status quo of parties, money, and politics. One survey found that the proportion of Americans saying the current Congress had achieved less than previous ones had climbed to 45 percent in 2006, double the number who said this in the 2002 or 1998 midterms, and higher than the number who expressed frustration with Congress in 1994 (38 percent). Republican leaders in Congress were blamed for the perceived failure, but Democratic leaders in Congress did not benefit from the criticism. More Americans disapproved than approved of the job Republicans were doing by a 53 percent to 30 percent margin but dissatisfaction with Democratic leaders was nearly as high (50 percent disapproved, 32 percent approved). In 2006, voters seemed distinctly disgruntled with the very nature of campaigns themselves.[2]

There is perhaps no area of American politics that has undergone as much change as the electoral system. In 1789, George Washington was elected unanimously by the electoral college. There were no political parties, and the mass media consisted of only a few newspapers with limited readership. The whole concept of campaigning would be largely foreign in such a system in which the president would be selected indirectly by electoral college delegates themselves indirectly selected by their various state legislatures. Senators, too, were selected by these state legislatures. Only members of the House of Representatives would be directly elected and then only by white men, and in twelve states only white men with property.

Today, candidates not only campaign for over 450,000 elected positions at the local, state, and national levels, they campaign, at least in most states, for their party's nomination for these offices. It is not uncommon for campaigns to run over a year or longer.

After their creation at the turn of the nineteenth century, political parties conducted all phases of the campaigns for office. They nominated their candidates; they funded the campaigns; and the parties were the principal communications link between the candidates and the voters. The parties held campaign rallies and worked behind the scenes to line-up support in the big urban centers of America. On election day, it was the party precinct workers who walked door-to-door getting out the vote. Party competition appears to have been the key in stimulating voter turnout. Competition between alternative parties gave citizens an incentive to vote and politicians an incentive to reach them and get their vote.[3] It was the competitive organizing activities of the Jeffersonian Republicans and the Federalists that first led to the democratic impulse to extend the franchise and the number of offices directly elected.

How different campaigns are run today! Beginning with the anti-party reforms of the Progressive Era, the parties' roles in campaigns have been greatly diminished. The civil service, direct primary, and nonpartisan elections have transformed the political landscape. Candidates are now nominated by voters casting ballots in primary elections in forty-two states. To win public support, candidates must turn to high-tech politics. Candidates need to be able to construct a meaningful message and take it to the public. Candidates pay enormous sums of money to conduct focus groups and public opinion polls to find out what issues most concern the American public. Once they get their message, the candidates need to communicate it to the most people at the least cost. Enter the mass media. Party organizations working door-to-door are simply no match for the slick and sophisticated technology of political advertisements, or for that matter a thirty-second soundbite on the evening news. The nomination secured, the candidate then moves on to the general election, where even more voters are involved and the mass media, therefore, all the more important.

All of this modern campaigning costs money and large amounts of it. A typical day on the presidential campaign trail involves moving more than 100 people, including the candidate, his staff, dozens of reporters, and security through stops in as many as six states per day. Working behind the scenes, the campaigns create virtual traveling towns, setting up hotel rooms, banquet halls, lighting, food, telephone lines, and plane flights, every day, seven days a week. The costs add up quickly. Renting a Boeing 727 goes for about $8,000 an hour. Setting up the lights at an event can cost as much as $25,000. When a campaign is in full swing, it is not unheard of to spend more than $200,000 a day. The political parties, while still important in fund-raising, cannot possibly raise all the money needed for the high-tech politics of polling, media events, and advertising so central to modern campaigns. Candidates today are entrepreneurs who increasingly have turned to the private sector for the resources necessary to run an effective campaign and win. Such resources may come from the candidate's own wealth, interest groups, corporations, or other individual donors. The way in which we finance campaigns places the candidate in a more central role. On election day, for most offices, a party label stands beside the candidate's name. But this label disguises the great number of changes that have fundamentally altered the electoral system of the United States, transforming it from a party-based to a candidate and media-centered system.

NOMINATING THE CANDIDATES

Historical Background

When the Constitution was being written, it was assumed by the framers that George Washington would be selected to be the first president of the new United States. In addition, it was largely assumed that the supporters of the new Constitution, the Federalists as they were called, would win most of the seats in the House and Senate, for to be anything other than Federalist was to be a traitor to the new government. Beyond these minimal assumptions, little else was known. The Constitution is completely silent on the subject of elections, choosing to leave it to each state to organize and control the elections. There was little thought given to how the nomination of future candidates would be conducted.

George Washington, upon becoming president, appointed Alexander Hamilton as Secretary of the Treasury and Thomas Jefferson as Secretary of State. Because Hamilton and Jefferson held divergent views on everything from foreign policy to a national bank to internal improvements, Jefferson soon quit the cabinet and began to organize the first political party, the Jeffersonian Republicans. Jefferson based his party in Congress, drawing together members who shared his political viewpoint. Hamilton, similarly, had his group of devotees in the House and Senate.

With the differences in political ideas apparent, the beginnings of party organization underway, democratic forces running strong, and Washington expressing no desire to seek a third term, the question soon arose how each party would nominate a candidate for the highest office of the presidency. By 1800, both the Federalists under Hamilton and the Republicans under Jefferson had established congressional caucuses that would nominate their party's candidate. These congressional caucuses were made up of men in the House and Senate sharing either the Federalist or Republican views.

The Caucus System

As the early 1800s progressed and party organization grew stronger and more complex, state party organizations began to develop state caucuses. These state party caucuses chose delegates that would participate in a national party convention, which would then nominate the party's presidential candidate. These national conventions quickly replaced the congressional caucuses as vehicles for nominating candidates. By 1830, the nomination process had become extremely complex with candidates having to be nominated at a variety of geographical levels, from the smallest electoral unit up to the national convention itself. The process began with local meetings, or caucuses, of party supporters to choose delegates to attend a larger subsequent meeting, usually at the county level. Most of the delegates selected in these local caucuses openly supported one of the presidential candidates seeking the party nomination. The process finally culminated in a state party convention with delegates selecting other delegates to the national party convention that will formally nominate the party's presidential candidate.

Today, one or both parties in sixteen states employ caucuses to select delegates to attend presidential nominating conventions. The Iowa caucuses, which are the first held, are similar to those in other states. The campaign in Iowa starts several months before the caucuses are actually held. In the election year 2004, presidential candidates spent over 1,000 days campaigning in Iowa. In early February, the party caucuses are held in private homes, schools, and churches. All who consider themselves party members can attend. They debate and vote on the candidates. The candidates receiving the most votes win delegates to later county and then state conventions. The number of delegates is proportional to the vote that the candidate received at the caucuses. The candidate must get at least 15 percent of the caucus vote in order to receive any delegates.

While Iowa is a small state and chooses only a handful of delegates to the party conventions, it is important as a bell weather of public opinion. The media widely cover these caucuses, looking to identify frontrunners in each of the two major parties. The winners of the Iowa caucuses attract not only media coverage but also the large donations that will allow them to continue to successfully campaign in the other state caucuses and primaries. Prior to the Iowa caucus in 2004, Howard Dean was considered the frontrunner for the Democratic nomination. When John Kerry won the Iowa caucus, he gained momentum that carried onto other state races and eventually the nomination.

The Primary System

Because there is no national legislation governing the selection of delegates to a national party convention, and because pressures for greater democracy and participation continued to grow throughout the early twentieth century, some states began to develop an alternative to the state caucus. In 1903, in response to reform movements seeking to end party controlled selection processes, the state of Wisconsin passed the first statewide primary law. Within only ten years, many states followed Wisconsin's lead.

In a presidential primary election, every presidential candidate who chooses to enter the state primary lists a slate of convention delegates who may, at least in some states, have promised to support his candidacy at the party's national nominating convention. Voters in that state then can choose between competing slates of national party convention delegates. In the presidential preferential primary, voters choose delegates who have not agreed to support any particular candidate.

A state primary may be either **open** or **closed**. A primary is considered closed when each voter must declare a choice of party before voting, either when registering or actually at the voting place itself. Party members in these closed primaries may only choose among those candidates on their party's ballot. The primary election is closed, then, to members of other parties. In the open primary, on the other hand, the voter receives ballots for all the parties and chooses which party election they want to vote in, right there in the voting booth on election day. A few states even have **blanket** primaries in which voters may choose candidates for various offices off different party ballots.

Whether their delegates are chosen in state **caucuses** as in Iowa or in primaries as in California, the convention system quickly worked to extend the number of people involved in the electoral process. In addition, the democratic forces that encouraged the creation of the primary system also led to more intense party competition along with efforts to extend the franchise, dropping the property qualifications for voting by 1840. Campaigns became festive affairs. For example, tens of thousands of men and women attended the Whig Party festival in Nashville in 1840. They carried torches, donned uniforms, chanted party slogans, and whipped themselves into a virtual frenzy of party sympathy.

The Entitlement Revolution

In the 1960s, new groups emerged on the scene, seeking greater representation in the American party system. In particular, the Civil Rights Movement began to make demands on the Democratic Party organization for greater representation and recognition. At the 1964 Democratic national convention, the Mississippi Freedom Democratic Party filed a challenge against an all white Mississippi delegation that had been selected through the Mississippi caucus system. The Mississippi Freedom Democratic Party charged that the Mississippi caucus system had systematically excluded blacks from registering to vote and from participating in the state party meetings.

The conflict at the 1964 Democratic national convention resulted in the 1968 Democratic convention requiring state parties to ensure that voters in each state, regardless of race, color, creed, or national origin, be given the fullest opportunity to participate in party affairs. Furthermore, in July 1967, a Special Equal Rights Committee established by the Democratic National Committee adopted unanimously a resolution urging the 1968 convention to replace any state delegation "not broadly representative of the Democrats of the state with a rival representative delegation."[4] This resolution led to the seating of the Mississippi Freedom Democratic Party delegates at the 1968 Democratic national convention held in Chicago.

The call for equal opportunity for black participation was matched by an even wider call for fuller participation on the part of all rank and file voters. It was not only the caucus system that was challenged; reformers began to look at the primary system as well. Before 1968, the primaries were nothing more than what Harry Truman called "eye wash." In fact, the election of 1952 proved Truman right. In that election year, Democratic Senator Kefauver sought to be the Democratic nominee. Kefauver, however, had angered and alienated the Democratic party organization with his Senate investigation of organized crime and subsequent embarrassment of Democrats in Illinois and Florida. Kefauver's standing was much higher with the American public who had watched the televised hearings. It was estimated that an average of 69.7 percent of American television sets in New York were watching the hearings, twice the number who watched the World Series game in October 1950.[5] The hearings were carried by television stations in twenty states.

At least in part because of this media attention, Senator Kefauver was able to win large victories in the primaries. He received over 257 delegates chosen in the various state primary elections; he

Riots outside the 1968 Democratic convention in Chicago influenced the party to reform its delegate selection procedures.

needed 616 delegates to win the Democratic nomination. At the Democratic convention, after four ballots, Kefauver lost the nomination to Adlai Stevenson who was the choice of the Democratic party organization but who had entered no primaries. Stevenson went on to be solidly defeated by Eisenhower in the general election, suggesting to many that primary voters might be better judges of candidates than those in the party organization.

In 1960, another Democrat, John F. Kennedy, used the primary system to challenge party leaders and secure the nomination. Kennedy was viewed by his party as a weak presidential hopeful. He was Catholic, and never had voters elected a non-Protestant to the White House. Kennedy was also seen as young and fairly inexperienced. It was not until he won the primary of West Virginia, a largely Protestant state, that Kennedy was seen as potentially electable.

Then came 1968. On November 30, 1967, a little-known Senator from Minnesota, Eugene McCarthy, announced his intention to challenge the incumbent president, Lyndon Johnson, for the Democratic party nomination. In the state of New Hampshire, the White House made an all-out effort to mobilize public support behind the incumbent president. The effort was not very successful with Johnson receiving less than 50 percent of the vote and McCarthy garnering 41.9 percent. Then on March 16, another insurgent candidate, Robert Kennedy, entered the race for the Democratic nomination. On March 31, Lyndon Johnson announced that he was pulling out of the race. His vice president and heir apparent, Hubert Humphrey, delayed his formal declaration of intent to seek the nomination until April 27, after all the final deadlines for the primaries had passed.

At the Democratic convention that year in Chicago, Humphrey won the nomination on the first ballot with 67 percent of the delegate vote. Even in fifteen primary states, 53 percent of the delegates voted for Humphrey abandoning the wishes of the voters in their state. In 1968, most states used some form of appointment in delegate selection. Either the Governor, the state party committee, or other state committees appointed all or some of the state's delegates to the party's national convention.

As in 1952, the candidate chosen by the Democratic national convention went on to be defeated in the general election. In the aftermath of defeat, the McGovern-Fraser Commission was organized by the Democratic Party to reform the delegate selection process to make it more representative of the rank-and-file voters in the party. The results were the extended use of the primary system and a more open and inclusive process in the states that continued to use the caucus system. The Republican Party has moved in a similar direction although less emphasis has been placed on making the delegate population demographically representative of the Republican voters. Once selected, by either state caucus or state primary, the delegates attend their party's national nominating convention in the summer before the November general election. Originally, the party conventions actually determined the nominee of the party. Today, the conventions merely ratify the decisions made in the state caucuses and primaries. The conventions have become extravagant media events that are used by the parties to whip up enthusiasm for the nominee and the party platform.

The most widely watched part of the convention is the last night when the keynote speaker gives an address reviewing the history of the party and promising a bright future for it. A party spokesperson who reviews the candidate's background and experience then places each candidate in nomination. The roll call of the states follows, formally nominating the party's presidential nominee. The presidential and vice presidential candidates give their acceptance speeches to much cheering. Those who fought for the nomination are often welcomed on stage in a show of party unity.

Special Interests and the Nominating Conventions

While the delegate selection process has become more open to the rank-and-file members of the parties, the party conventions themselves provide special privileges to the party leadership and the interest groups that support them. For example, one tradition at the national party conventions is the parties thrown for Members of Congress by special interest groups and corporations with business pending before Congress. Special interests sponsor these events to honor Members, who in many cases have direct influence over legislation affecting their industries.

Members of Congress take special advantage of the rules surrounding conventions, which exempt them from the federal ban on gift taking. A 1995 law forbids Members of Congress from taking gifts worth more than $50 from interest group lobbyists. However, Congress left the door open during the conventions by exempting themselves from the rule during special events. Members are not even required to disclose sponsors of their events and how much the sponsors gave.

Additionally, in the wake of the new ban on "soft money" enacted as part of the 2002 McCain-Feingold law (to be discussed later in this chapter), which prevents the national political parties from accepting unlimited contributions from special interests, corporate cash has instead been pouring into the coffers of the nonprofit host committees for the Democratic and Republican conventions. Despite McCain-Feingold, these donations are still completely unlimited.

In 2004, there was a constellation of corporate-sponsored parties surrounding the nominating conventions. In Boston, the home of the Democratic Convention in 2004, there was an exclusive $600,000 party at the ultra-hip Roxy nightclub featuring the Neville brothers. The party honoring

U.S. Representative Joe Baca (D – California) beams in the presence of law enforcement. Politicians actively seek the endorsement of groups likely to be popular with the voters.

the "Blue Dog" caucus of conservative Democrats in the House of Representatives was paid for by about 30 corporate sponsors including the Altria Group (the parent of Phillip Morris), Comcast (the cable giant), ConocoPhillips (the oil conglomerate), and Microsoft.

A few blocks away at the state Capitol, the Congressional Black Caucus honored the civil rights activist Frannie Lou Hamer. But even here corporate money added an incongruous note. Alongside a pencil-and-ink portrait of Hamer, the daughter of sharecroppers who risked her life and was brutally beaten for her civil rights activism, were banners prominently displaying the logos of Lockheed Martin and Verizon, the companies that underwrote the event.

Together, the two party committees raised more than $100 million from private sources—more than 12 times as much as they raised in 1992. This figure does not include the millions more that have been spent on hundreds of private parties. The effect of these convention party contributions: buying influence. The utility industry's Edison Electric Institute, for instance, which sponsored several pricey events during the Republican's 2000 convention, successfully lobbied Vice President Dick Cheney's energy task force to include a number of items from its legislative wish list in the Bush administration's energy plan, including new EPA regulations essentially exempting coal-burning utilities from installing pollution-control devices when making upgrades. In 2004, Edison hedged its bets by hosting nine events during the Democratic Convention in Boston.

Independent and Third-Party Nominees

Recent elections have seen strong independent candidates emerge: Ross Perot in 1992 and 1996 and Ralph Nader in 2000 and 2004. It is not easy for independent and third-party candidates to get on the ballot. State laws control access to the ballot, and Democratic and Republican legislators and governors make those laws. Unsurprisingly, the candidates of the Democratic and Republican

Parties are automatically placed on the ballot in all fifty states. Independent candidates, on the other hand, must demonstrate significant support to get on the ballot through petitions signed by voters.

Nominations for Congress and State Offices

Today, most candidates for major national and state offices are nominated through the primary election system. Thirty-seven states use primary elections to nominate candidates for all state and national offices. Primaries play at least some role in the nomination process in several other states.

Because partisan redistricting (discussed later in this chapter) has ensured that fewer general elections for the U.S. House of Representatives are meaningfully competitive, the primary election of the dominant party is often the most important race in many districts and money is now a key factor in determining primary election outcomes. An analysis of Federal Election Commission (FEC) campaign finance data for the 2006 primary elections shows that money played a key role in determining election outcomes and that most campaign contributions came from a small number of large donors. According to FEC data, major party congressional candidates who raised the most money won 92 percent of their primary races in 2006. Candidates who spent the most won 91 percent of the time. Winning candidates out-raised their opponents by a margin of 3.5-to-1, with the winners raising an average of $1.06 million and losers raising $304,000. This pattern held true for open seat races as well. The biggest fundraiser won 82 percent of the contests without an incumbent running for re-election in the district.

In the primary elections, the vast majority of campaign contributions come from a small number of large donors. FEC data indicate that while only 0.27 percent of voting-age Americans made a contribution to a candidate of $200 or more, these large donations accounted for 82 percent of individual contributions received by primary candidates. More than a quarter (29 percent) of the contributions came at or above the $2,000 level, while only 0.03 percent of voting-age Americans made a $2,000 contribution.

Many powerful incumbents have accumulated large war chests of campaign money which then further hinders electoral competition in the primary elections. Fully three quarters (76 percent) of 2006 congressional primary races featured only one candidate seeking his or her party's nomination, providing voters with no real choice on primary election day. One reason for this is that large financial advantages of incumbents discourage meaningful competition. Incumbent candidates began the 2006 election cycle with about $188 million in cash on hand, for an average of more than $432,000 per incumbent. The average incumbent Senator started his or her reelection campaign with $1.43 million already on hand.[6]

Campaigning for the Nomination

Voting turnout in primary elections tends to be relatively low, usually with less than one quarter of eligible voters participating. Still, almost 40 million citizens cast ballots in the Democratic and Republican primaries of 2004. Another half a million participated in state caucuses. The nomination process almost certainly requires candidates to reach millions of voters across the fifty states.

This has certain consequences for campaigning. First, the process takes time. Technically the selection process begins in February with the Iowa state caucuses. These are followed by the New Hampshire primaries. Even though only a very few delegates are selected in the small states of Iowa and New Hampshire, an exorbitant amount of media coverage and public attention attaches to them. The candidates victorious in these states will gain momentum from the early recognition as "winners."

In truth, the selection process begins way before February. Competitive candidates must raise huge sums of money to establish themselves as serious contenders. In 2000, George W. Bush was viewed as the likely Republican candidate way before Iowa and New Hampshire. This was because he had financial reserves unmatched by the other Republican hopefuls. Besides raising cash, the candidates test the waters before the actual selection process begins. In 2003, Senators Kerry, Lieberman, and Gephardt visited New Hampshire.

The second upshot of this lengthy, complex nomination process is that candidates win the nomination largely on the basis of the resources they can bring, on their own, to the campaign. The national party organization will usually refrain from backing one of their party's hopefuls over the others. There is little incentive for the party to play favorites so early in the game when so much is still uncertain. As a result, candidates are on their own to mobilize the money they need from individuals and interest groups willing to support their campaigns. Recent elections have yielded candidates who run against their party as anti-establishment "outsiders." Even incumbents Ronald Reagan and George Bush ran against their party, critical of what they called the "Washington insiders." Then, once victorious, such candidates are not likely to feel great loyalty to the party organization and, instead, may feel indebted to individual donors and powerful interest groups that may have been instrumental in their victory.

THE GENERAL ELECTIONS

By national law all 435 seats in the House of Representatives and one-third of the seats in the United States Senate must be filled every two years in the general election, held the first Tuesday after the first Monday in November of an even numbered year. In the years when a president is elected as well, the election is called a presidential election. In the years when no president is to be elected, the elections are called off-year congressional, or midterm, elections.

House Elections

Single-Member Plurality Elections

There is a series of steps involved in electing the House of Representatives that begins long before the November election of an even numbered year. The first step actually occurs every ten years: the United States Census. As mandated by the United States Constitution, every ten years an attempt is made to get an accurate count of every person residing in this country, legal and illegal (at least according to 1992 court decisions). Since 1929, the number of seats in the House has been set at

435; so, after the census, the total number of people living in the U.S. is divided by the number of seats, 435. This will yield a number, approximately 600,000, which is the number of people to be represented by each member of the House. The 435 seats are then apportioned to each of the states on the basis of its state population. For example, a state with the population of one million would be given two seats in the House. After the 2000 census, California was allotted 53 and Alaska 1. Washington D.C. has no seats in the House. After the state is told how many seats it has in the House, it must divide its state population into that number of congressional districts, each with approximately 600,000 people. This reshuffling that occurs every ten years is known as **reapportionment**.

In November, the nation votes as 435 separate congressional districts. Each district chooses one single member on the basis of which candidate gets the most votes, a plurality (not necessarily a majority). These elections are called **single-member plurality elections**.

The Framers of the American Constitution chose the single-member system to insure that the pluralist nature of American society would be represented at the national level. Rather than adopting the European system of multi-member proportional representation in which the national popular vote is represented proportionally in a national legislature, the American system allows each small district to produce a leader to represent the dominant interest in that district. The result of such a system is that the members of the House of Representatives are usually selected because they are perceived as serving *that* district. A House member is not intended nor expected to represent the interests of the nation as a whole. As a result, voters may decide to vote for one party for the House and a different party for the presidency. During the 1980s when Republicans controlled the White House and Democrats the Congress, many believed that perhaps voters perceived the Democrats as better able to serve their particular districts' concerns and the Republicans as better able to control the executive branch of the national government. During the Clinton administration, however, exactly the reverse has been the norm: a Democrat in control of the White House with Republicans in control of both chambers of Congress. The only pattern that is apparent is that the American voters seem to prefer **divided government**.

An additional upshot of the single-member plurality system is that a party's share of the popular vote need not necessarily be reflected in the number of seats that party has in the House. In fact, Republicans have won a smaller percentage of seats than votes in every House election since 1954. Why? One reason is that in single-member plurality elections, the candidate who gets even one more vote than the other candidate or candidates wins the election. So, if in 275 districts the Democrats win by a small margin of 51 percent to the Republicans 49 percent and in the remaining 160 districts the Republican candidates win with 90 percent to the Democrats 10 percent, more votes across all 435 districts will have been cast for the various Republicans but the final House delegation will consist of 275 Democrats and only 160 Republicans.

A second reason why party representation in the House may not mirror the popular vote is that some of the congressional districts have been gerrymandered by some of the state legislatures that are responsible for the drawing of district lines. **Gerrymandering** is the drawing of state district lines to benefit the political chances of one party's candidates over the other party's. Using lists of registered voters, which include the voter's party affiliation and place of residence, the political party that controls a state legislature could be tempted to draw the district lines so that their registered voters are a majority in as many districts as possible, while the opposing party's registered voters are lumped in the remaining few districts.

The result of such gerrymandering is that the opposition party will carry only the few districts where they have been isolated. Gerrymandering effectively wastes the opposition party's votes, since the party only needs a plurality. Although gerrymandering, historically, has been done by both parties, the Democrats have been in control of most of the state legislatures for most of this century and, as a result, Republicans have born the brunt of gerrymandering. In 1986, the Supreme Court heard a case that challenged gerrymandered congressional districts in Indiana. The Court ruled for the first time that redistricting for the political benefit of one group over another can be challenged on constitutional grounds.[7]

Criticisms of the Single-Member System

Many say that the American system is the worst ever invented.[8] Mathematicians first began to take the problems with plurality seriously in the years leading up to the French Revolution. In the 1770s, Jean-Charles Borda showed that pluralities pick the most popular candidate only in two-person races. In elections involving three or more candidates, the one with the plurality might easily lose when matched up against each of the other candidates one on one.

Plurality systems, used in most U.S. elections, hand victory to the candidate with the most votes even if that candidate falls short of a majority and even if the candidate is the person the

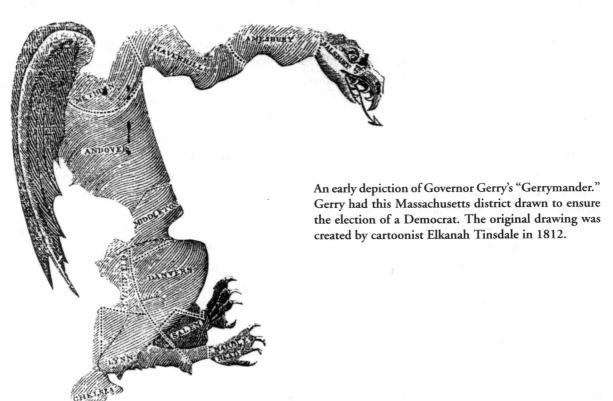

An early depiction of Governor Gerry's "Gerrymander." Gerry had this Massachusetts district drawn to ensure the election of a Democrat. The original drawing was created by cartoonist Elkanah Tinsdale in 1812.

majority likes least. The current system, then, can fail to reflect the wishes of most of the people much of the time.

In 1980, a plurality system gave conservative Republican Alfonse D'Amato a U.S. Senate seat even though two liberal candidates together had 55 percent of the vote to his 45 percent. The liberals split their votes between Republican incumbent Jacob Javits and Representative Elizabeth Holtzman, a Democrat. Almost certainly, Holtzman would have won in a run-off election, or under a different voting system. Northwestern mathematician, Donald Saari, makes the point: "Plurality is the worst because it has the highest likelihood of paradoxes. Of all the methods, it's the one where you can have the most people preferring A over B, yet B is the winner."[9]

Some are calling for a new system, approval voting. **Approval voting** allows everyone to cast one vote per candidate. A liberal voter in the 1980 New York Senate race could have, in this system, voted for Holtzman and Javits. The candidate approved of by most voters wins. Approval voting has its own problems, however. It tends to produce bland, mediocre winners who lack the sharp edges that may turn voters off.

An alternative solution would be **cumulative voting**, in which voters can pile up several votes for a single candidate they feel strongly about. Each voter would have as many votes as candidates running and distribute those votes among the candidates or give them all to one candidate. Many feel that this would give minorities more say in American elections, without creating race-based districts. Any group that has sufficient cohesion to vote as a bloc could greatly affect the outcome of an election. Cumulative voting has been around for over one hundred years and is widely used in the private sector to elect corporate boards of directors. It is also a system championed by C. Lani Guinier who was Clinton's nominee to head the civil rights branch of the Justice Department. Her nomination was withdrawn after her legal writings were criticized as *radical*.

The problem with all of these alternative plans is that since 1967, federal law has required that all states use single-member congressional districts. The law, passed in 1967, was designed to prevent minority votes from being diluted in at-large elections in Southern states. Ironically, scholars like Guinier now argue the rule actually works to impede minority representation. New legislation would be needed if change is to be made. A Washington based activist group, the Center for Voting and Democracy, has helped draft legislation recently introduced in Congress by Democratic Representative Cynthia McKinney of Georgia, an African American whose district prompted the Supreme Court ruling rejecting the use of race in drawing district lines. Her bill would permit states to experiment with alternative voting schemes.

Many who study the American system see it as the worst of all worlds. Indeed, the United States is the only democracy that gives the plurality winner all the power. And the system does so not just at the House level but at the electoral college level as well (discussed below). Robert Richie, the director of the Center for Voting and Democracy, says that "the current system is just a disaster for most voters and it's getting worse and worse."[10]

Senate Elections

Even though senators are elected by a statewide popular vote, their elections are just as likely to produce a split government, with one party in control of the Senate and another in control of the

White House. One reason is that, similar to the House, a voter may perceive his or her state's two senators to be representatives of his or her state, not the entire nation. Voters are less likely to think about national issues like foreign affairs and international trade than they are to think foremost of what a candidate can do for their state.

As in the House, incumbent members seeking re-election enjoy a significant advantage. Incumbents are known to use their office to deliver valuable goods and services to their districts, in the case of House members, and states, in the case of senators. Incumbents are prone to support pork-barrel legislation, laws that deliver the *bacon* to the district or state. Challengers have a much more difficult time of it. They can make promises, but they lack a record of delivery.

A second reason that Senate elections may produce a majority party different from that which controls the presidency is that Senate elections are staggered. Only one-third of the United States Senate is up for election in any two-year election. This results in exactly what the framers of the Constitution intended: a Senate that does not reflect the temporary passions of the moment. While the framers expected the House to be the repository of majority opinion, they designed the Senate to be a bastion to preserve the rights of minority viewpoints. While the majority may sweep the House and presidency, the Senate resists such popular tides. The result has often been divided government.

PRESIDENTIAL ELECTIONS

In contrast to both the House and Senate, the election of the president entails a two-step process.

The Electoral College

The Framers of the Constitution agreed that the president, being so singularly important, should be indirectly selected rather than directly elected by the voters. They further agreed that there would be a national body, the electoral college, that would select the president every four years. Agreement broke down, however, on the question of exactly how the states would be represented in this electoral college. Would small states have less representation or the same level of representation as the more populous states?

The final compromise created a formula for establishing representation in the electoral college. Each state gets a number of electoral college delegates, and, therefore, votes for president equal to the number of representatives that state has in the House plus an additional two for its two Senators. This formula pleases the large states because they will have a greater number of seats in the college. But it also pleases the smaller states in that a state, no matter how small its population, will have three electoral college delegates. Because the Twenty-third Amendment awards Washington, D.C. three electoral college votes, the total number in the electoral college comes to 538.

Each state legislature is designated by the Constitution to select the method of selection for electors to the electoral college. All states have written laws designating the political parties as the institutions that will in some way select the electors. The most common ways are party convention or state party committee. For example, in Kentucky, state statute says that each political party shall choose the method by which they select electors. Both the Democrats and Republicans have selected the party convention. At the party convention, each party selects the number of electors each state is constitutionally guaranteed. Only party faithfuls will be chosen, and they will only vote for the presidential candidate from their party. In Florida, the governor officially chooses the electors. However, he must choose only those electors selected by the parties' state executive committee.

Then on election day in November of a presidential year, state populations vote. Although the names of the presidential candidates appear on the ballot, voters are actually not casting a vote for a candidate. Rather, the voter is casting his or her ballot for the candidate's slate of electors. Each state's popular vote is then counted. The candidate that wins the plurality of the popular votes "carries" the state and wins all of its electoral votes. This means that all of that candidate's slate is elected to the electoral college. (There are two exceptions. In Maine two and in Nebraska three of the electoral votes are awarded by congressional district. The presidential candidate who carries each district wins a single electoral vote, and the statewide winner gets two additional electoral votes.)

In short, on the Tuesday in November, all that has transpired is the election of the 538 members of the electoral college. While the assumption is that these delegates will keep faith with the popular vote in their state, the electoral college delegates do not actually cast their ballots for president until December. At that time, the winning state slates travel to their various state capitals and cast their votes. Occasionally electors have broken from the popular vote. In 1988, for example, Margaret Leach, chosen as a Democratic elector by the voters in West Virginia, abandoned Michael Dukakis and voted instead for his running mate, Senator Lloyd Bentsen.[11] Usually, however, electors vote along the lines of their state's popular vote.

A candidate must receive a majority vote of the electoral college to become president. If none of the candidates receive these 270 votes, the presidential election is thrown to the House of Representatives. There each state delegation casts one vote, choosing between the top three candidates with the most electoral college votes. This has only happened twice, once in 1800 and again in 1824, both before the establishment of a stable two-party system.

The electoral college has several troubling aspects. The most worrisome is the possibility that the candidate who wins the most popular votes may not be elected president. This could happen if a candidate wins some states by a very large margin and loses by very narrow margins in the others. For example, if a candidate wins in the thirteen largest states with 51 percent of the vote and loses in the remaining states with only 10 percent of the vote, that candidate will become president although the other candidate would have received a greater number of popular votes. This has happened in three elections. In 1824, John Quincy Adams received fewer popular votes than Andrew Jackson. In that election, no candidate received a majority vote in the electoral college, and the House went on to choose Adams over Jackson. In 1876, Rutherford Hayes received fewer popular votes than his opponent, Samuel Tildon, but still won the presidency with 50.1 percent of the electoral college. In 1888, Grover Cleveland received 48.6 percent of the popular vote to Benjamin Harrison's 47.8 percent. Cleveland nevertheless lost to Harrison in the electoral college by a vote of 168 to 233. Most recently, in the election of 2000, George W. Bush won the presidency with 271 votes in the Electoral College even though he had fewer popular votes than his opponent Al Gore.

A second undemocratic feature of the Electoral College is that not all states require their electors to cast their votes for the candidate who won the state's popular vote. The **faithless elector** is one who casts his or her vote for a personal choice, even a candidate who was not on the ballot. While the Framers of the American Constitution wanted the Electoral College delegates to be independent, from today's perspective the faithless elector is problematic.

Another troublesome aspect of the electoral college is that it punishes third parties and their candidates. It is very difficult for a new, fledgling party to get more votes in any state than either of the two, well-established parties. It is not enough for a candidate to get votes; he has to get the most votes to get any representation in the electoral college.

This tends to breed a psychology among voters that they are throwing away their votes in voting for a third party candidate. Even more disturbing is that third parties that appeal widely across the nation, say Ross Perot's candidacy in 1992, are the most punished. Parties that have a

---

Table 6.1: Allocation of Electoral Votes based on the 2000 Census In Effect for the Elections of 2004 and 2008

Total: 538;   Majority Needed to Elect: 270

ALABAMA - 9	MONTANA - 3
ALASKA - 3	NEBRASKA - 5
ARIZONA - 10	NEVADA - 5
ARKANSAS - 6	NEW HAMPSHIRE - 4
CALIFORNIA - 55	NEW JERSEY - 15
COLORADO - 9	NEW MEXICO - 5
CONNECTICUT - 7	NEW YORK - 34
DISTRICT OF COLUMBIA - 3	NORTH CAROLINA - 15
FLORIDA - 27	NORTH DAKOTA - 3
GEORGIA - 15	OHIO - 20
HAWAII - 4	OKLAHOMA - 7
IDAHO - 4	OREGON - 7
ILLINOIS - 21	PENNSYLVANIA - 21
INDIANA - 11	RHODE ISLAND - 4
IOWA - 7	SOUTH CAROLINA - 8
KANSAS - 6	SOUTH DAKOTA - 3
KENTUCKY - 8	TENNESSEE - 11
LOUISIANA - 9	TEXAS - 34
MAINE - 4	UTAH - 5
MARYLAND - 10	VERMONT - 3
MASSACHUSETTS - 12	VIRGINIA - 13
MICHIGAN - 17	WASHINGTON - 11
MINNESOTA - 10	WEST VIRGINIA - 5
MISSISSIPPI - 6	WISCONSIN - 10
MISSOURI - 11	WYOMING - 3

Source: National Archives and Records Administration home page
URL: http://www.nara.gov /fedreg/elctcoll/vote2004.html

strong regional base, being concentrated in only certain states, like George Wallace's candidacy in 1968, have a much better chance of at least carrying a state or two and thereby receiving electoral college representation. Some might argue that in choosing a president for the *nation*, regional parties might be better discouraged than those that have a fairly wide national appeal.

Abolish the Electoral College?

Given these significant issues, some have called for the abolishment of the electoral college. There have been numerous proposals to revert to a direct, majoritarian popular vote. That none of these proposals has ever come close to adoption suggests that the electoral college does have its advantages.

To begin with, the original intent of the framers was to design a strong national government but one that allowed for state representation at the national level. In fact, there is very little evidence that the Constitution was concerned with the representation of individuals; rather, the Constitution is concerned with the representation of the dominant interest in each congressional district, in the case of the House of Representatives, and each state, in the case of the Senate and electoral college. Placed in this light, the electoral college today continues to function effectively just as the framers intended.

Another advantage of the electoral college is that it strengthens the mandate of the president. In our two-party system, most presidents have won with a fairly narrow margin of victory in the popular vote. Even in *landslides* like 1984, the president may win with only about 57 percent of the vote. The electoral college takes very narrow state margins of victory and turns them into state unanimity in the electoral college. Such amplification of the popular vote is especially important in elections like 1992 when the winning candidate may not have even won a majority of the popular vote. In 1992, Clinton received only 43 percent of the popular vote and in 2000, George Bush received fewer popular votes than Al Gore. The electoral college system, however, allowed both Clinton and Bush to say they had received a majority because, at least at the electoral college level, that was the case.

Finally, the electoral college, as noted above, strengthens the two-party system. A change in the electoral college would require a constitutional amendment. Because every existing amendment to the Constitution has been proposed by two-thirds of the House and two-thirds of the Senate, the Democrats and Republicans in Congress would have to vote to break their own lock on the presidency. This is not likely.

CAMPAIGNING IN THE GENERAL ELECTION

The Political Context

The most important structural feature of a general election is whether an incumbent is seeking re-election or whether it is an open election in which there is no incumbent running. Incumbents enjoy an enormous advantage at all levels but especially in House and Senate elections. House incumbents have historically been almost impossible to defeat, with 95 percent of them winning re-election. In the Senate, the incumbency rate is somewhat lower but still quite high. Incumbents enjoy such an advantage, at least in part, because of their ability to attract greater campaign contributions. Money is extremely important in modern campaigns.

Financing Campaigns

How Much Campaigns Cost

In 2004, over $3 billion was spent on campaigns and in the midterm elections of 2006, another $1.6 billion was spent. Campaigns have gotten dramatically more expensive with the increased reliance on the mass media and sophisticated polling technology. For example, there has been a 30 percent increase in the cost of airing a thirty-second commercial during prime time. Except for the presidential campaign in the general election, when federal government matching funds are available, all of this money must be raised by the candidates themselves. To understand where the money comes from, one must look at campaign finance regulations.

Regulating Campaign Finance

The way in which campaigns are financed in this country has changed dramatically over the last twenty-five years primarily because of changes in national campaign finance laws. Congress began to regulate campaign finance as early as the 1920s through a variety of federal corrupt practices acts. The first, passed in 1925, limited primary and general election expenses for congressional candidates. Then in the 1930s, Congress prohibited, by law, corporate and bank contributions. Then the Hatch Act (Political Activities Act) was passed in 1939 in another attempt to control political influence buying. The Hatch Act forbade contributions by government employees and individuals and companies receiving government funds, for example in the form of government contracts. In 1943, Congress went on to outlaw labor union contributions.

These early laws provided no avenue for enforcement. How could Congress know whether its laws had been violated? There was no effective way to make candidates fully disclose where they got their money or where they were spending it for that matter. The Watergate scandal of 1972 and the investigations that followed made it clear that abuse of the campaign finance system was rampant. It was discovered that large amounts of money had been illegally funneled to Nixon's committee to re-elect the president (CREEP). Congress acted quickly to prevent continued abuse of the system.

The Federal Election Campaign Act (FECA) of 1971 essentially replaced all past laws and instituted major reform. The law requires all candidates to fully disclose all contributions and expenditures in excess of $100. The effectiveness of this law was soon apparent. In 1968 before disclosure was strictly demanded, candidates reported spending $8.5 million. Only four years later, in 1972, the candidates reported to the FECA that they had spent $88.9 million.[12] The 1971 law also tried to limit the amount that each individual could spend of his own money in running for office. In *Buckley v. Valeo* the Supreme Court declared that provision of the law unconstitutional.[13]

In closing one loophole, that having to do with disclosing campaign finance information, the 1971 law opened another. The FECA said that it was permissible for corporations and labor unions to set up "separate, segregated funds . . . that could be used for a political purpose." This led to the creation of a large number of **PACs (political action committees)** that could now channel corporate, labor, and other interest group money to candidates. For a PAC to be legal, the money must be raised from at least fifty volunteer donors and must be contributed to at least five candidates in the federal election. Each corporation or each union is limited to one PAC.

In 1974, Congress passed another Federal Election Campaign Act. This law created the Federal Election Commission (FEC) to enforce compliance with the requirements of the act. Presidential candidates would be provided with public financing for the primaries and general elections if they agreed to limit their campaign expenditures to the amount prescribed by the law. In addition, the law limited individuals to campaign contributions of no more than $1,000 per candidate and a total of $25,000 in contributions in one year. Groups and PACs can contribute up to $5,000 per candidate in any election, primary and general. However, as discussed in Chapter 8, individuals and interest groups are not limited in the amount they can spend *on behalf of* a candidate. After every major attempt to regulate campaign finance, new ways to skirt the legal limits have emerged. Money in politics is like water: you squish it out of one place and it bubbles up somewhere else.

Soft Money Contributions to Political Parties

Candidates, PACs, and political parties have found ways to generate soft money, that is, campaign contributions to political parties that escape the rigid limits of federal election law. This loophole has allowed the parties to raise millions of dollars from corporations, interest groups, and individuals. As shown in Table 6.2, nearly four times as much soft money was raised in the 1999-2000 election cycle as in the 1993-1994 election cycle. The parties can spend this money on a variety of party-building activities, for example, on their conventions, for registering voters, and advertisements that promote the general party platform. The national party organizations also send a great deal of money to state and local party organizations, which then use it to support their own tickets.

Table 6.2

Soft Money Raised by Political Parties, 1994 to 2000

	1993-1994	1995-1996	1997-1998	1999-2000
Democratic Party	$45.6 million	$122.3 million	$92.8 million	$178.7 million
Republican Party	59.5 million	141.2 million	131.6 million	214.2 million
Total	105.1 million	263.5 million	224.4 million	392.9 million

In 2002, over 100 contributors gave over a $1 million to either or both of the political parties. The two largest campaign contributors to the Democratic Party were Saban entertainment, which gave a total of $10,852,000 and the American Federation of State, County, and Municipal Employees, which donated $8,851,705. The two biggest contributors to the Republicans were the National Association of Realtors with $4,126,913 and Microsoft Corporation with $3,765,105.

Independent Expenditures

Business corporations, labor unions, and other interest groups have discovered that it is legal to make **independent expenditures,** for example, on advertisements, in an election campaign if these expenditures are not coordinated with those of the candidate or political party. Although a 1990 United States Supreme Court decision, *Austin v. Michigan State Chamber of Commerce*, upheld the right of the states and the federal government to limit independent, direct corporate expenditures on behalf of the *candidates*, the decision did not stop business and other types of groups from making independent expenditures to support *issues*. In accordance with the 1976 *Buckley v. Valeo* decision, interest groups have a First Amendment right to advocate their positions. As a result, issue advocacy, especially spending unregulated money on advertising that promotes positions on issues rather than on candidates, has become an important campaign tactic in recent elections.

On Behalf Of Spending

The Supreme Court, in the 1996 case, *Colorado Republican Federal Campaign Committee v. Federal Election Commission*, ruled that political parties, interest groups, and individuals may also make independent expenditures on behalf of candidates, as long as they do so *independently* of the candidates. In other words, they may not coordinate such expenditures with the candidates' campaigns or let the candidates know the specifics of how party funds are being spent.

Another way corporations and other interest groups can maximize contributions to a candidate or party is by **bundling** their members' individual contributions together and delivering them together to the candidate or party. While these contributions will be reported to the FEC as individual donations, the candidate or party perceives them as a corporate or group contribution.

Campaign Finance Reform in 2002

In 2002, Congress approved the first major overhaul of the nation's campaign finance system in a quarter century, breaking a nearly decade-long impasse that thwarted efforts to reduce the influence of big money in American politics. The Bipartisan Campaign Reform Act (also known as McCain-Feingold) bans unrestricted soft money contributions to political parties, restricts end-of-campaign advertising by outside groups, and raises limits on direct contributions to $2,000 to a candidate, $5,000 to a PAC, and $25,000 to a political party. Corporations, unions, and other interest groups would still be allowed to pay for issue advertisements but not within 60 days before a general election and 30 days before a primary election.

New Loopholes in the Wake of the 2002 Campaign Finance Reform

Despite recent attempts to limit the flow of money into politics, campaign spending continues to skyrocket. According to the Center for Responsive Politics, the 2004 presidential and congressional campaigns collectively cost $3.9 billion, a 30 percent increase over 2000. This money is coming in through a variety of loopholes, some tried and true and some more newly minted.

Soft Money to State Political Parties

The McCain-Feingold reforms permit state party committees to continue to raise soft money and on June 22, 2002, the Federal Election Commission amended the Bipartisan Campaign Reform Act with a series of regulations that permit broader activities by state committees. One contributor alone, Steven Kirsch, gave a total of $3 million in soft money to state and candidate committees in 2000. Kirsch spread $2.1 million in six-figure chunks among nine different state Democratic Party committees, virtually all in key swing states in the 2000 presidential elections. Charles Lewis, director of the Center for Public Integrity, has said, "We have a stealth process here in the 21st century where you can't see who's doing what [at the state level]." State parties have become a largely unmonitored "back door" for vast amounts of money that do, in fact, strongly influence national elections. Not surprisingly, Steven Kirsch made an additional $1.2 million in contribution to state parties before the midterm 2002 elections.[14]

The 527 Organizations

When the Supreme Court upheld the McCain-Feingold ban on unlimited donations to political parties and other groups, so-called "soft money," it had no illusions about the difficulties faced in trying to reduce the role of money in politics. "Money, like water, will always find an outlet," wrote Justices John Paul Stevens and Sandra Day O'Connor.[15] For despite passage of the new campaign finance law in 2002, soft money is still finding a niche in elections. While the McCain-Feingold legislation approved in 2002 banned the parties from receiving unlimited contributions from unions, corporations, and individuals, the Democratic and Republican national committees together raised over $250 million by May 2004, more than what they collected during the same period in 2000 when soft money was allowed.

The soft money is now coming in through donations by independent groups, known as the 527s. These tax-exempt groups are organized under section 527 of the Internal Revenue Code to raise and disburse funds to influence the nomination, election, appointment or defeat of candidates for public office. On the face of the definition of what have become known as 527 organizations, they appear to be the same as PACs. And, in effect, a 527 is just a PAC by another name. However, there is one key difference. A 527 organization does not fall within the regulator realm of the Federal Election Commission and therefore is not subject to the same limits as the FEC regulated PACs. Unlike the PACs, the 527s are permitted to accept contributions in any amount from any source. The only requirement is that the 527 must make regular reports of its funding and expenditures to the Internal Revenue Service. These groups have stimulated federal campaign spending upwards of $3.9 billion in 2004, an increase of $900 million from 2000. Spending by 527 groups approximated $386 million in the 2004 election. The new campaign finance law did not curtail spending.

The 527s take donations and use the money to engage in a variety of campaign activities. For example, in 2004 these groups raised hundreds of millions of dollars that were then spent on attack campaign ads. In early August 2004, the Swift Boat Veterans for Truth (SBVT), an independent 527 group, launched a series of advertisements attacking Kerry's service in the Vietnam War and his anti-war protests when he had returned from that war. These veterans had served on swift boats during the Vietnam War. The first ad entitled "Any Questions?" cast doubt on Kerry's honesty about his wounds and courage in battle. The powerful advertisements drove Kerry's support downward.

Also in 2004, Representative Tom DeLay created a charity, Celebrations for Children Inc, and openly solicited funds to be used to pay for a luxury hospitality suite for big donors, a yacht cruise, VIP tickets to Broadway shows, a golf tournament, and a late-night party. For $500,000, a donor got a private dinner before and after the Democratic Convention with DeLay and congressional staff members. These functions had, before the McCain-Feingold law, been paid for out of soft money contributions. The donations now flowing to these newly created "charitable" foundations are even tax-deductible.

The 527s raise money primarily from very wealthy individuals. Their supporters include well-known billionaires like George Soros who contributed $23.7 million to the group America Coming Together. Lesser-known million-dollar donors include independent filmmaker Jeffrey Levy-Hinte, whose company Antidote Films produced such movies as "Thirteen" and "Laurel Canyon." At last count, 45 individuals have contributed a million dollars or more apiece to 527 organizations during the 2004 election cycle. Seventeen of the donors are on the Forbes list of the 400 richest people in America. Together, million dollar donors contributed about $617 million to the 2004 presidential campaign.

Issue-Related Advertisements

Finally, the most controversial provisions of the new campaign finance law have to do with the law's prohibition of issue-related advertisement that refers to any federal politician within 30 days of a primary election and 60 days of a general election.

The law's ban on last minute ads *only applies to corporations.* While many nonprofit "advocacy" groups, such as the Sierra Club and the ACLU, are corporations, they do not have to be. It is perfectly possible to form an unincorporated association and still get nonprofit tax status. If you are not incorporated, the law's ban on ads does not apply.

In 2006, unions, corporations, and wealthy individuals, pumping nearly $300 million into the unregulated 527 groups, funded dozens of aggressive and sometimes shadowy campaigns independent of the party organizations. The groups, both liberal and conservative, aired numerous TV and radio spots, all with no oversight by the Federal Election Commission. In 2006, by far the largest chunk of unregulated money came straight out of union treasuries and was used mostly to benefit Democrats. But conservatives fought back with multimillion-dollar donations. For example, in California, unregulated funds, mostly donated by New York developer Howard S. Rich, bankrolled an aggressive ad campaign for Proposition 90, which would limit the government's ability to seize private property. In Missouri, such money paid for a celebrity-studded TV ad opposing a ballot initiative on stem-cell research. In Ohio, a 527 ran some of the most provocative radio spots of the campaign season with an African American announcer accusing Democrats of "decimating our people" by promoting abortions of "black babies."[16]

Effects of the American Campaign Finance System

The Incumbency Advantage

More than 98 percent of House incumbents were re-elected in 2004, with most of them befitting from a huge fundraising advantage over their challengers. House incumbents had a more than 4-to-1 financial advantage over their challengers, with more than $391.7 million in campaign resources compared to $73.2 million for challengers. Incumbents have an even greater advantage in special-interest PAC fundraising, raising eight times the amount given to challengers. As Table 6.3 reveals, incumbents continued to enjoy a financial advantage in 2006.

Table 6.3

2006 Incumbency Financial Advantage

Senate

Type of Candidate	Total Raised	Number of Candidates	Average Raised
Incumbent	$350,097,220	31	$11,293,459
Challenger	$182,041,858	101	$1,802,395
Open Seat	$99,418,556	35	$2,840,530
Grand Total	$631,557,634	167	$3,781,782

House

Type of Candidate	Total Raised	Number of Candidates	Average Raised
Incumbent	$532,918,908	424	$1,256,884
Challenger	$175,465,632	627	$279,849
Open Seat	$153,100,297	265	$577,737
Grand Total	$861,484,837	1,316	$654,624

Based on data released by the FEC on Monday, December 18, 2006.

http://www.opensecrets.org/overview/incumbs.asp?cycle=2006

Selling Access and Influence

Americans have long worried that campaign contributions are a way for powerful individuals and groups to buy access to policy makers and to influence the policy making process. Concern with such influence peddling reached a crescendo immediately following the 1996 presidential election. President Clinton and the Democratic National Committee were heavily criticized for a series of 103 coffee klatches in the White House Map Room that were held for business executives and other supporters who had given over $27 million to the Democratic National Committee in 1995 and 1996. Revelations of these coffee klatches were soon followed by stories of well-healed donors who had spent the night at the White House apparently as a thank you for generous campaign contributions. The total amount of money contributed by those invited for the overnights is still not known but a partial guest list included Hollywood moguls Steven Spielberg and Lew Wasserman, who gave $300,000 and $335,000 to the Democratic National Committee. All total, close to nine hundred campaign contributors stayed overnight at the White House, many sleeping in the Lincoln Bedroom. Charles Lewis, executive director of Citizens for Public Integrity, an independent watchdog group with expertise in campaign finance, said: "Those numbers are staggering. It should be alarming to the American people that the president of the United States was using the national symbol of our democracy as a way station for fat-cat donors like a Holiday Inn or Motel 6."[17]

There is also evidence that campaign contributions allow powerful groups to influence public policy making. Airline interests, which successfully stopped efforts to pass a "Passenger Bill of Rights," gave more than $11 million in PAC and soft money contributions to federal candidates and the political parties from 1989 through June 30, 1999. Then, as momentum in Congress to pass a rights bill grew in 1999, airlines contributed an additional $1.3 million to parties and candidates during the first six months of the year. As a crucial committee vote on the passenger rights bill approached in June 1999, airlines delivered more than $131,000 in soft money contributions during the six days immediately preceding the vote and another $95,000 on the day of the vote. American Airlines alone gave $135,000 during that period, including $50,000 on the day of the vote.[18]

A Weakening of the Public Finance System

As campaign money flows in from individuals, corporations, and interest groups, the public financing system is faltering. The public financing program offers presidential candidates a monthly taxpayer-financed match of up to $250 for each private contribution they raise during the primary season, up to total grants of approximately $18.6 million. To qualify, candidates must raise at least $5,000 in each of twenty states and abide by other requirements, including overall, state-by-state, and personal spending limits. In 2004, almost all of the major candidates opted out of public financing in the primaries, freeing them to spend unlimited amounts. Howard Dean, one of the contenders for his party's nomination, was the first Democrat in history to forgo the taxpayer-financed system that encourages small donations by matching them with federal funds, freeing him to exceed the $45 million spending cap that comes with the public money. Dean said that he was forced to opt out to compete with President Bush who had already said that he would forgo matching funds and that he was aiming to raise at least $175 million before the Republican Convention. John Kerry also opted out because he intended to exceed the $50,000 personal spending limit imposed on candidates who accept public funds.

Increased Number of Personally Wealthy Candidates

The faltering of the public finance system is related to another effect of campaign finance laws is that candidates who are either personally wealthy or who can appeal to many small donors by mass mailings and television will have an advantage. A candidate with only modest means and little television appeal will find it much more difficult to raise the money needed to finance a campaign. Recent campaigns have seen very wealthy candidates spend considerable amounts of their own money running for office. Senator John Kerry boasts a family wealth in excess of $700 million. Senator Edward Kennedy has reported $8 million to $40 million in family trust funds, and Senator John D. Rockefeller has reported three trusts exceeding $80 million in value. Senator Jon Corzine of New Jersey reports holdings including $25 million to $50 million in stock in The Goldman Sachs Group plus a tax-free fund worth another $25 million to $90 million and the family of Senate Majority Leader Bill Frist started what is now HCA Inc., the country's biggest chain of for-profit hospitals. He lists assets including one blind trust of $5 million to $25 million, and two others worth $1 million to $5 million. To counter this trend, the Federal Election Commission in November 2002 agreed to let candidates pay themselves salaries using campaign donations. The aim is to encourage people who otherwise could not afford to give up their jobs to run and to scale back some of the advantages of incumbency.

Raising Campaign Money: A Distraction

Candidates are now forced to spend considerably greater amounts of time raising money. Particularly in congressional campaigns, which have no public funding, candidates must meet with many groups and many individuals to raise the money for a campaign. Insofar as many candidates for Congress are incumbent members of Congress themselves, these fund raising activities constitute a significant distraction from legislative duties. Additionally, because fund raising activities are so demanding on a politician's time and energy, candidates are increasingly finding it more efficient to stay in the nation's capital, working the fund raising party circuit. This means that trips home to their districts or states are made less frequently and constituents have, as a result, fewer opportunities to see their representatives. Such a focus on fund raising inside the belt of Washington, D.C., may work to insulate the politicians from the very constituents they seek to serve.

Abuse and Scandals: The Case of Enron

In just 15 years, Enron grew from nowhere to be America's seventh largest company, employing 21,000 staff in more than 40 countries. The firm's success, however, turned out to be an elaborate scam. Enron lied about its profits and stands accused of a range of shady dealings, including concealing debts so that they did not show up in the company's accounts. Enron executives lied about the profitability of the company and encouraged their employees to buy stock even as they themselves sold their stock knowing that it was inflated and would soon fall, which it did. While the executives sold their stock at its high, walking away with millions in stock profits, the Enron employees lost billions because their pensions were heavily invested in Enron's own stock. In December 2002, the company filed bankruptcy taking with it the lifetime savings of its employees and other investors.

A chorus of outraged investors, employees, pension holders, and politicians are demanding to know why Enron's failings were not spotted earlier. As the investigation unfolded in 2003, two principle culprits have been identified: a corrupt campaign finance system and an intricate web of relationships built up between the business community and politicians.

The Enron scandal has illustrated how widely the taint of large campaign contributions has spread. Enron spent a total of $5.8 million on federal elections over the past 12 years, 73 percent of the money going to Republicans. The company's donations went to 71 out of the 100 senators and 188 out of the 435 House members.

While hefty campaign contributions were forging a close working relationship between the Bush administration and Enron, other ties were also being developed. Fourteen top Bush administration officials held stock in Enron. Karl Rove, the president's senior adviser, listed more than $250,000 worth of Enron stock. Peter Fisher, the undersecretary of commerce who received more than a half-dozen phone calls from Enron executives in the months before the company's collapse, owned equities in the company as well. Additionally, Enron alumni fill prominent positions in the current Bush administration. The CEO of Enron, Kenneth Lay, worked for the Bush administration screening potential appointees to the Federal Regulatory Commission. President Bush's most prominent economic advisor, Larry Lindsey, and his point man on trade issues, Robert Zoelick, both served as Enron advisors. Secretary of the Army Thomas White was an Enron executive before joining the administration. So much influence did Enron wield with the Bush administration that Kenneth Lay could tell Curtis Herbert Jr., chairman of the Federal Energy Regulatory Commission, that he would be reappointed if he changed his views on electricity regulation. Mr. Herbert did not, and he was not.

The question at the center of the U. S. political stage now is what Enron got in return for its investment in politics. It appears that the campaign donations and close personal ties between Enron and government worked to insulate Enron from government attempts to regulate business dealings and allowed Enron to falsely conceal some of its debts. In 2002, Enron executives held a total of six meetings with Vice President Dick Cheney and his staff, who were responsible for the drawing up of one of the administration's most important initiatives, the energy plan, which advocates expansion and deregulation of U. S. production, including the opening up of the Arctic National Wildlife Refuge for oil drilling.

Enron is not unique in the annals of lobbyist interests prevailing over the public interest. From contracts for unneeded weapons to a banana trade war, the decisions often tend to come out in favor of the big campaign contributors. What makes the Enron case different is the drama of the huge implosion in full view of thousands of victimized employees and investors. As one journalist has written: "Enron's woes aren't really a scandal at all—instead they're a magnifying glass allowing us to see clearly exactly how government and business operate today."[19]

Many are calling for a congressional investigation into the links between Enron and a lax regulatory system that allowed the collapse of Enron to occur. But Enron's political contributions and political ties to those in high position are so extensive that finding anyone to investigate may be extremely difficult. To avoid any potential conflicts of interest, many public officials, including at least two federal judges, the Texas state attorney general, and the U. S. attorney general have recused themselves from Enron investigations. On the congressional side, it is virtually impossible to find a member who has not taken an Enron contribution. The House Commerce committee's investigation into Enron is expected to be one of the most far-reaching. But both the committee Chairman Representative Billy Tauzin, R-La., and the ranking Democratic member John Dingell of Michigan reported hefty contributions from Enron.

CAMPAIGN STRATEGIES AND TACTICS

Polling

A good place for any candidate to begin his campaign is with an identification of the electorate's concerns. To do this, candidates have in modern times increasingly turned to pollsters and political consultants.

Well-funded candidates may begin with focus groups. These groups usually consist of ten to twenty people selected because they are representative of certain groups that a candidate particularly wants to target in his campaign. These small focus groups, questioned at great length and depth, provide a way to identify the values and issue preferences of likely voters. Often a candidate's campaign consultants will then formulate "soundbites" on the basis of statements made in these focus group sessions. For example, in 1988, a focus group in Massachusetts repeatedly mentioned Willie Horton, a felon who had been given a furlough from prison during which he again committed a brutal crime. The Bush campaign used the furlough issue against Massachusetts Governor Michael Dukakis in the 1988 presidential campaign.

While focus groups are most useful in the early stages of the campaign, helping candidates identify issues of concern, other types of polls become more important as the campaign moves forward. A trend poll, for example, may be used to determine how well the candidate is doing and in what parts of the nation or state or district. In early October, tracking polls, using quick phone interviews of people on a daily basis, are used to make critical decisions about where the candidate should go and what he should try to convey.

Making the News

While polling helps the candidate tailor his message to the interests of the public, the candidate must also tailor his message to the needs of the news organizations. News values emphasize the dramatic, the conflict-laden, and the brief. Television, in particular, sees no value in airing long-winded statements by the candidates. Furthermore, most Americans have little interest in hearing them. Even newspaper readers are unlikely to read beyond the first paragraph of a story. As a result, candidates need to learn to speak in soundbites which are easily understood. They should be no longer than thirty seconds and preferably as short as ten seconds in length.

Candidate control of the soundbite is particularly important. If the candidate fails to set the *lead* for the story, the journalist may do so and may do so in a manner much less sympathetic to the candidate than the candidate would be to himself. One study has found that while visuals of the candidate are being aired, the news commentators voice overs are not as positive as the visuals themselves.[20]

Candidates also need to be concerned with news deadlines. It does little good for a candidate to make a major policy statement at 8:00 in the evening, too late for the national evening news, too stale for the next morning's breaking news. In fact, it may not be worth the candidate's trouble to make a policy statement at all. Given the media's preoccupation with image and the horserace aspects of a campaign, the candidate might be better to talk in generalities with good visuals running in the background.

The Tabloids

In 1992, the Twentieth Century Fund studied television coverage of that year's presidential campaign. They discovered the ascension of what they called the "new news." The new news consists of network morning shows, call-in talk shows, often with studio audiences, and other shows like *Larry King Live*, *MTV*, and *Oprah*. These tabloid shows allow the candidates to bypass the established press.[21]

In 1992, all three presidential candidates worked the tabloid talk circuit. Bill Clinton started the trend in January 1992 when he appeared on *60 Minutes* to dispel rumors of his alleged extramarital affair with Gennifer Flowers. In February, Ross Perot took to the *Larry King Live* to announce his candidacy. Gerry Brown, former Governor of California, appeared on the *Phil Donahue Show* where he fielded questions about his romantic relationship with singer Linda Ronstadt. One researcher has found that there were thirty-nine separate instances of presidential candidates appearing on tabloid programs between September 1 and October 19.[22]

Advertising

Studies of recent campaigns have found that most voters get their campaign information not from the news but rather from advertisements.[23] As will be discussed in Chapter 7, the increased sophistication of broadcast technology coupled with the use of multimodal techniques (for example, use of visuals and music) have enhanced the power of advertisements in molding public opinion.

Today, House candidates spend about 25 percent of their campaign budgets on advertising, and Senate candidates spend about 35 percent of theirs.[24] In the 2004 presidential election, George Bush and John Kerry spent approximately 60 percent of their budgets on advertising. From March through May 2004, the Bush campaign produced 17 commercials that together ran an estimated 70,000 times on local broadcasts in the campaign's most closely contested states and on national cable television. About 70 percent of the spots were critical of Kerry.[25] For example, the 30-second "Wacky" ad took a carnival tone as it played newsreel-like footage of the Keystone Kops and antique gas pumps to accuse Kerry of supporting higher gasoline prices. Polls suggested that these negative attack ads apparently worked in 2004. The University of Pennsylvania's National Annenberg Election Survey reported that voters in 18 states where the ads appeared the most viewed Kerry in a less favorable light.[26]

As the Democratic and Republican campaigns pounded each other through television commercials in 2004, some party strategists began to look beyond television and radio audiences to a whole new generation of Web surfers. Online industry experts have estimated that politicians spent over $25 million in 2004 on online ads in federal, state, and local campaigns. While that is a tiny fraction of the $1.3 billion that went to television, several factors point to an increasing role for online ads. The 2003 McCain-Feingold campaign finance reform law placed sharp limits on using campaign donations to pay for broadcast TV and radio ads, especially in the two months before an election. But the law was silent on the use of large checks from corporations, unions, and wealthy individuals, contributions known as "soft money," to finance Internet ads.

One of the newest and most effective political uses of the Web came from the 2004 Bush-Cheney campaign, which e-mailed six million supporters a link to an online ad portraying John Kerry as beholden to special interests. Aside from production costs for the ad, the ploy cost next to nothing. Yet it not only got the message in front of a million people, it led to the TV networks carrying long segments of the commercial. The Republican National Committee also placed banner and pop-up ads on about 1,400 sites starting March 19, 2004, attacking the Democratic nominee John Kerry for his vote against spending $87 billion for military operations and reconstruction of Iraq and Afghanistan. Several Democratic presidential contenders also experimented with online ads in 2004. Senator John Edwards promoted his advocacy of abortion rights and clean air in October 2004 on several websites, including WashingtonPost.com and CNN.com.[27]

The increased importance of advertising, especially negative advertising, and soundbite news coverage of campaigns may be related to recent trends in voting behavior. Recent elections have seen fewer people turning out to vote and a heightened level of indecision on the part of those who do vote. Voters appear to be making up their minds later in the campaign and, even when voting, express hesitancy and a lack of enthusiasm.

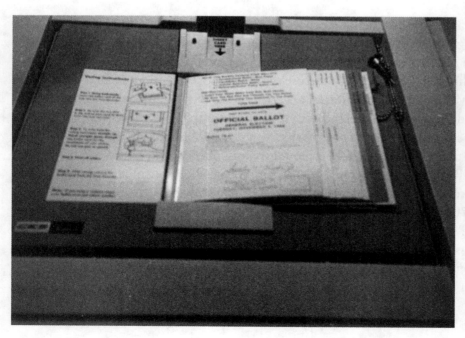

A typical punch type voting machine stands ready for the next voter. The voter merely needs to slip the ballot in at the top, turn the pages and punch out the designated spots with the attached pin.

Internet and High Tech Campaigning

In addition to online ads, campaigns are increasingly using e-mail to communicate with activists and raise money. In 2004, blogs, which are personal, frequently updated Web pages that typically contain short essays on a particular topic, played a significant role. During the 2004 presidential campaign, Howard Dean blazed the trail of electronic campaigning through his use of these Web blogs and aggressive use of online fundraising helped transform the obscure former Vermont governor into a frontrunner for the Democratic nomination.

The importance of the Internet in American campaigns is likely to grow in the future. More than 121 million American adults now use the Internet, according to Nielsen/Netratings. Additionally, Web users are more likely to vote and to show an interest in politics.[28] Today, every candidate has a blog and new blogs are being added daily. They are becoming an alternative news universe, giving everyone with a PC and a Web connection access to the sorts of political gossip that was once available only to reporters on the campaign press bus.

The Mechanics of Elections

The presidential election of 2000 will no doubt go down in history as one of the strangest. While it was the most expensive campaign in history, costing an almost unimaginable $1 billion, it produced no clear victor.

Hanging Chads, Pregnant Chads

In 2000, thousands of potentially valid votes were lost because ballot designs were confusing, counting methods were inconsistent, and, in some cases, election officials never looked at ballots that were rejected by machines. On more than 1700 ballots in Florida, the voters' choice for president was clear, but the ballot was rejected nonetheless. In an additional 5000 cases in Florida, voters' mistakes, apparently caused by confusing ballot design, made it impossible to determine the voters' intent.

The confusion surrounding the 2000 election outcome highlights an important but often ignored aspect of the American electoral process: state law and local policies determine the mechanics of elections, even national presidential elections. The Constitution gives the power to regulate elections to the states as part of the federal structure. In some parts of the country, votes are cast on automatic voting machines; in other places, paper ballots are used. Still other jurisdictions require voters to bubble in their choice. Finally, many voters vote by punching their vote on the punch cards that were the center of the controversy in the state of Florida in 2000.

The butterfly ballot, a form of the punch card, caused much confusion for voters in Palm Beach County, Florida. The county selected this ballot, not the state government or the national party organization. A butterfly ballot has the candidates' names on both sides of a vertical role of punch holes rather than on only one side. The odd format of the ballot made it difficult for the Palm Beach voters to determine which punch hole corresponded to which candidate. The butterfly ballot was used only in Palm Beach County. It is estimated that over three thousand votes were cast mistakenly in the county for Patrick Buchanan. The punch hole registering a vote for Buchanan was to the right of Gore's name on the ballot, leading some voters to punch it rather than the next hole. Other voters said they mistakenly voted for Buchanan, realized it, and then punched another hole for Gore. These ballots were all held invalid.

The question of whether votes should be recounted and, if so, how also emerged in 2000. Florida law mandated a recount because the state vote was so close. The first recount simply counted the ballots the same way they had been counted the first time with punch cards run through a counting machine. That recount registered several hundred more votes for Gore state-wide. Democratic voters in several punch card counties then called for a hand recount, claiming that machines fail to read *partially* punched holes, holes with the tiny piece of paper, called a chad, still hanging by one or more of its corners. Additionally, machines fail to read the voters' intent when the hole is not punched out at all but rather only indented, called a pregnant chad.

The election of 2000 has made it clear that voting in the United States is plagued with difficulties. A voting system even less reliable than the punch cards is the optical scanning system used in 15 of Florida's 67 counties and in many other states as well. That system in which ovals on paper ballots are filled in by pencil and scanned at a central county office resulted in 5.7 percent of all ballots being rejected and, therefore, not counted. The ballots, which were easy to examine with the naked eye, revealed a wide variety of problems. Florida election officials threw out 962 ballots on which voters penciled in the oval for Gore or Bush but also wrote the name of the candidate in the space labeled "Write-in candidate." In more than 100 cases, clear votes for Gore or Bush went uncounted because voters used pens rather than pencils. In 244 cases, ballots were rejected because voters tried to erase mistakes. On the other hand, in Bradford County, Florida, voters who made mistakes were given white stickers to place over their errors. When voters used more than one sticker, the counting machine threw them out. In 14 of the 15 counties, the ballot split the presidential candidates into two columns. In those counties, 4,268 voters mistakenly chose Bush or Gore in column one and another presidential candidate from the second column, which listed minor party candidates that a voter could have thought were running for other offices.[29.]

These mechanics have become the subject of fierce debates and litigation. The election laws of some states, including Texas' election law signed by then Governor George Bush, have standards for counting punch card ballots that allow hanging and pregnant chads to be counted. Florida, however, has no such law specifying how such ballots are to be counted. As a result, the Bush campaign sued in federal and state court to try to prevent the hand count in Florida. They were successful, with the Supreme Court of the United States agreeing that since there were no clear standards for a recount, the recount should not be done.

The mechanics of American elections have continued to be a subject of fierce debate and litigation following the election of 2004. In the state of Ohio, for example, the security of voting machines was called into question after a machine in Gahanna Ward at the New Life Church recorded 4258 votes for President Bush when only a total of 638 voters cast ballots and another machine in one precinct in Youngstown, Ohio, recorded a *negative* 25 million votes. There were other problems including the fact that voters in Franklin County, Ohio, had to wait five or six hours in order to vote.

POLITICAL PARTICIPATION IN ELECTIONS: THE WAXING AND WANING OF THE AMERICAN ELECTORATE

The Waxing of the American Electorate

At the time the Constitution was ratified, the right to vote was limited to taxpayers or property owners. By the administration of President Andrew Jackson (1829-1837), almost all of the states had extended the right to vote to all white males. Then after the Civil War and the Fifteenth Amendment, African Americans were given the constitutional right to vote. The Southern states, however, continued to find ways to disenfranchise Southern African Americans. Between 1915 and 1944, the Supreme Court overturned some of the most discriminatory of the rules: the poll tax (requiring payment to vote) and the grandfather clause (you could vote if your grandfather had had the right to vote). Still, a small proportion of Southern African Americans actually registered and voted.

It was not until the passage of the Voting Rights Act in 1965 that African-American participation in Southern elections would increase dramatically. This law suspended literacy tests and authorized the appointment of federal examiners who could order the registration of African Americans in states and counties where fewer than 50 percent of the voting-age population registered or had voted in the previous presidential election. The law also included criminal penalties for interfering with the right to vote. Additional efforts by Jesse Jackson have helped increase the voter registration among African Americans.

Though women were allowed to vote in some state elections, it was not until the Nineteenth Amendment in 1920 that women's suffrage was extended across the entire nation, doubling the size of the electorate. Then, the Twenty-sixth Amendment, ratified in 1971, gave the right to vote to eighteen-year-olds. Given these changes, the United States now has the widest voting rights of any country in the world.

The Waning of the American Electorate

Given this history of safeguarding and extending the right to vote, one would think that participation in elections would have risen over time. In fact, a smaller percentage of people vote today than in the latter part of the nineteenth century. Some argue that this decline is more apparent than real. Until the early twentieth century, voter fraud, for example, ballot-box stuffing, was common.[30] Also, the Australian ballot was introduced at the turn of the century. This ballot was to be cast in secret in private booths. This change also helped to reduce fraudulent voting.

Voter fraud, however, cannot explain the recent decline in voting turnout. Less than 40 percent of eligible Americans cast a vote in 2002 and less than 1 in 3 adults voted for the U.S. House member who represents their district. A recent study by the Institute for Democracy and Electoral Assistance found that in national elections since World War II, the United States ranks 103rd in voter participation out of 131 democracies.[31]

Explaining Turnout

While there are many reasons for not voting, one that appears common to all nonvoters is that politics offers few rewards and may exact some hardships. One must register to vote, read a long ballot and make sense of it, leave work to go vote, and even wait in lines to vote. All of this to cast a ballot that will surely not, in and of itself, effect the outcome of an election.

The people most likely to vote, then, tend to be people that have ways to reduce the costs of participating and/or increase the perceived benefits. Clear party differences, education, and family socialization of civic duty are all factors that can work to reduce the burden of voting. In countries with strong parties with clear ideological differences, voters may have an easier time making sense of the choices offered to them. The American parties are weak in comparison, often expressing similar policy positions. In such a weak party system environment, it is little wonder that many voters fail to perceive the significance of casting a ballot for one candidate over the other. While strong parties are one way to reduce the costs of voting, education is certainly another. People who are educated are in a much better position to process the ballot and understand the relevance of the choices being offered. Finally, coming from a family that has instilled a strong sense of civic duty is important as a motivating force.

Family socialization experiences may also work to clarify the rewards of voting. Some children grow up in an environment that stresses the importance of voting and the significance of the right to vote. Additionally, wealth and property ownership are tied to a person's ability to perceive that they have an immediate stake in the outcome of elections. People who own homes, have children in the school system, and who are paying income taxes are more likely to see that elections are important to their lifestyle and well being.

An additional reason for low voter turnout may be the lack of competition in congressional elections. Consider a few examples from the 2002 elections. First, the average victory margin in U.S. House races was 40 percent, meaning winners on average won more than 70 percent of the votes cast in their race. Fewer than 1 in 10 races were won by competitive margins of less than 10 percent. Second, 77 percent of House races are won in a landslide, defined as winning by at least 20 percent. Third, 99 percent of incumbents were re-elected, and two-thirds of them won their last two elections in landslides.

The non-competitiveness of congressional elections has contributed to an ongoing decline in voter participation. The states with the least competitive elections, heavily centered in the South, also have the lowest voter turnout. Obviously when powerful incumbents are faced with little or no challenge, they will not conduct the kind of energetic campaigns that might get voters to the polls.

The non-competitiveness of American electoral politics is due to several of the electoral features discussed in this chapter. The winner-take-all quality of single-member plurality elections amplifies the electoral power of the winner while discouraging voters of the opposition party in the district. Additionally, partisan methods of redistricting after every census allow state legislators to draw safe districts. The manner in which legislative districts are drawn is the single most powerful factor in who wins and loses legislative elections. In essence, the state legislators are choosing their constituents before the constituents choose them.

Increasing Turnout

From the above discussion it should be clear that turnout can be increased by reducing the cost, or the burden, of voting. In the United States the entire burden of registering to vote falls on the citizens. In most European nations, on the other hand, registration is done for you automatically by the government. Some states have moved to make registration easier. In some, people may register on the same day and at the same time as they vote. In 1993, Congress also took steps to simplify registration. The motor-voter bill requires states to allow people to register to vote when applying for a driver's license, at various state offices, and by mail. Of course, easing registration will not necessarily increase turnout. Voting itself may impose burdens. Elections, for example, are held on Tuesdays, a work day for most. In recent elections, a greater number of Americans used absentee ballots, which allowed the voter to fill out the ballot and mail it in by a certain date. Some states are also trying to reduce the "costs" of voting by providing an early voting period that includes the weekend.[32]

Turnout will also increase if more people see the benefits that flow from their participation. People who perceive an immediate stake in the outcome of an election are more likely to vote. Such a perception is more likely to develop as people increase their level of political literacy. Advertising campaigns to get out the vote, for example MTV's *Rock the Vote* campaign, may increase the perception that elections are important. Revitalized political parties, with clear platforms and re-invigorated methods to mobilize voters, could certainly also contribute to a renewed voter enthusiasm with the electoral process.

THE VOTERS: EXPLAINING VOTE CHOICE

In casting their ballots, voters are influenced by both long and short-term factors. A particular election does not exist in a vacuum. Voters bring with them a set of personal characteristics and a history of experiences with past candidates and issues. The current campaign then plays upon the stage of pre-existing ties. These predispositions, for many voters, are summarized by their partisan identification, a long-term attachment to one of the political parties. This party identification may be thought of as an anchor sunk in the past. A current campaign with its short-term forces of candidates and current issues may produce waves and swells that either may or may not be able to dislodge the partisan anchor.

Long-Term Forces: Group and Party Identification

Party identification is a general, long-term, psychological attachment to a political party. Early studies in the 1940s and 1950s found that most people expressed a long-term attachment to one or the other of the two political parties. Researchers found, furthermore, that these attachments were very stable over time, so stable that one could actually describe a social group profile for each party. What this means is that each of the parties was a coalition of groups that had, for relatively long periods, been tied to it. For example, upper-middle class Protestant voters have tended to call themselves Republican since the late 1800s, while Catholics, Jews, and other newer immigrant groups have disproportionately been tied to the Democratic Party. Loyalty to a party was, then, cemented by a larger group tie to the party, a tie passed down from one generation to another.

The early studies of voting behavior also found that this group identification with a party was an important determinant of the vote. About 40 percent of voters, in these early polls, would say that they had made up their mind for whom they would vote before the election campaign even began; and this intention was usually consistent with their party identification. Furthermore, on election day voters in the 1950s tended to cast a vote consistent with their long-term partisan identification, and over 60 percent even voted a straight ticket, remaining loyal to their party across national, state, and local offices.[33]

Today, the long-term ties to the political parties seem to be weakening. In 2004, for example, only 30 percent said that they had made up their minds before the campaign began and 44 percent said they would not decide until after the debates. Voters also exhibit greater volatility, often defecting from partisanship when casting their ballots. Since the middle of the 1960s, over 60 percent split their ticket, switching their votes from party to party.[34]

The greater amount of indecision evidenced in recent elections should not lead to the assumption that party identification is no longer an important determinant of vote choice for many individuals and groups in the electorate. In fact, 77 percent of those who called themselves Democrats actually voted for Kerry in November 2004. Seventy-three percent of the Republicans voted for Bush.

While party identification is, therefore, a strong determinant of the vote, there is some defection from this partisan identification. These defections, together with the vote decision of those who express no partisan predisposition (about 25 percent of the population) can be explained by short-term forces associated with a current campaign, its candidates, and issues.

Short-Term Forces: Issues and Candidate Image

Issues

Issues can be important determinants of vote choice. Some people may make a prospective vote decision, identifying the candidates' positions and determining which candidate is likely to serve the interests of the voters. Other members of the electorate may vote retrospectively, evaluating the current office holders and voting to reward or punish that office holder on the basis of his/her record in office. In general, studies have found that retrospective voting is much less demanding and, therefore, more likely to be the way in which voters use issues in voting.

Of all the issues that are likely to drive short-term electoral forces as well as defections from partisanship, the state of the economy is by far the most important. Studies have shown, however, that the voter's *perception* of the economy as a whole may be more important than the *actual* state of the voter's own pocketbook or for that matter the *actual* state of the economy itself.

In 2004, objective indicators suggested that the economy was rebounding after the slow economic growth after 2000. Inflation and interest rates were low, and the nation was not experiencing negative economic growth. President Bush repeatedly tried to make this argument on news programs throughout the fall campaign period. His message did not get through. Over half of the voters thought the nation as a whole had serious economic problems and John Kerry benefitted from these perceptions, getting the vote of 61 percent of these people as compared to bush's 39 percent.[35]

Issues other than economic may also be important. Immigration, crime, abortion, family values, and affirmative action have all recently played an important role in campaign politics. For example, the issue of gay marriage was extremely important in the 2004 election and in 2006, the War in Iraq was of paramount concern to voters. A *New York Times/CBS News* poll conducted just days ahead of the election confirmed that the handling of the War in Iraq was the most important issue in the 2006 midterm elections. It showed that only 29 percent of Americans approved of the Bush administration's handling of the Iraq war. The war was also considered the most important issue affecting their vote.[36]

Candidate Image

Studies have consistently found that candidate image is more important than the issue positions of the candidates. Even when the issues are very clear and the candidates stake out very different positions, for example in the election of 2004, image is still more closely related to vote choice than issues.[37]

While character issues have always been important in American campaigns, they seem to be becoming more central to the vote decision. In recent elections, character issues have been extremely important: Clinton's alleged extramarital affairs, his avoidance, while a college student, of the draft during the Vietnam War, his visit to the Soviet Union, and use of marijuana. Character issues need not always be negative. Leadership, honesty, and decisiveness are also characteristics that voters consider in selecting a candidate. Arthur Miller, in fact, found that along with concern about the deficit, the candidate's level of *caring* were the two strongest predictors of the vote.[38]

THE ELECTION OF 2004

In 2004, a majority of American voters rehired the 43rd president of the United States, George Bush, giving him 51 percent of the national vote and 286 Electoral College votes to his opponent, John Kerry, 48 percent of the national vote and 252 Electoral College votes. An understanding of the various structural features of American politics discussed in this chapter helps explain President Bush's victory.

Reelection campaigns are almost always won by the incumbent. In addition, incumbent presidents who have enjoyed a job approval rate of over 50 percent have never lost reelection. Bill Clinton had a 54 percent rating in 1996 and Ronald Reagan had a 59 percent job approval rating in 1984. On the other hand, George H. W. Bush, the 41st president of the United States and father of the current president, lost his bid for reelection with a presidential job approval rating that was around 40 percent the entire year before the election of 1992. According to the exit polls conducted on Election Day, November 2, 2004, 53 percent of voters approved of President Bush's handling of the presidency. Not surprisingly, then, he won the election even though John Kerry had mounted a strong and well-funded challenge.

Second, campaigns are usually won by the biggest spender. While John Kerry's campaign raised a record-breaking $50 million in the first three months of 2004, more than any candidate has ever raised in a single quarter, it was still less than the amount raised by the Bush campaign. Over the entire campaign, President Bush spent $210 million and John Kerry $120 million. These sums do not include the $150 million in public funds, $100 million spent by the parties for their conventions, the over $125 million spent by independent groups, and the hundreds of millions of dollars spent by the PACs.

A third structural feature that helped carry President Bush to a second term was a primary system that worked to President Bush's advantage. Following the 2002 midterm congressional elections, which gave the Republicans solid control of both the House and Senate, and the swift defeat of Iraq in April 2003, the president enjoyed a 71 percent job approval and, as a result, he stood unchallenged for his party's nomination. The Democratic nomination process, on the other hand, turned into a bruising battle that left John Kerry with scars he would be forced to carry into the general election campaign. Six major Democrats vied for the nomination: Senator John Kerry, Senator John Edwards, former Governor John Dean, House Minority Leader, Representative Richard Gephardt, Senator Joseph Lieberman, and former NATO commander Wesley Clark. While the Republicans stood united behind the president, the six Democrats engaged in internecine warfare as they fought their cases through the primary elections. Such primary battles tend to leave both the party and the eventually nominated candidate in a weaker position than a party that has stood united behind their single candidate.

Finally, while the long term structural aspects of American politics are extremely important in every election, there are also short term factors that provide the more immediate context of the election. In 2004, the incumbent president benefited from the absence of any single issue dominating voters' decision making. While 22 percent of voters cited moral values as influential, 20 percent mentioned the economy, 19 percent terrorism, and 15 percent Iraq, no issue was overwhelmingly salient for a majority of voters. The lack of a dominant issue in a campaign benefits the incumbent since no single issue is capable of coalescing voters into an angry opposition.

The three issues of war, terrorism, and moral values did come together in 2004 in a way that advantaged President Bush and overpowered the issue of a poor economy that might have worked to Kerry's advantage. The Iraq war and the lingering and painful memories of 9/11 heavily influenced the 2004 election. The election came during the process of transferring powers to an Iraqi civilian authority and many Americans, in exit polls, expressed a hesitancy to switch American administrations during this ongoing process. Additionally, terrorism continued to be a major concern for voters with a whole new group of voters being christened by the media as "security moms." While women have favored Democrats over Republicans in the recent past, 2004 saw a reversal of this gender gap. A poll taken in September 2003 showed that 64 percent of these "security moms" favored Bush's reelection, almost identical to the 66 percent of married men.[39] These soccer moms were also mobilized by moral issues that became salient primarily because of the gay marriage and stem cell research issues that dominated much of the news in 2003 and 2004.

In 2004, a powerful, well-funded, incumbent, with a job approval rating over 50 percent and unchallenged for the nomination, successfully used the issues surrounding the war, terrorism, and morals to energize the base of the Republican Party. The Democrats could count on those who lived in the large cities, urban residents, union members, single women, African Americans, and 18 to 24 year olds, voters who vote consistently for the Democrats. For Republicans, their base was to be found in the more rural areas, among farmers, small business owners, married couples, and religious conservatives. The suburbs and the small cities were turned into the battleground where swing voters would determine the outcome of the 2004 election. The victorious candidate in 2004 would prove to be the one who could mobilize these voters and get them to the polls. In the end, voters in these swing areas disproportionately gave their vote to the president, citing the issues of war, terrorism, and moral values.

Turnout in 2004

The 2004 campaign was marked by intense Get Out the Vote drives. The 527 groups, such as America Coming Together and Moveon.org aided the Democrats, spending upwards of $175 million on voter registration and activities to get voters to the polls. Republicans spent less money than the Democrats on such activities, approximately $125 million, yet mobilized a field organization of 1 million volunteers compared to the 250,000 working for the Democrats. The Republican strategy, known as the 72 Hour Campaign, referring to the final 3 days of the campaign, was tested in the congressional and local races in 2002 and then expanded in 2004 with statewide recruiting and voter registration drives. These registration drives were effective. By the end of the campaign, 143 million Americans were registered to vote compared to 132.5 million only four years earlier, an increase of 10.5 million.

Given how deeply divide the nation remained after the 2000 election, the candidate who could best mobilize voters would almost certainly win the election of 2004. President Bush was better able than John Kerry to mobilize the base of the Republican Party and swing voters. The Republican Get Out the Vote operation made the biggest difference in small cities, enabling the president to win both Ohio and Iowa. A very large increase in the voting turnout of Evangelical Christians also benefited the president. In 2000, Evangelicals comprised less than 14 percent of the electorate, in 2004, 23 percent! These voters gave Bush a 57-point margin over Kerry. The base of the Democratic Party, young voters, was not as successfully mobilized. While it is true that 20 million young voters cast ballots in 2004 as compared to 15.4 million in 2000, this increase was not enough to counteract the larger mobilization of the religious and those living in small cities and rural areas.

The Midterm Elections of 2006

The 2006 United States midterm elections were held on Tuesday, November 7, 2006. All United States House of Representatives seats and one third of the United States Senate seats were contested in this election, as well as 36 state governorships, many state legislatures, four territorial legislatures and other state and local races. The final result was a turnover of both the House of Representatives and the Senate from the Republicans to the Democrats, something that has not happened since Woodrow Wilson was president. Additionally, the Democratic Party won a majority of the state governorships and the U.S. House and Senate seats each for the first time since 1994, an election-year commonly known as the Republican Revolution. For the first time in the history of the United States, no Democratic incumbent lost, nor did Republicans capture any open House, Senate, or gubernatorial seat previously held by a Democrat.

The 2006 election saw many other firsts with Nancy Pelosi (D-California) becoming the first-ever female and first-ever Californian Speaker of the House and Harry Reid (D-Nevada) the first Mormon Senate Majority Leader. Keith Ellison (D-Minnesota) became the first Muslim ever elected to the U.S. Congress and Mazie Hirono (D-Hawaii) and Hank Johnson (D-Georgia) became the first Buddhists in a United States governing body.

CONCLUSION

Democracies rest on elections and popular participation in them. This is because true and peaceful competition that takes place in the electoral arena is a way for a society to reach decisions. At the same time such participation works to channel support for the democratically elected institutions of government. In the end, the stability of democratic regimes rests on mass support.

Some are coming to question the health and vitality of American electoral politics and, therefore, of the American form of government itself. As we saw at the beginning of this chapter, campaigns are increasingly expensive, and driven by advertising and poll technology. Yet substantive media coverage of campaigns and elections is declining, voter participation is at an historically low level, and congressional races are almost completely dominated by the incumbents who can use the vast resources of their office to discourage meaningful opposition. True competition is disappearing at a rapid rate.

As competition in the electoral arena declines, political conflict spills over to other arenas. Lowi and Ginsberg argue that unelected institutions are now at the epicenter of political conflict: the criminal justice system and courts and the mass media.[40] Between the early 1970s and the present, there has been a tenfold increase in the number of indictments brought by federal prosecutors against national, state, and local officials. In addition, there have been numerous investigations that have not resulted in indictments. The prominence of the courts has also been heightened by the great number of major policy issues that are being fought out in the courts. Abortion, women's rights, civil rights, and a host of environmental issues are currently being debated by judges and juries. The media, as well, have become prominent players in this nonelectoral politics. Today, investigative reporters are eager to publicize and expose official misconduct.

Not only has conflict spilled outside the electoral arena, the conflict has also intensified. We have had over two solid decades of divided government marked by intense battles between the legislative and executive branches. Perhaps because the partisan battles of today are not being fully decided through the elections that enjoy such low voter turnout, conflict continues to be fought out in acrimonious struggles between the branches of government. Neither Congress nor the president will concede defeat, both claiming to be the majority party. But unable to claim a solid electoral victory, both parties seek to discredit their opponents through other means. The Democratic controlled Congress conducted an extensive Iran-Contra investigation of the Reagan administration. A few years later, the Republican controlled Congress would give tit for tat with the Whitewater investigations of the Clintons.

In the end, the question is whether democratic politics can continue to function without voters. The strength of any institution is found in its ability to mobilize support. In the current atmosphere of weak political parties, candidate-centered mass media campaigns, and special interest group financing of campaigns, governmental fragmentation continues.

CHAPTER NOTES

[1]Andy Sullivan, "Congress campaign costs expected to set record," http://elections.us.reuters.com, Oct. 24, 2006.

[2]Erike Price, "The 2006 Midterm Elections—Even more decisive than we think," http://dangerous intersection.org, July, 1. 2006.

[3]Stanley Kelley, Jr., Richard E. Ayres, and William G. Bowen, "Registration and Voting: Puttin First Things First," *American Political Science Review* 61 (June 1967): 359-70.

[4]William Crotty, *Party Reform* (New York Longman, 1983), 13-25.

[5]Ibid.

[6]U.S. Pirg, "The Wealth Primary: The Role of Big Money in the 2006 Congressional Primaries," http://uspirg.org, Nov. 1, 2006.

[7]*Davis v. Bandemer*, 478 U.S. 109 (1986).

[8]Donald Saari, "Vetoing the Way We Vote," *Los Angeles Times*, 16 August 1995, A1.

[9]Ibid., A10.

[10]Ibid.

[11]Michael Nelson, ed., *Congressional Quarterly Guide to the Presidency* (Washington, D.C.: Congressional Quarterly Press, 1989), 1427.

[12]*Federal Election Commission*, "The First Ten Years: 1975-1985," Washington, D.C. Federal Election Commission, 14 April 1985, 1.

[13]*Buckley v. Valeo*, 424 U. S. 1 (1976).

[14]Mark Fineman, "Top 'Soft Money' Donor Does It 'Under the Radar,'" *The Los Angeles Times*, June 26, 2002, A1,13.

[15]"Politicking on Kids' Backs," *LA Times*, Feb. 18, 2004, B12.

[16]Stephen Simon, "Unregulated Groups Wield Millions to Sway Voters," *LA Times*, Oct. 30, 2006, A1.

[17]"Up to 900 Donors Stayed Overnight at White House," *Los Angeles Times*, 9 Feb. 1997,A33.

[18]Common Cause, "Airlines, Part II: Left at the Gate," www.commoncause.

[19]Julian Borger & David Teacher, "As Enron Scandal Spreads, U.S. Starts to Question Cash for Influence Culture," *The Guardian*, Jan. 16, 2002.

[20]Ann N. Cigler, Marion R. Just, and Timothy E. Cook, "Local News, Network News and the 1992 Presidential Campaign," paper presented at the annual meeting of the American Political Science Association, Washington, D.C., September 1993, 9.

[21]The Twentieth Century Fund, 1-800-President (New York Twentieth Century Fund Press, 1993), 31.

[22]Edwin Diamond, Martha McKay, and Robert Silverman, "Pop Goes Politics," American Behavioral Scientist 37 (November 1993): 258.

[23]Montague Kern, *30-Second Politics: Political Advertising in the Eighties* (New York: Praeger, 1989), 57.

[24]Sara Fritz and Dwight Morris, "Burden of TV Election Ads Exaggerated, Study Finds," *Los Angeles Times*, 18 March 1991, A1, A14.

[25]Nick Anderson, "Bush Campaign Cranks Up Attack Ads on Kerry," *LA Times*, June 8, 2004, A12.

[26]Nick Anderson, "Ad Experts Not Sold on Campaign Commercials," *LA Times*, May 10, 2004, A12.

[27]Nick Anderson, "Political Attack Ads Already Popping Up on the Web, *LA Times*, March 30, 2004, A15).

[28]Ibid.

[29]"Optical Scanners Topped Pregnant Chads as Most Flawed in Florida," *LA Times*, Jan. 28, 2001, A13.

[30]Morton Keller, *Affairs of State* (Cambridge, Mass.: Harvard Univ. Press, 1977), 523-24.

[31]"Dubious Democracy," http://www.fairvote.org/2002/overview.htm

[32]Kay Lehman Schlozmand, Sidney Verba, and Henry Brady, "Participation's Not a Paradox: The View from American Activists," *British Journal of Political Science* 25 (January, 1995), 1-36.

[33]Norman H. Nie, Sidney Verba, and John R. Petrocik, *The Changing American Voter* (Cambridge, Ma.: Harvard University Press, 1976), 29.

[34]Nie, Verba, and Petrocik, *Changing American Voter*, 52.

[35]Walter Volkomer, American Goverment (New Jersey: Pearson/Prentice Hall, 2004), 153.

[36]PBS, "Now: Sway the Course?" http://pbs.org/now/shows, November 3, 2006.

[37]Ibid.

[38]Miller, "Economic, Character, and Social Issues," 317.

[39]Alexsandra Starr, "'Security Moms': An Edge for Bush?" Business Week online, http://www.businessWeek.com, November 5, 2005.

[40]Lowi and Ginsberg, *American Government,* 571.

SUGGESTED READINGS

Bartels, Larry. *Presidential Primaries and the Dynamics of Public Choice.* Princeton, N.J.: Princeton University Press, 1987.

Burnham, Walter Dean. *Critical Elections and the Mainsprings of American Politics.* New York: Norton, 1970.

Piven, Francis Fox, and Richard A. Cloward. *Why Americans Don't Vote.* New York: Pantheon, 1988.

Salmore, Stephen, and Barbara G. Salmore. *Candidates, Parties, and Campaigns: Electoral Politics in America.* Washington, D.C.: Congressional Quarterly Press, 1989.

Sorauf, Frank. *Money in American Elections.* Glenview, Ill.: Scott Foresman, 1988.

Sundquist, James L. *Dynamics of the Party System: Alignment and Realignment of Political Parties in the United States. Rev. ed. Washington, D.C.: Brookings Institution, 1983.*

Wattenberg, Martin P. *The Rise of Candidate-Centered Politics: Presidential Elections in the 1980s.* Cambridge, Mass.: Harvard University Press, 1991.

Chapter Seven

THE MEDIA

On Friday, January 7, 2005, a bipartisan group of lawmakers called for an investigation into whether the Bush administration misused taxpayer funds by paying a prominent media pundit $240,000 to promote the president's new education policy. The No Child Left Behind Law, signed by the president in 2002, requires states to hold schools accountable for teaching reading and mathematics in elementary and middle schools in exchange for more federal education aid. The law became controversial when both Democrats and Republicans began to argue that the law fails to provide enough funding for the new policy. To help promote and explain the law, the Department of Education retained conservative news commentator, Armstrong Williams, as part of a million-dollar contract with the Ketchum public relations firm, to promote the No Child Left Behind Act with minority groups. Williams, who is African American, was hired by Ketchum in late 2003 to actively build support among minorities for the president's education plan. He repeatedly praised the program in numerous columns and on television without disclosing the payments.

The case of Armstrong Williams is only one example of government using taxpayer money to market its agenda to the American public under the guise of journalism. Public relations firms are increasingly used by government, receiving millions of dollars in contracts from federal agencies each year. The use of government funds to covertly influence public opinion surfaced as an issue in the 1980s, when the Reagan administration paid consultants to send op-ed pieces and letters to newspapers in support of its policies in Central America without disclosing the payments. During the Clinton era, Health and Human Services said it used actors to portray reporters in fake news segments designed to be distributed to television stations. Controversy has also more recently surfaced over video news releases produced by PR firms to disseminate to local TV stations. These releases include short segments on government programs and policies designed to be inserted into the nightly news reports. They include instructions to news anchors for suggested lead-ins to the segments and voice-over from actors who claim to be "reporting" on a subject. The news segments do not identify the source of the information as the U.S. government.

These allegations of illegal use of tax dollars to fund propaganda without explicit congressional approval and without disclosing the government's role constitute a fresh blow to a news media already racked by a series of scandals in 2004 that raised questions about both the independence and credibility of the American news media. During the presidential campaign of 2004, for example, Dan Rather of CBS had been forced to concede that he used falsified documents when he questioned President Bush's early National Guard record on *Sixty Minutes*. As a result of these scandals, a media once highly praised as an independent fourth-estate is now having its credibility questioned.

DEMOCRACY AND THE MASS MEDIA

In a democracy, communications must move in two directions: from government to citizens and from citizens to their government. In the United States, a technologically complex nation of over 280 million people, communication in either of these directions would be virtually impossible without mass forms of communication.

The Structure of the Mass Media

The term **mass media** covers the seven major channels of communication that carry messages to a mass audience.

Books

Over forty thousand books are published each year in the United States. While most of them are designed for entertainment, many others focus on public policy and government. In 1994, for example, speaker of the House of Representatives Newt Gingrich published his influential book, *To Renew America*.

Magazines

Close to ten thousand magazines are published each year in the United States, and the average American reads at least two a week. Again, many of these are solely for entertainment. Still, many others are specifically designed to address matters of political interest. *Time, Newsweek*, and *U.S. News and World Report* have a combined circulation of over 10 million readers. In addition, there are numerous magazines targeted at readers with particular ideological perspectives, for example, *Nation, New Republic*, and *The National Review*. Finally, there are many professional journals like the *American Political Science Review*.

Newspapers

Approximately 12,000 newspapers are regularly published in this country, with 1,800 in daily circulation. Approximately 70 percent of the American public claims to read a daily newspaper. In addition, most Americans receive weekly newspapers, as well as the local sheets circulated in small communities scattered across the nation.

Television

At one time, the three networks—ABC, NBC, and CBS—and their affiliates controlled the medium of television. Today, however, the networks are part of a much larger and more competitive market. The arrival of cable television has greatly increased the number of stations available to many in the United States. As of June 2006, the number of cable subscribers in the United States has grown to 78.7 million. It is little wonder that television is the medium most used and relied upon by the American public. The average household spends seven hours a day in front of the television set, and the average individual spends three hours a day watching TV. Americans say that they are most likely to get the news from television, and they tend to feel that television news is the most credible.

Radio

There are over ten thousand radio stations, divided between the AM and FM bands. The average American listens to the radio two-and-a-half hours a day. Today, talk radio programs like that of conservative Rush Limbaugh have become potent forces in the world of politics. Politicians and candidates use talk radio to interact with the American public. Ideologues on the left and the right compete for talk radio time to disseminate their particular views on the issues of the day. In 1996, Mario Cuomo created a liberal radio program as a counterpoint to Rush Limbaugh's more conservative program.

Records

Each year more than seven million records, tapes, and compact discs are sold in the United States. While CDs are primarily produced and consumed for enjoyment, many of the most popular songs have overtly political themes and messages. Rock concerts and rock artists often raise funds for politically charged causes such as AIDs, environment, world hunger, and so forth.

Motion Pictures

Twelve thousand theaters across the country show approximately 250 films a year. Many of these movies deal with political subjects, for example, Al Gore's *An Inconvenient Truth*, the 2005 hit, *Thank You for Smoking*, and in 2006, *Who Killed the Electric Car?*

The Internet

In recent years, the traditional news outlets have failed to expand their audiences despite the high level of interest in the war in Iraq, which has led to an increase in the amount of time Americans spend on the news. With other media trends flat, the steady growth in the audience for online news stands out. As of 2005, there are over 205 million Internet users in the United States, and Internet news, once largely the province of young, white males, now attracts a growing number of minorities. The percentage of African-Americans who regularly go online for news has grown by about half since 2000 (16 percent to 25 percent). The Internet population has also broadened to include more older Americans. Nearly two-thirds of Americans in their 50s and early 60s say they go online, up from 45 percent in 2000. Education continues to be the biggest single factor driving online news use, largely due to the continuing gap in Internet access. Fully half of college graduates regularly use the web for news, compared with just 18 percent of those who do not finish high school. Both men and women over age 40 without a degree are the least likely to go online for news with any regularity.[1]

Government Regulation of the Media

Thomas Jefferson wrote that "Our liberty depends on freedom of the press, and that cannot be limited without being lost."[2] Jefferson would be pleased with the amount of freedom enjoyed by the press today. Unlike journalists in many European and most African and Asian countries, journalists in the United States do not need a license to practice their trade. Stories do not have to be cleared with the government before publication and, in fact, the courts of this country have consistently ruled that there can be no prior restraint of the media.

The First Amendment does indeed give the media considerable freedom from governmental interference. Still, this freedom is not complete. There are very real constraints on the content of mass communications. One of the most important of these constraints takes the form of government regulation of three aspects of media operation.

Postwar Americans indulged themselves in flights of fancy. Television became the new entertainment medium.

Technical and Ownership Regulation

In the early years of radio, there was chaos. Stations would often broadcast on similar frequencies, thereby jamming each others' signals. The broadcasters petitioned the government to make some sense out of the cacophony. The result was that Congress passed the Federal Radio Act of 1927, which declared public ownership of the airwaves. The argument was that there was only a scarce number of airwaves, and these needed to be regulated in the interest of the American public. Accordingly, the law requires that private broadcasters obtain a license in order to use these airwaves.

Later, in 1934, Congress passed the Federal Communications Act, which created the Federal Communications Commission (FCC). The FCC has seven members, chosen by the president, with no more than four members being from the same political party. The members of the FCC serve a fixed term of seven years. They may not be removed by the president and can only be removed through impeachment by the House and conviction by the Senate. This makes the FCC an independent regulatory agency.

The FCC regulates all interstate and international communication by radio, television, cable, and satellite. The FCC is also charged by Congress to regulate the ownership of the mass media. In the 1940s, the FCC actively fought the concentration of media ownership. For example, an owner was limited to one of any type of broadcast medium, FM station, AM station, or TV station, in a single community.

In the 1950s the FCC loosened its ownership rules somewhat to allow a single owner to own up to seven AM, seven FM, and seven television stations across the nation. By the 1980s the number of television stations had more than quadrupled, and the number of radio stations had tripled. The FCC responded by further relaxing its ownership limits, allowing an owner to control up to twelve of each type of broadcast medium. The technological developments of the 1990s have continued to make the 1930s structure of communications regulation obsolete. In 1996, Congress overwhelmingly approved a major telecommunications act that seeks to replace government regulation with competition. The act removes the long-standing barriers between sectors of the telecommunications industry. For example, the new legislation abolishes the local phone monopolies and allows local companies to compete in offering long distance services.

On June 2, 2003, the Federal Communications commission relaxed decades-old restraints on the broadcast industry. In a bitter split along party lines, the Republican majority of the FCC, led by Chairman Michael K. Powell, voted 3 to 2 to relax rules that prevented TV stations from merging with local newspapers and restricted how many stations one company could own, both nationally and locally. The new rules repealed a 28-year-old ban on cross-ownership of TV stations and newspapers in all but the smallest media markets and one person or company would be able to own three TV stations up from two. This broad revision of ownership rules would clear the way for further consolidation by the biggest media conglomerates, enhancing the economic prospects of companies such as News Corp., Viacom Inc., and Tribune Co., parent of the *Los Angeles Times*. In Los Angeles, for example, Tribune would be permitted to continue its ownership of both the *Los Angeles Times* and KTLA Channel 5. Without the FCC's action, the company would have been required to divest itself of one of those properties by 2006, when the station's broadcast license comes up for renewal. Also under the new rules, broadcasters would be permitted to own stations reaching 45 percent of the nation's viewers, up from 35 percent. Taken together, the new rules would allow a single company to own the following media outlets in Los Angeles: the *Los Angeles Times*, KTLA, KCBS Channel 2, KCOP Channel 13, Time Warner Cable, KIIS-FM, KROQ-FM, KNX-AM, KFWB-AM, and KABC-AM. On September 3, 2003, however, the U.S. 3rd Circuit Court of Appeals issued an emergency order blocking the FCC's new rules from taking effect and an extended legislative debate over media ownership is now raging in Congress.

Regulation of Content

The First Amendment bars congressional interference with the press. But because broadcast channels are scarce, or at least were scarce until the arrival of cable and satellite technology, Congress has argued a right and need to regulate the content of the broadcast media. This congressional duty to regulate does not extend to the theoretically unlimited world of news print.

There are two principal restraints on broadcast content in effect today. First, the FCC requires a station that gives or sells air time to a candidate for any public office make an equal amount of time, under the same conditions, available to other candidates for that same office. This is called the **equal time provision**. Congress passed the law requiring the FCC to monitor compliance with this provision because it wanted to ensure a level and fair playing field for political debate in the United States. Congress, however, has never extended the equal opportunities rule to news coverage.

In 1949 the FCC created a second rule, the **fairness doctrine**, which required that stations provide opportunities for the expression of conflicting views on issues. Like the equal-time provision, the fairness doctrine was never applied to news coverage. In 1987, the FCC repealed the fairness doctrine because the growth of cable television made it unnecessary. Recent efforts on the part of Congress to enact the fairness doctrine into law have failed. Similarly, efforts to regulate the Internet have met with staunch opposition. Congress is currently considering regulating certain types of speech, for example obscenity, on the Internet.

The following sight is sure to bring a smile to the face of any protestor or candidate running for public office. Media attention is the one indispensable ingredient to success. The media can make or break candidates and causes.

There are three other legal restraints that place limitations on the content of both the print and broadcast media. Libel laws preclude the media's printing or airing of a story that unjustly and falsely damages a person's reputation. Obscenity laws limit the media's right to show obscene materials. Finally, there are laws limiting the media's access to classified information about intelligence operations.

In addition to the legal restraints, media content, especially in regard to the coverage of war, is also constrained by government pressure. During the Spanish-American War of 1898 and throughout World Wars I and II, journalists considered themselves part of the war effort. Beginning with the Korean and then Vietnam Wars, the press took an increasingly independent and critical view of the military. When the Vietnam War ended, many in the military blamed the press for "losing Vietnam." In 1983, the Pentagon barred all journalists from the initial invasion of Grenada. During this same period, the Reagan administration threatened to prosecute reporters for violating espionage laws.[4] Then in 1989, the Pentagon selected a dozen reporters to cover the invasion of Panama but restricted them to an airport until nearly all the fighting was over. Then during the first Persian Gulf War, the Pentagon accredited pools of journalists who had to first pass a military security review and who could then only interview military personnel with an escort present. News organizations filed suit charging the military with violating the First Amendment. Before the lawsuit against Gulf War press restrictions could come before a judge, however, Desert Storm ended. For the war in Iraq in 2003, the U.S. military devised new press rules. About 500 reporters (one-fifth of them from foreign countries) were placed, or "embedded," in military units. These embedded journalists have been given greater access to operational combat missions.[5]

Political Functions of the Mass Media

Entertainment

The news media in the United States are different from the media in other countries in that they are almost all private, for-profit corporate enterprises. This means that one of their principal functions is to make money for those who own them. These profits are tied to the media's ability to sell off their space, in the case of newspapers, or time, in the case of radio and television, to corporate advertisers called sponsors. Advertising revenues are directly related to the size of the audience, usually measured in terms of newspaper circulation or reader/viewer ratings. The ratings game, the need to attract large audiences, will even affect the content of the news and public affairs programs. The dramatic and sensational, the conflicted and the sordid, are more likely to attract large audiences.

Surveillance

Surveillance involves the press's role in the definition of what constitutes "news." The media are the gatekeepers, determining what the public sees, reads, and hears. It is the job of a journalist to sort through the enormous number of stories that might be considered as news and winnow them down, giving the audience a distilled, condensed version of reality.

Interpretation

But the news is nothing as simple as reality, or even parts of reality. The news is a story about reality told by a storyteller, a journalist. The media place events and people in a context, probing motives, causes, and effects. It is quite common for a newspaper or TV news program to run a segment that offers analysis and interpretation. In addition, there are whole programs devoted to such interpretative news reporting, for example, *60 Minutes, Nightline,* and *20/20.*

Watchdog

Traditionally, the American press has accepted responsibility for protecting the public from corrupt, incompetent, or deceitful politicians. In 2004, for example, the press reported the abuses of prisoners by U.S. soldiers in Iraq. Graphic photos of naked Iraqi prisoners forced into humiliating sexual poses were aired on national television news. Congress, forced by the airing of these photos to respond, launched hearings to discover why U.S. troops had behaved in such an illegal and horrible manner.

Socialization

The media are the principal purveyors of American culture, influencing particularly the young and recent immigrants. Studies have shown that children pick up most of their political information and many of their most basic values from the mass media.[7] Children who have the most exposure to mass communications tend to be better informed and have more political opinions than those who have less exposure.[8]

Persuasion and Propaganda

The mass media have long been looked at as vehicles to be used to persuade and mobilize mass publics. Governments, public officials, candidates, and interest groups have all, at one time or another, attempted to turn media coverage to their advantage. Advertisements and public information programs are examples of modern forms of propaganda. But all political campaigns involve propaganda designed to persuade and mobilize support.

Agenda Setting

Many believe that the media's power to persuade and change opinions is greatly overrated. They suggest instead that the media's primary power is the power to influence what the public thinks about rather than what they think. Issues prominently featured in the media, for example, become the issues that citizens think are most important. In 1990, on the twentieth anniversary of Earth Day, the television news featured many stories on the environment. Studies have shown that such coverage led many in the public to focus on environmental issues as a top priority. Certainly the media's coverage of Bill Clinton's 1992 campaign for the presidency helped to jettison the issue of health care onto the national political agenda.

Roosevelt was an outstanding media president.

THE INCREASED IMPORTANCE OF THE MODERN MASS MEDIA

The press has become the political intermediary in the American political system. This role has grown out of two modern, parallel developments. The first is the pervasiveness of the American media that has in turn led to the public's and politicians' increased reliance upon the press. The second is the movement of the press into an increasingly autonomous position, largely free from political controls.[9]

A Pervasive News Media

The media are more pervasive today than ever before. Daily newspaper circulation is at over 63 million copies. Weekly magazine circulation tops 53 million. National news magazines like *Time* and *Newsweek* enjoy a combined circulation of almost 10 million. Several daily national newspapers sell more than a million copies each weekday. The *New York Times* and the *Los Angeles Times*, for example, have grown by 25 percent in the past twenty years. The circulation of the *Wall Street Journal* has doubled during this period. The average length of a daily newspaper has also grown from 34 to 60 pages.[10] The number of newspapers has, however, declined, and this seems at least partly due to the increased number of electronic information sources.

Today there are over 1,500 television stations and over 10,000 radio stations. These stations are spending an increased amount of time covering the news.

In 1963, the three major networks—ABC, CBS, and NBC—devoted only eleven minutes daily to national news. By 1993, the amount of time on the networks devoted to news-type programming had increased to over three hours a day. This extensive televised coverage of the news has had its effect. Half of the American population says that they watch the evening news. In addition, most Americans find the televised news credible.[11] Twenty-four-hour-a-day news cable channels have only worked to increase the importance of televised news. News stations like C-SPAN and CNN and even MTV regularly broadcasts a news program aimed at younger audiences.

Public officials are also increasingly reliant on the American press. The number of journalists in Washington has tripled since the end of World War II to more than 10,000. The congressional press galleries accredit more than 5,000 journalists. The president alone is regularly accompanied by more than 100 journalists. The size of the press corps and its prestige require politicians to develop strategies to deal with the press corps. There are some 3,000 public information specialists working in federal agencies.

An Autonomous Press

The American press had its early beginnings as a partisan tool first of the American revolutionaries and then of the first political parties. Over the course of two centuries, however, the press has been transformed into a fiercely independent, autonomous profession, or as some call it, a "fourth estate."

Phase I: The Early Partisan Press

The first continuous newspaper in the United States was published in Boston by two brothers, John and Duncan Campbell.[12] The single-sheet Boston *Newsletter* began publication on April 24, 1704. By 1750, there were thirteen regular newspapers being printed in the colonies and gradually four-page papers replaced the single sheet.

The spread of the colonial press was actively encouraged by the government. In fact, these early papers were under the control of the British colonial government. Most papers carried on their mastheads "By Authority" and received a subsidy for publishing the proceedings of the colonial governments. Besides these subsidies, the papers were also sustained through lucrative government printing contracts. A final aspect of government control was to be found in the fact that the papers could be prosecuted for seditious libel if they included content seen as offensive to the colonial authorities.

During the Revolutionary War, the newspapers actively distanced themselves from the British colonial governments. The Stamp Act that had placed a tax on newspapers greatly angered the press, and as their anger made its way onto the pages of the papers, the press became the engine that would drive opinion against the British.

The press became further politicized during the fight over ratification of the new Constitution of 1787. The supporters of the Constitution sought to mobilize opinion through *The Federalist Papers* while the opponents of the new Constitution argued their case in the *Letters of a Federal Farmer*. This period of history is early evidence of the critical role the press plays in linking government and public opinion.

After the Constitution was ratified, the press remained partisan and politicized. Alexander Hamilton encouraged John Fenno, an ardent Federalist, to come to the nation's capital and establish a newspaper to serve as a voice for the administration of President Washington. Hamilton's encouragement of Fenno came primarily through the promise of government printing jobs. In response, the Jeffersonian Republicans cultivated Philip Freneau, urging him to publish a Republican journal, luring him with the promise of a government position, personal loans, and government printing contracts.

During the Jacksonian period, increased and intensified competition within and between the political parties led to an even greater party reliance on the press to mobilize electoral support. As the parties continued to subsidize and support the press through government printing contracts and patronage appointments, the number of newspapers burgeoned to over 12,000, with one copy for every fifteen people. Largely because of their financial dependence on the parties, the press remained intensely partisan during this period. The U.S. Census listed only 5 percent of all newspapers as "neutral" or "independent."

Phase II: The Penny Press and Yellow Journalism

After the Civil War, rapid breakthroughs in printing and communication technologies worked to give the press greater financial independence, thereby freeing it from its earlier partisan control. The high-speed rotary press meant lower costs and lower subscription rates. In addition, the invention of the telegraph carried with it the ability to disseminate information between cities at low cost. Growing numbers of people in the urban centers of the country provided a ready audience for the cheaper newspapers. When the suffrage was extended in the 1800s to nonproperty owning white males, this audience was not only ready but eager as well for political news. Finally, the commercialization and industrialization of America created a merchant class eager to reach mass audiences by way of advertising. The press was no longer dependent on the political parties. In the end, politicians themselves began to relinquish their partisan hold on the press as they found other ways to communicate with the public, in particular, strong party organizations geared to mass mobilization.

Together these developments worked to create a penny press with mass readership and much greater independence from partisan control. The editors of these newspapers often engaged in **yellow journalism,** focusing on sensationalism and scandal. Also during this period, an elite set of newspapers, including for example the *New York Times*, was developing. These newspapers were beginning to define their work as a profession, and the journalists working for these papers adopted a libertarian theory of the press.

The libertarian theory argued that journalists must print "the truth." It is not, according to libertarian theory, the job of the journalist to express his own viewpoint. Rather, the journalist is merely a conduit for the views of others. For example, it was not uncommon in the first half of the eighteenth century to find newspapers expounding the political philosophy of the owner of the newspaper. The press moguls of the nineteenth century, men like William Randolph Hearst and Joseph Pulitzer, had great influence on American government and society.

The libertarian theory of the press worked to the advantage of sitting presidents as well. During the period from 1870 through the middle of the 1960s, presidents in particular had greater access to press coverage and used the press as a bully pulpit to shape public opinion. It was generally accepted that in exchange for press access to politicians, certain topics would be off limits to the press corps. The private behavior of politicians and behind-the-scenes partisan machinations, for example, were taboo. Even John F. Kennedy's Addison's disease, for example, was left undiscussed in the press.[13]

Phase III: Investigative Journalism

In the middle of the 1960s, people began to see that big business was dominating many of the economic markets in the United States. It was little wonder that journalists soon began to look at the marketplace of ideas and recognize that this market too was dominated by established politicians often at the expense of other views. By the 1960s the prohibitive cost of starting a newspaper meant that the only way to get into the newspaper business was to buy out an existing one. Broadcasting further challenged the libertarian theory's assumption of an unlimited number of outlets for the expression of ideas. The technology of broadcasting made unlimited access impossible at the same time that it called for government regulation.

The Vietnam War, Watergate, and the Kerner Commission's criticism of media coverage of race relations worked to further call into question just how open a marketplace the press had ever been to any views other than those of the political establishment of public officials and established leaders. As a result, journalists began to articulate a new professional code of social responsibility. The professional press corps began to argue that the American public has a right to know the full story. If the full story does not spring from the mouth of officials, journalists have the responsibility to go behind the scenes and unearth the full story.

The result was the advocacy journalism of the late 1960s. Reporters felt justified in using journalism for what they perceived to be morally just causes: fighting corruption in government, disclosing environmental degradation, and unearthing examples of racial inequity. By the 1970s, advocacy journalism had given way to a new stage of adversarial journalism with the journalists actively challenging statements made by officials. The press acts as the opposition. The press's tradition of yellow journalism muckraking, the new technology of television, and the press's increasing access to alternative sources of information allowed the press to assume this role. In addition, the investigative, inside story made good sense economically; such stories filled with conflict and titillation built audiences that could then be sold to corporate advertisers.

Phase IV: Conglomerate Ownership of the Press

Today the news media are big business. The nine most influential national news organizations— ABC, CBS, NBC, *the New York Times, the Washington Post, the Wall Street Journal, the Los Angeles Times, Newsweek,* and *Time*—are all owned by corporations that rank among the five hundred largest in the United States.[14] Even more dramatic than the size of these media companies is the trend toward even greater concentration and at a very rapid rate. In 1981, a majority of the business in newspapers, radio, television, magazines, books, and movies was controlled by forty-six corporations. By 2007, ownership has become further consolidated into nine conglomerates. (AOL-Time Warner, Disney, Bertelsmann, Viacom, News Corporation, TCI, General Electric-NBC, Sony, and Seagram.)[15]

The trend towards increased concentration of media ownership is most evident with newspapers. Between 1960 and 1985, newspaper chains, that is, companies that own more than two daily newspapers in different cities, increased their share of total daily newspaper circulation from 46 to 77 percent.[16] Gannett Company, for example, owns *USA Today* as well as eighty-seven other dailies, and Knight-Ridder owns twenty-nine daily newspapers.

Ownership of radio and television stations is less concentrated but apparently only for the moment. The year 1995-1996 alone saw a number of huge conglomerate media mergers involving broadcasting. On July 30, 1995, the largest entertainment company in the world was created when Walt Disney Company agreed to buy Capital Cities/ABC Inc. for $19 billion in cash and stock. This second largest merger in U.S. history (after the $25 billion acquisition of RJR Nabisco by Kohlberg Kravis Roberts & Company in 1989) brings together the number one television distributor and network and the nation's premier producer of movies, creating a powerhouse with combined sales of $20.7 billion. On August 29, 1995, Time Warner announced its intention to buy Turner Broadcasting, which owns CNN, a merger that would create the largest media company in the world, a conglomerate with revenues of more than $18.7 billion. On August 1, 1995, CBS announced its intended merger with Westinghouse Electric Corporation. This merger at a cost of $5.4 billion will create the biggest TV, radio empire, with control over fifteen television stations and thirty-nine radio stations that reach over one-third of the country's listeners and viewers. Then on June 20, 1996, Westinghouse announced its imminent buy out of Infinity Broadcasting Corporation, bringing to Westinghouse an additional eighty-three radio stations. The government maintains that diversity of voices in the media is protected because of the proliferation of new technologies, from the Internet to satellites. As a result, Congress has further deregulated the telecommunications industry, and beginning in 1996, cable, radio, and television corporations underwent an even more radical wave of consolidation. Then, on January 10, 2000, American Online and the Time Warner conglomerate announced that they would merge into a $350-billion media empire.

Media concentration appears to be accelerating. In September of 2003, the Federal Communications Commission allowed Univision Communications Inc.'s $3.25 billion acquisition of radio

Ronald Reagan was one of the best with the media.

chain Hispanic Broadcasting Corp. Univision now controls two-thirds of the nearly $2.8 billion spent on advertising on Spanish-language television and radio. On October 7, 2003, General Electric merged its NBC assets with Vivendi Universal's entertainment operations, including movie studio Universal Pictures and the TV unit that owns three cable channels and produces the "Law and Order" franchise. NBC Universal, as the new company is called, posted sales of more than $13 billion in 2003. Then in 2006, Walt Disney announced that it would buy Pixar for $7.4 billion and newspaper publisher McClatchy acquired rival Knight-Ridder for $6.1 billion. Overall, there were 138 media mergers in the United States worth $48.1 billion in 2006. In short, the media are now huge corporate entities largely independent of political control. Their status as business enterprises will, no doubt, affect the news gathering process.

Phase V: Atomization of the Media

Despite the growing concentration of media ownership, a contrary trend, an atomization of the media, has also developed in recent years. Whereas concentration has led to a national media, atomization has fragmented the influence of this national media. The major newspapers and networks have lost their dominance, while other media, some not even considered news organizations, have started to play a greater role in American politics.

This trend is partly the result of technological changes. First, the national networks began to lose viewers to the local news stations. The local stations are now linked together via satellite and can thereby share coverage of national and international affairs. Next, the traditional stations lost viewers to the cable television, which because of their number can offer more, specialized programming. The offerings of cable television have become more focused. This "narrow casting" appeals to small segments of the audience in contrast to the networks' more generalized attempts to appeal to a mass audience. For example, C-SPAN provides live coverage of Congress and allows viewers to see and hear Congress at work.

There are other cable stations that cater to various racial and ethnic groups. A cable system in Los Angeles and New York is targeted to the Jewish population. A cable channel in California broadcasts in Chinese, one in Hawaii broadcasts in Japanese, and one in Connecticut and Massachusetts broadcasts in Portuguese. Stations in New York provide programs in Greek, Hindi, Korean, and Russian.

The Internet has led to additional news sites. Major newspapers can now be read on-line, as can several political magazines. Often these on-line services are at the forefront of the news. During the 2004 campaign, Web logs, or "blogs," played a critical role. Free Republic and the DailyKos are two of the ideologically driven Web logs that managed to attract hundreds of thousands of readers and helped shape the presidential campaign and contributed to a powerful grassroots mobilization of voters.

The trend toward atomization of the media is also a reflection of the increasing partisan polarization of the American electorate following the 2000 and the 2004 elections. This polarization is clearly reflected in the viewing habits of Americans. Since 2000, the number of people who regularly watch the Fox News Channel has increased by nearly half from 17 percent to 25 percent and the gains have been greatest among political conservatives. At the same time, CNN, Fox's principal rival, has a more Democrat-leaning audience than in the past. A nationwide poll, conducted in

April and May, 2004, has found that the audiences for Rush Limbaugh's radio show and Bill O'Reilly's TV program on Fox are overwhelmingly conservative and Republican. By contrast, audiences for some other news sources notable NPR, the NewsHour, and magazines like the *New Yorker*, the *Atlantic*, and *Harper's* tilt liberal and Democratic.[17]

The line between information and entertainment has been blurred. The trend toward atomization has worked to make politics more accessible to more people, but it has also made the news less factual. The newspapers and network news must compete with the more sensational coverage and so they too have become more focused on scandal, personalities, and entertainment-driven stories. Accuracy has suffered in the process. In an effort to attract viewers on election night in 2000, the networks prematurely predicted the victor in Florida to be Al Gore, then had to retract it and give the state to Bush, and then retract that and admit the race was too close to call. The public is largely at sea in this factual free-for-all. Without the help of trained, professional journalists, many are not able to separate truth from fiction.

THE NEWS GATHERING PROCESS

There are three main sets of factors that affect news decisions.

Personal Background and Values

Sociologist Herbert Gans has found that media personnel tend to be drawn disproportionately from middle and upper middle class backgrounds.[18] Today there are still very few minorities in the journalistic professions. It is perhaps not surprising that reporters tend to have values that correspond to their socioeconomic backgrounds. Studies have found that journalists tend to have a positive orientation to private business, emphasize individualism, and take moderate positions on political and social matters.[19] While some have suggested that journalists tend to be liberal, no such consistent ideological bias has ever been documented. Rather than being consistently liberal or Democratic, journalists might better be thought of as Progressive, reform-oriented, almost anti-partisan in approach.

Professional Values

Since the beginning of the 1900s, journalists have increasingly taken themselves seriously as professionals. The result has been the creation of journalistic societies, trade journals, and even a code of ethics to be followed. Reporters today follow certain standards of decency, refusing, for example, to print, say, or quote racial epithets. In addition, reporters depend on documentary practices such as reliance on reliable sources. Finally, since Watergate, journalists see themselves as social critics, crusaders for justice, ombudsmen for the disadvantaged. The post-Watergate generation of journalists takes a participatory stance. In Carl Bernstein's words: "The job of the press is not to follow Ronald Reagan's or George Bush's agenda, but to make its *own* decisions about what's important for the country.[20]

Organizational Factors

Perhaps more important than either personal background or professional considerations are the economic imperatives of the modern mass media. The news media, as noted above, are now part of larger conglomerates. These conglomerates often include non-media companies, and they are usually run by business executives that have little or no background in the media. The governing imperative of such conglomerates is to make a profit. To make a profit both newspapers and broadcasting must build an audience. This audience can then be sold to corporate advertisers, or sponsors.

Advertising is big business. Despite its lowest ratings in history, the broadcast industry experienced a banner year in 1994. Advertisers paid $31.2 billion to the networks and broadcast stations and an additional $4.6 billion to cable networks.

THE CONTENT OF THE NEWS: INFORMATIONAL BIASES

The Bias Debate

The media's growing importance has led to an increased concern over possible bias in media coverage of current events and people in the news. Left-wing critics claim that the press is simply a tool of "the establishment." Michael Parenti, for example, sees corporate ownership of the mass media as inevitably leading journalists in a pro-capitalist, pro-corporate posture.[21] These critics see all forms of mass communication as bolstering the establishment line. Even films are viewed as reinforcing capitalist dogma. There is an equal number of media critics on the right. They see the media as the tool of anti-government, anti-American "liberals." Journalists are viewed as advocates of a pro-welfare spending, anti-business, liberal agenda.

What critics on the left and right have failed to realize is the overriding influence of the economic pressures on the increasingly competitive mass media. A continually biased program is unlikely to attract a large audience. To ensure profits, the media must entertain the audience. The pressure to entertain and make money is far more determinant of media content than ideological purity. Both the networks and newspapers are experiencing stiffer competition—the networks from cable and the newspapers from human-interest tabloids. This increased competition in a field already driven by the profit motive works to produce a number of biases in media content.

Informational Biases

Infotainment

As discussed above, the first priority of the media is to build an audience. This means that even political matters will be played as "stories." The news tends to personalize, concentrating on individuals rather than institutions or process. For example, stories on the president commonly focus on some personal habit or trait of the person holding the office. Similarly, statistical data is often glossed over in favor of an illustration using an individual's story. For example, a jump in unemployment may be illustrated by an interview with someone standing in an unemployment line.

The media also attempt to build audiences through a focus on the dramatic, the visual, the exceptional. Violence is a central element of the news because it tends to be so visual. Change is emphasized over continuity, and news stories often follow certain intuitively understandable schema: good versus bad, rich versus poor.

Several authors have recently noted that audiences for news programs are built and maintained when the content of the news is brought to the lowest common denominator. Responding to the merger of Capital Cities/ABC with Disney, author Brian Stonehill, director of the Media Studies Program at Pomona College, argues that "the juvenile sets the tone for the culture, and the escapism of fun and games wins a shutout over the business of information."[22]

Negativity

An outgrowth of the media's need to entertain as well as its professional adherence to a watch-dog role, is a tendency to accentuate the negative aspects of American life. Journalists are intent upon publicizing the missteps of political leaders. The media's preference for "bad news" can be seen, for example, in the fact that the negative coverage of presidential candidates has risen steadily in recent decades and now exceeds the positive coverage. In 1960, less than 25 percent of the coverage of candidates was negative; in 2004, it was 58 percent.[23]

An agenda of problems, conflicts, and divisive issues now dominates the news. As journalist Meg Greenfield writes:

> "Out there"—wherever that is—people may be smiling or humming . . . but the world according to journalism is, on the contrary, a surprisingly bleak place. A Martian reading about it might in fact suppose America to be composed entirely of abused minorities living in squalid and sadistically run state mental hospitals, except a small elite of venal businessmen and county commissioners who are profiting from the unfortunates' misery.[24]

COVERAGE OF CAMPAIGNS

The informational biases built into the mass media can all be seen in the media's coverage of political campaigns. An agenda dominated by problems, divisive issues, and the "negative" dominates campaign coverage. Reporters seek to find the story behind the official story. A former editor of *The Washington Post* has said of reporters: "[They] want to be important players in the political process, not passive bystanders. They want to mix it up with the candidates, join the debate and defend the Republic as surrogates of the masses."[25] As a result, campaign coverage tends to follow a fairly set formula.

The Horserace

The media's proclivity toward the personal, the dramatic, and the divisive has led campaigns to be covered primarily as horseraces between competing sets of candidates. One study has found that 58 percent of all election news focused on the game. Another study found that 59 percent of CBS news coverage failed to contain even one issue sentence, and 55 percent of UPI news similarly failed. About five-sixths of all news stories referred to the competition rather than the issues. A study of local television during the final three months of California's 1998 gubernatorial campaign found that less than one-half of 1 percent of news time was devoted to the contest and that coverage was dominated by photo ops and horse-race speculations. On Oct. 29, 1999, a broad, bipartisan coalition of prominent Americans, including retired broadcaster Walter Cronkite and former Presidents Jimmy Carter and Gerald Ford, sent a letter urging 1400 TV station owners to devote five minutes a night in the month prior to the elections to candidate forums or mini-debates. Only nine said they would try.[26]

This fixation on the horserace may stem from the fact that many journalists were once campaign insiders. For example, ABC's Jeff Greenfield and George Will, NBC's Ken Bode, CBS's Diane Sawyer, *The News Hour with Jim Lehrer's* David Gergen, PBS's Bill Moyer, and *The New York Times's* William Safire were all campaign insiders before they were journalists. It is little wonder that these journalists see campaigns in terms of strategy and winning.[27]

Gaffes

In Washington, an off-the-cuff remark is referred to as a gaffe. A gaffe has been defined as the trouble a politician get into when he or she says what is actually being thought. The media often amplify the initial gaffe by repeatedly covering it, and the politician unwittingly further amplifies it by repeatedly apologizing over it. The end result is that such mistakes trap candidates in a spiral of controversy, getting them in ever deeper trouble.

In the modern age of technology, these campaign slips of the tongue have taken central stage, magnified because they are available via mouse click on websites like YouTube and replayed over and over by 24-hour cable news networks and radio talk show hosts eager for controversy. In the drive for ratings, foot-in-the-mouth syndrome has become the bane of candidates running for public office.

The campaigns of 2006 were filled with such slips of the tongue. Senator George Allen, for example, apologized for using the word "macaca" to describe a student of Indian descent who was dogging him with a video camera, and then went on to express regret for his youthful infatuation with the Confederate flag – which included wearing a rebel flag lapel pin for his Palos Verdes High School yearbook. And in what he said was a joke gone awry about the Iraq war, Senator John F. Kerry, the week before the off-year congressional elections, became the second would-be presidential candidate in one week to see his hopes dimmed because of a botched or unscripted comment. Appearing at a Democratic rally in Pasadena, California, Kerry told college students that they needed to study hard and try to do well in school because "if you don't, you get stuck in Iraq." Within two days, Senator Kerry was forced to issue a written apology.

Senators Allen and Kerry were apparently not the only candidates who got their feet stuck in their mouths. Steve Kagen, a Wisconsin Democrat running for the House, faced a similar problem with his media coverage. Arriving late to a campaign event after visiting an Indian reservation, he remarked, "We're on Injun time." He then went on to explain "They don't tell time by the clock." Banker Tramm Hudson, running in Florida's Republican primary for a House seat, told a Christian Coalition political forum: "Blacks are not the greatest swimmers or may not even know how to swim." Representative Steny H. Hoyer accused Maryland's Republican Senate candidate, Lieutenant Governor Michael Steele, an African American, of "a career of slavishly supporting the Republican Party." John Spencer, the Republican opponent of Hillary Clinton for the New York Senate seat, was asked by a journalist on October 18, 2006, whether he would attack Clinton in a forthcoming debate by using the "L word" – liberal. Spencer replied facetiously: "You know me, how words slip out. As long as I don't call her a lesbian, I'm OK." Oops.[28]

Coverage of the Incumbent

Incumbents running for re-election enjoy a number of advantages over their challengers, including a greater amount of media attention. Because the incumbent is in a position of power, the press corps is more likely to cover his or her actions. It is not unusual, for example, for the press to become almost fixated on a president's eating habits, holiday travels, and golf game, in addition to his discharge of the affairs of state. A recent study has found, however, that such abundant coverage is not always a good thing. Apparently journalists believe that because incumbents enjoy an advantage in terms of the amount of coverage, the press corps must balance this advantage by scrutinizing more carefully his or her actions.[29] Such intense scrutiny leads to more negative coverage. One study has found that in the presidential elections from 1960 through 1992, the incumbent president received consistently more negative coverage than did his challenger.[30]

COVERAGE OF THE PRESIDENT

All the informational biases discussed above lead the news media to fixate on the presidency. The president is one individual while the Congress is made up of 535 individuals. The presidency is dramatic; the Supreme Court is less so. In foreign affairs, the president is virtually the sole actor, and foreign affairs often involve a crisis likely to dominate the news agenda. Finally, that the president has sole responsibility for nuclear weapons, together with assassinations and assassination attempts, has heightened the press's interest in the health and well-being of the president.

This focus on the presidency is also stimulated by the White House itself. White House correspondents, numbering close to seventy-five, cover the White House as a regular beat and rely on information they receive from the president's own staff, information carefully crafted by the staff to control the direction of the story. The most frequent form such control takes is the press release, a prepared text distributed to reporters in the hopes that they will use it verbatim. A daily news briefing at 11:30 A.M. enables reporters to question the president's press secretary about these news releases and get film footage for the nightly television news. To no small extent, the correspondents are the captives of the White House press releases. Still, such intense scrutiny may set the president up for eventual negative coverage as his performance falls short of heightened expectations. One study found that 64 percent of all references to President Clinton by network news reporters was negative.[31]

COVERAGE OF CONGRESS

Most reporters in Washington are accredited to sit in the House and Senate press galleries, but only about four hundred cover Congress exclusively.[32] Most news about Congress comes from the numerous press releases issued by the members of Congress. In addition, C-Span now covers Congress live.

In general, Congress tends to receive less coverage than does the president, because of the informational biases of the media discussed above. Congress does not walk. Congress does not talk. Consequently, it is difficult to personalize the institution in the same way that the office of the presidency can be personalized. One study has found that over 60 percent of the *CBS Evening News* shows opened with a story that featured the president.[33] In addition, coverage of Congress has actually declined in recent decades. One study found that congressional stories on the network news dropped by two-thirds between the 1970s and 1980s.[34]

When the Congress can be made more personal and dramatic, it is more likely to get on the news. For six months after the 1994 election, the media riveted their attention on Speaker Gingrich and the new Republican majority in Congress. The Republican takeover of Congress was associated with the colorful personality of the Speaker and the brewing conflicts between the executive and legislative branches made for good news.

THE POLITICIANS RESPOND: THE MANAGEMENT OF NEWS COVERAGE

Shorter Campaign Speeches

Politicians have not been willing to sit by idly, leaving journalists in control of the news agenda. A group of political consultants, "spin doctors," have begun to play a central role in determining strategy, first at the presidential campaign level and then in more and more state and local races. These consultants attempt to tailor the politician's message to the needs of the news organizations for drama, personalization, and brevity. Increasingly, these consultants stage media events, situations that are simply too newsworthy for the media to pass up.

Candidates' and politicians' speeches are getting shorter and shorter. In the nineteenth century, hour-long speeches were the norm. Today, candidates deliver stump speeches in less than seventeen minutes. Politicians know that whatever they say is likely to be reduced to only a few seconds on the evening news. To control these few seconds of air time, candidates speak in soundbites, tricky little statements that are most likely to fill the media's need for drama and brevity. Candidate soundbites on CBS, NBC, and ABC have now dropped to under ten seconds. Soundbites like Walter Mondale's 1984 "Where's the beef" and George Bush's 1988 "Read my lips. No new taxes" are the stuff of modern campaigns. Clinton's 1996 "bridge to the future" and Dole's "just don't do it" are additional examples of soundbite politics.

Politicians also try to influence the media's interpretation of political events. Putting the appropriate **spin** on a story or event has become an art left to paid professionals, the **spin doctors**. For example, in 1996, Patrick Buchanan's campaign strategists tried to convince the media that coming in second behind Robert Dole in a Republican primary was actually a *victory*.

Presidential Debates

Candidates ideally would like to get as much free media coverage that they can control as possible. The presidential debates that have been regular features of presidential campaigns since 1960 offer the perfect setting for a candidate to warehouse his ideas with fairly little intervention on the part of journalists. In general, the political challenger has the most to gain from a debate. The challenger needs the attention, has little to lose, and gains the appearance of being presidential because of being on the same stage with the president himself. The incumbent president, on the other hand, has little to gain and may lose by making a mistake or appearing unprepared.

The debates are usually only an hour and a half in length, and usually no more than three debates are televised. The candidates can, however, extend the reach and importance of the debates by getting the news media to continue to discuss what occurred in the debates and perhaps show film footage from the debates repeatedly. Presidential debates have, therefore, also begun to turn on the production of effective, catchy soundbites. Traditional debate in the pre-radio age tended to focus, for a sustained period, on a single issue and tended to involve the real interchange of views. For example, the 1948 Dewey-Stassen debate was on the Mundt-Nixon bill outlawing the Communist Party. While radio did not kill such serious debate outright, it did insofar as the audience for radio expected to be entertained, expected messages to be brief, and expected to change the channel if any of their expectations were not met. Debates, in other words, had to be briefer and more entertaining. In 1856, Charles Sumner's eighty page *Crimes Against Kansas* speech was reprinted in its entirety, and almost one million copies were sold to people who actually read it! Bill Clinton's broadcast campaign messages in 1992, on the other hand, would not in their entirety even begin to approach that length. Today, in a ninety minute debate each candidate will actually speak for less than thirty minutes.

One of the most important features of the 2000 presidential debates was exclusivity. For the nation's scores of third-party presidential candidates, the debates are the political equivalent of not getting asked to the high school prom. While Pat Buchanan, Ralph Nader, and other third-party candidates sought to fight back through lawsuits and the Internet, they should not have taken their exclusion personally. Third-party candidates have been getting the debate brush-off since 1960, when Congress modified a 1934 law that required any broadcast station staging a debate to welcome all candidates. Congress suspended that rule to let Richard Nixon and John F. Kennedy square off by themselves in the first televised debates.

A special nonprofit commission selected by the Republican and Democratic hierarchy now controls the task of selecting who appears in the presidential debates. Not surprisingly, the bipartisan Commission on Presidential Debates, established in 1987, has set the bar higher than the current third-party candidates can jump, mandating they score at least 15 percent in nationwide polls. Only Ralph Nader came close in 2000 with 5 percent.

Political Advertisements

While politicians can never hope to control completely either the content or slant of their *free* news coverage, they can turn to paid political advertisements over which they can exert complete control over the message. Political advertisements have a long history in this country, but they have become increasingly central components of modern campaigns.

The new importance of political advertising has six sources. First, the primary election system used to choose nominees for public office requiring candidates to appeal directly to thousands, even millions, of voters. In the case of presidential primaries, candidates must reach voters in each of the thirty-eight separate states that employ primary elections. Second, advertisements now represent the biggest campaign expenditure in most campaigns. In 1952, only 30 percent of overall funds were so spent. For Ross Perot, who sought the presidency in 1992 and then again in 1996, 75 percent of his spending went to advertisements.[35] In 2000, candidates bought over $600 million in air time; that is six times as much, after inflation, as was spent in 1972.[36]

A third factor working to increase the importance of advertisements is that there are legal limits on how much candidates for certain public offices can spend on their campaigns. Such limits lead candidates to place a premium on reaching the most voters at the lowest possible cost. A fourth source of the centrality of advertisements in modern campaigns is found in the legal limits placed on how much money the Democratic and Republican National Committees and interest groups can donate to a candidate's campaign. However, one way around these limits is for interest groups and political parties to make and air an advertisement on behalf of the candidate. Such independent spending is not limited by federal campaign finance laws, and the Supreme Court in July 1996 ruled that parties and groups may spend unlimited amounts on behalf of candidates.[37] Similarly, the political parties can spend unlimited amounts on *party-building* activities that may include political advertisements seeking support for the party rather than one specific candidate. In the election of 2000, parties and independent groups spent over $342 million on ads. Independent groups deluged congressional and state races with more than 125 different groups running ads. The largest segment of the issue ads in 2000, about 24 percent, focused on health care, followed by the environment and gun control. The independent groups spending the most were backed by major industries. For example, Citizens for Better Medicare, a group founded largely by the pharmaceutical industry, spent $34 million on ads aimed at six competitive congressional races.[38]

The campaigns of 2006 continued this trend with candidates, parties, and their special interest supporters spending a record $2 billion on television ads, double the amount spent in the 2002 midterm elections and $400 million more than was spent on the presidential campaign of 2004.[39] Broadcasters are not charging more to run the ads. Rather the leap in revenue comes from special interest groups like the National Rifle Association, the Sierra Club, and various labor union coalitions. Seeing their ability to make soft money contributions to the parties being closed off by new campaign finance laws, these groups are turning their money and energies to issue ads.

The changing structure of the advertisements themselves may account for their increased importance. Today's television advertisements employ the rich multimodal properties of television. These advertisements use montage, music, and symbolism to create an entire mood. The soft focus, long shots, and slow music are the grammar of this mood. In addition, the increasing negativity built into modern advertisements has made them more powerful campaign tools. Not only have studies shown that people tend to remember negative messages better than positive ones, but also negative ads are dramatic, personal, conflict-laden, in short, news worthy. The news media often pick up soundbites taken from the advertisements and replay them on the evening news. For example, on September 4, 1991, CBS, NBC, ABC, and CNN all carried an excerpt from a conservative group called the Victory Committee urging Senate confirmation of Supreme Court nominee Clarence Thomas and attacking the integrity of his likely opponents, members of the Senate Judiciary Committee, and even one who was not on the committee. The news media thereby amplified and legitimized the negativity of the original advertisement, and they did so for free!

The trend toward greater negativity in advertising was clearly seen in the 2006 campaigns. In the midterm elections of that year, millions of dollars were spent on campaign ads that discredited opponents in the eyes of at-home viewers. From the much discussed Michael J. Fox on stem-cell research, to a lady who claims to have met a candidate at a Playboy party, the campaigns did whatever it took to get their message across. The Democratic National Committee ran an ad that asked if finding Osama bin Laden is a priority for the Bush administration or if the Al Qaeda leader is simply being used as a "scare tactic" before the upcoming elections. Meanwhile images of Al Qaeda leaders Osama bin Laden and Ayman al-Zawahiri and exploding bombs flashed across the screen in an ad from the Republican National Committee. The ad ended with this proclamation: "These are the stakes. Vote November 7th."[40]

Political advertisements may also carry subliminal messages that covertly influence viewers' attitudes. In 1990, for example, there was an ad made by the campaign of Senator Jesse Helms. Helms was running against Harvey Gantt, who is black. In the spot, the hands of a white man are seen crumbling a letter telling him he has been rejected for a job in favor of a minority applicant. Kathleen Hall Jamieson, director of the Annenberg School of Communications at the University of Pennsylvania, argues that there was a subliminal message contained in a black mark in the crumpled letter. In a focus group, some viewers told Jamieson the mark appeared to be the hand of an African-American person. Similarly, a 2000 Bush ad allegedly used subliminal messaging. The 30-second commercial ends with the words: "The Gore prescription plan: Bureaucrats decide," in white lettering on a black screen. In one frame, just before the ad closes, "rats," a fragment of the word "bureaucrat," appears in large white capital letters, superimposed over the phrase: "The Gore prescription plan." The Republican Party spent more than $2.5 million airing the ad in 35 media markets for two weeks in September. Political consultants working for both parties and advertising experts said they found it hard to believe the frame was an editing mistake.[41]

Finally, political advertisements may have become more important because they may be more informative than the news itself. In the month leading up to the 2006 mid-term elections, local television news viewers got considerably more information about campaigns from paid political advertisements than from news coverage. Local newscasts in seven Midwest markets aired 4 minutes, 24 seconds of paid political ads during the typical 30-minute broadcast while dedicating an average of 1 minute, 43 seconds to election news coverage. The analysis also shows that most of the news coverage of elections on early and late-evening broadcasts was devoted to campaign strategy and polling, which outpaced reporting on policy issues by a margin of more than three to one (65 percent to 17 percent).[42]

THE EFFECTS OF THE MASS MEDIA

What People Remember and Know

Although 86 percent of the American public say that it read or heard the news the previous day, very little information seems to have been transmitted. In the summer of 2002, fewer than half of the people questioned in a national survey knew which political party controlled the House of Representatives. On the other hand, three-fourths knew the names of the baseball teams playing in the World Series.[43] Furthermore, even though we have today more newspapers, magazines, television news programs and devote more time and space to the coverage of current events than ever before, there has been no concomitant growth in the amount of factual knowledge evidenced on the part of the American public. Similar surveys in 1967 and 1987 asked respondents to name their governor, representatives in the House, and head of their school district. Only 9 percent failed to name a single official in 1967 compared with 17 percent in 1987. The author of the study attributed the lower performance in 1987 to the public's increased reliance on television.[44]

Influencing Public Opinion

Documenting the effects of mass media on specific attitudes is difficult. Studies have found that prolonged, sustained media coverage on a single topic, especially in a crisis like war, can significantly influence mass opinions.[45] The same study found that of all the people expressing opinions on the news, for example the president, members of Congress, network commentators had the greatest influence on the audience. Other studies have found that even a single story can influence attitude change.[46]

Setting the Political Agenda

Evidence suggests that media coverage does heighten the audience's concern with certain topics over others. For example, studies have found that news coverage of crime has led to increased, in fact unrealistic, concern on the part of the mass public. Furthermore, the less knowledgeable a viewer is about political affairs, the more influenced he is by the agenda of the press.[47]

Cynicism, Alienation, and Declining Efficacy

The press's role in setting the political agenda also means that the increasingly sensational and negative topics covered in the news will dominate the public's agenda as well. Years ago, Michael J. Robinson attempted to document that the CBS documentary "The Selling of the Pentagon" produced antimilitary attitudes in the program's audience.[48] A more recent study has shown that the media attentive are more likely to pick up negative views of the economy.[49]

Other studies have found that those most attentive to the news experience reduced levels of political efficacy with feelings of political powerlessness and mistrust. One study concluded that "the presentation of news in a manner that conveys a high degree of political conflict or criticism leads to a sense of distrust and inefficacy among newspaper readers."[50]

Behavior

There is little consistent evidence that mass forms of communication can alter behavior. Recent studies attempting to link violence on television with violence in young adults have failed to find a clear causal relationship. What the mass media appear to be able to do is channel the behavior of people already predisposed to behave in a particular way. For example, news coverage and political advertisements may work to reinforce an individual's pre-existing partisan views, thereby further encouraging that individual to vote for the favored candidate. Another study has found a relationship between teenage suicide rates in troubled youths and media coverage of teenage suicide.[51]

CONCLUSION

This chapter has focused primarily on the role of the mass media in transmitting images and information to the citizenry of this country. The media are equally important transmitters of the citizens' views to those in government. Throughout history, journalists have suggested policy concerns and offered solutions to pressing problems. In doing so, the mass media have worked to bring issues of public concern to those in government. Today, the media have developed sophisticated methods to tap mass sentiments. Beginning in the 1800s, newspapers conducted straw polls to measure public opinion. These polls usually questioned subscribers but made no scientific attempt to get a random sample. By the middle of the twentieth century, the media began to conduct scientific polls and develop their own survey research divisions. Newspapers and broadcasters even team up to do extensive polling together. Virtually every day, the results of one major poll or another are published. During the 2000 campaign, CNN and *USA Today* reported a fresh poll daily from September 30 through the November election.

Recent developments suggest that the media link between governed and government will only become a more direct one in the future. Ross Perot, a candidate for the presidency in 1992 and again in 1996, has called upon government to employ electronic technology to construct a virtual town meeting. Perot himself set up satellite feeds from six different states to a central studio and invited thousands of people to attend the event. Using two-way television transmission, Perot could speak with the attendees and answer their questions. The technology for voting from the home is also already available. With either cable television lines or telephone connections, it is possible to cast a vote. Electronic democracy may be around the corner.

What still remains unclear is whether such an electronic democracy will succeed in being an informed democracy. While the parties and their candidates are spending ever-increasing amounts of money trying to get out the vote, fewer people seem to be interested. In 2000, only 17.5 percent of U. S. homes tuned into the Democratic National Convention and only 16 percent to the Republican National Convention. Both represented all-time lows based on Nielsen data going back to 1960. Nearly 30 percent of U. S. homes watched the conventions in 1960 on ABC, CBS, and NBC, when most TV viewers received only a handful of channels. Today, thanks to cable and satellite dishes, the average home has access to 60 channels. Still, Americans appear to be far more interested in entertainment than politics. Gore's acceptance speech at the Democratic National Convention was aired following ABC's popular quiz show *Who Wants to be a Millionaire?* An estimated 7.65 million viewers watched the speech on ABC. By way of comparison, that Thursday's edition of *Millionaire* exceeded the combined audience for the speech on ABC, CBS, and NBC, attracting 19.8 million viewers.[52]

CHAPTER NOTES

[1]The Pew Research Center, "News Audiences Increasingly Politicize," http://people-press.org, June 8, 2004, p.4.

[2]Quoted in Robert Kurz, "Congress and the Media: Forces in the Struggle Over Foreign Policy," in *The Media in Foreign Policy*, ed. Simon Serfaty (New York: St. Martin's, 1990), 77.

[3]Jay Peterzell, "Can the CIA Spook the Press?" *Columbia Journalism Review* (July/ August 1986): 18-19.

[4]Larry Speakes with Robert Pack, *Speaking Out: The Reagan Presidency From Inside the White House* (New York: Avon Books, 1989), 279.

[5]Constitutional Rights Foundation, "Online Lessons: War and the Media," http://www.crf-usa.org/Iraqwar html,2005,p.1.

[6]Jason DeParle, "17 News Executives Criticize U.S. for Censorship of Gulf Coverage," *New York Times*, 3 July 1991, 1.

[7]Sidney Kraus and Dennis Davis, *The Effects of Mass Communication on Political Behavior* (University Park: Pennsylvania State University Press, 1980), 127.

[8]Doris Graber, *Mass Media and American Politics* (Washington, D.C.: Congressional Quarterly Press, 1980), 127.

[9]Richard Davis, *The Press and American Politics* (New York: Longman, 1992), 6.

[10]Anthony Smith, "The Newspaper of the Late Twentieth Century: The U.S. Model," *Newspapers and Democracy* (Cambridge, Mass.: MIT Press, 1980), 17.

[11]Michael J. Robinson and Andrew Kohut, "Believability and the Press," *Public Opinion* 53 (Summer 1988): 174-189.

[12]Alfred McLung Lee, *The Daily Newspaper in America* (New York: Macmillan, 1937), 17.

[13]James MacGregor Burns, *John Kennedy: A Political Profile* (New York: Harcourt, Brace, 1960).

[14]Mark Hertsgaard, *On Bended Knee: The Press and the Reagan Presidency* (New York: Schocken Books, 1989), 77.

[15]Ask Questions.org, "A New Bridge to the Media," http://www.askquestions.org, Nov. 21, 2005.

[16]Hertsgaard, *On Bended Knee*, 78.

[17]The Pew Research Center, "News Audiences Increasingly Politicized," p.2.

[18]Herbert J. Gans, *Deciding What's News* (New York: Pantheon, 1979).

[19]Michael Parenti, *Inventing Reality* (1985).

[20]Carl Bernstein quoted in *Vanity Fair*, March, 1989, 106.

[21]Parenti, *Inventing Reality*.

[22]"The Mickey Moused Media," *Los Angeles Times*, 1 August 1995, B9.

[23]Thomas E. Patterson, *Out of Order* (NY:Vintage, 1994), 20.

[24]Meg Greenfield, "Why We're Still Muckraking," *Washington Post*, 20 March 1985, sec. 4, 1.

[25]Richard Harwood, "The Press Should Set The Agenda," Washington Post, 26 September 1988, sec. 4, 3.

[26]"Horserace Journalism," *LA Times*, Dec. 13, 1999, B6.

[27]Kathleen Jamieson, *Dirty Politics* (New York: Oxford University Press, 1992), 181-2.

[28]Johanna Neuman and Richard Simon, "Epidemic of Foot-in-mouth Afflicts Candidates This Year," *LA Times*, Nov. 2, 2006, A1, A15.

[29]Maura Clancey and Michael Robinson, "General Election Coverage: Part I," *Public Opinion* 7 (Dec/Jan 1985), 54.

[30]Michael Robinson, "The Media in Campaign '84: Part II: Wingless, Toothless, and Hopeless," *Public Opinion* 8 (February/March 1985): 48. Also see Thomas E. Patterson, Out of Order (New York: Knopf, 1995).

[31]William Glaberson, "The Capital Press vs. the President: Fair Coverage or Unreined Adversity?" *New York Times*, 17 June 1993, A11.

[32]Warren Weaver, "C-Span on the Hill: 10 Years of Gavel to Gavel," *New York Times*, 28 March 1989, A10.

[33]Michael Robinson and Margaret Sheehan, *Over the Wire and on TV* (New York: Russell Sage, 1983).

[34]S. Robert Lichter and Daniel Amundson, "Less News is Worse News: Television News Coverage of Congress, 1972-92," in *Congress, the Press, and the Public*, eds. Thomas Mann and Norman Ornstein (Washington,D.C.: American Enterprise Institute, 1994), 131-40.

[35]Darrell M. West, Air Wars (Washington, D.C.: Congressional Quarterly Press, 1993).

[36]"TV's Debt to Democracy," *LA Times*, Dec. 13, 1999, B6.

[37]*U.S. News and World Report*, 8 July 1996, 17.

[38]Jeff Leeds, "Studies Find Political Ad Spending Spree," *LA Times*, Nov. 20, 2000, A15.

[39]Tim Rutter, "Regarding Media: We pay the cost of campaign season," *The LA Times*, Nov. 4, 2006, A1.

[40]NPR.org, "As the Election Nears, the Ads Sling Mud," http://npr.org, Nov. 3, 2006.

[41]Jeff Leeds, "Republicans Try to Still Criticism of 'Rats' Ad," *LA Times*, Sept. 13, A18.

[42]Dennis Chaptman, "Study: Political Ad Time Trumps Election Coverage on the Tube," http://11news.wisc.edu, Nov. 21, 2006.

[43]Annenberg Survey: Most Americans Still Unfamiliar with Politics http://www.appcpenn.org/reports/2002/22000-2.

[44]Stephen Earl Bennett, "Trends in Americans' Political Information 1967-1987," *American Politics Quarterly* 17 (October 1989): 322-356.

[45]Benjamin Page, Robert Y. Shapiro, and Glen R. Dempsey, "What Moves Public Opinion?" *American Political Science Review* 81 (March 1987): 31.

[46]David L. Jordan, "Newspaper Effects on Policy Preferences," *Public Opinion Quarterly* 57 (Summer 1993): 191-204.

[47]Shanto Iyengar and Donald R. Kinder, *News That Matters: Television and American Opinion* (Chicago: University of Chicago Press, 1987), 33.

[48]Michael J. Robinson, "Public Affairs Television and the Growth of Video Malaise," *American Political Science Review* 70 (1976): 425-30.

[49]David E. Harrington, "Economic News on Television: the Determinants of Coverage," *Public Opinion Quarterly* 53 (Spring 1989): 17-40.

[50]Arthur Miller, Edie Goldenberg, and Lutz Ebring, "Type-Set Politics," *American Political Science Review* 73 (1979): 77.

[51]Madelyn Gould and David Shaffer "The Impact of Suicide in TV Movies," *New England Journal of Medicine* 315 (11 September 1986): 685-94.

[52]Brian Lowry, "An Issue Voters Can Agree on," *LA Times*, Sept 19, 2000, A16.

SUGGESTED READINGS

Ansolabehere, Stephen, Roy Behr, and Shanto Iyengar. *The Media Game: American Politics in the Television Age*. New York: Macmillan, 1993.

Auletta, Ken. *Three Blind Mice: How the TV Networks Lost Their Way*. New York: Random House, 1991.

Carter, T. Barton, Marc A. Franklin, and Jay B. Wright. *The First Amendment and the Fourth Estate: The Law of the Mass Media*, 5th ed. Mineola, New York: Foundation Press, 1991.

Donovan, Robert, and Ray Scherer. *Unsilent Revolution: Television News and American Public Life, 1948-1991*. New York: Cambridge University Press, 1991.

Entman, Robert. *Democracy Without Citizens: Media and the Decay of American Politics*. New York: Oxford University Press, 1989.

Graber, Doris A. *Mass Media and American Politics*, 5th ed. Washington, C.C.: Congressional Quarterly Press, 1996.

Jamieson, Kathleen Hall. *Packaging the Presidency: A History and Criticism of Presidential Campaign Advertising*. New York: Oxford University Press, 1992.

Parenti, Michael. *Inventing Reality: The Politics of Mass Media*. New York: St. Martin's Press, 1986.

Patterson, Thomas W. *The Mass Media Election*. New York: Praeger, 1980.

Chapter Eight

INTEREST GROUPS

For many, the Medicare/Prescription Drug Bill passed by Congress in 2003 represents a case study in how the government should not work. The law authorizes the government to spend $400 billion over ten years, beginning January 1, 2006, for a voluntary prescription drug program under Medicare. Under the new system, private insurance companies will compete to provide drug coverage to Medicare recipients through PPOs, HMOs, or other insurance policies. In the end, the legislation provides billions of dollars in subsidies to HMOs and other managed-care plans, paying them substantially more than it cost regular Medicare to provide the same services. How this bill became law is a story of interest group influence.

When Congress first took up the issue of prescription drugs, the drug industry began to draw up plans for raising millions of dollars to defeat any effort to reduce drug prices. For the drug industry, the financial stakes were huge and so the industry began to spend enormous amounts of money on campaign spending, lobbying, and advertising to influence the outcome of the legislation. The drug industry has made a reported $650 million in contributions to members of Congress in recent years, and many members of Congress have received donations totaling in the six figures from pharmaceutical interests.

No group was more active in its efforts than PhRMA. PhRMA increased its yearly budget 23 percent to $150 million in anticipation of the upcoming Medicare fight; industry protection in the Medicare reform bill was its top priority. PhRMA has long been known as one of Washington's most powerful lobbying forces. The trade group spent $16 million on lobbying in 2003 and if one includes lobbying spent by all of PhRMA's companies, the group spent at least $72.6 million lobbying in 2003, or roughly $135,701 per member of Congress.

PhRMA also capitalized on hiring former members of Congress and their staffs as part of its lobbying army. PhRMA lobbyists include former Representatives Vic Fazio, Vin Weber, and Bill Paxon. Other drug lobbyists include David W. Beier, former domestic policy advisor to Vice President Al Gore; Dave Larson, former health policy advisor to Senator Bill Frist; and Edwin A. Buckham, former chief of staff to Representative Tom DeLay. Through these lobbying efforts, the drug industry maintains a constant presence among policymakers. For example, in the weeks following the House and Senate's passage of their respective Medicare bills, pharmaceutical companies organized parties for congressional staffers who were working on the legislation. Staffers also were offered the opportunity to attend a "Rooftop Rendezvous" thrown by PhRMA and hospital trade groups. From start to finish, the $535 billion Medicare bill passed by Congress and signed into law by the president was a study in how powerful groups shut out opposing voices and the public good.[1]

Today it appears that senior citizens, low-income and disabled persons were dealt a hard blow when Congress passed this bill. While the bill funds $400 billion to the pharmaceutical companies, it reduces coverage for up to six million low income and disabled persons and may result in the loss of private employer-provided health insurance for as many as three million retirees.[2]

DEFINING INTEREST GROUPS

An **interest group** is an organization of people and or companies with specific policy goals, entering the policy process at several points. The key here is that an interest group is an *organization*. There are many people with many interests throughout the United States; but many, if not most, fail to organize with others to pursue their goals. In addition, many of the groups that do go on to get organized pursue private or social purposes. Groups only become political interest groups when they try to affect policies of local, state, and federal governments.

Interest Groups versus Political Parties

Political parties and interest groups are often easily confused because they both seek to influence policy; they are, however, distinct. Political parties nominate candidates for office and seek to gain office by aggregating groups into a coalition. In doing this, political parties often try to mute their policy positions to appeal to as many differing groups as possible. Interest groups, on the other hand, seek to articulate the specific viewpoint of the group. While it is true that some groups have a wider set of concerns than others, every interest group is concerned with representing the position or positions of the group. Usually, the interest group stands little to win from muting its position.

The Roles of Interest Groups

While political parties do mainly one thing, nominate candidates and run them for office, interest groups play several roles.

Representation

Perhaps the most important role performed by an interest group is representing the interests of its members. The Tobacco Institute promotes the interests of cigarette companies, and the Human Rights Campaign Fund works to advance the cause of gay and lesbian rights.

Political Participation

Interest groups provide people with an avenue to participate in politics. Many people feel that their vote is not very important. Still, these people may see strength in numbers and interest groups as the vehicle to express this strength.

Education

Interest groups expend a great deal of effort on educating their members, the general public, and government officials. It is quite common to see spokespersons for interest groups interviewed on television news programs or talk shows. Groups may also advertise both on television and in the newspapers. Interest groups may even try direct-mail campaigns to explain their viewpoints and mobilize support.

Agenda Building

By educating their members, the general public, and public officials, interest groups are seeking to set the agenda of issues that are to be actively debated by policy makers. In the 1970s environmental groups organized to get environmental issues onto the national agenda. In doing so, the environmental groups followed the path charted by the civil rights groups in the 1950s and women's groups in the 1960s.

Program Monitoring

Interest groups are not only concerned about what laws are passed; they are also concerned with the implementation of policy. Interest groups monitor how the government administers the programs that affect them. Sometimes the law may even require federal agencies to work with interest groups to ensure that their interests are taken into account. Clearly interest groups play several important roles in American politics. They shape policy outcomes through representation of their members, providing an avenue of participation, education, agenda setting, and the monitoring of government programs. Still, some groups may be more effective at fulfilling these roles than other groups. Some citizens may never see their interests represented. Some groups may mislead rather than educate officials and the public. Other groups may work to distort national priorities and programs to benefit their interests at the expense of the nation as a whole. To understand the inequities and inefficiencies of interest group politics, it is necessary to understand that some groups simply get better organized than others.

WHO IS ORGANIZED?

There is an astounding number of interest groups in the United States. *The Encyclopedia of Associations*, a voluntary government publication of national interest groups, lists over twenty-five thousand organizations working to affect public policy. The number of groups is matched by their incredible diversity. Everyone from the National Cricket Growers to the Flying Physicians is listed in the numerous volumes of the *Encyclopedia*. The multiplicity and obscurity of the groups disguise, however, some typical membership patterns.

Economic Interest Groups

Business Groups

Business groups are the most common type of interest group. Business groups account for approximately 20 percent of the organized interest groups in Washington. If one adds in lobbyists and law firms hired to represent business interests, business interests constitute up to 70 percent of all groups housed in the national capital.[3]

There are three distinct types of business organizations. The organization with the broadest membership is the peak business association. Peak associations attempt to speak for the entire business community. The Chamber of Commerce, for example, represents an assortment of local chambers of commerce and other groups. The National Association of Manufacturers (NAM) represents more than ten thousand manufacturing firms, and the Business Roundtable represents the country's two hundred largest corporations.

Businesses may also attempt to advance their interests through trade associations. These organizations represent companies in the same line of business. Mobil, Shell, and Texaco, for example, belong to the U.S. Petroleum Association.

Finally, many businesses try to influence public policy on an individual basis. Most large companies have offices in Washington or hire Washington lobbying firms to work with government officials in the making and implementation of policy.

While the Republican Party has traditionally favored business, in recent years the Democrats have also worked in the interests of the business community. The pro-business stance of the two parties reflects business's increasing financial contributions to both parties. In both 2000 and 2004 over 75 percent of the contributions to George Bush's campaign came from business interest groups. Businesses were also heavy contributors to Clinton in both 1992 and 1996. Once in office, President Clinton supported major international trade agreements, including "most favored nation" trading privileges with China. This was a major victory for business because labor and other groups had protested the serious human rights violations by China and the likelihood that the agreement will result in a loss of American jobs as firms transfer manufacturing to sites where labor costs are lower.

Organized Labor

Unions try to influence government policy across a wide array of issues. The minimum wage, safety regulations, health care, and civil rights issues are all of importance to the workers of America. The most important voice of organized labor is the AFL-CIO, which includes the Teamsters 1.4 million members, the American Federation of State, County, and Municipal Employees' 1.2 million members, the United Food and Commercial Workers International Union's 1 million workers, and the United Auto Workers 840,000 members.

The power of unions has waned over the years. The political influence of labor unions has waned considerably since the 1960s. One reason is that membership in unions continues to decline as a percentage of the workforce. Only 14 percent of the nonagricultural workforce belong to a union. Another reason for the declining membership is the loss of manufacturing jobs to foreign countries. Service jobs are now more numerous in the United States, and whereas manufacturing jobs have been highly unionized, service ones are not. Membership has also suffered because of antiunion business practices. Many businesses punish employees who advocate union activity. While illegal, such antiunion activities are rarely prosecuted.

Labor's political influence has also declined as states in the South and Southwest, where people have been historically hostile to unions, have gained population and representation in Congress, while the more heavily unionized northern states have experienced declining populations. The 2000 census shows that this trend is continuing to erode the power of unions.

To expand their membership, unions have been turning to the low-wage service sector. Labor won a major victory in 1999 when seventy-five thousand nursing employees voted to be represented by the Service Employees International Union, making it the third largest in the nation. Unions are also expanding into the ranks of high-tech and professional workers. Efforts are under way to organize computer specialists where they are highly concentrated in the Silicon Valley of California[4] Doctors employed by HMOs, as well as those in private practice, are also organizing into unions.

Unionism in America grew out of the strife between low-paid workers and the greed of capitalism. The struggle for unionization was long and bitter but was eventually won when the government recognized the right of workers to organize. Eugene Debbs is shown here addressing railroad workers. He and other union officials were jailed for disobeying a court injunction against the Pullman Strike of 1894.

César Chávez, a successful Hispanic leader, established the National Farmworkers Association that became the United Farm Workers.

Agriculture

There are two types of organizations representing agricultural groups. General farm interest groups, the biggest of which is the American Farm Bureau Federation, seek to represent the interests shared by most farmers. For example, the American Farm Bureau speaks for the interests of large farms while the National Farmers Organization and the National Farmers Union represent the interests of the smaller farmer.

A newer type of agricultural group is found in those that have organized around specific commodities. Today, almost every crop and type of livestock has a corresponding group. Pigs have the National Swine Improvement Federation. Lettuce greens have the National Leafy Greens Council.

Professional Associations

Professional associations represent occupations that usually involve extensive education and formal training and perhaps government licensing. The American Medical Association (AMA) and the American Bar Association (ABA) are two prominent examples of professional associations.

Citizen Groups

Unlike economic interest groups, citizen groups, often called **public interest groups**, work to promote their vision of the public good. Citizen groups exist for almost every issue but the most visible have been in the area of consumer protection and environmental policy making. Some groups advance broad agendas. For example, People for the American Way is a liberal interest group that pushes its position on issues from school prayer to abortion to censorship of the arts. Other citizen groups are single-issue groups that are organized around one specific issue, like abortion, saving the whales, or drunk driving.

Women's Groups

There are many groups organized to advocate women's equality. The National Organization for Women (NOW) is the largest of these groups with 250,000 members and chapters in all of the fifty states. In recent years the women's movement has divided between groups pushing an ideological agenda, such as NOW, which continues to focus on the issue of abortion, and more pragmatic groups, such as the National Women's Caucus, which seeks to elect women to public office regardless of their stands on specific issues. Another group, EMILY, is an organization that recruits, trains, and endorses pro-choice Democratic women candidates and then works to fund and elect them to public office. The organization holds seminars for candidates, campaign managers, and journalists. It has successfully elected five women to the Senate and thirty-four to the House. In 1994, EMILY was the largest contributor to the Democratic Party. In 2000, it spent over $12 million to get out the vote, and in 2004, its support of Governor Christine Gregoire was largely responsible for her 129-vote margin of victory in Washington State.

Religious Groups

Religious groups have become increasingly well organized. Conservative Christian groups have had a particularly large impact on American elections and politics. Christian groups were the major force behind the presidential candidacy of Pat Robertson in 1988. Following his inability to capture the Republican nomination, Robertson converted a mailing list of two million names into the Christian Coalition. The Coalition has sought to gain control of the Republican Party, and today has gained dominance, or at least leverage, in twenty state parties.[5] The Coalition is not as uncompromising on moral issues as it once was. Its backing in 2000 of George W. Bush for the Republican presidential nomination over several candidates more closely aligned with the religious right evidences its willingness to back more moderate candidates. The shift represents a desire to broaden the appeal of the Coalition. The group, however, remains the most powerful organization in the Republican Party.

Jewish groups have also been particularly well organized and politically active. Since its beginning in 1951, the Jewish pro-Israeli lobby has successfully influenced United States foreign policy, losing on only three key issues, all involving the sale of arms to Egypt and Saudi Arabia.

Gays and Lesbians

After World War II, the first gay rights groups organized to share information and fight police repression. During the 1960s, the gay rights movement became better organized and more visible. By 1972, gay rights issues were being addressed by politicians, and by 1973 the American Psychiatric Association removed homosexuality from its list of mental disorders. The election of Bill Clinton in 1992 was a crucial turning point for gay rights. He ended the federal policy treating homosexuals as security risks and invited gay activists to the White House for the first time. Today there are numerous gay groups. There are radical, confrontational groups like Queer Nation, but there are also more moderate, mainstream groups such as Human Rights Campaign (HRC) with a membership of 250,000.

The Elderly

Today, 12 percent of the nation's population is over sixty-five. Several groups, sometimes called the "gray lobby," represent their interests. Founded in 1958 to provide insurance for the elderly, the American Association of Retired Persons (AARP), with thirty-three million members, is the largest and of its most powerful interest groups. The AARP, through an active mail drive, attracts eight thousand new members every day. For only $10, anyone over fifty can join and gain access to the bounty of benefits provided by the organization, everything from auto and home insurance to car rentals.

With 1,800 employees and eighteen lobbyists, the AARP has become a potent political force. The goals of the AARP are primarily to preserve and expand government benefits to the elderly, which total about $14 billion each month.[6] Although programs for the elderly represent one-third of the budget, politicians are reluctant to touch them. Mindful of their political clout, President Clinton got the AARP to support his health-care reform by including long-term nursing home care. In 2003, the support of AARP's 35 million members helped the Republicans win passage of controversial Medicare legislation.

Several groups have formed to try to stem the power of the gray lobby. Groups such as Americans for Generational Equity and Children's Defense Fund are, however, smaller and less influential than AARP.

Environmental Groups

Earth Day 1970 marked the beginning of the environmental movement in the United States. The environmental movement today is large, well organized, and has the active support of most Americans. Some environmental groups, such as the National Audubon Society, Sierra Club, and the Natural Resources Defense Council, have permanent offices in Washington with a staff of highly skilled lobbyists. All experienced substantial growth in membership and finances during the 1980s, when the Reagan administration threatened to turn back the environmental protections of the 1970s.

Single-Issue Groups

Single-issue groups are distinguished by their concern for a single issue and their reluctance to compromise. The abortion issue has generated a number of single-issue groups. The National Right to Life Committee is supporting a constitutional amendment to ban all abortions. The committee works to elect candidates that favor such an amendment and defeat those who do not. In 2000, the organization activated its eight million members and contributed heavily on behalf of Republican candidates.

Foreign Governments

Foreign governments, foreign corporations, and citizens of foreign countries are also represented in Washington. Governments of the largest U.S. trading partners, such as Japan, South Korea, Canada,

Pro-choice is a single issue interest group.

and the European Union (EU) countries, maintain large research and lobbying staffs. Even smaller nations, such as those in Central America, engage lobbyists when legislation affecting their interests is under consideration by the Congress.

Government Interest Groups

Because the federal government in Washington controls most of the financial resources of the country and because the federal government gives grants of money to states and localities, state and local governments organize to lobby for these funds. In addition, the National Governors' Association, the National Association of Counties, and the National League of Cities all work to influence national policy on a wide array of issues affecting their levels of government.

Foreign governments may also be considered as interest groups when they work to affect U.S. policy making. In 1992, the governments of Croatia and Bosnia actively sought U.S. support for their wars with Serbia.[7] These foreign interests often hire former U.S. government employees to promote their interests in Washington.

COMMON FEATURES OF INTEREST GROUPS

While there are thousands of interest groups in the United States and while they come in all types and sizes, they share certain organizational features. First, every group must have a leadership and decision-making structure. The complexity of this structure will differ by group, but at a fundamental level, the group will need a staff including a public relations office, or a lobbying office, preferably in Washington, D.C. Second, the group must build a financial structure capable of sustaining the organization and funding group activities. Most groups require members to pay dues, and they often solicit additional funds through mailings and fundraising activities. Third, all groups must attract members to pay the dues and engage in group activities.

To attract such a membership, groups can offer three kinds of incentives. **Solidary incentives** involve the pleasure that members get from joining the group. Such incentives may include companionship and status. Parent-Teacher Associations and the Rotary Club are good examples of groups based principally on the provision of solidary incentives. **Material incentives** include anything that might make the group financially attractive to a member. The American Association of Retired Persons, for example, offers a grocery list of low-cost insurance, low-cost travel, and discounts in a variety of stores. These material incentives can only be obtained by people who join the group. The third type of incentive is the **purposive incentive**, the goals of the group. Some groups can attract members on the basis of passionate feelings about the group cause. Groups that rely primarily on their goals to attract members tend to be smaller groups where the purpose of the group involves a clear economic self interest. Groups with more amorphous purposes, for example, peace or solving world hunger, may have more difficulty arousing passion in their members for reasons discussed in the next section.

BIASES IN INTEREST GROUP FORMATION AND MAINTENANCE

The tremendous number and diversity of interest groups in the United States may disguise some inherent biases in the universe of interest group politics. The fact is that not all interests get organized and represented by groups. Neither are all groups that are organized equal in strength and influence. There are serious obstacles in the way of both interest group formation and interest group maintenance.

Obstacles to Interest Group Formation

The main obstacle to interest group organization is the problem of getting people to actually join the group, pay the dues, go to meetings and, in short, do the work. Many people may share a particular concern or interest; few will actually join the group. The reason that so few join the group is that all interest groups provide what economists call *collective goods*, benefits that will go not only to members of the group but nonmembers as well. Why go the full nine yards and work for the group when one can receive the benefits without expending the effort? In other words, interest groups are plagued by the age-old problem of free-riders, people who take the collective good without paying for it or working for it.

Some groups are faced with a greater free-rider problem than others. In 1965, in his book *The Logic of Collective Action*, Mancur Olson argued that interests shared by a larger number of people have a harder time getting organized than those shared by only a few people.[8] The reason, according to Olson, is that the larger the number of people sharing an interest the more likely each individual is to make the rational calculation that his or her effort is not needed and that someone will do the work of obtaining the collective good. For example, many people are concerned with a cleaner environment; yet, many refuse to donate time or money to the cause, not because they do not care but rather because they figure with so many other people out there concerned with the environment, there must surely be others who will do the work. Everyone will receive the benefits from a cleaner environment, but only a few will do the work. In a small group, however, members are more likely to see that if they fail to do the work, maybe no one will do the work. Consequently, maybe the collective good will not be obtained at all.

Additionally, when an interest is shared by a large number of people, it may often be the case that each individual member's share of the collective good is quite small. For example, a group called Heal the Bay works to clean up the Santa Monica Bay in southern California. While everyone would like a cleaner bay, each person's share of the bay is quite small, with many not living right on the coast or swimming in the bay regularly. On the other hand, in a small group the benefits may be very large. Say that one hundred people allegedly harmed by breast implants sue the manufacturer and receive thirty million dollars in damages. Quite obviously, the incentive to organize becomes stronger as the member's share of the collective good becomes larger.

The result of this collective good, free-rider problem is that many groups, particularly the larger ones, have a hard time tapping their potential membership. In the end, once organized, the groups may appear illegitimate and unrepresentative in that they have tapped such a small percentage of the population that should be concerned with the issue. Politicians tend to address issues only when they perceive the public to be fully aroused about and organized to pursue that issue. If a group has managed to organize only a bare fraction of those who should be sympathetic to the cause, politicians are likely to take a wait-and-see attitude.

What is important is that groups have a large *market share*, the number of members actually in the group compared to its potential membership. For years the American Medical Association (AMA) enrolled a very large percentage (more than 70 percent) of the nation's doctors as members. As its membership declined, however, so did the influence of the AMA.

Overcoming the Obstacles Through Interest Group Maintenance

After the publication of Olson's book, groups began to make serious efforts to attract and maintain their membership. One of the best ways for groups to attract members and keep them active in the group is to offer selective benefits, or one might think of them as noncollective goods, to only those who actually join the group. Such selective benefits can take any or all of three forms: material, solidary, and expressive benefits.

Material benefits are goods and services that come from belonging to a group. For example, the very well organized American Association for Retired Persons offers members a cornucopia of cheap travel rates, insurance benefits, and a monthly magazine. Similarly, the National Rifle Association's $25 annual membership fee entitles one to a magazine subscription, a shooter's cap, and eligibility to apply for a low-interest credit card. Fundraisers for public television often offer coffee mugs to those who make a contribution of a certain amount. Of course, selective benefits

Table 8.1

"The Power 25": The Influential Interest Groups

Rank	Group	Type
1	AARP	Citizen
2	American Israel Public Affairs Committee	Other (Foreign Affairs)
3	AFL-CIO	Union
4	National Federation of Independent Business	Business, Peak Association
5	Association of Trial Lawyers of America	Professional Association
6	National Rifle Association of America	Citizen
7	Christian Coalition	Citizen
8	American Medical Association	Business, Peak Association
9	National Education Association	Union
10	National Right to Life Committee	Citizen
11	National Association of Home Builders	Business, Trade Association
12	American Bankers Association	Business, Peak Association
13	National Association of Manufacturers	Business, Trade Association
14	American Federation of State, County & Municipal Employees	Business, Trade Association
15	Chamber of Commerce of the U.S.	Business, Peak Association
16	Veterans of Foreign Wars	Citizen
17	National Association of Broadcasters	Business, Trade Association
18	National Right to Life Committee	Citizen
19	Health Insurance Association of America	Business, Trade Association
20	Pharmaceutical Research & Manufacturers	Business, Peak Association
21	National Governors' Association	Government
22	Recording Industry Association	Business, Trade Association
23	American Legion	Citizen
24	National Association of Realtors	Business, Trade Association
25	International Brotherhood of Teamsters	Union

Source: *Fortune Magazine, August 2, 2006*

need not be material. Groups may also entice members with the **solidary benefits** of fun, camaraderie, and status. Other groups may offer **expressive benefits**, those derived from working for an interest group whose cause they see as just and right.

Selective goods are, however, expensive to provide. In each of the next 15 years, another 3 million Americans will reach age 50. Each one will get an invitation to join perhaps the most muscular political organization in the country, the American Association of Retired People (AARP). In May 2000, the organization unveiled a campaign to capture the loyalty of a generation of baby boomers with a series of selective goods. Not merely cruise discounts, but a new telephone hotline to put members in touch with experts who can help find a nursing home for a parent who has just suffered a stroke, or furnish a list of college scholarships for a high school senior. Not just auto rental coupons, but big savings on eye exams and glasses, perhaps even laser surgery. Not just motel promotions, but cut-rate subscriptions to AOL and savings on financial software programs and magazines. The provision of all these selective goods is expensive.

This provision siphons off money that the group might have otherwise used for political purposes like lobbying or campaign funding. Smaller groups, with less of a free-rider problem, are, therefore, at an advantage in that they do not have to spend money on these selective goods. In addition, business and trade groups, which often tend to be small, have the additional advantage in that their members have a clear economic self-interest. Such a clear self-interest may work to get the group organized making the provision of selective goods unnecessary.

Interest Group Bias

Although there are tens of thousands of interest groups organized in the United States, the interests of all the people are not equally represented. Studies have consistently shown that the affluent, the better educated, those with a clear self-interest, are far more likely to join groups, participate at high levels, and remain with the group. There are, of course, significant examples of poor, uneducated people getting organized. Cesar Chavez successfully organized farm workers into the United Farm Workers Union. Still, such cases are more the exception than the rule. As this chapter has discussed, groups with a large potential membership and groups that are organized around issues that may not be clearly related to the members' economic self-interest may face additional problems both in organization formation and maintenance. These groups are quite often those that attempt to speak for the poor, the consumers, the environment, and the disenfranchised.

Still, Fortune Magazine's Survey of the 25 most powerful pressure groups (Table 8.1) rebuts one of the oldest axioms of lobbying: that campaign contributions buy power in Washington. While donations are still crucial (and are often abused, as the recent revelations about "soft money" excesses in recent presidential elections show), they are not the only keys to the kingdom. True, three of the top ten organizations owe their high rankings to their substantial campaign contributions: the Association of Trial Lawyers of America (No. 5), the American Israel Public Affairs Committee (No. 2), and the American Medical Association (No. 8). But these days, interest organizations are valued more for the votes they can deliver. Most of the Power 25 have large numbers of geographically dispersed and politically active members who focus their energies on a narrow range of issues. In other words, they know their convictions and vote them. In this era of low voter turnout, that kind of commitment can mean the difference between victory and defeat in close elections, which translates into real heft on the legislative front. Few things are more important to a Congressman than getting reelected.

Fully half of the top ten groups in the FORTUNE survey were propelled there on the strength of their long-established grassroots networks. These kings of the town hall meeting are the American Association of Retired Persons (No. 1); the National Federation of Independent Business, better known as the small-business lobby (No. 4); the National Rifle Association (No. 6); the Christian

Coalition (No. 7); and the National Right to Life Committee (No. 10). This is not to say that money does not talk at all anymore. The AFL-CIO (No. 3) garnered great grades for both its grassroots and its campaign fundraising.

The affluence of an organization's members does not guarantee influence. Sometimes it has the opposite effect. In one of the most striking examples of the populist imperative, the only investor-related organization that made the Power 25 is the American Bankers Association at No. 12. The other financial services lobbies are washouts. The National Association of Securities Dealers is No. 83; the Public Securities Association, recently renamed the Bond Market Association, is No. 84; the Securities Industry Association is No. 47; and worst of all, the Investment Company Institute, the mutual fund industry trade association, languishes at No. 115. Of course these groups do more than try to affect laws and regulations; they also serve their own members. But one thing is for sure: Wall Street's stock is not as high in Washington as once thought.

In contrast, the groups with huge memberships that also have an intense self-interest in government payouts are disproportionately represented in the Power 25. These include the National Education Association (No. 9) and AFSCME, the American Federation of State, County, and Municipal Employees (No. 14), whose members rely on government for their paychecks. More to the point are the Veterans of Foreign Wars (No. 16) and the American Legion (No. 23), whose members not only get veterans' benefits but also have a patriotic pull on politicians. The lesson: It takes both time and more than a modicum of support from politicians in both political parties for an interest group to gain any real standing in the hidebound world of Washington.[9]

THE PROLIFERATION OF INTEREST GROUPS

Americans have long worried about this bias in interest group organization and activity. Even at the time of the writing of the Constitution, it was clear that divisions among the citizenry were inevitable, sown into the very fabric of a free society. Writing in 1787, James Madison warned that these "factions" could prove dangerous to the larger public interest as they attempted to control policy making on their own behalf. For Madison, tyranny by either a majority or minority was problematic.

According to Madison, only two solutions exist to cure the "mischief of faction." One is to do away with the very freedom that spawns the conflict between groups. This solution Madison rejected because it would destroy the foundation of the American experiment in self-government. The other solution would be encourage and nurture the factious nature of American society. Madison's vision was of a large, diverse nation with so many differences of opinion that domination by any one group would be unlikely. A group that might form on the basis of agreement on one issue would probably be internally divided by differences of opinion on other issues.

> Take in a greater variety of parties and interest [and] you will make it less probable that a majority of the whole will have a common motive to invade the rights of other citizens . . . [Hence the advantage] enjoyed by a large over a small republic.[10]

Unfortunately, some issues are not easily resolved. To dramatize their cause against "acid rain," members of Green Peace, an environmental group, hung banners from smokestacks in four different European countries to protest factory emissions.

Madison's constitutional theory was that a government must actually encourage the proliferation of interest groups to prevent tyranny by any one group. This theory is today called **pluralism**. The theory suggests that all interests are and should be free to pursue their goals through bargaining and compromising, accommodating the interests of other groups. Madison's solution may be seen at work today. Since the founding of this nation, groups have proliferated at a phenomenal rate. Today, the bias in favor of the wealthy, the educated, and the professional is somewhat mitigated by the recent expansion in the number of interest groups found in this country. Tyranny by any one group is made less likely in such an environment rich with interest group organization and activity. While this proliferation is partly a result of what Madison called a large republic, the seeds of the proliferation are also to be found in more modern developments.

Sources of Interest Group Proliferation

Increased Government Regulation

Before the Second World War, the national government played a relatively limited role in American life. After the war, the federal government began to regulate various sectors of the economy and society. In the 1970s, the reach of government regulation had extended to almost every nook and cranny of the country's life. In the 1940s and 1950s, laws were passed regulating the eight-hour work day, child labor, and minimum wages. In the 1960s, with President Lyndon Johnson's War on Poverty, additional laws were passed to regulate race relations. Such government regulations have a powerful politicizing effect, often igniting interest group organization and activity.

The greatest expansion in government regulation came in the 1970s when the national government moved into the areas of automobiles, oil, gas, education, and health care. A *New York Times* report notes that these regulations spawned increased interest group activity in all the regulated areas.[11] The first groups to organize were usually the affected industries, organizing to fight the regulations. But just as a pebble tossed into a pond sets off concentric circles, so did government regulation spawn growing interest group activity. New groups, often called **clientele groups**, soon sprang up to encourage the regulation and to influence the distribution of the benefits of regulation. A clientele group is a group or segment of society whose interests are directly affected or promoted by a government agency. The first clientele department was the Department of Agriculture established by Congress in 1862 to promote the interests of farmers.

Recently, despite serious concerns that U.S. chemical plants could be targets for terrorists, the chemical industry has successfully blocked legislation that would mandate more stringent security rules for chemical manufacturers and others. Following the September 11 attacks, the Environmental Protection Agency warned that 123 chemical plants across the country each contained enough toxic chemicals to kill or injure one million people, if terrorists attacked the facility, and that another 750 facilities could threaten more than 100,000 people. Due in part to the generous campaign donations from the chemical plants, neither Congress nor the White House, nor any federal agency, has been successful in closing this large hole in homeland security.

Court decisions and presidential actions may also stimulate interest group organizations. For example, when the Supreme Court stepped into the abortion controversy in 1973 with *Roe v. Wade*, pro-life groups were quick to organize. Then, the *Webster* case set off the pro-choice groups. Other issues, such as school prayer, flag burning, and the death penalty, have set off a similar pattern of group proliferation. Most recently, the Clintons set off a chain of interest group activity when they announced their intention of reforming the health-care system in this country, and the president appointed a health-care task force. The First Lady tried to shelter her task force from outside pressure by holding her meetings in secret. Hundreds of groups in the health-care field and insurance industries organized a massive lobbying effort nonetheless. Physicians, pharmaceutical companies, nursing groups, mental health professionals, chiropractors, Prudential Insurance Company, Aetna, and Cigna all entered the struggle over the direction of health-care reform. Perhaps, not surprisingly, no major reform has yet been legislated.

Postindustrial Changes and Public Interest Groups

The spread of affluence and education in the United States has led to a society that is capable of thinking of more than mere subsistence issues, a society that some have called **postindustrial**. On the other hand, countries plagued with constant poverty and endless wars are societies that may not spawn interest groups concerned with saving whales. In addition, agrarian, preindustrial nations are not faced with the technological complexities that would breed groups such as Mothers Against Drunk Drivers and consumer safety groups concerned with breast implants.

Postindustrial changes in the United States have generated a large number of interests, particularly among occupational and professional groups in the areas of science and technology. For example, genetic engineering associations have sprung up in the wake of recent DNA discoveries.

The excesses and errors of technology have also increased the number of groups in American society. Today there are dozens of groups organized to protect animal rights, including People for Ethical Treatment of Animals (PETA), Progressive Animal Welfare Society (PAWS), Committee to Abolish Sport Hunting (CASH), and the Animal Rights Network (ARN). Postindustrial affluence has freed discretionary income and channeled it towards these new causes.

Great numbers of new groups that have sprung up particularly in the affluent, professional, and college-educated sector of American society have led some to label this a "New Politics" movement.[12] The members fueling this New Politics had formative experiences rooted in the civil rights movement and the Vietnam War. Today, new politics issues include environmental protection, women's rights, nuclear disarmament, and gay rights.

A major result of the New Politics movement is the creation of "public interest" groups. These groups are not based on the economic self-interest of the members. Rather, the benefits to their members are largely ideological. Today, many public interest groups are important players in Washington politics. Most are environmental and consumer groups, but there are other groups that work on corporate accountability, good government, and poverty issues. Common Cause, the Sierra Club, the Environmental Defense Fund, and Greenpeace are all examples of public interest groups.[13]

Interest Group Friendly Laws and Actions

An additional stimulus to the New Politics groups, and group proliferation in general, has been the wide array of environmental and consumer laws that has opened up avenues for group participation in the policy-making process. Such legislative invitations to group participation have not always been the norm. Early in the twentieth century workers often found it hard to organize because business and industry used government-backed injunctions to prevent labor strikes. By the 1930s, prohibition of such injunctions in private labor disputes and the rights of collective bargaining were established and union formation flourished with government approval and protection. Recent campaign finance laws (discussed below) have also contributed to group proliferation.[14]

Government often intervenes directly in group creation. Since the 1960s, for example, the federal government has been especially active in providing start-up funds for groups. Interest group scholar Jack Walker found that nine citizens' groups out of ten received some outside funding in the initial stages of development.[15] For example, the Center for Substance Abuse and Prevention (CSAP), which is part of the Department of Health and Human Services, gives grants to hundreds of non-profit groups, financing after-school and summer youth programs, counseling for pregnant women, drug-free work place programs, and good nutrition workshops.

Cheaper Forms of Communication

After World War II great technological changes produced a variety of communication forms that would allow groups to reach their members more easily and facilitate their communication with government officials. Bulk mail rates and special phone rates reduced the costs of communication. These were followed by the FAX machine and the personal computer. Today, individuals and groups can communicate directly with public officials through the Internet and E-mail. Not only is such communication direct, it is immediate.

There are now also numerous computer mailing list companies that allow groups to target potential members. These companies assemble a bank of information about people including subscription lists, information put on warranty cards, and membership lists of other groups. A group trying to get laws to censor sex and violence in rock lyrics and videos, for example, might buy from such a company a subscription list of conservative readers of the magazine *National Review*. These people then can be contacted through the mail. These letters are personally addressed and the group message specifically tailored to the individual receiving the letter.

The Rise of Single-Issue Groups

The recent proliferation of interest groups has been fueled largely by a new type of group that first began to emerge in the 1970s: single-issue groups. These groups have three characteristics. First, they are concerned with only one issue. Second, their members are people new to politics. Finally, the group either will not or cannot compromise on the issue. The pro-life and pro-choice groups, Mothers Against Drunk Drivers, and the anti-nuclear proliferation groups are all examples of single-issue groups.

INTEREST GROUP METHODS AND STRATEGIES

Interest groups use four principal methods in their effort to influence policy making: electioneering, lobbying, mobilizing public opinion, and litigating.

Electioneering and Political Action Committees

Whenever and wherever people seek to influence decision making, the following is always good advice: get friends in the right places. Interest groups work very hard at doing exactly that. Given that in the United States 450,000 government officials get into office through elections, interest groups must affect election outcomes. There are many ways for groups and individuals to affect elections. They can man the phone banks on election eve; they can go door-to-door with campaign literature; they can vote. But the principal way in which interest groups affect elections today is through money. And the candidates are more than willing to play the game by taking it.

The Creation of Political Action Committees

The United States is the only country that expects its candidates for public office to raise virtually all the money necessary to run for office. Even in presidential elections, where there is public financing available, the candidates still work to raise additional millions of dollars. As campaign costs have escalated, candidates have had to mine as many sources of money as possible. Interest groups are one of those sources, and a lucrative one at that.

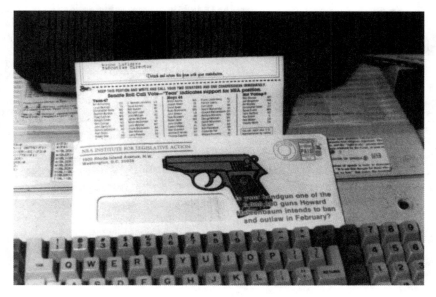

A PAC for the NRA sends letters to its constituents to update them on the voting behavior of their legislators. Notice the letter identifying which legislators supported NRA's position on a critical piece of legislation. Members are urged to write to their House and Senate legislators.

Before the early 1970s, national laws made it illegal for banks, corporations, labor unions, and businesses with government contracts to make campaign donations. While one result of these laws was to keep these groups at bay, the other result was that the laws allowed wealthy individuals to be the primary, if not sole, source of campaign money. So, in the 1970s Congress passed several laws to prevent "fat cat" donors from "buying" the loyalty of elected officials through the financing of their campaigns. The 1971 Federal Election Campaign Act limits individuals to $1,000 cash contribution per candidate. The law also, however, allows interest groups, including corporations, businesses, and labor unions, to set up **political action committees** (PACs), organizations that solicit campaign contributions from group members and channel those funds to candidates' campaigns. PACs are now the primary avenue by which interest groups contribute to federal election campaigns.

Federal campaign finance law limits PACs to cash contributions of no more than $5,000 per election, per candidate for national office. Under the law, primary, general, run-off, and special elections are all considered to be separate elections. As a result, a PAC may contribute $5,000 to each. In addition, the Supreme Court in the 1976 case of *Buckley v. Valeo* struck down as unconstitutional any attempt to deny individuals or groups the right to spend "on behalf of" a candidate. The Court argued that such spending was a form of "speech" and therefore protected by the First Amendment. The result is that PACs can spend unlimited amounts of money on in-kind services. For example, they can make advertisements and pay to have them aired. In 1992, the National Rifle Association's Political Victory Fund spent more than $100,000 on advertisements attacking Rep. Beryl F. Anthony, Jr. (D-Ark.) for having voted for a gun control bill. Anthony, a seven-term incumbent, lost his bid for re-election.[16]

The number of PACs exploded in the 1970s. Today, nearly 5,000 PACs are active in the electoral process.[17] Corporate PACs give the most money, followed in order by PACs representing trade, health associations, and labor.[18] Table 8.2 shows the top PACs in 2005-2006.

Table 8.2

Top PACs in 2005-2006

ALL | DEMS | REPUBS

PAC Name	Total Amount
National Assn of Realtors	$3,030,005
National Auto Dealers Assn	$2,376,600
National Beer Wholesalers Assn	$2,364,500
Intl Brotherhood of Electrical Workers	$2,311,650
Assn of Trial Lawyers of America	$2,114,500
American Bankers Assn	$2,047,774
Credit Union National Assn	$2,047,224
National Assn of Home Builders	$1,982,500
AT&T Inc	$1,972,515
United Parcel Service	$1,872,179

http://www.opensecrets.org/pacs/index.asp

The Effects of PACs and Campaign Contributions

PAC contributions benefit some candidates over others. Interest groups are pragmatic organizations. Given the high re-election rates in Congress, PACs favor the incumbents running for re-election. House incumbents collect nearly 13 times more money from PACs than the challengers receive.[20] Furthermore, more than half of the money raised by House incumbents comes from PACs.[21]

Incumbents feel the effects of PACs in other ways as well. A second effect of the privately financed campaign system in the United States is that politicians are distracted from their job of governing, with their energies siphoned off by having to raise the inordinate amounts of money needed to run an effective campaign. Candidates become entrepreneurs raising, in some cases, tens of thousands of dollars in a day's round of PAC cocktail parties, lunches, and dinners. A related problem is that incumbents running for re-election can raise money more efficiently by staying in Washington and working the PAC circuit of fund raisers. As a result, incumbents are spending less time at home with their constituents.

It might be expected that a third effect of PACs is that influence is being bought. While there is little evidence that PAC contributions actually buy the votes of politicians, there is evidence that PAC money can, and does, buy access. A member of Congress or one of the congressional staff is not likely to turn a deaf ear to a representative of an interest group that has donated generously to his or her campaign. The so-called Keating Five is a case in point. In this case, five senators, Alan Cranston (D-Calif.), Dennis DeConcini (D-Ariz.), John Glenn (D-Ohio), John McCain (R-Ariz.), and Donald Riegle (D-Mich.), came under the scrutiny of the Senate Ethics Committee. There were charges that these senators had sought to pressure the Federal Home Loan Bank Board to give lenient regulatory treatment to Lincoln Savings and Loan Association, headed by Charles Keating, a wealthy political contributor. The bank later failed, at a cost to government of more than $2 billion.[22] Buying access to politicians seems to be the main point of electioneering.

Senator Edward Kennedy once remarked that we "have the best Congress money can buy."[23] Congress, however, is not the only branch of government to be susceptible to PAC pressure; the executive branch also apparently plays the special interest game of access buying. After the 1996 election, a great number of questions were raised about the influence of special interest group money on the executive branch of government. At the epicenter of these campaign donations in 1996 was John Huang who worked as a fund-raiser for the Democratic National Committee. One study found that six firms contributed $100,000 or more and then were asked to join two oversees trade missions led by then Secretary of Commerce Mickey Kantor. Kantor's trade missions followed even larger ones led by his predecessor, the late Ronald H. Brown, which according to Republicans in Congress mixed government business with political fund-raising. Those participating in both sets of trade missions did meet with top government and industry officials in the host nations. Many major corporations had angled for the chance to go for there has been a succession of multimillion-dollar agreements and contracts arising out of these missions.[24]

Campaign donations do, then, appear to buy access to politicians and to policy-making. The campaign donations allow the donor to catch the politician's ear. This, then, leads to a second interest group method, lobbying.

Direct, or Inside, Lobbying

Once an interest group has access through campaign donations, the group will try to influence what those elected politicians do. Interest groups do this through **lobbying**, that is, pressuring through the provision of information, often highly technical in nature. Most politicians are inexpert in many of the policy areas they govern. They come to rely on the expert advice provided by interest groups.

The phrase *to lobby* originated in seventeenth-century England where people seeking to influence the government stopped members of the Parliament in a large lobby off the floor of the House of Commons. Perhaps because of this, lobbying is usually associated even in this country with Congress. But interest groups also lobby the executive branch of government. Executive branch lobbying focuses on senior staff aides in the White House and the various federal agencies. Even presidents are lobbied, and they, in fact, encourage lobbying activities through the Office of Public Liaison, an office whose express purpose is to communicate with interest groups.

The Federal Regulation of Lobbying Act defines a **lobbyist** as "any person who shall engage himself or pay any consideration for the purpose of attempting to influence the passage or defeat of any legislation of the Congress of the United States." There are different types of lobbyists. Some groups send one of their own members to Washington to lobby on the group's behalf. Such amateur lobbyists are often unfamiliar with the intricate workings of the Washington establishment and may find it difficult to gain access to the critical centers of power. A second type of lobbyist, the staff lobbyist, is a paid professional who works full time for a particular interest group.

Finally, groups may seek to hire a third type of lobbyist who has Washington experience, particularly Washington lawyers, former members of Congress, or former employees of executive branch agencies and departments. It is not uncommon for government officials to leave office and then become lobbyists. Federal law does prohibit members of Congress and executive branch officials from lobbying on matters they worked on while in government for one year after leaving office. Even so, 272 former members of Congress have registered as lobbyists since 1996 and 43 percent of members of Congress who left office since 1998 have become lobbyists.[25] Interest groups frequently hire former executive branch officials, as well. These professional lobbyists can cultivate their close working relationships with government policy makers. Interest group lobbyists bring pressure on government officials in a variety of ways.

Providing Information

Interest groups spend a considerable amount of time engaged in what is called **direct lobbying**. One study of Washington lobbyists found that 98 percent use direct contact with government officials to express their group's views.[26] Information is the key to direct lobbying. A lobbyist will, of course, try to present information that supports the interest group's position on an issue. Still, over the long term, lobbyists cannot afford to be perceived by policy makers as biased or untrustworthy. A lobbyist's access to a politician is only as good as the expert information he or she can provide. Lobbyists must maintain daily contact with politicians, providing them with information and data. Corporate groups, in particular, often have hundreds, even thousands, of personnel all equipped to provide mounds of information on a minute's notice.[27]

An innovation on the lobbying theme is the Christian Coalition's automated telephone bank, which it calls Hypotenuse. Executive director Randy Tate records a request to his membership, usually about the need to pass or defeat legislation. Hypotenuse then sends the audio message, along with a digitized call sheet, via modem, to personal computers around the nation. Those PCs, in turn, dial the preselected coalition leaders, deliver Tate's message, and thus spawn a wave of letter writing and phone calling from thousands of people who have already been trained in political action. The latest rage in lobbying is the Internet. NetRoots is dedicated to creating Websites for

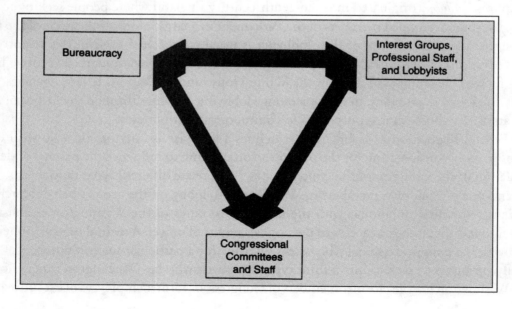

lobbying campaigns and its site on global warming, paid for by companies that oppose President Clinton's mandatory cutbacks in carbon emissions, provide predrafted E-mails from farmers, senior citizens, and small-business owners that read as if they were self-composed and can be launched directly to congressional representatives with the click of a mouse.

The Effects of Direct Lobbying

Lobbying often leads to the development of a close relationship between the interest group, the congressional committee involved in the policy area important to the group, and members of a bureaucratic department or agency responsible for the implementation of those policies. Such a tight relationship is referred to as an **iron triangle**, with three points: the interest group, the congressional committee, and the bureaucratic department or agency. These three points are mutually supporting. A committee member takes campaign donations from an interest group and is then lobbied by that group. The interest group also seeks out the bureaucracy as an ally who then can bring additional pressure on the congressional committee members. Remember also that there is often an exchange of personnel among the three points of the triangle. Many defeated or retired members of Congress join or form Washington law firms that are filled with lobbyists. For example, the Beer Institute's president is former GOP Representative Ray McGrath of New York. He lobbies Congress on behalf of the beer industry.[28]

The point is that at some point the interest of the interest group becomes the interest of the congressional committee members and bureaucrats. The relationship is referred to as *iron* because other than the three major players, everyone else is left out. The unorganized, those without lobbyists on Capitol Hill, those who lack expertise, are largely on the list of uninvited. In addition, presidents who come in with their own agenda for change may soon be faced with recalcitrant iron triangles. The president, in such cases, is usually the new boy in town, whereas the incumbent members of Congress, lobbyists, and career bureaucrats may have been part of the Washington establishment for twenty years or more. There is little reason to think that they will be willing to see or do things the president's way.

An example of an iron triangle is the military-industrial complex. This is a complex of relationships among manufacturers, the Department of Defense, and the Armed Services Committees in Congress. Even back in the 1940s, more than 1,400 officers, including 261 at the rank of general or its equivalent in the navy, had left the armed forces for employment by one of the hundred leading defense contractors.[29] This pattern was apparently at the heart of the military procurement scandal during the Reagan administration in 1988 when the news media and congressional investigators revealed that some defense contractors had systematically overcharged the pentagon for military hardware and supplies.

Regulating Lobbying

Lobbying is a form of speech and, therefore, protected by the First Amendment to the Constitution. In 1946, Congress passed the Federal Regulation of Lobbying Act, which requires groups and individuals seeking to influence legislation to register with the secretary of the Senate and the clerk of the House and to file quarterly financial reports. In 1954, in the case of *United States v. Harriss*, the Supreme Court upheld the 1946 law but limited its application to only lobbying involving direct contacts with members of Congress.[30] Not only was the 1946 law limited in its application, it was also very difficult to enforce.

In 1995, Congress unanimously passed a bill to broaden the definition of a lobbyist and tighten up registration and disclosure requirements. According to current law, a lobbyist is any person who spends at least 20 percent of his time lobbying, anyone who is paid at least $5,000 in any six-month period to lobby, or any corporation or group that spends more than $20,000 in any six-month period on their own lobbying staffs. The law covers those who lobby the executive branch and/or the legislative branch.

By law, lobbyists are required to register and to twice a year report the names of their clients, their income and expenditures, and the issues upon which they worked. Also under the law, tax-exempt, not-for-profit, groups (those to which people can make a tax deductible contribution) may not devote a "substantial part" of their activities to attempts to influence legislation. Tax-exempt, nonprofit groups that do substantially lobby are barred from receiving federal grants.

The regulations discussed above are limited in several respects. The registration and reporting requirements do not extend to grassroots organizations. Nor is there any enforcement organization to make sure there is compliance with the law. Congressional officials who suspect violations may refer them to the Justice Department for action. Fines for breaking the law may be as high as $50,000.

The Newest Trend in Lobbying: Supreme Court Nominations

The summer of 2005 saw the inauguration of a new trend, the nation's leading business lobbies campaigning for the confirmation of a Supreme Court nominee. The U.S. Chamber of Commerce and the National Association of Manufacturers put in place structures to review and consider endorsements of President Bush's nominee. Historically, judicial nomination fights have been the province of social activists and the American Bar Association and have not drawn active participation from business. There have been partisan battles over nominees, most famously the Reagan-era rejection of Robert H. Bork by Democratic senators and the organized left. But never before have interest groups prepared to spend millions of dollars on television and direct-mail-campaigns for or against a particular nominee. The addition of big business to the mix coincides with a shift in the way the judiciary is viewed by the public and leading interest groups. Federal courts were once largely seen as above the political fray. Now, judges and their decisions are routinely attacked by both conservatives and liberals.

Grassroots, or Outside, Lobbying: Going Public

Going public is a strategy that attempts to mobilize the widest and most favorable climate of public opinion. Whereas direct lobbying involves contact between a lobbyist and a politician, this grassroots lobbying uses rank-and-file members and other supporters to bring pressure on government. Such an outside strategy may include education campaigns, demonstrations, letter writing, and any other strategy that attempts to mobilize a large number of people to bring pressure on policy makers.

One way interest groups try to mobilize public opinion is by educating the public about issues. A group may send speakers armed with pamphlets to address gatherings of policy makers and other groups. A media campaign may prove even more effective. The pro-life groups have made considerable inroads into mass public opinion on abortion through their emotionally charged advertisements. In general, the great expense of media campaigns limits their widespread use to only those interest groups that have significant financial resources. The corporate sector appears to have the advantage here. Even as early as the 1930s, some were identifying a *new lobby* of public relations professionals.[31] The 1970s, however, saw a rapid rise in the sophisticated use of advertising to sway public opinion. During the oil crisis of the 1970s, Americans became increasingly restive over the escalating price of gasoline and the long wait to buy it. Eventually this resentment spilled over into hostility toward *big business* in general. The oil companies, particular Mobil and Chevron, began airing advertisements that were directed at soothing the sentiment of the American public. These advertisements were not designed to sell gasoline but rather to create a more sympathetic picture of corporations.

Interest groups may try to obtain free media coverage. Protests, sit-ins, and demonstrations are often specifically tailored for the evening news. One study by Jon Agnone, a sociologist at the University of Washington, compared the number of bills passed between 1960 and 1994 by the U.S. Congress with tactics used by "green" groups within the same year. The study showed that each protest raised the number of pro-environment bills passed by 2.2 percent, but that neither efforts at conventional lobbying on Capitol Hill nor the state of public opinion made any difference. The study concluded that direct action, like chaining oneself to a bulldozer or throwing paint over company executives, is more likely to influence environmental policy than talking to politicians.[32] Protest groups seeking amplification of their cause through the mass media should be aware, however, that they are dealing with a two-edged sword: they get media coverage, but it is negative. The early women's movement in the 1960s tried to attract media attention by burning their bras. Much of the resulting media coverage painted the early feminists as masculine man-haters. An additional problem with media attention is that it tends to be short-lived. It is difficult to keep a protest going long enough to get the government to recognize the issue and act on it. The civil rights movement shows that such movements can be kept alive, but it takes enormous organizational skills and charismatic leadership.

Litigating

Interest groups can also pursue the method of legal advocacy, trying to achieve goals through litigation. Interest groups can use the courts to affect public policy in any of three ways. First, the group may bring a suit on behalf of the group itself. Second, the group can finance suits brought by other individuals. In fact, groups sometimes actively seek test cases where they can challenge the constitutionality of existing laws or the ways in which they have been implemented. For example, in the 1950s, the National Association for the Advancement of Colored People was looking for a test case to challenge the racially segregated southern school system. Thurgood Marshall, a young attorney working for the NAACP, successfully litigated the case on behalf of the Browns. Finally, a group may also participate in the litigation process by petitioning the court for the right to file an *amicus curiae* ("friend of the court") brief that lays out arguments why the court should rule in favor of one of the parties to the case. A 1989 abortion case drew a record 78 such briefs. They were evenly divided between those who favored or opposed the right to abortion. In February 2003, however, that previous record was broken when over sixty groups filed friend-of-the-court briefs in defense of the University of Michigan's use of race-based affirmative action in their admissions policy.

The public interest groups spawned by the New Politics movement have been particularly active in the litigation process. The controversy over the completion of a dam being built by the Tennessee Valley Authority (TVA) is an example of New Politics litigation. The dam would have ruined the habitat for a small fish known as the snail darter. The Endangered Species Act at that time prohibited federal agencies from engaging in any actions that would "jeopardize the continued existence of an endangered or threatened species or . . . result in the adverse modification or destruction of [the species'] critical habitat." In *TVA v. Hill*, the Supreme Court held that the act made it an unqualified duty for agencies to refrain from taking actions that would harm the threatened or endangered species.[33]

Businesses and corporations have responded to the strong public interest movement by mobilizing their own forces. The 1970s and 1980s saw a massive increase in the number of businesses lobbying offices in Washington, and many trade associations head quartered elsewhere moved to Washington or opened branch offices there.[34] The result has been that many of the early victories of public interest groups have been overturned or muted by Congress or other court decisions. In the case of the TVA dam, after the Supreme Court decision, Congress amended the Endangered Species Act to soften the language and allow agencies like the TVA to weigh the costs of protecting a species against the benefits to be gained from proceeding with certain kinds of projects.

Protest and Civil Disobedience

Interest groups, often those that lack access or hold unpopular opinions, can protest. In the fall of 1999, for example, representatives from more than five hundred groups joined forces in protesting the World Trade Organization (WTO) at its Seattle meeting. The WTO represents 135 countries and has the authority to force countries to change their labor, environmental, and human rights laws that allegedly restrict trade among nations. The protestors charged the organization with responding more to the profit needs of the international corporations than those of the environment, working men and women, and the poor. The Sierra Club and Steelworkers joined together in a reenactment of the Boston Tea Party. They tossed steel imported from China, hormone-treated beef, and other goods into the sea.

Such protests are not new to this country. The 1960s saw the Vietnam War demonstrations and throughout the 1970s and 1980s, Greenpeace staged a number of protests. The civil rights movement provides an excellent example of the successful use of extended protest and civil disobedience. By peacefully protesting against legalized racial segregation in the South, the movement drew attention to the unequal treatment of African Americans.

Bribery

While there may be only a fine line between campaign donations and bribery, the line is nonetheless drawn by the legal code. Bribery involves the giving of cash gifts, worth over a certain amount, in exchange for a politician's promise to act in a certain way. The history of the United States has been punctuated with scandals involving interest groups bribing politicians. In the late 1970s, for example, the Washington bribery scandal, which came to be known in the press as Koreagate, rocked the country. A Korean businessman, Tong Sun Park, was at the center of legal and illegal favors involving at least two dozen members of the House and Senate. Congressman Richard Henna of California received $22,500 and the wife of Congressman Edwin Edwards of Louisiana received $10,000.

Bribery is probably not as widespread as many fear. It is a risky strategy for an interest group to pursue. As a result, it is mostly used to sustain a friendship rather than convert an enemy. In addition, bribery works best when the issue involved is fairly narrow, for example, involving a government contract. The bigger the issue, the more participants are likely to be involved and the more media coverage devoted to it. Bribery fares poorly in such an open arena of policy making.

Prospects for Reform

Even if the problem of illegal bribery is not overwhelming, when coupled with the legal system of campaign finance and PACs, perhaps some reform is needed. Some sectors of the interest group community do enjoy advantages over others. Such advantages may impede the equal opportunity of all groups to be heard in the political system. The Madisonian design, in other words, has not worked perfectly.

Allowing those who have the clearest self-interest and the resources to communicate and amplify their message may lead to inefficient and even bad policy-making. The Savings and Loan debacle of the 1980s and 1990s is a case in point. At the insistence of the Savings and Loans, President Bush and key members of Congress, all of whom had taken hefty contributions from the S&L industry, worked to deregulate the Savings and Loans. The industry was freed up to take depositors' money and invest it in high risk enterprises, like commercial real estate and junk bonds. When the Savings and Loans in many cases lost the money, the national government moved in to insure the deposits. The cost to taxpayers to date is in the billions.

To avoid such costly mistakes, some are calling for public financing of congressional elections. Other plans have suggested reducing the amounts that can be given to candidates. In May 1993, President Clinton introduced a set of proposals designed to diminish the role of private contributions in political campaigns. Under the Clinton plan, congressional candidates could voluntarily agree to spending limits that would entitle them to public campaign funds. At the same time, contributions by individuals to political parties, so called *soft money*, would be limited and contributions by PACs would be curtailed. The Republican controlled Congress immediately rejected the plan. However, the numerous campaign finance abuses of the 1996 campaign, including illegal contributions of foreign money and mounting evidence of influence peddling, have led to a renewed interest in reform.

CONCLUSION

This chapter opened with a discussion of the tobacco industry and their victory on the second-hand smoke issue. Still, as the chapter has noted, there are many groups in the United States, and public interest groups are increasing their presence and power on the stage of public policy making. Certainly the fight over tobacco is hardly over in this country. While the tobacco industry, the advertising industry, and the makers of smokeless tobacco have all been slugging it out in lawsuits against the FDA and lobbying members of Congress, a coalition of public health groups, the former head of the FDA, Dr. Kessler, and the Clinton administration have joined forces. On August 10, 1995, they proposed a new set of regulations governing the marketing and sale of cigarettes. Clearly, the issue of tobacco is not yet settled in the United States. In the game of interest group politics, battles may be won and lost, but the proliferation of groups and the struggles over policy making continue unabated. In fact, on Monday, February 10, 1997, thirty-five lawyers for the tobacco industry and twenty-five lawyers representing the government met in the U.S. District Court in Greensboro, North Carolina. U.S. District Judge William Osteen surveyed the litigators and said "It may be easier to introduce those who are not lawyers."[35] Ironically, David A. Kessler, the FDA Commissioner who dared to try to regulate the tobacco industry and who is involved in the lawsuit, could not get a nonsmoking room in the Greensboro Hilton.

CHAPTER NOTES

[1]Common Cause, "Democracy on Drugs," http://commoncause.org, May 18, 2004.

[2]Jan Erickson, "Harmful Medicare PrescRiption Drug Bill Passes," htp://now.org, winter 2003/2004.

[3]John T. Tierney and Kay Lehman Scholzman, "Congress and Organized Interests," in *Congressional Politics*, ed. Christopher J. Deering (Chicago: Dorsey Press, 1989), 198.

[4]Steven Greenhouse, "The Most Innovative Figure in Silicon Valley? Maybe This Labor Organizer," *New York Times*, November 14, 1999, p. 26.

[5]Sidney Blumenthal, "Christian Soldiers," *New Yorker*, July 18, 1994, p. 36.

[6]"Grays on the Go," *Time*, February 22, 1988, p. 69.

[7]Rochelle L. Stanfield, "Balkan Wars on K Street," *National Journal*, 15 August 1992, 1903-4.

[8]Mancur Olson, *The Logic of Collective Action* (Cambridge: Harvard University Press, 1965).

[9]Jeffrey H. Birnbaum, "Washington's Power 25," http://money.cnn.com Dec. 8, 2006.

[10]James Madison, *Federalist Paper No. 10* in *The Federalist Papers*, ed. Clinton Rossiter (NewYork: New American Library, 1961), 83.

[11]John Herbers, "Special Interests Gaining Power as Voter Disillusionment Grows," *New York Times*, 14 Nov. 1978, 1.

[12]Theodore J. Lowi and Benjamin Ginsberg, *American Government*, 3d ed. (New York: W.W. Norton, 1994).

[13]Andrew McFarland, *Common Cause* (Chatham, N.J.: Chatham House, 1984).

[14]Allan J. Cigler and Burdett A. Loomis, *Interest Group Politics* (Washington, D.C.: Congressional Quarterly Press, 1991).

[15]Jack L. Walker, "The Origins and Maintenance of Interest Groups in America," *American Political Science Review* 77 (June 1983): 390-406.

[16]Richard E. Cohen, "NRA Draws Bead on Incumbents," *National Journal*, 19 September 1992, 2134.

[17]Federal Election Commission, *FEC Releases 1992 Year-End Pac Count*, 23 January 1993, 1.

[18]Federal Election Commission, *PAC Activity Rebounds in 1991-92 Election Cycle-Unusual Nature of Contests Seen as Reason* 29 April 1993, 9.

[19]Ann Reilly Dowd, "Look Who' Cashing in on Congress," *Money*, December 1997, 130.

[20]"Political Action Committees," http://ap.grolier.com,2005.

[21]Frank Sorauf, *Inside Campaign Finance* (New Haven, Conn.: Yale University Press, 1992), 71.

[22]Nathaniel C. Nash, "Savings Unit Donations Criticized," *New York Times*, 29 June 29 1990, D4.

[23]Theodore J. Lowi and Benjamin Ginsberg, *American Politics*, 4th ed. (New York: W.W. Norton, 1996), 497.

[24]"Kantor Says Trade Trips, Big Donations Unrelated," *Los Angeles Times*, 13 February 1997, A1.

[25]Knight Ridder News, "Exiting Congressmen Cash in Years of Service for High-Paying Jobs," http://billingsgazette.com, Dec. 26, 2004.

[26]Key Lehman Schlozman, and John T. Tierney, *Organized Interest and American Democracy* (New York: Harper and Row, 1986), 50.

[27]John E. Chubb, *Interest Groups and the Bureaucracy* (Stanford, Ca.: Stanford University Press, 1983), 144.

[28]"Alcoholic Beverage Industry Lobbies for Bill to Gut Substance Abuse Agency Seen as Threat," *Wall Street Journal*, 14 August 1995, A12.

[29]*U.S. Congress, House of Representatives, 96th Congress, 1st Session, Report of the Subcommittee for Special Investigations of the Committee on the Armed Services* (Washington, D.C.: Government Printing Office, 1960), 7.

[30]*United States v. Harriss*, 347 U.S. 612 (1954).

[31]*Pendelton-Herring, Group Representation Before Congress* (New York: McGraw Hill, 1936).

[32]Wikipedia, "Interest Group," http://en.wikipedia.org,2006.

[33]*TVA v. Hill*, 437 U.S. 153 (1978).

[34]*Boston University School of Management, Public Affairs Offices and Their Functions* (Boston: Boston University School of Management, 1981), 8.

[35]"Washington Insight," *Los Angeles Times*, 12 February 1997, A5.

SUGGESTED READINGS

Berry, Jeffrey M. *The Interest Group Society*. Glenview, Ill.: Scott, Foresman/Little, Brown, 1989.

Cigler, Alan J., and Burdette Loomis, eds., *Interest Group Politics* 4th ed. Washington, D.C.: Congressional Quarterly Press, 1994.

Greider, William. *Who Will Tell the People?: The Betrayal of American Democracy*. New York" Simon and Schuster, 1992.

Lowi, Theodore J. *The End of Liberalism*. New York: Norton, 1969.

Olson, Mancur. *The Logic of Collective Action*. Cambridge, Mass.: Harvard University Press, 1965.

Schlozman, Kay Lebman, and John T. Tierney. *Organized Interest and American Democracy*. New York: Harper and Row, 1986.

Sorauf, Frank J. *Inside Campaign Finance: Myths and Realities*. New Haven: Yale University Press, 1992.

Stern, Philip M. *Still the Best Congress Money Can Buy*. Washington D.C.: Regnery Gateway, 1992.

Truman, David B. *The Governmental Process*, 2d ed. New York: Knopf, 1971.

Wilson, James Q. *Political Organizations*. New York: Basic Books, 1973.

Wright, John R. *Interest Groups and Congress: Lobbying Contributions, and Influence*. Boston: Allyn and Bacon, 1996.

Chapter Nine

THE CONGRESS

There has always been a close relationship between the Congress of the United States and the interest groups that try to affect legislation. The enormous campaign contributions funneled from the groups to the candidates running for the House and Senate buy access for the lobbyists to plead their case. Today, however, there appears to be an even closer relationship developing. One might say that it is almost like the interest groups and the members of Congress are family. Consider the following.

For more than a decade, the dietary supplements industry has counted on Senator Orrin G. Hatch to fend off tighter regulation of products such as ephedra, the controversial stimulant linked to more than 80 deaths, most recently a young Baltimore Orioles baseball player. Since at least 1992, Senator Hatch has played a decisive role in helping the industry fend off restrictive oversight by the Food and Drug Administration. Among other things, the Republican Senator from Utah co-wrote the 1994 law that lets supplement makers sell products without the scientific premarket safety testing required for drugs and other food additives. This law has proved a major obstacle to federal control of ephedra. Indeed, the Hatch-Harkin Act defined dietary supplements as a special category outside drugs and other food additives and did so in a way that has helped supplements mushroom into what the Nutrition Business Journal says is an industry with $17.7 billion in annual U.S. sales. Many of the companies are based in Utah, which describes itself as the "Silicon Valley of the supplements industry," and the supplements industry has given Senator Hatch its Congressional Champion award and a lifetime achievement citation.

Senator Hatch is the foremost defender of the diet supplements industry in Congress, and his support of the dietary supplements industry has not come cheap. He has received nearly $137,000 in campaign contributions over the last decade, according to the C enter for Responsive Politics. But the supplements industry has not only showered the senator with campaign money but has also paid almost $2 million in lobbying fees to firms that employed his son, Scott. From 1998 to 2001, while Scott Hatch worked for a lobbying firm with close ties to his father, clients in the diet supplements industry paid the company more than $1.96 million, more than $1 million of it from clients involved with ephedra.

Because stiffer rules now make it harder to direct cash to candidates, interest groups are finding other ways to put the politicians on their payroll. An increasingly popular maneuver in the age-old game of influence seeking in Washington is for a corporation or interest group to hire a member of a lawmaker's family as a lobbyist for their interest. At least 17 senators and 11 members of the House have family members who lobby or work as consultants on government relations, most in Washington, and often for clients who rely on the related lawmakers' goodwill.

When regional phone companies wanted Congress to make it easier for them to compete in the high-speed Internet market, they did what special interests usually do with billions of dollars at stake: They amassed an army of experienced lobbyists. But one of the so-called Baby Bells did not stop there. BellSouth also hired a pair of lobbyists distinguished by their family trees—John Breaux Jr. and Chester T. "Chet" Lott Jr. They are the sons of two of the most powerful men in America when it comes to telecommunications policy: Senator John B. Breaux (D-La.) and then-Senate Majority Leader Trent Lott (R-Miss.). Both fathers are senior members of the Senate commerce committee and its telecommunications subcommittee. The sons have banked thousands of dollars a month in BellSouth consulting and lobbying fees. In Breaux Jr.'s case, the total exceeds $280,000, and in Lott's, $160,000. The son of another heavy hitter on telecommunications, Representative W.J. "Billy" Tauzin (R-La.), was already on the BellSouth payroll, working in community relations. While their sons have been getting paid by BellSouth, Senator Breaux and Representative Tauzin have sponsored bills to loosen federal restrictions on Baby Bells that want to compete with cable companies in the high-speed Internet market. They failed on Capitol Hill, so the fathers are now pressing the Federal Communications Commission to lift those restrictions.

Former Senator Tom Daschle's (D-S.D.) wife, Linda, is one of the airline industry's top lobbyists. Her clients, Northwest and American Airlines, raked in a combined $1.1 billion from the post 9/11 government bailouts. Additionally, Linda was put on the payroll of L-3 Communications, a corporation that made baggage scanners that the Federal Aviation Administration had given a thumbs down to because it preferred a more accurate bomb-detecting device made by a rival company. Mrs. Daschle was hired to plead L-3's case to the government. This "pillow talk strategy" proved remarkably effective. Soon after Linda was put on the L-3 payroll, her spouse helped broker a deal in Congress that forced the FAA to purchase one scanner from L-3 for each one it bought from InVision, the rival company. Linda's lobbying firm was the recipient of close to $500,000 from L-3.

Another Senator, Ted Stevens, has channeled so much federal money into Alaska that so-called "Stevens money" is considered an engine that drives the state's entire economy. It has also furthered his son Ben's career as a consultant. When the senator helped direct $30 million in disaster relief funds to the Southwest Alaska Municipal Conference in 2000, the agency hired his son to mediate negotiations over how to divvy it up. A dozen Alaska interests benefiting from the senator's efforts have paid Ben Stevens at least $754,976 in consulting fees over the last three years, financial disclosure reports show.

The Senate ethics committee has taken up this issue. The committee, however, was chaired by Senator Reid who had more family members working for interests he supports than anyone else in Congress: three of his four sons, plus his son-in-law.[1]

THE ORIGIN AND POWERS OF CONGRESS

The Constitution and the Great Compromise

Perhaps because the framers of the Constitution believed that Congress would be the most powerful branch of the national government, the most contentious issue at the constitutional convention concerned the question of how the states would be represented in this national legislature. The small states, which had the most to fear from union, wanted equal representation in a one chamber legislature; this was put forth as the New Jersey Plan. The more populous states, on the other hand, supported the Virginia Plan that proposed a two chamber legislature. One of its chambers, the lower chamber, would have state representation on the basis of state population; this chamber would then select an upper chamber.

The final Connecticut Compromise created a **bicameral**, meaning two chamber, national legislature. The House of Representatives, the lower chamber, is apportioned to the states on the basis of state population. The United States Senate, the upper chamber, has equal state representation with each state having two senators, originally to be selected by their various state legislatures. While the House members serve only a two-year term and all seats are elected in every two-year election, the senators serve a six-year term, and only one third of the Senate is selected in any two-year election.

The Powers of the House and Senate

The Expressed Powers

The first seventeen clauses of Article I, section 8, specify most of the **enumerated powers** of Congress, powers expressly given to the national legislature by the Constitution. The most important of the domestic powers listed are the rights of Congress to collect taxes, to spend money, and to regulate commerce. The most important foreign policy power is the power to declare war. Other sections of the Constitution give Congress a wide range of additional powers. Article 1, section 5 gives Congress the power to establish rules for its own members. Article 1, section 7 gives it the power to override a presidential veto. Congress is also given the power to define the appellate jurisdiction of the Supreme Court (Article III, section 1), regulate relations between the states (Article I, section 10 and Article IV), and propose amendments to the Constitution (Article V). In addition, amendments to the Constitution have provided additional congressional power. The Twelfth Amendment, for example, requires Congress to certify the election of the president and vice president or to choose these officers if no candidate has received a majority of the electoral college vote. Congress may levy an income tax under the Sixteenth Amendment.

The House and Senate do have some responsibilities that they discharge on their own. Only the House of Representatives can originate revenue bills. Early colonial Americans had been sensitive about the issue of taxation without representation. As a result, the framers believed that money matters should be passed first by the House, the chamber that has representation on the basis of population, and only after that would the Senate address the issue. According to Article I, section 2 the House has the power to impeach a federal judge, the president, or vice president. To **impeach** means to bring up on charges, calling for a trial in the Senate. If two-thirds of the senators vote to convict, the federal official is then removed from office.

The Senate has the power to advise the president when he is appointing federal judges, ambassadors, and cabinet positions. In addition, the Senate can either vote to confirm or reject these appointments. The Senate also has the power to ratify or reject treaties negotiated by a president with a foreign nation.

The Implicit Power

Under Article I, section 8, the **elastic clause**, Congress has the power "to make all Laws which shall be necessary and proper to carrying into Execution the foregoing powers [of Article I], and all other Powers vested by this Constitution in the Government of the United States, or in any Department or Officer thereof." The open ended quality of the elastic clause has allowed Congress to define and redefine its powers over time and thereby alter the balance of power Congress shares with the president.

The Ebb and Flow of Congressional Powers

Because the framers of the Constitution feared tyranny emanating from any source, executive or legislative, they pitted Congress and the president against each other. For the first one hundred years, Congress clearly was the more dominant institution. Congress chose to use the powers outlined in Article I, section 8 and further extended its power by defining other activities as within its scope under the elastic clause. Even in foreign affairs, Congress exercised its muscle. The War of 1812 was planned and directed by Congress. After the Civil War, when President Andrew Johnson tried to interfere with congressional plans for Reconstruction, he was summarily impeached, though missed conviction in the Senate by one vote.

By the 1960s, however, congressional dominance was declining. The presidency became the stronger of the two branches. Franklin Roosevelt's "New Deal," Harry Truman's "Fair Deal," John F. Kennedy's "New Frontier," and Lyndon Johnson's "Great Society" had transformed American politics, placing the president in the center of the legislative process. Similarly, in foreign affairs, presidential initiative and direction took the country into both World Wars and then later wars in Korea and Vietnam.

The strength of either the presidency or the Congress as an institution is at least partly the result of the institution's ties to important groups in the American electorate. Until the administration of Franklin Roosevelt, people were more likely to see Congress as their representative institution. But Roosevelt's New Deal mobilized organized labor, farmers, African Americans, and key sectors of

American industry and tied their loyalty to the executive branch of government. Such electoral support was and continues to be empowering to the branch that can best mobilize it.

Events of the later 1960s and 1970s set the stage for a reassertion of congressional power. Groups that had not found the executive branch hospitable to their claims, now turned to the legislative branch to defend their interests. Environmental and consumer groups, along with civil rights and women's groups, pressed their claims upon Congress and, in doing so, provided a base for the reassertion of congressional power. It was inevitable that conflict would grow between the executive and legislative branches of government; and grow it did beginning during the Johnson administration.[2]

The most dramatic illustration of this growing tension was the congressional Watergate investigation that eventually led to the resignation of President Richard Nixon. But the tension between the branches has evidenced itself in other ways as well. Increasingly, Congress passed legislation mandating clear and specific action by the president, for example, the Wars Powers Act and the Endangered Species Act. Congress has also moved to increase its budgetary powers through the Budget and Impoundment Control Act of 1974 and the creation of the Congressional Budget Office (CBO).

More recently, Congress has asserted its power through the Iran-Contra investigation of President Reagan and the Whitewater investigation of President Clinton. The investigative power of the United States Congress is now institutionalized in a variety of oversight committees that are likely to continue to make the president's life difficult. In February 1997, for example, Representative Dan Burton (R-Ind.), chairman of the Government Reform and Oversight Committee, announced that his committee would be actively looking into the apparent irregularities in Democratic fundraising efforts during the 1996 campaign. On February 5, Burton's committee asked the White House for "all records relating to contacts with any prospective donors to the DNC (Democratic National Committee), Clinton-Gore and/or tax-exempt organizations."[3]

Differences Between the House and Senate

House	Senate
Larger (435 members)	Smaller (100 members)
Shorter term of office (2 years)	Longer term of office (6 years)
Less flexible rules	More flexible rules
Narrower constituency	Broader, more varied, constituency
Policy specialists	Policy generalists
Power less evenly distributed	Power more evenly distributed
Less prestige	More prestige
More expeditious in floor debate	Less expeditious in floor debate
Less reliance on staff	More reliance on staff
Less press and media coverage, but floor proceedings televised	More press and media coverage

The impeachment trial of President Andrew Johnson, who became president with the assassination of Abraham Lincoln, took place in the Senate.

The Era of Divided Government

By the end of the 1980s, divided government had become the norm in American politics, certainly at the national level and often in the state governments as well. Since 1975, the president's party has controlled the House of Representatives for only six years (1977-1980, 1993-1994) and the Senate for only ten years (1977-1986, 1993-1994). In such a state of divided government, it is hard to see either the president or Congress as the more powerful. A better understanding of the workings of the national government would be to see that any policy making is likely to be incremental, as Congress and the president inch their way toward common ground. Such common ground is largely to be found in symbolic politics.[4] Control of the deficit through budgetary ceilings and caps on spending is a way for both branches of government to appear to be doing something without really making substantive policy decisions.

The 107th Congress, elected in 2000, faced tremendous obstacles to its work due to the extremely small majority held by the Republicans in the House and the Democrats in the Senate. In the House consensus on legislative issues was possible because some twenty to thirty Democrats, calling themselves "Blue Dog Democrats," said that they were willing to work with the Bush administration. But, harmony in the Senate was much harder to achieve. Republican Senator Trent Lott, unseated as majority leader when Senator Jeffords defected and threw Senate control to the Democrats, had been quoted after the November 2000 election as making snide comments about newly elected Democratic Senator Hillary Clinton. If passing legislation in such a deeply divided Congress was difficult, it was virtually impossible to build the two-thirds majority needed to override a presidential veto. Both parties looked ahead to the election of 2002, hoping to increase their margin of control. In such an environment raising campaign funds proved crucial and largely accounted for the Republican victories in both 2002 and 2004 and the Democrats' success in 2006.

REPRESENTATION IN CONGRESS

Theories of Representation

While Article I, section 8, outlines the specific powers of Congress, the essence of all congressional powers is the quality of congressional representation. The United States Congress was created by the framers to be the branch of the federal government that represented the population. The question is what does *representation* mean? There are different theories as to what constitutes representation.

The Instructed-Delegate View of Representation

Some believe that legislators are duty bound to mirror the views of a majority of their constituents. The argument is that members of Congress are delegates with specific instructions from their voters at home on how to vote on critical issues. Delegates are not supposed to vote the party-line; nor are they to vote their conscience. For a member of Congress to be a delegate of his constituents, the constituents would have to hold well-formed views on the issues. In addition, they would have to have a clear-cut policy preference. Neither condition is likely to be found in reality. On many issues voters may not have enough information to formulate an opinion. On many other issues, there may be no majority opinion.

Several southern states elected African-American senators and representatives to Congress after African Americans gained voting rights in 1870.

The Trustee View of Representation

Edmund Burke argued that legislators must be free to vote as they see best.[5] Burke saw the legislator as a **trustee**, to do what he/she believed to be in the best interest of the society. Members, according to this theory, are expected to pursue the broad interests of the larger society and vote against the narrow interests of the constituents if these are in conflict with the needs of the greater society.

The Politico View of Representation

Studies have found that most members of Congress are neither pure delegates nor pure trustees.[6] Members of Congress try to combine both the delegate and trustee perspectives into a pragmatic mix, the so-called **politico** approach. Members from marginal districts, those in which the election was close, may tend to see themselves as obligated to vote as their constituents intend. Legislators from safer districts may feel more free to express their conscience. In addition, there may be times when the wishes of the voters are unclear or contradictory or cases in which constituents have no opinion; in such areas, the member may feel the need to act more as a trustee than a delegate. In any district, however, there are likely to be some issues on which constituents have pronounced opinions on which representatives feel they enjoy little latitude in supporting their constituents' preferences. For example, representatives from wheat, cotton, or tobacco districts will not be able to exercise great discretion on farm issues. Likewise, members from oil rich states can hardly risk being anything other than the advocates of the oil industries.

The Quality of Congressional Representation

When acting as either a delegate or a trustee, a member's ability to represent his or her district or state largely depends on two factors: descriptive representation and ties to a constituency.

Descriptive Representation

There are some who believe that the quality of representation in the United States Congress is dependent upon how descriptively representative the Congress is. The argument is that a legislature should be demographically similar to the general population.[7] If a high quality of representation really does hinge on descriptive representation, the Congress of the United States faces serious problems. The people we elect to Congress are not a cross section of American society. While nearly one-third of all workers in the United States are employed in blue collar jobs, most members are professionals, drawn primarily from business and legal backgrounds.[8] Only 22 percent of American families earn over $50,000 a year, yet 100 percent of the members of Congress earn over that amount. In 2001, annual congressional salaries were $141,300.00 In fact, 16 percent of the House and 33 percent of the Senate have assets of over a million dollars. Congress also underrepresents religious and racial minorities. Fully 93 percent of the House and 85 percent of the Senate are Christians. Eighty-seven percent of the House members and 96 percent of the Senators are white. Finally, while fully 51.9 percent of the population is female, only 11 percent of the House and 9 percent of the Senate are female.[9]

There is reason to believe that the descriptive characteristics of the members of Congress may affect the legislative process. Thirty-nine African Americans were elected to Congress in 1992. Almost immediately the Congressional Black Caucus, an organization of African-American members in the House, became an important force in the legislative process. The leader of the Black Caucus, Eddie Bernice Johnson, a Democrat from Texas, is considered the leader of a group often important in building the coalitions necessary to pass a piece of legislation. The Black Caucus has also been important on issues directly having an impact on the African-American community. President Clinton expressed his intention to nominate John Payton, a government lawyer from the District of Columbia, to be head of the civil rights division in the Justice Department. When members of the Black Caucus expressed their unease with such a choice, President Clinton backed away from the nomination.

Because women and minorities are still fairly new additions to Congress, their full impact has not been felt. Because the powerful leadership positions in Congress are assigned primarily on the basis of **seniority**, or length of service in the chamber or on a committee, it will take some years for women and minority members to achieve these highest leadership positions. Still, there are three African Americans currently chairing House committees. These members are able to initiate and channel legislation important to their constituents.

Constituent Ties

Evidence suggests that members of Congress do not need to look like their constituents to feel the pressure to serve those who live in their state or district. Members claim that they spend significant amounts of time and energy on addressing the individual level and state or district level needs of their constituents. When a member of Congress works on the statewide or district wide needs, it is often called **pork barrel**. When a member of Congress attempts to serve individual needs of a particular constituent it is commonly called **casework**.

Pork Barrel Legislation. Members of Congress cannot afford to systematically neglect constituency pressure emanating from groups within their district or state. Representatives from districts with defense industries, and perhaps thousands of jobs tied to those industries, are likely to feel the pressure to support defense spending that may end up funding a lucrative contract with one or more of these firms. A Senator from Florida knows that a vote for an increase in social security payments is a vote for the elderly, so many of whom live in his state.

Pork barrel legislation is very common in the United States Congress. Some have argued that pork barrel bills are the only ones that members of Congress take seriously because they are seen as so important to the members' chances for re-election. Often, controversial bills can only achieve passage by being filled with pet projects that mobilize the support of members of Congress and maybe even the president himself.

In 2005, Congress passed a $286.4 billion highway bill. In addition to funding the interstate highway system and other federal transportation programs, it set a new record for pork-barrel spending, earmarking $24 billion for a staggering 6,376 pet projects, spread among virtually every congressional district in the land. The enormous bill—1,752 pages long—passed 412 to 8 in the House and 91 to 4 in the Senate. The bill funneled upward of $941 million to 119 earmarked projects in Alaska, including $223 million for a mile-long bridge linking an island with 50 residents to the town of Ketchikan on the mainland. The bill also funded horse riding facilities in Virginia ($600,000), a snowmobile trail in Vermont ($5.9 million), parking for New York's Harlem Hospital ($8 million), a bicycle and pedestrian trail in Tennessee ($532,000), a daycare center and park-and-ride facility in Illinois ($1.25 million), dust control mitigation for rural Arkansas ($3 million), The National Packard Museum in Ohio ($2.75 million) and a historical trolley project in Washington ($200,000).

In 2006, Congress passed the $16 billion Foreign Operations Bill, which pays for everything from the Peace Corps to the aerial fumigation of Colombian coca. The 3,320-page bill includes $100,000 for goat-meat research in Texas, $549,000 for "Future Foods" development in Illinois, $569,000 for "Cool Season Legume Research" in Idaho and Washington, $63,000 for a program to combat noxious weeds in the desert Southwest, and $175,000 for obesity research in Texas. It was the biggest single piece of pork-barrel legislation in American history. The cost of such earmarks has tripled in the last 12 years, to more than $64 billion annually, and some lawmakers treat their share of the pork as personal accounts to dole out to constituents and campaign contributors.

On January 5, 2007, in the first one hundred hours of the 110th session of Congress, the new Democratic majority in the House of Representative imposed substantial new restrictions on earmarking. The new rules do not end the practice of packing legislation with pork but they do force legislators to attach their names to the pet items they slip into spending or tax bills and to certify that they have no personal financial stake in their earmarks.

Casework. There is fairly consistent communication between constituents and congressional offices. Even in the 1970s, the House and Senate post office handled nearly 100 million pieces of incoming mail.[12] Today, with the Internet, members are even more accessible to the mass public. House members claim that over a quarter of their time and nearly two-thirds of their staff members' time is devoted to working on the needs of individual constituents.[13]

Casework can take several forms. **Patronage** is a direct form of casework in which the member of Congress runs interference with a federal administrative agency seeking favorable treatment for a constituent or constituents. Patronage may even take the form of securing a government job for a constituent.

Casework can also take the form of a **private bill**, a proposal to grant some kind of relief or special privilege to the person named in the bill. Approximately 75 percent of the private bills introduced into Congress are concerned with helping foreign nationals who are unable to get permanent visas in this country.[14]

Congressional Elections

The process of electing members of Congress is decentralized. Congressional elections are controlled by individual state governments, which must, however, conform to the U. S. Constitution and national statute. The Constitution states that representatives are to be elected every second year by popular ballot, and the number of seats awarded to each state be established by a decennial census. Each state has at least one representative, with most congressional districts having close to six hundred thousand residents. Today, each state's two senators are elected by their state's voters for a six-year term. Only one-third of the senators are elected in any two-year election.

Congressional Reapportionment

By far the most complicated aspects of congressional elections are the issues of **reapportionment** (the allocation of seats in the House to each state after each census) and **redistricting** (the redrawing of the boundaries of the districts within each state). In 1962, in the case *Baker v Carr*, the Supreme Court held that reapportionment must not violate the Fourteenth Amendment principle that no state can deny to any person "the equal protection of the laws." Then in the 1964 case of *Wesberry v Sanders* the Court held that reapportionment must not violate the "one person, one vote" principle embodied in Article I, Section 2, of the Constitution, which requires that members of Congress be chosen "by the People of the several States." Prior to *Wesberry*, severe malapportionment had resulted in some districts containing two or three times the populations of other districts in the same state, thereby diluting the vote in the more populous districts. Today, districts are fairly equally populated, each district having approximately 600,000 people.

Gerrymandering

While the one person, one vote principle has dealt with the issue of district size successfully, the issue of how to draw the district boundaries has not yet been completely resolved. It is the job of each state legislature to divide its state's population into the number of congressional districts apportioned to it following the census. Many districts have been gerrymandered. A district is said to be gerrymandered when the dominant party in the state legislature alters its shape substantially in order to maximize its electoral strength at the expense of the legislature's minority party. Either concentrating the opposition party's voters in as few districts as possible or dispersing them thinly across many districts can achieve this.

In 1986, the Supreme Court heard the *Davis v Bandemer* case that challenged gerrymandered congressional districts in Indiana. The Court ruled for the first time that redistricting for the political benefit of one group could be challenged on constitutional grounds. The Court has gone on to declare as unconstitutional districts that are uneven in population or that violate norms of size and shape to maximize the advantage of one party.

Despite the Supreme Court's attempts to control gerrymandering, it continues to plague the drawing of congressional district lines. Following the 2000 census, after a protracted legislative struggle, the Republicans in Texas succeeded in drawing districts that benefit candidates of their party. Under the districting plan, the city of Austin, Texas is split three ways into a district that runs from North Austin to Houston, a district that runs from Southeast Austin to the Rio Grande, and a district that lumps San Marcos, South Austin, West Austin, New Braunfels, and Northern San Antonio together. After the 2004 election, unsurprisingly, Republicans won 21 of the 32 Texas congressional seats.

Racial Gerrymandering and "Minority-Majority" Districts

In the early 1990s, the Supreme Court actually began to encourage a type of gerrymandering that made possible the election of a minority representative from what is termed a "minority-majority" area. Under the mandate of the Voting Rights Act of 1965, the Justice Department issued directives to states after the 1990 census instructing them to create congressional districts that would maximize the voting power of minority groups, that is, create districts in which the minority voters were the majority. In 1995, these "minority-majority" districts were challenged, and the Supreme Court took the position that when race is the dominant factor in the drawing of congressional district lines, the districts are unconstitutional.

Candidates for Congress

Candidates for congressional seats are largely self-selected. They are likely to be people who have been active in local politics. Because congressional campaigns are expensive, candidates also must have access to substantial resources. The average cost of winning a Senate seat is now over $5 million and a House seat over $800,000.

Most candidates for Congress must win the nomination of their party through a direct primary, in which voters identified with their party choose among their party's candidates, picking the one they would like to see run against the opposing party in the general election. Because voter turnout tends to be very low in primary elections, those who do vote tend to be more ideological than those who stay home. As a result, Democratic candidates often take more liberal positions and Republican candidates more conservative positions, trying to appeal to the ideologues in their party. Later, in the general election when turnout is higher, these same candidates may have to moderate their views to attract the votes of independents, voters from the other party, and moderate voters in their own party.

The Costs of Congressional Campaigns

The 2006 midterm elections continued the trend in the ever-growing importance of money and incumbency in American elections. According to a post-election analysis by the nonpartisan Center for Responsive Politics, in 93 percent of House of Representatives races and 67 percent of Senate

To What Extent Does the House Mirror Society?

	Number in the House if it were representative of American society at large	Number in the 107th Congress	Number in the 108th Congress	Number in the 109th Congress	Number in the 110th Congress
Men	184	376	374	367	365
Women	226	59	61	68	70
Black	52	34	39	42	42
Hispanic	30	18	18	24	21
Poor	65	0	0	0	0
Lawyers	2	234	235	237	239
Under 45	300	140	141	140	140

races, the candidate who spent the most money won. The biggest spender was victorious in 398 of 428 decided House races and 22 of 33 decided Senate races. Additionally, 94 percent of House incumbents and 79 percent of senators won re-election.

The average cost of winning a 2006 House race was about $966,000 and $7.8 million for a Senate seat. The most expensive race in the country, as measured by the candidates' spending before Election Day, was the $45.7-million Senate race in New York—and it was not much of a contest. Incumbent Hillary Rodham Clinton, the Democrat, spent at least $35.9 million and won with 67 percent of the vote, defeating Republican John Spencer, who spent at least $4.8 million. Together, all federal candidates spent $1.2 billion. The national party committees reported spending an additional $710 million—$404.6 million by Republicans and $304.9 million by Democrats, and issue advocacy groups, commonly called 527 committees, chipped in at least $157.4 million to influence federal elections and issues, bringing the total cost of the 2006 federal election to approximately $2.8 billion. This makes 2006 the most expensive midterm election ever.

2006
Most Expensive Races

Senate

Raised		Spent	
1. New York Senate	$54,781,826	1. New York Senate	$40,749,449
2. Pennsylvania Senate	$42,671,931	2. Pennsylvania Senate	$37,767,899
3. Missouri Senate	$31,200,504	3. Missouri Senate	$27,886,361
4. Connecticut Senate	$30,923,381	4. Connecticut Senate	$26,160,754
5. Washington Senate	$29,144,639	5. Tennessee Senate	$24,803,651
6. Florida Senate	$26,528,947	6. Arizona Senate	$23,830,520
7. Arizona Senate	$26,120,870	7. Washington Senate	$22,548,549
8. Tennessee Senate	$25,060,960	8. Ohio Senate	$20,762,238
9. Virginia Senate	$21,690,179	9. Florida Senate	$18,854,236
10. Ohio Senate	$21,651,120	10. Nebraska Senate	$18,800,051

House

Raised		Spent	
1. Florida District 13	$8,114,464	1. Florida District 13	$7,819,586
2. Illinois District 8	$8,003,031	2. Illinois District 8	$7,347,698
3. Florida District 22	$7,911,857	3. Florida District 22	$7,114,737
4. New Mexico District 1	$7,224,389	4. Connecticut District 5	$6,199,766
5. Pennsylvania District 6	$6,543,060	5. New Mexico District 1	$6,173,098
6. Connecticut District 4	$6,292,318	6. Pennsylvania District 6	$5,443,882
7. Ohio District 15	$6,242,070	7. New York District 26	$5,441,720
8. Illinois District 6	$6,158,105	8. California District 50	$5,272,170
9. Connecticut District 5	$5,811,157	9. Illinois District 6	$5,199,555
10. Minnesota District 6	$5,799,854	10. Ohio District 15	$5,106,814

Based on data released by the FEC on Monday, November 13, 2006.

The Advantages of Incumbency

In 2006, the power of incumbency appeared even stronger than the power of money. In fact, the most important feature of any congressional election is the incumbency effect. The incumbency effect refers to the fact that since World War II, almost 95 percent of incumbent members of Congress have sought to be re-elected, and among those who seek re-election, more than 95 percent of them are re-elected. In the elections of 1998 and 2000, over 95 percent of incumbents were re-elected. There are several reasons why incumbents have an advantage over their challengers.

Visibility. Not only are incumbent members of Congress able to support pork barrel legislation and do casework, they are also positioned to be able to claim credit and advertise their constituent service. Senators and House members spend a significant amount of time and resources on cultivating media attention. The job of congressional press secretaries is to make sure the press is at media events and that copies of congressmen's and congresswomen's speeches are disseminated to the press. Today, members of Congress are increasingly developing direct lines to their local media markets, often bypassing the national press completely. These local news organizations are hungry for such direct news from Capital Hill and are likely to run the story unedited, guaranteeing favorable coverage of the members.

Members of Congress also make themselves visible through their free use of the postal system, the **franking privilege**. In recent years, members of Congress have sent out nearly 400 million pieces of mail.[15] In one year alone, members of Congress spend about $1.5 million on stamps, all at taxpayers' expense. These mailings quite commonly are used to remind the members' constituents of all the pork he/she is responsible for delivering to his/her constituents.

The Role of Gerrymandering in House Incumbency

Pork barrel, casework, and visibility are not the only explanations for the high rate of incumbent re-election. The way in which the House district lines are drawn may also work to the benefit of the incumbents. After the ten-year census, each state (at least those with more than one district) must divide itself into the number of districts apportioned to it on the basis of its state population. In most states, the state legislature draws these district lines. The party that controls the state legislature may be tempted to try to draw these lines for partisan advantage. This is called **gerrymandering**. The partisan advantage can be obtained by either concentrating the opposition party's voters in as few districts as possible or by diffusing the opposition party's voters across many districts always keeping them in the minority. In 1986, in the case of *Davis v. Bandemer,* the Supreme Court ruled that redistricting for the political benefit of one group could be unconstitutional. However, since that case, specific instances of gerrymandering have been difficult to prove in court and the practice continues.

Occasionally the gerrymandering system and the continuity in congressional membership that it ensures are overwhelmed by factors beyond their control, such as a seismic shift of party allegiances. This does not appear to have happened in 2006. Rather, in 2006, the Democrats managed to win in the approximately 50 districts that had not been gerrymandered so precisely. These are the only seats that tend to alternate between parties and in 2006 the Democrats took more of those competitive seats than the Republicans, thereby gaining control of the chamber as a whole.

Campaign Finance and Incumbency

For many years, researchers overlooked the role of campaign contributions in the re-election of incumbents. This was because studies have consistently found that there is no relationship between money spent on a campaign and winning the election. The big spender does not always win. In fact, incumbents win even when they spend less than their challengers. Because over 90 percent of incumbents will win re-election, they usually win whether they spend more or less than their opponent.

The problem with such studies is that they have focused on campaign *spending*. What they should look at is the relationship between money *raised* and winning, not money *spent* and winning. Incumbents enjoy an enormous advantage not enjoyed by their challengers: PAC money. Political action committees gave $137.4 million to House incumbents during the 2003-2004 election cycle, compared to a mere $24.4 million to the challengers.[16]

Even though incumbents raise more money than challengers, they do not necessarily spend all the money. Any unused campaign money goes into a **war chest**; this money can then be used for the following campaign or given to the incumbent's political party upon his retirement from Congress. Many incumbents have amassed significant war chests, so significant, in fact, that they may scare an opponent off. A significant number of congressional incumbents run unopposed, at least partly because their war chests are so daunting to a challenger. Obviously, if one runs unopposed, one will win. It is the money raised and amassed in huge war chests, but not necessarily spent, that may scare potential challengers out of the arena.

In 2006, despite the record expense to elect Congress, nearly one quarter of House races—111 in all—involved an incumbent with zero financial opposition. One senator, Richard Lugar (R-Ind.), faced no financial opposition, in 36 House races, the winning candidate ran completely unopposed, and another 5 winning candidates faced challengers who either spent no money or filed no reports with the FEC. One scholar has noted that "Congress may have changed hands, but overall this election was not competitive," Krumholz said. "Incumbents overwhelmed their opponents—or simply ran unopposed—because they had a huge cash advantage."[17]

The Issue of Term Limits

The enormous advantages enjoyed by incumbents have led many to call for mandatory term limits. Term limits are popular. Twenty-two states have passed laws limiting the number of terms for House members and Senators. Today, three fourths of all voters say they favor term limits.[18] In *U.S. Term Limits Inc. vs. Thornton*, however, the Supreme Court, by a vote of 5 to 4, declared that a state has no power to impose limits on the number of terms for which its members of the U. S. Congress are eligible either by amending its own constitution or state law. Because the Constitution explicitly addresses qualifications for both the House and Senate, the Court reasoned that the only way to change terms of office would be through the amendment process.

THE ORGANIZATIONAL STRUCTURES OF CONGRESS

Power in Congress is heavily decentralized. What limited leadership there is, comes in four forms: the party system, the committee system, the staff, and the caucuses.

The Formal Leadership of Congress: The Political Parties

Leadership in the House

Every two years, at the beginning of a new Congress, the members of each party gather to elect their House leaders. This gathering is usually referred to as the caucus, or conference. The elected leader of the majority party becomes the **speaker of the House**. House leadership is primarily exercised by the speaker. He presides over meetings in the House. He appoints members to joint committees and conference committees. He schedules legislation for floor action. He decides points of order and interprets the rules with the aid of the House parliamentarian. He refers bills and resolutions to the appropriate standing committees in the House. In 1975, the speaker's powers were enlarged by the House Democratic caucus, which gave its party's speaker the power to appoint the Democratic Steering Committee, which determines new committee assignments for House Democrats. A speaker may fully participate in floor debate, and he may vote, although in recent years, the speaker has only voted to break a tie.

After the speaker is selected, the House majority caucus then elects a **majority leader**. The majority leader is the spokesperson for the majority party in the House and generally acts as the speaker's first lieutenant. The majority leader also conducts most of the substantive and procedural floor debate.

The minority party goes through roughly the same process, selecting a **minority leader**. Like the majority leader, the minority leader is primarily responsible for maintaining party cohesion and acting as the party's spokesperson. The minority leader also speaks on behalf of the president if the president is of that party.

The formal leadership of each party also includes assistants known as **whips**. The whips assist the party leaders by transmitting information from the leaders to party members and by getting party members onto the floor when a vote is being called. Even before the vote is taken, the whips will have conducted polls of their party's members and communicated members' intentions to the leaders. Today, both the Republican and Democratic whips are elected by their party's caucus.

Next in line in importance for each party is its **Committee on Committees** whose tasks are to assign newly elected legislators to committees and deal with the requests of incumbent members for transfers from one committee to another. Members usually receive the assignments they want; and they usually request assignment on a committee related to the dominant interests in their districts.

Finally, every committee and subcommittee is chaired by a member of the majority party. In general, the most senior member, the one with the longest continuous service on that committee, is the chair. This is also true in the Senate.

Leadership in the Senate

The two highest-ranking leaders in the Senate are defined by the Constitution and are largely ceremonial. Under the Constitution, the vice president is the president of the Senate but rarely attends meetings of the Senate and may vote only to break a tie. The Constitution also allows the Senate to elect a **president pro tempore** to preside over the Senate in the vice president's absence. The president pro tem is a member of the majority party and usually is the member with the longest continuous service in the Senate.

The real leadership power in the Senate is exercised, as in the House, by the **majority floor leader**, the **minority floor leader,** and the whips, all elected by party caucus. These leaders have powers similar to their counterparts in the House. They schedule debate, make committee assignments, select members to the conference committees, mobilize the party vote, and act as their party's spokesperson. The Democratic leaders are more powerful than the Republican leaders in the Senate. This is because the Democratic floor leader is also the chairperson of all the following: the Democratic Conference (caucus), the Steering Committee (makes committee assignments), and the Policy Committee (schedules legislation for floor action).

PARTY LEADERS IN THE 110th CONGRESS, 2007-2009

Position	Incumbent	Party/State	Leader Since
House			
Speaker	Nancy Pelosi	D., Ca.	Jan. 2007
Majority leader	Steny Hoyer	D., Maryland	Jan. 2007
Majority whip	James Clyburn	D., S.C.	Jan. 2007
Chairperson of Republican Conference	Adam Putnam	R., Fl.	Jan. 2007
Minority leader	John Boehner	R., Ohio	Jan. 2003
Minority whip	Roy Blunt	R., Missouri	Jan. 2003
Chairperson of the Democratic Caucus	Rahm Emanuel	D., Il	Jan. 2006
Senate			
President	Dick Cheney	R., Wy.	Jan. 2001
President *pro tempore*	Robert C. Byrd	D., W.V.	Jan. 2007
Majority floor leader	Harry Reid	D., Nev.	Jan. 2007
Chairman of the Republican Conference	John L. Kyl	R., Ariz.	Jan. 2007
Minority floor leader	Mitch McConnell	R., Ky.	Jan. 2007
Chairperson of the Democratic Caucus	Harry Reid	D., Nev.	Jan. 2005
Majority Whip	Richard Durbin	D., Il.	Jan. 2007
Minority Whip	Trent Lott	R., Miss	Jan. 2007

Nancy Pelosi made history breaking the marble ceiling to become the first woman to serve as Speaker of the House of Representatives. For the last four years, Nancy has led the House Democrats with effectiveness leadership. Nancy was elected in 2003 as the first woman to lead a major political party in Congress. A recent study in the *Congressional Quarterly* found that "Democrats in the House were never more unified" than they were under in Pelosi in 2005 voting together a record 88 percent of the time. Nancy comes from a strong family tradition of public service. Her father served as Mayor of Baltimore for 12 years after representing the city for five terms in Congress. Her brother as served as Mayor of Baltimore. Nancy and her husband have five grown children and six grandchildren. Nancy brings to the Speaker's role 19 years of experience representing San Francisco in the House.

The Role of Money in Choosing Congressional Leadership

In 2006, the contest to become House majority leader was largely determined by money for while Representative John Murtha had the endorsement of Speaker-to-be Nancy Pelosi, Representative Steny Hoyer had a more powerful ally—money. Hoyer, the Maryland congressman who decisively won the high-profile position of Majority Leader on Nov. 16, 2006, contributed far more money to fellow House members than Murtha, and it paid off. In the 2006 election cycle, Hoyer gave other House candidates about $807,700 from his leadership political action committee (<u>AmeriPAC: The Fund for a Greater America</u>) and from his campaign committee. By contrast, Murtha, of Pennsylvania, gave away only $164,701 to other House candidates. Politicians establish leadership PACs to help fund the campaigns of their fellow party members. Raising money for others can help a lawmaker who aspires to a leadership position or committee chairmanship win chits with colleagues.

Those House Democrats who endorsed Hoyer tended to also get money from him. Of the 75 current and incoming members who publicly endorsed Hoyer, at least 40, or 53 percent, received contributions in the 2006 cycle from Hoyer's PAC, campaign, or both, for a total of $462,000. The average haul for those who got money from Hoyer was $11,550.

Party Discipline

A vote on which 90 percent or more of the members of one party take a particular position while at least 90 percent of the members of the other party take the opposing position is called a **party vote**. In the early 1900s, party votes accounted for nearly one-half of all votes in Congress. Today, they are very rare. Much more common is a weaker form of party voting in which the majority of a party votes one way, and the majority of the other party votes the other way. Such voting has increased in recent years.

Party discipline was short-lived during President Clinton's first term. During the spring 1993 *honeymoon* period, Senate Democrats gave the president unanimous support, resulting in strong party votes. By that summer, however, Democrats were less supportive of the president's programs. In August, Republicans in both the House and Senate voted unanimously against President Clinton's budget proposals. Then conservative Democrats deserted him as well. In the Senate, Vice President Gore had to cast the tie-breaking vote to give Clinton the narrowest of victories: 51 to 50.

Party discipline has been greater during the Bush presidency because the Republicans have control of the House and Senate as well as the White House. For example, during the first half of 2003, Congress devoted much of its time to debating tax and budget measures. Even though a large coalition of labor groups strongly opposed the budget crafted by the Republicans in Congress, in the end, the House and Senate passed the budget on largely party line votes.

While party discipline has been greater in recent years, the increased importance of religious and moral issues following the 2004 election has reduced the number of party line votes in the 109th session of Congress. Members of Congress have become increasingly polarized over such issues as stem cell research, same-sex marriage and abortion, much like their constituents. A recent study has found that on these issues members of Congress are more likely to vote on the basis of their personal convictions. These votes often conflict with others in their party.[19]

THE COMMITTEE AND SUBCOMMITTEE SYSTEM

The Work of Committees: Legislation and Oversight

In any institution as large as the United States Congress, a division of labor is necessary. Because most members of Congress have backgrounds in law or business, they cannot be expected to be experts on all the wide variety of issues on which they are asked to vote. Every year, thousands of bills are introduced into Congress. As a result, members must specialize in one or two issue areas of particular importance to their districts or states. They will then sit on committees and subcommittees dealing with these issue areas.

Most of the actual work of legislating is done by the committees and subcommittees within Congress. Committees usually control the fate of bills, particularly in three ways. First, the committee controls the scheduling of hearings and formal action on a bill and decides which of its subcommittees will act on the bill. A committee can hold up action on the bill and thereby virtually kill its chances to be considered by the entire chamber and passed into law. The only way to remove a bill from a House committee is through a **discharge petition**, signed by 218 members of the House. Such petitions are rare, with only twenty succeeding between 1909 and 1990.[20] Committees control the fate of a bill in a second way: they mark-up the bill. To mark-up means to alter the bill, essentially rewriting it. It is this marked-up version of the bill that will be submitted for consideration to the entire chamber, either House or Senate.

Committees exercise a third form of control over legislation: the committee vote, while not binding on the chamber, almost always determines the chamber's final vote. Committees and subcommittees make a formal report on proposed legislation. These reports are available from the

Government Printing Office. The committee's decisions can be reversed on the floor of the chamber, but this is highly unlikely. The whole point of a committee system is to allow for specialization and the effective division of labor.

The work of committees does not end when the bill goes to the entire chamber for consideration. Members of the committee act as floor managers of the bill, offering advice to other members and lining up support. Finally if there are any differences between the version of the bill passed by the House and the version passed by the Senate, it is the committee members who will be asked to serve on a conference committee whose duty it is to adjust the legislation into a compromise that, if the bill is to be passed, must be acceptable to a majority in both chambers.

Even after the legislation is passed into law, the work of the committees and subcommittees is not finished. Committee members remain active in their role of oversight, the process of monitoring the bureaucracy in its administration of policy. Oversight is accomplished primarily through committee hearings. At these hearings, agency heads, even cabinet secretaries, testify concerning their progress, or lack thereof, in administering the law and carrying out the will of Congress. Committee members and their staff question agency officials, probing particular areas that may seem problematic. If the committee feels the agency is not complying with either the letter or the spirit of the law, it may seek to cut the agency's budget to secure compliance with congressional intent.

The Committee System in the Era of Divided Government

Congress's oversight function has become especially visible in the modern era of divided government. In the 26 years since the Watergate scandal erupted, the same party has simultaneously controlled the White House and both Houses of Congress for only 6 years: during Jimmy Carter's one-term presidency and during the first 2 years of Clinton's first term.

The result has been to set off what amounts to guerrilla warfare between the executive and legislative branches. In 1973, the Senate established the Select Committee on Campaign Activities to investigate the misdeeds of the 1972 presidential campaign, otherwise known as the Watergate scandal. This was followed the next year by the House Judiciary Committee's hearings on the impeachment of President Nixon for his attempt to cover up the scandal. Shortly after the Judiciary Committee recommended these articles of impeachment, the president resigned.

In 1987, a special joint committee was established to investigate the Iran-Contra affair, which involved the Reagan administration's sale of arms to Iran and the diversion of some of the proceeds from the sale to the Contras, a rebel force fighting the Nicaraguan Sandinista government.

Then, in 1998, the Republican controlled House and Senate launched a series of investigations of the activities of Bill Clinton, his wife, and friends while he was Governor of Arkansas and then while president. While the congressional investigations originally concerned the Arkansas Whitewater land deal, they soon extended to issues of campaign finance abuse, and eventually to the probing of Clinton's relationship with a young White House staff member, Monica Lewinsky. House Minority Leader Richard A. Gephardt counted no fewer than 50 House committees investigating the executive branch of government. As of August, 1998, these committees had spent $17 million on inquiries into administration actions that Gephardt described as "politically motivated."[21]

Types of Congressional Committees

Standing Committees

The standing committee is the most important type of committee in Congress. These are permanent committees that specialize in a particular policy area. For example, the Banking, Finance, and Urban Affairs Committee in the House and the Banking, Housing, and Urban Affairs Committee in the Senate specialize in legislation dealing primarily with the banking industry. There are seventeen standing committees in the Senate and twenty-two in the House. In addition, these committees have subcommittees, 103 in the Senate and 139 in the House.

Typically, seventeen to twenty House members sit on each of these committees, with members sitting on an average of two standing committees. Members who serve on either the Appropriations, Rules, or Ways and Means Committee, however, can only serve on that one committee. Senators sit on two standing committees and one minor committee (either the Rules and Administration Committee or the Veterans Affairs Committee).

Standing Committees of the House and Senate

House	Senate
Agriculture	Agriculture, Nutrition and Forestry
Appropriations	Appropriations
Armed Services	Armed Services
Banking and Financial Services	Banking, Housing, and Urban Affairs
Budget	Budget
Commerce	Commerce, Science and Transportation
Education and the Workforce	Energy and Natural Resources
Government Reform	Environment and Publics Works
House Administration	Finance
International Relations	Foreign Relations
Judiciary	Governmental Affairs
Resources	Health, Education, Labor, and Pensions
Rules	Indian Affairs
Science and Technology	Judiciary
Small Business	Rules and Administration
Standards of Official Conduct	Small Business
Transportation and Infrastructure	Veterans' Affairs
Veterans' Affairs	
Ways and Means	

Select Committees

A select committee is a temporary committee created by Congress to fill a certain purpose. After they report to their chamber, they are disbanded. Select committees are often investigative committees, for example, those dealing with Watergate, Iran-Contra, and Whitewater.

Joint Committees

A joint committee is *joint* in several respects. It is created by the House and Senate, and it is made up of members from both chambers and from both political parties. Joint committees may be either temporary or permanent, but they always deal with very specific policy areas, such as economic policy or taxation.

Conference Committees

The conference committee is both a joint committee and a temporary committee. It is created by the House and Senate to work out a compromise in the case in which the House and Senate pass different versions of a bill. While only about 15 to 25 percent of all bills go to conference committee, almost all the most important and controversial ones will.

The House Rules Committee

The House Rules Committee is a uniquely powerful committee. It serves as a gatekeeper, structuring floor action. The Rules Committee sets the time limit on debate and decides whether and in what ways the bill can be amended from the floor.

Committee Membership

One of the first things newly elected members of Congress do upon arriving in Washington is to write to their parties' congressional leadership and the other members of their state delegation, indicating their committee preferences. Members seek to get on committees that will achieve three goals: re-election, influence in Congress, and the opportunity to make policy in areas they think are important.[22] Party leaders generally honor these requests because they want their party members to serve their constituents and thereby win re-election.

Each party in each chamber has its own particular way of making committee assignments. In the House, for example, the Democrats have the Steering and Policy Committee while the Republicans have their Committee on Committees. While these committees do have the authority to assign their party members to the committees and subcommittees, every committee must reflect the party balance of the entire chamber and every chair of every committee will be from the majority party in that chamber. In other words, if the Senate has, say, 60 Republicans and 40 Democrats, every committee and subcommittee in the Senate will have approximately 60 percent Republicans and 40 percent Democrats, and every chair will be a Republican.

Committee and Subcommittee Chairs

Until the 1970s, there was a simple rule for picking committee chairs: the seniority system. This system assigned the chair position to the committee member of the majority party who had the longest continued service on that committee. In the early 1970s, in the wake of the Watergate scandal, Congress faced a revolt staged by younger, newly elected members. Both parties moved to permit their party members to vote on committee chairs. Until 2002, however, seniority still remained the rule, although there were always significant exceptions.

Then after the 2002 election, the Republican leadership in the House announced that they would not be following the seniority principle in assigning the new committee chairs. Majority Leader Tom DeLay and Speaker Dennis Hastert chose the new chairs on the basis of who demonstrated fundraising ability and party loyalty. They chose five new members to fill vacant posts on the Armed Services, Resources, Government Reform, and Agriculture Committees, as well as the newly-created Homeland Security Committee. The five new chairs had donated more than $1 million to the national Republican Congressional Committee and had contributed nearly $500,000 more to House and Senate candidates through their candidate committees and leadership PACs in the 2002 election cycle.

There have been a series of reforms to somewhat reduce the power of the chairs. Chairs of a generation ago could bully members and bottle up legislation and succeed in killing it all together. Today's chairs are less able to control their committees decision-making processes.[23] They still are primarily responsible for scheduling their committees' hearings, hiring staff, appointing subcommittees, and managing committee bills once they are brought to the floor of the chamber.

The Staff System

More than 38,660 people are employed by the United States Congress. The average Senate office employs about thirty staff members but twice that number work for senators from the more populous states. House members employ about fifteen staff members.[24] These staffers handle constituent communications and deal with the details of legislative and administrative actions. Increasingly, staffers are responsible for formulating proposals, organizing hearings, dealing with interest group lobbyists, and advising the members for whom they work.

Besides their personal staff, Congress employs more than three thousand committee staffers. These employees are permanent and stay from one session of Congress to the next. Key pieces of important legislation have been proposed or altered by these committee staff members. Senator Robert Morgan (D-N.C.) has said, "this country is basically run by the legislative staffs of the Senate and House of Representatives."[25]

Congress has also created four different support institutions to enable Congress to oversee the actions of the executive branch, its administrative agencies, and the president himself. The Congressional Research Service does research on policy proposals. The General Accounting Office is Congress' financial watchdog over the bureaucracy, checking the departments and agencies to make sure they are spending the money appropriated by Congress in the way in which Congress meant it to be spent. The Office of Technology Assessment provides Congress with analyses of scientific or technical issues. The Congressional Budget Office assesses the economic implications and probable costs of proposed federal programs. Finally, a section of the Library of Congress acts as an information and fact-finding center for legislators and their staff members. It provides a computer based record of the content and status of major bills that can be accessed by members and their staff.

The Caucuses

Caucuses are groups of senators or representatives who share certain opinions, interests, or social characteristics. Some of the most important caucuses are the Congressional Black Caucus, the Congressional Caucus for Women's Issues, and the Hispanic Caucus. These three have actively sought to advance the interests of the groups they represent through the promotion of legislation and lobbying administrative agencies for favorable treatment. The Congressional Black Caucus now includes over forty members and has dramatically increased its role in the policy-making process.

There are also ideological caucuses such as the liberal Democratic Study Group, the conservative Democratic Forum (known as the *boll weevils*), and the moderate Republican Wednesday Group. There are also a large number of caucuses composed of legislators representing particular economic or policy interests such as the Travel and Tourism Caucus, the Mushroom Caucus, and the Concerned Senators for the Arts.

THE LEGISLATIVE PROCESS

For a bill to become law, it must pass through a series of steps in both the House and the Senate and be passed by a majority of both chambers in identical form. While flow charts may make the legislative process appear to be neat and tidy, the reality is far more complex and far messier. A bill may be introduced in one chamber, work its way through that chamber and then be taken up by the other chamber of Congress. Or a bill might be working its way through the two chambers simultaneously, though not necessarily at exactly the same stage in both. It is also not necessarily the case that the version of the bill in the Senate will be the same as the version in the House. In general, however, the steps discussed below must be completed within one two-year session of Congress. All sessions run from January of an odd year through December of the following even year.

Step One: The Bill is Introduced

The formal legislative process begins when a member of Congress introduces a bill. But before a bill can be introduced, a problem must be identified and a solution formulated. In short, the issue must get on the congressional agenda. An issue can exist for a time without becoming a *political* issue.

Issues get on the legislative agenda in a variety of ways. Certainly a sudden crisis can propel an issue to the forefront, for example, the bombing of the federal building in Oklahoma City. Sustained media coverage of an issue can also work the issue into the collective congressional consciousness. Presidents can also bring an issue to the fore, as President Clinton did with the issues of health care, welfare reform, and gays in the military. Interest groups are quite often instrumental in politicizing an issue, for example, Mothers Against Drunk Driving.

Of course, members of Congress themselves may be instrumental in advancing an issue to the legislative agenda, particularly in two situations. When the president is of one party and the other party controls both chambers of Congress, initiation of legislation is very likely to come from Congress itself. Before the election of 1994, the Republicans in Congress, led by Representative Newt Gingrich, laid out a Contract with America, outlining a legislative agenda that they promised to pursue if victorious in the 1994 election. The other situation that tends to encourage congressional initiation of legislation is when one or more members of Congress are seeking to be nominated as a candidate for the presidency. In 1995, Senator Robert Dole, considered the frontrunner for the Republican nomination, was eager to lead the legislative process.

Step Two: The Bill is Assigned to Committee

After a bill is introduced, in the House by a House member and in the Senate by a senator, it will be assigned to a committee that has jurisdiction over that policy area. The speaker of the House and the majority leader in the Senate are responsible for this assignation. While it is often very clear which committee should receive the bill, there are some cases when it is less than clear. In these situations the leaders can use their discretion to send the bill to a committee that will be friendly to it or to a committee that may be more hostile to the bill.

Once assigned to committee, the bill then will be further assigned to one of the committee's appropriate subcommittees. The subcommittee will do three things with the bill. First, the staffers of the committee members will conduct research on the issue, and the subcommittee may choose to hold hearings on the issue. The committee members will want to hear from people with expertise in the issue area. This group will likely include interest group lobbyists and bureaucrats from the executive branch department or agency involved in the issue area. These people will be asked to testify at the hearing.

When the subcommittee feels that it has sufficient information, it will hold meetings called **mark-up sessions**. The original bill will be marked-up, altered to reflect the information Congress gleaned from the hearing process. Finally, the subcommittee will vote on the bill. If passed, the bill will be sent by the subcommittee to its full committee. The full committee may accept the recommendation of its subcommittee or choose to hold its own hearings and prepare its own bill. It should be noted, however, that many bills will *die* in committee, with little or no consideration given to it. Many pieces are symbolic in that members of Congress introduce them to please some group in their constituency but expect nothing to be done on the bill. In a typical session of Congress, 95 percent of the roughly eight thousand bills introduced die in committee. In those cases when the committee has acted on the bill, the bill is ready to go to the floor of the chamber.

In the House, before the bill goes to the floor, it must go the House Rules Committee. The Rules Committee attaches a rule to the bill that will govern the floor debate in the House. The Rules Committee specifies the length of debate and decides whether amendments can be added from the floor and, if so, of what type.

HOW A BILL BECOMES A LAW

It is much easier to kill a bill than to pass one. Opponents of a bill must only defeat the bill once to kill it; in order to pass it, its proponents must continually secure passage at all different stages of the legislative process. A typical piece of legislation must pass both houses of Congress in the same language before it is sent to the President.

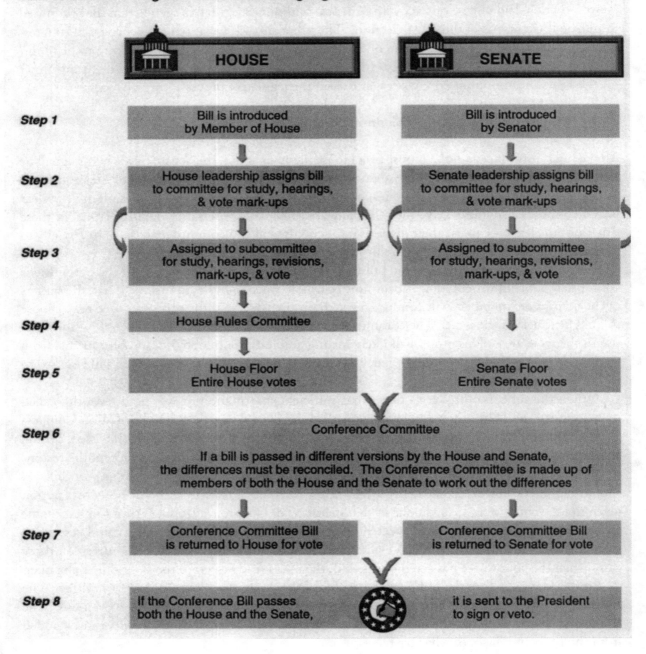

	HOUSE	SENATE
Step 1	Bill is introduced by Member of House	Bill is introduced by Senator
Step 2	House leadership assigns bill to committee for study, hearings, & vote mark-ups	Senate leadership assigns bill to committee for study, hearings, & vote mark-ups
Step 3	Assigned to subcommittee for study, hearings, revisions, mark-ups, & vote	Assigned to subcommittee for study, hearings, revisions, mark-ups, & vote
Step 4	House Rules Committee	
Step 5	House Floor Entire House votes	Senate Floor Entire Senate votes
Step 6	Conference Committee — If a bill is passed in different versions by the House and Senate, the differences must be reconciled. The Conference Committee is made up of members of both the House and the Senate to work out the differences	
Step 7	Conference Committee Bill is returned to House for vote	Conference Committee Bill is returned to Senate for vote
Step 8	If the Conference Bill passes both the House and the Senate,	it is sent to the President to sign or veto.

Before the bill can go to the floor, in both the House and Senate, it must be placed on the calendar. The majority and minority leaders, after consultation with committee chairs, the White House, and the leaders from the other chamber, place the bill on the calendar. Some bills are given an early date while others stay on the calendar from one session to the next.

Step Three: Floor Action

Debate in the House of Representatives is structured by the Rules Committee and the speaker of the House. The speaker can decide whether to grant recognition to a member. The time allotted by the Rules Committee for debate is usually controlled by the bill's sponsor and by its leading opponent. These two are usually the chairman of the committee to which the bill was assigned and the ranking minority member on that committee.

Debate on the floor of the Senate can only be structured by unanimous consent agreements to set the starting time and length of debate. If a senator wants to stop a bill from being passed, he or she may start a **filibuster**, speaking for as long as the member wants. The number of filibusters has risen dramatically in recent years, leading some to complain that there has been a trivialization of the filibuster. In 2005, a group of Republican senators led by Senate Majority Leader Bill Frist responded to the Democrats' threat to filibuster judicial nominees of President George W. Bush in order to prevent a vote on the nominations. They floated the idea of eliminating filibusters on judicial nominees by declaring current Senate rules allowing such filibusters unconstitutional. Senator Trent Lott, the senior Republican senator from Mississippi, named this plan the "nuclear option." Republican leaders later referred to the plan as the "constitutional option," though opponents and some supporters of the plan continue to use the term "nuclear option."

On May 23, 14 senators—seven Democrats and seven Republicans—led by John McCain and Ben Nelson brokered a deal to allow three of Bush's nominees a vote on the Senate floor while leaving two others subject to a filibuster. The seven Democrats promised not to filibuster Bush's nominees except under "extraordinary circumstances," while the seven Republicans promised to oppose the nuclear option unless they thought a nominee was being filibustered that wasn't under "extraordinary circumstances." "Extraordinary circumstances" was not defined in advance. The term is open for interpretation by each Senator, but the Republicans and Democrats will have to agree on what it means if any nominee is to be blocked. Senator John Kerry led a failed filibuster against Judge (now Justice) Alito in January 2006. This agreement was scheduled to expire at the end of the second session of the 109th congress (ends January 9, 2007).

If there is a filibuster, it can be ended under Senate Rule 22, debate may be ended through **cloture**. Sixteen senators must propose closing off debate. Then, after a two-day waiting period, sixty senators must vote for cloture for the debate to be ended. After cloture, each senator may speak for a maximum of one hour on a bill before a vote is taken.

The Senate of the United States is purposefully structured to allow intense minorities to block legislation. Whereas the House is the repository of majoritarianism, the Senate is the protector of the minority. The filibuster is only one of several techniques that allow for this minority veto. Under Senate rules, members are able to propose unlimited amendments to a bill. Each amendment must be voted on before the bill can come to a final vote. The introduction of new amendments can only be blocked by unanimous consent.

When debate is finished, a vote may be called. If a majority of the House votes for a bill, it is passed by the House. A majority vote in the Senate similarly passes the bill in that chamber. If there are any differences between the version passed by the House and the version passed by the Senate, then the bill is sent to a conference committee.

Step Four: The Conference Committee

It is often the case that a bill passed by the House will differ in significant ways from that passed by the Senate. In such cases, a conference committee is composed of the senior members of the committees and subcommittees that had had responsibility for the bills. The job of the conference committee is to work out a compromise version of the bill. When the bill gets out of conference, the House-Senate conference report must be approved on the floor of each chamber. Usually such approval is given readily. The bill can then be voted on. If it is passed by a majority of the House and a majority of the Senate, the bill then goes to the president.

Step Five: The President

When a president receives the bill, he may do any of three things with it. In the most usual situation he will sign the bill, in which case it becomes law. He may, on the other hand, choose to let the bill sit for ten days, excluding Sunday. On the tenth day, the bill becomes law without his signature. A president may choose to follow this course when he is presented with a bill that he does not approve of but for political purposes is willing to go along with Congress.

The third thing the president can do is **veto** the bill. The veto is the president's constitutional right to reject a piece of legislation passed by Congress. To veto a bill, the president must return it to the chamber in which it originated within ten days with his objections to the bill. Congress can try to override the president's veto, but such an override requires a two-thirds vote in both chambers. Overrides are very rare.

If Congress adjourns during this ten-day period in which the president may act, and the president has taken no action, the bill is considered **pocket vetoed**. A pocket veto cannot be overridden by Congress for the simple reason that Congress has adjourned.

For a brief period, the president also enjoyed the power of the **line item veto**. In 1996 President Clinton signed into law a bill passed by Congress authorizing the item veto that allows a president five calendar days following Congress' passage of a bill to notify Congress of his decision to "rescind" an item. This item veto applies to discretionary spending, new direct spending, and items of limited tax benefit. Congress has thirty days to override the president's item veto by a simple majority vote. In April 1997 U. S. District Court Judge Thomas P. Jackson declared the item veto authority unconstitutional because it violates the separation of powers.

Step Six: Oversight

Once Congress has passed a bill and the president has either signed it or allowed it to become law, the law must be put into effect. In the executive branch there are departments and agencies specifically responsible for executing the laws of the land. Members of Congress and their committees must oversee how these departments and agencies carry out the policies passed into law by Congress. This is the **oversight** function of Congress.

Congressional supervision of the executive branch bureaucracy takes several forms. First, no agency or department may exist (except for a few presidential offices and special commissions) without congressional approval. It is Congress that passes the **enabling legislation** that creates these agencies and empowers them. During the presidency of George Washington, Congress created three departments: Treasury, State, and War. Today, the bureaucracy has grown to over eighteen hundred departments, agencies, commissions, and government corporations, with a budget of over one and a half trillion dollars, and employing over five million people. While Congress cannot control all aspects of personnel selection, the Senate does have the constitutional power to advise and to consent to (or refuse to consent to) presidential nominations of top agency and department personnel.

The vast size of the bureaucracy does make oversight difficult. In addition, the legislative process itself complicates effective oversight. Congress tends to pass laws that are general outlines for policy development. Congress cannot anticipate all the possible applications of the law and so leaves much for the bureaucracy to fill in. On a typical weekday, agencies issue more than a hundred pages of new regulations. Determining how good a job a particular agency is doing will not be an easy job.

Congress also exercises oversight through its control of the budget. No money may be spent unless it has first been authorized and appropriated by Congress. **Authorization legislation** originates in a legislative committee and states the maximum amount of money an agency may spend on a given program. This authorization may be permanent, it may be fixed for a number of years, or it may be annual. Once funds have been authorized by Congress, they also must be appropriated. **Appropriations** are usually made annually and originate from the House Appropriations Committee and its various subcommittees. The Appropriations Committee may, and often does, appropriate less than was authorized.

Congress' oversight function does not stop once the money has been appropriated to the department or agency. In fact, Congress can actively participate in the activities of the bureaucracy. A congressional committee may obtain the right to pass on certain agency decisions. This is called **committee clearance**, and though the agency is not legally bound by the committee's decision, few agencies would risk angering the committee that largely controls its budget.

Perhaps the most visible and dramatic form of congressional oversight of the bureaucracy is the **investigation**. This investigative power of Congress is not mentioned in the Constitution but has been seen as implicit in the legislative powers of Congress. The Supreme Court has consistently upheld wide investigative powers.[26] As part of this investigative power, Congress may also hold committee hearings and investigations and gives these committees the power to subpoena witnesses, take oaths, cross-examine, compel testimony, and bring criminal charges for contempt and perjury. The most formal oversight methods include conducting a hearing or requesting a report on specific agency practices. An example of an investigation was the congressional inquiry into the Reagan administration's shipment of arms to the government of Iran.

Oversight may also be done more informally, through day-to-day contact between committee members and administrators in the executive branch. Congress has a large number of staff members working on oversight issues, as well as several specialized oversight offices, the congressional Budget Office, the Office of Technology Assessment, the Government Accounting Office, and the congressional Research Service of the Library of Congress.

DISILLUSIONMENT WITH CONGRESS AND DIVIDED GOVERNMENT

It is somewhat surprising that the institution designed to be closest to the people has spawned a fairly high level of disillusionment. There are several sources of this disillusionment.

Scandal

In 2007, 1 Senator, 8 Representatives, and 10 former members of Congress were under investigation by either the congressional ethics committees or by law enforcement authorities. In addition, at least two additional members of Congress were closely tied to an ongoing investigation, though not targets themselves. A staffer for Sen. Arlen Specter (R-Pa.), Vicki Siegel Herson, was under FBI investigation for allegedly helping her husband, a lobbyist, secure almost $50 million in Pentagon spending for his clients and Ben Stevens, the son of Sen. Ted Stevens (R-Alaska), faced an FBI probe surrounding his ties to VECO Corp., an Alaska-based oil services firm.

Gridlock

Since the early 1950s, the presidency has often been controlled by one party and Congress, either one or both chambers, by the other party. This split government has led to stalled legislation. The governmental **gridlock** was seen clearly during the Bush administration when the president vetoed forty-six pieces of legislation and Congress was able to override only once, and then only after the president had been weakened by losing the 1992 election. Many hoped that the gridlock would end after the 1992 election, when the Democrats controlled not only the White House but also both chambers of Congress. Such was not the case. By 1994, voters returned the country to divided government, turning Congress back over to the Republicans. Again, after the elections of 1996 and 1998, the White House and Congress would be controlled by different parties. And although the Republicans regained control of the Senate in 2002, their margin of control was very narrow, holding 51 seats to the Democrats' 48.

The 2006 Congressional Elections: A Return to Divided Government

In November 2006, the American electorate called for a change in congressional leadership resulting in the Democrats taking control of both chambers. Such peaceful power transitions in Washington, D.C., whether in the White House or in Congress, are one of the great hallmarks of the

American Republic. Still, while the composition of Congress changes at least somewhat after every election, changing the party leadership of even one of the chambers does not happen very often. The last time the House of Representatives changed from one party to another was twelve years ago. Prior to that, it was forty years for the next change.

In the House of Representatives such a change in party control is much more traumatic than in the Senate. The Senate lately has switched parties several times in the past decade as it is smaller and even more closely divided. Additionally, the Senate has rules of procedure that require a super-majority of 60 to bring any measure up for debate. Since no party has had more than 60 seats since the 1970s, a minority party Senator retains the power to withhold his/her vote and thereby preclude the chances of a supermajority vote. The House is not so collegial, and as a result, the majority party rules almost absolutely. Minority status offers very little legislative room in which to maneuver. This too may be too simplistic, as ideology can cross party lines. In the 1980's, for example, Republicans in the minority in the House were successful in gaining the support of a group of more conservative Democrats to move some legislative measures. Conservative Democrats (and Liberal Republicans) are not nearly as common today, however.

The most obvious impact of a change in party control of a chamber takes place on the floor in that the new majority party now has the votes to pass its own measures (assuming they can hold together). In the House, they also control the Rules Committee, which dictates what and how legislation will be debated on the floor. The most significant change, however, lies not on the floor but in the committees. Whole committees are re-formed. A committee with 21 members, 12 Republicans and 9 Democrats, now is reversed. Committee staff levels change too. Some Republicans may have to find a new committee to sit on and there will be many Republican staffers who will be looking for new jobs. A new Committee Chairperson will take charge of the committee, meaning they have control of hearing schedules, witnesses and the committee's agenda. This is a very significant shift in power in Washington.

The president, however, remains with his term in office continuing until January 20, 2009. For his first six years in office, President Bush had the luxury of having a Congress controlled by his own party. Following the 2006 elections, the president faces a Congress controlled by the other party. While the media have portrayed the president's plight as dismal, such divided government is quite common. President Clinton had to deal with the same situation and even faced impeachment by the Republican House of Representatives. Presidents G.H.W. Bush, Reagan, Ford, Nixon and Eisenhower all had to deal with hostile Congresses. A minority party member in Congress can take solace in the fact that the president is from his/her party and any bill from Congress needs his approval, so there is some significant influence they can exert on the majority.

In 2008, another presidential election will take place. Judging from the near exact split in the electorate between the parties, this transfer of power in Congress may become more common in the years ahead and the new era of divided government, which began on January 3, 2007 when the members of the 110th session of Congress took their seats, may continue for the foreseeable future.

CONCLUSIONS

The framers of the American Constitution hoped for a deliberative government, slow to act and resilient in the face of mob pressure. What we have today, largely because of the structure of Congress and the legislative process, is a politics best characterized as **incrementalism**. Incrementalism is policy making characterized by the *absence* of policies. Since the collapse of the New Deal party coalitions, politicians lack the strong electoral base that would enable them to pursue a bold legislative agenda. In addition, divided government has robbed both parties of being able to claim to be the majority party. In fact, whereas the Republicans once claimed to be the party of White House national leadership and the Democrats claimed to be the congressional party of constituent representation, they can no longer make such claims. After the 1994 elections, it was the Democrats that would control the White House and the Republicans the Congress.

As this chapter has suggested, Congress' power is tied to its ability to represent the people of this country. Until elections bring voters to the polls and produce clearer mandates, Congress is not likely to be able to rise above a stalled politics of incrementalism and symbolic politics. Presidential leadership is not likely to solve the governance problems the country faces because the presidency faces its own problems with a weak electoral base and divided government.

CHAPTER NOTES

[1] Janet Hook, "Jeffords Shifts Power in Senate," Los Angeles Times, May 25, 2001, A1.

[2] Theodore J. Lowi and Benjamin Ginsberg, *American Government*, 4th ed. (New York: W. W. Norton, 1996), 198.

[3] "Agency Probes Top Aide's Role in Fund-Raising," *Los Angeles Times*, 6 February 1997, A20.

[4] Lowi and Ginsberg, *American Government*, 749.

[5] Edmund Burke, *Burke's Politics*, ed. Ross J. H. Hoffman and Paul Levick (New York: A.A. Knopf, 1949).

[6] Roger Davidson, *The Role of Congressmen* (New York: Pegasus, 1977), 117.

[7] Hanna Fenichel Pitkin, *The Concept of Representation* (Berkeley: University of California Press, 1967), 60-91.

[8] Norman J. Ornstein, Thomas E. Mann, and Michael J. Malbin, eds., *Vital Statistics on Congress, 1993-94* (Washington, D.C.: Congressional Quarterly Press, 1994), 58-61.

[9] "The 105th Congress: A Study in Sameness," 19 January 1997, sec. 4, 5E.

[10] "Highway Bill Larded with Hometown Projects," *Champaign-Urbana News-Gazette*, March 30, 1999, p. A5.

[11] Lizette Alvarez, "Congress on Record Course For 'Pork' with Alaska in a Class of Its Own," *New York Times*, November 19, 1999, p. A28.

[12] *Congressional Quarterly, Guide to the Congress of the United States*, 2d ed. (Washington, D.C.: Congressional Quarterly Press, 1976), 588.

[13] John S. Saloma, *Congress and the New Politics* (Boston: Little, Brown, 1969), 184-85.

[14] *Congressional Quarterly Guide*, 229-310.

[15] *Congressional Quarterly Guide*, 588.

[16] "PAC Funding in Election 2000," http://cwx.prenhall.com/bookbind, 2000.

[17] Sheila Krumholz, "2006 Election Analysis: Incumbents Linked to Corruption Lose, but Money Still Wins," www.opensecrets.org, Nov. 8, 2006.

[18]James MacGregor Burns et al., *Government by the People*, 17th ed. (New Jersey: Prentice Hall, 1998), 305.

[19]*Bill Broadway, "In Congress, Religion Drives Divide,"* Washington Post, *August 28, 2004, B07.*

[20]*Congressional Quarterly*, Guide, 426.

[21]*The News Hour with Jim Lehrer*, August 25, 1998.

[22]Richard F. Fenno, Jr., *Congressmen in Committees* (Boston: Little, Brown, 1973), 1.

[23]Christopher J. Deering and Steven S. Smith, *Committees in Congress,* 3rd ed. (Washington, D.C.: Congressional Quarterly Press, 1997).

[24]The Tax Foundation, *Tax Features*, March, 1992, 6.

[25]Congressional Record, quoted in Lowi and Ginsberg, *American Politics*, 180.

[26]Edward S. Corwin, *The Constitution and What It Means Today*, 13th ed. (Princeton, N.J.: Princeton University Press, 1973), 151.

SUGGESTED READINGS

Aberbach, Joel D. *Keeping a Watchful Eye: The Politics of Congressional Oversight.* Washington: Brookings Institute, 1990.

Arnold, R. Douglas. *The Logic of Congressional Action.* New Haven, Conn.: Yale University Press, 1990.

Baker, Ross K. *House and Senate*, 2d ed. New York: W. W. Norton, 1995.

Congressional Quarterly, Inc. *Origins and Development of Congress*, 2d ed. Washington, D.C.: Congressional Quarterly Press, 1982.

Davidson, Roger H., ed. *The Postreform Congress.* New York: St. Martin's Press, 1991.

Dodd, Lawrence, and Bruce I. Oppenheimer, eds. *Congress Reconsidered*, 5th ed. Washington, D.C.: Congressional Quarterly Press, 1993.

Fenno, Richard F. *Congressmen in Committees.* Boston: Little, Brown, 1973.

Fenno, Richard F. *Homestyle: House Members in Their Districts.* Boston: Little, Brown, 1978.

Fiorina, Morris. *Congress: Keystone of the Washington Establishment.* 2d ed. New Haven, Conn.: Yale University Press, 1989.

Fisher, Louis. *The Politics of Shared Power: Congress and the Executive.* 3d ed. Washington, D.C.: Congressional Quarterly Press, 1993.

Light, Paul. *Forging Legislation.* New York: W. W. Norton, 1991.

Ornstein, Norman J., Thomas E. Mann, and Michael J. Malbin, *Vital Statistics on Congress 1995-1996.* Washington, D.C.: CQ Press, 1996.

Ripley, Randall. *Congress: Process and Policy*, 4th ed. New York: W. W. Norton, 1988.

Smith, Steven S., and Christopher Deering. *Committees in Congress.* 2d ed. Washington, D.C.: Congressional Quarterly Press, 1990.

Sundquist, James L. *The Decline and Resurgence of Congress.* Washington, D.C.: Brookings Institution, 1981.

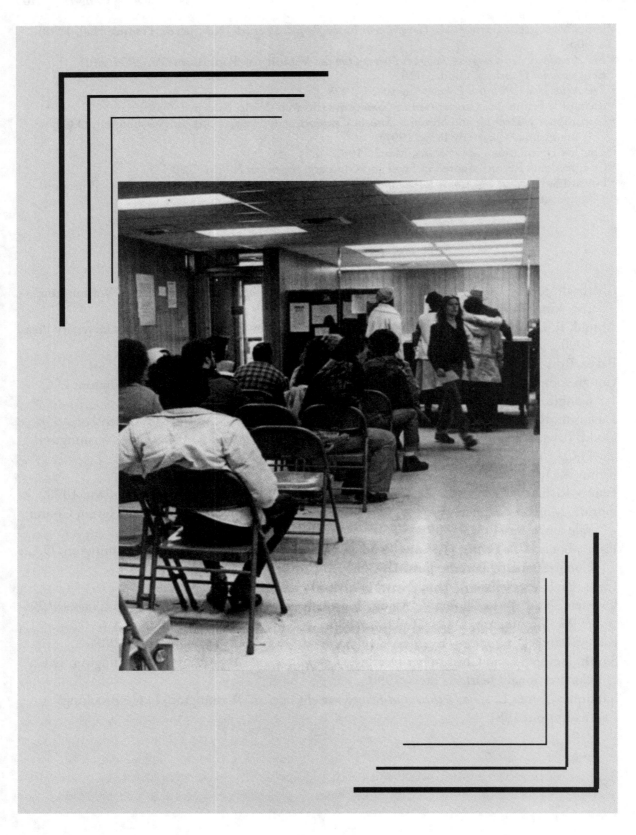

Chapter Ten

THE BUREAUCRACY

In the wake of Hurricane Katrina, red tape too often trumped common sense with a number of instances in which an overly inhibitive bureaucracy prevented an appropriate response to the disaster. Attempts to rescue stranded people by air were impeded by a turf war between FEMA, the FAA, and the military that led to an inability to identify the agency with authority. A mayor in one district tried to get supplies for his constituents who had been hit directly by the hurricane but when he called for help, he was put on hold for 45 minutes and was eventually told by a bureaucrat that he would write a memo to his supervisor. Evacuees on a boat from St. Bernard Parish could not find anyone to give them permission to dock along the Mississippi River and security forces turned them away at one port. A sheriff reported being told that he would not get the resources his office needed to do its job unless he e-mailed a request. Meanwhile, the parish remained flooded and without electricity. Perhaps the worst bureaucratic snafu was that the first responders to the Katrina crisis were hindered by a lack of interoperable communications. Communications problems had plagued the New York police and fire departments on 9/11 with the police and firefighters finding that they could not talk with each other. Four years later, despite billions spent on homeland security, state, federal, and local officials in Louisiana had the same problem

A long list of allegations has continued to surface that offers of personnel and material assistance to New Orleans and other areas affected by the storm were held up by bureaucratic red tape. One example of the criticisms that surfaced regarding the Bush administration's slow response to the damage wrought by Katrina came from Bill Richardson, governor of New Mexico and former Secretary of Energy under President Bill Clinton. Richardson told *NEWSWEEK* that on the Monday that Katrina hit New Orleans, he immediately authorized his state National Guard commander to dispatch 400 New Mexico guardsmen to the disaster area to help out Louisiana state forces. But according to a state official, a hold-up at the Pentagon meant that the New Mexico guardsmen did not actually fly to Louisiana until Friday morning, four days after Richardson authorized them to go.

Richardson said that when he asked his guard commander to explain the delay, he was told the New Mexico troops were not being allowed to travel to the region because of "federal paperwork," which the National Guard bureau at the Pentagon insisted had to be completed. According to Richardson, this paperwork included various authorizations and certifications as well as "transportation waivers." "I remember saying to [the New Mexico guard commander] it's going to be too late" by the time state guardsmen reached the disaster scene, Richardson recalled. An aide to the governor said that military officials later explained that the troops were not allowed to move until they had been assigned a specific mission to pursue once they got to the disaster region, and the mission assignment did not come through from the Pentagon until late Thursday. A spokesman for the National Guard Bureau at the Pentagon said the bureau worked "as quickly as possible" to move troops to the disaster area as part of "an orderly process."

National Guard troops from other states were not the only would-be rescue and recovery officials whose movement to the disaster scene appears to have been impeded by bureaucratic fumbling. According to a knowledgeable federal source, dozens of officers from one of the Homeland Security Department's own bureaus were also inexplicably delayed in being transported to the region. According to the source, investigators working for the Bureau of Immigration and Customs Enforcement, the plainclothes detective division of Homeland Security also known as ICE, were also put on standby to fly to the Gulf Coast within hours of the hurricane making landfall. However, the orders for the ICE agents to move to the region did not come from Homeland Security headquarters until a couple of days passed, leaving investigators puzzled about the reason for the delay.

In the end, Federal Emergency Management Agency Director Michael Brown was removed from his temporary appointment as top federal official on the scene of the disaster amid questions about his qualifications for the post—he had previously been a "commissioner" of the International Arabian Horse Association and had no background in emergency management. Brown resigned as FEMA chief and from his position as Homeland Security undersecretary. In a public appearance, President Bush acknowledged the faltering response by authorities to Katrina and said: "To the extent that the federal government didn't fully do its job right, I take responsibility."[1]

THE DEVELOPMENT OF THE BUREAUCRATIC STATE

Constitutional Beginnings

The Constitution does not specify the structure of the federal bureaucracy. The seeds of the modern administrative state, however, can be found in Article II, section 2, paragraph 2. The president is told that he may appoint, with the advice and consent of the Senate, "ambassadors, other public ministers and consuls, judges of the Supreme Court, and all other officers of the United States whose appointments are not herein otherwise provided for, and which shall be established by law."

The Constitution, then, gave both Congress and the president authority to devise and operate a bureaucracy. Congress has the power by law to create new agencies, and the president has the power to appoint (subject to Senate confirmation) the heads of the agencies.

The first Congress that met in 1789 created a simple bureaucratic structure consisting of three executive departments: the Department of State, the Department of War, and the Department of the Treasury. The first Congress also established the positions of the attorney general and postmaster general. The attorney general is the government's chief legal official, and in 1870 when Congress created the Department of Justice, the attorney general became the head of that department. The postmaster general is in charge of the Post Office.

All in all, the early bureaucracy was quite small. The original Department of State had only nine employees. Even by 1816, the federal bureaucracy employed fewer than five thousand people. The federal bureaucracy, however, grew rapidly thereafter. For the most part, the growth of the bureaucracy stems from the deep-rooted American belief that problems have solutions and progress can be made.

The Progressive Movement

In the early 1900s, a philosophy of political reform, Progressivism, began to call into question the dominant economic theory of the nineteenth century, laissez-faire. The theory of **laissez-faire** dictated a minimal role for the government in economic management. Business was viewed as largely autonomous, and government action was to be discouraged as obtrusive and unnecessary.

By the end of the nineteenth century it had become apparent that the laissez-faire, hands-off approach had allowed the emergence of huge oligopolies, dominating whole fields such as railroads. Gradually, people began to see the need for government involvement in at least parts of the economy. The question was which of the institutions of government would be responsible for protecting the marketplace from its own ogopolistic tendencies.

The answer given by the Progressives of the early twentieth century was the creation of the modern administrative state. Congress moved to create new bureaucratic agencies enabled to regulate specific industries. The Federal Trade Commission (FTC) was created in 1914 to protect consumers from unfair business practices especially in advertising and labeling. The Food and Drug Administration (FDA) was created in 1906 to regulate the purity and safety of foods and pharmaceuticals.

The New Deal and Social Welfare Legislation

The economic depression of the 1930s reaffirmed the nation's belief that government action was essential to economic stability and the financial security of individuals. The enormous effects of economic cycles on the population of the United States convinced most that any needed government intervention would have to come from the federal level of government. State governments were simply not equipped to deal with national economic cycles. As a result, it fell to Franklin Roosevelt and his New Deal legislative program to expand the scope of government action into areas of unemployment, electrical production, housing, and bank regulation. The Railroad Retire-

President Lyndon Johnson took on new commitments with programs of the Great Society.

ment Act of 1934 was the first federal attempt at an extensive security program. In 1935, the Social Security Act created a fund into which workers pay so that they will have income upon retirement. Today, Social Security pays over 93 million Americans every month with the average person receiving about $745 per month.[2]

World War II

By the 1940s, the federal government's role in regulating the economy was largely accepted as necessary. What was less clearly established was a permanent infrastructure of an administrative state. The New Deal involved many emergency boards and did not work to create a more permanent set of regulatory bodies.

World War II would lead to the creation of a permanent administrative state. During the war, the national government hired thousands of people. When the war ended, many of these people were absorbed into the civilian bureaucracy.

The Great Society and the Entitlements Revolution

By the end of the administration of President Lyndon Johnson, the size of the bureaucracy would reach its postwar peak, with 2.9 million civilian employees and an additional 3.6 million military personnel. In the 1950s, new problems had spawned new agencies to solve them. For example, in 1953, Congress created the Department of Health, Education, and Welfare (renamed the Department of Health and Human Services in 1979) to administer the nation's health, education, and assistance programs. Other departments and agencies were spawned in the 1960s when new interest groups began to press their claims on government. For example, Ralph Nader, a consumer activist, drew the public's attention to faulty automobile designs that posed a threat to the consumer. Congress responded in 1966 with the creation of the National Safety Agency (later renamed the Highway Traffic Safety Administration).

The programs of Lyndon Johnson's Great Society were a natural outgrowth of the public's growing sense that the government was responsible for the social welfare of the people. The government took on new commitments in the areas of aid to minorities and the poor. As a result, more and more groups began to see themselves as entitled to government protection. As the programs and their clientele groups grew in number, so did the bureaucratic agencies of the federal government.

Lobbying by Administrators

The budgets and staffs of bureaucratic departments and agencies have continued to grow as a result of activist bureaucrats seeking to defend their budgets and expand their authority. These administrators have often reinvented themselves to assure their continued existence. For example, after the collapse of the Soviet Union, the Department of Defense began to pressure Congress for budgets to do research on worldwide environmental degradation.[4] Similarly the Central Intelligence Agency (CIA) has recently defended their continued existence as necessary to the fight against the international drug trade. As a result, the national bureaucracy and federal spending has kept pace with the growth of the economy and society.

Ronald Reagan and Deregulation

America's acceptance of bureaucratic regulation developed slowly and never fully eclipsed a basic American dislike of government. Laissez-faire is deeply embedded in the very capitalist fabric of the American economy. Perhaps, then, it is unsurprising that as the bureaucratic state grew, uneasiness with it grew as well. By 1980, the American public was expressing disgust with the bureaucracy and government intervention. This disgust coalesced in support of Ronald Reagan in 1980 and then again in 1984.

President Reagan became the spokesperson for the belief that the national government was too involved in regulation, interfering in what should be the natural working of the business markets. Conservatives championed deregulation as a way to return unhampered efficiency to the marketplace.

Considerable deregulation was accomplished in the late 1970s and 1980s, most notably in the airline, trucking, financial services, and telecommunications industries.[5] In each of these areas, the government began to loosen the regulatory ties that were now seen as placing American industries in a less competitive posture in the now global economy. Some deregulation did lead to greater benefits for consumers. For example, in the case of the airlines, the Civil Aeronautics Board (CAB) had been determining fares and controlling access to routes. Some argued that such regulations actually reduced competition between airlines, thereby adversely affecting consumers.

Not all the deregulatory efforts, however, have proved so beneficial to the American economy or to American consumers. Some deregulation has led to horrific results. Savings and loans had been regulated by the national government up through 1988. The reasoning behind such regulation was that money is deposited in a savings and loan on the depositor's full faith that that money will be safe and will be returned on demand with interest. Many depositors come from the population of fixed income elderly retirees, seeking a secure investment.

The economic depression of the 1930s made it amply clear that such security may require some government regulation. As a result, the savings and loans came to be regulated in three ways. First, the savings and loans were told that they must keep a certain amount of the depositors' money "on deposit" in case depositors wish to withdraw funds. Second, the savings and loans were limited with the types of investments they could make with the depositors' money. Specifically, they were limited to making home loans, seen as the most secure because the home acts as collateral for the loan, can be repossessed and resold through foreclosure proceedings, and the depositors' money thereby recouped. Finally, the government insured the deposits just in case the savings and loans did lose the depositors' money in bad home loans.

The savings and loans ran profitably under such regulations until the 1970s when a number of competitors for depositors' money entered the picture. These new investment banking houses, free from government regulation, could promise the depositors greater interest on their money. As the financial market became more competitive, the savings and loans asked the government to ease the regulations and thereby allow them to compete more effectively with the investment banking houses.

Between 1980 and 1983, Congress approved a number of changes that significantly deregulated the savings and loans industry. In brief, Congress allowed the savings and loans to keep a Congress increased the insurance on deposits from $40,000 to $100,000.

While these changes began to reshape the savings and loans industry, the Reagan administration refused to allow the Federal Home Loan Bank Board, which was in charge of supervising the system, to hire the bank examiners it believed it needed to monitor the health of the system. As the real estate market began to slide, the savings and loans began to have trouble. Eventually, they were plunged into insolvency, and taxpayers had to cover the insured deposits to the tune of hundreds of billions of dollars.

More recently, energy companies were deregulated, and again disaster followed. When energy companies were deregulated, the belief was that a deregulated market would send cheaper and more reliable supplies of electricity coursing into homes and offices across the nation. What happened instead was that Enron Corporation, the vast energy trader at the center of the new freewheeling U.S. power markets, collapsed amid a blizzard of questionable financial deals. California, the first big state to deregulate its electricity market, watched its experiment in deregulation turn into a disaster, with intermittent blackouts and retail power rates as much as 40 percent higher than they were the year before. For the consumer, energy deregulation has been anything but good news. Unlike the deregulated telecommunications market, where fierce competition brought down prices while guaranteeing a reasonable level of reliability, the deregulated power market provided no real benefits and many costs. Consumers have been at the mercy of wholesale forces they often cannot understand and have few real options to switch service providers.

Many blame the catastrophic deregulation of energy companies on the campaign finance system. In the 2000 election cycle, the oil and gas sector contributed $15.4 million in contributions to the national party committees; electric utilities contributed $10.1 million more. Enron, alone, gave more the $1.4 million. Many believe that the Enron contributions exempted the company from oversight by the government agencies charged with protecting the interests of the employees, retirees, and shareholders. In other words, some say, the company paid the cop on the beat to take a nap.

Such debacles have fueled support of government regulations. Farmers continue to pressure for government subsidies administered by the Department of Agriculture. Labor unions want the protection offered to workers by the Occupational Safety and Health Administration. Defense contractors lobby for the lucrative government contracts of the Defense Department. In short, many Americans very much want the protections provided by the modern bureaucratic state. In light of such support, it is unlikely that any significant reduction in the size of the bureaucracy is likely in the near future.

Privatization of the Bureaucracy

As noted above, Congress, for over two decades, has been engaged in a bipartisan effort to shrink the size of government. But today, although fewer people appear on federal payrolls, more people than ever work for the U.S. government.

This seeming paradox has been achieved by hiring private contractors to perform many of the tasks previously performed by federal employees. The war in Iraq turned the spotlight on this shift. Government contractors are working in Iraq as prison interrogators, bomb defusers, and armed bodyguards for U.S. officials. They have landed lucrative contracts to rebuild infrastructure and to feed American troops. Paul Johnson, beheaded in June 2004 by Islamic militants in Iraq, worked as an engineer for Lockheed Martin. The four Americans whose bodies were mutilated by a mob in Fallouja worked for Blackwater Security, a "strategic support" firm that, among other things, was responsible for protecting U.S. administrator L. Paul Bremer III. More than one hundred other contract employees, including about forty Haliburton employees, have lost their lives while driving trucks, cooking dinner, or cleaning up damaged oil wells. It was a government contractor who issued student visas to two Sept. 11 hijackers and notified a Florida flight school of the issuance six months after they crashed their planes into the World Trade Center. In 2005, the United States spent $275 billion, more than 10 percent of the federal budget, buying goods and services from private contractors, often through contracts never fully opened to competitive bidding.

Nobody knows exactly how many contractors the government employs. Paul Light of the Brookings Institution estimates that the federal budget funds a "shadow government" of nearly 6 million contractors, about half of them in defense. That means contractors outnumber civil servants and military personnel by a ratio of 2 to 1.[6]

How did this privatization of the federal bureaucracy occur? President Ronald Reagan who sought to downsize what he saw as a bloated federal workforce launched the privatization. His mission has been embraced by every subsequent administration and, in 1998, was codified by Congress with the Federal Activities Inventory Reform Act. This law requires government agencies and departments to publish an annual accounting of which tasks under their auspices "are not inherently governmental functions" and could, therefore, be put out to private bid.

There are several concerns about the privatization of the federal workforce. First, these private contractors are driven solely by profit not the pursuance of the public good. Second, private contractors are not necessarily more efficient. In Iraq much of the $21 billion spent on reconstruction goes to high-priced foreign contractors rather than low-cost local labor. For example, non-Iraqi contractors charged $25 million to repaint 20 police stations, a job the government of Basra claims could have been done by local forms for $5 million. Finally, how should this growing army of workers be managed? Most of the contracts are not subject to competitive bidding and once they get the contract, the government is so dependent on them that it is virtually impossible to end the contract. These and other concerns will continue to fuel the debate about a privatized bureaucracy.

Budget Cuts and the Size of the Bureaucracy

In recent years, most change in the size of the bureaucracy has stemmed from budget cuts. The 105th session of Congress, controlled by Republicans, attempted to enact such cuts, some of which would be quite steep. The Environmental Protection Agency (EPA) was one of the hardest hit when Congress reduced its antipollution inspection programs.[7] These budget cuts, however, have been met with an outcry from the public and organized interest groups. Congress has been forced, in many cases, to reinstate the funds. The 105th Congress, in the end, retreated from its attempt to reduce the size of the EPA.

Budget cuts and attempts at deregulation have not significantly reduced the size of the federal bureaucracy. In fact, while federal employment has remained fairly stable, employment among federal contractors and consultants and in state and local governments has increased. In addition, the power of the federal bureaucracy has continued to grow in terms of its ability to make discretionary policy decisions. The number of regulations issued and the amount of money spent have risen much faster than the number of employees who write these regulations and spend the money. While the number of regulations dipped between 1980 and 1990, they have risen between 1990 and the present.

THE EXPANDING FUNCTIONS OF THE BUREAUCRATIC STATE

As the bureaucracy has grown in response to public demand for a greater number of services, so have its functions expanded. Today, the functions of the federal bureaucracy fall into four main categories. It is not uncommon for a federal department or agency to perform more than one of these functions, or even all of these functions.

National Maintenance

After the Constitution was ratified, Congress moved to create the beginnings of a bureaucratic state that could perform the basic functions essential to maintaining the country. Originally, three departments were created: the Treasury Department to collect tax revenue, the State Department to conduct relations with other countries, and the Department of War to defend the country militarily. Congress also created the Post Office to allow for communication across a fairly vast expanse of land. As long as the functions of the federal government were linked to national maintenance, the bureaucracy's growth occurred when the nation grew. So as new western territories were settled, Congress was moved to create the Interior Department in 1849 to manage these new territories.

Clientele Services

Toward the middle of the nineteenth century particular groups began to seek government services. Farmers, labor, and business were the first to press their claims. They were soon followed, however, by the poor, racial minorities, women, and veterans, to name only a few. Today, many of the departments at the federal level are specifically designed to serve the clientele needs of these groups: the Departments of Agriculture, Labor, Health and Human Services, Housing and Urban Development, Education, and Veterans Affairs.

Regulation

The federal government early on moved to regulate the economy. Prices of goods and services, the amount of competition in the marketplace, and the kinds of information that must be disclosed to consumers were all regulated by the national bureaucracy. In the 1960s, government regulation was extended into other areas. Congress has created agencies to regulate the quality of our air and water, our workplaces, and the safety of the goods we buy.

Income Redistribution

The fourth function of the federal bureaucracy is its most recent: the government's attempt to redistribute resources between groups in our society. Most redistributive efforts involve direct payments to individuals and groups. For example, Aid to Families with Dependent Children for many years involved cash subsidies paid to needy families. Similarly, the Social Security system makes cash payments to the elderly.

While many people think of these redistributive efforts as primarily going to the less privileged members of society, redistribution often goes to the wealthy as well. For example, the Department of Agriculture subsidizes farmers, many of whom are large corporate farmers. The Department of Defense gives lucrative government contracts to large corporations. Finally, Social Security payments go to the wealthy elderly as well as the poor elderly.

THE ORGANIZATION OF THE FEDERAL BUREAUCRACY

The federal bureaucracy includes four types of organizations: cabinet departments, independent agencies, regulatory agencies or commissions, and government corporations.

Cabinet Departments

Executive departments were the first bureaucratic organizations created by Congress, and they are now the biggest units of the executive branch bureaucracy. Today, there are fifteen departments, and they meet most of the federal government's responsibilities. These departments are headed by a single individual who, while appointed by the president with the "advice and consent" of the Senate, may be removed by the president acting alone.

The fourteen secretaries and the attorney general, who heads the Department of Justice, make up what has become known as the **cabinet**. In theory, the cabinet is meant to be the president's closest set of advisers. Historically, however, presidents have made little use of their cabinets, preferring instead to rely on the White House staff. Such a preference for the White House staff stems from the fact that the departments are created by Congress, funded by Congress, and overseen by Congress. The White House staff is more under the control of the president himself.

Each of the executive departments is quite large. As a result, the departments are further divided into many agencies, bureaus, and offices. For example, the Department of the Treasury oversees the U.S. Mint, the Bureau of Alcohol, Tobacco, and Firearms, the Secret Service, and the Internal Revenue Service.

The Fifteenth Department: The Department of Homeland Security

The creation of the department of Homeland Security is the most significant transformation of the U.S. government in over a half-century. The mission of the department is to prevent terrorist attacks within the United States, reduce America's vulnerability to terrorism, and minimize the damage and recover from attacks that do occur. The department has a clear organizational structure with four divisions: border and transportation security, emergency preparedness and response, chemical, biological, radiological, and nuclear countermeasures, and information analysis and infrastructure protection.

Independent Agencies

Independent agencies are not part of any executive department and their heads lack cabinet status. Independent agencies may be headed by a single individual or by a commission. These agencies have been created by Congress to perform a particular function. Some, like the Small Business Administration, provide a service; others (discussed in the next section), like the Environmental Protection Agency, perform a regulatory function. These agencies also vary in how closely they are tied to the president. Some, like the Central Intelligence Agency, are very directly under the influence of the president. Others, like NASA (National Aeronautics and Space Administration), are much less so.

Regulatory Agencies or Commissions

Even though the **regulatory agencies** are the second most important type of organization within the federal bureaucracy, after the cabinet departments, they are fairly recent creations of Congress. As noted earlier in this chapter, the national government did not begin to regulate economic and social affairs until the Progressive period of the late nineteenth century. The first independent regulatory commission, the Interstate Commerce Commission, was established in 1887.

All regulatory agencies perform the same basic function: they try to promote the public interest by writing and enforcing rules that regulate a sector of the economy or specific type of activity. The rules made by these agencies have the force of law.

Regulatory agencies may be either of two kinds. Some are actually bureaus housed within one of the fourteen departments. For example, the Food and Drug Administration is part of the Department of Health and Human Services. The Occupational Safety and Health Administration (OSHA) is housed within the Department of Labor. On the other hand, there are regulatory agencies that are independent of any department. The Federal Communications Commission (FCC), the Federal Aviation Agency (FAA), and the International Trade Commission (ITC) are all independent regulatory bodies.

Regulatory agencies and commissions tend to be much smaller than the fourteen departments. Also, the regulatory bodies are headed by a small number of commissioners (usually an odd number) appointed for a fixed term by the president with the consent of the Senate. The heads of the regulatory agencies are more removed from presidential control than are the heads of the departments because they serve staggered fixed terms. When a president comes into office, he will have to deal with commissioners appointed by a previous president. He will be able to appoint new commissioners only as vacancies open up.

While the regulatory agencies tend to be largely beyond the purview of the president, they are not independent of all types of political pressure. Client groups actively lobby the regulatory agencies to issue rules that are in their favor. For example, for most of its history, the Interstate Commerce Commission was closely tied to the interests of the railroad and trucking industries.

Government Corporations

Finally, Congress has created a small number of **government corporations** that provide public services that could be provided by the private sector. Government corporations are government-owned businesses that sell a service or a product to the public and thereby generate their own revenues. For example, the Postal Service, the Tennessee Valley Authority (TVA), and the Federal Deposit Insurance Corporation (FDIC) all charge for the service they provide whether it be stamps, electricity, or depositors' insurance. Some government corporations are headed by an individual; others have a plural leadership.

A disappointed office seeker assassinated President Garfield. Civil service positions began to replace the "spoils system."

WHO ARE THE BUREAUCRATS?

The national bureaucracy employs about 3 million civilian employees, accounting for 2.3 percent of the entire United States work force.[8] Most of these workers are today hired through the civil service process. Such was not always the case.

A Bureaucracy of Gentlemen

In the early years of the nation's history, service in the bureaucracy was considered the special purview of an elite class. Government office was seen as a prize to be awarded to men of experience, education, and wisdom. Presidents from the two major political parties, the Federalists and the Democratic-Republicans, appointed men drawn largely from these elite ranks.

The Spoils System

The **spoils system**, the practice of hiring and firing federal workers on the basis of party loyalty, was introduced in 1829 by Andrew Jackson. Under the spoils system, the "spoils" of government jobs were doled out by the victorious candidate to loyal campaign workers, friends, and even relatives. Such patronage following an election resulted in almost a complete turnover in government jobs.

By the early 1880s, the public was fairly cynical about the integrity and efficiency of a bureaucracy built upon party loyalty and nepotism. Public office was seen as the path to self-enrichment and corruption flourished. Finally, when President James Garfield was assassinated by a disgruntled campaign worker who was not awarded a job by Garfield, it became clear that a system based on merit was preferable to the spoils system.

The Civil Service

In 1883 Congress passed the **Pendleton Act**, which created the Civil Service Commission (now called the Office of Personnel Management). This commission makes sure that bureaucratic positions are filled on the basis of merit, not partisanship or cronyism.

In the beginning, only 10 percent of federal jobs were covered by the civil service system. Today, over 80 percent of federal employees fall within the purview of the civil service. Of these, approximately 60 percent are hired through the General Classification System, and another 25 percent are covered by the Postal Service System. Federal positions not covered by the civil service, those at the highest level of the bureaucracy, are appointed by the president with the advice and consent of the Senate.[9]

The line between civil servants and presidential appointees has been somewhat muted by the Civil Service Reform Act of 1978. This act creates the Senior Executive Service (SES), consisting of civil servants, today numbering about eight thousand, who have reached the highest level in their particular career path. The purpose of the SES is to allow these career bureaucrats to move into other positions that are usually reserved for appointees of the president. Individuals who join the ranks of the SES can be moved from one job to another by the sitting president.

Changes in the Demographic Composition of the Bureaucracy

Beginning as a "government by gentlemen," the bureaucracy has been slow to reflect the diversity of the expanding nation.[10] In the early 1970s, Congress moved to require the federal government to follow affirmative action guidelines in hiring. As a result of such guidelines, women now make up

50 percent of the federal work force and racial minorities make up an additional 26 percent. Still, at the highest level of the civil service, minorities are underrepresented.[11]

Presidential Appointees

While most of the bureaucratic positions are filled through the civil service, presidents may nominate a second category of bureaucrats called political appointees. To fill these positions, the president and his advisers solicit suggestions from politicians, businesspeople, and interest groups. Appointments to these positions offer the president a way to pay off political debts, reward campaign contributors, or reward voting blocs, for example women or African Americans, within his party. Often, the appointee may have strong ties to the interest groups whose interests he or she may be in charge of overseeing. For example, President George W. Bush chose Wisconsin Governor Tommy Thompson to head the Department of Health and Human Services. Thompson has traveled the world with tobacco lobbyists and raised tens of thousands of dollars in campaign contributions from tobacco interests. As Governor of Wisconsin, he was instrumental in delaying his state's entry into the lawsuit against tobacco companies.

WHERE ARE THE BUREAUCRATS?

Most of the national government's workers are employed outside Washington. Fewer than 350,000 (or about 12 percent) of career civilian employees work in the Washington area. The vast majority are scattered throughout the country and the world. In fact, nearly 20,000 federal civilian employees work in territories belonging to the United States, and another 100,000 in foreign nations. California, Texas, Florida, and several other states each house more than 100,000 civilian employees. Congress has every incentive to try to spread the jobs around. These jobs are "pork" for the members districts and states, "pork" that might help gain them re-election.

Many people believe that the welfare state now employs the greatest number of civilian employees. In reality, less than 15 percent of bureaucrats work in welfare agencies such as the Social Security Administration. The Department of Veterans Affairs employs twice the number of workers than these welfare agencies and nearly one-third of the civilian bureaucrats work for the army, the navy, the air force, or some other defense related agency.

WHAT BUREAUCRACIES DO

Bureaucracies implement policy. They take congressional, presidential, and sometimes even judicial pronouncements and develop procedures and rules to implement the policy goals outlined, often vaguely, in these pronouncements. In implementing policy, the bureaucracy comes to manage the day-to-day routines of government: training the armed services, delivering the mail, and building the country's roads. The sections that follow discuss the many ways in which the bureaucracy implements policy.

Policy Development

Members of the executive branch are often very involved in the development and drafting of legislation. Sometimes the initiative for such involvement may come from the bureaucracy, at other times from Congress. For example, Congress routinely asks agencies to respond to countless official and unofficial inquiries, some of which may lead to new legislation. Furthermore, congressional hearings on proposed legislation usually include members of the bureaucracy. Such expert testimony from the bureaucrats has considerable influence on congressional decision making.

All government agencies devote a considerable amount of their time and resources to research, and collecting and analyzing mounds of data. Some agencies, in fact, have such data collection as their principal task. The Bureau of Labor Statistics, for example, collects and publishes information about the economy while the Centers for Disease Control compile public health statistics.

Rule Administration

Cabinet departments, regulatory agencies, and government corporations are all creatures of Congress. Because the Constitution is silent as to the question of how the president shall faithfully execute the laws of the land, Congress has had to fill in the gaps. It is Congress that creates the different agencies and departments through enabling legislation that directly empowers the bureaucracy. Such enabling legislation cannot possibly describe every specific situation or contingency. As a result, Congress often leaves the bureaucracy with significant administrative discretion. Particularly in the areas of domestic and international security, Congress has afforded agencies enormous latitude.

Rule administration is the core function of the national bureaucracy. Departments and agencies carry out the policies of the Congress, the president, and even the courts. For example, the Environmental Protection Agency (EPA) is responsible for administering the multitude of laws passed by Congress to clean up the nation's air and water.

Rule Making and Regulation

The bureaucracy has a number of ways to carry out policy. The most common is through rule making. The bureaucracy issues regulations that are simply rules that govern the operation of government programs. These rules are the way in which the bureaucracy fleshes out the more general guidelines laid down by Congress in laws.

Regulations have the effect of law. For example, Congress passed the Nutrition Labeling and Education Act. The Food and Drug Administration (FDA) then needed to formulate rules to implement the law. The FDA has mandated that labels specifically list the nutritional content of food products. Because bureaucratic rules have the force of law, an agency must follow very detailed procedures in issuing these rules. For example, the agency must propose the rule by publishing it and giving all interested parties an opportunity to comment on the regulation.

Rule Adjudication

Many federal agencies are responsible for determining if the rules they administer have been broken, a process known as **rule adjudication**. Acting like a court, the agency provides the affected parties the opportunity to present arguments and evidence in a more-or-less formal hearing. In addition, more than twenty-five federal agencies employ administrative law judges to help them determine whether defendants have violated any relevant rules. Today, more than twenty-five federal agencies employ a combined total of nearly 1300 administrative law judges. As a greater number of federal agencies have gained responsibility for regulating economic activity, rule adjudication has grown in importance.[12]

Litigation

The most serious disputes between an agency and those affected by its decisions may end up in federal court. The courts have the authority to review all agency rules and decisions brought before them. In general, any party adversely affected by an agency decision has standing to bring suit. The 1970 Clean Air Act, for example, authorized three different types of suits: challenges to environmental protection agency rules and regulations, citizen suits seeking the performance of duties by the EPA, and enforcement suits against polluters.[13]

Program Evaluation

Congress, the civil service, and the president usually all require agencies to keep fairly detailed records of their various programs and to evaluate them on an ongoing basis. Both Congress and the president may also rely on outside consultants, analysts, and scholars for program evaluation.

THE POLITICAL RESOURCES OF THE FEDERAL BUREAUCRACY

Authority

The bureaucracy possesses authority because Congress passed legislation granting it and because other players recognize it by obeying its decisions.

Administrative Discretion

The power of a department or agency does not simply hinge on congressional delegations of power. Congress gives agencies great latitude to make policy; this is called **administrative discretion**. For example, Congress charges agencies with protecting the "public interest" but leaves them free to determine what specific policies will best serve the public. At times, Congress may be able to define the problem but may not be able to define a particular solution. Congress, then, leaves it to the bureaucracy to fill in the specifics. In 1988, the Department of Health and Human Services issued regulations that forbade family planning clinics that receive federal money to provide "counseling concerning the use of abortion as a method of family planning." When President Clinton came into office, his HHS secretary, Donna Schalala, used her administrative discretion to rescind this so-called gag rule.[14] Because Congress commonly gives only broad and vague directives to the bureaucracy, critics, like Theodore Lowi, charge that Congress delegates too much power to appointed administrators. Agencies also establish their power through exercising discretion in rule making.[15]

Rule Making

Agencies exercise their administrative discretion through rule making. **Rule making** is the bureaucracy's issuance of regulations that govern the operation of government programs. The power to issue these rules or regulations flows from the power of the bureaucracy to implement the programs and policies enacted into law by Congress. Because these regulations are authorized by Congress, they have the full effect of law. For example, after Congress enacted the Nutrition Labeling and Education Act, the FDA proposed rules requiring manufacturers of vitamins and dietary supplements to substantiate the health claims they make for their products on their labels.[16]

Expertise

When Congress grants power to a particular bureau or agency, it usually does so by way of a fairly broad and general grant of authority. Congress expects that bureaucrats, specialists in a particular area, will use their expertise in applying the laws in specific cases. Agencies gain considerable power, then, from the expertise of their employees. This expertise also allows the bureaucrats to be a considerable source for the development of policy proposals and the lobbying for them. Studies have found that many of the bills introduced into Congress have actually been drafted by members of the bureaucracy.

The fact that bureaucrats are hired, and can only be fired, through the civil service process contributes to their level of expertise. Most civil servants spend their entire career within one agency, gaining considerable expertise over the course of many years. Few members of Congress will ever develop this level of knowledge in one particular policy area. This gives the members of the federal bureaucracy a significant advantage in pressing their claims upon the legislative branch of government.

The expertise of the bureaucrats gives them a significant amount of independence from the political appointees who are their superiors. After all, the typical career bureaucrat will remain in the agency long after political superiors have been replaced. Their job security may allow the bureaucrats to resist the dictates of their bosses. Such bureaucratic resistance tends to frustrate not only the political appointee technically at the helm of the department but also the president who appointed him. Hear the frustration in President Richard Nixon:

> We have no discipline in this bureaucracy. We never fire anybody. We never reprimand anybody. We never demote anybody. We always promote the sons-of-bitches [who] kick us in the ass.[17]

Clientele Support

The groups and organizations affected by an agency's actions form its **clientele**. Many of the departments and agencies in the executive branch are specifically what political scientists call **clientele agencies**. These are agencies specifically designed by law to foster and promote the interests of certain groups.[18] For example, the Department of Labor and Commerce was created by Congress in 1903 "to foster, promote, and develop the foreign and domestic commerce, the mining, the manufacturing, the shipping, and fishing industries, and the transportation facilities of the United States."[19]

The power of an agency depends heavily on the power of its clientele. An agency that is actively supported by large, well-organized, and well-funded groups is much more likely to achieve its goals than is an agency with little or weak support. Interest groups can help the agency by bringing pressure on Congress and the president, for bigger budgets, greater powers, or new duties. As a result, congressional committees and subcommittees may become very important parts of an agency's clientele.

There tends to be regular communication between the agency, the clientele groups, and committee members in Congress. This routinized communication makes the agency a lobbyist on the group's behalf and the group a lobbyist on the agency's behalf. The result is the development of very close relationships between congressional committee members, clientele groups, and agencies. Such cozy relationships are often referred to as **iron triangles**.[20] These relationships tend to work to reinforce a particular program against drastic change or abolition at the hands of a hostile president.[21] Iron triangles make clientele agencies the hardest to change or coordinate. Generally, these agencies are able to resist external demands by vigorously defending their own prerogatives. Because of this resistance to change, Congress and the president have frequently been forced to create a new clientele agency rather than to try to convince an existing one to implement programs that the agency opposes.

328 / Chapter Ten

HOW BUREAUCRACIES MAKE DECISIONS

Political scientists have offered two alternative models to describe bureaucratic decision making.

The Rational-Comprehensive Model

The rational-comprehensive model of bureaucratic decision making suggests that bureaucrats follow a sequence of four steps:

1. Clear specification and prioritization of the goals to achieve along with their underlying values.
2. Identification of all alternative methods for achieving those goals.
3. Identification and evaluation, according to formal rules, of all the various outcomes likely to result from each method.
4. In each step, reliance upon information and analysis.

Bureaucratic policy implementation often does not conform to an ideal, rational process in which a problem is identified, various solutions weighed in terms of their costs and benefits, and the most effective, cheapest solution settled upon. Indeed, studies of how policy actually gets made in the federal bureaucracy suggest that the rational-comprehensive model may be far from reality.

The Incremental Model of Bureaucratic Decision-Making

In his classic article "The Science of Muddling Through," Charles Lindblom argues that a more prevalent model of bureaucratic decision making is the incremental model.[22] Bureaucrats work under the constraints of time and limited resources. Under such conditions, it may not be possible to research all the possible solutions to a problem. In the end, Lindblom suggests bureaucrats seek a solution in the modification of an already existing policy. In incrementally altering the status quo, policy making inches along one step at a time.

Incrementalism exhibits the following characteristics:

1. The problem itself may not be clearly defined. For example, take the problem of poverty. What is the problem to be solved? Feeding and housing people, preparing them for a job, or actually getting them a job? Often a problem is multi-faceted, and solving one aspect may make another aspect all the worse. For example, the provision of housing and food may work to discourage a poor person from seeking to get a job.

2. For a variety of reasons, only certain solutions are identified for serious consideration. First, policymakers may not know what to do about a particular problem. Second, it is often difficult to imagine doing things differently than the way you are currently doing them. As a result, radically different approaches to a problem are rarely considered. Finally, limited time and resources may make identification and analysis of all possible solutions unfeasible.

3. The values needed to assess the various solutions are unclear and unranked.

4. Policymakers tend to stop their analysis of solutions when they find one that is "good enough."

Incrementalism leads to a form of decision-making best described as just "muddling through." Rational, comprehensive, scientific analysis of a wide assortment of alternative policies is either not feasible or impossible. As a result, decision-makers make do with "good enough" as they make incremental changes to the status quo.

BUREAUCRATIC ACCOUNTABILITY

Big government, at least in the abstract, is unpopular with the public. The size of the federal bureaucracy is often equated with waste, remoteness, and incompetence. In the last twenty years, a period of "deregulation," more than 250 new federal agencies or bureaus have been created; fewer than two dozen have been disbanded. The government holds title to 400,000 buildings and rents 50,000 additional buildings. Many people believe that the national government has become an octopus, uncontrolled, uncontrollable, and largely unaccountable.

Presidential Control over the Bureaucracy

Presidents have never found it easy to exercise control over the bureaucracy, and civil service and other reforms have further insulated most government workers from the partisan politics inherent in both Congress and the presidency. An incoming president can appoint fewer than 1 percent of all executive branch employees, that is approximately three thousand people out of a bureaucracy that numbers in the millions.[23]

While it is true that the president nominates those who will fill the top policy-making positions in government, these appointments must be made with the advice and consent of the Senate. Additionally, most of these appointees are not personal friends of the president, nor do they tend to be drawn from the ranks of loyal campaign workers. Instead, most come from the sectors for which they will be responsible. For example, the top officials in the Department of Defense tend to have military backgrounds or experience in the defense industries. The Federal Communications Commission has often included people from the communications industry.

The American system of separated powers and checks and balances further exacerbates a president's ability to control the direction of the bureaucracy. The party winning a presidential election does not necessarily gain control of the national government. The president has limited time, limited political resources, and limited influence over the millions of decisions made by thousands of bureaucrats each day.

A president with a very clear agenda and a loyal White House staff may still be able to influence the direction of bureaucratic policymaking. During his two terms in office, Ronald Reagan and his White House staff gained effective control over the bureaucracy. The administration required that all major regulations of departments and agencies be approved by the Office of Management and Budget (OMB), which is part of the Executive Office of the President.

Congressional Control over the Bureaucracy

Congress, with an institutional staff of more than forty thousand, is more readily equipped to oversee the federal bureaucracy. It is Congress that creates the agencies, determines their organization and duties, and funds the budgets. In addition, Congress oversees the activities of the bureaucrats in appropriations hearings, special investigations, and congressional hearings. Finally, it is the Senate that confirms presidential appointments of high, cabinet-level officials.

Congress can significantly influence agency behavior by the statutes that it enacts. In the past, Congress has passed broad statutes that left much to the bureaucrats' discretions. Since the 1960s, however, Congress has attempted to restrict such agency discretion. Until 1983, Congress made increasing use of the **legislative veto**, a law that grants broad power to the executive branch but reserves for Congress the power to block the exercise of power in particular cases.

In 1983, in the *Chadha* case, the Supreme Court declared the legislative veto unconstitutional, ruling that the legislative veto violated the constitutional requirement of separation of powers among the branches of the federal government.[24] Even after the *Chadha* decision, Congress has continued to pass laws containing legislative vetoes. Congress has also rewritten some of the laws so as to require both Houses of Congress and a signature by the president.

Congress has also recently moved to tighten the financial reins on the bureaucracy. No money may be spent by the bureaucracy unless it has first been authorized and appropriated by Congress. In the past, many programs enjoyed permanent authorization. Today, most programs are permanently funded, for example Social Security and the hiring of military personnel. Increasingly, however, there has been a trend toward annual authorizations that enable Congress to strengthen its oversight of executive agencies and their spending. After the military procurement abuses of the 1980s, for example, Congress made Defense Department budgets for military equipment subject to annual authorizations.

Even after the funds have been authorized by Congress, they cannot be spent unless they are also appropriated by Congress. The House Appropriations Committee and its various subcommittees control appropriations. Because appropriations may be, and often are, for less than the amount authorized, Congress can at this second stage further control the budgets of the various bureaucratic departments and agencies.

The most visible and dramatic form of congressional oversight is the investigation. While the power to investigate is not mentioned in the Constitution, it is implicit in Congress' power to legislate. Congress may subpoena a person, compelling that person to come testify before Congress. If the person refuses, Congress may charge him or her with contempt and either vote to send the person to jail or refer the matter to a court for further action.

While it is apparent that Congress does exercise oversight over the executive bureaucracy, none of this is to say that Congress exerts significant control, only that it exerts more control than the president. Many charge that members of Congress actually benefit from the red tape associated with the national bureaucracy, gaining popularity and prestige from running interference with the bureaucracy and interceding on behalf of their constituents. In addition, many point to the fact that members of Congress, ever eager for re-election, avoid conflict by delegating sweeping authority to the agencies and bureaus.

Iron Triangles and Issue Networks

One reason that presidents and Congress often find it difficult to control bureaucracies is that the agencies have strong ties to interest groups, on the one hand, and to particular committees and subcommittees in Congress, on the other. As discussed in Chapter Eight, when agencies, groups, and committees come to depend on each other for support and information, they form what political scientists refer to as **iron triangles** or **subgovernments**.

The decisions reached by members of the iron triangle may not be easily controlled, or interfered with, by the president or Congress as a whole. As pointed out in Chapter Nine, Congress often defers to the decisions reached at the committee or subcommittee stage. Especially when an issue has little press coverage and, therefore, low visibility, decisions reached by the members of the iron triangle are likely to be final.

There is mounting evidence that the concept of iron triangles is overly simplistic, especially when applied to issue areas of higher visibility and greater conflict. In the modern period, as the number of interest groups and policy experts has expanded, congressional committees and bureaucratic agencies may be bombarded with competing demands from multiple sides of an issue. These relationships may be better characterized as fluid **issue networks**. Whether these relationships are iron or fluid, they still work to make congressional or presidential oversight over the bureaucracy difficult.[25]

REFORM AND REORGANIZATION

Some are calling for a complete overhaul of the civil service system. In an era in which term limits for elected government officials are gaining in popularity, perhaps it is not surprising that some are calling for term limits for career civil servants. Limiting their tenure is seen as a way to break up the iron triangles and bring new blood and breathe new life into the system.

These calls for reform are only the latest in a long string of efforts to rein in the federal bureaucracy. In 1946, Congress passed the **Administrative Procedures Act (APA)**, which requires that citizens have the opportunity to be heard concerning proposed rules or regulations to be issued by the executive branch bureaucracy. The APA also allowed citizens to appeal adverse decisions by the bureaucracy to the federal courts.

The increasing power of the federal executive branch also has led to concerns about the public's access to information. The **Freedom of Information Act** (FOIA), passed in 1967 and strengthened in 1974, was designed to address these problems. FOIA requires that government agencies make information "promptly available" to any person who asks for it. Some types of information are exempt: information that would compromise national security, law enforcement, personal privacy, or trade secrets.

Congress has also moved to open government meetings to the public. The **Sunshine Act** requires government agencies headed by commissions or boards to be open to the public. A similar law, the **Federal Advisory Committee Act**, applies this openness requirement to meetings involving executive officials and private citizens.

Congress has tried to make it easier for the bureaucracy to be held accountable through the 1989 **Whistle-Blower Protection Act**. This law says that agencies may not punish an employee who reports fraud, waste, corruption, or abuse on the part of their agency. This law also creates the Office of Special Counsel to help enforce the act. However, to date, very few employees have chosen to exercise their right to "blow the whistle" on their employer.

Finally, the Clinton administration has attempted to study the question of how a government agency might be more responsive to the citizens they serve. The National Performance Review led by Vice President Al Gore has conducted an extensive survey of government agencies to try to discover which agencies are efficient and responsive and which are not.

BENEFITS OF BUREAUCRACY

For all the complaining about big government, there are real and clear benefits of bureaucracy.

Managing Complexity

Life in modern America is complex. Government programs are increasingly sophisticated. Members of Congress are generalists usually not well equipped to deal with all the subtleties that new situations can entail. The tax code of the United States, for example, is nearly three thousand pages long. Only a well-staffed office of accountants can cope with such legal complexity.

Stability and Predictability

The stability and predictability of the federal bureaucracy allow citizens to more effectively grapple with their government. In addition, some communities, like the business community, rely on a certain amount of consistency in government rules, regulations, and programs. Constant reform would leave many in confusion.

CONCLUSION

Americans appear to have a love-hate relationship with their bureaucracy. On the one hand, the twentieth century has seen the size and scope of the executive branch bureaucracy grow dramatically. This growth appears to be an inevitable consequence of the growing technological complexity of modern America, and Americans are the first to say they want the services meted out by the various departments and agencies of the federal government. The Department of Agriculture performs vital services for farmers. The Departments of Education, Labor, Veterans' Affairs, and Commerce all have their clientele. The public as a whole admits the absolute necessity of a Food and Drug Administration to protect the safety of our foods and pharmaceutical drugs.

Still, Americans complain that the bureaucracy is inefficient and cold, unresponsive to even the most incessant demands. Most often Americans complain of bureaucratic red tape and waste. These problems are inherent in government institutions serving a population as large as that of the United States.

CHAPTER NOTES

[1]Bobby Jindal, "Katrina Bureaucratic Red-Tape," http://opinionjournl.com, Sept. 8, 2005.
[2]U.S. Bureau of the Census, *Statistical Abstract of the U.S., 1996* (Washington, D.C.: Government Printing Office, 1996).

3*Historical Statistics of the U.S.: Colonial Times to 1970* (Washington, D.C.: Government Printing Office, 1975), Vol. 2, 1107.

4Philip Shabecoff, "Senator Urges Military Resources Be Turned to Environmental Battle," *New York Times*, 29 June 1990, A1.

5Martha Derthwick, and Paul J. Quirk, *The Politics of Deregulation* (Washington, D.C.: Congressional Quarterly Press, 1985).

6Paul C. Light, "Fact Sheet on the New True Size of Government," Center for Public Service, Sept. 5, 2003, http://www.brookings.edu.

7John H. Cushman, Jr., "E.P.A. Is Canceling Pollution Testing Across the Nation," *New York Times*, 25 Nov.1995, 1.

8U.S. Bureau of the Census, Statistical Abstract of the United States, 1992 (Washington, D.C.: U.S. Government Printing Office, 1992), 331-381.

9U.S. Bureau of the Census, Statistical Abstract of the United States, 1995, 115th ed. (Washington, D.C.: Bureau of the Census, 1995), 350.

10Frederick C. Mosher, *Democracy and the Public Service*, 2d ed. (New York: Oxford University Press, 1982) 58-60.

11U.S. Bureau of the Census, Statistical Abstract, 1992, 332-33.

12Ann Crittenden, "Quotas for Good Old Boys," *Wall Street Journal*, 14 June 1995, 1.

13R. Shep Melnick, *Regulation and the Courts* (Washington, D.C.: Brookings Institute, 1989), 55.

14Marrion Burros, "F.D.A. Is Again Proposing to Regulate Vitamins and Supplements," *New York Times*, 15 June 1993, A25.

15Theodore J. Lowi, *The End of Liberalism*, 2d ed. (New York: W. W. Norton, 1979).

16Michael W. Spicer and Larry D. Terry, "Administrative Interpretation of Statutes," *Public Administration Review* 56 (January/February, 1996): 36-47.

17Richard Nixon to John Ehrlichman, presidential transcript published in *Washington Star News*, 20 July 1974, A1.

18Theodore J. Lowi and Benjamin Ginsberg, *American Government*, 3d ed. (New York: W. W. Norton, 1994), 274.

1915 USC 1501.

20Lowi, 276.

21Martin Shapiro, "The Presidency and the Federal Courts," in *Politics and the Oval Office*, ed. Arnold Meltser (San Francisco: Institute for Contemporary Studies, 1981), Chapter 8.

22Charles Lindblom, "The Science of Muddling Through," *Public Administration Review* 19 (Spring 1959): 19.

23Patricia Wallace Ingraham, *The Foundation of Merit* (Baltimore: John Hopkins University Press, 1995), 9.

24*Immigration and Naturalization Service v. Chadha*, 462 U. S. 919 (1983).

25Hugh Heclo, "Issues Networks and the Executive Establishment,": in *The New American Political System* ed. Anthony King (Washington, D. C.: American Enterprise Institute, 1978), 87-124.

SUGGESTED READINGS

Chub, John E. *Interest Groups and the Bureaucracy: The Politics of Energy.* Stanford, Calif.: Stanford University Press, 1983.

Downs, Anthony. *Inside Bureaucracy.* Boston: Little, Brown, 1967.

Fesler, James W., and Donald F. Kettl. *The Politics of the Administrative Process.* Chatham. N.J.: Chatham House, 1991.

Gore, Al. *Creating a Government That Works Better and Costs Less: The Report of the National Performance Review.* New York: Plume-Penguin, 1993.

Heclo, Hugh. *A Government of Strangers.* Washington, D.C.: Brookings Institution, 1977.

Skowronek, Stephen. *Building a New American State: The Expansion of National Administrative Capacities, 1877-1920.* New York: Cambridge University Press, 1982.

Wildavsky, Aaron. *The New Politics of the Budgetary Process*, 2nd edition. New York: HarperCollins, 1992.

Wilson, James Q. *Bureaucracy.* New York: Basic Books, 1989.

Chapter Eleven

THE PRESIDENCY AND LEADERSHIP

"For better or for worse, who gets to be President of the
United States makes a difference for our future."
James David Barber,
The Presidential Character, 1992

Write to: President George Walker Bush
           Office of the President
           The White House
           1600 Pennsylvania Avenue
           Washington, D.C. 20500

Salutation: Dear Mr. President:

Complimentary close: Sincerely yours,

Telephone: 202-456-1414
FAX: 202-456-2461
E-mail: www.whitehousegov/webmail

There are two major perspectives or ways of conceptualizing the U.S. presidency. It is, first of all, often conceptualized as a job. Like most other salaried executive positions (George W. Bush is the first president to receive a $400,000.00 salary.), it comes with a "job description" that sets forth the personal qualifications that the individual seeking the position must meet and provides a statement of the formal responsibilities the person selected for the job is expected to fulfill. The job description for the presidency is found in Article II of the Constitution.

Another way of thinking about the presidency places less emphasis on what a president is constitutionally required to do and more on who he is and how that affects what he does. The focus in this second, "non-constitutional," perspective is on the personal qualities of presidents and presidential leadership rather than on the institution of the presidency.

Neither of the two perspectives provides a complete picture. To understand what many consider to be the most important job and the most powerful person in the world today, this chapter then will examine both points of view.

THE PRESIDENCY

Qualifications: Formal and Informal

Article II of the Constitution establishes a minimum age of thirty-five to serve as president, but the average age has been fifty-five. The youngest president to date was Theodore Roosevelt, who was forty-two when he was inaugurated in 1901. The oldest was Ronald Reagan, who was sixty-nine when he began his first term (January 1981) and seventy-three when he began his second term (January 1985). If Bob Dole had won the 1996 election, he would have become, at age 73, the oldest first term president in history. Other qualifications for those seeking the office of the presidency include residency in the U.S. for at least fourteen years and "natural born" citizenship (Sec. 1, Clause 5). These are the "formal" or "legal" criteria that the framers of the Constitution believed would secure mature, experienced, and loyal Americans to fill the office of the presidency.

Although race, religion, and gender are not among the specified requirements, only white males have held the office, and the majority of these have been Anglo-Saxon, Protestants. In addition, most of the forty-three U.S. presidents began their terms with prior government experience as a governor, a senator, a representative, or as a vice president. Most, if not wealthy themselves, have had access to those who were wealthy and willing to help finance their election campaigns. Because these are "informal" qualifications, potential candidates are not legally bound by them. Thus, journalist Patrick Buchanan, who has never held an elected or appointive government position; former State Department official Alan Keyes, who is an African American; and Senator Arlen Specter, who is Jewish, have been among the serious contenders competing for the presidential nomination. Former Presidents William Jefferson Clinton and James Earl Carter, who were both Southern Baptists, also broke away from the historical tradition.

Getting Elected: The Electoral College

In addition to personal qualifications, the Executive Article of the Constitution also sets forth the procedure by which a president and vice president are to be elected (Section 1, Clause 3). Since the framers considered and then rejected the idea that the people would directly vote for president, the responsibility for the selection was to be that of their representatives, the electors, or, as they are more commonly and collectively referred to, the electoral college.

The procedure by which electors were to be chosen was left up to the individual states (Section 1, Clause 2). Some opted for having their legislature appoint the electors. Others relied on popular elections that were either statewide or by district. Some used a mixed system that required actions on the part of both the legislature and the voters. Whatever the method, the number of electors for each state was to equal the total number of its senators and representatives.

When the electors' joint ballot for president and vice president resulted in a tie between Thomas Jefferson and Aaron Burr in 1800, the selection process was modified in 1804 by the Twelfth Amendment to provide for a separate ballot for the president and for the vice president. This continues to be the way presidents are selected today.

Voters cast their ballots on Election Day for electors, even though their names may not appear on the ballot, rather than for a particular presidential candidate. The electors then cast their votes in their respective state capitols in December and select the president. All states, with the exception of Maine and Nebraska (which divide the Electoral College vote according to who wins in each congressional district), follow a winner-takes-all rule. This means that all of a states' electoral votes, except for that of an occasional **faithless elector** (one who follows personal choice rather than the wishes of state voters), go to the candidate who received the most votes in that state. The winner-takes-all rule also means that it is possible for a candidate to win the popular vote but lose the election. This actually occurred in 1824, in 1876, in 1888 and in 2000, and the results of the imaginary presidential election described below demonstrates how that happened.

In this imaginary election there are only three states, "Yours," which has a population of 50,000 and 50 electors; "Mine," which has a population of 35,000 and 35 electors; and "Theirs," which has a population of 20,000 and 20 electors. Using these numbers, assume that every person in each of these states votes for either the Democratic or Republican candidate as follows:

STATE	VOTE FOR DEMOCRAT	VOTE FOR REPUBLICAN	DEMOCRAT ELECTORAL VOTE	REPUBLICAN ELECTORAL VOTE
YOURS	40,000	10,000	50	0
MINE	15,000	20,000	0	35
THEIRS	9,000	11,000	0	20
TOTALS	64,000	41,000	50	55

The results of this election show that although the Democratic candidate with 64,000 votes was the people's choice, the electoral college—following the winner-take-all rule—selected the Republican candidate with his 41,000 votes. In actual elections a candidate must win a majority of at least 270 of the present total of 538 electoral votes.

Voters in large states with large numbers of electors generally prefer this system to a direct election. Candidates spend a lot of time and make many campaign promises to voters in those large states to secure those important electoral votes. After all, a win in the eleven largest states is all that is needed to obtain the needed majority. As one journalist bluntly put it, "Winning by a single vote in New York is worth more than winning by millions of votes in a dozen western states put together."[1]

It was not much more than a single vote that determined the outcome of the 2000 presidential election. After five weeks of intense legal disputes over the ballot count and partial recounts in the State of Florida, George Walker Bush was ultimately declared the winner of that state's twenty-five electors by only 537 votes. Those electoral votes brought his total to 271, just one more than is required to win the presidency. (Al Gore won 267.) Bush did not, however, win the national popular vote—Al Gore received 50,158,094 votes to Bush's 49,820,518 votes. Considering the numbers, it is not surprising that critics of the presidential election system (including former First Lady, Senator Hillary Rodham Clinton) immediately began to call for reform of what they consider to be an inherently undemocratic process.

A number of possible alternative methods, such as the district plan, the automatic plan, the proportional plan, and the direct-vote plan—which were discussed in an earlier chapter—have been suggested. However, to change the existing procedure would require a constitutional amendment and without the support of the large states it is unlikely that such an amendment would presently get the necessary three-fourths of the state legislatures to ratify it. At least for now, those seeking to occupy the oval office will have to plan their campaign strategies within the parameters set down in Article II and the Twelfth Amendment of the Constitution.

Presidential Powers and Duties: Given and Assumed

Powers Given

The first words of Article II give the president executive power, the power to carry out or administer the laws that Congress passes, and the duty to see that they are faithfully executed. Section 2, Clauses 1 and 2 of the Article list several additional powers the framers decided should be given to the president. These include the power to make treaties, "**with the Advice and Consent of the Senate**," to appoint Supreme Court justices, to appoint and receive Ambassadors, and to grant pardons to individuals convicted of federal offenses. They also include the responsibility of informing the Congress about the "State of the Union," and the powers—such as commissioning officers—associated with his role as "**Commander in Chief of the Army and Navy of the United States, and of the Militia [National Guard] of the several States.**"

In sum the list of given, or constitutional, presidential powers includes the power to:

- administer federal laws
- make treaties
- appoint federal officials
- receive ambassadors from foreign countries
- grant pardons
- inform the Congress about the state of the union
- serve as commander in chief

Powers Assumed

Looking at this limited list of formal powers, it becomes obvious that, however much the framers tried to limit them, the powers of the presidency have vastly increased over time. They have increased because Congress has gradually given the executive more to do (to submit an annual budget, for example), because the American people now expect him to take the legislative initiative in diverse matters such as health care and the environment, and because other world leaders often turn to him for economic or military assistance and guidance. They have also increased because so many of the men who have occupied the office have taken advantage of the opportunities, both domestic pressures and foreign crises, to do so by exercising what we have come to call their **emergency powers**.

The evolution of presidential power began immediately. It was George Washington (1789-1797) who, by issuing the 1794 Proclamation of Neutrality in the war between England and France, expanded the range of presidential decision-making into the area of foreign policy. This was an area that the framers expected to fall under congressional direction. It was Thomas Jefferson (1801-1809) who seized the opportunity to double the size of the country by purchasing Louisiana before getting congressional approval. It was Andrew Jackson (1829-1837) who went over the heads of the members of Congress, appealed directly to the people, and then, with their support, expanded the power of the president deep into the legislative process. Jackson was the first president to veto legislation not because he thought it was unconstitutional but because he did not like the policy.

With these early assumptions of foreign and legislative powers the stage was set for other presidents to follow suit and to increase them still further. James Polk (1845-1849) popularized the doctrine of "manifest destiny," which enabled him to declare war on Mexico and to add a half million square miles to the United States; Abraham Lincoln (1861-1865) bypassed both Congress and the Constitution and assumed enormous emergency powers during the Civil War; William McKinley (1897-1901) applied Polk's doctrine outside the country to acquire new economic markets for the U.S. (the beginning of American imperialism); and Theodore Roosevelt (1901-1909), who got Columbia to cede Panama and Panama to cede the Canal Zone to the U.S., intervened in Santo Domingo and Cuba and reformed the practices of big business and industry (railroads, mining, and meat) with a vengeance.

Roosevelt, the first president of the twentieth century and sometimes referred to as the first modern president, adhered to the philosophy that unless the Constitution explicitly stated that he couldn't do something, he could and would if he thought it was necessary. He expressed these sentiments candidly in a letter explaining that,

> while President I have **been** President, emphatically: I have used every ounce of power there was in the office and I have not cared a rap for the criticisms of those who spoke of my "usurpation of power"; for I knew that the talk was all nonsense and that there was no usurpation. I believe that the efficiency of this Government depends upon its possessing a strong central executive, and wherever I could establish a precedent for strength in the executive, . . . I have felt not merely that my action was right in itself, but that in showing the strength of, or in giving strength to, the executive, I was establishing a precedent of value.[2]

He did succeed in setting a precedent for the twentieth century presidents who followed him. In responding to events such as the Depression, World Wars I and II, the rise of Communism, the Cold War, the Korean War, the Vietnam Conflict and instances of domestic and foreign terrorism, they broke away from what Woodrow Wilson had referred to in the 1880s as "congressional government."[3] Wilson (1913-1921) and Franklin Delano Roosevelt (1933-1945) joined the growing list of presidents who helped to institutionalize presidential power and established its primacy. Political scientist James MacGregor Burns refers to the ascendancy of the institution of the presidency as "presidential government."

Presidential Roles

The evolutionary growth in the power of the presidency, it was observed many years ago by presidential scholar Clinton Rossiter, is reflected in "the staggering number of duties we have laid upon its incumbent."[4] The important presidential roles include both those which are formerly bestowed by the Constitution and some which were implied by the words "**he shall take Care that the Laws be faithfully executed**" (Article II, Section 3) and taken on by those who have held the office. Some of the major roles briefly described below, identified by Rossiter in his book *The American Presidency*, include: chief of state, chief executive, commander in chief, chief diplomat, and chief legislator.

Chief of State

This important role is an essentially "ceremonial" or a "symbolic" one, which is to say that as chief of state the president serves as a "figurehead" rather than as a "working head" of the U.S. government. In this role the president speaks and acts for all Americans in the U.S. and represents them in other countries. "He greets distinguished visitors from all parts of the world, lays wreaths on the tomb of the Unknown Soldier and before the statue of Lincoln, makes proclamations of thanksgiving and commemoration, bestows the Medal of Honor on flustered pilots, holds state dinners for the diplomatic corps and the Supreme Court, lights the nation's Christmas tree, buys the first poppy from the Veterans of Foreign Wars, gives the first crisp banknote to the Red Cross . . . rolls the first egg for the Easter Bunny, and in the course of any month greets a fantastic procession of firemen, athletes, veterans, Boy Scouts, Campfire Girls, boosters, hog callers, exchange students, and heroic school children."[5]

When President Bush delivered a televised address on the morning after the 2001 terrorist attacks in New York and Washington D. C. he was speaking both to all Americans and, in their behalf, to the rest of the world. He therefore used the collective term "we." "The United States of America will," he said, "use all our resources to conquer this enemy. We will rally the world. We will be patient. We'll be focused, and we will be steadfast in our determination."[6]

The president was again acting as chief of state in his visits to Mexico, Europe and Africa in an effort to demonstrate friendship. Needless to say, this role is extremely demanding on a president's time and energy. But a president who does not fulfill it to the people's satisfaction is not likely to win their enthusiastic approval or their votes.

Chief Executive: The Executive Office of the President, The White House Office, and The Cabinet

That the terms "president" and "chief executive" are so often used interchangeably indicates how closely a president is identified with this particular role. His job to **take Care that the Laws be faithfully executed**" is a constitutional directive to see to it that acts of Congress, federal court decisions, federal rules and regulations, and treaties are put into effect. In short, the president runs the executive branch of government. He is the "chief administrator." He is the government's equivalent to the Chief Executive Officer (CEO) of a major private corporation.

Like the CEO of a corporation the president is a "personnel manager." He has the power to hire and to fire, that is "to appoint" and "to remove from office." Instead of having to seek the approval of a corporate executive board, he appoints government personnel including Supreme Court justices, ambassadors, members of his cabinet, and members of boards and commissions with the advice and consent of the Senate.

George Washington predicted that "one of the most difficult and delicate parts of [his] Office" would be related to "nominations for appointments."[7] He was correct in that not all appointments do go smoothly. For example, Bush suffered the first major political setback of his yet to begin presidency on January 9, 2000, when he accepted a request from Linda Chavez that her name be withdrawn from consideration for the cabinet post of Secretary of Labor. Chavez, a conservation commentator, had failed to disclose during what some considered to be a too hasty vetting process that she had sheltered an illegal Guatemalan immigrant, Marta Mercado, in her home for two years (a felony), that the woman had occasionally done some cleaning in the Chavez home and that she was paid at least $1500 for the work (hiring an undocumented worker is also a violation of federal law.) Elaine Lan Chao, Bush's second choice for the post, was deemed more acceptable.

Alberto Gonzales, the president's selection to head the Justice Department in his second term was also considered by many to be an imprudent and highly controversial choice. Gonzales, White House counsel during Bush's first term in office, was criticized by both the media and by senators during his confirmation hearings for at least tacitly sanctioning the use of torture on prisoners at Abu Ghraib and Guantanamo.

To be sure, not all presidential appointments and dismissals generate as much attention as those described above. Presidents routinely appoint thousands of lesser officials, about two thousand out of the approximate total of three million civilian civil service employees, without any problems at all. While these appointments do not require the approval of the Senate, it has become customary in a practice known as **senatorial courtesy** for the president to yield some of the choices of agency heads and federal judges to the senators in his party. They generally select individuals from their respective states who might then feel that they owe their primary loyalties to the senators who chose them rather than to the president.

As burdensome as personnel matters may sometimes be, it has long been recognized that the presidency, just as a large corporation, cannot be run as a one-man shop. While he, as are all CEOs, is solely "responsible" for executing policy, he alone cannot see to it that the laws of Congress are carried out. "The President," according to the findings of a 1937 presidential committee report that is usually referred to as the Brownlow Report, "needs help."[8] After all, it concluded, things had changed in the executive office since the turn of the twentieth century when presidents could get by much of the time with just a few hours of work.

Stephen Hess, a researcher at the Brookings Institution and staff member in the Eisenhower and Nixon White House, explains that prior to World War I, Woodrow Wilson only worked for three or four hours a day. The remainder of his time was spent "happily and quietly, sitting around with his family."[9] The War, and later the Great Depression of the 1930s, changed all of that. The government began to grow, and it grew rather haphazardly.

The Executive Office of the President (EOP) It was both to cope with new responsibilities and to bring some order to the administration of policy that the Brownlow Report recommended that the executive branch be reorganized and enlarged to include an "Executive Office of the President (EOP)." That recommendation was gratefully accepted by President Franklin Delano Roosevelt, who explained:

> that no enterprise can operate effectively if set up as is the Government today. There are over 100 separate departments, boards, commissions, corporations, authorities, agencies and activities through which the work of the Government is being carried on. Neither the President nor the Congress can exercise effective supervision and direction over such a chaos of establishments, nor can overlapping, duplication, and contradictory policies be avoided.[10]

So it was that the EOP was established in 1939 by **Executive Order** (a presidential order that has the force of law) number 8248. The Executive Office has changed over time. Under Roosevelt it consisted of six administrative assistants, a National Resources Planning Board, the Liaison Office for Personnel Management, and the Office of Government Reports. As of now, the EOP consists of approximately forty thousand key federal executives and military leaders of which the top eight thousand, who hold policy and supporting positions, are presidential appointments. These forty thousand individuals staff positions in: The White House Office, The Office of the Vice President, Agencies of the Executive Office of the President, Presidential Advisory Organizations, The Executive Departments, Independent Agencies, and Quasi-Official Organizations.

When political writers and commentators speak of the "institutionalized" presidency, they are referring to the numerous and diverse offices, agencies, organizations, departments, and councils which constitute the EOP. The magnitude of this office provides an accurate reflection of the vast and growing responsibilities of a modern president and serves to remind us that while the final decision-making responsibility is his, much of the day to day preliminary work is by necessity carried out by the thousands of others who advise him.

The White House Office (WHO). Among the thousands of individuals in the EOP who assist the president are those in the White House Office. They are physically and often emotionally the closest to the president. The WHO consists of people—the number has varied from president to president—who provide such services as housekeeping, secretarial support, legal counseling, medical care, speech-writing, communication with the media and with the Congress, and a myriad of other functions needed to run the White House and assist the chief executive.

Frequently, as in Bush's case, the president's top assistants and advisors are his longtime acquaintances or close friends. The appointment of individuals with whom he has had a personal relationship has an "up" side—they are people who the president knows and whose judgments he trusts—but it sometimes has a "down" side as well—friends may be too protective and in the process of keeping the president "safe" inadvertently isolate him from people and information that he should have access to. It is said that this was the case in Richard M. Nixon's White House Office and contributed to his downfall.

Upon assuming office in 1969, Nixon appointed two of his California friends, which were dubbed by at least one political scientist as the "California mafia."[11] H.R. (Bob) Haldeman became Chief of Staff (the director of the White House Office) and John Erlichman was made Assistant to the President for Domestic Affairs. Because they knew the president and recognized that he was very much a loner, they organized and managed the White House with an eye to providing the seclusion that Nixon seemed to desire. In allowing them to centralize power, historian Arthur M. Schlesinger, Jr. suggests Nixon had made a fatal error. "He rarely saw most of his so-called personal assistants. If an aide telephoned the President on a domestic matter, his call was switched to Haldeman's office. If he sent the President a memorandum, Haldeman decided whether or not the President would see it. 'Rather than the President telling someone to do something,' Haldeman explained in 1971, 'I'll tell the guy. If he wants to find out something from somebody, I'll do it.' The result," Schlesinger concludes, "was the enthronement of unreality . . . . The White House became a world of its own, cut off from Washington and the nation."[12] In his role as Chief Executive, Nixon became a model of what not to do.

The Cabinet. The Constitution of 1789 makes no mention of a cabinet. The framers had specifically rejected the formation of such an advisory council. However, the wording of Section 2 of Article II makes it clear that the president could ask for the opinions of the "**principle Officer in each of the executive Departments**." With this instruction, it didn't take very long for a presidential cabinet to evolve. George Washington got the ball rolling in 1789 by inviting his attorney general and the secretaries of state, treasury and war to meet with him. Today the cabinet is one of the entrenched bodies in the Executive Office of the President, and its secretaries are among the first appointments made by a president-elect.

This is not to say that the cabinet, as a collective group, necessarily plays an essential role in advising the chief executive. As in all things, presidents run the gamut in their opinions of its utility. Some have found that within a short period after they appoint members of the cabinet, their appointees, such as those that head Agriculture, Labor, and Veterans Affairs, become stronger advocates for the departments they head rather than for the executive branch of government or for the general population. Nixon, who demanded the complete loyalty of his advisors, not surprisingly rebuffed his cabinet secretaries with the observation that "no [president] in his right mind submits anything to his cabinet."[13] Clinton, though less hostile than Nixon, followed most of his predecessors and only convened his cabinet seven times during his first year in office.

The Bush cabinet consists of fifteen **principle officers of the executive departments.** In making some of these appointments, including that of the Secretary of Defense, the Secretary of State, the Chairman of the Joint Chiefs of Staff, and the Executive Secretary of the National Security Council, the president's role as chief executive overlaps with that of his role of commander in chief.

Commander in Chief

It was the objective of the framers to place the military protection and the safety of the country in the hands of the national government rather than in those of the individual states. It was also their objective to place control over the military into the hands of a civilian. The Constitution in designating the president as **"Commander in Chief of the Army and Navy of the United States, and of the Militia [National Guard]"** accomplishes both of those objectives.

Still another objective, to ensure that the president was not an out-of-control warmonger, was accomplished by checking his power and leaving it to Congress to **"declare war** (Article I, Section 8, Clause 11)." Thus, as Madison wrote to Jefferson in 1798, "the constitution supposes, what the History of all Govts demonstrates, that the Ex. is the branch of power most interested in war, & most prone to it. It has accordingly with studied care vested the question of war in the Legisl."[14]

Although widely debated in *The Federalist Papers* (See Nos. 24-27 and 41) the framers did not specify in the Constitution just how much control the president was to have over the armed forces or how much direction he was supposed to provide, if any, in peacetime or, for that matter, in wartime. Apparently they didn't believe it would be very much—certainly not nearly as much as that of the British king. In the 69th *Federalist* Hamilton notes that while the king commands the military and naval forces, declares war and raises and regulates fleets and armies, the American president has only the "right to command the military and naval forces of the nation."

Since the Constitution is not much more specific than this, presidents have used their own discretion, sometimes acting in concert with the Congress, sometimes manipulating it, and sometimes bypassing that legislative body altogether. President James K. Polk (1845-1849) deliberately deployed U.S. troops in territory that was claimed by Texas and Mexico to provoke an attack by Mexico and to obtain congressional "recognition" of a state of war. Lincoln in waging the Civil War suspended the writ of **habeas corpus** (an order to bring a prisoner before a judge and explain why that individual is being held), instituted naval blockades of ports in the South, purchased military supplies, and enlarged the army and navy without congressional approval. "As commander-in-chief of the army and navy," he said, "in time of war I suppose I have a right to take any measure which may best subdue the enemy."[15]

Franklin Delano Roosevelt apparently agreed with Lincoln's supposition because he too stretched his role as commander in chief to the limits during World War II. Reminiscent of Lincoln, F.D.R. made it clear to the legislature on one occasion that "in the event that Congress should fail to act, and act adequately, I [FDR] shall accept the responsibility, and I will act."[16]

And act he did. His administration seized and ran industries deemed to be vital for the war effort, restricted consumer access to vital war materials such as gasoline, created scores of war-related defense agencies, and ordered the internment of about one hundred thousand Japanese Americans.

Harry Truman (1945-1953), who knew that there were eighty-seven historical instances in which American presidents had unilaterally sent military forces into combat, followed suit and, without consulting Congress, ordered troops into Korea. In more recent times, John F. Kennedy (1961-1963) orchestrated the invasion of Cuba; Lyndon B. Johnson (1963-1969) sent twenty-two thousand troops into the Dominican Republic and greatly expanded U.S. involvement in the war in Vietnam; Richard M. Nixon (1969-1974) ordered the invasion and the bombing of Cambodia; Jimmy Carter (1977-1981) sent troops into Iran to rescue American hostages; Ronald Reagan (1981-1989) invaded Grenada and Libya; George H. W. Bush (1989-1993) sent troops into Panama and Saudi Arabia; Bill Clinton (1993-2000) deployed U.S. forces to the Iraqi border, to Haiti, and to Kosovo, ordered the bombing of Serbian targets in Bosnia and Kosovo, and sent two aircraft carriers to the waters off Taiwan and George W. Bush (2001-2009) announced a new "preemptive" military strategy against enemies of the United States.[17]

The War Powers Resolution, passed by Congress in 1973, was an attempt to make it more difficult for presidents to initiate and to carry out these types of actions without congressional approval. The resolution requires that the president:

- consult, where possible, with the Congress before introducing U.S. forces into hostilities,
- submit a report to Congress, within forty-eight hours after introducing forces, explaining his actions,
- shall terminate the use of armed forces within sixty days unless Congress, declares war, or extends the sixty-day period, or there is an armed attack upon the United States.

Between 1973 when the Resolution was passed and 1995, there were thirty occasions where presidents had committed troops abroad. An analysis of their compliance to the provisions of the Resolution shows that it had been very low (No president had ever acknowledged the constitutionality of the resolution.) and that Congress had largely backed off from enforcing it.[18] It is not surprising then that Congress approved House Joint Resolution 114, which formally recognizes a president's right to act unilaterally, on October 16, 2002. The Resolution only requires that a president notify Congress, either before he orders an attack or within forty-eight hours, as to why a military action was (or needed to be) taken. It was Resolution 114, proposed by President Bush, which gave him the power to use military force in Iraq without having to first ask Congress for a declaration of war. Clearly we are still in an era of what Schlesinger called "presidential war," an era where presidents in their role as commander in chief are able to use military force to carry out their foreign policy objectives.

Chief Diplomat

Foreign policy objectives are carried out through diplomacy, as well as through the use of military force. The president, who heads the diplomatic corps, is the country's chief diplomat. The framers gave him this job because they understood that "the structural characteristics of the Presidency—unity, secrecy, decision, dispatch, superior sources of information—were . . . especially advantageous to the conduct of diplomacy."[19] In his role of chief diplomat the president may appoint diplomatic personnel and envoys, receive ambassadors, recognize foreign governments, negotiate treaties, make executive agreements, and hold summit meetings.

Appointing Diplomatic Personnel and Envoys. The Constitution (Article II, Section 2, Clause 2) states that the president "**shall appoint Ambassadors, [and] other public Ministers and Consuls.**" With approximately 190 sovereign countries in the world today the appointments to be made are so numerous that a president generally is only able to personally select candidates for the top posts, and he leaves it to his advisors to choose the remainder. Sometimes they fill the less important posts with senior foreign service officers who, unlike many political appointees, may already have extensive diplomatic experience.

Once selected, the Constitution states that it is then up to the Senate to confirm or deny confirmation to these presidential designees. The Senate, however, plays no confirmation role when a president decides to send a personal envoy, such as his wife, to a foreign country.

Receiving Ambassadors. In fulfilling his duties as chief diplomat the president not only appoints and sends ambassadors to represent the United States abroad he is instructed in Section 3 of Article II that it is also his duty to "**receive Ambassadors and other public Ministers**" from foreign governments. Every country has a certain protocol, or rules of etiquette to be followed, that it adheres to when formally receiving an ambassador. (See "Thomas Jefferson As Ambassador to France and as Chief Diplomat of the United States, p. 337.)

Recognizing Foreign Governments. There is nothing in the Constitution that explicitly gives a president the authority to grant recognition to the government of a foreign country. However, presidents, beginning with George Washington who received the French ambassador Edmond Genet, have done so based on the assumption that this is an **inherent power**, one that is inferred by the constitutional directive that the president appoints and receives ambassadors. In other words, when any country, including the United States, sends or receives the credentials of an official representative, the recognition of the legitimacy of that official's government is implied.

It is also implied that when a president withdraws or refuses to receive an ambassador, the recognition of a foreign government has been terminated or denied. Cuba, Iran, and the Republic of China (Taiwan) are among the countries that have had their legal recognition terminated by the United States.

Negotiating Treaties. As chief diplomat, the Constitution (Article II, Section 2, Clause 2) empowers the president to make treaties. Although a president does not do so without assistance, he has the exclusive authority to negotiate a treaty with another country. While the Constitution does call for the Senate to play an advisory role at some time either before or during the negotiations, they have been asked to do so only sporadically.

Presidents have generally accepted the constitutional instruction to secure Senatorial consent. So upon concluding negotiations, the document is presented to the Senate where it is either accepted "as is" by two-thirds of the membership, or it is modified. A modified treaty, such as the "Strategic Arms Limitation Treaty" (SALT II) to which the Senate attached twenty-three conditions, must then be returned to the president who may accept or reject the changes made by the Senate or withdraw the treaty from consideration. President Carter, who negotiated SALT II, opted to withdraw it.

Entering into Executive Agreements. An **executive agreement** is an understanding that is reached between the president and a foreign head of state or by their designees. These agreements have been used by contemporary presidents on such matters as "trade agreements, the annexation of territory, military commitments, and arms control pacts."[20] All of this and yet the Constitution makes no mention of them. As in the case of recognizing ambassadors, entering into an executive agreement is an inherent power.

THOMAS JEFFERSON AS AMBASSADOR TO FRANCE AND AS CHIEF DIPLOMAT OF THE UNITED STATES

Thomas Jefferson replaced Benjamin Franklin as the American Minister to France in 1784. He was a good one, in that he accomplished his main mission of negotiating credit and new markets for America. Jefferson was charmed by the French aristocracy but considerably less enchanted by some of their non-democratic diplomatic procedures.

David Humphreys, a secretary of the American commission, observed Jefferson's first meeting with King Louis XVI and later described one of these procedures. As he watched the ceremony in which Jefferson presented his credentials to the "rather fat" King who was "attended by one hundred Swiss guards," he observed the "somewhat ridiculous . . . rituals of bowing and hat removing, noting that every time Jefferson mentioned the name of either King or Queen in his prepared paper he took off his hat and the King and all his courtiers did the same."

When he became president, Jefferson, as his "rules for foreign ministers" indicate, would have none of this. Among his rules were the following three:

1. the Executive Government would consider every Minister "as the representative of his nation, and equal to every other, without distinction of grade,"

2. "no titles being admitted here, those of foreigners have no precedence,"

3. "at dinners in public or private, and on all occasions of social intercourse, a perfect equality exists between the persons composing the company, whether foreign or domestic, titled or untitled, in or out of office."

Needless to say, many foreign ministers were outraged by these rules.

Sources: Fawn M. Brodie, *Thomas Jefferson: An Intimate History* (Toronto, Canada: Bantam Books, Inc. 1975) 245; Claude G. Bowers, *Jefferson in Power: The Death Struggle of the Federalists* (Boston, Massachusetts: Houghton Mifflin Company, 1964), 37.

Executive agreements can take the form of written statements, or they can be verbal agreements. In either instance, they have the same legal standing as treaties—they are binding on the parties who enter them. Unlike a treaty, an executive agreement does not require either the advice or the consent of the Senate. It has therefore been used with increasing frequency by presidents who want to circumvent the confirmation process because they deem the likelihood of having a treaty ratified to be somewhat remote or because they want to keep their conduct of foreign policy a secret from Congress. (Frequencies are given in the table below.) Nixon, for example, entered a "secret" agreement with the president of South Vietnam in 1973, assuring him that the U.S. would provide full military support should North Vietnam invade the South. They did in 1975. By then Nixon was out of the White House, and the commitment was not met.

Table 11.1	Treaties and Executive Agreements, 1789-1998	
Period	Treaties	Executive Agreements
1789-1839	60	27
1839-1889	215	238
1889-1939	524	917
1940-1970	310	5,653
1971-1977	110	2,062
1978-1983	114	1,999
1984-1988	65	1,890
1989-1993	84	1,606
1994-1998	147	1,372

Source: Robert E. DiClerico, *The American President* (Upper Saddle River, New Jersey: Prentice Hall, 2000), 50.

The Congress has tried, without much success, to limit the use of executive agreements. In 1953 an amendment (the Bricker Amendment) to establish a congressional review of executive agreements was introduced but never came to a vote in the Senate; and the Case Act (1972), which requires the president to inform Congress within sixty days of all executive agreements entered into, has been successfully circumvented by presidents who choose to define their understandings with foreign governments as something other than an executive agreement.

Holding Summit Meetings. Summit meetings, still another example of an inherent power, are a form of personal diplomacy. They are the private, face-to-face meetings that take place between two or more leaders of the world's superpowers.

Little actual negotiation takes place at these meetings. Most of that is handled between lower-level diplomats before the summit even begins. These meetings, about such things as military, economic, and environmental concerns, give world leaders an opportunity to get to know one another. Ronald Reagan and Mikhail Gorbachev, Bill Clinton and Yizhak Rabin, and George W. Bush and Tony Blair are examples of the close relationships that sometimes develop. In addition, because they receive a lot of media attention, summits provide an excellent forum for leaders to promote themselves and their policies to the international community and the voters back home.

In conjunction with the other diplomatic powers discussed in this section, summit meetings have enabled presidents to steal much of the foreign policy thunder out from under the Congress. As if that was not enough, he has in his role of chief legislator also taken from them considerable legislative responsibilities.

Chief Legislator (Presidential/Congressional Relations)

What the framers wanted was for the Congress to propose and pass legislation and for the president to execute it. They also wanted to provide a check on legislative power and so they included the following instruction among the listed duties of the president: "**he shall from time to time give to the Congress Information of the State of the Union, and recommend to their Consideration such Measures as he shall judge necessary and expedient** (Article II, Section 3). This directive, in conjunction with the use of the veto and the responsibility to see to it that the laws are executed, has allowed for an immense expansion in the role that presidents were originally expected to play in the legislative process. Today, as the saying goes, "the president proposes and the Congress disposes."

Presidents as Legislators. The expansion in the legislative role of the president has occurred gradually. While some presidents have sought an active role in this area, others have seen their legislative role as being a passive one. There is a long run of nineteenth and early twentieth century presidents who, as inheritors of the old Whig beliefs (The Whig party was the successor to the Federalists [1832] and the predecessor of the Republicans [1860].), either had no desire—or resisted the temptation—to take the legislative initiative away from Congress.

Among those who adhered to the Whig philosophy of a presidency subservient to the Congress are: William Henry Harrison (1841), Zachary Taylor (1849-1850), Franklin Pierce (1853-1857), James Buchanan (1857-1861), Ulysses S. Grant (1869-1877), Benjamin Harrison (1889-1893), William McKinley (1897-1901), William H. Taft (1909-1913), Warren G. Harding (1921-1923), Calvin Coolidge (1923-1929), Herbert Hoover (1929-1933), and, more recently, Dwight D. Eisenhower (1953-1961). Each of these presidents conformed, with varying degrees, to the theory "that the presidency is limited strictly to following the Congress and adhering to the letter of the Constitution, that it could reasonably suggest fields in which legislation was required but no legislative program itself . . . ."[21]

This point of view gradually began to change after Theodore Roosevelt, who sent numerous legislative proposals over to the Congress, came into office in 1901. The pace of the change accelerated, and the legislative leadership of the president became more firmly established under Woodrow Wilson (1913-1921). It was Wilson who first submitted his recommendations and then went to the Congress in person to advocate in favor of them. Harry Truman (1945-1953) went even further than Wilson. He was the first president to submit to the Congress a whole legislative program, as opposed to individual proposals, at the beginning of each session.

A president today initiates as well as executes legislation. He sets forth a broad legislative agenda for Congress in his annual State of the Union address in January; he sends proposals for legislation to the Congress; he occasionally twists a few arms in trying to secure the passage of bills that he favors; and he vetoes any legislation that Congress sends to him for his signature that is not to his liking.

The Veto. The veto is one way a president has to say "I forbid"—which is what the Latin translation of the word veto means—the passage of a bill into law. Thus "the character of the veto power," as Taft once said, "is purely legislative."[22]

The procedures for two types of vetoes are set forth in Article I, Section 7, Clause 2 of the Constitution. The first way is for the president to return a bill without his signature and with his stated objections to the house in which it originated. The house at that point can either amend the bill and try again, or it can attempt to override the presidential veto. An override requires passage by a two-thirds majority of both congressional houses. The statistics in the table below reveal how rarely that majority is obtained. So a presidential veto virtually assures that the legislation will never be passed into law. For that reason sometimes even the threat of a veto is sufficient to cause Congress to make changes in legislation before they send it on to the president. Clearly that is what George W. Bush had in mind when he threatened to veto a reconstruction package for Iraq if part of it was made a loan.[23]

TABLE 11.2 PRESIDENTIAL VETOES AND OVERRIDES, 1932-2002

PRESIDENT	NUMBER OF BILLS VETOED (Regular and Pocket Vetoes)	NUMBER OF TIMES OVERRIDDEN
Roosevelt	635	9
Truman	250	12
Eisenhower	181	2
Kennedy	21	0
Johnson	30	0
Nixon	43	7
Ford	66	12
Carter	31	2
Reagan	78	9
Bush	46	1
Clinton	36	2
G. W. Bush	1	0

Source: Robert E. DiClerico, *The American President* (Upper Saddle River, N.J.: Prentice Hall, 2000), 95; Updated by the authors.

A second way that a president has to veto legislation, known as a **pocket veto**, is to hold on to it—not necessarily in his pocket—and if the Congress adjourns within ten working days after he has received it, the bill is automatically killed. It follows that pocket vetoes most often occur at the end of a legislative session when the Congress adjourns.

Whichever procedure a president uses, the veto applies to an entire bill. This "all or nothing" selection permits the Congress to attach a **rider**, an extraneous amendment that a president does not support, to a bill that he supports. So at times a president may either sign legislation, even when it has provisions that he does not particularly approve of, rather than see the whole bill go down in defeat, or he may veto legislation that he favors because he refuses to accept the rider.

Clinton, for example, vetoed two welfare reform bills (on December 6, 1995 and on January 9, 1996) because the Congress had coupled them with extreme changes in the Medicaid system, which he believed were "wrongheaded cuts" to which he would just not accede.[24] When the Medicaid provisions were decoupled from welfare reform in a third bill, Clinton announced on July 31, 1996, that he would endorse it. However, there were certain stipulations in the bill, such as excluding "legal" immigrants from getting most of the federal benefits and a cut of $24 billion dollars in the allotment of federal funds for food stamps, that he still did not condone.

The Federal Budget and Impoundment. The Constitution does not place the budget under the purview of the president. He has been brought into the process through his role as chief executive; by his power to veto spending bills; by the passage of the Budget and Accounting Act of 1921, which required the president to submit an Executive Budget (the Budget of the United States Government) to the Congress; and by the creation of the "OMB" the **Office of Management and Budget** (known from 1921 through 1971 as the Bureau of the Budget), one of the most important agencies assisting the president in the Executive Office of the President.

It is through the OMB that the president proposes funds for the programs and bureaucratic agencies that he supports. The OMB budgets money very much the way private corporations and citizens do. There is just so much available to allocate, and tradeoffs are often required. G. W. Bush recognized that tradeoffs would probably have to be made to fully fund the U. S. war against terrorism and, to make sure that Congress knew it too, he threatened to veto any bill that required "unnecessary" spending.

In making tradeoffs a president plays a part in the shaping of the federal budget and fulfilling his role as chief legislator. Every one of his executive agencies must clear any policy recommendation it wishes to present to the Congress with the OMB. Budgeting and policy making are, in a word, inseparable.

In addition to vetoing the budget or an appropriations bill, presidents also have the prerogative to just say no—that is, to refuse to spend the money that has already been appropriated by Congress. This power of refusal is called **impoundment**. A president might want to impound funds to save money, or he might want to impound funds as matter of policy because he believes, for example, that too much is being spent on defense, or on space exploration, or on the environment, or on any other program. Congress, under the authority of the Budget and Impoundment Control Act of 1974, has the final say on whether a president can delay or withhold spending.

Presidential Persuasion. Before resorting to the use of such techniques as the veto and impounding funds, a president can try to secure congressional support for his legislation by using persuasion. There are several "tools and tactics" that a president may opt for. Among those listed by DiClerico are:

- Status Conferral: flattering legislators by calling them on the telephone to thank them for their support, writing a personal letter, taking a picture with them, and so on.
- Legislative Assistance: offering to assist members of Congress to get their own legislation passed perhaps by agreeing to sign their bill when it reaches his desk.
- Programs, Projects, and Patronage: in exchange for support, a president may offer a representative such things as federal judgeships, federal contracts, and economic assistance for his/her district.

- Campaign Assistance: campaigning on behalf of the member or seeing that the party treasury gives generous support to the congressperson's campaign.
- Appeal to the Public: bringing pressure to bear on the Congress as a whole by taking his case directly to the American people.

Clearly a president has a wide range of options to choose from in his efforts to fulfill his role as chief legislator. However, while the options are available to all of them, not every president is equally successful.[25]

Success may be measured in a number of ways. It can be measured by the number of times his veto has been overturned [See table 11.2, p. 340.], the number of executive orders he issues, the volume of legislation he proposes, and the number of those proposals that are made to fulfill campaign promises.

Success can also be measured by public perceptions as reflected in the almost daily polls reported in the media and in the opinions of experts on the presidency. One authority on the subject, who suggests that it is a great oversimplification to give all the credit for legislative success to any one individual or to any one branch of the government, nevertheless names just four men for contributing to the image of the president as a strong legislator. The four, "credited with achieving landmark legislation and giving new direction to national policy," are: Theodore Roosevelt, Woodrow Wilson, Franklin D. Roosevelt, and Lyndon B. Johnson.[26]

Other Roles. The five presidential roles that have been the focus of the first part of this chapter have all been roles that the Constitution specified, however vaguely, were to be filled by the president of the United States. The responsibilities, and even the number of roles a president plays, have grown in number since 1789. Today, for example, a major role of the president is that of a politician. He is the head of his political party, and, as such, he is a **spin doctor** (gives the media favorable interpretations of his party's actions), a political campaigner for himself and for others running for election or re-election on the party ticket, and a major fundraiser.

Presidential Roles v. The Whole Picture

Just as medical students are expected to learn, to name and to describe the functions of various parts of the human anatomy and auto-tech students are expected to learn the parts and the workings of the components that make up a car, students of American government are expected to learn to identify the major presidential roles and to be aware of the responsibilities and the powers of the office of the president. However, learning just these things is not enough, for each of the examples above it can be said that the whole is larger than the sum of its parts.

Probably nobody expressed this sentiment about the presidency better than Clinton Rossiter who, after a lengthy and "piecemeal analysis of the Presidency" and its many roles, confessed:

> I feel something like a professor of nutritional science who has just ticked off the ingredients of a wonderful stew. The members of the audience may be clear in their minds about the items in the pot, but they have not the slightest notion of what the final product looks like or tastes like or will feel like in their stomachs. The Presidency, too, is a wonderful stew

whose unique flavor cannot be accounted for simply by making a list of ingredients. It is a whole greater than and different from the sum of its parts, an office whose power and prestige are something more than the arithmetical total of all its functions. The President is not one kind of official during one part of the day, another kind during another part—administrator in the morning, legislator at lunch, king in the afternoon, commander before dinner, and politician at odd moments that come his weary way. He is all these things all the time, and any one of his functions feeds upon and into all the others. He is a more exalted Chief of State because he is also Voice of the People, a more forceful Chief Diplomat because he commands the armed forces personally, a more effective Chief Legislator because the political system forces him to be Chief of Party, a more artful Manager of the Prosperity because he is Chief Executive.[27]

To get the whole picture of the presidency then one has to get beyond the roles that presidents play and take a closer look at the actors or players. This "non-constitutional" look at presidents focuses primarily on the leadership qualities of the men who have occupied the Oval Office.

LEADERSHIP AND LEADERS

One of the most daunting tasks facing anyone, including political scientists and other experts who write on the subject of leadership, is to define the term. So discouraging is it that some authors don't even make an attempt, and it is difficult to fault them. After all, as James MacGregor Burns, the author of the Pulitzer Prize winning book, *Leadership*, discovered, there were—as far back as 1978—at least 130 definitions of the word.[28]

In addition to an abundance of definitions there are also many different types of political leadership. Burns devotes a full chapter each to "Intellectual Leadership," "Reform Leadership," "Revolutionary Leadership," "Opinion Leadership," "Group Leadership," "Party Leadership," "Legislative Leadership," and "Executive Leadership." Other scholars have identified additional types so the list is seemingly an inexhaustible one.

The definitional and conceptual problems are not going to be resolved here. But an awareness of them should serve to remind the reader that any response to the question "What is leadership?" is both selective and tentative.

What is Leadership?

Leadership may be best understood by its absence. Imagine for example what would happen in a work situation where the boss informs the staff that she/he has something important to do and is, for the first time ever, leaving the office for the morning so that the workers will be entirely on their own. Before leaving, however, the boss tells them that while he/she is gone, they are to come up with some new ideas for increasing the company's sales and that their failure to do so will result in a decrease in their wages. What would happen? What feelings would these workers experience? Empirical studies have shown that most people who suddenly find themselves in circumstances where there is a "leadership vacuum"—a situation in which there is no one to answer their questions or provide instructions—often experience feelings of considerable anxiety.[29] It is because they are apprehensive, psychologically uncomfortable or uneasy that eventually one or more of the individuals in the leaderless group will be likely to step up, fill the vacuum, and act as the leader. "Leadership," as it has been observed, "is a necessary phenomenon in every form of social life."[30] At its most fundamental level, leadership is the ability to make others feel safe and secure by providing them with direction and guidance. This definition implies three things:

(1) It implies that leadership is a relationship. Leaders require followers—those who are to be directed and guided. Leadership, in short, implies followership;

(2) It implies that the ability to provide leadership is a special quality that an individual possesses. It has not yet been determined whether this quality is inborn or inherited, whether it is something that can be learned, or whether it is some combination of the two;

(3) It implies that not every individual who holds a position such as "boss" or "President of the United States" can provide direction and guidance. Such people are formal or nominal "heads" as opposed to "leaders."

Leadership and Headship

"**Headship**" according to Barbara Kellerman is a distinct type of leadership; it is **leadership by position.** "**Leadership**" is the term she reserves for the **relationship between leaders and followers.** As she explains it:

headship is associated with the "rights and duties of an office or status in a hierarchical structure, whether a formal organization or an informally stratified collectivity . . . . Leadership too, is associated with the one who shapes the actions of others. But the focus here is not on role, or position, but on the special relationship between leader and followers. Leaders, in contrast to heads, are accorded their authority spontaneously by group members who, it [sic] turn, follow because they **want** to rather than because they **must.**[31]

Every U.S. president is a leader or head simply because of his formal or constitutional position. But not every president is a leader in terms of his ability to inspire others to follow him. Some presidents have been notable failures in their attempts to provide the direction the American public has come to expect. Among the more recent presidents who have not measured up according to Robert Shogan, in his political bestseller on presidential leadership from 1948 to 1988 (from Truman to Bush) are Jimmy Carter (1977-1981) and George H. W. Bush (1989-1993.)[32]

Leadership Failures: Two Case Studies

Shogan argues that there are three key leadership qualities that ultimately determine whether a president will be a failure or a success in providing direction and guidance to his constituents. These interacting qualities are: ideology, values, and character. Ideology refers to a president's beliefs and his strategy for achieving his political objectives. Values are roughly equated with morality. They consist of private and public principles that guide a president's behavior. Character alludes to a president's temperament and inclinations.[33] Weakness in any of the three qualities might doom a presidency.

The Case of Jimmy Carter

Ideology. James Earl Carter, the thirty-ninth president of the United States, never fully articulated either his political beliefs or a strategy to achieve them for the American public. As a candidate, Carter defined himself predominantly as an "outsider." "This was equivalent to defining himself by what he was not. He was not from Washington, he was not a member of Congress, he was not a liberal, he was not a spokesman for any of the major interest groups in his party."[34] His biographer, Betty Glad, reached the same conclusion as Shogan had a decade earlier. "Where Carter differed in essence from his opponents," she observed, "was in his eagerness to appeal to everyone and in his refusal to connect his various individual stands in terms of some philosophic framework that would place him somewhere on the traditional spectrum of social and political values."[35]

Values. Jimmy Carter, a Southern Baptist, a born-again Christian, a lifelong faithful churchgoer, a Sunday School teacher, a peacemaker, an advocate for the poor, was and is a moral man. There has never been even the slightest hint of immoral behavior in his private or public life. Shogan reports hearing Carter tell a crowd of people in Concord, Massachusetts during the 1976 campaign that "There's a lot of things I will never do to get elected . . . . I will never tell a lie, make a misleading statement, or betray a trust. If I should ever betray a trust, don't support me."[36] He was never publicly accused of doing any of those things.

Given his strong moral and religious commitments, it is hardly surprising that Carter chose to publish his presidential memoirs under the title *Keeping Faith* or, as he reminisces in that work, that his inaugural speech focused "on those concerns that embodied [his] most important values—human rights, environmental quality, nuclear arms control, and the search for justice and peace."[37]

Character. Among Carter's often mentioned character or personality traits are his: intelligence, charm, perseverance, flexibility in choosing political strategies and rhetorical appeals, ambition, a tendency to exaggerate his record, single-minded determination, goodness, shyness, self-absorption and insecurity.[38] Some of these qualities, such as flexibility and single-mindedness, seem to be somewhat inconsistent with one another and probably reflect observations of Carter's behavior at different times or in different situations.

Of all the descriptions of the former president's character the most positive was that made by one of his speech-writers, James Fallows. The Carter that Fallows knew

> is unusually patient, less vindictive than the political norm, blessed with a sense of perspective about the chanciness of life and the transience of its glories and pursuits. [Fallows] left his service feeling that when moral choices faced him, he would resolve them fairly; that when questions of life and death, of nuclear war and human destruction were laid upon his desk, he would act on them calmly, with self-knowledge, free of interior demons that might tempt him to act rashly or to prove at terrible cost that he was a man . . . .[39]

President Jimmy Carter and Rosalynn Carter at the Inaugural Ball. January 20, 1977.
Photo credit: Jimmy Carter Library

If he "had to choose one politician to sit at the Pearly Gates and pass judgment on [his] soul," Fallows continued, "Jimmy Carter would be the one."[40]

Given this glowing testament, it is at first a bit difficult to understand why Carter's presidency failed, why he became the first incumbent president since Hoover lost to FDR in 1933 not to win re-election. To be sure external events, such as the fall of the Shah of Iran, the energy crisis, high inflation, and the seizure of the U.S. embassy in Iran coupled with the taking of American hostages, all contributed to Carter's downfall.

However, as Shogan is quick to point out, other presidents managed to survive such difficult circumstances whereas Carter could not. He could not because he never clearly stated his ideological position. The public did not know what Carter stood for or wanted; there was no vision to rally public support when there were problems. Carter faltered because values and character, without ideology, are not sufficient.

The Case of George Herbert Walker Bush

Ideology. George Herbert Walker Bush, the forty-first president of the United States, inherited a conservative mantle from his predecessor Ronald Reagan—one of the most ideological presidents in recent history—and did not embrace or hold on to it. To be sure, Bush had at times during his political career taken rather strong conservative positions. In the period that he was a member of the House of Representatives, he voted with the conservatives 83 percent of the time; he endorsed conservative Barry Goldwater rather than moderate Nelson Rockefeller during the 1964 Republican presidential primaries; he opposed the 1964 Civil Rights Act, Medicare, and the nuclear test-ban treaty; and he rejected the endorsement of the liberal Ripon Society during his own 1968 Senate campaign.[41]

George Bush had a record as a moderate as well. After moving to the political right in 1964, he had by 1966 moved far enough to the left to win the support of a respectable number of liberal Democrats. When he sought the presidency in 1980 and needed conservative support, Bush took a step away from his "excessive" liberalism and "tried to present himself as a moderate alternative to Reagan. The combined burden was not easy to carry."[42] When asked during that presidential campaign whether he thought of himself as a conservative or a moderate, Bush could only reply "I don't want to be perceived as either."[43]

However, as one newspaper later reported:

when Mr. Reagan chose him as his running mate . . . that sort of talk was quickly shelved. Mr. Bush quickly took on the ideological coloration of the Reagan Administration; not once during its whole eight years did he distance himself from any of its policies in any significant way. George Bush the Planned Parenthood advocate became George Bush the foe of abortion, for example.[44]

George Bush was apparently ideologically adrift long before he ever became president.

Values. Bush, as was Carter, was perceived as being a moral man, and his presidency too was unmarked by personal scandal. However, it was not as much moral propriety as it was loyalty that was the dominant value that guided Bush's actions.

Loyalty was the operative word: loyalty to family and to friends, loyalty to his Vice President Dan Quayle who he kept on the ticket in 1992 in spite of advice not to do so, loyalty to Nixon, loyalty to Reagan, loyalty to the Republican Party, and loyalty to the Central Intelligence Agency. "I make friends," Bush stated, "I believe in staying in touch with people. And I learn from them. Loyalty goes two ways, to them and from them. I pride myself on that."[45]

The loyalty was usually returned. Glad tells how Richard Nixon ordered his assistant John Erlichman to purge the politicians from his cabinet and then added "except George Bush. He'd do anything for the cause."[46] Bush did stand by him. He was one of the few individuals who accepted Nixon's proclamations of innocence right up to the last few hours before Nixon resigned from office.

Character. By temperament George Bush was congenial, optimistic, energetic, enthusiastic, and, as most presidents are prone to be, ambitious. He was also, although he disliked the characterization, a "patrician," a man of "breeding and cultivation" who was reared from birth to be self-reliant, self-disciplined, and self-contained. These admiral qualities were countered by others that were far less positive. Bush was perceived by many to be a "preppie" and a "wimp." This

perception was rooted partly in his proclivity to avoid conflicts within the organizations in which he worked and partly in his patterns of speech. When he talked of getting into "deep

President Bush meets with the Emir of Kuwait, Jabir Al-Ahmad Al Jabir Al-Sabah in the Office of the White House to discuss the situation in the Gulf. September 28, 1990. Photo credit: George Bush Presidential Library

doo doo," Bush sounded like a New England prep school boy. Aggressive language was a way of countering that image. His remark after his debate with Geraldine Ferraro [the democratic vice presidential candidate] in 1984—that "we kicked ass" last night—was one such episode . . . . The wimp charge was put to rest at this time by these devices.[47]

His wealthy upbringing also led to the charge, which was never really put to rest, that Bush was out of touch with the concerns and the problems of average Americans. His complacency about the faltering economy and his behavior during the 1992 election campaign did not do much to counter the charges of his indifference and his inability to empathize. On a stop at Orlando, Florida he was, for example, damaged by his expressions of astonishment over the electronic price scanners that are used at supermarket checkouts.[48] After all, not too many average citizens could identify with the president's surprise over technology that has been used in supermarkets and department stores for approximately two decades. The president, some thought, didn't seem to have a clue about how average citizens lived their daily lives.

There were other more serious criticisms of the president. Of these Bush was probably most severely reproached for not keeping his 1988 "read my lips—no new taxes" campaign pledge, and for not attempting to deal more definitively with the potential threat of further military incursions by Saddam Hussein, the Iraqi leader who invaded Kuwait at the end of the Gulf War. However, he might have withstood the heavy criticism he received about those decisions and been re-elected. Bush, just as Carter, was done in not so much by what he did as by what he didn't do.

What George Bush didn't do was to provide leadership. He asked Americans to "stay the course" and re-elect him for another four years, but he never told them exactly what the course was or would be. He never fully explained where it was that he wanted to take the country and how he planned to get there. Nor did he appear to think it was necessary to do so. In his autobiography, Bush wrote that the essence of presidential leadership was to have "faith in the system . . . confidence in the people . . . [and] optimis[m] about the future of the country . . . ."[49] He seems to have been unaware that voters, like tourists thinking about taking an ocean voyage, are not very likely to book passage on ship where the captain is known to navigate solely on the basis of his faith, confidence, and optimism rather than on a course that has been carefully chartered. So George Bush lost his bid for re-election in 1992.

Presidential Types

George Bush is a Republican, and Jimmy Carter is a Democrat. Although their party affiliations differ, as presidents, they nevertheless had something in common. Both of them had reputations as being moral men and both were unable to provide the direction and guidance that their constituents wanted. These personal qualities, in addition to others that they shared, enable scholars to speak of them, and any other presidents who have the corresponding attributes, as being the same "type."

It is as convenient to lump presidents together according to types as it is to categorize anyone else. It is much simpler to describe a friend as being the "intellectual" type than to provide a long list of "intellectual" behaviors (spends hours and hours doing homework, doing research at the library, writing poetry, reading *The Decline and Fall of the Roman Empire*, watching public television, etc.).

In addition to convenience, typing individuals (be they presidents or friends) also facilitates the making of accurate predictions about them. For example, one can reasonably predict that intellectual types will get good grades in school and that presidents who are typed as being ineffective leaders will—all things being equal—be less likely to get re-elected than those who do provide direction. There is nothing mystical about making these predications—the forecasts are simply based on what experience and observation have taught.

Barber's Presidential Typology

One of the best known presidential "**typologies**" in the discipline of political science is one that was developed by political psychologist James David Barber and published in his extraordinary book (Carter called it the best book on the presidency that he ever read.) entitled *The Presidential Character: Predicting Performance in the White House*.[50] This work, as its title implies, uses "character" or "the way [a] president orients himself toward life" as the basis for determining whether he will successfully perform or fulfill his leadership role. It is, as Barber says, a book that is "meant to help citizens and those who advise them cut through the confusion and get at some clear criteria for choosing Presidents."[51]

There are two criteria or "baselines" used to classify presidents. They are "activity" and "affect."

1. Activity: A president is typed by his level of activity, his energy, or how much time he spends on the job. Those who devote a lot of time are typed as "active," and those who do not are typed as "passive." Activity levels vary from president to president. "Lyndon Johnson," Barber reports, "went at his day like a human cyclone, coming to rest long after the sun went down. Calvin Coolidge often slept eleven hours a night and still needed a nap in the middle of the day. In between, the Presidents array themselves on the high or low side of the activity line."[52]

2. Affect: This baseline differentiates presidents according to how they (not the press or the voters) feel about what they do, that is whether they seem to enjoy doing the job. Those who seem to be having fun are typed as "positive" while those who are not are classified as "negative." Franklin Roosevelt, Barber says, was happy in the job—Richard Nixon was not.

These two criteria when mixed and matched in every conceivable combination, as the matrix below shows, produce an array of four different types. In other words, when there are two baselines each having two options (activity: active/passive and affect: positive/negative) the result is a 2 X 2 matrix that yields the following four presidential types.

AFFECT

	Positive	Negative
Active	Active Positive	Active Negative
Passive	Passive Positive	Passive Negative

(ACTIVITY)

Every president beginning with George Washington can be classified as one of these four types; however, the last edition of Barber's work, the fourth edition, concentrates on the character of the fifteen presidents from Taft through Bush (#41). They are typed as follows:

AFFECT

		Positive	Negative
Active		Active Positive	Active Negative
		FDR	Wilson
		Truman	Hoover
		Kennedy	LBJ
		Ford	Nixon
		Carter	
		Bush (George H. W.)	
Passive		Passive Positive	Passive Negative
		Taft	Coolidge
		Harding	Eisenhower
		Reagan	

(Left margin vertical label: A C T I V I T Y)

It is interesting that Barber's research revealed that each of our first four presidents fit into a different category: Washington was a passive-negative type; Adams was an active-negative; Jefferson was an active-positive; Madison was a passive-positive.[53] These men, as well as the fifteen presidents in the matrix above, were typed according to their levels of energy and enjoyment, but they also had, Barber found, other characteristics in common.

Active Positive: The Presidents Who Want to Achieve Results

There is a congruence, a consistency, between being very active and the enjoyment of it, indicating relatively high self-esteem and relative success in relating to the environment. The man shows an orientation toward productiveness as a value, and an ability to use his styles flexibly, adaptively, suiting the dance to the music. He sees himself as developing over time toward relatively well defined personal goals—growing toward his image of himself as he might yet be. There is an emphasis on rational mastery, and on using the brain to move the feet. This may get him into trouble; he may fail to take account of the irrational in politics. Not everyone he deals with sees things his way, and he may find it hard to understand why.

Active-Negative: The Presidents Who Want Power

The contradiction here is between relatively intense effort and relatively low emotional reward for that effort. The activity has a compulsive quality, as if the man were trying to make up for something or to escape from anxiety into hard work. He seems ambitious, striving upward and seeking power. His stance toward the environment is aggressive and he has a persistent problem in managing his aggressive feelings. His self-image is vague and discontinuous. Life is a hard struggle to achieve and hold power, hampered by the condemnations of a perfectionistic conscience. Active-negative types pour energy into the political system, but it is an energy distorted from within.

Passive-Positive: The Presidents Who Want Love

This is the receptive, compliant other-directed character whose life is a search for affection as a reward for being agreeable and cooperative rather than personally assertive. The contradiction is between low self-esteem (on grounds of being unlovable, unattractive) and a superficial optimism. A hopeful attitude helps dispel doubt and elicits encouragement from others. Passive-positive types help soften the harsh edges of politics. Their dependence and the fragility of their hopes and enjoyments make disappointment in politics likely.

Passive-Negative: The Presidents Who Emphasize their Civic Virtue

The factors [passive and negative] are consistent—but how are we to account for the man's **political** role-taking? Why is someone who does little in politics and enjoys it less there at all? The answer lies in the passive-negative's character-rooted orientation toward doing **dutiful** service; this compensates for low self-esteem based on a sense of uselessness. Passive-negative types are in politics because they think they ought to be. They may be well adapted to certain nonpolitical roles, but they lack the experience and flexibility to perform effectively as political leaders. Their tendency is to withdraw, to escape from the conflict and uncertainty of politics by emphasizing vague principles (especially prohibitions) and procedural arrangements. They become guardians of the right and proper way, above the sordid politicking of lesser men.[54]

Clinton Typed

Barber never typed the forty-second president, Bill Clinton. However others have used his typology to categorize the president and one of them, political psychologist Fred Greenstein, expressed the widely held view that Clinton's "outward characteristics seem almost to have been custom-made to illustrate . . . the active-positive character type."[55]

Activity: Energy Expended Doing the Job

Virtually anyone who followed the 1992 election campaign would have found it easy to classify Clinton—who spent up to eighteen hours a day shaking hands, kissing babies, and talking, talking, talking—as an active rather than a passive politician. Had there been any lingering doubts, his first year in the White House would have certainly laid them to rest.

Just a week and a half after his inauguration on January 20, 1993, it was observed that "Clinton is rattling the country," "activist government is here again," and Americans were warned to fasten

Prime Minister of Israel, Yitzhak Rabin, President Clinton, and Yasser Arafat, chairman of the Palestine Liberation Organization, shaking hands in an electrifying ceremony. September 1993. Photo credits: Clinton Presidential Materials Project

their seat belts.[56] Those seat belts remained fastened through the middle of his first year in office when his pace at the time was described by a columnist as being "frenetic":

> after a whirlwind first stretch that has lasted seven long months, President Clinton has finally gone on vacation today. He has left Washington weary; even worse, much of his support is exhausted. Not for two generations has a new President sought to do so much, so fast and so directly.[57]

A four-day vacation, termed an exercise in "exhaustive relaxation," which Clinton took at the end of his first year, led another reporter to remark that Bush (#41) was simply "frenetic" while Clinton is a "whirlwind."[58] On his second day of so-called rest and relaxation, for example, Clinton went horseback riding, jogged on the beach, played volleyball, posed for photographs, signed autographs, flew to Pasadena to attend a black-tie birthday celebration, partied until the early hours (It was said that he was the last to leave.) and ordered pizza from room service at 3:00 A.M.[59] The long days and the high levels of energy expended at work and at play never stopped. In President Clinton's penultimate year in office, 1999, he held a news conference in which he responded to the media's observation that because he was a lame duck president he was probably winding down.

Clinton stated that he still didn't mind hard work and long hours and, he observed,

> I don't feel myself winding down. I feel myself keying up. I want to do more. I want to try to make sure that I give the American people as much as I can every day. So I've got plenty of energy and I'll do whatever I'm asked to do.[60]

Clinton kept his word. On January 20, 2001, the morning of his last day in office, Clinton was busy at his desk in the Oval Office working on presidential pardons.

Affect: Enjoyment of the Job

It is reasonable to wonder how much fun the president was having during his long, hard work days. It seems that he was enjoying himself immensely. At least those that observed him on a daily basis, the press, thought so.

One of the classic stories from the early days of the Clinton administration, so illustrative of his enthusiasm for the job that it has been repeated more than once, centers on the president's appearance on a network television "town hall" hosted by Ted Koppel. A newspaper reporter who was there to witness the episode explains it this way. After receiving instructions from Koppel to "zip" right along in answering questions put to him by the audience

> Mr. Clinton nodded sympathetically, as he is wont to do, and then unleashed two and a half hours worth of highly detailed "first, secondly" and "let me just add this" and "I want to make this very clear" and "Can I say one thing real quick?" and "I would like to amend that answer" answers about his health care plan.

> The president was willing, actually "eager," to talk about any health matter—lumbago, massage therapy, chiropractors, malpractice suits, or bulimia.

> The president had promised to stay as long as anyone had a question—a promise that alarmed his staff, who envisioned the policy equivalent of the dance-marathon movie, "They Shoot Horses, Don't They?" "Do you want a Xanax?" said Robert Boorstin, a White House health policy aide, jokingly offering a tablet of the anti-anxiety medication to a reporter who planned to stay up as long as the President.

> Although his advisor on health care was in the audience to take on any technical questions that the president might have needed assistance with, Clinton never called on him. Long into the night he carried on solo.

> As Mr. Koppel looked on bemusedly, the increasingly hoarse President continued to take questions from people in the front rows during commercial breaks, even though his microphone was turned off . . . . Long after Mr. Koppel, who had a bad cold and kept checking his watch, looked like he was ready to be on his way, Mr. Clinton was still eagerly scanning

the crowd for questioners and jumping up from his black leather swivel chair to get a little roving room while he talked.

The television station finally cut the show at 12:15 A.M. but

the President continued to take questions from people who crowded around the stage for another 20 minutes . . . . He ignored his advisers . . . and his personal aides . . . who surrounded him like sheepdogs and, nipping, tugging and nudging, tried to herd him off the stage . . . . The President paid no attention to Mr. Koppel and Roone Arledge, the president of ABC News, who were waiting on stage to have their pictures taken with Mr. Clinton and to escort him to a private reception. He paid no attention to the ABC technician who reached under his jacket and took off his microphone. He was busy with a question from a woman . . . .

By 12:30 the president had been coaxed

over to the edge of the stage, close enough where they could actually pull him backstage without too much effort. But the President was still looking longingly at the crowd, hoping to make a few more points, to win a few more converts. His hoarse voice could be heard fading in and out on dozens of different aspects of the plan . . . .

Finally,

with one last tug from his advisers, the President was . . . backstage. But it did not stop there. He went up to his health care advisers . . . wanting to go over various points he had made . . . . The President, who did not get back to his hotel until the wee hours, seemed happy with his all-talk special. "He was having fun," explained [a media adviser]. [61]

Clinton is a "positive" president. The enjoyment of being president did not diminish even after his impeachment in December 1998. In a press conference held seven months, almost to the day, after that event, Clinton told the media "I love this job. I love it. Even on the bad days, all of a sudden you can do something good for the country, you can do something good for the future. I have loved doing this."[62] Enthusiasm, such as that demonstrated at the televised town hall meeting and at the news conference, cannot be easily faked. This kind of fervor is an integral part of his being, a part that has its roots deep in his distant past.

The Socialization of an Active-Positive President: William Jefferson Clinton

Hugh Sidey, a writer who observed and wrote about the presidents and the presidency for over fifty years, once explained that his subjects are analogous to "complex geologic formations." By that he meant that "they are created over the years as the various strata are deposited by heritage, by experience. They do not appear overnight at center stage, nudging nations this way and that. They are gentled by mothers, challenged by fathers, inspired by teachers, humbled by failure and assembled finally in the forge of continuous exposure to the world's realities."[63] This is just another way of saying that presidents, just as the rest of the population, are the products of their socialization. (See Chapter 4). Barber put it more succinctly. "The personal past," he said, "foreshadows the Presidential future."[64] That is very obvious in the case of Bill Clinton.

Origins. The baby born in Hope, Arkansas, on August 19, 1946, and named William Jefferson Blythe III was the son of a woman who had been widowed three months earlier. So Bill Clinton never knew his father. He lived with his mother in the home of his maternal grandparents. After his mother remarried in 1950, they set up a new household with Bill's stepdad, Roger Clinton, the name Bill later legally took as his own. Roger Clinton was a sometimes abusive alcoholic. As Bill grew older, he began to take on the role of family protector.

David Maraniss, the author of the Pulitzer Prize winning biography on the president entitled *First In His Class*, explains that it is not unusual for the eldest child of an alcoholic parent to take on the role of protector or "family hero."[65] In this capacity the child may either take charge and assume adult responsibilities or may, instead, serve as the family's "redeemer," bringing to it praise and rewards from the outside world.[66] Bill Clinton did both.

The Redeemer. Clinton was known as a "superachiever" in high school because of the numerous activities he participated in and honors he earned during those years. Among his many accomplishments, Bill played tenor saxophone in the school band and other performance bands, helped organize musical festivals all over Arkansas, was a devoted and active Boy Scout, served as president of his junior class and president of the Key Club and the Beta Club, was a member of the Student Council, the National Honor Society, and a leadership training organization called DeMolay, was accepted into the American Legion's Boys State, became a delegate to Boys Nation, was a semifinalist in the National Merit Scholarship competition, did volunteer work at a nonprofit treatment and research center in the hospital in which his mother was a nurse, and graduated fourth in a class of 363.[67]

Georgetown University, a Rhodes Scholarship at Oxford, Yale Law School, twelve years as Governor of Arkansas, and two terms as the President of the United States of America were to follow. Bill Clinton, the redeemer, did his family proud.

Predicting Presidential Performance. As the biographical sketch above indicates, Clinton has been a high-energy, enthusiastic person with a penchant for hard work ever since childhood. Knowing this, it would have been possible to predict that he would demonstrate these same attributes as president. As Barber explained,

The best way to predict a President's character, world view, and style is to see how he constructed them in the first place. Especially in the early stages, life is experimental; consciously or not, a person tries out various ways of defining and maintaining and raising self-esteem. He looks to his environment for clues as to who he is and how well he is doing. These lessons of life slowly sink in: certain self-images and evaluations, certain ways of looking at the world, certain styles of action get confirmed by his experience and he gradually adopts them as his own. If we can see that process of development, we can understand the product.[68]

Clinton acknowledged the importance of his early life in shaping his adult behavior in an interview. "The violence and dysfunction in our home made me a loner, which is contrary to the way people view me, because I'm gregarious, happy, all of that" the president said. "But I had to construct a whole life inside my mind, my own space . . . . I don't believe in psychobabble. You can overdo all that, but I think I have to be acutely aware that I grew up as a peacemaker, always trying to minimize the disruption."[69]

At times, Clinton learned, the best way to achieve harmony and end discord is to compromise, to listen, to accept, and even to borrow the ideas of others. As president, therefore, he has had no problem identifying himself as a "new kind of Democrat," one who could co-opt Republican ideas (the theme of family values and the crime issue) and incorporate liberal and conservative ideas into his policies. As a compromiser, it was also relatively easy for Clinton to back away from some of his policies. For example, in 1994 he backed off from his attempt to overhaul the entire health-care system by providing universal health care because he knew he wouldn't get his proposal through Congress; in its place he substituted smaller initiatives such as the transportability of health insurance from one job to the next and the continuance of health insurance for the newly unemployed, which did pass. Similarly, he signed a welfare reform bill into law in August 1996 even though he recognized that parts of the bill were "deeply flawed" because he believed it was the best he could get at the time and because he concluded that some change was better than no change at all.

These types of compromises could have been a surprise only to people who were unfamiliar with Clinton's early socialization. His presidential actions, including those that resulted in scandal, were entirely in keeping with the personality or character that was first shaped back in Hope, Arkansas.

George W. Bush Typed

At the time this is being written George W. Bush is in the middle of his second term of office as president. His presidential behavior to date and his past political style place him squarely into the passive-positive category of Barber's framework.

Activity: Energy Expended Doing the Job

George W. Bush is no Bill Clinton. He does not work into the wee hours of the morning. In fact, while Governor of Texas, he admitted that "my wife and I like to go to bed at nine P. M., earlier than our daughters, where we read and watch the news for awhile. But sometimes," he added, "I stay up late and type the girls' theme papers for them if they need help."[70] Nor does George W. Bush have the campaign stamina of his predecessor. When, for example, he was informed that his aides had scheduled two fundraisers and appearances at both a reading center and a baseball game for the same day (not an unusual agenda during a presidential campaign), he, according to one biographer, "went ballistic."

> What you're telling me is that because you guys [messed] up, I got to break my ass all day and won't get home until midnight?" Bush said. "We're going back to Plan A." The reading center and baseball game appearances were canceled, but the governor still didn't return to Austin until 11 P. M., resulting in a tired candidate departing the next day for Iowa.[71]

And so it was that on his very first campaign trip, before he had even officially declared that he was seeking the Republican nomination, Bush felt the need to account for his rather apparent fatigue by explaining to reporters that he

only got six hours sleep last night . . . . I need more than that."[72]

More often than not, he got it. And he got it in part by keeping his working day short. As reporter John Leland observed in an article comparing Bush's coasting manner ("he raised coasting to a form of personal expression") with Clinton's workaholic frenzied style ("leading the country as if it were the world's biggest aerobics class"), "as governor of Texas, he typically knocked off at 5 p.m. and still managed to schedule a couple hours during the day to exercise, play video games, get a massage or nap. He clipped the time he spent reviewing each scheduled execution from half an hour to 15 minutes. If briefings droned too long . . . Bush would point to his computer's solitaire program . . . . If this man stands for anything," Leland concludes, "it is for working only as hard as he has to."[73]

The schedule did not change radically when Bush became the chief executive. Frank Bruni, who has described the Bush presidency as "no-fuss, no-sweat, look-Ma-no-hands," makes note of the president's need for "restorative breaks" during the work day.[74] Bush acknowledged as much when he told a group of Democrats that he would answer some of their questions "and then I'm going to head home and take a nap."[75]

Affect: Enjoyment of the Job

If the biography of the president entitled *Shrub: The Short But Happy Political Life of George W. Bush* is at all accurate, Bush is enjoying his job.[76] According to his autobiography he certainly enjoyed being a student (Phillips Academy, Andover, Yale, Harvard—Yale fraternity brothers have likened him to the John Belushi character Bluto in the movie *Animal House*); forming his own oil company (Arbusto later renamed Bush Exploration Company); being a manager and general partner of the baseball team, the Texas Rangers; and holding the only other political position to which he was elected, the governorship of Texas.[77]

His memoir includes recollections about some of these pursuits. Bush recalls that "my friends and I found ways to have fun. I have always looked for the lighter side of life, and I did so at Andover."[78] And of the other "major endeavors" of his life Bush philosophizes, "baseball is a pursuit for optimists, just like drilling for oil or running for office. To come to the ballpark every day, you have to believe you can win. To drill another well after a dry hole, you have to believe this one will be successful. To run for office, especially after losing [a congressional race in 1978], you have to believe you can win."[79] Such optimism and sense of fun are trademarks of the "positive" character.

The enjoyment that Bush derives from the job comes from the "people" rather than the "policy-making" side of politics. In other words, he enjoys working a room, shaking hands, kissing babies, and slapping backs but does not enjoy long hours sitting behind a desk immersed in papers and in reading documents. These tasks, as the president explains, are delegated. "I put a lot of faith and trust in my staff. I look for people who are smart and loyal and who share my conservative philosophy. My job is to set the agenda and tone and framework, to lay out the principles by which we operate and make decisions, and then delegate much of the process to them. The final decision **often** [emphasis added] rests with me, but their judgment has a big influence."[80]

Even after the turbulent events that followed the September 11 attacks in the United States, the president maintained his "management" or "C.E.O." style of governing. (George W. Bush is the first U. S. president to hold an M.B.A. degree.) In a televised interview that aired in January 2002, when American troops were fighting in Afghanistan, the president was questioned about his "ease of mind" as compared with Presidents Johnson and Nixon who were "consumed" by Vietnam.[81] Bush explained it this way:

> It goes to show that the war [Vietnam] was not **managed** [emphasis added] properly. The president shouldn't be running the war. The generals run the war. The president sets the strategy. That's the lesson of Vietnam that I brought to this office.[82]

But was he having any fun during this demanding time? Bush said that he was enjoying himself and, true to his type, enthusiastically added that "I really, really like being the president."[83]

The Socialization of a Passive-Positive President: George W. Bush

George W. Bush, 53 years old when he took the oath of office for the presidency, was born on July 6, 1946 in New Haven, Connecticut. Two years after his birth his father, "poppy," graduated from Yale University and took a job that moved the family first to Odessa, Texas and eventually, after the birth of a second child, Pauline Robinson (nicknamed Robin), twenty miles northwest of Odessa to Midland. It was, George W. Bush's parents believe, Robin's death from leukemia in the spring of 1953 that played a large role in shaping their son's personality and, later in life, his political style. As biographer J. H. Hatfield tells it,

> when he was running for reelection as governor of Texas, George W.'s parents acknowledged that their eldest son's "back-slapping, wisecracking, occasionally teasing style" was developed as a child of seven, when his sister died, and he felt it was his responsibility to try and lift his parents out of their grief.[84]

George W. Bush had to deal with more than the death of his sister. He had to deal with growing up in a household headed by a powerful and politically prominent father. In tracing the Bush legacy one reporter noted that a young adult growing up in such a household tends to either flee or embrace the shadow of the powerful parent.[85] George W. Bush, who doesn't believe in psychoanalyzing himself, is somewhat uncomfortable with the notion that he has embraced and is following in his father's footsteps. As the following comments indicate many Bush observers disagree.

> When one steps back from any stage of Mr. Bush's life and examines his biography as a whole, one theme runs through each stage of his life: hero worship of his father, leading to

George H. W. Bush
with his four sons,
left to right: Neil,
George H.,
Jeb, George W.,
and Marvin. 1970.

an instinct to follow his father's trail. Many friends think that at some level, a driving force of George W.'s career has been an effort to honor his legacy and please his father, or at least to emulate him. Some acquaintances, though not all, even believe that this year's presidential bid is a culmination of that quest . . . . Some acquaintances believe that Mr. Bush's political career arose from a desire to avenge his father's defeat, although Mr. Bush dismisses the idea . . . "What makes him tick?" asked an old friend of both Bushes. "It's Daddy . . . . Daddy is the motivation—to please his dad."[86]

It is, in part, the "daddy" factor that may explain what has been called (depending on one's point of view) George W.'s "discipline" and "constancy" or his "stubbornness" and "inability to reverse course." For example,

the economic landscape changed, but Bush's faith in tax cuts has not. When he did reverse course, on campaign-finance reform or creating the Department of Homeland Security, he did so brazenly, without explanation or apology, that even caving was portrayed as an act of bold leadership. Above all, he has defended his decision to target Saddam Hussein even when some of the basic premises [weapons of mass destruction] of the war turned out to be wrong. He has continued to argue that he has set Iraq on the path to democracy even when others say its future is so much in doubt.[87]

As two journalists who sought to discover "why Bush doesn't budge" suggested, perhaps it was "the searing lesson of watching his father break a promise not to raise taxes and be fired for it."[88]

Presidential Types and Leadership

The potential that a candidate has to succeed in providing the direction and guidance that voters want varies according to which of the four categories or types of presidential character, identified by Barber, that he fits into.

Active-Negatives

Barber says: "the best prediction . . . is that the relatively grim, intensely striving, onward-and-upward-through-thick-or-thin type is particularly liable—given ultimate political power—to play out the drama to its psychological conclusion."[89] This character type, which is prone to adhere rigidly to a losing policy, is the most likely to bring himself down in defeat. (Richard Nixon and Lyndon Johnson are good examples of this.)

Passive-Negatives

Barber says: "The trouble with the passive-negative type in the Presidency is that he leaves untapped the energizing, initiating, stimulating possibilities of the role. He is a responder; issues are 'brought to his attention'—and there are too damned many of them. Under the flag of legitimacy, the nation unites—and drifts. Presidential dignity is restored at the cost of Presidential leadership."[90]

Passive-Positives

Barber says: "The passive-positive types are political lovers. Considering what politics does to some of them, they do not often wind up as lovers of politics, at least in its rougher aspects. Like the reluctant passive-negatives, they are responders, not initiators or pushers, but they go about their work with a different demeanor, an appearance of affectionate hopefulness . . . . The passive-positive type lives in a marketplace of affection, trading bright hellos for smiles in return. What threatens the fragile structure of that adaptation is conflict and particularly conflict at close quarters . . . . The passive-positive character is built around surfaces: when the surface begins to crack, collapse is imminent."[91]

Active-Positives

Barber says: "Their apparent happiness in what they do—as Presidents—stands out in contrast to the defenses other Presidents cling to. Each has shown in his own way these qualities: . . . . he is fully able to meet the challenges of the job . . . he learns quickly . . . . [he has] a sense of the future as possible . . . [and] a repertoire of habits. The active-positive President uses a variety of styles, moving flexibly among a number of modes of political action. Such a President seems to base his self-definition on ground deeper than the collection of stylistic approaches he has put together over the years. His style is a bag of tools, not a way of life."[92]

Although there are no guarantees, and there have been notable exceptions, such as Carter and Bush senior, of the four types of presidential character identified by Barber, active-positives are likely to provide the most effective political leadership.

CONCLUSION

Two major perspectives or ways of examining the presidency were discussed in this chapter. The presidency was first looked at as a job that is described, somewhat ambiguously, in Article II of the Constitution. That Article sets down the necessary qualifications for aspirants to the office, and it describes the process by which presidential elections are to be conducted. It also specifies the major presidential powers and duties. Presidential responsibilities are more commonly referred to simply as "roles." These roles, some aspects of which have only been implied in the words "he shall take Care that the Laws be faithfully executed" (Article II, Section 3), include: Chief of State, Chief Executive, Commander in Chief, Chief Diplomat, and Chief Legislator.

A second perspective taken by experts on the subject of the presidency is one that focuses on the person or the personality/character of the individual who does the job rather than on the job itself. From this point of view there is a clear distinction that can be made between leaders (men that have been elected to occupy the oval office and are leaders in name only) and leadership (the personal quality or ability of some of those men to provide direction and guidance). This distinction is sometimes expressed in terms of "headship" v. "leadership."

Leadership, according to Robert Shogan, consists of three interacting qualities: ideology, values, and character. All three, as was shown in the cases of Presidents Carter and George H. W. Bush, are necessary for success. James David Barber places his emphasis primarily on only one of these qualities—character. His contention is that the "active-positive" character type has the best potential as president to provide successful leadership.

It is useful for anyone who reads about and studies the presidency to try to keep in mind that the two perspectives are like the two sides of a coin: virtually impossible to divide and, if separated, without much practical value.

CHAPTER NOTES

[1]Lloyd Robinson, *The Stolen Election: Hayes versus Tilden—1876* (New York: Doubleday & Company, Inc., 1968), 118.

[2]Roosevelt to George Otto Trevelyan, June 19, 1908, *The Letters of Theodore Roosevelt*, ed. Elting E. Morison (Cambridge: Harvard University Press, 1952), vol. 6, 1087; quoted in James MacGregor Burns, *Presidential Government: The Crucible of Leadership* (New York: Avon Books, 1965), 73, n. 29.

[3]Woodrow Wilson, *Congressional Government* (New York: Houghton, Mifflin and Co., 1885.)

[4]Clinton Rossiter, *The American Presidency* (New York: New American Library, 1956), 10.

[5]Ibid., 11.

[6]*The New York Times*, 13 September 2001, 16(A).

[7]Quoted in Arthur Bernon Tourtellot, *The Presidents on the Presidency* (Garden City, N.Y.: Doubleday & Company, Inc., 1964), 137.

[8]President's Committee on Administrative Management, *Administrative Management in the Government of the United States* (Government Printing Office, 1937), 5.

[9]Stephen Hess, *Organizing the Presidency* (Washington, D.C.: The Brookings Institution, 1976), 1-2.

[10]Franklin Delano Roosevelt, "Message on Reorganizing the Executive Branch, January 12, 1937," in Tourtellot, 124.

[11]Fred I. Greenstein, "The Need for an Early Appraisal of the Reagan Presidency, in *The Reagan Presidency: An Early Assessment*, ed. Fred I. Greenstein (Baltimore, Maryland: The Johns Hopkins University Press, 1983), 12.

[12]Arthur M. Schlesinger, Jr., *The Imperial Presidency* (Boston, Massachusetts: Houghton Mifflin Company, 1973), 222-223.

[13]Richard M. Pious, *The Presidency* (Boston, Massachusetts: Allyn and Bacon, 1996), 277.

[14]Schlesinger, 5.

[15]Tourtellot, 328.

[16]Edward S. Corwin, *Presidential Power and the Constitution: Essays*, ed. Richard Loss (Ithaca, New York: Cornell University Press, 1976), 113.

[17]The "National Security Strategy of the United States," October 2002.

[18]Robert E. DiClerico, *The American President*, (Englewood Cliffs, New Jersey: Prentice-Hall, 1995), 38-45.

[19]Schlesinger, 7.

[20]Michael Nelson, ed., *Congressional Quarterly's Guide to the Presidency* (Washington, D.C.: CQ, 1989), 510.

[21]Tourtellot, 185-187.

[22]Ibid., 245.

[23]October 2003.

[24]*The New York Times*, 1 August 1996, 22 (A).

[25]DiClerico, 87-92.

[26]Harold M. Barger, *The Impossible Presidency: Illusions and Realities of Executive Power* (Glenview, Illinois: Scott, Foresman and Company, 1984), 100.

[27]Clinton Rossiter, *The American Presidency*, revised ed. (New York: Harcourt, Brace & World, Inc., 1960), 41.

[28]James MacGregor Burns, *Leadership* (New York: Harper & Row, Publishers, 1978), 2.

[29]See Michael B. Binford, "Decision Making and Participation: An Exercise," *News: For Teachers of Political Science* 41 (Spring 1984): 26-27.

[30]Robert Michels, *Political Parties: A Sociological Study of the Oligarchical Tendencies of Modern Democracy* (New York: The Free Press, 1962), 364. Michels, a sociologist who studied the behavior of political elites, refers to this phenomenon of the need for leadership in all organizations, even the most democratic ones, as the "iron law of oligarchy."

[31]Barbara Kellerman, "Leadership as a Political Act," in *Leadership: Multidisciplinary Perspectives*, ed. Barbara Kellerman (Englewood Cliffs, New Jersey: Prentice-Hall, Inc., 1984), 70-71.

[32]Robert Shogan, *The Riddle of Power: Presidential Leadership from Truman to Bush* (New York: A Dutton Book, 1991).

[33]Ibid., 6-7.

[34]Ibid., 205.

[35]Betty Glad, *Jimmy Carter: In Search of the Great White House* (New York: W.W.Norton & Company, 1980), 312.

[36]Shogan, 198.

[37]Jimmy Carter, *Keeping Faith: Memoirs of a President* (Toronto, Canada: Bantam Books, 1982), 20.

[38]Glad, 488-493; Shogan, 207-211.

[39]James Fallows, quoted in James David Barber, *The Presidential Character: Predicting Performance in the White House* (Englewood Cliffs, New Jersey: Prentice Hall, 1992), 447.

[40]Ibid.

[41]Betty Glad, "How George Bush Lost the Presidential Election of 1992," in *The Clinton Presidency: Campaigning. Governing, & the Psychology of Leadership*, ed. Stanley A. Renshon (Boulder, Colorado: Westview Press, 1995), 33; Shogan, 264.

[42]Shogan, 265.

[43]Ibid., 259.

[44]R.W. Apple Jr., "In His Various Defining Moments, Has Bush Clearly Defined Himself?" *The New York Times*, 23 February 1992, Section 4, 1.

[45]Shogan, 269 and 272.

[46]Sidney Blumenthal, *Pledging Allegiance: The Last Campaign of the Cold War* (New York, HarperCollins, 1993), 62; quoted in Glad, "How George Bush Lost the Election," 31.

[47]Glad, "How George Bush Lost the Election," 25.

[48]Ibid., 22.

[49]George Bush, *Looking Forward: An Autobiography* (New York: Doubleday, 1987), 193.

[50]James David Barber, *The Presidential Character: Predicting Performance in the White House*, 4th ed. (Englewood Cliffs, New Jersey: Prentice Hall, 1992.)

[51]Ibid., 1.

[52]Ibid., 8.

[53]Ibid., 10.

[54]Ibid., 9-10.

[55]Fred I. Greenstein, "Political Style and Political Leadership: The Case of Bill Clinton," 144.

[56]Thomas L. Friedman, "Ready or Not, Clinton Is Rattling the Country," *The New York Times*, 31 January 1993, Sec. 4 (1).

[57]Douglas Jehl, "Weary Clinton Takes Break From His Own Frenetic Style," *The New York Times*, 15 August 1993, 1 (A).

[58]Michael Kelly, "Clinton's 4-Day Holiday: Exhaustive Relaxation," *The New York Times*, 1December 92, 9 (B).

[59]Ibid.

[60]"Excerpts from President Clinton's Wide-Ranging News Conference." *The New York Times*. 22 July 1999, 17 (A).

[61]Maureen Dowd, "On Health, Clinton Finds Heaven Is in the Details," *The New York Times*, 25 September 1993, 1(A) and 8(A).

[62]Ibid.

[63]Hugh Sidey, preface to *George Bush: An Intimate Portrait*, by Fitzhugh Green (New York: Hippocrene Books, 1989), xii.

[64]Barber, 11.

[65]David Maraniss, *First in His Class: A Biography of Bill Clinton* (New York: Simon & Schuster, 1995), 38.

[66]Ibid.

[67]Charles F. Allen and Jonathan Portis, *The Life and Career of Bill Clinton: The Comeback Kid* (New York: Carol Publishing Group, 1992), 11-12; George Carpozi, Jr., *Clinton Confidential: The Climb to Power* (Del Mar, California, Emery Dalton Books; 1995), 21-22; Meredith L. Oakley, *On the Make: The Rise of Bill Clinton* (Washington, D.C.: Regnery Publishing, Inc., 1994), 32-33.

[68]Barber, 7.

[69]Todd S. Purdum, "The Incumbent as a Riddle: William Jefferson Clinton," *The New York Times*, 29 August 1996, 13 (B).

[70]J. H. Hatfield, *Fortunate Son: George W. Bush and the Making of an American President* (New York: Soft Skull Press, 2000), 167.

[71]Ibid., 276.

[72]Ibid., 275.

[73]John Leland, "To Loaf or Not to Loaf," *The New York Times Magazine*, 17 December 2000, 26.

[74]Frank Bruni, "Presidency Takes Shape With No Fuss, No Sweat," *The New York Times*, 10 February 2001, 1(A).

[75]Ibid.

[76]Molly Ivins and Lou Dubose, *Shrub: The Short But Happy Political Life of George W. Bush* (New York: Vintage Books, 2000).

[77]Bill Minutaglio, *First Son: George W. Bush and the Bush Family Dynasty* (New York: Times Books, 1999), 95.

[78]George W. Bush, *A Charge to Keep: My Journey to the White House* (New York: Perennial, 2001), 21.

[79]Ibid., 197.

[80]Ibid., 103-4.

[81]NBC. 23 January 2002. "The Bush White House: Inside the Real West Wing." Tom Brokaw.

[82]Ibid.

[83]Ibid.

[84]Hatfield, 22.

[85]Nicholas D. Kristof, "A Father's Footsteps Echo Throughout a Son's Career," *The New York Times*, 11 September 2000, 16 (A).

[86]Ibid., 16 (A).

[87]Nancy Gibbs and John F. Dickerson, "Inside the Mind of George W. Bush: For This President, The Essence of Wisdom Lies In Knowing When Not To Change," *Time*, September 6, 2004, p. 28.

[88]Ibid.

[89]Barber,122.

[90]Ibid., 193.

[91]Ibid., 195 and 223.

[92]Ibid., 267.

SUGGESTED READINGS

Barber, James David. *The Presidential Character: Predicting Performance in the White House*, 4th ed. Englewood Cliffs, N.J.: Prentice Hall, 1992.

Barger, Harold M. *The Impossible Presidency: Illusions and Realities of Executive Power.* Glenview, Ill.: Scott, Foresman and Company, 1984.

Burns, James MacGregor. *Leadership.* New York: Harper & Row, Publishers, 1978.

_____. *Presidential Government: The Crucible of Leadership.* New York: Avon Books, 1965.

George, Alexander L., and Juliette L. George. *Presidential Personality and Performance.* Boulder: Westview Press, 1998.

Hinckley, Barbara. *The Symbolic Presidency: How Presidents Portray Themselves.* New York: Rutledge, 1990.

Jacobson, Gary C. *A Divider, Not a Uniter: George W. Bush and the American People.* New York: Pearson Education, Inc., 2007.

Pious, Richard M. *The Presidency.* Boston, Mass.: Allyn and Bacon, 1996.

Renshon, Stanley A., ed. *The Clinton Presidency: Campaigning, Governing, & the Psychology of Leadership.* Boulder: Westview Press, 1995.

Rossiter, Clinton. *The American Presidency.* New York: Harcourt, Brace & World, Inc., 1956.

Schlesinger, Arthur M. Jr. *The Imperial Presidency.* Boston, Mass.: Houghton Mifflin Company, 1973.

Chapter Twelve

THE JUDICIARY

Our court system is vast and encompasses both the state and federal judiciaries. It is also part of a larger process, the law enforcement system. This chapter specifically focuses on the process and procedures of the federal court system. However, in this process, it is noteworthy to mention that Americans have become exposed to all elements of the law enforcement process through television.

Television has exposed Americans to a myriad of images related to their system of justice: drive-by shootings, overcrowded prisons, plea bargaining, legal technicalities, high profile court dramas, victim rights, civil rights, corporate fraud, and the war on drugs. The elements of the justice system are so interrelated that it is often difficult to determine who does what to whom. Implementing the process often requires action from such disparate participants that range in scope from lawmakers to law-enforcement officers to the justices who interpret the law. Although all are essential to the process, it will be our goal in this chapter to sort out what role the courts actually play in our system of justice.

The American public is both fascinated and frustrated with its judicial process. These two feelings are so interconnected that they have possibly established a cause and effect situation that has created a love/hate relationship with the court system. Fascination has, in fact, produced frustration.

Historically, the public has been fascinated with the judicial system. This has been true whether the dramas have been fiction or nonfiction. Many of the most popular drama series on television have produced fictional courtroom scenarios, for example, *Perry Mason, Law and Order* and its several spin-offs and more recently the trials of pop culture personalities such as Anna Nicole Smith. The American public has also eagerly followed sensational real life courtroom dramas such as the Scopes Monkey Trial, the Ethel and Julius Rosenberg's treason trial, and, more recently, the trial of the American Taliban, John Walker Lindh. The advent of television has made it easier for Americans to satisfy their fascination with the legal process by providing almost instant and total access to the elaborate procedures of the judicial system. Television cameras in the courtroom have become an everyday occurrence virtually bringing the judicial process into every American family's living room, which has fostered a feeling of knowledge and familiarity about it. High profile court proceedings, such as the O. J. Simpson and Scott Peterson murder trials, dominated the airwaves for months.

Easier access to the judicial process has heightened the public's fascination with it. However, ironically, this also has increased the public's frustration with the court system. A recent Gallop Poll survey indicated that only 6 percent of the population had total confidence in the criminal justice system, 38 percent responded they had some confidence in the criminal justice system, 38 percent had very little confidence, and 4 percent had no confidence at all in the system. Although the poll does not single out the courts, it reveals the population is dissatisfied with the entire process of justice. Frustration may stem from two sources: easy access to the system created by the visual media and the "mystification" of the judicial process by the legal system itself.

First, easy access to the judicial process initially was meant to provide the public with more information about it. Knowledge about the process would, in turn, produce a feeling of familiarity; however, it often had the opposite effect. Although television provided more opportunities to view the judicial system in action, the information provided has not always been accurate. Instead of providing strictly factual information, the media often placed its own "spin" on a trial, resulting in an oversimplified portrayal of a very complex system. Instead of providing substantive information, the visual media has for the sake of ratings presented a perception of the judicial process created in its own image. This perception has often left Americans with a sense of security that they possess complete and accurate information of the inner workings of the judicial system, when in actuality, they merely possess a media image of the judicial process. This perception can actually cause frustration and a sense of alienation. Instead of bringing the judicial system closer to the people, it is now farther away than ever.

Second, Americans' frustration with their courts can often be traced to their basic lack of understanding of the judicial process, often perpetuated by the judicial system itself. The court system is enshrouded in tradition. At first glance, the physical appearance of the courtroom and its officers denote pomp and circumstance that often is very threatening to the average citizen. For example, the judge, who still wears the traditional robe as a symbol of authority, requires the entire room to stand when he/she enters the room as a sign of respect. Instead of providing a user friendly atmosphere, the courtroom often produces one of intimidation.

The judicial process is so foreign to the average citizen that it is extremely difficult to navigate without the help of legal professionals. Many unsavory jokes are often made about lawyers. However, it is often impossible to resolve a legal issue without one simply because an attorney knows the rules of the system and the average citizen does not. The reason for this is complex but centers on the fact that the judicial system has integrated into its tradition a vast and often imposing set of regulations and procedures. The jargon used by the officers of the court is often court specific, its meaning often difficult to comprehend within an everyday context. Often faced with the consequence of losing life, liberty, or property, people are faced with a mysterious judicial maze that they cannot maneuver themselves. They are forced to rely on legal professionals to resolve legal problems whose consequences might have an affect on the rest of their lives.

The Scopes trial caught the attention of the entire world. John Thomas Scopes, a twenty-four-year-old high school teacher, was charged with being in violation of a Tennessee statute, which forbade the teaching of Charles Darwin's theory of evolution. Merchants were selling books outside the courtroom.

Americans rely on the court system to administer justice for crimes against society and its citizens fairly and without prejudice; however, exactly what is justice and how is it to be administered? Is justice what television has defined it to be in its many courtroom dramas both fictional and nonfictional? Is the American public presented with unrealistic presentations of how the judicial system is to work supported by unrealistic myths perpetuated by our political culture? How can the average citizen measure if the judicial system is in actuality an effective institution capable of supporting a democratic process in the twenty-first century?

Today there exists a discussion both within the legal community and the society at large about the possibility of reorganizing the existing judicial structure. To participate in such a discussion, it would be helpful to examine where we have been to see where we might be going. It will be our goal in this chapter to demystify the court system by examining the Constitution to determine what it originally intended the judicial system to accomplish. This process will involve looking at the intentions of the framers of the Constitution, examining the structure of the court system, and evaluating how the courts have developed over the past two hundred years. Were the courts designed to administer justice, and, if so, exactly what is justice within the context of the American political culture and judicial system?

Judicial Foundations

The United States is a common law country based on the common law system of Great Britain. This distinguishes it from most of the rest of Europe, which has accepted Roman law as the basis for their legal systems. The American jurisprudence system today is a fusion of British tradition and American resourcefulness and creativity. English law was an amalgam of different political cultures, transforming its jurisprudence system over hundreds of years. It is the traditional unwritten law of England, based on custom and usage, which began to develop over a thousand years before the founding of the United States. It is interesting to note that during the medieval period when women had little power, the best of the pre-Saxon compendiums of the common law was reportedly written by a woman, Queen Martia, wife of a king of a small English kingdom. Queen Martia's work was translated into the emerging English language by King Alfred (849-899 CE) considered by many historians to be the father of Great Britain.

For centuries England's legal system had been based on local authorities. One of the most significant events that transformed not only the British legal system but the entire culture occurred in 1066 when the Anglo-Saxon population was conquered by the Norman, William the Conqueror. Although the Normans integrated Anglo-Saxon tradition into its governmental structure, their introduction of feudalism, a social and political organization, into the British system forever altered the fabric of its governmental institutions.[1] The feudal system required more centralization than existed in England prior to William's conquest. Consequently, William and his successors found it necessary to implement unifying measures in a country that was more often than not governed by local authorities. One of the instruments the Norman rulers used to accomplish unification was the judicial system known as the King's Court or *Curia Regis*.[2]

Two fundamental concepts evolved from the King's Court: ***stare decisis*** and **common law**. Today, these concepts stand as the cornerstones of the English and American judicial system. ***Stare decisis***, to stand on decided cases, is based on the theory that the legal system is not a set of isolated judicial decisions but rather a series of judgments, each one serving as a building block for the next. The King's Court attempted to establish a uniform set of procedures based on a general philosophy that would apply to all citizens throughout the realm. As the court became more established, it required a more elaborate system of record keeping; consequently, the more important cases were gathered and recorded in yearbooks. These decisions were then used as precedents for future decisions, creating principles or a **common law** for all judges to follow.[3]

In effect, William the Conqueror combined the best of Anglo-Saxon law with Norman law, which ultimately resulted in what we know today as English common law and by the fourteenth century legal decisions and commentaries on common law began providing precedents for the courts and lawyers to follow. The common law became the basic law of most U.S. states and for the foundation of federal law in large part due to the *Commentaries on the Laws of England*, completed by Sir William Blackstone in 1769, which became every American lawyer's ultimate legal guide. Today almost all common law has been enacted into statutes with the exception of Louisiana, which is still influenced by the Napoleonic Code because of its historical connection to France.[3]

Constitutional Convention

The basic legal tenets inherited from the British system were practiced on a state by state basis under the Articles of Confederation; however, since the Articles of Confederation did not provide for a federal judiciary, these tenets were often applied inconsistently throughout the United States. The delegates at the constitutional convention realized that just as feudalism required a more centralized judicial system in England, the governmental structure they were constructing would also require a more unified judiciary capable of developing an effective system of **common law**.

The concept of a central judicial system generated spirited debate among the delegates. Two questions were involved in this debate: first, should a federal judiciary be included in the new governmental structure, and, second, if the answer to the first question was "yes," what form would it take? The first question produced very little debate, because a general consensus quickly developed among the delegates that a central judiciary was an essential element in a viable and stronger national government. It had become clear to them that the state courts were incapable of administering uniform judgments or common law specifically in those matters that dealt with national issues. On the basis of past experiences, the delegates were particularly concerned with the state court's ability to interpret the new constitution in a uniform fashion. Consequently, Article III of the new constitution established an independent federal judiciary whose power was vested in one Supreme Court.

After stipulating that the "judicial power shall be vested in one supreme Court," the convention turned its attention to the second question, the nature of the structure of the national judiciary. The question was simple; the answer was not. Central to the question was the subject of "inferior," or additional, federal courts. Inferior does not necessarily denote the status of the courts but rather their supplementary nature. Should inferior federal courts be constructed to augment the Supreme Court thereby creating not only a federal judiciary but also a federal judicial system? Expanding the federal judiciary could seriously alter the distribution of power between the legislative and executive branches of the federal government, as well as the relationship between the federal and state governments.

The delegates weighed how a federal judicial system would affect the separation of powers and checks and balances among the branches of the national government, as well as the relationship between the national and state governments. First, inferior courts would establish a "system" of federal courts that had the potential by its very size to exercise more extensive political power than would the "one" Supreme Court. This could go a long way in establishing the judicial branch as an equal governing power with the other two branches of the federal government. Second, extending federal judicial power by creating inferior courts would also solidify the strength of the federal government vìs a vìs the states. A national judicial system, coupled with Article VI of the Constitution stating that "This Constitution and the Laws of the United States . . . shall be the supreme Law of the Land; and the Judges in every State shall be bound thereby," creates the possibility that the states, as well as their courts, would at the very least in a more tenuous position if not relegated to a subordinate role in governing.

The debate among the delegates was fierce. The position against inferior courts was effectively argued by many delegates. Two champions of this position were Roger Sherman from Connecticut and John Rutledge of South Carolina. Roger Sherman used a fiscal argument in pleading his case, stating that inferior federal courts would be a major financial burden for the national government. He believed that the states should be responsible for the major financial burden of the jurisprudence system. John Rutledge had different concerns. He did not want the inferior courts to overstep their boundaries and interfere with issues that he perceived as solely "state" problems. Therefore, state courts should hear all cases on **original jurisdiction**, and the national courts should be reserved only for the right of **appeal** from the state courts. This would ensure that the national judiciary would hear only matters the state considered of national significance. He represented the position that the appeal process of the national judiciary is all that would be necessary to secure national rights and uniformity of judgment.

The case for inferior federal courts was also strong and arguments for them were led by such prominent delegates as James Madison. Edmund Randolph from South Carolina also supported "a national court system," believing that state courts could not be trusted with the administration of national laws. Alexander Hamilton, a staunch supporter of a strong national government albeit a late convert to the concept of a strong central judiciary, proposed that inferior courts should exist but that they must be constructed by Congress.

Hamilton's idea became central to forging the compromise that finally ended the delegates' heated debate. Instead of delaying the convention over the issue of designing a federal court system, the delegates resolved that they would leave that job to Congress. They decided there could be federal inferior courts but only if Congress would "ordain and establish" them. However, this compromise did not satisfy Governor Morris, Chairman of the Committee on Style, the committee designated to construct the language of the Constitution. Morris was extremely frustrated over the lengthy discussion concerning federal inferior courts; he wanted to ensure passage of Article III without further debate. He believed the most expedient way to accomplish this objective was to incorporate the compromise and then write the judicial article in the most ambiguous language possible assuming that this would allow the delegates to interpret Article III anyway they pleased. Lack of specifics would give them less to squabble about.

The delegates easily passed Article III with all its ambiguities. However, this expedient resolution had its consequences. The carefully sculpted ambiguous language designed to halt debate on the judicial system in 1787 left the mission of the courts and its relationships to the other institutions of government open to interpretation. Ending a debate has seemingly facilitated an endless one.[4]

CONGRESS AND THE COURTS

Inferior Courts

Congressional power to create inferior federal courts and determine their jurisdiction has virtually defined the relationship between these two seemingly independent yet interrelated branches of government. The first Congress moved quickly to exercise its power and establish inferior courts. Under the guidance of William Patterson and Oliver Ellsworth, both delegates to the Constitutional Convention and future Supreme Court justices, a congressional committee hammered out the first judiciary act, the **Judiciary Act of 1789**. This act established important precedents for the existing structure of the federal court system.[5]

Congress established two types of inferior courts: Article III, **judicial courts**, and Article I, **legislative courts**. Both types of courts receive their names from the articles of the Constitution from which Congress derives its power to establish them. Congress has the explicit power to create judicial courts. Articles III states that Congress shall create such inferior courts as they "may from time to time ordain and establish." Articles III, judicial courts, were the first ones to be established, and they were created to exercise the judicial power of the national government to administer justice within constitutional guidelines. Most people are more familiar with Article III courts than Article I courts, as they provide the basic framework of the federal court system. The judicial courts currently include the federal district courts and court of appeals. Over the years, the growth in population has necessitated that Congress increase the number of these courts. Today, legislation has established twelve courts of appeals and ninety-four district courts.[6]   However, although the number of courts has increased, the basic structure of the judicial courts has not. The structure remains virtually unchanged since the early days of the republic. Today's federal district courts and courts of appeal are essentially derivatives of the original courts established by the first Congress.

Congress' power to establish Article I courts is implied rather than explicit. They derive this power from Article I, Section 8, and it is a combination of an explicit grant of power and the "necessary and proper" clause, or implied powers clause. Article I, Section 8 stipulates that Congress shall have the power "to constitute Tribunals inferior to the supreme Court" and also "to make all Laws which shall be necessary and proper for carrying into Execution the foregoing Powers." Article I, or legislative courts, differs from Article III courts in that although they are involved in adjudication, they do not technically exercise the judicial power of the United States. Legislative courts are usually designed to deal with specific issues or to administer specific congressional statues. For example, in 1988, Congress established the Court of Veterans Appeals to review decision made by the Department of Veterans Affair. Article I courts could be given nonjudicial duties, which might be inappropriate to vest in an Article III court. Article I courts also include federal district courts located in U.S. territories in Guam, Northern Marianas, and the Virgin Islands as well as the United States Court of Military Appeals, the U.S. Court of Federal Claims, United States Tax Court, and the Court of International Trade.[7]

It is often difficult to determine whether a court is a legislative or a judicial court. Except for the Supreme Court of the United States, which is constitutionally designated as an Article III court, Congress decides whether a court will function as either an Article I or Article III court. Legislative courts enjoy less independence than do judicial courts, as their activities are specifically monitored by Congress. Congress has the authority to enact laws regulating the conduct of Article I courts and the means by which their judgments are enforced. Article I judges also do not enjoy the same "good behavior" tenure that is constitutionally guaranteed to Article III judges. Congress usually designates that legislative judges serve for a fixed term although they could and have in the past legislated that in particular circumstances Article I judges be bestowed "good behavior" tenure.[8]

Checks and Balances

As discussed in Chapter 2, checks and balances is a concept that is interwoven into the entire fabric of the Constitution. The ability of Congress to create courts that eventually fall under the judiciary's jurisdiction is one excellent example of the intricate system of constitutional checks and balances. However, the relationship between Congress and the judiciary is much more complicated than that and extends far beyond the powers we have already discussed. The relationship between these two branches of government goes beyond the explicit "checks" and gives great insight into the often "hidden" or implicit substance of constitutional checks and balances.

The Constitution's ambiguous language in Article III as to the specific structure of the courts left the door open for Congress to define its role vis-à-vis the judicial branch. Inferior federal courts were not the only judicial congressional creation. Congress' ability to legislate the structure of the

TABLE 12.1 LEGISLATIVE COURTS

U.S. Claims Court—handles cases in which there is a monetary claim for property damage against the national government.

U.S. Court of International Trade—deals exclusively with cases involving disputes over trade laws and agreements.

U.S. Court of Military Appeals—reviews courts-martial in which military personnel are either discharged for "bad conduct" or given prison sentences of one year or more. It is up to the court to decide which cases to review. However, the discharge of generals or admirals must automatically be reviewed, as well as any case in which the sentence is a penalty of death.

U.S. Tax Court—examines the rulings of the Internal Revenue Service in regard to its assessments of income, gifts, tax evasion, etc.

U.S. Court of Appeals for the Federal Circuit—handles appeals from Claims Court and Court of International Trade, plus patent appeals and patent infringement cases.

U.S. Court of the District of Columbia—hears criminal and civil cases in Washington, D.C.

U.S. Territorial Courts—hear criminal cases and civil suits for territories of the United States (Guam, Puerto Rico, Virgin Islands, Mariana Islands).

U.S. Bankruptcy Court—handles cases of bankruptcies in which there is a federal question.

U.S. Foreign Intelligence Surveillance Court—reviews applications for electronic surveillance by foreign governments and their agents in the United States and its territories.

courts has done more than merely "create more courts." Beginning with the Judiciary Act of 1789, Congress has managed to legislate a significant role for itself in the affairs of the judicial system to include the workings of the Supreme Court. This legislation has served as a "check" on the power of the Supreme Court.

One such "check" has included the structure of the Supreme Court. The Judiciary Act of 1789 originally established that there would be six seats on the Supreme Court. Congress altered the number of Supreme Court justices more than six times during the nineteenth century, ranging from as few as five members to as many as ten. The current Supreme Court consists of nine justices, which was established by Congress in 1869. However, this has not been without debate or challenge. Since 1869, there have been several attempts to change the number of justices on the Supreme Court, the most famous of which occurred in 1937. President Franklin Roosevelt attempted to use his executive power to "pack" the Supreme Court with justices more favorable to his

New Deal. He asked Congress to pass a law requiring the appointment of one additional justice for each sitting justice over the age of seventy. This would have immediately increased the size of the Court to fifteen members all of whom would be appointed by Roosevelt and would be sympathetic to his political agenda. Congress denied Roosevelt's request, and the number of Supreme Court justices remained at nine. In this instance, the intricate system of checks and balances not only limited the executive branch but effectively "checked" and "balanced" the power of all three branches of the national government.

Separation of Powers

Often there is a fine line between the concepts of checks and balances and separation of powers; however, separation of powers is readily apparent in the relationship between Congress and the federal judiciary in the area of fiscal responsibility. The Constitution bestows upon the Supreme Court the power to exist but does not empower it with any funds to operate. Consequently, the Supreme Court cannot function as an independent entity as it must rely on another institution for its funding. This is true of the other courts as well. Article I grants Congress the power to appropriate money or the "power of the purse"; therefore, Congress determines exactly how many funds will be allocated to the federal judiciary. In this instance, separation of powers mandates the continued interdependence of these two institutions.

All the judiciary's budget requests are subjected to full review by the congressional appropriations committee and finally full congressional approval, as it is simply considered as one part of the entire budgetary package voted on by Congress. The judicial branch must justify its expenditures to Congress just as other bureaucracies, such as the Pentagon, are required to do. However, the federal judiciary, one of the three main branches of government, represents only 2/10s of 1 percent of the federal budget.[9] This is in contrast to the Pentagon's budget that currently absorbs approximately 20 percent of the federal budget.[10] However, according to the *Newsletter of the Federal Courts*, dated February 2007, Congress approved a 4.9 percent increase over 2006. Much of this is needed to fund operating increases to include rent, electricity, building repairs and salaries. Specifically, judges in the federal system have not seen a significant increase in their pay since the early 1990's. Former Chief Justice Rehnquist had asked for increased federal judiciary pay for the last 20 years. His replacement Chief Justice John G. Roberts has also taken up the cause. Chief Justice Roberts devoted his annual year-end report on the state of the nation's courts to just one issue, albeit one he said has "now reached the level of a constitutional crisis and threatens to undermine the strength and independence of the federal judiciary." Roberts stated that in real terms federal judicial pay has decreased 24 percent over the past decade resulting in federal judges leaving for higher paying jobs in the private sector. The question is will Congress be able to rectify the funding issue within the federal judiciary with continuing rising costs in other areas such as defense and health care.

Structure of the Federal Court System

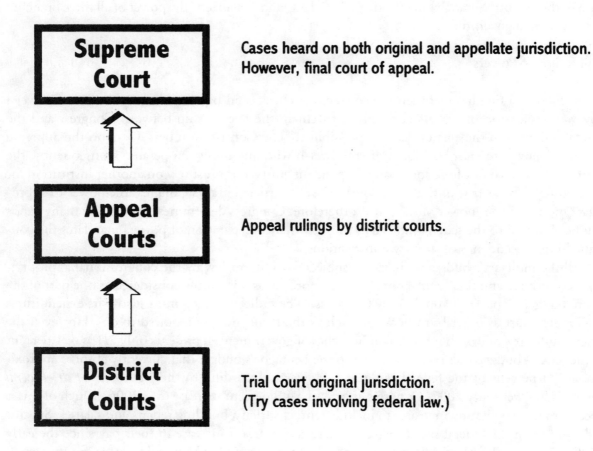

Supreme Court — Cases heard on both original and appellate jurisdiction. However, final court of appeal.

Appeal Courts — Appeal rulings by district courts.

District Courts — Trial Court original jurisdiction. (Try cases involving federal law.)

*District & Appeals Court include both Article I and Article III Courts.

Article I district courts include the courts in the territories of Guam, Virgin Islands, and the Northern Mariana Islands as well as the special legislative courts such as the Tax Court and the Court of Military Appeal.

*Another route to the Supreme Court is via the State Courts. Each State Court System is an independent parallel structure to the federal system. The traditional "bridge" or way over to the federal courts is via the 14th Amendment.

FEDERAL COURT STRUCTURE

Federalism

Federalism, power shared between the national and state governments, has produced an elaborate **dual court system** consisting of a vast network of federal and state courts. Within any state there exists two parallel court systems, state and federal, neither of which is superior to the other. Some situations dictate that state courts have jurisdiction; others necessitate federal jurisdiction; while still other situations will require joint jurisdiction. For example, if two citizens of Illinois are engaged in a dispute over the terms of a contract signed in Illinois, the case would fall under the exclusive jurisdiction of the Illinois state courts. A law suit involving more than $75,000 and citizens of different states would be within the jurisdiction of both the federal courts and the state courts of either the plaintiff's or defendant's state. A case arising under the Sherman Antitrust Act, an 1890 national antimonopoly law, would fall under the exclusive jurisdiction of the federal courts.[11]

Federal/State: Common Ground

The dual court system is by nature complex. Jurisdiction is often difficult for the nonlegal professional to discern, and complex court procedures fill law libraries across the country. Each individual state court adjudicates the laws of that individual state in a manner prescribed by its state law albeit within the context of federal guidelines. Because of the complexity of the dual system and the individual nature of the state courts, the chapter will focus exclusively on the national judiciary. However, although state courts do not fall within the scope of this chapter, some general statements can be made regarding the nature and functions of the judicial system, both federal and state.

In principle, the judicial system is an adversarial one in which the courts provide an arena for two parties to bring their conflict before an impartial judge and, in certain circumstances, a jury to weigh the merits of their case. The task of the judge is to apply the law to the specifics of the case to determine which party is legally correct. Justice will be determined not in terms of who is morally right or wrong, good or evil, but, rather, which party is legally correct. This concept coupled with the "due process" clause of the Fifth and Fourteenth Amendments to the Constitution, as well as the "equal protection" clause of the Fourteenth, defines justice in the United States. If the rules have been followed and equally applied to all, then under the U.S. legal system, justice has been served.

At both levels, federal and state, there are two basic kinds of cases, criminal and civil. Criminal cases are ones in which the government brings suit against an individual charging that he/she violated a specific statute of law that results in criminal charges warranting punishment by the government. In a criminal case, the accused, if found guilty, owes restitution to the government. In a civil case, there are no criminal charges that demand securing governmental punishment. Rather, two individual parties seek the court's assistance in resolving a dispute between them. The parties, one of which may be the government, asks the court to define the relationship between them using the guidelines established by statutory law, *stare decisis*, and common law. Restitution is made to the other party in the suit.

The bulk of judicial cases commence at the state level. The vase majority of all criminal and civil cases involve state law and are tried in state courts. Although the percentage of civil cases is not as high, 98 percent of all criminal cases are heard in state courts. Of the millions of cases heard by the courts last year, only 259,000 were heard in federal district courts. Consequently, the majority of people, if they find themselves in court, will do so at the state level.[12]

Federal Courts: District Courts

Since Article I courts' jurisdiction is often narrowly constructed, the focus of the remainder of this chapter will be on Article III, federal courts. State courts will only be discussed if they relate to the federal system and/or the Constitution.

The current federal court system is actually a three-tier system consisting of the federal district courts, federal appeal courts, and the Supreme Court. The first tier consists of the federal **district courts**. Today, there are ninety-four district courts legislated by Congress that are located within the fifty states, the District of Columbia, the Commonwealth of Puerto Rico, and the territories of the United States, including Guam, the U.S. Virgin Islands, and the Northern Mariana Islands. All the district courts except those located in U.S. territories are considered Article III courts. District courts located in the territories are considered by Congress to be Article I courts. A large district may be divided into several divisions and may require several different locations where cases are heard. Each district court contains a bankruptcy unit.

The district courts are designed to function as the federal trial court where most federal cases begin and end. As such, the jury system is used. In federal criminal cases, there are usually twelve jurors and from one to six alternate jurors. In federal civil cases there are from six to twelve jurors. Unlike criminal cases, civil cases do not have alternate jurors. The jurors will decide guilt or innocence during a trial. The U.S. Constitution guarantees trial by jury only in federal criminal cases (Article III, Sec. 3 and the Sixth Amendment) and civil litigation (Seventh Amendment). However, in *Duncan v. Louisiana,* 1968, the Supreme Court extended to the states, citing the Fourteenth Amendment, the right to trial by jury in criminal prosecutions. The Supreme Court has to date failed to extend jury privileges to state civil trials.[13] Over 80 percent of the cases heard by the court are civil rather than criminal in nature because most criminal cases involve state laws and are resolved in state courts. District court trials are presided over by a single federal justice whose job it is to examine the facts of the case and apply the laws of Congress and the precedents established by the higher courts to each trial.

There is another type of jury, the grand jury, which is guaranteed by the Constitution in all federal cases. Amendment V states "No person shall be held to answer for a capital or other wise infamous crime, unless on a presentment or indictment of a grand jury . . . ." Unlike the standard jury described above, which is used in district court trials, the grand jury is not to determine the guilt or innocence of a person but rather decide whether or not there is enough evidence to justify issuing an indictment to bind someone over for trial. In this way the grand jury provides a check on the judicial system against hasty or political prosecutions. The U.S. Supreme Court in *Wood v. Georgia* stated that the grand jury, has been regarded as a primary security to the innocent against hasty, malicious and oppressive persecution, it serves the invaluable function in our society of standing between the accuser and the accused . . . to determine whether a charge is founded upon reason or was dictated by an intimidating power or by malice and personal ill will.[14]

Courts of Appeal

The **courts of appeal** make up the second tier of the national judiciary. Today, congressional legislation sets the number of courts at thirteen. Since federal law provides that every individual has a right to appeal his or her case, these courts have very little discretion over the cases that they hear. However, only approximately 10 percent of the cases heard in lower courts ever reach this level. Twelve of the thirteen appeals courts have a geographic jurisdiction, including the Court of Appeals for the District of Columbia, which has the distinction of hearing many cases involving the federal regulatory agencies. The District of Columbia court contains a special section that on the request from the Attorney General of the United States selects independent prosecutors to head federal investigations. Many of these investigations are familiar to the American public and have been more than a thorn in the side of various White House administrations such as "Watergate" during the Nixon years and "Whitewater" and "Monicagate" during the Clinton administration. The last court of appeals was established by Congress in 1982; the Court of Appeals for the Federal Circuit was created to deal with specialized subjects such as patents and copyrights.

By definition an appeals court is designed to hear appeals of decisions previously rendered by the district courts, Article I courts, and some federal administrative agencies. The court of appeals' function is really quite different from that of the district court. Since it is not to function as a "trial court," it does not utilize a jury system nor does it determine the guilt or innocence of an individual. It does not hold another "trial" to examine or reexamine evidence presented at a lower court. Rather, a panel of three federal judges considers the record of the lower courts to assure that during the trial phase of the process an individual received a fair trial. The justices determine such issues as whether the trial judge correctly applied a law and/or the Constitution during the actual court proceeding. Although the justices have little discretion over the cases they hear, the prescribed function of these courts allows the judges more discretion in their rulings than at the district court level. The appeals court judges are required to "interpret" the law and extend it, which can often result in new legal "**precedents**."

INFERIOR COURT JUDGES/SELECTION PROCESS/SEPARATION OF POWERS AND CHECKS AND BALANCES

As Article III judges, District and Court of Appeals judges must be nominated by the president and confirmed "with the advice and consent of the Senate." These appointments, although for a constitutional term of "good behavior," are in reality life-time appointments, theoretically so that once appointed, the judges will make decisions unfettered by political pressure. Today the average tenure of a federal judge is approximately 24 years, or six presidential terms; judges appointed in their

30s or 40s can theoretically serve for much longer. Therefore, thoughtful consideration is critical in examining judicial nominees as to who they are and what they believe as once confirmed federal misjudgments fitness are difficult to remedy.[15]

Much has been written regarding this process at it relates to the selection of Supreme Court justices, the specifics of which are discussed in the next section. Currently, however, an unusual amount of media coverage has focused on the judicial appointments of inferior court justices. Historically, the media has not given much coverage to this process as it was usually viewed as either much less glamorous or much more mundane than an appointment of a "Supreme" to the high court. However, since the days of Adams and Jefferson, the selection of inferior court justices has always proven to provide a fertile ground for partisan ideological wrangling.

There is less concern and debate over the judges appointed to the District Courts. District court judges, except for those who preside over territorial district courts, are considered Article III judges. However, the very nature of their job as "trial judges" limits the discretion district court judges are capable of exercising in their case rulings much more so than the judges at the other two levels of the federal court system. As Article III judges, they are also appointed by the president and confirmed by the Senate and serve for terms of "good behavior." However, the selection process used by the president to nominate candidates for these courts is quite different from the process used for the other two levels of the federal courts. Since there are so many district court appointments, currently 675 district court judgeships, the president uses a process called **senatorial courtesy**. Although the president formally nominates the judicial candidate, the nomination usually originates with a senator or senators from the president's party from the state in which there is a vacancy. Unless the candidate is deemed unqualified by the Committee on the Federal Judiciary of the American Bar Association or considered personally or politically repugnant to the president, the candidate is appointed and confirmed.

Using the American Bar Association (ABA) to evaluate judicial candidates is a fifty-year-old tradition that dates back to the Eisenhower administration. Although not as old as senatorial courtesy, which dates back to the Washington administration (1789), it has become firmly entrenched in the judicial appointment process. That process has recently been abandoned by the Bush administration. Upon entering office, Bush said that he would not use the American Bar Association to screen candidates for the federal bench. The ABA has long been considered by many Republicans to be too bias towards liberal judicial candidates. Democrats contend that ending the ABA's historic role in the selection process could not only slow Senate confirmation of Bush's appointees but also threaten the entire tradition of senatorial courtesy. Democrats, unlike Bush, will continue to rely on the ABA's evaluations.[16] This presents the possibility that two entirely different lists of candidates for judicial appointments, one Democrat and one Republican, will be constructed. Appointments to the federal bench now, more than ever, could be based on ideology rather than merit. This confrontation only exacerbated the bitterness that existed between the two parties in the Senate over judicial appointments. The ideological rivalry between Senate Republicans and the Clinton administration left one hundred judgeships unfilled.

President Bush, however did not believe his judicial agenda would suffer the same fate as Clinton's as the 2004 election returned a strong Republican majority to the Senate. The Republicans believed they had enough votes to thwart any ideological power struggle. However, it was business as usual in the Senate and judicial confirmations of less than mainstream nominees were carefully scrutinized and their credentials challenged by the now minority party, the Democrats. The most vicious battles for appointments were to the Courts of Appeal. These candidates demanded more attention from the president and from the Senate as the Courts of Appeal are viewed as a stepping stone for more prestigious appointments, including the Supreme Court. These judges are also viewed as policy-makers and considered by many to be the keeper of the moral consciousness of the country. Therefore, senatorial courtesy is not invoked, and the appointment process is personally scrutinized by the president before the nomination is presented to the Senate for confirmation. The Bush Administration, to date, has refused to utilize the American Bar Association to evaluate potential judicial appointments for the Courts of Appeal vacancies.

Since 2001, the Senate Democrats have successfully held up 10 of the 57 Bush nominees for the Courts of Appeal. Normally, a candidate's nomination is blocked in the Senate Judiciary Committee; however, due to the Republican's solid control of this committee, the Democrats resorted to the filibuster as their procedural weapon of choice. A filibuster is a Senate procedure, glamorized in the 1939 movie *Mr. Smith Goes to Washington* starring Jimmy Stewart, which allows for unrestricted debate from the floor of the Senate. It is so effective because it takes a cloture vote of 60 votes, (three-fifths of the Senate) in order to stop one.

The filibuster has been used by both parties to block confirmation of judges. Defenders of the filibuster say that it has always been a tool used by the minority party to slow down the process in the Senate in order to protect minority rights, which is the cornerstone and safeguard for any democratic society. According to Senator Byrd from West Virginia:

> One of the things that makes the United States Senate the unique upper body that it is is the ability to talk at great length. And there have come times when the protection of a minority is highly beneficial to a nation. Many of the great causes in the world were at first only supported by a minority. And it's been shown time and again that the minority can be right. So this is one of the things that's so important to the liberties of the people. As long as a people have a forum in which members can speak at length, the people's liberties will be safe.[17]

In the case of the 10 stalled Bush nominees, the Democrats have viewed these individuals as unacceptable to the mainstream of the American public. They view the ideological stances of these individuals as counter to the civil liberties agenda hard fought and won over the past forty years. Many Democrats have argued that the Republicans are using these nominations to reach out to certain constituents, namely Evangelical Christians, which have increasingly become an important part of the Republican coalition. Confirming these individuals would put them in positions of setting social policy for decades to come, ironically something that strict constructionist President Bush has argued judges should not do from the bench.

Opponents of the filibuster have argued that it thwarts majority rule, delays or kills needed nominations, brings the Senate into disrepute, and permits small minorities to extort unwarranted concessions supported by Senate majorities.[18] Republicans argue that judges are the only non-elected constitutional officers. As a check and balance the Constitution grants the president power to nominate and the Senate power to confirm (or not) these nominations. Since the 2004 elections returned a Republican president to office and a Republican majority to the Senate, blockage of these confirmations is tantamount to thwarting the democratic process and denying the American public the spoils of their electoral process.

Although blocking judicial nominations is not new in American history, these debates have taken an unusual twist. In the current debate over nominees to the Courts of Appeal, the filibuster itself has become an issue. What makes it unusual is the fact that this procedural rule used in the Senate since its inception has become wrapped in religious and nationalistic rhetoric. Recently, April 24, 2005, was declared "Justice Sunday: Stop the Filibuster Against People of Faith," by the Family Research Council, a Washington-based Christian lobbying group and organizer of the event. The use of the filibuster was now cast as an issue of faith. More than 2000 people and reporters from 25 news organizations gathered at Highview Baptist Church in Louisville, Kentucky to denounce Senate Democrats as being "against people of faith" for blocking 10 of President Bush's judicial nominations.[19] This meeting was nationally simulcast to more than 500 radio stations, 130 other churches and the Internet. The "Justice Sunday" telecast included a four-minute videotaped speech by Senate Majority Leader Republican Bill Frist.[20]

"Justice Sunday" was highly criticized and condemned by leaders of several major religious denominations to include the Presbyterian Church (USA), and the Washington-based Religious Action Center on Reform Judaism. The National Council of Churches USA issued a statement, "To brand any group of American citizens as anti-Christian simply because they differ on political issues runs counter to the values of both faith and democracy."[21] Critics of "Justice Sunday" held a rally at the Central Presbyterian Church across town. The organizers of this counter event said that Senator Frist and his allies were exploiting religion for political purposes.

Interestingly, at a time when Republicans were in a minority in the Senate, they also used the filibuster to stop nominations, most notably, the non-confirmation of Abe Fortas to Chief Justice of the Supreme Court.[22] The Democrats then threatened to change the rules. However, the issue of the use of the filibuster was not constructed in religious rhetoric. Is all of this business as usual in the confirmation process? Is there a new twist in this 200 year old confirmation battle to introduce the filibuster as some form of a faith based initiative? There are two questions that might be significant for the judicial selection process. First, now that the Democrats have taken back control of the Senate in the election of 2006, will the Republicans feel the need to use the filibuster in order to block judicial appointments to lower federal courts they believe are not ideologically appropriate? Second, how well will the separation of powers and checks and balances be maintained by the majority for the minority or vice versa and how best to ensure dialogue through the process.

THE SUPREME COURT

The Supreme Court is the only court prescribed by the Constitution in Article III; therefore, unlike the other federal courts that can be either created or dissolved by Congress, it must exist in some form. Its ability to exist independent of Congress places it at the pinnacle of the federal court system. Its unique position firmly establishes the Supreme Court not only as the most prestigious of all of our courts but also the most controversial. Much of the controversy surrounding the Supreme Court stems from its ability to make policy using the concept of judicial review. The Court has increased its own decision-making power through its establishment of the "incorporation doctrine," which has essentially nationalized the Bill of Rights on a case by case basis at the discretion of the Court. Many of these cases are discussed in chapters 13 and 14, which focus on civil liberties and civil rights.

Judges of the Supreme Court

The Framers of the Constitution intended that the justices of the Supreme Court be isolated from the political process as much as possible, which today excludes them from engaging in such political activities as raising election funds, tending to the needs of special interest groups, and seemingly endless campaigning. It might then be concluded that this would politically insulate the justices, removing them from the passions and persuasions of the political arena. However, this isolation has often had the opposite effect, producing perhaps the most political of all the institutions of government crafted at the Constitutional Convention. The Constitution positioned the Court above the roar of the crowd and the accountability of "the people"; however, it did not remove it from the political fray. Instead of participating in the traditional electoral politics that is experienced within a very broad popular framework by the other two branches of the federal government, the Court has been subjected to a much narrower political fray of "institutional" politics. The Constitution created a Supreme Court that is an elitist, almost aristocratic, institution whose personnel, at least for the appointment process, are virtually required to be totally reliant on the politics of the other two branches of the federal government.

How did an institution designed to be isolated from politics become such a political animal? The expedient and so often necessary compromises forged at the constitutional convention significantly influenced the current structure and consequently the present substance of our governmental institutions. For example, the vague language of Article III crafted by Governeur Morris's Committee on Style was designed to eliminate any more discussion of the judiciary. In so doing, numerous clauses in Article III leave the Court's structure open for interpretation and lays fertile ground for the seeds of political action to be planted and nurtured. Two omissions in Article III have had profound effects on the politics of the Court. First, it made no provisions for qualifications for personnel serving on the Court. Second, it established the term of office to be set for "good behavior," which is more commonly thought of as a lifetime appointment. The language in Article III contrasts sharply to the language in Article I, legislative branch, and Article II, executive branch. Both of these articles stipulate that the personnel holding office in these two branches of government are required to fulfill very specific qualifications including age and citizenship requirements and serve for a specified period renewable only by reselection.

Selection Process

The selection process itself excludes any direct input from the people as the justices are appointed by the president and confirmed by the Senate. Careful scrutiny reveals that this process under the original Constitution actually distanced the Court farther from the democratic process than is realized at first glance. The two institutions involved in the process of selecting justices were themselves intended not to be directly selected by the people: the president selected by the electoral college and the Senate selected by their state legislatures. Today, tradition and constitutional changes have altered the method of selection for both the president and the senators making them more assessable to the people. Although the judicial selection process is still out of the direct reach of the American public, these changes have brought the justices one step closer to the democratic process. However, another element, outside of the scope of Constitution, and one of those unforeseen consequences, which is responsible for increased public input into the judicial selection process, is the use of television in confirmation hearings. This more than anything else has "democratized" the judicial confirmations.

Tradition has dictated that the appointment process is the personal prerogative of the president. However, the Constitution requires that the president navigate the political landmines of the Senate to secure a judicial appointment. As mentioned in the previous section, the justice selection process to the Supreme Court have been given much more media coverage than those nominated to the inferior courts. However, the agenda has been the same for both levels of courts. One is just more high profile than the other. Presidents have always coveted the opportunity to appoint justices to the Supreme Court, as they have used this appointment to put forward their own ideological and political perspectives. This process then enables the president to make his political agenda public through his nomination. Therefore, a conservative president would tend to put forth a conservative nominee to fill a Court position; liberals would do the same. Strengthening the Court with like-minded individuals hopefully insures that their own ideological conviction will be translated into a political agenda that would be given favorable consideration by the Court both during their administration and in the justiciable future.

More often than not, the Senate has deferred to the president, rejecting only 29 of 137 nominations ever sent to it. However, recent confirmation hearings have demonstrated that this procedure is not merely a rubber stamp of the president's nominee. Two of these hearings that were given extensive media coverage turned into bitter political battles centering both on the ideology and the personalities of the nominees: Clarence Thomas, nominated by George Bush in 1991 and Harriet Miers, nominated by his son, George W. Bush, in 2005.

The two nominations had very different outcomes as Thomas was confirmed and Miers was not. Thomas' confirmation hearings illustrate two concepts discussed earlier: first, immediate and public access to the proceedings by television; second, the role the judiciary plays in the separation of powers and checks and balances. Thomas's hearings were played out on national television. He was not thought of particularly well within the legal community as he did not have an extensive judicial resume.

Thomas, an African American, was nominated to replace the retiring Thurgood Marshall, the first African American appointed to the Court. During his tenure on the Court, Justice Marshall had more than distinguished himself; he had set the bar extremely high for his successor. As only the second African American ever nominated to the Court, race and the political issues surrounding it played a major role in the nomination hearings. The first part of the hearings focused primarily on Thomas' ideological perspective, which reflected the conservative viewpoint of limited judicial participation in public policy. His views on racial issues, such affirmative action and racial quotas, were highly scrutinized by the Senate.

However, what became more central to the hearings were questions surrounding Thomas' personal behavior that turned the confirmation hearings into a major media event. Some people might effectively argue that his Senate hearings digressed into a "sleazy" political spectacle that shook the confidence of the American public not only in the nomination process but in the Senate itself. Anita Hill, a Yale law school graduate, alleged that Thomas had sexually harassed her when she worked for him at the Equal Employment Opportunity Commission. Hill was cool and calm on television and made an effective witness against Thomas. The hearings then placed not only Thomas' behavior in question but the entire issue of sexual harassment in the workplace. Thomas was immediately put on the defensive. He not only denied the charges waged against him by Hill but attempted to divert attention away from the issue of sexual harassment by focusing on the issue of race, calling the hearings a "high-tech lynching" of an "uppity" black man. As the proceedings continued, the press coverage became more intense. Various groups began to mount campaigns both for and against Thomas in their attempt to influence public opinion that would result in asserting political pressure on senators to "correctly" cast their ballot. The two major groups to mount campaigns were African Americans and women's organizations, the former pressing for confirmation, the later for rejection. This put the Democratic Senate between a rock and a hard place, because they were caught in a bitter conflict between two of their core constituent groups. Thomas won the media battle. At the end of the confirmation hearings 61 percent of men and 57 percent of women supported his confirmation.[23]

This confirmation hearing produced both a winner and a loser. The winner was Thomas, who won his nomination as the Senate finally confirmed him by a vote of 52 to 48, which was the closest confirmation vote of a Supreme Court justice in over 100 years. The loser was the Senate, the institution constitutionally mandated to confirm presidential appointments. The Senate Judiciary Committee responsible for the hearings consisted of thirteen white men. They were accused of being inept at handling the timely and pressing issues of gender and race in twentieth century America. They tap danced around several of the major issues of our time choosing to give both

Thurgood Marshall, distinguished African-American civil rights lawyer, was chief counsel for the *Browns* in the *Brown v. Board of Education* case.

issues only cursory coverage that in the end not only damaged the nomination process to the Supreme Court but forever placed into question whether the Senate was capable of successfully handling such sensitive questions in a mature fashion.

More recently, it was President George W. Bush and the executive office that came under intense scrutiny and political fire with the nomination of Harriet Miers to the Supreme Court in 2005. In 2005, Supreme Court Justice Sandra Day O'Connor announced her retirement from the Court. Aft first, President Bush nominated John Roberts to fill the position, but the death of Chief Justice William Rehnquist led to Roberts' nomination as Chief Justice instead. He was easily confirmed for that position by a vote of 78-22. Roberts was not seen as an ideologue and openly sought to emulate the legendary John Marshall's consensus-building style.

Bush's second choice for O'Connor's position was Harriet Miers, an old friend of the president, who had previously served as his personal lawyer. At the time of her nomination to the Supreme Court, Miers was serving as White House counsel. She headed the search committee that had originally marked Roberts for O'Connor's position; however, when he was repositioned as Rehnquist's replacement, Miers was nominated instead. The decision came amid suggestions that Bush look for a candidate outside the appellate court system, the route taken by Roberts, following a recommendation from Democratic Senator Harry Reid. While Reid was the Minority Leader in the Senate and openly supported the Miers nomination, Bush's opponents attacked her as a crony, a charge that was particularly damaging after the Hurricane Katrina disaster relief effort was mismanaged under the leadership of a clearly under qualified head of the FEMA, considered to also be a "crony" of the Bush administration. Her opponents questioned her judicial acuity as she had never served as a judge and were concerned that her background as former head of the Texas State Bar Association and as a Dallas city council member provided neither significant background for the high court nor provided few clues into her judicial philosophy.

Meanwhile conservatives also had questions about Miers, complaining that she did not have a clear voting record on key issues such as abortion since she did not serve in the appellate court system. This divided Bush's supporters as Miers could not demonstrate to the right-wing of the Republican Party that her ideology was conservative enough for a life-time appointment to the Supreme Court. If confirmed, she was to take the place of O'Connor who was noted as the "swing" vote on the Court. If the conservatives could put into place one of their own, they believed that many social issues, such as abortion, gay marriages, and prayer in school, would be decided in their favor by the new "conservative swing" vote. Democrats and Republicans alike had asked for documents she had worked on as the White House top council hoping to uncover clues into Miers' ideological preferences. President Bush refused to release these papers, as he believed this would compromise the executive branch and executive privilege. A political firestorm ensued primarily led from the conservative ideologues within the Republican Party. Harriet Miers was forced to withdraw her nomination.

Samuel Alito was nominated in October 2005 to now fulfill Justice O'Connor's position. Following the Miers controversy, Alito's confirmation hearings in January 2006 came as something of an anti-climax. Although Democrats were worried that Alito would become a conservative ideologue like Justices Scalia and Thomas, Alito was confirmed 58-42. Not as close as Thomas's confirmation but certainly not demonstrating an overwhelming body of bipartisan support.

Both the Thomas' and Miers' hearings demonstrated the influence of media coverage and the affect greater public access to the Senate has made on the Court selection process. It also brings us full circle to the conclusion that the Supreme Court is not only a political institution but that it is caught in the politics of the executive and legislative branches.

Good Behavior

To secure judicial independence, the Constitution stipulates that Supreme Court judges, as well as other Article III judges, serve for a term of "good behavior," which insulates the judges from external public pressure such as direct interest group pressures and the election process. Article III also attempts to provide protection from internal institutional pressure by prohibiting Congress from decreasing judge's salaries while they are in office. This permits the judges to render decisions they deem proper without the threat of financial reprisals from other branches of the government. These protections stem from the colonial opposition to royalist judges under the English Crown. One of the grievances listed in the Declaration of Independence as a justification for the Revolutionary War was that King George III had "made Judges dependent on his will alone."[24]

Although "good behavior" has for all practical purposes evolved into a lifetime appointment, the question remains "what is good behavior?" Can judges be removed for "bad behavior," and exactly what would this be? Article II is very clear about what is an impeachable offense for other constitutional officers, stipulating "The President, Vice President and all officers of the United States, shall be removed from Office on Impeachment for, and Conviction of, Treason, Bribery, or other High Crimes and Misdemeanors." Some argue that the "good behavior" language in Article III implies that judges may be impeached for offenses that go beyond those stipulated for other constitutional officers. This vague concept of "good behavior" might translate into impeachment charges for such activities as the failure to perform their judicial duties, vices such as alcoholism, or other conduct that brings the judicial office into disrepute. Impeachment charges could be more "loosely constructed" for judges than for other constitutional officers. Interestingly, Thomas Jefferson, usually considered a strict constructionist when it came to interpreting the Constitution, supported "loose construction" of judicial impeachment. As president, Jefferson allegedly threatened Chief Justice John Marshall with impeachment proceedings if the Supreme Court ruled against his administration in *Marbury v. Madison* (1803). However, for all practical purposes impeachment is more of an implied rather than a real threat as the House of Representatives rarely exercises its power to bring charges against constitutional officers, particularly against federal judges. Although Supreme Court justices have been threatened with impeachment proceedings, only Samuel Chase (1796-1811) had charges filed against him. The Jeffersonians charged Chase with "intemperate and inflammatory political harangues," delivered with the "intent to excite the fears and resentment of the . . . people . . . against the Government of the United States."[25] The charges were not sustained. Lower tiered judges have not fared as well and in rare circumstances have been impeached by the House and tried and convicted by the Senate for misbehavior that fell short of treason, bribery or other "crimes and misdemeanors."[26]

Demographics of the Court

The demographics of the justices on the Supreme Court need to be considered as an input into their decision-making. As discussed, justices are nominated by the president for their ideological perspectives, and although each justice has been labeled as either a conservative or a liberal, it can be argued that their similar backgrounds have produced very similar ideological characteristics. The process of legal education and professional training coupled with the defining elements associated with an individual's social class makes it unlikely that dissidents would be appointed to the Court. These ideological characteristics are evident in the rulings of the Court, which will be explored later in the section on judicial activism. Reflecting their socioeconomic class, except for the rarest of circumstances and during particular time periods, most notably the 1960s and 1970s, the justices have more often identified with the interests of the slave-owners rather than the slaves, the propertied and landowners rather than with the indigent, and the industrialists rather than the workers.[27]

There have been only 110 judges who have served on the Supreme Court, and over the past two hundred years these justices have shared very similar backgrounds. Although more recent appointments have slightly altered the demographics of the Court, with few exceptions, the justices have been white, Anglo-Saxon, Protestant males from the upper socioeconomic class. Minorities have been obviously underrepresented. All except two of the justices have been white. The only other ethnic group to be represented have been African Americans. Thurgood Marshall was appointed in 1967, and Clarence Thomas was nominated to replace him in 1991. Women have also been underrepresented. Although today women comprise over 50 percent of the population, only two women have ever been appointed to the Supreme Court, Sandra Day O'Connor in 1981 and Ruth Bader Ginsburg in 1993. More than 90 percent of the Supreme Court justices have been from socially prominent, politically influential upper-class families.[28] Several Catholics have served on the Court, and the first Jewish justice, Louis Brandeis, was appointed in 1916. Two of the Clinton appointees were Jewish. And today, five of the nine sitting judges are Catholic.

The career paths leading to the Supreme Court have varied, but the justices have all shared one common trait and that is their educational background. They are all lawyers who have had a traditional legal education. This tradition began with George Washington who believed it was essential that justices to the Supreme Court belong to the legal profession. All of his Court nominees were lawyers, and this tradition has continued to this day.[29] The attorneys who become Supreme Court justices more often than not receive their legal education at the finest law schools in the country. More than two-thirds of them have received their legal training at Ivy league or other prestigious law schools.[30]

The Court and Its Traditions

The Supreme Court is steeped in tradition and does not lack in pomp and circumstance. The Supreme Court first assembled on February 1, 1790, in the Merchants Exchange Building in New York City, then the nation's capital. Although the location of the court has changed, in many respects it resembles the same institution that met in 1790. One legal historian has called it, "the first Court still sitting."

Table 12.3: Background of Supreme Court Justices

Occupational Position before Appointment

Private legal practice	25
State judgeship	21
Federal judgeship	30
U.S. Attorney General	7
Deputy or Assistant U.S. Attorney General	2
U.S. Solicitor General	2
U.S. Senator	6
U.S. Representative	2
State Governor	3
Federal executive posts	9
Other	3

Religious background

Protestant	83
Roman Catholic	13
Jewish	6
Unitarian	7
No religious affiliation	1

Age on Appointment

Under 40	5
41-50	32
51-60	59
61-70	14

Political Party Affiliation

Federalist (to 1835)	13
Democrat-Republican (to 1828)	7
Whig (to 1861)	1
Democrat	44
Republican	44
Independent	1

Educational Background

College graduate	94
Not a college graduate	16

Sex

Male	108
Female	2

Race

Caucasian	108
Other	2

Source: Congressional Quarterly, *Congressional Quarterly's Guide to the U.S. Supreme Court*, (Washington, D.C.: Congressional Quarterly Press, 1996) and author's update.

Table 12.4

The Supreme Court, 2007

Name	Birth Year	Appointment Year	Political Party	Law School	Appointment President	Religion
John Paul Stevens	1920	1975	R	Chicago	Ford	Nondenominational Protestant
Antonin Scalia	1936	1986	R	Harvard	Reagan	Catholic
Anthony Kennedy	1936	1988	R	Harvard	Reagan	Catholic
David Souter	1939	1990	R	Harvard	Bush	Episcopalian
Clarence Thomas	1948	1991	R	Yale	Bush	Catholic
Ruth Bader Ginsburg	1933	1993	D	Columbia	Clinton	Jewish
Stephen Breyer	1938	1994	D	Harvard	Clinton	Jewish
John Roberts*	1955	2005	R	Harvard	Bush	Catholic
Samuel Alito	1950	2006	R	Yale	Bush	Catholic

*Chief Justice

As is customary in American courts, the nine justices are seated by seniority on the bench. The Chief Justice occupies the center chair; the senior Associate Justice sits to his right, the second senior to his left and so on, alternating right and left by seniority. Since at least 1800, it has been traditional for justices to wear black robes while in Court.

Initially, all attorneys wore formal "morning clothes" when appearing before the Court. Senator George Wharton Pepper of Pennsylvania often told friends of the incident he provoked when, as a young lawyer in the 1890s, he arrived to argue a case in "street clothes." Justice Horace Gray was overheard whispering to a colleague. "Who is that beast who dares to come in here with a gray coat?" The young attorney was refused admission until he borrowed a "morning coat." Today, only Department of Justice and other government lawyers, who serve as advocates for the United States government, follow the tradition of formal dress. Quill pens have remained part of the courtroom tradition. White quills are place on counsel tables each day that the Court sits, as was done at the earliest session of the Court. The "Conference handshake" has been a tradition since the days of Chief Justice Melville W. Fuller, (1888-1910). When the justices assemble to go on the bench each day and at the beginning of the private conferences at which they discuss decisions, each justice shakes hands with each of the other eight. Following Chief Justice Fuller's tradition, the practice is a reminder that a difference of opinion on the Court does not preclude overall harmony of purpose.[31]

Jurisdiction of the Supreme Court

Jurisdiction is the authorized power of a court to hear a case and to exercise judicial review. The jurisdiction of the Supreme Court derives from three sources: the Constitution, congressional legislation, and the Court's interpretation of what is meant by the first two sources.[32]

The Supreme Court has both **original and appellate jurisdiction**. In 1979, in *California v. Arizona* the Supreme Court stated, "Original jurisdiction of the Supreme Court is conferred by the Constitution, is self-executing and needs no legislative implementation." However, **original jurisdiction** is neither mandatory nor constitutionally exclusive.[33] Although Congress cannot eliminate the Supreme Court's power of original jurisdiction, it can dilute it by legislating concurrent jurisdiction to other courts, which it has effectively done. Currently the Supreme Court only exercises the exclusive power of original jurisdiction over suits involving disputes between states. Very little of the work of the Supreme Court involves cases heard on original jurisdiction. In recent times they hear only one or two cases a year on original jurisdiction.

The bulk of the Court's work is done on **appellate jurisdiction**, which is the ability to hear the decided decisions of a lower court. Unlike original jurisdiction that is constitutionally mandated, all appellate jurisdiction is legislated by Congress. Although Congress has the power to restrict the Supreme Court's jurisdiction, it cannot specify how a court should decide a particular case. Unlike an appeal to the second tier of the system, the appeals court, no one has an automatic "right" of appeal to the Supreme Court. Consequently, only a small percentage of cases reach the Supreme Court. Not only does a person not have a right to an automatic appeal but in 1989, Congress legislated that the Supreme Court would have almost total discretion over the cases that they heard. Consequently, only approximately 5000 cases are annually appealed to the Supreme Court, and of those only about 150-200 are actually heard.

Case Criteria

Case selection begins to define the very nature of the Court's public policy-making ability. However, unlike either the legislative or executive branches of government, which can be proactive in the field of public policy, the Supreme Court is reactive. Although the Court has almost carte blanche in selecting its cases, it is not restricted to how and when they may render judicial decisions that ultimately result in public policy. The Court does not seek to take judicial action. It is passive and remains so until a case is brought before it. It only renders judicial decisions, first, if it "must" and, second, if it "chooses."

The Supreme Court operates within a prescribed setting and is subject to certain limitations. Before a case can be considered for selection, it must fulfill certain requirements to get its foot in the door. First, the Court can only decide real legal cases and controversies. Second, a person may not just file a lawsuit to enact judicial power whenever he/she perceives a grievance. Rather, a person must have standing to sue, which means a legal reason for being before the Court. Finally, a case must be nonpolitical in nature. All of these requirements are what the Court interprets them to be, and it should be remembered that they are constantly in flux resting on the very precedents the Court itself establishes.

First, the Court requires that the litigants involved in a lawsuit must have a legal question that can only because of its adversarial nature be resolved by the Court. The case must be real and not deal with a hypothetical question or situation. The Supreme Court will not render an advisory decision based on "what could be" if "this or that" were to happen. It also will not give an opinion on issues not presented in an actual lawsuit. This position was established very early in our history when the Court denied two requests for advisory opinions. The first request was in 1790 by Secretary of Treasury Alexander Hamilton on the national government's power to assume state Revolutionary War debts and the other in 1793 by Secretary of State Thomas Jefferson for an interpretation of certain treaties and international law. Chief Justice John Jay held that it would be improper for the Court to judge such matters because the president had a cabinet that could determine such questions. The Supreme Court has maintained this position throughout history stating in *Muskrat v. United States* (1911) that it is inappropriate "to give opinions in the nature of advice concerning legislative action, a function never conferred upon it by the Constitution and against the exercise of which this court has steadily set its face from the beginning.[34]

Although the concept of **standing to sue** is constantly changing, in general it requires that a person, organization, or corporation must be able to demonstrate either direct past or immediate injury within the context of a legally protected interest. A speculative or abstract interest by an uninvolved party is not sufficient to invoke judicial power. The interest must again be real and not hypothetical. A person must expect that Court action will bring a positive decision that will result in obtaining relief from that injury. It is insufficient to use the Court to vindicate or clarify one's own position. Nor is it enough to show a general desire to prevent Congress from acting unconstitutionally or to keep the president from exceeding his authority. A person cannot claim that a law is merely unconstitutional but that they have personally suffered injury from the unconstitutional law.[35] Recently, in 1997, the Court declined to hear arguments regarding the constitutionality of the line-item veto because the six U. S. senators who brought the case did not have "standing" before it. The Court ruled that they had not suffered any personal injury. However, in June 1998, in *Clinton v. New York City* the Supreme Court in a 6-3 ruling struck down the line-item veto as unconstitutional. In this instance, unlike the Senators, the Court perceived that the city of New York did have standing to sue regarding this issue.

Finally, the Court may decline to hear a case because it considers it to involve a "political question" that could best be resolved by another branch or institution of government. Since the Supreme Court is itself a political institution, this criteria is at best a puzzle whose pieces are held in the hands of the sitting justices. Political questions are what the Court deems them to be, and there seems to be no end to what is "not a political question." Staying out of the political fray had its origin in *Marbury v. Madison* (1803) when Marshall observed that the Court had an obligation to decide solely on the rights of individuals. However, almost everything that deals with the rights of the individual at some point becomes political in nature. It becomes a matter of how the Court defines the problem. For example, in 1962, in *Baker v. Carr*, the Court decided to redefine what is a "political" question when the Court determined that malapportionment of legislative districts did violate the equal protection clause of the Fourteenth Amendment. This was only the first of many legislative apportionment cases culminating in a 1996 case stating that race may not be the predominant criteria in deterring legislative boundaries.[36] In a more recent case dealing with apportionment, in April 2001, the Court ruled in what some perceived of as a political battle that the drawing of North Carolina's 12th legislative district did not violate whites' voting rights. This is the fourth time this district has been in litigation over claims that race was the main factor in its configuration.[37]

Final Selection and Hearing

The Supreme Court usually conducts its business in one annual session called a term, which begins the first Monday in October. The term lasts until the Court has finished its business, which is usually sometime in June or July. The first thing on the Court's agenda is to determine exactly which cases it will decide to hear.

It is important that if a case is to be heard by the Supreme Court that all procedures are properly followed. These procedures are often complex and very precise. First, a case must be correctly routed to the Supreme Court. This may occur in several ways, the most common of which is passage through the federal court of appeals. The Supreme Court becomes the federal court of last appeal for these cases. The majority of the remainder of the cases come directly from state supreme courts, as the case of *Bush v Gore*. These cases previously have been tried in state courts because they originally involved violations of state statutes. However, to reach the Supreme Court, one of the litigants must contend that an important federal issue is at stake as well.

Next, a litigant will request the Supreme Court grant their case a **writ of *certiorari***, which is an order by the Supreme Court requiring a lower court to send the records of a case to it for review. Granting a writ of cert would mean that the Supreme Court had agreed to hear the case. This is a very serious matter and not considered lightly. Granting a **writ of *certiorari*** is not a matter of right but of judicial discretion. A petition for a **writ of *certiorari*** will be granted only for compelling reasons, and the justices have almost total discretion over which writs they will grant. There is a **Rule of Four** that requires that at least four of the nine justices must vote to hear a case. These votes are cast in a secret conference known as the **cert conference**, attended only by the justices, and the actual vote is usually not made public. If the Court chooses not to hear a case, the writ will be denied, and the previous court decision will stand as the final decision.

Once the Court has decided to hear a case, it is scheduled for both written and oral arguments. These arguments are not designed to present new evidence. Rather, as an appeals court, the Supreme Court uses the facts already presented at the lower trial court. Its job is to interpret that information within the context of legal precedents and the Constitution.

In presenting a case before the Court, except in rare instances, each side is allowed a thirty-minute argument. During this time, the attorneys summarize their already received extensive written briefs emphasizing their most compelling points. The justices may interrupt the lawyer's presentation at any time and ask him/her to clarify a point in his/her argument or pose pertinent questions and/or seek additional information. After twenty-five minutes, a white light comes on, and the attorney knows that he/she has only five more minutes of argument remaining. At the end of five minutes, a red light signals the end of the argument. The lawyer must stop speaking even if it is in midsentence. The oral argument is over.

The justices then discuss the case at a closed meeting called a **case conference**. It is here that they discuss the case and determine whether the lower court decision is to be reversed or confirmed.

It is in these conference meetings that laws are interpreted and reinterpreted, new precedents established, and the Constitution is defined and redefined. After a complete discussion of the case, a vote is taken, and the opinion of the Court will be expressed in a written document. Who writes the opinion of the Court is very important, because it becomes the **precedent** for future cases.[38]

There are four kinds of written opinions for any particular case: unanimous opinion, majority opinion, concurring opinion, and dissenting opinion.[39] Although **unanimous** opinions occur, such as in *Brown v. Board of Education* (1954), they are very rare. The other three types of written opinions are much more common and consequently worth more attention. The **majority** opinion is extremely important, because it reflects the sentiments of the "majority" of the Court. By tradition, the Chief Justice, if he is in the initial majority, can assign himself or another member of the majority to write the opinion. When the Chief Justice is not in the majority, the senior justice in the majority makes the assignment. While one justice is writing the majority opinion, other justices may be writing **concurring** opinions. These opinions are written by the justices who agree with the conclusion of the Court but wish to either make or emphasize a point that was not done so in the majority opinion. A concurring opinion may also be written by a justice in the majority if he or she agrees with the decision of the Court but reaches this decision for a different reason than the rest of the justices. The last opinion, the **dissenting** opinion, is written by justices who are not in the majority. There may be one or several different dissenting opinions expressed, each reached and written for completely different reasons. These dissenting views are very important, because they are often used as a basis for argument to appeal and establish new precedent at a later date.[40]

The process of granting cert, hearing arguments, and writing opinions takes months. The judges are not only deciding individual litigant's claims but defining the Constitution, which is binding on all of us. The Court is determining public policy. Once this process is completed, the justices determine how much of their decision and reasoning for it they will make public. There is usually a flurry of Court pronouncements towards the end of the session usually in June or July. The complete versions of the Court cases are available for perusal in law libraries and more recently on the Internet.[41]

JUDICIAL POLICY MAKING

Judicial activism, the ability of the court to construct public policy, is considered by some citizens and legal scholars alike to be an extremely controversial power. The controversy tends to focus on two central issues. First, judicial policy making is not an explicit constitutional grant of power, and, as such, perhaps the federal courts have over stepped their boundaries. Second, since the judges are not selected directly by the people, are the actions of the court "democratic" within the context of what is normally considered to be the "democratic" process? The very nature of judicial activism is often considered undemocratic because both the judges and the decisions they render, unlike the personnel and policies of either the executive or legislative branches, are not directly accountable to the people.

Critics of judicial activism, including President Bush, tend to be politically conservative and usually paint this judicial power as a tool used by liberals to craft progressive social and fiscal policy that otherwise would be unacceptable to the general public and, therefore, undemocratic in nature. However, political and consequently judicial activism has no ideological boundaries, and what is often overlooked is the real construction of the policy decisions rendered by the Court. The historical record of the Supreme Court has demonstrated that with a few exceptions, more often than not, its judicial activism has been conservative, not liberal, in nature, reinforcing the existing status quo rather than initiating progressive changes. The Supreme Court has had the power to define the Constitution and has chosen to do so by constructing a "speedbump" for progress. Its decisions more often than not have either slowed down social change, reflecting the policies of the existing power structure, or rendered decisions that merely reflected inevitable social changes. Although there are many policy areas that reflect conservative activism, one of the most obvious is the area of race relations. Cases such as *Dred Scott v Sanford* (1857) and *Plessy v Ferguson* (1896) were conservative in nature. The former upheld the interests of the slave-owners and plantation elite instead of those of the slaves while the later effectively established an apartheid system in the United States maintaining the interests of the existing white power structure. Both of these decisions were significant in legally constructing a two-tiered system based on race, creating serious if not irreversible barriers for race relations in the United States. The Court did not drive over the very speedbump they created until 1954 when they rendered their unanimous decision of school desegregation in *Brown v. Board of Education*.

Brown v Board of Education (1954) reversed *Plessy v Ferguson* jolting the American public over the "speedbump" almost one hundred years after the Civil War and driving in a new era of civil rights. This decision, considered to be a landmark progressive decision that altered the social fabric of the United States, reflected the civil rights struggle that had been active since the days of the constitutional convention. It legitimized a civil rights movement that began the day slavery was accepted as a legal institution in the United States. *Brown* finally reversed decisions such as *Plessy v Ferguson*, which had successfully maintained the status quo of the white power structure in the United States both before and after the Civil War.

Judicial policy-making derives from many sources. First, who is sitting on the Court determines how actively the Court will engage in policy-making and what direction that policy will take. Second, Congress legislated that the Supreme Court have the power of judicial discretion or control over what cases they will or will not hear. Last, the Supreme Court can exercise both its explicit and implicit grants of constitutional power, specifically the powers of judicial review and judicial interpretation. We have already examined the first and second aspects of judicial policy-making in previous sections of this chapter so all that is left for us to explore are the policies of judicial review and judicial interpretation.

Judicial Review

At the heart of the Supreme Court's authority and prestige rests the principle of **judicial review**, which is the power to declare unconstitutional any state or federal law, judicial ruling, or executive action that it believes is in conflict with the Constitution. The study of the American Constitution then becomes largely a study of the judicial decisions of the Supreme Court as it interacts with the other branches of government, as well as with the states. Alexander Hamilton once remarked that he believed that the judicial branch of government would be the "least dangerous" because it lacked sufficient power to affect policy making. However, many scholars contend that judicial activism fostered by the Court's ability to implement the concept of judicial review has resulted in judicial supremacy. Judicial review has negated Hamilton's early vision of the Court.

Although some form of judicial review was bantered about at the constitutional convention, no action was taken to incorporate such a power into Article III. The origin of judicial review then does not directly stem from any enumerated judicial power in the Constitution but rather from implied powers effectively argued by Chief Justice John Marshall in *Marbury v Madison* in 1803. This case is the most important case ever rendered by the Supreme Court as it establishes itself as a viable and equal branch of the federal government with the executive and legislative branches.

The case of *Marbury v Madison* reflected the raging political battle between the Federalists and the Jeffersonians or Antifederalists. This struggle generated a legal situation that was to be resolved in the courts. The Supreme Court seized this political opportunity to define itself and, in so doing, established the concept of judicial review. The political struggle between the Federalists and Antifederalists was destined to affect the future of the new republic as it was instrumental in defining the power relationships among the three branches of the federal government. It also went a long way in legitimizing the concept of national supremacy, which was extremely important in establishing a framework for the concept of federalism.

Marbury v Madison

Federalist President John Adams lost his re-election bid to the Antifederalist Thomas Jefferson in the election of 1800. Congress was also now controlled by the Antifederalists. The Federalists considered the results of this election to be disastrous because many of them considered Thomas Jefferson, a Southerner and an ardent states' righter, to be a threat to the existing national institutions. Before leaving office, the Federalists did what they could to protect the national government from the clutches of Thomas Jefferson and his political cronies. Since the Federalists had lost control of the executive and legislative branches, the only national institution left was the judiciary. They proceeded to "pack" it with Federalists. First, President Adams appointed Secretary of State John Marshall as the new Chief Justice of the Supreme Court. He was immediately confirmed by the Senate. Then the outgoing Federalist controlled Congress enacted the Circuit Court Act,

John Marshall (on the left) and
James Madison (on the right).

creating sixteen new circuit court judges and decreased the size of the Supreme Court so that the new president could not replace the departing Justice Cushing.[42] Congress also created forty-two new justices of the peace positions in the District of Columbia. Adams nominated Federalists for all these new judicial positions, and the Senate quickly confirmed them. However, according to the Judiciary Act of 1789, to complete a judicial appointment, the Secretary of State must officially deliver the commission. Time ran out before all the commissions could be delivered, and John Marbury was one of the individuals who had received an appointment but had not been delivered his commission.

The Antifederalists took office, and the new president, Thomas Jefferson, was furious to find out that on their way out of office the Federalists had packed the judicial branch. The AntiFederalist Congress quickly repealed the Circuit Court Act passed by the outgoing Congress, and Jefferson immediately ordered his new Secretary of State, James Madison, to cease delivering the undelivered judicial commissions for the District of Columbia.

Jefferson's mandate to Marshall left Marbury without his judicial appointment. Marbury believed that James Madison was in violation of the Judiciary Act of 1789 that required him to deliver judicial appointments. Marbury believed Marshall should be forced to fulfill his duties and deliver the commission. The only way that Marbury could accomplish this was to file suit against Madison asking the Court to grant him a *writ of mandamus*, which is a court order directing a public official to fulfill his/her duties or otherwise be in contempt of court. Marbury filed his suit directly with the Supreme Court. He claimed that Congress in Section 13 of the Judiciary Act of 1789 extended the power to issue writs of mandamus to the Supreme Court on original jurisdiction.

This case put both John Marshall, a staunch Federalist and now Chief Justice of the Supreme Court, and the Supreme Court in a tenuous position. He was caught in the middle of a political battle that effected the prestige and status of the Supreme Court. Jefferson had already informed Marshall that if he issued Marbury the writ he sought, his personal political career was in jeopardy. If Marshall did not issue Marbury the writ, more importantly the status of the Court vis-à-vis the executive and legislative branches was at stake. Both the Congress and the president had been manipulating the judicial branch, creating courts, repealing them, appointing judges, and then refusing to fulfill congressional mandates and deliver their commissions. Failure by the judicial branch to require the executive and legislative branches to fulfill the letter of the law would forever put them in an inferior position to the other two branches of government.

Marshall looked for a way out of the political battle while establishing the Supreme Court as a viable national institution. Marshall writing the opinion for a unanimous Supreme Court decision said that they would, if they could, issue a writ of mandamus to Secretary of State James Madison. Marshall stated, "The Supreme Court shall have the power to issue writs of mandamus in cases warranted by the principles and usages of law, to persons holding office under the authority of the United States."[43] However, the Court could not issue the writ to Madison because Marbury did not have "standing" before the Supreme Court. Marbury should have brought his case to a lower federal court first and then the Supreme Court would have heard the case on appeal. Marshall countered Marbury's claim that Section 13 of the Judiciary Act of 1789 gave him standing before the Supreme Court on original jurisdiction by striking down Section 13 of the Judiciary Act of 1789 as unconstitutional. Marshall claimed that the Constitution established the original jurisdiction of the Supreme Court, not Congress. The Constitution stipulated that the Court's original jurisdiction extended to cases "affecting ambassadors, other public ministers and consuls, and those to which a state is party," and since Marbury did not belong to any of those categories, he could not address the Supreme Court on original jurisdiction. Marshall went on to reason that Congress had enacted a statute that altered and conflicted with the Constitution and since the Constitution was the supreme law of the land, the law must be struck down. Further, it is the duty of the Supreme Court to say what the Constitution means and, if necessary, to strike down laws that conflict with it.[44]

Marshall was extremely clever and an astute politician. He knew exactly what had been accomplished in *Marbury v Madison,* and he also knew exactly how far he could push Jefferson and the legislative branch. While usurping an enormous amount of power for the Court, he simultaneously diffused a potential constitutional crisis between the Court and the executive branch. The Supreme Court declared that Marbury had no standing to sue before the Court. Therefore, the Court had no authority to require the executive branch to perform any action. Jefferson, though enraged by the Court's decision, let sleeping dogs lie. The Court had declared its power of judicial review thereby establishing the Court as one among equals with the other branches of government while at the same time saving face for the executive branch because it did not have to comply with any of the Court's mandates.

The decision of *Marbury v Madison* was a huge political victory for the Court. However, there was a quick and angered response to the opinion of the Court. Particularly angered by the decision was Thomas Jefferson whose administration was not only challenged but who had never personally believed in the concept of judicial review. In fact, Jefferson continued to be an opponent of judicial review not only during the remainder of his presidency but to the end of his life. Writing in 1819 to Spencer Roane, a Virginia state judge, Jefferson explained, "Each of the three departments has equally the right to decide for itself what its duty under the Constitution, without any regard to what the others may have decided for themselves under a similar question."[45]

Marshall's constitutional arguments appear plausible and although withstanding the test of time, they have long been reviewed and disputed by legal scholars. Many would not only dispute the merit of the constitutional arguments of the case but would go further to conclude that the Court used a legal dispute to resolve a political problem. Critics have gone on to argue that the Constitution is only the supreme law of the land because it is derived from the people; therefore, only the most accountable and responsive institutions to the people, the Congress and the president, have a right to interpret the Constitution. The supreme law of the people should be held in trust by those most accountable to the people. Following this argument to its logical conclusion, the least accountable branch of the government entrusted itself with the job of protecting the supreme law of the people.[46]

Marbury v Madison was the first Supreme Court decision to declare a law passed by a legislative body to be unconstitutional. Article III stipulates that the "judicial Powers shall extend to cases and controversies arising under this Constitution." Therefore, Marshall reasoned that Article III implies that the judiciary shall have the power to decide constitutional questions. Article VI makes it clear that the Constitution is the "supreme law of the land" therefore any law contrary to the Constitution must be nullified because all laws must fall within the framework of the document.

Marshall concluded that since the Constitution is the supreme law of the land and since the judiciary shall have the power to decide constitutional questions, it naturally follows that the Supreme Court implicitly has the power of judicial review, which allows them to determine whether a law is in compliance with the Constitution. The Court must first determine whether a law is constitutional before it can determine whether it should be enforced.

Although it would take decades of usage and tradition to establish this power, under Marshall's leadership the Court was successful in creating itself as the "keeper of the constitutional conscious." However tenuous Marshall's argument might appear to be, one of the reasons that judicial review has not been seriously challenged by the other branches of government is that the Court has used its power sparingly. In fact, the Court did not declare another act of Congress unconstitutional until it rendered its 1857 *Dred Scott v Sanford* decision. The Court has remained passive and therefore seemingly apolitical only rendering decisions on cases brought before it by an individual litigant wishing to resolve a legal matter. For the most part the Court has upheld the laws of Congress and consequently the agendas of the executive branch thereby making it not only an equal partner but a credible ally as well.[47]

Judicial Interpretation

Judicial interpretation is a key component to judicial review. Judicial review is always considered within the context of the "opinion of the court." The Court has established some guidelines that are meant to restrain judicial action in the area of constitutional review. Although they are not always followed, here are some key points usually observed by the Court:
- Do not decide a constitutional issue unless it is absolutely necessary to depose a case.
- Whenever there is a choice, interpret a law in such a way as to render it constitutional.
- If it is necessary to make a constitutional ruling, restrict it as narrowly as possible and do not anticipate or decide issues not immediately before the Court.
- Whenever state law is unclear and is susceptible of an interpretation that will preserve its constitutionality, abstain from deciding the case until state judges have ruled on the law.[48]

Bush v Gore

The Supreme Court decision, *Bush v Gore*, rendered in December 2000, clearly brings into focus how really "undefined" and transient the relationships are that are only "vaguely" established by such constitutional concepts such as separation of power, checks and balances, judicial review, and judicial interpretation. The Court chose to enter the political fray of the presidential election 2000 when it agreed to hear arguments from the Bush campaign for a request for a stay of the Florida Supreme Court order, mandating hand recounts of disputed ballots. The Court not only issued a stay of the recount but also agreed to hear Bush's appeal of the Florida Supreme Court's constitutional authority to mandate the recount in the first place.[49]

On December 12, 2000, the Court by a 5-4 margin declared that the presidential vote recount in Florida must be terminated. Seven justices decided that the manual recount procedures approved by the Supreme Court of Florida violated the "equal protection" clause of the Fourteenth

Amendment of the Constitution. A bare Court majority (5-4) held that there was insufficient time for Florida to adopt new constitutional procedures and complete a new recount in order to use the results by December 12, the deadline set by Congress to grant electors "safe harbor," unchallenged acceptance to cast their votes in the Electoral College election.[50]

The Court by its own rules establishes what cases it will hear. By accepting the case, the Court believed that it had an institutional responsibility to bring legitimacy to the process of electing a president. In so doing, the Court expended an enormous amount of political capital and called into question its legitimacy as an independent and nonpartisan institution. Not only did the conservative majority in the Court open itself up to criticism of "playing favorites" and "throwing the election" to Bush, it possibly usurped the constitutional power of Congress. If not overt usurpation, then, at the very least, a redefinition of the concepts of separation of powers and checks and balances. Much as been written challenging the Court's decision to terminate the recount on the basis of an equal protection violation, particularly because the Rehnquist Court has not been especially known as an "equal protection" Court. Many scholars believe that "equal protection" was not the issue. Rather, the fundamental legal question centered on the problem of election deadlines. Many of those who opposed the Court's decision did so on the grounds that the dispute over electoral deadlines should be resolved elsewhere in the political process, in this case, Congress. Justice Breyer makes an elegant argument for this in his dissent.

> "The Constitution and federal statues themselves set forth a road map of how to resolve disputes about electors, even after an election as close as this one. The Twelfth Amendment commits to Congress the authority and responsibility to count electoral votes . . . A federal statue, the Electoral Count Act, enacted after the close of the 1876 Hayes-Tilden presidential election, specifies that, after states have tried to resolve disputes (through "judicial" or other means), Congress, is the body primarily authorized to resolve remaining disputes."[51]

The legislative history of the Electoral Count Act clearly shows its intent to commit the power to resolve such disputes to Congress, not the Supreme Court. However, is the Electoral Count Act as clear as Justice Breyer contends or does it simply put into question the ever-unresolved and ever-shifting relationships between the three branches of government and the national government and the states. Is the Court to be a political entity and, if so, how is the selection process for justices to the Court to be removed from the political process? The Constitution created the guidelines by which to establish the parameters of political power and left the Supreme Court to interpret them. Their decisions, particularly the more controversial ones such as *Bush v Gore*, will always appear to be political in nature.

CONCLUSION

Justice is often portrayed by a blindfolded woman holding a set of scales meant to symbolize that justice is blind in weighing the precarious balance between right and wrong. However, what exactly is weighed on those scales? Were they meant to balance good and evil or right and wrong, resulting in a system of retribution or revenge? Is this delicately balanced system of justice crafted so that all people who do bad things will be punished? The answer to what is to be balanced is up to the courts.

The precarious balance of justice is established by a set of rules derived from the concepts of *stare decisis* and common law as developed and interpreted by the courts. Using these rules the Court attempts to weigh the rights of the individual versus the rights of society. If the rules have been followed in facilitating this balance then justice has been served. However, the rules constantly change, and the delicate balance between the individual and society constantly shifts back and forth as it is difficult for the Court to maintain an equilibrium. Political scientist, John Domino, contends there is no formula for this balance and that the Court, much like the blindfolded woman, must search in the dark to find the answers. It relies on the Constitution, tradition, public safety, national security, and public standards of decency and morality.

The Court has constantly attempted to resolve twentieth and now twenty-first century political, economic, and social problems using a vague, almost ambiguous, set of guidelines handed down from the eighteenth century.[52] How should the Constitution be interpreted in the modern world? Were the vague notions of the judiciary designed at the constitutional convention enough to guide our judicial system today? There are obviously no easy answers to any of these questions even though they are sometimes presented that way to us on the evening news. The hardest question of all is whether the American public is comfortable with the judicial process and the question of twenty-first century justice.

CHAPTER NOTES

[1]The European feudal system was a reaction to the breakdown of centralized government in Europe during the Middle Ages. The lack of centralization had created major famines and the constant threat of invasion from foreigners. To counter these forces, the weak sought protection from those that were stronger. This produced a social, political and economic system based on land and a bond of reciprocity between those who worked the land and those owned it.

[2]Clayton Roberts and David Roberts, *A History of England: Prehistory to 1714*, Volume I, 3d edition, (Englewood Cliffs, New Jersey: Prentice Hall, 1991), 65-89.

[3]Frederic A. Youngs, Jr. Henry L Snyder and E. A. Reitan, *The English Heritage*, 2d edition,(Arlington Heights, Illinois: Forum Press, Inc., 1988),54.

[4]I would like to acknowledge Brian James Stewart for his research of the discussion of the federal judiciary at the constitutional convention. The historical information he gathered regarding this issue largely stems from two major sources. Ralph Mitchell, *CQ's Guide to the U.S. Constitution*, (Congressional Quarterly, 1988), and Robert J. Wagman, *The Supreme Court: A Citizens Guide*, (New York: Phares Books, 1993). Mr. Stewart also used several supplemental sources in his research. Christopher Collier and James Lincoln Collier, *Decision in America*, (New York: Random House, 1986), and Bernard Schwartz, *A History of the Supreme Court*, (Oxford University Press, 1993).

[5]Robert J. Wagman, *The Supreme Court: A Citizens Guide*, (New York: Phares Books, 1993), 39.

[6] J.W. Peltason, Corwin & Peltason's *Understanding the Constitution*, 13th edition, (Fort Worth:Harcourt Brace College Publishers, 1994), 140.

[7] Ibid., 141.

[8] Ibid.

[9] "Judiciary Seeks Exclusion from Line-item Veto," The Third Branch, February Issue, 1997, 2. HYPERLINK http://www.uscourts.gove/ttb/february/linettb.html http://www.uscourts.gov/ttb/february/linettb.html,

[10] Peverill Squire and others, *Dynamics of Democracy*, (Madison: Brown & Benchmark Publishers, 1995), 396.

[11] Peltason, 143.

[12] "2000 Year End Report of the Federal Judiciary," 1.

[13] Ibid., 632.

[14] Ibid.

[15] Herman Schwarz, "Senate Rules Meltdown," *The American Prospect*, March 27,2005.

[16] Joan Biskupic, "Bush to Change Screening of Judges," *USA Today*, March 22-25, 2001, 1.

[17] Walter J. Oleszek, *Congressional Procedures and the Policy Process*, (Washington, D.C.:CQ Press, 2004), 239.

[18] Ibid, 240.

[19] Andres Wolfson, "Justice Sunday to Air Tonight," *The Courier Journal*, April 24, 2005, p.1

[20] Ibid.

[21] Ibid.

[22] Biskupic.

[23] Dye, 338.

[24] David M. O'Brien, *Constitutional Law and Politics*, Volume One, 2nd edition (New York: W.W. Norton, 1994), 25.

[25] Gary B. Nash and others, eds., *The American People: Creating a Nation and a Society*, (New York: Harper Row, 1986), 302.

[26] Peltason, 144.

[27] Michael Parenti, *Democracy for the Few*, (New York: St. Martin's Press, 1995), 290.

[28] Dye, 54.

[29] Robert J. Wagman, *The Supreme Court: A Citizens Guide*, (New York: Phares Books, 1993), 43

[30] Dye, 54

[31] The section of the *Court and Its Tradition* was taken from a booklet prepared by the Supreme Court of the United States and published with funding from the Supreme Court Historical Society. www.supremecourt.gov

[32] O'Brien, 98.

[33] Peltason, 150.

[34] O'Brien 100.32. Ibid., 101.

[35] Ibid.

[36] Ibid.

[37] "Voting District Uphold," *National Public Radio, All Things Considered, Coverage of the Supreme Courts 2000-2001 Terms*, www.npr.org/news/specials/supremecourt/index.html..

[38] Bob Woodward and Scott Armstrong, *The Brethren: Inside the Supreme Court* (New York: Avon Books, 1979), xii.

[39] Bardes, 427.

[40] Kermit Hall, 607.

[41] Bob Woodward, xii.

[42] Daniel A. Farber, William N. Eskridge, Jr. and Phillip P. Frickey, *Constitutional Law: Themes For the Constitution's Third Century*, (St. Paul: West Publishing, Co.,), 61.

[43] Peltason, 28.

[44] John C. Domino, *Civil Rights and Liberties: Toward the Twenty-first Century*, (Harper Collins College Publishers), 5.

[45] O'Brien, 39.

[46] Peltason, 28-30.

[47] Domino, 5.

[48] Peltason., 36.

[49]"*Bush v Gore*: The Supreme Court's Misguided Foray into Presidential Politics," www.uslaw.com/library/article/ article, 1-4.
[50]Ibid, 2-3.
[51]Ibid.
[52]Domino, 6.

SUGGESTED READINGS

Farber, Daniel A., Williams N. Eskridge, Jr., and Philip P Frickey. *Constitutional Law: Themes for the Constitution's Third Century*. St. Paul: West Publishing, Co., 1993.

Garvey, John H., and T. Alexander Aleinikoff. *Modern Constitutional Theory: A Reader*, 2d edition. St. Paul, Minn.: West Publishing Co., 1991.

Goldman, Sheldon. *Picking Federal Judges*. New Haven, Ct.:Yale University Press, 1997.

Hall, Kermit, ed. *The Oxford Guide to the United States Supreme Court Decisions*. New York: Oxford University Press, 1999.

Rossum, Ralph A. and G. Alan Tarr. *American Constitutional Law, Volume I & II*, 5th edition, Boston: Bedford/St. Martin's Press, 1999.

Savage, David G. *Turning Right: The Making of the Rehnquist Court*. New York: Wiley, 1992.

Wagman, Robert J. *The Supreme Court: A Citizen's Guide*. New York: Phares Books, 1993.

Woodward, Bob, and Scott Armstrong. *The Brethren: Inside the Supreme Court*. New York: Avon Books, 1979.

Chapter Thirteen

CIVIL LIBERTIES

While the debate over the context of the new constitution was brewing in Philadelphia, Thomas Jefferson wrote to his dear friend James Madison that "while there were many things about the proposed Constitution that please him, first among the things he did not like was 'the omission of a bill of rights, providing clearly, and without the aid of sophism, for freedom of religion, freedom of the press, . . . and trials by jury in all matters of fact triable by the laws of the land. . . .'"[1] At the end of his letter, Jefferson stressed that a Bill of Rights was absolutely necessary because "it is what the people are entitled to against every government on earth, ... and what no just government should refuse. . . ."[2] Our rights to speak freely, to practice our religious beliefs, to gather with others, to redress our government without fear of imprisonment, to have a fair public trial, and so on are embodied in the Bill of Rights. The framers guaranteed these rights to **all** citizens by attaching the Bill of Rights to the supreme law of the land—the United States Constitution. "Our nation was founded on the idea that all men are created equal, that they are endowed by their Creator with certain inalienable rights, and that governments are instituted among men to secure the rights nature gives. From the beginning, Americans have believed that if their country was about anything, it was about personal freedom and the rights that helped secure it."[3]

The framers went a step further to ensure that no level of government could strip citizens of their protected rights. In 1789, the United States Congress passed the **Judiciary Act**, which among many provisions gave the newly created Supreme Court the power of judicial review. The key to understanding the longevity of those unalienable rights called civil liberties rests in part with the

Supreme Court's use of judicial review. This chapter focuses on the creation, interpretation, and subsequent preservation of the civil liberties enumerated in the Bill of Rights.

However, the preservation of our civil liberties does not and should not rest wholly upon the shoulders of the nine justices of the Supreme Court. The governed, that is the citizens, bear an equal burden. The constraints placed upon the governing emphasize that laws are man-made. "Americans are much given to saying with pride—with more pride, perhaps, than understanding— that they live under a government of laws and not a government of men. But laws, of course, are man-made. The Constitution of the United States itself, the supreme law of the land, was framed by mortal men. Ordinary mortals legislate in Congress, administer the laws in the executive branch of the government, and interpret the laws in the judicial branch. These laws were not delivered to us on tablets from Mount Sinai; they are not self-executing; and there are inevitable conflicts about the application and construction of them."[4] Consequently, this chapter also explores the roles played by ordinary citizens such as Ernesto Miranda, Steven Engle, Dollree Mapp, and Clarence Gideon in reminding the governing of their responsibility to preserve, protect, promote, and defend those precious civil liberties enumerated in the Bill of Rights.

The continuing quest to preserve and, in some circumstances, to expand the scope of civil liberties has been oftentimes derailed by events that have seriously threatened the viability of the United States. At the beginning of the Civil War, President Abraham Lincoln issued orders curtailing selective civil liberties such as the *writ of habeas corpus*. President Franklin Roosevelt signed the order that placed American citizens of Japanese extraction into detention camps for the duration of World War II. President George W. Bush was confronted with the same challenge that these two presidents had to face. The tragic international terrorists' attacks of September 11, 2001, placed this nation into a perilous threatened state of emergency. Prompted by the Bush administration, Congress enacted legislature granting more police powers to federal law enforcement agencies that do, to some degree, seriously challenge the scope of American civil liberties. The Preamble of the United States Constitution charges the national government with the tasks to "provide for the common defense" and to "promote the general welfare" of the American people. When the future of the nation is challenged, it is the responsibility of the nation's leaders to do whatever is necessary to protect the American people from threats to their survival, while at the same time trying to avoid the erosion of those precious individual freedoms and civil liberties the framers gave to us in the Bill of Rights. This chapter examines the steps taken by the Bush administration to meet the challenge of international terrorism.

THE CONCEPT OF CIVIL LIBERTIES

In 1215, English noblemen gathered in Runnymede to force their king to sign a pledge guaranteeing the preservation of certain privileges and rights to all Englishmen, regardless of rank and bloodline. They boldly declared that the pursuits of life, liberty and property were **unalienable rights**. They recognized that these are basis fundamental rights "derived from natural law, which all people have and which cannot be taken away or transferred."[5] The **Magna Carta** was the initial quest of Englishmen to end the arbitrary rule of their monarchs who governed under the **divine right theory** of kings. This concept of kingship rested on "the notion that monarchs rule by the will of, indeed in place of God. Since God created this situation, any effort to change it would be considered sinful, because it is through kings that God works his will on men."[6] In his *Two Treaties on Government*, John Locke joined the ranks of John Stuart Mill and Jean J. Rousseau, who firmly believed that civil liberties were indeed unalienable rights "that belong to individuals by the nature of humanity, and which cannot be taken away without violating that humanity."[7] The framers subsequently changed Locke's list of unalienable rights to life, liberty, and the pursuit of happiness.

Although concerned about the protection of individual freedoms, the framers did not include a Bill of Rights into the original document. "James Madison, for example, argued that since the Constitution was one of strictly enumerated powers, the federal government was necessarily prevented from passing legislation that would trample individual rights."[8] Besides, the newly formed thirteen states had already written constitutions containing protections of individual rights and freedoms. It was the Anti-Federalists in their quest to defeat ratification of the Constitution that made the omission of the Bill of Rights the major argument against adopting the document. "Within hours of the delegates signing the Constitution, George Mason published a pamphlet entitled *Objections to This Constitution of Government*, the central theme of which was that the absence of a 'declaration of rights' made the Constitution unacceptable. Without limitations, Mason believed, the federal government would infringe the basic rights of the citizenry. '[T]he laws of the general government,' Mason warned, 'being paramount to the law and constitution of the several States, the Declaration of Rights in the separate States are no security.'"[9]

Once the new Congress convened under the newly adopted Constitution, James Madison led the charge to adopt a Bill of Rights. It is interesting to note that "the first ten amendments to the federal Constitution contain twenty-seven separate rights. Six of these rights, or about 20 percent, first appeared in the Magna Carta. Twenty-one or about 75 percent had their initial formulation in colonial documents written before the 1689 English Bill of Rights. Even more impressive, all but the Ninth Amendment could be found in several of the state constitutions written between 1776 and 1787."[10] Essentially, the Bill of Rights corrected many of the abuses levied by the British government over its own citizens. Throughout its history, England has a blemished record of denying speedy trials, jury trials, reasonable bail, *writ of Habeas Corpus*, protections from cruel punishment, freedom of religion practices and beliefs, freedom of speech, and so on. The framers were quick to recognized how important protecting these basic rights were to the successfulness of a democratic government. The permanency of these rights was assured with the adoption of **Article VI (Supremacy Clause)** that declared the Constitution and all subsequent amendments to the document as the supreme law of the land. Any state or local law deemed in conflict with the spirit and meaning of the Constitution would be declared an unconstitutional act. Therefore, the framers guaranteed to the governed that the governing would not undo what they had created.

However, the framers were concerned that the absolute and unrestrained individual pursuit of unalienable rights would severely jeopardize the concept of a unified civil society. It was a question of absolute individual rights versus the creation of governmental restraints on the pursuit of those rights for the protection of society. The framers rationalized that "if we were to live in a truly 'civil' society, we must agree to respect the rights of others and subject our activities to reasonable restrictions enacted for the good of society."[11] Consequently, religious freedom is not an absolute right.

Table 13.1

The Bill of Rights

Amendment I - Congress shall make no law respecting an establishment of religion, or prohibiting the free exercise thereof; or abridging the freedom of speech, or of the press; or the right of the people peaceable to assemble, and to petition the Government for a redress of grievances.

Amendment II - A well-regulated militia, being necessary to the security of a free State, the right of the people to keep and bear arms, shall not be infringed.

Amendment III - No soldier shall, in time of peace be quartered in any house, without the consent of the owner, nor in time of war, but in a manner to be prescribed by law.

Amendment IV - The right of the people to be secure in their persons, houses, papers, and effects, against unreasonable searches and seizures, shall not be violated, and no warrants shall issue, but upon probable cause, supported by oath or affirmation, and particularly describing the place to be searched, and the persons or things to be seized.

Amendment V - No person shall be held to answer for a capital, or otherwise infamous crime, unless on a presentment or indictment of a Grand Jury, except in cases arising in the land or naval forces, or in the militia, when in actual service in time of war or public danger; nor shall any person be subject for the same offense to be twice put in jeopardy of life or limb; nor shall be compelled in any criminal case to be a witness against himself, nor be deprived of life, liberty, or property, without due process of law; nor shall private property be taken for public use, without just compensation.

Amendment VI - In criminal prosecutions, the accused shall enjoy the right to a speedy and public trial, by an impartial jury of the State and district wherein the crime shall have been committed, which district shall have been previously ascertained by law, and to be informed of the nature and cause of the accusation; to be confronted with the witnesses against him; to have compulsory process for obtaining witnesses in his favor, and to have the assistance of counsel for his defense.

Amendment VII - In Suits at common law, where the value in controversy shall exceed twenty dollars, the right of trial by jury shall be preserved, and no fact tried by a jury, shall be otherwise reexamined in any Court of the United States, than according to the rules of the common law.

Amendment VIII - Excessive bail shall not be required, nor excessive fines imposed, nor cruel and unusual punishments inflicted.

Amendment XI - The enumeration in the Constitution, of certain rights, shall not be construed to deny or disparage others retained by the people.

Amendment X - The powers not delegated to the United States by the Constitution, nor prohibited by it to the States, are reserved to the States respectively, or to the people.

Amendment(s) Pertaining to Application of Civil Liberties

Amendment XIV - All persons born or naturalized in the United States, and subject to the jurisdiction thereof, are citizens of the United States and of the State wherein they reside. No state shall make or enforce any laws which shall abridge the privileges or immunities of citizens of the United States; nor shall any State deprive any person of life, liberty, or property, without due process of law; nor deny to any person within its jurisdiction the equal protection of the laws.

One cannot be arrested because his/her religious beliefs are socially unacceptable. However, a citizen can be arrested when his/her pursuit of religious beliefs breaks a law or causes damage to another individual. Also, freedom of speech is not an absolute right to say whatever an individual wishes to say. Freedom of speech ceases to be a protected right when one's words become fighting words that create a clear and present danger to others. **Reasonable restrictions** are the logical and rational curtailments enacted by government upon the absolute unrestrained pursuit of unalienable rights in order to guarantee the protection of those rights to all members of a civil society.

The phase "reasonable restrictions" is essential to understanding the relationship of government at all levels to the United States Supreme Court. The framers never provided a clear-cut guideline for legislating reasonable restrictions on civil liberties. For example, the Second Amendment guarantees the right to bear arms. However, the framers did not define what constitutes an acceptable weapon or did they explain under what conditions weapons can be legally used. What is reasonable bail? What constitutes a fair trial? Under what conditions can a witness declare protection from prosecution under the Fifth Amendment? The lack of clear cut guidelines has produced problems for lawmakers. Too often the national Congress and state legislative houses have passed what they considered to be reasonable laws only to have the United States Supreme Court declare these actions as unreasonable restraints upon protected civil liberties. The interpretation of the intent of the Bill of Rights and the determination of "reasonable restrictions" has been left to the federal court system through **judicial review**. The power of judicial review "authorizes the Supreme Court to hold unconstitutional, and hence, unenforceable any law, any official action based upon a law, any other action by a public official it deems—upon careful reflection and in line with the inherent tradition of the law and judicial restraint—to be in conflict with the Constitution."[12]

The initial question confronting the United States Supreme Court was whether certain provisions of the Bill of Rights were enforceable upon just the national government or applicable to all levels of government. In *Barron v Baltimore* (1833), Chief Justice John Marshall ruled that the first ten amendments to the United States Constitution were enforceable only on the actions of the national government. Marshall believed that "the Constitution was ordained and established by the people of the United States for themselves, for their own government, and not for the government of the individual states . . . . The powers they conferred on this government were to be exercised by itself; and the limitations on power, if expressed in general terms are . . . necessarily applicable to the government created by the instrument. They are limitations of power granted in the instrument itself: not of distinct governments framed by different persons and for different reasons."[13]

The passage of the Fourteenth Amendment with its provisions of equal protection and due process paved the path for the United States Supreme Court to reverse its original decision outlined in *Barron*. In *Gitlow v New York* (1925), Gitlow challenged the ruling of the New York State Supreme Court that declared his use of the *Communist Manifesto* in classroom lectures as subversive and unconstitutionally protected speech. The United States Supreme Court's ruling in this case is significant for two reasons. First, the Court applied the phrase "**clear and present danger**" used initially in its ruling in *Schenck v United States* (1919), as its litmus test for determining the fine line between protected and unprotected speech. Second, and most importantly, the Court clearly expressed its desire to apply the Bill of Rights to the states through the Fourteenth Amendment.

The justices rationalized that "for present purposes we may and do assume that freedom of speech and of the press which are protected by the First Amendment from abridgment by Congress are among the fundamental personal rights and liberties protected by the due process clause of the Fourteenth Amendment from impairment by the states."[14]

However, the United States Supreme Court did not and has not yet ruled that the entire Bill of Rights is applicable to all levels of government, particularly the states. Since the *Gitlow* case, the United States Supreme Court has used a piece-meal and often confusing practice of **selective incorporation**. In other words, justices *selectively* apply the due process clause of the Fourteenth Amendment to the states when the constitutional issue tied to the Bill of Rights appeals to the Court's interests. The Court has incorporated the First Amendment's establishment clause (usually referred to as the separation of church and state doctrine) to the states as well as issues involving cruel and unusual punishment, right to counsel, and double jeopardy, among others. "Those provisions that remain unincorporated are: 1) grand jury indictments (Fifth Amendment), 2) trial by jury in civil cases (Seventh Amendment), 3) the excessive bail and fines prohibitions (Eighth Amendment), 4) the right to bear arms (Second Amendment), and 5) the safeguard against involuntary quartering of troops in private homes (Third Amendment)."[15] Historically, liberal jurists favor expanding incorporation whereas conservative jurists, including the current Chief Justice of the Supreme Court John Roberts, reframe from expanding the scope of the Court's jurisdiction into state affairs.

Due Process

The application of **due process** is a particularly important consideration in any issue concerning civil liberties and civil rights. Due process involves "the procedural safeguards guaranteed to those who would be deprived of life, liberty, or property because they are accused of criminal wrongdoing."[16] The Fifth and Fourteenth Amendments forbid both the national and state governments from denying to any person life, liberty, and property without due process of the law. Today the application of due process extends beyond the criminal court room to issues involving the employment and termination process, voting rights, and so on. "The concept of due process of law and its application to our federal and state governments is based an extensive reservoir of *constitutionally expressed and implied limitations upon governmental authority*, ultimately determined by the judicial process, and upon those basic notions of fairness and decency which govern, or ought to govern, the relationships between rulers and ruled."[17]

The law involves the concepts of procedural and substantive due process. **Substantive due process** refers "to the *content or subject matter* of a law or ordinance; that is, whether what it deals with what it is trying to accomplish, *contextually* conforms to due process of the law. On the other hand, **procedural due process**-as the most litigated of the two-refers to the manner in which a law, an ordinance, administrative practice, or judicial task is carried out; that is, whether the procedures employed by those who are charge with the application of the law or ordinance violate *procedural* due process, regardless of the substance of the former."[18] Laws must be equally enacted and enforced. Yet, some enactments are so vague in content that people of common intelligence must guess as to their meaning and application. Government cannot hold citizens accountable for obeying laws that provide nebulous enforcement guidelines to law enforcement personnel, judges, juries, and, of course, the citizens themselves. Second, laws must be clearly written whereby all parties understand what the law means. For example, in 1971 the United States Supreme Court heard arguments in *Coates v Cincinnati* that posed both procedural and substantive issues involving a Cincinnati city ordinance. Dennis Coates and several companions were arrested for violating a city ordinance that made it illegal for three or more persons who assembled on any street corner, sidewalk, or vacant lot to display any behavior that was deemed annoying to persons passing by. The United States Supreme Court ruled this ordinance as an unconstitutional act for several reasons. First, the ordinance was both procedurally unenforceable and too vague in content and substance. Without properly defining what constituted "annoying behavior," both citizens and law enforcement personnel were confused as to the differences between acceptable and unacceptable behavior. Like the appreciation of art, the definition of annoying behavior is a subjective one. Individual interpretation of annoying behavior leads to discriminatory application of the ordinance. Second, the ordinance was a direct violation of the right to assemble as guaranteed by the First Amendment to the United States Constitution. Again, the power of judicial review rescued the citizen from unfair and unconstitutional treatment.

The Importance of the First Amendment

The First Amendment to the United States Constitution addresses the fundamental civil liberties granted to the American people. This amendment states that "Congress shall make no law respecting an establishment of religion, or prohibiting the free exercise thereof; or abridging the freedom of speech, or of the press; or the right of the people peaceably to assemble and to petition the Government for a redress of grievances." An analysis of the interpretation and application of reasonable restrictions clearly illustrates the roles the federal court system, legislative houses, interest groups, and the people have in establishing acceptable limits for exercising these freedoms.

Freedom of Religion

The phrase "Congress shall make no laws respecting the establishment of religion" is called the **establishment clause**. The framers did not want government to sponsor one religion over others nor to advocate one religious practice over other practices. The framers justified their actions by emphasizing century old problems the English government had when it sponsored one religion over other religions and the horrible loss of life and property resulting from religious conflicts. The tendency for one religious group to believe that their teachings and practices should take the preeminent position over other beliefs and practices has led to religious conflicts and a breakdown of religious tolerance for centuries. "The bitter memories of religious intolerance suffered by American colonists before coming to America can be seen in a statement in 1774 by the First Continental Congress declaring that the Church of England [Anglicanism] was '. . . a religion that has deluged [England] in blood, and dispersed bigotry, persecution, murder, and rebellion through every part of the world.'"[19]

Banished from the Massachusetts colony for his religious beliefs, Roger Williams "steadfastly maintained that religion was something personal, something defined by an individual's relationship with his or her god. It could not—should not be—coerced by anyone, especially kings, magistrates, or the decree of governments. Forcing someone to worship according to the Christian faith was antithetical to Christ's own teachings."[20] Subsequently, the choice of one's religious beliefs and practices would rest with the individual, not government. The framers opted to separate church or religious issues from government by incorporating the **separation of church and state doctrine** into the First Amendment. United States Supreme Court Justice Hugo Black once wrote that the First Amendment's Establishment Clause meant that "neither a state nor the Federal Government can set up a church. Neither can pass laws which aid one religion, aid all religions, or prefer one religion over another. Neither can force nor influence a person to go to or to remain away from church against his will or force him to profess a belief or disbelief in any religion. No person can be punished for entertaining or professing religious beliefs or disbeliefs, for church attendance or nonattendance. No tax in any amount, large or small, can be levied to support any religious activities or institutions, whatever they may be called, or whatever form they may adopt to teach or practice religion. Neither a state or the Federal Government can, openly or secretly, participate in the affairs of any religious organizations or groups and vice versa. In the words of Jefferson, the clause was intended to erect a wall of separation between Church and State."[21] The United States Supreme Court has become the champion for ensuring that this fragile wall separating church from state remains intact by steadfastly preserving the right of individuals to hold diverse religious beliefs and practices without recrimination.

The use of public funds to promote education in public, private, and parochial schools has challenged the Supreme Court's desire to maintain a complete separation of government from religion. In 1947, the Supreme Court heard arguments in *Everson v Board of Education of the Township of Ewing*, questioning the constitutionality of a New Jersey state law that provided public funding to qualifying parents to offset the costs of public transportation for their children to and from public and private schools. Everson filed a suit challenging the use of public funds to send children to parochial schools as a violation of the Establishment Clause. In rendering their 5 to 4 decision in favor of the funding program, the justices applied the **child benefit theory** whereby public funding can be provided to students who attend both public and private or parochial schools as long as it is the child, rather than the school, that benefits from the funding. Justice Black argued that the New Jersey law "does no more than provide a general program to help parents get their children, regardless of their religion, safely and expeditiously to and from accredited schools."[22] President Lyndon Johnson applied the same argument when he signed into law the Elementary and Secondary Education Act of 1965. This legislation was the first major infusion of federal money into the nation's private and public schools. The Court's ruling in *Lemon v Kurtzman* (1971) established the guidelines for subsequent religious-based issues. The *Lemon* case addressed two state programs that provided state funding for private schools. Pennsylvania's plan allocated state funds to private schools for instructional salaries, textbooks, and instructional materials used for nonreligious classes. The Rhode Island state legislature provided a 15 percent pay increase to teachers in private schools teaching nonreligious classes. The Court ruled both of these programs as unconstitutional violations of separation of church and state. The resulting **Lemon Test** is a three-part test that determines whether the law's purpose is basically secular; whether the law's primary effect neither advances nor inhibits religion; and whether the law excessively entangles church and state. For example, in **Mitchell v Helms** (2000) the United States Supreme Court upheld a Louisiana law providing public funding for instructional equipment to include computers, maps, books, etc., to both public and private schools as long as it is "in a secular neutral non-ideological way."[23] The Supreme Court also upheld a lower court's ruling in favor of a 1997 Arizona law granting a tax credit up to $500 for donations to parochial and private school scholarship and tuition assistance programs. Once again, the money is donated to a program benefiting students and is not directed to any particular school.

In response to the declining quality of the nation's public school systems, the Republican Party, guided by members of its conservative wing, advocated voucher programs whereby parents could choose to transfer their children from low performing public schools to higher rated public, private, and parochial schools. To offset additional tuition, textbook, and transportation costs, parents would receive taxpayer funded vouchers. For example, the Ohio state legislature adopted a pilot program for children attending public schools in Cleveland. "The program gave parents $2,250 per child in tuition vouchers to be used in about 50 schools."[24] Initially, both federal and state courts viewed the use of public money to send students to private and parochial schools as a violation of the separation of church and state doctrine. In 1995, a lower federal appeals court ruled the Ohio voucher program unconstitutional on the grounds that it "has the effect of advancing religion through government-sponsored religious indoctrination."[25] Voucher advocates appealed this decision to the United States Supreme Court. Declaring that the "Ohio program is entirely neutral with respect to religion," the United States Supreme Court ruled in its 2002 session that the Cleveland voucher program is constitutional.[26] "Justice Sandra Day O'Connor; writing a concurring opinion with the majority of the Supreme Court, said she was 'persuaded that the Cleveland voucher program affords parents of eligible children genuine non-religious options' consistent with separation of church and state protections."[27]

Perhaps the most controversial religious issue addressed by the United States Supreme Court is prayer in the public school systems. In 1962 and 1963, the United States Supreme Court heard two cases challenging government sponsored prayer in the classroom. In **Engle v Vitale** (1962), Steve Engle challenged a 1951 decision of the New York State Board of Regents to approve a brief prayer for recital in the public schools. In 1958, the New Hyde Park School District required their students to recite the prayer each day in every class. Engle protested on the grounds that his two children were required to recite the prayer. Engle charged that an official prayer mandated to be recited in the public schools violated both the First Amendment's guarantee of freedom of religion and the separation of church and state doctrine. The United States Supreme Court ruled 8 to 1 in favor of Engle. Justice Black wrote "that by using its public school system to encourage recitation of the Regents' prayer, the State of New York has adopted a practice wholly inconsistent with the Establishment Clause. *There can, of course, be no doubt* that New York's program of daily classroom invocation of God's blessing as prescribed in the Regents' prayer is a religious activity. It is a solemn avowal of divine faith and supplication for the blessing of the Almighty. . . [T]he constitutional prohibition against laws respecting an establishment of religion must at least mean that in this country it is no part of the business of government to compose official prayers for any group of the American people to recite as part of a religious program carried on by government."[28]

Students in public schools have always prayed, especially around test time. But, the Court objects to sponsorship or encouragement of prayer by public-school authorities. The Court has ruled that prayer can not be an attempt on the part of the government to promote religion.

The companion case was the *School District of Abington Township v Schempp* (1963). In this case, a Pennsylvania law required the verbal reading of ten verses from the Bible at the beginning of each school day in all public schools. Children could be excused from this exercise with parental consent. The Schempp family objected to the readings because their Unitarian faith did not interpret the meaning of the Bible in the same manner as other religions. They also felt that their children were the subject of ridicule because they were sent out into the hallway during the readings. Ruling 8 to 1 in favor of Schempp, the United States Supreme Court decided that the Biblical readings constituted a religious ceremony, an unconstitutional act in the public schools.

In both cases, the United States Supreme Court never ruled that prayer in the public schools was unconstitutional. However, the advocacy of one's religious belief over other religious beliefs (*Schempp*) and the promotion of one religious practice over other practices by a governing body (*Engle*) were unconstitutional actions violating the separation of church and state. Since the *Engle* and *Schempp* rulings, the United States Supreme Court has addressed several cases concerning prayer in the nation's public schools. In 1985, for example, the Court heard arguments in *Wallace v Jaffree*. The primary issue focused on the implementation of an 1981 law passed by the Alabama State legislature which stated that "at the commencement of the first class of each day in all grades in all public schools the teacher in charge of the room in which each class is held, may announce that a period of silence not to exceed one minute in duration shall be observed for meditation or voluntary prayer, and during any such period no other activities shall be engaged in."[29] On behalf of his three children, Ishmael Jaffree charged that the Alabama law was an unconstitutional act in violation of the First Amendment's guarantee of religious freedom. Initially, a federal district court judge upheld the Alabama law. However, the federal appellant courts overturned the lower court's ruling. In a 6 to 3 decision, the United States Supreme Court upheld the appellant court's decision. Justice Paul Stevens stressed that "the legislation [was] enacted for the sole purpose of expressing the State's endorsement of prayer activities for one minute at the beginning of each school day. The addition of 'or voluntary prayer' indicates that the State intended to characterize prayer as a favored practice. Such an endorsement is not consistent with the establishment principle that the government must pursue a course of complete neutrality toward religion."[30]

In 1992, the United States Supreme Court ruled in *Lee v Weisman* that clergy-led prayer at public school graduation ceremonies is a violation of the separation of church and state doctrine.

"That ruling allowed prayer at school graduation ceremonies only if school officials instructed students to keep them non-sectarian and non-proselytizing."[31] The Supreme Court also addressed the issue of student-led prayers at high school football games. Students attending the Santa Fe School District in Texas decided to continue the tradition of a pre-game prayer conducted by a member of the student body over the stadium's public address system. Two parents sought legal action to end public pre-game prayers. The 5th United States Circuit Court of Appeals ruled that student-led prayers were an unconstitutional violation of the First Amendment's Establishment Clause. The justices ruled "that while limited prayer may be appropriate at such solemn events as graduation, football games are hardly the sober type of annual event that can be appropriately solemnized with prayer."[32] The United States Supreme Court subsequently concurred with the appellate court's ruling. In a 6 to 3 decision, Justice Paul Stevens stated that "we [the Courts] recognize the important role that public worship plays in many communities, as well as the sincere desire to include public prayer as part of various occasions as to mark those occasions' significance. But such religious activities in public schools, as elsewhere, must comport with the First Amendment."[33] The United States Supreme Court has consistently upheld the belief that voluntary prayer is legal; however, involuntary prayer is not!

The current trend is to allow "a moment of silence" or "a moment for self reflection" to be used in the public school systems. This policy underscores voluntary self reflection without mentioning the word prayer. The constitutionality of a "moment of silence" was upheld by the United States Supreme Court during its 2001 session when the justices declined to address a challenge to a lower court's affirmation of Virigina's "moment of silence law." "For nearly 25 years, Virginia law allowed school districts the choice of holding a moment of silence for 60 seconds. . . But in 2000, the state's legislature and governor changed the law to require that all schools take part in the moment."[34] The Virginia law clearly met the Supreme Court's litmus test since it is "a moment of silence law that is clearly drafted and implemented so as to permit prayer, meditation, and reflection within the prescribed period, without endorsing one alternative over the others . . .[because it does] not favor the child who chooses to pray over the child who chooses to meditate or reflect."[35]

Traditionally, the United States Supreme Court has held that religious practices are constitutional as long as the activity is lawful and does not violate the personal rights or the property of others. The Supreme Court, for example, upheld the use of animal sacrifices as a bona fide religious ceremony in its ruling in ***Church of the Lukumi Babbalu Aye v Hialeah*** (1993). In ***West Virginia State Board of Education v Barnette*** (1943), the Supreme Court ruled that the state's law requiring all teachers and pupils in the public schools to participate in a daily flag salute ceremony or face expulsion from school clearly violated the religious rights of members of the Jehovah Witnesses. Writing for the majority, Justice Jackson stated that "to sustain the compulsory flag salute, we are required to say that a Bill of Rights which guards the individual's right to speak his own mind, left it open to public authorities to compel him to utter what is not in his mind."[36] The United States Supreme Court reaffirmed a lower court ruling upholding a Maryland law requiring public schools to close on Good Friday. The state's law was challenged by a teacher who is Jewish on the grounds that the closure law "sends a message of inclusion to Christian schoolchildren and a message of exclusion to their Jewish, Muslim, and non-believing classmates."[37] The Court upheld an Indiana state law designating Good Friday as a state holiday. The justices concurred that "Indiana does not celebrate the religious aspects of Good Friday; for Indiana, the holiday has absolutely no religious significance. To Indiana, Good Friday is nothing but a Friday falling in the middle of the long vacationless spring—a day that employees should take off to rejuvenate themselves."[38] In a wide variety of rulings on complex issues ranging from school prayer to state-funded public/private education voucher programs, the United States Supreme Court has consistently upheld that the "**exercise clause** protects our right to believe or not to believe in any religious doctrine, prohibits all government regulation of religious beliefs; forbids the government from compelling us to worship; prohibits the punishment of religious beliefs that the government believes to be false; and denies to the state the power to grant benefits or place burdens on the basis of religious beliefs or status."[39]

Freedom of Speech

The right to express one's opinions is a sacred privilege to all Americans. Although we may not like what some people say and do, we do respect their rights to express their viewpoints. Any government action slightly resembling censorship is met with sharp criticism. Lawmakers do not want to repeat the backlash the Federalist Party received in 1798 when it ventured into the realm of censorship with the passage of four laws commonly known as the **Alien and Sedition Acts**. Their rationale for suppressing free speech was deeply rooted in the developing revolution in France. They viewed the overthrow of the French monarchy "as the degeneration of legitimate government into mob rule, particularly during the 1793 and 1794 bloody 'Reign of Terror' when counterrevolutionaries lost their lives on the guillotine. Federalist fears deepened as they watched the new French republican government encourage wars of liberation and conquest in Belgium, Switzerland, Holland, and on the Italian peninsula. In 1798 rumors spread about a possible French invasion of America, one that allegedly would be supported by American traitors and a large number of French émigrés that grew to more than 20,000."[40] The **Naturalization Act** extended the immigrant residency requirement for citizenship from five to fourteen years. The president was empowered through both the **Alien Act** and **Alien Enemies Act** to arrest and subsequently expel all aliens deemed to be a threat to the security of the nation. The most objectionable law was the **Sedition Act,** which made it "illegal to publish or utter any statements about the government that were 'false, scandalous and malicious' with the 'intent to defame' or to bring Congress or the president into 'contempt or disrepute.'"[41] Several journalists were tried and convicted of violating the Sedition Act. The legality of the Sedition Act was one of the primary issues in the presidential election of 1800 as Republican candidate Thomas Jefferson denied Federalist candidate John Adams a second presidential term of office. Jefferson subsequently repealed the Sedition Act and pardoned those convicted of violating it.

Lawmakers and jurists alike have consistently protected the rights of Americans to express their opinions. However, we do not have the absolute right to say or do whatever we want to do. The United States Supreme Court has distinguished protected speech from unconstitutional breaches of freedom of speech. **Pure speech** is "speech without any conduct."[42] A person's words are constitutionally protected as long as those words do not pose a harm to others. The United States Supreme Court distinguished acceptable from unacceptable speech in its ruling in *Schenck v United States* (1919). Schenck had been convicted by a lower court for violating the Espionage Act of 1917 by distributing Socialist-inspired leaflets encouraging men to resist the draft imposed at the height of World War I. Ruling unanimously against Schenck, the United States Supreme Court ruled that his actions created a "clear and present danger" to others. Justice Holmes wrote:

> We admit that in many places and in *ordinary times* the defendants in saying all that was said in the circular would have been within their constitutional rights. *But the character of every act depends upon the circumstances in which it is done. . . .* The most stringent protection of free speech would not protect a man in *falsely* shouting fire in a theatre and causing a panic. It does not even protect a man from an injunction against uttering words that have all the effects of force. . . . *The question in every case is whether the words used are used in such circumstances and are of such a nature as to create a clear and present danger that they will bring about the substantive evils that Congress has a right to prevent.* When a nation is at war many things that might be said in time of peace are such a hindrance to its effort that their utterance will not be endured so long as men fight and that no Court could regard them as being protected by any constitutional right.[43]

Words that present a clear and present danger are unconstitutional. Collectively these words are called **fighting words**. The United States Supreme Court defines fighting words as words that by their very nature inflict injury upon those to whom they are addressed. For example, an individual speaking out against injustice is using his constitutional right to freedom of speech. If that same speaker calls a police officer a derogatory name and incites the crowd to attack the police officer, the speaker's words have ceased to be constitutional and become fighting words, thus creating a clear and present danger. The speaker can now be held accountable for the violent reactions of the audience.

Symbolic speech is "the use of symbols, rather than words, to convey ideas."[44] The turmoil of Vietnam in the late 60s and early 70s filled the United States Supreme Court's docket with cases involving the use of symbolic speech. In *Tinker v Des Moines School District* (1969), the Supreme Court ruled that the wearing of black arm bands as a silent protest against the war by high school students did not present a clear and present danger. Furthermore, the Supreme Court ruled in *Cohen v California* (1971) that the wearing of a jacket bearing an inappropriate four-letter word against the draft was a protected right. However, the Supreme Court does not consider a violation of a law to be a constitutionally protected expression of free speech. In *United States v O'Brien (1968),* the Supreme Court, for example, upheld O'Brien's conviction for burning his draft card in protest against Vietnam. Although O'Brien's protest was constitutionally protected, his actions of destroying government documents (draft cards) was not afforded the same protection. The tragedy of the Vietnam War continues to plague our nation. Recently, a Vietnamese immigrant was harassed by his neighbors in the Little Saigon section of Westminster, California, for publicly displaying a picture of the late North Vietnamese leader Ho Chi Minh. The state's highest court ruled that Tran's display was a constitutionally protected right to free speech. "'Mr. Tran's display is undisputedly offensive and engenders hatred,' the judge said. 'However, these symbols are part of political speech, which Mr. Tran has a right to express even if the context of that expression is offensive.'"[45]

The burning of the American flag evokes the strong emotions of the American people. However, the United Sates Supreme Court has held the burning of the flag in protest as a protected expression of speech. In ***Street v New York*** (1969), the United States Supreme Court reversed a lower court's conviction of Street for defacing and burning the flag. Street's defiant actions followed the 1960 ambush shooting of James Meredith in Mississippi. Likewise, during the 1984 Republican National Convention held in Dallas, Texas, Gregory Johnson headed a political protest against President Reagan. Following their march, Johnson set fire to an American flag soaked in kerosene. No bystanders were physically injured. Johnson was arrested for the desecration of the American flag, convicted of a Class A misdemeanor, sentenced to one year in prison, and fined $2,000. The Texas Court of Criminal Appeals overturned Johnson's conviction on the grounds that flag burning was protected by the First and Fourteenth Amendments to the United States Constitution. The state of Texas petitioned the United States Supreme Court to reverse this ruling on the basis that burning the flag presented a threat to clear and present danger as well as caused the destruction of a national symbol. In a close 5 to 4 decision, the Supreme Court ruled in ***Texas v Johnson*** that Johnson's actions were constitutionally protected under the First Amendment. "With two of the high court's most conservative members, Justices Scalia and Kennedy, moving over to the liberal trio of Justices Brennan, Marshall, and Blackmum, the Court thus declared unconstitutional flag desecration laws in forty-eight states and the federal government set off a firestorm of protest."[46] Stressing that burning the American flag is not under normal circumstances socially acceptable, Justice Brennan wrote: "Our decision is a reaffirmation of the principles of freedom and inclusiveness that the flag but reflects, and of the conviction that our toleration of criticism such as Johnson's is a sign and source of our strength. We do not consecrate the flag by punishing its

Not all areas of free speech are protected. The Court has ruled that some practices are clearly illegal. Here, Goddard C. Graves, 22, burns his selective service classification card in front of the local draft board office as a protest against the Vietnam War. Although this gesture of symbolic speech is prohibited, a ruling by the Court gave such protection to burning the American flag.

The Court stated, "We do not consecrate the flag by punishing its desecration, for in doing so we dilute the freedom that this cherished emblem represents."

desecration, for in doing so we dilute the freedom that this cherished emblem represents."[47] In 1989, Congress thought it had afforded the American flag the appropriate protection with the passage of the Federal Flag Protection Act, only to have it declared unconstitutional by the Supreme Court a year later.

The anti-Vietnam War protests of the 60's and 70's have resurfaced with the George W. Bush administration's invasion of Iraq. The fear of potential terrorist acts on American soil has moved the Federal Bureau of Investigation (FBI) and the Department of Homeland Security to closely monitor the formation and in particular, the tactics used by anti-war groups. Since the initial military invasion, "the FBI has run post-9/11 counter-terrorism investigations into animal rights, environmental, and antiwar groups, including Roman Catholic peace activists, People for the Ethical Treatment of Animals, and Greenpeace . . . . [and] dramatically expanded its use of 'national security letters', formal requests for Americans' phone records, E-mail, and financial transactions. Historically, such letters were used rarely; today, however, the FBI reportedly issues over 30,000 of these letters a year, without review by any court. Defense Department intelligence operatives are keeping tabs on groups protesting the Iraq war and military recruiting efforts."[48] The FBI's actions clearly demonstrate that in the time of war or threats to national security, the line separating protected from unprotected speech is blurred. Recalling the infiltration tactics used by the Nixon administration during the height of Vietnam, Anthony Romero, executive director of the American Civil Liberties Union, stated "the FBI is dangerously targeting Americans who are engaged in nothing more than lawful protest and dissent. The line between terrorism and legitimate civil disobedience is blurred, and I have a serious concern about whether we're going back to the days of [J. Edgar] Hoover."[49] Of course, this nation can ill-afford a repeat of events that occurred at Kent State University on May 4, 1970. Across the nation, college students were demonstrating against the Vietnam War and, in particular, President Nixon's decision to bomb Cambodia. The governor of Ohio vowed to "use 'every force possible' to maintain order and drive the protestors out of Kent.

He called them 'worse than the brown shirts and the communist element, and also the nightriders and the vigilantes. They are the worse type of people we harbor in American.'"[50] The governor called in the National Guard to break up the protest and bring calm back to the campus. On that fateful day, the guardsmen were supposed to peacefully disperse the crowd from the college's Commons area. After throwing gas canisters at the students, the guardsmen retreated only to have angry students follow them. Suddenly, "28 guardsmen wheeled and fired on students. At 12:55 p.m., 61 shots from M-1 rifles rained down the hill [near the Commons] for 13 seconds . . . . Four students lay dead in the parking lot, and nine others were wounded."[51]

Freedom of speech is unconstitutionally protected when its use deliberately harms the character and reputation of another person. **Slander** is verbal malicious attacks against another person. On the other hand, **libel** is defamation of character in print or by other visual presentations. The reasonable restrictions involving slander and libel revolve around the intent of the initiating party. In 1964, the United States Supreme Court addressed the issue of libel in its decision in *New York Times v Sullivan*. Sullivan, a Montgomery, Alabama police commissioner, was awarded $500,000 in damages by a lower court to settle his lawsuit against the *New York Times* for printing an advertisement containing false statements charging his police force with brutality and discrimination against African Americans. The United States Supreme Court reversed the lower court decision. The *New York Times* was deemed not accountable for several reasons. First, public officials are natural targets for verbal and printed attacks. Second, erroneous statements are often unavoidable. If the media was held accountable for every erroneous statement it made, the courts would be flooded with libel and slander cases. Third, and most importantly, the Supreme Court ruled that "even false statements about official conduct, therefore, enjoy constitutional protection, unless they were made with actual malice; that is with the knowledge that they were false or with a reckless disregard of whether or not they were false."[52] The mere printing of false statements is not libel unless those statements were printed with a reckless disregard for the truth, for the sole purpose of maliciously harming the reputation of an individual.

Obscenity

If art is in the eyes of the beholder, the same standard applies to determining what is or is not obscene. According to the United States Constitution, we do have the freedom to express ourselves in both word and deed. Paintings, motion pictures, advertisements, dance forms, sculpture, and literature are modes of expression. Judging a work as art or as obscenity should be a personal decision. However, too often it is left to the courts to determine what constitutes obscenity and to establish the criteria for reasonable restrictions. In *Roth v United States* (1957), Justice Brennan drew a fine line in distinguishing the difference between constitutionally and unconstitutionally protected creative expression. Writing for the majority, Brennan pointed out that "the First Amendment was not intended to protect every utterance . . . . All ideas having even the slightest redeeming social importance—unorthodox ideas, controversial ideas, even ideas hateful to the prevailing climate of opinion—have the full protection of the guaranties unless excludable because they encroach upon the limited area of more important interests. But implicit in the history of the First Amendment is the rejection of obscenity as utterly without redeeming social importance . . . It has

Adult book stores, such as this one, have been the battlefield for many local communities. Although the Supreme Court has ruled that it is unconstitutional to ban them, zoning ordinances restricting them to certain areas is permissible.

been well observed that such utterances are no essential part of any exposition of ideas, and are of such slight social value as a step to truth that any benefit that may be derived from them is clearly outweighed by the social interest in order and morality. . . . We hold that obscenity is not within the area of constitutionally protected speech or press."[53] Chief Justice Earl Warren believed that precisely defining obscenity was "the Court's must difficult area of adjudication. What is 'obscenity' to some is mere 'realism' to others; what is 'lascivious' in the eyes of one reader is merely 'colorful' in those of another; what is 'lewd' to one parent may well be 'instructive' to another."[54] In *Miller v California* (1973), the United States Supreme Court ruled that actions or objects can be deemed obscene only if they meet all three of the following criteria:

1. Whether the average person, applying contemporary community standards, would find that the work taken as a whole, appeals to the prurient interest.

2. Whether the work depicts or describes, in a patently offensive way, sexual conduct specifically defined by the applicable state law.

3. Whether the work taken as a whole, lacks serious literary, artistic, political or scientific value.[55]

Reasonable restrictions tell us that the personal possession of obscene materials by an adult is a protected right. However, the sale and distribution of sexually explicit materials to minors are a crime. Child pornography is a crime. Erotic dancing by an adult, however, is a form of expression legally protected by the First Amendment. Basically for the majority of the obscenity cases argued in the nation's courts, the distinction between legal and illegal activities is determined primarily by the age of the participating parties.

Freedom of the Press

A free press is essential to democratic governments. Citizens do have the right to know what their government is or is not doing. The United States Supreme Court has protected the sanctity of the fourth estate, the press. In 1931, the Supreme Court established the boundary line of "**no prior restraint**" in its decision in *Near v Minnesota* The editor of the *Saturday Press,* Jay Near, was well known for using his paper to express his "anti-Semitic, anti-Catholic, anti-labor, and anti-black viewpoints. In addition, in a series of articles, Near charged that Minneapolis police and prosecutors were in collusion with Jewish gangsters involved in gambling, bootlegging, and racketeering.[56] The county attorney decided to "stop the presses" by accusing Near of being in violation of a Minnesota public nuisance law prohibiting the publishing of materials deemed to be "malicious, scandalous and defamatory."[57] Ruling in favor of Near, the Supreme Court's decision mandated that the only time government can legally bar the press from publishing a story is when such an action poses a real and eminent threat to national security. For example, it would have been a threat to national security for the press to publish in advance the exact date and time of the dropping of nuclear bombs on Japan during World War II or to divulge the schedule for sending scud missiles into Iraq during the Gulf War. It is not a breach of national security to publish information about these activities after the fact.

The concept of no prior restraint was held to close scrutiny when the United States Supreme Court heard arguments in *New York Times v United States* (1971). The case centered on the actions of Daniel Ellsberg, a temporary federal employee who discovered a cache of secret government documents detailing the coverup by the federal government regarding the United States' initial entry into the Vietnam conflict. Ellsberg was a trusted ally to the paper's reporters since he occasionally provided background information for storylines. Ellsberg voluntarily offered the seized documents to the *New York Times* and the *Washington Post.* After publishing the first excerpts from the documents, both newspapers were placed under federal court ordered injunctions to stop the presses. The federal government claimed that publishing these sensitive documents presented a threat to national security, even though the United States was heavily involved in the Vietnam conflict.

The United States Supreme Court ruled against the federal government's actions. Justice Black credited the papers' bold actions to print the documents by stating, "in my view, far from deserving condemnation for their courageous reporting, the *New York Times,* the *Washington Post*, and other newspapers should be commended for serving the purpose that the framers saw so clearly. In revealing the workings of government that led to the Vietnam War, the newspapers nobly did precisely that which the Founders [Framers] hoped and trusted they would do."[58] The Supreme Court also decided that the purported threat to national security was non-existent since the event had already happened. Ellsberg, however, still suffered the consequences of his actions by being convicted of stealing government documents. Although we may not always agree with the articles published in our daily newspapers or aired on the television and radio waves, any action towards censorship is viewed by the majority of Americans as a violation of freedom of the press.

Although the First Amendment initially extended constitutional protections to the print media, the rise of the electronic media to include television, cable, and internet accessibility has expanded the application of "freedom of the press." Established in 1934, the **Federal Communications Commission (FCC)** sets the programming and broadcasting guidelines for the majority of the nation's television and radio stations. In 1996, Congress passed the **Telecommunications Act** requiring cable stations that did not abide by the FCC's programming guidelines for airing sexually explicit programs only at late-night hours to completely block out their signal to protect children from watching these programs. In a 5 to 4 decision, the United States Supreme Court ruled that the Telecommunications Act was an unconstitutional infringement upon the stations' protected First Amendment rights to freedom of expression and press. In 1997, the Supreme Court ruled that the **Communications Decency Act** was an unconstitutional infringement upon users of the internet. The act banned the electronic transmission of any materials deemed indecent to minors. "This was the first time that the highest court had contemplated the status of the key medium of the next century. Instead of regarding the Net with caution the court usually shows while exploring new frontiers, the justices went out of their way to assure that this most democratic of mediums would receive the highest level of protection. Internet speakers will not be shackled with the regulations that limit content on television and radio; instead, they will enjoy the freedom granted to printed matter."[59]

Dr. Daniel Ellsberg, antiwar activist who was arrested for releasing the secret "Pentagon Papers," holds an impromptu news conference outside a federal building in Boston while his wife, Patricia, waits behind him. Daniel Ellsberg was indicted for espionage, theft, and conspiracy. His case was dismissed on the grounds of government misconduct.

Assembly and Association

A basic civil liberty granted to all American citizens is the right to associate with others and to assemble or to join their ranks if we so choose to do so. The freedom of association is just as important to a free society as the freedoms of speech, redress, and religion. Our history, however, has been severely tainted by the actions of racial supremacy groups, such as the Klan, skinhead groups, the American Nazi Party, and so on. Periodically, the United States Congress has tried to limit the scope of these organizations by holding individual members accountable for criminal actions spurned by their affiliations with these groups. These congressional acts, however, are oftentimes in direct conflict with the original intentions of the framers. The authors of the Bill of Rights never intended for governing authorities at any level to legislate whether citizens could affiliate with certain groups deemed in conflict with our nation's fundamental principles. Sanctioning membership in the local PTA while arresting an individual for joining a white supremacist group is unconstitutional. In addition, the entire membership of a group cannot be held criminally liable when the actions of one of its members results in a criminal act. Once again, it is the United States Supreme Court through its right of judicial review that has applied reasonable restrictions to the rights of assembly and association.

In 1969, the United States Supreme Court heard arguments in ***Brandenburg v. Ohio,*** a landmark case that set the stage for subsequent rulings in assembly-related cases. Charles Brandenburg, leader of a local Ku Klux Klan (KKK) chapter, invited a television station to film several Klan rallies. The films contained excepts from his speech in which he stated that "if our president, our Congress, our Supreme Court, continues to suppress the white, Caucasian race, it's possible that there might have to be some revengence taken."[60] No violent action resulted from his speech. Brandenburg, however, was arrested and convicted of violating Ohio's Criminal Syndicalism Act, prohibiting the advocacy of terrorism. The United States Supreme Court overturned Brandenburg's conviction because the Ohio statute was designed "to punish mere advocacy and to forbid on pain of criminal punishment, assembly with others merely to advocate the described type of action. Such a statute falls within the condemnation of the First and Fourteenth Amendments."[61]

The price of free society! The Court has ruled that the constitutional right to free speech and assembly apply to all citizens regardless of how offensive their beliefs might be to the majority.

Antiwar demonstrations can be well attended and quite vocal.

The question of assembly arose once again in 1978 with the emotionally charged case, *Village of Skokie v National Socialist Party.* The National Socialist Party, also known as the American Nazi Party, wanted to hold a public march through the predominately Jewish suburb of Skokie, Illinois. Since the majority of the suburb's residents were either survivors or had lost relatives in the Nazi concentration camps of World War II, they were furious and petitioned their city council to deny the group a parade permit. Denied the permit, the Nazi Party filed a challenge on the grounds that their First Amendment rights had been violated. The Illinois state courts refused to allow the march on the grounds that it might create a clear and present danger to the residents of Skokie. The United States Supreme Court reversed all lower court rulings on the grounds that a mere presumption of violence is not a valid reason to deny the group's constitutional right to march. In this particular case, the jurists thought that the "use of the swastika is a symbolic form of speech entitled to First Amendment protection. Its display on uniforms or banners by those engaged in peaceful demonstrations cannot be totally precluded solely because that display may provide a violent reaction by those who view it. Particularly this is true where, as here, there has been advanced notice by the demonstrators of their plans so that they have become, as the complaint alleges, 'common knowledge' and those to whom sight of the swastika banner on uniforms would be offensive are forewarned and need not view them."[62] This decision was a reasonable restriction accommodating to both parties. Although the Nazi Party decided to bypass Skokie and march through downtown Chicago, they retained their constitutional right to stage a public march as long as they applied for the proper permits. For those who would have been offended by the message of the marchers, their protected rights not to watch the march were preserved!

The rise of teenage gangs has prompted municipal governments across the country to implement curfew laws designed to restrict teenagers' accessibility to gang-related activities. These city ordinances mandate that unsupervised juveniles cannot be allowed on city streets after a predetermined time period. In 1999, the United States Supreme Court essentially gave municipal governments a green light to continue curfew laws. The same court, however, ruled that an anti-gang ordinance crafted by the Chicago, Illinois, city council was unconstitutional. Enacted in 1992, the ordinance allowed the Chicago police to disperse and/or arrest individuals "if they stood or sat around in one place with no apparent purpose in the presence of a suspected gang member."[63] Over a three-year period, the Chicago police used this ordinance to arrest approximately 43,000 individuals subjected to a maximum fine of $500 and six months in the city jail. In *Chicago v Morales*, the United States Supreme Court ruled 6 to 3 that this ordinance was a violation of the First Amendment's right to association and assembly. Writing in support of the majority, Justice John Paul Stevens noted that "the ordinance allowed the police to order people to move on without inquiring into their reasons for remaining in one place. . . It matters not whether the reason that a gang member and his father, for example, loiter near Wrigley Field is to rob an unsuspecting fan or just to get a glimpse of Sammy Sosa leaving the ballpark. Friends, relatives, teachers, counselors, or even total strangers might unwittingly engage in forbidden loitering if they happen to engage in idle conversation with a gang member."[64] The Supreme Court further ruled that the vagueness of the Chicago city ordinance posed both substantive and procedural due process problems by giving the police too much discretion in predetermining the intent of those individuals participating in a sidewalk gathering.

Protecting the Rights of the Accused

The American judicial system artfully created by the framers is firmly based on the **adversary system** whereby the accused is innocent until proven guilty. The burden of proof is placed squarely on the shoulders of the prosecution who must establish beyond a **reasonable doubt** that the accused did indeed commit a crime. Regardless of the severity of the crime, the accused has the same protected civil liberties as any other American citizen, until the accused has been declared guilty by a jury of his peers. "The Constitution strongly emphasizes the protection of rights of defendants in the criminal process. The original document contains no fewer than seven provisions specifically addressed to this matter—these are in keeping with the Founder's [Framers] concern to protect minorities (in this case, unpopular defendants) from the tyrannical excesses of an aggrieved or outraged majority . . . . The Bill of Rights places an even greater stress on criminal procedure. Of the twenty-three separate rights enumerated in the first eight amendments, thirteen relate to the treatment of criminal defendants."[65] The protection of the rights of the accused was needed to reverse the historical pattern governments used to abuse its citizens. The history of Europe is tainted by arbitrary arrests, imprisonment without benefit of trial, horrific punishment methods, and so on. The framers realized that citizens should be protected from criminals. However, even criminals, particularly those *accused* of a criminal action, should be treated in a humane and fair manner.

The initial problem was applicability of those amendments relating to the accused on state criminal laws. The states were charged with establishing their own criminal procedures. Article III of the United States Constitution gave the federal court system extremely limited original jurisdiction in both criminal and civil matters. Despite the passage of the Fourteenth Amendment's provision of due process and equal protection, the United States Supreme Court was extremely reluctant to require the states to incorporate protections for the accused as detailed in the Bill of Rights into their state judicial procedures. "In its earliest interpretation of the Fourteenth Amendment, the famous *Slaughterhouse Cases* of 1873, the Supreme Court reaffirmed Marshall's opinion in *Barron* that the guarantees in the Bill of Rights and the Fourteenth Amendment were not construed to apply to the states."[66] However, the Supreme Court opted for selective incorporation of pretrial rights. The landmark case cementing the states to compliance with the "fundamental rights" guaranteed in the Bill of Rights was *Palko v Connecticut* (1937).

Frank Palko was originally indicted and tried on a first-degree murder charge. However, the jury found Palko guilty of a second-degree murder charge and gave him a life sentence without parole possibilities. The state appealed the decision to the Connecticut Supreme Court of Errors. This court subsequently overturned the original decision and ordered a new trial. Palko was tried again on a first-degree murder charge, convicted, and handed the death sentence. Palko petitioned the United States Supreme Court to overturn his latest conviction as a violation of the Fifth Amendment's protection against double jeopardy and the Fourteenth Amendment's guarantee of due process. The Supreme Court ruled against Palko. However, Justice Benjamin Cardozo's "carefully crafted opinion has long been regarded as a catalyst in the nationalization of the rights of the accused, as it established categorically that the states were obligated to the fundamental imperatives of the Bill of Rights through the Fourteenth Amendment. Cardozo distinguished rights that are fundamental—the very essence of a scheme of ordered liberty—from rights that are not quite so fundamental . . . . Fundamental rights must always be applied to the states, whereas, others may be applied to the states only when state action violates the due process clause of the Fourteenth Amendment."[67] Subsequent Supreme Court rulings conform with Cardozo's position.

The framers firmly believed that no one should be arbitrarily arrested and allowed to waste away in prison without knowing the charges against them. A guaranteed constitutional right, a *writ of Habeas Corpus* is "an order to an incarcerating official to bring a person held in custody before the court to determine if the person is being held lawfully."[68] Basically, the accused is brought before a judge or magistrate within a short time after arrest. The accused and the presiding court official are informed of the charges against the accused by the arresting officer. The accused is then given the opportunity to explain his/her actions. If the presiding court official finds the arresting officer's actions valid, the accused will be held for further confinement or granted bail options. If the arresting officer does not provide a valid reason for the arrest, the presiding court official will release the accused.

The question of whether accused persons can waive their constitutionally protected rights to self-incrimination even though the accused is unaware of their rights in the first place was addressed by the United States Supreme Court in *Miranda v Arizona* (1966). Ernesto Miranda was arrested and questioned about the kidnapping and rape of an eighteen-year-old girl. During interrogation, Miranda signed a confession with a statement waving his constitutional protection against self-incrimination. However, Miranda did not understand or had prior knowledge of the United States Constitution, the Bill of Rights, or his protected rights. Miranda did not even speak English fluently. The arresting officers argued that they assumed Miranda was aware of his protected right to remain silent and voluntarily waived that right. The confession was admitted as evidence during the trial. Miranda was convicted and sentenced to twenty to thirty years in prison. The United States Supreme Court ruled 5 to 4 that Miranda's rights had been violated. Chief Justice Earl

Warren "made it clear that the prosecution may not use a statement against the accused elicited during custodial interrogation 'unless it demonstrates the use of effective safeguards to secure' his or her constitutional rights, and they must be made known to the accused. Interrogation could proceed if the accused 'voluntarily, knowingly, and intelligently' makes a waiver of the rights to which he or she is entitled."[69] The Supreme Court mandated that law enforcement verbally apprised an arrested suspect of the following rights prior to questioning:

1. He must be told he has the right to stay silent.
2. He must be told anything he says may be used against him in court.
3. He must be told he has the right to have an attorney with him before any questioning begins.
4. He must be told that, if he wants an attorney but cannot afford one, an attorney will be provided for him free.
5. If, after being told this, an arrested suspect says he does not want a lawyer and is willing to be questioned, he may be, provided he reached his decision "knowingly and intelligently."
6. If, after being told all his rights, a suspect agrees to be questioned, he can shut off the questions any time after they have started, whether or not he has an attorney with him.[70]

In addition, law enforcement must operate on a more than reasonable assumption that the accused understands English. If not, the arresting officers should postpone questioning until an interpreter can be present. Once these warnings are given, the accused may opt to stop answering questions at any time; halt an interrogation until legal representation is present; or voluntarily waive his rights.

The *Miranda* case was revisited by the United States Supreme Court in a case questioning whether a section of a federal anti-crime law, allowing voluntary confessions without benefit of *Miranda* protections, could be used as evidence during a trial. The Supreme Court reaffirmed the necessity of *Miranda* in a 7 to 2 decision. Chief Justice William Rehnquist commented that "*Miranda* announced a constitutional rule that Congress may not supersede legislatively. We decline to overrule *Miranda* ourselves. *Miranda* has become embedded in routine police practice to the point where the warnings have become part of our national culture."[71]

The Fourth Amendment protects citizens from unreasonable searches and seizures. The English concept that a "man's home is his castle" was first addressed in the Magna Carta. In 1763, William Pitt declared before the British Parliament that "the poorest man may, in his cottage, bid defiance to all the forces of the Crown. It may be frail; its roof may shake; the wind may blow through it; the storm may enter, the rain may enter, but the King of England may not enter; all his force does not cross the threshold of the ruined tenement."[72] Despite the reassuring words of Pitt, the Crown continued to conduct invasive searches through the use of general warrants. These search documents were issued without probable cause, allowing English custom agents to seize whatever they deemed of value to compensate for delinquent taxes. In the American colonies, the **Townshend Acts** of 1767 granted colonial courts the power to use general warrants. At a 1772 Boston Town Meeting, colonists complained that:

"Thus our houses and even our bed chambers, are exposed to be ransacked, our boxes, chests and trunks broke open, ravaged and plundered by wretches, whom no prudent man would venture to employ even as menial servants; whenever they are please to say they suspect there are in the house wares for which the duties have not been paid. Flagrant instances of the wanton exercise of this power have frequently happened in this and other sea port towns. By this we are cut off from that domestic security which renders the lives of the most unhappy in some measure agreeable. Those Officers may under colour of law and the cloak of a general warrant break thro' the sacred rights of the domicil, ransack mens houses, destroy their securities, carry off their property, and with little danger to themselves commit the most horred murders."[73]

After declaring their independence from England, several of the newly formed states addressed the issue of searches and seizures in their state constitutions. These documents outlawed the use of general warrants, opting instead for courts to issue specific warrants detailing both the items subjected to the search and possible seizure, as well as the rationale for the search. For example, the tenth article of the 1776 Pennsylvania constitution states "that the people have a right to hold themselves, their houses, papers and possessions free from search and seizure, and therefore, warrants without oaths or affirmations first made, affording a sufficient foundation for them, and whereby any officer or messenger may be commanded or required to search suspected places, or to seize any person or persons, his or their property, not particularly described are contrary to that right, and ought not to be granted."[74] Consequently the framers used the guidelines established in these early state constitutions when they penned the Fourth Amendment to the United States Constitution.

Although Americans fear rising crime and demand swift action against violators, the United States Supreme Court has exercised reasonable restrictions in delineating proper from improper searches and seizures, and the effects a search has on the fate of the accused. "As far back as 1886, in *Boyd v United States*, the Court in effect, tied the Fourth Amendment to the Fifth Amendment's self-incrimination provision, indicating that the two 'run almost into each other.' An unreasonable search and seizure, the Court felt, is in reality a 'compulsory extortion' of evidence that could result in compulsory self-incrimination."[75] The key to understanding the logic of the Supreme Court's rulings rests with the interpretation of probable cause and the application of the exclusionary rule.

Under normal circumstances, police officers should obtain a search warrant issued by a magistrate prior to conducting the search. Officers must demonstrate **probable cause**, that is, a reasonable assumption that a crime has or will be committed. The suspicion of the execution of a criminal act compels the search and possible seizure of evidence. A proper warrant must describe the places to be searched and the items to be seized. The **exclusionary rule** means "that evidence which is otherwise admissible may not be used in a criminal trial if it is a product of illegal police conduct."[76] One of the landmark cases tying probable cause to the exclusionary rule is *Mapp v Ohio* (1961).

In May 1957, three Cleveland police officers arrived at Dollree Mapp's residence after receiving a tip that she was harboring a wanted fugitive. After twice refusing to admit the police without a search warrant, the officers forcibly gained entry, physically assaulted her, and handcuffed her. The search did not produce the sought after fugitive. However, Mapp was arrested and subsequently convicted of possession of the obscene materials the officers seized during their search. The United States Supreme Court overturned Mapp's conviction. Speaking for the majority, Justice Tom C. Clark wrote that "all evidence obtained by searches and seizures in violation of the Constitution is, by that same authority [Amendment Four], inadmissible in a state court and since the Fourth Amendment's right of privacy has been declared enforceable against the States through the Due Process Clause of the Fourteenth, it is enforceable against them by the same sanction of exclusion as is used against the Federal Government."[77] Since its initial ruling, the Supreme Court has revisited several of the issues raised by the *Mapp* case, particularly involving permission to enter, unannounced entries, and searches conducted without a warrant. In a 5-4 decision, the Court recently ruled that "yes, the so-called knock-and-announce rule is violated when police fail to announce their presence and wait a reasonable amount of time before entering someone's home and what they find once they're inside. But no, that violation isn't sufficiently related to what they find during a search to justify banning drugs, guns or any other evidence that's uncovered from later criminal proceedings."[78] The Court also ruled that police officers after viewing a violent melee through a window did not need a warrant to enter the residence to break up the fight. Chief Justice John Roberts wrote: "the role of a peace officer includes preventing violence and restoring order, not simply rendering first aid to casualties; an officer is not like a boxing (or hockey) referee, poised to stop a bout only if it becomes too one-sided."[79] The question over consent to search without a warrant resulted in a 5-3 decision in favor of the homeowner. Initially, the police were granted permission by one of the residents, only to have the other resident refuse. "A warrantless search of a shared dwelling for evidence over the express refusal of consent by a physically present resident cannot be justified as reasonable."[80]

The Court has heard numerous cases involving searches and seizures conducted outside the protection of a person's home. For example, Steven Dewayne Bond was a passenger on a Grayhound Bus that was stopped at an immigration checkpoint in California. A random squeezing of his luggage convinced agents that Bond was carrying controlled substances. Upon opening the bag, the agents discovered a package of methamphetamine. Bond was subsequently convicted of drug possession. Bond's attorneys argued that the random squeezing of the luggage constituted an illegal search and seizure. The Supreme Court concurred. The Supreme Court dealt another blow to law enforcement ruling that police officers cannot search people and their vehicles after issuing a routine traffic citation. Local police officers in Iowa searched Patrick Knowles' car after he was given a traffic ticket. The search of the vehicle revealed that Knowles was carrying marijuana. Although recognizing the necessity for searching suspects after their arrests for dangerous weapons, the Supreme Court ruled that in this situation, no arrest occurred, therefore, the search was illegal. Therefore, "absent probable cause and/or a warrant, police may not conduct a full-blown search of motorists and their vehicles after pulling them over and ticketing them for speeding or other minor traffic violations."[81] The United States Supreme Court has oftentimes ruled on the side of law enforcement. During its 2004-2005 session, the Court ruled that during routine traffic violation stops, law enforcement could legally use drug-sniffing dogs to detect possible possession of illegal substances. In support of the Court's 6-2 decision, Justice Paul Stevens wrote that "a dog sniff conducted during a concededly lawful traffic stop that reveals no information other than the location of a substance that no individual has any right to possess does not violate the Fourth Amendment."[82]

The United States Supreme Court also has taken a dim view of law enforcement inviting television crews and journalists to come along for the ride. "In a 1999 unanimous decision, the Court curbed 'ride along' practices by ruling that police can be sued for letting reports and photographers accompany them on raids of private homes."[83] Chief Justice Rehnquist ruled that these searches violated both the Fourth Amendment's prohibition against unreasonable searches and seizures as well as "the centuries-old principle of respect for the privacy of the home."[84] The police can continue to invite members of the press to observe arrests and searches. However, the media cannot enter the suspect's residence.

The right to counsel is guaranteed by the Sixth Amendment. However, not every person accused of a criminal action can afford an attorney nor are they guaranteed that their legal representation will provide an adequate defense. The United States Supreme Court addressed the issue of court appointed legal representation in capital criminal cases in *Powell v Alabama* (1932). Powell and six other African-American youths were arrested, indicted, tried, and given the death penalty for the rape of two Anglo women. The trials began six days after their arrests with two tried at a time in proceedings lasting only a day. The Supreme Court ruled overwhelmingly that all of the defendants were blatantly denied their rights of due process and equal protection of the law because: "(1) they [the defendants] were not given fair, impartial and deliberate trials; (2) they were denied the right of counsel, with the accustomed incidents of consultation and opportunity of preparation of trial; and (3) they were tried before juries from which qualified members of their own race were systematically excluded."[85] Lacking financial resources, the defendants were provided court-appointed attorneys on the day of their trials. Echoing the sentiments of his fellow justices, Justice Sutherland wrote that "in light of the facts—the ignorance and illiteracy of the defendants, their youth, the circumstances of public hostility, the imprisonment and close surveillance of the defendants by the military forces, the fact that their friends and families were all in other states and communication with them necessarily difficult, and above all, that they stood in deadly peril of their lives—we think the failure of the trial court to give them reasonable time and opportunity to secure counsel was a clear denial of due process."[86]

In *Escobedo v Illinois* (1964), the question before the United Sates Supreme Court was whether legal representation should be present during the interrogation of the defendant by law enforcement officials. Danny Escobedo and three others were arrested for the fatal shooting of his brother-in-law. Initially, Escobedo was released after fourteen and a half hours of questioning without the presence of legal representation. Escobedo was rearrested, and despite the requests of both the defendant and his lawyer, legal representation was not present during that interrogation period. Consequently, Escobedo did make incriminating statements that led to his indictment and conviction. Escobedo petitioned the United States Supreme Court to overturn his conviction on the belief that his Sixth Amendment right to counsel had been violated. "Justice Arthur Goldberg's opinion for the majority stressed the need for counsel when the police action shifts from the investigatory to the accusatory stage, that is, when the focus is directed on the accused and the purpose of interrogation is to elicit a confession."[87] The Supreme Court overturned Escobedo's conviction.

One of the most high profile cases heard by the United States Supreme Court was *Gideon v Wainwright* (1963). Clarence Gideon was arrested for burglarizing a pool hall. Gideon could not afford to hire an attorney. His plea for a court appointed attorney was denied since the Florida courts granted these requests only to defendants accused of capital criminal charges. Gideon pleaded not guilty, conducted his own defense, and, of course, was found guilty. From his prison cell, Gideon submitted to the United States Supreme Court one of the rarely accepted hand-written briefs. The Supreme Court overturned Gideon's conviction. The decision in this case "extended the absolute right of indigents to have counsel assigned in all criminal cases—save those involving certain misdemeanors—by making the Sixth Amendment's requirements of the Assistance of Counsel obligatory upon the states via the due process of the law clause of the Fourteenth Amendment."[88] Gideon was retried and acquitted.

Unfortunately, few states have implemented effective indigent-defense programs. "More than 40 years after the Supreme Court ruled that competent counsel was a fundamental right of all Americans accused of crimes, the American Bar Association says thousands of indigent defendants still navigate the court system each year without a lawyer, or with one who doesn't have the time, resources, or interest to provide effective representation."[89] Consequently "some poor defendants serve jail time longer than the law requires or plead guilty to crimes they didn't commit just to get out of jail. A few receive the death penalty or life in prison because their court-appointed lawyers were incompetent, lazy, or both."[90] Without federal funding, state and county governments are left to their own devises in appointing local attorneys to represent the poor.

American society is still debating whether the death penalty is a violation of the Eighth Amendment's prohibition against cruel and unusual punishment. After winning independence, the states created penitentiaries as viable substitutes to punish violent criminals. Michigan and Wisconsin abolished the death penalty in the 1840s while other states restricted its use and banned public executions. Today the death penalty is just as controversial as it was in the eighteenth century. The United States Supreme Court has vacillated over the appropriateness of the death penalty. In 1972, the Court ruled in *Furman v Georgia* that the use of the death penalty in this particular case was a violation of the Fourteenth Amendment. "Although the Court never decided that execution was necessarily cruel and unusual punishment, the justices outlawed mandatory death sentences and approved a two stage process for capital cases, with guilt determined first and

The gas chamber of San Quentin Prison was hermetically sealed by twisting the wheel affixed to the iron door. The executioner stood by the lever at the upper right, looking into the gas chamber through blinds slanted so that he could see the victim but the victim could not see him.

punishment fixed later by predetermined standards."[91] The *Furman* decision promoted states to reevaluate their capital punishment laws and resulted in a virtual moratorium of the death penalty. The Court reversed its decision against the use of the death penalty in 1976, giving the green light for states to reintroduce the use of capital punishment. The number of executions rose dramatically. Recent death penalty related decisions rendered by both the federal district courts and the Supreme Court indicate a change in prospective once again towards restricting the use of capital punishment. U.S. District Judge Jed Rakoff declared the 1994 Death Penalty Act unconstitutional. His ruling effectively halted the use of the death penalty in federal cases. The judge's ruling was based on the fact "that the best available evidence indicates that on one hand, innocent people are sentenced to death with materially greater frequency than was previously supposed and that, on the other hand, convincing proof of their innocence often does not emerge until long after the convictions."[92] Although the Supreme Court has not once again declared the death penalty unconstitutional, three of its most recent decisions placed limitations on its use. In a 6-3, the Court ruled that the execution of mentally handicapped inmates was an unconstitutional violation of the Eighth Amendment's prohibition against cruel and unusual punishment. During its 2002 session, the jurists ruled that juries, not judges, must determine whether a convicted murderer should receive the death penalty. Affirming the 7-2 decision, Justice Ruth Bader Ginsburg stated that "the Constitution guarantees a trial by jury, and that right extends to weighing whether a particular killing merits death or life in prison."[93] In 2005, the Supreme Court ruled in a 5-4 decision that the execution of juveniles was indeed cruel and unusual punishment. In support of the majority opinion, Justice Anthony Kennedy wrote: "The . . . national consensus here—the rejection of the juvenile death penalty in the majority of the states; the infrequency of its use even where it remains on the books; and the consistency in the trend toward abolition of the practice—provide sufficient evidence that today our society view juveniles, in the words . . . used respecting the mentally re-

Former Governor George Ryan (R. IL) (left) and Senator Dick Durbin (D. IL) (right) at a news conference. On Saturday, Jan. 11, 2003, Former Gov. George Ryan cleared Illinois' death row, commuting 167 condemned inmates' sentences in the broadest attack at the death penalty in decades. Ryan's decision came three years after he temporarily halted state executions to examine the system's fairness. George Ryan said, "I had to act. Our capital system is haunted by the demon of error—error in determining guilty, and error in determining who among the guilty deserves to die."

tarded as 'categorically less culpable than the average criminal.' Once the diminished culpability of juveniles is recognized, it is evident that the penological justifications for the death penalty apply to them with lesser force than to adults. The age of 18 is the point where society draws the line for many purposes between childhood and adulthood. It is, we conclude, the age at which the line for death eligibility ought to rest."[94] In 2006, the Supreme Court opened the door for death row inmates to challenge their sentences through DNA testing. Calling for a new trial, Justice Kennedy wrote "that the DNA evidence, combined with other errors in the case, made it quite probably that [Paul Gregory] House could convince jurors of his innocence" of committing a murder that happened twenty years ago.[95]

While the debate continues over the use of the death penalty, violent crimes continue to plague the nation's cities. Several states have opted to impose longer prison terms without the possibility of parole in hopes the knowledge of spending years and years in prison will be an effective deterrent to committing a criminal act. President Clinton introduced the concept of "three strikes and your out" mandating that an individual convicted of a third felony would receive an automatic life prison sentence, regardless of the nature of the crime. Clinton also signed the "Aimee's Law" whereby "a murderer, child molester or rapist released before serving 85 percent of his or her sentence, or before his or her jail term passes the national average for the offense, then commits the same crime in a different state, the original jailing state will have to pay for the new investigation and incarceration with its federal crime funds."[96] During its 2004-2005 session, the United States Supreme Court gave judges more latitude in determining sentencing options when it ruled the Sentencing Reform Act unconstitutional. Passed by Congress twenty years ago, this act established mandatory sentencing guidelines. Basically, "judges could increase or decrease the prescribed sentences because of aggravating or mitigating factors—a gun was used in the crime, for example, or the defendant served in the military—but they didn't have much flexibility. And with prosecutors allowed to preset evidence at sentencing that they didn't have to put forward at trial, defendants had even less leverage."[97] Now, federal judges will be able judge on their own without the influence of the United States Congress whether or not the circumstances involved in the commission of a felony merits a stiffer sentence.

The appeals process has also been revisited with several states enacting laws limiting the accessibility of the convicted to the court system. In the past, those convicted of a crime in a state court could seek a direct appeal to a federal court if that individual received the death penalty or could demonstrate that his/her constitutionally protected rights were violated at some point from arrest to conviction. In 1999, the United States Supreme Court ruled 6 to 3 that those convicted of crimes in state courts must initiate their appeals at the state-court level. "Writing for the majority, Justice Sandra Day O'Connor said that as long as a state has given its supreme court the choice to review a case, federal courts should require state inmates make use of the available process to give the state court a chance to exercise its discretionary jurisdiction."[98] The inmate still has the option to begin the appeal process at the federal court level only if the state courts refuse to hear the case. United States Supreme Court justices further restricted the appeals process to death row inmates. The issue involved a provision of the Anti-Terrorism and Effective Death Penalty Act that shorten the time between conviction and execution. In a 5 to 4 decision, Justice O'Connor stated that "the law requires a hands-off approach by federal judges unless a state court clearly is wrong about some

Supreme Court precedent or unreasonably applies that principle to the facts of the prisoner's case."[99] The Supreme Court sent a clear message that defense attorneys can use the federal courts only if the state court system has clearly violated the constitutional rights of the accused. "This decision makes clear that the *writ of habeas corpus* is not to be used as a device to go judge-shopping, running the same marginal claims past multiple sets of judges."[100]

The Sixth Amendment to the United States Constitution entitles those accused of committing a criminal offense to be judged by a jury of one's peers. The majority of the nation's state and federal courts select twelve members from a panel of potential jurors. These individuals are charged with weighing the evidence and, subsequently, rendering a verdict of guilt or innocence. The concept of the jury system emerged in England after the Norman invasion. Determining the method of proving one's guilt or innocence has taken numerous avenues. Prior to the arrival of William the Conqueror, "under Saxon law, if you could carry several pounds of glowing red-hot iron in your bare hands for nine steps or walk barefoot over nine red-hot plowshares without getting any blisters, you were not guilty. . . In Britain, Africa and parts of Asia, plunging your arm into boiling water, oil or lead without the usual results proved your innocence. Water was also knowledgeable stuff. The innocent sank; the guilty floated and could be fished and dealt with."[101] In some instances, the Saxons dismissed the hot irons and opted for a rudimentary jury composed of twelve people. The practice of the twelve-member jury is credited to Morgan of Glamorgan, Prince of Wales. In 725 A.D., he wrote: "For as Christ and his Twelve Apostles were finally to judge the world, so human tribunals should be composed of the king and twelve wise men."[102] The jury system, however, has posed serious questions as to whether a panel of twelve can be a truly fair and impartial group capable of rendering a decision based solely on the evidence presented during the trial without injecting their own biases and emotions into their deliberations.

The rulings of the United States Supreme Court have upheld and preserved the rights of the accused. Both state and federal courts have been more inclined to grant **changes of venue** for high profile cases to ensure a fair trial for the accused. The federal trial of those accused of the tragic bombing of the federal building in Oklahoma City was moved to another federal district court. The judge believed that finding a fair and impartial jury in the Oklahoma district was an impossible task. The O. J. Simpson murder trial revealed the problems of jury selection and sequestering juries for long periods of time.

Protection of Property and Privacy

In *Democracy in America*, Alexis de Tocqueville observed that "in no other country in the world is the love of property keener or more alert than in the United States and nowhere else does the majority display less inclination toward doctrines which in any way threaten the way property is owned."[103] Once again, the framers desired to reverse the historical patterns of governments using arbitrary measures to seize private property for political purposes. The Articles of Confederation failed miserably to protect the rights of property owners to transact their business without undo interference from individual state governments. It was the business community and property owners that compelled the framers to meet in Philadelphia in the first place. Consequently, the framers created a document that specifically granted constitutional protections for the right to own, use, rent, invest, and contract for property with the minimal interjection of government. After all, the free enterprise system is based on the concept of private property ownership.

Article I, Section 10 of the United States Constitution prohibits the states from passing any laws that impair the obligation of contracts. Known as the **Contract Clause**, this provision was designed to prevent state governments from passing laws that would expand a debtor's right not to pay an obligation or to back out of a contractual agreement. However, the Constitution did not give property owners the exclusive right to do whatever they wanted to do with their property. Property ownership and property rights evoke the classic struggle of the individual or private needs against the collective good of the community or public needs. It has been the task of state and federal courts under the guidance of the United States Supreme Court that have selectively applied the concept of reasonable restrictions to property issues.

The United States Supreme Court began gradually to restrict the exclusiveness of the contract clause in the 1880s by subjecting contracts to reasonable police powers designed to protect the health, safety, welfare, and, in some instances, the morals of the public. In ***Home Building and Loan Association v Blaisdell*** (1934), the Supreme Court ruled that contracts between two or more parties could be modified by state laws to prevent social and economic catastrophe. Subsequent rulings have upheld federal regulations ranging from worker safety standards to the proper disposal of hazardous substances by property and business owners. City and county ordinances can determine whether a home owner can paint his residence a certain color or fix the site location of sexually explicit businesses and establishments selling liquor, and so on. These actions are constitutional as long as these restrictions are not unreasonable application of police powers.

The framers also recognized the necessity for government to seize or to use private property for the collective benefit of the community or the nation. The United States Constitution specifically grants the power of **eminent domain** to the federal government. However, the property owner must receive just compensation for the loss of his/her property. The states and other subgovernmental units received the right of eminent domain through the Fourteenth Amendment. The use of reasonable restrictions is key to understanding the scope of eminent domain. Governments need privately held lands to build additional government buildings, public schools and hospitals, to expand the nation's transportation systems and airways, and so on. But, the rights of property owners must be recognized and justly compensated for their losses. During its 2006 session, the Supreme Court ruled that governments can use eminent domain to condemn lower valued residential property as blighted or a slum in order to allow a private business to develop the land into higher valued residential property such as townhouses. The Court, however, did not give the green light for every property developer by giving state governments the right to ban this practice. Several states have already enacted legislation restricting the use of eminent domain for private gain.

Privacy issues are tied directly to the Fourth Amendment's protection from unreasonable searches and seizures particularly when law enforcement enters a private residence. In ***Boyd v United States*** (1886), the United States Supreme Court decided that "the Fourth and Fourteenth Amendments extend to all invasions on the part of the [federal] government and its employees of the sanctity of a man's home and the privacies of life. It is not the breaking of his doors, the rummaging of his drawers, that constitutes the essence of the offense, but it is the invasion of his indefeasible right of personal security, personal liberty, and private property."[104] However, the Supreme Court did not address this issue seriously until technological advancements gave law enforcement the capability to use wiretapping and sophisticated surveillance tools to enhance their efforts to apprehend potential lawbreakers. In *Olmstead v United States* (1928), the Supreme Court applied reasonable restrictions to the right to privacy and gave law enforcement a boost by ruling that wiretapping was not a breach of the Fourth Amendment. At the height of the Prohibition Era, Ray Olmstead and several of his cohorts were convicted of violating the National Prohibition Act for their bootlegging activities. The federal government introduced wiretapped conversations between the defendants as their primary incriminating evidence. The Supreme Court justified its ruling against Olmstead with the rationalization that "if a person installs a telephone for the purpose of projecting his or her voice outside of the home, then the person gives up an expectation of privacy in the conversation."[105]

However, the United States Supreme Court did not give law enforcement the green light to spy on American citizens at will. In *Silverman v United States* (1961), the Supreme Court ruled that law enforcement eavesdropping on conversations in private residences through the pipes of a heating system was an unconstitutional violation of the Fourth Amendment. The use of electronic listening and recording devices in public telephone booths drew the ire of the Supreme Court. In *Katz v United States* (1967), Justice Potter Stewart wrote "that when a person enters such a booth, closes the door behind him, and pays a toll to make a call, he is entitled to assume that the words he utters into the mouthpiece will not be broadcasted to the world."[106] Corrective legislation was passed with the 1968 Omnibus Crime Control and Safe Streets Act, which granted limited use of wiretapping and bugging devices for investigative purposes. This legislation allowed warrantless use of listening devices for forty-eight hours for emerging investigations involving organized crime or threats to national security. Although subsequent legislation has expanded the use of listening devices, the courts do weigh the absence of a warrant when judging admissibility of evidence against the accused.

Privacy issues extend to a wide variety of subjects from drug testing, alternative lifestyles, reproductive freedom, and so on. However, the increased use of drugs has prompted businesses and insurance companies to push for drug-free working environments through random drug testing. Although the use of drugs is extremely detrimental to the survival of our society, some Americans believe that random blood sampling and supervised urination is a gross violation of one's dignity and an invasion of privacy. It's a basic question of protecting the rights of the individual to privacy or the intrusion into a person's lifestyle to preserve the safety of the public. In a series of decisions, the United States Supreme Court did rule that testing for drugs or alcohol by penetrating the skin is a search under the Fourth Amendment (*Terry v Ohio*, 1968), as well as the use of breathalyzer tests on suspected drunken drivers (*California v Trombetta*, 1984). Despite the cries of civil libertarians, the Rehnquist Court ruled 6-3 in favor of mandatory drug testing in *Skinner v Railway Labor Executives Association* (1989).

The United States Supreme Court could be confronted by extremely complicated privacy issues caused by advanced high-tech computer systems and breakthroughs in genetic testing. Computer hackers are capable now of accessing information about an individuals' buying habits, credit history, and medical problems. How can the average citizen protect his privacy when potentially damaging information is only an access code away? Who do you sue? The person who accessed the data in the first place or the company that gathered it and made it so readily available? Advanced genetic testing has the capability to chart a person's medical history through generational genetic patterns. Should the right to know whether you have a defective gene that will eventually give you cancer be held in strict confidence, or should it be publicly revealed to potential insurance carriers and employers? Could this information create a new form of discrimination whereby healthy individuals will be denied employment, long-term loans, and health insurance because their medical profile indicates a generational genetic pattern of heart disease?

Homeland Security and the Preservation of Civil Liberties

The American people enjoyed a vast range of personal freedoms before September 11, 2001. Basically, we went as we pleased without the fear of government intrusion into our personal lives. All of that, however, changed as those hijacked planes plunged into the towers of the World Trade Center and the Pentagon. A reasonable person understands that the government has to take extraordinary measures in the time of a threatening crisis to preserve and protect both the nation and its people. Urged by President George W. Bush, the United States Congress granted the executive branch sweeping security-related powers to apprehend those responsible for the attacks, root out domestic and foreign-based terrorist organizations, and protect this country from future attacks. The Bush administration justified its request by declaring that the nation was at war with international terrorism. A state of war does allow the national government to place extraordinary restrictions on civil liberties. As the American people, however, begin to deal with the tragedy of September 11, questions are arising about the extent of the Bush administration's efforts to curtail constitutionally guaranteed civil liberties under the guise of security-related measures. "Although couched in terms of which civil liberties will be sacrificed to keep this country safe, the conflict being waged in courts and political corridors represents a sort of national identity crisis. Americans are being asked to choose between the values that this nation has embraced since it crafted the U.S. Constitution 215 years ago."[107] Has this administration overstepped its constitutional authority by placing time-honored civil liberties in jeopardy? What role will the United States Supreme Court exercise in reversing these legislative acts? Can we return to the best of both worlds and once again become a secure nation whereby individual citizens can continue to go about their daily business as they please without government interference?

Signed into law in 2002, specific provisions of the Patriot Act gives federal agents "more leeway to wiretap phones, lets investigators track e-mail and internet connections, allows secret searches of terror suspects' property, enhances the ability of federal agencies to share data, includes legislation to fight international money laundering, and increases terror-related penalties."[108] Set to expire in 2006, several key elements of the Patriot Act were extended by Congress after several weeks of heated debate in both houses. Through an executive order, Bush approved the use of military tribunals rather than traditional judicial courts to try terrorists. "The sweeping document, patterned after similar actions taken by FDR and Abraham Lincoln, gives the government the power to try, sentence—and even execute—suspected foreign terrorists in secrecy, and under special rules that would deny them constitutional rights and allow no chance to appeal."[109]

Throughout the nation's history, the curtailment of certain civil liberties has occurred during national crises. For example, the United States Congress passed the **Smith Act** in 1940. The law made it illegal to organize or knowingly become a member of any organization that advocated by force or violence the overthrow of any agency or branch of the United States government. Primarily targeting the Communist Party and anyone sympathetic to its ideology, the Smith Act was the catalyst for the Red Scare and the era of McCarthyism that resulted in a witch hunt of anyone criticizing the government and its officials. Initially the Court endorsed the Smith Act until 1957, when justices began to realize the hypocrisy of their actions. The granting of constitutional rights to others while denying those rights to members of groups that were feared for their issues and thoughts was, in itself, an unconstitutional act. Gradually, the United States Supreme Court overturned the majority of the provisions of the Smith Act.

After suspending the *writ of habeas corpus*, President Lincoln approved the use of military tribunals for thousands of suspected traitors and Confederate captives. "In 1866, the Supreme Court took a strong stand against the use of military justice. 'The Constitution . . . is a law for rulers and people, equally in war and peace, and covers with the shield of its protection all classes of men, at all times, and under all circumstances,' the justices wrote in *Ex parte Milligan,* a decision that declared military tribunals unlawful as long as civil courts were open."[110] One hundred and forty years later, the Supreme Court once again struck down a president's use of military tribunals. Basically, the Court ruled that Bush's plan to use military tribunals to try suspected terrorists violated "U.S. military law and the Geneva Conventions. In a 5-3 ruling, the justices also rejected an effort by Congress to strip the court of jurisdiction over *habeas corpus* appeals by detainees at the prison camp in Guantanamo Bay, Cuba."[111]

Lower federal appellate courts have already challenged several of the anti-terrorist provisions enacted by the Bush administration. For example, the 6th U.S. Circuit Court of Appeals ruled against holding secret deportation hearings for those accused of being terrorists. Other U.S. District Judges have challenged the right of the Justice Department not to release the names of and the charges against individuals detained in federal prisons since September 11. After co-chairing a commission on national security issues in 1999, former U.S. Senator and one time presidential candidate Gary Hart commented that "I don't think we will reach a perfect balance between security and liberty. We haven't done it in 225 years. That's why we have courts."[112]

Meanwhile, several local communities have passed resolutions and ordinances restricting the intrusion of federal authorities into criminal activities that have usually been the exclusive jurisdiction of local law enforcement agencies. The Amherst, Massachusetts city fathers enacted a measure that orders "city personnel not to help federal or state officials in activities that could be considered in violation of civil rights or liberties."[113]

CONCLUSIONS

The framers seized the moment to craft a document suitable to a democratic government by advancing the causes of freedom, individualism, and equality. "That Constitution erected a fortification for freedom. It furnishes safeguards against ourselves, against our passions and extravagances. It set forth in a Bill of Rights those 'unalienable rights,' which no Congress, no government, no majority of the people could invade or violate."[114] The framers also created a federal court system charged with the heavy burden of defending this document from those desiring to weaken it or to deny protected rights to others. With judicial review, the Supreme Court has become the definitive authority and ultimate defender of the Constitution and the Bill of Rights. However, the preservation of freedom, individualism, and equality has not been an easy task to accomplish. "There remains intense controversy over the definition, scope, and application of these values. For one thing, in particular circumstances these values may and do collide and conflict with each other. Individualism, for example, may conflict with what many might think is necessary to safeguard the 'public interest' or to promote the 'general welfare.' Then again, suppose these values are denied by government itself (and others) to particular individuals. How and to what extent should government intervene to rectify the damage that has been done? And might such intervention itself be viewed as an encroachment upon these very values, e.g., individual freedom? These questions continue to pose a dilemma for American politics and politicians."[115]

CHAPTER NOTES

[1]"The Bill of Rights: Amendments I-X," Milton R. Konvitz, ed., *An American Primer,* Daniel J. Boorstin, ed., (Chicago, Illinois: The University of Chicago Press, 1966), 171.

[2]Ibid., 172.

[3]Gary L. McDowell, "Rights Without Roots," *The Wilson Quarterly,* (Vol. XV, No. 1, Winter, 1991), 71.

[4]Alan Barth, *The Rights of Free Men: An Essential Guide to Civil Liberties*, James E. Clayton, ed., (New York: Alfred A. Knopf, 1987), 111-112.

[5]Jay M. Shafritz, *HarperCollins Dictionary of American Government and Politics*, (New York, New York:HarperCollins Publishers, Inc., 1992), 291.

[6]Ibid., 186.

[7]Leon W. Blevins, *Texas Government in National Perspective*, (N. J.: Prentice-Hall, 1987), 221.

[8]Kermit L. Hall, "Framing the Bill of Rights," *By and For the People: Constitutional Rights in American History,*Kermit L. Hall, ed., (Ill.: Harlan-Davidson, Inc., 1991), 17.

[9]Ibid., 18.

[10]Ibid., 17.

[11]John C. Domino, *Civil Rights and Liberties: Toward the 21st Century*, (New York: HarperCollins College Publishers, Inc., 1994), 2.

[12]Henry J. Abraham and Barbara A. Perry, *Freedom & The Court: Civil Rights and Liberties in the United States,* 8th ed., (Lawrence, Kansas: The University Press of Kansas, 2003), 3-4.

[13]Lucius J. Barker and Twiley W. Barker, Jr., *Civil Liberties and the Constitution*, 6th ed., (Englewood Cliffs, N. J.: Prentice-Hall, 1990), 13.

[14]Ibid.

[15]Kermit L. Hall, "Introduction," *By and For the People: Constitutional Rights in American History*, Kermit L. Hall, ed. (Ill.: Harlan-Davidson, Inc., 1991), 8.

[16]Domino, 132.

[17]Abraham, 109.

[18]Ibid.

[19]Thomas R. Hensley, Christopher E. Smith and Joyce A. Baugh, *The Changing Supreme Court: Constitutional Rights and Liberties* (St. Paul, Minnesota: West Publishing, Co., 1997), 132.

[20]"Liberty for the Soul," *American History*, (Vol. 42, No. 1, April, 2007), 27.

[21]Hensley, 141.

[22]Ibid., 139-140.

[23]Anjetta McQueen, "Religious Schools Get Public Aid," *San Antonio Express-News* (Thursday, June 29, 2000), 12A.

[24]Gary Martin, "High Court Oks School Vouchers," *San Antonio Express-News*, (Friday, June 28, 2002), 12A.

[25]Jodie Wilgaren, "Judge Rips Vouchers for Parochial Schools," *San Antonio Express-News*, (Tuesday, December 21, 1999), 10A.

[26]Martin, "High Court Oks School Vouchers," 1A.

[27]Ibid., 12A.

[28]Abraham, 310.

[29]Hensley, 162.

[30]Ibid., 163.

[31]J. Michael Parker and Cecilia Balli, "Justices to Tackle Football Prayers," *San Antonio Express-News* (Tuesday, November 16, 1999), 1A.

[32]Terri Langford, "District Asks Supreme Court to Review School Prayer Issue," *San Antonio Express-News* (Friday, July 9, 1999), 8B.

[33]Gary Martin, "6-3 Ruling in Texas Lawsuit Criticized by Conservatives," *San Antonio Express-News* (Tuesday, June 20, 2000), 4A.

[34]Mark Helm, "Silent Nod Given to 'Silence' Law," *San Antonio Express-News*, (Tuesday, October, 30, 2001), 10A.

[35]Hensley, 164.

[36]Ibid., 206.

[37]Joan Biskupic, "Court Allows Good Friday School Closing Law," *San Antonio Express-News* (Wednesday, January 19, 2000) 8A.

[38]Richard Carelli, "Good Friday Ruled Good Day Off," *San Antonio Express-News*, (Tuesday, March 7, 2000), 5A.

[39]Domino, 87-88.

[40]Larry Gragg, "Order vs. Liberty," *American History* (Vol. XXIII, No. 4, October, 1998), 26.

[41]Ibid.

[42]Susan Welch, John Gruhl, Michael Steinman, John Comer, and Susan M. Rigdon, *American Government*, 5th ed., (St. Paul, Minn.: West Publishing Co., 1994), 450.

[43]Abraham, 178.

[44]Welch, 454.

[45]Cynthia Webb, "Court Sides with Man Over His Display of Ho Chi Minh Picture," *San Antonio Express-News* (Thursday, February 11, 1999), 8A.

[46]Abraham, 196.

[47]Domino, 47.

[48]David E. Kaplan, "The Eyes Have It," *U.S. News & World Report*, January 9, 2006, 22.

[49]Eric Lichtblau, "FBI Keeps Tabs on War Protests," *San Antonio Express-News* (Sunday, November 23, 2003), 10A.

[50]Charles Phillips, "A Day To Remember: May 4, 1970," *American History*, (Vol. 39, No. 2, June, 2004), 18.

[51]Ibid.

[52]Ralph A. Rossum and G. Alan Tarr, *American Constitutional Law: Cases and Interpretations*, (New York: St. Martin's Press, 1983), 383.

[53]Hensley, 381.

[54]Abraham, 231.

[55]Domino, 67.

[56]Hensley, 326.

[57]Ibid.

[58]Rossum, 418.

[59]Steven Levy, "On the Net Anything Goes," *Newsweek*, July 7, 1997, 28.

[60]Rossum, 397.

[61]Ibid., 398.

[62]Ibid., 418.

[63]Aaron Epstein, "Anti-Gang Loitering Ordinance Rejected," *San Antonio Express-News* (Friday, June 11, 1999), 1A.

[64]Ibid., 1A and 20A.

[65]Rossum, 469.

[66]Domino, 133-134.

[67]Ibid., 138.

[68]Hensley, 895.

[69]Barker, 263.

[70]Abraham, 142.

[71]Mark Helm, "Miranda Warning: Court Upholds 'The Right to Remain Silent,'" *San Antonio Express-News* (Tuesday, June 27, 2000), 1A.

[72]Leonard W. Levy, "Origins of the Fourth Amendment," *Political Science Quarterly*, (Vol. 114, No. 1, Spring, 1999), 80.

[73]Ibid., 92.

[74]Ibid., 93.

[75]Barker, 249.

[76]Domino, 140.

[77]Abraham, 69.

[78]Stephen Henderson, "Court Comes Down on Cops' Side," *San Antonio Express-News*, (Friday, June 16, 2006), 1A.

[79]Gina Holland, "Justices Say Cops Can Enter Homes to Stop Violence," *San Antonio Express-News*, (Tuesday, May 23, 2006), 4A.

[80]David G. Savage, "Court Slams A Door on Cops," *San Antonio Express-News*, (Thursday, March 23, 2006), 1A.

[81]Ibid., 159.

[82]Jan Crawford Greenburg, "High Court Expands Police Right to Search," *San Antonio Express-News*, (Tuesday, January 25, 2005), 1A.

[83]Abraham, 159.

[84]Laurie Asseo, "Televised Raids A Violation of Privacy Rights," *San Antonio Express-News* (May 25, 1999), 4A.

[85]Rossum, 521.

[86]Ibid., 522.

[87]Barker, 268.

[88]Abraham, 138.

[89]Kit R. Roane, "When The Poor Go To Court," *U.S. News & World Report*, January 23, 2006, 34.

[90]Ibid.

[91]Domino, 98.

[92]Delvin Barrett, "Federal Death Penalty Halted," *San Antonio Express-News*, (Tuesday, July 2, 2002), 3A.

[93]Anne Gearan, "Justices Give Jury Last Say On Executions," *San Antonio Express-News*, (Tuesday, June 25, 2002), 6A.

[94]Marco Robbins, "Justices Rule Teen Killers Can't Be Put To Death," *San Antonio Express-News*, (Wednesday, March 2, 2005), 6A.

[95]Stephen Henderson, "Killers Get New Way to Avoid Needle," *San Antonio Express-News*, (Tuesday, June 13, 2006),6A.

[96]Jesse J. Holland, "Crime Package Approved; Will Turn Up Heat on States," *San Antonio Express-News* (Thursday, October 12, 2000), 6A.

[97]Mitch Frank, "Judge for Themselves," *Time*, (January 24, 2005), 31.

[98]Linda Greenhouse, "Court Limits Inmate Appeals," *San Antonio Express-News* (June 8, 1999), 1A and 6A.

[99]Richard Carelli, "Justices Make Death Row Appeals Tougher," *San Antonio Express-News* (Wednesday, April 19, 2000), 6A.

[100]Ibid.

[101]Barbara Holland, "You Swear That You Will Well and Truly Try?", *Smithsonian*, (Vol. 25, No. 12, March, 1995), 110.

[102]Ibid., 108.

[103]Alexis de Tocqueville, *Democracy in America*, J. P. Mayer, ed., (Gordon City, New York: Doubleday and Co., Inc., 1969), 638-639.

[104]Domino, 190.

[105]Ibid.

[106]Barker, 569.

[107]Maro Robbins, "Are Civil Liberties At Risk?", *San Antonio Express-News*, (Thursday, September 5, 2002), 1A.

[108]Gary Martin, "Bush Hails New Terror Law," San Antonio Express-News, (Saturday, October 27, 2001), 4A.

[109]"Justice In The Shadows," *Newsweek*, November 26, 2001, 39.

[110]Andres Curry, "Liberty and Justice," *U.S. News & World Report*, December 10, 2001, 53.

[111]John O'Neil and Scott Shane, "High Court Strikes Down Gitmo Military Tribunals," *San Antonio Express-News*, (Friday, June 30, 2006), 1A.

[112]Robbins, 9A.

[113]Michael Janofsky, "Patriot Act Chafes Some Local Governments," *San Antonio Express-News*, (Friday, December 27, 2002), 14A.

[114]Barth, 122.

[115]Barker, 10.

SUGGESTED READINGS

Abraham, Henry J. *Freedom and the Court: Civil Rights and Liberties in the United States*, 4th ed. New York: Oxford University Press, 1982.

Abraham Henry J., and Barbara A. Perry, *Freedom & the Court: Civil Rights & Liberties in the United States,* 8th ed., Lawrence, Kansas: University Press of Kansas, 2003.

Baker, Lucius, and Twiley W. Barker, Jr. *Civil Liberties and the Constitution.* 6th ed. Englewood Cliffs, N. J.: Prentice-Hall. 1990.

Barth, Alan. *The Rights of Free Men: An Essential Guide to Civil Liberties.* James E. Clayton, ed. New York: Alfred A. Knopf, 1987.

Domino, John C. *Civil Rights and Liberties: Toward the 21st Century.* New York: Harper Collins College Publishers, Inc., 1994.

Hall, Kermit L. ed. *By and For the People: Constitutional Rights in American History.* Arlington Heights, Ill.: Harlan Davidson, Inc., 1991.

Hensley, Thomas R., Christopher E. Smith and Joyce A. Baugh, *The Changing Supreme Court: Constitutional Rights and Liberties*, St. Paul, Minnesota: West Publishing Co., 1997.

Hickok, Eugene W., ed., *The Bill of Rights: Original Meaning and Current Understanding*, Charlottesville, Virginia: University Press of Virginia, 1996.

Rossum, Ralph A., and G. Alan Tarr. *American Constitutional Law: Cases and Interpretations.* New York: St. Martin's Press, 1983.

Signing of the Civil Rights Act of 1964.

Chapter Fourteen

CIVIL RIGHTS

On September 15, 1963, four young African-American girls in Birmingham, Alabama, decided to make a last minute visit to their deserted church's basement lounge after Sunday school. A dynamite bomb planted outside the church by members of the Ku Klux Klan (KKK) exploded killing 11-year-old Denise McNair, 14-year-olds Cynthia Wesley, Carole Robertson and Addie Mae Collins and injuring twenty others. Although the Federal Bureau of Investigation (FBI) quickly identified four Klansmen as the likely suspects, it took 39 years before the final suspect was tried and convicted of the bombing. Basically, "the killers of the girls hid for decades inside a brittle silence that cracked only when they boasted among kin and people they believed held the same hatred."[1]

In the early hours of June 2, 1998, James Byrd left a family gathering to begin his walk to his home in Jasper, Texas. As he walked along a dark road, three white ex-cons with ties to an in-prison white supremacy group, stopped and offered Byrd, an African American, a ride. Accustomed to hitch hiking, Byrd willingly accepted their offer and got into the bed of their truck. Byrd never made it home that night. Instead, the three men beat him unconscious, chained him to the tailgate of the truck, and dragged him to his death. The Jasper police subsequently found what was left of Byrd. He was decapitated with every bone in his torso broken. Body parts, including his dentures, were scattered over a two and a half mile stretch of the roadway. The three were captured, charged, and subsequently convicted of first-degree murder. Two received the death penalty. On Friday, April 28, 2000, an Anglo male randomly opened fire in several suburban Pittsburgh, Pennsylvania communities. "The gunman fatally shot a person of Indian descent at an Indian grocery store, two employees at a Chinese restaurant and a black [African American] man at a martial arts school. A Jewish woman who lived next door to the suspect's parents was found dead in her home."[2] He also shot out the glass doors of a nearby synagogue and painted the outside walls with swastikas. With the exception of one of the victims, the suspect did not know these people nor did they do anything to provoke him. They were simply at the wrong place at the wrong time. These killings were racially motivated by the suspect's hatred of minorities. Although incidents of this caliber are extremely isolated tragedies, what happened at that church in Birmingham, on that dirt road in Jasper, and on those streets in Pittsburgh reminded all of us that racism still haunts a nation that was founded, in part, on the sacredly revered Declaration of Independence that boldly proclaims that "all men are created equal." Yet, nothing is further from the truth. For thousands of years, the history of humanity has been continuously marred by periods of horrific and, far too often, deadly indignities leveled by individuals upon their fellow human beings. For over two hundred years, United States lawmakers from George Washington to George W. Bush have struggled to erase the blemishes of previous conditions of servitude, racial hatred, and gender discrimination only to be confronted by a new wave of racism, sexism, and intolerance. For this country, the quest for equality for all is a tale of short-lived victories followed by devastating failures and extremely painful setbacks.

For many Americans, the civil rights movement of the 1960's and 70's did awaken the social consciousness of this nation to the destructiveness of racism. Yet, the awakening failed to solve the problems. "Once integration was regarded as the supreme goal of the civil rights movement. Opening America's neighborhoods and schools and workplaces to minorities, we believed, would end racial inequalities. But almost fifty-plus years after the civil rights movement began with Rosa Parks and the Montgomery bus boycott, and after no small amount of progress has been made, profound racial divisions remain, mired in arguments over everything from class to crime, from education to birthrates. A once indomitable government seems paralyzed in a policy bog of its own, unable to grasp the scope of the problem, much less purpose solutions."[3] The obvious shortcomings and failures of the public policy process to address racial discrimination are seen in the faces of those the laws were supposed to help. Far too often minorities feel that the scales of justice move too slowly to bring those accused of civil rights violations to justice. For example, in 1966, the bullet-riddled body of Ben Chester White, an African-American farmhand, was found in Pretty Creek, near Natchez, Mississippi. Three known Klansmen were arrested with one actually confessing to the murder. All three were acquitted in state courts. In 2003, the federal government reopened the case, charging 72-year-old Ernest Avants, the only defendant still living, with the crime. The federal government discovered a loophole. "For years his [Avants] acquittal of state murder charges in the 1960s had shielded him from new prosecution. But White's body was found on federal land, in a national forest, enough to get around double jeopardy and give federal prosecutors jurisdiction."[4] Another tragic case was the 1964 slayings of James Chaney, 21, an African American from Mississippi and his two white companions from New York. They were three young men traveling through the Deep South trying to register potential African-American voters. Although more than a dozen well-known Klan members were involved in the slayings, only a few were actually charged, tried and convicted. "One of the men who was convicted, Sam Bowers—the Neshoba County Klan's Imperial Wizard—later said that he was 'quite delighted to have the main instigator of the entire affair,' meaning [Edgar Ray] Killen, 'walk out of the courtroom a free man.'"[5] Although Killen was never charged with the crimes in the state courts, he was tried on federal-civil rights violations in 1967, but acquitted by an all-white jury. In 2005, the state of Mississippi officially charged 79 year-old Killen with three counts of murder. It has taken 40 plus years to bring the man responsible for instigating these murders to justice. The Justice Department has also reopened the 1955 murder of 14-year-old Emmett Till, "an African American boy from Chicago who was in Mississippi visiting relatives, allegedly whistled at the wife of a white man, Roy Bryant. Four days later, Bryant and his half-brother J. W. Milam, yanked Emmett from his bed in the dead of the night, threw him in the back of their truck, and beat him beyond recognition with a Colt .45 before tying a metal fan to his neck, shooting him, and throwing his body in a river."[6] Of course, both men were charged and acquitted of the murder. "A few months later, the two men, protected by the double-jeopardy doctrine that prevents a person from being tried twice for the same crime, gloated about getting away with the murder in an interview with *Look* magazine."[7] Although both men have died, the Justice Department is investigating the possibility that Bryant and Milam were not the only ones involved in this tragic slaying.

The frustrations and disappointments experienced by this nation's minority group populations are further fueled by the perception that their lawmakers and their government also move too slowly to enact the proper corrective legislation with enough governmental muscle to end racial discrimination. The lofty words of the Declaration of Independence and the Constitution declaring equality for all are meaningless to those confronted with racial hatred, poverty, inadequate educational opportunities, and the stark realization that the American dream of riches and success belongs to someone else.

Any discussion of civil rights must also encompass the struggles of American women to gain an equitable footing with their male counterparts. Incidences of gender-based discrimination are just as offensive as racial discrimination. Charges of sexual harassment are prevalent. Women are still struggling with wage disparity issues as their male counterparts continue to earn more than they do in comparable positions. Although few disputed the need to reform the welfare state, national women's organizations were adamantly opposed to the rhetoric of welfare reform that openly attacked, belittled, and blamed low income single parent women for the faults of the welfare system.

While women and minorities are seeking redress through the courts and legislative Houses, some Americans believe that an over zealous government has gone too far by arbitrarily granting special treatment for minorities and women to the detriment of its Anglo male citizens. Although the majority of all Americans support the concepts and philosophy of civil rights and are themselves

Rosa Parks refused to give up her seat to a white man on a Montgomery, Alabama, bus that led to a citywide bus boycott.

law-abiding citizens, a small group of white supremacists and militants have become extremely vocal and, in some cases, violent in venting their anger against politicians, lawmakers, and government. The fear that government is systematically stripping away their rights while giving preferential treatment to minorities, women, and immigrants has materialized into white backlash attacks against affirmative action, civil rights laws, and immigration policies. On April 19, 1995, a nine-story federal government building in Oklahoma City was blown apart, killing 168 men, women, and children. The primary suspects were affiliated with a predominately white-male state militia group angry over the intrusion of government into their private lives. Both Timothy McVeigh and Terry Nickols were tried and convicted for their involvement in the Oklahoma disaster. Members of another militia group were arrested in West Virginia after their plans to blow up national and state government buildings were discovered. Unfortunately, every state has at least one white supremacist militia organization, and, of course, the Klan is still a viable organization.

The challenge before government at all levels is to protect and uphold the rights and privileges of all its citizens. On June 14, 1997, President Bill Clinton introduced his plan to end racial strife in a speech delivered at the University of California—San Diego. Entitled "One America in the 21st Century: The President's Initiative on Race," the president's plan had five goals: "to articulate the President's vision of a just, unified America; to inform the nation about the facts surrounding race in this country; to promote a constructive dialogue and work through the difficult issues of race; to encourage leadership at the federal, state, and local community levels to help bridge racial divides; and to identify policy and program recommendations and solutions to critical areas such as education and economic opportunity."[8] On paper, this seemed to be a simple charge for a country founded on the democratic principles of equality and freedom. However, racial tolerance, gender equality, and political and social acceptability have eluded this country for over 200 years. Men and women of diverse races, nationalities, and beliefs have and will in all likelihood continue to battle against racial and gender discrimination, physical and verbal abuses, and threats just to gain the right to have a job at a decent and fair wage, to hold and purchase property, to receive an equitable educational opportunity, and to participate in the full spectrum of the political process. Their struggles will continue because we as a nation have finally realized that equality is one of the most difficult public policy issues confronting this country. The inability of this nation's people to achieve racial and gender equality is deeply rooted in the historical, political, and cultural development of this nation. Of course, government has and probably will continue to pass laws mandating equality laden with sanctions to be leveled against those who choose not to comply with the laws. However, government cannot legislate attitude changes. Laws cannot change attitudes no matter how hard lawmakers try. This chapter focuses on the development and theories of racism and prejudice and the struggles of those targeted with the slurs and repercussions of racism. This chapter also examines the actions government has taken to address the issues of racism and gender discrimination in this country.

Civil Rights and Racism

Civil rights are collectively known as "the acts of government intended to protect disadvantaged classes of persons or minority groups from arbitrary, unreasonable, or discriminatory treatment."[9]

Government at all levels has the authority to pass laws and statutes designed to protect citizens against prejudicial and discriminatory actions caused by other citizens. Basically, these laws protect us from each other. Essentially a learned behavior, **prejudice** is "a feeling or act of any individual or any group in which a prejudgment about someone else or another group is made on the basis of emotion rather than reason."[10] **Discrimination** is an action precipitated by prejudice against an individual or group. The two terms are connected. Therefore, "prejudice is an *unfavorable attitude* towards people because they are members of a particular racial or ethnic group and that discrimination is an *unfavorable action* toward people because they are members of a particular racial or ethnic group."[11]

There are two forms of discrimination. The most obvious form is **de jure discrimination** whereby a *purposeful action* adversely impacts one group over another group. The creation of "all white" communities across this country was accomplished through a series of government ordinances backed by personal threats and reprisals to keep minority groups out of certain cities and towns. However, **de facto discrimination** is an *undeliberate action* adversely impacting one group over another group. For example, white flight to the suburbs created racially segregated neighborhoods, located primarily in economically depressed and deteriorating central business districts. No laws or deliberate actions were taken to force Anglo residents to leave their inner city neighborhoods. These individuals simply possessed the resources and the desire to relocate. The question of whether the adverse action was a result of de facto or de jure discrimination usually arises over a multiplicity of issues ranging from legislative redistricting and reapportionment issues to public school financing problems.

Before delving into the theories of racism, it is important to understand the vital role the United States Supreme Court has taken in promoting and protecting civil rights as the means of eradicating the damages wrought by prejudice, discrimination, and racism. "When the race controversy attained a degree of no longer an ignorable public concern at the highest governmental level in the late 1940s, it was the judicial branch of the government, with the Supreme Court at its apex, which led the other branches in tackling the problem. While it probably did not lead eagerly or joyously, a people's rightful claims could no longer be ignored merely because the political, in particular, the legislative branch refused then to become involved beyond the most cursory of levels, and in fact consistently passed the problems on to the Court. It is an intriguing question how much strife might have been spared and how much understanding might have been engendered had the elective branches of the government provided the decisive leadership with which they are charged and, as subsequent events proved, of which they are capable when pressed."[12] For example, the 1960s civil rights movement actually began when the Supreme Court completely dismantled the nearly century-old concept of separate but equal in its landmark ruling in *Brown v the Board of Education of Topeka, Kansas* (1954). The pattern appears to be that once the federal bench renders a decision concerning civil rights, it then becomes the responsibility of the legislative and executive branches to enact the much needed corrective legislation.

Unfortunately, the only public policy options normally open to lawmakers are the alleviative, preventive, and punitive. (These policy options are discussed in detail in Chapter 15.) The civil rights acts were designed to prevent incidences of racial discrimination from spreading by penalizing violators with both civil and criminal sanctions. The suffering of those adversely impacted by acts of discrimination is alleviated by civil monetary determinations as well as criminal sanctions, particularly acts that violate a person's civil rights. The purpose of affirmative action is two fold. First, it alleviates those adversely impacted by racial discrimination by sanctioning actions to reverse previous conditions of discrimination in the workplace. Second, affirmative action like civil rights laws prevents further damage by providing punitive sanctions against violators. (**Affirmative actions** are the formalized efforts on the part of government to remedy previous incidences of past discrimination particularly in the employment and political processes.) The curative approach is not a viable option at this point due to the deeply rooted attitudes of racism and discrimination that have been and continue to be instilled through the cultural and social development of all population groups.

Theories of Racism

For centuries, humanity has been emboiled in a great debate over whether equality is achievable in multicultural societies. Colonized by immigrants, the United States population is a mixture of people hailing from various countries who brought their cultural values, folkways, and mores to America's shores. Americans oftentimes try to convince themselves that their multicultural society is a melting pot of diversity that speaks with one voice. This nation's continual struggle to achieve racial and cultural equality reveals a country that speaks with many voices, oftentimes in conflict with each other. Europe is currently experiencing its own struggles with multiculturalism. "Only fifty years ago, a collection of distinct nations that were mostly linguistically and culturally homogenous, Europe has become a multicultural stew, one that has grown all the faster with the collapse of the Soviet Union, the removal of trade barriers and blurring of national borders, and the desire of the poor in Asia, Africa and the Middle East to seek a better life. Increasingly, those who say they have done their best to adapt socially and culturally in their adopted countries complain they're kept at arm's length by the majority, tolerated at best, marginalized, mocked and attacked at worst."[13] Not every European openly embraces the concept of multiculturalism. Even the ancient Greeks clearly divided their societies by granting citizens a full spectrum of political, social, and economic privileges while denying those same rights to noncitizens. Slaves fared worse. An advocate of equality, Aristotle "on the other hand was sure that all men possessed reason, but thought that the distinguishing mark of slaves was that they possessed only so much of the power of reason as to enable them to understand their masters, without being able to reason for themselves; and he concluded that manual workers ought not to participate in government on the grounds that their lives denied them the opportunity to cultivate the qualities essential to wisdom."[14] Embedded in Aristotle's words are four of the prevailing rationalizations for racism: nativism, the superior/inferior concept, the economic theory of racism, and the concept of racial separation. An examination of each concept reveals the basis for racism in America.

The concept of **nativism** is based on the belief that only those born on their country's soil should reap the benefits of their birthrights. The first generation of English colonists born in America quickly established themselves as the natives of this country. The original immigrants now became the **host culture** for subsequent immigrants. For example, the United States Constitution recognizes the lofty status of the native culture by declaring that only a native-born person can be president. Alexis de Tocqueville observed this distinct separation between the native-born and others by noting that in the United States "the first that attracts attention, and the first in enlightenment, power, and happiness is the white man, the European, man 'par excellence,' below him come the Negro [African Americans] and the Indian."[15] Eventually, the host or native culture becomes very protective of its superior position, seeing any intrusion of an outside culture as a threat to their livelihood and survival.

The concept of nativism surfaced in the 1790s as Americans began their quest to preserve and protect their culture by advocating English-only and pressing for anti-immigration laws. "In the flush of their newfound freedom, the Americans began to view all foreigners—even those from England—as possible carriers of anti-republican beliefs that might threaten the new nation. They tended to suspect that the Catholics might be monarchist subversives and that anyone French might attempt to ferment the kind of unrest that had led to the French Revolution."[16] The cries against increased immigration were coupled with violence, racial slurs, and harassment towards immigrants, particularly the Irish and Catholics.

Around 1850 a national organization called the Secret Order of the Star Spangled Banner was formed in New York. Renamed the Order of United Americans, lodges were formed in every state, with approximately 960 organizations in New York alone. "Only native-born male citizens of the Protestant faith, born of Protestant parents, reared under Protestant influence and not united in marriage with a Roman Catholic, could actually join a lodge."[17] The nativist movement developed into the Know-Nothings, a third political party launched in 1854. In their first campaign effort, "they elected more than a hundred Congressmen, eight governors and thousands of local officials, including the mayors of Boston, Philadelphia and Chicago. They won control of state legislatures in a half dozen states, from New Hampshire to California, and made a strong showing in a dozen more from New York to Louisiana."[18] In 1856, the party ran Millard Filmore for president. His electoral defeat was the swan song for the Know-Nothing movement. However, the party's primary anti-immigrant policy continues to play a key role in American politics. Today, the debate on immigration reform echoes the same concerns expressed in the 1790's as congressional proposals include efforts "to restrict immigration, limit the rights of immigrants, and increase the length of time needed to become a naturalized citizen."[19]

Closely related to nativism, the **superior/inferior** explanation for racism is based on the belief that one group or culture is genetically, intellectually, and culturally more superior than any other group. Thus, the superior group becomes the natural choice to rule over the inferiors. Adolph Hitler viewed the Germanic race as the genetically superior race. His desire to create an Aryan nation served as his justification for his horrific actions against Jews during the 1930s and 1940s. In *Mein Kampf*, Hitler envisioned a new world order dominated by the Aryan or Germanic race whereby races would be divided into three groups: "the culture-creating or Aryan race; the culture-bearing races which can borrow and adopt but cannot create; and the culture-destroying race, namely, the Jews."[20] The culture-creating race is destined to rule over the genetically inferior races. In addition, advocates of this theory believe that members of certain white "races" are destined to rule not only over the nonwhite races but over the other white races as well. Under this more specific version of the doctrine of white supremacy, "the tall, blond, blue-eyed peoples of northern and western Europe were the modern remnants of a talented race called the Nordics (or Teutons), who were descended from the ancient Aryans of India. The Nordics were said to have a special talent for political organization that enabled their members to form representative governments and create just laws; hence, the Nordic portion of the White race was destined to rule over all races, including the shorter "alpine: and the darker-skinned "Mediterranean" portion of the White race."[21]

The superior/inferior concept of racism is often justified as a benevolent action to protect a perceived inferior race from self-destruction. In 1732, prominent slaver John Barbat wrote "that the slave's conditions in his own country were so appalling that it was a kindness to ship him to the West Indies and more considerate masters, not to mention the inestimable advantage they may reap of becoming Christians, and saving their souls."[22] This is basically the same rationale used by the Spanish conquistadors and missionaries for the enslavement of Native American tribes in Central and Latin America. The white South African apartheid policies were based on the notion that black Africans were historically and genetically too inferior to survive on their own. Armed with the lofty challenge of saving souls and protecting those incapable of protecting themselves, the self-proclaimed superior races have been able to conquer and, subsequently, control the fortunes of those deemed inferior.

In his book, *Jim Crow America*, Jim Conrad states that racism is purely an economic issue, not a culturally or genetically based concept. For example, in the United States it was the overwhelming desire for land, natural resources, and gold that compelled Anglo Americans to use whatever means available to them to acquire these precious treasures. "Greed had come to America, along with democracy, and greed was built into the hearts and minds of millions of whites who were the products of the past, not the creators."[23] Native American tribes were the initial targets because they possessed vast rich fertile land holdings. The discovery of gold on Indian land just intensified the greed factor. In 1863, representatives from the federal government met with Nez Perces tribal leaders to negotiate the purchase of approximately 90 percent of their reservation lands located in the territory that would become the states of Washington, Oregon and Idaho. Signed by only a handful of the tribal leaders, the federal government "agreed to pay the Nez Perces $265,000 for the ceded land. In his report to the Commissioner of Indian Affairs in Washington, Superintendent Calvin Hale announced the signing of the treaty as a great victory for the government: 'The amount thus relinquished is very nearly six million of acres, and is obtained at a cost not exceeding eight cents per acre . . . In the tract of country there is much that is exceedingly valuable, by reason of its gold and silver mines, whilst many of its valleys, and much of its uplands, will be found desirable and necessary for agricultural and grazing purposes'."[24] The original Spanish-Mexican landowners in Texas and California saw their vast acreage gradually forced from them by Anglo-American settlers through a creative combination of legal and illegal tactics. African-American slaves were brought to this country to enhance the economic viability of the Southern planter just as immigrants were openly welcomed to this land to toil in the factories.

Once these groups become economically depressed and totally dependent upon their benefactors, Native Americans, slaves, Hispanics, and immigrants alike were denied accessibility to the two tools that could liberate them—education and voting rights. Minorities, in particular, were constantly reminded of their inferior status by a series of laws known as **Jim Crow**, which successfully built a wall of separation between them and Anglo Americans. According to Conrad, racial explanations are overshadowed by the prevailing economic issue. "The issue comes down to pennies, then, and so it has been since the time when slave traders marched into Africa, handed out a few bottles of rum, and walked off with a hundred or so human commodities. The profit was enormous . . . . Twenty-five cents in the hands of two white men is twenty-five cents less in the hands of a African-American laundress. Magnify that in terms of the economic process intensively at work in all Southern states, and almost as sharply operative in the north, and you can put an arrow through the heart of Jim Crow.[25] The economic theory also fuels anti-immigrant sentiments. When the economy slumps and job security is questionable, some Americans see the flow of immigrants as a threat to their own economic viability. Another traditional economic argument for halting immigration is the belief that immigrants keep the wage system depressed by accepting jobs that pay at or below minimum wage levels.

Another perspective of racism is **separation**. Immigrants, for example, usually lived among members of their own culture, forming their own cities within a city such as China Town, Little Italy, and so on. Within their own neighborhoods, they felt more secure in speaking their own language and adhering to their own traditions and beliefs. Separation was further encouraged with the denial of interracial and intercultural marriages. The creation of cluster neighborhoods or zones was enforced by invisible lines and barriers backed by social, economic, and political laws, customs, and mores on the part of all parties involved. Immigrant groups themselves were just as eager to avoid intrusions into their cultures just as much as the host Anglo cultures wanted to protect their own lifestyles and livelihoods. However, separation from other cultures creates isolation and can lead to the fear of other cultures. "The minute society separates people from each other by color or class, it sets in motion diverse economic, psychological, and cultural processes. Society builds two antithetical cultures side by side. They can be different economies and different cultures separated by a railroad track or a picket fence, and one can then pit one culture against the other and make each group hate and misunderstand the other."[26] Once races and cultures have been separated from each other for generations, it is easy to see why the feelings of prejudice, mistrust, and suspicion would develop. In part, the desire of lawmakers to integrate the various races has been only marginally successful in this country because of a long history of cultural and racial separations.

Racism in America

Of course, we cannot overlook the obvious. All people, regardless of their own racial and cultural identity, harbor to some extent prejudices against others. These acquired habits have become as much a part of our own roots and traditions as patriotism and nationalism are to every American. It should be clearly understood that not every Anglo American is a racist nor is every member of a minority group a victim of racial discrimination and hatred. Regardless of their individual racial background, the majority of the American people have learned to transcend past discriminatory practices by coming to terms with their own prejudices.

However, there are some individuals who harbor intense hatred towards others. Their vocal and sometimes violent displays of their hatred divide rather than unite the American people. Minority population groups, immigrants, and homosexuals are the primary targets. Recently, the World Organization Against Torture USA released their findings on racism in America:

"While officially sanctioned segregation has been eliminated, de facto segregation and persistent racial discrimination continue in parts of our society. . . . The true extent of contemporary racism remains clouded by ignorance as well as differences of perception. While most whites [Anglos] do not believe there is much discrimination today in American society, most minorities see the opposite in their life experiences."[27]

Furthermore, the report challenged lawmakers to confront this nation's racial problems. The agency stressed that "there have been increasing demands, especially by developing countries, that while the U.S. must continue to focus attention on human rights violations abroad, we need to do more to recognize and address situations of human rights non-compliance in our own country."[28]

The increase in the number of racially motivated crimes has created a new category of criminal offenses—hate crimes. Both the federal and state governments tract officially reported hate motivated criminal activities. In 2003, of the 7,531 reported incidents that resulted in 9,166 victims of hate crimes, 3,859 were racially based criminal actions followed by 1,033 ethnically/national origin related, 1,343 religiously based, 1,246 sexual orientation, and 46 disability-related criminal acts. For the same period, California led in the number of reported hate-based crimes with 1,472. Although all of the fifty states reported hate crimes, the states with over 200 incidents in 2003 were Arizona, Florida, Indiana, Maryland, Massachusetts, Michigan, Minnesota, New Jersey, New York, Ohio, Texas, Virginia and Washington.[29] These figures illustrate only the reported incidents whereby an individual violated the rights and property of others purely on the grounds of hatred. The increase in the number of hate crimes has prompted state and national lawmakers to introduce hate-crime bills. At the end of his administration, President Clinton urged Congress to pass legislation adding "crimes motivated by sexual orientation, gender or disability to the list of offenses already covered under a 1968 federal law, and allow federal prosecutors to pursue a hate crime case if local authorities refuse to press charges."[30] The legislation passed the Senate but failed to receive a favorable nod from the House. The major problem with hate crimes legislation is determining actually what differentiates a crime motivated by hate over another motive. Legislative houses must also heed the warnings of the United States Supreme Court. The Court ruled in a 5 to 4 decision, that "juries, not judges, must decide whether someone charged with a hate crime was motivated by bias and therefore can be given a higher maximum sentence."[31]

Several law enforcement units have been practicing their own form of racial discrimination known as **racial profiling**. This practice is based on the assumption that criminals possess certain common traits and characteristics that separate them from the law-abiding citizen. Armed with a profile of those most likely to commit a crime, law enforcement officers in several states have been stopping innocent drivers, subjecting them to vehicle searches, and, in some instances, harassing them simply because they possess physical characteristics associated with the criminal element. Racial profiling has been aimed at minorities, primarily African Americans. In New Jersey, the actions of the state police resulted in a multi-million dollar settlement to four young minority students who were illegally stopped by state troopers on the suspicion that they were drug dealers. New Jersey's state law enforcement had been using racial profiling since 1989. In addition, the 9th U.S. Circuit Court of Appeals overturned the United States Border Patrol's use of racial profiling against Hispanics. The justices defended their decision by pointing out that "stops based on race or ethnic appearance send the underlying message to all our citizens that those who are not white

[Anglo] are judged by the color of their skin alone. Such stops also send a clear message that those who are not white [Anglo] enjoy a lesser degree of constitutional protection—that they are in effect assumed to be potential criminals first and individuals second."[32]

An examination of the struggles of Native Americans, Hispanics, African Americans, women, and immigrants to achieve the same civil rights granted by the Framers to white male citizens reveals that this country has yet to reverse racism and discrimination. There is much left to be done. At the 1848 Seneca Falls Convention, Frederick Douglass reminded the audience of the ultimate goal of civil rights when he declared that "right is of no sex, truth is of no color."[33] Obviously, this objective has yet to be accomplished.

Native Americans

No racial group has suffered more humiliation, destruction, abuse, and discrimination from the "white man's" ways than the American Indian. Where once hundreds of thousands of Indians inhabited this land, today there are only "562 distinct tribes with federal recognition, and scores of others recognized only locally or not at all."[34] Basically, Native Americans fell victim to the economic theory of racism justified by the superior-inferior concept. The North American Indians became the target of intense hatred from the very beginning of the colonial experience since they possessed what American settlers desired most—rich fertile lands. The arrival of the first English colonists to the shores of the James River in 1607 initiated this over 400-year-old relationship as the settlers carved out of the virgin forests the Jamestown colony. Predictably, Native Americans viewed the white man's encroachment into their lands as a threat to their culture, livelihood, and, ultimately, their survival. Consequently, the settlers were subjected to continuous attacks from members of the Powhatan chiefdom, a confederative alliance consisting of nearly 30 different tribes. After seven years of attacks and counterattacks, the colonists captured Pocahontas, daughter of the chief. Both sides unofficially agreed to end the warfare. However, "hostilities persisted until a peace settlement in 1632. But colonial expansion continued, gobbling up Powhatan land. Opechancanough [Pocahontas' uncle] retaliated again in 1644 in a final spasm of attacks, killing more than 500 colonists."[35] Since few Native Americans were agriculturalists, the white man's way of developing the land destroyed it for the Native American's nomadic hunting lifestyle. Native American tribes initially sought to negotiate with Anglo-American settlers. Native Americans saw more and more of their lands taken from them with each new wave of colonists. "Eradication and land grabs were embraced by Virginians George Washington and Thomas Jefferson when they were president, policies that had their origins in Virginia early in the 17th century. The Indians called Washington "Conotacarious'—devourer of villages. He ordered the destruction of Indian villages in New York state during the Revolutionary War and warned other tribes he would do the same thing to them if they fought the Americans."[36] Tribal leaders quickly realized that the only viable option left for Native Americans was to fight to keep what was theirs by launching violent counter-attacks against the advancing covered wagons.

The initial public policy response from the United States government was to relocate various tribes first to the west of the Mississippi and then to lands further beyond. The negotiation process began in earnest at the end of the French and Indian War, fought between 1754 and 1761. Pontiac, an Ottawa chief, convinced the tribal leaders of the Hurons, Potawattomis, Chippewas, Delawares, Kickapoos, Shawnees, and other tribes to join forces to drive the English out of America. Confronted with the might of the British military, Pontiac sued for peace by signing the Proclamation of 1763, which declared that: (1) all land west of the crest of the Appalachian mountains was "Indian Country"; (2) any settlers west of the Appalachian who had not acquired a legal title to their land from the Indians must return to the colonies; and (3) all future land purchases from the Indians must be conducted in public meetings attended by representatives of the king.[37] As anticipated, colonists openly violated the treaty by establishing more settlements in "Indian Country." After winning independence, the United States government continued the British tradition of signing treaties with tribal leaders to hold the peace with the intention of eventually violating treaty provisions. Treaties between the United States government and the Iroquois, Delawares, Wyandots, Chippewas, Ottawas, Shawnees, Cherokees, Choctaws, Chickasaws, Seminoles, Cheyenne, Navajo, and so on were openly violated by the zeal of **manifest destiny**, the belief that the Anglo-American's destiny was to own all of the land between the Atlantic and Pacific Oceans. However, uprooting whole tribes from their sacred ancestral lands and forcing them to walk hundreds of miles to reach these territories only served to accelerate the tension and mistrust between the United States government and Native American tribal leaders. The Jackson administration signed approximately ninety-four treaties demanding tribal relocations. The **Trail of Tears** resulted in the forced relocation of the Cherokees, Choctaws, Creeks, Chickasaws, and Seminoles from East of the Mississippi to Indian territory on the opposite side of the river simply because gold was discovered in Georgia in 1829. The Seminoles, in particular, posed serious problems for the government's relocation schemes. In retaliation of the **Indian Removal Act** (1830), the Seminoles launched their own

war against the United States known as the Second Seminole War. Eventually, "the United States removed 3,800 Seminoles to Indian Territory, but at a terrible price. The war lasted for an interminable seven years, 1,500 American soldiers died, and the cost has been estimated at between $20,000,000 to $60,000,000—significantly more than the United States paid for the entire Louisiana Purchase only fifty-two years earlier. Worst, perhaps, was the national embarrassment caused by the war. The U.S. Army, in its first real showing since the War of 1812, was shocked at the ferocity of the Seminole assault and never recovered from its initial surprise. The result was an immense loss of face, internationally and domestically, which could have been avoided or at least postponed."[38]

Native Americans began to fight back with violent attacks against settlers. Realizing that a peaceful settlement was impossible, the federal government gave its army the green light, in effect, to exterminate those tribes who refused to relocate. Lawmakers justified their actions by portraying Indians as savage killers bent on brutally attacking and scalping innocent settlers whose only desire was to carve out a better life for themselves and their families by moving West. In 1862, the United States Army was ordered to begin the extermination of the Mescalero Apaches. Granted leniency, approximately 400 tribe members were located to Bosque Redondo, a remote area in the New Mexico territory. The Navajos were next. "Well over half the estimated 12,000 Navajos eventually were rounded up. They first went to Fort Canby, near present-day Window Rock, Arizona, where many died of exposure and dysentery. Survivors were sent off in groups to march 300 miles to Bosque Redondo. . . Some who could not keep up the pace, including the elderly, children and pregnant women, were shot by soldiers. . . In all, nearly 3,000 Navajos died at Bosque Redondo."[39] The slaughter of Indians during the Plains War ensued. On January 29, 1863, the United States calvary under the leadership of Col. Patrick O'Connor attacked a Shoshone tribe at Bear Creek, near present day Salt Lake City, Utah. "Connor lost 14 of his 200 men. An estimated 270 to 400 Shoshones died, two-thirds of them women and children. No more than 60 escaped or survived."[40] Tribe after tribe saw its mighty braves, women, and children killed by bullets, diseases, and starvation. The Battle of Bear River was "much more grim than better-known Indian massacres at Sand Creek in Colorado Territory, where 133 Cheyennes were killed by troopers on Nov. 28, 1864, and at Wounded Knee, S. D., where soldiers slaughtered 153 Sioux on Dec. 28, 1890."[41]

Placed on reservations, Native Americans became the victims to the whims of lawmakers as they vacillated between policies advocating **cultural assimilation** and **separation**. Assimilation meant that reservation Indians were to become "civilized" by adopting to the white man's society and culture. "The Bureau of Indian Affairs (BIA) agents, who supervised the reservations, tried to root-out Native American ways and replace them with white dress and hairstyles, the English language, and the Christian religion."[42] In the 1930s, the federal government, however, reversed its assimilation policy by urging a return to tribal identities. But, irreversible damage had been done as Native Americans did not know who they were or where they belonged in American society.

For this country's Native Americans, the road to political, social, and economic parity with their Anglo brothers and sisters has been a tragic uphill battle with very few victories along the way. Table 14.1 illustrates some of the important events that have had positive and negative impacts on Native Americans. For example, Native Americans did not become United States citizens until 1924, a privilege denied to them by the framers.

One of the primary issues for Native Americans is reclaiming ownership of or at least royalties from their ancestral lands. In 1887, the United States Congress passed the **Dawes Severalty Act** as a concerted effort to break up large reservation holdings that bond Native Americans to their tribes. "Rather than allotting reservation lands to tribal groups, the act allowed the president [of the United States] to distribute these lands to individuals. Private property, the framers of the bill reasoned, would undermine communal norms and tribal identity and encourage Indians to settle down and farm as white men did."[43] However, the land redistribution scheme merely took Indian lands held supposedly in trust by the Bureau of Indian Affairs from public oversight to private ownership. "Within 20 years of the Dawes Act, Native Americans had lost 60 percent of their lands. The federal government held the profits from land sales 'in trust' and used them for 'civilizing' missions."[44]

Recent federal legislation coupled with favorable federal court rulings have given Native Americans more control over their lands and, subsequently, their own futures. In particular, the federal courts have rendered favorable decisions in cases involving treaty violations by the federal government. The Oneida Indian Nation has been battling in court since 1920 seeking compensation from the state of New York over 250,000 acres located between Utica and Syracuse, land the tribe claims was stolen from them. "The federal government first signed a treaty reserving some 270,000 acres for the Oneidas in 1794, after tribe members fought British troops and reportedly lugged 600 bushels of corn hundreds of miles to George Washington's starving troops at Valley Forge. Congress, however, specified that all future purchases of Indian lands could proceed only with federal consent. The Oneidas signed some 27 treaties with New York State over the years, but only one of the state's treaties received federal approval. Eventually, the Oneidas' lands in the state dwindled to a single 32-acre tract."[45] In 1985, the United States Supreme Court ruled that the initial 1794 treaty was a binding document. The Blackfeet are also challenging the BIA's withholding of trust money from the sale or lease of Indian lands dating back to 1820. Through numerous treaties, Native Americans were supposed to receive just compensation for the seizure of their lands. However, while the majority of this nation's Native Americans are either below or one step away from the poverty level, the federal government through the BIA has been denying them royalties on their lands for over one hundred years. Indian culture and traditions did gain recognition when Congress passed legislation protecting Indian burial grounds and artifacts. Native Americans are gradually reclaiming their lands and their culture and artifacts in a long arduous battle through the nation's courts.

Crow leader Chief Plenty Coups once warned his tribe to "learn to associate with the white man, learn his ways, get an education. With an education, you are his equal, without it, you are his victim."[46] Few have followed his advice. According to the 2000 census, there are approximately 4,119,301 American Indian and Alaska Natives in the United States. The largest tribes are the Cherokee with 729,533 members, the Chippewas with 149,699, the Choctaws with 158,774, the Navajo with 298,197, and the Sioux with 153,360.[47] With few exceptions, the majority of the nation's Native Americans live at or below the poverty level. Educational opportunities, especially for Native Americans living on reservations, are limited. Confronted with high public school drop out rates, the number of Native Americans completing higher education degree programs is dismal.

Table 14. 1

Significant Events for Native Americans

Date	Event
1778	The newly formed United States negotiates its first treaty with an Indian nation promising future statehood to the Delawares.
1787-1789	The United States Constitution gives the federal government the exclusive authority to regulate trade and commerce with Indian tribes.
1809	Treaty of Fort Wayne secures 2.5 million acres from Indians for Anglo-American settlement in Ohio and Indiana.
1813-1814	The Creek Wars end with treaty agreements relinquishing all lands held by the Creeks in the Southeast to the American government.
1817-1818	First Seminole War.
1820-1824	Kickapoos resist removal from Illinois territory.
1824	Bureau of Indian Affairs established under the War Department.
1830	Congress passes the Indian Removal Act.
1835-1842	Second Seminole War.
1853-1856	United States government obtains 174 million acres of Indian lands through treaties.
1854	United States Indian Affairs Commission ends the Indian Removal Policy.
1855-1858	Third Seminole War.
1861-1863	Mangas Colorados and Cochise lead Apache uprising.
1862	Smallpox kills 200,000 Indians in the Northwest Coast.
1863-1866	Navajo Wars in New Mexico and Arizona.
1866	United States Congress declares Indian land as right-of-way for construction of the Trans-Continental Railroad.
1876-1877	Sioux Wars waged by Sioux, Cheyenne and Arapaho under Sitting Bull and Crazy Horse.
1881-1886	Apache resistance under Geronimo.
1885	The last great herd of buffalo are exterminated.
1887	Congress passes the General Allotment Act or the Dawes Act.

1924	Congress grants citizenship to Native Americans.
1926	National Council of American Indians is formed.
1928	Charles Curtis, Kansas Indian and United States Senator, is elected vice president under Herbert Hoover.
1934	Congress passes United States Indian Reorganization Act, reversing United States practice of land allotment by establishing tribal self government and landholding.
1965	Congress passes Voting Rights Act ensuring suffrage to all Native Americans.
1968	Passage of the American Indian Civil Rights Act extending civil liberties outlined in the Bill of Rights to Indians living on reservations.
1969-1971	Members of Red Power movement occupy Alcatraz Island to call attention to the plight of Native Americans.
1973	Members of American Indian Movement and 200 armed Oglala Sioux occupy site of Wounded Knee Massacre on Pine Ridge Reservation in South Dakota for 71 days.
1978	Congress passes American Indian Freedom of Religion Act.
1988	Congress passes Indian Gaming Regulatory Act, allowing Indians to operate casinos on their reservations under guidelines established by the states.
1990	Congress passes Native American Graves Protection and Repatriation Act.
1999	President Bill Clinton becomes the first president to visit an Indian reservation since President Franklin Roosevelt included a stop at a Cherokee reservation while on vacation in North Carolina in 1936.
2004	National Museum of the American Indian opens in Washington, D.C.

Of the 632,192 associate degrees awarded in 2003, only 7,462, representing 1.2 percent of the total number of earned degrees, were awarded to American Indians and Alaskan Natives. During the same period, 9,816 or 0.7 percent of awarded bachelor's, 2,837 or 0.6 percent of awarded master's degrees, 196 or 0.4 percent of awarded doctor's degrees, and 582 or 0.7 percent of awarded first professional degrees were earned by American Indians and Alaskan Natives.[48] With limited education, Native Americans are confronted with a limited opportunity to secure higher paying career field job opportunities.

African Americans

The economic prosperity of the pre-Civil War South was the result to a large degree by the back-breaking toil of African-American slaves and their descendents who worked in the fields from sun up to sun down either bent over picking cotton, wielding a machete cutting sugar cane, or standing in ankle-deep water planting and harvesting rice. Most Southerners rationalized the exploitation, brutality, injustice, and degradation of slaves with the "old assumptions of Anglo-Saxon superiority and innate African inferiority, white supremacy, and Negro [African American] subordination."[49] The institution of slavery completely controlled the fate of the slave from birth to death. Slaves were part of their owner's properties just like the house, the fields, and the furniture. Citizenship, voting privileges, property ownership, and education were systematically denied to African Americans, even to those born on American soil. Frederick Douglass once remarked that "whatever of comfort is necessary for him [the slave] for his body or soul that is inconsistent with his being property, is carefully wrested from him, not only by public opinion but by the laws of the country . . . . He [the slave] is deprived of education. God gave him an intellect; the slaveholder declares it shall not be cultivated."[50] The denial of education, even the simplest forms of reading and writing, reinforced the concept of the superior/inferior relationship by making the slave more dependent upon his master and, thus, less likely to be disobedient or to run away.

Slavery was first introduced to the colonies in 1619 when a few Black Africans were brought to the new world to harvest Jamestown's tobacco crop. "Within a decade after South Carolina's 1691 adoption of a comprehensive slave code, other Colonies had laws defining and regulating human chattel."[51] Aided by a lucrative cross-Atlantic slave trading industry, the slave system grew rapidly. "By the eve of the [American] Revolution, slave-holding was deeply rooted in all of those Colonies, with New York City, among colonial cities, standing second only Charleston, S.C., in its population of slaves."[52] The emerging slave system was economically attractive to both the agricultural interests in the South and the developing textile industries in the North. Although several of the framers opposed the institution of slavery on moral grounds, economic reality prevented the abolition of the system, opting instead to ban the exportation of new slaves into the country by 1808. "By as early as 1815, cotton was America's most valuable export, and the worth of the people who harvested the product grew apace with cotton's steadily growing value. 'By the eve of the Civil War, the dollar value of slaves was greater than the dollar value of all of America's banks, railroads, and manufacturing combined."[53] Unable to halt the spread of slavery in the traditional Southern states, the abolitionist movement convinced Congress to limit the spread of slavery into new territories seeking statehood with the passage of the **Missouri Compromise** in 1820.

The fate of the Missouri Compromise was determined by the United States Supreme Court's decision in ***Dred Scott v Sanford*** (1857). First, the Court invalidated the Missouri Compromise of 1820 as an unconstitutional intrusion into state affairs. Second, it ruled that Dred Scott, a slave, did not have the right to sue the government because he was not a citizen of the country. Third, Scott was still considered to be a slave since the Court affirmed that slaves were the property of their owners, and only their owners could release them from their bondage.

The man who would eventually abolish slavery echoed superior/inferior sentiments against slaves in a speech delivered in 1858 at a Republican Party function. Abraham Lincoln stated: "I will say then that I am not, nor ever have been in favor of bringing about in any way the social and political equality of the white [Anglo] and black [African American] races, [applause]—that I am not nor ever have been in favor of making voters or jurors of Negroes [African Americans], nor of qualifying them to hold office, nor to intermarry with white [Anglo] people, and I will say in addition to this that there is a physical difference between black [African American] and white [Anglo] races which I believe will forever forbid the two races living together on the terms of social and political equality. And inasmuch as they cannot so live, while they do remain together, there must be the position of superior and inferior, and I as much as any other man, am in favor of having the superior position assigned to the white [Anglo] race."[54] During the Civil War, free African Americans living in the Northern states were initially denied the right to join the military effort. "The hardest problem for black [African American] men was not in being brave, it was in getting a chance to fight at all. At every step, they were confronted with racial scorn and fear, created by the long existence of slavery itself."[55] In 1862, Congress passed the Militia Act, enabling African Americans to join the warfront. However, African Americans received less than half of the standard soldier pay and were denied any officer and command positions. At the end of the war, "some 180,000 black [African-American] solders served in the Union Army, about 10 percent of its total strength; 2,800 were killed in battle, 34,000 died of disease in the field, and twenty-one were awarded the Medal of Honor for bravery."[56] Given such sentiments, it is no wonder that the struggle of African Americans to achieve social, economic, and political equality and social acceptability has been a courageous and valiant story.

The end of the Civil War brought limited social, economic, and political relief to former slaves. Economic viability was difficult, if not immediately impossible. Few knew how to read or write. Few had ventured far from their plantations. Once emancipated, few knew how to survive on their own. During the final months of the Civil War, General William Sherman attempted to entice southern African Americans to join the union cause by offering to each family forty-acres of prime farmland in Georgia and South Carolina. He also promised to lend them Army mules. Congress also allocated approximately 850,000 acres of southern soil to the Freedman's Bureau. In turn, the bureau was supposed to help former slaves make the transition from slavery to freedom by giving them land. Few received any land since President Andrew Johnson used his executive muscle to allow former Confederates to quickly reclaim their properties. In 1865, the United States Congress

The Supreme Court decided that Dred Scott was not a citizen of the United States.

finally outlawed slavery with the passage of the **Thirteenth Amendment**. Former slaves were granted citizenship with the passage of the **Fourteenth Amendment** and voting privileges with the **Fifteenth Amendment**. The **Civil Rights Act of 1866** granted former slaves the rights to own property, file lawsuits, and make contractual agreements. Initially, the Republican-dominated Congress used these three constitutional amendments and the Civil Rights Act to punish defeated members of the **Confederate States of America**. Known as the **Radical Republicans**, these individuals desired to topple the Southern aristocracy by placing former slaves into policy-making roles. Across the South, former Confederate officials, soldiers, and any one who supported the Southern cause lost their rights to vote and to run for elective office. Consequently, citizenship and voting privileges enabled former slaves to run for public office. "Every session of the Virginia General Assembly from 1869 to 1891 contained black [African American] members. Between 1876 and 1894 North Carolinians elected fifty-two blacks [African Americans] to the lower house of their state legislature, and between 1878 and 1902, forty-seven blacks [African Americans] served in the South Carolina General Assembly . . . . Southern states elected two blacks [African Americans] to the U. S. House of Representatives after Reconstruction, the same number elected during Reconstruction. Every Congress but one between 1869 and 1901 had at least one black [African American] member from the South."[57]

"Yet despite these enactments, despite the mandates of Amendment Fourteen, and despite the language of the Fifteenth Amendment of 1870 which on its face seemed to assure to blacks [African Americans] the privilege of the ballot, neither the myth of white supremacy nor the fact of color prejudice was wiped out."[58] The Southern states struck back at the federal government by enacting a series of legislative acts and city ordinances known as black codes or **Jim Crow laws** that denied freedoms and political rights to African Americans. National lawmakers soon realized "that you cannot change the mores of a people by law, and since the social segregation of the races is the most deep-seated and pervasive of the Southern mores, it is evident that he who attempts to change it by law runs risks of incalculable gravity."[59] Jim Crow laws began to have an impact on African-American accessibility to the ballot box, blocking full political participation. The **grandfather clause** required passing a **literacy test** for those potential voters whose grandfathers could not vote before 1867. Variations of the grandfather clause were incorporated into the state constitutions of South Carolina, Louisiana, North Carolina, Alabama, Virginia, Georgia, and Oklahoma. The **poll tax**, a state mandated voting fee, was enacted in Florida, Tennessee, Arkansas, and Texas. The Democratic Party's **white only primary** effectively eliminated African-American participation, since in most general races, the opposition party did not run a candidate. This tactic was adopted in South Carolina, Arkansas, Georgia, Florida, Tennessee, Alabama, Mississippi, Kentucky, Texas, Louisiana, Oklahoma, Virginia, and North Carolina. "The effectiveness of disenfranchisement is suggested by a comparison of the number of registered black [African American] voters in Louisiana in 1896, when there were 130,334 and in 1904, when there were 1,342. Between the two dates the literacy, property, and poll tax qualifications were adopted. In 1896, black [African American] registrants were in a majority in twenty-six parishes—by 1900 none."[60] During the early part of the nineteenth century, the North Carolina political scene was dominated by the Democratic Party that systematically disenfranchised all Republicans—both Anglo and African American—by crafting a new voter registration procedure requiring all potential voters to read the Constitution to a voter registrar's satisfaction.

Jim Crow laws also socially separated Anglos from African Americans. Immediately following the election of 1884, "the rumor, when it struck, was deemed as vile as any that had ever hit the nation's capitol. A 'colored man' [African American], people were whispering, had attended a White House function. Grover Cleveland swiftly responded. "It so happens," the President assured the nation, "that I have never in my official position, either when sleeping or walking, alive or dead, on my head or my heels, dined, lunched, or supped or invited to a wedding reception any colored [African American] man, woman, or child."[61] The mean-spiritedness of Jim Crow pervaded legislative houses across this nation. The Virginia state legislature passed a 1912 ordinance mandating segregated residential districts. The law made it "unlawful for any colored [African American] person to move into a white district, or a white [Anglo] person to move into a colored [African American] district. This act [did] not preclude persons of either race employed as servants by persons of the other race from residing on the premises of the employer."[62] In the Southern states, the segregation of the races was conducted under the **separate but equal** policy. "They [African Americans] were either excluded from railway cars, omnibuses, stage coaches, and steamboats or assigned to special 'Jim Crow' sections; they sat, when permitted, in secluded and remote corners of theaters and lecture halls; they could not enter most hotels, restaurants, and resorts, except as servants; they prayed in 'Negro [African American] pews' in white [Anglo] churches, and if partaking of the sacrament of the Lord's supper, they waited until the whites [Anglos] had been served the bread and wine. Moreover, they were often educated in segregated schools, punished in segregated prisons, nursed in segregated hospitals, and buried in segregated cemetaries."[63] Almost all the Southern states passed laws requiring railroad stations to have separate waiting rooms and segregated cars. Public facilities had separate drinking fountains, restrooms, swimming pools, and parks.

"There was nothing particularly secretive about either public or private discrimination; it was simply a way of life."[64] These tactics effectively created African-American ghettos and slum areas whereby African Americans were kept economically, socially, and politically depressed. In smaller towns, an invisible line successfully separated African Americans from Anglos. The term "living on the wrong side of the tracks" indicated the societal status of the resident. Both the white and black communities felt the adverse impact of Jim Crow. Civil rights advocate James Meredith stressed that "you can't forget that whites in the South were as unfree as any black. White supremacy was official and legal—it was enforced by judges and the law people—and a white that failed to acknowledge and carry out the mandate of white supremacy was as subject to persecution as any black."[65]

Ironically, the United States Supreme Court upheld Jim Crow laws in hearing a case that originated in Louisiana. Originally a French colony, Louisiana was far more liberal in its treatment of African Americans than her sister states. "New Orleans began experimenting with integrated public schools—the only Southern city to do so. Blacks [African-Americans] served with whites [Anglos] on juries and public boards. New Orleans had an integrated police department with a color-blind municipal pay scale... Between the years 1868 and 1896, racial intermarriage was made legal, and Louisiana elected 32 black [African-American] state senators and 95 state representatives. It had the only black [African-American] governor in U.S. history before the late 1980's."[66] With the end of Reconstruction, the power of the Radical Republicans in the South began to erode as former

Confederates, armed with their voting rights, reestablished the Democratic Party power base in the South. Louisiana began to join her fellow southern sisters by implementing Jim Crow laws. In 1890, the Louisiana legislature passed the **Separate Car Act,** mandating separate accommodations for Anglo and African-American patrons. "Under its terms any railway company that did not provide separate coaches for blacks [African Americans] and whites [Anglos] could be fined $500. Except for nurses attending children of the other race, individual whites [Anglos] and blacks [African Americans] would be forbidden to ride together or risk a $25 fine or 20 days in jail."[67] Opposition to the law saw African Americans and the railroad companies on the same side of the fence. Railroad executives rationalized that "it was going to cost money to build and run extra cars-for the bill implied that if a half-empty "white" [Anglo] car was waiting, even if only one black [African American] passenger showed up, he or she would have to have a whole separate-but-equal vehicle made available. For a city [New Orleans] that had for so long seen so much racial mixing, railway conductors would now have to decide who was white [Anglo] and who was black [African American]—a touchy business, especially since some wives and husbands would not be allowed to ride together."[68] Opposition groups decided to test the validity of the law. Homer Plessy, who was one-eighth African American, was purposely selected by the East Louisiana Railroad to sit in the "white" section of the railway car headed from New Orleans to Covington. Railroad officials believed the uproar of Plessy's arrest would convince the courts that the law was unconstitutional. When ordered to give up his seat, Plessy refused and was arrested. Plessy sued, believing that the Louisiana law violated the Thirteenth and Fourteenth Amendments to the United States Constitution. The United States Supreme Court's 1896 ruling in *Plessy v Ferguson* resulted in a 7 to 0 vote against Plessy. In defense of its decision, the Court maintained that "a statute that made a legal distinction between the races on the basis of color did not destroy the legal equality of the races or create a condition of slavery; it merely reflected the social distinctions based on color that existed in society. Furthermore, while the object of the Fourteenth Amendment was to enforce the absolute legal and political equality of the two races, it was not intended to abolish distinctions based upon color or enforce social equality and the 'commingling' of the two races upon terms unsatisfactory to either."[69] This ruling gave state legislative houses the ability to continue passing laws separating the races, providing the segregated accommodations or services were basically in principle equal. The United States Supreme Court also struck down the **Civil Rights Act of 1875,** prohibiting private discrimination in accommodations, transportation, and public places of amusement. The Court's decision was based on the premise that the Fourteenth Amendment applied to state or public actions, not to private activities. "This meant that the federal government, lacking the means and will, pretty well got out of the business of making sure that the new civil rights laws were applied in the South."[70]

African Americans were "kept in their place" through the intimidation of the **Ku Klux Klan (KKK).** The Klan emerged in the South during the Reconstruction era and remained a strong presence in Southern politics until the late 1920s. Garbed in white robes and hoods, Klansmen used a variety of scare tactics against defiant African Americans and whites [Anglos] sympathetic to the plight of African Americans. Burning crosses, public tar and featherings, floggings, and lynchings were used throughout the South to remind African Americans of their inferior status. Scores of Asians, Native Americans, Hispanics and even Anglos were lynched throughout the United States.

However, the practice was more predominately used as a scare tactic against the African-American community in the southern states. Thurgood Marshall once commented that "even in Mississippi a Negro [African-American] will get a trial longer than 42 minutes, if he is fortunate enough to be brought to trial."[71] In some southern communities, African Americans could be arrested for petty offenses, such as not stepping off the sidewalk to make way for an Anglo pedestrian. Far too often, "justice" for African-Americans was a lynch mob, not a jury of twelve impartial men and women. "In the past two decades of the nineteenth century more than 2,500 blacks [African Americans] were lynched in the South. Another thousand or so were murdered in this way in the first decade and a half of the new century."[72] It was the efforts of the **Association of Southern Women for the Prevention of Lynching** that finally gained public support of state laws prohibiting lynching. During its 2002 term, the United States Supreme Court heard arguments in a case concerning the Klan's continued practice of burning crosses as a means of intimidating African Americans. Known for his quiet demeanor on the bench, Justice Clarence Thomas, the Court's only African-American member, decried that "this [the Klan's activities] was a reign of terror, and the cross was a symbol of that reign of terror. Isn't that significantly greater than intimidation or a threat? . . . We had almost 100 years of lynching and activity in the South by the Knights of Camellia and the Ku Klux Klan. It was intended to cause fear and to terrorize a population."[73]

Jim Crow also meant that African Americans were prohibited from moving into white neighborhoods by the restrictive covenant, redlining, and steering techniques. A **restrictive covenant** was a provision in a mortgage contract that forbade the buyer from eventually selling the house to a member of a minority race. If such a sale occurred, the property could revert back to the original owner. Another ploy was to increase the selling price of the property based upon the interested party's race, placing the sale price at a prohibitive cost. **Steering** was the practice of just showing properties to minorities located in solely minority residential areas, thus keeping them away from already segregated white [Anglo] neighborhoods. **Redlining** was the tactic used by financial institutions to deny loans to individuals wanting to purchase property in a racially changing neighbor-

The Ku Klux Klan was politically strong in the South. Action was directed at African Americans and white sympathizers.

hood. The loan would either be denied outright or the interest rate would be substantially increased to discourage the potential borrower.

African Americans began to challenge Jim Crow laws and acts of discrimination by forming community and nationally based organizations. In 1909 a well-known African-American scholar, W. E. B. DuBois, founded the **National Association for the Advancement of Colored Persons** (NAACP). Groups leading the charge for equality for African Americans included the Congress of Racial Equality (CORE), and the Southern Christian Leadership Conference (SCLC), founded by the late Dr. Martin L. King, Jr., in 1956.

The modern civil rights movement drew national attention to the adverse discriminatory practices of Jim Crow when Mrs. Rosa Parks [an African American] was arrested for refusing to give up her seat on a Montgomery, Alabama bus to a white [Anglo] person; four African-American students at the North Carolina Agricultural and Technical College sat peacefully at a lunch counter at Woolworth's while employees refused to serve them and bystanders hurled racial insults and food at them; and Dr. Martin L. King, Jr., led protesters in peaceful, nonviolent demonstrations throughout the South. When asked why she refused to give up her seat, Rosa Parks said "that my feet were hurting, and I didn't know why I refused to stand up when they told me. But the real reason of my not standing up was I felt that I had a right to be treated as any other passenger. We had endured that kind of treatment for too long."[74] Honored as the "Mother of the Civil Rights Movement", Mrs. Parks continued her fight for equal treatment. She once noted that "without vision, the people will perish, and without courage and inspiration, dreams will die-the dream of freedom and peace."[75]

A new term began to emerge from the protesters—**integration**. "One cannot be close to the problem very long without hearing that word. *Integration* is what the Negro [African American] has not got. He is on the outside, and he wants to be on the inside. He is not allowed to play or live or work as others and he wants to play, live, and work as others. He occupies a negative position, and desires the positive. The principle of integration (and its opposite, non-integration) cuts a pattern through the nation just as widespread but far more complex than the transportation system over which the trains roll, planes fly, farm wagons crawl, and people walk."[76] The demand for inclusion from a group excluded from the political, social, and cultural environment of mainstream America for over two hundred years could no longer be ignored or dismissed. One by one the repressive practices of Jim Crow began to be challenged and successfully overturned by the federal courts. The actions of the United State Supreme Court awakened the United States Congress to pass a series of civil rights acts, which provided voting rights and desegregation of public accommodations and public schools to correct past abuses.

The first major civil rights bill since Reconstruction, the **Civil Rights Act of 1957**, created the United States Commission on Civil Rights and the Civil Rights Section of the Justice Department. The federal government was now empowered to obtain injunctions to halt illegal voting activities. The **Civil Rights Act of 1960** authorized federal appointed voter referees to conduct voter registration drives and to monitor federal elections in areas with historical patterns of voting problems. The **Civil Rights Act of 1964** prohibited discrimination in public accommodations and employment practices. Discriminatory housing practices to include restrictive convenants, redlining and steering were prohibited with the passage of the **Civil Rights Act of 1968**.

The United States Supreme Court began to curtail discriminatory voting practices as early as 1927. In *Nixon v Herndon*, the Supreme Court invalidated the Texas White Primary Law of 1924, which mandated that "in no event shall a Negro [African American] be eligible to participate in a Democratic primary election in the State of Texas, and should a Negro [African American] vote in a Democratic primary election, such ballot shall be void and election officials shall not count the same."[77] Defiantly, the Texas Democratic Party continued the white-only primary by declaring the party a private club capable of establishing its own membership criteria. The United States Supreme Court finally dealt the fatal blow to this practice by ruling in *Smith v Allwright* (1944) that the Texas Democratic Party was not a private club but an agent of the state, subject to state and federal mandates. As a state agency, the party could no longer deny voting privileges to any qualified voter for any election.

The poll tax was outlawed with the passage of the **Twenty-fourth Amendment** to the United States Constitution. In *Guinn v United States* (1915), the United States Supreme Court invalidated Oklahoma's grandfather clause as a direct violation of the Fifteenth Amendment. The literacy test was dismantled in a piecemeal fashion. The **Civil Rights Act of 1964** required states to accept a sixth grade education as meeting voter literacy and testing requirements. Minor errors on the test or voter registration card, such as abbreviations, could not be used to deny voting privileges. The **Voting Rights Act of 1965** suspended the use of discriminatory literacy tests. A 1970 amendment to the Voting Rights Act completely eliminated the literacy requirement.

Jim Crow also extended to the military. During World War II, for example, African Americans were denied officer and leadership roles. Supervised by Anglo officers, African-American soldiers were far too often segregated into their own camps, barracks, mess halls, and even latrines. "More than a million blacks [African Americans] served in that war, of the more than 16 million U.S. military personnel. Most were assigned to construction, transportation, service or support units."[78] On July 26, 1948, President Harry Truman issued **Executive Order No. 9981**, which desegregated the military by mandating "equality of treatment and opportunity for all persons in the armed forces without regard to race, color, religion or national origin."[79] However, the military was reluctant to desegregate its facilities much less to promote African Americans into command and officer positions. Of course, off base, African-American military personnel were subjected to the same discriminatory practices as their non-military counterparts.

The demise of the "separate but equal" doctrine began with the certainly separate but definitely unequal conditions in public schools and colleges across the nation. Segregated education even garnered international attention. The United States Secretary of State commented that "the segregation of school children on a racial basis is one of the practices which has been singled out for hostile foreign comment in the United Nations and elsewhere. Other peoples cannot understand how such a practice can exist in a country which professes to be a staunch supporter of freedom, justice and democracy."[80] For example, Herman Sweatt, an African-American mail carrier from Houston, Texas, wanted to attend the University of Texas Law School. Sweatt was denied admission because of his race. His only option was to attend the Texas State University for Negroes, an academically inferior school when compared to the University of Texas. In *Sweatt v Painter* (1950), the United States Supreme Court ruled that Sweatt should not be forced to attend a racially separated inferior school. "By ruling that the term *equal* applied not only to tangible factors, such as

Chief Justice Earl Warren ruled for a unanimous Court in the desegregation decision in 1954.

university buildings, books, and faculty, but to intangible qualities such as institutional reputation and opportunity to interact with a cross-section of the legal profession, the Court made it more difficult for states to maintain and justify separate but equal or 'dual' school systems."[81] A similar ruling was made that same year in *McLaurin v Oklahoma State Regents*. The University of Oklahoma did not have a separate graduate school for African Americans. The university would admit African Americans on a segregated basis, meaning that African Americans sat in totally segregated classes and facilities from white students. The Court ruled against the university's policy.

In 1954, the United States Supreme Court handed down its "separate but equal" shattering ruling in *Brown v the Board of Education of Topeka, Kansas*. Eight-year-old Linda Brown was refused admittance to an all-white public school located just five blocks from her home because of her race. Instead, she was forced to attend an African-American school located twenty-one blocks from her home. The *Brown* suit was one of four filed by African-American families confronted with similar situations in South Carolina, Virginia, and Delaware. Basically, African-American children were forced to attend poorly equipped, inadequately staffed, and seriously underfunded African-American public schools. The question before the Court was whether the Fourteenth Amendment's equal protection clause extended to public schools. The United States Supreme Court ruled unanimously with Brown concluding that "*in the field of public education the doctrine of 'separate but equal' has no place. Separate educational facilities are inherently unequal . . .* The plaintiffs and others similarly situated for whom the actions have been brought are, by reason of the segregation complained of, *deprived of the equal protection of the laws guaranteed by the Fourteenth Amendment.*[82] The *Brown* decision dismantled the philosophical basis of Jim Crow. However, public schools, colleges, and universities reluctantly and defiantly opened their doors to African-American students. Orval Faubus, governor of Arkansas, openly defied desegregation of Little Rock's four high schools by closing them down for the entire 1958-59 academic year, leaving approximately 3,700 public school students to make their own arrangements. "Some families sent their children to private schools, many of them newly minted during the 'crisis.' Others enrolled in correspondence courses. In what amounted to a nationwide diaspora, many were shipped off to live with relatives. . . . the Lost Year blew apart high school sports teams, theater troupes, debate squads and college preparation plans. Today, Little Rock's high schools have no graduating classes of 1959."[83] To counter the governor's actions, federal authorities decided to force desegregation by enrolling nine African-American students into Little Rock's Central High School. With the assistance of the United States Army, the nine were finally admitted into the door of the high school. Their school year, however, was not a pleasant experience. "The nine students were bombarded with racial hatred. The U.S. Department of Justice had assigned a bodyguard to each of them, but white [Anglo] students still harassed them. They were body-slammed into lockers, attacked in gym

The mule-drawn wagon bearing the body of Dr. Martin Luther King, Jr. moves up Auburn Avenue toward downtown Atlanta after funeral services for the slain civil rights leader. Winner of the Nobel Peace Prize and a staunch supporter of nonviolence, Dr. Martin Luther King, Jr. was assassinated in Memphis, Tennessee, on April 4, 1968.

class, tripped in the hallways, and push down stairs. And the name calling was incessant. So were the death threats."[84] By 1960, the federal government realized that it had to assume a more forceful role in desegregating public schools and facilities. "In Louisiana, Mississippi, Alabama, Georgia, and South Carolina there has been no change at all. In Florida, Arkansas, Tennessee, North Carolina and Virginia, only an occasional school district has allowed white [Anglo] and colored [African American] children to sit in the same classrooms. Texas, Oklahoma, Missouri, Kentucky, West Virginia, Maryland, Delaware, and the District of Columbia range, however, from extensive to complete desegregation of schools."[85] Consequently, the enforcement of desegregation was accomplished through court mandated busing and federal threats of denial of federal money to schools participating in discriminatory practices. Subsequent court decisions and legislative acts mandated desegregation of all public facilities and accommodations. The now outlawed practices of separate but equal proved to be very costly to the South, both in budgetary dollars and public image as the rest of the country began to see the impact of their discriminatory practices. One observer noted that Jim Crow laws "compels the South to have to buy two of everything, two schools, two toilets, two communities, two worlds."[86]

The victories won by civil rights leaders in the 1960s should not be underestimated. Civil rights activists were murdered for their efforts to register African Americans to vote in the Deep South. Martin L. King, Jr., Malcolm X, Medger Evers, and many others were slain because their quest for African-American equality was viewed by some as too revolutionary for mainstream America. The Civil Rights Movement of the 60s has resulted in more African Americans registering, voting, and running for public office. Douglas Wilder, for example, became the first African-American governor in the country when he was elected to the top executive post in Virginia. Retired Commander of the Joint Chiefs of Staff, Colin Powell, who was heavily recruited by both political parties to run for the presidency in 1996 and 2000, was selected by President George W. Bush to become the nation's only African American Secretary of State. At the beginning of his second term of office, George W. Bush accepted Powell's resignation and name Condoleezza Rice as his replacement, making her the first African-American woman to serve as the nation's Secretary of State. Although not the first African American to make a bid for the White House, Freshman Illinois Senator Barack Obama is an announced candidate for the 2008 Democratic Party's presidential nomination. Table 14.2 is a selected listing of significant events and achievements for African Americans.

Yet, these political achievements are overshadowed by the plight of this nation's African-American citizens. The battle cries of integration and the politics of inclusion have yet to produce promised economic and social changes. In particular, the African-American community is continuously battling high poverty, dropout and unemployment rates coupled with the rising number of African-American youths incarcerated in the nation's prison systems. Recognizing the growing number of minorities, particularly African Americans, tried and convicted in federal courts, President Clinton's Attorney General Janet Reno pointed out that "minorities are over-represented in the federal death penalty system as both victims and defendants, relative to the general population. Crime is often the product of social ills and harsh conditions, such as poverty, drug abuse and lack of opportunity, that disproportionately affect minorities. So long as those conditions remain, we will continue to see disparities in the number of minorities in the criminal justice system."[87] In

2004, 1,985,000 families constituting 22.3 percent of African American families and 8,801,000 persons representing 24.5 percent of all African Americans lived below the poverty level. For them, the promise of the "American Dream" of home ownership and economic stability is just that, an elusive dream. The 2004 medium family income for blacks (African Americans) was $34,369 in comparison to $55,768 for whites (Anglos). Additionally, 1,729,000 or 10.4 percent of all African Americans in the civilian labor force were unemployed.[88]

Table 14.2
Significant Events for African Americans

Date	Event
1619	The first African slaves arrive in Virginia.
1831	William Lloyd Garrison begins publishing *The Liberator*, an abolitionist newspaper. Nat Turner leads rebellion in Virginia, resulting in the deaths of 57 white men, women, and children. Turner was executed for his role.
1832	Garrison organizes the New England Anti-Slavery Society.
1833	Lewis Tappan, Theodore Weld and William Garrison establish the American Anti-Slavery Society, a national organization opposing slavery.
1851	Sojourner Truth gives her "Ain't I A Woman?" speech at the women's rights convention held in Akron, Ohio. Myrtilla Miner opens the first school to train African-American women to be teachers.
1852	Harriet Beecher Stowe publishes *Uncle Tom's Cabin*.
1855	In *Missouri v Celia, a Slave,* an African-American woman is declared to be property without the right to defend herself against her master's continuous acts of rape. She was eventually executed for murdering her master. Fighting breaks out in Kansas, known as "Bloody Kansas."
1857	The U.S. Supreme Court rules in *Dred Scott v Sanford* that slaves are not citizens; therefore, they do not have the right to sue. This case nullifies the Missouri Compromise.
1862	Mary Jane Patterson is the first African-American woman to receive a full baccalaureate degree from Oberlin College.
1863	Lincoln issues his Gettysburg Address to include the Emancipation Proclamation.
1865	Congress passes the 13th Amendment abolishing slavery. Lee surrenders. Lincoln is assassinated. The Freedmen's Bureau is founded to assist newly freed slaves. Black codes enacted across the southern states.
1866	The 14th Amendment granting citizenship to former male slaves is passed by Congress. The Civil Rights Bill of 1866 is passed over President Johnson's veto. The Ku Klux Klan is organized.
1867	African Americans vote in Southern elections.

1870   The 15th Amendment, expanding voting rights to former male slaves, is officially ratified.

1875   Civil Rights Act of 1875, guaranteeing desegregated public facilities, passes Congress. This law will be ruled as unconstitutional by the Supreme Court in the *Civil Rights Cases*, 1883.

1896   The National Association of Colored Women, founded by Margaret Murray Washington, unites several African-American women's groups under one organization. Mary Church Terrell serves as its first president. In *Plessy v Ferguson*, the Supreme Court upholds the separate but equal doctrine.

1909   The National Association for the Advancement of Colored Persons (NAACP) is formed with W. E. B. Dubois as its first president.

1935   Mary McLeod Bethune organizes the National Council of Negro Women as a lobbying group for African-American women. Key agenda items focus on fighting job discrimination, racism & sexism.

1939   Marian Anderson gives a concert at the Lincoln Memorial.

1954   *Brown v Board of Education of Topeka, Kansas.*

1955   Montgomery Bus Boycott in response to Rosa Parks being arrested for refusing to give up her bus seat to a white person. The boycott is staged from December 5, 1955 to December 21, 1956. The Interstate Commerce Commission bans segregation on interstate travel. Emmett Till is killed on August 28.

1956   Tallahassee Bus Boycott begins on May 27. The boycott ends in March 1958. Autherine Lucy is admitted to the University of Alabama. The Southern Manifesto is presented.
The Supreme Court upholds the use of busing for desegregation of public schools. Martin L. King, Jr.,'s home is bombed as well as the Shuttlesworth home.

1957   Southern Christian Leadership Conference is formed. Protests begin at the Little Rock Central High School. The protests end in May 1959. The first civil rights bill since 1875 passes through Congress.

1960   Greensboro sit-in occurs on February 1, followed by sit-ins and boycotts all over the South and in some Northern cities. Civil Rights Act of 1960 signed.

1961   Freedom Rides occur during the summer. Federal courts order Hunter and Holmes to be admitted to the University of Georgia.

1962   James Meredith enters the University of Mississippi. John Kennedy federalizes Mississippi State Troopers to protect Meredith. Los Angeles riots occur on April 27 followed by the Ole Mississippi riots in October.

1963   University of Alabama desegregation crisis occurs as George Wallace attempts to block federal troops sent by the president. John Kennedy meets with civil rights leaders for the March on Washington, August 28. Medgar Evers and John Kennedy are killed.

1964   Title VII of the Civil Rights Act barring employment discrimination by private employers, employment agencies, and unions is enacted. Martin L. King, Jr., awarded Nobel Prize. The 24th Amendment to the U.S. Constitution, banning the poll tax, is ratified. Race riots occur in New York, New Jersey, Chicago, and Philadelphia. Goodman, Schwerner, and Chaney killed on June 24.

1965	Lyndon Johnson enacts Executive Order 11246 calling for the federal government to take affirmative action in overcoming employment discrimination. Voting Rights Act signed into law. Malcolm X is killed. Race riots in Watts.
1968	Martin L. King, Jr., and Robert Kennedy are assassinated. Riots at the Democratic Convention.
1971	Shirley Chisholm (D-NY) is the first African-American woman elected to the U.S. Congress.
1972	Barbara Jordan (D-TX) becomes the first African American elected to U.S. Congress from a southern state.
1984	The nonpartisan National Political Congress of Black Women is founded by Shirley Chisholm to address women's rights issues and to encourage political participation.
1988	Rev. Barbara Harris becomes the first female African-American bishop of the Episcopal Church.
1990	The number of African-American women elected to office increased from 131 in 1970 to 1,950 in 1990.
1992	Carol Moseley-Braun (D-Ill). becomes the first African-American woman elected to the U.S. Senate.
2000	Colin S. Powell becomes the first African American to serve as the nation's Secretary of State and Condoleezza Rice becomes the first woman and African American to serve as the National Security Advisor.
2005	Condoleezza Rice becomes the first African-American woman to serve as the nation's Secretary of State.

The Hispanic Experience

Other victims of discrimination, racial hatred, prejudice, and stereotyping are Hispanics, Americans of Mexican and Spanish descent. When most Americans voice their concerns over illegal immigration, their attention is focused to the Mexican national crossing the Rio Grande in the Southwestern states or the international border into California. Anti-immigration advocates fail to mention that other nationalities have come to this country illegally. In addition, we should not forget that "the Spanish Mexicans of the Southwest are not truly an immigrant group, for they are in their traditional home.[89] Hispanics are the fastest growing minority group in the United States. Despite their booming population, Hispanics have been victimized by the very same philosophy of Anglo superiority that was used against African Americans. Hispanics continue to struggle against the adverse impact of dire poverty that in some areas is close to third world poverty conditions with inadequate housing coupled with a lack of indoor plumbing and sewer systems. Denied adequate educational opportunities, far too often Hispanics are employed at minimum wage or lower scale positions. In addition, Hispanics are routinely denied adequate health care and social services and reside in segregated low income and depressed tax based neighborhoods. There are still far too many towns and cities in the Southwest where an invisible line separates the Anglo side of town from the "Mexican" district, rendering Hispanics to the status of second class citizens. Low levels of voter turnout and political efficacy have hampered the efforts of Hispanics to reverse these dismal trends.

The "Hispanic" community also suffers from stereotyping that fails to recognize the cultural diversity of those called "Hispanics." "The label Latino or Hispanic covers people who come from two dozen countries and who can claim mixtures of Spanish, Portuguese, Indian, African, Italian, German and Italian ancestry."[90] Basically the Hispanic community is composed of three culturally, socially, and politically diverse groups who live in different areas of the country. "Mexican-Americans, who make up almost two-thirds of the Hispanics in the United States, are concentrated in the Southwest. Cuban-Americans live primarily in South Florida. Puerto Rican Americans have settled mostly in the Northeast, particularly in New York City and New Jersey."[91] Politically, Mexican-Americans promote liberal Democratic candidates while Cuban-Americans are known to cast a bloc vote for conservative Republican candidates.

The growing distrust between Hispanics and Anglo Americans began in earnest with the colonization of Texas. Unable to settle Texas with families from Spain and Mexico, both governments opened up the region to Anglo Americans through a land grant program known as the empresario system. Initially welcomed into the region, Anglo Americans soon began to take advantage of their hosts by openly defying the Mexican government. The aftermath of the inevitable Texas Revolution made the already fragile relationship deteriorate further as Hispanics encountered "the wrath of Anglos, who considered them a conquered people and an alien race and who persecuted them with impunity."[92] Although there are several explanations for the racial tensions between Hispanics and Anglos, the economic theory of racism was evident in the settlement of the Southwestern states and California. Like the Native American tribes, Spanish and Mexican landowners held a precious commodity Anglo Americans wanted—vast landholdings. Anglo American settlers guided by a government bent on achieving its manifest destiny cast an envious and greedy eye upon those vast parcels of land that were granted by the Spanish monarchy to the economic elites or Creoles. Gradually, Anglo Americans used a variety of schemes to seize these lands.

Meanwhile, the non-economic elite Hispanics, known as **Mestizos,** became the primary labor force in building the nation's railroads, working in the mines extracting precious natural resourses, toiling in the fields picking agricultural crops, or riding fence on cattle ranches, relegated to a life of picking fruits and vegetables, herding cattle or laboring at unskilled or semiskilled jobs at exceptionally low wages, Hispanics workers were needed for their muscles, not their minds. Testifying before the House Immigration and Naturalization Committee in 1920, then Congressman John Nance Garner from Uvalde, Texas, stated: "I believe I am within the bounds of truth when I say that the Mexican man is superior laborer when it comes to grubbing land. . . And I may add that the prices that they charge are much less than the same labor would be from either the Negro [African-American] or the white man and for the same time they do . . . a third more—they produce a third more results from their labor then either the Negro [African-American] or white man would do."[93] Unfortunately, Hispanics were subjected to the same Jim Crow laws and acts of wanton discrimination as those levied against African Americans. "For roughly 75 years after the end of the war between Mexico and the United States, Mexican Americans in the Southwest contended with segregation in the public schools, segregation and discrimination in public facilities such as restaurants, movie theaters, swimming pools, and barbershops; primary election procedures that prevented them from exercising their right to vote; and discrimination in housing. They also suffered discrimination in the administration of justice that prevented them from serving on juries and treated violence against them as so common as to pass almost unnoticed."[94]

The story of the farmer laborer or **compensino** in the Southwest and California is a tragic one. The movement of Mexican labor into the United States picked up stream during World War I. "In California, the demand for workers in the citrus, melon, tomato, and other industries increased sharply, encouraging Mexicans to come across the border to perform these necessary tasks. The other southwestern states were similarly affected. Workers were needed in Texas to tend the cotton, spinach, and onion crops and in Arizona, New Mexico, and Colorado to raise vegetables, forage crops, and sugar beets."[95] Since these are not yearly crops, the term "seasonal" or "migratory" workers was used to describe this Mexican labor force. At the turn of the twentieth century, approximately 85 percent of Hispanics living in Texas were employed as farm workers, ranch hands, and tenant farmers. Tenant farmers worked the landowner's fields from sun up to sun down in return for extremely low wages, a one-room shack, and a small plot of land to grow their own vegetables. The future of tenant farmers rested squarely upon the shoulders of the landowner, who could at any time raise rents, restrict planting, or relocate and remove the tenant from his property. Whether stationary or migratory, the farm workers of today toil in the fields picking and harvesting crops in the same bent over position assumed by their fathers and grandfathers. Living conditions are in some instances akin to third world poverty. Job security is just as nonexistent as ample health care and education. Severe weather destroys both crops and jobs. In the mid 1960s, the late César Chávez began organizing campesinos into the **United Farm Workers Union (UFW)**. This organization brought national attention to the living and working conditions of farm workers in Texas and California by its series of protests and strikes over the picking -of lettuce and grapes. "In the 1970s, they [the campesinos] still faced lamentable working conditions. Most fields lacked restrooms, and since modesty compelled women to delay their bodily functions for hours, they suffered from disproportionately high levels of kidney infections. Wages remained as low as $2 or $3 for a typical day of field labor. Diseases such as typhoid, typhus, dysentery, and leprosy afflicted farm workers to a degree unknown to other Texans. Infant mortality rates among the compesinos

Chávez was a leader for the Hispanic farm workers.

in South Texas were among the highest in the United States at that time, and the life expectancy for field hands hovered around forty-nine."[96]

The success of the United Farm Workers Union has helped to produce corrective legislation designed to improve the lifestyle of farm workers. They can now apply for unemployment and workers compensation benefits. Their children can now attend schools offering half day class schedules to accommodate those students who must spend a portion of their day working along side their parents. State health laws now mandate that growers provide clean drinking water and field restrooms. Although the wage scale has gradually increased, farm workers still are not fairly compensated for a hard day's work. "Picking a 50-pound bag of onions earns a farm worker $1.20 (market price is $6 per bag)... The rate for harvesting a 10-gallon bucket of jalapeno peppers is $1. When they work watermelon, cantaloupe, lettuce and cabbage fields, they can earn minimum wage. Clearing a large field of weeds might pay $500. UFW leaders say a 'respectable wage' would be $8 an hour."[97] Farm workers still do not have collective bargaining rights, life insurance, health care, or protection against hazardous pesticides and chemicals. Growing up in migrant farm labor camps, Chávez knew first hand the problems confronting Hispanic farm workers. Although he dedicated his life to organizing workers and conducting voter registration drives, Chávez strongly believed that political empowerment alone could not fully uplift Hispanics from their plight. In a 1973 interview, Chávez stated:

> But political power alone is not enough. Although I've been at it for some twenty years, all the time and the money and effort haven't brought about any significant change whatsoever. Effective political power is never going to come, particularly to minority groups unless they have economic power. And however poor they are, even the poor people can organize economic power.
>
> Political power by itself, as we've tried to fathom it and to fashion it, is like having a car that doesn't have any motor in it. It is like striking a match that goes out. Economic power is like having a generator to keep that bulb burning all the time. So we have to develop economic power to assure a continuation of political power .... As a continuation of our struggle, I think we can develop economic power and put it into the hands of the people so they can have more control over their own lives, and then begin to change the system. We want radical change. Nothing short of radical change is going to have an impact on our lives or our problems. We want sufficient power to control our own destinies. This is our struggle. It is a lifetime job. The work for social change and against social injustice is never ended.[98]

The untimely death of Chávez has left a leadership void in the Hispanic community. "Many Hispanics regard[ed] Chávez as akin to Mohandas Gandhi in India and Martin Luther King Jr., in the United States because of his belief nonviolent protests lead to social change."[99] On November 28, 2000, the Hispanic community lost another hero—United States Congressman Henry B. Gonzalez. He too devoted his life's work to the Hispanic community. Although more Hispanics are being elected to state and national legislative houses, there has been no one to rise to the occasion as a viable replacement for Chávez or Gonzalez. Conducted by the Latino Coalition, a recent poll revealed that "Hispanics are so short of national leaders in the United States that [then] Mexican President Vicente Fox beat out slim U.S. competition as their most admired Latino leader. . . Three quarters of the 1,000 Hispanic respondents in the poll failed to name any Hispanic when asked: 'Which national Latino political leader, living today, do you most admire?'"[100]

César Chávez's dream of economic empowerment for Hispanics has yet to develop. In 2003, approximately 1,441,000 representing 7.7 percent of all Hispanics in the civilian labor force were unemployed.[101] The total number of Hispanic families and persons living below the poverty level continues to increase. In 2003, 1,792,000 or 19.7 percent of Hispanic families and 8,549,000 or 21.8 percent of Hispanic individuals lived below the poverty level.[102] There is an obvious connection between poverty and the lack of an education. In 2003, only 5,456,000 of Hispanics age twenty-five and older, have complete their high school programs, while 44,199,00 Anglos and 6,445,000 African-Americans have done so. On the college level, only 11.9 percent of Hispanics age twenty-five or older have obtained a four-year or high college degree, compared to 27.7 percent of Anglos and 17.0 percent of African Americans.[103]

The Hispanic community has been in some respects adversely impacted by illegal immigration of Mexican nationals to the United States. In the Southwestern border states, it is still a daily task for Immigration and Naturalization Service agents to round up illegals who crossed over the border or swam across the Rio Grande and send them back home. Mexican nationals are also buying their way into the United States by hiring a coyote to smuggle them across the border. The trip can prove to be deadly. Far too often illegals are crammed into un-air conditioned vehicles, semi-tracker trailers, and railroad cars. Fearful of being captured by border guards, coyotes will often abandon the vehicle or the railroad car, leaving the illegals locked inside. If the border agents do not find them soon enough, illegal immigrants usually die of heat-related illnesses or starvation. The simple solution would be to hire more agents and seal up the border. But, the issue of illegal immigration and the exploration of possible solutions is far more complicated and more difficult to solve. In part, the number of illegals from Mexico is directly tied to the Mexican economy. Although Mexico is improving its economic footing, the wealth is still distributed to a very small percentage of Mexico's people. Mired in third and fourth world poverty, Mexican nationals see even a below minimum wage job in the United States as their only means to feed, clothe, and educate their children.

There are, however, several misnomers and misconceptions about Mexican immigration into this country. First, the advocates of anti-immigration laws always point a finger at the Hispanic community as the source of this country's immigration woes. While immigrants were entering this country in the thousands from Europe, relatively few Mexican nationals entered the country as permanent residents for nearly fifty years after the signing of the Treaty of Guadalupe Hidalgo, ending the Mexican War. "For one period, in fact, between 1886 and 1893, there are no official records of immigration from Mexico into the United States."[104] The increase flow of immigrants has been seen in periods of economic upheavals and political discords in Mexico. For example, "in the latter years of the nineteen century and extending into 1910 were the distressful conditions many faced under the dictatorship of President Profirio Diaz. The rural poor were forcibly removed from their common lands by ambitious land barons and faced a dismal life of peonage on

Table 14.3

Significant Events for Hispanic Americans

Date Event

1845   Texas is admitted into the United States.

1846   The United States declares war on Mexico.

1848   The Treaty of Guadalupe Hidalgo ends the war with Mexico. The United States purchases Mexican territories held in the Southwest for $15 million with the promise of respecting the property rights of Mexicans living now in the U. S. and allowing them to become citizens.

1897   Mexican-American Miguel A. Otero is appointed governor of New Mexico.

1900   More than 125 Spanish-language newspapers are in circulation in the U. S. to include one of the first *El Mississippi*, published in New Orleans.

1910   The Mexican Revolution brings Mexican nationals to the U. S. for safety and employment. Mexican immigrants become a source of cheap farm labor in the Southwest.

1918-21 More than 50,000 Mexican nationals are recruited to combat a labor shortage in the Southwest.

1921   The Sons of America is organized in San Antonio, Texas, to fight for equality and raise awareness of Mexican-Americans' rights as U. S. citizens.

1924   The Immigration Act of 1924 establishes guidelines for the admission of Mexican workers, collecting a head tax on each. More than 89,000 enter the U. S. on permanent visas while others enter illegally to avoid the fees.

1928   The *Confederacion de Uniones Obreras Mexicanas* (CUOM) is formed to organize all Mexican workers in the U. S. to fight for wage parity and an end to racial discrimination. Octaviano Larrazola (NM) is the first Mexican American elected to the U. S. Senate.

1929   The League of United Latin American Citizens (LULAC) forms in Corpus Christi, Texas, to help Mexican Americans assume their rightful places as U. S. citizens and to fight discriminatory practices.

1930   LULAC organizes its first school desegregation case in Del Rio, Texas, but looses the case.

1931   Female Mexican-American garment workers in Los Angeles, California, are unionized by labor organizer Rose Pesotta.

1939   El Congreso del Pueblo de Habla Espanola (The Spanish Speaking People's Congress) is founded by Lusia Moreno. This working-class organization aims to secure basic rights for all Spanish-speaking people in the U. S. by forming a unified labor movement to combat poverty and discrimination. Mexican Americans in Beeville, Texas, desegregate the local high school.

1942   The bracero program begins, allowing Mexican nationals to work in the Southwest as a source of cheap agriculture labor. The program ends in 1964. Approximately, 300,000 Mexican-American men served in WWII with 17 awarded the Congressional Medal of Honor.

1946	LULAC supports a class-action suit by Gonzalo Mendez against several school districts in California. The Federal District Court rules that segregation in these school districts is unconstitutional. Andres Morales becomes the first Mexican American to be elected to a city council in California since the 19th century.
1947	The Community Service Organization (CSO) is established in Los Angeles to encourage voter registration and grass-roots political support for Mexican Americans.
1953-58	The U. S. Immigration Service arrests and deports over 3.8 million persons of Mexican descent during Operation Wetback. Many U. S. citizens are deported unfairly.
1961	Henry B. Gonzalez (D-Tex) is the first Mexican American elected to the U. S. House of Representatives from Texas. He retired from the House in 1998.
1962	César Chávez organizes the National Farm Workers Association (NFWA) in Delano, California.
1965	César Chávez and the NFWA begin a grape boycott, targeting Schenley Industries and the Di Giorgio Corporation.
1967	Corky Gonzales writes the epic poem "I Am Joaquin." The Mexican-American Legal Defense and Education Fund (MALDF) is formed. The Brown Berets are established in Los Angeles, California.
1972	La Raza Unida holds its national convention in El Paso, Texas.
1974	Willie Velasquez forms the Southwest Voter Registration and Education Project. MANA, the Mexican-American Women's National Association, is established as a feminist activist organization. By 1990, MANA chapters operate in 16 states.
1975	The 1965 Voting Rights Act is extended to the Southwest.
1992	Lucille Roybal-Allard (D-CA) becomes the first Mexican-American woman elected to the U. S. House of Representatives.

the rural estates. . . . The Mexican Revolution which broke out in 1910 and lasted until 1920 also became a catalyst for migration. Mexicans fled to the United States to escape the horrors of war or reprisals from the feuding factions."[105] Second, the United States government has not always cast a negative eye at the Mexican national worker. For example, the United States experienced a dramatic decrease in cheap farm laborers during and immediately after World War II. The United States government contracted with the Mexican government to bring agricultural workers into the United States. The **Bracero program** allowed farm workers to enter the country under the following conditions: "free transportation and food; guarantees concerning wages, working conditions, and housing; and the right of Mexican officials to make inspections and to investigate workers' complaints."[106] The program ended in 1964 as growers sought ways to bypass the program by hiring illegal Mexican nationals at wages far below those offered through the Bracero contracts.

Third, illegal immigration, particularly from Mexico, has resulted in "white fear," a new concept of the economic theory of racism. **White fear** is the feeling "of becoming a member of the new minority as the existing minority becomes a majority within the social community."[107] The potential loss of economic viability, and social and political clout fuels the fires of those advocating stronger anti-immigration laws. Expressing their fears that the continuous flow of both legal and illegal Mexican immigrants across the Rio Grande will eventually take jobs away from American workers and depress the wage market, white fear advocates created a system of political and economic barriers against Hispanic citizens. Particularly in the Southwestern states, Hispanics were kept from developing any political muscle to flex at city, state, or national legislative houses. Redistricting plans ensured that Hispanics were grossly under-represented in legislative houses while at-large city council elections precluded the election of Hispanic candidates. While statistics do not support their claims against Mexican nationals, the cries of white fear accelerate whenever the American economy slumps or job security becomes questionable. Basically, "as long as there was a shortage of cheap labor, the 'Mexicans' were welcomed and praised as cooperative, uncomplaining workers; but when economic times were bad, 'American' officials wanted the 'Mexicans' to go 'home.'"[108] The Mexican nationals' threat to American job security is in itself a misnomer since the majority of Mexican nationals are seasonal workers toiling at jobs few Americans want in the first place.

Beginning with the election of Ronald Reagan, anti-immigration advocates joined forces with the conservative wing of the Republican Party and gained the upper-hand in promoting immigration reform legislation. A series of 1997 immigration laws made it more difficult for both foreigners to seek political asylum and legal immigrants to bring immediate family members into the country. Particularly after September 11, the federal government was granted more authority to deport immigrants who arrived without proper documentation. All job applicants are required to provide proof of work eligibility and citizenship status. Beginning in January 2004, the Bush administration made it more expensive to become a legal worker or a citizen by increasing the fees to apply for citizenship; to apply, replace or renew a permanent residency card, also known as a green card; to petition to bring in a fiancé or family member into the country; and to be fingerprinted. A key element of the Bush administration has been to discourage illegal immigration while at the same time, provide foreign nationals the opportunity to work legally in the United States under a guest worker program similar to the Bracero program. An ill-fated attempt introduced by Senators John McCain (R-Arizona) and Edward Kennedy (D-Massachusetts) would have allowed workers who have illegally worked in the country for six years or more, to apply for green cards and eventually gain citizenship. Anti-immigration advocates successfully got Congress to approve the building of a fence along the Mexico/United States border. Since the founding of this nation, immigration laws have been constitutionally focused at the federal level. "A 1986 federal law forbids states from enacting stricter criminal or civil penalties for illegal immigration than those adopted by Congress."[109] However, the inability of Congress to pass immigration reform, coupled with the changing pattern of illegal immigration from the traditional border-states to regions from the Midwest, Rocky Mountains to New England, has moved state legislative houses to enact their own versions of immigration reform. "More than 550 bills relating to illegal immigration were introduced in statehouses this year [2006], and at least 77 were enacted. . . . State bills aimed at illegal immigration . . . have included measures on education, employment, drivers' licenses, law enforcement, legal services and trafficking."[110] Armed anti-immigration groups have voluntarily set up camp long the Mexican border to "help" the federal government capture illegal immigrants. Perhaps the tide of state initiatives is beginning to ebb. In a 2006 decision, the United States

Supreme Court signaled that federal law, not state laws, guide the nation's immigration and deportation policies. In an 8-1 decision the Court ruled in favor of an immigrant who had violated a South Dakota law making a deportable offense to possess illegal substances. "The issue before the Supreme Court was the interpretation of the federal Immigration and Nationality Act, which says immigrants found guilty of aggravated felonies are subject to deportation. Conduct that's felony under state law but a misdemeanor under the Controlled Substances Act isn't a felony for purposes of immigration."[111] Whether enacted by Congress or state legislative houses, anti-immigration legislation designed to punish illegal immigrants has the propensity to have an adverse impact on legal minority population groups, particularly Americans of Hispanic origin.

The key to Hispanic empowerment does begin within the political arena. In the 1970s, a small group of students from St. Mary's University in San Antonio, Texas, led by Jose Angel Gutierrez founded a third political party movement dedicated to the causes of the Hispanic community. **La Raza Unida** (LRU) began in the South Texas Rio Grande Valley, a predominately agricultural area stretching south of San Antonio to the Mexican border. The majority of the region's Hispanic population are farm workers who toil in the fields picking fruits and vegetables, earning at or below minimum wages. The party began at the lowest political level by winning positions on the Crystal City, Texas, city council and school board. Founded in 1968, the National Council of La Raza provides a cadre of lobbyists to promote Hispanic issue concerns in state and national legislative houses. "In 30 years it [the National Council of La Raza] has grown to include 200 affiliates in 37 states."[112] Hispanic organizations such as the **League of United Latin American Citizens** (LULAC) and the **Mexican-American Legal Defense and Educational Fund** (MALDF) keep the social, economic, and political needs of the Hispanic community alive by conducting voter registration drives, recruiting and supporting Hispanic candidates, and lobbying legislative and executive houses across the country. Outdated discriminatory redistricting plans have been successfully challenged in federal courts, and the corrective legislation embodied in the Voter Rights Act and subsequent amendments have provided bilingual ballots and materials. In 1968, the late Willie Velasquez, another graduate of St. Mary's University, founded the **Southwest Voter Registration Project** (SVRP) and organized voter registration drives throughout Southwest Texas, California, Arizona, and New Mexico.

No Hispanic had ever served in a cabinet level position until President Ronald Reagan appointed Lauro Cavazos as Secretary of Education and President Clinton appointed Henry Cisneros and Frederico Pena to his team. President George W. Bush has appointed several Hispanics to high ranking positions including Alberto Gonzales to attorney general. Hispanic empowerment is also hampered by a lack of cooperation among Hispanics. "Even activists acknowledge that Hispanic potential has been sapped by the group's overall political apathy and its inability to knit together Mexican-Americans, Cuban-Americans, Puerto Ricans, and other factions . . . . Hispanics don't have any issues they can come together on . . . . The only things they really have in common are that they tend to be Catholic, speak Spanish, have generally the same skin color, and have some of the same cultural values. Other than that they are very different and distinct groups."[113] Hispanic political clout, however, is beginning to exert its presence. Traditionally, Hispanics joined the ranks of African-American voters in their solid support of Democratic candidates. In the 2000 presidential election, Hispanics voted 2 to 1 for Al Gore over George W. Bush. However, the Hispanic vote is becoming more difficult to predict. A recent poll indicates that "among registered Latinos [Hispanics], about half, or 49 percent, identify as Democrats, with 20 percent saying they are Republican and 19 percent independent."[114] The Democratic Party continues to draw a large percentage of the Hispanic vote due to the party's positions on immigration, education, the economy, and health care. The Hispanic vote cannot be taken for granted. The increase in Hispanic voting clout "should serve as a cautionary note to anyone in political life that campaigning in this community is a lot more than speaking Spanish."[115] The Hispanic community, however, must begin to exert more of a solid presence in the political arena and actively recruit and, subsequently, elect more Hispanic candidates to public office to ensure that the quest so eloquently voiced by the late Cesar Chávez will not fall upon deaf ears.

Gender Issues

In 1776, Abigail Adams warned her husband John Adams to: "Remember the Ladies, and be more generous and favorable to them than your ancestors. Do not put such unlimited powers into the hands of the Husbands. Remember all Men would be tyrants if they could. If particular care and attention is not paid to the Ladies, we are determined to ferment a Rebellion, and will not hold ourselves bound by any Laws in which we have no voice, or Representation."[116] Unfortunately, the framers chose to ignore her warnings, opting instead to deny women basic rights guaranteed to men through the United States Constitution. In 1995, women across this nation celebrated the seventy-fifth anniversary of the passage of the **Nineteenth Amendment** to the United States Constitution, granting women suffrage rights. While civil rights struggles have been focused primarily on minority groups, we cannot overlook the tremendous and arduous task women of this nation faced to not only vote but to own property, apply for credit, get an education, earn a decent wage, and even serve on a jury. These basic rights should have been guaranteed to all American citizens, male and female, when the framers pinned both the Constitution and the Bill of Rights.

For centuries, however, gender-based discrimination fueled by paternalistic attitudes has kept women in subservient roles. It was women of all creeds and colors who worked side by side their male counterparts to build this nation. Yet, they realized from the very beginning that they had very few civil rights that fell under the protection of the Bill of Rights, no meaningful voice in the political arena, and only a marginal role in society. In 1872, ardent feminist Victoria Woodhull decided to take on incumbent President Ulysses S. Grant and Horace Greeley for the race for the White House. The first woman to run for the presidency, Woodhull's time was "a much more difficult one for women, who then had almost no rights to property or person. If a married woman worked, her wages were given directly to her husband. She could not dispose of her property upon death. If she divorced, she automatically forfeited custody of her children. Women could not enter universities, law schools or medical schools. They could not vote. Most significantly, women had no control over their own bodies: There were no laws to protect them from physical abuse at the hands of their husbands or fathers, although some states stipulated the size of the objects that might be used to inflict discipline . . . . Men were allowed all means of sexual license, but a woman who committed adultery was subject to a jail sentence."[117] Although improvements have been made, women not only in the United States but across the globe are still battling against those historical and cultural barriers that continue to keep them in a subservient role, usually one step behind their male counterparts.

The **paternalistic attitude** of male superiority over women is supported by the myth that women are just too fragile mentally and physically to survive the rigors of life by themselves. Women need a "knight in shining armor" to protect them from harm and unpleasantness. The Southern plantation system went a step further by placing women on pedestals. Frail and fragile like a treasured piece of fine bone china, women became the objects of worship, requiring the constant watchful protective eye of their husbands and fathers. The frontier experience with its encouragement of rugged individualism played right into the hands of paternalism by creating the "macho" male role. In 1873, Supreme Court Justice Joseph Bradley wrote:

"Man is, or should be, woman's protector and defender. The natural and proper timidity and delicacy which belongs to the female sex evidently unfits it for many of the occupations of civil live. The constitution of the family organization, which is founded in the divine ordinance, as well as in the nature of things, indicates the domestic sphere as that which properly belongs to the domain and functions of womanhood. The harmony . . . of interests and views which belong, or should belong, to the family institution is repugnant to the idea of woman adopting a distinct and independent career from that of her husband. . . The paramount destiny and mission of woman are to fulfill the noble and benign offices of wife and mother."[118]

Justice Bradley's beliefs were enhanced with the contention that the biological differences between the sexes rendered men stronger and more capable than women. "The case of women, though seldom expounded in explicit detail, was based on analogous connections of assumption and achievement, and in both instances, biological structure, genetics, and the chemistry of the body were to yield definitive explanations of the differences. . . . It was not until the twentieth century that more than the merest handful of sceptics or malcontents declined to draw what seemed the common sense conclusion from the fact that there were female saints, but no female theologians, that there was female intuition, but no female philosopher, female musicians but few female composers, no female Rembrandt but innumerable nineteenth century lady colourists. Men-and-women-extrapolated from the biological facts of childbearing, lactation, comparative size and strength, and related characteristics to the entire range of abilities and qualities attributed or denied to the female sex were thus using a method that was strikingly analogous to that employed in making biological race distinctions."[119] Paternalistic attitudes toward women resulted in repressive laws, social barriers, restrictive employment opportunities, and denial of education. Oddly, single women had more rights and freedoms than married women. "The very being of woman was suspended during marriage or at least incorporated into that of her husband, under whose wing she maintained her legal status."[120] State legislative houses passed laws prohibiting women from selling or borrowing against her own private property without her husband's permission. Women could not on their own enter into contracts, apply for loans and credit, witness a will, sue, or serve on a jury. The Texas Constitution once contained an amendment barring women from purchasing a refrigerator without prior approval from their spouses.

With very few exceptions, women did not venture forth into the world of politics until the beginning of the Abolitionist movement in the 1830s. However, antislavery organizations did not openly embrace or offer leadership roles to women. A disgusted Sarah Grimke wrote the president of the Boston Female Anti-Slavery Society that "all history attests that man has subjugated woman to his will, used her as a means to promote his selfish gratifications, to minister to his sensual pleasure, to be instrumental in promoting his comfort; but never has he desired to promote her to the rank she was created to fill. He has done all he could to debase and enslave her mind; and now he looks triumphantly on the ruin he has wrought, and says, the being he has thus deeply injured is his inferior."[121] The plight of women prompted Lucretia Mott and Elizabeth Cady Stanton to organize the first Women's Rights Convention held at Seneca Falls, New York, in 1848. Their penning of the **Declaration of Sentiments and Resolutions** declaring women equal to men set the stage for the Women's Suffrage Movement. Stanton was adamant about gaining the right to vote for women. She argued "to have drunkards, idiots, horse racing rum-selling rowdies, ignorant foreigners, and silly boys fully recognized [with voting privileges], while we ourselves are thrust out from all the rights that belong to citizens, is too grossly insulting to be longer quietly submitted to. The right is ours. We must have it."[122] The United States Supreme Court gave the emerging movement a chance to vent its frustrations when the Court ruled in *Minor v Happersat* (1875) that the Fourteenth Amendment to the United States Constitution did not give women the right to vote. The quest for a constitutional amendment to reverse the Court's decision solidified an emerging feminist movement to the cause of suffrage.

Ardent feminists, Elizabeth Cady Stanton and Susan B. Anthony, founded *The Revolution*, a weekly newspaper focusing on feminist issues. Stanton and Anthony also formed the **National American Women Suffrage Association** while Lucy Stone organized the **American Woman Suffrage Association**. Francis Perkins Gilman took on the economic issues confronting women. The incidents of the mistreatment of workers, particularly women, were too frequent to be ignored. "Far from gaining in personal freedom, women were increasingly the victims of the factories and workshops; competition no doubt drove their employers to exploit their defenseless positions on the labour market just as the need for subsistence, the absence of special qualifications, and the lack of alternatives drove innumerable young women into the factories and garment-making shops."[123] Women garment workers joined women of all classes in massive demonstrations as the New York Women's Trade Union League staged strikes in 1909.

Lacking cohesive leadership, women's organizations needed a board-base issue to draw the various factions together. The **Temperance Movement** in the 1900s helped to solidified women behind the desire to rid the nation of alcohol. Their efforts resulted in the passage of the **Eighteenth Amendment** and the Prohibition Era. Meanwhile, a new suffrage leadership was emerging under Dr. Anna Howard Shaw, Carrie Chapman Catt, and Alice Paul, founder of the Congressional Union, which later became the **Woman's Party**. Although several states allowed women to vote in statewide and local elections, women did not have voting rights in national elections. Both Paul and Chapman organized daily marches and protests in front of the White House to jar a reluctant President Woodrow Wilson to assert pressure for the passage of a woman's suffrage amendment. Women's organizations began lobbying Wilson immediately after he took office in 1913. In his 1916 re-election effort, Wilson advocated giving women the right to vote. However, once re-elected, he changed his mind. Members of the National Woman's Party met with Wilson on January 9, 1917, only to be rebuffed in their efforts. "The next morning the White House picketing began. The press described the pickets as 'Silent Sentinels.' Nearly every day, rain or shine, whenever Congress was in session, they were there. They stood essentially motionless, holding large purple, white, and gold banners. 'How long must women wait?' some banners asked. 'President Wilson, what will you do for woman suffrage?'"[124] To break the monotony of daily protests, Alice Paul had "theme days" whereby the messages on the banners would be changed on a daily basis. Finally Wilson caved in. Approved by Congress in 1919, the **Nineteenth Amendment** was ratified by the required number of states by August 1920. The suffrage movement involved a complex array of political, social, and economic issues. Women were scorned, publicly and socially humiliated, arrested, jailed and even killed in their struggle to reverse the stranglehold of paternalism. Conditions in the jails were horrible. "The cells at the workhouse in Occoquan, Virginia, were small, dark and rat-infested. Bedding hadn't been cleaned in almost a year; the staff handled it only with rubber gloves. The suffragists held contests to see who had the most mealworms in her food. For extended periods the women were allowed no visitors or legal counsel. All mail was censored . . . Dorothy Day, 20, the future founder of the Catholic Worker Movement, had her arms twisted and was violently thrown against a iron bench. Dora Lewis, 55, was knocked unconscious. Lucy Burns, identified as a Woman's Party leader, was beaten and left handcuffed to her cell bars with her hands above her head."[125] Alice Paul was arrested for protesting in front of the White House. Staging a protest hunger strike, Paul was forced-fed simply because the White House feared the repercussions her death would have on the American public and, ultimately, political careers. "Hoping to discredit her by having her diagnosed as mentally ill, the warden moved her to the psychopathic ward, where the screams of patients and a flashlight shined in her face every hour, kept her awake."[126] Once they were released from prison, the women continued their fight to gain social, economic, legal, and political equality with their male counterparts.

With the exception of the war years of the 1920s and 1940s, employment opportunities for women were limited to a few low paying positions usually available to just single women. In most states, female public school teachers had to resign their positions when they married. In the 1920s, women gained in the job market by replacing men who were fighting overseas. However, the Depression Era reversed this trend as women were deliberately fired to open up job opportunities for unemployed men. World War II again gave women a chance for employment as they replaced men in industrial and manufacturing positions. Today, the economic necessity of the two-household income has substantially increased the number of females in the workforce.

Despite countless litigations and legislative acts correcting previous adverse actions, women are still confronted by a multiplicity of job-related discriminatory practices. The **pay equity** issue addresses the problem that women earn less than their male counterparts employed in comparable positions. Women, as a whole, earn less since they hold the majority of clerical and secretarial positions, collectively known as **pink collar** jobs. Across the board, men earn more than women. A man with only a high school diploma will earn approximately $33,266 per year compared to $21,659 for a woman with the same high school diploma. A woman with a bachelor's degree employed in a similar position to her male counterpart with the same education earns only $38,447 per year while he brings home $63,084. The professional category includes doctors, lawyers, engineers, scientists, and so on. Once again, women earn on an average of $72,445 per year while men in comparable positions earn an average yearly paycheck of $136,128.[127] Whether they are Anglo, African American, or Hispanic, women in all of these categories earn less than men. Although job promotability and mobility opportunities for women have increased substantially, women are still victims of the **glass ceiling**, which prohibits them from becoming the CEO or president of the firm. A military career for a woman is still a controversial issue particularly when the discussion focuses on whether women should be assigned to combat duty. Initially, women enter the military in hopes of building a career by moving up the promotional ladder. However, the majority of this nation's female military personnel were traditionally confined to office duty and nursing. The bulk of the command positions are still held by men. Across the broad spectrum of occupational categories, there are still significantly fewer women than men in charge of making the policy decisions for corporate America.

Of course, the increased incidences of sexual harassment in the workplace are a continuing problem for women. *All* workers should be able to work in an environment free of intimidations and threats. Sexual harassment, in particular, is a difficult issue since there is not clear definition what exactly constitutes an act of sexual misconduct. In addition, women are concerned about child-care issues that may prohibit their rise up that corporate ladder. The majority of this nation's women "must still find a way to survive the uncaring institutions, the exploitative employers and the deep social inequities the successful few have not got around to challenging."[128]

However, the woman's movement like other social movements has failed to maintain a consistent and cohesive battlefront. In the 1920s, "the newly political liberated womanhood of America made no move to disturb the social order; they arranged themselves instead along lines already marked out by the structure and economic interests of a society dominated by men. What was more surprising, and disappointing to those who had hoped for real alterations among the roles in American society, was the limping and limited manner in which women attempted to move into positions occupied by men throughout industry or the professions. Leaders of the suffrage movement did not see their duty now as that of inspiring a diffused and dispersed multitude of followers . . . ."[129] True to form, the woman's movement declined after winning the suffrage battle only to re-emerge in the 1960s under new leadership and new issues—reproductive freedom and women's liberation. The feminist movement achieved its goal when the Supreme Court upheld reproductive freedom of choice in *Roe v Wade* (1973). The women's movement began to decline in the 1980s, only to re-emerge in the 1990s with the issue of electing more women to public office. In the 1992 "Year of the Woman," women did succeed in increasing their numbers in state and national elective offices.

However, the feminist movement has yet to address the problems confronting the average woman and those women who are undereducated and living in poverty. The separate sisters—"women in minority groups; women in 'traditional' women's jobs; women who stay at home to raise children; elderly, rural, some poor and younger women—acknowledge their debt to feminism's early battles. But they charge that the feminist movement has failed to broaden its base and remains made up largely of white, highly educated women who have not adequately addressed the issues that matter to them: child care rather than lesbian and abortion rights, economic survival rather than political equality, the sticky floor rather than the glass ceiling."[130] In addition, women's organizations like minority groups have not established a consistent proactive record. They join to battle an issue and then disperse. Their success hinges on pursuing a proactive diverse array of issues that will unite women of diverse races and incomes rather than just reacting to a problem area.

Table 14.4

Significant Events for American Women

Date	Event
1848	The first women's rights convention is held in Seneca Falls, New York on July 19 and 20. A *Declaration of Sentiments and Resolutions*, setting the agenda for the women's movement, was adopted.
1850	The first national women's rights convention is held in Worcester, Massachusetts with over 1,000 attending. Annual conventions were held through 1860.
1851	Sojourner Truth gives her speech "Ain't I a Woman?" at the women's rights convention in Akron, Ohio.
1853	Antoinette Brown is the first American woman ordained as a minister in a Protestant Church.
1855	Lucy Stone becomes the first woman on record to keep her own name after marriage. Women who followed her example were called "Lucy Stoners."
1866	The American Equal Rights Association is founded. This is the first organization in the United States advocating national suffrage rights for women.
1868	Sorosis, the first professional club for women, is founded. The Working Women's Protective Union in New York is founded by middle- and upper-class women to lobby for laws protecting women workers. Elizabeth Cady Stanton and Susan B. Anthony begin publishing *The Revolution*, a women's periodical.
1869	Women shoe stitchers from six states form the Daughters of St. Crispin, the first national women's labor organization. The first woman suffrage law in the United States passes in the territory of Wyoming. Susan B. Anthony and Elizabeth Cady Stanton form the National Woman Suffrage Association as Lucy Stone establishes the American Woman Suffrage Association.
1870	For the first time in the history of jurisprudence, women serve on juries in the Wyoming Territory. Iowa becomes the first state to admit a woman to the bar.
1872	Congress passes an equal pay law for women federal employees. Susan B. Anthony is arrested, tried, found guilty, and fined $100 for registering and voting in the presidential election.
1874	The United States Supreme Court rules in *Bradwell v Illinois* that states can restrict women from any professional career "to preserve family harmony and uphold the law of the Creator." The Woman's Christian Temperance Union is founded by Annie Wittenmyer.
1875	The Supreme Court rules in *Minor v Happersett* that the 14th Amendment does not give women the right to vote.
1878	The Susan B. Anthony Amendment, granting suffrage to women, is introduced into Congress.
1884	Belva Lockwood, presidential candidate of the National Equal Rights Party, becomes the first woman to receive votes in a presidential election.
1909	Women garment workers strike in New York City for better wages and working conditions.

1913   5,000 suffragists parade in Washington, D. C., drawing away from newly-elected President Wilson's arrival.

1917   Jeanette Rankin of Montana becomes the first woman elected to the U. S. Congress. In January, suffragists begin a silent vigil in front of the White House.

1919   The House of Representatives and the Senate pass the woman suffrage amendment.

1920   On August 26, the 19th Amendment to the Constitution is ratified, giving American women citizens the right to vote.

1923   An equal rights amendment is introduced in Congress.

1924   Nellie Tayloe Ross of Wyoming becomes the first woman elected governor of a state.

1926   Bertha Knight Landes is the first woman elected mayor of a sizable U. S. city (Seattle).

1932   The National Recovery Act forbids more than one family member from holding a job, resulting in many women losing their jobs. Hattie Wyatt Caraway (Louisiana) is the first woman elected to the U. S. Senate.

1933   Frances Perkins becomes the first woman to serve on a president's cabinet.

1948   Margaret Chase Smith (R-Maine) becomes the first woman elected to the U. S. Senate in her own right. In 1964, she is the first woman to run for the presidency in the primaries of a major political party.

1963   The Equal Pay Act, establishing equal pay for men and women performing the same job duties, passes Congress.

1964   Pasty Mink (D-Hawaii) becomes the first Asian-American woman elected to the U. S. Congress.

1966   The National Organization for Women (NOW) is founded as a civil rights organization for women.

1970   Betty Freidan organizes the first Women's Equality Day, August 26, to mark the 50th anniversary of women's right to vote. The Equal Rights Amendment is reintroduced into Congress.

1971   The National Women's Political Caucus is founded to encourage women to run for public office.

1973   The Supreme Court rules in *Roe v Wade* that women have a right to an abortion. This overturns 46 state laws banning the procedure.

1974   The Equal Credit Opportunity Act prohibits sex discrimination in all consumer credit practices. Ella Grasso (Connecticut) becomes the first woman to win election as governor in her own right.

1975   The Supreme Court rules in *Taylor v Louisiana* that states cannot prohibit women from serving on juries.

1977   Congress passes the Hyde Amendment, eliminating federal funding for low-income women's abortions. By 1995, only 13 states still provide public funding for abortions.

1981	Sandra Day O'Connor becomes the first woman appointed to the U. S. Supreme Court. In 1993, Ruth Bader Ginsburg was appointed to the bench.
1982	The Equal Rights Amendment fails to secure ratification. Over 900 women hold positions as state legislators, compared with 344 a decade ago.
1984	Geraldine Ferraro (D) becomes the first woman vice presidential candidate of a major political party.
1986	The U. S. Supreme Court declares sexual harassment as a form of illegal employment discrimination.
1992	The Year of the Woman results in 24 women elected to the House of Representatives and 6 to the Senate, including Lucille Roybal-Allard (D-CA), the first Mexican-American woman in the House; Nydia Velazquez (D-NY), the first Puerto Rican woman elected to the House; Carol Moseley-Braun (D-IL), the first black woman elected to the Senate; Barbara Boxer and Dianne Feinstein (D-CA), the first two women elected to the Senate from the same state. Janet Reno becomes the nation's first woman attorney general.
1997	Madeleine Albright is appointed Secretary of State, becoming the first woman to hold that position.
2001	President Bush names Gail Norton to head the Interior Department, Christine Whitman to head the Environmental Protection Agency, and Condoleezza Rice an African American, as his National Security Advisor.
2005	President Bush names Condoleezza Rice as his Secretary of State.
2007	Nancy Pelosi (D-CA) becomes the first woman Speaker of the House of Representatives.

The Homosexual Community

The Bill of Rights guarantees basic freedoms for all Americans including those who choose alternative lifestyles. Historically, homosexuality has not been widely accepted as a viable alternative to a heterosexual lifestyle. Members of the gay and lesbian community have opted to protect themselves from social stigmas by hiding their sexual orientations from the heterosexual world. "Coming out" by openly admitting their homosexuality has oftentimes led to being branded as social outcasts. The high profile murders of two openly gay men serve as a reminder that the homosexual community continues to be the target of discriminatory practices driven by prejudice and hatred. A student at the University of Wyoming, Matthew Shepard was a patron at the Fireside Lounge in Laramie, Wyoming. He was approached by two men who convinced Shepard that they too were homosexual. Shepard willingly left the bar with these two individuals. However, Shepard's trust in his new friends was tragically flawed. Robbed of $20, beaten repeatedly with a .357 magnum pistol that caused six skull factures, Shepard was found eighteen hours later tied to a fence in subfreezing temperatures. He died shortly after. Both men were arrested and convicted of Shepard's murder. At their trials, defense lawyers attempted to justify the murder as a gay panic response. "The gay panic or homosexual panic defense is built on a theory that a person with latent homosexual tendencies will have an uncontrollable, violent reaction when propositioned by a homosexual."[131] Also a homosexual, Jack Gaither met a similar fate in Alabama. As he was leaving a gay facility, two men attacked him and drove him to a remote area. Gaither was beaten to death with an ax handle and his body was burned on a pile of old tires. The individuals charged and subsequently convicted of these crimes were motivated by their hatred towards those whose sexual orientations deviated from the norm.

United States Supreme Court Justice Harry Blackmun once wrote that "only the most willful blindness could obscure the fact that sexual intimacy is a sensitive, key relationship of human existence, central to family life, community welfare, and the development of human personality. The fact that individuals define themselves in a significant way through their intimate sexual relationships with others suggests, in a Nation as diverse as ours, that there may be many 'right' ways of conducting these relationships, and that much of the richness of a relationship will come from the freedom an individual has to *choose* the form and nature of these intensely personal bonds."[132] The First Amendment to the United States Constitution guarantees to every American the freedom to choose the direction of their lives to include sexual orientation.

During his first term of office, President Clinton addressed the issue of discriminatory practices against homosexuals in the military. Although lacking definitive evidence that homosexual orientation was detrimental to a successful military career, the military was systematically eliminating gays and lesbians from its ranks through harassment, early discharges, and threats of court-martials. President Clinton offered a compromise policy of "don't ask, don't tell" as a means of eliminating the harassment of gay and lesbian military personnel. Homosexuals are allowed to remain in the military as long as they do not reveal their sexual orientation or engage in homosexual acts.

The United States Supreme Court entered into the realm of gay issues when it heard arguments over whether a homosexual man could serve as a scoutmaster for a Boy Scout troop. In a 5 to 4 decision, the Court upheld the organization's right to deny gays from serving as troop leaders. Chief Justice William Rehnquist wrote that "requiring the organization [Boys Scouts of America] to have a gay scoutmaster would force it to send a message, both to the youth members and the world, that the Boy Scouts accepts homosexual conduct as a legitimate form of behavior."[133] The Court, however, appears to be sending mixed messages. In 1996, the Supreme Court ruled that a Colorado constitutional amendment prohibiting local governments from protecting the rights of homosexuals was an unconstitutional act. In a 6 to 3 decision, the justices reasoned that the Colorado law "identifies persons by a single trait and then denies them protection across the board."[134] The Court emphasized that state laws cannot treat homosexuals as second-class citizens.

Disabled Americans

Unfortunately, disabled Americans have been the targets of discriminatory practices that have denied them social acceptance, personal mobility, and economic viability. Some have disabilities so severe that they cannot care for themselves, much less hold a job. Historically, care for the disabled fell upon individual family members and private charities and institutions. State and local governments provided few, if any, means of assistance. The national government did not provide substantial support for disabled Americans until 1920 with the passage of the **Vocational Rehabilitation Act**. The **Social Security Act** provided federal income-support for the disabled. It was not until

1948 that a special presidential commission was established to explore the problems confronted by the disabled.

For the disabled, normal errands can be extremely frustrating, oftentimes, impossible to achieve. Although corrective legislation has been passed at federal, state, and local levels, the laws are only marginally successful in addressing disability concerns. The United States Constitution prohibits any level of government from passing **ex post facto** laws. Once passed, legislation is enforceable for present actions, not for actions that occurred before the law was passed. For example, the **Architectural Barriers Act** (1970), the **Rehabilitation Act** (1973), and the **Americans with Disabilities Act (ADA)** (1990) require that all new public buildings must be handicapped accessible. These laws, however, cannot mandate that buildings constructed prior to the legislation must be reconfigured to accommodate the disabled. The legislation can only strongly encourage owners of existing public buildings to provide *reasonable but affordable* accommodations. Transportation issues were initially addressed with the passage of the **Urban Mass Transportation Act** in 1970. This act required that state and local governments must ensure that their transportation systems are handicapped accessible.

Title VII of the **Civil Rights Act of 1964** initially barred employment discrimination based on race, color, national origin, religion, and sex. Subsequent legislation has expanded the parameters to include age (individuals over the age of 40), Vietnam era veterans, and the handicapped. "The aim of the civil rights legislation is to prohibit any considerations of disability-related characteristics unless they can be shown to affect ability to perform the job."[135] The law prohibits employers from using any action that treats disabled employees differently from non-disabled employees. "**Disparate treatment** refers to actions in which employers treat people with disabilities differently. **Disparate impact** results when the standards for employment have the effect of excluding people with disabilities on the basis of standards or tests that are not directly related to determining the skills or experience necessary to perform the job."[136]

The major flaw of the ADA law is the legislation's inability to clearly define what constitutes a disability and to set clear-cut direction for reasonable accommodations for the disabled. "In defining the disabled population, the act not only includes anyone with a physical or mental impairment that substantially limits one or more of the major life activities but also includes anyone with a record of having such an impairment or anyone who is perceived as having such an impairment."[137] The issue of reasonable accommodations is oftentimes confusing to employers. For example, what reasonable accommodations should an employer provide to employees who suffer from mental impairments, chronic illnesses, or a bad back? How reasonable should employers be?

While lawmakers and jurists argue over what constitutes a disability, disabled Americans are earning far less than their non-disabled counterparts. In order to lead productive lives, disabled Americans must be able to earn the same paycheck as the non-disabled. Of course, no legislation can change the negative attitudes and stereotypes that are used against the disabled.

CONCLUSION

The public policy process has tried to respond to the needs of minority population groups and women by removing many of the political, economic, and social barriers that kept the doors of success locked for so long. Yet, those doors are still partially closed to the vast majority of this nation's poor women and minorities. The punitive direction of social service and welfare programs is demeaning, discriminatory in application, and ineffective in raising people out of their poverty. Hailed as the answer to ending poverty, educational opportunities for low income women and minorities are often second-rate, resulting in low paying employment possibilities. Washington politicians talk of ending affirmative action, cutting federal student loan programs, slashing low income health-care programs, and so on. In addition, the plight of the poor is far too often neglected by those very same organizations claiming to represent all members of their targeted groups. In essence, minority and women's organizations won rights for some but left others behind. A growing middle-class of women and minorities often fight for "their" issues, disregarding the problems confronting their entire minority or gender group. Equality before the law and society itself will not become a reality as long as some groups and individuals are treated unequally.

Corrective legislation is, of course, part of the solution. However, the leadership of minority and women's organizations must fulfill their obligations by actively pursuing an all inclusive agenda in the political arena. Lawmakers favorable to minority and women's issues cannot continue to promote legislation in hostile political environments without the full support of the groups they are trying to help. Low voter turnout among minority and female population groups feeds right into the hands of those legislators seeking to hold the line and, in some instances, roll back the clock on civil rights and liberties for minorities and women. These groups cannot afford compliancy.

Frederick Douglass once wrote that the "so-called race problem cannot be solved by keeping the Negro [African-American] poor, degraded, ignorant and half-starved . . . It cannot be solved by keeping the wages of the laborer back by fraud . . . It cannot be done by ballot-box stuffing . . . or by confusing Negro [African-American] voters by cunning devices. It can, however, be done, and very easily done... Let the white [Anglo] people of the North and the South conquer their prejudices . . . Time and strength are not equal to the task before me. But could I be heard by this great nation, I would call to mind the sublime and glorious truths with which, at its birth, it saluted a listening world . . . Put away your race prejudice. Banish the idea that one class must rule over another. Recognize... that the rights of the humblest citizen are as worthy of protection as are those of the highest, and . . . your Republic will stand and flourish forever."[138] Although speaking on behalf of the African-American community, Douglass' words apply to all who have suffered from discrimination and prejudice. The United States Constitution and the Bill of Rights protects the civil rights of all Americans, not just a few. The framers charged the nation's leaders with the task of preserving these civil rights for generations to come. As previously mentioned, presidents and governors can compel legislative houses to pass laws ranging from banning discrimination and to outlawing hate motivated crimes. However, Douglass' challenge transcends laws. All Americans regardless of their race, gender or sexual orientation, must practice what Douglass preached—put away your prejudices.

CHAPTER NOTES

[1]Rick Bragg, "Justice At Last," *San Antonio Express-News* (Thursday, May 23, 2002), 10A.

[2]Todd Spangler, "Race Tied to Fatal Shooting," *San Antonio Express-News* (Saturday, April 29, 2000), 1A.

[3]Mini Swartz, "Vidor in Black and White," *Texas Monthly*, (December, 1993), 135.

[4]Rick Bragg, "Klansman Faces Trial in '66 Mississippi Slaying", *San Antonio Express-News* (Sunday, January 26, 2003), 14A.

[5]Tim Pagdett, "Long Wait for Justice", *Time* (January 17, 2005), 53.

[6]Justine Evers, "In Pursuit of Justice", *U.S. News & World Report* (May 24, 2004), 62.

[7]Ibid.

[8]Judith A. Winston, "One America in the 21st Century: The President's Initiative on Race," *The National Voter* (The League of Women Voters, March/April 1998), (6-7), 6.

[9]John C. Domino, *Civil Rights and Liberties: Toward the 21st Century*, (New York: HarperCollins Publishers, 1994), 2.

[10]Leon C. Blevins, *Texas Government in National Perspective*, (New Jersey: Prentice-Hall, 1987), 255-256.

[11]S. Dale McLemore and Harriet D. Romo, *Racial and Ethnic Relations in America*, 7th ed., (Boston, Mass.: Pearson Education, Inc., 2005), 47-48.

[12]Henry J. Abraham and Barbara A. Perry, *Freedom & the Court: Civil Rights & Liberties in the United States,* 8th ed., (Lawrence, Kansas: The University Press of Kansas, 2003), 367-368.

[13]Kevin Cullen, "Europe Scowls At Immigrants," *San Antonio Express-News* (Friday, December 29, 2000), 26A.

[14]J. R. Poole, *The Pursuit of Equality in American History*, (Los Angeles, Calif.: University of California Press, 1978), 6-7.

[15]Alexis de Tocqueville, *Democracy in America*, Translated by George Lawrence, J. P. Mayer, ed. (Garden City, New York: Doubleday and Company, Inc., 1969), 317.

[16]McLemore, 118.

[17]Robert Wernick, "The Rise and Fall of a Fervid Third Party," *The Smithsonian* (November, 1996), 152.

[18]Ibid., 154.

[19]McLemore, 115.

[20]George H. Sabine, *The History of Political Thought*, 3d ed. (New York: Holt, Reinhart and Winston, 1961), 906.

[21]McLemore, 117-118.

[22]Joseph E. Harris, *Africans and Their History*, 2nd ed. (New York: New American Library Penguin, Inc., 1987), 18.

[23]Earl Conrad, *Jim Crow America*, 2d. ed., (New York: Duell, Sloan and Pearce, 1947), 27.

[24]David Vachon, "Chief Joseph Refuses to Sell Tribal Lands", *Old News*, March, 2004, 1.

[25]Conrad, 27-28.

[26]Ibid., 94.

[27]Sonya Ross, "Fed Report Eyes Racism," *San Antonio Express-News* (Friday, September 22, 2000), 4A.

[28]Ibid.

[29]U.S. Bureau of the Census, *Statistical Abstract of the United States: 2006*, 125th ed., (Washington, D.C., 2005), Tables 305 and 306, 200.

[30]Soyna Ross, "Hate Crimes Targeted," *San Antonio Express-News* (Thursday, September 14, 2000), 4A.

[31]Laurie Asseo, "Only Juries Can Decide Motive in Hate Crimes," *San Antonio Express-News* (June 27, 2000), 4A.

[32]Henry Weinstein, "Court Bars Racial Profiling on Border," *San Antonio Express-News* (Wed., April 12, 2000), 19A.

[33]Richard Conniff, "Frederick Douglass Always Knew He Was Meant to be Free," *The Smithsonian*, (February, 1995), 116.

[34]Thomas Hayden, "Modern Life", *U.S. News & World Report* (October 4, 2004), 46.

[35]Bill Baskervill, "Indians Say 'No Thanks,'" *San Antonio Express-News* (Thursday November 23, 2000), 3AA.

[36]Ibid.

[37]McLemore, 291.

[38]Floyd B. Largent, Jr., "The Florida Quadmire," *American History*, Vol. XXXIV, No. 4, October, 1999, 42.

[39]Anthony Dellafora, "Center May Preserve Story of 'Long Walk,'" *Dallas Morning News* (Sunday, March 8, 1998),45A.

[40]"U.S. May Soon Admit Battle Was Massacre," *The Express-News*, (Sunday, March 11, 1990), 6A.

[41]Ibid., 6A.

[42]Susan B. Welch, John Gruhl, Michael Steinman, John Comer, and Susan M. Rigdon, *American Government*, 5th ed. (St. Paul, Minn.: West Publishing Co., 1994), 505.

[43]Gary B. Nash and Julie Roy Jeffrey, *The American People: Creating A Nation and A Society*, 5th ed., (New York, New York: Addison-Wesley Educational Publishers, Inc., 2001), 546.

[44]Ibid.

[45]David Whitman, "A Court Fight Truly Off the Reservation," *U.S. News & World Report* (April 5, 1999), 42.

[46]"Our Century: The Oldest Living Crow Indian," *U.S. News & World Report*, (August 28/September 4, 1995), 97.

[47]*Statistical Abstract of the United States: 2006*, 125th ed., Table, 38, 42.

[48]Ibid., Table 287, 186.

[49]C. Van Woodward, *The Strange Career of Jim Crow*, 3rd. ed. (New York: Oxford University Press, 1974), 11.

[50]Conrad, 109.

[51]Jay Tolson, "The Complex Story of Slavery", *U.S. News & World Report*, February 14, 2005, 66.

[52]Ibid., 66-67.

[53]Ibid., 67.

[54]Woodward, 21.

[55]Jack Fincher, "The Hard Fight Was Getting Into the Fight At All," *Smithsonian*, Vol. 21, No. 7, October, 1990, 46.

[56]Ibid.

[57]Woodward, 54.

[58]Abraham, 374.

[59]Woodward, 104.

[60]Ibid., 85.

[61]"A Farewell to 'Mr. Civil Rights'," *U. S. News & World Report*, (February 8, 1993), 10.

[62]Conrad, 98.

[63]Woodward, 18-19.

[64]Abraham, 375.

[65]Carolyn Kleiner Butler, "Down In Mississippi", *Smithsonian*, Vol. 35, No. 11, February, 2005, 24.

[66]Keith Weldon Medley, "The Sad Story Of How 'Separate But Equal' Was Born," *Smithsonian*, Vol. 24, No. 11, February, 1994, 106.

[67]Ibid., 108-109.

[68]Ibid., 112.

[69]Domino, 226.

[70]Medley, "The Sad Story of How 'Separate But Equal' Was Born," 108.

[71]David Uhler, "Jim Crow Was A Loser in Korean War," *San Antonio Express-News* (Sunday, June 4, 2000), 1A.

[72]Paul Finkleman, "Race and the Constitution," *By and For the People: Constitutional Rights in American History*, Kermit L. Hall, ed., (Illinois: Harland Davidson, Inc., 1990), 155.

[73]Gregg Holland, "Quiet Justice Speaks Out on Cross Burning", *San Antonio Express-News* (Thursday, December 12, 2002), 4A.

[74]Bree Fowler, "'Mother of the Civil Rights Movement' Dies", *San Antonio Express-News*, (Tuesday, October 25, 2005), 1A.

[75]Ibid.

[76]Conrad, 156.

[77]Abraham, 420.

[78]Uhler, 1A.

[79]Ibid.

[80]Woodward, 132.

[81]Domino, 227.

[82]Abraham, 396.

[83]Scott Parks, "The Little Rock Nine: School Integration Battle Changed Lines Of Players in Central High Drama," *Dallas Morning News* (Sunday, September 21, 1997), 45A and 56A.

[84]Ibid., 56A.

[85]Alan Barth, *The Rights of Free Men: An Essential Guide to Civil Liberties*, James E. Clayton, ed., (New York: Alfred A. Knopf, 1987), 172.

[86]Conrad, 207.

[87]Michael J. Sniffen, "Gaps Found in Federal Death Penalty," *San Antonio Express-News* (Wednesday, August 21, 2002), 1A.

[88]*Statistical Abstract of the United States: 2006*, 125th ed., Table 36, 39.

[89]McLemore, 227.

[90]Mark Helm, "Diversity Among Hispanics Make For Political Disunity," *San Antonio Express-News* (Tuesday, October 13, 1998), 1A.

[91]Ibid.

[92]Arnold DeLeon, "Los Tejanos: An Overview of Their History," *The Texas Heritage*, Ben Procter and Archie McDonald, eds., 1st ed., (Ill.: Harlan Davidson, Inc., 1980), 134.

[93]Arnold DeLeon, *Mexican-Americans in Texas: A Brief History*, (Ill.: Harlan Davidson, Inc., 1991), 67.

[94]McLemore, 243.

[95]Ibid., 236-237.

[96]DeLeon, *Mexican-Americans in Texas: A Brief History*, 134.

[97]Hector Saldana, "United They Stand," *San Antonio Express-News* (Sunday, March, 31, 2002), 5J.

[98]"An Interview," *Voice of Diversity: Perspectives on American Political Ideals and Institutions*, Pat Andrews, ed., (Guilford, Conn.: The Dushkin Publishing Group, Inc., 1995), 164-165.

[99]Mark Helm, "Soldiers Blazed The Trail to Political Prominence," *San Antonio Express-News* (Sunday, October 11, 1998), 17A.

[100]Stewart M. Powell, "Hispanic Political Leaders Are Scarce," *San Antonio Express-News* (Wednesday, August 21, 2002), 1A.

[101]*Statistical Abstract of the United States: 2006*, 125th ed., Table 40, 43.

[102]Ibid.

[103]Ibid., Table 37, 40-41.

[104]McLemore, 223.

[105]DeLeon, *Mexican-Americans in Texas: A Brief History*, 66.

[106]McLemore, 238-239.

[107]Blevins, 259.

[108]McLemore, 238.

[109]Erick Schelzig, "States' Immigration Laws May Not Pass Court Test", *San Antonio Express-News*, (Sunday, August 20, 2006), 8A.

[110]Ibid.

[111]Pete Yost, "High Court Slaps Leash on Booting Immigrants," *San Antonio Express-News*, (Wednesday, December 6, 2006), 7A.

[112]Helm, 17A.

[113]Tim Lopes, "Hispanic Muscle Going Unflexed," *The Houston Chronicle*, (Sunday, April 16, 1995), 6A.

[114]Gary Martin, "Latino Vote Bloc Hard to Pin Down," *San Antonio Express-News* (Friday, October 4, 2002), 18A.

[115]Ibid.

[116]Paula Petrek, "Women and The Bill of Rights,"*By and For the People: Constitutional Rights in American History*, Kermit L. Hall, ed., (Ill.: Harlan Davidson, Inc., 1991), 133.

[117]Barbara Goldsmith, "The Woman Who Set America on Its Ear," *Parade Magazine*, *The San Antonio Express-News* (Sunday, March 8, 1998), 14-15.

[118]Domino, 252.

[119]J. R. Poole, 296.

[120]Paula Petrek, 134.

[121]Poole, 301.

[122]Rynder, 25.

[123]Ibid., 307.

[124]"The Object at Hand," *Smithsonian*, Vol. 23, No. 12, March, 1993, 30.

[125]Ibid., 32.

[126]Ibid.

[127]*Statistical Abstract of the United States: 2006*, 125th ed., Table 217, 148.

[128]Barbara Ehrenreich, "Sorry Sisters, This Is Not A Revolution," *Time*, (Fall, 1990), 15.

[129]Poole, 309-310.

[130]"Separating the Sisters," *U. S. News & World Report*, (March 28, 1994), 49.

[131]Steven K. Paulson, "Witness Says Victims Propositioned Him," *San Antonio Express-News* (Saturday, October 30, 1999), 6A.

[132]Thomas R. Hensley, Christopher E. Smith and Joyce Baugh, *The Changing Supreme Court: Constitutional Rights and Liberties*, (St. Paul, Minnesota: West Publishing Co., 1997), 831.

[133]Laurie Asseo, "Justices Say Scouts Can Ban Gay Leaders," *San Antonio Express-News* (Thursday, June 29, 2000), 1A.

[134]"The New Civil Rights Battle," *U.S. News & World Report*, June 3, 1996, 29.5

[135]Nancy R. Mudrick, "Employment Discrimination Laws for Disability: Utilization And Outcome," *The Annals of the American Academy of Political and Social Science*, Vol. 549, January, 1997, 55.

[136]Ibid., 56.

[137]Marjorie L. Baldwin, "Can the ADA Achieve Its Employment Goal?", *The Annals of the American Academy of Political and Social Science*, Vol. 549, January, 1997, 40-41.

[138]Coniff, 127.

SUGGESTED READINGS

Abraham, Henry J., and Barbara A. Perry, *Freedom & the Court: Civil Rights & Liberties in the United States,* 8th ed., Lawrence, Kansas: University Press of Kansas, 2003.

Barth, Alan. *The Rights of Free Men: An Essential Guide to Civil Liberties.* James E. Clayton, ed. New York: Alfred A. Knopf, 1987.

Conrad, Earl. *Jim Crow America.* 2d ed. New York: Duell, Sloan, and Peace, 1947.

Domino, John C. *Civil Rights and Liberties: Toward the 21st Century.* New York: HarperCollins Publishers, 1994.

McLemore S. Dale, and Harriet D. Romo, *Racial and Ethical Relations in America*, 7th Ed., Boston, Mass.: Pearson Education Inc. 2005.

Tocqueville, Alexis de. *Democracy in America.* Translated by George Lawrence, J. P. Mayer, eds. Garden City, N. Y.: Doubleday and Company, Inc., 1969.

Woodward, C. Van. *The Strange Career of Jim Crow.* 3rd ed. New York: Oxford University

Conrad, Earl. *Jim Crow America.* 2d ed. New York: Duell, Sloan, and Peace, 1947.

Chapter Fifteen

PUBLIC POLICY

Residents along the Gulf Coast area are well aware of the typical hurricane season—the beginning of June to usually the end of September. Every year, the National Hurricane Center announces the predicted number of storms, the category levels, and a list of alternating male and female names for each storm. Hurricanes can range from the least potentially dangerous Category 1 to the extremely dangerous Category 5 with its 175 plus mile per hour winds—the "big one." Despite a cadre of sophisticated weather equipment and well-trained meteorologists, predicting the path of where a hurricane will strike is extremely difficult. Far too often, Mother Nature has the final say on where a hurricane will eventually make landfall. Once the projected path is mapped out, potential hurricane victims take the usual precautions of nailing plywood boards to the windows, purchasing bottled water, food, candles, and flashlight batteries, and packing a few items just in case they will have to evacuate for a day or two until the storms quickly blow ashore with their high winds, rain, storm surges, and potential tornados, break apart into tropical storms, and move further inland. Depending upon the potential severity of the storm, some residents will evacuate while others will opt to "ride it out." Gulf Coast residents can usually count on the majority of the hurricanes to range between categories one to three with only one or two potential category four storms. The 2005 hurricane season was anything but typical. The number of hurricanes far exceeded the chosen names from A to Z. Officials had to resort to using the Greek alphabet of Alpha, Beta, Gamma, etc. And on August 29, 2005, the rare "big one" named Katrina headed, as predicted it would, straight for the approximately 455,000 residents of New Orleans, Louisiana.

Founded in 1718 by the French, New Orleans established itself as a showcase of Southern charm and hospitality. The image of New Orleans was one of wealth—tree-lined streets, French buildings with wrought iron balconies, large Southern plantation style mansions, etc. Tourists flocked to the city especially during Mardi Gras. In reality, New Orleans has always been an easy target for the "big one." The city is located "atop a Mississippi River delta that stretches out past the end of North America, fading from hard ground to a blot of mud, grass, and water. It's a malleable place without clear boundaries, a land between earth and sea—belonging to neither and alternately claimed by both."[1] Periodically, the city was flooded by tropical storms and hurricanes. The answer to protecting the city from catastrophic flooding was a series of "earthen levees to protect it from the Mississippi River to the south and Lake Pontchartrain to the north."[2] However, the levees could not stop the inevitable erosion of the coastline. "When New Orleans was founded, it was 10 to 12 feet higher and it was 100 miles from the coast. Now it's the coast."[3] When Katrina hit, New Orleans was already 10 feet below sea level surrounded by the levees. Basically, New Orleans sits in the bottom of a bowl. "And it's the very reason the Red Cross listed a direct hurricane hit on New Orleans as the nation's most deadly natural-disaster threat a few years ago."[4] If just confronted with the hurricane, the city would have sustained millions of dollars in damages, but it would have survived. It was the combined efforts of Katrina and the breeching of those levees that flooded the city for weeks and turned the showcase of Southern charm and hospitality into a leveled war zone similar to what was left of Dresden, Germany after continuous bombing by U.S. warplanes during World War II. Frankly, "Katrina knocked one of the nation's largest cities back to the Stone Age— no electricity, no phone system, no water, no sanitation, no commerce," no way out, and no immediate substantial help on the way from any level of government.[5]

As Katrina's high winds and storm surges tore apart New Orleans and its levees, as well as areas stretching from Louisiana to Mississippi, it also severely and painfully exposed the inability of government at all levels to alleviate the suffering of the victims of Katrina's wrath. Those who had the time and the financial means did leave the area. However, the majority of the area's poor, sick and elderly simply did not have a way out without some form of public assistance. Like the majority of our nation's cities, city leaders in New Orleans did not have a full-scale evacuation plan in place. For days on end, Americans across the country watched the tragedy of the Gulf Coast as report after report showed the starving, thirsty and, in some cases, dying residents of New Orleans sitting on expressway overpasses in stifling heat waiting for someone to rescue them. Thousands of people were sitting on top of their roofs waving white pieces of cloth and signs hoping to attract the attention of an occasional helicopter hovering overhead to take them to safety. News footage showed the desperation of people using makeshift boats to ferry themselves and those they could rescue to the Superdome. "Official shelters became hellholes, with unsanitary conditions and mob rule. The Superdome swelled to 26,000 desperate homeless people; 15,000 broke into the city convention center, creating their own society in the hot and dark hall."[6] Eventually, the high winds tore a hole in the Superdome's roof, rendering an already unbearable situation impossible. "In the local hospitals, doctors and nurses trapped with thousands of patients had to decide who got medicine and who got hooked up to life-saving ventilators in hot, dark wards as supplies of water, food and medicine dwindled. By the end of the first week, doctors were forced to decide between intravenously feeding themselves or their patients."[7] To add insult to injury, another major hurricane Rita would tear into the same area and East Texas approximately one month later.

Once help arrived, the call went out to cities across the country to *temporarily* house approximately 2.5 million displaced Gulf Coast residents.[8] The federal government through the Federal Emergency Management Agency (FEMA) guaranteed that cities would be reimbursed for all expenses. "In cities stretching from Atlanta [Georgia] to San Antonio [Texas], good will has often given way to crude reality of absorbing a traumatized and sometimes destitute population. In Baton Rouge, which added 100,000 to a pre-Katrina population of 225,000, residents bemoan the loss of the city's small-town feel and worry that trailer-park settlements will become permanent fixtures of blight. In Dallas, the city housing authority began offering rent vouchers to some of its 20,000 evacuees, only to become quickly overwhelmed and fail to pay landlords, prompting a number of eviction notices. But perhaps no city has been as convulsed as Houston, which took in the greatest number of survivors [approximately 150,000]. As some see it, the city is suffering from compassion fatigue."[9] In San Antonio, evacuees were housed in a former air force base, a vacant shopping mall and abandoned factories. For far too many, a *temporary* relocation has become *permanent*.

Meanwhile, the façade of a competent federal system was crumbling before our very eyes as city leaders were at odds with state and federal officials and agencies. Federalism is built on the understanding that government at all levels must work with each other to successfully address the needs of its citizens. Unfortunately, behind the scenes bickering, finger pointing, miscommunications, or, in some instances, no communication led to inordinate delays in meeting the crisis in New Orleans and the affected Gulf Coast areas. Simply, when people needed their government the most, it failed them miserably. When relief did arrive, it was too late and too little. Weeks later, "even as the around-the-clock relief effort winds down—with planes, helicopters, boats, barges, ferries and more than 2,000 buses having taken tens of thousands of people out and another fleet bringing tons of relief in—bitterness rivals floodwaters as the lingering legacy of Katrina."[10] Himself slow to respond, President George W. Bush held a nation-wide broadcast from New Orleans on September 13, 2005. "Katrina exposed serious problems in our response capability at all levels of government," Bush said. "And to the extent the federal government didn't fully do its job right, I take responsibility. I want to know what went right and what went wrong."[11]

Although the wrath of Katrina and Rita has passed, the rebuilding process has barely begun. In New Orleans, "the city has lost more than half its population. Water and electrical services are still out in some areas, garbage collection is spotty, many schools and hospitals are still closed, and the city buses don't run regularly or on time. Whole blocks still look as though they were bombed. On a sultry afternoon in late August [2006], along Florida Avenue near the now repaired Industrial Canal, gawkers stopped to photograph a house sitting on top of a car."[12] Few of the 2.5 million evacuees have returned to their homes, opting to remain in their adopted cities. The majority of the cities who opened their arms to evacuees are still waiting for their full reimbursements from the federal government. Far too many of Gulf Coast hurricane victims are still waiting for their FEMA trailers. The rebuilding process has been further slowed by the on-going battles between insured homeowners and their insurance companies over what hurricane-related damages are covered under their policies. The rebuilding of the levees to offset the next Category 5 hurricane is mired in Washington budgetary politics. With the majority of its residents scattered over forty-nine states, the Secretary of State of Louisiana flew coast-to-coast trying to contact as many of its former residents as possible just to make sure that they knew where they could vote in the November 2006 general elections. Meanwhile, the finger pointing in Washington continues as Congress launches a series of investigations and hearings. Forced to resign his position, former FEMA director Michael Brown has been a target of several congressional inquiries. One hearing was so contentious that "at several points, Brown's face turned red and he slapped the table. 'So, I guess you wanted me to be the superhero, to step in there and take everyone out of New Orleans,' he said. 'What I wanted you to do is do your job and coordinate,' Rep. Christopher Shays, R-Connecticut replied."[13] The situation reminds one of the classic fairy tale of Humpty Dumpy, with one twist—all of the king's horses and all of the king's men can't put New Orleans back together again!

Despite their best efforts, no governing body can pass legislation to stop the destructive nature of a hurricane. However, government at all levels surely can enact laws and policies that provide prudent and effective evacuation and relief efforts. In the aftermath of Katrina and the on-going problems in Iraq, a disillusioned American public now strongly distrusts this government that was created by lawmakers promising what they could not deliver in the first place, much less legislate through the public policy process. Why does this happen so frequently?

It would be so easy just to place the blame totally on Congress, the president, or in the case of Katrina, a governor or a mayor. Although public policy is itself a product of politics, the blame for policy failures cannot be solely contributed to "politics as usual." The primary cause of poorly written and ineffective public policies is the inability of both legislative houses and members of executive branches alike to follow the public policy process from start to finish. The majority of this nation's laws and city ordinances suffer from crippling design flaws that ultimately result in policy failures.

Most lawmakers propose legislation with good intentions in mind. For example, the New Deal legislation of Franklin Roosevelt's administration that produced the modern welfare state was founded on the principles of government helping those in financial need. The Great Depression, caused by the 1929 crash of the stock market, put millions of hardworking Americans and their families out of work and one step away from starvation and potentially irreversible financial ruin. State and local governments, as well as private charities, simply did not have the resources to meet the needs of the destitute. Roosevelt reasoned that a compassionate government should without question address the needs of its people.

However, good intentions do not necessarily produce skillfully crafted and successfully implemented public policies. In the 1980s and 1990s, it became clearly evident that the welfare state created by President Franklin Roosevelt had deteriorated to the point that politicians from all political parties advocated reforming it with the ultimate goal of actually eliminating the bulk of its income support programs. A bureaucratic nightmare, the welfare system produced an economically disadvantaged underclass that became almost totally dependent upon the "system" for survival. The hardworking and over-tax-burdened middle class resented a welfare system that continuously needed more tax dollars for its programs, while failing to deliver on its lofty promise to eliminate poverty. Public opinion shifted from favoring a benevolent government intent on providing for everyone faced with adverse economic hardships to one that provided for only those who were not only truly desperate but willing to work for their share of the dole. The welfare system, as originally conceived, broke down. However, the welfare reform package finally enacted during the Clinton administration has not adequately addressed the needs of the nation's poor. Just establishing stiffer eligibility requirements and time limits for services does not mean that former recipients of government-sponsored income support programs have raised their income levels to the point that they no longer need government assistance. In some instances, the poor are in a worse situation because of welfare reform.

In the 1970s, Americans were awakened to the state of their deteriorating environment. Lawmakers responded by enacting corrective legislation covering an array of environmental concerns from cleaner air and water to protection of endangered plants and wildlife. Once again, good intentions did not produce effective policies. Business and industry see environmental laws laden with costly impact statements, threats of litigation, fines and penalties as cost prohibitive and unnecessary impediments to the economic viability of the free market system. On the other hand, environmentalists believe that the existing laws are just halfhearted attempts to address a potentially irreversible problem. They criticize the government for doing too little too late to save our planet. Public opinion is also divided. The average American citizen is concerned about the environment. All agree that something must be done to ensure a cleaner environment or the future of this planet may be in serious jeopardy. However, these same citizens are fearful that the expense of producing environmentally safe consumer products will be cost prohibitive. They are also concerned as to the extent of the personal sacrifices they may be asked to make to preserve the environment. Both sides are not pleased with the existing laws. What went wrong?

This chapter explores the public policy process from the inception of the concept to its final evaluation as a means of discovering exactly what goes wrong with the majority of the public policy initiatives created by the legislative and executive branches at all levels of government from the national to the city/county level. In actuality, the "process" of public policy is a series of steps that must be equally weighed in importance. Overlooking just one step can condemn a potentially successful legislative action to failure before it is even written. Public policy is more than a legislative act. The final product is the embodiment of the prevailing political, economic, social, and cultural philosophies of the time. The answers to who makes public policy begins with the average citizen and ends on the desk of the president to await its fate. While the wheeling and dealing between party leaders, legislators, and the president continues, the average citizen must pay close attention to their actions because the outcome of their decisions impacts everyone. "Public polices in a modern, complex society are indeed ubiquitous. They confer advantages and disadvantages, cause pleasure, irritation, and pain, and collectively have important consequences for our well-being and happiness. They constitute a significant portion of our environment. This being so, we should know something about public policies, including how they are formed, budgeted, implemented and evaluated."[14] Eventually, the prudent student of government will conclude that "politics is about policy. The decisions that government makes are the end result of a complex process. Many potential issues never get discussed seriously by political leaders; and policy is not necessarily determined even for those issues on which serious debate takes place. Even after policies have been announced, the politics of the policy process continues, as efforts may be made to shape implementation of program."[15] The creation of the policy is often more important than the policy itself. The success or failure of a policy initiative hinges more on how it was created, budgeted, implemented, and evaluated than the problem or issue the policy was intended to address. The process of creating public policy extends to all items of domestic and foreign policy issues and considerations. This chapter explores how to create a policy masterpiece while avoiding a policy disaster.

PUBLIC POLICY DEVELOPMENT

The term **policy** is defined as "a relatively stable, purposive course of action followed by an actor or set of actors in dealing with a problem or matter of concern."[16] Policy, therefore, is not just a statement concerning a problem or issue. It is a purposeful action designed to reach a defined goal or objective. Policy originates in both the private and public sectors with one major exception. Created by governmental bodies, **public policy** can be defined as "an officially expressed intention backed by a sanction, which can be a reward or punishment."[17] Governing institutions at all levels make public policy. Laws, edits, rules, and ordinances are public policy initiatives created by governing bodies in response to the demands of the citizens for authoritative action deemed necessary to address a public concern, issue, or need. Consequently, "public policy has an authoritative, legally coercive quality that the policies of private organizations do not have."[18] If citizens obey and follow the policy directives of their government, they are rewarded for their obedience. Contrary, citizens who disobey the laws of their government will be punished by a sanction, fine, imprisonment, or any combination thereof.

The development of public policy at any level of government is based upon four fundamental principles. First, public policy initiatives created in a democratic government are the products of conflict and accommodation. As evidenced by the day to day bickering between legislative and executive leaders, "all forms of political organization have a bias in favor of the exploitation of some kinds of conflicts and the suppression of others because organization is the mobilization of bias. Some issues are organized into politics while others are organized out."[19] The result, the policy directive, is a compromise between various factions and key governmental actors. Regardless of the issues before a legislative house, "there is opposition to virtually every policy proposal, and agreement is reached only after bargains have been struck and compromises have been agreed on."[20] Political bickering is a given in the creation of public policy. It is an extremely high stakes game with every interested and effected party desiring to be a winner, not a loser.

Second, public policy is a series of policy outputs and outcomes. "**Policy outputs** are the things actually done by agencies in pursuance of policy decisions and statements."[21] Far too often, the policy outputs are different from what policy makers initially envisioned. For example, the policy establishing the income tax created a progressive tax program whereby everyone would pay their proportionate share towards taxes. Those with higher incomes would pay a higher amount of tax in comparison to those with lower incomes. However, the policy output created a regressive income tax plan. By allowing deductions for certain expenditures and investments, taxpayers in the highest income brackets are actually paying less towards their income tax obligations than taxpayers whose earnings are in the lower income brackets.

Policy outcomes are" the consequences for society, intended or unintended, that stem from deliberate governmental action or inaction."[22] For example, the civil rights acts were enacted to disband discriminatory actions against minorities, particularly African Americans, in all areas including employment, voting, housing, education, and public accommodations. The implementation of these laws lead to profound and oftentimes violent upheavals to the political, social, and cultural traditions embraced by American society. Laws designed to eliminate discrimination by encouraging desegregation often resulted in sit-ins, race riots, violent protests, and race-related killings that further eroded the fragile relationship between the Anglo and African-American communities. The resulting lesson painfully learned by lawmakers and jurists alike was that legislative acts alone cannot change longstanding attitudes and beliefs.

Third, there is a distinct difference between decision-making and policy-making. **Decision-making** "involves making a discrete choice from among two or more alternatives," whereas, **policy-**

Taxpayers have lofty desires for the space program. America won the race to place a man on the moon. Watching the lift-off of the first American in space. (L-R) Vice President Johnson, Arthur Schlesinger, Adm. Arleigh Burke, President Kennedy and Mrs. Kennedy, White House, Office of the President's Secretary. May 5, 1961.. Photo credit: Cecil Stoughton, White House/ JFK Library

making "typically encompasses a flow and pattern of action that extends over time and includes many decisions, some routine and some not so routine."[23] Decisions are made on a daily basis, often without the benefit of a deliberation process. To be effective, policy decisions must be treated as purposeful deliberative actions resulting from an intense and often, lengthy planning process. Quick decisions on the part of lawmakers can have disastrous policy results.

Fourth, the taypayer demands that lawmakers create policies that are both cost-effective and successful in achieving intended goals and objectives, subsequently, "the need is to design realistic goals that embrace a balance between efficiency and effectiveness."[24] Efficiency and effectiveness are often diametrically opposed to each other. For example, the national space program is an expensive project. Americans expect the space program to launch space shuttles, build space stations, and explore the galaxy at the cheapest cost possible. The taxpayers' expectations are lofty desires that cannot be fulfilled by lawmakers. There can be a balance between efficiency, effectiveness, and cost. However, in the case of the space program and other government programs, the quality and quantity of the service are questionable when the budget alone guides the policy decision process.

Who Makes Public Policy?

There is a multiplicity of key actors in the public policy process. Each actor plays an essential role in the creation, implementation, and evaluation of a policy directive. The interplay between the actors is politics at its best and worst.

Public opinion does play a vital role in determining the scope and response of policy issues and outcomes. Basically, public opinion is collectively "those public perspectives or viewpoints on policy issues that public officials consider or take into account in making decisions."[25] Elected officials do listen to public opinion. Input from concerned citizens is essential to a democratic government. Citizens express their concerns through public opinion polls and, most importantly, the ballot box. Despite the oftentimes fickleness of public opinion, it is a truism in politics that those "elected public officials who totally ignore public opinion and do not include it among their criteria for decisions, should any be so foolish, are likely to find themselves out of luck at election time."[26] However, public opinion is hard for lawmakers to gage on a long-term basis since it is so unpredictable. Surveys reveal that public opinion can change from staunchly supporting a policy decision to hostility against it. The public unrealistically wants immediate actions from their lawmakers that miraculously address their concerns. A disappointed public can turn government on its backside without mercy. The key issues that definitely helped the Democrats win control of both the House and the Senate in the November 2006 general elections were the Bush administration's Iraq policy coupled with the inability of the Republicans to deal with pressing domestic issues such as Katrina and to appropriately respond to the congressional page scandal surrounding Mark Foley, a long-term Republican Congressman. Basically, "the American public does not seem to feel that the government copes very well at all. Congress has been portrayed as unproductive and spineless, unwilling to tackle the tough problems that require discipline or sacrifice."[27]

Interest groups play an extremely important role in the policy process. The 1960s saw the rapid rise of liberal citizen groups advocating a wide range of issue positions from anti-war protests to voting rights, equal opportunity, and environmental concerns. Today, a wide range of citizen or social movement groups have impacted public policy decisions in "defense and foreign affairs; health care policy pertaining to AIDS and abortion; environmental protection; and the rights of various groups including women, gays, the handicapped, the homeless, and racial and ethnic minorities."[28] The Framers were concerned that interest groups would eventually fragment and destroy the collective spirit of community and nationalism. In actuality, the growth of interest groups has strengthened the democratic nature of the political system. "The rise of liberal citizen groups was largely responsible for catalyzing an explosion in the growth of all interest groups. Efforts to limit the impact of liberal citizen groups failed, and the policy-making process became more open and more participatory."[29] Openness demanded that lawmakers change their approach towards interest groups. "Policymaking moved away from the closed subgovernments, each involving a relatively stable and restricted group of lobbyists and key government officials to much broader policymaking communities. Policymaking in earlier years is typically described as a product of consensual negotiations between a small number of back-scratching participants."[30] Once confined to closed-door meetings, congressional hearings are now fully open to the public through the watchful eyes of the media. Cable television networks now offer continuous daily broadcasts of congressional committee hearings. The media has helped to keep those once closed doors wide open to the public.

The past forty years have also witnessed a change in the tactics traditionally used by social movement groups. The 1960s style of haphazardly organized protest movements, massive rallies, sit-ins, and, sometimes, violent displays of behavior have been replaced by well-organized "going public" media campaigns; professionally trained lobbyists sitting side by side those representing economic and business interests; well-financed and highly visible political action committees capable of raising large sums of money for candidates garnering the groups' public endorsements; a cadre of well-prepared attorneys poised to use litigation through the courts whenever the legislative side of government fails to push their causes; and a well-organized structure of locally-based chapters guided by a strong national organization capable of mobilizing its membership on a very short notice. Today, citizen or social movement interest groups resemble a corporate structure.

It has also become more difficult for lawmakers to successfully fulfill the requests of social movement groups since many of these organizations are apt to pursue narrowly defined ideological issues such as abortion, school prayer, environmental concerns, and so on. The traditional public policy approach rested on the belief that consensus is a compromised product of conflict and accommodation with each participant able to claim a partial victory. Unfortunately, lawmakers find compromise oftentimes impossible when working with groups that take an "all or nothing" approach. "Democracy requires adequate representation of interests as well as institutions capable of addressing difficult policy problems. For policy makers who must balance the demand for representation with the need for results, the key is thinking creatively about how to build coalitions and structure negotiations between large groups of actors."[31] Far too often, the agenda items of social movements are in direct conflict with the business and economic interests of this country, placing lawmakers in a perilously difficult and often impossible position of trying to broker a compromise.

There are noticeable pros and cons to interest group involvement in the public policy arena. "On the positive side, interest group politics create a dynamism, often through conflict, that draws out diversity in policy proposals, a diversity producing innovation and social change. Interest groups also provide access for the public to effect government decision-making . . . . On the negative side, interest groups fighting for their special goals can fragment the policy process. This struggle reduces the leadership's capacity to direct citizen demands toward an effective solution, promoting instead a compromise that may partially satisfy each group but not resolve the initial issue."[32]

Political parties exert their influence directly on public policy issues by electing lawmakers. It is the elected official's primary responsibility to his/her political party to actively pursue the agenda outlined in their party's platform. The leadership of legislative houses is controlled by the political parties. Loyalty to one's political party and its agenda can mean a key committee assignment for a legislator. Unlike interest groups, political parties are board-based umbrella organizations pursuing a multiplicity of diverse policy items. "Generally, parties have a broader range of policy concerns than do interest groups; hence, they act more as brokers than as advocates for particular interests in policy formation."[33]

The credibility of a political party rests solely with the ability of its elected party members to enact public policy on behalf of their party. The intense competition between the Democrat and Republican Parties in the 1980s resulted in a congressional gridlock as both parties dug in their heals, refusing to compromise between themselves and the White House. President Clinton expressed his frustrations with the congressional gridlock by commenting that "America is at a crossroads. One path leads to continual partisan conflict where nothing is really resolved and each decision simply sets the stage for the next fight. The other path leads to national unity, a unity built on true solutions and real common ground."[34] Unfortunately, President Clinton's dream of unity will not emerge in the near future. Armed with an ideological shield crafted of supposedly unbreakable metals, both political parties are slugging it out with each other over every issue of concern. As the result of the 2002 midterm and the 2004 general elections, President George W. Bush had the luxury of Republican majorities in both the House and the Senate. The final two years of the Bush administration is confronted with a Congress controlled by the other party, a potentially hostile Congress. Particularly in the Senate, several members from both parties are announced candidates for the 2008 presidential nomination from their respective parties. Any president confronted with a hostile Congress has to be able to use exceptionally keen political skills to guide his legislative agenda through these legislative houses or gridlock between the two will rear its ugly head again.

Since both the president and members of Congress are popularly elected representatives of their respective political parties, the roles they play in the development of public policy are paramount throughout the process. As lawmakers, they must take on issues concerning the few and transform them into policies potentially benefiting the many. The framers compounded the complexity of this task by creating a two-house (bicameral) legislature charged with different focuses. The House of Representatives was designed to serve regional needs. Members of the House are obligated to pursue issues beneficial to his/her constituents. A congressperson voting against a legislative act potentially beneficial to his/her constituents could pay a career-ending price on election day. In contrast, senators are focused more on the needs of the nation as a whole. However, they too must ensure that what benefits the whole will to some degree benefit the state they represent. Basically, "representatives tend to be known as subject matter 'specialists' while senators tend to be 'generalists.' If the Senate has been the nation's great forum, a representative said, then the House has been its workshop."[35]

Sometimes enacting what is morally and ethically correct conflicts with what is politically correct. Members of Congress are also members of their respective political parties and their ideological positions. It is a duty of congressional party leaders to constantly remind members of their party loyalties wherever a key vote is on the floor.

Since the executive is bound constitutionally to work with the legislature, the president oftentimes finds himself in the middle of the congressional fray. In 1936, President Franklin Roosevelt, a Democrat, remarked on a comment made by his Republican cousin: "Theodore Roosevelt said, 'Sometimes I wish I could be president and Congress too.' Well, I suppose if the truth be told, he is not the only president that has had that idea."[36] Franklin Roosevelt was merely echoing the frustrations all presidents have had in their dealings with the legislative branch. Executive-legislative relationships do shape the course of public policy. Legislatively successful presidents have developed a strong positive working relationship with their Congresses. Of course, the relationship is far smoother if the president's political party holds the majority of the seats in both houses. Nevertheless, presidents do exercise influence at all levels of the legislative process to include the ultimate threat and/or use of the veto.

Beginning with George Washington, every resident of the Oval Office wants future generations to know his particular impact on American history. "It has been a habit of presidents to try to write their own history, to establish themselves as a legitimate embodiment of America's past and shaper of America's future."[37] A president's legacy is seen through the legislation passed during his administration. Therefore, it is imperative that the president and his White House staff play a vitally important role in the development and eventual implementation of public policy. Presidents officially inform Congress about their policy agendas through their yearly delivery of the State of the Union message. Realizing they have only four or if lucky eight years in office, presidents are prone to promise too much in the beginning, only to see their lofty expectations reduced by Congress into piecemeal legislative victories. Richard Nixon appeared to be totally prepared for the reality of Washington, D.C. However, "for a man with a perfect resume to become president—military officer, congressman, senator, vice-president for eight years—it was surprising how much Nixon's views on policy making changed in the first two years of his administration."[38] Initially, Nixon advocated complete and expedient elimination of the Great Society programs that were the cornerstone of the Johnson administration. He quickly found himself at odds with his staff over the appropriate approach his administration should take with Congress. "Thus, the administration's initial problem was not deciding what its policies were, instead it was converting campaign policy positions to the 'bullet proof' presidential messages and detailed draft legislation that can achieve major changes in public policy."[39] Nixon quickly found out what every president has discovered, that Congress is reluctant to approve quick sweeping changes advocated by the White House. Instead, they prefer to take several small steps rather than one large leap. After pressure from congressional Republicans and the White House staff, a staff person noted that "a consensus emerged that the president [Nixon] should launch relatively few initiatives, because we could not afford many; we needed to be bold, but we needed to get results; and we needed to communicate a focused approach."[40]

However, the congressional incremental approach can be extremely frustrating for presidents. For example, in 1946, President Harry Truman was determined that he would desegregate all branches of the military's officer corps. Truman was facing pressure from civil rights organizations to fulfill his campaign promises. "Harry Truman was crude and ineloquent, but he made tough decisions and got them mostly right (a view that stands up well)."[41] Bypassing Congress and his own party's congressional leadership, Truman took the initiative by issuing an executive order. Truman's action changed the leadership core of the nation's military branches. Traditionally, African Americans and other minority military personnel were limited to non-leadership roles. Truman's desegregation plan provided the impetus for minorities to strive for officer positions. Colin Powell was able to become the first African American to be named the Chairman of the Joint Chiefs of Staff, and ultimately, Secretary of State in part because Harry Truman could not wait for Congress to drag its collective feet. With or without the blessings of Congress, presidents can and do exert a tremendous impact on the direction of this nation's domestic and foreign policy initiatives.

The media has a direct role in public policy by bringing sensitive issues to the public's attention. It is estimated that two-thirds of the American public rely upon television as their sole source of news and information. The media does play a key role in shaping public opinion. The key for government agencies and elected officials is to learn how use the media to their advantage. "President Bill Clinton, for one, showed extraordinary talent at using direct televised presidential addresses and nationally televised 'town meetings' to reach citizens in the studio audience and nationwide audiences who witnessed and identified with this direct interaction. . . . some commentators have observed that part of President Clinton's skill in influencing (and some would say misleading) public opinion about his sexual affairs later aggravated his legal and constitutional problems—and as with his State of the Union address during his trial, helped him survive those challenges."[42]

Traditionally, **bureaucrats** were viewed as mere implementors of public policy with little impact on the development of policy directives. This perspective has changed dramatically. "Although it was once common doctrine in political science that administrative agencies only carried into effect, more or less automatically, policies determined by the 'political' branches of government, now it is axiomatic that politics and administration are blended, and that administrative agencies are often significantly involved in the formation of public policies. This is particular apparent, given the concept of policy as encompassing what government actually does over time concerning a problem or situation."[43] Consequently, bureaucracies do shape public policy. Bureaucratic agencies begin their influence at the initial stages of policy development. Lawmakers are not experts on every policy issue. They rely upon bureaucratic agencies to provide research and testimony before committee hearings. Their input can determine the course of action Congress will eventually take on a policy issue. However, federal agencies will also flex their muscles to block unfavorable legislation by actively lobbying members of Congress and soliciting the support of key interest groups. In addition, bureaucracies can make or break policy initiatives simply by the manner in which agencies implement a new policy directive. Bureaucrats can control the fate of any law since the majority of the congressional legislation leaves implementation schemes totally in the hands of the responsible federal agency.

President Reagan holds a National Security Council meeting on the Persian Gulf with National Security Advisor Colin Powell in the Oval Office. April 18, 1988.

Many federal, state, and local laws have been overturned by the federal courts. The **judiciary** does make public policy whenever it declares a law unconstitutional. **Article VI** of the United States Constitution called the **Supremacy Clause** has been interpreted to allow the United States federal courts to rule any law passed at any level of government as unconstitutional when that law conflicts with the spirit and meaning of the United States Constitution. The power of **judicial review** has compelled government at all levels to reconsider its course of public policy options. A judge's gavel makes public policy!

The Supreme Court's 1954 ruling in *Brown v Board of Education of Topeka, Kansas*, began the modern civil rights movement. The United States Congress and state legislative houses began to pass laws reversing over one hundred years of discriminatory practices aimed at minorities. The *Roe v Wade* (1973) decision overturned about forty-six state laws prohibiting elective abortion procedures. In 2005, the Supreme Court has handed down two significant rulings involving criminal procedures used by state courts nationwide. First, the Court declared the federal sentencing guidelines established by Congress two decades ago as unconstitutional. Basically, "the Supreme Court said making the guidelines mandatory violated a defendant's Sixth Amendment right to a jury trial because they call for judges to make factual decisions that affect prison time. Under the ruling [of the Supreme Court] the guidelines are now only advisory; federal judges are free to sentence convicted criminals as they see fit, but they may be subject to reversal if appeals courts find them 'unreasonable.'"[44] The Supreme Court also ruled that the application of the death penalty to defendants under the age of eighteen is a violation of the Eighth Amendment's prohibition against cruel and unusual punishment. Their decision "spared 72 inmates nationwide, although it will take days, weeks and even longer before state courts or parole boards formally commute the individual death penalties into life sentences."[45] As the nation's court-of-last-resort, there can be no appeals of the body's decisions.

In summary, the key actors in the public policy process are the public, interest groups, political parties, the media, the bureaucracy, the courts, and elected officials. All of these actors play a key role in shaping public policy. All public policy is a byproduct of conflict, consensus, accommodation, and compromise among these essential policy actors.

What is the Purpose of Public Policy?

Governments enact public policy in response to the public's demand to address an identified concern, issue, or problem. Usually the approach that was originally taken by government failed to accomplish its stated goals and objectives. Hopefully, corrective public policy will present a new alternative or change from the traditional approach. Also, government may not have had to respond to this policy concern before. The framers did not address such issues as the environment, air traffic, radio and television programming issues, and so on. In the early 1800s, the environment was not an issue, much less a potential threat to the survival of mankind.

Through public policy, government at any level must be able to enforce legislative acts either through sanctions, fines, or imprisonment for noncompliance. "Consequently, it must be clearly understood that all public policies are coercive, even when they are motivated by the best and most beneficent of intentions . . . . For us, the coercive element in public policy should instill not abso-

President Bush signing the Americans With Disabilities Act in the Rose Garden of the White House.
July 26, 1990. Photo credit: George Bush Presidential Library

lute opposition but a healthy respect for the risks as well as the good that may be inherent in any public policy."[46] In other words, public policy through its enforcement mechanisms, modifies our behavior and, in some cases, changes our perspectives. Few of us like to drive the posted speed limit. But we definitely modify our driving habits to the mandated speed when we see the police car in front of us since we all want to avoid a costly ticket.

The primary purpose of law enforcement is to serve as a visible deterrent to crime. Criminal statutes and civil fines and penalties are attached to each criminal activity to warn an individual of the consequences of his/her criminal actions. The problem confronting law enforcement is the same problem faced by the Environmental Protection Agency, the Immigration Service, Internal Revenue Service, and any other government agency charged with enforcing a government policy. Basically, how can government ensure that the penalties for noncompliance are severe enough to mandate compliance and deter a would be violator? As we will discover, government at all levels has failed to find the absolute deterrent penalty.

Governments can use a variety of tools besides laws to force behavior modifications. The direct approach is through contracting and licensing. **Government contracts** contain mandates that the recipient must enact or face losing the contract. A federal housing contract, for example, will specify the types of approved building materials, construction methods, inspection criteria, and so forth to include compliance with federal laws, such as the Equal Employment Opportunity Act, Occupational Safety and Health Act, Americans with Disabilities Act, and wage and labor laws. To enforce these requirements, each segment of the construction project must be open to inspection by federal agents before the next phase can begin. Noncompliance means loss of existing and, perhaps, future contracts. The contract mandates ensure that taxpayer money will produce a properly constructed product at the best possible price.

A **license** is "a privilege granted by government to do something that it otherwise considers to be illegal."[47] A license compels behavior modification by forcing the recipient to comply with industry or professional standards. Noncompliance can mean revoking the license and denying the recipient to practice his/her own profession. The threat of removing the license should ensure proper professional conduct. Teachers, doctors, lawyers, and even plumbers and hairdressers must be licensed by their state governments to practice their trades.

Particularly in the foreign policy arena, nations such as the United States, are more apt to use sanctions rather than full-scale warfare as a viable option to force weaker nations to comply with their demands. **Sanctions** are "the penalties meted out as consequences of illegal conduct."[48] Sanctions can range from economic restrictions on exports and imports, suspension of diplomatic ties, to limited military intervention. For example, the United States government severed all diplomatic ties with Cuba following Castro's rise to power in 1959. In addition, the United States issued an economic embargo prohibiting any shipments of cigars and sugar from the island nation into American ports. Sanctions, however, must be used with caution. "In absence of an international executive to enforce the law, the imposition of sanctions depends upon the degree of consensus in the international community and on the willingness of each member of the state system to accept responsibility to uphold the law. To be effective in specific cases, sanctions must create more hardship for the offending state than is created for the states applying the sanctions."[49] Severe sanctions can be an effective short-term plan to modify the offending nation's behavior as long as the entire international community abides by them. Gulf War I was fought by the international community against Iraq's invasion of Kuwait. Suffering a humiliating defeat, Iraq was placed under severe sanctions levied by the United Nations. The Iraqi government could only sell a predetermined amount of oil with the understanding that the generated revenues could be used only for food and medical necessities. The Iraqi government tried every conceivable way to circumvent the sanctions while at the same time, showing media coverage of the adverse impact the imposed sanctions were having on the Iraqi people. Years of economic sanctions did not produce the anticipated goal of crippling the Iraqi government. As evidenced in Iraq, sanctions have not proved to be a viable long-term option in addressing international problems.

Indirectly, every citizen's spending habits are governmentally controlled through taxing, banking, and pricing policies. The on-going military action in Iraq coupled with political unease throughout the Middle East resulted in a shortage of crude oil throughout international markets. In the United States, the price of a gallon of regular grade gasoline quickly rose to over four dollars in some areas of the country. The rapid increase in the price of gasoline forced drivers to use their vehicles less frequently than when gasoline prices were lower. Drivers began to conserve fuel opting for either carpooling or using public transportation. Once the prices went down, drivers reverted back to their old ways.

An economic stimulus involves the manipulation of interest rates. An increase in mortgage and consumer loan rates will force people to think twice before purchasing a new home or automobile. Conversely, government can encourage increased consumer buying by just lowering the prime interest rate, decreasing taxes, or increasing IRS deduction amounts. The Carter administration attempted to lure Americans into saving more money by increasing the interest rates on savings and checking accounts.

Government can modify our use of certain products and public services by charging us a fee. **User fees** or charges or "specified sums that consumers of a government service pay to receive that service."[50] The United States Park Service assesses a higher user fee for those individuals utilizing the nation's parks. The Service wanted to provide additional protection to wildlife and parklands by reducing the number of visitors and campers to these sites. Park rangers used to charge a fee for each vehicle that entered a park, regardless of the number of individuals in the vehicle. The new regulations stipulate that each person in the vehicle will pay a fee to use the parks. The per-person fee has accomplished its intended purpose of reducing the number of visitors. User fees provide governments at all levels with the mechanisms to control the use of the service while at the same time providing additional revenue for the maintenance of that service.

The Public Policy Process

The development of public policy is "analogous to biological natural section. In what we have called the policy primeval soup, many ideas float around, encountering new ideas, and forming combinations and recombinations . . . . Through the imposition of criteria by which some ideas are selected out for survival while others are discarded, order is developed from chaos, pattern from randomness. These criteria include technical feasibility, congruence with values of community members, and the anticipation of culture constraints, including a budget constraint, public acceptability, and politician's receptivity."[51] The **process** to developing the policy is the key to creating effective policy initiatives. The task confronting lawmakers is a difficult one. However, "legislators and other policy formulators can go a long way toward assuring effective policy implementation if they see that a statute incorporates a sound technical theory, provides precise and clearly ranked objectives, and structures the implementation process in a wide number of ways so as to maximize the probability of target group compliance. In addition, they can take positive steps to appoint skillful and supportive implementing officials, to provide adequate appropriations and to monitor carefully the behavior of implementing agencies throughout the long implementation process, and to be aware of the effects of changing socio-economic conditions and of new legislation (even in supposedly unrelated areas) on the original statute."[52] Lawmakers can make good laws if they are totally committed to the process from the start to the finish. The process involves eight crucial steps. Each step is critical to the success of the policy initiative and must be afforded equal attention. If one step is marginally treated or overlooked, the policy initiative, no matter how necessary, will fail. Bad ineffective public policy is the result of poor planning. The process begins with the difficult task of identifying the problem and ends with an evaluation of the resulting policy initiative.

Problem Identification

The first step confronting lawmakers is to identify the problem. A **policy problem** is "a condition or situation that produces needs or dissatisfaction among people and for which relief or redress by governmental action is sought."[53] Not all issues and concerns expressed by the general public will become policy problems requiring redress by government. For too often, city halls are faced with the ire of one citizen who wants council to pass an ordinance addressing his one particular concern, a concern that may not be an issue for anyone else. For example, Mrs. Brown claims that her trash cans are being periodically damaged by city trash crews. She calls her councilperson demanding that city leaders pass an ordinance fining garbage workers for abusing garbage containers. Of course, she is the only one making this request. City Council members simply cannot do this because identified "public problems are those affecting a substantial number of people and having broad effects, including consequences for persons not directly involved. Such occurrences as dirty air, unwholesome food, the practice of abortion, urban traffic congestion, crowded prisons, and global warming are conditions that may become public problems if they produce sufficient anxiety, discontent, or dissatisfaction to cause many people to seek governmental remedies."[54]

Generally, public policy problems fall into one of two categories, namely foreign and domestic, however, foreign policy decisions can positively and negatively impact domestic considerations and vice versa. For example, President Jimmy Carter decided to punish the former Soviet Union over its invasion of Afghanistan by cancelling its wheat shipments to the Soviets. The Soviet Union had been experiencing severe grain shortages caused by over ten years of crop failures. The United States Department of Agriculture purchased wheat from American farmers only to ship it free to the Soviets. Cash-strapped farmers were relieved that their surplus grain stored in silos had finally found a buyer. The subsequent grain embargo cost farmers dearly and created a domestic policy embarrassment for the Carter administration. This breakdown in the wall of separation between domestic and foreign policy has produced **"intermestic issues,"** that is, "those issues (such as trade, finance, pollution, energy, terrorism, human rights, etc.) which overlapped the foreign and domestic policy boundaries."[55] Lawmakers are confronted with the realization that their actions on internal or domestic issues effect foreign policy matters and vice versa. Consequently, the public policy arena has become more complex.

There is also a noticeable difference between substantive and procedural problems. **"Procedural problems** relate to how government is organized, and how it conducts its operations and activities. **Substantive problems** are concerned with the actual consequences of human activity, whether it involves free speech, the sale of used cars or environmental pollution."[56] Each problem area demands unique policy directives to address their issues and concerns.

Too often legislation treats what the problem causes without actually solving the problem. "The effort to define a problem by identifying the causes of broad conditions rests on a certain conception of cause. In this conception, any problem has deep or primary causes that can be found if one only looks hard enough and does careful research.... Once 'the' cause is identified, policy should seek to eliminate it, modify it, reduce it, suppress it, or neutralize it, thereby eliminating or reducing the problem."[57] The contributing factors or **causal factors** should be the targets of legislative action if lawmakers want to solve the problem.

The solution to crime is not just arresting more people and building more jails. Today, the United States has a record number of prisons; court dockets are teeming with new criminal cases; more people are being arrested; and convicts are serving longer sentences without parole. The crime rate is declining for some offenses. However, crime has not been eliminated. The actual criminal act is the result or the "disease" stemming from a multiplicity of complex causal factors.

The solution to crime rests, in part, with adequately identifying the causal factors that motivated that person to commit a crime.

Oftentimes, lawmakers believe they have identified the correct casual factors only to find out that they have wasted their energies by focusing on something that is closely associated with the problem but is not the cause of the problem in the first place. For example in the fourteenth and seventeenth centuries, the Bubonic Plague, or Black Death, killed thousands of people in Europe and England. Initially, lawmakers were convinced that the disease was being spread by rats. The public policy decision was to kill the rats and destroy the homes and personal belongings of the dead. The Plague, however, remained. Lawmakers overlooked the cause of the disease. True, rats and their fleas spread the disease to humans, but the real culprit was the living style of the citizens. Residents threw trash out into the streets, and personal waste was pitched into open sewers. The rats and their fleas were thriving in the debris. The solution to curing the disease was to eliminate the cause by encouraging healthier personal habits and proper sanitation procedures. Through corrective legislation backed by sanctions, the personal and sanitation habits improved as the rats, their fleas, and the disease disappeared.

The same situation applies to New Orleans. As previously mentioned, Katrina was not the first and will not be the last hurricane to flood the city. Subjected to frequent damaging flooding, "each generation engineered defenses against high water, only to see them washed away. Then—whether because they wanted to defy nature, prove their ingenuity, or simply forget about the risks—they started over."[58] City leaders believed that it was the barriers that created the flooding because they were not high enough to prevent the surging water from flowing over the top. The solution was simply to add enough feet to the existing barriers in hopes of preventing the next flood. By the time Katrina roared into New Orleans, the city's "landscape was carved up like a jigsaw puzzle, embedded with concrete, steel, pipes, and electronics. Suburbs stretched for miles. Around this urban blotch sat hundreds of miles of earthen levees, concrete-and-steel floodwalls, gates, and locks—their highs carefully calculated to repel all but the highest floods. An intricate web of canals, pipelines, and pumps was built to expel any water that got in."[59] By merely building a wall to hold back the floodwaters, the experts either failed to see or opted to ignore the casual factors that placed this city and its residents in harms way. Despite the city's historic proximity to the coastline, placing it at near or below sea level, city leaders for decades encouraged suburban growth by enacting city building ordinances for residential and commercial construction that edged the people of New Orleans closer and closer to those levee walls. A maze of row-to-row houses with concrete streets connecting them only encourages flowing water to continue its journey. In hindsight, suburban growth should have been centered on higher ground away from the levees, leaving the areas near the levees as green belts capable of absorbing water and subsequently minimizing the damage. Before Katrina, experts had expressed the same concerns. "'It's not rocket science; its [the levee system] concrete and steel.' Environmental groups, meanwhile, lobbied for more than a decade to restore southeastern Louisiana's vanishing wetlands, which once provided New Orleans with a robust, natural hurricane buffer. They got nowhere."[60]

Another consideration is the distinct difference between a crisis situation and a problem. The policy responses are significantly different for both situations. A crisis situation demands an immediate short-term response from government. In the case of an advancing hurricane, prudent evacuation plans must be executed to remove people, their pets, and livestock from rising waters. Temporary housing, food, and clothing for the displaced, heavy equipment to clear roadways and re-store public utilities, clean drinking water, medical services, and so on are the prudent and neces-sary responses required to address the crisis. As evidenced in New Orleans, the city's evacuation plan failed miserably. In an attempt to avoid a similar disaster, Governor Rick Perry of Texas decided to order a full-scale evacuation of the Texas Gulf Coast to include Houston days before the anticipated landfall of Rita, estimated to be another "big one." Inland cities were notified to begin the process of receiving evacuees as Perry placed on readiness the necessary emergency response units and heavy equipment needed to move into the potential storm-damaged areas once the hur-ricane passed through. However, what Texas state officials overlooked were the "little things" nec-essary to evacuate one of the nation's largest cities. Fleeing residents jammed the roadways, creating a snail-paced traffic jam. Everything was in short supply from bottled water, food, and gasoline. Both motorists and gas stations along the route ran out of fuel. Stalled cars impeded the path to safety as tempers flared. As Governor Perry soon realized, no evacuation plan is perfect! Once the crisis passed, state lawmakers must now deal with the problem. In the case of the Gulf Coast region, it is how to effectively minimize the catastrophic lost of life and costly property damage caused by the hurricane season. This involves an in-depth analysis hopefully producing a long-term solution. When lawmakers treat problems as crises, the problems will never be adequately addressed or solved.

Lawmakers must also avoid the trap of allowing public opinion to turn a problem into a crisis. Public outcry is not necessarily a crisis situation. The senseless tragic bombing of a federal building in Oklahoma City, Oklahoma, was caused by two individuals marginally associated with a para-military anti-government group. Likewise, James Byrd, an African American, was dragged to his death by three men advocating the racial hatred espoused by the Klu Klux Klan. The existence of these anti-government and racial hatred groups is a problem, but not a crisis. Although the ideo-logical foundations of these groups are objectionable to the majority of the American people, the United States Constitution does guarantee the right of association. The document does not distin-guish between acceptable and unacceptable groups. This nation's lawmakers can not overreact by passing legislation forbidding association with racially objectionable groups. The rationale ap-proach is to hold individuals legally accountable when their actions, whether they be guided by their affiliation to a racial supremacy group, caused harm to individuals or their property.

Panic and fear set in immediately after the terrorist attacks at the World Trade Center and the Pentagon. The average American citizen turned to his/her lawmakers to prudently enact laws to protect them from future attacks. The quest for the Bush administration is to enact appropriate legislative responses to guard against future terrorist attacks **without** violating the rights and privi-leges guaranteed to all Americans by the United States Constitution's Bill of Rights. Regardless of the severity of the problem, lawmakers must be able to calm public fears and act rationally in addressing our country's problems.

Agenda Building

Once the causal factors have been identified, an agenda, or action plan, must be developed. The agenda is the embodiment of the philosophical and technical approaches to an identified policy issue. For example, Democrat and Republic lawmakers agree that the nation's health care system is in critical condition; Americans are paying too much of their hard earned income into tax programs; the minimum wage needs to be increased; and the national debt is too high. Each political party, however, has different philosophical approaches to these issues. Consequently, each party follows a different agenda.

An effective agenda should attack all the identified causal factors at the same time. Doctors have realized that bombarding one side of a cancerous tumor with heavy doses of radiation and chemotherapy will halt the growth of the tumor on just the treated side while the untreated side continues to grow. The same holds true for public policy. By treating and curing just one symptom, policy makers allow the other symptoms to grow stronger. The drug policies passed during the Reagan administration desired to end the importation of drugs into the country. Instead of focusing on all international drug sources, the agenda focused primarily on Columbia. Columbian drug trafficking was substantially slowed. However, the flow of drugs continued as other international drug operatives assumed the Columbian share of the market.

> "In the issue of death and injuries resulting from drunk driving, both our laws and our cultural beliefs place responsibility with the drunk driver. There are certainly alternative ways of viewing the problem: we could blame vehicle design (for materials and structure more likely to injure or kill in a crash); highway design (for curves likely to cause accidents); lack of ambulance service or nearby hospitals; lax enforcement of drunk-driving penalties by police; or even availability of alcoholic beverages . . . Even when there is a strong statistical and logical link between substance and a problem—such as between alcohol and car accidents, handguns and homicides, tobacco and cancer deaths, or cocaine and overdose deaths—there is still a range of places to locate control and impose sanctions . . . . In the case of alcohol, we have traditionally seen drinkers as the cause and limited sanctions to them, although sellers have more recently been made to bear the costs. In lung cancer deaths, we have blamed the smoker primarily, but to the extent that people have sought to place blame elsewhere, they have gone after cigarette manufacturers, not sellers or tobacco growers. With handgun homicides, we have limited blame to the user of guns, rather than imposing sanctions on either the seller or manufacturers."[61]

Regardless of the issue, the answer to solving the problem rests with identifying all of the factors that caused the problem in the first place and holding each factor equally accountable for its actions. Again, the good intentions of lawmakers fail to achieve anticipated results when they overlook that effective public policy must attack the entire problem from all sides.

Action plans must contain well defined goals and objectives to ensure that all of the involved parties have a clear understanding of the intent of the policy directive. A **goal** is the end result of an action. For example, the ultimate goal of the Medicare program is to ensure that elderly and permanently disabled citizens are provided with government-sponsored health care. **Objectives**, on the other hand, are the strategies used to obtain the desired goals. Clearly defined and precise goals and objectives are an essential ingredient to the successful implementation of a policy directive just as a set of blueprints is to a homebuilder. "Statutory objectives that are precise and clearly ranked in importance serve as an indispensable aid in program evaluation, as unambiguous directives to implementing officials, and as a resource available to supporters of those objectives both inside and outside the implementing agencies."[62]

Action plans must also include measurable and attainable goals and objectives. Far too often, lawmakers attempt to sell their ideas as wondrous miracle cures. How many times have voters heard their leaders pledge that their proposed policy or program will completely eradicate a problem, only to see the policy fall disastrously short of its objectives. For example, President Lyndon Johnson's War on Poverty program was designed to eliminate poverty. Johnson's pledge was a lofty, unreasonable, and unattainable goal. Lawmakers should be honest and realistic with their constituents. An anticrime package designed to achieve a 5 percent reduction in crime each year over a five-year period has a better chance of seeing this goal achieved and/or exceeded over a policy with the lofty goal of eliminating all crime within a five-year period.

Formulation of Policy

The formulation process involves more than just designing the programs and the policy responses needed to address agenda items. Lawmakers must first determine the policy approach, and the type of policy option, as well as whether the responsibility for the resulting programs should be assigned to the public or private sector.

Usually, lawmakers opt for one of four policy approaches: punitive, alleviative, preventive, and, the rarely used, curative. The selection of the policy approach will fluctuate depending upon the prevailing political philosophy of lawmakers, public opinion, the severity of the deprivation and/or damage, and the status of the nation's economy.

The **punitive approach** rests upon the premise that the problem arose from self-inflicted causal factors. For example, there is a belief that poverty is usually a self-inflicted result of an individual's failure to achieve economic viability. Guided by the concepts of Social Darwinism and the free market theory, the belief holds that poverty is "the product of moral or character deficiencies in the individual. If people were poor, it was their own fault" and, subsequently, their responsibility alone to rise above their economic deprivation.[63] The punitive approach recognizes their economic needs while, at the same time, punishing the poor for their misfortunes. For social service programs, the usual approach has been an attempt to distinguish the deserving from the undeserving poor. Means-tested programs require applicants to demonstrate that they are indeed deserving of the benefits of the government program.

The same approach has been used in a wide range of policy issues including environmental concerns. The majority of the environmental laws are designed to identify and punish violators. Few environmental laws award businesses, industries, and individuals for not polluting. The punitive approach is a reactionary response to an existing problem. The primary objective of the punitive approach is to *punish* violators, not *solve* problems.

The **alleviative approach** seeks to relieve the suffering caused by the policy problem without adequately addressing the problem itself. For example, the New Deal programs were designed as temporary measures to relieve the suffering of economic deprivation caused by the Great Depression. The Roosevelt administration believed that temporary federally funded social programs would stop the suffering while the economy recovered on its own. "The designers of the Social Security Act in 1935 assumed that needs-tested public assistance would wither away as younger workers

The most significant reform enacted in 1935 was the Social Security Act.

became fully covered by social insurance—an expectation that was shattered by changing demographics, steadily expanding welfare rolls, and more generous benefits during the postwar period."[64] Unable and, in most respects, unwilling to face the actual causes of poverty and eventually attempt to cure it, lawmakers opted for the easy way out. Relieving or alleviating the suffering of the effected parties is an excellent short-term policy alternative that should never be used as a long-term policy commitment. The same observation can be made for the majority of the social service programs enacted by the federal government. Building more prisons merely alleviates the suffering criminals inflict upon society. Providing the homeless with overnight temporary shelters and three square meals a day simply alleviates the suffering of hunger. Merely easing the pain does not cure the disease. In addition, the alleviative approach is extremely costly to taxpayers who demand that their dollars actually eliminate the policy problem.

The third option is the **preventive strategy**. This alternative adverts actually curing the problem by just preventing it from getting worse. The farm price subsidy programs were designed to prevent farmers and food processors from losing more money. The program was based on the assumption that by controlling the supply of the product, the price of the product would be stabilized. The Social Security program was designed to prevent retired workers from falling into poverty by creating a self-funded insurance program for workers. Medicare and medigap insurance programs were designed to prevent senior citizens from falling below the poverty level due to medical expenses. Social preventive policy schemes have successfully built a safety net from the ills of poverty for retired workers, the elderly, and disabled Americans while successfully avoiding the task of curing the potential income deprivations confronting these citizens. Again, the preventive strategy should be treated as a short-term response that realistically will not meet the long-term goal of eliminating the problem.

The most difficult and, subsequently, the least used policy option is the **curative approach**. The primary objective of this option is to eliminate or cure the problem. The bulk of today's problems can be solved eventually or, at least, dramatically reduced in scope and adverse impact. It is possible, for example, to eliminate some types of crime and to successfully protect the environment from future pollution. However, the ultimate success of the curative approach is dependent upon several factors. First, this approach can be used only after a deliberative assessment has been made that correctly identifies the factors that created the problem in the first place. Second, the curative approach mandates a long-term policy commitment. Crime cannot be solved in a five, ten, or even a twenty year period. Long-term solutions also need non-partisan support. This is exceptionally difficult to achieve in a democratic environment whereby periodic elections can unseat incumbent administrations. Reasonable goals are essential to the acceptance and ultimate success of any curative policy initiative.

Most lawmakers opt for a combination of the punitive, alleviative, and preventive approaches. For example, the Clean Water Act is designed to prevent future pollution to our nation's water supply by mandating quality standards while using the alleviative option to relieve the suffering and damage caused by previous incidences of water pollution. The punitive approach to the Clean Water Act includes a series of criminal and civil sanctions to be levied on those who participate in pollution activities. The curative approach, however, is seldom used.

Decision-makers must also select the type of policy required to meet anticipated goals and objectives. Domestic policy alternatives include distributive, redistributive, and regulatory options.

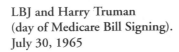

**LBJ and Harry Truman
(day of Medicare Bill Signing).
July 30, 1965**

Distributive policies are "governmental actions that convey tangible benefits to individuals, groups or corporations."[65] The most commonly used form of distributive policy is the subsidy. **Subsidies** are "simply government grants of cash and other commodities."[66] However, subsidies must be used correctly to achieve anticipated results. Initially, the gift of the subsidy is given with few strings or conditions attached. For example, the Department of Agriculture gives Farmer Brown a cash payment for not planting turnips. The recipient continues to receive the subsidy to the point that Farmer Brown becomes financially dependent upon receiving the yearly payment. Once dependency is established, government can now begin to add more stringent conditions to the gift. The coercive arm of government will now threaten to reduce and/or actually revoke the gift if Farmer Brown fails to meet the new conditions. The dependency factor usually results in compliance! Subsidies can range from agricultural payments to partial or full payments to low income individuals to offset rent expenses. The United States government uses a wide range of subsidies such as cash payments, military arms and equipment, and humanitarian aid in cementing its relationships with foreign countries.

On the other hand, a **redistributive policy** is "a conscious attempt by the government to manipulate the allocation of wealth, property, rights, or some other value among broad classes or groups in society."[67] Those policies are often called Robin Hood programs since the wealth of the affluent is given to the economically disadvantaged. The federal grant programs of the 1960s and 1970s were designed to reallocate federal tax revenues to the poorer states under the premise that the wealthier states could afford their own infrastructure programs. Consequently, economically strapped states, such as Arkansas, received large federal cash outlays to rebuild its highways, bridges, airports, and so on. The welfare system is another example of redistributive policy. The popularity of redistributive policies is directly tied to the economy. When the economy is in a healthy growth pattern, the wealthier states rarely balk about these initiatives. However, a depressed economy renders Robin Hood schemes exceptionally unpopular.

Finally, lawmakers may opt to use regulatory actions to address a domestic issue or problem. **Regulatory actions** are "governmental actions that extend government control over particular behavior of private individuals or businesses."[68] Initiated in 1887 with the creation of the Interstate Commerce Commission, the federal government has used regulatory actions to exert its influence into virtually every segment of the economy from banking to the environment. To insure regulatory compliance, each act is accompanied by a series of punishing civil, criminal, and monetary sanctions. As evidenced in our discussion of environmental issues, businesses, corporations, farmers, and ranchers, as well as property owners, have come to resent the federal mandates attached to federal regulatory legislation. Lawmakers should realize by now that regulatory policies laden with costly mandates followed by extremely punitive sanctions do not lead to effective public policy that is openly embraced by the regulated party.

In addressing foreign policy concerns, lawmakers generally mold their policy decisions into one of three policy options. The decision may involve a **crisis policy response**. This option is used when "the perception of a threat to national security cuts across normal channels of decisions."[69] Due to the sensitivity and the potential threat to national security, crisis issues are centered in the executive branch of the government. As evidenced by the Cuban Missile Crisis, President Kennedy involved only a few key members of his cabinet in formulating his response to the presence of Soviet missiles in Cuba.

Although the executive branch has more latitude in foreign policy concerns, both the legislative and executive branches are involved in the formulation of foreign policy issues. **Strategic defense policy** is "oriented toward foreign policy and international politics, and it involves the units and uses of military force, their strength, and their deployment."[70] The initial decision to send troops rests with the president. The continual deployment of those troops will involve congressional action, particularly when the time limits under the War Powers Act have expired. The formulation of the policy response involves more than just sending troops into hostile territories. For example, the deployment of troops into Bosnia was only one piece of a complex American foreign policy initiative aimed at ending the civil war in former Yugoslavia.

Congress assumes a larger role in foreign policy when the issue requires the use of a **structural defense policy**. This option is "oriented toward foreign policy and international politics, and it involves decisions about the procurement, allocation, and organization of men, money, and material that constitute the military forces."[71]

Lawmakers must consider which sector of the economy, namely, public or private, will be responsible for the implementation of the program. Traditionally, government services and policies have been the sole responsibility of government or the public sector. Each new major piece of legislation led to the creation of another federal agency and the hiring of more government employees. The outcry to cut the federal deficit, reduce spending, and balance the budget has led lawmakers to consider another option. The current move is towards privatization that reassigns some functional areas from the public or government sector to the private sector through contracting. Technically, **privatization** is "a general effort to relieve the disincentives toward efficiency in public organizations by subjecting them to the incentives of the private market."[72] Privatization has gained supporters who believe this scheme will save the government money in personnel and equipment costs, while at the same time, relieving government of the burdens of providing a service to the public. Enthusiastic proponents would like "to privatize the full gamut of public assets and services, including many forms of public provisions such as public schools, national parks, public-transport infrastructure, and prisons, whose origins and rationale fall comfortably within the gambit of the classical liberal state. In privatization they believe they have found a sovereign remedy against all ailments to the body politic, good for stimulating economic growth, improving the efficiency of services, slimming down the state, and expanding individual freedom, including the opportunities to disadvantaged minorities, too."[73] Despite lofty expectations, privatization should be used sparingly and with extreme discretion. The drawbacks of privatization include loss of control over that functional area. Government will bear the responsibility and the blame when things go wrong whether the problem is handled by the public or private sector. Second, government can not privatize all functions due to the sensitivity of the function. For example, local governments would be very foolish and irresponsible to contract to the private sector all of its law enforcement functions.

The actual formulation of public policy also involves all the key actors. Once an idea evolves into a proposed piece of legislation, all potentially effected parties are set for action. "As the formulation process moves toward the decision stage, some proposals will be rejected, others accepted, still others modified; differences will be narrowed; bargains will be struck, until ultimately, in some instances, the final policy decision will be only a formality. In other instances, the question will be in doubt until the votes are counted or the decision is announced."[74] The formulation phase is the most politically heightened step in the process of developing public policy.

Budgeting

The proper preparation of a budget is a crucial step in the development of public policy initiatives. A **budget** is a "technical document in the form of a detailed balance sheet that identifies expenditures and revenues for all government activities."[75] The budget is the embodiment of the national government's prevailing fiscal policies. Basically, **fiscal policy** is "public policy that concerns taxes, government spending, public debt, and management of government money."[76] The preparation of a budget entails the estimation of expected expenditures and calls upon the skillful talents of budget makers to find the funding sources needed to pay for these items. For example, state governments are using everything from lotteries, casino gambling, horse racing, state income taxes, and a full array of fines, fees, and special taxes to fund their activities. The budget is also a political document, indicating in dollar amounts to specified budget categories the prevailing political ideologies of lawmakers. "If politics is regarded as conflict over whose preferences are to prevail in the determination of policy, then the budget records the outcomes of this struggle."[77]

Agenda items must reflect budgetary reality. Attainable goals and objectives must be affordable. An improperly budgeted program is doomed for several reasons. First, lawmakers may grossly underestimate the cost of the program. Usually this happens on long-term projects. The cost projections for each year should be increased to adjust for increases in salaries, equipment, materials, maintenance, and customary expenses. "Financial resources are perhaps particularly problematic in labor-intensive service delivery programs and in regulatory programs with a high scientific or technological component, where implementing agencies often lack the funds to engage in the research and development necessary to examine critically the information presented by target groups and, in some cases, to develop alternative technologies."[78] A poorly funded program means that targeted service areas will shrink considerably, rendering the program a failure. Testifying at a congressional hearing, former FEMA director Michael Brown blamed service cuts in his agency's budget as a major contributing factor to FEMA's inability to properly respond to the Katrina disaster. "Brown presented a portrait of a federal disaster-response system that has been hampered in recent years by funding shortfalls and a demoralized staff. He said he'd privately warned administration officials well in advance of the hurricane that the agency was dangerously over stretched. . . . He said FEMA has lost 500 staff positions in recent years. And he said homeland security had diverted $30 million from money appropriate this year [2005] for FEMA and redirected it to other agencies."[79] Governors across the Gulf Coast expressed concerns as to whether or not the federal government had the funds to offset the costs for disaster relief and rebuilding. Charging that all of the attention has been focused on New Orleans because of Katrina, Governor of Texas Rick Perry openly "criticized the federal response to the storms, saying states slammed by Katrina are getting more generous help than his state, which bore the brunt of Hurricane Rita. . . . Total spending on the devastated region is heading toward the $100 billion mark, but considerably more will needed, said Govs. Bob Riley, R-Ala., Kathleen Blanco, D-La., Haley Barbour, R-Miss., in addition to Perry."[80] Second, lawmakers are extremely skeptical of appropriating large sums of money for an unproven project. The program must look good enough on paper and promise long lasting results to garner full budgetary treatment. Congress was already skeptical of the Army Corps of Engineers's plans to shore-up and expand the height of the New Orleans levee system even before the disaster struck. "Decreases in funding for hurricane protection began four years ago and have come fast and furious since then. This year [2005], representatives from Louisiana asked for $27.1 million for hurricane protection, saw the request slashed by the White House, but managed to nudge it back up to nearly $6 million. . . . Funding for the levee walls had been cut by 75 percent, compared with five years ago—despite the fact that the levees in some areas had sunk by a foot or more, through a process known as 'subsidence,' rendering them inadequate to protect the city's neighborhoods even from Category 3 storms."[81] Third, the voters can influence the budgeting process. Voters always want top quality services while at the same time demanding budgetary cuts.

A priority in the budgeting process is whether to **dedicate** or **earmark** funds to certain budgetary items. States more often than the national government use dedicated budgetary strategies to fund highways, public education, and so on. Dedicating does ensure that the money will be used for its intended purpose. However, once revenue is dedicated it cannot be transferred to another budget item or used to offset an unexpected crisis.

A sometimes ominous term associated with the budgeting process is porkbarreling. **Porkbarrel politics** is "the use of political influence by members of Congress to secure government funds and projects for their constituents."[82] A congressperson's job includes fighting for federal funds for projects and needs within his/her legislative district.

Taxation has become the traditional means for governments to acquire revenue. A **tax** is a "compulsory contribution for a public purpose rather than for the personnel benefit of an individual."[83] Tax dollars are returned to the citizens in the form of public services. Citizens constantly demand increases in services. However, the majority of Americans are weary of paying taxes and do not support too many politicians and lawmakers advocating tax increases. In developing a tax program, lawmakers must select a plan that will provide a reliable ample source of revenue with a minimal affect on the taxpayers' pocketbooks.

There are several key factors that lawmakers must consider in considering the type of tax they wish to levy on citizens. First, **elasticity** is "an economic criterion applied to a tax which refers to the tax's ability to generate increased revenue as economic growth or inflation increases."[84] A highly **elastic tax** will expand and/or contract proportionally with economic growth or stagnation. Elastic taxes are reliable and predictable sources of revenue. The income tax is the best example of an elastic tax. As a person's income increases, his/her tax burden increases.

A tax is tagged as **inelastic** when it does not generate increased revenues in proportion to economic growth. Sales taxes are inelastic taxes. The sales tax rate is fixed. It does not matter what the individual's income level is, the amount of tax is fixed on the item. An individual whose income is $100,000 will pay the same amount of tax on an item of clothing as an individual earning $10,000 who purchases the same item.

Lawmakers must take into account the potential **reliability** of the tax as a source of revenue. A tax that meets its anticipated level of revenue is a better program than a tax that is highly unpredictable in revenue returns. "Sales, property and income taxes are reliable because experts can predict with only a small margin of error future economic growth and activity upon which taxes are based. Severance taxes on energy production can be unreliable because the income they generate is affected by rapidly changing and unpredictable international political forces."[85]

Tax accuracy and reliability go hand in hand. Governments must have adequate revenue sources to accurately predict income generation. Revenue may be lost if the measurement tool to assess tax values is inadequate or antiquated. Accurate tax sources are essential to economic security. The Internal Revenue Service depends upon employers accurately submitting W-2 wage information to both the IRS and the employee. The "honor system" is an extremely unreliable revenue reporting source as some taxpayers purposefully would not report their current earnings.

How much money a tax will ultimately produce is called the **tax yield**. The cost of administering the tax program and eventually collecting the tax can effect the yield of the tax. "Taxes that return substantial sums of money at minimal costs are preferred to taxes that require large outlays for moderate revenues."[86] The easiest taxes to administer and collect are income and sales taxes. These taxes produce a higher yield over property taxes. Property taxes are costly to administer because property must be assessed for its tax value on a regular basis.

The **tax effort** is "a measure of whether, given a state's economic situation, it is taxing above or below its capacity to raise revenue."[87] In other words, states with strong track records of economic growth have the potential to raise ample revenues at average tax rates, if willing to do so.

The **visibility** of a tax is an important political consideration for lawmakers. Although very reliable revenue sources, income and property taxes are highly visible. The taypayer receives an income tax form and a property tax bill in the mail. To add salt to the wound, taxpayers are constantly reminded to pay those taxes on time or face costly late charges, fines, imprisonment, or loss of property. On the other hand, sales taxes are low visibility taxes since the majority of consumers do not keep records of sales tax expenditures. Politicians usually prefer low visibility tax programs.

The **application** of the tax program is another major consideration for budget makers. The primary categories for budget expenses are operating costs and capital expenditures. **Operating expenses** are yearly expenses needed to run government. These items would include salaries, benefits, equipment, rent, utilities, supplies, and so on. **Capital expenses** are multi-year or amortized expenses. A new mainframe computer system or a new building is an expense allocated over five, ten, or thirty year periods. It is essential that reliable revenue sources be used to fund operating expenses.

There are four types of taxes government may access on its citizens. A **progressive tax** is "one that increases the tax burden for upper-income people while reducing it for lower-income people."[88] Income, property, and corporate taxes are progressive tax programs. The national government relies heavily on income and corporate taxes; whereas, most state, county, and city governments rely on property taxes.

In contrast, a **regressive tax** "increases the tax burden for lower-income people while reducing it for upper-income people."[89] Sales, excise, and energy taxes are regressive taxes since they adversely affect incomes of middle and lower class individuals. The national government uses a wide variety of regressive tax programs such as taxes on cigarettes, alcohol, and so on.

Advocated by President Ronald Reagan, **proportional taxes** impose equal tax burdens regardless of one's income level. Reagan believed in a flat tax rate on income with no deductions. Subsequently, a 5 percent tax rate would produce the same tax burden regardless if one's income was $10,000 or $100,000 per year.

Finally, the tax system can follow a **benefit principle system**. "Under this principle, those who reap more benefits from government services should shoulder more of the tax burden than people who do not avail themselves of service opportunities to the same degree."[90] Municipal governments impose a wide range of user fees to offset the costs of maintaining their roads and public transportation systems.

Tax equity or the fairness of the tax is another major consideration for lawmakers. As long as the taypayer believes the tax is fairly applied and justifiable, he/she will pay the tax. However, this country separated itself from England in part over inequitable taxes imposed on the colonists. The principle of fairness in taxation cannot be overlooked by lawmakers seeking re-election.

The selection of the budget strategy is also vital to the planning process. There are several budgetary strategies available to budget makers. The **incremental process** has been the traditional budgetary approach. It is virtually an automatic process whereby federal agencies receive marginal budget increases or decreases with each new budget cycle. Federal agencies merely submit their budget requests with a built-in increase. Without much review, budget makers would normally accept the budget request. However, there are several potentially severe drawbacks to using the incremental system. "There is little attempt to evaluate program results or compare across different program areas in a given fiscal year. Such systematic evaluation would require a number of factors not readily available to most state (or federal) agencies: clear agreement on programmic objectives, reliable methods of measuring progress towards those objectives, and personnel skilled in methods of policy analysis."[91] Second, the incremental system encourages federal agencies also to inflate their budget requests and to spend all of their allocated money during the fiscal year. "Typically, administrators ask for more money than they actually need, believing that those appropriating the money will automatically cut budgetary requests. Also they tend to spend all funds that are allocated for a specific time, such as a fiscal year, because to return funds can lead to a reduction of funds during the next budgetary period."[92]

Experimental budgetary strategies include the **planning program budgeting (PPB)** concept with a cost benefit analysis feature. The focus is on programs, not line item allocations. "Agencies were obliged by PPB to define each activity's objectives and to indicate how the budget amounts related to the objectives, how to accomplish the objectives in alternative ways, and whether the objectives were being accomplished."[93] The cost benefit is a built-in feature.

Zero-based budgeting is similar to PPB. It is a program based strategy. However, each agency's budget has to be totally rewritten with each budgetary cycle starting from zero. Agencies submit their budgetary requests every year as if they were just beginning their operations. Zero-based budgeting has lost some of its appeal since it is a very complicated process for all parties involved.

Political Implications

Regardless of the policy issue, all lawmakers must consider the potential political implications of their actions. Each legislative action will provide benefits to one group and hardships to another. One of the fundamental keys is to hurt those who cannot politically hurt you. For example, Democrats and Republicans ran their 1994 and 1996 election campaigns on the need for welfare reform. By pointing out the failure of the program plus examples of fraud and abuse, politicians scored with the middle class voter at the expense of those lower income groups most likely to be welfare recipients. Why? Voter statistics indicate that the poor usually do not vote in large enough numbers to be an electoral threat. A well-crafted public policy initiative adversely hurts those groups who are too politically weak to hurt lawmakers.

All presidents have been keenly aware that their foreign policy decisions are often more visible and potentially harmful to their political careers. Few Americans are concerned about foreign aid packages or the shipment of grains to foreign countries. Once a president commits American forces to a foreign soil, the American public pays close attention. A failing war effort will ruin the re-election opportunities for an otherwise popular president. For example, Lyndon Johnson decided not to seek re-election based primarily on his administration's failure to bring the Vietnam War to a successful conclusion. He knew he would not win the election. Perhaps the election of 1980 would have had a different outcome if President Jimmy Carter's mission to rescue the hostages in the American embassy in Iran had been successful.

The political implications for a congressperson are long lasting since each vote becomes public record. The congressperson's opposition will not let the public forget those votes perhaps cast years ago that run against the grain of current public opinion. Interest groups and political action committees do review congressional voting records to ensure that both endorsed candidates and individuals requesting endorsement have been true to the bottom line issues of their groups. Far too often incumbent candidates must justify their actions for voting for or against controversial legislative items such as abortion, school prayer, gun control, and so on.

Adoption/selling

A policy must be sellable to the recipient and, if required, the group targeted to fund the program. Politicians must package their programs by emphasizing the good benefits and downplaying any potential negatives. Poor salesmanship can destroy a perfectly well designed program. For example, the failure of the Clinton administration to convince Americans that the administration's health-care reform package was the best option available was caused by poor marketing on the part of the White House. The president's staff did not adequately combat the concerns of opposition forces espousing the ills of national health-care programs nor did they successfully sell the positive points of the plan such as universal coverage, no pre-existing illness clause, and so on. Consequently, the opposition gained the upper hand and quickly defeated the plan. The lesson learned is that effective public policy must have the support of public opinion behind it. If not, it will fall short of its anticipated goals and objectives.

As previously stated, public opinion and support for public policy actions are a series of peaks and valleys. On the 2000 campaign trail, George W. Bush advocated sharing the nation's budgetary surplus with taxpayers by lowering income tax rates and providing a one time tax refund to every American taxpayer. The perceivably overtaxed American voter was elated that meaningful tax relief could become a reality. After the 2000 election, the Bush administration followed through on its promise. However, "after receiving 86 million tax rebate checks worth almost $40 billion in the past year [2001], Americans still have doubts about who gains."[94] Although the majority of American taxpayers believe that the current taxing structure needs an overhaul, the Bush tax rebate program did not garner overwhelming support for several reasons. First, candidate Bush made a lofty promise of a tax rebate without revealing how much would be refunded nor which taxpayers would qualify for the rebate. After the election, the Bush administration stated that all single taxpayers would receive $300 while married couples who filed a joint return would receive a $600 rebate. In actuality, the majority of the nation's taxpayers received less than what was promised. Many taxpayers received no rebate. Individuals who owed outstanding taxes were excluded as well as the poorest Americans whose incomes fell below taxable income scales. Therefore, the tax rebate and the proposed reduction in income tax rates for all Americans was perceived as just another tax break for the nation's wealthy. Second, the Bush administration was convinced that tax rebates would be used to buy new goods and services that would generate economic growth. Unfortunately, the maximum refund amount of $300 was not enough of a stimulus to prompt Americans to buy higher end consumer goods. The majority of individuals who received rebates used the money to pay outstanding debts. Third, the inability of the Bush administration to properly sell their tax rebate program soured many Americans against additional tax rebates and tax reductions. "In fact, four in five think cuts generally benefit someone else. . . The public also is decidedly more sympathetic to congressional candidates who place a higher priority on balancing the budget than they do on cutting taxes—with three-fourths preferring the budget-balancers and only a fourth supporting the tax-cutters."[95]   It is remarkable that a policy effort designed to give tax dollars back to taxpayers actually resulted in taxpayers wanting their tax dollars to be used to balance the budget! In reality, those tax rebates coupled with the Bush administration's commitment in Iraq are, in part, responsible for the nation's current budget deficit problems.

The selling process is an ongoing process extending throughout the life-cycle of the public policy initiative. Supporters of both foreign and domestic policy directives must not forget that "a statute, no matter how well it structures implementation, is not a sufficient condition for assuring target group compliance with its objectives. Assuring sufficient compliance to actually achieve those objectives normally takes at least three to five, and often ten to twenty, years. During this period, there are constant pressures for even supportive agency officials to lose their commitment, for supportive constituency groups and sovereigns to fail to maintain active political support, and for the entire process to be gradually undermined by changing socioeconomic forces."[96] Lawmakers must not overlook that targeted groups adversely affected by a policy directive will gain the upper hand in the battle for public opinion support if left unchecked. "There is a general tendency for organized constituency support for a wide variety of programs— including environmental and consumer protection, as well as efforts to aid the poor—to decline over time, while opposition from target groups to the costs imposed on them remains constant or actually increases. This shift in the balance of constituency support for such programs gradually becomes reflected in a shift in support among members of the legislature as a whole and the committees in the relevant subsystem(s).[97] Candidates espousing the negatives of an existing policy effort, once elected, will introduce measures to reform or dismantle that policy effort. Particularly in foreign policy, the waxing and waning of public support and subsequent congressional actions has resulted in the United States flip flopping in its relations with foreign countries. These governments are confused and, far too often, become suspicious of the everchanging policies of the United States government. Consistency in foreign policy is extremely difficult to achieve.

Implementation

Despite the well advertised policy flops, governments can and do successfully implement many of its public policy initiatives. Successful implementation ensures that policies will achieve their anticipated results well within their budgetary constraints. Paul Sabatier and David Mazmanian believe that policies can be successful if the following conditions are met:

1. The program is based on a sound theory relating changes in target group behavior to the achievement of the desired end-state (objectives).

2. The statute (or other basic policy decision) contains unambiguous policy directives and structures the implementation process so as to maximize the likelihood that target groups will perform as desired.

3. The leaders of the implementing agencies possess substantial managerial and political skill and are committed to statutory goals.

4. The program is actively supported by organized constituency groups and by a few key legislators (or the chief executive) throughout the implementation process, with the courts being neutral or supportive.

5. The relative priority of statutory objectives is not significantly undermined over time by the emergency of conflicting public policies or by changes in relevant socioeconomic conditions that undermine the statute's "technical" theory or political support.[98]

A successfully implemented policy directive is not achieved by accident or through sheer luck. It takes a staff committed to executing all the required steps according to the designated time table by using all the necessary tools including budget, personnel, and equipment. Lawmakers can certainly help the implementation process by first clearly delineating the levels of responsibility and, most importantly, the measurements of accountability to be followed by the agency designated to oversee the implementation of the policy directive. Bureaucrats can make or break a good policy simply by the manner in which they phase in the implementation process. "Any new program requires implementing officials who are not merely neutral but also sufficiently committed and persistent to develop new regulations and standard operating procedures and to enforce them in the face of resistance from target groups and from public officials reluctant to make mandated changes."[99] Far too often legislatively created programs have failed due to the lackluster and haphazard actions of bureaucratic agencies.

Second, successful programs correctly anticipate the demand for the service and adequately allocate resources to meet the demand. Resources include personnel, equipment, site location, and revenue. For example, opening a new facility to handle food distribution to a low income group with one clerk in a building located in a higher income neighborhood is missing the targeted service group. This is poor allocation of resources and a waste of money.

Third, long-term policy initiatives are multiple year phased in projects. Each phase must be implemented to produce anticipated goals and objectives. It can take as long as ten to twenty years before even a well-crafted policy can fulfill its goals and objectives. Unfortunately, "an overemphasis on pragmatism can produce a focus on immediate results rather than long term or enduring programs."[100] Impatience on the part of the average American citizen can ruin a perfectly designed long-term plan. The tendency is to implement one or two phases and use a half implemented program as the sole measurement of the success or failure of the entire program. Also, a change in administrations and party leadership could conceivably prevent a program from achieving full implementation. A newly elected Democrat president is unlikely to continue to carry out policies initiated by a Republican president and vice versa.

Evaluation

The final stage of the policy process is a complete and honest evaluation of the policy and resulting programs. Essentially, "governments cannot make rational policy choices unless they can evaluate whether programs attain their objectives. Without evaluation, they cannot know which programs are successful, which administrative practices work, and even which groups of employees are competent."[101]

Every program should be effectively evaluated to determine its successes or failures. "At a minimum, policy evaluation requires that we know what we want to accomplish with a given policy (policy objectives), how we are trying to do it (programs), and what, if anything, we have accomplished toward attainment of the objectives (impacts or outcomes, and the relation of the policy thereto). And, in measuring accomplishments, we need to determine not only that some change in real-life conditions has occurred, such as a reduction in the unemployment rate, but also that it was due to policy actions and not to other factors, such as private economic decisions."[102]

Unfortunately, it took the fury of a Category 5 hurricane to expose the vulnerability of government at all levels to provide the resources needed to bring a timely and appropriate assistance to the residents of New Orleans and the Gulf Coast area. Every level of government bears a share of the blame. One congressional report entitled "A Failure of Initiative," called the government response to Katrina a "litany of mistakes, misjudgments, lapses, and absurdities."[103] The report is critical of both Mayor Nagin and especially Governor Kathleen Blanco for "not issuing a mandatory evacuation order earlier. Once the order was issued, much of the evacuation proceeded smoothly, the report says, but evacuation plans fell short for the poor and the sick. The failure to completely evacuate those who couldn't do so themselves, said the report 'led to preventable deaths.'"[104] Whether it be a military branch or a bureaucratic agency, chain-of-command should not be violated. However, FEMA director Michael Brown did not have a solid working relationship with his immediate supervisor, Michael Cherthoff, Secretary of Homeland Security. "It was revealed in Senate hearings that Brown was calling the White House directly during the crisis—and ignoring Chertoff, his boss because Brown thought calling Chertoff would have 'wasted my time.'"[105] Lack of communication and coordination between the different levels of government further complicated rescue and relief efforts. For example two days after the storm hit New Orleans, "Federal Emergency Management Agency official Philip Parr and the Louisiana National Guard were prepared to evacuate the wretched men, women, and children huddling in the Superdome, using Chinook and Black Hawk helicopters. They had worked through the night finalizing the plan, but just hours before they were set to begin, they were told to stop. The Guard had learned that active-duty troops, under the command of Gen. Russel Honore, were planning to airlift the evacuees out of the dome. Louisiana Gov. Kathleen Babineaux Blanco had requested Honore's help; neither thought to tell FEMA about the plan. The result: the miserable people in the dome would have to wait an additional 24 hours between the evacuation began."[106] Meanwhile, a power struggle developed between the White House and the Governor's office over who was to take charge. Prudently, Blanco exercised her option to request federal assistance on August 29, the day the hurricane hit. President Bush did send approximately 7,000 active-duty military with the promise of more to come. Relationships between the two became testy to the point that on the evening of September 2, "Blanco received a fax from the White House asking that she sign a letter requesting a federal takeover. Bush Chief of Staff Andrew Card said the president planned a news conference to announce the changes the next morning."[107] However, Blanco refused to sign the order. A former governor himself, President Bush still pushed the issue that the federal government, not state governments, should be in charge of major catastrophes. Calling for a supportive rather than controlling role for the federal government, the National Governors Association reiterated that "governors are responsible for the safety and welfare of their citizens and are in the best position to coordinate all resources to prepare for, respond to and recover from disasters."[108] Hopefully the evaluation process will eventually lead to corrective measures that address the above mentioned problems.

CONCLUSION

The planning process is a series of eight steps beginning with problem identification and culminating with an in-depth evaluation process. As previously stated, each step is equally vital to the development of cost effective, administratively effective, and goal achievable public policy initiatives. It takes a well thought out action plan to create good public policy. As we examine public policy issues, we should remember how the planning process was applied in addressing these concerns.

CHAPTER NOTES

[1]John McQuaid and Mark Schleifstein, "A Disaster Long in the Making," *U.S. News & World Report*, September 4, 2006, 45.
[2]Roy Bragg, "Storm of the Century," *San Antonio Express-News*, (Sunday, September 11, 2005), 5N.
[3]Ibid., 4N.
[4]Dan Gilgoff, "Understanding Katrina," *U.S. News & World Report*, September 12, 2005, 27.
[5]Bragg, "Storm of the Century," 4N.
[6]Ibid.
[7]Ibid.
[8]Arian Campo-Flores, "Katrina's Latest Damage," *Newsweek*, March 13, 2006, 26.
[9]Ibid., 27.
[10]Bragg, "Storm of the Century," 4N.
[11]Gary Martin, "I Take Responsibility," *San Antonio Express-News*, (Wednesday, September 14, 2005), 1A.
[12]Evan Thomas, Jonathan Darman and Sarah Childress, "New Orleans Blues," *Newsweek*, September 4, 2006, 31.
[13]Lara Jakes Jordan, "Ex-FEMA Boss at Eye of Storm," *San Antonio Express-News*, (Wednesday, September 28, 2005), 1A.
[14]James E. Anderson, *Public Policymaking: An Introduction*, 5th ed., (Boston, Mass.: Houghton Mifflin Company, 2003), 1.
[15]Steven A. Peterson and Thomas H. Rassmussen, *State and Local Politics*, (New York: McGraw-Hill, Inc., 1994), 199.
[16]Anderson, 5th ed., 2.

[17]Theodore J. Lowi and Benjamin Ginsburg, *American Government: Freedom and Power*, 4th ed., (New York: W. W. Norton & Co., 1996), 607.

[18]Anderson, 5th ed., 5.

[19]Ibid., 95.

[20]David C. Saffell, *State and Local Government: Politics and Public Policies*, 4th ed., (New York: McGraw-Hill, Inc., 1990), 239.

[21]Anderson, 5th ed., 248.

[22]Ibid., 249.

[23]Ibid., 14.

[24]Gerry Riposa and Nelson Dometrius, "Studying Public Policy," *Texas Public Policy*, Gerry Riposa, ed., (Dubuque, Iowa: Kendall/Hunt Publishers, 1987), p. 11.

[25]Anderson, 5th ed., 130.

[26]Ibid., 132.

[27]Jeffrey M. Berry, "Citizen Groups and the Changing Nature of Interest Group Politics in America," *The Annals, The American Academy of Political and Social Science*, (Newbury Park, Calif.: Sage Publications, 1993), Vol. 528, July, 1993, 41.

[28]Thomas R. Rochon and Daniel A. Mazmanian, "Social Movements and the Policy Process," *The Annals*, The American Academy of Political and Social Science (Newbury Park, California: Sage Publications, 1993), Vol. 528, July, 1993, 76.

[29]Barry, 31.

[30]Ibid., 34.

[31]Ibid., 41.

[32]Riposa, 9.

[33]Anderson, 5th ed., 60.

[34]_____ "Analysts say budget battle in about rich v poor," *The Dallas Morning News*, (Sunday, January 7, 1996), 18A.

[35]Walter K. Olezek, *Congressional Procedures and the Policy Process*, 3rd ed., (Washington, D.C., The Congressional Quarterly, 1989), 25-26.

[36]*Treasury of Presidential Quotations*, Caroline Thomas Hornsberger, ed., (Chicago, Illinois: Follett Publishing Co., 1964), 263.

[37]Michael Barone, "The Politics of Negation," *U.S. News & World Report*, February 20, 2006, 40.

[38]Edward L. Harper, "Domestic Policy Making in the Nixon Administration: An Evolving Process," *Presidential Studies Quarterly*, (New York, New York: The Center for the Study of the Presidency, 1996), Vol. XXVI, No. 1, Winter, 1996, 41.

[39]Ibid.

[40]Ibid., 47.

[41]Barone, "The Politics of Negation," 40.

[42]James L. Garnett, "Administrative Communication (Or How To Make All the Rest Work): The Concept of Its Professional Centrality", *Public Administration: Concepts and Cases*, Richard Stillman, II, ed., 8th ed., (Boston: Mass.: Houghton Mifflin Company, 2005), 260.

[43]Anderson, 5th ed., 52-53.

[44]Hope Yen, "Ruling on Sentences Has Judges Scratching Their Heads", *San Antonio Express-News*, (Friday, January 28, 2005), 12A.

[45]Marco Robbins, "Jutices Rule Teen Killers Can't Be Put To Death," San Antonio Express-News, (Wednesday, March 2, 2005), 1A.

[46]Theodore J. Lowi and Benjamin Ginsburg, *American Government: Freedom and Power*, 3rd ed., (New York: W. W. Norton & Co., 1994), 620.

[47]Lowi, 611.

[48]Jack O. Plano and Roy Olton, *The International Relations Dictionary*, (New York, New York: Holt, Reinholt and Winston, Inc., 1969), 265.

[49]Ibid.

[50]Jay M. Shafritz, *The HarperCollins Dictionary of American Government and Politics*, (New York, New York: HarperCollins Publishers, Inc., 1992), 590.

[51]Peterson, 190-91.

[52]Paul Sabatier and Daniel Mazmanian, "The Conditions of Effective Implementation: A guide to Accomplishing Policy Objectives", *Public Administration: Concepts and Cases*, Richard Stillman, II., ed., 4th ed., (Princeton, New Jersey: Houghton Mifflin Company, 1988), 387.

[53]Anderson, 55-56.

[54]Ibid., 81.

[55]Richard Maidment, and Anthony McGrew, *The American Political Process*, (Beverly Hills, Calif.: Sage Publications, Inc., 1981), 135.

[56]James E. Anderson, *Public Policy Making*, (New York: Paeger Publishers,1975), 57.

[57]Deborah A. Stone, *Public Paradox and Political Reason*, (New York: HarperCollins College Publishers, 1988), 147.

[58]McQuaid, "A Disaster Long in the Making," 45.

[59]Ibid.

[60]Gilgoff, "Understanding Katrina," 28.

[61]Stone, 162-163.

[62]Sabatier and Mazmanian, 380.

[63]Randall W. Bland, Alfred B. Sullivan, Robert E. Biles, Charles P. Elliott, Jr., and Beryle E. Pettus, *Texas Government Today*, 5th ed., (Pacific Grove, Calif.: Brooks/Cole Publishing Co., 1992), 432.

[64]Sar A. Levitan, "How the Welfare System Promotes Economics Security," *Political Science Quarterly*, (New York: The Academy of Political Science), Vol. 100, No. 3, Fall, 1985, 453.

[65]Randall B. Ripley, and Grace A. Franklin, *Congress, the Bureaucracy and Public Policy*, (Homewood, Ill.: The Dorsey Press, 1976), 16.

[66]Theodore J. Lowi, and Benjamin Ginsburg, *American Government: Freedom and Power*, 4th ed., (New York: W. W. Norton & Co., 1996), 610.

[67]Ripley, 18.

[68]Ibid.

[69]Ibid., 19.

[70]Ibid.

[71]Ibid.

[72]Robert W. Bailey, "Uses and Misuses of Privatization," *Prospects for Privatization*, Steve H. Hanke, ed., (New York: The Academy of Political Science, 1987), Proceedings, Vol. 36, No. 3, 138.

[73]Paul Starr, "The Limits of Privatization," *Prospects for Privatization*, Steve H. Hanke, ed., (New York: The Academy of Political Science, 1987), Proceedings, Vol. 36, No. 3, 124.

[74]Anderson, 5th ed., 119.

[75]Bland, 329.

[76]Ibid, 332.

[77]Aaron Wildansky, "Budgeting as a Political Process," *Public Administration: Concepts and Cases*, Richard J. Stillman, II, ed., 4th ed., (Princeton, N.J.: Houghton Mifflin Company, 1988), 346.

[78]Sabatier and Mazmanian, 381.

[79]Jordan, "Ex-FEMA Boss at Eye of Storm," 15.

[80]Andrew Taylor, "Perry Rattles Congress' Cage, Demands More Rita Money," *San Antonio Express-News*, (Wednesday, March 8, 2006), 5A.

[81]Gilgoff, "Understanding Katrina," 28.

[82]Grier D. Stephenson, Jr., Robert J. Bresler, Robert J. Friedrich, and Joseph J. Karlesky, *American Government*, 2d ed., (New York: HarperCollins Publishers, 1992), G15.

[83]Eugene W. Jones, Joe E. Ericson, Lyle C. Brown, and Robert S. Trotter, Jr., *Practicing Texas Politics*, 8th ed., (New York: Houghton Mifflin Co., 1992), 433.

[84]Nelson C. Dometrius, "Government Revenues and Expenditure Policy," *Texas Public Policy*, (Dubuque, Iowa: Kendall/Hunt Publishing Co., 1987), 33.

[85]Ibid., 34.

[86]Ann O'M. Bowman, and Richard C. Kearney, *State and Local Government*, (Boston: Houghton Mifflin Co., 1990), 374.

[87]Susan B. Hansen, "The Politics of State Taxing and Spending," *Politics in the American States: A Comparative Analysis*, Virginia Gray, Herbert Jacob and Robert Albritton, eds., 5th ed., (New York: HarperCollins Publishers, Inc., 1990), 348.

[88]John J. Harrigan and David C. Nice, *Politics and Policy in States and Communities,* 8th ed., (New York, New York: Pearson Education, 2004), 306.

[89]Ibid.

[90]Bowman, 374.

[91]Hansen, 362.

[92]Leon W. Blevins, *Texas Government in National Perspective*, (New Jersey: Prentice-Hall, Inc., 1987), 317.

[93]Harrigan and Nice, 257.

[94]Will Lester, "Tax Rebates Haven't Sold 4 in 5 Americans on Cuts," *San Antonio Express-News* (Wednesday, April 3, 2002), 12A.

[95]Ibid.

[96]Sabatier and Mazmanian, 383.

[97]Ibid, 384.

[98]Ibid., 379.

[99]Ibid., 381.

[100]Nelson C. Dometrius, "The Texas Policy Environment," *Texas Public Policy*, Gerry Riposa, ed., (Dubuque, Iowa: Kendall/Hunt Publishers, 1987), 18.

[101]Harrigan and Nice, 254.

[102]Anderson, 1st ed., 134-135.

[103]Angie C. Marek, "A Post-Katrina Public Flaying," *U.S. News & World Report*, February 27, 2006, 62.

[104]Ibid.

[105]Ibid., 64.

[106]Ibid., 62.

[107]Spencer S. Hsu, Joby Warrick andRob Stein, "Louisiana Gov., White House Wrestled for Control," *San Antonio Express-News*, (Monday, December 5, 2005), 10A.

[108]Pam Easton, "Perry Wants Feds to Defer to States When Disaster Hits," *San Antonio Express-News*, (Tuesday, April 4, 1006), 5B.

SUGGESTED READINGS

Anderson, James E., *Public Policymaking: An Introduction*, 5th edition, Boston, Mass.: Houghton Mifflin Company, 2003.

Harrigan, John B. and David C. Nice, *Politics and Policy in States and Communities,* 8th edition, New York, New York: Pearson Education, 2004.

Mainment, Richard, and Anthony McGrew. *The American Political Process*, Beverly Hills, Calif.: Sage Publications, Inc., 1981.

Peterson, Steven A., and Thomas H. Rassmussen. *State and Local Politics*. New York: McGraw-Hill, Inc., 1994.

Saffell, David C. and Harry Basehart, *State and Local Government: Politics and Public Policies,* 8th edition, Boston, Mass.: McGraw-Hill Companies, 2005.

Stillman, Richard J. II., ed., *Public Administration: Concepts and Cases*, 8th edition, Boston, Mass.: Houghton Mifflin Company, 2005.

Stone, Deborah A. *Public Policy Making*. New York: Praeger Publishers, 1975.

Chapter Sixteen

SOCIAL SERVICES

The election of Ronald Reagan to the White House began the re-examination of an issue that stirs the consciousness of every American, namely poverty. It is ironic that a nation so blessed with natural resources, ingenuity, and wealth has millions of its citizens who are living below the poverty level, roaming the streets during the day with absolutely no place to call home, or living in fear that they are just one step away from falling into the dismal black hole of poverty. Politicians and elected officials from George Washington to George W. Bush have had to wrestle with this national problem. Despite the efforts of state legislative houses and Capitol Hill, the poor have yet to find the right road leading them to a better life and economic security. Where did we go wrong? Why does the American Dream of promised riches and success continue to elude millions of Americans? These tough questions have yet to be answered.

In the late 1980s, heavily overburdened state legislative houses began to question the ability of the welfare state created by Franklin Roosevelt's think tank to meet the needs of the impoverished, while at the same time pleasing taxpayers whose hard earned dollars funded the system. Politicians and lawmakers agreed that the welfare system needed major repair work simply because it was not working. The all too simple solution was to turn a blind eye to the millions of Americans in financial need by slashing billions of federal dollars from welfare programs that had been providing a safety net against the harshness of poverty since 1935. Yet, this option is not a viable solution. Governments merely washing their hands of welfare programs will not miraculously erase poverty or eliminate the suffering and deprivation. In 1996, a reluctant President Clinton signed a sweeping welfare reform law that significantly changed the welfare system created by President Franklin Roosevelt. Initially, it appeared that the reform package was fulfilling its expectations. The number of welfare recipients declined as a healthy economy produced more job opportunities for the nation's poor. Already in a noticeable slump, the nation's economy declined significantly after September 11, 2001, leading to massive layoffs and the outsourcing of jobs to foreign countries coupled with increased requests for unemployment compensation and, of course, welfare benefits. Prior to September 11, 5,692,000 or 4.0 percent of the civilian labor force was unemployed, a relatively low unemployment rate in comparison to previous double-digit years. By the end of 2004, 8,149,000 or 5.5 percent of the nation's civilian labor force was unemployed.[1] Every attempt to revamp the nation's welfare system has been based on the hopes that reform efforts would lower the poverty rate by providing the tools necessary to permanently remove individuals from their dependency upon the dole. However, this nation has been plagued with double-digit poverty rates for decades. For example, in 2003, 35,861,000 Americans representing 12.5 percent of the population lived below the poverty level.[2] The eligibility rate for many federal and state income support programs is set at 125 percent of the poverty level. Consequently, 48,687,000 Americans or 16.9 percent of the nation's 2003 population were eligible for a government sponsored service or income support program.[3]

While this nation's leaders are so critical of the failures of other countries to address their poverty-related issues, our lawmakers have failed for over two hundred years to adequately come to grips with the human side of this nation's poverty-related problems. The politics of poverty directly affects millions of faces from all races, ages, and genders that may well fare worse under the new programs and funding options crafted in congressional and executive committee rooms. It is this human face of poverty that this nation cannot morally or consciously ignore. We, as citizens, must also remember that poverty involves more than just statistics on a chart or a dollar figure on a budget line. For every number on a chart, bell-curve, or bar graph there is a face of a man, woman, or child who, with few exceptions, found themselves impoverished through no direct fault of their own.

The solution to poverty lies in an extremely complex and painfully difficult re-examination of the American social and economic consciousness. The framers of the Constitution recognized government's burdensome responsibility of meeting the needs of **all** of its citizens whether rich or poor by charging government with the task of providing for and promoting the general welfare. While liberals and conservatives continue to argue over the proper philosophical approaches to solving poverty and congressional Democrats and Republicans hurl insults at each other, the sad reality is that the number of poverty-stricken Americans continues to increase as the gap between rich and poor widens. In addition, millions of Americans are employed at minimum or below minimum wage jobs without the benefits of life insurance, pension plans, and health-care coverage for themselves or their family members. Rock bottom poor roam the streets, seeking shelter at night in crowded shelters or the parks and alleys of our nation's streets. As it tore apart the city of New Orleans and portions of the Gulf Coast, hurricane Katrina also exposed the depth of decades-old chronic poverty. "'I hope we realize that the people of New Orleans weren't just abandoned during the hurricane,' Sen. Barack Obama said . . . on the floor of the Senate. 'They were abandoned long-ago—to murder and mayhem in the streets, to substandard schools, to dilapidated housing, to inadequate health care, to a pervasive sense of hopelessness'"[4] Unfortunately, it took a Category 5 hurricane to remind us that America does indeed have a poverty problem. In reality, the United States is a rich nation for the privileged few and a poor one for millions. Poverty does not discriminate in its choice of victims, nor is anyone completely safe from its stranglehold.

This chapter examines the depth of poverty confronting this nation as well as the difficult tasks faced by lawmakers to address the underlying causal factors that lead to poverty and economic deprivation. Since the founding of this country, lawmakers have attempted to address only the **immediate** needs of the poor. The resulting legislative actions have only marginally alleviated the suffering of many, but not all of the poor, and have failed miserably to solve the problems of poverty. This chapter explores the policy actions pursued by all levels of government in their valiant but unsuccessful attempts to fulfill their obligations and challenges of promoting the general welfare. Of course, no discussion of the issue of poverty would be complete without exploring the current health-care crisis confronting not only the poor of this nation but all Americans.

THE VOCABULARY OF POVERTY

Poverty is "the state of condition of being poor by lacking the means of providing material needs or comforts."[5] One of the major problems confronting lawmakers is the actual determination of the number of people who are actually living in poverty. "The current formula was created by President Lyndon Johnson to keep score in his 'war on poverty' and has remained unchanged since 1965."[6] The number will fluctuate depending upon the measurement tool or factor used to determine economic deprivation. For years, policy makers have used a loose definition of the **poverty level** or threshold to determine actual numbers as well as benefit eligibility. "Based on the assumption that poor families spend one-third of their income on food, the United States Social Security Administration sets an official poverty line at three times the amount of income needed to eat according to a modest food plan."[7] This numerical figure is adjusted annually for inflation. Poverty levels are established for a wide range of variables. Table 16.1 details the poverty thresholds for an individual to nine or more family members from 1990 to 2003. In 2003, the poverty levels were $8,825 for an individual over the age of 65; $14,680 for a family of three; and $18,810 for a family of four. The highest range was $37,656 for a family of nine or more persons. Each year the income levels are only marginally increased, hardly reflecting the increased costs of food, shelter and clothing. For example, the change in the poverty level between 2000 and 2003 for a family of four was an increase of only $1,206.

Both liberals and conservatives believe that the current method of determining the poverty level needs to be changed to reflect a more realistic measurement tool of deprivation. "Conservative critics of the official definition point out that it [the poverty level] is based on cash income and does not count family assets or 'in-kind' (non-cash) benefits from government such as food stamps, medical care, and public housing. If poverty rate calculations include these factors, the 'net poverty' rate is lower than the official rate; fewer people are considered poor."[8] On the other hand, liberals contend that "taxes, work expenses, child care costs, and medical expenses paid by consumers from their own pocket should be deducted from cash income."[9] By using these factors, the number of individuals living below the poverty level would increase.

Poverty levels can also be determined in absolute and relative terms. **Absolute poverty** is defined as "the minimum subsistence income needed to survive deprivation."[10] This determination is based on the cost of a modest income outlay for food, shelter, and clothing. The federal government currently measures poverty in absolute terms, using food as the primary factor. However, this approach is inelastic with marginal adjustments made only for increases in inflation. **Relative**

poverty compares an individual's income to the nation's overall standard of living. This elastic approach takes into account the ups and downs of the nation's economic growth and prosperity. As the standard of living increases, the gap between rich and poor widens, producing an increase in the number of persons whose incomes fall below the poverty level. An adverse economic situation would shrink the gap between rich and poor, resulting in a reduction in the total number of people living below the poverty level.

There are several subcategories of impoverishment. The **working poor** are usually undereducated high school dropouts who are either employed full time or part-time at minimum or below minimum wage positions. Their salaries do not generate enough income to place them above the poverty level. Some of these are holding two or more part-time jobs at the same time. For the nation's working poor "every little setback is a crisis to them; unkindness or fear immobilizes them. Depression, low self-esteem and hopelessness all combine to make them exceptionally fragile. Supporting two kids on the minimum wage requires a lot of togetherness, not to mention sheer stamina. Fighting one's way through the welfare bureaucracy to get the help to which one is entitled is a challenge for someone with a college degree with a lot of self-confidence; try doing it after

Table 16.1

Weighted Average Poverty Thresholds by Size of Unit: 1990-2003[1]
(in dollars)

Size of Family Unit	1990	2000	2003
One Person (unrelated individual)	$6,652	$8,791	$9,393
Under 65 Years	6,800	8,959	9,573
65 Years and Over	6,268	8,259	8,825
Two Persons	8,509	11,235	12,015
Householder Under 65 Years	8,794	11,589	12,384
Householder 65 Years and Older	7,905	10,418	11,133
Three Persons	10,419	13,740	14,680
Four Persons	13,359	17,604	18,810
Five Persons	15,792	20,815	22,245
Six Persons	17,839	23,533	25,122
Seven Persons	20,241	26,750	28,544
Eight Persons	22,582	29,701	31,589
Nine Or More Persons	26,848	35,150	37,656

[1]Poverty levels for nonfarm families
Source: *Statistical Abstract of the United States: 2006*, 125th ed., (Washington, D.C.: United States Census Bureau, 2005), Table 695, page 453.

an eight-hour workday with no transportation, especially if your English isn't good and you are terrified of authority. (Offices open 9 to 5, with long waiting periods, endless forms and proof of income and assets required.) 'Catch-22' is not a trite phrase for poor Americans—it's a way of life."[11] An expense beyond the stretch of their paychecks is health care. Part-time workers do not receive health care and pension benefits beyond social security and worker's compensation unless they work over 37.5 hours per week at one job site. A full time minimum wage job will guarantee health care and life insurance benefits for the worker. However, the cost of dependent care is usually totally or partially the responsibility of the worker, often at cost prohibitive premiums.

In the 1990s, a new subcategory of the working poor emerged under the label of **hyperpoor**. These individuals have annual incomes that total less than half of the official poverty level. In 2002, approximately 8,169,000 men and 16,335,000 women earned less than $5,000 per year.[12] Many of the nation's mentally and physically handicapped Americans fall into this category. In addition, the hyperpoor include those individuals who are not technically homeless but who must rely upon family members and friends to augment their costs for food and housing. Oftentimes, undereducated and unskilled legal and illegal immigrants fall into this category. For example, in South Texas, individuals who lack the skills to hold regular jobs, gather early every morning at a designated site whereby small building, paving, and construction contractors and farmers can seek a crew of laborers for a day's work. These individuals, known as day laborers, are paid a small wage in cash after their employer drops them off at the pickup site after the day's tasks are completed.

The **nonworking poor** include those individuals receiving unemployment compensation, the unemployed without benefits, the homeless, the totally disabled/mentally ill, and the elderly whose incomes fall below the poverty level. An accurate accounting of the nonworking poor is difficult to determine. The unemployment rate, for example, is supposed to indicate the total number of jobless Americans. However, the unemployment rate is an unreliable measuring tool since it only accounts for the unemployed who are currently receiving some form of unemployment compensa-

Many of the homeless manage to eke out only a miserable existence.

tion. It cannot account for those individuals whose benefits have been depleted even though they are still unemployed or for those who did not qualify for unemployment compensation.

Technically, any individual lacking shelter is considered to be homeless. The National Alliance to End Homelessness estimates that 744,313 people experienced some form of homelessness in 2004.[13] The tally, however, would be higher if the counts included those who are unable to afford housing but are living "rent free" with family and friends.

The **feminization of poverty** recognizes the increase in the number of single-parent families headed by a female whose income falls below the poverty level. Since the 1960s, there has been a dramatic steady increase in the number of female-headed households. This rise in matriarchal families is attributed to the increase in the number of divorces, separations, out-of-wedlock pregnancies, and individual choices opting for non-traditional independent living styles. Usually these women are too undereducated and underskilled for the higher paying job market. Consequently, they are employed at the lowest ranking positions at minimum wage or slightly higher without immediate opportunity for promotion or advancement. Stereotypically, the feminization of poverty is seen as a minority out-of-wedlock teenager who drops out of high school, never to return again. This generalization overlooks that the ranks of poor women with dependent children that includes those who completed high school and married shortly afterward. After years of marriage, these women now find themselves divorced without marketable job skills beyond low paying service-sector positions, struggling to support their children on a paltry sum of child support from their ex-husbands. Basically, "the U.S. labor market has always failed women who have little formal education and sporadic job experiences. Low-income women are still segregated into low-paying occupations, despite the vast improvements for college-educated women."[14] As single parents, these women must oftentimes make the difficult decisions between meeting the needs of their children and their employment-related responsibilities. "Employers, especially those who employ low-wage workers, will not tolerate workers who come in late because a school bus did not show up, miss days because there was no child care or a kid was sick, or worry about their children at 3 p.m. instead of doing their work."[15] These women are also confronted with rising costs for day care, health care, and other living expenses. In 2003, the median family income of married-couple families with one income was $41,122 compared to $26,550 for female householders with no husband present.[16]

Another subcategory of poverty distinquishes the permanently or persistently poor from the marginally or temporarily poor. The determination is based on an individual's income level over a ten-year span. A person is considered **permanently** or **persistently** poor when his/her income has been below the poverty level for eight years or longer within the ten-year period. Individuals whose incomes are below the poverty level for less than two years within the same ten-year span, are **temporarily** or **marginally** poor. Of course, each group has a different set of needs to overcome their financial deprivations. The persistently poor require long-term housing, extensive job training and educational programs, food, and other financial assistance. The temporarily poor, however, need short-term assistance such as unemployment compensation, health-care benefits, and perhaps food stamps and shelter while seeking another job. However, most social programs crafted at both the national and state levels tend to be "one size fits all" plans that truly do not meet the unique needs of both groups.

A Profile of America's Poor

The concept of the American Dream is based on the belief that anyone in the United States can become a rich person if he/she gets an education, works hard and takes advantage of any and every opportunity to improve one's economic status. In reality, the rags to riches story happens to only a very few. The majority work hard and try their best to climb up that corporate ladder, only to see the American Dream happening to someone else. Basically over the past twenty-five years, "median family incomes have risen by less than 1 percent a year—for a total of 18 percent overall—but median incomes for the top 1 percent have gone up more than 10 times faster—by an astounding 200 percent."[17] The rich are getting richer and poor are getting poorer! Table 16.2 illustrates the changes in aggregate family income from 2000 to 2003. The figures clearly indicate that over the past three years, the percentage of aggregated income shared by lower- and middle-income earners has decreased while the upper income earners have seen their share of the pie increase. "Some 85 percent of the nation's wealth now resides in the hands of the richest 15 percent of American families. The bottom 50 percent of families, on the other hand, claim only 2.5 percent of house-hold net worth. . . The average net worth of the richest 10 percent of American families rose to $861,000 [in 2005], a 6.5 percent increase over 2001. What happened to the typical family in the bottom 25 percent? Net worth actually fell, by 1.5 percent."[18] How did this happen?

Basically, lower- and middle-class Americans continue to find themselves with less and less income for basic necessities such as rent, clothing, food, transportation, day care and health care. A major contributing factor is the disparity in wage treatment. The minimum wage has not been increased since 1997. A job at $5.15 per hour simply does not pay the bills nor leave disposal income for consumer goods and services. Those earning above minimum wage have seen their salaries increased by a mere 2 to 3 percent per year. For the majority of America's workforce, "wages have not kept pace with the cost of living, except at the top. In 1965, CEOs [chief executive officers] made 24 times as much as the average worker; by 2003, they earned 185 times as much."[19] The controversy over increasing the minimum wage was a key campaign issue in the November 2006 midterm elections. Leading the charge, Sen. Ted Kennedy (D-Massachusetts) has proposed increasing the minimum wage to $7.25 per hour. "If there is one message from this election that emerged loud and clear, it's that no one who works for a living should have to live in poverty,' Kennedy said."[20] Several states have already enacted a living wage standard for either their state employees or, in some cases, all of their employees that pays well above the standard minimum wage.

The gap between rich and poor is further widened by this nation's dependency upon state and federal income taxes and regressive tax programs that place a heavier tax burden upon middle and lower income groups. Sales, property, and excise taxes, as well as user fees, consume a greater chunk of the paychecks earned by the average American worker than those whose wages place them into the upper income brackets. One of the perpetual indictments leveled against the poor is that they do not pay their fair share in taxes that, in turn, help to fund the social services programs that they ultimately use. Statistics, however, dispel this myth. For example, in 2003, a family of four with an annual income of $25,000 paid an average of $1,816 or 7.3 percent of their income in state and local taxes. For families with annual incomes of $50,000, their yearly tax burden to state and local

Table 16.2

Share of Aggregate Income 2000-2003

Income Bracket	2000 Income	Percent of Total	2003 Income	Percent of Total
Lowest Fifth	$ 25,636	4.3%	$ 24,117	4.1%
Second Fifth	43,795	9.8%	42,057	9.6%
Third Fifth	65,563	15.5%	65,000	15.5%
Fourth Fifth	97,952	22.8%	98,200	23.2%
Fifth Fifth		47.4%		47.6%

Source: *Statistical Abstract of the United States: 2006*, 125th ed., (Washington, D.C.: United States Census Bureau, 2005), Table 680, page 464.

taxes was $4,172 or 8.4 percent of their total income.[21] Although the majority of the nation's states do not require that the lowest income individuals pay state income taxes, nineteen states continue to tax the income of the poorest of its residents. "Six of those states tax people who have so little money that even if they doubled their income, they still officially would be classified as poor . . . Kentucky imposes the heaviest income tax burden on poor families, followed closely by Alabama and Hawaii."[22] If tax burdens were taken into the computation of the poverty level, the number of impoverished and needy would increase substantially.

Poor and lower-middle income Americans are confronted with the task of finding affordable housing. The majority of the nation's poor are forced to live in rental properties, relying on government subsidized housing to offset the costs. In 2002, federal and state government allocated $35,566,000,000 in housing benefits to lower-income Americans. Approximately, 3.3 million Americans received monthly low-income housing assistance through the Section 8 programs funded by the federal government while another 1.2 million received monthly income support for low-rent public housing from both federal and state governments.[23] A recently released government study shows "that a record 5.4 million poor families spend more than half their income on housing.[24] Finding affordable livable housing is becoming extremely difficult as the price of residential properties continue to rise. For too many Americans, the dream of owning a new or even a pre-owned home is cost prohibitive.

The impoverished and homeless of this nation are further adversely affected by the stereotypical myths about poverty that far too often cloud the perceptions of lawmakers and the general public. The myth portrays the poor as shiftless, lazy, able-bodied men and women who simply refuse to fend for themselves, opting instead for a life of dependency upon the government's generosity. The homeless are seen as filthy unkept winos and bums who roam the streets panhandling for money to fund their addictive habits. The media has for the past fifty years helped to create the image of impoverishment. In the 1960s, the poor were portrayed as rural Anglos living in the mountainous isolated areas of Appalachia. Pictures documented the poor as living in one-room shacks without electricity or indoor plumbing. The stereotype changed in the 1980s as the poor were portrayed as primarily African Americans living in rundown urban areas called the ghettoes. Stereotypes help to shield Americans from the reality and complexity of poverty. The majority of Americans are actually in denial about homelessness, impoverishment, and poverty. **Denial** is defined as "the inability to recognize a problem in the face of compelling evidence."[25] The majority of Americans are in denial as to the historical depth of our nation's poverty problem. Far too often seen as a third-world country's problem, Americans simply can not continue to ignore the fact that this nation's poverty level is "the highest in the developed world and more than twice as high as in most other industrialized countries, which all strike a more generous social contract with their weakest citizens. Even if the real number is lower that 37 million [in the United States], that's a nation of poor people the size of Canada or Morocco living inside the United States."[26] Across the board, census statistics shatter the myths and reveal the problem and the reality that poverty strikes the very young and old of this nation in every hamlet from the East to West Coast and definitely cuts across all racial barriers.

The Census Bureau tracts the total number of persons by race whose incomes fall below the poverty level. Peaking at 15.1 percent in 1993, the poverty rate gradually declined as a healthy economy produced more job opportunities for the nation's lower-income persons. In 2003, approximately 35,861,000 persons had incomes falling below the poverty level. Historically, the percentage of poverty stricken Anglos (Whites) has been consistently lower than rates for Hispanics and Blacks (African-Americans). The total number, however, of Anglo (White) individuals living below the poverty level continues to be higher than the combined totals for Blacks (African-Americans) and Hispanics. In 2003, 24,272,000 Anglo (White) individuals representing 10.5 percent of all Anglos (Whites) earned wages below the poverty level compared to 8,781,000 or 24.4 percent of Blacks (African-Americans), 1,401,000 or 11.8 percent of Asian and Pacific Islanders, and 9,051,000 or 22.5 percent of Hispanics.[27] The same trend holds for poverty rates for families by race. In 1993, 12.3 percent, representing 8,393,000 families lived below the poverty level. After 1992, the nation's family poverty rates declined and continued to range between 11.6 to 9.2 percent. For example, 2003 census figures indicate that 7,607,000 or 10 percent of the nation's total families had incomes below the poverty level, a 2.3 percent decrease over 1993 figures.[28] Once again, the family poverty rates for Anglo (White) families is 9.4 percent, considerably lower than the Black (African-American) family poverty rate of 31.3 percent and 27.3 percent of Hispanic families, but numerically, 5,058,000 Anglo (White) families live in poverty in comparison to 1,986,000 Black (African-American) and 1,925,000 Hispanic families.[29]

The fate of our nation's children is directly tied to their parent's income status. The poverty rates for children under the age of eighteen over a twenty-three year period, indicates a high of 22.0 percent in 1993 followed by steady, but marginal declines. In 2003, 12,340,000, representing 17.2 percent of all children under the age of eighteen were living in poverty conditions. The percentages for both Black (African-American) and Hispanic children in poverty continues to be alarming. In 2003, 33.6 percent of Black (African-American) and 29.5 percent of Hispanic children lived below the poverty level.[30] Regardless of their racial orientation, all of these children are at risk for constant illnesses and poor diet. "Hungry children are more than four times as likely to suffer from frequent colds, ear infections, and headaches. Hungry children miss school because of sickness more often, and they go to the doctor almost twice as often."[31] Nutritionists have proven that hunger does have a direct affect on a child's ability to retain knowledge. These at-risk children are likely to become tomorrow's high school dropouts, saddled with the same dismal employment opportunities and substandard wage earnings that keep their parents mired in poverty.

Tragically, far too many children born in poverty do not live to reach adulthood. "Poor diet is closely related to low birth weight, which is a factor in the deaths of infants during their first twelve months. Twenty-three other developed nations have lower infant-mortality rates than the United States."[32] Recent figures indicate a slight decline in the nation's infant mortality rate. In 1950, 104,000 or 29.2 of every 1,000 babies under the age of one died. Medical advancements to include pre-natal care programs have greatly decreased infant mortality rates. Consequently, in 2003, 28,000 or 6.9 of every 1,000 babies under the age of one died.[33] Infant morality rates for minority children are still higher than those for Anglo children. The Centers for Disease Control report that "infant death rates are significantly higher for black [African American] babies, who were 21/2 times more likely to die than were Anglo babies."[34] Children raised in poverty as also more apt to become victims of criminal activities and gang-related deaths than children raised outside of poverty's grasp. In the ghettoes and low-income neighborhoods across this nation, "high crime rates are the norm, as are underground economies fueled by drugs, prostitution, and African-American markets in goods of all kinds. Most disturbing is the daily body count of young African-American men who are victims of drug wars, gang killings, and the hunger for material possessions so perverse that children kill each other over $100 sneakers and $20 drug debts."[35] The children born and reared in poverty have become the forgotten faces of the cruel reality of economic deprivation and social isolation found in the deteriorating neighborhoods of our nation's cities. "Residents of these wastelands become the victims of a nation unable to cope with what appeared to be ever-expanding misery, joblessness, poverty, crime, drugs, alcohol, and connect all of these with homelessness."[36]

The two primary keys to removing oneself from the shackles of endless poverty are education and economic viability. The two go hand and hand. Unfortunately, this nation is confronted with a consistently high number of teenagers who opt not to complete their high school educations. High dropout rates coupled with low test scores in reading, mathematics and English have resulted in state legislative houses assuming a more pro-active role in the administration of traditionally locally controlled public school districts. As the governor of Texas, George W. Bush demanded more accountability from the state's public schools. A cornerstone of his presidency, Bush pledged that the reforms he implemented in Texas were well suited for all of the nation's public schools. He vowed that his plan would indeed leave "no child left behind." However, standardized testing scores in mathematics, reading and English reveal that many children, particularly minority children, are being left further and further behind the learning curve. "Despite concerted efforts by educators, the test-score gaps are so large that, on average, African American and Hispanic students in high school can read and do arithmetic at the average level of Anglos in junior high school. The gaps between African Americans and whites are showing very few signs of closing."[37] Initially, it appeared that federal and state reform efforts were working. In 1995, 3,393,000 Americans between the ages of 14 and 24 dropped out of their high school programs. By 2003, 3,734,000 youths dropped out, resulting in a 1.5 percent decrease over 1995 figures.[38] Although experiencing a slight decline, the dropout rate for minorities continues to be alarming. In just 2003, approximately 84,000 Hispanics between the ages of 14 and 17, 627,000 between the ages of 18 and 21, and 726,000 between the ages of 22 and 24 had dropped out of high school. The combined dropout rate in 2003 for all Hispanic youths was 19.6 percent. Approximately 63,000 Black (African-American) youths between the ages of 14 and 17, and 276,000 between the ages of 18 and 21, and 269,000 between the ages of 22 and 24 dropped out of high school. The combined dropout rate for all Black (African-American) youths was 9.7 percent. Although the Anglo (White) dropout rate of 8.3 percent is lower than the dropout rates for Hispanics and Blacks (African-Americans), approximately, 2,875,000 Anglo (White) youths opted not to complete high school.[39] Ironically, it is the job market that is a leading fact to high school dropout rates. In 2004, 29,847,000 youths between 16 and 24 years of age were employed. Unfortunately, only 8,283,000 were still enrolled in public or private high schools.[40]

The trend for some begins with a part-time job so they can either help their financially strapped parents or save to purchase items for themselves. The part-time job soon begins to conflict with the grind of school responsibilities. Gradually, the teen opts to work more hours and sacrifice school-related time. The possibility of a full time job even at minimum wage can be attractive to a youth living in the vise grip of poverty. Many of these individuals will eventually return to school to get a GED certificate and possibly enroll in a community college. Another factor to consider is whether or not students who did graduate from high school are actually taking the next step by enrolling in college. In 2003, approximately 2,677,000 seniors received their high school diplomas or GED equivalency, but only 6.9 percent actually enrolled in a two- or four-year college or university within twelve months of completing their public school education.[41] However, the four-year degree completion rates for minority students continue to be alarmingly low. In 2003, 1,348,503 college students were awarded bachelors degrees. While 994,234 Anglos (Whites) walked the stage, only 124,241 Blacks (African-Americans) and 89,030 Hispanics received their four-year degrees.[42] Obviously, the level of one's education does have a direct bearing on life-long wage earning capabilities. In particular, "Hispanic educational progress will affect the nation's economic health. Over 25 years, the Anglo working age population is expected to decrease by about 5 million, but the number of working-age Hispanics is projected to rise by 18 million."[43]

Poverty also affects the nation's elderly. In 2003, 3,552,000 or 10.2 percent of the nation's total population over the age of sixty-five had incomes below the poverty level despite the fact that they were employed and/or receiving some form of government-sponsored assistance.[44] These figures would be substantially higher if senior citizens were not receiving Social Security and Medicare benefits. However, lawmakers are concerned that the present Social Security system will not be able to meet the income needs of an expanding senior population with potential life expectancies into their eighties and nineties.

A category of poverty that cannot be overlooked is this nation's homeless population. As previously stated, an accurate accounting of the homeless is virtually impossible. The United States Census Bureau attempted in the 1990 and the 2000 tally to include figures for the homeless. Usually, estimates include those who are living in the streets or in shelters. The numbers vary depending on how one defines the parameters of "homeless." Another factor is the nomadic lifestyle of the homeless. According to the Homelessness Research Institute of the National Alliance to End Homelessness, "in January 2005, an estimated 744,313 experienced homelessness:

- 56 percent of homeless people counted were living in shelters and transitional housing, and shockingly, 44 percent were unsheltered.
- 59 percent of homeless people counted were single adults and 41 percent were persons living in families.
- In total, 98,452 homeless families were counted.
- 23 percent of homeless people were reported as chronically home-less, which, according to HUD's [Housing and Urban Development] definition, means that they are homeless for long periods or repeatedly and have a disability.
- A number of states had high rates of homelessness, including Alaska, California, Colorado, Hawaii, Idaho, Nevada, Oregon, Rhode Island, and Washington State. In addition, Washington, DC had a high rate of homeless people."[45]

Among the ranks of the homeless are Vietnam veterans and the elderly. These individuals do not qualify for disability and Social Security benefits simply because they do not have an address! A post office box or community shelter is not considered to be a viable address. Although many of the homeless would qualify for food stamps, they simply cannot use them effectively. Without shelter, they cannot carry or store a large amount of perishable food items or can goods. Only a handful of restaurants and fast-food chains will accept food stamps. In 1996, Congress attached a work requirement for food stamp recipients. According to the law, "able-bodied adults without children are required to work for at least 20 hours a week to get food stamps for more than three months out of a three-year period."[46] The majority of the homeless are either too physically or mentally impaired to hold a job or lack employable skills. Even if they did qualify for food stamps, they are limited to purchasing food that is already prepared since most shelters do not have cooking areas for public use. These individuals are caught in a "Catch 22" situation with no viable solution in sight. The homeless also include families. The profile is basically the same.

The average American citizen is perplexed about the plight of the homeless. "On one hand, many people want to reach out and help these destitute and troubled men, women, and children; on the other, they are frustrated because, despite so many public and private efforts, nothing has eliminated or even decreased homelessness."[47] "For a brief period in the 80s, homelessness was the chic issue of the pretty people. It was worthy of galas and fund-raisers and cover stories. Now, as a cause, it has fallen on hard times, and the glamour crusades have moved to new fronts. But homelessness is a problem that is not going away. There are more homeless this year than last, and the number keeps growing. The new welfare overhaul our politicians are so proud of is sending more poor people into the streets . . . . There is now a growing threat. Some cities are in the midst of an effort to criminalize homelessness."[48] Once tolerant city councils are passing ordinances removing homeless persons from their makeshift housing in parks and under expressway underpasses; arresting panhandlers for loitering; and charging winos with public drunkenness. The city council in Asheville, North Carolina enacted an ordinance "barring aggressive panhandling with fines of up to $500 and up to 20 days in jail for people with at least five prior misdemeanors. . . . Orlando [Florida] barred people from sitting or lying on downtown sidewalks, with violators fined $500 and sent to jail for 60 days. Panhandling was restricted to 'blue boxes' drawn on downtown sidewalks."[49]

Statistics reveal that the poverty stricken are either very young or very old. The majority of the children living in poverty are being raised in single-parent female-headed households. We also know that poverty adversely affects more Anglo individuals and families than other racial groups, although a larger percentage of ethnic minorities live in impoverished conditions. Studies indicate that homelessness can strike anyone at any time, particularly those surviving from paycheck to paycheck. Nor can one overlook the possibility of being unemployed. The economic downturn beginning in 2001 changed the traditional stereotype of the unemployed from the blue-collar factory worker to the white-collar manager. The safety net programs of the traditional welfare system have kept millions from becoming mired in poverty. This is the real picture of poverty. The faces of those living in poverty are not just skid row bums, hobos, and winos. They are, in reality, a cross section of American society.

The Philosophy and Politics of Poverty

The latest round of welfare reform initiatives enjoyed widespread bipartisan support with the Democrat and Republican Parties making it a major campaign issue since the rise of Ronald Reagan in the 1980s. However, their zeal for reform revealed that both political parties were, and still are, sharply divided over the philosophical nature of the concept of welfare and welfare reform. In 1996, lawmakers argued over every aspect of the welfare system from methodical approaches to funding options. The resulting package of reform measures received mixed reviews as critics on both sides of the political spectrum level criticisms and complaints while vowing to enact corrective legislation to address identified program weaknesses. Against the backdrop of a sagging economy, Democrats continue their traditional cry to increase government funding for social service programs as President George W. Bush advocates the conservative Republican complaint that the current welfare law should be strengthened.

Republican Party leaders openly advocate the traditional conservative belief that economic deprivation is the inevitable result of an individual's failure and, in some cases, laziness to avail one's self of the free market's promise of economic viability and riches. They strongly believe that the American Dream of economic success is like the brass ring at the carnival. The ring can be grabbed by anyone who possesses the talent, determination, and desire to grab it. It's the individual who makes the choice between success and failure, not the economy or any other outside factor. Conservatives concede that the competitive nature of capitalism will naturally award the brass ring to only a select few because they possess a higher level of competitive skills over others. This competitive edge is often explained by Charles Darwin's concept of the survival of the fittest. Subsequently, "life's circumstances will always put some people into poverty, but the people with initiative will overcome their poverty."[50] Most conservatives, therefore, believe that government should play an extremely limited role in aiding the impoverished with benefits limited to the deserving poor, to the physically and mentally impaired, or to those of advanced age unable to compete and survive.

Extreme conservatives uphold that all welfare programs have failed miserably because the impoverished themselves are just too culturally and intellectually deficient to use government-sponsored programs and benefits to lift themselves out of their poverty. In *The Unheavenly City*, Edward C. Banfield argued that economic deprivation is an inwardly acquired trait that eventually evolves into a culture of poverty. Therefore:

> extreme present-orientedness, not lack of income or wealth, is the principal cause of poverty in the sense of the 'culture of poverty.' Most of those caught up in this culture are unable and unwilling to plan for the future, to sacrifice immediate gratifications in favor of future ones, or to accept the disciplines that are required in order to get and to spend. Their inabilities are probably culturally given in most cases.[51]

It followed, according to this line of reasoning, that the welfare state created by Franklin Roosevelt merely sustained the culture of poverty by making benefit recipients dependent upon the government for their survival.

The election of Ronald Reagan to the White House gave anti-welfare conservative Republicans the opportunity to lay the philosophical groundwork that produced the welfare reform legislation passed by the 104th Congress. A strong advocate of the competitiveness of the free market feature of capitalism, Reagan continuously blamed the welfare system for instilling dependency by robbing benefit recipients of their dignity and self-reliancy. "At the heart of President Reagan's opposition to federal welfare initiatives lies the suspicion that the poor are morally different from the nonpoor— that they do not share the values and aspirations of working Americans, that they do not respond to the incentives and opportunities of the market in the same way as the more prosperous do."[52] Republican-led legislative acts at state and national levels are designed to redirect the poor back to the conservative concept of the proper work ethic by tightening benefit eligibility requirements, limiting benefits, and requiring recipients to work, while at the same time slashing federal budgetary dollars traditionally allocated for social service programs.

The liberal perspective is that:

> those who are living in poverty have not individually created their poverty any more than those who are prosperous have individually produced their wealth. The fine line between success and failure represents one of the most sensitive and complex unsolved phenomena of the era of space, conglomerates and megalopolises. The future . . . of this nation may well rest upon the effectiveness with which the political and economic leadership recognizes and provides for the needs of the less fortunate.[53]

The Democratic Party became the standard bearer for the liberal perspective with the election of Woodrow Wilson to the presidency. Every Democratic president since has to some degree promoted government sponsored programs to meet the needs of impoverished and lower-income Americans with programs ranging from federally insured student loans to food stamps and Medicaid.

Liberals base their position on three major premises. First, they believe that the historical pattern of economic prosperity followed by devastating recessions, high inflation, and depressions have placed the American worker in constant economic peril. It's the fickleness of the economy and the inability of government to respond to economic upheavals that cause poverty and deprivation. Second, statistics support the liberal contention that far too many hard working Americans are losing economically as the rich become richer and the poor only become poorer. Liberals believe that government has the obligation to assist workers in reversing this trend. They stress that without the intervention of government, "the gap between rich and poor would tend to widen in an advanced economy, generating more unacceptable disparities and straining the fabric of an open, free, and democratic society."[54] Third, liberals believe that economic, social, and political equality for all Americans can be realized only through the efforts of the government. Consequently, the safety net created by President Franklin Roosevelt was designed "not only to seek to prevent extreme deprivation among the most disadvantaged, but also to attempt to cushion the impact of economic misfortune and uncertainty on the more advantaged and affluent members of society. The resulting 'safety net' has been remarkably successful in shielding diverse segments of the population from the full brunt of the vagaries and hardships implicit in a free market economy."[55] Affirmative action legislation helped to open the economic doors to disadvantaged Americans, particularly minorities and women. The Voting Rights Act passed during Lyndon Johnson's term in the White House extended voting privileges to the disenfranchised. The liberal perspective underscores inclusion and equal opportunities to the have nots in their struggles to become haves.

The welfare system and the never ending quest to reform it involves a wide range of interested parties. Of course, welfare recipients are extremely concerned that the elimination of benefits will just deepen rather than help them to overcome their suffering. After all, they are the ones in the "economic bubble" whereby any hint of an economic downslide could cost them their jobs. Requiring welfare recipients to work in order to keep their benefits only works if the jobs they are qualified for are available to them. However, the poor are, in most instances, the silent voices in the public policy process simply because they really do not participate. Few vote or even voice their concerns at public meetings or congressional hearings. The poor do not have the powerful advocates and lobbyists that other interest groups use to affect the public policy process. Yet, their survival may very well hinge on the actions of others who have very little first hand knowledge of the plight of the poor beyond statistical and budgetary reports. The poor were not consulted about the direction and scope of welfare reform.

The elderly have voiced their concerns about the future of Social Security, Medicare, and health-care reform. They want assurances from the national government that the Social Security system is financially sound for themselves and for future generations. Health-care reform has seniors worried as the federal government threatens to cut billions from Medicare programs. They fear that cuts in Medicare coverage will lead to inadequate health care. The lobbyists representing the **American Association of Retired Persons (AARP)** are constantly watching legislative actions at both the state and national level. Talks about health-care reform have disabled veterans worried that their federally funded health-care benefits will be severely cut or eliminated, thereby, leaving the majority of them without any form of health-care coverage. Women's organizations play an important role as they see welfare and health-care reform adversely affecting low-income women and children. They are fearful that any additional reform efforts will result in "a whole new world of hurt coming. A world where you scare people. You confuse them. You threaten to take their benefits and make them scared for their children. And its OK to do this because they are just lazy welfare moms anyway."[56] Far too often, lawmakers and politicians alike from both political parties have used demeaning rhetoric towards the recipients of public assistance programs, particularly women.

The providers of public welfare and health-care assistance are equally concerned whenever lawmakers threaten to reform the system. For example, extreme cuts in the food stamp program can adversely impact the nation's farmers and ranchers. It is their food products that are eventually sold in the nation's supermarkets to cash and food stamp carrying patrons. Any discussion of health-care reform is closely watched by the owners of the nation's drug companies and health-care providers. Cuts in Medicare and Medicaid are keenly watched by the **American Medical Association (AMA)**, the **American Hospital Association (AHA)**, and other health-care-based interest groups. State and federal cost containment efforts mean less money for health-care providers. Consequently, hospitals may face severe employee layoffs and budgetary constraints for new equipment, innovative procedures, and research. The victim of over zealous health-care reformers will be the patient. Health-care providers are worried that reform means a drastic and tragic loss of quality health care for their patients. The elderly, the impoverished, the children, the disabled veterans, the care providers, the farmers, and so on are the key players involved in the legislative battles over welfare and health-care reform. They have a vested interest either personally or professionally in any legislation involving public assistance and health-care interests. Often at odds with each other, the push for reform has the recipients and the providers of health care and social services on the same side as they desire to see that any reform measure adequately protects their interests.

The Historical Development of the Welfare State

Throughout the history of humankind, civilizations have always recognized their responsibility to address the needs of the deserving poor while at the same time holding an unpleasant distaste for those deemed to be undeserving of their charitable efforts.

> Most people in all cultures enjoy the feeling of helping others, and most cultures consider charity a community or religious duty or a measure of good character. But a distaste for freeloaders also characterizes many cultures. The violator may appear to not really need the help, or to use the help in a bad way, or to not work hard. The giver then feels taken in and may become hostile and resentful. But if the recipient is truly needy and unable to help himself or herself—a child, for example, or a handicapped person—the giver no longer feels exploited or concerned about freeloading. Those mixed feelings about giving and sharing have surrounded aid to the needy for centuries in most cultures.[57]

The distinction between the deserving and undeserving poor has pervaded every public policy initiative addressing this nation's poor since its founding. "The first American settlers understood the relationship between work, survival and dependence. The original colonists came from a broad cross section of English society that included many of England's wandering homeless, vagrants, bona fide criminals, lunatics, and misfits of all sorts."[58] Public sympathy was extended to the aged, the sick, the disabled, and the temporarily impoverished due to economic downturns and job loss.

It was a community responsibility to help those in true need. The able-bodied, however, received harsh treatment. "As Cotton Mather put it, 'For those who indulge in idleness, the express command of God unto us is, that we should let them starve.'"[59] The English poor laws served as a foundation for the colonial response to poverty and homelessness. Although programs varied from colony to colony, "there were four basic responses to poverty: auctioning off the poor ('selling' them to the lowest bidder, who agreed to care for and maintain them with public funds), contracting the poor (placing them in private homes at public expense), outdoor relief (basic assistance given outside the confines of a public institution), and the poorhouse (public institutions, also known as indoor relief)."[60]

After the Revolutionary War, the newly created states usually opted for outdoor relief assistance aimed primarily to assist long-term community residents confronted with a serious injury, illness, or death of the breadwinner. Pensions were established for war widows and orphans. Local tax dollars supported relief programs as the national government played practically no major role in social service programs. To offset costs, local authorities used several options including "'binding out' (indenturing the poor to families needing laborers or servants), 'farming out' (requiring men to work for wages that were in turn used for their support), and arrangements similar to modern foster care whereby indigents were placed in homes where they received care or where their children were apprenticed to craftsmen to learn trades."[61] Charges of fraud and abuse, as well as the growing belief that outdoor relief programs were undermining the fabric of American society, led to a new alternative—the poorhouse or **almshouse**.

The poorhouses took the poor, the mentally ill, and the criminal element off the streets. It was believed that "institutional life would not only protect the individual from corrupting influences but also allow the individual to reform."[62] Although popular in the 1820s and 1830s, poorhouses soon became just as distasteful as outdoor relief. Despite reform efforts, poorhouses were targeted by Progressive reformers for their deplorable conditions. Report after report revealed that "graft, corruption, and brutality were common; alcohol was smuggled in; inmates came and went; filth and disorder prevailed; criminals, alcoholics, women, mothers, children, and infants were mixed together. Mortality rates were high."[63] There were no state regulatory laws governing the operation of orphanages and poorhouses. There were, with few exceptions, no requirements for periodic onsight inspections. Poorhouses and orphanages received little monetary support from state treasuries. Dependent upon private donations, orphanages and poorhouses farmed out their residents as laborers for farmers, ranchers, and businessmen and as servants for private residences. Workers' earnings went directly to the orphanage or the poorhouse to help offset operational costs. The only viable options to the poorhouse were shelters provided through religious or private charity groups, outdoor relief, or an innovative form of the poorhouse called the **settlement house**.

Settlement houses were community centers located in the poor districts of major cities. These centers would provide guidance, services, and basic skills training to anyone living within the neighborhood. Settlement workers were usually recent college graduates from middle and upper class families who lived in the settlement houses. "The settlement house movement unabashedly promoted bourgeois values and habits—instructing the poor in everything from art appreciation and home economics to the importance of establishing savings accounts. To children in poverty, it offered recreation, books, clubs, as well as a sense of the history of American democratic institutions. It approached thousands of the urban poor, particularly children and teenagers, with a message of inclusion in the larger world beyond the slums."[64] Similar to those operating in London, the first American settlement house, known as the **Neighborhood Guild**, was opened by Dr. Stanton Coit in the Lower East Side of New York in 1886. By the turn of the century nearly a hundred settlement houses had been opened throughout the United States. The most notable centers were Jane Addams' **Hull House** in Chicago (1889), Robert A. Woods's South End House in Boston (1892), and Lillian Wald's Henry Street Settlement in New York (1893). Settlement houses were only marginally successful since their reliance upon private donations could not keep up with the cost of maintaining the houses much less meeting the demands of the ever increasing number of impoverished Americans.

The states were extremely ill-prepared for the economic deprivation caused by the crash of the Stock Market in 1929. Millions of hardworking Americans were suddenly unemployed. Their savings were gone since banks were not required to insure their deposits. The city streets were soon crowded with Depression Era homeless. Private charity-sponsored soup kitchens and breadlines could not feed all the hungry. As state coffers dwindled, governors began to turn toward the federal government for assistance and, most importantly, money. The United States Congress enacted the **New Deal** proposals of President Franklin Roosevelt, which included work programs under the **Civilian Conservation Corps**, the **Works Progress Administration**, the **Emergency Relief Administration**, and the **National Youth Corps**. These programs were jointly funded by the national and state governments with the bulk of the funding coming from Washington, D.C.

The current welfare system began in earnest when the United States Congress passed the **Social Security Act of 1935**. This landmark piece of legislation established two major insurance programs geared towards protecting the elderly and the unemployed from slipping into poverty. The **Old Age Insurance** program created a self-funded insurance plan providing pensions and benefits for the elderly and disabled; the **Unemployment Insurance** program assisted workers temporarily laid off their jobs. The Social Security Act also created several public assistance programs including **Old**

Jane Addams in Chicago
working at Hull House.

Age Assistance, Aid to the Blind, and **Aid to Dependent Children** (later changed to **Aid to Families with Dependent Children**). The bulk of the New Deal policies were designed as alleviative and preventive actions, that is, temporary public assistance to relieve the suffering while protecting millions more from falling into poverty. These temporary fixes almost became permanent fixtures.

The nation's next major assault on poverty occurred when President Lyndon Johnson introduced his **War on Poverty** program in the 1960s. In a speech delivered on May 22, 1964 at the University of Michigan, President Johnson not only declared war on poverty but introduced his concept of the **Great Society:**

> "The Great Society rests on abundance and liberty for all. It demands an end to poverty and racial injustice, to which we are totally committed to in our time. But that is just the beginning. The Great Society is a place where every child can find knowledge to enrich his mind and to enlarge his talents. It is a place where leisure is a welcome chance to build and reflect; not a feared cause of boredom and restlessness. It is a place where the city of man serves not only the needs of the body and the demands of commerce but the desire for beauty and the hunger for community. It is a place where man can renew contact with nature. It is a place which honors creation for its own sake and for what it adds to the understanding of the race. It is a place where men are more concerned with the quality of their goals than the quantity of their goods."[65]

FDR at the Grand Coulee Dam in Washington. October 2, 1937

Grand Coulee Dam on the Columbia River in Washington, which created a 150-mile long lake. Together with the Bonneville Dam (also on the Columbia), the Grand Coulee gave the Pacific Northwest the cheapest electricity in the nation and created the potential for significant economic and population growth. TheBonneville and Grand Coulee Dams made the state of Washington the largest per capita recipient of New Deal funds. The benefits of this dam building program, in terms of economic development and population growth, did not come to fruition until the post-World War II years.

The Johnson administration opted for a curative approach to solving poverty by retaining several of the alleviative and preventive plans created by New Deal initiatives and creating a wide variety of programs designed to address and, hopefully, eliminate poverty. The whole program was based on the belief that poverty could be eliminated by providing the poor with the essential tools needed to lift themselves out of their economic deprivation. An inadequate educational opportunity and the lack of proper job training programs were viewed as two of the primary reasons why many Americans were confronted with a lifetime of at or below minimum wage jobs with extremely limited opportunities for advancement.

The **Economic Opportunity Act of 1965** established the Office of Economic Opportunity designed to coordinate all federal initiatives with state and local governments. The War on Poverty was this nation's first major assault designed to eliminate poverty. The package of antipoverty measures also included programs to enhance the quality of life for the needy through such initiatives as the **Model Cities** program. Federal dollars were allocated for the construction of low-income housing units throughout the nation's economically depressed inner cities. Revitalization plans were encouraged as a means of revamping depressed central business districts in hopes of attracting higher paying job opportunities to inner cities.

The architects of the New Deal and the War on Poverty programs established the pattern for all subsequent social service initiatives. First, the federal government and state legislative houses realized that the complexity of poverty with its ever increasing numbers of impoverished Americans was beyond the limited abilities of the states to handle totally on their own. The horror story of states scrambling to meet immediate needs of the Depression Era unemployed could not be repeated again. Consequently, the federal government would create the policy response and target a specific service group for benefit coverage. While this provided nationally based responses to national issues and problems, the federal government's role deprived the states of their rights to create their own programs. Consequently, few state lawmakers have created innovative public assistance programs independent of the federal government.

Second, program funding was either totally or partially provided by the federal government. Leaving the states off-the-hook, the federal government allowed the states to become totally dependent upon federal funding to assist their state's impoverished. State legislatures could create budgets with the lowest allocations possible for social service programs knowing that the federal government would foot the bill.

Third, the states would continue to receive federal funding only if they complied with the minimal requirements set by the federal government. For example, each state was required to create a separate state agency to administer each federal program. The federal government assumed the majority of the responsibility for funding the program while leaving the administrative chores to the individual states. However, the creation of a multiplicity of state agencies merely complements the fragmentary and decentralized organization of state governments creating duplication of services, mounds of red tape, and little accountability on the part of state agencies.

Fourth, the federal government permitted the states to set their own eligibility requirements, benefit amounts, service delivery options, and punitive sanctions for abuse as long as the states followed the minimal eligibility and benefit standards set by the federal government. Consequently, the majority of state programs use the punitive public policy approach by just tightening the eligibility requirements every year to guarantee that only the truly deserving receive assistance. Each year, stiffer penalties are attached to each program to guard against fraud and abuse. Unfortunately, the zeal to attached punitive sanctions has cast a suspicious eye on anyone seeking government assistance. "Programs for the poor are stigmatized in numerous ways: surveillance of recipients for possible cheating throws suspicion on all recipients [and] surveillance of recipients for moral standards throws suspicion on all recipients."[66] Statistics reveal a discrepancy between those in economic need and those receiving government-sponsored assistance. Many needy Americans simply do not apply for assistance because of the stigmatized image associated with "welfare."

Finally, benefit allocations vary from state to state. States can opt to pay only the minimal benefit amount, which is usually totally funded by the federal government, or they can add-on their own allocation to the minimum. "In general, programs tend to be most generous in states with wealth, strong labor unions, high voter turnout by poor people, and liberal political beliefs or cultures. The generous states are found disproportionately in the Northeast, Midwest, and Pacific regions, and the least generous states tend to be in the South, Southwest, and Rocky Mountain regions."[67]

The Programs of the Welfare State Entitlements:
Social Security and Unemployment Compensation

Initially, both **Social Security** and **unemployment compensation** were marketed as temporary programs. Today, they are viewed by some as absolute guaranteed rights for American workers. Millions of retired American citizens believe that they "toiled for years to send Uncle Sam a mountain of dollar bills. These taxes went into individual accounts with their names and Social Security numbers emblazoned on them; now, seniors are simply withdrawing what is rightfully their own."[68] Yet, "Social Security has never been an insurance program, it has never been a contract that we make with ourselves to fund our own retirement, and our tax money is not set aside in a trust fund, as advertised. Nor are our benefits tied to how much we paid in taxes. Most people get back many times what they put in, even after interest is accounted for. To be precise, Social Security is an intergenerational transfer of money from workers to non-workers. Kind of like welfare. Exactly like welfare."[69] The United States Supreme Court settled the issue by its 1960 ruling in *Flemming v Nestor* that Social Security is not a guaranteed right. Justice John Harlan noted that Social Security was "designed to function into the indefinite future, and its specific provisions rests on predictions as to expected economic conditions, which must inevitably prove less than wholly accurate, and on judgments and preferences as to the proper allocation of the nation's resources which evolving economic and social conditions will of necessity in some cases modify."[70]

Social Security is funded through payroll taxes paid by employees and employers. Workers are eligible to receive benefits as early as age 55 if they are deemed unemployable due to permanent disabilities. The benefit amount is based on the individual worker's work history, including length of employment as well as salary history. Those retirees that worked the majority of their adult lives at higher paying jobs will receive a higher benefit amount over those who worked just as long but at lower paying jobs. In 2004, retired workers received an average monthly benefit of $955, retired workers with wives $1,585, disabled workers $894, and widows and widowers $920.[71] Usually

Social Security recipients receive a yearly cost of living adjustment ranging between 2 to 3 percent. However, the monthly benefits plus a marginal yearly adjustment simply leave little disposable income for expenses beyond the essentials of food, shelter and clothing. Therefore, the monthly benefits for the average retired worker are not enough to maintain a comfortable lifestyle. Many elderly receive just enough in benefits to put them into the **safety net**, just one perilous step away from poverty.

Initially, seniors were subjected to an earnings penalty that required the government to deduct $1 in Social Security benefits for every $3 dollars earned by seniors under the age of 70. It was estimated that "more than 800,000 lost part or all of their benefits because of the earnings limit."[72] Once the Social Security recipient turned 70, he or she could earn as much as they could without any reductions in benefits. In 2000, President Clinton signed legislation removing the earnings penalty. Now seniors regardless of their age, can continue to work full or part-time jobs without the fear of losing their full Social Security benefits.

If Social Security was a true pension program, retirees would receive benefits equal only to what they initially paid into the plan. Social Security, however, guarantees benefits for the life of the retired worker with survivor benefits for their female spouses of 50 percent of the original benefit. Consequently, there is a point where Social Security ceases to be a pension and becomes an entitlement or public assistance payment. **Entitlements** are "benefits provided by government to which recipients have a legally enforceable right."[73] Social Security, Medicare, veteran's benefits, and military retirement are entitlement programs.

The survival of Social Security has lawmakers searching for remedies to keep the program soluble and intact. Currently, the total amount of employee/employer contributions is sufficient to provide benefits for today's retirees. Yet, statistics do indicate an alarming increase in the number of retirees living longer with an offsetting decrease in wage earners. "The Social Security system faces rising gaps between revenues and promised benefits starting in 2017 and an exhaustion of trust fund assets in 2041."[74] Proposals to save Social Security include elimination of the mandatory retirement age, reducing annual cost-of-living adjustments (COLAs), reducing benefits for high-income beneficiaries, increasing the Social Security payroll tax, increasing the amount of earnings subject to the payroll tax, taxing Social Security like a private pension program, establishing individual accounts, allowing workers to invest a portion of their potential Social Security benefits, and, if all else fails, reducing or actually cutting benefits. Since its inception, politicians have been leery of advocating any substantial reform of the Social Security program. However, George W. Bush launched his 2004 campaign and began his second term of office with the determination to revamp the entire Social Security system. Underscoring that Social Security is in a crisis situation, Bush's reform package hinged on the belief that American workers should be able to invest a percentage of their Social Security earnings into private investment accounts.

Unemployment compensation was designed to be a temporary entitlement benefit for temporarily displaced workers. Mandated by the federal government, the states determine eligibility requirements, benefit allocations, and benefit time frames. Not every unemployed worker automatically receives unemployment benefits. In most states, individuals who have been involuntarily separated from their employment through no fault of their own will receive full benefits. However, in several states, voluntary separations and terminations by employee actions result in reduced payments or no benefits at all. Recipients are required to continue to search for work or lose their benefits. Generally, it is extremely difficult for unemployed recipients to make financial ends meet. This is particularly problematic for the higher-end of the salary scale employee who loses his/her job. In 2004, the average weekly unemployment benefit was $263. Massachusetts offers $351, the highest weekly unemployment benefit among the fifty states. The lowest benefit of $172 per week is offered by Mississippi.[75] The United States Congress can extend the benefit period during severe economic downturns. In 2002, the state of the sluggish economy moved Congress to enact a 13-week extension to the normal 26-week benefit allocation. The lack of economic growth, however, did not generate enough jobs to enable the unemployed to successfully find work. By December 2002, Congress was faced with the task of deciding whether to grant another extension. Congress, however, adjourned for the Christmas break without approving it. Subsequently, approximately 1 million jobless workers temporarily lost their benefits. Deemed as a "Scrooge," Congress quickly passed the extension once they returned from their holiday vacation.

Public Assistance Programs

The bulk of state and federal public assistance programs are means-tested plans providing in-kind services or cash transfer benefits. **Means-tested eligibility** is based upon the applicant's documented inability to provide for his/herself the desired benefit because of depressed income levels. Basic welfare and Supplemental Security Income (SSI) are two of the cash-transfer programs available to the needy. Each program is available to those who meet the qualifications. For example, the federally funded **Supplemental Security Income** program was designed to provide cash payments to lower income elderly, the blind, disabled adults, and children. To qualify, recipients must have incomes below 185 percent of the poverty level. **In-kind programs** are means-tested services providing "assistance that has a cash value even though it is not received in cash."[76] Subsidized public housing and day care, Medicare, special supplemental program for Women, Infants, and Children (WIC), food stamps, and legal services are examples of in-kind assistance programs.

The **Food Stamp Program** was developed in 1964 as part of President Johnson's War on Poverty package. The program is designed to provide an in-kind exchange of coupons for food items to offset nutritional deficiencies and hunger among America's needy. Administered by the Department of Agriculture through state and county public assistance agencies, the program is totally funded by the national government to include two-thirds of state and county administrative costs. The stamps are supposed to be used to buy staple products, not items that cannot be consumed such as paper products, household cleaners, and so on.

The Census Bureau defines **food secure** as "a household that had access at all times to enough food for an active healthy life for all household members, with no need for recourse to socially unacceptable food sources or extraordinary coping behaviors to meet their basic food needs. **Food insecure** households had limited or uncertain ability to acquire acceptable foods in socially acceptable ways. Food insecure households with hunger were those with one or more household members who were hungry at least sometime during the period due to inadequate resources for food."[77] Food stamps have become a household necessity for the nation's impoverished and low-income wage earners simply because their paychecks cannot be stretched far enough to cover rent, day care, utilities, and medical costs, plus the monthly grocery bill. Statistics indicate that "the average hungry household is only able to spend 68 cents per person per meal, which turns out to be nearly a third of their gross monthly income."[78] In 2004, 23,900,000 individuals received food stamps while 2,397,000 children participated in public/private school lunch programs. The Census Bureau also reported that in 2003, 12,583,000 representing 11.2 percent of the nation's households were food insecure.[79] This program, however, is criticized for being too costly and riddled with abuses and fraud. The coupon system does allow recipients to receive cash change when the grocery bill is less than the face value of the coupon. Some recipients have sold their stamps to someone else or have exchanged them for items not covered under the program. However, the majority of the recipients do not abuse the benefit nor do they participate in fraud. Across the nation, cities and community organizations have established food banks for those individuals who are hungry but either do not qualify for food stamps, are too embarrassed to apply for them, or do not have enough food stamps to last through the month.

The **Special Supplemental Program for Women, Infants and Children,** commonly known as **WIC,** was created to provide nutritional food staples to pregnant women, breastfeeding mothers, mothers up to six months after giving birth, and children under the age of five. In 2004, WIC provided food to 7,900,000 people each month at a yearly estimated cost of $3,561,000,000.[80] Funded by the federal government, this program is administered by the Food and Nutrition Service of the Department of Agriculture with assistance from state and county public agencies. Recipients receive vouchers for food items including milk, iron-fortified infant formula, cheese, eggs, fruit juice, cereals, peanut butter, and beans. The WIC program provides immunizations and prenatal care for free or at a nominal fee. The WIC program has been very successful in reducing health-care costs by treating infants with low birth weights.

The Reform Bandwagon

The political climate of the 1980s and 1990s compelled state legislative houses across this country to enact their own welfare reform initiatives. With few exceptions, state lawmakers took a punitive approach by placing time limits on benefits, requiring recipients to seek work, stiffening eligibility requirements, and placing stronger punitive measures to curb abuse. Although an advocate of welfare reform, President Clinton reluctantly signed into law the **Personal Responsibility and Work Opportunity Act** on July 31, 1996. His signature ushered in the long-awaited package of welfare reform initiatives destined to revamp the system established over 50 years ago. In some respects, this legislation merely duplicated several of the punitive measures already adopted by several states. The legislation's major provisions include:

A) Limiting lifetime welfare benefits to five years.
B) Requiring the head of household to find work within two years or the entire family will lose its benefits.
C) Mandating that at least half of all single parents in any state be employed or involved in work-related activities such as school or job training by the year 2002 or the noncomplying state will lose a part of its federal block grant money. However, the new federal law prevents

state governments from penalizing women on welfare who are unable to secure day care for their children under six years of age.

D) Limiting all childless adults between 18 and 50 years of age to three months of food stamps during a three-year period. Workers who have exhausted their three month supply of food stamps can apply for an additional three months if they are laid off their jobs during the three-year period.

E) Requiring unwed teenage mothers to live with their parents and attend school to receive benefits. Furthermore, the law does give the states the latitude to deny benefits to teenage mothers who do not meet the new requirements and to children born while the mother is receiving benefits.

F) Prohibiting food stamps and cash aid to anyone convicted of felony drug charges. However, pregnant women and adults in drug programs are exempt.

G) Denying food stamps and cash benefits to legal immigrants. Individual states, however, can provide Medicaid benefits for legal immigrants already living in the United States.

H) Prohibiting future legal immigrants from receiving Medicaid benefits during their first five years of residency in the United States.

The federal government did soften the punitiveness of the reform package by inserting provisions for exemptions; establishing funding requirements on the states designed to prevent states from eliminating all of their social service programs; and providing additional federal funds to offset potential economic crises such as recessions and periods of high unemployment. Each state is allowed hardship exemptions up to 20 percent of their current welfare cases. This provision ensures a continuation of benefits for the elderly and disabled citizens. The states are also prohibited from dramatically slashing their state budgetary allocations for social service programs. States must maintain their social service budgets at 80 percent of their 1994 levels or face severe reductions in their federal funding. The federal law does provide additional federal funding to states with high unemployment rates or fast-growing populations. The implementation process of this new legislation was designed to be gradually phased in to ease welfare dependent recipients off the system with a minimal amount of economic suffering.

Welfare Reform – Is It Working?

The success of any welfare reform package is tied directly to the nation's economic ups and downs. Initially, one could declare welfare reform a success. Statistically, more poverty-level Americans were removed from the public dole. More were finding employment. But, the question of whether the poor were truly benefiting from welfare reform still plagued lawmakers. Were the income gains of the poor meaningful enough to ensure that they were, as promised, never again to seek public assistance for their daily survival? Were the job opportunities viable ones that would eventually lead to salary increases and possible promotions? Was the economy strong enough in the long run to ensure that the poor were no longer the likely victims of economic downturns?

The initial setting for welfare reform could not have occurred at a better time. The United States economy was booming. The service sector generated an ample number of positions for those with marginal and limited job skills. The majority of service sector jobs, however, are basically minimum wage positions with very little opportunity for meaningful salary increases and, unless the worker receives additional job training and education, little or no hope for advancement. Earning six to eight dollars an hour at a full time job brings home only an annual income of $12,480 to $16,640 before payroll tax deductions. These salaries do not provide enough income to cover the costs for rising rents, day care, food, clothing, and, most importantly, health care.

Welfare reformers hoped that by requiring welfare recipients to work at least 30 hours per week, lower income workers would be able to afford reasonable day care. Recent studies, however, reveal that "a rising share of children, particularly black [African-American] children in cities are turning up in non-parent households, left with relatives, friends or foster families without their mothers or fathers."[81] Oftentimes, working mothers must rely upon family members to care for their preschool age children. Although not trained as professional day care providers, grandparents, aunts, fathers, and other relatives usually provide free babysitting services.

The warning signs of a failing welfare reform effort were evident before the economy began its decline following the events of September 11, 2001. In particular, the income levels of households headed by single women declined under the revamped welfare system. By 1999, "the poorest 20 percent of these families lost an average of $577 per year, with incomes falling to $8,047 annually. Typically, these are families that left welfare but had not made up lost benefits with wages. The situation was particularly bad for the poorest 10 percent, who lost an average of $814 per year."[82] A report issued in January 2001, revealed the dismal reality that "nationally, about 40 percent of former welfare recipients aren't working."[83]

Unfortunately, as low-income workers earn more, they become less eligible for benefits. State agencies across the country have seen a rise in the number of people seeking emergency food supplies from food banks. "More than half of the people seeking emergency food were members of families; two-thirds of the adults were employed. More than one-third of the homeless are families with children. That may be fueled partially by welfare-reform efforts in states, which have placed people in jobs generally paying less than $10,000 a year."[84] Food banks are having a difficult time keeping up with the demand. During times of prosperity, many Americans simply do not see the need to donate food and clothing to charitable agencies. A food bank spokesperson lamented that "rather than look at their stock market portfolios, it would be helpful if more Americans would look at their neighbor."[85] Also with the rising costs of housing, cities across the country are seeing more full time workers who are homeless.

Basically, this latest attempt to revamp the welfare system has failed once again to adequately address the needs of the nation's poor. Relying solely upon the take home pay of a low paying job simply does not provide enough income to adequately cover the costs of food, shelter, clothing, day care, and health insurance to this nation's lower-income citizens. If the original intent of welfare reform was to reduce the number of people on public assistance, one can say the program was initially a success. But, if the original intent of welfare reform was to provide the poverty-stricken with the tools to achieve the self-sufficiency required to obtain the income necessary to be above the poverty level over the long term, then the program has been a failure. As previously mentioned, any economic down turn can be devastating to this nation's poor. "What if, for poor families, this truly is as good as it gets?"[86]

Health-care Reform

As this country moves into the new millennium, lawmakers have yet to adequately address this nation's health-care crisis. Currently, the United States is the only highly industrialized nation in the world without a universal coverage national health-care plan. Instead, Americans rely upon a combination of private insurance and health-care providers and publicly funded programs for the nation's poor and elderly. Both public and private health-care plans are simply not working. The number of uninsured Americans continues to increase year after year. The majority of these individuals once enjoyed employer-paid health insurance plans. However, the sluggish economy of 2001 caused many businesses to layoff workers, slash benefit packages, and, eventually, file for bankruptcy. Based on 2003 figures, the United States Census Bureau estimated that 44,961,000 persons representing 15.6 percent of all Americans do not have health care benefits. Of the 44.9 million uninsured, 8,373,000 are children under the age of eighteen. California has the highest number of uninsured with 6,499,000, including 1,196,000 uninsured children. Texas ranks second with 5,374,000 uninsured persons to include 1,264,000 children under the age of eighteen.[87] The rapidly rising cost of insurance programs is just as alarming as the growing number of the nation's uninsured. "The cost of private health insurance is increasing at an annual rate in excess of 12 percent. Individuals are paying more out of pocket costs and receiving fewer benefits."[88] The majority of the nation's workers do receive some form of employer-paid health insurance. However, the cost of dependent care is oftentimes beyond the reach of the worker's paycheck.

The sad reality is that "being uninsured for even a year appears to diminish a person's general health."[89] The insured can afford yearly physicals to include mammograms, Pap smears, colon exams, diabetes and cholesterol screenings, and so on. "A lack of insurance translates annually into 360 to 600 premature breast cancer deaths, 1,200 to 1,400 deaths among HIV-infected adults and 1,400 premature deaths due to undertreated hypertension."[90] For those with health care coverage, the quality of the coverage far too often determines the course of treatment options. A recent study revealed that "women on Medicaid were 41 percent more likely to be diagnosed with breast cancer at the late stage and were 44 percent less likely to receive radiation."[91] Furthermore, a recent report prepared by the American Journal of Public Health points out that "more than 886,000 deaths could have been prevented from 1991 to 2000 if African Americans had received the same care as whites. The study estimates technological improvements in medicine—including better drugs, devices and procedures—averted only 176,633 deaths during the same period. That means 'five times as many lives can be saved by correcting the disparities (in care between whites and blacks) than in development new treatments."[92]

A report released by the World Health Organization ranks the United States as the top spender in per capita health-care costs at $3,724 but places the United States in 37th position in overall performance. The group rated France, Italy, San Marino, Andorra, Malta, Singapore, Spain, Oman, Austria and Japan as the top ten nations in providing quality health-care services to its citizens.[93] The organization justified their ranking by pointing out that "while good at expensive, heroic care, Americans are very poor at the low-cost preventive care that keeps Europeans healthy."[94] Containing the costs of health care has become a serious problem for health-care providers. "Within a decade, an aging America will spend one of every five dollars on health care. . . The nation's total health care bill by 2015: more than $4 trillion. Consumers will foot about half the bill, the government the rest. . . . Overall, the analysts forecast a 7.2 percent annual increase in health care costs over the coming decade. That's in line with the 7.4 percent increase in 2005. The overall economy is projected to grow at a rate of only 5.1 percent over the coming decade, which means health care will eat up even more of private and governmental budgets."[95] Clearly, the programs sponsored by federal and state governments are failing to provided adequate affordable care for our nation's seniors and lower-income Americans while the private sector is providing health benefits to those who can afford the soaring costs. Basically, what can lawmakers do to provide good affordable health-care coverage for all Americans? Is it possible to reverse the increasing numbers of the uninsured?

The two basic publicly funded programs are Medicaid and Medicare. A jointly funded federal and state program, **Medicaid,** was created in 1965 as part of the War on Poverty. Medicaid was designed to be a preventive health-care system whereby a child with a cold would receive the medication necessary to prevent that cold from developing into a potentially life-threatening illness mandating more costly health-care services. Medicaid is an in-kind program with the payment given directly to the provider of the service. Medicaid spending consists of direct payments issued for outpatient and inpatient care services, hospital care, nursing home services, and long-term care facilities. Since the patients receive no direct cash payments, charges of fraud, overpricing, and unnecessary medical treatments must be rightfully levied at the health-care provider.

Initially providing benefits to only those receiving AFDC or SSI benefits, Congress began to extend Medicaid coverage to other parties. In 1972, Congress provided benefits for nursing home and intermediate care facilities for the treatment of the mentally ill. Coverage for prenatal, obstetrics, and follow up medical care for one year for pregnant women was added in 1986. By 1988, states were required to extend Medicaid coverage for one year after families became ineligible for AFDC benefits to allow time for personal economic recoveries. Congress lowered the original eligibility requirements to include children up to age six. In 1990, Congress extended the coverage to include children up to age eighteen. Despite welfare reform efforts, 2003 census figures reveal a Medicaid enrollment of 35,394,000 Americans representing 12.3 percent of the nation's total population. Approximately, 15,103,000 of plan participants have incomes below the poverty level while the remaining 20,291,000 earn incomes slightly above the poverty level.[96]

In 2003, Medicaid costs were $87,000,000,000 for hospital care, $26,100,000,000 for physician and clinical services, and an additional $51,000,000,000 for nursing home care.[97] Congress responded to these rising costs by cutting both Medicaid appropriations to the states and severely questioning reimbursement requests from Medicaid health-care providers to include insurance companies, hospitals, and physicians. While the cost of services is increasing, the amount of money reimbursed to physicians accepting Medicaid patients has decreased. Consequently, health-care providers began not to provide health services to those individuals with just Medicaid insurance coverage. While the bulk of the costs is covered by the federal government, state governments must also shoulder a portion of the cash outlays. As governors attempt to balance their state budgets against declining revenue streams, they must deal with the reality that "Medicaid now is a larger component of total state spending than elementary and secondary education combined."[98]

Although Medicaid provides insurance coverage to the nation's impoverished, it does not cover children raised in families whose incomes are too high too qualify for Medicaid coverage but are still too low to afford the premiums for dependent care coverage. In 1997, the United States Congress enacted the **Children's Health Insurance Program (CHIP)** to provide free low-cost health insurance to the nation's uninsured children. The program is funded by the federal government but implemented by state governments. Despite allocating millions of dollars to state governments, CHIP got off to a shaky start because state agencies either dragged their feet or simply opted not to use the money. While many eligible children still remain without coverage, 6,058,900 were enrolled as of 2004. In total, the federal government paid $4,600,700,000 in plan reimbursable costs at the end of 2004. Still leading the nation in the total number of uninsured children, Texas is trying to close the gap. By the end of 2004, the state had enrolled 650,900 children, an increase of 519,800 over 2000 enrollment figures.[99]

Medicare was supposed to be the nation's health-care plan that extended coverage to all Americans. The ensuing battle between those conservatives against national health care and the liberal camp promoting it resulted in a program that provides coverage primarily to America's elderly. Liberals hoped that over time coverage would be expanded in an incremental fashion with children first, followed by pregnant women and other groups, until the goal of universal coverage was ultimately achieved. "All Medicare enthusiasts took for granted that the rhetoric of enactment should emphasize the expansion of access, not the regulation and overhaul of United States medicine. The clear aim was to reduce the risks of financial disaster for the elderly and their families, and the clear understanding was that Congress would demand a largely hands-off posture towards doctors and hospitals providing the care that Medicare would provide."[100] Without Medicare, the majority of senior citizens using Social Security as their sole source of income, would not be able to afford health care and prescription costs. However, the success of Medicare as the solution to seniors' health-care needs is questionable.

Coverage is automatically granted to all persons over 65 who have paid Social Security taxes during their working lives and to their spouses. Funded totally by the federal government, the Medicare plan is administered by the Social Security Administration. The program essentially provides two plans of health-care coverage. Part A, commonly known as HI, provides mandatory hospitalization coverage. Part B permits participants to purchase through beneficiary premiums and general tax revenues coverage for doctor's fees and other medical expenses including prescription drugs. In 2004, approximately 41,700,000 Americans comprised of 35,400,000 seniors and 6,300,000 disabled persons were enrolled in Medicare.[101] By the end of fiscal year 2004, Medicare benefits paid out an estimated $301,488,000,000 for a wide variety of hospital care facilities and physician services.[102]

In fulfillment of his 2000 campaign promise to fix the health-care system, George W. Bush convinced Congress in 2003 to pass **Medicare Prescription Drug, Improvement and Modernization Act**. Hailed as "the most sweeping change to Medicare since its founding in 1965," the primary purpose of the legislation was to bring the accelerating costs of prescription drugs under control.[103] A controversial piece of legislation, Republican leaders were able to gradually garner the support of the American Association of Retired Persons (AARP) into its camp. The organization's leadership felt that although the bill had major flaws, it was a baby step in the right direction to addressing the rising costs of medical care and prescription drugs. Many AARP members were outraged, resorting to canceling their memberships and tearing up their cards. Major provisions include the following:

A. Increasing the premium of the Part B Medicare Plan whereby individuals with incomes greater than $80,000 would pay a larger premium. The size of the premium increase would be on a sliding scale, topping out at 80 percent for people whose incomes are above $200,000.

B. Gradually raising the deductible to $110 by 2005.

C. Private firms will administer the dug benefit on a regional basis. The federal government would provide $12 billion in subsidies to private insurers that choose to offer basic health insurance. Preferred provider organizations would allow their patients to see any doctor.

D. Beginning in 2010, traditional Medicare will face competition from private plans in six metropolitan regions. The goal is to enroll 25 percent of Medicare participants into these plans. For those who remain in traditional Medicare, premium increases would be capped at 5 percent a year and waived for low-income seniors.

E. New benefits include coverage for initial doctor's appointments and screening for diabetes and cardiovascular disease.

F. Cutting payments for home health agencies.

G. Allowing people with high-deductible health insurance to shelter from taxes $1,000 a year for individuals and $2,000 for couples.[104]

The most controversial section of the legislation deals with prescription drugs. On paper, the new approach appears to be simple. The drug portion of Medicare is known as Plan D. "In addition to a monthly premium, seniors must pay for the first $250 in annual costs for covered drugs, the standard deductible. When the year's drug costs reach $251, consumers start paying out of pocket 25 percent of the cost and keep paying until their contributions hit $2,250. Then comes the infamous '**doughnut hole**' in which Part D enrollees are responsible for the entire cost of drugs between $2,251 and $5,100. Above that, catastrophic coverage must kick in, whereby seniors shell out just a small portion (5 percent of the cost or a co-pay of a few dollars) of their annual drug costs."[105] In other words, the entire process begins again on January 1st of each year. Seniors can opt to stay with their current Medicare managed-plan, their company retiree plan or opt for a private insurance carrier that offers a medical plan with prescription drug coverage. Basically, "the government is subsidizing dozens of private insurers to offer their own plans (many are offering more than one), which have to meet or exceed the federal government's drug benefit standard. The plans will either be stand-alone prescription drug plans (PDPs) to supplement Medicare's existing medical coverage (or a private plan with drug coverage) or will be part of a more comprehensive Medicare private health plan like a health maintenance or preferred provider organization."[106] However, purchasing a drug plan has proven to be a very confusing process. "With a choice of more than 70 cards around the country, signing up for the benefits takes some help. 'No one tells you what's going on,' complains the senior who suffers from diabetes and arthritis and takes several medications. 'Sure, we older folks need help with prescription costs, but not this way. What a mess!'"[107] Realizing the confusion, many major drug store chains hired insurance specialists to be at the drug counters to assist seniors in selecting a plan. Far too often, seniors are finding out that their annual drug costs have fallen into the doughnut hole when they go to the pharmacy to pick up a prescription thinking they only have to pay a co-pay but instead, are given a bill for the full amount. "They may be asked to pay $75 to $125 or more for a drug they have been receiving for a co-payment of $20 or $30."[108] Unable to pay the full amount, seniors are once again faced with the choice that this reform package was supposed to fix. The choice is counting the number of pills one can afford, regardless of the medical necessity of taking the full amount of pills for the prescribed period of time.

Still in its initial implementation stage, the future of the Medicare reform package is at best, on shaky ground. The critics are lining up in expressing their displeasure. For example, "the Alliance for Retired Americans, which represents some 3 million retired union workers, said Congress had 'failed older Americans' by passing legislation that would open the doors to Medicare privatization, enrich the pharmaceutical and insurance industries and prohibit Medicare from negotiating for lower drug prices."[109]

This leaves the elderly with two choices. First, they can purchase **medigap insurance** to supplement Medicare coverage. Supplemental insurance usually pays 80 percent or better of the costs not covered by Medicare once the policyholder's expenses exceed deductible amounts. Second, those unable to afford medigap insurance must just limit their health-care options to what they can afford with Medicare.

Obviously, the task is to find an affordable health-care plan that adequately addresses insurees' needs while controlling the costs of providing the services. There are several viable health-care options; however, all have serious drawbacks. Employers still offer group insurance packages that are totally or partially paid by the employer with low cost dependent coverage for immediate family members. However, group plan rates are determined by the dollar value of claims filed against the group plan. Accelerating claims prompted insurance carriers to place restrictions on coverage through pre-existing illness clauses, second opinion mandates, and higher premiums.

Managed-care plans appeared to be a palatable compromise between private-sector health plans and publicly administered universal coverage. **Health maintenance organizations (HMOs)** are prepaid health-care systems emphasizing preventive medical services that should avoid costly long term serious illnesses. There are several hybrids of the HMO. A **preferred provider organization (PPO)** permits plan members to choose from a preapproved list of doctors providing medical services at predetermined fees. Members can use out-of-plan physicians by paying higher co-payments. The **point of service (POS)** program charges members a higher premium and copayment for using non-HMO approved health services. An **independent practice association (IPA)** is a group of physicians affiliated to HMOs through contracts as providers of health-care services. The HMO reimburses the doctors through an annual fixed sum amount of a pre-visit fee for each plan member. HMO's seemed to be an attractive alternative to seniors, low-income Americans, and employers seeking more affordable health-care coverage. Plan participants would pay a nominal monthly fee for medical coverage. Patients would pay a $5 to $10 fee for each visit to the doctor. Prescription drugs would cost patients a nominal set fee for each trip to the pharmacy. In return, plan participants would be unable to select their own doctors, opting instead for the organization's primary-care doctor, a salaried employee of the health-care organization. "Usually an internist or family practitioner, this physician is a combination guide and gatekeeper, steering patients through the system—ordering tests, prescribing drugs, providing routine treatment, referring to specialists."[110] Costs were contained as long as the patient was treated solely by the primary-care physician.

However, costs began to soar as these doctors were ordering more expensive medical procedures, and referring more and more patients to specialists. The owners of managed-care facilities decided to operate these facilities as profit making enterprises. Therefore, costs had to be contained. The solution was for management to become the gatekeeper of the primary-care physician by exercising approval authority over every medical procedure and specialist referral. Doctors soon began to question the capability of an office manager to make life saving decisions that only should be made by a physician.

Initially, managed health-care providers were receiving ample reimbursement for services rendered to Medicare patients. Seniors, in particular, liked HMOs because they experienced little out-of-pocket expenses for prescriptions and physician visits. As a means of trimming federal outlays for Medicare, Congress opted to begin allocating funds for only those medical services and procedures deemed absolutely necessary. In addition, Medicare would only reimburse a portion of the costs. Managed health-care facilities retaliated by denying services to Medicare patients. Potentially millions of seniors have been dropped from their HMOs. "Without an HMO option, senior citizens must return to the traditional fee-for-service Medicare program, with its higher monthly premiums, no drug coverage and only 80 percent coverage for doctor and hospital costs."[111]

Despite the charges of abuse, overcharging, and fraud, medicaid is the only health insurance the "deserving poor" have and will probably ever have. Denying health care and emergency treatment to the disadvantaged is against every principle this country was founded upon. People should not be allowed to die simply because they can not afford medical care. Health-care reform must involve more considerations than just the budget! A step in the right direction was taken in 1996 with the passage of legislation allowing already covered workers to gain immediate health-care coverage after a change of job even if they have a pre-existing condition. Uninsured new employees must be covered within twelve months of hire. The measure also provided for tax-deductible medical savings accounts primarily for the self-employed and those employed by small companies unable to offer group plans. However, this legislation does not, nor was it intended to, reform the health-care system. Unlike welfare reform, corrective health-care initiatives are likely to follow a long-term incremental pattern that gradually retools the system.

CONCLUSION

Can the federal government and state legislative houses turn a blind eye to this nation's poor, old, disabled, and sick? The answer is a resounding no. Should government and society provide the incentives and avenues for the impoverished to be less dependent upon the dole and gain self-sufficiency and economic security? Yes, of course. For too long government at all levels has taken the path of providing assistance that just attempts to ease the suffering and prevent it from becoming worse. However, the suffering has not been eased enough. The fear of more becoming poor has not abated, nor has the costs of maintaining the welfare system decreased at all. We are still a frustrated nation! Morally, we cannot stand by and do nothing for starving, impoverished, elderly, and disabled citizens. Financially, we cannot afford to provide for all of their needs. The heart stretches out but the wallet cannot keep up with the pace. We do not yet have the definitive answer to cure the nation's ills that produce poverty and homelessness.

CHAPTER NOTES

[1]U.S. Census Bureau, *Statistical Abstract of the United States: 2006*, 125th ed., (Washington, D.C.: 2005), Table 610, 409.

[2]Ibid., Table 693, 472.

[3]Ibid.

[4]Jonathan Alter, "The Other America: An Enduring Shame," *Newsweek*, September 19, 2005, 42.

[5]*The American Heritage Dictionary of the English Language: New College Edition,* (Boston: Houghton Mifflin Co., 1982), 1027.

[6]Louis Uchitelle, "Census Bureau May Raise Poverty Level," *San Antonio Express-News* (Monday, October 18, 1999), 7A.

[7]John J. Harrigan and David C. Nice, *Politics and Policy in States and Communities,* 8th ed., (New York, New York: Pearson Education, Inc., 2004), 332.

[8]Randall Bland, Alfred B. Sullivan, Robert E. Biles, Charles P. Elloitt, Jr., and Beryl E. Pettus, *Texas Government Today*, 5th ed. (Pacific Grove, Calif.: Brooks/Cole Publishing Co., 1992), 431.

[9]"Committee to Recommend Broader Definition of Poverty," *The Dallas Morning News*, (Sunday, April 30, 1995), 4A.

[10]Harrigan, 332.

[11]Molly Ivins, "The Working Poor Have Names, Faces," *San Antonio Express-News* (Monday, January 3, 2000), 5B.

[12]*Statistical Abstract of the United States: 2006*, 125th ed., Table 685, 466.

[13]Mary Cunningham and Meghan Henry, "Homelessness Courts," The Homelessness Research Institute of the National Alliance to End Homelessness, January, 2007, 3.

[14]Randy Albelda, "Fallacies of Welfare-To-Work Policies," *The Annals*, The American Academy of Political and Social Science, Vol. 577, September, 2001, 66-78, 72.

[15]Ibid., 72-73.

[16]*Statistical Abstract of the United States: 2006*, 125th ed., Table 682, 465.

[17]Mortimer B. Zuckerman, "Rich Man, Poor Man," *U.S. News & World Report*, June 12, 2006, 72.

[18]Ibid.

[19]Alter, 45.

[20]Kevin Freeking, "Democrats Planning to Launch Major Bid to Boost Minimum Pay," *San Antonio Express-News*, (Friday, November 17, 2006), 8A.

[21]*Statistical Abstract of the United States: 2006*, 125th ed., Table 443, 301.

[22]David Clay Johnston, "Study Says 19 States Tax People Living Below the Poverty Level," *San Antonio Express-News* (Sunday, March 7, 1999) 22A.

[23]*Statistical Abstract of the United States: 2006*, 125th ed., Table 543, 362.

[24]Frank McCoy, "In An Age of Plenty, A Search for Shelter," *U.S. News & World Report,* April 10, 2000, 28.

[25]Baum, 3.

[26]Alter, 44.

[27]*Statistical Abstract of the United States: 2006*, 125th ed., Table 693, 472.

[28]Ibid., Table 698, 474.

[29]Ibid.

[30]Ibid., Table 694, 472.

[31]"Portrait of a Poor City: The Facts of Life," *San Antonio Light,* (Sunday, August 18, 1991), 6.

[32]Ibid.

[33]*Statistical Abstract of the United States: 2006*, 125th ed., Table 72, 64.

[34]Laura Mechler, "Life for Nation's Kids Is Better," *San Antonio Express-News* (Friday, July 12, 2002), 12A.

[35]Baum, 45.

[36]Ibid.

[37]Sam Dillion, "Studies See Little Progress for No Child Left Behind," *San Antonio Express-News*, (Monday, November 20, 2006), 4A.

[38]*Statistical Abstract of the United States: 2006*, 125th ed., Table 259, 173.

[39]Ibid.

[40]Ibid., Table 583, 391.

[41]Ibid., Table 263, 174

[42]Ibid., Table 287, 186.

[43]Deborah Kong, "College Dropout Rate for Hispanics Studied," *San Antonio Express-News* (Friday, September 26, 2002), 21A.

[44]*Statistical Abstract of the United States: 2006*, 125ᵗʰ ed., Table 696, 473.

[45]Cunningham and Henry, 3-4.

[46]Philip Brasher, "Advocates Allege Homeless Unfairly Denied Food Stamps," *San Antonio Express-News* (Wednesday, November 24, 1999) 7A.

[47]Ibid., 11.

[48]John Grisham, "Somewhere for Everyone," *Newsweek* (February 9, 1998), 14.

[49]Robert Tanner, "Cities Pushing Back At Pushy Panhandlers," *San Antonio Express-News* (Sunday, December 22, 2002), 22A.

[50]Harrigan, 337.

[51]Edward C. Banfield, *The Unheavenly City*, (Boston: Little, Brown, and Company, 1970), 125-126.

[52]Sar A. Levitan, "How the Welfare System Promotes Economic Security," *Political Science Quarterly*, (The Academy of Political and Social Science, Vol. 26, No. 3, Fall, 1985, 449.

[53]Edward J. Harpham, "Welfare Reform in Perspective," *Texas At the Crossroads: People, Politics and Policy*, Anthony Champagne and Edward J. Harpham, eds., (College Station, Texas: Texas A & M University Press, 1987), 283.

[54]Levitan, 453.

[55]Ibid., 447-448.

[56]Helen O'Neill, "Welfare Well Drying Up," *Houston Chronicle*, (Sunday, June 9, 1996), (4A-5A), 5A.

[57]Linda Gordon, "Who Deserves Help? Who Must Provide," *The Annals*, The American Academy of Political and Social Science, Vol. 577, September 2001, 12-24, 14.

[58]Baum, 92.

[59]Joel F. Handler, *The Poverty of Welfare Reform*, (New Haven, Conn.: Yale University Press, 1995), 12.

[60]Ibid.

[61]Baum, 92.

[62]Handler, 14.

[63]Ibid., 16.

[64]Howard Hysock, Fighting Poverty the Old-Fashioned Way," *The Wilson Quarterly*, Vol. XIV, No. 2, Spring, 1990, 78-9l, 80.

[65]"Lyndon Baines Johnson, President of the United States, 1963-1969: The Great Society," *Documents of Texas History*, Ernest Wallace, David M. Vigness and George B. Ward, eds. (Austin, TX: State House Press, 1994), 289-290.

[66]Gordon, 16

[67]Harrigan, 342.

[68]Susan Dentzer, "You're Not As Entitled as You Think," *U.S. News & World Report*, (March 20, 1995), 67.

[69]Joel Achenbach, "Why Poorer Classes Foot The Social Security Bill," *San Light* (Sunday, June 2, 1990) L1.

[70]Michael Barone, "Future Shock," *U.S. News & World Report*, June 13, 2005, 38.

[71]*Statistical Abstract of the United States: 2006*, 125ᵗʰ ed., Table 537, 364.

[72]"'Earnings Penalty' Removal Endorsed," *San Antonio Express-News* (Sunday, February 20, 2000) 13A.

[73]Jack C. Plano and Milton Greenburg, *The American Political Dictionary* (Orlando, Florida: Harcourt, Brace and Jananovich College Publishers, 1993), 489.

[74]Barone, 38.

[75]*Statistical Abstract of the United States: 2006*, 125ᵗʰ ed., Table 549, 370.

[76]Harrigan, 347.

[77]*Statistical Abstract of the United States: 2006*, 125ᵗʰ ed., Table 199.

[78]Colin Greer, "Something Is Robbing Our Children of Their Future," *Parade Magazine, San Antonio Express-News*, (Sunday, March 5, 1995), 6.

[79]*Statistical Abstract of the United States: 2006*, 125ᵗʰ ed., Tables 560 and 199, 375 and 134.

[80]Ibid., Table 560, 375.

[81]Nina Bernstein, "More Kids Living Without Parents," *San Antonio Express-News* (Monday, July 27, 2002), 8A.

[82]Laura Meckler, "Report: Poor Hurt By Welfare Reform," *San Antonio Express-News*, (Sunday, August 22, 1999) 6A.

[83]Ellen Goodman, "Success of Welfare Reform Hides Poverty," *San Antonio Express-News* (Friday, January 5, 2001) 5B.

[84]Richard Wolf, "Survey Pegs Part of Crisis on Wages," *San Antonio Express-News* (Thursday, December 16, 1999) 17A.

[85]Ibid.

[86]Goodman, 5B..

[87]*Statistical Abstract of the United States: 2006*, 125ᵗʰ ed., Table 143, 109.

[88]Robert Pear, "Panel Says Health Care Is In Critical Condition," *San Antonio Express-News* (November 20, 2002), 6A.

[89]Ceci Connolly, "Lack of Insurance Is Unhealthy," *San Antonio Express-News* (Wednesday, May 18, 2002), 18A.

[90]Ibid.

[91]"Breast Cancer More Deadly for Poor," *San Antonio Express-News* (Wednesday, April 3, 2002), 13A

[92]January W. Payne, "Study Says Unequal Care Kills Thousands," *San Antonio Express-News*, (Tuesday, December 28, 2004), 2A.

[93]Lauren Neergaard, "U.S. Ranked 37th On Health Care," *San Antonio Express-News* (June 21, 2000) 4A.

[94]Ibid.

[95]"No Cure Seen For Rising Medical Bills," *San Antonio Express-News*, (Wednesday, February 22, 2006), 2A.

[96]*Statistical Abstract of the United States: 2006*, 125th ed., Table 135, 106.

[97]Ibid., Table 125, 101.

[98]Paul Belluck, "Governors Fighting Medicaid Limits," *San Antonio Express-News*, (Sunday, December 26, 2004), 6A.

[99]*Statistical Abstract of the United States: 2006*, 125th ed., Table 138, 107.

[100]Ted Marmar and Julie Beglin, "Medicare and How It Grew...Grew...and Grew... and Grew...," *The Dallas Morning News*, (Sunday, June 25, 1995), 12J.

[101]*Statistical Abstract of the United States: 2006*, 125th ed., Table 132, 105.

[102]Ibid., Table 133, 105.

[103]Travis E. Poling and Gary Martin, "Medicare Rewrite Is not A Cure-All," *San Antonio Express-News*, (Friday, December 26, 2003), 1A.

[104]Ibid., 14A.

[105]Katherine Hobson, "How The Plan Works," *U.S. News & World Report*, November 7, 2005, 74.

[106]Ibid., 72.

[107]Rose Mary Burge, "Medicare Drug Plan Causing Headaches," *San Antonio Express-News*, (Saturday, May 29, 2004), 1A.

[108]Robert Pear, "Medicare Drug Plan's 'Doughnut Hole' A Shock for Some," *San Antonio Express-News*, (Sunday, July 30, 2006), 3A.

[109]Vicki Kemper, "New Era Dawns for Medicare," *San Antonio Express-News,* (Wednesday, November 26, 2003), 1A.

[110]"Managing Managed Care," *U.S. News and World Report*, (July 24, 1995), 58.

[111]Galewitz, 11A.

SUGGESTED READINGS

Banfield, Edward C. *The Unheavenly City*. Boston, Mass.: Little, Brown and Co., 1970.

Baum, Alice S., And Donald W. Burnes, *A Nation in Denial: The Truth About Homelessness*. Boulder: Westview Press, 1993.

Handler, Joel F. *The Poverty of Welfare Reform*. New Haven, Conn.: Yale Univ. Press, 1995.

Heidenheimer, Arnold, Hugh Helco, and Carolyn Teich Adams, *Comparative Public Policy: The Politics of Social Choice in America, Europe, and Japan*, 3d ed., New York: St. Martin's Press, 1990.

Chapter Seventeen

THE ENVIRONMENT

When the colonists first landed in the New World, they stepped upon the shores of their new homeland awe-strucked by the sight before them. Here was a land rich beyond their expectations. Abounding with the richness of natural resources, America offered millions of acres of virgin forests and wilderness teeming with a vast array of plants and wildlife. Rivers and streams were crystal clear, revealing plentiful stocks of fish. All of this beauty was crowned by clear blue skies. To Native Americans, the earth was the center of their universe. They worshiped and praised her lands and seas. They honored her creatures, plants, mountains, forests, and rivers. They revered her moon, sun, stars, and skies. They feared her anger that was so often vented in violent storms, harsh winters, and dry summers. They treasured the land. "The Indians stressed the web of life, the interconnectedness of land and man and creature."[1] Unfortunately, the European mindset viewed natural resources quite differently from Native Americans. "Chief Luther Standing Bear of the Oglala Sioux put it this way: 'Only to the white [Anglo] man was nature a wilderness and only to him was the land 'infested' with 'wild' animals and 'savage' people. To us it was tame. Earth was bountiful and we were surrounded with the blessing of the Great Mystery."[2] The beauty of this land was soon jeopardized with the continuous flow of new settlers bringing technological advancements to the emerging agricultural and industrial sectors of the New World. "Successive generations of immigrants have come to this country in search of economic opportunity. They arrived from Ireland and Germany in 1850, from Italy and Russia in 1920, and from Haiti and Mexico in 1990. Their hard work transformed abundant natural resources into a cornucopia of material wealth but at a cost of declining environmental quality. We have depleted the fertility of our soils, cut down primeval forests, and used water supplies faster than they can be replenished. Our fields produce meat, milk, and vegetables, but the nation's streams are polluted when fertilizer, pesticide, and animal waste residues run off the land. Factories convert raw materials into appliances, plastic products, and paper, but they also dump waste materials into the air and water."[3] Today, over one hundred years of industrialization with its all too familiar smokestacks have made this country materially wealthy beyond one's expectations but environmentally damaged almost beyond the hopes of repair. The legacy of the twentieth century will include the tragic vocabulary of environmental damage: ozone alerts, smog, pollution, acid rain, deforestation, endangered species, and hazardous wastes. The challenge before the new millennium is to finally solve the puzzle of how man and nature can co-exist without destroying each other.

The task is even more daunting when one realizes that environmental damage is not just an American problem. It is an international concern that affects every single country, rich and poor alike. "During the 1990s, the United State Nation's reports, 2.4 percent of the world's forests were lost, almost all in tropical Africa and Latin America. The estimated area—220 million acres—is larger than Venezuela. Nearly one-third of coral reefs were seriously degraded, and 60 percent of the world's oceans have been overfished. In a U. N. report, scientists say species extinction is unrivaled since the dinosaurs were wiped out 65 million years ago. Example: One in four mammals risks extinction within 30 years."[4] The human side of environmental damage is overwhelming. Across the globe, "more than 3 million die every year from the effects of air pollution, and 2.2 million people die from contaminated water."[5] Experts also estimate that the world's population will reach nearly "9 billion by 2050, with more than 95 percent of that growth occurring in developing nations. To feed, house, and otherwise provide for people's needs and aspirations will tax natural resources and ecological systems throughout the world. Some estimates indicate that if current forms of development continue, the world could see a five- to ten-fold increase in economic activity over the next 50 years, including an enormous jump in energy use."[6] Although certainly not a third world country, China is a primary example of a nation trying to "catch up" to her industrial giant sisters. The transition from a primary agricultural society to an industrial one has allowed the Chinese to successfully compete in world-wide markets. The emerging Chinese middle-class is now demanding higher-end consumer goods and services to include American-style homes built from wood and concrete and luxury automobiles. Building contractors in China are willing to pay premium prices for American building materials, especially lumber and concrete, placing a considerable strain on the United States commercial and residential construction markets. The Chinese thirst for oil, and gasoline has driven up world-market prices. "China has signed deals totaling more than $7 billion for stakes in oil and gas fields in Kazakhstan, Nigeria and Syria. A state-controlled company reportedly is considering a $2 billion bid for yet another Kazakh property. The worldwide buying spree helped net at least 3.5 million barrels per day of imported oil last year [2005]—enough to make China the world's third-leading consumer of foreign oil. Chinese demand is forecast to more than double by 2025, to 14.2 million barrels a day from the current 7 million a day."[7] However, there is a considerable downside. "Pollution is pervasive in China, as anyone who have visited the smog-chocked cities can attest. On the World Bank's list of 20 cities with the worst air, 16 are Chinese."[8]

Confronted with its own laundry list of environmental concerns, American lawmakers and citizens alike are still searching for the solution that will enable industry to provide us with the goods and services we are dependent upon without causing further damage to the air we breathe and the water we drink. To date, this quest has proven to be extremely difficult to accomplish. The desire to strike a balance between the constitutionally protected rights of property owners and the preservation of the environment evokes strong sentiments and hotly contested debates that sharply divide public opinion. On the one hand, property owners should be able to use and dispose of their property as they choose without undo interference from government. On the other hand, the desire to preserve society and its quality of life does depend upon the maintenance of an ecosystem free of pollution and contamination whereby plant and wildlife can successfully coexist with humankind. In every legislative house at *all* levels of government, there are constant battles between environmentalists and property owners over everything from location of parks to hazardous waste dumps. The issue whether to cut trees to make way for a new mall or business park can wreak havoc at a city council meeting. Part of the problem rests with us, average American citizens. "Although Americans express a general desire to protect their environment, they are reluctant to sacrifice their standard of living to slow the rate of natural resource use and to reduce pollution. As they implement federal environmental rules, state and local governments have been careful to protect local economic interests from being harmed seriously by environmental interests."[9] This chapter examines both the policy options available to lawmakers as well as future policy choices against the backdrop of an American society struggling to face the reality of the damage their actions have done to the quality of their environment.

Environmental issues and policy considerations are still in the infancy stage when compared to centuries-old poverty-related issues. Environmental politics did not emerge in the United States until the early 1970s when the country's consciousness was awakened to accept the truth that their century-old wanton and abusive habits had produced an extensive array of severe and, in some instances, irreversible damage. All the nation's waterways were to varying degrees polluted with run-offs from pesticides, fertilizers, chemicals, and industrial and municipal wastes. Rural residents were urged to boil their drinking water to ward off the ingestion of harmful substances. Lead-based paint, which had been the only paint base available for decades, was now labeled as a contributing cause of respiratory diseases and cancer. The once clear blue skies were suddenly noticed for their grayish and brownish hues caused by the spewing of polluting byproducts from the smokestacks of the nation's major industrial areas. The nation's coastal areas were hit with severe oil spills that spoiled tourist and resort areas and killed countless numbers of animal and marine life. Forests and wetlands became the victims of progress as bulldozers and dredgers drained swamplands and chopped whole stands of trees to make way for business and residential construction projects. Ozone alerts began to warn people with chronic respiratory ailments to remain indoors due to dangerously high levels of smog and air pollution. It was discovered during the 1970s that farm workers were the victims of deadly skin cancers acquired through years of hand-harvesting fruits and vegetables heavily sprayed with pesticides. The examples are too numerous to mention within the scope of this chapter. Consequently, this chapter focuses on the extent of the environmental damage to our nation's air, water, coastal areas, wetlands, wildlife, forests, and the problems associated with the disposal of nuclear, hazardous, and solid waste materials.

This chapter also presents a balanced approach by examining both sides of the issue. Traditionally, business and industry have fought regulatory laws that pose a threat to their livelihood. Environmental laws are, with few exceptions, laden with severe punitive actions against violators. Business leaders feel that they have been unfairly targeted and unduly punished for using acceptable traditional industrial production methods that have only now been deemed harmful to the environment. They have a valid argument that cannot be ignored by lawmakers. Antipollution devices are expensive. The increased cost of producing a product is passed onto the American consumer who is always searching for the best product at the cheapest price possible. Yes, these laws are expensive to implement. Irate property owners, business leaders, and anti-big government groups are constantly lobbying Congress to relax environmental restrictions and reduce punitive fines. Environmental groups also have a vital concern. Environmental damage must be curtailed or the future of this planet is in serious jeopardy. In *The Human Home*, British writer J. A. Walker wrote: "How are Americans to restore the environment to its proper position as an essentially political issue, over which reasonable people will disagree . . . ? How can we regain the attitude of those earlier ages which saw the natural world as pointing to the divine without itself being divine? How can we cherish our environment without making a fetish of it?"[10] Thus, the mission of environmental advocates is a noble one—protect the balance between humankind and nature. This chapter explores the role that lobbyists/advocates on each side of the environmental issue play in the creation and subsequent implementation of environmental legislation.

FEDERAL AND STATE ROLES IN ENVIRONMENT POLICIES

The reserved powers clause of the Tenth Amendment delegated to the states those governing powers not specifically granted to the national government. Consequently, the states were initially responsible for addressing environmental concerns. The national government played only a marginal role. Historically, government at all levels did not involve themselves with environmental issues with the exception of a natural disaster. For example, the Johnstown Flood of 1889 gained national attention as over 2,200 residents of several small Pennsylvania towns were tragically swept away after the collapse of a man-made earthen dam. The tragedy, however, did not result in any corrective legislative actions from Congress nor were actions taken against those responsible for building the dam. The cries of the nation's earliest environmentalists fell upon deaf ears. Former United States Minister to Turkey, George Perkins Marsh, wrote *Man and Nature* in 1864, a novel depicting the destructiveness of deforestation. Marsh believed that "man is everywhere a disturbing agent. Wherever he plants his foot, the harmonies of nature are turned to discords . . . It is certain that a desolation, like that which has overwhelmed many once beautiful and fertile regions of Europe, awaits an important part of the territory of the United States . . . unless prompt measures are taken to check the action of destructive causes already in operation."[11] Marsh's words were instrumental in motivating a group of bird watchers to form the **American Forestry Association (AFA)**, an interest group promoting conservation of the nation's forests. An avid naturalist, John Muir once commented that "pollution, defilement, squalor are words that never would have been created had man lived conformably to Nature. Birds, insects, bears die as cleanly and are disposed of as beautifully . . . The woods are full of dead and dying trees, yet needed for their beauty to complete the beauty of the living. . . . How beautiful is all Death!"[12] In 1892, Muir founded the Sierra Club "to lead city people into the mountains, where he hoped that they would learn to see granite peaks and glacial valleys as he did."[13] A realist, "Muir believed that the retreats where he and others felt such strong emotion were worth defending against the forces of technology and economic development."[14] Consequently, the Sierra Club would evolve into the preeminent political force devoted to the protection of the environment. It was individuals, not national, state, or local governments, that took the early steps to rein in the destruction of the environment. Whether it be George Marsh, John Muir, Al Gore, Teddy Roosevelt, Rachel Carson, or Bill Clinton, it should be noted that "nearly every aspect of environmentalism since the founding of the AFA has demonstrated the same pattern: a charismatic and influential individual who discerns a problem and formulates a public concern; a group that forms itself around him/her or around his/her ideas and exerts educational pressure on the Congress; legislation that creates some new kind of reserve—national park, national forest, national monument, national wildlife sanctuary or wilderness area; and finally, an increasingly specific body of regulatory law for the protection of what has been set aside."[15]

The first notable piece of federal legislation concerning the environment, was the **Refuse Act** passed in 1899. This legislation required that potential dumpers of waste materials into navigable rivers had to obtain a permit from the Army Corps of Engineers prior to dumping. Due to sixteen years of constant pressure from the AFA, Congress finally responded with the passage of the **General Revision Act** in 1891, granting the President of the United States the authority to promote the general welfare by setting aside forest lands for preserves and parks. Presidents Benjamin Harrison, Grover Cleveland and Teddy Roosevelt did exercise this right by "putting 43 million acres of forest, mainly in the west out of reach of the loggers."[16] Another pioneer environmentalist, George Bird Grinnell, was a boyhood friend of Teddy Roosevelt. Owner of *Forest and Stream*, Grinnell "carried on an impassioned campaign against market hunters, poachers and women who wore feathers on their hats; and he and the Audubon societies (he formed the first one in 1886) can be credited not

Theodore Roosevelt meets with conservationist John Muir in the Yosemite Valley. Roosevelt succeeded in making preservation of America's natural resources an important issue.

only with the **Park Protection Act** of 1894, forbidding hunting within the national parks. . ."[17] As the nation's first "environmental president" Roosevelt believed that "the Nation behaves well if it treats the national resources as assets which it must turn over to the next generation increased, and not impaired in value."[18] In 1903, Roosevelt established the nation's first wildlife sanctuary, Pelican Island. In 1905, he founded the **United States Forestry Service.** In 1906, Roosevelt signed into law the **Antiquities Act.** The initial intent of the legislation was to protect archeological sites in the Southwest from grave robbers. This legislation, however, empowered the President of the United States to set aside for federal protection any monument or sites, including forests, considered to be precious or threatened. When Roosevelt took office, the nation's only national park was Yellowstone. By 1916, however, there were thirteen national parks. "The **National Park Act** [1916] gave these reserves their stated purpose, public enjoyment, public use *without impairment,* and created the National Park Service to carry it out."[19] When Teddy Roosevelt left office, the zeal for environmentalism went underground. With the exception of the New Deal's Civilian Conservation Corps and the Works Progress Administration in the 1930s, no major environmental legislation was passed until the 1960s.

The issue of environmental quality surfaced in the early 1960s as public awareness began to focus less on the economy and more on the quality of the environment. This shift in values occurred in part because a "period of sustained prosperity following World II brought about a fundamental intergenerational shift in value priorities within Western societies. Citizens became less preoccupied with basic material needs and began to place a higher priority on the quality of their lives. This value shift appears to have been most pronounced among people in white-collar and service occupations—a growing segment of all Western populations . . . . Post-materialists place particularly high value on protection of the environment and a life-style that is high-quality but simple."[20] Policymakers also realized that the states lacked the initiative and the resources to address emerging environmental concerns. "They [the states] could not afford to develop the technical expertise on pollution issues; they had no jurisdiction over pollution generated in other states upstream or upwind; and polluting industries could threaten to move their operations elsewhere to escape compliance with strict environmental rules."[21] Consequently, the individual states needed the muscle of the federal government to establish the guidelines for legislative and, if necessary, legal action to halt environmental damage.

Rachel Carson gave the emerging environmental movement a shot in the arm when her book, *Silent Spring,* was published in 1962. In her novel, the earth and all of humankind is destroyed not by an invading army from outer space but by the wanton use of synthetic chemicals such as DDT, heptachlor, aldrin, and chlordane. Carson weaves her tale of environmental doom around her thesis that:

the unique speed of human actions, combined with the introduction of synthetic chemicals for insect control, would accelerate the occurrence of resistance mutations to such a degree that invincible insects would swagger across the Earth. Industrial alchemists would then fashion ever-stronger portions in a frantic attempt to stop the superbugs. Armed with mutated immunity the superbugs would defy the new poisons; as farmers grew desperate, pesticides would be sprayed indiscriminately. The superbugs would escape unharmed, but indiscriminate spraying would wipe out the crops, flowers, and "friendly" insects farmers hoped to encourage. The battle would end in less than a human generation, with favored species vanquished at every turn. Once the earthworm, a key friendly species, fell extinct from excess spraying of poisons, the food chain of songbirds would be destroyed forever. The next year would come a silent spring.[22]

Placing the blame for the ruin of earth squarely on the backs of all mankind, Carson declares that "the 'control of nature' is a phrase conceived in arrogance, born of the Neanderthal Age of biology and philosophy, when it was supposed that nature exists for the convenience of man."[23] *Silent Spring* did for the environmental movement what *The Jungle* did in promoting a stunned national government to move against the meat packing industry with the passage of the **Pure Food and Drug Act.** The federal government responded by passing laws placing controls and bans on DDT, other pesticides, and herbicides.

The United States Congress was jarred into action. In 1963, it passed the **Clean Air Act** giving the federal government a powerful, and to date, permanent role over state and local governments in the creation, implementation, and enforcement of environmental public policy issues. Another pioneering environmentalist, Howard Zahnister, executive director of the Wilderness Society, saw fifteen years of work finally result in the 1964 passage of the **Wilderness Act.** This legislation defined **wilderness** "as an area where the earth and its community of life are untrammeled by man, where man himself is a visitor who does not remain."[24] Congress declared approximately 9.1 million acres as wilderness falling under the protection of the federal government.

The environmental issue became a volatile political concern in the 1970s. Both presidential candidates, Edmund Muskie(D) and Richard Nixon(R), campaigned for rapid and severe federal responses to clean up environmental damage, punish violators, and protect the environment from further damage. During his tenure in the White House, President Nixon was instrumental in convincing Congress to pass "a remarkable series of acts, including the revised Clean Air Act of 1970; the sweeping National Environmental Policy Act of 1970, which created the Environmental Protection Agency and the Council on Environmental Quality and required environmental impact statements for all construction projects affecting land owned by the federal government; the Federal Water Pollution Control Act of 1972; and the Endangered Species Act of 1973."[25] Regardless of political philosophy and party loyalties, every presidential candidate since has advocated protection of the environment. For example, President Jimmy Carter stated that "most of the environmental damage which now occurs can be prevented. The additional cost of responsible surface mining, or preventing oil spills, or cleaning auto and power plant emissions is low, compared to the costs to society and future generations if we fail to act . . . . To maintain environmental quality, and to improve the quality of life for our people is an essential goal, and in its pursuit, we must act responsibly . . . . It makes little sense, if we are concerned about the quality of life, to talk about having to choose between employment and the environment or between enough energy and environmental quality."[26] Reminding the American public of their responsibility to the environment, Carter underscored that "in developing a national energy policy, the government should not try to do the job alone. . . . With the energy crisis, as with other crises, we have met as a nation, government, industry and the public must all do our part."[27] Support for preventive legislation gained public endorsement. "In a survey conducted by the *New York Times* in 1989, an astonishing 80 percent of those polled agreed with the proposition that 'Protecting the environment is so important that requirements and standards cannot be too high, and continuing environmental improvements must be made regardless of cost.'"[28]

Environmental issues were certainly a leading campaign topic during the 2000 presidential elections. Vice President Al Gore had already demonstrated his pledge to promote pro-environmental legislation if he were to be elected to the White House. Then candidate George W. Bush echoed his own commitment to a cleaner environment despite the fact that his vice presidential candidate Dick Cheney was the immediate past president of Halliburton, one of the nation's leading oil and gas producers. Bush promised that if elected he would, along with other environmental actions, seek regulations on carbon dioxide emissions from power plants. His proposal included declaring sulfur dioxide, nitrogen oxide, mercury and carbon dioxide as pollutants subject to regulation by the Environmental Protection Agency. After assuming the office, President Bush reversed his campaign promise by telling Congress that he would not require the EPA to regulate carbon dioxide emissions from power plants. In addition, the Bush administration withdrew United States participation in the Kyoto Agreement. Environmentalists, Democrats, and moderate Republicans are concerned about Bush's proposal to shift the responsibility of enforcing environmental laws from the federal government to state governments. They cite studies indicating that the majority of the states "have failed to report violations of federal pollution laws, allowed major industrial polluters to operate without proper permits and failed to conduct basic emissions tests of industry smokestacks" as evidence to support stronger, not weaker, federal authority over environmental regulations.[29] Others question his selection of individuals deemed as too "pro-business" to head key environmental posts within his administration. Critics claim that "from his first days in Washington, President Bush has built an environmental record marked by extraordinary controversy, with decisions that have outraged environmentalists while drawing praise from industry trade groups and political conservatives. In the view of the administration and its supporters, Bush's solutions to problems such as global warming and mercury pollution reflect pragmatism and a preference for consensus over confrontation. Opponents say Bush's policies unabashedly favor industry at the expense of the environment."[30] Although the majority of his predecessors could not be labeled as "Environmental Presidents," Bush definitely has taken a uniquely controversial and, perhaps, confrontational approach to environmental concerns. The next resident of the White House must deal with the sobering reality that the ill effects of global warming are upon us. Declaring that it is already occurring, the world's leading climate experts have pinpointed mankind as the very likely culprit. "The phase 'very likely' translates to a more than 90 percent certainty that global warming is caused by people's burning of fossil fuels. That was the strongest conclusion to date, making it nearly impossible to say natural forces are to blame."[31] How hot will it get? The experts think "temperature rises of 2 to 11.5 degrees Fahrenheit by 2100 . . . . On sea levels, the report projects rises of 7-23 inches by the end of the century. An additional 3.9-7.8 inches are possible if recent surprising melting to polar ice sheets continues."[32]

Today, April 20 is celebrated as Earth Day to remind us of what has been done and what legislation still needs to be enacted to protect this environment. Table 17.1 details the major pieces of environmental legislation passed by Congress. The majority of the legislation passed at both the national and state levels is designed with a ten- or twenty-year life cycle, whereby the initiating governing level must decide whether to extend the legislation for another life cycle. Against this backdrop, environmentalists can never rest easy that public opinion, office seekers, and lawmakers will be on their side whenever these legislative items are before Congress.

The Air We Breathe

The survival of the earth's inhabitants is very dependent upon the quality of the air they breathe. **Air** is basically a "mixture of nitrogen (78.084 percent), oxygen (20.948 percent), argon (0.934 percent), carbon dioxide (0.032 percent), and traces of neon, helium, krypton, hydrogen, xenon, methane, and vitreous oxide."[33] Each element performs an essential function: nitrogen, oxygen, and carbon dioxide are essential for the survival of plant and animal life; oxygen is a basic element necessary for higher forms of life; carbon dioxide plays a key role in photosynthesis and food production; ozone, a byproduct of oxygen, protects life forms from dangerous ultraviolet light; and so on. Even the slightest contamination of these elements jeopardizes the quality of the air all forms of life breathe.

Air pollution is defined "as a group of chemical compounds that are in the wrong place or in the wrong concentration at the wrong time."[34] Air pollution is caused by the release of **suspended particulates** such as ash, smoke, dust, soot, and liquid droplets into the air by the burning of fuels, agricultural practices, and industrial processes. Sulfur dioxide (SO_2) is a particularly harmful substance created by the release of sulfur-based fuels from the burning of coal and oil. On the other hand, carbon monoxide (CO) is released when fuels such as gasoline are not burned completely.

Air pollution also consists of toxic air pollutants that are released into the air during the manufacturing processes used by refineries, chemical plants, and dry cleaners. Toxins are also produced by the burning of lead-based gasoline. The combination of all of these components of air pollution may form into smog, haze, or acid rain. **Smog** occurs when "nitrogen oxides (Nox) produced by burning fuel and volatile organic compounds (VOCs) escape to the atmosphere."[35] Producing a hazy dirty brown cloud, smog is the end product of the mixing of over one hundred various compounds with sunlight and heat. **Ozone** is a primary ingredient of smog. Many of the nation's major cities have ozone alert days urging residents to prevent further damage by not gassing up the car or mowing the lawn during alert hours while at the same time warning those with respiratory ailments and allergies to remain indoors. Similar to smog, **haze** refers to "wide-scale, low-level pollution that obstructs visibility."[36] In the 1980s, scientists discovered that the average American was unknowingly contributing to air pollution problems simply by using everyday products containing chlorofluorocarbons or CFCs. These elements belong to "a family of inert, nontoxic, and easily-liquefied chemicals used in refrigeration, air conditioning, packaging, and insulation or as solvents or aerosol propellants."[37] In combination with other chemicals, "CFC's have been linked to depletion of the stratospheric ozone layer, located between 6 and 30 miles above Earth, which shields life on the surface from dangerous ultraviolet radiation. Chemically stable and unreactive, CFCs rise to the stratosphere, where they are broken down by intense ultraviolet light. The freed chlorine atoms can destroy as many as 100,000 ozone molecules before being inactivated. In this way, CFCs reduce the capacity of the ozone layer to block ultraviolet radiation from penetrating to the surface of the Earth. CFCs are also a major greenhouse gas, contributing to possible climate change."[38]

Table 17.1

Selective List of Federal Environmental Laws

Air Pollution Control Act (1955) - Provided federal funding for air-pollution control research projects.

Air Quality Act (1967) - Created nationwide federal air quality regions and set acceptable pollution levels for each region. Required that all state and local governments must develop their own standards for air-quality or follow federal mandates.

Antiquities Act (1906) — Authorized the President of the United States to set aside by proclamation sites to include national monuments and parcels of land that are objects of historical and scientific interests.

Asbestos Hazard Emergency Response Act (1986) — required the EPA to conduct inspection and removal of asbestos-containing materials from the nation's public schools.

Atomic Energy Acts (1946 and 1954) — created the nation's civilian nuclear energy programs.

Clean Air Act (1963) - Provided federal funding and assistance to local and state governments in their efforts to establish air pollution control programs.

Clean Air Act Amendments (1965) - Set federal pollution standards for automobile exhaust emissions.

Clean Air Act Amendments (1970) - Empowered the Environmental Protection Agency to establish national air pollution standards; restricted the discharge of major pollutants into the lower atmosphere; mandated that automobile manufacturers reduce emissions of nitrogen oxide, hydrocarbon, and carbon monoxide by 90 percent.

Clean Air Act Amendments (1990) - Established formulas for the development of anti-polluting gasoline fuels for use in the nation's smoggiest cities; mandated further emissions reductions of carbon monoxide and exhaust emissions by year 2003; placed additional restrictions on toxic pollutants.

Clean Water Act (1972) — also known as the **Federal Water Pollution Control Act Amendments of 1972**, the federal government's major program overseeing the quality of all surface water.

Clean Water Act (1974) (known as the Safe Water Drinking Act) - Set federal safe drinking water standards for all water suppliers servicing more than 25 people.

Coastal Zone Management Act (1972) — created the Office of Ocean and Coastal Resource Management to give federal grants to states for the development of their plans to preserve coastal areas and estuarine sanctuaries.

Comprehensive Environmental Response, Compensation, and Liability Act (1980) - Established the federal-level Superfund to clean up toxic waste sites.

Endangered Species Act (1973) - Empowered the Departments of Interior and Commerce to purchase land and water for the sole purpose of protecting, restoring, and propagating endangered species; established an identification and listing system for endangered and threatened species.

Energy Policy and Conservation Act (1975) – created the nation's Strategic Petroleum Reserve to offset future oil and gas shortages in emergency situations.

Federal Hazardous Liquid Pipeline Safety Act (1979) - Set federal guidelines for the transportation of hazardous liquids by pipelines.

Federal Insecticide, Fungicide and Rodenticide Act (1947) – authorized the registration and labeling of pesticides used as agricultural chemicals.

Federal Land Policy and Management Act (1976) – empowered the Bureau of Land Management to oversee the leasing of federally held lands for livestock grazing.

Federal Natural Gas Pipeline Safety Act - Set federal guidelines for the transportation of natural and other gases by pipelines.

Federal Water Pollution Control Act (1948) - Established federal standards for the treatment of municipal wastes prior to discharge. (Revised in 1965 and 1967)

Federal Water Pollution Control Act Amendments (1972) - Mandated national water quality standards and goals for the rehabilitation of polluted waters into safe water sources for recreational and fishing purposes.

Fish Conservation and Management Act (1976) - Restricted foreign fishing in U. S. territorial waters.

General Revision Act (1891) – Authorized the President of the United States to establish forest reserves on public land.

Lacey Act (1900) - Outlawed interstate exportation or importation of wildlife harvested or possessed in violation of federal laws.

Marine Mammal Protection Act (1972) - Prohibited the killing and importation of whales and nearly all marine mammals.

Migratory Bird Conservation Act (1929) - Empowered the federal government to purchase land for waterfowl refuges.

Migratory Bird Hunting Stamp Act (1934) - Required hunters over age 16 to purchase a stamp or license before hunting migratory waterfowl.

Migratory Bird Treaty Act (1918) - Prohibited the hunting or injury of wild birds migrating between the United States, Britain, and Mexico.

National Energy Act (1978) – deregulated the pricing of natural gas; encouraged alternative energy sources such as solar and geothermal; granted tax credits for home insulation; and encouraged conservation efforts in home-related products and motor vehicles

National Environmental Policy Act (1969) - Mandated the establishing of the Council for Environmental Quality, and the Environmental Protection Agency.

National Forest Management Act (1976) – established stricter guidelines for the harvesting and selling of timber and placed limits on clear-cutting of forests.

National Park Act (1916) – Stated that the purpose of national parks was to guarantee public enjoyment and public use without impairment. This legislation established the National Park Service.

National Wildlife Refuge System Improvement Act (1997) – underscored the need for wildlife protection and the creation of programs supporting wildlife-dependent recreation.

Nuclear Waste Policy Act (1982) – mandated the construction of federally-supervised permanent disposal sites for nuclear waste.

Oil Pollution Act (1990) – passed immediately after the Exxon *Valdez* oil spill; required all oil companies to create and submit oil spill contingency plans and to train their employees on containment efforts.

Park Protection Act (1894) – Prohibited hunting in national parks.

Pittman-Robertson Act (1937) - Allocated revenue for state wildlife conservation efforts from the collection of excise taxes on rifles, shotguns, ammunition, and archery equipment.

Refuse Act (1899) - Mandated issuance of a permit for dumping of refuse into any navigable waterway.

Resource Conservation and Recovery Act (1976) - Granted federal control over hazardous wastes; prohibited the creation of new dumping sites without prior permission; mandated the upgrade of existing open dumps to sanitary landfills or face closure.

Solid Waste Disposal Act (1965) - Provided federal assistance to state and local governments for the establishment of guidelines for solid waste disposal activities.

Surface Mining Control and Reclamation Act (1977) – placed strict guidelines for strip mining projects to include the restoration of areas subject to strip mining.

Toxic Substances Control Act (1976) – empowered the EPA to identify, register, evaluate and regulate all commercially used chemicals that posed an "unreasonable risk."

Water Quality Act (1965) - Set federal standards for the discharge of harmful substances into water sources.

Wilderness Act (1964) – Authorized a "hands-off" protection for special areas carved out of the national forest, national park and Bureau of Land Management lands.

Another type of air pollution, **acid rain**, is a "complex chemical and atmospheric phenomenon that occurs when emissions of sulfur and nitrogen compounds and other substances are transformed by chemical processes in the atmosphere, often far from the original source, and then deposited on earth in either a wet or dry form. The wet form, properly called 'acid rain,' can fall as rain, snow, or fog. The dry forms are acidic gases and particulates."[39] Acid rain was a contributing factor to a cooling of relations between the United States and Canada during the Reagan administration. The Canadian government threatened to stall a lucrative trade agreement unless the United States took measures to curtail acid rain pollution. Created in the United States, the polluting effects of acid rain were crossing into Canada destroying crops and deteriorating buildings and national monuments, as well as polluting Canadian air.

The various elements that create air pollution are both collectively and individually harmful to human beings. Ozone pollution causes respiratory ailments including shortness of breath, premature aging of the lungs, eye irritation, nasal congestion, and asthma, as well as reduced resistance to infections. Eye and throat irritation, cancer, and bronchitis are directly linked to long-term exposure to particulate matter. Both sulfur dioxide and nitrogen dioxide cause respiratory tract infections and damage to both the lung tissue and immune system. Carbon monoxide severely impairs, often with fatal results, the blood's ability to carry oxygen. It can also cause severe damage to the nervous, cardiovascular, and pulmonary systems. Brain damage and mental retardation can be caused by exposure to lead.

Traditionally throughout the hot summer months, farmers, ranchers, and homeowners particularly in the Southwest and Western sections of the country cast a hopeful eye at any cloud that could bring much needed rain to rescue their crops, their livestock, and their lawns from withering and dieing. State and local governments have resorted to cloud seeding as a means of jump-starting the rain making process. Weather experts usually point to the El Nino and El Nina weather cycles as the primary culprits for prolonged periods of drought conditions followed by short-lived monsoon like flooding. Scientists, however, have recently cast a suspicious eye towards air pollution as a likely contributor to drought conditions. A new study "for the first time, seems to provide direct evidence that tiny particles in industrial pollution cause physical changes in clouds that prevent water from condensing into raindrops and snowflakes."[40] Although the report concedes that definitely pinpointing the source of the pollution that caused the lack of meaningful precipitation is extremely difficult due to changing wind currents, scientists strongly believe that "it is a physical, rather than a chemical process that blocks formation of rain and snow. Industrial plants spew particles formed by fuel combustion that are much smaller than the water droplets normally found in clouds. The small pollution particles inhibit the cloud's water droplets from coalescing into large drops to create rain. Smaller water droplets also are slower to freeze, reducing the ice particles in clouds. In types of clouds that are short-lived, the lack of larger droplets reduces, or even eliminates, the precipitation."[41]

Initially, the federal government believed that air pollution and its subsequent cleanup were the responsibility of the states. Opting for a marginal role, the United States Congress passed the **Air Pollution Control Act** of 1955. This law enabled the federal government to provide funding to those states conducting research on air pollution. The **Clean Air Act** of 1963 provided a $95 million grant-in-aid program to assist state governments in setting their own air quality standards.

The United States Congress marginally expanded its role in 1965 by mandating federal emissions standards for hydrocarbons and carbon monoxide for new motor vehicles. The federal regulations were issued in 1966 for the 1968 model year. Congress was still "reluctant to give any real regulatory power to federal officials, however, even though the states were doing relatively little and many air pollution problems transcended state boundaries."[42] The **Air Quality Act** of 1967 went a step further by authorizing the creation of approximately 247 metropolitan air quality regions for the sole purpose of establishing their own air quality standards and developing plans to meet their anticipated goals. For the first time, the United States Congress used a punitive policy approach by authorizing the then Department of Health, Education, and Welfare to force noncomplying states to use federal standards or face lose of federal funds. However, this law proved to be very ineffective. "By 1970, no state had put into place a complete set of standards for any pollutant and the federal government had designated less than one-third of the metropolitan air quality regions that had been projected."[43]

In his State of the Union message delivered in 1970, President Richard Nixon decided to "get tough" with the states by proclaiming both the need for comprehensive federal air quality standards and expanded federal authority to implement the actions required to meet those standards. The **Clean Air Act** of 1970 bore a lofty aim "to protect and enhance the quality of the nation's air resources so as to promote the public health and welfare and the productive capacity of its population."[44] This law empowered the newly created **Environmental Protection Agency (EPA)** to establish **national ambient air quality standards (NAAQS)** for ozone, carbon monoxide, sulfur dioxide, particulate matter, nitrogen dioxide, and lead. Areas would be designated as **attainment** if air quality met federal standards. Areas failing to meet the standards for one or more NAAQS would be designated as **nonattainment**. Once the EPA announced the standards, states had nine months to develop their implementation plans. In turn, the EPA was to ensure that each plan included monitoring requirements, emission limitations for the six elements, provisions for periodic inspection of sites, and the testing of motor vehicles, as well as a state budgetary commitment to enforce air pollution standards. In addition, motor vehicle emissions of carbon monoxide and hydrocarbons were to be reduced by 90 percent beginning with the 1975 models. Nitrogen oxide emissions were to be cut by 90 percent by 1976. The EPA was granted enforcement power to include leveling fines from up to $10,000 per day for anyone removing a pollution control device to $25,000 per day for each violation of pollution. The investigative tools given to the EPA included injunctions to halt polluting activities pending legal actions. For the first time, citizens could file suits against both the polluter and the EPA for failure to respond to reported incidences of air pollution.

Despite heated debate from all sides of the issue, it was the Nixon administration that garnered public and political support for this legislation. However, the president's aim was to oversee the enactment of legislation that accomplished the goals of both protecting the environment and shielding America's business and industry from unreasonable regulations and penalties. "Part of its motivation [the Nixon administration] was a concern that regulation in some states but not in others, put regulated industries at a competitive disadvantage. Industry representatives also lobbied for one set of federal standards rather than a variety of state provisions. They prevailed on Congress to prohibit the states from imposing more aggressive regulation than provided in the Clean Air Act of 1970."[45] This initial "get tough" policy was further compromised by subsequent amendments to the Clean

Air Act that year after year granted waivers to automobile manufacturers that successfully blocked full implementation of the stronger emissions standards. Amendments passed in 1977 did threaten to deny federal funding for highway and sewage treatment projects to those states not in compliance with the Clean Air Act. However, the federal government opted to avoid taking such actions.

Although the Reagan administration sought to weaken it, the George Bush administration did enact a series of amendments to the **Clean Air Act** in 1990. This package included a mandatory production phaseout of chlorofluorocarbons, carbontetrachloride, methyl chloroform, and hydrochlorofluorocarbons, all major contributors to ozone pollution. Vehicle manufacturers were required to reduce harmful emissions and to improve emissions control devices. The gasoline companies were required to produce cleaner burning fuels. Industry was required to reduce emissions levels of both sulfur dioxide and nitrate oxide in an attempt to reduce acid rain levels. The 1990 amendments targeted 250 hazardous pollutants for emissions reductions of 90 percent by 2003. In 1993, diesel engine trucks were added to the list of motor vehicles subjected to emissions control standards.

The air pollution laws passed since 1970 have produced a mixed-bag of results. From 1970 to 1991, "emissions levels of many pollutants have dropped: lead by 96 percent, sulfur dioxide by 28 percent, particulates by 61 percent."[46] However, more Americans are driving personal vehicles, resulting in noticeable increases in ozone, carbon monoxide, and nitrogen oxide emissions levels thus offsetting any decreases. A well-known urban historian, the late Lewis Mumford, once commented that Americans "had adopted the cloverleaf as the national flower."[47] The invention of the automobile enabled Americans to freely travel across the country. However, the automobile's continued success is dependent upon a unique combination of fossil fuels commonly known as gasoline, rubber tires, and miles upon miles of asphalt and concrete roadways. Urban sprawl and highways go hand in hand. "Two million homes are built each year—and with them comes the proliferation of superstores, strip malls, and office parks. Badly planned and not planned, they turn up in the wrong places, allowed by the wrong building and zoning codes. Supported by the infrastructure of the automobile, from highways to sewage lines, and by subsidies for big oil and tax relief for developers, these trophies of highway-fed economic growth consume two million acres of productive farmland a year, according to the American Farmland Trust, and uncounted acres of woods and wetlands."[48] As early as 1991, congressional leaders recognized the necessity of encouraging alternative means of transportation to offset the polluting ways of the personal automobile culture. The **Intermodal Surface Transportation Efficiency Act** allocated $155 billion over a six-year period to "encourage foot power, bike power, mass transit, and other transportation alternatives. Two billion dollars from the act would support transportation-related 'enhancement' projects: fixing up a train station, for instance, or rehabilitating a bridge. . . Further the act mandated an additional billion dollars to Congestion Mitigation Air Quality funds, supporting a broad and vital array of projects ranging from buying alternative-fuel buses to laying light rail lines to organizing ridesharing."[49] Reliable and rapid mass transportation systems do help to reduce the number of commuters using personal vehicles. The majority of the nation's sophisticated mass transportation systems are concentrated in a handful of large metropolitan cities such as New York and Chicago. In most cities, the bus line with its reputation for unreliable service is the mass transportation system. Consequently, Americans will continue to be dependent upon their personal vehicles as their primary source of reliable transportation.

However, the cost of owning and fueling a personal vehicle is becoming more expensive as the price at the pump continues to increase. The solutions are either the development of cheaper but less powerful alternative fuels or the discovery and extraction of new sources of traditional fossil fuels. Experts believe that 40.5 billion barrels of oil can be recovered within the continental United States with an additional 76 billion barrels in nearby offshore sites, such as the Gulf of Mexico, the Alaskan shoreline, etc.[50] Since the Clinton presidency, Congress and environmentalists have been battling over drilling for oil in Alaska's Arctic National Wildlife Refuge. "A 1998 U.S. Geological Survey assessment still used today concluded it's almost certain there are at least 5.6 billion barrels of recoverable oil and possibly as much as 16 billion barrels (a 5 percent likelihood) beneath the refuge's 1.5 million-acre coastal plain."[51] Fearful of the encroachment of oil derricks and tanker trucks, environmentalists want to keep the pristine area preserved for endangered and protected species. Oil companies, on the other hand, believe "there is enough oil in the refuge to supply every drop needed by New Hampshire for 315 years or Maine for 299 years. It's enough oil for the nation's capitol for 1,710 years."[52] Throughout his presidency, George W. Bush, a former owner of a oil company, has been a strong advocate of drilling in the Alaskan refuge while at the same time, developing alternative fuels as the solutions to decreasing America's dependency upon foreign oil markets.

A primary source for the nation's on-going problem with air pollution is industries heavily involved in chemical, oil and gas production, and refining businesses. Corpus Christi, Texas, for example, is well known for its natural beaches along the Gulf of Mexico. While tourism is big business, the city's largest employers are six refineries located all in a row on a 10-mile corridor known as Refinery Row. These six refineries employ 23,000. Although these companies have spent millions on devices to control their pollution, "there are days when the pungent smell of rotten eggs, caused by hydrogen sulfide, wafts over neighborhoods. On some occasions when the flares [located on top of the refinery pipelines to burn off excess gas] burn, inky black smoke spreads across the sky, drifting wherever the wind takes it. Residents wake up on some mornings to find their vehicles coated with ash."[53] Once the area's residential properties were prime real estate. Today, these neighborhoods support a dependent minority underclass that simply cannot afford to move elsewhere. Finding a buyer for one's home is not a viable option since given a choice, few would want to live right next door to a polluting oil refinery. Although the area's benzene levels are within the EPA's parameters for compliance, the levels are among the highest in Texas. Refinery worker accidents are common. "In the past five years, twenty industrial explosions to gas line breaks to chemical releases—in Nueces County [the county seat for Corpus Christi] caused more than $74 million in damages, injured 30 people and killed two workers."[54] Work-related accidents in chemical plants are not uncommon. The U.S. Chemical Safety and Hazard Investigation Board reports that "since 1998, an average of five plant workers have been killed every month in the United States by explosions or leaks of chemicals. . . There is at least one chemical accident some-where in the nation everyday."[55]

In some areas, the quality of the nation's air is questionable. For example in 1997, the Clinton administration instructed the EPA to toughen air quality rules by requiring "states to meet more stringent reductions in smog-causing ozone and in microscopic soot."[56] Instead of complying with the new regulations, several cities opted to sue over the right of the federal government to set higher standards. Representatives of the oil and gas industry argued before the United States Supreme Court "that the EPA should consider the cost of compliance in setting air-quality standards."[57] The justices saw it differently siding with the tougher EPA air quality standards.

Recognizing the importance of reducing air pollution, the George W. Bush presidency is relying less on the muscle of federal enforcement and more on the private business sector to reduce harmful levels of air pollution. Coal-fired power plants are no longer required to install anti-pollution devices whenever they upgrade their equipment. In addition, the EPA "issued a final set of revised enforcement rules governing the nation's refineries, which will give them new flexibility to make repairs without fear of prosecution under the Clear Air Act."[58]

Global Warming

"The earth's atmosphere works like a greenhouse: It traps solar radiation, making life on earth possible. **Climate change** describes a rise in the earth's temperature caused by an increase in the concentration of certain gases, especially carbon dioxide."[59] Although not alarmists, both climate experts and environmentalists have expressed serious concerns that the future of the earth's greenhouse is being severely compromised to the point that the damage may not be reversible. They warn of **global warming** or the **greenhouse effect** that occurs when "methane, carbon dioxide, and certain other air pollutants increase, trapping heat in the earth's atmosphere and gradually warming it."[60] If their predictions are correct, "the results could be devastating: rising oceans, ferocious hurricanes, and prolonged droughts."[61] So far, the evidence clearly indicates that the earth is, indeed, getting warmer. According to the National Academy of Sciences, "average surface temperatures have climbed about 1.4 degrees Fahrenheit since the 20th century, coinciding with spiking atmospheric levels of carbon dioxide which have ballooned 35 percent over the same period. Levels of methane, a far more potent heat-trapping gas, have jumped 152 percent since the pre-industrial age.... Model projections show temperatures jumping anywhere from 2.7 to 10.7 degrees Fahrenheit over the next 100 years."[62] Higher temperatures mean that the polar ice caps are melting. It is predicted that "by the end of this century, Arctic temperatures could reach as high as 130,000 years ago, when the oceans were 13 to 20 feet higher than now."[63] What happens in Greenland and Antarctica does have an impact elsewhere. For example, experts believe that approximately one-third of the coral reefs in the Caribbean waters are dying due to global warming and rising sea temperatures. "The mortality that we're seeing now is of the extremely slow-growing reef-building corals. These are corals that are the foundation of the reef . . . We're talking colonies that were here when Columbus came by have died in the past three to four months. Some of the devastated coral never can be replaced because it only grows the width of a dime per year."[64] The potential demise of the coral reefs means economic ruin for the tourist industries in Puerto Rico and the Virgin Islands.

Realizing that global warming is an international problem involving all nation states, approximately 160 nations, including the United States, signed the Kyoto Protocol to the 1992 UN Framework Convention on Climate Change. The agreement "establishes a framework for addressing the release of greenhouse gases. [It] requires industrialized nations to reduce emissions of carbon dioxide by a specified amount within a particular timeframe so as to meet the overall goal of stabilizing atmospheric concentration of gases that contribute to climate change."[65] The Clinton administration enacted measures to ensure that the United States would meet its obligations to reduce greenhouse emissions. In March 2001, however, the United States became the only industrialized nation to withdraw from the accord. The Bush administration justified its actions by stating "the agreement would weaken the U.S. economy and create inequities by exempting developing nations from the treaty's requirements. In its place the administration called for additional scientific research and urged U.S. companies to set voluntary targets for reduction in greenhouse gas emissions."[66] Bush's actions caused a major rift with world leaders and environmentalists. Meanwhile, it is well known that "America belches up more greenhouse gases than any other country; 5.8 billion metric tons of carbon dioxide in 2003 alone, thanks mostly to autos burning gasoline and power plants consuming coal."[67]

The Water We Drink

On paper, the United States has an abundant supply of surface water, totally 259,287 square miles consisting of 79,018 square miles of inland surface water, 42,241 square miles of coastal waters and 60,251 square miles of water in the Great Lakes.[68] In reality, the United States has regions with an over abundant supply of water offset by areas that face yearly droughts and water shortages. Also, major rivers and lakes have been used as the dumping sites for industrial and municipal wastes. Americans use "about 338 billion gallons of fresh water per day for all uses, or about 1,400 gallons per capita, more water than any other industrial country. About 10 percent of that water is used for public tap supplies, 11 percent is used by industry, 38 percent is used to cool electric power-generating plants, and 41 percent is used for irrigated agriculture."[69] The demand for fresh plentiful water increases in proportion to the growth in population. Biologically, humans are composed of 80 percent water! People need water to survive. Unfortunately, Americans have wasted their water resources for far too many years. Today, most Americans are unaware that "when you fill your bathtub, you use 36 gallons of water. When you do your family laundry, you use 35 to 50 gallons. Shaving takes a gallon if you work from a full basin; 5 to 10 if you just let the water run."[70] Yet, it is extremely difficult to persuade Americans to conserve water particularly in areas with plentiful surface water and ample rainfall. Conservation and preservation of *clean* water are essential to human survival.

Again, government at *all* levels was extremely reluctant to recognize the damage caused by dumping wastes into the nation's waterways. The federal government did recognize the need for sewage treatment plants by enacting a 1948 law providing federal funds to local communities. It was not until 1965 that Congress mandated that states applying for these federal dollars had to establish clean water standards as a criterion for grant consideration. By the 1970s, incidences of severe water pollution could no longer be ignored. For all practical purposes, Lake Erie was "dead, with garbage and rotting fish regularly washing onto beaches and runoff of fertilizer and raw sewage causing massive algae blooms that starved fish of oxygen. The Cuyahoga River [in Cleveland, Ohio], which feeds Erie, was so polluted with oil, logs, sewage and every other kind of garbage that it caught fire on June 22, 1969. The walleye in Erie contained so much toxic mercury that the government banned its consumption. Cormorants were born horribly deformed by pesticides, local populations of peregrine falcons have been driven toward extinction by DDT, and lake trout in

Michigan and Huron were wiped out by over-fishing."[71] The majority of the nation's waterways located near heavy and medium-sized industrial plants were heavily polluted. "Before 1972, at least 18,000 communities regularly dumped their untreated raw sewage into rivers and lakes. Food, textile, paper, chemical, metal, and other industries discharged 25 trillion gallons of waste water each year."[72] The federal government's response was the passage of the **Water Pollution Control Act** (also known as the **Clean Water Act**) in 1972. This legislation established guidelines for nationwide water pollution standards.

One of the problems with water pollution is determining the origination of the pollution and the identity of the polluting party. The Clean Water Act did draw a distinction between nonpoint source and point-source pollution. **Point-source pollution** is defined as "pollution that can be traced to a specific point of introduction into the water."[73] Any industry visibly dumping industrial waste into a waterway could be cited for point-source pollution. **Nonpoint source pollution** is "pollution whose specific point of entry into the water cannot be traced."[74] A river or stream could be heavily polluted with run-offs from fertilizers and pesticides originating from several farms and ranches located along that waterway. Determining the identity of the guilty party is extremely difficult, if not impossible.

The Clean Water Act also created the **National Pollution Discharge Elimination System (NPDES)** whereby all businesses and industries must file for a permit prior to discharging and dumping any effluents into a waterway. Municipalities were required to install more sophisticated treatment units into their sewer systems as a means of purifying waste water. The Clean Water Act gave the administration and enforcement duties to the EPA, which, in turn, passed these responsibilities on to the states. States were required to establish separate state agencies to handle water pollution problems. In addition, the states were given the latitude to pass their own legislation as long as state-mandated standards did not undermine federal restrictions and penalties. Federal and state guidelines mandate that all surface water be tested for "aesthetic parameters (taste and odor, floating debris and settleable solids); radiological parameters; toxic parameters; nutrient parameters (such as nitrogen and phosphorus); temperature; salinity; and dissolved oxygen for unclassified waters."[75] These tests should indicate the presence of harmful substances such as arsenic, lead, toxaphene, and chromium. The Clean Water Act was renewed in 1977, 1987, and 1997.

The Clean Water Act has produced some positive results. "From 1972 to 1982, the amount of **biochemical oxygen demand (BOD)** (the amount of oxygen needed by bacteria to breakdown a specific amount of organic matter) declined by 46 percent at municipal sewage treatment plants and by at least 71 percent in industrial discharges."[76] Progress in cleaning up the nation's waterways has met with marginal success. According to the EPA's biennial *National Water Quality Inventory* report issued in 2002, "61 percent of the surveyed river and stream miles fully supported all uses set by states and [Native American] tribes, with 39 percent found to be impaired to some extent as well as 45 percent of lakes. The same survey found that 51 percent of the nation's estuaries were impaired, as were fully 78 percent of Great Lakes nearshore waters (generally because of persistent toxic pollutants in the food web and habitat degradation and destruction).[77] Rivers are classified as **impaired** when they can't support aquatic life or are unsafe for fishing or swimming. In 2000, the National Wildlife Federation conducted its own analysis of the progress state governments were making in cleaning up their rivers. Using a grading scale of A to F, the group announced that no state's actions merited an "A" for excellence. The group assigned "Bs" to six states, "Cs" to six, and "Ds" to eighteen. Eighteen states (Washington, Idaho, California, New Mexico, Texas, Nebraska, Minnesota, Iowa, Missouri, Arkansas, Louisiana, Mississippi, Alabama, Georgia, Virginia, New York, Alaska, and Hawaii) received "Fs."[78] Basically, EPA sources have determined that "the biggest source of water quality problems in rivers and streams comes from agriculture in the form of nutrients (farm fertilizers and animal wastes), pesticides, and suspended solids. Large animal feedlots favored by agribusiness have been a particular target of environmentalists, forcing the EPA and the Agricultural Department to issue new rules in 2002 to reduce that source of water pollution. . . Other major sources of impairment are hydrologic and habitat modification (e.g., loss of wetlands), urban runoff, forestry, municipal sewage treatment plants, storm sewers, and industry."[79]

Dams have also been identified as a contributing factor to water pollution. Damming rivers seemed to be the perfect solution to an area's drought conditions particularly in the West and Southwest regions of the United States. The Army Corps of Engineers provided a helping hand in determining the site location and size of the dam. "For nearly a century local water districts and Congress have regarded any Western rivers that flowed to the sea unimpeded as a colossal waste—a waste of water that could be captured for farming and urban development, a waste of potential hydropower, a waste of potential recreation sites that could be created by backing up the great rivers into lakes. To harness the water, federal and state agencies, as well as private developers, have built more than 600 major dams this century [20th]."[80] Damming a river does successfully prevent water from eventually spilling into the ocean. However, it also destroys natural habitat for sea creatures, animals, birds and plants. Damming also provides recreational spots for fishermen and outdoorsmen. However, it destroys the natural runoff patterns for rain. Far too often disastrous floods are caused by the inability of water to runoff naturally from properties. Now the Army Corps of Engineers is leading the charge to tear them down.

Oceans are also heavily polluted. "Throughout the world, important water bodies—especially the oceans—have become virtual waste bins for the tons of plastic products dumped daily by commercial fishermen, military vessels, merchant ships, passenger liners, pleasure boats, offshore oil and gas drilling operations, the plastics industry and sewage treatment plants."[81] While the sun is coming up over the ocean's horizon, it is tragic to realize that the first sight one has in the morning is the fleet of front end loaders making their daily sweep of the trash either thrown on by people or washed up on shore by the evening tide. Because oceans usually fall under international laws, few nations have enacted legislation designed to protect their shorelines from trash and pollution. The victims are the birds and sea creatures who must wade through the piles of garbage.

In 1974, the United States Congress passed the **Safe Water Drinking Act** with the promise of guaranteeing to all Americans a plentiful and healthy supply of drinking water. This legislation set federal standards for all suppliers of drinking water serving more than twenty-five people. **Drinking water** is defined as "all water distributed by any agency or individual, public or private, for the purpose of human consumption or which may be used in the preparation of foods or beverages or for the cleansing of any utensil or article used in the course of preparation or consumption of food or beverages for human beings. The term also includes all water supplied for human consumption or used by an institution catering to the public."[82] The law was amended in 1986 with the provision that water suppliers test for dozens of chemicals and bacterial substances and notify their customers when water supplies did not meet federal standards. The amendments also banned the use of lead pipes in public water systems. In 2006, President Bush signed into law the latest round of amendments to the Safe Drinking Water Act.

Despite federal and state laws, the federal government still cannot guarantee a safe drinking water supply. Far too many communities must boil their water to remove unwanted substances. The renowned United States Center for Disease Control and Prevention warned those individuals with weakened immune systems, such as AIDS, and chemotherapy patients to either use bottled or boiled water. Groundwater is still in grave jeopardy of contamination from pesticides, human, animal and industrial wastes, home cleaning products, and gasoline. In addition, municipal governments across the country are confronting costly problems with fixing and or replacing leaking and rupturing water mains and sewer systems. A ruptured sewer main can lead to the introduction of harmful substances, such as pathogens, into the drinking water system. City governments can no longer ignore taking "action on the fissures spreading in the 700,000 miles of pipes that deliver water to U.S. homes and businesses. Three generations of water mains are at risk: cast-iron pipes of the 1880s, thinner conduits of the 1920s, and even less sturdy post-World War II tubes. Cost estimates range from the EPA's $151 billion figure to a $1 trillion tally by a coalition of water industry, engineering, and environmental groups. The AWWA [American Water Works Association] projects costs as high as $6,900 per household in some small towns."[83]

Several municipalities are taking action to protect their drinking water supplies. Cities such as Dayton, Ohio, and San Antonio, Texas, are using restrictive and/or no-development zoning laws to protect their underground aquifer systems. In Dunedin, Florida, residents angry over the rust in their tap water, pressured city leaders to build a new water treatment plant with membrane-filtration systems.

Oil Spills and Toxic Wastes

The world's latest major oil spilled occurred in November 2002, as the Bahamian-registered *Prestige*, carrying 77,000 tons or 20 million gallons of Alaskan crude oil, broke apart and sunk off Spain's northwestern coast. The majority of the ship's cargo leaked from its ruptured tanks and spoiled approximately 93 miles of pristine Spanish coastline. In 1989, Americans were horrified as the Exxon *Valdez* went aground on Alaska's pristine Prince William Sound, spilling its cargo of crude oil over 900 square miles. The black goo spoiled shorelines, killed millions of marine animals and fish, and destroyed the fishing industry for several seasons. Three more major oil spills occurred that year. The Greek tanker, *World Prodigy*, struck a reef in Narragansett Bay, Rhode Island, dumping 420,000 of No. 2 fuel oil into the waterway. "In Delaware where the Uruguayan tanker, *Presidente Rivera*, ran aground and spilled 300,000 gallons of heavy No. 6 oil, about 70 percent had been cleaned up. The smallest of the spills, which occurred when a barge collided with a cargo ship in the Houston Ship Channel and released 250,000 gallons of heavy crude, was almost completely recovered."[84] The *Valdez* was one of the most costly oil spills in the nation's history. In 2001 alone, 7,559 oil spills occurred just in United States waters.

Obviously not every oil spill is preventable, but the majority of them can be avoided. Faced with the reality that only 10 percent of oil spilled is usually recovered, one would assume that the federal government would have taken extraordinary measures to keep disastrous oil spills to the bare minimum. However, interest group politics driven by the major oil producers has successfully prevented the federal government from taking severe punitive criminal and civil actions against violators. For example, then United States Senator Lloyd Bentsen introduced in 1989 a bill requiring all domestically owned oil tankers to use a triple hull structure around the oil storage tanks. Although public opinion sided with Bentsen, particularly after the *Valdez* episode, the legislation was defeated on the grounds that it was a costly unnecessary mandate against both big and small oil firms that would ultimately result in higher prices at the pump. The major oil companies had already served notice that if the bill passed, they would simply bypass the legislation by contracting out to foreign tanker companies to ship their oil. As merely the contracting party, the oil companies could transport their oil more cheaply while at the same time avoiding costly litigation if the tanker spilled its load. Our beaches, marine life, and, in some instances, economic viability is in jeopardy every time one of these tankers enters into America's waters.

The proper identification, storage, and disposal of hazardous, nuclear, and solid and municipal wastes are problems confronting all levels of government. Nuclear energy is a cost-effective method of supplying electricity to homes. Yet, scientists have yet to develop a safe method for the disposal of radioactive materials, much less obsolete nuclear reactors. The Industrial Revolution introduced manufacturing processes that produced toxic byproducts. For over one hundred years, it was an acceptable practice to dump these hazardous substances into waterways and vacant lots. The United States government is just as guilty as the nation's industrial giants. Beginning in the mid-1980s, Congress and the White House began searching for ways to save money. They decided that with the end of the Cold War and the collapse of the Soviet Union the United States government no longer needed a large standing army supported by thousands of civil servants. The answer was to begin closing down American military bases. However, the Pentagon and lawmakers soon realized that the money they were going to save in closing the bases was small in comparison to the money they were going to be spending to clean up the hazardous materials housed and, unfortunately, dumped on these military bases. In California, McClellan Air Force Base is still in the process of being converted from public to private hands. "Decades of dumping, leaks and spills at the base have left the heavily used aquifer contaminated with chlorinated solvents and fuels that will take more than 30 years to clean up . . . McClellan hasn't fully assessed the extent of its contamination and doesn't expect to have its final cleanup systems in place until 2014. Cleanup is not expected to be finished until 2034. The projected cleanup tab for the 64-year old base is $984 million with $300 already spent."[85]

In addition to military installations, commercial nuclear power plants have their own problems disposing of their high-level radioactive wastes. "By 2002, the United States had accumulated about 40,000 metric tones of high-level wastes, chiefly spent fuel from power plants. The DOE [Department of Energy] has estimated that the nation will have about 59,000 metric tons by the year 2025, assuming that no additional nuclear power plants are built. The spent fuel rods remain highly dangerous for thousand of years. Most of the radioactivity decays quickly, but enough remains that the EPA standards for disposal of such waste specify 10,000 years of isolation from the biosphere to protect public health and the environment."[86]

The dilemma confronting the EPA is the location of sites for the disposal of radioactive waste materials. The fear of a potential disaster evokes strong emotions from citizens as government officials seek to find dump sites. Oftentimes politics enters into the picture. For example in September 1998, the United States Congress granted final approval for the Texas Low-Level Radioactive Waste Disposal Compact, known as the Sierra Blanca project. Located near the Mexican border in a remote area of West Texas, the dump site would have housed radioactive waste from decommissioned nuclear power plants and industrial and medical facilities located in Maine and Vermont. Located in an impoverished and overwhelmingly Hispanic community with little political clout at the state or national capitols, the Sierra Blanca dump site drew national attention as opponents accused Congress of environmental racism. "'This isn't just a Texas issue. This is a national civil rights issue,'" The late United States Senator Paul Wellstone, D-Minn., the compact's leading Senate critic, said at an anti-dump rally. "'It seems like almost every single time . . . we try to decide where to put an incinerator or a nuclear waste dump site, it's always the path of least resistance.'"[87] A federal judge finally put the brakes on the Sierra Blanca project. The controversy over Sierra Blanca is not an isolated incident. The United States Senate approved a plan endorsed by President George W. Bush to build a nuclear waste dump in the Yucca Mountains located in the Nevada desert. The site is approximately 90 miles from Las Vegas. Both environmentalists and Nevada lawmakers opposed the plan and sought legal action to stop it. Although Americans enjoy the benefits of nuclear power, they are extremely fearful of nuclear accidents, particularly when the discussion of a potential site is their neighborhood!

Today, it is known that the disposal of nuclear and industrial byproducts must be properly stored and ultimately disposed of to prevent hazardous spills and contaminations; and individuals must dispose of their solid wastes and trash in a nonpolluting and responsible manner. However, the proper disposal of these materials is extremely costly and demands sacrifices from all participating parties. The federal government took the lead by setting the guidelines for the identification, monitoring, and disposal of solid and industrial waste products in 1976 with the passage of the **Toxic Substance Control Act**. The EPA was empowered through this legislation to establish testing procedures for new chemical substances before they could be sold. The EPA also authorized federal and state authorities to ban the sale of any harmful substances. The law specifically prohibited the sale of toxic polychlorinated biphenyls (PCB) not contained in closed systems. On January 1, 2000, the Clinton administration imposed tighter reporting rules on the use of toxic substances. The old rules required "release reports by companies that manufacture or process more than 25,000 pounds or use more than 10,000 pounds of toxic chemicals a year. The new rules require reports by companies that use 100 pounds a year, or, for some especially dangerous chemicals, 10 pounds a year."[88] The **Resource Conservation and Recovery Act** of 1976 established the process for the disposal of hazardous wastes. The act also defines **solid waste** as "any garbage, refuse, sludge from a waste treatment plant, water supply, treatment plant or air pollution control facility and other discarded materials, including solid liquid, semi-solid, or contained gaseous material resulting from industrial, municipal, commercial, mining, and agricultural operations."[89] Federal laws have produced a "cradle to grave" tracking system with both federal and state rules prohibiting "the unauthorized discharge of wastes to groundwater or surface water, creation of any nuisance or public-health problems, and the disposal of waste at unauthorized locations."[90]

Both federal and state laws prohibit the transportation of any hazardous materials through municipal areas. The risk of a derailment or traffic accident is minimized by redirecting vehicles and railcarriers carrying hazardous substances to rural routes. However, the potentiality of an accident resulting in the release of toxic and harmful substances into rivers, waterways, soil, and the air is still a tragic reality. All parties involved in the storage and disposal of toxic and hazardous materials must record the site with the appropriate county offices as well as file monthly and yearly reports.

The average American throws away tons of garbage every year. **Municipal solid waste** is defined as "solid waste resulting from or incidental to municipal, community, commercial, institutional, and recreational activities including garbage, rubbish, ashes, street cleanings, dead animals, abandoned automobiles, and all other solid waste other than industrial waste."[91] Once it was perfectly acceptable to pile up the trash in landfills and trash dumps, pitch it out the window to the streets below, or simply burn it in the privacy of one's backyard. With every American contributing 4.4 pounds per day, it is estimated that 236,200,000 tons of municipal solid waste was generated in 2003.[92] Although federal and state laws set guidelines for the disposal of these products, the ultimate responsibility falls squarely upon the shoulders of city and county governments. The laws establish extremely strict regulations covering a wide range of municipal waste activities, including the size of the landfill and the height of the trash piles. Site location is an extremely delicate situation since no one wants a landfill in their backyard. However, the trash can be piled only as high as the federally mandated level. Cities can apply for a variance to buy time until a new site can be located. There is just too much trash and too little landfill space to dump it on. In addition, reclamation of landfills is virtually worthless since it is unlikely that anyone would want to build their homes or businesses on a filled-in landfill that may emit harmful vapors and odors.

Communities have adopted volunteer recycling programs for newspapers, paper products, glass, plastics, and aluminum cans. However, converting recycled products into reusable goods is still an expensive venture. Although environmentally aware, the average American consumer is reluctant to purchase higher priced recycled products. Another alternative is incineration whereby unsorted trash is burned. Although incineration does reduce the need for landfill space, the process of burning mass amounts of trash does pose potential harmful effects to air quality. Site selection proposals for incineration plants produce heated battles between angry residents vehemently opposed to having smokestacks release byproducts from burning trash over their homes and city leaders desperate to find cost effective trash disposal methods. Advanced incineration systems include mass burn combustors, modular combustion systems, refuse-driven fuel combustors, and waste-to-energy plants. Obviously, this nation's major cities are facing an uphill battle unless cost-effective and environmentally safe alternative trash disposal methods are adopted within the immediate future.

Superfund Programs

Since the cost of properly disposing and cleaning up hazardous, solid, and municipal wastes is often too expensive for the violators to bear alone, the **Comprehensive Environmental Response Compensation and Liability Act** established a federally funded Superfund in 1980. The Superfund operates on a "'polluters pay' principle under which seven-eighths of the Superfund's budget comes from a special tax on chemicals and oils that are believed to cause much hazardous waste."[93] An identified hazardous waste site qualifies for Superfund assistance once it is officially placed on the EPA's National Priority List. As of 2004, the EPA had officially listed 1,286 sites within the United States with an additional sixteen located in Guam, Puerto Rico and the Virgin Islands.[94] Administered by the EPA, the balance of the superfund in 2005 was $1,567,000,000.[95] The **Emergency Planning and Community Right-to-Know Act** passed in 1986 requires local businesses to notify communities about the types of hazardous substances they use and how these products were being stored, used, and disposed. The **Pollution Prevention Act** (1990) expanded reporting guidelines to include both the amount of waste recycled and the amount of waste not produced because of antipollution devices. The **Community Right-to-Know-More Act** (1991) requires public disclosure of how much of a hazardous chemical is used to produce a particular product.

It is questionable whether state and federal Superfund programs are effective tools in cleaning up hazardous waste sites. The federal Superfund program appears to spend the bulk of its budget on legal and administrative costs rather than on cleanup and disposal activities. Cited violators can postpone cleanup activities for years by tying up the EPA in lengthy and very costly legal battles. State-created Superfunds have fared worse than the federal initiative. Natural resource energy dependent states, such as Texas, pass strict laws with only marginal intentions of enforcing them.

Forest and Wetland Conservation

The EPA defines **wetlands** as "areas that are inundated or saturated by surface or groundwater often enough or for a long enough period to support vegetation adapted for saturated soils."[96] The wetlands play a fundamental role in maintaining the balance of nature since "among other functions, they reduce flood and storm damage, provide wildlife and fish habitat, help improve water quality by filtering run-off, protect drinking water sources, and provide recreation opportunities."[97] By contrast, **deepwater habitats** are "permanently flooded land lying below the deepwater boundary of wetlands. Deepwater habitats include environments where surface water is permanent and often deep, so that the water, rather than air, is the principal medium within which the dominant organisms live, whether or not they are attached to the substrate."[98] Unfortunately, the wetlands have become the victims of a growing population's demand for residential, recreational, and commercial construction. Initially, both the federal and state governments encouraged the dredging and filling of wetland properties to the point that "about half of the 200 million acres of wetlands in the contiguous 48 states at the time of the European colonization have been lost."[99] "Twenty-two states have lost over one-half of the wetlands they had in the nation's earliest years, and seven of those—California, Indiana, Ohio, Missouri, Kentucky, Illinois, and Iowa—have lost more than 80 percent. Nationally, between the mid-1950s and the mid-1970s, an estimated 458,000 acres a year of marches, swamps, and other ecologically important wetlands were lost to development, highways, and mining. The rate slowed to about 290,000 acres a year lost by the mid-1980s, and the EPA and the Fish and Wildlife Service maintain that the net rate slowed further, to about 58,000 acres per year."[100] The desire of government to protect and preserve wetlands is a classic case of government's charge to promote the "public good" clashing head-on with the treasured rights of private property ownership since over 3/4's of all wetlands is held in private hands.

There are, however, several federal and state laws establishing guidelines for the use and disposition of wetlands property. Section 404 of the Clean Water Act requires the issuance of permits to any interested party involved in the draining and/or filling of wetlands. The U.S. Army Corps of Engineers is the primary agency charged with the issuance of these permits and with periodic inspection of the sites. A provision of the 1990 **Farm Bill** requires that farmers and ranchers receiving U.S. Department of Agriculture benefits and subsidies must protect any wetlands located on their property. In addition, the **Wetlands Reserve Program** provides cash incentives to property owners as a means of encouraging preservation efforts. These legislative enactments, however, have failed to halt the gradual erosion of these precious habitat areas.

The nation's forests are also in peril as more and more acres of trees are cut every year. The lumber is used to build homes and businesses. The pulp is processed into the billions of reams of paper and paper products used every day. Forests play an essential role in the maintenance of a healthy clean environment, as well as provide natural habitats for a wide range of plant and animal life. "At the time of white settlement, approximately, 1.1 billion acres of forest thrived in the United States, covering 49 percent of the landscape. From the 1600s to 1920, 370 million acres of forests (34 percent) were cleared, leaving 730 million acres today. Only 10 to 15 percent of today's forests have never been cut."[101] Management of publicly owned forests falls under the jurisdiction of the United States Forest Service. These forests are used for recreation, timber harvest, wildlife habitat, watershed protection, and wilderness and range management. President Bill Clinton used his authority as outlined in the Antiquities Act of 1906 to add another 58,518,000 acres for protection by the federal government.[102] Through his executive order, these lands are now protected from future road building, private development, oil and gas exploration, and drilling and logging. The Bush administration was taken aback by Clinton's actions and called upon the federal courts to overrule Clinton's midnight hour use of the Antiquities Act. As a candidate, Bush openly advocated the exploration and possible drilling of oil from the Alaskan wilderness as a means of decreasing the nation's dependency upon foreign oil. The 9th Circuit Court of Appeals, however, ruled in favor of President Clinton. The ruling "prohibits virtually all road building in roadless parcels of 5,000 acres or more, acreage that covers a third of America's national forest or 2 percent of the nation's land mass."[103] The ruling includes Alaska's 17-million acre Tongass National Forest.

Endangered Species

Passed in 1973, the **Endangered Species Act (ESA)** is still one of the most controversial of the federally enacted environmental laws. The law empowers the U.S. Fish and Wildlife Service to prohibit the harassing, collection, capture, and hunting of any species determined to be threatened or in danger of extinction. The ESA defines **endangered species** as "one in danger of becoming extinct throughout all or a significant part of its natural range; whereas, a **threatened species** is "one likely to become endangered in the foreseeable future."[104] As of 2005, the ESA listed 1,077 species of mammals, birds, reptiles, amphibians, fish, snails, clams, crustaceans, insects and arachnids as well as 749 varieties of plants as either endangered or threaten species.[105] However, environmentalists believe the law is not strong enough in protecting species from the encroachment of progress. Viewing it as a reactionary program, they believe that "ideally, the ESA should serve as an emergency room for species on the decline, but only if we also practice preventive medicine by helping healthy populations of wildlife before they get into trouble."[106] They point to the few successes such as the American Bald Eagle, the alligator, and so on and compare these to the growing list of extinct and so-to-be extinct species.

Opponents believe the law goes too far by placing the value of one animal or bird above economic progress, jobs, and property rights. On the Gulf Coast, fishermen complained that using turtle excluder devices, or break-away nets, would severely hamper the shrimping business, placing smaller trollers out of business. Protecting the habitat of the California gnatcatcher, a small, blue-gray bird, has land developers crying foul. In Texas, the Edwards Underground Recharge Zone is the only breeding habitat for the rare blind catfish. The Fish and Wildlife Service and other environmentally charged federal agencies and the federal court system are still debating how to protect this fish while drought-prone South Texas seeks to meet the water needs of its residents. The list of complaints goes on and on.

Despite the critics, the ESA is "the one legal mechanism in the United States that can force communities to balance conservation with development."[107] The ESA has been successful in slowing the rate of extinction since "sixty U.S. endangered species are now increasing in number or expanding their ranges, including species once reduced to a few individuals, such as the whooping crane, red wolfe, and black-footed ferret."[108] And, those shrimpers on the Gulf Coast actually improved their catch by using those nets. The logging business in the Pacific Northwest has lost more jobs due to automation and a growing timber industry in the Southeastern part of the United States than to the protection of the spotted owl.

POLICY OPTIONS AND THE POLITICAL CLIMATE

Particularly with environmental issues, policy options are limited. The curative policy approach is not a viable option since existing environmental damage cannot be substantially reversed, much less cured. The alleviative approach can be used to address property or health-related problems caused by previous incidences of environmental damage. However, this option is viable only if the source of the pollution can be identified. For example, an area's residents are experiencing high incidents of lung-related illnesses caused by bacteria in the water supply. Medical experts believe the source of the problem is the one river that runs through this community. However, the water in this river has been contaminated for years as the five to six major industries located on its banks have dumped their industrial byproducts into it. Determining who is responsible for the pollution and ultimately liable for damages is almost impossible. In addition, liability for pollution-related damage is questionable since the majority of the laws have "grandfather" clauses that protect businesses and individuals from litigation for polluting activities that happened before the laws were passed.

Consequently, lawmakers turn to the preventive and punitive approaches. Every environmental law seeks to prevent future damage by punishing those who pollute with strict penalties and with criminal sanctions to deter would-be polluters. "Interestingly, the government of the United States, whose political and legal culture is the most protective of private property rights, takes the most confrontational position towards private polluters of any nation. Its laws are the strictest, giving administrators the least discretion in their dealings with industry."[109] However, the evidence clearly indicates that this nation continues to have a serious environmental problem. It is clear that "the strictness of laws and procedures in the United States has not necessarily produced better results than in other countries that take a more conciliatory stance towards industry."[110] If the laws are strong in verbiage and punitive penalties, why does this nation continue to have an evergrowing environmental problem? The answer rests with an evaluation of (a) the effectiveness of the EPA and other federal agencies; (b) the policy approach used to produce regulations; (c) the lack of incentives to encourage nonpolluting activities; (d) the inability to enforce regulations in a timely and consistent manner; and (e) an often hostile political climate.

Created in 1970 with the passage of the **Environmental Protection Act**, the **Environmental Protection Agency (EPA)** was initially charged with overseeing air and water pollution problems. The role of the EPA has been expanded to include hazardous wastes, pesticides, noise pollution, and, in part, endangered species. The EPA monitors potential environmental damage by requiring all federal agencies to file an **impact statement** detailing any potential harm a project might cause to the environment, as well as proposing solutions to prevent undo environmental damage and potential efforts on the part of a project's sponsors to maintain and hopefully enhance the productivity of the environment. The EPA has the power to make or break a project. If irreversible harm will occur, the EPA should and will cancel a project. Usually, the EPA opts to attach additional requirements or **mandates** to a project in hopes of avoiding environmental damage. The mandates may indirectly lead to the demise of a project simply because they add to project costs. The EPA also reserves the right to inspect all aspects of the construction to ensure compliance.

The EPA has become the enemy to many construction firms, land developers, property owners, state and local governments, environmentalists, and lawmakers and politicians from both sides of the political spectrum. These groups usually have few kind words for the EPA and its impact statements, mandates, and regulations. First, critics believe that the command and control approach used by the EPA is "excessively rigid and insensitive to geographical and technical differences and for being inefficient."[111] Rural areas, for example, are subjected to the same standards as heavily populated urban areas.

The EPA's command and control approach also permits the agency to set the compliance guidelines but turns enforcement over to a myriad of state and federal agencies. This strategy severely compromises the effectiveness of the EPA. First, states may and do pass their own environmental laws. "Generally, the states are not precluded from enforcing criteria more strigent than those required by federal laws, and are given considerable leeway to follow enforcement interpretations which may not be fully consistent with those applied at the federal level."[112] Some states do pass environmental laws that are considerably more strict in scope as well as laden with far more punitive measures than federal sanctions. On the other hand, some states opt for a minimalist approach by barely enforcing federal guidelines. Second, the EPA is not the sole implementator of environmental laws and regulations. The agency shares its authority with a myriad of federal agencies including the Fish and Wildlife Service, the Corps of Engineers, the Interior Department, the National Park Service, and so on. The states have overlapped this fragmented approach by creating numerous state agencies with duplicated functions. A business trying to comply with the various rules often deals with too many agencies, each requiring the submission of duplicated reports, paperwork, and procedures. Although on paper the EPA did set national standards, the individual states have wreaked havoc with them, leaving everyone involved in a state of confusion.

The Science Advisory Board leveled another criticism of the EPA by calling it "a largely 'reactive' agency, insufficiently oriented toward opportunities for the greatest risk reduction . . . . The board also called upon the EPA to pursue a much broader agenda than it has in the past, and to take responsibility for protecting the environment, not just for implementing environmental law by addressing the most serious risks, whether or not agency action is required by law."[113] Basically, the EPA has done very little to prevent damage since it appears to react after the damage has been done!

The policy approach with its emphasis on punitive sanctions is a major point of disagreement to business, industry, and property owners. "The implementation process for environmental laws in the United States is by far the most formalized, rule-oriented, and adversarial—in a word, confrontational."[114] The EPA emerges not as a friend to business but as a sinister rule-laden monster fixated with complicated rules and procedures that are burdensome and often too costly for business to bear. Far too often, environmental issues are decided by judges, not the EPA or its complicated rules. "Regulations are based on collected evidence marshalled by the contending sides and interpreted according to specific procedures that are open to appeals and legal challenges at all stages. The rule-making process is typically long and contentious, often ending in litigation."[115] It can take years of legal action to adjudicate one case. Meanwhile, the accused polluters can continue their polluting ways while the attorneys battle it out in the courts.

The rules themselves are just as reactive. The United States Constitution prohibits the enactment of ex post facto laws. Consequently, laws are enforceable and penalties are binding only for future violations. For example, both federal and state laws mandate that all injection or underground wells and surface pits be plugged and/or filled upon completion of extraction activities. Yet, these laws do not apply to wells drilled before the laws were passed. Natural resource-rich states have thousands of abandoned gas, oil, and water wells left unplugged and pits left unfilled. A small town in Texas lost a whole school bus load of children who drowned when their bus was hit by a truck, pushing the bus into a water-filled abandoned gravel pit. The owner of the pit was not liable since the pit was created before the legislation to fill it was passed.

Perhaps the business community would be more cooperative if the EPA and other environmental agencies would offer incentives to those who voluntarily exceed federally mandated compliance levels. "A factory might be able to reduce its emissions by 70 percent rather than the required 50 percent at little additional cost, but the factory most likely will not do the additional cleanup—its goal is to minimize the cost of product, not to provide a cleaner environment for society."[116] Could not the EPA and other federal and state agencies encourage more conservation through the development of environmentally safe production methods by offering incentives towards research and rewards for results rather than just punishing the violators?

The EPA's enforcement track-record has been described as being mired in lengthy and costly litigation that results in lenient cleanup schedules and few fines. Too often the EPA's targets are small and medium-sized businesses and industries who can not afford the daily fines much less the expensive legal fees to fight a lengthy court room battle with the federal government. Larger firms, however, can afford to tie up the EPA for years while they continue to pollute the environment. Basically, the EPA is "reluctant to enforce standards against large companies with political clout or small profit margins, especially industries crucial to the nation's economic health. To take action against a large industry requires significant political will all the way up to the White House."[117] The failure of environmental agencies to take on the giants has ruined their effectiveness, tarnished their reputations, and left small businesses with a justifiable charge of foul play.

The political climate is particularly important in the development and implementation of environmental policies. Public sympathy does support the cause of environmentalists. It would seem reasonable to assume that since public opinion is solidly behind protecting the environment, that lawmakers could easily address this issue. However, like so many other issues, fickle public opinion can change rapidly. The urge to clean up the environment waxes and wanes when the words "sacrifice," "cost," and "accountability" enter into the picture. In general, the American public is not committed to long-term sacrifice without seeing immediate tangible results capable of encouraging them to continue their efforts.

"We associate environmentalism with the burgeoning of grassroots citizen participation in the 1960s throughout the Western countries. As motivating issues, nuclear power and other environmental concerns were second only to the Vietnam War in their power to mobilize middle-class citizens."[118] Today, environmental groups continue to pursue their bottom-line issues. Preeminent groups include the Sierra Club, Wildlife Federation, Environmental Defense Fund, National Resources Defense Council, Greenpeace, and the radial Greens group. Their message advocating a cleaner environment is soundly backed by the visible evidence and statistical data detailing environmental damage. However, the tactics they use often adversely impact their effectiveness. The environmental movement had difficulties "incorporating itself into national politics, largely because its goals and styles did not fit that of traditional party politics."[119] Consequently, environmental groups rely upon protests, demonstrations, and mass arrests to get their point across. Doomsday predictions by environmentalists have led some to label them as extremists who are willing to sacrifice the economic viability of this country to protect the environment from the encroachment of progress. "Environmentalists' perchant for doomsaying is coming back to haunt them. By overstating evidence, by presenting hypotheses as certainties, and predictions as facts to create a sense of urgency, scientist-activists have jeopardized their own creditability."[120]

Environmental groups, like the majority of the nation's interest groups, attract advocates from upper- and middle-income classes who view the value of the environment differently from their lower-income counterparts. "The economically secure are more willing to close down polluting factories. They are more willing to ban logging operations in order to preserve wilderness areas and to pay extra for canned goods in order to reduce the cannery's waste emissions into a river."[121] The affluent can afford to make these sacrifices without seriously compromising their social and economic viability. The poor may be sympathetic to environmental concerns; however, they cannot afford to make personal sacrifices. To them, environmentalists and their causes mean factory and business closings and loss of jobs. To the mechanic, factory worker, oil field worker, and so on "their jobs depend upon exploiting environmental resources; their first priority is to maintain a healthy growing economy, and keep factories operating even if emissions pollute the air; feeding one's family and paying the rent are of primary importance; an unpleasant smell in the air is of relatively little concern. Smoke means jobs."[122] It is obvious why the average American factory worker does not embrace the message of environmentalists.

Although the Democratic Party has been more receptive in embracing environmental causes and the cry for stronger federal regulations, the party still must deal with political reality. Among the voting population are those who are adversely affected by strict environmental policies. The Republican Party is well known for its opposition to governmental regulation, particularly environmental laws. Their cries to end the role of big government meddling into the affairs of business, industry, and private property owners win support nationwide. Yet, the Republican Party cannot afford to be too "anti." Both parties are guilty of wanting "to please the voting public by jumping on the 'ecological band wagon' while not alienating the business interests so dominate in the pollution problem and yet so essential to their political successes."[123] The safest course of action for both parties is to pursue a moderate position by avoiding extreme positions on both sides of the issue.

Thirty-plus years of Earth Day celebrations and bitter political arguments over the environment has resulted in the development of a multi-billion dollar environmental industry. In 2004, the industry generated $240,800,000,000 in revenue and employed 1,501,600 workers in environment-related businesses and industries.[124]

Environmental issues are further complicated by the inclusion of the international community. Policy-makers in the United States must work closely with other countries to ensure a steadfast commitment that protecting the environment is essential to the world's survival, not just the United States. The relationship between United States lawmakers and the international community is a fragile one. Not all nations have the resources that the United States has to deal with environmental concerns. Nor can the United States afford to "lord over" other countries by trying to dominate the policy responses. In addition, the environment, unlike other policy issues such as poverty, transportation, education, and so on, is a problem that the United States cannot address by itself. What happens in the Brazilian rain forest, for example, directly has an impact on environmental efforts in the United States. Effective international environmental policies can only become a reality with a solid and unified front from the international community.

CONCLUSION

In the United States, the collective "we," the industrialists, business people, workers, consumers, politicians, lawmakers, and so on have polluted our communities, our countries, and our planet. We are to blame for polluting the air, watersupply, and waterways. We have allowed our quest for progress and modernization to jeopardize plant and wildlife and to deplete the forests and wetlands. The problem is how can the collective "we" put this wanton destruction to a screeching halt. Obviously, no one is pleased with the current strategy of passing strict regulatory laws backed with costly punitive sanctions. Environmentalists view these enactments as an ineffective tool in combating environmental damage while the opposing camp is embodied in lengthy legal battles as they attempt to ward off both the regulations and the regulators. The current federal and state laws may be strong in verbiage and intent but are weak in implementation, in fair and just enforcement, and in results. No one factor, including the environment itself, is winning the war. The collective "we" can save the environment by not placing the blame on each other but by collectively beginning to make the sacrifices needed to preserve our planet.

CHAPTER NOTES

[1] Wallace Stenger, "It All Began With Conservation," *Smithsonian*, Vol. 21, No. 1, April, 1990, 35.

[2] Ibid.

[3] Steven A. Peterson and Thomas H. Rausmussen, *State and Local Politics*, (New York: McGraw-Hill, Inc., 1994), 241.

[4] Joseph B. Verrengia, "Goal Is To Save The Earth And Its People," *San Antonio Express-News* (Sun., Aug. 25, 2002), 18A.

[5] Ibid.

[6] Michael E. Kraft, *Environmental Policy and Politics,* 3rd ed., (New York, New York: Pearson Education, Inc., 2004), 2-3.

[7] Peter Enav and Elaine Kurtenbach, "China's Increasing Energy Thirst Is Shaking Up the Old Oil Order," *San Antonio Express-News*, (Sunday, June 11, 2006) 24A.

[8] Jim Yardley, "China Pollution Takes Deadly Toll on Poor," *San Antonio Express-News* (Sunday, September 12, 2004), 26A.

[9] Peterson, 261.

[10] Peter Borelli, "Environmental Philosophy," *Major Problems in American Environmental History*, Carolyn Merchant, ed., (Lexington, Massachusetts: D. C. Heath, 1993), 567.

[11] Stenger, 38.

[12] Borelli, "Environmental Philosophy," 560.

[13] Steven Stoll, *U.S. Environmentalism Since 1945: A Brief History with Documents*, (Boston, Massachusetts: Bedford/St. Martin's, 2007), 8.

[14] Ibid.

[15] Stenger, 39.

[16] Ibid.

[17] Ibid, 39.

[18] *Treasury of Presidential Quotations*, Caroline Thomas Harsberger, ed., (Chicago: Follett Publishing Co., 1964), 41.

[19] Stenger, 40.

[20] Arnold Heidenheimer, Hugh Helco, and Carolyn Teich Adams, *Comparative Public Policy: The Politics of Social Choice in America, Europe, and Japan*, 3rd ed., (New York, New York: St. Martins Press, 1990), 316.

[21] Peterson, 251.

[22] Gregg Easterbrook, *A Moment On the Earth: The Coming Age of Environmental Optimism*, (New York, New York: Penguin Books, USA, Inc., 1995), 79-80.

[23] Stephen Klaidman, "Muddling Through," *The Wilson Quarterly*, Vol. XV, No. 2, Spring, 1991, 74.

[24] Stegner, 43.

[25] Stoll, 19.

[26] *The Presidential Campaign 1976: Jimmy Carter*, Vol. I, Part 1, (Washington, D.C.: United States Government Printing Office, 1978), 662 & 664.

[27] Ibid., 663-664.

[28] Klaidman, 73.

[29] Eric Pianin, "Bush Eyes Giving EPA Role To States", *San Antonio Express-News* (Sunday, July 22, 2001), 7A.

[30] Joby Warrick and Juliet Eilperin, "Bush Land Policy Seen Favoring Energy Over Ecology", *San Antonio Express-News* (Sunday, September 26, 2004), 7A.

[31]Seth Borenstein, "Global Warming Likely Is Our Fault," *San Antonio Express-News*, (Friday, February 2, 2007), 1A.

[32]Ibid.

[33]Gary C. Bryner, *Blue Skies, Green Politics: The Clean Air Act of 1990*, 1st ed., (Washington, D.C.: CQ Press, 1993), 41.

[34]Ibid., 42.

[35]*The 1993 Information Please Environmental Handbook*, compiled by the World Resource Institute, (New York, New York: Houghton Mifflin Co., 1993), 88.

[36]Bryner, 42.

[37]Ibid., 188.

[38]Kraft, 35.

[39]Bryner, 187.

[40]Marla Cone, "Study Says Pollutant Suppress Rain, Snowfall," *San Antonio Express-News* (Sunday, March 12, 2000), 8A.

[41]Ibid.

[42]Klaidman, 81.

[43]Ibid.

[44]Ibid., 83.

[45]Ibid., 84.

[46]Ibid.

[47]Jane Holtz Kay, "Moving In The Right Direction," *Preservation*, Vol. 49, No. 3, May/June, 1997, 53.

[48]Kay, 54.

[49]Ibid.

[50]H. Josef Herbert, "Nobody Knows How Much Oil Refuge Holds," *San Antonio Express-News*, (Tuesday, December 20, 2005), 5A.

[51]Ibid.

[52]Ibid.

[53]John Tedesco, "Clearing the Air on Refinery Row," *San Antonio Express-News*, (Saturday, October 7, 2000) 8A.

[54]Ibid.

[55]Marianne Lavelle, "Blasts, But Not From the Past," *U.S. News & World Report*, July 17, 2000, 18.

[56]H. Josef Hebert, "Appeals Court Block on Clean Air Rules," *San Antonio Express- News* (Saturday, Oct. 30, 1999) 11A.

[57]Laurie Asseo, "Justices Fume At Air Claims," *San Antonio Express-News* (Wednesday, November 8, 2000) 6A.

[58]Eric Pianin, "Pollution Rules Are Blasted," *San Antonio Express-News* (Saturday, November 22, 2002), 3A.

[59]Stoll, 17.

[60]Susan Welch, John Gruhl, Michael Steinman, John Comer, and Susan M. Ridgon, *American Government*, 5th ed., (Minneapolis, Minnesota: West Publishing Co., 1994), 615.

[61]Bret Schulte, "Turning Up The Heat", *U.S. News & World Report*, April 10, 2006, 34.

[62]Ibid., 35.

[63]"Concern About Polar Ice Melt, Rising Seas Become More Heated," *San Antonio Express-News*, (Friday, March 24, 2006), 1A.

[64]Seth Borenstein, "Hot Water, Disease Kills Coral Reefs That Columbus Saw," *San Antonio Express-News*, (Friday, March 31, 2006), 10A.

[65]Kraft, 267.

[66]Ibid., 274.

[67]Schulte, 34.

[68]U.S. Census Bureau, *Statistical Abstract of the United States: 2006*, 125th ed., (Washington, D.C., 2005), Table 347, 221.

[69]*The 1993 Information Please Environmental Handbook*, 36.

[70]Ibid., 37.

[71]Peter Annin and Sharon Begley, "Great Lake Effect," *Newsweek*, July 5, 1999, 52.

[72]Welch, 615.

[73]John J. Harrigan and David C. Nice, *Politics and Policy in States and Communities,* 8th ed., (New York, New York: Pearson Education, Inc. 2004), 443.

[74]Ibid.

[75]*Texas Environmental Law Handbook*, Debra Baker, Eva M. Fromm, and Lance L. Shea, eds., 2nd ed., (Rockville Maryland: Government Institutes, Inc., 1990), 21.

[76]*The 1993 Information Please Environmental Handbook*, 38 & 40.

[77]Kraft, 37.

[78]Christopher Anderson, "Dirty Water," *San Antonio Express-News* (Thursday, April 6, 2000) 1A.

[79]Kraft, 38.

[80]Andrew Murr and Sharon Begley, "Dams Are Not Forever," *Newsweek*, November 17, 1997, 70.

[81]Michael Weisskopf, "Plastic Reaps A Grim Harvest In the Oceans of the World," *Smithsonian*, Vol. 18, No. 12, March, 1988, 59.

[82]*Texas Environmental Law Handbook*, 80.

[83]Marianne Lavelle and Joshua Kurlantzick, "The Coming Water Crisis," *U.S. News & World Report*, Aug. 12, 2002, 24.

[84]Barbara Rudolph, "Whose Mess Is It?", *Time*, July 10, 1989, 42.

[85]Jerry Needham, "The McClellan Monster," *San Antonio Express-News* (Saturday, October 21, 2000), 15A.

[86]Kraft, 46.

[87]Michelle Mittelstadt, "Radioactive Waste Dump Foes Take Case to Washington," *San Antonio Express-News* (Wednesday, September 2, 1998), 7A.

[88]William C. Mann, "Clinton Airs Tougher Rules for Toxic Pollution," *San Antonio Express-News* (Sun., Oct. 31, 1999), 13A.

[89]*Texas Environmental Law Handbook*, 102.

[90]Ibid., 101.

[91]Randy Lee Loftis, "Texas Environment: State of Neglect," *The Dallas Morning News* (Sunday, November 24, 1991),3N.

[92]*Statistical Abstract of the United States: 2006*, 125th ed., Table 363, 229.

[93]Harrigan, 439-440.

[94]*Statistical Abstract of the United States: 2006*, 125th ed., Table 369, 23296

[95]Ibid., Table 370, 233.

[96]Elana Cohen, "Protecting Wetlands: Creating A Sense of Stewardship," *The National Voter*, (Washington, D.C.: League of Women Voters of the United States, June/July, 1996), 15.

[97]Ibid.

[98]*Statistical Abstract of the United States: 2006*, 125th ed., Table 353, 225.

[99]Cohen, 15.

[100]Kraft, 39.

[101]*The 1993 Information Please Environmental Handbook*, 176-177.

[102]John Heilpirn, "Court Again Slaps Limits on Use of National Forests," *San Antonio Express-News* (Sun., Dec. 15, 2002), 11AA.

[103]Ibid.

[104]*Statistical Abstract of the United States: 2006*, 125th ed., Table 373, 234.

[105]Ibid.

[106]*The 1993 Information Please Environmental Handbook*, 159.

[107]Ibid.

[108]Ibid.

[109]Heidenheimer, 310.

[110]Ibid.

[111]Bryner, 20.

[112]J. Gordon Arbuckle, etal., *Environmental Law Handbook*, 111th ed., (Rockville, Md.: Government Institute, Inc., 1991), 8.

[113]Bryner, 32.
[114]Heidenheimer, 323.
[115]Ibid.
[116]Peterson, 259.
[117]Welch, 614.
[118]Heidenheimer, 310.
[119]Ibid.
[120]"The Doomsday Myths," *U.S. News and World Report*, December 13, 1993, 81.
[121]Peterson, 243.
[122]Ibid.
[123]"Wilbourn E. Benton, *Texas Politics: Constraints and Opportunities*, 5th ed., (Chicago, Illinois: Nelson-Hill, 1984), 375.
[124]*Statistical Abstract of the United States: 2006*, 125th ed., Table 372, 234.

SUGGESTED READINGS

Esterbrook, Gregg, *A Moment on the Earth: The Coming Age of Environmental Optimism*, New York, New York: Penguin Books USA, 1995.

Harrigan, John J., and David C. Nice, *Politics and Policy in States and Communities*, 8th ed., New York, New York: Pearson Education, Inc., 2004.

Heidenheimer, Arnold, Hugh Heclo, and Carolyn Teich Adams. *Comparative Public Policy: The Politics of Social Choice in America, Europe, and Japan*. 3rd ed. New York: St. Martin's Press, 1990.

Klaidman, Stephen. "Muddling Through," *The Wilson Quarterly*. Spring, 1991, Vol. XV, No. 2, pp.73-82.

Kraft, Michael E., *Environmental Policy and Politics*, 3rd ed., New York, New York: Pearson Education, Inc., 2004.

Peterson, Steven A. and Thomas H. Rausmussen. *State and Local Politics*. New York: McGraw-Hill, Inc., 1994.

Chapter Eighteen

FOREIGN POLICY

> To probe the foreign policies of nations is to inquire into extraordinarily broad and complex range of phenomena. Involved are nothing less than the internal life and external needs—the aspirations, attributes, culture, conflicts, capabilities, institutions, and routines—of large groups of people who have somehow managed to achieve and maintain a social, legal and geographic identity as a nation-state.   James N. Rosenau[1]

This chapter establishes theoretical concepts for the understanding of American foreign policy decision-making at the beginning of the twenty-first century. Many of these concepts are universal and relate to any one of the more than 190 countries in the community of nation-states. Recent significant events have had an impact on American foreign policy. It is important to both acknowledge and define these events as they relate to the conceptual framework.

September 11, 2001

On the morning of September 11, 2001, America experienced a national tragedy that became the symbol for the U.S. world-wide War on Terror. Nineteen members of Osama bin Laden's **Al Qaeda** terrorist network, led by Muhammed Atta, hijacked four American jetliners. Three of the four planes crashed into important symbols of American power and prestige: the two towers of the World Trade Center and the Pentagon, killing over 3,000 people. The fourth plane crashed in the western Pennsylvania countryside after passengers apparently thwarted the terrorists who were directing the plane to another target. These terrorists' attacks were of an unprecedented scale and audacity that revealed a massive, sophisticated plot and an operation of such proportions to be well beyond what most Americans could envision, apparently including our leaders and intelligence experts.

Immediately following the attack, U.S. decision makers began to fashion a response. On September 20, 2001, President Bush committed his administration and the nation to a complex and dangerous campaign of undefined scope and duration that would redefine post cold war foreign

Historians will certainly view the destruction of the World Trade Center in New York City, on September 11, 2001, as a turning point in American foreign, as well as domestic policy.©Danny C. Sze Photography

policy for years to come. In a televised speech before a joint session of Congress, President Bush presented his plan to the American people. America was waging a global war against terrorism. This "war on terrorism" would begin with Al Qaeda, but it would not end there. The Bush administration stated that it would "shut down" terrorist operations around the world. In the process, it would make no distinction between terrorists and the nations that harbor them. He stated, "From this day forward, any nation that continues to harbor or support terrorism will be regarded by the United States as a hostile regime."

In his speech, Bush made it clear that the United States would use all resources necessary to hunt down bin Laden and bring him to justice. That night, President Bush presented an ultimatum to the **Taliban** government in Afghanistan, the government the United States held responsible for shielding bin Laden, to either turn him over to the United States or it would share his fate. It refused, and military action was taken. Afghanistan was the first target in "the war against terrorism," commencing with Operation Enduring Freedom, which began October 7, 2001. The Taliban government fell quickly and was replaced by a regime friendly to the United States led by President Hamid Karzai. To date, Osama bin Laden's whereabouts are not known, but many of his followers have been killed or captured. However, as recently as February 2007, much concern has been raised over progress in stabilizing the Karzai regime in Afghanistan. Evidence continues to surface of a resurgence of the Taliban in Afghanistan and Pakistan. More U.S. troops have been deployed to the region and during 2006-2007 fighting has intensified. The September 11 attack continues to be the justification for U.S. military actions in the Middle East.

Terrorism

America's seeming naiveté about terrorism came to an abrupt halt on September 11, 2001. For most Americans, prior to that attack, terrorism was an abstract concept, something that happened to someone else, somewhere else. Although Americans had previously experienced acts of terrorism, including two in 1993, the bombing of the Federal Building in Oklahoma City and the previous less deadly attack on the World Trade Center. Timothy McVeigh, an American, was found guilty and executed for the former, and an Egyptian, Umar Abd al-Rahman, was convicted and is currently serving a life sentence in the latter. The general perception was that these were random acts committed by unstable individuals who were identified, caught, and brought to justice.

Terrorism, however, is a political act. It is normally defined as acts of violence that are perpetuated to specifically target noncombatants for the purpose of inducing widespread fear that will make governments change their policies. These acts of violence are usually committed in unconventional ways, and conventional rules of military engagement are not commonly used. The violent nature of the terrorist acts often obscures the terrorist's political agenda, and it is often difficult to distinguish dispassionately between the acts and their purposes. Ultimately, terrorism becomes the political tool of last resort to induce political change.

Although it makes little difference to its victims, terrorist acts can either represent a strategy for achieving political goals or as a tactic that is part of a broader strategy intended to reach particular ends.[2] Although this distinction may seem peripheral to the overall goal of understanding the dynamics of terror, it is not. The attack on New York City and Washington D. C. by Al Qaeda were part of a strategy designed to create terror in the hearts of Americans until the United States accepted their demands. In this sense, terror was in and of itself the broader plan. There are, however, many examples of the tactical use of terror by states, including the United States. The United States has often been charged with committing acts of terror tantamount to those used by professional terrorists, for example, the nuclear bombing in 1945 of civilian targets, namely, the cities of Nagasaki and Hiroshima in Japan. Hundreds of thousands of civilians were either killed or wounded in these attacks. When these cities were bombed, a legal state of war existed between the attacking state and those that were attacked. Therefore, the dropping of the bombs was seen as tactical, part of the broader strategy of the military defeat of Japan without having to mount an all out invasion force. Instilling terror in the civilian population was not in and of itself a goal.[3]

Reactionary Muslim terrorists of the Al Qaida organization, led by Osama bin Laden, crashed an American Airlines flight into the Pentagon with the resulting destruction seen here.

Since September 11, 2001, the United States has focused on small groups of terrorists that may or may not be supported by governmental money and military backing. Terrorism, however, is by no means the exclusive purview of shadowy private groups of individuals. States practice terrorism in tactical ways all the time, and it is considered an act of war or maintaining social order within a society. To name just a few in the twentieth century, the Ottoman Empire instituted systemic terror against Armenia in the years before World War I, Hitler instituted systematic terror on the Jews in Germany and Eastern Europe, the Khmer Rouge in Cambodia in the 1970's cleansed its own population in an attempt to rebuild society, and Saddam Hussein used chemical weapons to kill the inhabitants of Kurdish villages in 1987.

The sponsorship of terrorism, therefore, lies along a continuum of levels of involvement by the governments of countries. At one end of the continuum are instances of direct state sponsorship, where governments may use parts of their formal governmental apparatus. For example, in El Salvador the secret police were used to terrorize their own population. In other instances, the state may commission individuals or groups that are not otherwise connected to the state to carry out terrorist acts on their behalf. For example, the Libyan dictator Muammar Qaddafi during the 1970's and 1980's was accused of operations such as the bombing of an airliner over Lockerbie, Scotland.

The other extreme is the complete absence of governmental participation where terrorist groups act without the encouragement, assistance, or solace of any formal nation-state. Usually, such privately based movements are very small and isolated, and their scope is very limited, for example, Timothy McVeigh's bombing of the Oklahoma City Federal Building.

Between these two extremes is the third form of sponsorship—state sanctioned terrorism. This form is found most prominently in the Middle East, where terrorist organizations are not arms of any government taking direct orders on whom to attack, how or why, but these groups are shielded from outside interference and harassment by governments sympathetic to the terrorist's cause, such as the Taliban support of Al Qaeda in Afghanistan.[4]

It is apparent that in using this continuum that terrorism can mean almost any act of violence, and that a terrorist becomes increasingly difficult to distinguish. Often, the best that can be said is that terrorism is in the eye of the beholder. In the spirit of "one man's terrorist is another man's freedom fighter," Ronald Reagan, regarding the Contra fighters that were opposing the government in Nicaragua, once proclaimed: "I am a Contra." To the British government in 1776, the American revolutionaries were perceived as terrorists. It then becomes the purview of the foreign policy decision-makers to differentiate between what is terrorism and what is not.

Al Qaeda and Osama bin Laden

Al Qaeda, "The Core," is the first transnational terrorist group of the twenty-first century, confronting the world with a new kind of threat. It is a radical Islamic organization that forms a worldwide network of individual cells all professing a broad based ideology centered on returning Muslims to the true faith, which is based on the Koran and Hadith. This is a very reactionary ideology attempting to go back to the way things were in the seventh century during the time of Muhammed. Once accomplished, these countries would establish a Pan-Islamic union of states. Al Qaeda is the first of its kind in the Middle East, differing from previous terrorist organizations that tended to have nationalistic agendas that were geographically confined, such as the Egyptian Islamic Jihad.

Although Osama bin Laden is currently the Emir General of Al Qaeda, Abdullah Azzam originally founded the group in 1985 in Afghanistan. Azzam conceptualized the modern idea of jihad to stabilize and organize the diverse mujahidin forces to drive the Soviets out of Afghanistan. The successful formulation and articulation of this doctrine of jihad mobilized Afghans and Arab volunteers into a viable fighting force that was capable of taking on one of the superpowers and winning. The Soviets were forced out of Afghanistan in 1989. The United States, as part of its cold war foreign policy strategy, aided the mujahidin with money and arms to undermine the Soviets.

Azzam and bin Laden had a different perception of the goals of the Al Qaeda organization after the Soviets were expelled from Afghanistan. Azzam believed that Al Qaeda funds should only be used in Afghanistan, and he issued a decree, a fatwa, stating that using jihadist funds to train in terrorist tactics would violate Islamic law.[5] He believed that the organization should channel its energies into creating a large army of mujahidin capable of fighting on behalf of oppressed Muslims worldwide. Azzam believed that you built support for the organization through radical rhetoric rather than indiscriminate killing. Osama bin Laden, in contrast, wanted to establish terrorist camps throughout Afghanistan and create a worldwide network of cells that would eventually topple apostate, fake—not true to Islam, Muslim governments, such as the royal family in Saudi Arabia, who sided with the United States and Israel. It is believed that shortly after that decree, bin Laden had Azzam assassinated. With Assam's death the organization was freed from the constraints of Azzam's limited vision, and the Al Qaeda organization of today is really the creation of bin Laden.

When the Soviets withdrew from Afghanistan in 1989, bin Laden was one of the few surviving senior mujahidin who organized and supported the anti-Soviet campaign at a strategic level. Privately, bin Laden took credit for the expulsion of the Soviets from Afghanistan, and he firmly believed that it was the actions of the mujahidin, primarily supported by the Muslim world, that led to the collapse of the Soviet Union and the ending of the cold war. He also believed that the U.S. had achieved its goal of becoming the sole global superpower on the backs of the mujahidin and always considered the United States "ungrateful" because it took credit for the fall of communism and the end of the cold war.[6]

After the Soviets left Afghanistan, bin Laden returned to Saudi Arabia. About this time, on the pretext of supporting a group of Kuwaiti revolutionaries opposed to the ruling Sabah family, Iraq invaded Kuwait on August 2, 1990 and occupied its oil fields. As the Saudi royal family discussed inviting U.S. troops to repel the Iraqis and establish a presence in their country, bin Laden approached them with an alternative plan. He proposed to forge an anti-Saddam Hussein Arab coalition to defeat the Iraqis by enlisting 5,000 mujahidin veterans who were still in Afghanistan. His proposal was rejected, and the U.S. troops were invited to put troops on Islam's sacred ground. Bin Laden was humiliated both by the Saudi royal family and the United States.[7]

From that point on, bin Laden had four goals and has dedicated Al Qaeda to fulfilling them. First, remove the apostate government from Saudi Arabia and all other Islamic states, such as Egypt and Iraq. These governments are either secular governments or puppets of Israel and the United States. Their rulers must be overthrown. Second, remove the United States from the Islamic holy lands. Third, Israel must cease to exist. Fourth, establish a Pan-Islamic, not Pan-Arab, state in the Middle East capable of standing up to the West.

Until 2001, his organization had operated terrorist camps out of Afghanistan where they were shielded by the Taliban government. His organization is secret and elite and has cells all over the world. Although thousands of young men went to Afghanistan to train in the camps, approximately 3,000 were chosen to be Al Qaeda fighters. Al Qaeda's organization is both vertical and horizontal. The vertical organization consists of an Emir General, currently Osama bin Laden, a shura, consultative council, and four committees: military, finance, public relations and Islamic studies. Horizontally, the organization is constructed of individual cells whose members are unknown to each other.[8] These cells carry out operations independently or with the prior knowledge, financing and permission from the shura and Emir General. Although the idea for the attack on the United States originated in the Hamburg, Germany cell of Al Qaeda, it is believed that it was approved of and financed by the shura and Emir General.

War with Iraq

The War on Terror was the centerpiece for The Bush Doctrine. This doctrine established a strategy for pre-emptive action against hostile states and terrorist groups alleged to be developing weapons of mass destruction (WMD). It posited that the United States would never allow its military supremacy to be challenged in the way that it was during the cold war. As the only remaining superpower, the Bush Doctrine maintained that it will act unilaterally if it found that the United State's interests conflicted with internationalism, the United Nations, or treaty obligations and negotiations. Bush enacted his doctrine on a smaller scale when his administration ignored the Kyoto Protocol, withdrew from the ABM Treaty, and refused to the sign the Landmines Treaty. On March 19, 2003, Iraq felt the full force of the Bush Doctrine when the United States, as leader of the "coalition of the willing," spearheaded a pre-emptive attack against Iraq. The attack was predicated on the now known false assumption that Iraq possessed weapons of mass destruction. The goal was to facilitate a regime change in Iraq ousting Saddam Hussein from power and installing an interim government friendly to America. In the best of all possible worlds, the new government in Iraq would become a functioning democracy.

The Road to Baghdad and war with Iraq did not begin with September 11, but, rather, has been a long one with many twists and turns. Examining a chronology of those events will find that the Bush Doctrine and the Road to Baghdad began almost a decade before it was implemented. The strategy was devised by members of previous Replication administrations, most notably President Reagan and President George H. W. Bush (the first Bush administration). They defined themselves as neo-conservatives and their policy as the Project for the New American Century. The chairperson was William Kristol, editor of *The Weekly Standard*, and former chief-of-staff to Vice President Dan Quayle. Members of this group later controlled important foreign policy decision-making positions within the current George W. Bush administration, including Donald Rumsfeld, Secretary of Defense, Paul Wolfowitz, Deputy Secretary of Defense, and Richard Perle, chairman Defense Policy Board. As of Spring 2007, all of these individuals no longer hold positions in the administration, however, the combined influence they exerted over the previous decade in the area of foreign policy in the United States was significant. They were the main architects of the War in Iraq.

The Road to Baghdad

- **1991**

After Operation Desert Storm, President Bush encouraged Iraqis to rise up against Saddam Hussein, and if they did, the United States would help them. A rebellion soon occurred, but the Bush administration ordered U.S. troops not to intervene. At this juncture President Bush backed off of the concept of a regime change and opted for a strategy of containment, tough UN inspections, economic sanctions, and no-fly zones to protect the Kurds.

- **1992**

The failed uprising was a defining movement for men such as Wolfowitz. As under secretary of defense policy (the Pentagon's third-highest ranking civilian), he drafted an internal set of military guidelines called "Defense Planning Guidance." In his draft he argued for a new military and political strategy in a post cold war world. Containment was obsolete. America should speak loudly and carry a big stick. And, if America had to act alone, so be it.

- **1993-1998**

Between 1993 and 1998, Iraq continually pushed the envelope with UN weapons inspectors until finally in December 1998, the inspectors withdrew claiming that any more action on their part would prove useless. Iraq had failed to comply with UN directives to allow the inspectors to find and destroy any nuclear, chemical, or biological weapons.

- **1998**

In an open letter to President Clinton, the Project for New American Century argued for a much stronger U.S. global leadership exercised through "military strength and moral clarity." Included in the letter is support to remove Saddam Hussein from power in that they did not believe the policy of "containment" was effective. The letter urged Clinton in his State of the Union address to do the following:

> *enunciate a new strategy that would secure the interests of the U.S. and our friends and allies around the world. That strategy should aim, above all, at the removal of Saddam Hussein's regime from power. We stand ready to offer our full support in this difficult but necessary endeavor.*[1]

Among the signatories to this letter included Donald Rumsfeld, Paul Wolfowitz, Richard Perle, and William Kristol.

- **1999**

While the U.N. Security Council issued a resolution creating a new Iraqi disarmament commission, George W. Bush established an exploratory committee for a presidential campaign. As governor of Texas, he had little hands-on foreign policy experience and called on previous members of his father's and Reagan's administrations to advise him in this area, including Wolfowitz and Rumsfeld. He also enlisted the services of several pragmatic realists including Colin Powell and Condoleezza Rice. All will end up in the new Bush administration in positions to impact foreign policy. These two groups opposed each other in their approach to the new world order proposed by the Bush Doctrine. Eventually Wolfowitz and Rumsfeld won the debate.

- **September 11, 2001**

- **September 20, 2001**

Bush included a tough new passage about punishing those who harbored terrorists in his speech to the nation. To those in his inner circle, including Rumsfeld and Wolfowitz, the president's words set the tone and the direction for the Bush administration's policy on Afghanistan and Iraq. Two days later, Wolfowitz expanded on the president's words. He seemed to signal that the U.S. will enlarge its campaign against terror to include Iraq. He states before a Pentagon briefing,

> *I think one has to say it's not just simply a matter of capturing people . . . but removing the sanctuaries, removing the support systems . . . ending states who sponsor terrorism . . . And that's why it has to be a broad and sustained campaign.*[2]

Colin Powell and others were alarmed by what they viewed as Wolfowitz's inflammatory words about "ending states." The rift in the administration was clearly visible.

- **January 29, 2002**

In his State of the Union speech, President Bush listed Iraq, Iran and North Korea and stated, "States like these and their terrorist allies constitute an axis of evil, arming to threaten the peace of the world." This was a clear signal of policy. He had divided the world into good and evil and made a case for not just eliminating the terrorists but those states the administration considered evil.

- **June 2002**

In a graduation speech at West Point, Bush cited the realities of a new post cold war era and outlined a major shift in national security tactics. The containment tactics of his father's administration were outdated for the twenty-first century. The new Bush administration's foreign policy would move from containment to pre-emptive action. He stated "Our security will require all Americans to be forward-looking and resolute, to be ready for preemptive action when necessary to defend our liberty and to defend our lives."[3] During his speech, President Bush also called for an American hegemony,

> *America has and intends to keep, military strengths beyond challenge.*

These two policies, American hegemony and pre-emptive action were policies that Wolfowitz promoted in 1992 and the Project for the New American Century proposed to Clinton in 1998. It appeared only a matter of time before the United States was on the Road to Baghdad.[4]

- **October 11-12, 2002**

Over the wishes of men such as Cheney, Rumsfeld and Wolfowitz, Bush now turned to a domestic audience for approval of his new policy. Powell had convinced him that it was prudent to seek not only congressional support for any action with Iraq but also the international community. On October 11-12, Bush cleared the congressional hurdle securing a joint resolution to use force against Iraq. The House vote was 296-133; the Senate was 77-23.

> *The President is authorized to use the Armed Forces of the United States as he determines to be necessary and appropriate in order to . . . Defend the national security of the United States against the continuing Threat posed by Iraq . . . enforce all relevant United Nations Security Council Resolutions regarding Iraq.*[5]

- **November 8, 2002**

Heeding Powell's advice, Bush took his case to the international community; his political vehicle was the Security Council of the United Nations. On November 8, 2002, the Security Council unanimously passed Resolution 1441, which threatened Iraqi President Saddam Hussein with "serious consequences" if he did not disarm. However, it also required U.N. inspectors to return to Iraq and see whether Hussein had disarmed. By the end of November, experts began work in Iraq under the auspices of the November 8 resolution.[6]

- **December-March 7, 2003**

Saddam Hussein contended that he had, in fact, disarmed. To show good faith, he opened Iraq to U.N. inspectors. The Bush administration contended that Hussein was lying and was simply creating a "willful charade" to trick the U.N. and the world. This debate continued for several months as the arms inspectors continued to give increasingly positive reports regarding their findings within Iraq.

It became increasingly evident that the Bush administration was not satisfied with any reports from the inspector and that nothing less than a regime change was acceptable to the United States. Serious opposition mounted within the Security Council with regards to the use of force. In a news conference on March 6, 2003, Bush made it clear that the United States would disarm Iraq even if the U.N. Security Council voted against a resolution authorizing force. Bush said he would seek a council vote to put countries on record to "let the world know where they stand" on Saddam.

On March 7, the Security Council heard a report from Hans Blix that Iraq was improving its cooperation and that disarmament could be done in months. France threatened to veto any U.N. resolution authorizing force. In spite of the inspector's reports and France's threat to veto,

President Bush gave Hussein an ultimatum to give up banned weapons by March 17 or face military action.

- **March 17, 2003**

The United States knew it did not have the nine votes in the Security Council to authorize force against Iraq. Bush withdrew the proposed resolution and announced that time had run out for diplomacy.

- **March 19, 2003**

The War with Iraq commenced.

- **April 2005**

Cost of war to reach $207 billion at the end of FY 2005. Over 150,000 U.S. and coalition troops remain in Iraq and Afghanistan indefinitely.

According to the Pentagon, 1,546 U.S. military have died; over 13,000 wounded.

Iraqi casualty numbers are not kept by the U.S. governmental sources. Such information is gathered by foreign sources and human rights organizations. As such, the numbers differ significantly depending on what source is quoted. There is an Iraqi death toll range from 12,000-20,000; 20,000-35,000 wounded.

Elections were held in Iraq in January 2005. A 275-member Transitional National Assembly was elected. Its main task is to draft Iraq's new constitution, which will be presented to the Iraqi people in October 2005. Under the new constitution, Iraq is scheduled to elect a permanent government in December 2005. Despite elections, insurgency continues unabated, and there is a daily death count in Iraq of U.S. soldiers, Iraqi combatants and civilians.

Prime Minister Ibrahim al-Jaafari is in the process of naming ministers to his Cabinet. Currently Jaafari failed to appoint permanent ministers to the important posts of oil, defense, industry and human rights. Disputes over how to distribute power among various ethnic and religious groups has accounted for this delay. As delays continue, tensions mount.

Bush administration admits that Saddam Hussein did not have weapons of mass destruction (WMD) prior to invasion and occupation of U.S. troops.

Oil prices reached historic high of $58/barrel. Gasoline prices rise significantly in the United States.

A 2005 *ABC News/Washington Post* poll finds that since the start of the war President Bush's wartime job approval ratings has dropped 27 percent. Immediately following the end of the main fighting it was 77 percent; currently it is 50 percent. His approval specifically on Iraq in 2003 was 75 percent; currently it is 39 percent, a career low.

- **October 2005**

Special Iraqi Tribunal begins trial against Saddam Hussein for his crimes against humanity and genocide, specifically for the mass killings of 148 Iraqi Shiite following a failed assassination attempt against him.

- **March 2006**

Estimates of the cost of the war cause debate both in and out of Congress. The cost of the war is going to be much more than estimated. The war costs approximately $200 million dollars a day. Costs could go well over $1 trillion dollars.

- **March 15, 2006**

The United States Institute for Peace (USIP) launched the Iraq Study Group. It was a bi partisan study group co-chaired by James A. Baker, III and Lee Hamilton. Its mandate was to conduct a forward-looking, independent assessment of the current and prospective situations on the group in Iraq, its impact on the surrounding regions and consequences for U.S. interests. Three organizations supported USIP in facilitating this study: the Center for Strategic and International Studies (CSIS), The Center for the Study of the Presidency (CSP) and the James A. Baker III Institute for Public Policy at Rice University.

- **March 19, 2006**

On the eve of the third anniversary of the Iraq invasion, President Bush yesterday promised to "finish the mission" with "complete victory," urging the American public to remain steadfast but offering no indication when victory may be achieved.

- **April 14, 2006**

Six retired generals call for the resignation of Defense Secretary Donald Rumsfeld. President Bush continues to express support for his Secretary of Defense.

- **April 19, 2006**

Oil prices soar to $72/barrel.

- **June 15, 2006**

American deaths since the invasion of Iraq reached 2,500.

- **November 5, 2006**

An Iraqi court sentences Saddam Hussein to death for his crimes against humanity.

- **November 7, 2006**

In what was widely viewed as a repudiation of Bush's Iraq policies, the war in Iraq being the number one campaign issue, Republicans lose control of both House and Senate.

- **November 8, 2006**

Secretary of State Donald Rumsfeld resigns and President Bush nominates former CIA Director Robert Gates to fill the position.

- **December 6, 2006**

Iraq Study Group issues its final report. Among its recommendations were the following:
1) A planned gradual withdrawal of U.S. combat troopers with a goal of bringing the bulk of American troops home by early 2008
2) Launch a diplomatic offensive to quickly engage Syria, Iran and the leaders of insurgents in negotiations on Iraq's future.
3) Work toward resolving the long-standing Arab-Israeli conflict to ease hostility through the Middle East.
4) The U.S. should provide $5 billion a year in economic aid and work faster to implement assistance programs, giving U.S. officials more flexibility to quickly fund or eliminate programs. It encouraged greater international investment in Iraq's oil industry, its management and its security.

- **December 30, 2006**

Saddam Hussein is executed.

- **December 31, 2006**

U.S. military deaths since the start of the war reach 3,000.

- **January 10, 2007**

President Bush ignored the recommendations of the Iraq Study Group and unveiled his new retooled war strategy in a prime-time address from the White House. His new plan, "The Surge," would send over 20,000 more American troops to Iraq.

- **April 2007**

House of Representative and Senate pass supplemental war spending bills authorizing over $100 billion new expenditures for war in Iraq. However, attached to bills are timetables requiring specific troop withdrawals from Iraq. The House and Senate bills are currently in different forms and must go to Conference Committee to reconcile differences. President Bush has threatened to veto any bill that ties his hands as Commander in Chief of the Armed Forces and calls for specific troop withdrawals.

Speaker of the House Nancy Pelosi traveled to Syria to meet with Syrian President Bashar Al Assad claiming, "the road to Damascus is a road to peace." Speaker Pelosi was highly criticized by the White House for her trip claiming that Syria supports the Hamas and Hezbollah, two groups on the U.S. terrorist list. Pelosi is the highest-ranking official to visit Syria since Secretary of State Colin Powell in 2003.

U.S. death toll in Iraq 3294 killed, over 26,000 wounded.

Iraqi civilian death count is uncertain but external agencies such as Amnesty International estimate it to be between 60,000 and 100,000.

Sources:

1. The War Behind Closed Doors: Chronology: The Evolution of the Bush Doctrine, 1-7, www.pbs.org/wgbh/pages/frontline/shows/iraq/etc/cron.html.
2. "Chronology to war in Iraq," Associated Press, the.honoluluadvertiser.com/article/223/Mar/20/In/In29a.html.
3. Information for Iraq War updates taken from several sources to include ABC News, Pentagon news briefs, White House press releases, BBC, Amnesty International and Human Rights Watch, *Washington Post,* The Law Library of Congress, The Iraq Study Group, The United States Institute for Peace, *New York Times*.

Footnotes:

[1] Project for the New American Century, January 26, 1998, www.newamericancentury.org.
[2] The War Behind Closed Door, Chronology: The Evolution of the Bush Doctrine, p7, www.pbs.org/wgbh/pages/frontline/shows/iraq/etc/cron.html.
[3] President Bush Delivers Graduation Speech at United States Military Academy, press release, www.whitehouse.gove/newsreleases.
[4] Ibid.
[5] "Text of resolution authorizing U.S. use of Force," *USA Today*, October 11, 2002, 11A.
[6] "Security Council Tightens Iraqi Disarmament Regime," U.N. Security Council Resolution 1441, usinfo.state.gov/topical/pol/terror/0211803.htm

NATIONAL INTERESTS

In 1648, the Treaty of Westphalia established the current international order. The foundation for today's system is the independent country and/or nation-state. Since scholars disagree as to the correct terminology, country and **nation-state** will be used interchangeably in this chapter. Each state is a sovereign entity, an independent political unit, vested with a legal status and equity with all other states. Sovereign states are responsible for their own decision-making and are not required to answer to a higher authority. Consequently, state sovereignty created a world order based on a decentralized system of individual nation-states each pursuing their own national interests. Foreign policy is the process of pursuing these interests within the international community. It ultimately functions as a link between the internal activities of a nation-state and the world outside it.[9]

National interests are the sum total of a state's goals and objectives, and they represent the decision-makers' ordering of a country's priorities. In reality, national interests are essentially whatever decision-makers deem them to be. Its definition is inherently broad allowing policy-makers great latitude in determining exactly what constitutes "national interests" and what actions will be taken to achieve them. According to Walter Lippmann,

National interest has been identified with every conceivable thing that people are interested in. Once the national interest in Europe was that the Catholic religion should be spread. Then it was the Protestant religion. And then it was that the woolen traders should have a good market and then it was that nations should get gold to inflate their currencies. National interests can mean any one of these things.[10]

Lippmann's quote suggests that the leaders of a state pursue a wide variety of private and public objectives, some concrete, some abstract, and very often in conflict.[11] His quote indicates that these interests are pursued within a framework of contextual awareness that indicate change over time, place, and culture. Interests are defined and redefined to reflect the internal political culture of a state as well as the prevailing international social, political, and economic circumstances.

National interests are divided into two categories: vital and secondary. **Vital interests** are of the utmost importance and are defined as objectives for which countries will go to war. A state usually defines these interests as securing existing territorial borders and/or the maintenance and protection of its international credibility and prestige. The Bush administration defined U.S. vital interests as a preemptive strike against Iraq to force a regime change. President Bush coupled Hussein's defiance of U.N. resolutions and the possibility that Iraq might possess weapons of mass destruction to the security of U.S. territorial borders. **Secondary interests** are everything else and the "stuff" of which diplomatic negotiations and compromise are made. This includes the myriad of issues debated by the international community including such concerns as fishing rights in international waters, trade agreements such as the North American Free Trade Agreement (NAFTA), and environmental issues, for example, correct disposal of biological and chemical weapons and maintenance of the rainforests.

The pursuit of a state's vital national interests inevitably places individual nation-states on a natural collision course with each other, which if unchecked has a great possibility of resulting in conflict. Consequently, foreign policy is largely a country's ability to pursue their interests while effectively engaging in conflict management. Successful conflict management would mean peaceful coexistence and cooperation. This would require states to formulate mutually compatible foreign policies that depend on defining mutually compatible vital interests. For example, although the U.S. and U.S.S.R. were adversaries during the cold war, they defined a mutually compatible vital interest as the avoidance of nuclear war and mutual destruction.

Security

Security is the sum total of a state's vital interests, and it is the centerpiece of a country's foreign policy. It is a relative condition that can never be completely realized because it can only be attained within the context of another state's vital interests. These interests often conflict and, when they do, they create a **security dilemma**. For example, arms acquired by State A for defensive or security purposes may be perceived by State B as offensive and therefore a threat to its vital interests. In response, State B bolsters its own defenses and builds up its military arsenal. State A perceives State B's buildup as offensive rather than defensive. The quest for security on the part of both State A and B has created an arms race resulting in a proliferation of weapons. Tensions mount, and the possibility for conflict increases. In this instance, the quest for security actually resulted in more insecurity that exacerbated the cycle of arms proliferation. This, in turn, increased the need for greater security, resulting in an increased arms buildup. The pursuit of security often has produced the opposite effect: insecurity.

The nuclear arms race during the cold war is the ultimate example of a security dilemma or "security" gone awry. The **cold war** was a conflict between the United States and the Soviet Union following W.W. II that lasted until the Soviet Union collapsed in 1991. Each country sought to establish international **hegemony**, the ability to dominate the international order politically, socially, and economically. To this end, however, the combatants in this conflict did not actually fight each other with bullets but rather engaged in political strategies and manipulations that would affect practically every country in the world.[12]

During the cold war, the U.S. and U.S.S.R. engaged in a foreign policy of **mutual assured destruction**, or **MAD**, that created a balance of terror. The philosophy behind the "balance of terror" was that the idea of a nuclear exchange was so horrible that it encouraged stability and the avoidance of war. In the process of maintaining the "balance of terror," each state manufactured thousands of nuclear warheads, weapons of mass destruction, capable of causing nuclear holocaust and the destruction of the planet. In the early 1980s, the United States possessed over 9,000 nuclear warheads in its strategic arsenal. This translates into approximately 50,000 megatons of nuclear power that is equivalent to about fifteen tons of dynamite for every person on earth. The Soviet Union had 7,000.[13] In the late 1980s the United States and the former Soviet Union each deployed about 11,000 strategic warheads. The ultimate result of this policy was that neither nation felt more secure.[14]

The end of the cold war led to the concept of mutual security and the end of defining national interests solely in mutually exclusive terms. Instead, nation-states began to define their vital interests in terms of mutually compatible security needs. There were two main reasons for this. First, globalization and the proliferation of technology led to the concept of interdependence, requiring nations to redefine their national interests in more global terms. Second, the cold war and the "balance of terror" not only exacerbated the breakup of the Soviet Union but bankrupted the two superpowers in the process. Neither of the major powers or other individual nations were capable of singularly assuring their own security. For example, because of its reliance on foreign oil imports, U.S. security is intricately tied to the vital interests and security of the Middle East. This was evident in 1991 when Iraq invaded Kuwait. The United States engaged in military maneuvers, the Gulf War, to re-establish what it considered the security of the region. However, the United States did not attempt to resolve the security problems of the Middle East in a unilateral fashion. It could neither financially or politically sustain such an action. Consequently, the U.S. defined the Iraqi invasion of Kuwait as a global security issue and stated that a joint effort by the "community of nations" was required to resolve the problem. The United States relied on the financial and political backing of other nation-states, such as Japan, that also defined their vital interests in terms of security in the Middle East.

A decade later, as we have seen by the United States' willingness to go to war with Iraq, that it clearly defines its vital interests in terms of the security of the Middle East. However, unlike his father, the new Bush administration was not successful in convincing the world community that Saddam Hussein was a global security issue. Countries that had clearly defined their security and vital national interests with those of the United States no longer did so. Consequently, in 2003, the

United States decided to take unilateral action to secure its interests in the region defying many of its allies and the consensus of the international community. Unlike the Gulf War, the United States had to sustain virtually the entire cost of the current war with Iraq, both financially and politically. Although the United States forged a "coalition of the willing," to back its efforts, most of its forty countries, such as Bulgaria and Cameroon, were either unable or unwilling to send troops or money to sustain the military campaign. Great Britain, America's staunchest ally in the Iraqi war, supplied a significant amount of troops and money. However, by the Spring of 2007, the "coalition of the willing" had begun to dissolve and even Great Britain had established a timetable to withdraw its troops from Iraq. It is clear that in the new millennium the United States is willing to define its interests unilaterally even if they appear to diverge from the world community in matters of mutual security.

Security has many components and at the end of the cold war, the world community redefined its mutual security interests in terms other than military, for example, issues of global warming and disease control. Much like his decision to act unilaterally in the Middle East, the Bush administration has tended to do so in these matters as well. For example, the Kyoto Protocol, negotiated under his father's administration and signed in 1998 by President Clinton, was ignored by the present administration. The Protocol, signed by eight-four other countries, was designed to reduce greenhouse gas emissions by 7 percent to reduce global warming. The Bush administration stated that Kyoto Protocol conflicted with the United States' national interests of boosting domestic energy production and stimulating the economy.

It is too soon to tell whether the Bush administration will change its position on the Kyoto Treaty. Until recently the Bush administration refused to acknowledge the human component in global warming. Without this recognition, the Bush administration has seen no reason to solve a natural global climate change with a human solution. However, there has been an ever increasing popular acceptance of scientific data that acknowledges the human element of global warming. This has been championed and popularized by former Vice President Al Gore. His recent movie, *An Inconvenient Truth,* on the subject of global warming, won an Oscar for the Best Documentary in 2006. He has also been nominated for a Nobel Peace Prize for his work on environmental issues and recently returned after six years to testify before Congress outlining the problems of global warming and what humans must do in order to contain the problem. It has been difficult in light of Al Gore's spotlight on the issue for the Bush administration to continue to deny the impact of the human component of global warming. The question still remains whether President Bush will take action to honor our commitment to the Kyoto Treaty before he leaves office.

Diseases, such as AIDS, know no national borders but seriously threaten the security of nation-states. Currently at least 1 out of 4 individuals in sub-Sahara Africa is infected with HIV, and everyday 5,500 people in this region die from AIDS-related complications. Currently UNAID, a joint UN and World Bank organization, estimates that there are 42 million people infected with HIV worldwide, and by 2010, 60 million individuals will have contracted the disease. However, a new intelligence report revised that estimate upwards citing the fact that the HIV virus has spread more quickly than expected in countries such as India, China and Russia. The report of the National Intelligence Council predicts that by 2010, there could be anywhere between 75 million and 100 cases of HIV worldwide.[15]

The Clinton administration attempted to pursue a policy to limit the spread of this disease. Former Secretary of State Warren Christopher, Secretary of State during the first Clinton administration, observed during his Senate confirmation hearings that "we face a world where borders matter less, . . . a world that demands we join other nations to face challenges that range from overpopulation to AIDS, to the very destruction of our planet's life support system."[16] Perhaps international pressure on the pharmaceutical companies to sell AIDS drugs to Africa at a medical rate will facilitate mutual security interests for the world community. In May 2001, the United Nations established a global fund to fight the AIDS epidemic in Africa. President Bush committed 200 million dollars as seed money for this fund. The African states believed that the Bush administration's seed money was merely symbolic. Shortly after Bush took office, a high administration official questioned the wisdom of trying to save the lives of Africans who had contracted HIV. Officials said then that money should be spend on preventing the spread of the disease in Africa but would it would be wasted on expensive anti-AIDS drugs because African health systems were not equipped to dispense the medicine properly. However, in an abrupt change of policy, Bush surprised even many of his Republican colleagues when in his 2003 State of the Union Address called on Congress to spend 15 billion over the next five years to help countries in Africa and the Caribbean fight the pandemic. In his speech, the president proposed supplying drugs to 2 million HIV infected people and caring for 10 million others. A senior administration official said that this pledge "far outstrips anything that has been done in the past by any government in AIDS treatment."[17] Although the Bush administration claims that it will honor its original commitment, to date funds have been authorized but not appropriated. The current budget crisis has put this item on the backburner.

Models for Decision-Making

Rosenau's quote at the beginning of this chapter describes the complexity of foreign policy-making. It is so complex that it is often difficult to discern the reason or motivation for any particular foreign policy decision. Individual decisions are often difficult to analyze because the individual components of foreign policy are interrelated and often hard to isolate and distinguish. Consequently, political scientists have spent much time and effort developing increasingly more sophisticated means by which to examine foreign policy. This has enabled policy analysts greater insight into the decision-making process.[18]

This approach goes beyond the traditional historical outlook that tends to focus on individual circumstances rather than patterned tendencies in decision-making. Although it is useful to be familiar with the facts of world politics—who did what to whom and when—it is equally, if not more significant, to analyze the facts and discern if there are patterns of recurring elements in the decision-making process. For example, it is of less interest to know the steps whereby a country acquired nuclear weapons than to understand why it did. In examining the cold war, it is more significant to ask, "Why did the United States and Soviet Union engage in a "balance of terror?" Was the "balance of terror" predictable, and, if so, what common elements lend itself to this conclusion? Using this approach, it is possible to predict future behavior of individual nation-states as well as how other nations might react to their policies.[19]

Many political scientists, most notably Charles Kegley and Eugene Wittkopf, use a funnel of causality to examine the foreign policy process of any nation-state, including that of the United States. The funnel illustrates that the output or public policy is a dependent variable. It is dependent on the input. The sources of inputs are independent variables that may either influence or constrain a decision-maker in the policy process. The inputs are divided into two major categories: external, international or foreign, and internal, or domestic.

The second category of inputs is internal and influence or constrain a decision-maker from within his/her nation-state. This category is subdivided into four major areas: society, government, role, and individual. The governmental level of analysis examines the structure of governmental institutions and their affect on a decision-maker's ability to make public policy. For example, a dictator would be less constrained by governmental institutions than would a president in a constitutional democracy. The societal level examines the cultural norms that exist within a society that may or may not constrain a decision-maker. These norms are wide in scope and may range from evaluating the impact of religion on foreign policy decisions to the role the media plays in a society.

Role theory posits that the positions and the processes, rather than the characteristics of the people who decide, influence the behavior and choices of those responsible for making foreign policy. Each role or position carries with it social and psychological demands and expectations that shape perceptions of how it should be performed.[20] Therefore, the role or position of president carries with it certain expectations that constrains the president's decision-making. The individual level of decision examines the leaders themselves and discusses the particular personality characteristics and ideology that they bring to the policy process. How do their personal aspirations, anxieties, convictions, memories, and experiences influence foreign policy?[21] What does George W. Bush, the individual, bring to decision-making?

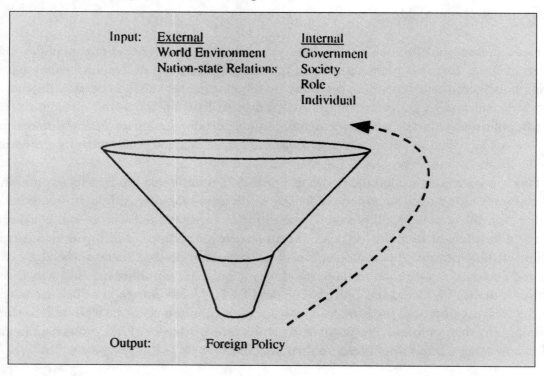

Patterns of Behavior

Over time, it appears that U.S. policy-makers have identified national interests in very different ways to reflect changing internal and external circumstances. However, upon closer scrutiny, it becomes clear that this has not been the case. Instead, American leadership has been relatively consistent in defining U.S. national interests and has exhibited remarkably patterned behavior in developing foreign policy objectives including the current Bush Doctrine. Consequently, although the world has changed dramatically since the Constitution was ratified in 1789, the basic tenets of American foreign policy have not. Apparent changes in U.S. foreign policy have resulted from the need to alter the tactics required to secure the objectives of U.S. national interests rather than any significant alteration in the national interests themselves. Tactics have changed but the fundamental premises on which they are built have not. Therefore, it is useful in studying American foreign policy to think in terms of persistent goals and somewhat more variable tactics.[22]

The patterns of foreign policy-making are often obscured by the day-to day variations in the tactical application of long range policies and the persistent media coverage of current events. Current event coverage of foreign policy often tends to emphasize the individual administration's decisions without placing them in an historical context. The decision-makers themselves tend to present their own policies as unique to favorably position themselves for the sake of elections as well as for the history books. The presentation of individual tactical developments in the foreign policy area often gives the illusion that there have been significant changes in foreign policy when, in fact, the decision-makers are often merely reinventing the wheel.

Consistent policies

Three underlying themes have consistently underpinned U.S. foreign policy: U.S. ideological superiority, its desire to shape world events through its promotion as a world power, and its quest for stability and security through the maintenance of the status quo. First, U.S. decision-makers have based their policies on their own **ethnocentric** construct of the world political environment. U.S. policy-makers have always perceived that the country held a special place in the world political arena both politically and ideologically. Decision-makers consistently and self-righteously proclaimed that the U.S. possessed an innate virtue and innocence and based its policies on the premise that the nation had a special mission in the world. American decision-makers appear to share a belief that the American ideals and ideas can and should solve all the problems of the world and that it is their mission to apply these ideals abroad. This view was made very clear when Secretary of State Donald Rumsfeld, in an October 2001, *New York Times* interview stated that the tragedy of 9/11 has given the United States "the opportunity to refashion the world." In the view of Kegley and Wittkopf, this ethnocentric view "is just a short step from messianic crusading."[23]

Second, the U.S. has exhibited a desire to shape world events. However, within this broad construct, American policy-makers have historically vacillated between **isolationism**, withdrawing from the world, and **internationalism**, the ability and need to reform it. This has resulted in rhythmic cycles of introversion and extroversion that take approximately twenty-five to thirty years to run their course.[24] What is noteworthy is that even periods of isolationism were driven by

American ideological superiority. This was particularly acute during the isolationist or introversion movement of the 1920s and 1930s. According to historian Louis Hartz, an absolute national morality "is inspired either to withdraw from 'alien' things or to transform them; it cannot live in comfort constantly by their side."[25] Consequently idealism in the form of ideological superiority has contributed to the cyclical swings between introversion and extroversion evident in America's diplomatic history.

Today, it appears the pendulum of U.S. foreign policy has clearly swung to the side of internationalism and extroversion in its pursuit of ideological superiority. The global war on terror combined with the Bush Doctrine's policy that justifies unilateral pre-emptive self defense measures clearly places ideological concerns above pragmatic political solutions. This was very clear in the way that the Bush administration rejected the proposals put forth by the bi-partisan Baker-Hamilton Commission, aka the Iraq Study Group, in December 2006. This group was coordinated by the United States Institute for Peace after the increase in sectarian violence in Iraq in March 2006. The Iraq Study Group challenged major principles of the handling of the war in Iraq stating that "current U.S. foreign policy was not working." The study concluded that a new approach was needed and urged the Bush administration to launch a diplomatic offensive in the Middle East that would include Syria and Iran in the negotiations over Iraq's future. Syria and Iran had been previously isolated as "terrorist states" by the Bush administration. Although President Bush claimed to consider the findings of the group, his actions did not support his rhetoric. Instead of changing policy in Iraq as indicated by the Iraq Study Group, President Bush "stayed the course" and increased troop deployment in early 2007 to Iraq in what he called "The Surge." The underlying ideological superiority of the current policies has stalled pragmatic political solutions.

Third, the world's leading revolutionary nation in the eighteenth century became the leading protector of the **status quo** in the twentieth century. After its own revolution, the United States consistently feared and fought change because it had become a status quo power. It wanted to maintain stability to foster its existing position in the world. Consequently, the United States opposed movements and revolutions that fostered the concepts of democracy and prosperity, particularly if the revolutions were not ideologically compatible with the U.S. vision of the world. Nowhere is this more evident than in U.S. foreign policy towards Central America. No region in the world is more tightly integrated into the United States economic and security system than Central America. Virtually every country in Central America experienced revolutions including Nicaragua, El Salvador, and Guatemala. In all cases, the United States opposed the revolutions and opted to support the existing regimes to maintain the status quo even when these regimes were blatantly authoritarian and engaged in human rights violations. The official reason for supporting oppressive regimes, particularly in Central America, was that the internal revolutionary movements were not really "democratic" in nature. During the cold war, revolutions were easy to oppose once they were described as "communist" in nature. Although U.S. response to nationalist revolutionary movements was always one of moral outrage, its foreign policy was predicated on maintaining its economic and political superiority in a region. The United States was clearly defining what was democratic and what was not. It defined in terms of its own moral superiority and ethnocentric construct. Economic and political interests are often obscured by the rhetoric of moral superiority. Revolutionary instability would threaten U.S. economic and political interests and consequently the "vital" interests of the United States.[26]

Patterned "National Interests"

These three themes or constructs have significantly affected the way in which U.S. decision-makers define national interest. Over time they have used these interests as a basis for decision-making that has established a recognizable pattern of "national interests." Early U.S. policy-makers defined national interest as **manifest destiny**, the belief that it was the destiny of the United States to spread across the continent. This resulted in foreign policy decisions such as the Louisiana Purchase of 1803 and the Indian removal policies of the Jackson administration, both of which demonstrated the ideological superiority or "moral destiny" of the United States. Twentieth century decision-makers expanded the definition of manifest destiny to include the moral imperative of halting the worldwide spread of communism. This new definition of national interests resulted in such foreign policy as the military actions in Korea and Vietnam during the cold war.

Since W.W.II, the United States has clearly developed internationalist policies designed to perpetuate its ideological superiority. After W.W.II, the United States emerged as a superpower. The U.S. assumed a role of global responsibility, executing it with an almost missionary zeal. From the end of W.W.II until the collapse of the Soviet Union in 1991, U.S. vital interests were defined in terms of the containment of communism. Since W.W.II, for the better part of forty years, the U.S. perceived communism as a monolithic ideological system diametrically opposed to the U.S. belief system. U.S. decision-makers believed the communist ideology dictated world domination and must be eliminated. The construct of U.S. ideological superiority vìs a vìs the Russians shaped U.S. foreign policy for over fifty years.

The disintegration of the Soviet Union signaled the end of the cold war. U.S. decision-makers were forced to refocus their attention in the area of foreign policy. They did this without fundamentally altering its patterned behavior. Although the world political environment had been significantly altered, U.S. decision-makers remained relatively constant in preserving their ethnocentric construct within which they defined their vital interests. U.S. decision-makers continued to define their foreign policy objectives in terms of ideological superiority. For example, at the end of the Gulf War with Iraq in 1991, President George Bush proclaimed that there was a new world order and the United States would be the leader of this new world order.

> But in the wake of the cold war, in a world where we are the only remaining superpower, it is the role of the United States to marshal its moral and material resources to promote a democratic peace. It is our responsibility —it is our opportunity to lead.[27]

President Bush's speeches after September 11, 2001, clearly divided the world into two camps, good and evil. These two camps seem to have replaced the capitalist and communist spheres of the cold war. The "coalition of the willing" implies that any country willing to fight with the U.S. against evil could share the moral high ground. The group responsible for the Project for the New American Century, many of whom were significant policy-makers within the Bush administration, defined the organization as follows:

> it is a non profit educational organization dedicated to the proposition that American leadership is good both for America and for the world.[28]

U. S. foreign policy based on moral and ideological superiority has often been used to disguise its economic policies. Often these policies are one in the same. These policies have a long history and extend to multiple regions of the world. Walter LaFeber, in his book, *Inevitable Revolutions,* clearly outlines U. S. foreign policy in Central America. He contends that U. S. foreign policy was not accidental in this region of the world but rather well-considered and designed to foster its economic interests. LaFeber demonstrates that U. S. policies developed slowly between the 1820s and 1880s, reaching its maturity rapidly during the 1940s and 1950s.[29] At the core of these policies in Central America was U.S. ideological superiority based on an undaunted belief in the continuation of capitalism as both an economic and political system. The U. S. demonstrated its unwavering willingness to achieve these policy objectives by using both overt and covert military maneuvers in such places as Honduras, El Salvador, and Nicaragua.

Although LaFeber focuses only on U. S. foreign policy in Central America, it is clear that subsequent decision-makers not only continued to use this construct after the 1950s in this region but did not hesitate to extend its use to other parts of the world. President George H. Bush demonstrated his commitment to securing U. S. economic interests disguised in terms of moral superiority when he used force in both Panama and Iraq. In Panama, Bush secured U. S. trading and economic interests in the Panama Canal and in Iraq, cheap oil. Both the invasion of Panama in December of 1989 and the Gulf War in 1991 were justified not in economic terms but rather in moral ones. Couching U. S. economic interests in moral rhetoric enables U. S. policy-makers to kill two birds with one stone. It allowed them to secure U. S. capitalist interests while placating the American public that all is being done with the best of intentions.

President Clinton was not as militarily aggressive in his pursuit of protecting U.S. economic interests; however, he validated LaFeber's basic assumptions when he declared in a speech before the United Nations in September 1993, "our overriding purpose must be to expand and strengthen the world's community of market-based democracies." In pursuit of this policy, the Clinton administration had been willing to ignore human rights violations of other countries in order to secure their markets, for example, China. The United States is extremely interested in capturing Chinese markets and consequently has been willing to overlook its record on human rights since the student uprising at Tiananmen Square in 1989 to its present treatment of Tibet.

And today what are the economic interests of the United States in Iraq? It is difficult to separate the invasion of Iraq with U.S. oil interests. Saddam Hussein was sitting on the second largest oil reserve in the world. Of all the reasons the administration offered for removing Saddam, from terrorism to weapons of mass destruction, it seldom publicly mentioned oil. Yet critical to the American economic agenda is the fear that an Iraq armed with nuclear weapons could dominate or hold hostage a region through which flows an estimated 30 percent of the world's oil and natural gas. The fundamental issue was that the day after Saddam Hussein was removed from power, the Iraqi oil industry was up for grabs, and it will depend upon the government of Iraq to decide how it will dispense that resource. Right now, the new government of Iraq is sustained by the occupation forces of the United States. Certainly, after democracy is secured, American oil companies will be in a very strong position to control the Iraqi oil fields.[30] The rhetoric and tactics may have changed from the early 1800s but U.S. strategic "national interests" have not. The old world order of manifest destiny and the new world order appear remarkably similar.

EXTERNAL INFLUENCES

World Structure

The structure of the world system and the political position the United States has assumed within it is a major determinant in its foreign policy decision-making. The international system reflects the power relationships that exists between the nation-states. Since America's inception, external power relationships can be historically categorized into a balance of power system, unipolar, bipolar, bipolycentric, and a recent return to the balance of power system. A **pole** is a major center of political power.

Balance of Power

Before W.W.II, the United State's decision-makers operated within the European **balance of power** system. This system relied on the premise that no individual state should become too powerful. Each state viewed its vital interests in terms of maintaining the global system's political and military equilibrium. Failure to accomplish this goal could result in world domination by a superpower. For example, America entered W.W.I on the side of the British, French, and Russians against the German and Austro-Hungarian and Ottoman empires when the territorial ambition of Germany was about to achieve hegemony in Europe. The destruction of the European balance of power and the possibility that Germany would become a superpower was seen as a threat to American vital interests, and it acted accordingly. The U.S. was willing to go to war to protect its vital interests.

W.W.II demolished the European balance of power system. The European centers of powers, for example, Germany, France, and Great Britain, were either like Germany, militarily defeated, or as France and Great Britain, politically and economically bankrupt. A new paradigm, model or way of viewing the world, began to develop. At the center of the paradigm was **ideology**, a consistent way of thinking about man and society. Ideology, not political "balance," was at the center of nation-states' power relationships. The two major ideologies around which the new global system was organized were communism and capitalism. As the chieftain of the capitalist ideology, the U.S. played a dominant role in the new global system

Unipolar

The end of W.W.II ushered in a unipolar system with the U.S. as the sole source of power. Comparatively speaking, the U.S. had emerged unscathed from W.W.II. Unlike the European powers that were emotionally drained and physically decimated, America prospered. In fact, W.W.II had transformed the American economy. Its gross national product (GNP) rose 72 percent between 1941 and 1944, agricultural production increased by 25 percent, and civilian consumption of goods and services rose by 20 percent.[31] The health of the U.S. economy placed it in the unique position as the only power capable of exercising control over global affairs. Not only was the United States capable but it was also willing to do so. Consequently, for one brief moment in its history, the United States emerged as the dominant power in the world. Not only was it a superpower, it was the only superpower. Ironically, this situation would have been intolerable under the old European balance of power system. The global system had been altered, and this change would affect U.S. foreign policy. The change would be more one of tactics, however, rather than strategy as the U.S. expanded its concept of manifest destiny to include ideology as well as territory.

Bipolar

A bipolar structure consists of two opposing states or coalitions that preserve the balance of power within the international community.[32] This international system developed shortly after W.W.II, as the unipolar structure disappeared almost as soon as it was recognized. By 1949, the Soviet Union had successfully challenged the hegemony of the U.S. and established itself as a superpower. This created a bipolar global system of power that lasted until around 1962. Many scholars contend that the Cuban Missile Crisis in 1962 marked the demise, if not the end, of the bipolar system.

Within the framework of the bipolar structure, the United States pursued a policy of containment of the Soviet Union. The United States meant to contain the existing territorial boundaries of the Soviet Union in Western Europe while ideologically containing it everywhere else in the world. This policy and the Soviet's action and reaction to it created a political and economic power struggle based on ideological superiority that virtually affected every country in the world. The focal point of the bipolar system is the superpower, so their actions and interactions are of paramount importance. The superpowers establish the rules and/or conventions of the bipolar system, and they are understood by all albeit not always adhered too. The rules of the system are extremely rigid and are designed to maintain the superpowers in their positions of power. They are dictated by the superpowers and administered in a hierarchical manner, from the top down. Violations of the rules upset the system and create instability.

By definition, the two superpowers are stronger than any of their allies or friends and therefore cannot be restrained by them. The two superpowers considered themselves as adversaries necessitating secondary, less powerful, states to form an alliance or allegiance with one or the other. This created two blocs of nations, one aligned with the United States, the other with the Soviet Union. Power was so concentrated in the hands of the superpowers that it was necessary for the other states to look to the superpowers for protection. Although the relations between the superpowers and the weaker states were hierarchical, it was also reciprocal. Ideological commitment, at least superficially, was a prerequisite for entry into one bloc or the other. The secondary states would economically, politically, and ideologically support the superpower and the pursuit of its vital interests, often to the detriment of their own. In return, the superpower would offer protection from the other pole of power. For example, during this time, nuclear weapons were not extremely sophisticated. They did not have the capacity to travel a great distance. For example, the United States did not have the capacity to launch a nuclear missile at the heart of the Soviet Union from Iowa. It required a closer launching facility, a forward missile base. Consequently, the United States and the Soviet Union used their client states, or allies, as forward missile bases from which to strike the other pole.

The bipolar system required that a country be in one camp or the other. It was very difficult to remain neutral in this system and virtually impossible to straddle the fence although several states such as India made a valiant effort to do so. It was a given that the Eastern European states would belong in the Soviet bloc and the Western European states were part of the U.S. bloc. The Warsaw

Pact, the Eastern bloc, and NATO (North Atlantic Treaty Organization), the Western bloc, were the formal alliances that served as the lynchpins for this political division. However, the rest of the world was not so easily divided. Consequently, Asia, Africa, and South America were constantly engaged in a power struggle between the Soviet Union and the United States. Countries such as Korea, Vietnam, Zaire, and Chile were all battlegrounds in the struggle for power between the two superpowers. It was here that the superpowers engaged in covert, clandestine or secret, activities, paramilitary operations, and proxy wars. Almost all civil wars during the cold war era occurred in the **Third World**, developing or preindustrial states, where the number of casualties ran into the tens of millions. This pattern continues today even though the international power system has been altered.[33] More than 80 percent of the conflicts in the post-cold war world have taken place in the Third World countries largely due to the destruction of their political infrastructures and the amount of weapons distributed to them by the superpowers during the bipolar period. The bipolar system was a perfect example of the zero-sum game described earlier in the book. Whatever one power won, the other power lost.

Since the guidelines of the bipolar system are strict, there is little room for flexibility on the part of the actors. The basic rule for behavior in a bipolar structure was to oppose any unilateral attempt by the adversary to upset the balance of power. If the opponent pushes, push back. The constant search for allies and friends and the attempts to undermine the opposing bloc while preventing defections from one's own meant that there were frequent crises, occasional limited wars, and a mutually reinforcing fear.[34] All of these actions challenged the basic concept of security of both the Soviet Union and the United States. All the events in the world were "linked" to each other in the zero-sum game of the superpowers. During this time, the United States pursued a foreign policy based on absolute security where none existed. The result of this policy was the constant threat of nuclear war resulting from an arms race based on mutual destruction.

Foreign aid was a favored policy instrument used by the United States both to woo nations to their circle of influence and to prevent defection from existing allies to the Soviet bloc. Between the end of the Korean War and 1990, the United States expended over $200 billion in foreign economic aid.[35] During the 1950s and 1960s, foreign aid was designed to transform poorer countries into urbanized industrial societies. There was a major concern that poverty in these Third World countries had created very unstable social and political institutions. This instability could lead to revolutionary movements that might adopt communism as the ideological tenet and the Soviet Union as a political model. However, because the objective of the United States was to stop the advance of communism, foreign aid was usually distributed in the form of military aid. The major portion of American aid in the 1950s and 1960s was military aid to support the armies of allied nations around the Sino-Soviet periphery including nationalist China, South Korea, South Vietnam, Pakistan, and Turkey.[36] These military expenditures often produced the opposite effect, undermining the economic, political, and social infrastructures of Third World countries while building up the military. This did not create the democratic industrialized society that the United States had hoped but rather established dictatorial oppressive regimes that were able to rule their citizens through intimidation based on the weapons they had acquired through U.S. foreign aid packages. The United States continued to support these regimes, for example, Chile, Guatemala, and Zaire, as long as they remained in the U.S. bloc.

Bipolycentric

As mentioned earlier, the Cuban Missile Crisis of 1962 is usually cited as the end of the tight bipolar system. The world system assumed a looser structure as the superpowers stepped back from the nuclear precipice and eventually pursued a policy of détente. **Détente** meant the initiation of many linkages of trade, finance, travel, and cultural exchanges not only between the superpowers but between their client states. These exchanges produced substantial reductions in both the tightness and exclusivity of the bipolar system.[37] There were several reasons for the change in the global system including major advances in technology, nationalist movements in the Third World, the proliferation of nation-states, and the declining importance of ideology in power relationships. First, major catalysts in this change were the technological advances in weapon systems that allowed the United States and the Soviet Union to give up their forward weapons bases in client states. Intercontinental ballistic missals or ICBM's enabled the superpowers to strike at their targets from their own territories.

Second, nationalist movements in Asia and Africa effectively ended the European colonial system that had dominated the world for over 100 years. After W.W.II over 100 new countries gained independence more than tripling the previous number of nation-states. The perspectives and demands of these new countries changed the focus of the world political and economic debate.

Third, the new nations that emerged after W.W.II were more concerned with pragmatic political problems, such as the accumulation of capital and industrialization, than they were with ideology. Consequently, they preferred to remain ideologically "nonaligned" to either superpower and adopted a "moral neutrality between the two blocs."[38] Economic and political transnational organizations such as the Organization of African Unity and Organization of Petroleum Exporting Countries (OPEC), developed to promote their own agendas and challenge the bipolar system. The Third World countries had used the cold war and the bipolar system to their advantage. They knew that they could not materially affect the outcome of the cold war so they used their nonalignment to maximize their own gains while minimizing their costs. The strategy stimulated keen efforts by each of the two superpowers to woo the uncommitted to its own side while preventing their alignment with the other. Nonalignment in effect enabled developing nations to play one side against the other to gain advantage for themselves.

One of the major U.S. foreign policy tools has traditionally been foreign aid. This is aid that is essentially non-military in nature. However, the amount of aid given and the recipients of that aid have fluctuated over time depending on how U.S. interests were defined. Therefore, U.S. foreign aid in the 1950's and 60's was significantly different from that of today's.

As the world structure changed, so did the form of U.S. foreign aid. Since World War II, the United States had been the leading source of aid to developing countries. As the United States pursued their policy of "containment" of the Soviet Union, foreign aid was thought to "win friends and win more friends." However, it became clear during the bi-polar system of securing friends and deterring enemies (zero-sum game) many decision-makers realized that "instant" economic development and industrialization was unrealistic. The efforts were always disappointing, perhaps because they were never really aimed at development but containment. It became evident that the money did not necessarily buy allies or woo states away from the Soviet bloc. The United States became disenchanted with those who kept biting the hand that fed them. As the bipolar system loosened and the superpowers engaged in détente, the accumulation of secondary states in the form of formal blocs became less pressing. Consequently, what foreign aid was given was targeted at specific strategic areas. For example, beginning in the 1980s, 40 percent of all U.S. aid went to Israel and Egypt. And although the percentage of dollars fluctuates over time, to date, Israel and Egypt are the two major recipients of U.S. foreign aid.[39] During the nineties, U.S. foreign aid significantly declined.

The U.S., once the largest donor of foreign aid, had by the mid 1990s shrunk its aid to a mere 0.15 percent of GDP (gross domestic product), placing it last among the twenty-one industrial nations.[40] Although it contributed the most in terms of total dollars, countries such as Japan and Canada spent more on a per capita basis than did the United States. However, since September 11, 2001, the United States has attempted to renew its commitment to use foreign aid as a constructive policy tool and close the foreign aid spending gap. It was apparent to some policy-makers that this effort was necessary as they realized that global poverty was one of several central components that generated animosity towards the United States. It was believed that these feelings were one of several factors that contributed to fostering terrorist groups and violent political agendas in other parts of the world.[41] Although only a slight increase, the United States now commits 0.22 percent of its GDP to foreign aid (Japan, 0.28 percent, Canada 0.34 percent).[42]

Today: System in Transition

For fifty years, U.S. foreign policy was driven by its relationship with the Soviet Union. However, by 1991, the Soviet Union had fallen; consequently, the cold war was over. Some U.S. decision-makers claimed that the disintegration of the Soviet Union was caused by two significant factors: U.S. ideological superiority and the relentless "containment" policies implemented by policy-makers during the cold war. However, as appealing as this explanation may be to the leadership and the public in the United States, there is no one interpretation or set of conditions that completely explains the demise of the Soviet Union. Rather, it is a combination of the change in leadership in the Soviet Union, domestic political and economic decay, its invasion of Afghanistan, and bankruptcy caused by the arms race perpetuated by the cold war policies of both the United States and Soviet Union. Whatever combination of factors led to its demise, the Soviet Union was no longer a "pole" in the global system, and power relationships in the world political arena were significantly altered. The United States has had to refocus its foreign policy of containment and redirect its energies and resources elsewhere.

The cold war not only depleted the assets of the Soviet Union, but it diminished the power and resources of the United States. Fifty years ago the United States stood at the helm of a unipolar system as the only superpower. It was unquestionably the dominant military and economic power in the world. And although it is still the greatest military power on earth, determined to fulfill its manifest destiny, it no longer is the political and economic force it once was. Its economic power has significantly decreased since W.W.II. Immediately following W.W.II, the U.S. controlled approximately 50 percent of the world's gross national product. Today, it is less than half that number. Perhaps just as troubling is the climbing U.S. balance of trade and the fact that before W.W.II, the United States was a creditor nation; today it is the world's largest debtor country.[43] In the economic arena, the European Union and countries such as Japan and China have successfully challenged the U.S. for world markets.[44] Today, in this period of transition, there are multiple poles of power: military, economic, or some combination of both.

In the post cold war era, the United States has attempted to define its vital interests in terms of mutual security. However, as the memory of the cold war waned, so too did the political power of the United States. Old political loyalties to old superpowers had faded, and countries now sought new pragmatic relationships.

This has presented serious challenges to U.S. political capital in the world arena. It is no longer the undisputed leader of an ideological bloc of nations capable of maintaining loyalty through economic and political manipulation. Different tactics needed to be employed to accomplish the same objectives, For example, the political power the United States maintained in a bipolycentric world made it easier for President George H. Bush to politically secure an international consensus and form a coalition to go to war against Saddam Hussein. By 2003, the United States did not possess the position politically in the world that it had in 1991. Different methods of diplomacy were needed to convince the international community that its mutual security was vested in ousting Saddam Hussein; it was not accomplished. George W. Bush was not able to rally the world to go to war against Saddam Hussein as his father had done.

The United States remains, however, the undisputed military power in the world. It appears that without its former political and economic clout, the United States will use this tool to re-establish its dominance in the world. President Bush's goal is to re-establish the United States to its former status as the undisputed world power, returning to a unipolar world system much like the one that existed shortly after World War II based on ideological superiority. Bush wasted no time in "announcing his administration with authority," in the international arena. His early actions are characterized by unilateral adversarial cold war tendencies solely aimed at protecting U.S. interests.

On January 29, 2002, in his State of the Union Address, President Bush defined foreign policy objectives in terms of good and evil He proclaimed that Iraq, Iran and North Korea were part of an "axis of evil." He stated in his address that "states like these and their terrorist allies constitute an axis of evil arming to threaten the peace of the world." Since then he has invaded Iraq in what now seems to be intractable war, engaged both North Korean and Iran in brinkmanship like policies over nuclear weapons and future nuclear capabilities and isolated many of U.S. traditional allies in the process. In other areas of the world, President Bush retrogressively revamped U.S. foreign policy selling arms to Taiwan, thereby re-establishing the concept of a "two-China" policy abandoned by the Nixon administration and has pushed for his National Missile Defense System as the cornerstone of his defense policy, in spite of Russian and European opposition. The present Bush administration continues to snub the international community in the areas of environmental and health issues, the Kyoto Protocol and the Landmines Treaty. In all of these policies, the Bush Doctrine of unilateral pre-emptive action has changed the tactics, albeit not the strategy, of foreign policy-making since the bipolycentric construction of the world political system. It is too soon to assess whether the Bush administration will be successful in its attempt to re-establish the U.S. as the world's only superpower or creating a unipolar system or if like a Phoenix, a new power system will emerge from the ashes of the past. Perhaps a non-ideological balance of power system will develop among other countries to offset the U.S. attempt to establish itself as the ideological leader of the neoconservatives vision of a "new world order."

INTERNAL INFLUENCES

Governmental Constraints

The foreign policy of the United States is constrained by the structure of the government whose parameters and powers are defined in the Constitution. The Constitution designates the formal policy-maker institutions and establishes the framework for their relationship. As with all other constitutional powers previously discussed in other chapters, powers in the Constitution are both formal and informal, explicit and implicit, and have fluctuated through interpretation and reinterpretation by those in power.

Formal Powers

As discussed, separation of powers and checks and balances are two of the fundamental principles that underpin the Constitution and, consequently, the entire governing process. Adherence to these principles are strikingly evident in the constitutional grants of power in the area of foreign policy. The Constitution formally divides power in this area between the president and Congress. Each branch performs a different function in the area of foreign policy decision-making thereby separating the powers while at the same time implementing the concept of checks and balances and providing both Congress and the president the authority to "check" each other's power.

Much of our foreign policy focuses on the military and its ability to wage war and keep peace. Consequently, who and how our vital interests are defined in this area are major constitutional considerations.

The President. The framers of the Constitution originally intended that the legislative branch would be the most powerful. However, in the area of foreign policy, as in other aspects of policy-making, the executive has become the dominant branch of government rendering the legislative branch to a secondary position. Three specific grants of power to the executive branch in Article II of the Constitution make the president the major actor and principal policy-maker in the area of foreign policy. All three grants of power either explicitly or implicitly stipulate that foreign policy officially be made in the name of the president. First, Article II, Section 1, states "The executive Power shall be vested in a President of the United States of America." This section gives the president an implied power not enumerated in the Constitution. The power cannot be specifically defined because its scope is broad and largely depends on circumstances. Constitutional expert, J.W. Peltason, describes this section of the Constitution as an enormous grant of informal power to the executive branch particularly in the area of foreign policy:

> Although not so broad, this executive power is akin to the prerogative formerly claimed by the English crown to act for the public good "without the prescription of the law" and "sometimes even against it." The president can issue proclamations of neutrality... make executive agreements with foreign nations, and take emergency action to preserve the nation, although such powers are not specifically granted to the president by the Constitution.[45]

In 1936, a Supreme Court case, the *United States v Curtiss-Wright Export Corp.* supports this observation. Justice Sutherland, writing his opinion in this case for a unanimous Court, described a special role for the president in the area of foreign affairs. Quoting John Marshall, Sutherland wrote that, "The President is the sole organ of the nation in its external relations, and its sole representative with foreign nations."[46]

Second, Article II, Section 3 solidifies the president's position as the major player in foreign policy-making by granting him the power to "receive Ambassadors and other public Ministers." This has been interpreted to mean that the president is the only constitutional officer who can officially speak for the United States to foreign governments. Foreign governments may speak to the United States only through the president or his agent. The president's power to receive ambassadors extends to recognizing new states or governments.[47]

The third and final grant of authority is the power to make war and its antithesis, the ability to maintain peace through conflict management. The framers of the Constitution who had declared their independence from England in 1776 were extremely distrustful of standing armies and a king or executive who would send troops to the colonies to suppress their rebellion. Consequently, the framers divided the power to wage war between the president and Congress so that no one individual could control the power of war and peace. Article I, Section 8 grants Congress the formal authority to declare war. However, Article II, Section 2, states that "The President shall be Commander in Chief of the Army and Navy of the United States, and of the Militia of the several States, when called into actual Service of the United States." This ensures civilian supremacy over the military and makes the president ultimately responsible for decisions on all matters of military strategy during times of war and peace.

Historically, the president has exercised the nation's war-making powers. Since 1789, U.S. forces have engaged in military actions with foreign governments over 150 times, but Congress has only declared war on five of these occasions: the War of 1812, the Mexican War, the Spanish-American War, W.W. I, and W.W. II. Congress did not declare war on Iraq; it authorized the president to utilize force within the constraints of the War Powers Act.

George Washington quickly recognized when he was president that there was a need for a strong chief executive who could respond quickly to military threats to the vital interests of the nation. In defending the new Constitution, the *Federalist* papers construed the president's war powers narrowly, implying that the war-making power of the president was little more than the power to defend against imminent invasion when Congress was not in session. However, it was not long until the executive branch extended its authority in foreign policy and executed its power as commander-in-chief without consulting with Congress. Although Vietnam is usually used as the ultimate example of the use of a president's war-making power, the use of presidential power in sending troops without the consent of Congress was based on many precedents in U.S. history, for example, John Adams fought a war against the French without a congressional declaration of war and Thomas Jefferson fought the Barbary Coast pirates.[48]

The Congress. The Constitution actually grants Congress more farther-reaching foreign policy powers than it gives the president. However, its implementation of these powers is another story and, as previously stated, Congress has played a secondary role to the executive. First, although the Constitutional Convention declared the president to be the commander in chief of the armed forces, it divided the war powers of the United States between the president and the legislature by granting to Congress in Article I, Section 8 the power to "provide for the common defense . . . to declare war . . . to raise and support armies . . . to provide and maintain a navy . . . to make rules for the government and regulation of the land and naval forces." Second, the Constitution also granted to Congress the power of the purse and the ability to control funds for foreign-policy initiatives such as foreign aid and funding military actions. Third, the Senate has the power to ratify treaties with foreign powers. The Constitution states that the president shall have the power "by and with the Advice and Consent of the Senate, to make Treaties, provided two thirds of the Senators present concur." Although its authority over treaties, war, and money place Congress in a commanding position with regards to foreign policy-making enabling it to set overall policy, the reality is quite different.[49]

Historically Congress has had little success in either exercising its right or curtailing the ever-increasing president's predominant role in controlling our military forces and ultimately our foreign policy. As previously mentioned, presidents have engaged in military actions not only without a formal congressional declaration of war but also often without its consent. The ultimate modern example of "hostilities" was the Vietnam "conflict" that resulted from protecting our vital interests during the cold war. Presidents Eisenhower, Kennedy, and Johnson ordered U.S. forces into Vietnam to protect U.S. economic and political interests although the action was explained in terms of freedom and democracy. The U.S. was gradually drawn into the conflict, and by the height of its involvement in the late 1960s, President Johnson had committed over 550,000 troops to fight in Vietnam. By the end of the war, over 50,000 combat troops had died, all without a formal declaration of war by Congress.

This episode in U.S. history deeply disturbed congressional members because in hindsight they felt duped by successive executive administrations, particularly the Johnson administration. This prompted Congress to re-evaluate the war-making balance that existed between it and the president that the legislative branch believed had tipped too much in favor of the executive branch. Congress was determined to constrain the war-making power of the president thus limiting his power as a decision-maker in the area of foreign policy. In 1973, Congress passed the **War Powers Act** over President Nixon's veto. In so doing, Congress exercised its ability to check the power of the president and restore the balance of power between the two branches in the area of "war-making." The Resolution stipulated that presidents must consult with Congress whenever possible prior to using military force and to withdraw forces after sixty days unless Congress declares war or grants an extension.[50]

There have been many problems with the War Powers Act, not the least of which is that subsequent presidents have considered this resolution to be unconstitutional. Their position was given validity when in 1983, the Supreme Court in *INS v Chadha*, ruled that legislative vetoes were unconstitutional. The War Powers Act could be considered to be a legislative veto since Congress is actually vetoing a presidential act after he/she has already deployed troops. Besides the constitutional problem presented by the War Powers Act, several presidents have simply been unwilling to adhere to the reporting requirements and fine print of the law. This occurred when President Reagan sent troops into Lebanon and President Bush sent them to Saudi Arabia.[51] It appears the same can be said for President Bush's policies in Afghanistan and Iraq vìs a vìs the War Powers Act.

The "power of the purse" has given Congress some ability to check the power of the executive in matters of foreign policy. Since Congress has the exclusive power to appropriate funds for foreign as well as domestic programs, the president must at least submit its foreign policies to congressional financial scrutiny. Two areas in which Congress exercises this authority are foreign aid and military expenditures. This is no small matter since both of these areas are considered not only to be major instruments of foreign policy but, in many instances, the centerpiece of U.S. international credibility.

First, Congress frequently exercises its power of the purse by not only cutting the president's foreign aid requests but by also placing conditions and restrictions on particular requests.

> Part of the reason for this penchant is that foreign aid cuts, unlike many other areas of the budget, are unlikely to adversely affect local constituents' interests. Moreover, Congress characteristically "earmarks" foreign aid funds for particular countries. Special-interest groups and ethnic lobbies are important in determining who gets how much, with the result that flexibility in the president's use of this long-standing policy instrument is severely impaired."[52]

Second, Congress implements its "check" on the president's foreign policy by its micromanagement of the defense budget. Individual members often use military spending as a tool of political campaigning and often focus on programs not policies, particularly if those programs might help their constituents.

> The same parochialism that motivates members of Congress to serve on committees fuels Congress's micromanagement of the defense budget, as members are alert to the impact of defense spending on their constituencies."[53]

President Bush currently believes that Congress is micromanaging his defense budget. The failed war in Iraq was one of the critical issues during the congressional elections of 2006 that enabled the Democrats to take over both the House of Representatives and the Senate. Consequently, both houses of Congress are in a position to flex their constitutional foreign policy making muscles. This has currently engaged Congress and President Bush in a power struggle over military funding of the war in Iraq. Despite repeated veto threats, both the House and the Senate have approved enormous supplemental war spending bills that contain a schedule for eventual withdrawal of American soldiers from Iraq. President Bush needs the almost $100 billion dollars to continue military operations in Afghanistan and Iraq: however, President Bush refuses to be tied to any timetable for troop withdrawal dictated to him by Congress.[54] Although currently unresolved, it is sure to be an issue during the congressional and presidential campaigns of 2008. In the constitutional struggle over the foreign policy issue of war, will Congress or the president prevail? Or, as perhaps the Constitution intended, a check and balance on both of these branches of government will require them to compromise to find a middle ground rather than a high ground.

Bureaucracies. Both Congress and the president utilize bureaucracies and their staffs to formulate and implement foreign policy. In Congress, the committees and their staffs perform a major role in decision-making and in the oversight process of their policies and their budgets. Many congressional committees have jurisdiction over and responsibilities in foreign affairs. For example, the Senate Judiciary Committee is responsible for issues relating to immigration. The major committees responsible for foreign affairs are the Foreign Relations Committee and the Armed Services Committee; in the House of Representatives, the major committees are the International Relations Committee and the Armed Services Committee. Both houses have Intelligence Committees that are responsible for policies that affect the intelligence community and covert activities.

Although Congress's committee system fosters parochialism, and its members are more often than not concerned with the domestic problems of his/her constituents, foreign policy committees are high profile and are plum appointments for anyone seeking national attention or recognition. National recognition in the area of foreign affairs often increases the power and prestige of an individual Congressperson that in the long run will aid their local constituents.

The president's foreign policy team is made up of members of his/her cabinet and its departments, the military, and the intelligence community. The major departments involved in foreign policy are State, Defense, and Treasury. These departments are composed of individuals who are appointed as well as merit civil service career employees. The Joint Chiefs of Staff has traditionally represented the military establishment. The new cabinet department, the Office of Homeland Security, is now a major player in foreign policy making. The department was created to coordinate the efforts of the disparate bureaucracies, including the traditional intelligence agencies, such as the Central Intelligence Agency (CIA) and the Federal Bureau of Investigation (FBI) to thwart future terrorist attacks. This is no easy task as organizations such as the CIA and FBI maintained very specific tasks and turfs and were not used to sharing information. The 9/11 Commission created by Congress to investigate the terrorists attacks of September 11 found that there were institutional and structural deficiencies within the intelligence community, to include the FBI and CIA. Of particular concern was the inability of these institutions to communicate not only with each other but also within their own organizational structures. These failures were significant in Al Qaeda's ability to penetrate our security.

All these separate institutions form a foreign policy establishment that is vast in number and scope. It is the president's responsibility to evaluate their input and coordinate their efforts to develop a consistent and effective foreign policy. In 1947, the National Security Council (NSC) was created for that purpose. The NSC is headed by the National Security Advisor (NSA). The most prominent and influential NSA was Henry Kissinger, who concurrently served as Secretary of State and National Security Advisor during the Nixon administration. He virtually controlled foreign policy. Other members of the NSC are the president, vice president, the secretary of defense, and the secretary of state as well as other presidential appointments.

Over the years the foreign policy establishment has become just that, an establishment. It has tended to represent the status quo or the existing norm incorporating the traditional views and world visions of the governing elite fostering the ideas of U.S. ideological superiority and its desire to recreate the world in its own image.[55] This has led to a strong resistance for self-examination. It has usually taken a crisis such as 9/11 for bureaucracies to engage in introspection. Foreign policy is institutionalized through the bureaucratic structure established and utilized by Congress and the president. The establishment has created a continuity of thinking in the realm of foreign policy that has resulted in habitual ways of thinking and conflict management that have severely limited the number of options available to decision-makers. This has created great stability in the process of decision-making but has often stifled creativity in the process. Old ways of thinking create old patterns of decision-making and behavior. Radical departure from existing policy structures is rare, if any, and foreign policy decision-making has become incremental. Long range goals have been avoided, and policy innovations have been rare. Consequently, the pattern of foreign behavior, while occasionally appearing on the surface to change, has been marked by a preference for gradual adaptation rather than fundamental change.[56]

Societal Level

The U.S. political culture is diverse and can be defined as a multicultural pluralistic society. However, within this context the majority of individuals have been socialized to share the core political values of liberty, equality, and democracy. Domestically, how these values are constructed and implemented are hotly and endlessly debated issues; in the area of foreign affairs they tend to frame the foundations of U.S. moral superiority and sense of nationalism. Since the political culture supports the civil liberties expressed in the Bill of Rights including freedom of speech, assembly, and press, foreign policy issues are debated in a relatively open manner using the newest vehicles of political information, such as the Internet.

The nature of the U.S. political culture encourages a myriad of societal inputs that influence decision-makers in the area of foreign policy. However, since foreign policy issues are often closely interconnected to domestic concerns, it is often difficult to distinguish the decision-makers and/or their motivation. For example, in 1993, the United States signed the North American Free Trade Agreement (NAFTA) with Canada and Mexico. This agreement not only addressed critical foreign relationships with countries bordering the United States but serious domestic issues as well, such as business profits versus workers' rights in the areas of job security and wages. In 2001, the impact of NAFTA is still unclear and so are Americans' feelings about it. In a new poll by the University of Maryland, only 43 percent of Americans supported freer trade with "low-wage countries," which lowered their tariffs, compared with the 66 percent who supported freer trade in general. These figures have dented American political commitment to free trade. President Clinton attempted to get congressional backing for "fast-track" authority to negotiate trade treaties. When the attempt collapsed, trade unions, environmentalists, and many congressional members celebrated. This same coalition has helped bring talks on a global foreign-investment accord to a halt.[57]

Today, closely connected to the issue of free trade and NAFTA is the question of immigration. On September 11, 2001 the U.S.-Mexico border was virtually shut down. U.S. border inspectors were put on a Level 1 alert, defined as a "sustained, intensive, antiterrorism operation." The virtual shutdown of the border signaled that security can trump trade.[58] This issue presents itself as a double-edged sword and cuts both ways as both a domestic as well as a foreign policy issue. The question of whether the United States has lost control of its borders, most notably its southern one, is becoming more important in the area of public opinion and ultimately campaigning.

Public Opinion

The premise of democratic theory—that the American people will make informed policy choices—does not hold up well under scrutiny. That most Americans do not posses even the most elementary knowledge about their own political system, much less international affairs, is an inescapable fact. Moreover, people's "information" is often so inaccurate that it might better be labeled "misinformation."[59]

Three important characteristics of American public opinion in the area of foreign policy are as follows: the low level of interest in and knowledge of foreign affairs, the volatility of opinion on specific issues, and the long-term stability of fundamental attitudes regarding a world view.[60] First, polls regularly document that Americans are ignorant about foreign affairs. For example, in 1985, 28 percent of those surveyed thought that the Soviet Union and the United States found each other in World War II; 44 percent did not know the two were allies at that time. And in 2004, after numerous high profile reports refuted the claim that Iraq had weapons of mass destruction before the Iraq war, and even after the Bush administration itself had disavowed the allegation as a rationale for the war, over 70 percent of Republicans, 50 percent of independents and 30 percent of Democrats still embraced that view.[61] However, the absence of knowledge regarding foreign affairs does not stem from any deficiency in the U.S. educational institutions. Rather, it stems from disinterest. Public ignorance is a function of public inattention. People are more concerned with domestic matters that they perceive affect their daily lives. Individuals do not view foreign affairs in this light and, consequently, choose not to educate themselves on such matters.[62]

Second, public opinion can be volatile. The public tends to react to specific issues when something is "in the news." For example, an issue that has been receiving increasing news coverage is the flow of undocumented workers into the United States from Hispanic countries, most notably from Mexico. This has occurred as immigration has been presented both as a domestic issue, jobs and domestic resource distribution as well as a foreign policy issue, security. Over time, surveys have generally found that immigration has been a second tier priority, falling behind major national security and domestic concerns, such as the war in Iraq or the condition of the U.S. economy. This appears to have changed in 2006 as the issue of immigration has rapidly gained in significance to the American public. Two surveys done by PEW, one in March 2006, the other in May 2006, reflect the rising national profile of this issue. The poll conducted in March 2006 recorded that only 4 percent of Americans volunteered immigration as the biggest problem confronting the country. When the survey was again conducted in May, the number had risen to 10 percent.[63]

How the media presents events is significant to public opinion. The public reacts to the media presentation, not necessarily the facts of the situation. In particular, the visual media tends to present foreign affairs as isolated incidents, not as extensions of an historical process. Events are presented out of context in a rather disjointed fashion accounting for much of the volatility in public opinion. This is particularly evident in the opinion polls regarding the war with Iraq as most Americans daily watch events unfold on television. A Gallop poll on March 29, 2003, found that 62 percent of the American public viewed that the "war was going well." Two days later, on March 31, 2003, the Gallop poll found the only 34 percent of Americans found the "war was going well." It is also apparent from polls that the public loses patience with policy decisions over time, especially those that involve U.S. troop commitments. A Gallop poll administered in November 2004 reflects that 55 percent of those that responded supported President Bush's actions as president, only 42 percent disapproved The same poll was administered in February 2007 and only 37 percent of the respondents approved of President Bush's actions while 59 percent disagreed.

Finally, although Americans are uneducated about the specific events or facts regarding foreign affairs and their opinions can be volatile regarding specific issues, their attitudes regarding the role of the United States in international affairs has remained fairly stable over time. Americans have a clear idea about the direction they want their decision-makers to go but spend little time or energy on the specific tactics, leaving those up to the policy-makers.

Americans have always vacillated between isolationism and internationalism. However, since W.W.II, the American public has been consistently internationalist. Although the Vietnam War has led some to retreat from this position, it has also created a new strand of internationalism. This new twist on traditional internationalism has produced some inconsistencies in how Americans view the world. This coupled with the uncertainty of the post-cold war era world has produced some competing foreign policy goals that have been reflected in public opinion:

1) Americans favor global activism but oppose sending economic and military aid to other nations.

2) Americans desire peace through strength but are wary of international institutions.

3) Americans fear nuclear weapons and their proliferation and support efforts to reach negotiated arms agreements with the nation's present and former adversaries.

4) Americans oppose the use of force abroad; yet, they back presidents when they choose force of arms and prefer military victory to limited war.

5) Americans worry about the impact of free trade on their jobs; yet, many are willing to open the United States to broader involvement in the world political economy.[64]

6) Americans favor global activism but prefer multilateralism over unilateralism

7) They support preemptive war at least "sometimes" but reject the view that the United States should assume the role of global policeman.[65]

The post cold war era requires that American public opinion respond to new information. The public does, however, acknowledge moral imperatives in the world and, if convinced, will follow presidential leadership in the use of troops. Regarding the war with Iraq, a Gallop poll administered on April 4, 2003, reported approximately 7 out of 10 Americans supported military action. Interestingly, the same poll discovered that this support was seriously split along racial lines. Of those polled who were identified as white, 78 percent supported military action, whereas among those who were identified as African American, only 29 percent supported it. Dr. Sam Hoff, a political science professor at Delaware State University, explained the gap in support. His researched indicated that many "African Americans still have bitter feelings about the way the draft was run during the Vietnam era." There is a belief in the African-American community that the draft was elitist and that a larger proportion of blacks than whites died in Vietnam.[66]

It is important, however, in discussing public opinion that polls are often difficult to interpret simply because they do not deal with perplexity. Polls insist upon a yes or no response, which is worth remembering when evaluating the high numbers who support the war in Iraq. Those polls are accurate and informative, but they do not measure ambiguity, doubt, contradiction, uncertainty, or inner turmoil. Considering that one or another of those emotions commonly besets most human beings when making tough decisions, this is not a small deficiency. In real life, people are often "sort of for something," or "reluctantly in favor." Polls could measure these uncertainties but it usually takes more time and costs more money and so it is rarely done. This does not mean that the recent polls are wrong. It only means that real public opinion is more complex than polls can measure.[67]

Demographics/Gender Gap

Gender is a demographic factor that has begun to affect the U.S. political arena. Women are participating in ever larger numbers in the political process both at the voting booth and as decision-makers. In 1996, women showed their political power at the voting booth as "soccer moms" were credited for Bill Clinton's re-election. Early in the 2000 campaign, the gender gap was alive and well. Al Gore led among women by ten points while George W. Bush led men by the same amount, resulting in a twenty point gap. That was a little larger than in the past; in 1996 the gap was seventeen points and has averaged thirteen points every since 1980. In 2004, however, the gap had somewhat closed as exit polls showed women only 7 percent more likely to have voted for John Kerry than President Bush. In general, women demonstrate greater support for a more activist government and stronger and more viable social programs; consequently, in a broad sense, believe the Democratic Party is better attuned to the concerns of women.[68]

How will gender affect foreign policy? The foreign policy establishment has traditionally been a bastion of male culture. Women have, however, begun to crack the glass ceiling in the higher echelons of foreign policy decision-making. In 1997, Madeleine Albright was confirmed as the first female Secretary of State; in 2001 Condoleezza Rice, the first woman National Security Advisor and today Secretary of State. However, by and large, foreign policy remains dominated by men and this culture had constructed a foreign policy paradigm that used military strength and force as the ultimate weapons of influence. Women tend to have different views regarding these matters. Beginning in 1980, surveys demonstrated that women were more opposed to the use of force and to taking risks with the environment than men. Women's aversion to the use of military force contributed to their greater support of the dovish Jimmy Carter in 1980 over the hawkish Ronald Reagan.[69] In December 1990, American men were fairly evenly split on whether attacking the Iraqi forces in Kuwait was a good idea; women opposed it by a margin of 73 percent to 22 percent. Although there is still a gap between women and men regarding military action, Gallup polls on the 2003 war with Iraq have consistently shown that women support the president's actions in larger numbers than were previously thought. Prior to the war, women opposed unilateral action in large numbers focusing on the issue of collective action. Once the invasion occurred, however, the numbers showed a surprising amount of support for military action. In a poll completed March 28, 2003, 78 percent of men favored the war and only 20 opposed it; among women, 66 percent favored the war with Iraq and 32 percent opposed it. These findings are often explained in the context of a woman's role in the family and society. Typically women have been relegated to subordinate positions in foreign policy matters; consequently, they sought to weaken or eliminate coercion, conflict, and violence. Men tended to view "security" in terms of a zero-sum game. Someone must win and someone must lose. Women tended to view it as freedom from all fear and oppression. The women's definition of security does not require distinct winners and losers but rather allows for the possibility that everyone could be "secure."[70] These new poll results might indicate that women believed that their homes and security were threatened by recent terrorist's attacks and believed that the war with Iraq would go a long way to remedy their feelings of insecurity. Or as columnist Ellen Goodman contends:

> I am impatient with the idea that women are genetically programmed to be more nurturing or peaceful. We share with men an equally strong desire for personal and national security, evidenced after Sept. 11 . . . As we break down the double standard, do women rally to the old single standard which was male? Or can we help create a new one? And if the differences between men's and women's lives disappear, will it make a difference?[71]

It is too early to draw any conclusions regarding the affect of gender on foreign policy, but it is not to soon to ask whether or not, the increased feminine influence in the decision-making process may redirect the structure of world politics so that power and domination, force and conflict are not the key considerations of decision-makers in the area of foreign policy? The answer may well depend on two factors: whether the differences between men and women's lives actually disappear and women become "insiders," in the area of foreign policy making, and whether security is actually a gender issue or a human one.

Impact of public opinion

The most important questions are not necessarily the competence or the interest of the public in foreign affairs, but rather how and when does public opinion influence foreign policy decision-making. For the most part, public opinion in the United States validates the decisions of the policy-makers. It does this in two significant ways. First, public opinion provides the boundaries for permissible action by setting broad limits of constraint. There are certain limits within which the public allows their leaders to act before they suffer retribution at the polls.[72] This usually provides great latitude for U.S. decision-making in the area of foreign policy. For example, the United States had been involved in Vietnam either covertly or overtly since W.W.II. Yet, it was decades before mainstream America began to question the wisdom of U.S. decision-makers. It was not until the Tet Offensive in 1968 that the American public became acutely aware of the blatant discrepancies and outright lies formulated by the Johnson administration. By this time, U.S. policy-makers had committed over 500,000 American ground troops to Vietnam. In 1968, Lyndon Johnson realized he had gone beyond the limits that public opinion would tolerate regarding the Vietnam War. Although he did not lose an election, criticism of his policies in Vietnam became so great, he chose not to run for a second term.

Second, public opinion only sets the broad parameters within which decision-makers operate; rarely does it influence the specific tactics employed by them. Public opinion does not normally take shape until after some foreign event has occurred. Therefore, decision-makers attempt to gain public support for their actions after the fact. Government leaders tend to direct public opinion where they want it to go; decision-makers tend to lead public opinion rather than follow it. After

After 444 days the Iranian hostage crisis ended, but it destroyed Carter's chances for re-election.

"being led," the public tends to validate their decision-makers' policies thereby giving the impression that the decision-makers were actually following the public's wishes. Those in power did, however, learn at least one important lesson from the Vietnam era; over time, acquiring and maintaining public support for the broad concepts of foreign policy makes implementing the specific tactics much easier and far less controversial. For example, President Bush Sr. ran an effective public relations campaign prior to the Gulf War to secure public support for his actions against Saddam Hussein. After securing general support for the Gulf War, the military was able to implement whatever specific tactics were necessary to secure their objective. The present Bush administration attempted to do the same for his regime change in Iraq but was not as adept as accomplishing this as his father. Unlike in 1991, in 2003, there were massive demonstrations in almost every large American city and foreign capital protesting not only the specific policy of the war with Iraq, but also the concept of war in general. However to date, these protests have had no impact upon governmental policy even though by 2006 a clear majority of Americans did not believe the war was worth it. The Democrats were able to capture (take over the majority of seats) in both the House of Representatives and the Senate in 2006 in large part by focusing on the administration's mishandling of the war in Iraq.

In general, public opinion tends to be supportive of the president in his foreign policy initiatives. The masses will defer to and look for leadership from the executive in this area.[73] This is particularly true so long as the leader is "doing something." His actions may be hawkish or dovish, willing to use force to resolve conflicts or introduce peace initiatives to manage conflict. In the short run, the action itself is of less consequence than the ability "to act." When the president shows leadership and takes the lead in foreign policy initiatives, the public tends to initially "rally around the flag" exhibiting and embracing their nationalist sentiments. Almost all presidents have experienced this phenomena. Both Clinton and Bush initiated hawkish activities and saw their popularity soar; Jimmy Carter fostered peace initiatives and saw the same result.

> George W. Bush's approval rating in 2003 increased 15 percent from 53 to 68 percent once he actually commenced military action against Iraq.[74]

> Bill Clinton's popularity with the American people spurted eleven percentage points following the June 1993 American cruise missile attack on Iraqi intelligence headquarters in Baghdad and nine points following the occupation of Haiti a year later.

> George Bush's popularity climbed by eighteen points following the initiation of military action against Iraq in January 1991.

> Jimmy Carter's popularity jumped by thirteen points following the Camp David Middle East accords in September 1978.[75]

Interest Groups

Several different types of interest groups attempt to influence decision-makers in the area of foreign policy: organized economic groups, organized ethnic groups with strong attachments to and interest in the country of their national origin, and human rights organizations.[76]

Economic

The largest and most powerful of the organized economic groups are the multinational corporations. Multinational corporations (MNC's) have created controversy because they are transnational and, consequently, do not owe any allegiance to any nation-states; yet, they put pressure on governmental decision-makers to secure policies favorable to their interests. The individuals who run multinational corporations tend to view policies in terms of its corporate interests rather than "state" policies, and the bottom line is always what political circumstances would best further their profit margin.

Although large corporations have always influenced U.S. foreign policy, for example, United Fruit Company in Central America, globalization of the economy has not only allowed for but encouraged the growth of multinational corporations. Consequently, favorable political circumstances have promoted the significant growth in the number of these organizations. As their numbers have grown, so have their influence. At the close of the twentieth century, the UN estimated that more than 53,000 MNC's and their 450,000 foreign affiliates had global assets in excess of $13 trillion and global sales of more than $9.5 trillion. This volume of foreign investments and sales accounted for more than one-fifth of the world's economy and one-third of its exports. The top one hundred multinationals own nearly $2 trillion of assets outside their home countries and a quarter of the world's stock. They also employed over seventy-three million people worldwide.[77] With this kind of economic power, multinationals sometimes challenged the ability of sovereign states to control their own economies and their own fates.[78]

Multinational corporations may also alter the power relationships in the political arena in their home and host countries by changing the relative size and power of social groups. For example, they increase the size of the labor force in some industries and expand the middle class in others. The political demands of these groups increase as their numbers increase. Their interests often become intertwined with the interests of the multinational corporations and these may or may not coincide with the interests of the state. As individual's interests become more and more interconnected with the "corporation" and disassociated from the state, decision-makers are forced to give more and more and more consideration to the foreign policy demands of the multinationals.[79]

Ninety per cent of all MNC's home offices are located in the developed world. Historically the United States had been the home country for most multinational corporations; however, currently Germany heads the list, followed by Japan. Together these countries account for nearly 40 percent of all parent corporations. Although a MNC's "home" country tends to be in the developed world, much of its business is conducted in the "host" countries of the Third World of Asia, Africa, and South America. To operate both in their home and host countries, which means to make a profit, American multinational corporations need a stable and predictable political environment. Their economic power enables them to lobby decision-makers in the U.S. to initiate foreign policies that ensure that these conditions exist. Often these conditions are secured at a high price to the populations of the host nations. Examples of this are numerous in the Third World. Countries such as Nicaragua, El Salvador, and Somalia have suffered economic oppression at the hands of MNC's.

Multinational Influence/Chile

Although the United States has redirected much of its "energy" to the oil companies who have interests in the Middle East, it is important to examine how its relationship with MNC's in the past have impacted the Americas.

The political events that occurred in Chile during the Nixon administration is a classic example of a multinational corporation's ability to influence U.S. foreign policy. The U.S. intervened in the internal affairs of Chile on behalf of a multinational corporation that culminated in the 1973 coup d'état that toppled the Allende government, the first popularly elected Marxist regime in Latin America. The events that occurred in Chile combined implementing Washington's global strategy with the international interests of International Telephone and Telegraph (ITT) and other multinational corporations, such as Kennicott Copper.

U.S. foreign policy towards Chile was formulated at the highest level, the National Security Council. Henry Kissinger was the National Security Advisor (NSA), and he directed all of U.S. foreign policy during the Nixon administration. Kissinger envisioned the countries of the world as being "linked." He believed that all points of conflict in the world existed in a single continuum that connected the U.S.S.R. and the U.S. less on the merits of each case than on the balance of world power and the relationship between the two main poles of power. According to this concept, the events in Chile did not exist in a vacuum; rather, the U.S. could hold Chile up to the Soviet

Union to show the extent of its global power. Governmental interests became fused with those of multinational consortiums and large capital investment companies in order to facilitate this claim. Chile was seen as a client state in the zero-sum game between the Soviet Union and the U. S.[80] According to Kissinger, we should not,

> delude ourselves that an Allende take-over in Chile would not present massive problems for us, and for democratic forces and for pro-U.S. forces in Latin America and indeed for the whole Western Hemisphere.[81]

International Telephone and Telegraph (ITT) tried to protect its interest in the profitable Chiltelco telephone company by seeking to prevent the election of Salvador Allende, an avowed Marxist, as president of Chile. ITT was concerned that if he was elected, MNC's would be nationalized by the government. If this happened, corporate executives believed their company would lose its lucrative monopoly over the communication networks. ITT's efforts to undermine Allende included giving monetary support to his political opponents. Its efforts were unsuccessful, and Allende was elected president. Once Allende was elected, it changed its tactics to have him forcibly removed from office. It needed the help of the U. S. government to accomplish this task. ITT effectively lobbied the U.S. government into disrupting the Chilean economy. The United States instituted a policy of economic strangulation in the hopes that the Chilean people would be so economically deprived that they would rise up and overthrow the government. When this strategy failed, the Chilean military, backed by the CIA and with arms purchased largely from the U.S. government, overthrew the Allende government and replaced it with a U.S. backed military dictatorship that lasted over fifteen years.[82]

Ethnic Groups

Ethnic populations that live in the United States but maintain sentimental, economic, or political ties with their homelands are another type of interest group that attempt to influence foreign policy. These populations sometimes want the U.S. government to influence and/or intervene in the politics of other countries to facilitate a particular policy. Americans of Irish descent are unusually vigilant regarding American policies toward Ireland and Northern Ireland. Ireland is a republic; however, Northern Ireland is part of Great Britain. Until recently, the U.S. government unconditionally supported British policies in Northern Ireland. However, the Clinton administration under pressure from both high ranking Democrats, for example, Senator Edward Kennedy and Irish interest groups, such as Americans for a New Irish Agenda, successfully changed traditional U.S. policy and allowed Jerry Adams, the popularly elected president of Sein Fein, which is the political arm of the Irish Republican Army (IRA), to enter the United States, thereby giving tacit recognition to the Irish independence movement. The Clinton administration actively supported the 1998 Easter Peace Agreement that may eventually bring peace and independence to Northern Ireland. Unlike Clinton, President Bush did not put Northern Ireland high on his foreign policy agenda. In April 2004 Bush met in Belfast, Northern Ireland with Prime Minister Tony Blair in what some analysts viewed as a "payback" for Blair's undaunted support in Iraq. The British and Irish governments had been pressing local parties for months to make a new round of concessions designed to keep Northern Ireland's 1998 peace accord moving forward. White House officials predicted that Bush's visit would not only come at a pivotal time in the peace process but would also help his friend, Tony Blair.[83]

Human Rights

Other types of organizations that attempt to influence decision-makers are human rights organizations. Many of these are transnational. One of the largest of these is Amnesty International. Amnesty International (AI) is dedicated to the protection of human rights independent of an individual's country or origin or political affiliation. Amnesty International conducts international investigations and publicizes instances of human rights abuses. It often comes into direct conflict with the State Department, which has the statutory mandate to produce a list of countries that are human rights abusers. The State Department list is usually shorter than Amnesty International in that it constructs its list based on geopolitical considerations and how important a country is to the United States, regardless of its human rights record. Congress often uses the Amnesty International list as a tool to check the State Department and, consequently, the policies of the executive in the area of foreign policy.[84]

The Media

Although there are many societal inputs, the last one we will examine is the role the media plays or does not play in influencing foreign policy. The major media influence is television, and it has basically become a governmental tool used by political elites to maintain the status quo. It functions as the gate-keeper of the news and, consequently, sets the political agenda for the American public.

Television

In the past, interest in foreign policy was confined to the elite who largely relied on the print media for their information. Television changed all that by opening foreign policy coverage to the masses.[85] The war in Vietnam forever altered the way foreign policy was presented to the American public as the war was literally fought, by way of television, in American's living rooms as well as in the jungles of Southeast Asia. More recently, Americans have been able to view around the clock coverage of Operation Desert Storm and the 2003 war with Iraq.

During the Gulf War (1991) the news media believed it was hampered in its reporting by the Pentagon. A number of reporters in the field complained that the information they received was managed by the Pentagon through very carefully constructed news briefings. In response to this "flip board" and "pointer" analysis of the war, the Pentagon authorized "embedding" 500 reporters with coalition fighting forces during the 2003 Iraq War. This enabled the reporters to report combat action as it occurred. The reporters literally became part of the unit in which they were "embedded."

This form of news reporting was highly controversial as it put the reporters in a position of actually being part of a military operation. Obviously, their lives were dependent on its success or failure. Reporters were no longer observers but participants in the war. Questions were raised as to whether reporters could remain impartial under these conditions. Americans, however, reacted very positively to this new kind of reporting. Results of a Los Angeles Times Survey in April 2003, found that 55 percent of those polled favored embedded reporting, 37 percent were against and 8 percent did not know. There was no significant gender gap in these responses. Men and women equally approved of embedded reporting.

Although Americans receive most of their news regarding foreign policy from television, unless it somehow relates to the United States, they are basically disinterested in it. Given the choice, the American public would rather watch entertainment or domestic news. All media sources, including television, cover foreign policy to some extent, but their role is limited for two major reasons. First, the media must place most of its emphasis on domestic issues because that is what the people are interested in watching. Second, the government can limit the media's coverage of certain sensitive stories, as it did with the war in Afghanistan in 2001. The aftermath of the September 2001 terrorist attacks made some foreign coverage more relevant to Americans; however, much of the coverage focused on domestic issues or American concerns overseas.[86] Rarely are Americans concerned with the big picture of foreign policy issues; rather, their focus tends to be only on American interests within the world environment. Americans were less concerned with the results of the Iraqi elections as they related to the region but in a more personal sense as to what this would mean to American troop deployment.

Gate-keeper and Agenda Setting

Television serves as the gate-keeper of the news because it determines what the American public will view. The news stories are controlled by corporate America in that it is the top network executives at the television networks who determine which stories will be aired and which stories will not. These executives are a small fraternity of privileged men. The gatekeeping role is especially pronounced in foreign affairs, as the menu of foreign affairs coverage offered to the American people comes from remarkably few sources.[87] Most news about world events is collected by four major wire services: American-owned Associated Press (AP), Reuters (British), the French Agency France-Press (AFP), and ITAR-Tass, which replaced the Soviet news agency Tass in 1992. Besides these worldwide organizations, coverage is also served by syndicated news collected by major American papers, including the *New York Times,* the *Washington Post,* and the *Los Angeles Times.* The print press foreign correspondent corps is joined by correspondents from ABC, CBS, NBC, and CNN. Doris Graber contends that gatekeeping provides adequate information but that it lacks depth and breadth. "It stereotypes and oversimplifies, and it often distorts facts in the interest of timeliness."[88]

Gate-keeping and agenda-setting provides support for government policies. The media usually accepts the official designations of who America's friends and enemies are and interprets their motives accordingly. For the most part, news stories support the prevailing American stereotypes about the world including the concepts of U. S. moral superiority. Preoccupation with the developed powers reinforces many Americans' beliefs about the importance or over-importance of these countries. Conversely the portrayals of less developed countries and the stereotypes produced about them led Americans to reinforce their image about them that they are incapable of handling their own internal affairs.[89] Since they are incapable of this, the U. S. must use both its military and moral superiority to sustain world peace and order. Public opinion is both responsive to events and susceptible to manipulation, policy-makers have embraced television in an effort to generate policies. Consequently, television is now the principal means elites use to communicate to the masses and maintain the status quo in foreign policy making.[90]

ROLE/INDIVIDUAL LEVEL OF ANALYSIS

> Traditionally the study of world politics has been approached from either the nation-state or global viewpoint.... Too often in this theoretical shuffle, the individual and the meaning of human political action are lost.
>
> Robert Isaak

The systems approach to foreign policy analysis is a tool developed to evaluate individual policy-makers' decisions. To use this tool correctly, a wide assortment of inputs within the foreign policy structure must be evaluated. Only then can an accurate assessment regarding the entire process be made. However, this assessment is actually a montage of images using various camera angles to develop a complete picture. The first stage of our analysis required that the camera lens be set on a "wide angle" to view decision-making within the broadest context, the global environment. Now, the last stage of our analysis, requires a narrower focus. The camera angle needs to be adjusted from the panoramic "big picture" to a "close-up" portrait shot. In the final analysis, foreign policy decisions are made by people, either as individuals or as a part of a group.[91]

Earlier in the chapter, we discussed how levels of analysis or types of inputs were all interconnected. These elements of decision-making were often blended so that it was difficult to evaluate one without the other. There were distinct connections between the global and societal factors and between the governmental and the global inputs. However, nowhere is the connection stronger and often more difficult to discern than the connection between the role factor and the individual level of analysis. It is often difficult to divorce the individual from the role he or she plays.

Perception is the key to understanding the role/individual level of foreign policy making because perception defines reality. History is a carefully constructed perception of reality that is filtered through a national camera lens to develop and foster national identities. These identities then become the reality. Individual decision-making is then carried out within this framework. Clearly countries see "reality" differently and their individual leaders define their vital interests within that vision. The U.S. consistently defines its interests within its own world view that has led to its patterned behavior in foreign policy decision-making discussed in the first section of this chapter. It reflects U.S. moral superiority and the desire to create the world in its own image. For example, Russian history books construct a substantially different view of the cold war than do U.S. history books based on their perceptions of the "facts." Iranian President Ahmadinejad and North Korean President Kim Il Sung, both leaders of President Bush's self described "axis of evil," construct a very different reality of nuclear power and the United States for their people than is presented to the American public. In each case, the decision-maker's view of reality resulted in brinkmanship diplomacy, the threat of using violence to resolve conflicts.

The understanding and responses of a decision-maker are not determined by the objective facts of a situation but, rather, their image of it.[92] Policy-makers, whether their views are filtered through national, elite or bureaucratic lenses, believe *they* see the world correctly and that *other* policy-makers do not. Each nation and its leadership can justify its perceptions and policies using an impressive construct of historical facts and analyses. After all, a fact is a fact. Actually, a fact is only a fact once it is placed within an individual's perceptual framework that is influenced by personal experiences, beliefs, and interpretations of history.[93] An individual's image of what is perceived is often more important than what is factual. Decision-makers employ selective vision in determining what facts they will or will not use. These facts tend to be consistent with an individual's world view.[94] This allows the decision-maker to understand the world within his or her own perceptional framework. The situation becomes what the decision-maker perceives it to be. According to Robert Isaak:

> All human beings move through life with theories in their heads that color their vision, whether they know it or not. A story is told about a drunk who is asked why he is looking under a certain streetlight for a key. "Because there is more light here," he replies. We all have our own idea of where to look for the most light to explain everyday reality as we experience it.[95]

It is at the decision-maker level of analysis that the idiosyncratic characteristics of individuals are examined. The lens of the camera has zoomed in so close that we are able to examine the psychological foundations of human nature. Personality determines perception; consequently, a person's needs, desires, and personal dreams and demons play a part in foreign policy-making. In the words of the famous comedian, Flip Wilson, "the devil made me do it," may "in fact" be the perceptional basis for a real decision.

Role Theory

Role theory posits that all human behavior is constrained and molded by the role an individual performs in that system. That role is often determined by the formal position that a person holds within society. Each position or role carries with it certain expectations, responsibilities, and demands of how it should be performed. Pressures to conform to the image of the position modify how an individual will act when performing the functions of the role. These images are assumed to influence the behavior of anyone who fills that position. Therefore, every individual acts similarly to others who have occupied the same position. Conformity is especially evident in formal roles, such as are found in governmental positions, where norms governing performance are backed by legal obligations and sanctions as well as social pressures.[96]

As discussed earlier, the president is the chief foreign policy decision-makers. As such, it would be appropriate to examine the role that that position constructs. The office of the president requires an individual to fulfill formal and informal expectations or roles. The role individuals assume, formally and informally, within these other governmental positions, will ultimately constrain the individual empowered to perform the formal role of president of the United States. Formally, the position of the U.S. president requires him to be the commander and chief of the armed forces and, as such, to determine the parameters of war and peace. To perform this function, the president is bound by governmental constraints such as the role Congress plays in foreign policy as well as international treaties to which the United States is a party. It also requires the president to "receive Ambassadors and other public Ministers." As previously discussed in the governmental level of analysis, this requirement has been interpreted to mean that the president is the only constitutional officer who can officially speak for the United States to foreign governments. The president will often use other formal institutions such as Congress and the Department of State to implement this function.

U.S. presidents are also expected to perform an informal role. They are expected to exhibit strong leadership qualities and direct foreign policy initiatives; the president is expected to act "presidential." In the previous section, it was observed that in the short run, "the action itself is of less consequence, than the ability to act." In the past, the traditional American perception of what the role of the president *should* be and how the duties *should* be performed had been constructed in a sexist manner. Although there have been female heads of state in other countries, most notably former Prime Minister Margaret Thatcher, Americans have always been reluctant to accept the idea that a female could "act" presidential and perform the appropriate duties. In 1984, Senator Walter Mondale, the Democratic presidential candidate selected Congresswoman Geraldine Ferraro as his vice-presidential running-mate. Unlike any other previous male candidate for that position, Ferraro was constantly plagued with questions regarding her leadership ability and/or whether she would be capable of "pushing the button" and dropping the bomb. Today, over twenty years later, as Senator Hillary Clinton positions herself to be the Democratic nominee for president in 2008, political pundits and newscasters still pose the question, "is American ready for a female president?"

Rational Policy-Making

Americans believe that their foreign policy is made for them by their decision-makers in a rational manner. In its simplest form, rational behavior can be defined as purposeful behavior and rationality as the ability to relate means to an end.[97] This implies that foreign policy will be reached in a deliberate manner to maximize the nation's vital interests. Rational decision-making is made by individuals who respond to an international event using the best information available, weighing the options and choosing the best response out of a myriad of alternatives to realize the nation's goals. According to Charles Kegley and Eugene Wittkopf, rational decision-making requires a sequence of intellectual steps that are extremely stringent and often impossible to fulfill:

1) **Problem recognition and definition.** Objectivity requires full information about the actions, motivations and capabilities of other actors as well as the state of the international environment and trends within it. The search for information must be exhaustive and all the facts relevant to the problem have to be gathered.

2) **Goal Selection.** Those responsible for making foreign policy have to determine what they want to accomplish . . . . This requires the identification and ranking of all values in a hierarchy from most to least preferred including such values as security, democracy, freedom, and economic well-being.

3) **Identification of Alternatives**. Rationality requires the compilation of an exhaustive list of all available policy options. This requires an estimation of the costs associated with each alter native.

4) **Choice**. Rationality requires selecting the best alternative from the competing options. This requires analyzing which alternative has the best chance of achieving the desired goal. For this, policymakers need to conduct an extensive means-ends, cost-benefit analysis.[98]

Do U.S. decision-makers act rationally in making foreign policy decisions? Since rational decision making requires a means-end relationship, the question is, "Do policy-makers select the best available means for achieving a given end?" Anything less would not be acceptable. It would be virtually impossible for Americans to believe that when then stakes are so high, such as nuclear war, that their decision-makers would act in any other manner.[99]

> The notion of rational policy making is . . . comforting. Political leaders also try to cultivate public images of themselves as decisive, unfettered by subconscious psychological drives, able to manage the stress and burden of their position, endowed with boundless energy, and prepared to guide the country safely through crises while pursuing the nation's best interest.[100]

There are many barriers to formulating a completely rational foreign policy and implementing it. The president is ultimately held accountable for the foreign policy agenda; however, he is not solely responsible for developing it. The ability of the president to formulate rational foreign policy is largely dependent on the capacity of others to perform their roles rationally. This scenario leaves a lot of room for error.

It may be reasonable to hypothesis that U.S. decision-makers do not attempt to make foreign policy in an irrational manner. However, even with the best intentions, there are many barriers that prevent policy-makers from following the four steps of rational decision-making. First, U.S. decision-makers are bound by their own perceptions of reality. Their world view and construct of history limits the criteria by which they interpret and implement Kegley and Wittkkopf's four steps of rational decision-making. Second, full information about the "actions, motivations and capabilities of other actors," is simply not available to U.S. decision-makers. Some of its unavailability stems from the fact that decision-makers are simply unwilling to filter full information through their belief system. It is not possible for U.S. decision-makers to evaluate Third World revolutions, for example, Nicaragua, from a Third World perspective. American decision-makers are bound by their own cultural constructs, one of which is to maintain stability and the status quo. This is the antithesis of revolutionary movements. At other times, institutions such as the Central Intelligence Agency (CIA) have their own agenda in presenting information to decision-makers, for example, The Bay of Pigs invasion of Cuba. The CIA had been covertly training anti-Castro exiles to invade Cuba and overthrow the Castro government. The CIA then had a vested interest in the mission's success and painted an overly optimistic picture of the ease at which the invasion could be accomplished to President Kennedy. Kennedy was misled by the CIA information and approved the mission. It ultimately failed and proved to be an embarrassment not only to his administration but to the country as a whole.

Third, decision-makers determine goals and objectives in a hierarchical fashion. This means that goals such as security, democracy, freedom, and economic well-being will be prioritized. However, these objectives are not always mutually exclusive; consequently, they often cause conflict in the domestic political arena as well as the international one. This results in often inconsistent and contradictory foreign policy. The goals of democracy and economic well-being are not always consistent. In fact, they often conflict. Decision-makers often rationalize these conflicts. For example, while U.S. decision-makers espouse the notion that the "U.S. is the beacon of democracy" in the world, they have supported both politically and economically oppressive regimes in other parts of the world, for example, the death squads in El Salvador. American decision-makers have rationalized their policies in El Salvador claiming that they were stopping communism and keeping the world safe for democracy. The death squads used to "protect the world for democracy" are the antithesis of the democratic process. Economic considerations have allowed decision-makers to evaluate the communist government in China in a significantly different light than the communist government in Cuba. As mentioned earlier, American policy-makers have overlooked Chinese human rights violations, for example, Tibet, to gain their markets. On the other hand, the United States has imposed an economic boycott on Cuba since the beginning of the Castro regime claiming that it was necessary because of its human rights violations.

Fourth, collecting an exhaustive list of all available policy options and weighing the cost/benefit relationship for each one takes time. Some foreign policies need to be made quickly, for example, the taking of American hostages and/or responding to terrorist threats or attacks. Other circumstances might lead decision-makers to delay making decisions until it is too late to do an extensive study of all the alternatives. There are myriads of reasons why a decision-maker might defer making decisions ranging from unfavorable public opinion to personal denial of the existence of a problem on the part of a decision-maker. Finally, the decision-maker needs to assess the means/end equation and determine what choice among the competing options has the best chance of achieving the desired goal. In this process short term goals might be sacrificed for long term goals. Another consideration is that all policy options cannot be weighed because all are not presented. Presidents usually do not identify all of their own options. They are usually presented with a "short list" of feasible alternatives by their advisors. Their advisors filter out various options for a myriad of reasons. A president cannot consider what he or she does not know.[101]

Are all foreign policy decisions rational? If they are rational, are they good? These are the questions that decision-makers wrestle with and for which the public must hold them accountable.

Great Individuals in History?

> One of the most unsettling things for foreigners is the impression that our foreign policy can be changed by any new president on the basis of the president's personal preference"
> Former Secretary of State Henry Kissinger, 1979

One of the most debated questions in the area of foreign policy making is whether an individual can make a substantive difference in policy. Historians sometimes refer to this as the "great man in history" theory. The very fact that men such as Napoleon, Hitler, Lenin, or Roosevelt existed make history what it is today. These men framed the events of history. Other historians and scholars have suggested that these men were merely caught up in history. If these men had not existed, others would have risen to the challenge. Since the president is the dominant decision-maker in foreign policy, the question is, "whether or not the president's personality and personal idiosyncrasies alter policy?" Does each president and his own personality "quirks" alter the actual policies or does his personality distinguish simply on the basis of style?

No two individuals are identical so it would be easy to theorize that a president's personality would certainly make an impact on decision-making. Lengthy in-depth psychobiological studies have been done on many of the presidents to determine whether their personalities had an impact on their foreign policy. For example, it has been proposed that Woodrow Wilson and his League of Nations failed because of his pathological idealism.[102] Wilson's approach to political issues involving power and control resulted in an unwillingness to compromise with political opponents. Wilson's intractable nature stemmed from the consequences of his childhood relationship with his father. It has been theorized that his need to dominant others stemmed from his competition with and repressed feelings of hostility towards his father.[103] The question is, "whether or not the U.S. Senate would have ratified the League of Nations if another president would have been in office." This question is difficult to quantify.

James Rosenau argues that the "strength of idiosyncratic factors can be assessed only in relation to the variables that underlie foreign policy and, in all likelihood, their relative importance will tend to be inversely related to that of other variables" He contends that the more developed and more institutionalized or structured a nation-state is the less important idiosyncratic factors of personality will have on foreign policy making; the less structured and less institutionalized a society, the more impact they will have. Since the United States is highly structured and highly institutionalized, a president's personality will have a small impact on foreign policy-making. In the United States, the difference in policy-making is a matter of style rather than content. Rosenau contends:

> What is striking about American foreign policy under Harry S. Truman, Dwight David Eisenhower, John Fitzgerald Kennedy, Lyndon Baines Johnson, Richard Milhous Nixon and Gerald R. Ford, for example, is not its discontinuities, but its continuity: not the differences among the emphases that these six postwar Presidents brought to foreign policy, but the similarity of their postures toward the external world.[104]

CONCLUSION

The original premise of the chapter was that there were clear patterns in U.S. foreign policy-making that were underpinned by a distinct belief system centering on U.S. moral superiority and its desire to make the world over in its own image. If this is true, then the "hero-in-history" theory for the U.S. is too simple. Foreign policy is much more complicated than that and the decision-makers much more constrained. Different individuals often, if not always, pursue their predecessors' policies and respond to international events in a consistent manner. American policy-makers routinely display a propensity for incremental change, perpetuation of established routines of thought and action, and the preservation of established policies. Personal characteristics influence the style rather than the substance. The overall thrust of American foreign policy remains highly patterned and fixated on the past.[105]

CHAPTER NOTES

[1]James N. Rosenau, Kenneth W. Thompson, and Gavin Boyd, *World Politics: An Introduction*, (New York: The Free Press, a Division of Macmillan Publishing Co., Inc., 1976),1.

[2]Donald M. Snow, *September 11, 2001: The New Face of War?* (New York: Longman, 2002), 3-5.

[3]Ibid 9-15.

[4]Ibid.

[5]Rohan Gunaratna, *Inside Al Qaeda: Global Network of Terror* (New York: Columbia University Press, 2002), 22.

[6]Ibid.

[7]Ibid, 27.

[8]Ibid, 54-72.

[9]Bruce Russett, and Harvey Starr, *World Politics: The Menu for Choice*, 5th ed. (New York: W.H. Freeman and Co., 1996), 54.

[10]Walter Lippmann, Interview, Oct. 10, 1971. I received a copy of Lippmann's interview at a seminar on American Foreign Policy at the University of Louisville, Fall, 1984.

[11]Russett and Starr, 167.

[12]The Soviet Union of the cold war period no longer exists. It collapsed in 1991 and has been replaced with the Russian Federation, which consists of eleven of the fifteen former Soviet republics. These republics formed the Confederation of Independent States. Although in practice, the Soviet Union no longer is a viable political entity, for identification purposes, many scholars still tend to refer to the former Soviet Union as the "Soviet Union." Alternatively, scholars refer to the former Soviet Union as Russia.

[13]Charles W. Kegley, Jr. and Eugene R. Wittkopf, *American Foreign Policy: Pattern and Process* 2nd ed., (New York: St. Martin's Press, 1982), 91.

[14]Barry B. Hughes, *Continuity and Change in World Politics: Competing Perspectives*, (Upper Saddle River, N. J.: Prentice Hall, 1997), 149.

[15]"Intelligence Study Raises Estimate of AIDS Spread," *Washington Post*, October 1,2002, A07.

[16]Charles W. Kegley, Jr. and Eugene R. Wittkopf, *American Foreign Policy: Pattern and Process*, 5th edition, (New York: St. Martin's Press, 1996), 154.

[17]Mike Allen and Paul Blustein, "Unlikely Allies Influenced Bush to Shift Course on AIDS Relief," *Washington Post*, January 30,2003, A01.

[18]Rosenau, 15.

[19]Ibid., 3.

[20]Kegley, 1996, 464.

[21]Ibid., 503.

[22]Charles W. Kegley, Jr., and Eugene R. Wittkopf, *American Foreign Policy: Pattern and Process*, (New York: St. Martin's Press, 1991), 4.

[23]Kegley, 1996, 46.

[24]Ibid., 41

[25]Ibid., 47

[26]Walter LaFeber, *Inevitable Revolutions: The United States in Central America,* (New York: W.W. Norton, 1984), 13-18.

[27]Kegley, 1996, 70.

[28]"Statement of Principle," Project for the New American Century, www.newamericancentury.org.

[29]LaFeber, 18.

[30]John Stossel, "Spoils of War," October 4, 2002, www.abcnews.com.

[31]Kegley, 1996, 162.

[32]John Spanier, and Robert L. Wendzel, *Games Nations Play* (Washington D.C.: CQ Press, 1996), 121.

[33]Kegley, 1996, 170.

[34]Spanier, 121.

[35]Kegley, 1996, 187.

[36]Spanier, 372.

[37]Russett and Starr, 103.

[38]Kegley, 1996, 188.

[39]Paul R. Viotti and Mark V. Kauppi, *International Relations and World Politics: Security, Economy, Identity*, (New Jersey: Prentise Hall, 2007), p. 408.

[40]Spanier, 372-374.

[41]Michael Lind, *The American Way of Strategy* (New York: Oxford University Press, 2006).

[42]Data and Statistics on Foreign Aid Contributions, Organization for Economic Cooperation and Development, 2006.

[43]Benjamin Ginsberg, Theodore J. Lowi, and Margaret Weir, *We the People: An Introduction to American Politics*, (New York: W.W. Norton & Company, 1997), 733.

[44]Causes of Poverty, Facts and Stats, www.globalissues.org

[45]J.W. Peltason, *Corwin & Peltason's Understanding the Constitution*, 13th edition, (Fort Worth: Harcourt Brace College Publishers, 1994, 113.

[46]Ibid., 114.

[47]Ibid., 113.

[48]Thomas R. Dye and Harmon Zeigler, *The Irony of Democracy: An Uncommon Introduction to American Politics*, (Belmont, Calif.: Wadsworth Publishing Co., 1993), 254-255.

[49]Kegley, 1996, 439.

[50]George C. Edwards, Martin P. Wattenberg, and Robert L. Lineberry, *Government in America: People, Politics and Policy*, 7th ed., (New York: Longman, 1997), 610.

[51]Peltason, 124.

[52]Kegley, 1996, 439

[53]Ibid., 454.

[54]"Congress Approves War Funding: Pressures Bush to Withdraw Troops," OMB Watch, www.ombwatch.gov

[55]Kegley, 1982, 6.

[56]Ibid.

[57]Helen E. Purkitt, ed., "World Trade: Fifty Years On," *World Politics, Annual Edition 99/00, 20ᵗʰ edition,* (Guilford, Connecticut: Dushkin/McGraw-Hill, 2000), 49.

[58]*American Foreign Policy Annual Editions, 07/08,* (Iowa: McGraw Hill), 2007/2008, p. 65.

[59]Kegley, 1996, 265.

[60]Hughes, 183.

[61]Eugene R. Wittkopf and Christopher M. Jones, *American Foreign Policy: Pattern and Process*, (United States: Thomson, 2007), p. 252

[62]Ibid.

[63]"The State of American Public opinion on Immigration in Spring 2006: A Reviewe of Major Surveys," PEW Hispanic Center, May 17, 2006, www.pewhispanic.org.

[64]Kegley, 1996, 264.

[65]Wittkopf, p. 250.

[66]Victor Greco, "Race divides Americans'war feelings," April 4, 2003. www.delaware online.com and Jeffrey Jones, "Blacks Showing Decided Opposition to War," *The Gallup Organization*, March 28,2003, www.gallup.com.

[67]Jon Margolis, "Public opinion is the blind leading the blind," *Chicago Tribune*, April 8, 2003, Section 2, 4.

[68]Daniel Merkle, "The Gender Gap's Back: What Causes Political Battle of the Sexes?" April 14, 2000, www.abcnews.go.com/sections/politics

[69]Norrander, 169.

[70]Hughes, 199.

[71]Ellen Goodman, "Can women break the war rut," *Washington Post Writers Group*, March, 26, 2003, www.workingforchange.com.

[72]Spanier, 236.

[73]Ibid., 264-265.

[74]Jim Bencivenqa, "Protestors Hit the Streets," April 3, 2003, The Christian Science Monitor, www.csmonitor.com.

[75]Kegley, 1996, 277.

[76]Ginsberg, p. 720.

[77]Charles W. Kegley, Jr. and Eugene R. Wittkopf, World Politics: Trend and Transformation (Boston: Bedford/St.Martins, 2001), 226.

[78]Charles W. Kegley, Jr. and Eugene R. Wittkopf, World Politics: Trend and Transformation, 6th edition, (New York: St. Martin's Press, 1997), p. 191.

[79]Russett and Starr, p. 17.

[80]Armando Uribe, The Black Book of American Intervention in Chile, (Translated from the Spanish by Jonathan Casart), (Boston: Beacon Press, 1974) p. 87.

[81]Ibid, p. 60.

[82]Ibid, Chapters, 1-3.

[83]John Murray Brown, "Blair to meet Bush in Belfast new week in payback," Financial Times, www.financialtimes.com.

[84]Donald M. Snow and Eugene Brown, *Beyond the Water's Edge: An Introduction to U.S. Foreign Policy*, (New York: St. Martin's Press, 1997), p. 236.

[85]Doris A. Graber, *Mass Media and American Politics*, 5th edition, (Washington D.C. CQ Press: A Division of Congressional Quarterly, Inc., 1997), p. 367.

[86]Christine Barbour and Gerald C. Wright, *Keeping the Republic: Power and Citizenship in American Politics,* 2nd ed.(Boston:Houghton Mifflin, 2003), 681.

[87]Kegley, 1996, 319.

[88]Graber, 342-356.

[89]Ibid.

[90]Kegley, 1996, 323.

[91]Russett and Starr, 219.

[92]Kegley, 1996, 503.

[93]Spanier, 270.

[94]Ibid., 271.

[95]Robert Isaak, *Individuals and World Politics*, 2nd ed. (Monterey, Calif.:Duxbury Press, 1981), ix.

[96]Kegley, 2nd edition, 1982, 438-440.

[97]Russett and Starr, 222.

[98]Kegley, 1996, 467.

[99]Ibid., 466.

[100]Ibid., 266.

[101]Ibid., 472.

[102]Isaak, 86.

[103]Russett and Starr, 255.

[104]Rosenau, 29.

[105]Ibid., 533.

SUGGESTED READINGS

Brisard, Jean-Charles and Guillaume Dasquiè. *Forbidden Truth: U.S.-Taliban Secret Oil Diplomacy and the Failed Hunt for Bin Laden.* (New York: Thunder's Mouth Press/Nation Books,2002).

Gunaratan, Rohan. *Inside Al Qaeda: Global Network of Terror.* (New York: Columbia University Press, 2002).

Khapoya, Vincent. *The African Experience: An Introduction.* Englewood Cliffs, N. J.: Prentice Hall, 1994).

LaFeber, Walter. Inevitable Revolutions. (New York: WW Norton and Company, 1984).

Logevall, Fredrik, ed. Terrorism and 9/11: A Reader. (Boston: Houghton Mifflin Co., 2002).

Mayer, Jeremy D. *American Media Politics in Transition.* (Boston: McGraw-Hill, 2007).

Rossiter, Clinton, and James Lare. The Essential Lippmann: A Political Philosophy for Liberal Democracy. (Cambridge, Mass.: Harvard University Press, 1982).

Snow, Donald M., and Eugene Brown. *Beyond the Water's Edge: An Introduction to U.S. Foreign Policy.* (New York: St. Martin's Press, 1997).

Uribe, Armando. Translated from the Spanish by Jonathan Casart. *The Black Book of American Intervention in Chile.* (Boston: Beacon Press, 1974).

APPENDIX A

Declaration of Independence

Congress, July 4, 1776

When, in the course of human events, it becomes necessary for one people to dissolve the political bonds which have connected them with another, and to assume, among the powers of the earth, the separate and equal station to which the laws of nature and of nature's God entitle them, a decent respect to the opinions of mankind requires that they should declare the causes which impel them to the separation.

We hold these truths to be self-evident: That all men are created equal; that they are endowed by their Creator with certain unalienable rights; that among these are life, liberty and the pursuit of happiness; that, to secure these rights, governments are instituted among men, deriving their just powers from the consent of the governed; that whenever any form of government becomes destructive of these ends, it is the right of the people to alter or to abolish it, and to institute new government, laying its foundation on such principles, and organizing its powers in such form, as to them shall seem most likely to effect their safety and happiness. Prudence, indeed, will dictate that governments long established should not be changed for light and transient causes; and accordingly all experience hath shown that mankind are more disposed to suffer, while evils are sufferable, than to right themselves by abolishing the forms to which they are accustomed. But when a long train of abuses and usurpations, pursuing invariably the same object, evinces a design to reduce them under absolute despotism, it is their right, it is their duty, to throw off such government, and to provide new guards for their future security. Such has been the patient sufferance of these colonies; and such is now the necessity which constrains them to alter their former systems of government. The history of the present King of Great Britain is a history of repeated injuries and usurpations, all having in direct object the establishment of an absolute tyranny over these states. To prove this, let facts be submitted to a candid world.

He has refused his assent to laws, the most wholesome and necessary for the public good.

He has forbidden his governors to pass laws of immediate and pressing importance, unless suspended in their operation till his assent should be obtained; and, when so suspended, he has utterly neglected to attend to them.

He has refused to pass other laws for the accommodation of large districts of people, unless those people would relinquish the right of representation in the legislature, a right inestimable to them, and formidable to tyrants only.

He has called together legislative bodies at places unusual, uncomfortable, and distant from the depository of their public records, for the sole purpose of fatiguing them into compliance with his measures.

He has dissolved representative houses repeatedly, for opposing, with many firmness, his invasions on the rights of the people.

He has refused for a long time, after such dissolutions, to cause others to be elected; whereby the legislative powers, incapable of annihilation, have returned to the people at large for their exercise; the state remaining, in the mean time, exposed to all the dangers of invasions from without and convulsions within.

He has endeavored to prevent the population of these states; for that purpose obstructing the laws for naturalization of foreigners; refusing to pass others to encourage their migrations hither, and raising the conditions of new appropriations of lands.

He has obstructed the administration of justice, by refusing his assent to laws establishing judiciary powers.

He has made judges dependent on his will alone, for the tenure of their offices, and the amount and payment of their salaries.

He has erected a multitude of new offices, and sent hither swarms of officers to harass our people and eat out their substance.

He has kept among us, in times of peace, standing armies, without the consent of our legislatures.

He has affected to render the military independent of, and superior to, the civil power.

He has combined with others to subject us to jurisdiction foreign to our constitution, and unacknowledged by our laws, giving his assent to their acts of pretended legislation:

For quartering large bodies of armed troops among us;

For protecting them, by a mock trial, from punishment for any murder which they should commit on the inhabitants of these states;

For cutting off our trade with all parts of the world;

For imposing taxes on us without our consent;

For depriving us, in many cases, of the benefits of trial by jury;

For transporting us beyond seas, to be tried for pretended offenses;

For abolishing the free system of English laws in a neighboring province, establishing therein an arbitrary government, and enlarging its boundaries, so as to render it at once an example and fit instrument for introducing the same absolute rule into these colonies;

For taking away our charters, abolishing our most valuable laws, and altering fundamentally the forms of our governments;

For suspending our own legislatures, and declaring themselves invested with power to legislate for us in all cases whatsoever.

He has abdicated government here, by declaring us out of his protection and waging war against us.

He has plundered our seas, ravaged our coasts, burned our towns, and destroyed the lives of our people.

He is at this time transporting large armies of foreign mercenaries to complete the works of death, desolation and tyranny already begun with circumstances of cruelty and perfidy scarcely paralleled in the most barbarous ages, and totally unworthy the head of a civilized nation.

He has constrained our fellow-citizens, taken captive on the high seas, to bear arms against their country, to become the executioners of their friends and brethren, or to fall themselves by their hands.

He has excited domestic insurrections among us, and has endeavored to bring on the inhabitants of our frontiers the merciless Indian savages, whose known rule of warfare is an undistinguished destruction of all ages, sexes, and conditions.

In every stage of these oppressions we have petitioned for redress in the most humble terms; our repeated petitions have been answered only by repeated injury. A prince, whose character is thus marked by every act which may define a tyrant, is unfit to be the ruler of a free people.

Nor have we been wanting in our attentions to our British brethren. We have warned them, from time to time, of attempts by their legislature to extend an unwarrantable jurisdiction over us. We have reminded them of the circumstances of our emigration and settlement here. We have appealed to their native justice and magnanimity, and we have conjured them, by the ties of our common kindred, to disavow these usurpations, which would inevitably interrupt our connections and correspondence. They, too, have been deaf to the voice of justice and of consanguinity. We must, therefore, acquiesce in the necessity which denounces our separation, and hold them, as we hold the rest of mankind, enemies in war, in peace friends.

We, therefore, the representatives of the United States of America, in General Congress assembled, appealing to the Supreme Judge of the world for the rectitude of our intentions, do, in the name and by authority of the good people of these colonies, solemnly publish and declare, that these United Colonies are, and of right ought to be, FREE AND INDEPENDENT STATES; that they are absolved from all allegiance to the British crown, and that all political connection between them and the state of Great Britain is, and ought to be, totally dissolved; and that, as free and independent states, they have full power to levy war, conclude peace, contract alliances, establish commerce, and do all other acts and things which independent states may of right do. And for the support of this declaration, with a firm reliance on the protection of Divine Providence, we mutually pledge to each other our lives, our fortunes, and our sacred honor.

JOHN HANCOCK

BUTTON GWINNETT	THOS. NELSON, JR.	RICHD. STOCKTON
LYMAN HALL	FRANCIS LIGHTFOOT LEE	JNO. WITHERSPOON
GEO. WALTON	CARTER BRAXTON	FRAS. HOPKINSON
WM. HOOPER	ROBT. MORRIS	JOHN HART
JOSEPH HEWES	BENJAMIN RUSH	ABRA. CLARK
JOHN PENN	BENJA. FRANKLIN	JOSIAH BARTLETT
EDWARD RUTLEDGE	JOHN MORTON	WM. WHIPPLE
THOS. HEYWARD, JUNR.	GEO. CLYMER	SAML. ADAMS
THOMAS LYNCH, JUNR.	JAS. SMITH	JOHN ADAMS
ARTHUR MIDDLETON	GEO. TAYLOR	ROBT. TREAT PAINE
SAMUEL CHASE	JAMES WILSON	ELBRIDGE GERRY
WM. PACA	GEO. ROSS	STEP. HOPKINS
THOS. STONE	CAESAR RODNEY	WILLIAM ELLERY
CHARLES CARROLL OF CARROLLTON	GEO READ	ROGER SHERMAN
GEORGE WYTHE	THO. M'KEAN	SAM'EL HUNTINGTON
RICHARD HENRY LEE	WM. FLOYD	WM. WILLIAMS
TH. JEFFERSON	PHIL. LIVINGSTON	OLIVER WOLCOTT
BENJ. HARRISON	FRANS. LEWIS	MATTHEW THORNTON
	LEWIS MORRIS	

APPENDIX B

The Constitution of the United States of America

PREAMBLE

We the people of the United States, in order to form a more perfect union, establish justice, insure domestic tranquility, provide for the common defense, promote the general welfare, and secure the blessings of liberty to ourselves and our posterity, do ordain and establish this Constitution for the United States of America.

ARTICLE I.—THE LEGISLATIVE ARTICLE

Section 1. All legislative powers herein granted shall be vested in a Congress of the United States, which shall consist of a Senate and a House of Representatives.

House of Representatives: Composition, Qualification, Apportionment, Impeachment Power

Section 2. The House of Representatives shall be composed of members chosen every second year by the people of the several States, and the electors in each State shall have the qualifications requisite for electors of the most numerous branch of the State Legislature.

No person shall be a Representative who shall not have attained to the age of twenty-five years, and been seven years a citizen of the United States, and who shall not, when elected, be an inhabitant of that State in which he shall be chosen.

Representatives and direct taxes shall be apportioned among the several States which may be included within this Union, according to their respective numbers, *which shall be determined by adding to the whole number of free persons, including those bound to service for a term of years and excluding Indians not taxed, three-fifths of all other persons.* The actual enumeration shall be made within three years after the first meeting of the Congress of the United States, and within every subsequent term of ten years, in such manner as they shall by law direct. The number of Representatives shall not exceed one for every thirty thousand, but each State shall have at least one Representative; *and until each enumeration shall be made, the State of New Hampshire shall be entitled to choose three, Massachusetts eight, Rhode Island and Providence Plantations one, Connecticut five, New York six, New Jersey four, Pennsylvania eight, Delaware one, Maryland six, Virginia ten, North Carolina five, South Carolina five, and Georgia three.*

When vacancies happen in the representation from any State, the Executive authority thereof shall issue writs of election to fill such vacancies.

The House of Representatives shall choose their Speaker and other officers; and shall have the sole power of impeachment.

Passages no longer in effect are printed in italic type.

Senate Composition: Qualifications, Impeachment Trials

Section 3. The Senate of the United States shall be composed of two Senators from each State, *chosen by the legislature thereof,* for six years; and each Senator shall have one vote.

Immediately after they shall be assembled in consequence of the first election, they shall be divided as equally as may be into three classes. The seats of the Senators of the first class shall be vacated at the expiration of the second year, of the second class at the expiration of the fourth year, and of the third class at the expiration of the sixth year, so that one-third may be chosen every second year; and if vacancies happen by resignation or otherwise, during the recess of the legislature of any State, the Executive thereof may make temporary appointments until the next meeting of the legislature, which shall then fill such vacancies.

No person shall be a Senator who shall not have attained to the age of thirty years, and been nine years a citizen of the United States, and who shall not, when elected, be an inhabitant of that State for which he shall be chosen.

The Vice President of the United States shall be President of the Senate, but shall have no vote, unless they be equally divided.

The Senate shall choose their other officers, and also a President *pro tempore*, in the absence of the Vice President, or when he shall exercise the office of President of the United States.

The Senate shall have the sole power to try all impeachments. When sitting for that purpose, they shall be on oath or affirmation. When the President of the United States is tried, the Chief Justice shall preside: and no person shall be convicted without the concurrence of two-thirds of the members present.

Judgment in cases of impeachment shall not extend further than to removal from the office, and disqualification to hold and enjoy any office of honor, trust or profit under the United States; but the party convicted shall nevertheless be liable and subject to indictment, trial, judgment and punishment, according to law.

Congressional Elections: Time, Place, Manner

Section 4. The times, places and manner of holding elections for Senators and Representatives shall be prescribed in each State by the legislature thereof; but the Congress may at any time by law make or alter such regulations, except as to the places of choosing Senators.

The Congress shall assemble at least once in every year, and such meeting *shall be on the first Monday in December, unless they shall by law appoint a different day.*

Powers and Duties of the Houses

Section 5. Each house shall be the judge of the elections, returns and qualifications of its own members, and a majority of each shall constitute a quorum to do business; but a smaller number may adjourn from day to day, and may be authorized to compel the attendance of absent members, in such manner, and under such penalties, as each house may provide.

Each house may determine the rules of its proceedings, punish its members for disorderly behavior, and with the concurrence of two-thirds, expel a member.

Each house shall keep a journal of its proceedings, and from time to time publish the same, excepting such parts as may in their judgment require secrecy; and the yeas and nays of the members of either house on any question shall, at the desire of one-fifth of those present, be entered on the journal.

Neither house, during the session of Congress, shall, without the consent of the other, adjourn for more than three days, nor to any other place than that in which the two houses shall be sitting.

Rights of Members

Section 6. The Senators and Representatives shall receive a compensation for their services, to be ascertained by law and paid out of the treasury of the United States. They shall in all cases except treason, felony and breach of the peace, be privileged from arrest during their attendance at the session of their respective houses, and in going to and returning from the same; and for any speech or debate in either house, they shall not be questioned in any other place.

No Senator or Representative shall, during the time for which he was elected, be appointed to any civil office under the authority of the United States, which shall have been created, or the emoluments whereof shall have been increased, during such time; and no person holding any office under the United States shall be a member of either house during his continuance in office.

Legislative Powers: Bills and Resolutions

Section 7. All bills for raising revenue shall originate in the House of Representatives; but the Senate may propose or concur with amendments as on other bills.

Every bill which shall have passed the House of Representatives and the Senate, shall, before it become a law, be presented to the President of the United States; if he approve he shall sign it, but if not he shall return it with objections to that house in which it originated, who shall enter the objections at large on their journal, and proceed to reconsider it. If after such reconsideration two-thirds of that house shall agree to pass the bill, it shall be sent, together with the objections, to the other house, by which it shall likewise be reconsidered, and if approved by two-thirds of that house, it shall become a law. But in all such cases the votes of both houses shall be determined by yeas and nays, and the names of the persons voting for and against the bill shall be entered on the journal of each house respectively. If any bill shall not be returned by the President within ten days (Sundays excepted) after it shall have been presented to him, the same shall be a law, in like manner as if he had signed it, unless the Congress by their adjournment prevent its return, in which case it shall not be a law.

Every order, resolution, or vote to which the concurrence of the Senate and House of Representatives may be necessary (except on a question of adjournment) shall be presented to the President of the United States; and before the same shall take effect, shall be approved by him, or being disapproved by him, shall be repassed by two-thirds of the Senate and House of Representatives, according to the rules and limitations prescribed in the case of a bill.

Powers of Congress

Section 8. The Congress shall have power

To lay and collect taxes, duties, imposts and excises, to pay the debts and provide for the common defense and general welfare of the United States; but all duties, imposts and excises shall be uniform throughout the United States;

To borrow money on the credit of the United States;

To regulate commerce with foreign nations, and among the several States, and with the Indian tribes;

To establish an uniform rule of naturalization, and uniform laws on the subject of bankruptcies throughout the United States;

To coin money, regulate the value thereof, and of foreign coin, and fix the standard of weights and measures;

To provide for the punishment of counterfeiting the securities and current coin of the United States;

To establish post offices and post roads;

To promote the progress of science and useful arts by securing for limited times to authors and inventors the exclusive right to their respective writings and discoveries;

To constitute tribunals inferior to the Supreme Court;

To define and punish piracies and felonies committed on the high seas and offenses against the law of nations;

To declare war, grant letters of marque and reprisal, and make rules concerning captures on land and water;

To raise and support armies, but no appropriation of money to that use shall be for a longer term than two years;

To provide and maintain a navy;

To make rules for the government and regulation of the land and naval forces;

To provide for calling forth the militia to execute the laws of the Union, suppress insurrections, and repel invasions;

To provide for organizing, arming, and disciplining the militia, and for governing such part of them as may be employed in the service of the United States, reserving to the States respectively the appointment of the officers, and the authority of training the militia according to the discipline prescribed by Congress;

To exercise exclusive legislation in all cases whatsoever, over such district (not exceeding ten miles square) as may, by cession of particular States, and the acceptance of Congress, become the seat of the government of the United States, and to exercise like authority over all places purchased by the consent of the legislature of the State, in which the same shall be, for erection of forts, magazines, arsenals, dock-yards, and other needful buildings;—and

To make all laws which shall be necessary and proper for carrying into execution the foregoing powers, and all other powers vested by this Constitution in the government of the United States, or in any department or officer thereof.

Powers Denied to Congress

Section 9.   *The migration or importation of such persons as any of the States now existing shall think proper to admit shall not be prohibited by the Congress prior to the year 1808; but a tax or duty may be imposed on such importation, not exceeding $10 for each person.*

The privilege of the writ of habeas corpus shall not be suspended, unless when in cases of rebellion or invasion the public safety may require it.

No bill of attainder or ex post facto law shall be passed.

No capitation, or other direct, tax shall be laid, unless in proportion to the census or enumeration herein before directed to be taken.

No tax or duty shall be laid on articles exported from any State.

No preference shall be given by any regulation of commerce or revenue to the ports of one State over those of another; nor shall vessels bound to, or from, one State, be obliged to enter, clear, or pay duties in another.

No money shall be drawn from the treasury, but in consequence of appropriations made by law; and a regular statement and account of the receipts and expenditures of all public money shall be published from time to time.

No title of nobility shall be granted by the United States; and no person holding any office of profit or trust under them, shall, without the consent of the Congress, accept of any present, emolument, office, or title, of any kind whatever, from any king, prince, or foreign state.

Powers Denied to the States

Section 10. No State shall enter into any treaty, alliance, or confederation; grant letters of marque and reprisal; coin money; emit bills of credit; make anything but gold and silver coin a tender in payment of debts; pass any bill of attainder, ex post facto law, or law impairing the obligation of contracts, or grant any title of nobility.

No State shall, without the consent of the Congress, lay any imposts or duties on imports or exports, except what may be absolutely necessary for executing its inspection laws: and the net produce of all duties and imposts, laid by any State on imports or exports, shall be for the use of the treasury of the United States; and all such laws shall be subject to the revision and control of the Congress.

No State shall, without the consent of Congress, lay any duty of tonnage, keep troops or ships of war in time of peace, enter into any agreement or compact with another State, or with a foreign power, or engage in war, unless actually invaded, or in such imminent danger as will not admit of delay.

ARTICLE II.—THE EXECUTIVE ARTICLE

Nature and Scope of Presidential Power

Section 1. The executive power shall be vested in a President of the United States of America. He shall hold his office during the term of four years, and, together with the Vice President, chosen for the same term, be elected, as follows:

Each State shall appoint, in such manner as the legislature thereof may direct, a number of electors, equal to the whole number of Senators and Representatives to which the State may be entitled in the Congress; but no Senator or Representative, or person holding an office of trust or profit under the United States, shall be appointed an elector.

The electors shall meet in their respective States, and vote by ballot for two persons, of whom one at least shall not be an inhabitant of the same State with themselves. And they shall make a list of all the persons voted for, and of the number of votes for each; which list they shall sign and certify, and transmit sealed to the seat of government of the United States, directed to the President of the Senate. The President of the Senate shall, in the presence of the Senate and House of Representatives, open all the certificates, and the votes shall then be counted. The person having the greatest number of votes shall be the President, if such number be a majority of the whole number of electors appointed; and if there be more than one who have such majority, and have an equal number of votes, then the House of Representatives shall immediately choose by ballot one of them for President; and if no person have a majority, then from the five highest on the list said house shall in like manner choose the President. But in choosing the President the votes shall be taken by States, the representation from each State having one vote; a quorum for this purpose shall consist of a member or members from two-thirds of the States, and a majority of all the States shall be necessary to a choice. In every case, after the choice of the President, the person having the greatest number of votes of the electors shall be the Vice President. But if there should remain two or more who have equal votes, the Senate shall choose from them by ballot the Vice President.

The Congress may determine the time of choosing the electors, and the day on which they shall give their votes; which day shall be the same throughout the United States.

No person except a natural-born citizen, *or a citizen of the United States at the time of the adoption of this Constitution*, shall be eligible to the office of President; neither shall any person be eligible to that office who shall not have attained to the age of thirty-five years, and been fourteen years a resident within the United States.

In case of the removal of the President from office or of his death, resignation, or inability to discharge the powers and duties of the said office, the same shall devolve on the Vice President, and the Congress may by law provide for the case of removal, death, resignation, or inability, both of the President and Vice President, declaring what officer shall then act as President, and such officer shall act accordingly, until the disability be removed, or a President shall be elected.

The President shall, at stated times, receive for his services a compensation, which shall neither be increased nor diminished during the period for which he shall have been elected, and he shall not receive within that period any other emolument from the United States, or any of them.

Before he enter on the execution of his office, he shall take the following oath or affirmation: —"I do solemnly swear (or affirm) that I will faithfully execute the office of President of the United States, and will to the best of my ability preserve, protect, and defend the Constitution of the United States."

Powers and Duties of the President

Section 2. The President shall be the commander in chief of the army and navy of the United States, and of the militia of the several States, when called into the actual service of the United States; he may require the opinion, in writing, of the principal officer in each of the executive departments, upon any subject relating to the duties of their respective offices, and he shall have power to grant reprieves and pardons for offenses against the United States, except in cases of impeachment.

He shall have power, by and with the advice and consent of the Senate, to make treaties, provided two-thirds of the Senators present concur; and he shall nominate, and by and with the advice and consent of the Senate, shall appoint ambassadors, other public ministers and consuls, judges of the Supreme Court, and all other officers of the United States, whose appointments are not herein otherwise provided for, and which shall be established by law: but the Congress may by law vest the appointment of such inferior officers, as they think proper, in the President alone, in the courts of law, or in the heads of departments.

The President shall have power to fill up all vacancies that may happen during the recess of the Senate, by granting commissions which shall expire at the end of their next session.

Section 3. He shall from time to time give to the Congress information of the state of the Union, and recommend to their consideration such measures as he shall judge necessary and expedient; he may, on extraordinary occasions, convene both houses, or either of them, and in case of disagreement between them, with respect to the time of adjournment, he may adjourn them to such time as he shall think proper; he shall receive ambassadors and other public ministers; he shall take care that the laws be faithfully executed, and shall commission all the officers of the United States.

Section 4. The President, Vice President and all civil officers of the United States shall be removed from office on impeachment for, and on conviction of, treason, bribery, or other high crimes and misdemeanor.

ARTICLE III.—THE JUDICIAL ARTICLE

Section 1. The judicial power of the United States shall be vested in one Supreme Court, and in such inferior courts as the Congress may from time to time ordain and establish. The judges, both of the

Supreme and inferior courts, shall hold their offices during good behavior, and shall, at stated times, receive for their services a compensation which shall not be diminished during their continuance in office.

Jurisdiction

Section 2. The judicial power shall extend to all cases, in law and equity, arising under this Constitution, the laws of the United States, and treaties made, or which shall be made, under their authority;—to all cases affecting ambassadors, other public ministers and consuls;—to all cases of admiralty and maritime jurisdiction;—to controversies to which the United States shall be a party;—to controversies between two or more States;—*between a state and citizens of another state*;—between citizens of different States;—between citizens of the same State claiming lands under grants of different States, and between a State, or the citizens thereof, and foreign states, citizens or subjects.

In all cases affecting ambassadors, other public ministers and consuls, and those in which a State shall be party, the Supreme Court shall have original jurisdiction. In all the other cases before mentioned, the Supreme Court shall have appellate jurisdiction, both as to law and fact, with such exceptions, and under such regulations, as the Congress shall make.

The trial of all crimes, except in cases of impeachment, shall be by jury; and such trial shall be held in the State where said crimes shall have been committed; but when not committed within any State, the trial shall be at such place or places as the Congress may by law have directed.

Treason

Section 3. Treason against the United States shall consist only in levying war against them, or in adhering to their enemies, giving them aid and comfort. No person shall be convicted of treason unless on the testimony of two witnesses to the same overt act, or on confession in open court.

The Congress shall have power to declare the punishment of treason, but no attainder of treason shall work corruption of blood, or forfeiture except during the life of the person attained.

ARTICLE IV.—INTERSTATE RELATIONS

Full Faith and Credit Clause

Section 1. Full Faith and credit shall be given in each State to the public acts, records, and judicial proceedings of every other State. And the Congress may by general laws prescribe the manner in which such acts, records and proceedings shall be proved, and the effect thereof.

Privileges and Immunities; Interstate Extradition

Section 2. The citizens of each State shall be entitled to all privileges and immunities of citizens in the several States.

A person charged in any State with treason, felony or other crime, who shall flee from justice, and be found in another State, shall on demand of the executive authority of the State from which he fled, be delivered up, to be removed to the State having jurisdiction of the crime.

No person held to service or labor in one State, under the laws thereof, escaping into another, shall, in consequence of any law or regulation therein, be discharged from such service or labor, but shall be delivered up on claim of the party to whom such service or labor may be due.

Admission of States

Section 3. New States may be admitted by the Congress into this Union; but no new State shall be formed or erected within the jurisdiction of any other State; nor any State be formed by the junction of two or more States, or parts of States, without the consent of the legislatures of the States concerned as well as of the Congress.

The Congress shall have power to dispose of and make all needful rules and regulations respecting the territory or other property belonging to the United States; and nothing in this Constitution shall be so construed as to prejudice any claims of the United States, or of any particular State.

Republican Form of Government

Section 4. The United States shall guarantee to every State in this Union a republican form of government, and shall protect each of them against invasion; and on application of the legislature, or of the executive (when the legislature cannot be convened) against domestic violence.

ARTICLE V.—THE AMENDING POWER

The Congress, whenever two-thirds of both houses shall deem it necessary, shall propose amendments to this Constitution, or, on the application of the legislatures of two-thirds of the several States, shall call a convention for proposing amendments, which, in either case, shall be valid to all intents and purposes, as part of this Constitution, when ratified by the legislatures of three-fourths of the several States, or by conventions in three-fourths thereof, as the one or the other mode of ratification may be proposed by the Congress; *provided that no amendment which may be made prior to the year one thousand eight hundred and eight shall in any manner affect the first and fourth clauses in the ninth section of the first article*; and that no State, without its consent, shall be deprived of its equal suffrage in the Senate.

ARTICLE VI.—THE SUPREMACY ACT

All debts contracted and engagements entered into, before the adoption of this Constitution, shall be as valid against the United States under this Constitution, as under the Confederation.

This Constitution, and the laws of the United States which shall be made in pursuance thereof; and all treaties made, or which shall be made, under the authority of the United States, shall be the supreme law of the land; and the judges in every State shall be bound thereby, anything in the Constitution or laws of any State to the contrary notwithstanding.

The Senators and Representatives before mentioned, and the members of the several State legislatures, and all executive and judicial officers, both of the United States and of the several States, shall be bound by oath or affirmation to support this Constitution; but no religious test shall ever be required as a qualification to any office or public trust under the United States.

ARTICLE VII.—RATIFICATION

The ratification of the conventions of nine States shall be sufficient for the establishment of this Constitution between States so ratifying the same.

Done in Convention by the unanimous consent of the States present, the seventeenth day of September in the year of our Lord one thousand seven hundred and eighty-seven and of the Independence of the United States of America the twelfth. In witness whereof we have hereunto subscribed our names.

GEORGE WASHINGTON
President and Deputy from Virginia

New Hampshire
JOHN LANGDON
NICHOLAS GILMAN

Massachusetts
NATHANIEL GORHAM
RUFUS KING

Connecticut
WILLIAM S. JOHNSON
ROGER SHERMAN

Virginia
JOHN BLAIR
JAMES MADISON, JR

South Carolina
J. RUTLEDGE
CHARLES G. PINCKNEY
PIERCE BUTLER

New York
ALEXANDER HAMILTON

New Jersey
WILLIAM LIVINGSTON
DAVID BREARLEY
WILLIAM PATERSON
JONATHAN DAYTON

Pennsylvania
BENJAMIN FRANKLIN
THOMAS MIFFLIN
ROBERT MORRIS
GEORGE CLYMER
THOMAS FITZSIMONS
JARED INGERSOLL
JAMES WILSON
GOUVERNEUR MORRIS

Delaware
GEORGE READ
GUNNING BEDFORD, JR.
JOHN DICKINSON
RICHARD BASSETT
JACOB BROOM

Maryland
JAMES MCHENRY
DANIEL OF ST. THOMAS JENIFER
DANIEL CARROLL

North Carolina
WILLIAM BLOUNT
RICHARD DOBBS SPRAIGHT
HU WILLIAMSON

Georgia
WILLIAM FEW
ABRAHAM BALDWIN

THE BILL OF RIGHTS

The first ten Amendments (the Bill of Rights) were adopted in 1791.

AMENDMENT I.—RELIGION, SPEECH ASSEMBLY, AND PETITION

Congress shall make no law respecting an establishment of religion, or prohibiting the free exercise thereof; or abridging the freedom of speech, or of the press; or the right of the people peaceably to assemble, and to petition the government for a redress of grievances.

AMENDMENT II.—MILITIA AND THE RIGHT TO BEAR ARMS

A well-regulated militia being necessary to the security of a free State, the right of the people to keep and bear arms shall not be infringed.

AMENDMENT III.—QUARTERING OF SOLDIERS

No soldier shall, in time of peace, be quartered in any house without the consent of the owner, nor in time of war, but in a manner to be prescribed by law.

AMENDMENT IV.—SEARCHES AND SEIZURES

The right of the people to be secure in their persons, houses, papers, and effects, against unreasonable searches and seizures, shall not be violated, and no warrants shall issue but upon probable cause, supported by oath or affirmation, and particularly describing the place to be searched, and the persons or things to be seized.

AMENDMENT V.—GRAND JURIES, SELF-INCRIMINATION, DOUBLE JEOPARDY, DUE PROCESS, AND EMINENT DOMAIN

No person shall be held to answer for a capital, or otherwise infamous crime, unless on a presentment or indictment of a grand jury, except in cases arising in the land or naval forces, or in the militia, when in actual service in time of war or public danger; nor shall any person be subject for the same offense to be twice put in jeopardy of life or limb; nor shall be compelled in any criminal case to be a witness against himself, nor be deprived of life, liberty, or property, without due process of law; nor shall private property be taken for public use without just compensation.

AMENDMENT VI.—CRIMINAL COURT PROCEDURES

In all criminal prosecutions, the accused shall enjoy the right to a speedy and public trial, by an impartial jury of the State and district wherein the crime shall have been committed, which district shall have been previously ascertained by law, and to be informed of the nature and cause of the accusation; to be confronted with the witnesses against him; to have compulsory process for obtaining witnesses in his favor, and to have the assistance of counsel for his defense.

AMENDMENT VII.—TRIAL BY JURY IN COMMON LAW CASES

In suits at common law, where the value in controversy shall exceed twenty dollars, the right of trial by jury shall be preserved, and no fact tried by a jury shall be otherwise reexamined in any court of the United States, than according to the rules of the common law.

AMENDMENT VIII.—BAIL, CRUEL AND UNUSUAL PUNISHMENT

Excessive bail shall not be required, nor excessive fines imposed, nor cruel and unusual punishments inflicted.

AMENDMENT IX.—RIGHTS RETAINED BY THE PEOPLE

The enumeration in the Constitution, of certain rights, shall not be construed to deny or disparage others retained by the people.

AMENDMENT X.—RESERVED POWERS OF THE STATES

The powers not delegated to the United States by the Constitution, nor prohibited by it to the States, are reserved to the States respectively, or to the people.

PRE-CIVIL WAR AMENDMENTS

AMENDMENT XI.—SUITS AGAINST THE STATES
[Adopted 1798]

The judicial power of the United States shall not be construed to extend to any suit in law or equity, commenced or prosecuted against one of the United States by citizens of another State, or by citizens or subjects of any foreign state.

AMENDMENT XII.—ELECTION OF THE PRESIDENT
[Adopted 1804]

The electors shall meet in their respective *States*, and vote by ballot for President and Vice President, one of whom, at least, shall not be an inhabitant of the same State with themselves; they shall name in their ballots the person voted for as President, and in distinct ballots the person voted for as Vice President, and they shall make distinct lists of all persons voted for as President, and of all persons voted for as Vice President, and of the number of votes for each, which lists they shall sign and certify, and transmit sealed to the seat of the government of the United States, directed to the President of the Senate;—the President of the Senate shall, in the presence of the Senate and House of Representatives, open all the certificates and the votes shall then be counted;—the person having the greatest number of votes for President shall be the President, if such number be a majority of the whole number of electors appointed; and if no person have such majority, then from the persons having the highest numbers not exceeding three on the list of those voted for as President, the House of Representatives shall choose immediately, by ballot, the President. But in choosing the President, the votes shall be taken by States, the representation from each State having one vote; a quorum for this purpose shall consist of a member or members from two-thirds of the States, and a majority of all the States shall be necessary to a choice. And if the House of Representatives shall not choose a President whenever the right of choice shall devolve upon them, before *the fourth day of March* next following, then the Vice President shall act as President, as in the case of the death or other constitutional disability of the President.

The person having the greatest number of votes as Vice President shall be the Vice President, if such a number be a majority of the whole number of electors appointed; and if no person have a majority, then from the two highest numbers on the list the Senate shall choose the Vice President; a quorum for the purpose shall consist of two-thirds of the whole number of Senators, and a majority of the whole number shall be necessary to a choice. But no person constitutionally ineligible to the office of President shall be eligible to that of Vice President of the United States.

CIVIL WAR AMENDMENTS

AMENDMENT XIII.—PROHIBITION OF SLAVERY
[Adopted 1865]

Section 1. Neither slavery nor involuntary servitude, except as a punishment for crime whereof the party shall have been duly convicted, shall exist within the United States, or any place subject to their jurisdiction.

Section 2. Congress shall have power to enforce this article by appropriate legislation.

AMENDMENT XIV.—CITIZENSHIP, DUE PROCESS, AND EQUAL PROTECTION OF THE LAWS
[Adopted 1868]

Section 1. All persons born or naturalized in the United States, and subject to the jurisdiction thereof, are citizens of the United States and of the State wherein they reside. No State shall make or enforce any law which shall abridge **the privileges or immunities** of citizens of the United States; nor shall any State deprive any person of life, liberty, or property, without **due process of law**; nor deny to any person within its jurisdiction the **equal protection of the laws.**

Section 2. Representatives shall be apportioned among the several States according to their respective numbers, counting the whole number of persons in each State, excluding Indians not taxed. But when the right to vote at any election for the choice of Electors for President and Vice President of the United States, Representatives in Congress, the executive and judicial officers of a State, or the members of the legislature thereof, is denied to any of the male inhabitants of such State, being twenty-one years of age and citizens of the United States, or in any way abridged, except for participation in rebellion, or other crime, the basis of representation therein shall be reduced in the proportion which the number of such male citizens shall bear to the whole number of male citizens twenty-one years of age in such State.

Section 3. No person shall be a Senator or Representative in Congress, or Elector of President and Vice President, or hold any office, civil or military, under the United States, or under any State, who, having previously taken an oath, as a member of Congress, or as an officer of the United States, or as a member of any State legislature, or as an executive or judicial officer of any State, to support the Constitution of the United States, shall have engaged in insurrection or rebellion against the same, or given aid or comfort to the enemies thereof. Congress may, by a vote of two-thirds of each house, remove such disability.

Section 4. The validity of the public debt of the United States, authorized by law, including debts incurred for payment of pensions and bounties for services in suppressing insurrection or rebellion, shall not be questioned. But neither the United States nor any State shall assume or pay any debt or obligation incurred in aid of insurrection or rebellion against the United States, or any claim for the loss or emancipation of any slave; but all such debts, obligations and claims shall be held illegal and void.

Section 5. The Congress shall have power to enforce, by appropriate legislation, the provisions of this article.

AMENDMENT XV.—THE RIGHT TO VOTE
[Adopted 1870]

Section 1. The right of citizens of the United State to vote shall not be denied or abridged by the United States or by any State on account of race, color, or previous condition of servitude.

Section 2. The Congress shall have power to enforce this article by appropriate legislation.

AMENDMENT XVI.—INCOME TAXES
[Adopted 1913]

The Congress shall have power to lay and collect taxes on incomes, from whatever source derived, without apportionment among the several States, and without regard to any census or enumeration.

AMENDMENT XVII.—DIRECT ELECTION OF SENATORS
[Adopted 1913]

Section 1. The Senate of the United States shall be composed of two Senators from each State, elected by the people thereof, for six years; and each Senator shall have one vote. The electors in each State shall have the qualifications requisite for electors of (voters for) the most numerous branch of the State legislatures.

Section 2. When vacancies happen in the representation of any State in the Senate, the executive authority of such State shall issue writs of election to fill such vacancies: Provided, that the Legislature of any State may empower the executive thereof to make temporary appointments until the people fill the vacancies by election as the Legislature may direct.

Section 3. This amendment shall not be so construed as to affect the election or term of any Senator chosen before it becomes valid as part of the Constitution.

AMENDMENT XVIII.—PROHIBITION
[Adopted 1919; Repealed 1933]

Section 1. *After one year from the ratification of this article the manufacture, sale, or transportation of intoxicating liquors within, the importation thereof into, or the exportation thereof from the United State and all territory subject to the jurisdiction thereof, for beverage purposes, is hereby prohibited.*

Section 2. *The Congress and the several States shall have concurrent power to enforce this article by appropriate legislation.*

Section 3. *This article shall be inoperative unless it shall have been ratified as an amendment to the Constitution by the legislatures of the several States, as provided by the Constitution, within seven years from the date of the submission thereof to the States by the Congress.*

AMENDMENT XIX.—FOR WOMEN'S SUFFRAGE
[Adopted 1920]

Section 1. The right of citizens of the United States to vote shall not be denied or abridged by the United States or by any State on account of sex.

Section 2. The Congress shall have power to enforce this article by appropriate legislation.

AMENDMENT XX.—THE LAME DUCK AMENDMENT
[Adopted 1933]

Section 1. The terms of the President and Vice President shall end at noon on the 20th day of January, and the terms of the Senators and Representatives at noon on the 3rd day of January, of the years in which such terms would have ended if this article had not been ratified; and the terms of their successors shall then begin.

Section 2. The Congress shall assemble at least once in every year, and such meeting shall begin at noon on the 3rd day of January, unless they shall by law appoint a different day.

Section 3. If, at the time fixed for the beginning of the term of the President, the President-elect shall have died, the Vice President-elect shall become President. If a President shall not have been chosen before the time fixed for the beginning of his term, or if the President-elect shall have failed to qualify, then the Vice President-elect shall act as President until a President shall have qualified; and the Congress may by law provide for the case wherein neither a President-elect nor a Vice President-elect shall have qualified, declaring who shall then act as President, or the manner in which one who is to act shall be selected, and such persons shall act accordingly until a President or Vice President shall have qualified.

Section 4. The Congress may by law provide for the case of the death of any of the persons from whom the House of Representatives may choose a President whenever the right of choice shall have devolved upon them, and for the case of the death of any of the persons from whom the Senate may choose a Vice President whenever the right of choice shall have devolved upon them.

Section 5. Section 1 and 2 shall take effect on the 15th day of October following the ratification of this article.

Section 6. This article shall be inoperative unless it shall have been ratified as an amendment to the Constitution by the Legislatures of three-fourths of the several States within seven years from the date of its submission.

AMENDMENT XXI.—REPEAL OF PROHIBITION
[Adopted 1933]

Section 1. The eighteenth article of amendment to the Constitution of the United States is hereby repealed.

Section 2. The transportation or importation into any State, Territory, or Possession of the United States for delivery of use therein of intoxicating liquors, in violation of the laws thereof, is hereby prohibited.

Section 3. This article shall be inoperative unless it shall have been ratified as an amendment to the Constitution by conventions in the several States, as provided in the Constitution, within seven years from the date of submission thereof to the States by the Congress.

AMENDMENT XXII.—NUMBER OF PRESIDENTIAL TERMS
[Adopted 1951]

Section 1. No person shall be elected to the office of President more than twice, and no person who has held the office of President, or acted as President, for more than two years of a term to which some other person was elected President shall be elected to the office of President more than once. But this article shall not apply to any person holding the office of President when this article was proposed by the Congress, and shall not prevent any person who may be holding the office of President, or acting as President, during the term within which this article becomes operative from holding the office of President or acting as President during the remainder of such term.

Section 2. This article shall be inoperative unless it shall have been ratified as an amendment to the Constitution by the legislatures of three-fourths of the several States within seven years from the date of its submission to the States by the Congress.

AMENDMENT XXIII.—PRESIDENTIAL ELECTORS FOR THE DISTRICT OF COLUMBIA [Adopted 1961]

Section 1. The District constituting the seat of Government of the United States shall appoint in such manner as the Congress may direct:

A number of electors of President and Vice President equal to the whole number of Senators and Representatives in Congress to which the District would be entitled if it were a State, but in no event more than the least populous State; they shall be in addition to those appointed by the States, but they shall be considered for the purposes of the election of President and Vice President, to be electors appointed by a State; and they shall meet in the District and perform such duties as provided by the twelfth article of amendment.

Section 2. The Congress shall have power to enforce this article by appropriate legislation.

AMENDMENT XXIV.—THE ANTI-POLL TAX AMENDMENT
[Adopted 1964]

Section 1. The right of citizens of the United States to vote in any primary or other election for President or Vice President, for electors for President or Vice President, or for Senator or Representative in Congress, shall not be denied or abridged by the United States or any State by reason of failure to pay any poll tax or other tax.

Section 2. The Congress shall have power to enforce this article by appropriate legislation.

AMENDMENT XXV.—PRESIDENTIAL DISABILITY, VICE-PRESIDENTIAL VACANCIES
[Adopted 1967]

Section 1. In case of the removal of the President from office or his death or resignation, the Vice President shall become President.

Section 2. Whenever there is a vacancy in the office of the Vice President, the President shall nominate a Vice President who shall take office upon confirmation by a majority vote of both Houses of Congress.

Section 3. Whenever the President transmits to the President pro tempore of the Senate and the Speaker of the House of Representatives his written declaration that he is unable to discharge the powers and duties of his office, and until he transmits to them a written declaration to the contrary, such powers and duties shall be discharged by the Vice President as Acting President.

Section 4. Whenever the Vice President and a majority of either the principal officers of the executive departments or of such other body as Congress may by law provide, transmit to the President pro tempore of the Senate and the Speaker of the House of Representatives their written declaration that the President is unable to discharge the powers and duties of his office, the Vice President shall immediately assume the powers and duties of the office as Acting President.

Thereafter, when the President transmits to the President pro tempore of the Senate and the Speaker of the House of Representatives his written declaration that no inability exists, he shall resume the powers and duties of his office unless the Vice President and a majority of either the principal officers of the executive department{s} or of such other body as Congress may by law provide, transmit within four days to the President pro tempore of the Senate and the Speaker of the House of Representatives their written declaration that the President is unable to discharge the powers and duties of his office. Thereupon Congress shall decide the issue, assembling within forty-eight hours for that purpose if not in session. If the Congress, within twenty-one days after receipt of the latter written declaration, or, if Congress is not in session, within twenty-one days after Congress is required to assemble, determines by two-thirds vote of both Houses that the President is unable to discharge the powers and duties of his office, the Vice President shall continue to discharge the same as Acting President; otherwise, the President shall resume the powers and duties of his office.

AMENDMENT XXVI.—EIGHTEEN-YEAR-OLD VOTE
[Adopted 1971]

Section 1. The right of citizens of the United States, who are eighteen years of age or older, to vote shall not be denied or abridged by the United States or by any State on account of age.

Section 2. The Congress shall have power to enforce this article by appropriate legislation.

AMENDMENT XXVII.—VARYING CONGRESSIONAL COMPENSATION
[Adopted 1992]

No law varying the compensation for the service of the Senators and Representatives shall take effect until an election of Representatives shall have intervened.

APPENDIX C

PRESIDENTIAL ELECTIONS

Year	Name	Party	Popular Vote	Electoral College Vote
1789	George Washington	Federalist	—	69
1792	George Washington	Federalist	—	132
1796	John Adams	Federalist	—	71
	Thomas Jefferson	Democratic-Republican	—	68
1800	Thomas Jefferson	Democratic-Republican	—	73
	John Adams	Federalist	—	65
1804	Thomas Jefferson	Democratic-Republican	—	162
	Charles C. Pinckney	Federalist	—	14
1808	James Madison	Democratic-Republican	—	122
	Charles C. Pinckney	Federalist	—	47
1812	James Madison	Democratic-Republican	—	128
	George Clinton	Federalist	—	89
1816	James Monroe	Democratic-Republican	—	183
	Rufus King	Federalist	—	34
1820	James Monroe	Democratic-Republican	—	231
	John Quincy Adams	Democratic-Republican	—	1
1824	John Quincy Adams	Democratic-Republican	108,740	84
	Andrew Jackson	Democratic-Republican	153,544	99
	William Crawford	Democratic-Republican	46,618	41
	Henry Clay	Democratic-Republican	47,136	37
1828	Andrew Jackson	Democrat	647,286	178
	John Quincy Adams	National Republican	508,064	83
1832	Andrew Jackson	Democrat	687,502	219
	Henry Clay	National Republican	530,189	49
	Electoral votes not cast		2	
1836	Martin Van Buren	Democrat	765,483	170
	William Henry Harrison	Whig	550,816	73
	Hugh White	Whig	146,107	26
	Daniel Webster	Whig	41,201	14
	Total for the 3 Whigs		739,795	113
1840	William Henry Harrison	Whig	1,274,624	234
	Martin Van Buren	Democrat	1,127,781	60
1844	James K. Polk	Democrat	1,338,464	170
	Henry Clay	Whig	1,300,097	105
1848	Zachary Taylor	Whig	1,360,967	163
	Lewis Cass	Democrat	1,222,342	127

Year	Name	Party	Popular Vote	Electoral College Vote
	Martin Van Buren	Free-Soil	291,263	—
1852	Franklin Pierce	Democrat	1,601,117	254
	Winfield Scott	Whig	1,385,453	42
	John P. Hale	Free-Soil	155,825	—
1856	James Buchanan	Democrat	1,832,955	174
	John Frémont	Republican	1,339,932	114
	Millard Fillmore	Whig-American	871,731	8
1860	Abraham Lincoln	Republican	1,865,593	180
	John C. Breckinridge	Democratic	848,356	72
	Stephen Douglas	Democrat	1,382,713	12
	John Bell	Constitutional Union	592,906	39
1864	Abraham Lincoln	Unionist (Republican)	2,206,938	212
	George McClellan	Democrat	1,803,787	21
	Electoral votes not cast		81	
1868	Ulysses S. Grant	Republican	3,013,421	214
	Horatio Seymour	Democrat	2,706,829	80
	Electoral votes not cast		23	
1872	Ulysses S. Grant	Republican	3,596,745	286
	Horace Greeley	Democrat	2,843,446	
	Thomas Hendricks	Democrat	—	42
	Benjamin Brown	Democrat	—	18
	Charles Jenkins	Democrat	—	2
	David Davis	Democrat	—	1
1876	Rutherford B. Hayes	Republican	4,036,572	185
	Samuel Tilden	Democrat	4,284,020	184
	Peter Cooper	Greenback	81,737	—
1880	James A. Garfield	Republican	4,453,295	214
	Winfield S. Hancock	Democrat	4,414,082	155
	James B. Weaver	Greenback-Labor	308,578	—
1884	Grover Cleveland	Democrat	4,879,507	219
	James G. Blaine	Republican	4,850,293	182
	Benjamin Butler	Greenback-Labor	175,370	—
	John St. John	Prohibition	150,369	—
1888	Benjamin Harrison	Republican	5,447,129	233
	Grover Cleveland	Democrat	5,537,857	168
	Clinton Fisk	Prohibition	249,506	—
	Anson Streeter	Union Labor	146,935	—
1892	Grover Cleveland	Democrat	5,555,426	277
	Benjamin Harrison	Republican	5,182,690	145
	James B. Weaver	People's	1,029,846	22
	John Bidwell	Prohibition	264,133	—
1896	William McKinley	Republican	7,102,246	271
	William J. Bryan	Democrat	6,492,559	176
	John Palmer	National Democratic	133,148	—
	Joshua Levering	Prohibition	132,007	—
1900	William McKinley	Republican	7,218,491	292
	William J. Bryan	Democrat	6,356,734	155

Year	Name	Party	Popular Vote	Electoral College Vote
	John C. Wooley	Prohibition	208,914	—
	Eugene V. Debs	Socialist	87,814	—
1904	Theodore Roosevelt	Republican	7,628,461	336
	Alton B. Parker	Democrat	5,084,223	140
	Eugene V. Debs	Socialist	402,283	—
	Silas Swallow	Prohibition	258,536	—
	Thomas Watson	People's	117,183	—
1908	William Howard Taft	Republican	7,675,320	321
	William J. Bryan	Democrat	6,412,294	162
	Eugene V. Debs	Socialist	420,793	—
	Eugene Chafin	Prohibition	253,840	—
1912	Woodrow Wilson	Democrat	6,296,547	435
	William Howard Taft	Republican	3,486,720	8
	Theodore Roosevelt	Progressive	4,118,571	86
	Eugene V. Debs	Socialist	900,672	—
	Eugene Chafin	Prohibition	206,275	—
1916	Woodrow Wilson	Democrat	9,127,695	277
	Charles E. Hughes	Republican	8,533,507	254
	A. L. Benson	Socialist	585,113	—
	J. Frank Hanly	Prohibition	220,506	—
1920	Warren Harding	Republican	16,143,407	404
	James M. Cox	Democrat	9,130,328	127
	Eugene V. Debs	Socialist	919,799	—
	P. P. Christensen	Farmer-Labor	265,411	—
	Aaron Watkins	Prohibition	189,408	—
1924	Calvin Coolidge	Republican	15,718,211	382
	John W. Davis	Democrat	8,385,283	136
	Robert La Follette	Progressive	4,831,289	13
1928	Herbert C. Hoover	Republican	21,391,993	444
	Alfred E. Smith	Democrat	15,016,169	87
	Norman Thomas	Socialist	267,835	—
1932	Franklin D. Roosevelt	Democrat	22,809,638	472
	Herbert C. Hoover	Republican	15,758,901	59
	Norman Thomas	Socialist	881,951	—
	William Foster	Communist	102,785	—
1936	Franklin D. Roosevelt	Democrat	27,752,869	523
	Alfred M. Landon	Republican	16,674,665	8
	William Lemke	Union	882,479	—
	Norman Thomas	Socialist	187,720	—
1940	Franklin D. Roosevelt	Democrat	27,307,819	449
	Wendell Willkie	Republican	22,321,018	82
1944	Franklin D. Roosevelt	Democrat	25,606,585	432
	Thomas E. Dewey	Republican	22,014,745	99
1948	Harry S. Truman	Democrat	24,179,345	303
	Thomas E. Dewey	Republican	21,991,291	189
	Strom Thurmond	Dixiecrat	1,176,125	39
	Henry Wallace	Progressive	1,157,326	—
	Norman Thomas	Socialist	139,572	—
	Claude A. Watson	Prohibition	103,900	—

Year	Name	Party	Popular Vote	Electoral College Vote
1952	Dwight D. Eisenhower	Republican	33,936,234	442
	Adlai Stevenson II	Democrat	27,314,992	89
	Vincent Hallinan	Progressive	140,023	—
1956	Dwight D. Eisenhower	Republican	35,590,472	457
	Adlai Stevenson II	Democrat	26,022,752	73
	T. Coleman Andrews	States' Rights	111,178	—
	Walter B. Jones	Democrat	—	1
1960	John F. Kennedy	Democrat	34,226,731	303
	Richard M. Nixon	Republican	34,108,157	219
	Harry Byrd	Democrat	—	15
1964	Lyndon B. Johnson	Democrat	43,129,566	486
	Barry Goldwater	Republican	27,178,188	52
1968	Richard M. Nixon	Republican	31,785,480	301
	Hubert H. Humphrey	Democrat	31,275,166	191
	George Wallace	American Independent	9,906,473	46
1972	Richard M. Nixon	Republican	47,170,179	520
	George McGovern	Democrat	29,171,791	17
	John Hospers	Libertarian	—	1
1976	Jimmy Carter	Democrat	40,830,763	297
	Gerald R. Ford	Republican	39,147,793	240
	Ronald Reagan	Republican	—	1
1980	Ronald Reagan	Republican	43,904,153	489
	Jimmy Carter	Democrat	35,483,883	49
	John Anderson	Independent candidacy	5,719,437	—
1984	Ronald Reagan	Republican	54,455,074	525
	Walter F. Mondale	Democrat	37,577,137	13
1988	George Bush	Republican	48,881,278	426
	Michael Dukakis	Democrat	41,805,374	111
	Lloyd Bentsen	Democrat	—	1
1992	Bill Clinton	Democrat	43,727,625	370
	George Bush	Republican	38,165,180	168
	Ross Perot	Independent candidacy	19,236,411	0
1996	Bill Clinton	Democrat	45,628,667	379
	Bob Dole	Republican	37,869,435	159
	Ross Perot	Independent candidacy	7,874,283	0
2000	George W. Bush	Republican	49,820,518	271
	Albert Gore Jr.	Democrat	50,158,094	267
2004	George W. Bush	Republican	58,900,000	286
	John Kerry	Democrat	55,400,000	252

APPENDIX D

Members of the Supreme Court of the United States

Chief Justices	State App't From	Appointed by President	Service
Jay, John	New York	Washington	1789-1795
Rutledge, John*	South Carolina	Washington	1795-1795
Ellsworth, Oliver	Connecticut	Washington	1796-1799
Marshall, John	Virginia	Adams, John	1801-1835
Taney, Roger Brooke	Maryland	Jackson	1836-1864
Chase, Salmon Portland	Ohio	Lincoln	1864-1873
Waite, Morrison Remick	Ohio	Grant	1874-1888
Fuller, Melville Weston	Illinois	Cleveland	1888-1910
White, Edward Douglass	Louisiana	Taft	1910-1921
Taft, William Howard	Connecticut	Harding	1921-1930
Hughes, Charles Evans	New York	Hoover	1930-1941
Stone, Harlan Fiske	New York	Roosevelt F.	1941-1946
Vinson, Fred Moore	Kentucky	Truman	1946-1953
Warren, Earl	California	Eisenhower	1953-1969
Burger, Warren Earl	Virginia	Nixon	1969-1986
Rehnquist, William H.	Virginia	Reagan	1986-2005
Roberts, John G., Jr.	Maryland	Bush, G. W.	2005-

Associate Justices	State App't From	Appointed by President	Service
Rutledge, John	South Carolina	Washington	1790-1791
Cushing, William	Massachusetts	Washington	1790-1810
Wilson, James	Pennsylvania	Washington	1789-1798
Blair, John	Virginia	Washington	1789-1796
Iredell, James	North Carolina	Washington	1790-1799
Johnson, Thomas	Maryland	Washington	1791-1793
Paterson, William	New Jersey	Washington	1793-1806
Chase, Samuel	Maryland	Washington	1796-1811
Washington, Bushrod	Virginia	Adams, John	1798-1829
Moore, Alfred	North Carolina	Adams, John	1799-1804
Johnson, William	South Carolina	Jefferson	1804-1834
Livingston, Henry Brockholst	New York	Jefferson	1806-1823
Todd, Thomas	Kentucky	Jefferson	1807-1826
Duvall, Gabriel	Maryland	Madison	1811-1836
Story, Joseph	Massachusetts	Madison	1811-1845
Thompson, Smith	New York	Monroe	1823-1843
Trimble, Robert	Kentucky	Adams, J. Q.	1826-1828

*ActingChief Justice; Senate refused to confirm appointment.

McLean, John	Ohio	Jackson	1829-1861
Baldwin, Henry	Pennsylvania	Jackson	1830-1844
Wayne, James Moore	Georgia	Jackson	1835-1867
Barbour, Philip Pendleton	Virginia	Jackson	1836-1841
Catron, John	Tennessee	Jackson	1837-1865
McKinley, John	Alabama	Van Buren	1837-1852
Daniel, Peter Vivian	Virginia	Van Buren	1841-1860
Nelson, Samuel	New York	Tyler	1845-1872
Woodbury, Levi	New Hampshire	Polk	1845-1851
Grier, Robert Cooper	Pennsylvania	Polk	1846-1870
Curtis, Benjamin Robbins	Massachusetts	Fillmore	1851-1857
Campbell, John Archibald	Alabama	Pierce	1853-1861
Clifford, Nathan	Maine	Buchanan	1858-1881
Swayne, Noah Haynes	Ohio	Lincoln	1862-1881
Miller, Samuel Freeman	Iowa	Lincoln	1862-1890
Davis, David	Illinois	Lincoln	1862-1877
Field, Stephen Johnson	California	Lincoln	1863-1897
Strong, William	Pennsylvania	Grant	1870-1880
Bradley, Joseph P.	New Jersey	Grant	1870-1892
Hunt, Ward	New York	Grant	1873-1882
Harlan, John Marshall	Kentucky	Hayes	1877-1911
Woods, William Burnham	Georgia	Hayes	1880-1887
Matthews, Stanley	Ohio	Garfield	1881-1889
Gray, Horace	Massachusetts	Arthur	1882-1902
Blatchford, Samuel	New York	Arthur	1882-1893
Lamar, Lucius Quintus C.	Mississippi	Cleveland	1888-1893
Brewer, David Josiah	Kansas	Harrison	1889-1910
Brown, Henry Billings	Michigan	Harrison	1890-1906
Shiras, George, Jr.	Pennsylvania	Harrison	1892-1903
Jackson, Howell Edmunds	Tennessee	Harrison	1893-1895
White, Edward Douglass	Louisiana	Cleveland	1894-1910
Peckham, Rufus Wheeler	New York	Cleveland	1896-1909
McKenna, Joseph	California	McKinley	1898-1925
Holmes, Oliver Wendell	Massachusetts	Roosevelt T.	1902-1932
Day, William Rufus	Ohio	Roosevelt T.	1903-1922
Moody, William Henry	Massachusetts	Roosevelt T.	1906-1910
Lurton, Horace Harmon	Tennessee	Taft	1910-1914
Hughes, Charles Evans	New York	Taft	1910-1916
Van Devanter, Willis	Wyoming	Taft	1910-1937
Lamar, Joseph Rucker	Georgia	Taft	1911-1916
Pitney, Mahlon	New Jersey	Taft	1912-1922
McReynolds, James Clark	Tennessee	Wilson	1914-1941
Brandeis, Louis Dembitz	Massachusetts	Wilson	1916-1939
Clarke, John Hessin	Ohio	Wilson	1916-1922
Sutherland, George	Utah	Harding	1922-1938
Butler, Pierce	Minnesota	Harding	1923-1939

Sanford, Edward Terry	Tennessee	Harding	1923-1930
Stone, Harlan Fiske	New York	Coolidge	1925-1941
Roberts, Owen Josephus	Pennsylvania	Hoover	1930-1945
Cardozo, Benjamin Nathan	New York	Hoover	1932-1938
Black, Hugo Lafayette	Alabama	Roosevelt F.	1937-1971
Reed, Stanley Forman	Kentucky	Roosevelt F.	1938-1957
Frankfurter, Felix	Massachusetts	Roosevelt F.	1939-1962
Douglas, William Orville	Connecticut	Roosevelt F.	1939-1975
Murphy, Frank	Michigan	Roosevelt F.	1940-1949
Byrnes, James Francis	South Carolina	Roosevelt F.	1941-1942
Jackson, Robert Houghwout	New York	Roosevelt F.	1941-1954
Rutledge, Wiley Blount	Iowa	Roosevelt F.	1943-1949
Burton, Harold Hitz	Ohio	Truman	1945-1958
Clark, Tom Campbell	Texas	Truman	1949-1967
Minton, Sherman	Indiana	Truman	1949-1956
Harlan, John Marshall	New York	Eisenhower	1955-1971
Brennan, William J., Jr.	New Jersey	Eisenhower	1956-1990
Whittaker, Charles Evans	Missouri	Eisenhower	1957-1962
Stewart, Potter	Ohio	Eisenhower	1958-1981
White, Byron Raymond	Colorado	Kennedy	1962-1993
Goldberg, Arthur Joseph	Illinois	Kennedy	1962-1965
Fortas, Abe	Tennessee	Johnson L.	1965-1969
Marshall, Thurgood	New York	Johnson L.	1967-1991
Blackmun, Harry A.	Minnesota	Nixon	1970-1994
Powell, Lewis F., Jr.	Virginia	Nixon	1972-1988
Rehnquist, William H.	Arizona	Nixon	1972-1986**
Stevens, John Paul	Illinois	Ford	1975-
O'Connor, Sandra Day	Arizona	Reagan	1981-2006
Scalia, Antonin	Virginia	Reagan	1986-
Kennedy, Anthony M.	California	Reagan	1988-
Souter, David H.	New Hampshire	Bush, G. H. W.	1990-
Thomas, Clarence	Georgia	Bush, G. H. W.	1991-
Ginsburg, Ruth Bader	New York	Clinton	1993-
Breyer, Stephen G.	Massachusetts	Clinton	1994-
Alito, Samuel A., Jr.	New Jersey	Bush, G. W.	2006-

Notes: The acceptance of the appointment and commission by the appointee, as evidenced by the taking of the prescribed oaths, is here implied; otherwise the individual is not carried on this list of the Members of the Court. Examples: Robert Hanson Harrison is not carried, as a letter from President Washington of February 9, 1790 states Harrison declined to serve. Neither is Edwin M. Stanton who died before he could take the necessary steps toward becoming a Member of the Court. *Chief Justice Rutledge is included because he took his oaths, presided over the August Term of 1795, and his name appears on two opinions of the Court for that Term.

[The foregoing was taken from a booklet prepared by the Supreme Court of the United States.]

**Elevated.

GLOSSARY

Absolute Poverty - The minimum subsistence income needed to survive deprivation.

Acid Rain - Complex chemical and atmospheric phenomenon that occurs when emissions of sulfur and nitrogen compounds and other substances are transformed by chemical processes in the atmosphere, often far from the original source, and then deposited on earth in either a wet or dry form.

Ad Hoc Committee - A temporary special legislative committee formed to perform a specific task.

Ad Valorum Tax System - Property tax assessment based on the fair market value of the property.

Adversary System - The judicial principle that one is innocent of a criminal act until proven guilty.

Affirmative Action - The formalized effort on the part of government to remedy previous incidences of past discrimination particularly in the employment and political processes.

Aid to the Blind - A financial assistance program created through the New Deal to provided assistance to the nation's blind citizens.

Aid to Dependent Children - A New Deal program designed to provide financial assistance to parents of children whose incomes fall below the poverty level. This program became the primary plan for the welfare system. Its name was changed to **Aid to Families With Dependent Children**.

Air - A mixture of nitrogen, oxygen, argon, carbon dioxide with traces of neon, helium, krypton, hydrogen, xenon, methane, and vitreous oxide.

Air Pollution - A group of chemical compounds that are in the wrong place or in the wrong concentration at the wrong time.

Alien and Sedition Acts - A series of four laws passed during John Adams' administration restricting freedom of press and speech and the rights of immigrants.

Alleviative Approach - A public policy option that seeks to relieve the suffering caused by the policy problem without adequately addressing the problem itself.

Almshouse - Another term for poorhouse.

Al Qaeda - "The Core," is the first transnational terrorist group of the twenty-first century, confronting the world with a new kind of threat. It is a radical Islamic organization that forms a worldwide network of individual cells all professing a broad based ideology centered on returning Muslims to the true faith, which is based on the Koran and Hadith.

Amendatory Veto - A type of veto used by the governors of Montana and Illinois whereby the governor can increase or decrease appropriations made by the legislature without further action from the legislature.

Americans with Disabilities Act (1990) - Federal legislation mandating equal opportunities in employment, housing, and accommodations to disabled persons.

Annexation - The process by which cities incorporate adjacent land into their municipal boundaries.

Appellate Jurisdiction - A case is originally heard in another court first and then remanded to another court on appeal. The Supreme Court has both original and appellate jurisdiction.

Apportionment - The process by which the total number of seats in a legislative body is distributed within a state's boundary.

Approach - An orientation, perspective, or way of looking at political phenomena, for example, the traditional or the behavioral approach.

Architectural Barriers Act (1970) - Federal legislation mandating that newly constructed public buildings must be accessible to handicapped persons.

Article VI - An article of the United States Constitution mandating that the constitution is the supreme law of the land. See Supremacy Clause.

Articles of Confederation - The first constitution of the United States adopted in 1777.

Association of Southern Women for the Prevention of Lynching - A woman's organization that lead the battle to end mob-rule dominated lynchings.

At-Large Election - A city- or county-wide election.

Attorney General - The legal counsel for state governments.

Authority - Legitimate or accepted power in a democracy.

Baker v Carr (1962) - The United States Supreme Court decision mandating that reapportionment of state legislative houses must guarantee the principal of "one man, one vote."

Balanced Budget - Budgetary strategy whereby anticipated revenues equal anticipated expenses.

Balance of Power - A global system based strictly on power relationships. In this system, the ultimate goal is to maximize your own power while ensuring that no other country becomes too powerful.

Balance of Terror - The idea that a nuclear holocaust was so abhorrent that it encouraged stability and the avoidance of war.

Barron v Baltimore (1833) - United States Supreme Court ruled that the Bill of Rights was enforceable only upon the actions of the national government.

Benefit Principle System - Based on the principle that those who reap more benefits from government services should shoulder more of the tax burden than people who do not avail themselves of service opportunities to the same degree.

Beyond a Reasonable Doubt - The criteria for determining guilt or innocence in a criminal case.

Bicameral - A two-house legislature.

Biennial Session - A legislative sessions that meets once every two years.

Bill - A legislative proposal formally introduced for consideration.

Biochemical Oxygen Demand - The amount of oxygen needed by bacteria to breakdown a specific amount of organic matter.

Bipolar System - A global system in which power is concentrated in the hands of two main sources of power and they maintain the balance of power in the international community. Between 1947-1962, the international community experienced a bipolar system with the Soviet Union and the United States as the two main sources of power.

Bipolycentric - An international system that took the place of the bipolar structure. The bipolycentric system was much more fluid than the bipolar one, and it allowed the secondary actors and/or client states much more independence from the Soviet Union and the United States.

Boyd v United States (1886) - The United States Supreme Court tied the Fourth Amendment's protection against unreasonable searches to the Fifth Amendment's protection against self-incrimination.

Bracero Program - A federal government sponsored agreement between the United States and Mexico to hire Mexican nationals as agricultural workers.

Brady Bill - A congressional law mandating that state law enforcement agencies conduct criminal background checks prior to allowing an individual to purchase a handgun.

Brown v Board of Education - A 1954 Supreme Court decision that reversed the 1896 *Plessy v Ferguson* decision. The Court, in a unanimous decision, ruled that segregation in public schools was inherently unequal and violated the Fourteenth Amendment and equal protection. This case ended legal segregation in the United States and was the impetus for the modern civil rights movement. This case effectively placed the protection of civil rights under the authority of the national government rather than the states.

Budget - Technical document in the form of a detailed balance sheet identifying expenditures and revenues.

Bureaucracy - The collective term for government agencies.

Cabinet - The attorney general and the thirteen principle officers of the executive departments that provide advise to the president upon his request.

California v Trombetta **(1984)** - The United States Supreme Court ruled breathalyzer tests constitute a legal search and are not a violation of protected privacy rights.

Capital Expenses - Multi-year or amortized expenses.

Casework - A collective term for the services performed by legislators and congresspersons and their staffs at the request of and on behalf of their constituents.

Cash Transfers - Direct payments to program recipients.

Caucus - A meeting of like-minded people.

Central Business District (CBO) - The core of a city.

Cert Conference - Conference at which the Supreme Court justices decide whether to hear a case. Four of the nine justices must agree to hear a case.

Change of Venue - The right of a judge to change the location of a trial to afford the defendant a fair and impartial trial.

Chief Diplomat - The role of the president in which his job is to appoint diplomatic personnel and envoys, receive ambassadors, recognize foreign governments, negotiate treaties, make executive agreements, and hold summit meetings.

Chief Executive - The role of the president in which his job as the head of the executive branch of the government is, according to the Constitution, to "take Care that the Laws be faithfully executed."

Chief Legislator - The role of the president in which his job consists of setting forth a broad legislative agenda in his annual State of the Union address, sending proposals for legislation to the Congress, making efforts to secure the passage of bills that he favors, and vetoing legislation not to his liking.

Chief of State - The ceremonial or symbolic role of the president in which he serves as a "figurehead" rather than a "working head" of the government.

Child Benefit Theory - The notion that public funding can be provided to students who attend private, public and parochial schools as long as it is the child, rather than the school, that benefits from the funding.

Children's Health Insurance Program (CHIP) - A federally funded health care plan for children whose parents cannot afford health care even though their incomes are above the poverty level.

Church of the Lukumi Babbalu Aye v Hialeah **(1985)** - The United States Supreme Court ruled that the church's practice of animal sacrifice was constitutionally protected under the First Amendment's guarantee to religious freedom.

City - A municipal corporation chartered by the state.

City Charter - Organic law of home rule cities detailing the structure, powers, and responsibilities of local government.

City/County Consolidation - The combining or merging of separate city and county governments into one governing unit.

City of Trenton v State of New Jersey **(1913)** - United States Supreme Court decision upholding Dillon's Rule.

Civil Law - Focuses on disputes between citizens such as whether or not one has violated a contract, whether or not one person has wronged another (for instance, through negligence), divorce proceedings, and the like.

Civil Rights - Acts of government intended to protect disadvantaged classes of persons or minority groups from arbitrary, unreasonable, or discriminatory treatment.

Civil Rights Acts (1866) - Federal legislation granting former slaves the rights to own property, file lawsuits and make contractual agreements.

Civil Rights Act (1875) - Federal legislation prohibiting private discrimination in accommodations, transportation, and public places of amusement. This law was declared unconstitutional by the United States Supreme Court's ruling in *Plessy v Ferguson*.

Civil Rights Act (1957) - Federal legislation establishing the United States Commission on Civil Rights and the Civil Rights Section of the United States Justice Department.

Civil Rights Act (1960) - Federal legislation authorizing the use of federal voter referees to conduct voter registration drives and to monitor federal elections in areas with historical patterns of voting problems.

Civil Rights Act (1964) - Federal legislation prohibiting discrimination in public accommodations and employment practices. The law also established a sixth grade education as meeting voter literacy and testing requirements.

Civil Rights Act (1968) - Federal legislation prohibiting discrimination in housing practices.

Civilian Conservation Corps. (CCC) - A New Deal program designed to hire the unemployed to work rural areas.

Classified Charter - A city charter plan that draws a distinction between large and small cities by giving more independent governing authority to larger metropolitan areas.

Clear and Present Danger - The criteria established by the United States Supreme Court in *Schenck v United States* (1919) to determine whether or not spoken words or symbolic displays violate the First Amendment's guarantee of freedom of speech.

Client States - During the bipolar structure, client states and/or allies that were committed to one bloc or the other. Each client state relied on the main pole of power for protection from the other power.

Coates v Cincinnati (1971) - United States Supreme Court ruling that a city ordinance denying three or more individuals to gather in a public place was an unconstitutional violation of the First Amendment's guarantee to freedom of assembly and association.

Cohen v California (1971) - The United States Supreme Court ruled that the wearing of a jacket bearing an inappropriate word against the draft was a constitutionally protected right to freedom of speech.

Cold War - Term used to describe the relationship between the United States and the Soviet Union between 1945 and 1991.

Commander in Chief - The role of the president in which he serves as the civilian head of U.S. military forces.

Commission - A form of city government whereby elected commissioners serve as the governing body.

Commissioners Court - A type of county government composed on a county judge and at least four commissioners.

Common Law - Judge-made law originating in England from decisions based on prevailing customs.

Compensino - A farm laborer.

Concept - Words or names used to symbolize or represent ideas.

Concurrent Majorities - John C. Calhoun is usually credited with being the champion of concurrent majorities in order to protect the interests of the South prior to the Civil War. Concurrent majorities virtually give state governments veto power over the national government. In contrast to majority rule, Calhoun believed that each region of the country should be able to sustain veto power over the majority. This would ensure the rights of minorities. Calhoun's theories can be seen in the modern-day "devolution revolution."

Concurrent powers - Constitutional powers that are simultaneously shared by the national and state governments, for example, the power to tax. However, in the process of implementing concurrent powers the state does not have the right to thwart national policy.

Concurrent Resolution - A legislative action passed by a simple majority in both Houses that requires the approval of the president or governor.

Confederation - It is a system of government that is a subset of federalism.

Conference Committee - A special joint legislative committee composed of members from both Houses to reconcile differences over similar pieces of legislation.

Connecticut Compromise - It is also known as the Great Compromise. It was a compromise reached at the constitutional convention between the New Jersey Plan and Virginia Plan. It established a bicameral legislature, the House of Representatives and the Senate. The House of Representatives was to be based on population; the Senate on equal representation of states.

Constitution - It is the supreme law of the land. It creates institutions of government and sets the parameters of political power.

Containment - U.S. foreign policy designed to physically restrain the Soviet Union in Europe and the ideology of communism throughout the world.

Coroner - Officer of the county that certifies the causes of death and manages the county morgue.

Council-Manager - A form of city government in which the city council appoints a professional administrator or manager to act as the chief executive.

County - A major unit of local government in the United States that exists as a principal agency for the state and as a unit for local governance.

County Board - The governing body of county government. (See Commissioners Court)

County Clerk - A county's official record keeper for all vital statistics to include birth and death certificates, marriage licenses, divorce and child custody records, mortgages, deeds, wills, and so on.

County/District Attorney - A county's chief prosecutor for criminal activities.

County/District Courts - The first level of trial courts for felony cases at the state level.

County Sheriff - The chief law enforcement officer for county governments.

County Tax Assessor/Collector - An elected county official responsible for assessing and collecting property taxes levied against residential and commercial properties.

Court of Appeal - These courts are the second of the three tiers of the national court system and are designed to hear cases on appeal from the district court. They do not determine guilt or innocence of an individual but decide whether they received a fair trial at the district level.

Criminal Law - The code that regulates the conduct of individuals, defines crimes and provides punishment for violators.

Crisis Policy Response - A foreign policy option used when the perception of a threat to National security cuts across normal channels of decisions.

Curative Approach - A public policy option designed to solve an identified problem.

Dayton Accords - Dayton, Ohio, 1996. U. S. brokered peace agreement that attempted to end hostilities between the warring factions in the former Yugoslavia.

Dealignment - Traditional constituents defect from two national political parties.

Decision-making - The choice of an alternative from among a series of alternatives.

Dedicated Revenues - Constitutionally mandated budgetary allocations to a particular budget line item.

De Facto Discrimination - An undeliberate action adversely impacting one group over another group.

Defense of Marriage Act (1996) - A federal law mandating that the individual states do not have to recognize same-sex marriages as a legal union.

De Jure Discrimination - A purposeful action that adversely impacts one group over another group.

Democracy - A political regime in which the power base is constitutionally given to the people. (See "Regime.")

Derrickson v City of Danville - The United Sates Supreme Court ruling mandating that the city's at-large city council elections underrepresented the African-American community.

Dillon's Rule - An 1868 court decision detailing the control state governments can exercise over county and municipal governing units.

Direct Democracy - A type of democracy, sometimes referred to as a participatory democracy, in which the people make the political decisions and laws by which they are governed.

Discrimination - Unfavorable action towards people because they are members of a particular racial or ethnic group.

Disparate Impact - Standards used in employment practices that have the effect of excluding people with disabilities on the basis of tests or standards that are not directly related to the skills or experience required to perform the job.

Disparate Treatment - Actions in which employers treat people with disabilities differently from others.

Distributive Policies - Governmental actions that convey tangible benefits to individuals, groups, or corporations.

District Court - They are the first of three tiers of the national court system, and they are designed to function as the trial court.

Districting - The process of drawing boundaries on a map that delineate the geographic areas-the districts-from which representatives will be elected.

Divine Right Theory of Kings - The concept of kingship based on the notion that monarchs rule by the will of, indeed, in place, of God.

Dove - An individual who is prone to not using military solutions to foreign policy problems.

Dred Scott v Sanford (1857) - United States Supreme Court decision nullifying the Missouri Compromise of 1821 and stipulating that slaves were not citizens of the United States and therefore, could not sue the government in a court of law.

Drinking Water - All water distributed by any agency or individual, public or private, for the purpose of human consumption or which may be used in the preparation of foods or beverages or for the cleansing of any utensil or article used in the course of preparation or consumption of food or beverages for human beings.

Dual Court System - Network of national and state courts.

Due Process - The procedural safeguards guaranteed to those who would be deprived of life, liberty, or property because they are accused of criminal wrongdoing.

Earmarked - Another term for dedicated revenues.

Economic Opportunity Act (1965) - Federal legislation establishing the Office of Economic Opportunity as the coordinator for all federal anti-poverty initiatives with state and local governments.

Elasticity - An economic criterion applied to a tax that refers to the tax's ability to generate increased revenue as economic growth or inflation increases.

Elector - An individual who casts a ballot for the president and the vice president according to the wishes of the majority of state voters. (See "Faithless Elector.")

Elite Theory of Democracy - One of several explanations of who has power in a political community. It holds that power resides primarily with the relatively few people who have the most of one or more of the fundamental values such as wealth, prestige, education, etc.

Emergency Power - An inherent power given to the president to facilitate his ability to act swiftly in times when a national crisis, particularly in the area of foreign affairs, may necessitate an immediate decision or response.

Emergency Relief Administration - A New Deal agency designed to provide food, shelter and clothing to the nation's unemployed during the Great Depression.

Empirical - Knowledge that is derived from and tested by the senses, especially systematic observations.

Endangered Species - One in danger of becoming extinct throughout all or a significant part of its natural range.

Engle v Vitale (1962) - United States Supreme Court decision mandating that involuntary prayer in the public schools was an unconstitutional violation of the First Amendment's guarantee to religious freedom.

Entitlements - Benefits provided by government to which recipients have a legally enforceable right.

Epistemology - A branch of philosophy that examines the origins and nature of human knowledge and the methods that are used to acquire it.

Escobedo v Illinois (1964) - The United States Supreme Court ruled that an individual can request legal counsel when the interrogation process turns from exploratory to accusatory.

Establishment Clause - The First Amendment to the United States Constitution granting religious freedoms and separating church related matters from state or governmental matters.

Ethnocentric - View of the world from one's own cultural perspective.

Everson v Board of Education of the Township of Ewing (1947) - The United States Supreme Court ruled that giving public tax dollars to low-income parents to offset the cost of children's transportation to and from public and parochial schools was not a violation of the separation of church and state doctrine.

Exclusionary Rule - Evidence that is otherwise admissible may not be used in a criminal trial if it is a product of illegal police conduct.

Executive Office of the President (EOP) - The numerous offices, agencies, organizations, departments, and councils that provide administrative assistance to the president.

Executive Order - An edict or decree from a president that has the force of law.

Exercise Clause - Another term for Establishment Clause.

Explicit Powers - Explicit or enumerated powers are powers of the national government that are specifically designated in the Constitution, for example, Article I, Section 8 lists the specific powers of Congress. Strictly adhering to the specific grants of power is known as strict construction of the Constitution.

Faithless Elector - An individual who follows personal choice, rather than the wishes of state voters, in casting a ballot for the president and the vice president. (See "Elector.")

Federalism - A system of government where power is shared between two or more units of government. This means that power is decentralized and there are different points of power within government that have power and authority over the same people and the same territory.

Felony - A serious crime punishable by death or imprisonment in a penitentiary for a year or more.

Feminization of Poverty - The increased number of single-parent families headed by a female whose income falls below the poverty level.

Fighting Words - Words that by their very nature inflict injury upon those to whom they are addressed.

Fiscal Policy - Public policy concerning taxes, government spending, public debt, and management of government money.

Food Stamp Program - A federally funded program in the 1960s providing coupons to those whose incomes were below the poverty level to purchase food items.

Funnel of Causality - Analytical tool used by political scientists to examine foreign policy decision-making.

Furman v Georgia (1972) - The United States Supreme Court ruled that the death penalty was a violation of the Fourteenth Amendment's guarantee of due process and equal protection of the law.

Game Theory - A behavioral approach to the study of politics that focuses on the decision-making process. (See "Approach.")

Gannett v DePasquale (1979) - The United States Supreme Court upheld a lower court ruling barring members of the press and the public from pretrial hearings.

Gatekeeper - An individual or institution who is in a position to control the flow of information.

Gentrification - The process whereby upper-middle income whites (Anglos) move into inner-city neighborhoods and rehabilitate the properties.

Gerrymandering - The purposeful drawing of legislative districts to favor one group or one political party over other groups or political parties.

Gibbons v Ogden - A Supreme Court decision in 1824 that essentially empowered the national government to develop a national economy. This case went a long way in establishing the nationalists' position and the concept of national supremacy by validating Congress' power to use the "commerce clause" in the Constitution to regulate interstate and foreign commerce.

Gideon v Wainwright (1963) - The United States Supreme Court ruled that all persons accused of committing a crime have a constitutional right to legal counsel.

Gitlow v New York (1925) - The Supreme Court was not involved in First Amendment cases until fairly recent times. In 1925, *Gitlow v. New York,* the Court stated that the Fourteenth Amendment made the First Amendment applicable to the states. This was the beginning of the incorporation doctrine of the Supreme Court.

Glass Ceiling - The practice of denying women accessibility to upper management positions.

Global Warming (greenhouse effect) - The effect of increasing amounts of methane, carbon dioxide, and certain air pollutants resulting in trapping heat in the earth's atmosphere and gradually warming it.

Government - The people and the institutions who make and enforce political decisions.

Grand Jury - A panel charged with reviewing evidence in a case to determine whether or not a case should be forwarded for trial.

Grandfather Clause - A Jim Crow law requiring that individuals whose grandfathers could not vote before 1860 to pass a literacy test as a requirement for voting; ruled unconstitutional by the United States Supreme Court in *Guinn v United States* (1915).

Group Theory of Democracy - One of several explanations of who has power in a political community. It holds that power resides primarily with interest groups.

Guinn v United States 1915) - The United States Supreme Court ruled that Oklahoma's use of the grandfather clause to preclude African Americans from voting was an unconstitutional violation of the Fifteenth Amendment of the United States Constitution.

Hawk - An individual who is prone to using military solutions to foreign policy problems.

Haze - Wide-scale, low-level pollution that obstructs visibility.

Hegemony - One country establishes political and/or military dominance over others.

Health Maintenance Organizations (HMOs) - Prepaid health-care systems emphasizing preventive medical services.

Home Building and Loan Association v Blaisdell (1934) - The United States Supreme Court ruled that contracts between two or more parties can be modified by state laws to prevent social and economic catastrophe.

Home Rule - Usually granted to large municipal areas, the ability or power of a municipal corporation to develop and implement its own charter.

Home Rule Charter - A city charter allowing a city to choose among a number of options, its own form of government.

Homeless - A term used to describe those individuals who lack permanent shelter.

Horizontal Federalism - Interstate relationships in accordance with Article IV (Full faith and credit clause) of the United States Constitution.

Housing Act (1937) - Congressional legislation providing for federal funding for the construction of low-income apartments in inner-city areas.

Hyperpoor - A term used to describe those individuals whose annual incomes are less than half of the official poverty level.

Ideology - A consistent way of thinking about man and society.

Impact Statement - A report detailing any potential harm a project might cause to the environment, the possible solutions to prevent undo environmental damage, and potential efforts on the part of the project sponsors to maintain and hopefully enhance the productivity of the environment.

Impaired Rivers - A waterway that cannot support aquatic life.

Implied Powers - These powers are not specifically granted in the Constitution but are reasonably inferred from the explicit grants of power. Implied powers stretch the boundaries of the Constitution. The "necessary and proper" clause, the last paragraph of Article I, Section 8, states that Congress has the power to "make all laws necessary and proper for carrying into execution" the powers of Article I, Section 8. When the national government implements its implied powers, it is often known as loose construction of the Constitution.

Impoundment - The refusal of a president to release or spend money that has been appropriated by Congress in the federal budget.

Incorporation Doctrine - The Fourteenth Amendment nationalized the Bill of Rights. The Supreme Court began to incorporate the first ten amendments into the Fourteenth so that whatever the national government was forbidden to do, the states could not do either.

Indian Removal Act (1830) - Federal legislation mandating the forced relocation of Native American tribes from east to west of the Mississippi River.

Indirect Democracy - A type of democracy, sometimes referred to as a representative democracy, in which the people elect others to make political decisions and laws for them. (See "Republic.")

Inelastic Tax - A tax program that does not generate increased revenues in proportion to economic growth.

Infrastructure - The collective term for roads, buildings, sewers, water supply systems, and similar structures essential for a municipality to operate.

Inherent Power - This is a special classification of constitutional power in the area of foreign affairs. It is neither an explicit nor implied grant of power but rather grows out of the very existence of the Constitution. These powers exist simply because the national government exists. For example, in the field of foreign affairs, since the United States is one sovereign power, the national government is the only government that can act for it.

Inherited Powers - These are powers the national government inherited from tradition including the British Parliament and early state legislatures.

Initiative - A set of procedures through which residents in a state or local community may propose new legislation or an amendment to the constitution.

In-Kind Programs - Means-tested services providing assistance that has a cash value even though it is not received in cash.

Integration - The practice of desegregating public schools, public accommodations, residential areas, and so on.

Interim Committee - A standing committee of a state legislative house that continues to meet when the legislature is not in session.

Intermestic Issues - Those issues such as trade, finance, pollution, energy, terrorism, human rights, etc., which overlap foreign and domestic policy boundaries.

Internationalism - Country's foreign policy constructed to actively engage in world arena. This engagement includes the philosophy of reconstruction and reforming present world political environment in a country's own image.

Isolationism - Country's foreign policy constructed to withdraw it from international arena.

Issue Network - A set of organizations that share expertise in a policy area and interact with each other over time as relevant issues are debated.

Jihad - Holy war.

Jim Crow - A series of economic, political, and social laws enacted in the southern states to deny African Americans access to employment, social activities, and political rights including voting privileges.

Joint Committee - A legislative committee composed of members from both legislative Houses.

Joint Resolution - A legislative action passed by a majority in both Houses of Congress or a state legislature requiring the president's or governor's signature for approval.

Judicial Court - Article III inferior courts.

Judicial Review - The power of the courts to hold unconstitutional and unenforceable any law, any official action based upon a law, any other action by a public official it deems (upon careful reflection and in line with the taught tradition of the law and judicial restraint) to be in conflict with the Constitution.

Judiciary Act of 1789 - First congressional act passed that specifically dealt with its power to create inferior courts.

Katz v United States (1967) - The United States Supreme Court ruled that wiretapping a public phone is a violation of the constitution's guarantee to privacy.

La Raza Unida - A third political party movement dedicated to the concerns of the Hispanic community.

Leadership - The ability to make others feel safe and secure by providing them with direction and guidance.

Lee v Weisman (1992) - The United States Supreme Court ruled that public schools could use a clergy-led prayer at graduation ceremonies only if the prayer was non-sectarian and non-proselytizing.

Legislative Courts - Article I inferior courts.

Lemon Test - The criteria established by the United States Supreme Court to determine governmental violations of the separation of church and state doctrine.

Lemon v Kurtzman (1971) - The United States Supreme Court established the criteria for judging whether or not government actions or legislative acts violated the separation of church and state doctrine.

Libel - Defamation of character in print or by other visual presentations

License - A privilege granted by government to do something that it otherwise considers to be illegal.

Lieutenant Governor - In forty-two states, the second highest ranking state executive officer.

Line-item Veto - A governor's authority to disapprove an appropriated amount without vetoing the entire bill. (The United States Congress did grant this authority to the president; however, the United States Supreme Court ruled it as an unconstitutional grant of power.)

Literacy Test - A written or oral examination to determine whether or not an individual possessed the required intelligence to vote.

Magna Carta - A document written in 1215 by English noblemen placing restrictions upon the authority of their king.

Main Street Project – Municipal rehabilitation project created by the National Trust for Historical Preservation to maintain historically significant properties.

Majoritarian Theory of Democracy - One of several explanations of who has power in a political community. It holds that power resides primarily with the people or citizens who take the majority position on a given issue.

Mal-apportionment - A districting plan whereby legislators from some districts represent more people than legislators from other districts.

Mandates - Legislative orders arising from statutes, court decisions, and administrative orders that demand action from a subordinate government.

Manifest Destiny - The concept that the United States was destined because of its innate superiority to govern the North American continent.

***Mapp v Ohio* (1961)** - The United States Supreme Court established the exclusionary rule whereby evidence obtain in an illegal search is inadmissible in court.

Marbury v Madison - An 1803 Supreme Court decision that established the concept of judicial review.

Mayor-Council System - A city council system of urban government with a separately elected executive (mayor) and an urban legislature (the city council) usually elected in a partisan ward (or district) elections

Matrix - A rectangular array of information.

McCulloch v Maryland - A landmark Supreme Court decision in 1819 that established both the concepts of national supremacy and implied powers. The Court maintained that the national government had the "implied power" to establish a national bank and that the state governments did not have the right to thwart national policy.

McLaurin v Oklahoma State Regents (1950) - The United States Supreme Court ruled that segregated facilities at public universities was an unconstitutional violation of the Fourteenth Amendment of the United States Constitution.

Means-tested Programs - Eligibility based upon the applicant's documented inability to provide for his/herself the desired benefit because of depressed income levels.

Medicaid - Government-sponsored health-care program for individuals whose incomes fall below the poverty level.

Medicare - Government-sponsored health-care program for individuals over 65 years of age regardless of income level.

Medigap Insurance - Supplemental health-care coverage.

Method - The process by which political knowledge or information is acquired, for example, the scientific method. Methodology is a branch of epistemology. (See "Epistemology.")

Miller v California (1973) - The United States Supreme Court established the criteria for obscenity.

Minor v Happersat (1875) - The United States Supreme Court ruled that the Fourteenth Amendment to the United States Constitution did not give women the right to vote.

Minority Vote Dilution - The process of dividing large minority populations into several legislative districts to prevent them from electing candidates from their own minority group.

Minority Vote Packing - The purposeful drawing of legislative districts whereby large minority population groups are placed into one or two legislative districts.

Misdemeanor - A minor criminal offense.

Mitchell v Helms (2000) - The United States Supreme Court ruled that a Louisiana state law providing public funding for instructional equipment to public and private schools was not a violation of the separation of church and state doctrine.

Model Cities Program - A federal program created in the 1960s to encourage urban areas to provide low-income housing units.

Multinational Corporation (MNC) - A corporation whose business ventures and investments are transnational.

Municipal Bonds - A bond program used by governments to fund major capital improvement programs to include roads, drainage, convention facilities, and so on.

Municipal Courts - City courts with limited jurisdiction over traffic-related cases; also known as traffic courts.

Municipal Solid Waste - Solid waste resulting from or incidental to municipal, community, commercial, institutional, and recreational activities including garbage, rubbish, ashes, street cleanings, dead animals, abandoned automobiles, and all other solid waste other than industrial waste.

Mujahidin - Guerrilla fighters responsible for expelling the Soviets from Afghanistan in 1989.

Nation-state - Political term for "country"; Denotes political and territorial sovereignty.

National Ambient Air Quality Standards (NAAQS) - The attainment levels established by the Environmental Protection Agency for air quality standards.

National Association for the Advancement of Colored Persons (NAACP) - A predominately African-American group founded by W. E. B. Dubois to address social, economic, and political discrimination against African Americans.

National Youth Core - A federally fund New Deal program to put unemployed youths to work during the Depression Era.

National Interest - It is the sum total of a state's goals and objectives and represents the decision-makers' ordering of a country's priorities.

National Supremacy - It is the concept that the Constitution is supreme to the national government and the national government is supreme to the states. The foundations for national supremacy are found in Article IV of the Constitution in the national supremacy clause.

Nativism - The belief that only those born on their country's soil should reap the benefits of their birthrights.

***Near v Minnesota* (1931)** - The United States Supreme Court established the rule of "no prior restraint" regarding the freedom of the print media to publish news items.

Nebraska Press Association v Stuart (1976) - The United States Supreme Court overturned a gag order issued by a district court as a violation of First Amendment's guarantee to freedom of the press.

New York Times v Sullivan (1964) - The United States Supreme Court ruled that the *New York Times* was exercising its constitutionally protected right to freedom of the press when it printed a story about a Montgomery, Alabama police commissioner.

New York Times v United States (1971) - The United States Supreme Court ruled that the *New York Times* and the *Washington Post* were constitutionally protected by the First Amendment's guarantee to freedom of the press when they published sensitive data concerning the United States' involvement in Vietnam.

Nixon v Herndon (1927) - The United States Supreme Court ruled that the Texas White Primary Law of 1924 was unconstitutional.

No Prior Restraint - The ability of the print media to publish without government interference.

Nominal Definition - A description that indicates how a concept is to be used.

Non-Point Source Pollution - Pollution whose specific point of entry into the water cannot be traced.

Non-Working Poor - A term used to describe unemployed individuals whose incomes fall at or below the poverty level.

Old Age Assistance Program - A New Deal program designed to assist the nation's elderly during the Depression Era.

Old Age Insurance - A program created by the Social Security Act of 1935 providing a self-funded insurance for the nation's elderly and disabled.

Olmstead v United States (1928) - The United States Supreme Court ruled that wiretapping was not a violation of the Fourth Amendment's protection against unreasonable searches and seizures.

Operating Expenses - Yearly expenses needed to run government such as salaries, benefits, equipment, rent, utilities, supplies, etc.

Original Jurisdiction - The court in which a case is first heard, usually a trial court. However, the Constitution grants the Supreme Court original jurisdiction in certain circumstances.

Outputs - Tangible manifestations of public policies, the things actually done in pursuance of policy decisions and statements.

Ozone - A primary ingredient of smog.

Palko v Connecticut (1937) - United States Supreme Court ruling distinguishing fundamental rights from non-fundamental rights.

Party Disassociation - Citizens not only do not align themselves with one or the other of the two national parties but rather see political parties as superfluous in the political process.

Paternalistic Attitude - The belief of male superiority over women.

Pay Equity - The term used to recognize that women earn less than their male counterparts employed in comparable positions.

Personal Responsibility and Work Opportunity Act (1996) - Federal legislation initiating reform of the welfare system.

Pink Collar Job - Collective term applied to secretarial and clerical jobs usually held by women.

Plessy v Ferguson - An 1896 Supreme Court decision that provided the constitutional foundations for apartheid in the United States. The Court validated the Jim Crow laws that had been passed after Reconstruction and the concept of "separate but equal" facilities for whites and blacks when it upheld a Louisiana statute that required railroads to provide "equal but separate accommodations for the white and colored races."

Pluralism - The view that competition and subsequent negotiation and bargaining among multiple centers of power is the key to understanding how decisions are made.

Pocket Veto - Upon receiving a bill from Congress the president takes no action and, if Congress adjourns within the following ten working days, the bill is automatically killed.

Point of Service (POS) - A health care program charging members a higher premium and co-payments for using non-HMO approved physicians and health services.

Point-Source Pollution - Pollution that can be traced to a specific point of introduction into the water.

Pole - In foreign policy, a term to designate a center of power.

Policy - A proposed course of action of a person, group or government within a given environment providing obstacles and opportunities which the policy was supposed to utilize and overcome in an effort to reach a goal or realize an objective or purpose.

Policy Making - A pattern of action, extending over time and involving many decisions, some routine, and some not so routine.

Policy Outcomes - The consequences for society, intended or unintended, that flow from the action or inaction by government.

Political Culture - The predominant political beliefs, attitudes, and values collectively shared by a people at a given time.

Political Machine - Political party organizations in large cities effective in turning out the vote for their candidate. Political patronage is often used by the machine as an inducement for party loyalty.

Political Party - A political party is a linkage institution that connects people to government. In the best of all possible worlds it translates the needs of the people into governmental policy.

Political Patronage - The hiring and firing of individuals for governmental jobs based on party loyalty and electoral support.

Political Science - The academic discipline devoted to the systematic study of political phenomena. (See "Politics.")

Political Spectrum - The range of political beliefs from the left (communism) to the right (fascism).

Political System - A government and its domestic and international environments.

Political Socialization - The process by which an individual acquires political beliefs, attitudes, and values and by which a political culture is passed down from one generation to another over time. (See "Political Culture.")

Politics - Anything related to the making of governmental decisions: the authoritative allocation of values for a society (Easton) or who gets, what, when, how (Lasswell).

Poll Tax - A voting fee; overturned with the passage of the Twentieth Amendment to the United States Constitution.

Porkbarrel Politics - The use of political influence by members of Congress to secure government funds and projects for their constituents.

Poverty - The state or condition of being poor by lacking the means of providing material needs or comforts.

Poverty Level - Based on the assumption that poor families spend one third of their income needed to eat according to a modest food plan.

Powell v Alabama (1932) - The United States Supreme Court ruled that those accused of a crime must be guaranteed their rights of due process and equal protection as guaranteed by the Fourteenth Amendment to the United States Constitution.

Power - A relationship in which an individual or a country gets what it wants from another, using the promise or the threat of sanctions.

Precedent - A court ruling bearing upon subsequent legal decisions made in similar cases.

Precinct - Local electoral units.

Preferred Provider Organization (PPO) - A health care system where plan members select from a pre-approved list of doctors providing medical services at predetermined fees.

Prejudice - Feeling or act of any individual or any group in which a prejudgment about someone else or another group is made on the basis of emotion rather than reason.

Presidential Types - Presidents that share the same personal qualities and are categorized according to these common attributes.

Preventive Approach - A public policy option designed to prevent future damage without adequately solving the problem that caused the damage.

Primary Election - Intraparty election used by political parties to select a candidate to run in the general election.

Privatization - General effort to relieving the disincentives toward efficiency in public organizations by subjecting them to incentives of the private market.

Probable Cause - A reasonable assumption that a crime has or will be committed.

Probate Courts - County-district level courts charged with filing wills and settling the distribution of a deceased's property and belongings.

Problem - Condition or situation that produces a human need, deprivation, or dissatisfaction, self identified or identified by others, for which relief is sought.

Procedural Due Process - The manner in which a law, ordinance, an administrative practice, or judicial task is carried out.

Progressive Tax - A tax that increases the tax burden for upper-income people while reducing it for lower-income people.

Proportional Representation - Representatives are not necessarily selected from specific geographic regions or districts. Rather, each political party receives representation in proportion to the amount of votes cast. In contrast to the single-member district, this is not a winner-take-all system.

Proportional Taxes - Tax programs that impose equal tax burdens regardless of one's income level.

Public Opinion - The shared views, beliefs, or attitudes of a segment of a population.

Public Policy - An officially expressed intention backed by a sanction, which can be a reward or punishment.

Punitive Approach - A public policy option designed to punish the recipients of the benefit by placing stiff eligibility requirements and sanctions for abuse.

Pure Speech - Speech without any conduct.

Racial Profiling - the practice of law enforcement using stereotypes of the criminal element to determine if individuals should be subjected to searches, seizures, and if necessary, arrests.

Realignment - Shift in constituent base of two national political parties.

Reasonable Restrictions – The logical and rational curtailments enacted by government upon the absolute unrestrained pursuit of unalienable rights to guarantee the protection of those rights to all members of a civil society

Recall - A set of procedures through which residents in a state or local community may remove an elected official from office.

Redistributive Policies - Conscious attempts by government to manipulate the allocation of wealth, property, rights, or some other value among broad classes or groups in society.

Redlining - Practice used by financial institutions to deny loans to individuals desiring to purchase properties located in racially changing neighborhoods.

Referendum - A set of procedures through which residents in a state or local community may indicate their approval or disapproval of existing or proposed legislation and/or changes to their constitution

Regime - A way of governing (democracy, communism, fascism, etc.)

Regressive Tax - A tax that increases the burden for lower-income people while reducing it for upper-income people.

Regulatory Actions - Government actions that extend government control over particular behavior of private individuals or businesses.

Relative Poverty - Measurement of the poverty level by comparing an individual's income to the nation's overall standard of living

Republic - A country which has an indirect or representative form of democracy at the national level of government. (See "Indirect Democracy.")

Reserved powers - The Tenth Amendment to the Constitution explicitly states that powers not explicitly granted to the national government are reserved to the states. The proponents of states' rights use this amendment to support their position.

Resolution - A congressional or legislative action that deals entirely within the prerogatives of one house or the other.

Restrictive Covenant - A provision in a mortgage loan contract forbidding the buyer of a home from eventually selling the house to a minority.

Reynolds v Sims **(1964)** - United States Supreme Court ruling that redistricting plans for state Senates must guarantee the principle of "one man, one vote".

Reynolds v United States **(1879)** - The United States Supreme Court upheld a federal law outlawing the practice of polygamy.

Rider - An extraneous amendment attached to a bill by Congress.

Roe v Wade **(1973)** - The United States Supreme Court ruled that a woman's choice to have an abortion is a protected Constitutional right.

Roth v United States **(1957)** - The United States Supreme Court ruled that obscenity is not constitutionally protected by the First Amendment's guarantee to freedom of speech.

Ruiz v Estelle **(1980)** - United States Supreme Court decision ruling that triple bunking in state prisons was an unconstitutional act.

Sanctions - The penalties meted out as consequences of illegal conduct.

Schenck v United States (1919) - The United States Supreme Court decision to apply the term "clear and present danger" to differentiate constitutionally protected from unconstitutionally protected speech.

School District of Abington Township v Schempp (1963) - The United States Supreme Court ruled that the reading of the Bible in a public school constituted an unconstitutional sponsorship of one religious practice over other practices.

Secondary interests - Interests for which a country will not go to war but rather negotiate a settlement.

Security - It is the sum total of a nation-state's vital interests, and it is the centerpiece of a country's foreign policy.

Selective Incorporation - The process used by the United States Supreme Court to apply certain rights guaranteed in the Bill of Rights to state actions.

Senatorial Courtesy - The practice in which a president yields the choice of an agency head or federal judge to a senator in his party.

Separate But Equal - The practice used to segregate public schools, public accommodations, housing, etc., initially upheld by the Supreme Court in *Plessy v Ferguson* (1896); overturned by the United States Supreme Court in *Brown v Board of Education* (1954).

Separate Car Act (1890) – A Louisiana state law mandating that railroads had to provide separate rail cars for Anglos and African-American passengers.

Separation – the belief that each racial or cultural group should live in isolation of other racial and cultural groups

Separation of Church and State Doctrine - As outlined in the First Amendment, the practice of separating religious issues from governmental control or sponsorship.

Settlement Houses - Community centers located in the poor districts of major cities designed in the 1880s to address the needs of urban poor.

Shaw v Reno (1993) - United States Supreme Court decision ruling that racial gerrymandering is unconstitutional.

Shura - Consultative council of Al Qaeda.

Silverman v United States (1961) - The United States Supreme Court ruled that law enforcement violated Silverman's Fourth Amendment rights when they used the pipes of his heating system to eavesdrop on his conversations.

Single-member district - The political system is divided into districts and the people of that district will select one person to represent them. It is a winner-take-all system.

Slander - Verbal malicious attacks against another person.

Smith Act (1940) - A federal law outlawing the right to organize or associate with any member belonging to any organization advocating the overthrow of any agency or branch of the United States government.

Smith v Allwright (1944) - The United States Supreme Court ruled that political parties were agents of state government and therefore, could not deny voting or membership privileges to any qualified voter for any election.

Smog - An air quality problem occurring when nitrogen oxides produced by burning fuels and volatile organic compounds escape into the atmosphere.

Social Security Act (1935) - Federal legislation creating a income support program for the nation's retired citizens funded through payroll taxes.

Solid Waste - Any garbage, refuse, sludge from a waste treatment plant, water supply, treatment plant or air pollution control facility, and other discarded materials, including solid liquid, semi-solid, or contained gaseous material resulting from industrial, municipal, commercial, mining, and agricultural operations.

Special Supplemental Program for Women, Infants and Children (WIC) - A federally funded program providing nutritional food staples to pregnant women, breastfeeding mothers, mothers up to six months after giving birth and children under the age of five whose individual or family incomes are at or below the designated poverty level.

Spin Doctor - Serving as a politician and the head of a political party, a president attempts to give the media favorable interpretations (spin) of his own, and his party's actions. This role is also played by his political campaign advisor.

Sprawl - The outward extension of a new low-density residential and commercial development from the core of the city.

Standing Committees - Permanent committees within a legislative house, i.e., Budget Committee, Foreign Relations Committee, and so on.

Standing to sue - A legal reason to be before a court.

Statistics - A mathematical method used by some political scientists to analyze data.

Status Quo - Present public policy. What is right now.

Steering - The practice of showing real estate properties to minorities located only in minority neighborhoods thus steering them away from more affluent neighborhoods.

Strategic Defense Policy - Policy response oriented toward foreign policy and international politics involving the use of military force.

Street v New York (1969) - The United States Supreme Court ruled that the burning of the American flag was a constitutionally protected right under the First Amendment's guarantee to freedom of speech.

Structural Defense Policy - Policy response oriented toward foreign policy and international politics involving decisions of procurement, allocation, and organization of military forces.

Subsidies - Government grants of cash or other commodities.

Substantive Due Process - The content or subject matter of a law.

Superior/Inferior Theory of Racism – The concept that one group or culture is genetically, intellectually, and culturally more superior than any other group.

Supplemental Security Income (SSI) – A federally funded program providing cash payments to lower income elderly, the blind, and disable adults and children.

Supremacy Clause - Article VI of the United States Constitution mandating that the Constitution is the supreme law of the land.

Supreme Court - The Supreme Court is the only national court that is guaranteed under Article III of the Constitution. Although it serves as a court of original jurisdiction, it is most often the last court of appeal.

Survey - A method used by some political scientists to collect data about the attitudes and beliefs held by a sample of the population.

Sweatt v Painter (1950) - The United States Supreme Court ruled that the practice of allowing African Americans to attend racially separated inferior schools was an unconstitutional violation of the Fourteenth Amendment.

Symbolic Speech - Use of symbols, rather than words, to convey ideas.

Systems Analysis - A behavioral approach to the study of politics that focuses on the relationship that exists between a government and its environments. (See "Approach" and "Political System.")

Taliban - government in Afghanistan responsible for shielding Osama bin Laden. The Taliban government has since fallen and been replaced by interim President Hamid Karzai, a regime friendly to the United States.

Tax - A compulsory contribution for a public purpose rather than for the personal benefit of an individual.

Tax Equity - Fairness of tax application.

Technique - The specific set of procedures adhered to in the process of acquiring political knowledge.

Temperance Movement - The organized effort to forbid the production, sale, and consumption of alcohol.

Terry v Ohio (**1968**) - The United States Supreme Court ruled that testing for drugs or alcohol by penetrating the skin is not a violation of the Fourth Amendment's protection against unreasonable searches.

Theory - An explanation of some aspect of politics.

Third World - Preindustrial or developing states.

Threatened Species - A species that is likely to become endangered in the foreseeable future.

Tinker v Des Moines School District (**1969**) - The United States Supreme Court ruled that the wearing of arm bands in protest of the Vietnam War was a protected right to freedom of speech.

Trail of Tears - the 1829 forced relocation sponsored by the United States government of the Cherokees, Choctaws, Creeks, Chickasaws and Seminoles from their traditional lands east of the Mississippi to new lands west of the Mississippi.

Unalienable Rights - Fundamental rights derived from natural law which all people have and which cannot be taken away or transferred.

Unemployment Insurance – A federally funded program providing financial assistance to unemployed workers.

Unfunded Mandate – An order from a higher level of government upon a subordinate level of government to perform a particular task without receiving the additional revenue or resources needed to perform the task.

Unicameral - A one-house legislature.

United Farm Workers Union - A labor organization founded by the late Cesar Chavez to address the concerns of migrant farm workers.

United States v O'Brien **(1968)** - The United States Supreme Court ruled that the burning of draft cards was an unconstitutional act in violation of the First Amendment's guarantee to freedom of speech.

Unitary - A system of government where power is centralized.   It vests all power in the central government.

Urban Renewal Program - A federally financed program designed to clear blighted inner city areas and redevelop them with a mixture of commercial and residential properties.

Veto - The return of a bill to Congress without a presidential signature and with his stated objections. (See "Pocket Veto.")

Village of Skokie v National Socialist Party **(1978)** - The United States Supreme Court ruled that the denial of a parade permit to the American Nazi Party violated the organization's constitutionally protected right to assemble.

Vital Interests - Interests for which a country will go to war.

Vocational Rehabilitation Act (1920) - Federal legislation providing financial assistance to disabled Americans.

Voting Rights Act (1965) - Federal legislation suspending the use of literacy tests to determine voting qualifications.

Wallace v Jaffree **(1985)** - The United States Supreme Court ruled that Alabama's law requiring a moment for voluntary prayer violated the First Amendment's guarantee to freedom of religious beliefs.

War on Poverty - The collective term used for President Lyndon Johnson's programs to address poverty-related issues during the 1960s designed to create a **Great Society**.

War Powers Act - Legislation passed by Congress in 1973 designed to limit the president's ability to "make war" without their consent.

West Virginia State Board of Education v Barnette (1943) - The United States Supreme Court ruled that the school district's mandatory flag salute violated the religious rights of school children belonging to the Jehovah Witnesses.

Westbury v Sanders (1964) - United States Supreme Court decision mandating that the United States House of Representatives implement the concept of "one man, one vote: in its redistricting plans.

White Fear - Feeling of becoming a member of a new minority as the existing minority becomes a majority within the social community.

White Flight - The movement of white (Anglo) residents from central cities to the suburbs.

White House Office (WHO) - The people who run the White House and assist the chief executive in a variety of functions including speech writing and secretarial services.

White Only Primary - A tactic used by the Democratic Party in southern states to deny African Americans the right to vote in primary elections; overturned by the United States Supreme Court in *Smith v Allwright* (1944) and *Nixon v Hernon* (1924).

Wilderness - An area where the earth and its community of life are untrammeled by man, and where man himself is a visitor who does not remain.

Woman's Party - A third party movement founded by Alice Paul to address the concerns of women.

Working Poor - The term used to describe those individuals who are employed at jobs paying at or below the poverty level.

Works Project Administration (WPA) - A federally funded Depression Era New Deal program providing jobs to the nation's unemployed.

Writ of *Certiorari* - Order by the Supreme Court requiring a lower court to send the records of a case for it to review.

Writ of Habeas Corpus - A direct order to the person detaining another and commanding him to produce a body of the person or persons detained.

Writ of Mandamus - a court order directing a public official to fulfill his/her duties or otherwise be in contempt of court.

Index